THE NEW INTERNATIONAL COMMENTARY
ON THE
NEW TESTAMENT

General Editors

NED B. STONEHOUSE
(1946–1962)

F. F. BRUCE
(1962–1990)

GORDON D. FEE
(1990–2012)

JOEL B. GREEN
(2013–   )

The Letters to

TIMOTHY

and

TITUS

PHILIP H. TOWNER

WILLIAM B. EERDMANS PUBLISHING COMPANY
GRAND RAPIDS, MICHIGAN / CAMBRIDGE, U.K.

Published 2006 by

Wm. B. Eerdmans Publishing Co.

2140 Oak Industrial Drive N.E., Grand Rapids, Michigan 49505 /

P.O. Box 163, Cambridge CB3 9PU U.K.

www.eerdmans.com

Printed in the United States of America

21   10 9

Library of Congress Cataloging-in-Publication Data

Towner, Philip H., 1953-

The letters to Timothy and Titus / Philip H. Towner.

p.   cm.

Includes bibliographical references and index.

ISBN 978-0-8028-2513-1 (cloth: alk. paper)

1. Bible. N.T. Pastoral Epistles — Commentaries.   I. Title.

BS2735.53.T69   2006

227'.83077 — dc22

2006006711

For Rev. Dr. Walter McGregor Dunnett,
with gratitude and affection

CONTENTS

CONTENTS

THE FIRST LETTER TO TIMOTHY

CONTENTS

THE LETTER TO TITUS

INDEXES

EDITOR'S PREFACE

When I first agreed to succeed the late F. F. Bruce as editor of this series of commentaries, there were three volumes that had not yet been published (Matthew, the Pastoral Epistles, Jude–2 Peter), and this was to be my first task as editor. For a variety of reasons, it is now a decade and a half later, and the present volume (happily) is the first of these three now to see the light of day (and there is good hope for the other two within a couple of years). So as editor it is my delight finally to write an "Editor's Preface" for one of the three "missing" volumes.

It is also a distinct privilege to introduce this volume to the church and academy. Some forty years after the original contract had been issued for this volume by the original editor, Professor Ned Stonehouse, but for several reasons had not come to fruition, Dr. Towner first approached me in 1990 about the possibility of his writing this commentary. In the meantime Phil had been a colleague for a year as a Visiting Professor at Regent College, where we struck up a very cordial and lasting friendship. So it was with special joy that I was able in 1995 to turn to Phil and invite him into the series. But in accepting the offer, he also indicated that, besides his working full time as a translation consultant with the United Bible Societies, he also had a couple of other projects on his plate.

Those who use this commentary will be glad that I waited. Phil wrote his doctoral dissertation on some theological and ethical aspects of these letters, which was published in 1989 and has become an important part of the literature. Meanwhile, having worked closely with Professor I. Howard Marshall (his *Doktorvater*) on the latter's International Critical Commentary volume, Dr. Towner now had had plenty of experience working through the text yet one more time with great care. In the meantime he has also published widely on various aspects of these letters, and in so doing has developed his own approach and understanding of the so-called Pastoral Epistles.

Here is a commentary that was therefore a delight to edit. Having written a shorter commentary on these letters two decades ago, I found myself learning much from this volume. Dr. Towner here offers a genuinely new, and stimulating, option for understanding these letters as ultimately from within the Pauline mission itself. Without being dogmatic or argumentative, he has engaged the scholarly community with his own distinctive insights into the possible meaning of these letters within that mission. It is a pleasure to commend it to the church and academic community.

I am therefore pleased to commend this volume to the church and the academy for their learning and listening to what the Spirit would say to the churches of the twenty-first century.

GORDON D. FEE

AUTHOR'S PREFACE

It is fair to ask authors of new commentaries to explain why on earth they are adding to the many volumes already available. In my case, a convergence of two histories suggests a reason. First, this particular volume in the New International Commentary on the New Testament series had never been done — a gap existed, and I was asked to fill it. Second, my personal history with these New Testament letters provides some background, while it also sharpens that initial question to why *I* would want to write this commentary. It has its origins in work I did more than two decades ago at the University of Aberdeen in Scotland. Since that time, work related to the letters to Timothy and Titus has steadily occupied some part of my time. Early publishing exercises — a few journal articles, a monograph based on my Ph.D. dissertation, and a shorter commentary — flowed from doctoral research. I had a more extensive commentary in mind when I. Howard Marshall invited me back to Aberdeen to assist him in the writing of the International Critical Commentary volume on the Pastoral Epistles. During that period, Gordon Fee invited me to write the present commentary. Even after two years of intensive collaboration on a scholarly commentary, I remained convinced that there was more to be said about these New Testament letters, or at least more that I wanted to say. And so, finally, the present work has emerged.

But in view of that ICC project, on which I rely in many ways (see the notes), it is important to mention very briefly, and without spoiling any surprises, a few of the elements that will make this commentary distinct (see further the Introduction). First, the sense of uneasiness Professor Marshall and I shared concerning the view of authorship termed "pseudonymity" continues to be reflected in the present work. But I have pushed to a different place in my interrogation of the intractable and monolithic (and yet unproven) scholarly consensus (again, see the Introduction).

Second, I have taken a fresh look at the settings of the letters in their political, social, religious, and ecclesiastical contexts. Of particular interest is influence from prevalent cultural movements and stories that may have affected life and perceptions in Ephesus and Crete. Some might warn that creativity in such scholarly exercises can run to excess; but I would rather insert the usual caveats into my reconstructions than to risk missing some useful clue to interpretation that might otherwise not have come to light.

Third, the Old Testament has not normally figured largely in the interpretation of the letters to Timothy and Titus. Yet within Pauline studies it has never been clearer that the story of Israel as told in the Jewish Scriptures (in Greek for Paul) is the fabric of the worldview that the apostle seeks to share with his churches. Studies in intertextuality have shown that New Testament writers access these Scriptures in ways much more subtle than overt quotation, and do so quite intentionally to draw hearers and readers across story boundaries to find themselves within (and evaluated by) God's redemptive narrative. The reasons for doing so can be quite startling. I have paid special attention to intertextuality throughout the commentary.

A similar sort of engagement in the cultural stories that shape worldviews can be detected in Paul's letters. The possibility that this engagement intends not just to draw on current concepts and language to facilitate communication (i.e., for purposes of contextualization) but rather to challenge, oppose, and subvert prevalent notions makes investigation of linguistic and conceptual parallels mandatory. The author of these three letters did not employ the language of "epiphany," "godliness," "Savior," and the like, nor draw on the dominant features of benefaction and patronage simply because they were current. In fact, they were prominent in propagating and promoting the imperial cult, and Pauline use of such material to communicate the gospel was designed to force an intellectual confrontation that would expose the Roman hegemony for what it was. I have explored this type of riposte, and its relevance for interpretation, at various points in the commentary.

Thus, following these several routes (among others), I aim to bring out the vital message and theology of Christian existence, the church, and its mission in the world found in the letters to Timothy and Titus. I stand on the shoulders of many scholars who have gone before me, and have sought to treat them fairly and apply them well. But I have chosen to be selective in my interaction with the scholarly literature. I do not intend the footnotes to serve as inventories of scholarship on this view or that. Rather, I cite authors because they add something enlightening to the discussion, the background, the language, or the culture, or sometimes because they pose an interesting alternative that is worth considering.

Recent English commentaries (e.g., those of Marshall, Johnson, and Mounce) have processed fairly thoroughly the text-critical findings of J. K.

Elliott and B. M. Metzger on these letters. I have therefore chosen not to duplicate these efforts by exploring every variant in the Greek text, and rather to restrict my discussions to those points where textual variants significantly affect exegetical conclusions.

I owe thanks to so many people who have contributed in one way or another to this project. Let me begin with two scholars and friends. I am deeply indebted to Dr. I. Howard Marshall. First as his research student and later as his colleague and collaborator, I was given the opportunity to carry out research on various aspects of the letters to Timothy and Titus. The experience gained in working with him prepared the way for the present book. I am also profoundly grateful to Dr. Gordon Fee for inviting me to write this book, for the friendship and fellowship that developed through the process, for his patience and encouragement when progress was slow, and for his thorough and incisive interaction with the drafts. These two Christian gentlemen and brothers have never been slow to invest themselves in their students and colleagues, and my life is far richer for their generosity.

Another to whom I am deeply indebted is Milt Essenburg of Eerdmans. He has stood tirelessly in the gap, ensuring that errors were caught and expressions were clear. And I have valued his insight, expertise and encouragement.

It would certainly be remiss of me to fail to thank my class of advanced Greek students at Denver Seminary. In the autumn of 2004, they read parts of the final draft, offered comments, spotted errors, and engaged my ideas with their usual mix of patience, scepticism, good humor, and open-mindedness. I am especially grateful to Brian Bennett, a member of this outstanding class, who chauffeured me to and from the airport countless times, and at a crucial moment introduced me to "Napoleon Dynamite." Another former student, Samuel Thomas (now a UBS colleague), deserves thanks for his last-minute help with one of the indexes.

Members of our house group(s) at Messiah Episcopal Church, St. Paul, Minnesota, prayed for the completion of this book. Thank you, Julie and Paul Saxton, Robin and Jim Morical, Carol Meinders, Debbie and David Reynolds, Sheri and Mark Hank, and Leslie and John Winter.

My wife Anne, who gave generously of her time to help with the Bibliography and Indexes, and my daughters Rebekah and Erin have been a huge part of this adventure. May the Lord bless you richly in all that you do, just as he has blessed me through the presence of each of you in my life.

Finally, it gives me great pleasure to dedicate this book to Rev. Dr. Walter M. Dunnett. From the days of my undergraduate studies, he has been a model of academic excellence and Christian maturity, and I am very grateful for the role he has played in my life. I have him to thank for introducing me to I. Howard Marshall, via the New International Greek Testament Commentary volume on Luke, as well to the importance of "the primary sources." He kindly and expertly read through the completed draft, and I am thankful for his contribution.

PHILIP H. TOWNER

ABBREVIATIONS

I. GENERAL ABBREVIATIONS

acc.	accusative
act.	active
adj.	adjective
ad loc.	*ad locum* (at the place)
adv.	adverb
aor.	aorist
B.C.E.	before the common era
bk.	book
c.	*circa* (around)
C.E.	the common era
cf.	*confer* (compare)
ch(s).	chapter(s)
comp.	comparative
conj.	conjunction
dat.	dative
diss.	dissertation
ed.	edition, edited by
e.g.	*exempli gratia* (for example)
esp.	especially
et al.	*et alii* (and the others)
etc.	*etcetera* (and the rest)
fem.	feminine
fig.	figurative
frag.	fragment
freq.	frequently
fut.	future
gen.	genitive

Gk.	Greek
i.e.	*id est* (that is)
impv.	imperative
indic.	indicative
inf.	infinitive
lit.	literally
LXX	Septuagint
masc.	masculine
mid.	middle
MS, MSS	manuscript(s)
Mt.	Mount
MT	Masoretic Text
NA	Nestle-Aland
n.	note
neut.	neuter
nom.	nominative
n.p.	no place
n.s.	new series
NT	New Testament
obj.	object
opt.	optative
OT	Old Testament
P.	Papyrus
PE	Pastoral Epistles
par(s).	paragraphs
perf.	perfect
pers.	person
pl.	plural
pred.	predicate
pref.	preface
prep.	preposition
pres.	present
pron.	pronoun
q.v.	*qui vide* (which see)
refs.	references
rel.	relative
repr.	reprinted
rev.	revised
sc.	*scilicet* (namely)
sg.	singular
subj.	subjunctive
subst.	substantive

s.v.	*sub vide* (under which)
Tebt.	Tebtunis
Tg.	*Targum*
trans.	translated by
UBS	United Bible Societies
unpub.	unpublished
v., vv.	verse, verses
v.l.	*varia lectio* (variant reading)
vol.	volume
vs.	versus

II. TRANSLATIONS AND PARAPHRASES

CEV	Contemporary English Version
GNB	Good News Bible
KJV	King James Version
NEB	New English Bible
NIV	New International Version
NJB	New Jerusalem Bible
NKJV	New King James Version
NLT	New Living Translation
NRSV	New Revised Standard Version
REB	Revised English Version
TEV	Today's English Version
TNIV	Today's New International Version

III. APOCRYPHA

Add Esth	Additions to Esther
Bar	Baruch
Bel	Bel and the Dragon
Ep Jer	The Epistle of Jeremiah
1 Esdr	1 Esdras
Jdt	Judith
Macc	1, 2, 3, and 4 Maccabees
Sir	Wisdom of Sirach
Sus	Susanna
Tob	Tobit
Wis	Wisdom of Solomon

IV. DEAD SEA SCROLLS

1QapGen	*Genesis Apocryphon*
1QH	*Thanksgiving Hymns*
1QM	*War Scroll*
1QpHab	*Pesher Habakkuk*
1QS	*Rule of the Community*
1QSa	*Rule of the Congregation*
CD	*Damascus Document*

V. MISHNAIC AND RELATED LITERATURE

B. Meṣ.	*Baba Meṣ'ia*
Giṭ.	*Giṭṭin*
Ker.	*Kerithot*
Menaḥ	*Menaḥot*
Ned.	*Nedarim*
Qidd.	*Qiddushin*
Sanh.	*Sanhedrin*
Soṭa	*Soṭa*
Yebam.	*Yebamot*
Yoma	*Yoma*

VI. OTHER RABBINIC WORKS

Gen. Rab.	*Genesis Rabbah*
Exod. Rab.	*Exodus Rabbah*
Midr. Ps.	*Midrash on the Psalms*
Pirqe Abot	*Pirqe Abot*
Pirqe R. El.	*Pirqe Rabbi Eliezer*
Sipre Deut.	*Sipre Deuteronomy*

VII. TARGUMIC WORKS

Pal. Tg.	*Palestinian Targum*
Tg. Ps.-J.	*Targum Pseudo-Jonathan*

VIII. GENERAL PUBLICATIONS

AB	Anchor Bible
ABD	*Anchor Bible Dictionary*
AnBib	Analecta biblica
BAGD	W. Bauer, W. F. Arndt, F. W. Gingrich, and F. W. Danker, *A Greek-English Lexicon of the New Testament* (2d ed.)
BBB	Bonner biblische Beiträge
BBR	*Bulletin for Biblical Research*
BDAG	W. Bauer, F. W. Danker, W. F. Arndt, and F. W. Gingrich, *A Greek-English Lexicon of the New Testament* (3d ed.)
BDF	F. Blass, A. Debrunner, and R. W. Funk, *A Greek Grammar of the New Testament*
BET	Beiträge zur evangelische Theologie
Bib	*Biblica*
BibInt	*Biblical Interpretation*
BibLeb	*Bibel und Leben*
BJRL	*Bulletin of the John Rylands Library*
BT	*Bible Translator*
BTS	*Bible et terre sainte*
BWANT	Beiträge zur Wissenschaft vom Alten und Neuen Testament
BZ	*Biblische Zeitschrift*
CBQ	*Catholic Biblical Quarterly*
CH	*Church History*
ConNT	*Coniectanea neotestamentica*
DLNTD	*Dictionary of the Later New Testament and Its Developments*
DPL	*Dictionary of Paul and His Letters*
EDBT	*Evangelical Dictionary of Biblical Theology*
EDNT	*Exegetical Dictionary of the New Testament*
EKKNT	Evangelisch-katholischer Kommentar zum Neuen Testament
EQ	*Evangelical Quarterly*
ExpTim	*Expository Times*
FRLANT	Forschungen zur Religion und Literatur des Alten und Neuen Testaments
HBT	*Horizons in Biblical Theology*
HTKNT	Herders theologischer Kommentar zum Neuen Testament
HR	*History of Religions*
IBS	*Irish Biblical Studies*
ICC	International Critical Commentary
Int.	*Interpretation*

IvEph	H. Wankel et al., eds., *Die Inscriften von Ephesus* (Bonn: Habelt, 1979-84).
JAAR	*Journal of the American Academy of Religion*
JBL	*Journal of Biblical Literature*
JRelSt (JRS)	*Journal of Religious Studies*
JSNT	*Journal for the Study of the New Testament*
JSNTS	Supplemental Volume to *Journal for the Study of the New Testament*
JTS	*Journal of Theological Studies*
LSJ	H. G. Liddell, R. Scott, H. S. Jones, and R. McKenzie, *A Greek-English Lexicon*
LTP	*Laval théologique et philosophique*
MM	J. H. Moulton and G. Milligan, *The Vocabulary of the Greek New Testament*
MTS	Marburg Theological Studies
NICNT	New International Commentary on the New Testament
NIDNTT	*The New International Dictionary of New Testament Theology*
NIGTC	New International Greek Testament Commentary
NovT	*Novum Testamentum*
NovTSup	Supplement to *Novum Testamentum*
NTD	Das Neue Testament Deutsch
NTOA	Novum Testamentum et Orbis Antiquus
NTS	*New Testament Studies*
OTP	J. H. Charlesworth, ed., *Old Testament Pseudepigrapha*
PG	J.-P. Migne, ed., Patrologia Graeca
PGL	G. W. H. Lampe, *Patristic Greek Lexicon*
PWSup	Supplement to A. F. Pauly and G. Wissowa, *Realencyclopädie der classischen Altertumswissenschaft*
QD	Quaestiones Disputatae
RB	*Revue biblique*
ResQ	*Restoration Quarterly*
RGG	*Religion in Geschichte und Gegenwart*
RNT	Regensburger Neues Testament
RST	Regensburger Studien zur Theologie
SB	Stuttgarter Bibelhefte
SBJT	*Southern Baptist Journal of Theology*
SBLDS	SBL Dissertation Series
SE	*Studia Evangelica*
SNTSMS	Society for New Testament Studies Monograph Series
SNT(SU)	*Studien zum Neuen Testament (und seiner Umwelt)*
ST	*Studia theologica*

StrB	H. Strack and P. Billerbeck, *Kommentar zum Neuen Testament*
SNT	Studien zum Neuen Testament
SUNT	Studien zur Umwelt des Neuen Testaments
TANZ	Texte und Arbeiten zum neutestamentlichen Zeitalter
TCGNT	B. M. Metzger, *A Textual Commentary on the Greek New Testament*
TDNT	*Theological Dictionary of the New Testament*
TLZ	*Theologische Literaturzeitung*
TLNT	*Theological Lexicon of the New Testament*
TrinJ	*Trinity Journal*
TynB	*Tyndale Bulletin*
TZ	*Theologische Zeitschrift*
VC	*Vigiliae christianae*
WBC	Word Biblical Commentary
WMANT	Wissenschaftliche Monographien zum Alten und Neuen Testament
WUNT	Wissenschaftliche Untersuchungen zum Neuen Testament
ZBNT	Zürcher Bibelkommentar/Neues Testament
ZNW	*Zeitschrift für die neutestamentliche Wissenschaft*

BIBLIOGRAPHY

WORKS OF REFERENCE

Elliott, J. K. *The Greek Text of the Epistles to Timothy and Titus.* Studies and Documents XXXVI. Salt Lake City: University of Utah Press, 1968.

Hennecke, E. *New Testament Apocrypha,* Vol. 1: *Gospels and Related Writings; Volume 2: Writings Related to the Apostles; Apocalypses and Related Subjects.* Edited by W. Schneemelcher. Eng. trans. edited by R. McL. Wilson. Philadelphia: Westminster, 1963-65.

Holmes, M. W., ed. *The Apostolic Fathers: Greek Texts and English Translations.* Grand Rapids: Baker, 1999.

Llewelyn, S. R., et al., eds. *New Documents Illustrating Early Christianity,* Vol. 3. Grand Rapids: Eerdmans, 1978-98.

Malherbe, A. J. *The Cynic Epistles: A Study Edition.* SBL Sources for Biblical Study 12. Atlanta: Scholars, 1977.

Metzger, B. M. *A Textual Commentary on the Greek New Testament.* Rev. ed. New York: United Bible Societies, 1975.

The New Testament in the Apostolic Fathers. By the Oxford Society of Historical Theology. Oxford: Clarendon, 1905.

COMMENTARIES

Arichea, D. C., and H. A. Hatton. *Paul's Letters to Timothy and Titus.* UBS Handbook Series. New York: United Bible Societies, 1995.

Barrett, C. K. *The Pastoral Epistles.* New Clarendon Bible. Oxford: Oxford University Press, 1963.

Bassler, J. M. *1 Timothy, 2 Timothy, Titus.* Abingdon New Testament Commentaries. Nashville: Abingdon, 1996.

Bernhard, J. H. *The Pastoral Epistles.* Cambridge Greek Testament. Cambridge: Cambridge University Press, 1899.

Brox, N. *Die Pastoralbriefe.* RNT. Regensburg: Verlag Friedrich Pustet, 1963.

Calvin, J. *The Second Epistle of Paul the Apostle to the Corinthians and the Epistles to Timothy, Titus, and Philemon.* Translated by T. A. Smail. Calvin's New Testament Commentaries. Carlisle: Paternoster, 1996.

Chrysostom. *The Homilies of St John Chrysostom on . . . Timothy, Titus, and Philemon.* Translated by J. Tweedy. Oxford: J. H. Parker/London: Rivington, 1853 (references in the Commentary are to PG 62).

Collins, R. F. *1 and 2 Timothy and Titus: A Commentary.* The New Testament Library. Louisville: Westminster John Knox, 2002.

Davies, M. *The Pastoral Epistles.* Epworth Commentaries. London: Epworth, 1996.

Dibelius, M., and H. Conzelmann. *The Pastoral Epistles.* Hermeneia. Philadelphia: Fortress, 1972.

Easton, B. S. *The Pastoral Epistles.* London: SCM, 1947.

Ellicott, C. J. *Commentary on the Pastoral Epistles.* London: Longmans, 1861, 1883.

Fee, G. D. *1 and 2 Timothy, Titus.* New International Biblical Commentary. Peabody, MA: Hendrickson, 1988.

Guthrie, D. *The Pastoral Epistles.* Tyndale New Testament Commentaries. London: Tyndale, 1957, 1990.

Hanson, A. T. *The Pastoral Epistles.* New Century Bible Commentary. London: Marshall Pickering, 1982.

Hasler, V. *Die Briefe an Timotheus und Titus.* Zürich: Theologischer Verlag, 1978.

Hendriksen, W. *New Testament Commentary: Exposition of the Pastoral Epistles* London: Banner of Truth, 1959.

Holtz, G. *Die Pastoralbriefe.* Theologischer Handkommentar zum Neuen Testament. Berlin: Evangelische Verlagsanstalt, 1965, 1972.

Holtzmann, H. J. *Die Pastoralbriefe kritisch und exegetisch bearbeitet.* Leipzig: W. Engelmann, 1880.

Houlden, J. L. *The Pastoral Epistles.* Penguin New Testament Commentary. Harmondsworth: Penguin, 1976; reprinted London: SCM, 1989.

Hultgren, A. J. *I-II Timothy, Titus* (and R. Aus, *II Thessalonians*). Augsburg Commentary on the New Testament. Minneapolis: Augsburg, 1984.

Jeremias, J. *Die Briefe an Timotheus und Titus.* NTD. Göttingen: Vandenhoeck und Ruprecht, 1934, 1963.

Johnson, L. T. *The First and Second Letters to Timothy.* AB 35A. Garden City, NY: Doubleday, 2001.

―――. *Letters to Paul's Delegates: 1 Timothy, 2 Timothy, Titus.* The New Testament in Context. Valley Forge, PA: Trinity Press International, 1996.

————. *The Pastoral Epistles.* Knox Preaching Guides. Atlanta: John Knox, 1987.

Karris, R. J. *The New Testament Message — The Pastoral Epistles.* Dublin: Veritas, 1979.

Kelly, J. N. D. *A Commentary on the Pastoral Epistles.* Black's New Testament Commentaries. London: A. & C. Black, 1963.

Knight, G. W., III. *Commentary on the Pastoral Epistles.* NIGTC. Grand Rapids/ Carlisle, UK: Eerdmans/Paternoster, 1992.

Knoch, O. *1. und 2. Timotheusbrief, Titusbrief.* Die Neue Echter Bibel. Würzburg: Echter, 1988, 1990.

Lock, W. *The Pastoral Epistles.* ICC. Edinburgh: T&T Clark, 1924, 1952.

Marshall, I. H. *The Pastoral Epistles.* ICC. Edinburgh: T&T Clark, 1999.

Martin, R. P. "1, 2 Timothy and Titus." In J. L. Mays, ed. *Harper's Bible Commentary.* San Francisco: Harper, 1988.

Merkel, H. *Die Pastoralbriefe.* NTD. Göttingen: Vandenhoeck und Ruprecht, 1991.

Mounce, W. D. *The Pastoral Epistles.* WBC 46. Dallas: Word, 2000.

Oberlinner, L. *Die Pastoralbriefe,* Erste Folge. *Kommentar zum Ersten Timotheusbrief.* HTKNT. Band XI/2. Freiburg: Herder, 1994.

————. *Die Pastoralbriefe,* Zweite Folge. *Kommentar zum Zweiten Timotheusbrief.* HTKNT. Band XI/2. Freiburg: Herder, 1995.

————. *Die Pastoralbriefe,* Dritte Folge. *Kommentar zum Titusbrief.* HTKNT. Band XI/2. Freiburg: Herder, 1996.

Parry, R. *The Pastoral Epistles.* Cambridge: Cambridge University Press, 1920.

Quinn, J. D. *The Letter to Titus.* AB 35. Garden City, NY: Doubleday, 1990.

Quinn, J. D., and W. C. Wacker. *The First and Second Letters to Timothy: A New Translation with Notes and Commentary.* Grand Rapids: Eerdmans, 2000.

Roloff, J. *Der Erste Brief an Timotheus.* EKKNT. Zürich/Neukirchen-Vluyn: Benziger/Neukirchener, 1988.

Schlatter, A. *Die Kirche der Griechen im Urteil des Paulus.* Stuttgart: Calwer, 1936, 1962.

Scott, E. F. *The Pastoral Epistles.* Moffatt New Testament Commentary. London: Hodder and Stoughton, 1936, 1957.

Simpson, E. K. *The Pastoral Epistles.* London: Tyndale, 1954.

Spicq, C. *Les Épîtres Pastorales.* Études Bibliques. Paris: J. Gabalda, 1948, 1969.

Stott, J. R. W. *Guard the Gospel: The Message of 2 Timothy.* Leicester: InterVarsity Press, 1973.

Towner, P. H. *1-2 Timothy and Titus.* Downers Grove, IL/Leicester: InterVarsity Press, 1994.

Weiser, A. *Der zweite Brief an Timotheus.* EKKNT XVI/1. Düsseldorf: Benziger, 2003.

GENERAL BIBLIOGRAPHY

Aalen, S. "A Rabbinic Formula in 1 Cor. 14,34." *SE* 2 (1964): 513-25.

Aland, K., and B. Aland. *The Text of the New Testament.* 2d ed. Grand Rapids: Eerdmans, 1989.

Allan, J. A. "The 'in Christ' Formula in the Pastoral Epistles." *NTS* 10 (1963): 115-21.

Aune, D. E. *The New Testament in Its Literary Environment.* Philadelphia: Westminster, 1987.

———. "Prolegomena to the Study of Oral Tradition in the Hellenistic World." Pp. 59-106 in *Jesus and the Oral Gospel Tradition.* Edited by H. Wansbrough. Sheffield: Sheffield Academic, 1991.

———. *Prophecy in Early Christianity and the Ancient Mediterranean World.* Grand Rapids: Eerdmans, 1983.

Balch, D. L. *Let Wives Be Submissive: The Domestic Code in 1 Peter.* Atlanta: Scholars, 1981.

Baldwin, H. S. "Appendix 2: αὐθεντέω in Ancient Greek Literature." Pp. 269-305 in *Women in the Church: A Fresh Analysis of 1 Timothy 2:9-15.* Edited by A. J. Köstenberger, et al. Grand Rapids: Baker, 1995.

———. "A Difficult Word: αὐθεντέω in 1 Timothy 2:12." Pp. 65-80 in *Women in the Church: A Fresh Analysis of 1 Timothy 2:9-15.* Edited by A. J. Köstenberger et al. Grand Rapids: Baker, 1995.

Balsdon, J. V. P. D. *Roman Women.* Westport: Bodley Head, 1962.

Barr, J. *Biblical Words for Time.* London: SCM, 1969.

Barrett, C. K. *The Signs of an Apostle.* Philadelphia: Fortress, 1972.

Bartchy, S. S. *ΜΑΛΛΟΝ ΧΡΗΣΑΙ.* SBLDS 11. Atlanta: Scholars, 1973.

Barth, M. *Ephesians.* Vol. 2. Garden City, NY: Doubleday, 1974.

Bartsch, H.-W. *Die Anfänge urchristlicher Rechtsbildungen: Studien zu den Pastoralbriefen.* Hamburg: Reich, 1965.

Bassler, J. M. "The Widow's Tale: A Fresh Look at 1 Tim 5:3-16." *JBL* 103 (1984): 23-41.

Bauckham, R. *Jude, 2 Peter* WBC 50. Waco: Word, 1983.

Baugh, S. M. "A Foreign World: Ephesus in the First Century." Pp. 13-52 in *Women in the Church: A Fresh Analysis of 1 Timothy 2:9-15.* Edited by A. J. Köstenberger et al. Grand Rapids: Baker, 1995.

Baur, F. C. *Paulus der Apostel Jesu Christi.* 2 vols. 2d ed. Leipzig: Fues, 1866-67; reprinted Osnabrück: Zeller, 1968.

———. *Die Sogenannten Pastoralbriefe des Apostels Paulus aufs neue kritisch untersucht.* Stuttgart: Cotta, 1835.

Beale, G. K. "The Origin of the Title 'King of Kings and Lord of Lords' in Revelation 17.14." *NTS* 31 (1985): 618-20.

Beasley-Murray, G. R. *Baptism in the New Testament.* London: Macmillan, 1962.

Betz, O. "Felsenmann und Felsengemeinde: Eine Parallel zu Mt. 16,17-19 in den Qumrantexten." *ZNW* 48 (1957): 49-77.

Blackburn, B. L. "The Identity of the 'Women' in 1 Timothy 3.11." Pp. 303-19 in *Essays on Women in Earliest Christianity.* Vol. 1. Edited by C. D. Osburn. Joplin, MO: College Press, 1993.

Bleich, D. *The Double Perspective: Language, Literacy, and Social Relations.* New York: Oxford University Press, 1988.

Blomberg, C. L. *Neither Poverty nor Riches.* Grand Rapids: Eerdmans, 1999.

Bockmuehl, M. N. A., *Revelation and Mystery in Ancient Judaism and Pauline Christianity.* WUNT 2.36. Tübingen: J. C. B. Mohr (Paul Siebeck), 1990; reprinted Grand Rapids: Eerdmans, 1997.

————. "Das Verb φανερόω im Neuen Testament." *BZ* 32 (1988): 87-99.

Boer, W. den. *Private Morality in Greece and Rome.* Leiden: Brill, 1979.

Bousset, W., and H. Gressmann. *Die Religion des Judentum im späthellenistischen Zeitalter.* Reprinted. Tübingen: Mohr (Siebeck), 1966.

Bradley, K. R. *Slavery and Society at Rome.* New York: Cambridge University Press, 1994.

Braun, H. *Qumran und das Neue Testament.* Tübingen: J. C. B. Mohr (Paul Siebeck), 1966.

Brewer, D. I. "1 Corinthians 9:9-11: A Literal Interpretation of 'Do Not Muzzle the Ox.'" *NTS* 38 (1992): 554-65.

Brox, N. "Amt, Kirche, und Theologie in der nachapostolischen Epoche: Die Pastoralbriefe." Pp. 120-33 in *Gestalt und Anspruch des Neuen Testaments.* Edited by J. Schreiner. Wurzburg: Echter, 1969.

————. "Historische und theologische Probleme der Pastoralbriefe des Neuen Testaments: Zur Dokumentation der fruhchristlichen Amtsgeschichte." *Kairos* 11 (1969b): 81-94.

————. "Die Kirche, Saule, und Fundament der Wahrheit: Die Einheit der Kirche nach den Pastoralbriefen." *BK* 18 (1963): 44-47.

————. "Zu den personlichen Notizen der Pastoralbriefe." *BZ* 13 (1969): 76-79.

Bruce, F. F. *The Canon of Scripture.* Downers Grove, IL: InterVarsity Press, 1988.

Burkhardt, H. *Die Inspiration heiliger Schriften bei Philo von Alexandrien.* Giessen/Basel: Brunnen, 1988.

Burton, E. D. W. *A Critical and Exegetical Commentary on the Epistles to the Galatians.* ICC. Edinburgh: T&T Clark, 1921.

————. *Syntax of Moods and Tenses in New Testament Greek.* 3d ed. Edinburgh: T&T Clark, 1898/1976.

Campbell, A. "'Do the Work of an Evangelist.'" *EQ* 64 (1992): 117-29.

Campbell, R. A. *The Elders: Seniority within Earliest Christianity.* Studies of the New Testament and Its World. Edinburgh: T&T Clark, 1994.

————. "Identifying the Faithful Sayings in the Pastoral Epistles." *JSNT* 54 (1994): 73-86.

————. "Καὶ μάλιστα οἰκείων — A New Look at 1 Timothy 5.8," *NTS* 41 (1995): 157-60.

Campenhausen, H. von. "Polycarp von Smyrna und die Pastoralbriefe." Pp. 197-252 in *Aus der Frühzeit des Christentums: Studien zur Kirchengeschichte des ersten und zweiten Jahrhunderts*. Tübingen: J. C. B. Mohr (Paul Siebeck), 1964.

————. *Ecclesiastical Authority and Spiritual Power in the Church of the First Three Centuries*. London: A. & C. Black, 1969.

Collins, J. N. *DIAKONIA: Reinterpreting the Ancient Texts*. New York: Oxford University Press, 1990.

Collins, R. F. "The Image of Paul in the Pastorals." *LTP* 31 (1975): 147-73.

————. *Letters That Paul Did Not Write: The Epistle to the Hebrews and the Pauline Pseudepigrapha*. Good News Studies 28. Wilmington, DE: Michael Glazier, 1988.

Craig, W. L. "The Bodily Resurrection of Jesus." Pp. 60-70 in *Gospel Perspectives*. Vol. I. Edited by R. T. France and D. Wenham. Sheffield: JSOT, 1980.

Cranfield, C. E. B. "Changes of Person and Number in Paul's Epistles." Pp. 280-89 in *Paul and Paulinism*. Edited by M. D. Hooker and S. G. Wilson. London: SPCK, 1982.

————. *A Critical and Exegetical Commentary on the Epistle to the Romans*. Vol. I. ICC. Edinburgh: T&T Clark, 1975.

Crites, S. "The Narrative Quality of Experience." *JAAR* 39 (1971): 291-311.

Dahl, N. A. "The Particularity of the Pauline Epistles as a Problem in the Ancient Church." Pp. 261-71 in *Neotestamentica et Patristica*. NovTSup 7. Leiden: Brill, 1962.

Dalbert, P. *Die Theologie der hellenistisch-judischen Missionsliteratur unter Ausschluss von Philo und Josephus*. Hamburg: H. Reich, 1954.

Dalton, W. J. *Christ's Proclamation to the Spirits*. Rome: Pontifical Biblical Institute, 1965.

Danker, F. W. *Benefactor: Epigraphic Study of the Graeco-Roman and New Testament Semantic Field*. St. Louis: Clayton, 1982.

Daube, D. *The New Testament and Rabbinic Judaism*. London: Athlone, 1956.

Dautzenberg, G., H. Merklein, and K.-H. Muller, eds. *Die Frau im Urchristentum*. QD 95. Freiburg: Herder, 1983.

Davies, M. *The Pastoral Epistles*. New Testament Guides. Sheffield: Sheffield Academic Press, 1996.

Davies, R. E. "Christ in Our Place: The Contribution of the Prepositions." *TynB* 21 (1970): 71-91.

Davies, S. L. *The Revolt of the Widows: The Social World of the Apocryphal Acts.* Carbondale, IL: Southern Illinois University Press, 1980.

Deichgräber, R. *Gotteshymnus und Christushymnus in der frühen Christenheit.* Göttingen: Vandenhoeck & Ruprecht, 1967.

Deissmann, A. *Light from the Ancient East.* Reprint. Peabody, MA: Hendrickson, 1927/1995.

DeSilva, D. A. *Honor, Patronage, Kinship, and Purity.* Downers Grove, IL: InterVarsity Press, 2000.

————. *An Introduction to the New Testament.* Downers Grove, IL: InterVarsity Press, 2004.

Dey, J. *PALINGENESIA.* Münster: Aschendorff, 1937.

Dodd, C. H. "New Testament Translation Problems, II." *BT* 28 (1977): 112-16.

Donaldson, T. L. *Paul and the Gentiles: Remapping the Apostle's Convictional World.* Minneapolis: Fortress, 1997.

Donelson, L. R. *Pseudepigraphy and Ethical Argument in the Pastoral Epistles.* Hermeneutische Untersuchungen zur Theologie 22. Tübingen: J. C. B. Mohr (Paul Siebeck), 1986.

Donfried, K. "Paul as Σκηνοποιός and the Use of the Codex in Early Christianity." Pp. 249-56 in *Christus Bezeugen: Festschrift für Wolfgang Trilling zum 65 Geburtstag.* Edited by K. Kertelge et al. Leipzig: St. Benno, 1989.

Donfried, K. P., and I. H. Marshall. *The Theology of the Shorter Pauline Letters.* Cambridge: Cambridge University Press, 1993.

Doriani, D. "Appendix I: History of the Interpretation of 1 Timothy 2." Pp. 213-67 in *Women in the Church.* Edited by A. J. Köstenberger. Grand Rapids: Baker, 1995.

Dover, K. J. *Greek Popular Morality in the Time of Plato and Aristotle.* Berkeley: University of California Press, 1974.

Duff, J. "P[46] and the Pastorals: A Misleading Consensus?" *NTS* 44 (1998): 578-90.

Dunn, J. D. G., *Baptism in the Holy Spirit.* London: SCM, 1970.

————. "Jesus — Flesh and Spirit: An Exposition of Romans 1.3-4." *JTS* n.s. 24 (1973): 40-68.

————. *Jesus and the Spirit.* London: SCM, 1975.

————. *Romans 1–8.* WBC 38A. Dallas: Word, 1988.

————. *Romans 9–16.* WBC 38B. Dallas: Word, 1988.

————. *The Theology of Paul the Apostle.* Grand Rapids: Eerdmans, 1998.

Dupont, J. Συν Χριστῷ: *L'union avec le Christ suivant Saint Paul.* Bruges: Nauwelaerts, 1952.

Eckstein, H.-J. *Der Begriff* Syneidesis *bei Paulus.* Tübingen: Mohr, 1983.

Edwards, R. B. *The Case for Women's Ministry.* London: SPCK, 1989.

————. "The Christological Basis of the Johannine Footwashing." Pp. 367-83 in

Jesus of Nazareth: Lord and Christ. Edited by J. B. Green and M. Turner. Grand Rapids: Eerdmans; Carlisle, UK: Paternoster, 1994.

Ehrman, B. D. *The Orthodox Corruption of Scripture: The Effect of Christological Controversies on the Text of the New Testament.* New York: Oxford University Press, 1993.

Eichhorn, J. G. *Historisch-kritische Einleitung in das Neue Testament.* Vol. 3. Leipzig: Weidmanischen Buchhandlung, 1812.

Ellingworth, P. "'Men and Brethren . . .' (Acts 1.16)." *BT* 55, no. 1 (2004): 153-55.

———. "The 'True Saying' in 1 Timothy 3,1." *BT* 31 (1980): 443-45.

Ellis, E. E. "'The Ends of the Earth' (Acts 1:8)." *BBR* 1 (1991): 123-32.

———. *Pauline Theology: Ministry and Society.* Grand Rapids: Eerdmans, 1989.

———. *Prophecy and Hermeneutic in Early Christianity.* WUNT 18. Tübingen/Grand Rapids: J. C. B. Mohr (Paul Siebeck)/Eerdmans, 1978.

———. "The Silenced Wives of Corinth (1 Cor 14.34-35)." Pp. 213-220 in *New Testament Textual Criticism: Its Significance for Exegesis.* Edited by E. J. Epp and G. D. Fee. Oxford: Oxford University Press, 1981.

Engberg-Pedersen, T., *Paul and the Stoics.* Edinburgh: T&T Clark, 2000.

Epp, E. J. "The Eclectic Method in New Testament Textual Criticism: Solution or Symptom?" Pp. 141-73 in *Studies in the Theory and Method of New Testament Textual Criticism.* Edited by E. J. Epp and G. D. Fee. Grand Rapids: Eerdmans, 1993.

Fee, G. D., "Christology and Pneumatology in Romans 8:9-11 — and Elsewhere: Some Reflections on Paul as a Trinitarian." Pp. 312-31 in *Jesus of Nazareth: Lord and Christ.* Edited by J. B. Green and M. Turner. Grand Rapids: Eerdmans; Carlisle, UK: Paternoster, 1994.

———. *The First Epistle to the Corinthians.* NICNT. Grand Rapids: Eerdmans, 1987.

———. *God's Empowering Presence: The Holy Spirit in the Letters of Paul.* Peabody, MA: Hendrickson, 1994.

Ferguson, E. *Backgrounds of Early Christianity.* Grand Rapids: Eerdmans, 1987.

———. "Canon Muratori: Date and Provenance." Pp. 677-78 in *Studia Patristica* 17. Edited by E. A. Livingstone. New York: Pergamon, 1982.

Finley, M. I. *Ancient Slavery and Modern Ideology.* New York: Viking, 1980.

Fiore, B. *The Function of Personal Example in the Socratic and Pastoral Epistles.* AnBib 105. Rome: Pontifical Biblical Institute, 1986.

Foerster, W. "ΕΥΣΕΒΕΙΑ in den Pastoralbriefen." *NTS* 5 (1958-59): 213-18.

Fowl, S. E. *The Story of Christ in the Ethics of Paul.* JSNTS 36. Sheffield: JSOT, 1990.

Fridrichsen, A. "Zu APNEOMAI im Neuen Testament insonderheit in den Pastoralbriefen." *ConNT* 6 (1942): 94-96.

Fuller, J. W. "Of Elders and Triads in 1 Timothy 5:19-25." *NTS* 29 (1983): 258-63.

Gamble, H. Y. *The New Testament Canon: Its Making and Meaning.* Philadelphia: Fortress, 1985.

Gärtner, B. *The Temple and the Community in Qumran and the New Testament.* SNTSMS 1. Cambridge: Cambridge University Press, 1965.

Gayer, R. *Die Stellung der Sklaven in den paulinischen Gemeinden und bei Paulus.* Frankfurt: Lang, 1976.

Gielen, M. *Tradition und Theologie neutestamentlichen Haustafelethik.* BBB 75. Frankfurt: Anton Hain, 1990.

Gill, D. W. J. "Achaia." Pp. 448-53 in *The Book of Acts in Its First Century Setting,* Vol. 2. *The Book of Acts in Its Graeco-Roman Setting.* Edited by D. W. J. Gill and C. Gempf. Grand Rapids: Eerdmans, 1994.

Gnilka, J. *Der Philipperbrief.* 4th ed. Freiburg: Herder, 1987.

Goodwin, M. J. "The Pauline Background of the Living God as Interpretive Context for 1 Timothy 4.10." *JSNT* 61 (1996): 65-85.

Goppelt, L. *A Commentary on 1 Peter.* Grand Rapids: Eerdmans, 1993.

———. *Theology of the New Testament.* Vol. 2. Grand Rapids: Eerdmans, 1982.

Gordon, R. P. "Targumic Parallels to Acts XIII and Didache XIV 3." *NovT* 16 (1974): 285-89.

Grayston, K., and G. Herdan. "The Authorship of the Pastoral Epistles in the Light of Statistical Linguistics." *NTS* 6 (1959-60): 1-15.

Greeven, H. "Propheten, Lehrer, Vorsteher bei Paulus: zur Frage 'Amter' im Urchristentum." Pp. 306-61 in *Das kirchliche Amt im Neuen Testament.* Edited by K. Kertelge. Darmstadt: Wissenschaftliche Buchgesellschaft, 1977.

Grudem, W. A. *The Gift of Prophecy in 1 Corinthians.* Washington, D.C.: University of America Press, 1982.

Gülzow, H. *Christentum und Sklaverei in den ersten drei Jahrhunderten.* Bonn: Habelt, 1969.

Gundry, R. H. "The Form, Meaning and Background of the Hymn Quoted in 1 Timothy 3:16." Pp. 203-22 in *Apostolic History and the Gospel.* Edited by W. W. Gasque and R. P. Martin. Exeter: Paternoster, 1970.

Gunther, J. J. *St Paul's Opponents and Their Background.* NovTSup 35. Leiden: Brill, 1973.

Guthrie, D. *New Testament Introduction.* Downers Grove, IL: InterVarsity Press, 1970.

Hanson, A. T. *Studies in the Pastoral Epistles.* London: SPCK, 1968.

———. "The Use of the Old Testament in the Pastoral Epistles." *IBS* 3 (1981): 203-19.

Harding, M. *Tradition and Rhetoric in the Pastoral Epistles.* Studies in Biblical Literature 3. New York: Peter Lang, 1998.

Harris, M. J. *Jesus as God: The New Testament Use of* Theos *in Reference to Jesus.* Grand Rapids: Eerdmans, 1992.

Harrison, P. N. *The Problem of the Pastoral Epistles.* Oxford: Oxford University Press, 1921.

Hasler, V. "Epiphanie und Christologie in den Pastoralbriefe." *TZ* 33 (1977): 193-209.

Hauerwas, S. *A Community of Character.* Notre Dame, IN: University of Notre Dame Press, 1981.

————. "On Doctrine and Ethics." Pp. 21-40 in *The Cambridge Companion to Christian Doctrine.* Edited by C. E. Gunton. Cambridge: Cambridge University Press, 1997.

Haufe, G. "Gnostische Irrlehre und ihre Abwehr in den Pastoralbriefen." Pp. 325-39 in *Gnosis und Neues Testament.* Edited by K.-W Tröger. Gütersloh: Mohn, 1973.

Haykin, M. A. G. "The Fading Vision? The Spirit and Freedom in the Pastoral Epistles." *EQ 57* (1985): 291-305.

Hays, R. B. *Echoes of Scripture in the Letters of Paul.* New Haven: Yale University Press, 1989.

————. *The Moral Vision of the New Testament.* San Francisco: HarperCollins, 1996.

Hegermann, H. "Der geschichtliche Ort der Pastoralbriefe." Pp. 47-63 in *Theologische Versuche 2.* Edited by J. Rogge and G. Schille. Berlin: Evangelische Verlagsanstalt, 1970.

Hemer, C. J. "Alexandra Troas." *TynB* 26 (1975): 79-112.

————. *The Book of Acts in the Setting of Hellenistic History.* Edited by C. H. Gempf. WUNT 49. Tübingen: J. C. B. Mohr (Siebeck), 1989.

————. "The Name of Paul." *TynB* 36 (1985): 179-83.

Hengel, M. *The Atonement.* Philadelphia: Fortress, 1981.

————. *Between Jesus and Paul.* London: SCM, 1983.

————. *Crucifixion.* Philadelphia: Fortress, 1977.

————. *Jews, Greeks, and Barbarians.* London: SCM, 1980.

————. *The Pre-Christian Paul.* Philadelphia: Trinity Press International, 1991.

————. *Property and Riches in the Early Church.* Philadelphia: Fortress, 1974.

Herr, T. *Naturrecht aus der kritischen Sicht des Neuen Testaments.* München: F. Schöningh, 1976.

Hill, D. *Greek Words and Hebrew Meanings.* Cambridge: Cambridge University Press, 1967.

————. *New Testament Prophecy.* London: Marshall, Morgan & Scott, 1978.

Holland, N. *The Dynamics of Literary Response.* New York: Oxford University Press, 1968.

————. *5 Readers Reading.* New Haven, CT: Yale University Press, 1975.

Holmes, J. M. *Text in a Whirlwind: A Critique of Four Exegetical Devices at 1 Timothy 2.12-15*. JSNTS 196. Sheffield: Sheffield Academic, 2000.

Holmgren, B. *Paul and Power.* Philadelphia: Fortress, 1978.

Holz, T. "Zum Selbstverständnis des Apostels Paulus." *TLZ* 91 (1966): 321-30.

Horbury, W. *Jewish Messianism and the Cult of Christ.* London: SCM, 1998.

Horsley, R. A. "Gnosis in Corinth: 1 Corinthians 8.1-6." *NTS* 27 (1980-81): 32-51.

——, ed. *Paul and Empire.* Harrisburg, PA: Trinity Press International, 1997.

Hort, F. J. A. *Judaistic Christianity.* Cambridge and London: Macmillan, 1894.

Hurley, J. B. *Man and Woman in Biblical Perspective.* Leicester: Inter-Varsity Press, 1981.

Ilan, T. *Jewish Women in Greco-Roman Palestine.* Peabody, MA: Hendrickson, 1996.

Jaeger, W. *Paideia: The Ideals of Greek Culture.* Vol. 1. 2d ed. New York: Oxford University Press, 1945.

Jeremias, J. *Abba.* Göttingen: Vandenhoeck & Ruprecht, 1966.

Jewett, R. *Paul's Anthropological Terms.* Leiden: Brill, 1971.

Johnson, L. T. *The Letter of James.* AB 37A. Garden City, NY: Doubleday, 1995.

——. "The New Testament's Anti-Jewish Slander and the Conventions of Ancient Polemic." *JBL* 109 (1989): 419-41.

——. *Scripture and Discernment.* Nashville: Abingdon, 1996.

——. "II Timothy and the Polemic against False Teachers: A Reexamination." *JRelSt* 6-7 (1978): 1-26.

——. "The Social Dimensions of *Sōtēria* in Luke-Acts and Paul." Pp. 520-36 in *The SBL 1993 Seminar Papers.* Edited by E. H. Lovering. Atlanta: Scholars, 1993.

Judge, E. A. *Rank and Status in the World of the Caesars and St Paul.* New Zealand: University of Canterbury Press, 1982.

Käsemann, E. *Essays on New Testament Themes.* London: SCM, 1964.

——. *Exegetische Versuche und Besinnungen.* Erster Band. Göttingen: Vandenhoeck & Ruprecht, 1960.

——. *New Testament Questions of Today.* Philadelphia: Fortress, 1969.

Kamlah, E. *Die Form der katalogischen Paränese im Neuen Testament.* WUNT 7. Tübingen: J. C. B. Mohr (Paul Siebeck), 1964.

——. "ΥΠΟΤΑΣΣΕΣΘΑΙ in den neutestamentlichen Haustefeln." Pp. 237-43 in *Verborum Veritas: Festschrift für G. Stählin.* Edited by E. Bocher and K. Haacker. Wuppertal: Brockhaus, 1970.

Karris, R. J. "The Background and Significance of the Polemic of the Pastoral Epistles." *JBL* 92 (1973): 549-64.

——. "The Function and *Sitz im Leben* of the Paraenetic Elements in the Pastoral Epistles." Unpublished diss. Harvard University, 1971.

Keener, C. S. *Paul, Women and Wives.* Peabody, MA: Hendrickson, 1992.

Kelsey, D. H. "Biblical Narrative and Theological Anthropology." Pp. 121-43 in *Scriptural Authority and Narrative Interpretation.* Edited by G. Green. Philadelphia: Fortress, 1987.

Kertelge, K. *Gemeinde und Amt im Neuen Testament.* München: Kösel, 1972.

Kidd, R. M. "Titus as *Apologia:* Grace for Liars, Beasts, and Bellies." *HBT* 21 (1999): 185-209.

————. *Wealth and Beneficence in the Pastoral Epistles.* SBLDS 122. Atlanta: Scholars, 1990.

Kirk, J. A. "Did 'Officials' in the New Testament Church Receive a Salary?" *ExpTim* 84 (1972-73): 105-8.

Kittel, G. "Die γενεαλογία der Pastoralbriefe." *ZNW* 20 (1921): 49-69.

Knight, G. W., III. *The Faithful Sayings in the Pastoral Letters.* Kampen: J. H. Kok, 1968.

————. "ΑΥΘΕΝΤΕΩ in Reference to Women in 1 Timothy 2.12." *NTS* 30 (1984), 143-57.

Koester, H. *History and Literature of Early Christianity,* Vol. 2: *Introduction to the New Testament.* Philadelphia: Fortress, 1982.

Köstenberger, A. J. *Studies in John and Gender.* New York: Peter Lang, 2001.

————. "Women in the Pauline Mission." Pp. 221-47 in *The Gospel to the Nations: Perspectives on Paul's Mission.* Edited by P. Bolt and M. Thompson. Leicester, UK: Inter-Varsity Press, 2000.

Köstenberger, A. J., et al., eds. *Women in the Church: A Fresh Analysis of 1 Timothy 2:9-15.* Grand Rapids: Baker, 1995.

Kramer, W. *Christ, Lord, Son of God.* London: SCM, 1966.

Kretschmar, G. "Der paulinische Glaube in den Pastoralbriefen." Pp. 113-40 in *Glaube im Neuen Testament.* Edited by F. Hahn and H. Klein. Biblisch-Theologische Studien 7. Neukirchen-Vluyn: Neukirchener, 1982.

Kroeger, R. C., and C. C. Kroeger. *I Suffer Not a Woman: Rethinking 1 Timothy 2:12 in Light of Ancient Evidence.* Grand Rapids: Baker, 1992.

Küchler, M. *Schweigen, Schmuck, and Schleier: Drei neutestamentliche Vorschriften zur Verdrängung der Frauen auf dem Hintergrund einer frauenfeindlichen Exegese des Alten Testaments im antiken Judentum.* NTOA 1. Freiburg: Universitätsverlag, 1986.

Läger, K. *Die Christologie der Pastoralbriefe.* Hamburger Theologische Studien 12. Münster: Lit, 1996.

Lane, W. L. "1 Tim iv.1-3: An Instance of Over-Realized Eschatology?" *NTS* 11 (1964-65): 164-67.

Lau, A. Y. *Manifest in Flesh: The Epiphany Christology of the Pastoral Epistles.* WUNT 2.86. Tübingen: J. C. B. Mohr (Paul Siebeck), 1996.

Lee, E. K. "Words Denoting 'Pattern' in the New Testament." *NTS* 8 (1962-63): 167-73.

Lestapis, S. *L'énigme des Pastorales.* Paris: Gabalda, 1976.

Lightfoot, J. B. *The Apostolic Fathers: Clement.* Vol. 1. London: Macmillan, 1890.

———. *Biblical Essays.* London: Macmillan, 1893.

Lightman, M., and W. Zeisel. "Univira: An Example of Continuity and Change in Roman Society." *CH* 46 (1977): 19-32.

Lincoln, A. T. *Paradise Now and Not Yet.* SNTSMS 41. Cambridge: Cambridge University Press, 1981.

Lindemann, A. *Paulus im ältesten Christentum: Das Bild des Apostels und die Rezeption der paulinischen Theologie in der frühchristlichen Literatur bis Marcion.* Tübingen: J. C. B. Mohr (Paul Siebeck), 1979.

Lippert, P. *Leben als Zeugnis: Die werbende Kraft christlicher Lebensführung nach dem Kirchenverstandnis neutestamentlicher Briefe.* Stuttgarter biblische Monographien 4. Stuttgart: Katholisches Bibelwerk, 1968.

Lips, H. von. *Glaube–Gemeinde–Amt: Zum Verständnis der Ordination in den Pastoralbriefen.* FRLANT 122. Göttingen: Vandenhoeck & Ruprecht, 1979.

———. "Die Haustafel als 'Topos' im Rahmen der urchristlichen Paränese: Beobachtungen an Hand des 1 Petrusbriefes und des Titusbriefes." *NTS* 40 (1994): 261-80.

Lohfink, G. *Die Himmelfahrt Jesu.* München: Kösel, 1971.

Lohse, E. *Colossians and Philemon.* Hermeneia. Philadelphia: Fortress, 1971.

———. *Die Ordination im Spätjudentum und im Neuen Testament.* Göttingen: Vandenhoeck & Ruprecht, 1951.

———. "Die Ordination im Spätjudentum und im Neuen Testament." Pp. 501-23 in *Das kirchliche Amt im Neuen Testament.* Edited by K. Kertelge. Darmstadt: Wissenschaftliche Buchgesellschaft, 1977.

Lührmann, D. "Epiphaneia: Zur Bedeutungsgeschichte eines griechischen Wortes." Pp. 185-99 in *Tradition und Glaube.* Edited by G. Jeremias et al. Göttingen: Vandenhoeck & Ruprecht, 1971.

———. "Neutestamentliche Haustafeln und antike Ökonomie." *NTS* 27 (1980-81): 83-97.

Lütgert, W. *Die Irrlehrer der Pastoralbriefe.* Beiträge zur Forderung christlicher Theologie 13:3. Gütersloh: W. Bertelsmann, 1909.

MacDonald, D. R. *The Legend and the Apostle: The Battle for Paul in Story and Canon.* Philadelphia: Westminster, 1983.

McDonald, J. I. H. *Kerygma and Didache: The Articulation and Structure of the Earliest Christian Message.* SNTSMS 37. Cambridge: Cambridge University Press, 1980.

McDonald, L. M. *The Formation of the Christian Biblical Canon.* Revised and expanded ed. Peabody, MA: Hendrickson, 1995.

MacDonald, M. Y. *The Pauline Churches: A Socio-Historical Study of Institu-*

tionalization in the Pauline and Deutero-Pauline Writings. SNTSMS 57. Cambridge: Cambridge University Press, 1988.

McEleney, N. J. "The Vice Lists in the Pastoral Epistles." *CBQ* 36 (1974): 203-19.

McKay, K. L. "Aspect in Imperatival Constructions in New Testament Greek." *NovT* 27 (1985): 201-25.

McNamara, M. *The New Testament and the Palestinian Targum to the Pentateuch.* Rome: Pontifical Biblical Institute, 1978.

Malherbe, A. J. "'In Season and out of Season': 2 Timothy 4:2." *JBL* 103 (1982): 23-41.

———. *The Letters to the Thessalonians.* AB 32B. Garden City, NY: Doubleday, 2000.

———. "Medical Imagery in the Pastoral Epistles." Pp. 19-35 in *Texts and Testaments: Critical Essays on the Bible and Early Church Fathers.* Edited by W. E. March. San Antonio: Trinity University Press, 1980.

———. *Moral Exhortation: A Greco-Roman Sourcebook.* Philadelphia: Westminster, 1986.

———. *Paul and the Popular Philosophers.* Minneapolis: Fortress, 1989.

———. *Social Aspects of Early Christianity.* Philadelphia: Fortress, 1977, 1983.

Malina, B. J. *The New Testament World: Insights from Cultural Anthropology.* Revised ed. Louisville: Westminster/John Knox, 1993.

Marshall, I. H. "Brothers Embracing Sisters." *BT* 55, no. 3 (2004): 303-10.

———. "The Christology of the Pastoral Epistles." *SNT(SU)* 13 (1988): 157-77.

———. "Faith and Works in the Pastoral Epistles," *SNT(SU)* 9 (1984): 203-18.

———. "Salvation, Grace, and Works in the Later Writings in the Pauline Corpus." *NTS* 42 (1996): 339-58.

Meade, D. G. *Pseudonymity and Canon: An Investigation into the Relationship of Authorship and Authority in Jewish and Earliest Christian Tradition.* WUNT 39. Tübingen: J. C. B. Mohr (Paul Siebeck), 1986.

Meeks, W. A. *The First Urban Christians: The Social World of the Apostle Paul.* New Haven: Yale University Press, 1983.

———. "The Image of the Androgyne: Some Uses of a Symbol in Earliest Christianity." *HR* 13 (1974): 180-204.

Meier, J. P. "*Presbyteros* in the Pastoral Epistles." *CBQ* 35 (1973): 323-45.

Merk, O. "Glaube und Tat in den Pastoralbriefen." *ZNW* 66 (1975): 91-102.

Merz, A. *Die fiktive Selbstauslegung des Paulus: Intertextuelle Studien zur Intention und Rezeption der Pastoralbriefe.* NTOA/SUNT 52. Göttingen: Vandenhoeck & Ruprecht, 2004.

Metzger, B. M. *The Canon of the New Testament: Its Origin, Development, and Significance.* Oxford: Clarendon, 1987.

———. *The Text of the New Testament.* 2d ed. New York: Oxford University Press, 1968.

Metzger, W. *Die letzte Reise des Apostels Paulus*. Stuttgart: Calwer, 1976.

———. "Die *neōterikai epithymiai* in 2 Tim 2.22." *TZ* 33 (1977): 129-36.

Michel, O. "Grundfragen der Pastoralbriefe." Pp. 83-99 in *Auf dem Grunde der Apostel und Propheten: Festgabe für Theophil Wurm*. Edited by M. Loeser. Stuttgart: Quell, 1948.

Moltmann, J. *The Coming of God*. Translated by M. Kohl. Minneapolis: Fortress, 1996.

———. *The Crucified God*. New York: HarperCollins, 1991.

———. "Hope and Reality: Contradiction and Correspondence." Pp. 77-86 in *God Will Be All in All: The Eschatology of Jürgen Moltmann*. Edited by R. Bauckham. Minneapolis: Fortress, 2001.

Moore, A. L. *The Parousia in the New Testament*. NovTSup 13. Leiden: Brill, 1966.

Morris, L. *The Apostolic Preaching of the Cross*. 3d ed. London: Tyndale, 1965.

Mott, S. C. "Greek Ethics and Christian Conversion: The Philonic Background of Tit. II, 1.14 and III, 3-7." *NovT* 20 (1978): 22-48.

Moule, C. F. D. *An Idiom Book of New Testament Greek*. 2d Ed. Cambridge: Cambridge University Press, 1959.

———. "The Problem of the Pastoral Epistles: A Reappraisal." Pp. 113-32 in *Essays in New Testament Interpretation*. Cambridge: Cambridge University Press, 1982. Originally in *BJRL* 47 (1965): 430-52.

Moxness, H. "Honor and Shame." Pp. 19-40 in *The Social Sciences and New Testament Interpretation*. Edited by R. L. Rohrbaugh. Peabody, MA: Hendrickson, 1996.

Müller-Bardorff, J. "Zur Exegese von 1 Tim 5:3-16." Pp. 113-33 in *Gott und die Götter*. Edited by G. Delling. Berlin: Evangelische Verlagsanstalt, 1958.

Mullins, T. Y. "Benediction as a New Testament Form." *Andrews University Seminary Studies* 15 (1977): 59-64.

Munck, J. *Paul and the Salvation of Mankind*. London: SCM, 1959.

Munro, W. *Authority in Paul and Peter: The Identification of a Pastoral Stratum in the Pauline Corpus and 1 Peter*. SNTSMS 45. Cambridge: Cambridge University Press, 1983.

Murphy-O'Connor, J. "Lots of God-Fearers? *Theosebeis* in the Aphrodisias Inscription." *RB* 99 (1992): 418-24.

———. *Paul: A Critical Life*. Oxford: Clarendon, 1996.

———. "2 Timothy Contrasted with 1 Timothy and Titus." *RB* 98 (1991): 403-18.

Nauck, W. "Die Herkunft des Verfassers der Pastoralbriefe: Ein Beitrag zur Frage der Auslegung der Pastoralbriefe." Unpublished Diss. Gottingen, 1950.

———. "Probleme des frühchristlichen Amtsverständnisses." *ZNW* 48 (1957): 200-220.

Nebe, G. *'Hoffnung' bei Paulus*. Göttingen: Vandenhoeck & Ruprecht, 1983.

Neumann, K. *The Authenticity of the Pauline Epistles in the Light of Stylo-statistical Analysis.* Atlanta: Scholars Press, 1990.

Niccum, C. "The Voice of the Manuscripts on the Silence of Women: The External Evidence for 1 Cor 14:24-25." *NTS* 43 (1997): 242-55.

Oberlinner, L. "Die 'Epiphaneia' des Heilswillens Gottes in Christus Jesus: Zur Grundstruktur der Christologie der Pastoralbriefe." *ZNW* 71 (1980): 192-213.

O'Brien, P. T. *Colossians, Philemon.* WBC 44. Waco, TX: Word, 1982.

——— . *Commentary on Philippians.* NIGTC. Grand Rapids: Eerdmans, 1991.

——— . *Gospel and Mission in the Writings of Paul.* Carlisle: Paternoster, 1995.

——— . *Introductory Thanksgivings in the Letters of Paul.* Leiden: Brill, 1977.

O'Callahan, J. "1 Tim 3,16; 4,1.3 en 7Q4?" *Bib* 53 (1972): 362-67.

Ollrog, W.-H. *Paulus und seine Mitarbeiter.* WMANT 50. Neukirchen-Vluyn: Neukirchener, 1979.

Osburn, C. "ΑΥΘΕΝΤΕΩ (1 Timothy 2:12)." *ResQ* 25 (1982): 1-12.

Osiek, Carolyn. "Family Matters." In *Christian Origins,* Vol. 1: *A People's History of Christianity.* Edited by R. A. Horsley. Minneapolis: Fortress, forthcoming.

Osiek, C., and D. L. Balch. *Families in the New Testament World: Households and House Churches.* Louisville, KY: Westminster John Knox, 1997.

Padgett, A. "Wealthy Women at Ephesus: I Tim 2:8-15 in Social Context." *Int* 41 (1987): 19-31.

Page, S. "Marital Expectations of Church Leaders in the Pastoral Epistles." *JSNT* 50 (1993): 105-20.

Patzia, A. G. *The Making of the New Testament.* Downers Grove, IL: InterVarsity Press, 1995.

Pax, E. *ΕΠΙΦΑΝΕΙΑ: Ein religiongeschichtliche Beitrag zur biblischen Theologie.* München: K. Zink, 1955.

Payne, P. B. "Libertarian Women in Ephesus: A Response to Douglas J. Moo's Article, '1 Timothy 2:11-15: Meaning and Significance.'" *TrinJ* 2 (1981): 169-97.

Perrin, N. "The Use of *(para-)didonai* in Connection with the Passion of Jesus in the New Testament." Pp. 204-212 in *Der Ruf Jesu an die Antwort der Gemeinde.* Edited by E. Lohse et al. Göttingen: Vandenhoeck & Ruprecht, 1970.

Petersen, W. L. "Can ΑΡΣΕΝΟΚΟΙΤΑΙ Be Translated by 'Homosexuals'? (1 Cor 6:9; 1 Tim 1:10." *VC* 40 (1986): 187-91.

Peterson, E. *HEIS THEOS.* Göttingen: Vandenhoeck & Ruprecht, 1926.

Pfitzner, V. C. *Paul and the* Agon *Motif.* NovTSup 16. Leiden: Brill, 1967.

Pietersma, A. *The Apocryphon of Jannes and Jambres the Magicians.* Leiden/New York/Köln: E. J. Brill, 1994.

Pilch, J. J., and B. J. Malina. *Handbook of Biblical Social Values.* Peabody, MA: Hendrickson, 1998.

Porter, S. F. "What Does It Mean to Be 'Saved by Childbirth' (1 Timothy 2.15)?" *JSNT* 49 (1993): 87-102.

Price, S. R. F. "Rituals and Power." Pp. 47-71 in *Paul and Empire.* Edited by R. A. Horsley. Harrisburg, PA: Trinity Press International, 1997.

————. *Rituals and Power: The Roman Imperial Cult in Asia Minor.* Cambridge: Cambridge University Press, 1984.

Prior, M. *Paul the Letter Writer and the Second Letter to Timothy.* JSNTS 23. Sheffield: JSOT, 1989.

Prumm, K. "Herrscherkult und Neues Testament: Ein Beitrag zum sprachlichen Problem der Pastoralbriefe und zur Frage nach den Wurzeln des paulinischen Christusbekentnisses ΚΥΡΙΟΣ ΙΗΣΟΥΣ." *Bib* 9 (1928): 3-25, 129-42, 289-301.

Puech, É. "Des fragments grecs de la Grotte 7 et le Nouveau Testament? 7Q4 et 7Q5, et le papyrus Magdalen grec 17 = P⁶⁴." *RB* 102 (1995): 570-84.

Quinn, J. D. "The Holy Spirit in the Pastoral Epistles." Pp. 35-68 in *Sin, Salvation, and the Spirit.* Edited by D. Durken. Collegeville, MN: Liturgical Press, 1979.

————. "The Last Volume of Luke: The Relation of Luke-Acts to the Pastoral Epistles." Pp. 62-75 in *Perspectives on Luke-Acts.* Edited by C. H. Talbert. Edinburgh: T&T Clark, 1978.

————. "Paul's Last Captivity." Pp. 289-99 in *Studia Biblica 3.* Edited by E. Livingstone. JSNTS 3. Sheffield: Sheffield Academic Press, 1979.

————. "P⁴⁶ — the Pauline Canon?" *CBQ* 36 (1974): 379-85.

Rapske, B. *The Book of Acts in Its First Century Setting,* Vol. 3: *The Book of Acts and Paul in Roman Custody.* Grand Rapids: Eerdmans, 1994.

Reicke, B. "Chronologie der Pastoralbriefe." *TLZ* 101 (1976): 81-94.

Reumann, J. "'Stewards of God': Pre-Christian Religious Application of *Oikonomos* in Greek." *JBL* 77 (1958): 339-49.

Richards, E. R. *The Secretary in the Letters of Paul.* Tübingen: Mohr-Siebeck, 1991.

Ridderbos, H. *Paul: An Outline of His Theology.* Grand Rapids: Eerdmans, 1975.

Riesner, R. *Paul's Early Period.* Grand Rapids: Eerdmans, 1998.

Roberts, C. H., and T. C. Skeat. *The Birth of the Codex.* Oxford: Oxford University Press, 1983.

Robinson, J. A. T. *Redating the New Testament.* London: SCM, 1976.

Robinson, T. A. "Grayston and Herdan's 'C' Quantity Formula and the Authorship of the Pastoral Epistles." *NTS* 30 (1984): 282-88.

Rogers, G. *The Sacred Identity of Ephesos: Foundation Myths of a Roman City.* London: Routledge, 1991.

Roloff, J. *Apostolat–Verkündigung–Kirche.* Gütersloh: Mohn, 1965.

—————. "Pfeiler und Fundament der Wahrheit." Pp. 229-47 in *Glaube und Eschatologie*. Edited by E. Grässer and O. Merk. Tübingen: J. C. B. Mohr (Paul Siebeck), 1985.

Rudolph, K. *Gnosis: The Nature and History of an Ancient Religion*. Edinburgh: T&T Clark, 1983.

Ruppert, L. *Jesus als der leidende Gerechte?* SB 59. Stuttgart: Calwert, 1972.

Sand, A. "Witwenstand und Ämterstruktur in den urchristlichen Gemeinden." *BibLeb* 12 (1971): 193-97.

Sanders, J. T. *The New Testament Christological Hymns*. Cambridge: Cambridge University Press, 1971.

Schlarb, E. *Die gesunde Lehre: Häresie und Wahrheit im Spiegel der Pastoralbriefe*. Marburg: Elwert, 1990.

—————. "Miszelle zu 1 Tim 6.20." *ZNW* 77 (1986): 276-81.

Schleiermacher, F. *Über den sogenannten ersten Brief des Paulos an den Timotheos*. Berlin: Realschulbuchhandlung, 1807.

Schmithals, W. "The *Corpus Paulinum* and Gnosis." Pp. 107-24 in *The New Testament and Gnosis*. Edited by A. H. B. Logan and A. J. M. Wedderburn. Edinburgh: T&T Clark, 1983.

Schnackenburg, R. *The Church in the New Testament*. London: Burns and Oates, 1974.

Schoedel, W. R. *Ignatius of Antioch*. Hermeneia. Philadelphia: Fortress, 1985.

—————. *Polycarp, Martyrdom of Polycarp, Fragments of Papias*. The Apostolic Fathers, Vol. 5. Camden, NJ: Nelson, 1965.

Scholer, D. M. "Women's Adornment: Some Historical and Hermeneutical Observations on the New Testament Passages." *Daughters of Sarah* 6, no. 1 (1980): 3-6.

Schrage, W. *The Ethics of the New Testament*. Philadelphia: Fortress, 1988.

—————. "Zur Ethik der neutestamentlichen Haustafeln." *NTS* 21 (1975): 1-22.

Schreiner, T. R. "An Interpretation of 1 Timothy 2:9-15: A Dialogue with Scholarship." Pp. 105-54 in *Women in the Church: A Fresh Analysis of 1 Timothy 2:9-15*. Edited by A. J. Köstenberger et al. Grand Rapids: Baker, 1995.

Schroeder, D. "Die Haustafeln des Neuen Testaments: Ihre Herkunft und theologischer Sinn." Unpublished diss. University of Hamburg, 1959.

Schubert, P. *Form and Function of the Pauline Thanksgivings*. Berlin, A. Töpelmann, 1939.

Schürer, E. *The History of the Jewish People in the Age of Jesus Christ* (175 *BC-AD 135*). Revised and edited by G. Vermes, F. Millar, M. Black, and P. Vermes. Edinburgh: T&T Clark, 1973-87.

Schüssler Fiorenza, E. *In Memory of Her: A Feminist Theological Reconstruction of Christian Origins*. London: SCM, 1983.

Schwarz, R. *Bürgerliches Christentum im Neuen Testament?* Klosterneuburg: Österreichisches Katholisches Bibelwerk, 1983.

Schweizer, E. *Church Order in the New Testament.* London: SCM, 1961.

Seeberg, A. *Der Katechismus der Urchristenheit.* München: C. Kaiser, 1903/1966.

Sell, J. *The Knowledge of the Truth — Two Doctrines.* Frankfurt: Lang, 1982.

Selwyn, E. G. *The First Epistle of St. Peter.* London: Macmillan, 1946.

Sherwin-White, A. N. *Roman Society and Roman Law in the New Testament.* Oxford: Oxford University Press, 1963.

Simonsen, H. "Christologische Traditionselemente in den Pastoralbriefen." Pp. 51-62 in *Die paulinische Literatur und Theologie.* Edited by S. Pedersen. Århus: Forlaget Aros, 1980.

Skeat, T. C. "'Especially the parchments': A Note on 2 Tim 4.13." *JTS* n.s. 30 (1979): 173-77.

Spicq, C. "Pélerine et vetements (A Propos de II Tim IV.13 et Act. XX.33)." Pp. 389-417. *Mélanges E. Tisseront,* Vol. 1. Civitas Vaticana, 1964.

Stanley, D. M. *Christ's Resurrection in Pauline Soteriology.* AnBib 13. Rome: Pontifical Biblical Institute, 1961.

Stelzenberger, J. Syneidēsis *im Neuen Testament.* Paderborn: Schöningh, 1961.

Stenger, W. *Der Christushymnus 1 Tim 3,16.* RST 6. Frankfurt: Lang, 1977.

Stettler, H. *Die Christologie der Pastoralbriefe.* WUNT 2.105. Tübingen: J. C. B. Mohr (Paul Siebeck), 1998.

Stowers, S. K. "Social Typification and the Classification of Ancient Letters." Pp. 76-89 in *The Social World of Formative Christianity and Judaism.* Edited by J. Neusner and H. C. Kee. Philadelphia: Fortress, 1988.

Strobel, A. "Der Begriff des 'Hauses' im griechischen und römischen Privatrecht." *ZNW* 56 (1965): 91-100.

Stuhlmacher, P. *Das paulinische Evangelium.* Vol. 1. Göttingen: Vandenhoeck & Ruprecht, 1968.

Tachau, P. *'Einst' und 'Jetzt'.* Göttingen: Vandenhoeck & Ruprecht, 1972.

Theissen, G. *The Social Setting of Pauline Christianity.* Philadelphia: Fortress, 1982.

Thielman, F. *Paul and the Law.* Downers Grove, IL: InterVarsity Press, 1994.

Thiering, B. "*Mebaqqer* and *Episkopos* in the Light of the Temple Scroll." *JBL* 100 (1981): 59-74.

Thiessen, W. *Christen in Ephesus: Die historische und theologische Situation in vorpaulinischer und paulinischer Zeit und zur Zeit der Apostelgeschichte und der Pastoralbriefe.* TANZ 12. Tübingen/Basel: Francke, 1995.

Thiselton, A. C. *The First Epistle to the Corinthians.* NIGTC. Grand Rapids: Eerdmans, 2000.

———. "The Logical Role of the Liar Paradox in Titus 1:12, 13: A Dissent from the Commentaries in the Light of Philosophical and Logical Analysis." *BibInt* 2 (1994): 207-23.

———. "Realized Eschatology at Corinth." *NTS* 24 (1978): 510-26.

Thrall, M. E. *2 Corinthians.* Edinburgh: T&T Clark, 1994.

———. "The Pauline Use of ΣΥΝΕΙΔΗΣΙΣ." *NTS* 14 (1967): 118-25.

Thurston, B. B. *The Widows: A Women's Ministry in the Early Church.* Minneapolis: Fortress, 1989.

Towner, P. H. "Can Slaves Be Their Masters' Benefactors? 1 Timothy 6:1-2a in Literary, Cultural, and Theological Context." *Current Trends in Scripture Translation* 182/183 (1997): 43-50.

———. "Christology in the Letters to Timothy and Titus." Pp. 219-44 in *Contours of Christology in the New Testament.* Edited by R. N. Longenecker. McMaster New Testament Studies 7. Grand Rapids: Eerdmans, 2005.

———. "Feminist Approaches to the New Testament." *Jian Dao* 7 (1997): 91-111.

———. "The Function of the Public Reading of Scripture in 1 Tim 4:13 and in the Biblical Tradition." *SBJT* 7 (2003): 44-54.

———. "Gnosis and Realized Eschatology in Ephesus (of the Pastoral Epistles) and the Corinthian Enthusiasm." *JSNT* 31 (1987): 95-124.

———. *The Goal of Our Instruction.* JSNTS 34. Sheffield: Sheffield Academic, 1989.

———. "Mission Practice and Theology under Construction (Acts 18-20)." Pp. 417-36 in *Witness to the Gospel: The Theology of Acts.* Edited by I. H. Marshall and D. Peterson. Carlisle, UK: Paternoster/Grand Rapids: Eerdmans, 1998.

———. "The Old Testament in the Letters to Timothy and Titus." In *Commentary on the Use of the Old Testament in the New Testament.* Edited by G. K. Beale and D. A. Carson. Grand Rapids: Baker, forthcoming.

———. "Pauline Theology or Pauline Tradition in the Pastoral Epistles: The Question of Method." *TynB* 46, no. 2 (1995): 27-314.

———. "Piety in Chinese Thought and in the Biblical Tradition: *Li* and *Eusebeia.*" *Jian Dao* 5 (1996): 95-126.

———. "The Portrait of Paul and the Theology of 2 Timothy: The Closing Chapter of the Pauline Story." *HBT* 21, no. 2 (1999): 151-70.

———. "The Present Age in the Eschatology of the Pastoral Epistles." *NTS* 32 (1986): 427-48.

———. "Romans 13:1-7 and Paul's Missiological Perspective: A Call to Political Quietism or Transformation?" Pp. 149-69 in *Romans and the People of God: Essays in Honor of Gordon D. Fee on the Occasion of His 65th Birthday.* Edited by S. K. Soderlund and N. T. Wright. Grand Rapids: Eerdmans, 1999.

———. "Structure and Meaning in Titus 3:1-8." Unpublished paper, 1994.

Trebilco, P. *The Early Christians in Ephesus from Paul to Ignatius.* WUNT 166. Tübingen: J. C. B. Mohr Paul Siebeck, 2004.

Trites, A. A. *The New Testament Concept of Witness.* SNTSMS 31. Cambridge: Cambridge University Press, 1977.

Trummer, P. "*Einehe* nach den Pastoralbriefen: Zum Verständnis der Termini *mias gynaikos anēr* und *henos andros gynē.*" *Bib* 51 (1970): 471-84.

———. "Mantel und Schriften (II Tim 4,13): Zur Interpretation einer persönlichen Notiz in den Pastoralbriefen." *BZ* 18 (1974): 193-207.

———. *Die Paulustradition der Pastoralbriefe.* Beiträge zur biblischen Exegese und Theologie 8. Frankfurt: P. Lang, 1978.

Turner, M. *The Holy Spirit and Spiritual Gifts Then and Now.* Carlisle, UK: Paternoster, 1996.

Turner, N. *A Grammar of New Testament Greek,* Vol. 3: *Syntax.* Edited by J. H. Moulton et al. Edinburgh: T&T Clark, 1963.

———. *A Grammar of New Testament Greek,* Vol. 4: *Style.* Edited by J. H. Moulton. Edinburgh: T&T Clark, 1976.

van Bruggen, J. *Die geschichtliche Einordnung der Pastoralbriefe.* Wuppertal: Brockhaus, 1981.

van Unnik, W. C. "Die Rücksicht auf die Reaktion der Nicht-Christen als Motiv in der alchristlichen Paränese." Pp. 307-22 in *Sparsa Collecta.* Vol. 2. Leiden: Brill, 1980.

Vermes, G. *An Introduction to the Complete Dead Sea Scrolls.* Minneapolis: Fortress, 1999.

Verner, D. C. *The Household of God: The Social World of the Pastoral Epistles.* SBLDS 71. Chico, CA: Scholars, 1983.

Vielhauer, P. Oikodomē: *Aufsätze zum Neuen Testament.* Band 2. Munich: Kaiser, 1979.

Viviano, B. T. "The Genre of Matt. 1–2: Light from 1 Tim. 1:4." *RB* 97 (1990): 31-53.

Vögtle, A. *Die Tugend- und Lasterkataloge im Neuen Testament.* Neutestamentliche Abhandlungen 16, no. 4/5. Münster: Aschendorff, 1936.

Volf, M. *Exclusion and Embrace.* Nashville: Abingdon, 1996.

Wagner, G. *Pauline Baptism and the Pagan Mysteries.* London: Oliver & Boyd, 1967.

Wagener, U. *Die Ordnung des "Hauses Gottes": Der Ort von Frauen in der Ekklesiologie und Ethik der Pastoralbriefe.* WUNT 2.65. Tübingen: J. C. B. Mohr (Paul Siebeck), 1994.

Wainwright, J. J. "*Eusebeia:* Syncretism or Conservative Contextualization." *EQ* 65 (1993): 211-24.

Wallace, D. B. *The Basics of New Testament Syntax.* Grand Rapids: Zondervan, 2000.

Warfield, B. B. *The Inspiration and Authority of the Bible.* 2d ed. Phillipsburg, NJ: Presbyterian and Reformed Publishing, 1980.

Warkentin, M. *Ordination — A Biblical-Historical View.* Grand Rapids: Eerdmans, 1982.

Webb, W. J. *Slaves, Women, and Homosexuals: Exploring the Hermeneutics of Cultural Analysis.* Downers Grove, IL: InterVarsity Press, 2001.

Wegenast, K. *Das Verständnis der Tradition bei Paulus und in den Deuteropaulinien.* WMANT 8. Neukirchen-Vluyn: Neukirchener, 1962.

Weidinger, K. *Die Haustafeln: Ein Stück urchristlicher Paränese.* Untersuchungen zum Neuen Testament 14. Leipzig: Hinrich, 1928.

Wendland, P. "Σωτήρ: Eine religionsgeschichtliche Untersuchung." *ZNW* 5 (1904): 335-53.

Wengst, K. *Christologische Formeln und Lieder des Urchristentums.* Gütersloh: Mohn, 1973.

Westerholm, S. "The Law and the 'Just Man' (1 Tim 1, 3-11)." *ST* 36 (1982): 79-95.

Wilder, T. L. *Pseudonymity, the New Testament, and Deception.* Lanham, MD: University Press of America, 2004.

Wilshire, L. "The TLG Computer and Further References to ΑΥΘΕΝΤΕΩ in 1 Tim 2:12." *NTS* 34 (1988): 120-34.

Wilson, S. G. *Luke and the Pastoral Epistles.* London: SPCK, 1979.

Windisch, H. "Zur Christologie der Pastoralbriefe." *ZNW* 34 (1935): 213-38.

Winter, B. W. *After Paul Left Corinth: The Influence of Secular Ethics and Social Change.* Grand Rapids: Eerdmans, 2001.

———. *Philo and Paul among the Sophists.* 2d ed. Grand Rapids: Eerdmans, 2002.

———. "*Providentia* for the Widows of 1 Timothy 5.3-16." *TynB* 39 (1988): 83-99.

———. *Roman Wives, Roman Widows: The Appearance of New Women and the Pauline Communities.* Grand Rapids: Eerdmans, 2003.

———. *Seek the Welfare of the City: Christians as Benefactors and Citizens.* Grand Rapids: Eerdmans, 1993.

Wire, A. C. *The Corinthian Women Prophets.* Minneapolis: Fortress, 1990.

Witherington, B., III. *Conflict and Community in Corinth.* Grand Rapids: Eerdmans, 1995.

———. *The Paul Quest.* Downers Grove, IL: InterVarsity Press, 1998.

———. *Women in the Earliest Churches.* SNTSMS 59. Cambridge: Cambridge University Press, 1988.

Wolter, M. *Die Pastoralbriefe als Paulustradition.* FRLANT 146. Göttingen: Vandenhoeck & Ruprecht, 1988.

Wright, D. F. "Homosexuals or Prostitutes: The Meaning of ΑΡΣΕΝΟΚΟΙΤΑΙ (1 Cor 6:9; 1 Tim 1:10)." *VC* 38 (1984): 125-53.

———. "Translating ΑΡΣΕΝΟΚΟΙΤΑΙ (1 Cor 6:9; 1 Tim 1:10)." *VC* 41 (1987): 396-98.

Wright, N. T. *What Saint Paul Really Said.* Grand Rapids: Eerdmans, 1997.

Yinger, K. L. *Paul, Judaism, and Judgment according to Deeds.* SNTSMS 105. Cambridge: Cambridge University Press, 1999.

Young, F. *The Theology of the Pastoral Letters.* New Testament Theology. Cambridge: Cambridge University Press, 1994.

Ziesler, J. A. *The Meaning of Righteousness in Paul.* SNTSMS 20. Cambridge: Cambridge University Press, 1972.

INTRODUCTION

I. INTRODUCTION AND AGENDA

1 Timothy, 2 Timothy, and Titus have been known as "the Pastoral Epistles" (PE) from about the eighteenth century,[1] but as early as the second century they had been grouped together within the broader Pauline corpus.[2] In the course of NT interpretation, this grouping has undeniably had some adverse consequences. There are, however, good reasons for considering these three letters together — they are unique within the Pauline corpus — though this by no means permits interpreters to ignore the historical and literary individuality of the letters. First, they are the only Pauline letters addressed to individual coworkers rather than to churches. Second, their subject matter distinguishes them from other Pauline letters, though this criterion must be applied carefully, for it applies to any individual Pauline letter in relation to another. Third, at the linguistic and conceptual levels there appear to be significant points of both dissimilarity and similarity when compared to the other Pauline letters. These are indispensable observations for a proper understanding of these letters to coworkers within the Pauline ministry, but for the most part their net effect in modern scholarship has been to isolate these letters from the other Pauline letters and consign them rather rigidly to their own corpus. Consequently, fourth, as the "PE," these three letters have struggled in recent times for a place in discussions about Pauline theology.

As a methodological and hermeneutical starting point, this commen-

---

1. See the discussion in D. Guthrie, *New Testament Introduction* (Downers Grove, IL: InterVarsity Press, 1970), 584; in reference to P. Anton, *Exegetische Abhandlung der Pastoral-briefe Pauli an Timotheus und Titum* (ed. J. A. Maier; 1753-55); cf. R. F. Collins, *Letters That Paul Did Not Write: The Epistle to the Hebrews and the Pauline Pseudepigrapha* (Good News Studies 28; Wilmington, DE: Michael Glazier, 1988), 88.

2. This is the implication to be derived from Irenaeus, on which see below: II. A. Reception and Canonicity, 4-7.

tary proposes to discard the concept that lies behind much of the present understanding of the letters as the "PE" and the nomenclature itself — except as a reference to readings and interpretations that assume the corpus status of the three letters — and to read the letters first of all as distinct literary productions. But before this alternative way of reading can be introduced, and in preparation for it, it is essential to trace the fortunes of these letters in recent scholarship, where the letters have tended to stand or fall as a group. Before turning to this and other elements of introduction, the agenda and organization of an introduction that will read the letters individually should be discussed.

It is standard practice in writing of commentaries to provide an introduction to the particular biblical writing to be considered. This allows for discussion of the numerous matters that form the background of the writing (historical, social, literary, theological, etc.) that might shed light on interpretation. And it allows the biblical writing to be placed within an interpretive framework established mainly by the consensus of modern scholars. Consequently, both historical and contemporary issues form the context of a present-day interpretation of a biblical writing. In the case of the letters to Timothy and Titus, however, certain decisions about how to organize an introduction become more complex.

The reason for this is the dominance of a particular approach to these letters taken both by those who regard them as authentic and especially by those who regard them as pseudonymous works written at some point after Paul. This may be called the tendency to read them as a corpus — a three-volume work in which no one of the three parts can be read apart from the other two, and in which observations in any one part may be taken as immediately applicable to the interpretation of the remaining two. This sort of corpus reading, as we will see below, has some merit, but only in the sense that literary and conceptual elements common to these three letters but missing from the other Pauline writings suggest a second contextual horizon beyond that of the individual letter that might shed light on interpretation. But the limitations inherent in this corpus approach far outweigh any benefits for interpretation to be derived from it. And the adoption of this way of reading is so closely linked with a set of assumptions about the nature of these three letters that it has also shaped the way introductions to commentaries have been written.

Corpus readings of these three letters have called for corpus introductions. There is no denying that there are historical reasons for their being gathered together. They are the only letters to coworkers, and by reason of length they occur in the canon together near the end of the Pauline corpus. Less obvious interpretive reasons behind the corpus reading include the assumption of some conservative scholars that while authentic the letters nonetheless come after the other Pauline letters that can be placed within the chronological framework of Acts or the other Pauline letters. The similar decision of the majority view that the letters are post-Pauline serves equally to reinforce the corpus effect.

The assumption of this commentary, shared with others, is that the letters to Timothy and Titus appear as three separate letters written by Paul to his coworkers, Timothy and Titus. There are, moreover, no compelling reasons to read them as other than distinct pieces of correspondence. But if the long-term effects of their being corpus read are to be neutralized, the question is how best to "introduce" the letters in a way that places them into the series of context frames necessary to proceed with their interpretation and exposition as individual letters.

An ideal way to do this in a single volume devoted to the three letters might be to provide first of all a general introduction. This would treat global matters, such as a history of interpretation and a description and assessment of approaches to the letters by recent scholarship. Matters related to historical setting, occasion, and theology might then be left to specific introductions preceding each commentary treatment of the individual letters.[3] For two reasons, however, I have chosen not to follow this course. The first is a practical concern. I am aware that introductions normally occur at the front, and I am concerned that especially introductions to theological and situational aspects of the letters might just get lost in a novel rearrangement. Second, and more significant in my opinion, is that I regard the individual letters as retaining at the same time a degree of interrelationship (see below), so that certain linguistic and conceptual elements are in fact in a very qualified way continuous. This continuity never infringes on any of the letters' uniqueness and independence (cf. the Thessalonian or the Corinthian letters). Consequently, in order to attempt to describe the cluster nature of the letters to coworkers in terms of unity and diversity, I have chosen to locate the introductory discussions in a single Introduction that precedes the individual treatments of the letters.

II. THE LETTERS TO TIMOTHY AND TITUS IN THE EARLIEST CENTURIES

In seeking to place a NT letter into historical context, it might seem best chronologically to begin with a consideration of the Greek text that forms the

---

3. Cf. the excellent model in Johnson, 13-99, 135-54, 319-30. Conversely, the three-volume work of Oberlinner, though perfect in format for introducing the letters as discrete writings — with an individual volume allowed for treatment of each letter — nevertheless treats introductory matters as global matters at the front of the first volume.

basis of our modern translations. In the absence of the original text, however, we rely on later copies and an eclectic reconstruction that is much later still. Before describing the sources from which our translations are made, we will consider the history of the early reception and use of these letters, for it is through the church's early use and attestation of them that we gain insight into its perception of their authority as apostolic writings.[4]

A. RECEPTION AND CANONICITY

Modern interpreters give varying degrees of weight to the status accorded to the letters to Timothy and Titus in the ancient church. These letters obviously found their way into the canon, but how early were they attested as Pauline and authoritative? The evidence is questionable at points since it is sometimes impossible to tell whether an early Christian writer's language reflects knowledge of these letters or simply uses common phraseology. Nevertheless, the evidence from Polycarp (c. 110-35)[5] and *1 Clement*[6] (their use of language and casual quotations) suggests strongly that these letters were known and used by these early witnesses. Polycarp's knowledge and use of the Pauline corpus as a whole further suggest that the letters to Timothy and Titus were regarded as part of that collection. Irenaeus (c.120/140-200/203) attributes 1 Timothy to "the apostle."[7] Clement of Alexandria (c. 150-211) cites 1 and 2 Timothy and Titus.[8] Consequently, it seems safe to say that the status accorded these letters to coworkers beyond the early Fathers, by the later second century and afterwards, is not problematic.[9] Most notably they

---

4. In view of the full discussions in, e.g., Johnson, 20-26; Marshall, 2-8, I will make no attempt here to reproduce exhaustively the early evidence.

5. Polycarp, *To the Philippians* 4.1 (referring to 1 Tim 6:7, 10); cf. 5.2 (= 1 Tim 3:8-13), on which see W. R. Schoedel, *Polycarp, Martyrdom of Polycarp, Fragments of Papias* (The Apostolic Fathers, vol. 5; Camden, NJ: Nelson, 1965), 4-5; D. A. Hagner, *DLNTD* 86.

6. See *1 Clement* 2.7; 60.4; 61.2 (which texts employ language reminiscent of Titus 3:1; 1 Tim 2:7; 1 Tim 1:17, respectively). For the possibility that Ignatius and the author of the *Epistle of Barnabas* also knew the letters to Timothy and Titus, see *The New Testament in the Apostolic Fathers* (by the Oxford Society of Historical Theology; Oxford: Clarendon, 1905), 37-40. But cf. Johnson, 20 n.16.

7. *Against Heresies* 1.pref. (citing 1 Tim 1:4); see also 4.16.3 (citing 1:9); 5.17.1 (citing 2:5); 3.1.1 (citing 3:15); 1.23.4 and 2.14.7 (citing 6:20).

8. *Stromateis* 1.1 (citing 1 Tim 5:21); 1.9 (citing 6:3-5); etc.; 4.7 (citing 2 Tim 1:7-8); 1.10 (citing 2:14); etc.; *Exhortation* 1 (citing Titus 2:11-13; 3:3-5).

9. See the discussion in F. F. Bruce, *The Canon of Scripture* (Downers Grove, IL: InterVarsity Press, 1988), 176.

are included in the Muratorian Canon, which makes their acceptance by the late second century almost certain.[10]

Marcion's omission of the letters to Timothy and Titus from his "canon" is often cited as a reason for caution in addressing the question of their authoritative status in the second century. According to a statement by Tertullian, Marcion rejected these letters from his authoritative collection;[11] assuming that this is an accurate statement, we are left to decide whether he did so because they contained teaching that was inimical to his program[12] or whether he regarded them as sub-Pauline, but the former is most likely. Some explain the omission as an indication that his copy of Paul's writings did not contain them[13] (though they already existed), or that he did not know of them because they had not yet been produced.[14] While Marcion's activity (which included a rather high-handed and selective use of Scripture) was the sort that inspired the church to confirm the boundaries of the canon, his relevance for the question of the early status of the letters to Timothy and Titus is negligible. From Tertullian's comment, we know that the letters were already in existence by the time of Marcion, and the wider tendency to reject the letters (at least those to Timothy) because of antiheretical themes[15] suggests that Marcion's omission was intentional even if his precise reasoning for this remains obscure.

On the whole, the indicators confirm that the three letters were known and used — as Pauline writings — prior to the time of Polycarp (110-35; possibly by the time of *1 Clement*) and consistently afterward through the early centuries of the church.[16] This observation does not settle the question

10. On this matter, see Bruce, *Canon,* 158-69; and for a second-century date, see E. Ferguson, "Canon Muratori: Date and Provenance," in *Studia Patristica* 17 (ed. E. A. Livingstone; New York: Pergamon, 1982), 677-78.

11. Tertullian, *Against Marcion* 5.21. See the discussion in B. M. Metzger, *The Canon of the New Testament: Its Origin, Development and Significance* (Oxford: Clarendon, 1987), 159; Marshall, 7-8.

12. E.g., L. T. Johnson, *Letters to Paul's Delegates* (Valley Forge, PA: Trinity Press International, 1996), 24.

13. E.g., Bruce, *Canon,* 131, 138.

14. E.g., H. Y. Gamble, *The New Testament Canon: Its Making and Meaning* (Philadelphia: Fortress, 1985), 42; L. M. McDonald, *The Formation of the Christian Biblical Canon* (rev. and expanded ed.; Peabody, MA: Hendrickson, 1995), 157, 141. For the view that Polycarp wrote these letters against Marcion (which is extremely unlikely in view of the evidence that Polycarp actually cited 1 Timothy), see Hans von Campenhausen, "Polykarp von Smyrna und die Pastoralbriefe," in idem, *Aus der Frühzeit des Christentums* (Tübingen: Mohr [Siebeck], 1964), 197-252; H. Koester, *History and Literature of Early Christianity,* vol. 2: *Introduction to the New Testament* (Philadelphia: Fortress, 1982), 297-308.

15. Cf. Clement, *Stromateis* 2.11.

16. See Johnson, 22-26.

of their authorship, but it does suggest that the knowledge about these three letters available to the early Fathers did not cause them to dispute their authenticity. Furthermore, both Polycarp's positive use and Marcion's rejection of them point to a significantly earlier origin for them than the modern consensus (see below) would generally allow. It is highly unlikely that letters written at the turn of the century could, after just a decade or two or three, have been mistaken as coming from the Pauline mission. Whether they could have knowingly been received as pseudonymous letters at that later period is another question. In any case, the evidence of early second-century reception and use (let alone the still earlier attestation possible in the case of *1 Clement*) has not been adequately accounted for by the majority, pseudonymity view.

Beyond this the letters to Timothy and Titus were not only acknowledged as Pauline but they were used in concert with the rest of the letters attributed to Paul. This pattern may well suggest a corrective to current tendencies to isolate the letters — as if they were written after Paul to resurrect Pauline theology for a later church — or to limit their application, as "pastoral" letters, to matters of leadership and church order. As I will argue in the commentary, in these letters Paul addresses an array of issues similar to those in his longer letters to churches (esp. comparable is 1 Corinthians). In any case, in the evidence from the early centuries there is no indication that these letters, though recognized as especially useful for matters of church discipline, and drawn on in the polemics against heretics, had spun off into some completely different orbit from the rest of the Pauline letters. The Muratorian Canon does, however, distinguish these letters to coworkers (along with Philemon) from his seven letters to churches as letters to individuals concerned with matters of church discipline.[17]

The final matter to be considered in relation to the early evidence is the problem posed by the papyrus known as P[46] (c. 200), which contains all of the Pauline letters (including Hebrews) except 2 Thessalonians, 1 Timothy, 2 Timothy, Titus, and Philemon. The papyrus is missing its last seven leaves, and the argument is often made that while this might account for the missing letter to the Thessalonians (and perhaps Philemon), there would not have been sufficient space for all five missing letters to be included. Various explanations are offered. Some suggest that P[46] contained only Paul's letters to churches, and other papyri (lost) were devoted to the letters to individu-

---

17. Cf. discussion in Johnson, 25. There is much to be learned from the reception and use of these letters in subsequent periods of church history, which until the nineteenth century fairly uniformly regarded them as Pauline and authoritative. Johnson, 26-42, shows how approaches to them developed, with refinements in method (and the expected idiosyncrasies too), as their status as canonical Scripture continued to be affirmed.

6

als.[18] Against this others propose that P[46] did in fact contain the whole Pauline corpus, or at least that the scribe intended this; his tendency to increase the number of characters per page as the writing progressed, combined with the possibility that pages were added to the original number,[19] in any case makes it impossible to judge from the omission whether the scribe knew of the letters or how he may have regarded them. No firm conclusions about the dating and/or canonicity of the letters to Timothy and Titus can be based on what cannot be known about P[46].[20]

B. TEXT AND TRANSLATION

In the NICNT commentaries, it is standard practice to provide a translation of the biblical text under consideration as an orientation and aid to readers. Rather than add to the proliferation of English translations by supplying one of my own, I have chosen to include the text of the TNIV. On the one hand, the NIV, which the TNIV revises, is widely read and regularly used or consulted by a large number of those who make up the readership of this series. On the other hand, as a revision of the NIV the TNIV deserves to be tested in the context of a close and thorough exegetical inspection of the text. Along with discussion of and comparison with a number of English translations, the commentary will regularly take up those points where study of the Greek text seems to warrant correction of the supplied translation. Consequently, the base text from which the exegesis is carried out is that of the Nestle-Aland[27] (= UBS[4]).

While they do not assume that the text supported by NA[27] is indisputably certain, a sufficient number of scholars who have chosen to pay close attention to the matter of establishing the text have gone before me that I have decided not to discuss text-critical problems exhaustively.[21] Discussion of textual problems is limited to those that have particular significance for interpretation or that shed light on scholarly disagreement.

18. See J. D. Quinn, "P[46] — the Pauline Canon?" *CBQ* 36 (1974): 379-85; Johnson, 17-18; cf. Jeremias, 4. For the various negative views, see J. Duff, "P[46] and the Pastorals: A Misleading Consensus?" *NTS* 44 (1998): 578-90.

19. Duff, "P[46] and the Pastorals."

20. See further Marshall, 6-7. Cf. N. A. Dahl, "The Particularity of the Pauline Epistles as a Problem in the Ancient Church," in *Neotestamentica et Patristica* (NovTSup 7; Leiden: Brill, 1962), 261-71.

21. See esp. J. K. Elliott, *The Greek Text of the Epistles to Timothy and Titus* (Studies and Documents XXXVI; Salt Lake City: University of Utah Press, 1968); B. M. Metzger, *A Textual Commentary on the Greek New Testament* (rev. ed.; New York: UBS, 1975), 639-56; Marshall; Johnson; Johnson, *Letters to Paul's Delegates;* Mounce.

The Greek text assembled by the methods employed by the committees behind the NA and UBS editions represents a theoretical "construct." The aim of scholars operating with the variously weighted criteria (external vs. internal evidence; earliest to latest witnesses; shorter reading, harder reading, etc.)[22] is to reconstruct from the earliest and best-attested witnesses a NT text that (ideally) reflects the original form in which it was written. The problem, of course, is that while the text given by, for example, NA[27] represents a majority agreement based on the application of the eclectic text principles, it does not reflect the form of a text that was ever actually known to be used by a church.[23]

In the case of these three letters, two papyri, the earliest from about 200 C.E., the latest nearer 700 C.E., contain parts of the letter to Titus (P[32], Titus 1:11-15; 2:3-8; P[61], 3:1-5, 8-11, 14-15). The situation with regard to papyrus support of the letters to Timothy is less certain,[24] with the first complete texts of the letters found in the uncial Codex Sinaiticus (fourth century), followed by Codex Alexandrinus (fifth century).[25] What appears to be a meager showing of support for these letters to coworkers is less reflective of their early provenance, use, acceptance, and authoritative status and more reflective of the precarious state of this sort of evidence. As Johnson points out, one needs to bear in mind that an undisputed Pauline letter such as 2 Corinthians, although occurring in P[46], appears elsewhere in no other extant papyri: "Arguments from silence are always hazardous, and nowhere more so than in the case of MS evidence. The absence of 1 and 2 Timothy

---

22. For an introduction to the methodology and witnesses to the Greek NT text, see B. M. Metzger, *The Text of the New Testament* (2nd ed.; New York: Oxford University Press, 1968); E. J. Epp, "The Eclectic Method in New Testament Textual Criticism: Solution or Symptom?" in E. J. Epp and G. D. Fee, eds., *Studies in the Theory and Method of New Testament Textual Criticism* (Grand Rapids: Eerdmans, 1993), 141-73; K. Aland and B. Aland, *The Text of the New Testament* (2d ed.; Grand Rapids: Eerdmans, 1989).

23. See the discussion of this phenomenon in Johnson, 19.

24. See Elliott, *The Greek Text,* 13, who claims papyrus evidence for 1 Tim 1:4-7, 15-16; cf. Johnson, 16 n. 9, for comment, and note his reference to B. D. Ehrman, *The Orthodox Corruption of Scripture: The Effect of Christological Controversies on the Text of the New Testament* (New York: Oxford University Press, 1993). For the unlikely view that the Greek Qumran fragment 7Q4 has parts of 1 Tim 3:16–4:3, see J. O'Callaghan, "1 Tim 3,16; 4,1.3 en 7Q4?" *Bib* 53 (1972): 362-67; the assessment in É. Puech, "Des fragments grecs de la Grotte 7 et le Nouveau Testament? 7Q4 et 7Q5, et le papyrus Magdalen grec 17 = P[64]," *RB* 102 (1995): 570-84; and the discussion in Marshall, 10-11.

25. Thereafter, see the Codices Ephraemi Rescriptus (fifth century), Codex Bezae Cantabrigiensis (D; fifth century), G (012, ninth century), H (015, sixth century), I (016, fifth century), K (017, ninth century). For fuller lists of the MSS attestation of the letters to Timothy and Titus, see Marshall, 10; Elliott, *The Greek Text,* 13-14; Aland and Aland, *The Text of the New Testament,* 107-28, 246.

from NT papyri has no significance either for the dating of the letters or for their authenticity."[26]

Although patristic citations of and allusions to the biblical texts are sometimes a less precise and more disputable source of attestation, these three letters to coworkers are more in evidence in the writings of the early Fathers (see discussion above) than in the papyri. From the level of reception and use apparent in these authorities, it is safe to say that the letters were in circulation, as Pauline letters, despite the fact that the evidence of their preservation as complete texts comes first in the important fourth-century Codex Sinaiticus. It probably follows that their inclusion in Sinaiticus (et al.) was at least partly a function of decisions about their usefulness, authority, and apostolicity made at the patristic stage of the church's history.

III. READINGS OF THE LETTERS IN THE MODERN ERA: INTERPRETIVE OPTIONS AND THE AUTHORSHIP QUESTION

After considering the early reception of the letters and the shape of the text that informs our exegesis, the natural next step might seem to be an evaluation of the composition and contents of the letters and their interrelationship.[27] However, questions about the authenticity of these letters and the subsequent development of interpretive schemes leading to the modern consensus have so influenced the way they are read that a description of the state of interpretation and some assessment of the consensus must precede an evaluation of the letters themselves.

Much can be learned about the churches' attitude toward these letters from the record of pastoral and scholarly reflection on them throughout the centuries. A most thorough assessment is given by L. T. Johnson, who, after considering the recognition and use of these letters in the early Fathers, surveys the commentators from the fourth century to the twentieth century.[28] He traces developments in the approach to these letters along with refinements in method, and the emergence of some peculiarities as well.

No attempt need be made here to repeat such a study, but two of Johnson's observations should be summarized. First, until about the nineteenth century, the letters to Timothy and Titus went relatively unchallenged as letters from Paul the apostle to his coworkers. Their status as canonical Scrip-

26. Johnson, 18.
27. Cf. the organization of introductory topics in Marshall, 1-40.
28. Johnson, 26-54.

ture was never seriously in doubt. What comes to light through the succession of commentaries is the way in which their authors' own cultural and philosophical frameworks conditioned their exposition of the letters for the church.[29] The letters were found to address matters concerning pastoral care of the church, church discipline, administration, and order, and they were regarded as rules of special significance for those in pastoral ministry.

Second, several notable scholars and exegetes discerned, as any who read the letters as they portray themselves will, that, for instance, Timothy is not the sole addressee of 1 Timothy but that much of what is conveyed to him is intended for the church in which he is being directed to minister. And on occasion the purpose of this letter could be seen to be that of authorizing Timothy as an apostolic delegate for work in a context where that authority might be challenged. The letters were naturally read in the context of the Pauline mission and the Pauline corpus, and attempts were made to locate Paul as he wrote the letters, and to understand the local situations to which he was writing.[30] This may all seem like the stuff of a first-year course on the interpretation of NT letters, but the twists and turns that would come especially in the nineteenth century effectively overlooked the understanding of these letters in the preceding centuries of church history.

A. THE TRADITIONAL PARADIGM AND ITS STATUS TODAY (THE MINORITY INTERPRETATION)

It was in the nineteenth century, with the work of F. D. E. Schleiermacher, J. G. Eichhorn, and F. C. Baur,[31] that the Pauline authorship of the letters to Timothy and Titus came seriously into question. Since the time of Baur, and especially in the twentieth century, proponents of the traditional interpretation such as D. Guthrie, J. N. D. Kelly, G. D. Fee, G. W. Knight, and W. D. Mounce have challenged the mainstream interpretation by insisting that Paul in one way or another wrote the PE.[32] Their treatments offer every possible

---

29. Cf. esp. Johnson's discussion of Thomas Aquinas's treatment (35). On Calvin's bias against women (1 Tim 2:11) and against the "papists," see Johnson, 38.

30. See Johnson, 41, for discussion of J. D. Michaelis's *Introduction to the New Testament* (4th ed.; London: Rivington, 1823).

31. F. Schleiermacher, *Über den sogenannten ersten Brief des Paulos an den Timotheos* (Berlin: Realschulbuchhandlung, 1807); J. G. Eichhorn, *Historisch-kritische Einleitung in das Neue Testament* (Leipzig: Weidmanischen Buchhandlung, 1812); F. C. Baur, *Die sogenannten Pastoralbriefe des Apostels Paulus aufs neue kritisch untersucht* (Stuttgart: Cotta, 1835).

32. Details of publication may be found in the Bibliography; commentators are indicated by their last name and page number.

contact between these letters and the undisputed Pauline writings in evidence of their authenticity. Every effort is made to fit the teaching of the letters (on theology, the Christian life, the church, ministry, etc.) into the teaching of the main Pauline writings that were written to churches.

The various approaches taken by those who maintain authenticity could be organized in various ways. But a chief obstacle to this interpretation is the assumed historical placement of Paul when the letters were written. Two main solutions prevail.

1. The Second Imprisonment Theory

Using the movements of Paul as charted by Luke in Acts as a starting point, most scholars have resorted to the theory that Paul must have been released from a "first" Roman imprisonment (i.e., that indicated in Acts 28). The theory creates the space needed for the travels and ministry indicated by 1 Timothy and Titus, but unmentioned in Acts, to take place. 2 Timothy depicts Paul after he has been rearrested, which locates this final letter of the apostle in his second Roman imprisonment when his execution is anticipated. In this way, the three letters may be consigned to a fairly narrow space of time.[33]

Support for a release from a first Roman captivity and subsequent missionary activity is drawn indirectly from *1 Clement* 5.7, which mentions the tradition of Paul's travels to the far west. If this means Spain instead of Rome,[34] according to the statement of Paul's westward ambitions (Rom 15:24), then the author presumably implies some sort of knowledge about a release of Paul not mentioned by Luke. The tradition of Paul's visit to Spain is also mentioned in the Muratorian Canon and the apocryphal *Acts of Peter* 1.1. Later Eusebius (*Ecclesiastical History* 2.22) also indicates unambiguous knowledge of the tradition of Paul's release from a first Roman imprisonment, as well as of Paul's eventual death at the hands of Nero when he came to Rome a second time.

The question in all of this is the reliability of the tradition. For one thing, Paul's aspiration to continue westward, signaled in Romans and echoed in the later tradition, needs to be squared with his additional mission activities after his release from his first Roman imprisonment that actually take him eastward. Too much should probably not be made of this, since in Philemon 22 the prisoner Paul is thinking about visiting Asia. Fee suggests that Paul's westward plans had changed, which would account for the movements implied in 1 Timothy and Titus,[35] even if it places some stress on the

---

33. See J. B. Lightfoot, *Biblical Essays* (London: Macmillan, 1893), 421-37; modern proponents include Guthrie; Knight; Fee.
34. See E. E. Ellis, "'The Ends of the Earth' (Acts 1:8)," *BBR* 1 (1991): 123-32.
35. Fee, 4.

westward direction of the later tradition. Certainty is not possible; the scenario of a release from a first Roman imprisonment should not be too quickly dismissed.

J. Murphy-O'Connor, who rejects the authenticity of 1 Timothy and Titus, reads 2 Timothy as authentic and reflecting on Paul's second and terminal Roman imprisonment. Somewhere between the imprisonment reflected in Philippians (and Acts 28), Paul obtained release, made a brief but unsuccessful trip to Spain, and then returned through Macedonia to minister for a while in Asia. Paul returned to Rome after Nero had made things hard for the Christian community, was imprisoned again, wrote to Timothy (2 Timothy), and was eventually martyred.[36] While little of this squares with the movements mentioned in 1 Timothy and Titus, Murphy-O'Connor avoids this difficulty by ruling them out of bounds.

W. Metzger's detailed reconstruction, which places 2 Timothy in the context of Paul's second and final Roman imprisonment and makes use of all the names and movements indicated in the three letters, illustrates well the space created for the interpreter by positing his release and resumption of ministry.[37] There is no (or very little) hard data on which to evaluate the hypothesis. While attempts such as this that strive for too much thoroughness in tying up the loose ends may possibly strain credulity, the basic hypothesis that accounts for the historical location of Paul in these letters by positing a release and second Roman imprisonment remains a possibility. The greatest challenge is probably the uncertainty of the evidence on which the release from his first Roman imprisonment is grounded.

2. Locating the Letters within the Acts Framework

An alternative approach has been taken by some who place the movements of Paul reflected in 1 Timothy and Titus within the Acts framework, aligning the (only) Roman imprisonment of Paul indicated in 2 Timothy with Acts 28. Specific reconstructions differ in details,[38] and some are more delicate than others, but proponents are agreed that the letters are authentic. At the heart of the matter is the assumption that Acts contains gaps in the description it provides of the Pauline mission and churches.

36. J. Murphy-O'Connor, *Paul: A Critical Life* (Oxford: Clarendon, 1996), 356-71.

37. W. Metzger, *Die letzte Reise des Apostels Paulus* (Stuttgart: Calwer, 1976), and see Marshall, 69-70, for further discussion.

38. Thus cf. B. Reicke, "Chronologie der Pastoralbriefe," *TLZ* 101 (1976): 81-94; J. A. T. Robinson, *Redating the New Testament* (London: SCM, 1976); S. de Lestapis, *L'énigme des Pastorales* (Paris: Gabalda, 1976); J. van Bruggen, *Die geschichtliche Einordnung der Pastoralbriefe* (Wuppertal: Brockhaus, 1981); Johnson, 65-68.

J. van Bruggen's detailed reconstruction will illustrate the method. Paul wrote 1 Timothy and Titus during his third missionary journey (Acts 18:23–21:15). 2 Timothy belongs to the time of the Roman imprisonment introduced in Acts 28. Luke is silent about Timothy's assignment in Ephesus and Titus's in Crete. Van Bruggen suggests that a gap exists in the Acts account between 19:20 and 21. In this gap, Paul will have made a round-trip from Ephesus to Corinth and back again, which movement divides Paul's Ephesian ministry into two stages. These two stages and the movements between Ephesus and Corinth may be supported by the Corinthian letters. Stage one was about two years (and three months) in length (Acts 19:8-20); stage two (19:21-40), with a broadened scope of work in Ephesus and Asia, is suggested by the summary reference to three years in 20:31. 2 Cor 1:8 (reflecting on stage-two ministry in Asia = Acts 19:23-40), together with 1 Cor 15:32 and 16:8 (where stage-one Ephesus is in view), supports the two-stage reflection of Paul's Ephesian work. According to van Bruggen, references to a "third" visit to Corinth in 2 Cor 12:14 and 13:1 force the question of the timing of Paul's second visit (see 2 Cor 13:2). 1 Corinthians and Acts 18 assume only one visit thus far. But in 1 Cor 4:18-19 an upcoming visit emerges that is probably also in view in 16:5-11 — a proposed stop as part of a fuller travel itinerary that involves a round-trip beginning and ending at Ephesus that (from just after Pentecost in May to the following spring when sea travel became possible again) would cover about a year. Van Bruggen inserts this year-long period of travel into the gap between stages one (19:8-20) and two (19:21-40). He further suggests that Luke implies knowledge of the movements in 19:29, where he mentions Paul's Macedonian travel companions in reference to the Ephesian riot. This is possible confirmation of a trip to Macedonia, which aligns 1 Cor 16:5 and 1 Tim 1:3 as references to the same trip.

Within the scenario, where do Timothy's and Titus's movements come in? First, 1 Cor 16:10 (around Ephesus prior to the round-trip) implies that Timothy, dispatched to Corinth (1 Cor 4:17), has not yet returned. Once he returned, Paul gave him instructions to remain in Ephesus and went himself to Macedonia and Corinth (1 Tim 1:3). Problems with opponents had already begun (1 Cor 15:32). When Paul writes to Timothy (i.e., 1 Timothy from Macedonia or Achaia), he gives instructions to meet this need and indicates his plans to return to Ephesus (1 Tim 3:14).

Titus may have been dispatched to Crete from Ephesus before Paul began the round-trip. Titus 1:5 (see the commentary), which seems to place Paul in Crete with Titus, may mean nothing more than that Paul "assigned" Titus to the Cretan duties and location. Paul perhaps wrote to Titus sometime after he wrote 1 Timothy (Titus 3:12 suggests that his plans were more stable than when he wrote 1 Tim 3:14). By this time his earlier plans to winter in

Corinth (1 Cor 16:6) had changed because of the painful confrontation in Corinth (2 Cor 2:1), leaving his schedule open for a trip to Nicopolis.

Acts 19:21-22 resumes the story (stage two of Paul's Ephesian ministry) after Paul has completed the round-trip. The summary includes mention of Paul's future plans and describes stage two more broadly as activity carried out "a little longer in Asia." After his return to Ephesus, the riot broke out, bringing that stage to a conclusion.

Assigning 2 Timothy to the same Roman imprisonment that produces the more optimistic letters of Philippians, Colossians, and Philemon could be seen as problematic for this reconstruction. In addition to the change of tone, Timothy is with Paul in the writing of these Prison Epistles but absent in the case of 2 Timothy. But the optimistic tone and the three Prison Letters may belong to the earlier, two-year period of Roman house arrest (Acts 28:30), during which presumably Timothy accompanied Paul (cf. the reference to Roman believers because Timothy knew them; 2 Tim 4:21). There would have been sufficient time for Timothy to have been sent back to Ephesus/ Asia, during which period things turned stressful for Timothy and bleak for Paul.

Far more restrained is Johnson's variation on this approach. He points out the same factors: both Luke's and Paul's recountings of details of travel and work contain gaps, and we have no idea why Luke would choose to omit certain things that seem so intrinsic to Paul's telling of the story (e.g., problems in Corinth, or the activity of Paul as a letter writer). Critics essentially imagine only that the movements indicated by 1 Timothy and Titus are incapable of reconciliation with the Acts or Pauline frameworks because of ill-advised assumptions about the literary objectives of either of them. Johnson tentatively suggests that these two letters might belong to the stage of Paul's work indicated in the early verses of Acts 20, just after the riot but where Paul is obviously still engaged in work and travel in Asia and Macedonia.

Consequently, among those belonging to the traditional paradigm, who maintain the authenticity of the letters to Timothy and Titus, two historical reconstructions attempt to create the space necessary to fit the three letters into the historical mission of Paul. Questions and difficulties do not disqualify the traditional paradigm — the pronouncement of disqualification has come more from the louder voice of the critical modern consensus than from a superior reconstruction. But the advantage of exercising restraint in attempting to account for the details can be seen. In any case, the measures taken in such reconstructions reflect the seriousness with which the traditional paradigm is seeking to give an account of itself to its detractors. And the extensive introductions of recent commentators who take seriously the historical settings of the letters provide ample proof of the way the winds have been blowing. To start with the assumption that the letters are what they purport to be is to start with the minority position today. On a much smaller scale than the discussions offered in the critical commentaries, we must explore this matter further and report on the state of the discussion today.

B. THE MODERN PARADIGM (THE MAJORITY INTERPRETATION)

1. The Modern Paradigm and Its Methodology

If pride of place in this Introduction must for history's sake go to the traditional interpretation, the powerful influence of the developing majority interpretation on a wide range of scholars over the years requires a somewhat more detailed assessment. The influence of especially Baur in the nineteenth century and Martin Dibelius in the twentieth can still be felt in the most recent studies of the letters to Timothy and Titus. Baur endowed NT scholarship with a rigid dialectical paradigm whereby early, genuine Paul could be identified primarily by the Jew/Gentile debate and later writings by its resolution (or absence) and "early catholic" tendencies.

At the root of the rejection of Pauline authorship lie a number of notable differences between the PE and the main letters of Paul that have evolved into a monolithic critique. Dibelius's listing remains characteristic,[39] though other representatives of this view will stress the elements in different degrees, and with increasing frequency the distance of the letters from Paul is simply assumed and no longer demonstrated.

(1) The external evidence (see above) is often argued to be weak, with absence of the letters from Marcion's canon and from P^{46} cited as evidence of their problematic status.

(2) The heavy concentration of polemical argument is held to be unlike the undisputed Pauline letters. Parallels have been drawn instead with the combative writings of the philosophical schools. Moreover, when compared with the polemical passages that do occur in the earlier Paul (Galatians 3–4; 2 Corinthians 10–13), the argumentation is held to be differently constructed and accented. Extended theological argument is thought to be absent from the PE, which instead favor *ad hominem* attacks on opponents.

(3) The PE reflect situations and mission movements that cannot be reconciled with the situations and movements indicated in the undisputed Pauline letters and Acts.

39. Dibelius and Conzelmann, 1-5.

15

(4) The church order set out in 1 Timothy and Titus, which is variously construed as a developed system of bishops (or perhaps a single bishop), elders, a college of elders, deacons, deaconesses, and widows, is completely unlike the authority structure envisioned in letters such as 1 Corinthians or Romans. Equally, the pneumatic, Spirit-lcd and -empowered ministry characteristic of Paul's discussions in the Corinthian situation is held to have disappeared in the situation reflected in the PE. As it is classically argued, the later period is characterized by institutionalization and structure, and what charismata remain have been transferred to the offices.

(5) Less popular now but still in evidence is the view that the letters evince an ethic no longer rooted in a vital theological tension. Rather, with the shift away from the original Pauline eschatological and theological elements, and with salvation now linked to the great established church, ethical teaching strives to inculcate a Christianity that maintains a peaceful coexistence in the world — seeking compatibility instead of conflict, credibility rather than a mission confrontation. This "bourgeois" Christianity is linked to an alleged diminishment of eschatological hope; as an interpretive paradigm, *christliche Bürgerlichkeit* ("Christian good citizenship") dominated the scholarly discussion of the PE in the 1970s to the 1990s.

(6) Finally, the vocabulary and style of the Pastorals are held to diverge so drastically from the those of main Pauline letters (Romans, Galatians, 1 and 2 Corinthians) that only non-Pauline authorship can account for the difference. Terms that dominate in the theology of the letters (e.g., "godliness," "sound teaching," "epiphany") and a distinctive penchant for Greek ethical language place the PE into a different category from the Pauline letters. Statistical studies have pointed to the higher frequency of *hapax legomena* when compared with the undisputed Paul;[40] connectives and particles common to the undisputed Paulines are absent from the PE; the language of the PE shows a greater attraction for certain later Hellenistic Jewish writings like *4 Maccabees* and *Testaments of the Twelve Patriarchs* than, as with the "earlier" Pauline writings, the LXX.

---

40. For our purposes, the following references are most representative: P. N. Harrison, *The Problem of the Pastoral Epistles* (Oxford: Oxford University Press, 1921); K. Grayston and G. Herdan, "The Authorship of the Pastoral Epistles in the Light of Statistical Linguistics," *NTS* 6 (1959-60): 1-15; and critique by T. A. Robinson, "Grayston and Herdan's 'C' Quantity Formula and the Authorship of the Pastoral Epistles," *NTS* 30 (1984): 282-88; cf. K. Neumann, *The Authenticity of the Pauline Epistles in the Light of Stylo-statistical Analysis* (Atlanta: Scholars, 1990). See the discussions in Roloff, 28-31; Marshall, 59-66.

In terms of style or genre, 1 Timothy and Titus have been placed alongside documents that take up community organization in various ways (in Qumran, *The Manual of Discipline* [1QS] and *The Damascus Document* [CD]; in the early postapostolic period, see *the Didache,* and later, in the third and fourth centuries, the *Didascalia Apostolorum* and the *Apostolic Constitutions*) or the Pseudo-Socratic writings. 2 Timothy has been compared with the testamentary literature contained in, for example, *Testaments of the Twelve Patriarchs, Testament of Job,* and *Testament of Moses.* The "testament" typically comprised the testimony of a patriarch on the verge of death that amounted to an ethical charge given to the children of the patriarch, which writing then was intended as an authoritative traditional witness to shape the present-day community.

While each item in the list is capable of other explanations, as we shall see, they do nevertheless form the basis of the critique of the modern consensus. From this starting point (often working with Baur's reconstruction of history), the PE were set into the second century as if into concrete.[41] Dibelius's influence could be seen everywhere — that the letters projected a general view, divorced from any particular historical situation, of a Christianity that for all practical purposes had become secularized.[42]

Thus what can indeed be called the majority interpretation assumed its distinctive proportions as the essential critical ingredients listed above were combined and recombined in numerous scholarly presentations. Confident assertions emerged. (1) The PE are pseudonymous, and doubts about this need no longer be seriously entertained.[43] (2) The letters form a unique literary corpus within the NT, which reflects a more fully developed theological and ecclesiastical situation than the genuine Paul. (3) Their provenance is an early second-century church setting, in which the expectation of Christ's return is no longer an evident influence for life. (4) This changed outlook had forced the church to adjust to living in relationship to the society

41. F. C. Baur, *Paulus der Apostel Jesu Christi* (2 vols.; 2d ed.; Leipzig: Fues, 1866-67; repr. Osnabrück: Zeller, 1968), 2:108-16; cf. the refinements in the application of H. J. Holtzmann, *Die Pastoralbriefe kritisch und exegetisch bearbeitet* (Leipzig: W. Engelmann, 1880), 84-252.

42. Dibelius and Conzelmann, *The Pastoral Epistles.*

43. See L. R. Donelson, *Pseudepigraphy and Ethical Argument in the Pastoral Epistles* (Tübingen: Mohr [Siebeck], 1986). If one explores the introductions to Roloff, Oberlinner, Weise, Hultgren, Houlden, Hasler, Merkel, Bassler, and Collins, one is immediately struck by the complete lack of anxiety over the issue of establishing or verifying pseudonymity as the likely view of authorship. It is simply regarded, as Johnson suggests, as "conventional wisdom."

in which it found itself; in this environment, the church's challenge had become that of maintaining the continuity of the gospel in this postapostolic time, and the appearance of heretics heightened that challenge.

While these elements form the core of the general consensus, recent more nuanced investigations of the PE as post-Pauline writings exhibit agreement on three additional conclusions that define the present state of the majority opinion. First, the teaching of the PE represents a coherent theological and ethical argument that may be thought to address a real church or churches somewhere in time. Second, the differences and distinctiveness of the "Pastor's" theology underscore the distance and discontinuity of the PE from the authentic Paul. Accordingly, differences discovered far outweigh any points of contact with the early and undisputed Paulines. And these differences are typically regarded as "findings" upon which a theory of the relation of the PE to Paul can be built. Paul was absorbed with the Jew/Gentile problem and with works of the law and faith, but in the PE such things are no longer relevant, and their dominant issues of succession and transmission of the gospel and ecclesiology are foreign to the earlier Paul. The differences are too great; Pauline theology has clearly spun off into a completely new orbit. Consequently, the third common element of the consensus is the conclusion that these letters belong to a late period when the transition from third- to fourth-generation Christianity was occurring (Timothy and Titus being reduced to fictive figures from the past).

Within this critical paradigm, the theology of the PE, then, has to be understood in terms of Pauline tradition *(Paulustradition),* not Pauline theology.[44] By co-opting Paul's name, the pseudepigrapher implies that he understands his task to be to interpret Paul. He knows Paul's letters, as his use of them indicates. He assumes that his readers also have knowledge of the Pauline correspondence. As an interpreter, he does not aim to supplant the

---

44. The view is held widely among English-speaking scholars; see Bassler, *1 Timothy, 2 Timothy, Titus;* F. Young, *The Theology of the Pastoral Letters* (Cambridge: Cambridge University Press, 1994); Donelson, *Pseudepigraphy and Ethical Argument in the Pastoral Epistles.* But the most substantial work at the exegetical level is still to be found in the German commentaries and monographs; J. Roloff, *Der erste Brief an Timotheus* (EKKNT 15; Zürich: Benziger, 1988); L. Oberlinner, *Die Pastoralbriefe: Erste Folge; Kommentar zum ersten Timotheusbrief* (HTKNT XI/2; Freiburg/Basel/Wien: Herder, 1994); N. Brox, *Die Pastoralbriefe* (RNT 7; Regensburg: F. Pustet, 1969). Less detailed commentaries such as those of V. Hasler (*Die Briefe an Timotheus und Titus (Pastoralbriefe)* [ZBNT; Zürich: Theologischer Verlag, 1978]) and H. Merkel (*Die Pastoralbriefe* [NTD 9/1; Göttingen: Vandenhoeck & Ruprecht, 1991]) confirm that the consensus is that the PE are second-century or late-first-century documents that will be understood only with this in mind. Significant monographs and detailed articles provide grist for this particular mill.

genuine Pauline letters and so eliminate the influence of Paul. Rather, he will appeal to the firm basis of the Pauline gospel (using the name of the apostle) to provide solutions to the new problems of his situation. The author does not create his own theology, as concepts such as "the deposit" *(parathēkē)* show (1 Tim 6:20; 2 Tim 1:12, 14); he has consciously limited his own task to interpreting Paul for later practical situations for which the already existing Pauline letters to churches lack the necessary practical teaching.[45]

An interpretation working from this pseudonymous angle cannot simply refer to the "occasion" of the writing, as is done in works that take personal and historical references in the NT letters at face value. Instead one finds in the current expressions of the consensus view various attempts to create a profile of the author (who produced this Pauline tradition) and his community — the "real" audience. Numerous permutations may be found in the scholarly literature. But some of the more typical descriptions place the author (and his church) at a point of crisis or change in which Paul needs to be reinterpreted for the new situation.[46] The nature of this crisis or change is explained variously. The earliest reconstructions tended to pit the author against heretical interest groups in the church who had taken up Pauline theology as a way of backing such things as asceticism and emancipation among women and slaves. Or spun differently, as is more the current fashion, the author can be seen as reacting against women who have risen to leadership positions — who in fact are truer to Paul's original gospel-freedom impulse than even the later Paul himself was able to be. As the argument goes, the author's preference, and his solution, is to stabilize the church by returning it soundly to the patriarchal values associated with the household and enshrined in the NT household code tradition — by bringing back into line unruly teachers, women, and young widows who have as-

45. See G. Kretschmar, "Der paulinische Glaube in den Pastoralbriefen," in F. Hahn and H. Klein, eds., *Glaube im Neuen Testament* (FS H. Binder) (BTS 7; Neukirchen-Vluyn: Neukirchener, 1982), 135-36; M. Harding, *Tradition and Rhetoric in the Pastoral Epistles* (Studies in Biblical Literature 3; New York: Peter Lang, 1998), especially concentrates on the literary and rhetorical forms in which "the Pastor" accesses, interprets, and actualizes the "Pauline tradition."

46. See M. Y. MacDonald, *The Pauline Churches: A Socio-Historical Study of Institutionalization in the Pauline and Deutero-Pauline Writings* (SNTSMS 60; Cambridge: Cambridge University Press, 1988). The theory is developed in greater detail in the German literature: Roloff, 23-39, 376-82; Oberlinner, XLII-L; P. Trummer, *Die Paulustradition der Pastoralbriefe* (BET 8; Frankfurt: Lang, 1978); M. Wolter, *Die Pastoralbriefe als Paulustradition* (FRLANT 146; Göttingen: Vandenhoeck & Ruprecht, 1988), 11-25, 245-56. Most recent is A. Merz, *Die fiktive Selbstauslegung des Paulus: Intertextuelle Studien zur Intention und Rezeption der Pastoralbriefe* (NTOA/SUNT 52; Göttingen: Vandenhoeck & Ruprecht, 2004), esp. 195-375.

sumed roles and entered into activities that threaten the author's conservative categories.[47]

As I view the scholarly situation, there are gains and losses. While the majority view's more recent conclusion that the PE present a coherent theology and a real setting in history might be an improvement over the older view that regarded the letters as simply a haphazard collection of traditions and Pauline memorabilia (as well as rather lame forgeries), it has evolved into a monolithic, rigid interpretive framework that rests on assumptions and creative reconstructions. These assumptions shape the interpretive methodology of the consensus; and this determines and in some ways restricts the understanding of the theology of these letters that results. What needs to be shown here is that the key assumptions and the methodology are neither airtight nor particularly compelling when objectively considered.

2. Assessing the Modern Paradigm

The effectiveness of the majority approach may be questioned on the level of broad assumptions and on the level of its treatment of specific issues of interpretation, though almost always these two matters are closely bound together. Several characteristic features of the pseudonymity view will be considered below.

a. Pseudonymity

Clearly, the most all-encompassing assumption is a particular view of the phenomenon called pseudonymity.[48] Its application to the authorship problem of the PE can be seen as a solution that sought a middle ground between the earliest critical view — in which a judgment of non-Pauline authorship

---

47. With some variation, see, e.g., the D. R. MacDonald, *The Legend and the Apostle: The Battle for Paul in Story and Canon* (Philadelphia: Fortress, 1983); E. Schüssler-Fiorenza, *In Memory of Her: A Feminist Theological Reconstruction of Christian Origins* (New York: Crossroad, 1983), 288-91; Bassler; U. Wagener, *Die Ordnung des "Hauses Gottes": Der Ort von Frauen in der Ekklesiologie und Ethik der Pastoralbriefe* (WUNT 2.65; Tübingen: Mohr [Siebeck], 1994); see the commentary at 2:9-15; 5:11-15; Merz, *Die fiktive Selbstauslegung des Paulus*, 245-375.

48. See esp. R. Bauckham, *Jude, 2 Peter* (WBC 50; Waco, TX: Word, 1983), 158-62; Donelson, *Pseudepigraphy and Ethical Argument in the Pastoral Epistles;* D. G. Meade, *Pseudonymity and Canon: An Investigation into the Relationship of Authorship and Authority in Jewish and Earliest Christian Tradition* (WUNT 39; Tübingen: J. C. B. Mohr [Paul Siebeck], 1986); T. L. Wilder, *Pseudonymity, the New Testament and Deception* (Lanham, MD: University Press of America, 2004); see discussions in Marshall, 79-83; Mounce, cxxiii-cxxvii.

meant "forgery" and at best a reduced authority within the canon — and the unpalatable conservative insistence on authenticity. Existence of the practice of pseudonymity in the ancient world is well documented. And studies of the phenomenon in Greco-Roman and Jewish cultures have shown that it was a literary means of drawing on ancient authoritative voices to address current situations, and, most significantly, that the process was accepted and understood by the communities and free from allegations of deception.[49]

However, this understanding and use of the device are better attested in Intertestamental Judaism and in the Greco-Roman philosophical schools than in early Christianity,[50] and the widespread assumption drawn from this wider practice for the composition of the PE is problematic. In the first place, the indication from those who were first confronted with pseudonymous or pseudepigraphical apostolic writings is that they were not accepted as benign, well-intentioned writings but as substandard fakes to be rejected.[51] Secondly, in the case of the Jewish (especially) and Greco-Roman examples of pseudonymous writings that bore authority, the time between the ancient co-opted author and the receiving community could be considerable. But in the case of the PE there simply does not exist the amount of time between the apostle and the supposed later receiving church for the theory to work. In Paul's day, letters written by others in his name were challenged as fraudulent (2 Thess 2:2). In subsequent generations letters written in Paul's name but known to be otherwise were excluded from the canon.[52] Yet during this period the letters to Timothy and Titus were generally received and used as Pauline and authoritative (the heretical Marcion and a few others, of course, dismissed them; see above).

What has happened in the case of the majority interpretation is that a known practice that applies in certain circumstances has also been assumed to apply in the case of the PE. This assumption, it has to be said, is not only far from proven but in fact remains quite problematical. Yet in much of NT scholarship it has passed into the realm of the unassailable, reliable "facts" upon which the consensus view is founded.

49. Donelson, Meade, and esp. Wilder (who insists that in the Christian context, anyway, with an awareness of pseudonymity went the assessment of deception) will need to be compared.

50. See Donelson, *Pseudepigraphy and Ethical Argument in the Pastoral Epistles,* 11-12; Wilder, *Pseudonymity;* cf. Marshall, 82-83.

51. E.g., Tertullian, *On Baptism* 17.

52. Notably *3 Corinthians; The Letter to the Laodiceans; Letters of Paul and Seneca.*

b. Illegitimate Historical Disjunctions

Within this category are several planks in the majority view that are wobbly indeed. A first problem is the way in which apostolic authorship has been denied[53] on the basis of questionable criteria.[54] On the historical level, the matter of locating the letters to Timothy and Titus within the Pauline ministry attested by the undisputed letters and Acts is a genuine problem, but it is not necessarily an insoluble one. The question is whether the only way out of the difficulty is to follow the majority interpretation into the second century.

If we compare for a moment the traditional way of dealing with this and the route taken by the majority view, we find an interesting correspondence. Each side assumes that Paul's movements in 1 Timothy and Titus cannot be reconciled with the chronology provided by Luke in Acts and by Paul's letters to churches. As a consequence, many proponents of authenticity have proposed a release and second arrest theory, on the basis of the later traditions that Paul was released from a first Roman imprisonment and preached in Spain, after which he was rearrested and executed (see above). For proponents of the majority view, negotiating the apparent disjunction is easier. It is assumed that any such historical coloring is simply part of the letters' fiction. The letters might bear some historical connection with post-Pauline Ephesus or Crete, or they might not; but either way, the constructed "context" of the letters' composition can be adjusted as need be.

There is a third way of considering these letters in relation to Paul that does not begin with the assumption of a disjunction. Some, as we've seen, attempt to place the three letters to coworkers within the known travels of Paul.[55] This approach begins with the acknowledgment that Luke's and Paul's accounts of mission movements contain gaps and chronologies are incomplete, and this is a significant observation and an indisputable fact. The problems begin, however, when reconstructions seek to place the movements indicated by 1 Timothy and Titus into those gaps with too much precision (see above). But we will explore this option further below.

What seems highly questionable is whether the place to start "locating" the letters to Timothy and Titus in relation to Paul's letters to churches and historical mission is with the assumption of a disjunction. Is it necessary to assume that references to geography and mission movements in 1 Timothy and Titus cannot be reconciled with the historical Pauline mission? Paul and Luke would in fact seem to challenge the assumption. Not only does Paul

---

53. And in some cases affirmed — the methodology of the traditional interpretation could also stand some fine-tuning.

54. See the excellent discussion in Johnson, 78-90; idem, *Paul's Delegates,* 21-26.

55. See n. 38 above.

mention activities and adventures that have escaped Luke's attention or interest (2 Cor 11:23-29), but the sweep and imprecision of Lukan summary statements open up numerous possibilities (e.g., Acts 20:1-3). This means that there are indeed considerable gaps in the record. The nature of the documents may caution against attempting too much precision in offering reconstructions, but being limited to provisional explanations is no reason to dismiss the effort.[56] Perhaps these three letters should test previously accepted notions of Pauline chronology and movement; the nature of the data from Acts and Paul is not such as should rule out the attempt.

c. Illegitimate Literary Disjunctions

On the literary level, it has been assumed that the undisputed letters of Paul represent a more or less fixed Pauline "style." This is misleading for at least two reasons. First, it is possible that more than one hand or mind was involved in writing at least some of Paul's letters to churches. His use of amanuenses is acknowledged by all. But in fact our actual knowledge of the writing situation and process is incomplete, and the idea that Paul wrote or dictated his letters all in one go, without various kinds of input from his colleagues, is possibly far too simplistic. Second, the letters of Paul that no one disputes are not uniform in style, and, as Johnson insists, "style" must be considered from a first-century perspective, not a modern Western one.[57] An ancient Hellenistic writer adopted the style that suited the occasion; the argument that Paul's style is shaped by his personality (a modern notion) does not apply. Some of Paul's letters employ diatribe, others do not; some employ what seems akin to Jewish midrash style, others do not. The occasion or need determined the style adopted. What must be asked with regard to the letters to Timothy and Titus is what "style" best suited the situations Paul sought to address, and what stylistic options may have been open to him, whether or not he exercised these options in the letters to churches.

The assumptions selected for consideration, and the questions raised about them, are of the type that might require some reshaping of the traditional interpretation. Yet they pose a greater challenge to the majority view, which concludes that the letters are pseudonymous. Whatever advantages this view appears to offer by positing a pseudonymous follower of Paul as author — thus accounting for Pauline similarities and differences all at once — are really imaginary in view of the serious flaws in assumptions and methodology. At this point, some additional loose bricks in this majority foundation can be identified, some of which need to be explored further.

56. A point well made by Johnson, *Paul's Delegates,* 11.
57. See Johnson, 60, and sources cited.

First, the case for pseudonymity as a model for the composition of the letters to Timothy and Titus has been questioned already. But with it go some further assumptions that are individually suspect. For example, in general the majority view takes a considerably simplistic view of the three letters as a corpus. A corpus reading of the letters is essential to the theory, but it has always been difficult to fit Titus into such a scheme. This corpus approach to the letters ignores the specificity and uniqueness of each letter (see below).

Second, as we saw above, there is good evidence of a fairly early and uniform acceptance of these letters by Clement (c. 95) and Ignatius (c. 115). And the impression gleaned from these early witnesses seems to indicate that the apostolic age had been closed for some time. If these letters were regarded as apostolic, their distance from the witnesses makes the assumption of pseudonymity problematic. Attempts to place the PE into the second century do not acknowledge the very real historical problems of doing so (see above), and the failure of the view to address the problems reveals a methodological flaw and a unilateralism that is objectionable.

Third, behind the conclusion of non-Pauline authorship and the eventual evolution of pseudonymity is the insistence that the PE are different from the undisputed Pauline letters. Here we encounter another illegitimate disjunction. It is far too convenient for the majority view to elevate the areas of alleged Pauline dissimilarity as evidence of discontinuity while dismissing the points of similarity as part of a fiction. This is a methodological flaw. On this same basis any undisputed Pauline writing could be found wanting. In fact, little attention is given to the dissimilarity that exists between any individual Pauline letter when stacked up against some set or cluster of the others. This way of treating the evidence skews the assessment in the necessary direction. But it is hardly a fair treatment of the evidence. There are a number of significant points at which the letters to Timothy and Titus reflect what is clearly an organic connection with Paul's other letters (see the commentary at 1 Tim 1:19-20; 2:8, 11-14; 5:17-18; 2 Tim 1:7-8; 2:11; Titus 2:14; 3:5-7). There will always be ways to "explain" away these discrete "similarities," but when they are coupled with broader shared themes and tendencies that permeate the undisputed Paul, the case is strengthened for a unified mind behind the writings compared. At the same time, the dissimilarities that are allowed to overrule are often assessed on the basis of a skewed compilation of data.[58]

58. As Johnson, *Paul's Delegates,* 11-12 (and throughout the commentary), pointed out in relation to statistical studies, the allegedly "non-Pauline" vocabulary (i.e., absent from the selection of Pauline letters deemed to reflect "the way Paul wrote") tends to occur in passages taken up with heresy or other topics not addressed in the authoritative sample; cf. the comments in M. Prior, *Paul the Letter-Writer and the Second Letter to Timothy* (JSNTS 23; Sheffield: Sheffield Academic Press, 1989), 29-32; D. A. deSilva, *An Introduction to the New Testament* (Downers Grove, IL: InterVarsity Press, 2004), 737-38.

It is typical to compare the letters to Timothy and Titus with a restricted "mini-Pauline corpus," minus Colossians, Ephesians, and 2 Thessalonians.[59] If these three letters were added to the sample, the index of dissimilarity would drop significantly.

Fourth, and again falling out from the assumption of pseudonymity, is the question of the adequacy of the social and ecclesiastical reconstructions given in support of this theory of composition. It need only be said that the author/community profiles introduced above, while possible, bear little resemblance to anything known to have existed. There is a lack of any evidence for the putative Pauline school or community that might have had the authority in the eyes of the later church to accomplish such a literary feat, unless the three letters themselves are counted as evidence of its existence.[60] On the sliding scale from plausibility to implausibility, this should at least move the theory of pseudonymity somewhere to the middle and require it to be given at best "provisional" status. But this seems not to be an acknowledged weakness for the view that is now simply assumed.

C. THE SEARCH FOR A HISTORICAL MIDDLE GROUND: "ALLONYMITY"

I. H. Marshall finds himself caught somewhere in the middle ground. On the one hand, he is convinced that the language of the letters (vocabulary, connective particles, elements that might be attributed to style) distance them too far from the undisputed letters to attribute them equally to Paul. On the other hand, he feels that the teaching of the letters and situations they address conform reasonably to what might be expected in the time following closely on his death. He is also unconvinced by the case for pseudonymity.

To navigate this treacherous middle ground, Marshall suggests the term "allonymity"[61] to define an authorial process that might close the gap between the apostle and the author who co-opts his name, in a way that allows escape from the allegations of deception and falsehood in the process. He explains that either the student or follower of Paul edits the notes of the deceased apostle, or he steps into the shoes of the dead apostle and carries the master's teaching forward for future generations in a manner that is faithful to earlier apostolic intentions, even if the key of the theological score has

59. See P. H. Towner, "Pauline Theology or Pauline Tradition in the Pastoral Epistles: The Question of Method," *TynB* 46.2 (1995): 287-314; Johnson, 82.

60. See the excellent discussion in Johnson, *Paul's Delegates,* 21-33.

61. Marshall, 83-84; cf. J. D. G. Dunn, *DLNTD* 977-84; Easton, 21; the classic fragments theory is that of Harrison, *The Problem of the Pastoral Epistles.*

been transposed. Examples of this might be found in the philosophical schools, and some aver that Colossians and Ephesians represent letters of the same type. The view allows that the letters to Timothy and Titus, and 2 Timothy especially, may well contain authentic Pauline fragments that a follower worked into the three letters after Paul's death. At some point between the time of their writing and early circulation and the time of the Fathers who first mention them, the "allonymous" authorship of the letters was forgotten and the earliest witnesses attribute them to the apostle.

Considering the shortcomings of the standard view of pseudonymity and the problems that exist for Pauline authorship, "allonymity" is not an unattractive alternative. The gains may be seen in the respect shown for the basic historical shape of the letters — Ephesus and Crete become real destinations, Timothy and Titus may have had some real role in relation to the situations they depict, and the letters may well have originated in the shadows of Paul's death. But there remains a rather undeniable "if" in this whole proposition. This solution explains the dissimilarities with Pauline style and theology and retains for the letters an unsullied (if slightly derivative) apostolic authority *if* the procedure, code-named "allonymity," was in fact regarded as acceptable in the early church that first received the "allonymous" letters. Marshall cites the fortunes of Hebrews, with its confused links to Paul, as an example of a letter that acquired canonical status even though its links to the apostle were lost. But, of course, given the anonymity of the letter to the Hebrews, the analogy is not perfect.

At this point in time, given the nature of the evidence in support of it and the fact that the earliest attestation of the letters is Pauline (along with those of Colossians and Ephesians), the "allonymity" hypothesis remains a not implausible solution to the authorship problem. It improves significantly on pseudonymity, but the jury continues to deliberate.

It is not possible to prove the authenticity of the letters to Timothy and Titus. The problems raised are on both the literary and the historical levels. The question is whether a reasonable case can be made that places them within the Pauline orbit. At this point, while we await further evidence of "allonymity," I will assess some of the more crucial literary and historical issues before framing a hypothesis that locates the letters within Paul's mission ministry.

IV. READING THE LETTERS IN HISTORICAL CONTEXT

A. THE LITERARY CHARACTER OF THE LETTERS TO TIMOTHY AND TITUS

The concern here is chiefly with the way in which the nature of these letters as compositions has been understood and the way in which their interrelationships should be explained.

1. The Unity and Individuality of the Letters

The most widely held view of the letters' composition and interrelationship is that one author wrote them all. From time to time this has been challenged, usually along the lines argued by J. Murphy-O'Connor to the effect that 2 Timothy was written by Paul, 1 Timothy and Titus by someone else.[62] But this sort of argument faces daunting challenges. First, the language shared among the three letters includes key terms such as *eusebeia* and *epiphaneia,* and numerous ethical terms (see the Excursuses) in a way that immediately suggests a single author.[63] Second, the letters' way of presenting theology and ethics reflects a unified approach and a single dominant mind.[64] Third, the evidence of continuity that links the letters to Timothy and sets them off in some respects from Titus — such as personalia, themes and concerns, and language (e.g., *parathēkē,* 1 Tim 6:20; 2 Tim 1:12, 14) — strongly indicates that these two letters share a single author.

2 Timothy is more personal and is often held to be more like a "typical" Pauline letter than 1 Timothy and Titus — the latter are closer to one another than to 2 Timothy in character, genre, and purpose. Such differences are hardly unexpected, however, if the likely influence of the different situations addressed and the changed circumstances of the writer presupposed by the letters are taken into account. Additionally, recent evaluation of the literary forms of these writings within a wider range of stylistic options open to Paul and his contemporaries (see below), along with considerations of the complexity of the process behind the composition of Paul's letters, suggests that perhaps other differences are partly a matter of the forms in which the author chose to write.

---

62. J. Murphy-O'Connor, "2 Timothy Contrasted with 1 Timothy and Titus," *RB* (1991): 403-10; idem, *Paul: A Critical Life,* 356-59; cf. Prior, *Paul the Letter-Writer,* 168.

63. See Marshall, 1-2; Oberlinner, *Erster Timotheusbrief,* xxii-xxiii.

64. See P. H. Towner, *The Goal of Our Instruction* (JSNTS 34: Sheffield: Sheffield Academic Press, 1989).

Two questions emerge from these initial decisions about the letters' unity. First, to what extent are they to be considered as a group, a three-part corpus that was written to be interpreted as a single piece? Second, how are they to be related to the rest of the Pauline writings? As we saw above, it is characteristic of the majority interpretation to read the letters as a distinctly unified corpus. The pseudonymous theory requires it,[65] but this is a most disadvantageous conclusion for the interpretation of the letters.[66] The inevitable outcome of this assumption is that one letter will be read as the interpretive guide to another, and local elements in the letters are then disregarded as having little or no significance for interpretation.

An intentional corpus reading of the letters is unwarranted. First, there are no internal clues to suggest that they originated from the same place or time, or that they are to be read as a single literary unit. From a general perspective, the letters read as separate messages, and where language and themes overlap, each letter nevertheless employs them to achieve unique literary objectives.

1 Timothy manifestly treats a situation in which in various ways false teaching has troubled a church that has existed for some time. The solution is to reassert the sound apostolic gospel, resist unruly behavior (2:8-15; 5:9-15; 6:1-2), maintain strong leadership in the church (3:1-13; 5:17-25), pay attention to prayer and other aspects of orderly worship (2:1; 4:13), and model the life of godliness that others must take up.

The letter to Titus is in many ways similar, but the needs of the Cretan churches are rather different. In the face of both opposition and the lingering Cretan influence on life, the coworker was to set in place strong leadership (1:5-9) and ensure that life lived in the ordinary context of the household was demonstrably Christian (2:1-10). In that setting, the public image of the church is the specific focal point (3:1-2, 8), and reversing cultural habits in the behavior of Christians is the key to shoring up its public profile. The theological basis given for the ethical instruction (2:11-14; 3:5-7) makes clear that the behavior enjoined was to be understood as the appropriate out-

65. Roloff, 43-45; see also Young, *The Theology of the Pastoral Letters,* 136-41; Trummer, *Paulustradition der Pastoralbriefe,* 72-78, 97-105. J. D. Quinn represents the extreme example of this approach: he maintained that the PE together comprised Vol. 3 of Luke's writings: "The Last Volume of Luke: The Relation of Luke-Acts to the Pastoral Epistles," in C. H. Talbert, ed., *Perspectives on Luke-Acts* (Danville, VA: Association of Baptist Professors of Religion, 1978), 62-75; idem, *The Letter to Titus* (AB 35; New York: Doubleday, 1990), 17-21.

66. The logical problem that immediately challenges any such corpus theory of composition is the letter to Titus: as it is, its existence in the "corpus" simply disrupts what might have been a rather believable two-part fiction. Roloff, 44, is aware of the difficulty, though he is unable to resolve it.

working of the grace of God in human relationships in various forms of godliness (*eusebeia;* 2:12; see commentary).

2 Timothy shares themes and language that occur in 1 Timothy and Titus, and the heresy of Ephesus is a continuing concern (2:14-18; 3:1-9). But this letter is far more personal and deeply concerned with Timothy's personal welfare and faithfulness. It begins by reminding Timothy of his relationship with Paul and his similar calling. He is to follow Paul's model (1:11-13; 2:8-10; 3:10-17; 4:6-7) as he prepares to join Paul. Both in coming to Rome to be with Paul and in continuing the apostle's ministry, Timothy will encounter suffering (1:8; 2:3; 3:12; 4:5). Paul's tone is one of finality; Timothy must get to Rome before the end, and, presumably, from there carry the mission on to completion. Within the NT it is 2 Timothy that concludes the Pauline story.

The individuality of the letters seems evident. Yet equally evident are certain linguistic and conceptual elements that traverse the three letters,[67] linking them with one another and distinguishing them slightly from the rest of the Pauline writings. These elements of continuity should not be overstressed, but they nevertheless justify recognizing that the three letters form a second important contextual horizon, one ring out from the individual compositions themselves, within which the meanings of language and concepts can be explored. Consequently, unless there are compelling reasons to do otherwise, after following all leads in the letter itself, we ought to look to Titus, for example, to understand language and argumentation in 1 Timothy. Afterward, we may move outward to the next horizon of the rest of the Pauline writings, which differ more noticeably in terms of situation, style, and language. In other words, in reading the letters to Timothy and Titus we must acknowledge both their individuality and their unity and interrelationship.

But there will be compelling reasons to read phrases, texts, and passages of these letters within other literary contexts. Most notably, Paul frequently engages OT texts in addressing his coworkers and through them the churches under their charge. While the reason he does so will, at least in part, be detectable within the immediate literary horizon of the letter (or even within the co-text), exploration of the materials and story accessed by intertextual echo will be necessary for Paul's intended meaning, motivation, and application to be discerned.[68] Less frequently Paul sets elements of these

---

67. Note, e.g., leadership concerns in 1 Timothy and Titus and the way in which these are expressed, and the presumed location of these two letters within the Pauline mission; personalia and the presence of heresy link the two letters to Timothy.

68. See P. H. Towner, "The Old Testament in the Letters to Timothy and Titus," in D. A. Carson and G. K. Beale eds., *Commentary on the Use of the Old Testament in the New Testament* (Grand Rapids: Baker, forthcoming). See the commentary at 1 Tim 2:5, 8, 13-15; 4:3-4; 5:18-20; 2 Tim 2:7, 19; 3:8, 11; 4:14, 16-18; Titus 2:14; 3:4-6.

compositions into a literary relationship with his own writings or proclamation,[69] and with the Jesus tradition either directly[70] or as it has been transposed in the church's growing tradition.[71] And the attempt must also be made
to measure the pulse of his language and the intention of his message against
what is known to have been the current coded language and thrust of the
dominant stories broadcast by the cultural political/religious powers.[72]

Yet this way of reading applies to all individual compositions. Any
part of a composition is first to be read on the basis of the composition to
which it belongs; additional relevant contextual horizons will surely exist
and must be considered in the proper balance. The point to be made in the
case of these three letters is that the corpus status thrust upon them by the
modern paradigm is as unwarranted as it is simplistically understood. The interrelationships are more subtle, and each letter's individuality and independence are more fundamental to a fair reading of its message.

Johnson's term to describe the letters' simultaneous individuality and
attraction is "cluster." He applies it appropriately to other groupings of Pauline letters (1-2 Corinthians; 1-2 Thessalonians; Ephesians-Colossians;
Romans-Galatians) — groupings in which writings that are clearly individual letters nevertheless bear historical, linguistic, and thematic affinity for
one another. Apart from an authorship hypothesis that requires a corpus or
trilogy conclusion, a term like "cluster" seems a better way of describing the
interrelationship of the letters to Timothy and Titus.

The canonical organization of these letters was according to length,
starting with letters to churches and followed by letters to individuals.[73] From
the standpoint of the part of the Pauline story they tell, it is undoubtedly best
to regard the developments to be moving historically from 1 Timothy and
Titus[74] to 2 Timothy. The relationship between 1 Timothy and 2 Timothy is
clear enough. Titus is to be placed earlier than 2 Timothy because of the interests it shares with 1 Timothy and the picture it presents of a Paul for whom

69. See on 1 Tim 2:6; 2 Tim 1:7; 2:11; Titus 2:14; 3:4-6.
70. See on 1 Tim 5:18; 6:19; 2 Tim 2:12.
71. See on 1 Tim 1:20; 5:20; Titus 3:10.
72. See on 1 Tim 3:16; 6:14; 2 Tim 4:14-16; Titus 1:12; 2:11-13.
73. See H. Y. Gamble, "Canon, New Testament" (B.2.a), n.p., *ABD on CD-ROM.*
Version 2.1a. 1995, 1996, 1997.
74. Which of these two letters is actually first is impossible to tell — although Titus addresses a more primitive situation than that of Ephesus, it may still have followed
1 Timothy. Those convinced that the letters are not directly from the hand of Paul but are
based on and to some degree constructed from authentic Pauline fragments generally find
these in greater abundance in 2 Timothy. On this view, 2 Timothy is thought to be
compositionally prior to 1 Timothy and Titus, though in terms of historical settings depicted the situation might be reversed (cf. Easton, 17-18; Marshall, 1-2).

imprisonment is not a factor. In any case, 2 Timothy purports to be the last letter of Paul.[75]

2. The Literary Character of the Letters

1 and 2 Timothy and Titus give the impression of being personal letters. But they contain a curious combination of materials. Sayings and theological pieces that stand out within their contexts occur in greater proportion than elsewhere in Paul. When we add the way these letters shift from personal to public advice, we have a set of literary features that gives these letters to co-workers a shape that is distinctive within the broader Pauline corpus. Of course this peculiarity has also raised endless suspicions about authorship among interpreters. On the basis of the nature of the contents alone, the letters are argued to be some distance from the authentic Paul. And the alternation between public and private address seems to some precisely what should be expected of pseudonymous letters in which "Timothy" and "Titus" serve merely fictional literary purposes in letters designed to encourage later churches to cherish the apostle and receive his teaching in adapted form. One scholar formulates the dilemma in this way: "The Pastorals claim to be personal letters from the apostle Paul to his two co-workers . . . but . . . they do not seem to be what they claim to be."[76] This problem needs to be addressed. But we turn first to the materials themselves.

The materials occurring in the letters probably came from a variety of sources. 1 Tim 3:1-13 and Titus 1:5-9 possibly reflect the reworking of codes developed to regulate the selection of overseers/elders and deacons. It is not certain where they originated, and the proposals range from composition in ecclesiastical circles (possibly the church at Rome)[77] to the secular domain.[78] As I will attempt to show in the commentary, whatever sources might lie behind these "codes," Paul has adapted them carefully for inclusion in these letters. And this adaptation will shed more light on interpretation.

The early church's common ethical teaching was the source of Paul's "household code" style of instruction: 1 Tim 2:8-15; 5:1-2; 6:1-2; Titus 2:1–3:8. In writing 1 Timothy and Titus, Paul adapts the form that in broader NT use originally addressed the Christian household. The original application of the device from secular ethics to Christian use reflects the conviction that just

---

75. See P. H. Towner, "The Portrait of Paul and the Theology of 2 Timothy: The Closing Chapter of the Pauline Story," *HBT* 21.2 (1999): 151-70.

76. J. D. Miller, *The Pastoral Letters as Composite Documents* (SNTSMS 93; Cambridge University Press, 1997), 1.

77. See E. E. Ellis, *Pauline Theology: Ministry and Society* (Grand Rapids: Eerdmans, 1989), 107-11, esp. 111.

78. E.g., Dibelius and Conzelmann, 50-51.

as the household was regarded as the epicenter of social life in the Greek and Roman world, so too in the Christian community the household is to provide the first authentic reflection of Christian faith and godliness. Additional instructions, according to socioeconomic or official categories, concerning widows (1 Tim 5:3-16), elders (5:17-25), and the wealthy (6:17-19), may be patterned after the household code, and it is likely that these themes and teaching were also current outside the Pauline orbit.

Theological material, such as hymns, creeds, baptism and (perhaps) ordination vows, and other preaching formulas, had accumulated over time. Such materials are often thought to be employed in 1 Tim 1:15-16; 2:3-6; 3:16; 2 Tim 1:9-10; 2:8-13; Titus 2:11-14; 3:5-7. But again in each case the evidence of special shaping for present literary and community needs makes clear that Paul has made the items his own, and in some cases he possibly creates them himself (see the commentary).

The so-called "trustworthy saying" formula is one of those literary peculiarities that link the three letters together into a cluster. It sometimes appears to have a more theological thrust (1 Tim 1:15; 2 Tim 2:11; Titus 3:8) and sometimes a more ethical thrust (1 Tim 3:1; 4:9).[79]

In the discussion above, I introduced the need at times to read the letters against other writings. Here those other writings can be considered sources upon which Paul drew. As we saw, these include the Jesus tradition and sayings from OT and Intertestamental Wisdom and apocryphal writings. However, Paul was not slow to cite and adapt secular wisdom if the situation called for it,[80] for its popular appeal and motivational value would lend impact to his discourse. He also seems to have occasionally cited, adapted, or in some sense redeployed his own earlier teaching themes or compositions. Although this latter tendency is normally viewed as prime evidence of post-Pauline authorship, one has to wonder whether this might not rather be typical of an authentic Paul writing to coworkers who knew his materials. If, as I will argue in the commentary, a recurring issue is opposition to Paul's authority and gospel in the churches to which Timothy and Titus are sent, then it is all the more reasonable for Paul to guide his coworkers in the task of correction by alluding to elements of what had become the Pauline gospel.

A dominant feature of the letters to Timothy and Titus is their deployment of an array of well-known terminology current in Hellenistic ethics. One of many instances is the triad of virtues that appears in Titus 2:12, which correspond to the Greek cardinal virtues: "self-controlled, upright, and godly." These terms and the comparative frequency of their occurrence, and

---

79. G. W. Knight III, *The Faithful Sayings in the Pastoral Letters* (Grand Rapids: Baker, 1979).

80. See on 1 Tim 6:7-10; Titus 1:12.

others such as the dominant term *eusebeia* ("piety" or "godliness"), are part of what creates the gravitational force that pulls the letters together uniquely within the broader Pauline corpus. Again, many see this literary "innovation" as evidence of non-Pauline authorship and of a secular dip of the Christian moral barometer. But such an interpretation is far from evident because the theological basis he supplies for his ethics makes clear that this Paul does not endorse a secular ethic. Instead for various reasons he has chosen to articulate his view of authentic Christian living in unmistakably Hellenistic language.[81] It is the reason for using the language, not the language itself, that determines meaning and intention.

The question is how to account for this diversity of materials and their oscillation between public and private concerns. For a time it was popular with some scholars to conclude that these writings represent early examples of the form known as a "church order." This type of document combined various traditional materials and catechisms that could be read aloud and easily memorized by new believers preparing for baptism, or by men about to become ordained ministers. Others, noting the mixture of personal and public materials, argue for their "composite" nature.[82] In either case, the fictional roles of "Timothy" and "Titus" are thought to be verified by the overt public intention of the letters. Such solutions demand that the letters belong to a time subsequent to Paul's ministry. 2 Timothy, however, with its much more personal tone and different interests, becomes the odd one out.

The question is whether there are not other literary antecedents that might explain the shape of the letters. This feature of combining disparate elements in a single document has also been found to characterize other types of writing known to have been current in Paul's time. C. Spicq, who maintained the authenticity of the three letters, broke decisive ground in comparing these letters with a range of Greek government documents of the ancient era: decrees, mandates, and memoranda.[83] He focused on the tendency of the PE to alternate between public and private concerns, on the situation of a superior addressing a subordinate, and on parallels with the ethical language employed.[84]

---

81. See Towner, *Goal,* 143-68; S. C. Mott, "Greek Ethics and Christian Conversion: The Philonic Background of Titus 2.10-14 and 3.3-7," *NovT* 20 (1978): 22-48; Quinn, 282-91. See the commentary at 1 Tim 2:2, 9-10; 3:2-7; 5:9-10; 6:11; Titus 1:6-8; 2:2-10, 12; 3:3; etc.

82. Miller, *The Pastoral Letters.*

83. See not only his discussion in the 1969 (fourth) edition that is consulted throughout this commentary, but also his earlier conclusion from 1947 (first ed.).

84. Spicq, 35-36: he also brought to the attention of NT scholars the work done on the third-century-B.C.E. papyrus known as P. Tebt. 703. With this heavily reconstructed text, Spicq constructed a literary background for the letters that could account for the mix of ordinances, decrees, administrative emphases, and apparent elements of personal ethics.

But he was not inclined to establish a specific genre template for the PE from among the network of ancient texts with which he compared them.

This latter task was taken up by B. Fiore and M. Wolter. Fiore examined the Hellenistic diplomatic documents and noticed certain similarities with the PE (the form of the writing, a superior addressing a subordinate who represents him, the public character, and a degree of mixture of official decree and exhortation),[85] as well as differences. And in view of the latter, he found a closer resemblance to the pseudepigraphical letters of Socrates and his students and Seneca's *Moral Epistles.*

Wolter took the matter further, making a helpful generic distinction that placed 1 Timothy/Titus into one category and 2 Timothy into another. Through his thorough study of possibly relevant written forms surrounding the time of the PE,[86] he concluded that 1 Timothy and Titus were similar in form and function to the body of royal correspondence known as *mandata principis* (mandates of a ruler). Comparable features include the alternation between third-person plural imperatives (public instructions or decrees) and second-person singular imperatives (addressed to the subordinate-delegate entrusted to bear the message and to serve among the wider group of addressees).[87]

What seems less certain, especially in view of the recent examination carried out by M. M. Mitchell,[88] is whether the further refinement in this genre search made by Johnson can be accepted without some qualification. Johnson went back to one of the documents (P. Tebt. 703 — a third-century-B.C.E. Ptolemaic "memorandum"), of which a rather crucial section is heavily reconstructed,[89] and identified it as the genre template of the "*mandata principis* letters."[90] The main issue here is whether the *mandata principis* documents belong to the letter genre (Johnson), to which 1 Timothy and Titus with their epistolary openings and closings clearly belong, or should be

85. B. Fiore, *The Function of Personal Example in the Socratic and Pastoral Epistles* (AnBib 105; Rome: Pontifical Biblical Institute, 1986), 81-84.

86. Wolter, *Paulustradition,* 156-80.

87. Wolter, *Paulustradition,* 164-70, 178-80.

88. M. M. Mitchell, "PTebt 703 and the Genre of 1 Timothy: The Curious Career of a Ptolemaic Papyrus in Pauline Scholarship," *NovT* 44 (2002): 344-70.

89. The foundational work on this document, and the creative reconstruction, upon which Spicq, Fiore, and Johnson rely, is that of M. Rostovtzeff (see *The Tebtunis Papyri,* vol. 3, part 1, ed. A. S. Hunt and J. G. Smyly, with assistance from B. P. Grenfell, E. Lobel, and M. Rostovtzeff [London: Cambridge University Press, 1933], 66-102). Mitchell ("PTebt 703," 344-54) has challenged Rostovtzeff's translation and reconstruction, as well as Johnson's use of the term "letter" to describe its genre: memorandum is the more accurate term.

90. Johnson, 139-42 (142).

otherwise classified (Mitchell).[91] Some refinement of Johnson's specification may well be in order. But in any case, as Wolter concluded,[92] the characteristics of the mandate documents make this body of writings a helpful parallel to 1 Timothy and Titus: communication of mandates/decrees, the superior-subordinate relation between the writer and the bearer of the letter, the mix of public (third-person plural imperatives) and private (second-person singular imperatives) instruction. And the *mandata* documents were available in Greek in the Imperial provinces. If the *mandata* are not generically epistolary in form, there are nonetheless examples in the correspondence of Pliny and Trajan in which royal mandates are communicated within the context of letters.[93] Such a coalescing of literary elements into a broader letter form may show something of the process by which 1 Timothy and Titus were written,[94] but it is not yet clear that there existed something as firm as a mandate-letter genre that might have served as a template.

Consequently, the mandate writings (from a ruler to a subordinate to be installed or assigned to work in a receiving context) help us to understand the combination of elements (public and private) that occurs in 1 Timothy and Titus.[95] While the existence of the *mandata principis* does not settle the authorship question (anyone, Paul or a pseudepigrapher, could have formulated the letters), neither does the unique shape of the letters in comparison with the undisputed letters to churches preclude the possibility that Paul could have designed such letters to his subordinate delegates.[96]

2 Timothy has often been regarded as the least problematic of the three in the matter of authenticity. However, its association with 1 Timothy and Titus generally tips the scales in favor of pseudonymity. Most recently, the letter has been compared with the testament genre by which a letter might be presented as the last message of a dying religious leader to a faithful follower (cf. Acts 20:17-35). This type of letter is thought to be typically characterized by pseudonymity.[97] While some aspects of the genre present a compelling comparison to 2 Timothy, the impression in the letter that Paul is still alive reduces the likelihood of this connection.

91. Mitchell ("PTebt 703," 363) notes that neither Fiore nor Wolter names the *mandata principis* "letters."

92. Wolter, *Paulustradition,* 164-70 (and notes) for examples of the form.

93. Mitchell ("PTebt 703," 363-64) points this out. See the discussion in A. N. Sherwin-White, *The Letters of Pliny* (Oxford: Clarendon, 1966), 590-91.

94. Cf. the combination of epistolary, prophetic, and apocalyptic elements that went into the writing of Revelation; see R. Bauckham, *The Theology of the Book of Revelation* (Cambridge: Cambridge University Press, 1993), 1-17.

95. See also Marshall, 12.

96. Johnson, 137-42; idem, *Paul's Delegates,* 107-8.

97. Wolter, *Paulustradition,* 222-41; Bassler, 22-23.

Johnson suggests that another genre bears a closer resemblance. The parenetic style of letter was meant to encourage pursuit of what was deemed acceptable conduct in common situations of life and avoidance of that which was regarded as unacceptable conduct. Typical of such letters is the use of example for imitation (a father showing the way for a son), diversity of content, and brief admonitions that are strung together. 2 Timothy is closely similar in many ways. Paul fashions himself as Timothy's father. He calls to mind for Timothy models to be imitated. And he issues practical admonitions to concretize the model. Although the polemical discourse carried on against opposing teachers in 2 Timothy diverges from the parenetic form, Paul's use of it shows affinity for another style of exhortation, also current in his day. The protreptic style was designed to win someone over to a superior point of view or pursuit.[98] Applied to the polemical element of 2 Timothy, what emerges is a running discourse, with pauses and resumptions, through which Paul is able to contrast his own exemplary model of faithfulness and orthodoxy with the godless beliefs and behavior of the opponents. This element then functions in concert with the parenetic element to underline the distinctions between right and wrong, godly and godless, in a way that guides Timothy in what he is to pursue and avoid.

While we can only guess why Paul would have chosen to craft letters to his delegates in these ways, we can make suggestions. First, the church situations and ministering roles that 1 Timothy and Titus depict may have made incorporation of *mandata principis* elements most suitable. As for the ethical language employed in the letters, Johnson posits that both Timothy and Titus almost certainly had access to a Greek education (Acts 16:1; Gal 2:3). If so, both the literary elements and the strongly Hellenistic language would likely have been appreciated by the coworkers. Furthermore, the circulation of *mandata* in Greek in the provinces would ensure equally that letters akin to this body of writings would be effectively received by the communities in which the delegates were to take up posts.[99]

---

98. For descriptions and examples of both styles, see A. J. Malherbe, *Moral Exhortation: A Greco-Roman Sourcebook* (Philadelphia: Westminster, 1986), 121-29; for discussion of the relevance for 2 Timothy, see Johnson, 320-34; idem, *Paul's Delegates,* 37-41.

99. Cf. Johnson, *Paul's Delegates,* 29-31.

B. READING THE LETTERS AS LETTERS: THE HISTORICAL CHARACTER OF THE LETTERS TO TIMOTHY AND TITUS

1. Ephesus and Crete: Cities and Churches

1 Timothy identifies Ephesus as the location of the church in which Timothy has been assigned to work (1:3). The city's pre-Christian history goes some way toward explaining its dominance in the Pauline mission.[100] Originally a seaport, modern Ephesus is located several miles inland. Its history and name date back to c. 1100 B.C.E. and a founding by indigenous Asians (Amazons, according to the traditions). Greeks came to occupy the city and surrounding environs from very early times, and made the place known for the worship of Artemis, with whom they replaced worship of a female deity by local inhabitants. Both its geography, with a strategic harbor, and its worship of Artemis made Ephesus a prominent and wealthy city in the centuries before the Christian era. In the six or so centuries preceding our era, the city saw and survived the shifts of political power from the Lydian King Croesus to Persian to Greek to Roman influences. Never really independent, the city's Greek inhabitants staked their fortunes on their ability to accommodate the long and changing cast of rulers that came to power. The Greek ethos predominated, but ideals such as democracy and equality (often linked to the great Greek city of Athens) were less determinative for Ephesian life.

In the late first century B.C.E., Augustus's quelling of rebellion in Rome brought the *pax Romana* to Asia. Augustus visited Ephesus and recognized the city as the provincial capital. By the time Paul came on the scene, among Asian cities Ephesus was in the ascendancy. Its population numbered about 100,000, and its economy was robust. Moreover, it was known for its theater on the western slope of Mt. Pion (going back to the second century B.C.E., and enlarged in the time of Claudius, 41-54 C.E., and further modified through the reigns of Nero and Trajan) and the Artemesion (the temple of Artemis). The temple's history predates the fourth century B.C.E. and includes a rebuilding after its destruction by an arsonist. In its glory, it was the largest building in ancient times, according to Pausanias (4.31.8; 7.5.4). It formed the center of civic and religious life in Ephesus and was its chief symbol of cultural identity.

---

100. See esp. P. Trebilco, *The Early Christians in Ephesus from Paul to Ignatius* (WUNT 166; Tübingen: Mohr [Siebeck], 2004), 11-52; H. W. Hoehner, *Ephesians: An Exegetical Commentary* (Grand Rapids: Baker, 2002), 78-92; H. Koester, ed., *Ephesos: Metropolis of Asia* (Valley Forge, PA: Trinity Press International, 1995); S. M. Baugh, "A Foreign World: Ephesus in the First Century," in A. J. Köstenberger et al., eds., *Women in the Church* (Grand Rapids: Baker, 1995), 13-52.

The life of Ephesus was as religiously complex as that of any other Imperial Asian city. Emperor worship had come to the fore after a long and complicated period of gestation throughout the Greek and Roman eras. While Ephesus failed to acquire the distinction of being the temple warden of Emperor Tiberius, mainly because of its distinction as the temple warden of Artemis, emperor worship had come to be part of the city's identity as an Imperial capital. Luke's retelling of Paul's interaction with the Artemis worshipers (Acts 19) may not tell the whole story of Ephesus's religious life, but it demonstrates the central place occupied by the Artemis cult in the apostle's day. Not only were the goddess's devotees ardent in their worship, but the cult itself was at the center of commercial activity in the city. The cult was flexible enough to absorb the interests of numerous other local cults and to reshape itself accordingly. Ephesus was apparently known for the practice of magic, sorcery, and soothsaying, practices that found room in most or all of the pagan religions.

Consequently, the city in which Timothy was assigned to represent the apostle was a large and diverse one. Dominant religious features such as the Artemis cult should, of course, not be ignored (see the commentary at 1 Tim 3:16), but the presence and relevance of other vital concerns should also be considered in discussions of background. The most dominant among these is the factor of the church itself that existed in Ephesus. According to Luke's account in Acts, Paul came to Ephesus only after earlier aspirations were frustrated by the leading of the Spirit (Acts 16:6). Finally, however, following a long period of ministry in Corinth (18:1-17), Paul with his coworkers arrived for a brief stay in Ephesus (18:18-21), and a brief period of ministry, in the synagogue, ensued. He left Priscilla and Aquila in place as he himself departed for Syrian Antioch. During the interval of his absence, Apollos arrived in Ephesus, was taught more accurately the Christian faith, and began his own less-well-understood ministry in the Ephesus-Corinth theater. Paul's return to Ephesus (Acts 18:23; 19:1; c. 53 C.E.) marked the launch of his second long-term period of ministry in a city. The same pattern as in Corinth, of movement from the synagogue to a neutral setting, is notable. And Paul was in Ephesus (with some travel elsewhere in Asia and Greece) for about three years. His ministry was marked by works of the Spirit and by great success (19:10-11). But Luke emphasizes the opposition that arose surrounding the encounter of Paul's gospel and Artemis worship. Conversions to Christianity were hurting the silver trade, so closely associated with the cult. A riot resulted in which many under Demetrius's leadership squared off against the Christian movement centered in Paul's ministry. The church itself, which included Jews and Gentiles, represented an urgent threat to the well-being of Artemesian Ephesus.

There are some ambiguous indications that the church itself was experiencing instability. In writing from Ephesus, Paul would refer to his encounter with "wild beasts in Ephesus" (1 Cor 15:32) and "many adversaries" (16:9), all of which may be further commented on in the "affliction to the point of death" in 2 Cor 1:8-9. The references are disputed, but there is every chance that Paul referred not simply to the riot (a confrontation between belief and unbelief as Luke portrays the scene), nor to an otherwise unknown imprisonment,[101] but rather to human opponents within the Ephesian Christian context.[102] Acts 20:18-38 recounts Paul's final meeting with the Ephesian elders, in which Paul makes reference to savage attacks by "wolves" and false teaching by some among the believers. While it is given a prophetic shape, one wonders whether the account is not more of a commentary on the events in Ephesus that would later call forth 1 Timothy. Rev 2:6 is another ambiguous piece of data in the Ephesian story. But in keeping with the Lukan and Pauline reflections of the situation in Ephesus, it stresses community struggle, the need for perseverance in truth, the presence of false teachers, and the need to withstand their influence, with the stakes being the demonstration of genuine Christian commitment and purity of the faith.

It is less clear how to define the local situation of 2 Timothy. Certain concerns, interests, and personalia reflect continuity with 1 Timothy and suggest that the link with Ephesus still exists. But the thrust of the letter (Paul's own changed situation in Rome and the need for handing over the ministry to Timothy) veils the historical setting somewhat. Timothy is depicted as reeling from the battle and perhaps disheartened by the failure of the corrective measures enjoined in 1 Timothy. But the false teaching and opponents who spread it still form the backdrop to personal parenesis to Timothy (e.g., 2:14-26; 3:10; 4:1-5), though preparing the community for his departure to Paul (2:1-7) has now changed the tone.

Crete[103] enters Luke's Pauline travelogue in Acts 27 (vv. 7, 12, 13, 21; see "Cretans" in 2:11), where Paul visited en route to Rome. The only other Pauline association with this island country comes in the letter to Titus. Here Paul's instructions assume that his mission has already made inroads into the cities of the island, but the story as told by Luke is silent on this development. The island is located in the Mediterranean Sea, south of Greece and Asia Minor on a north-south line bisecting the Aegean Sea. One of the last strongholds to resist Roman domination, it finally came under

101. Cf. G. S. Duncan, *St. Paul's Ephesian Ministry* (London: Hodder and Stoughton, 1929).

102. See esp. the discussion in Johnson, 143.

103. In addition to the references to sources and discussion in the commentary at 1:5, see B. W. Winter, *Roman Wives, Roman Widows: The Appearance of New Women and the Pauline Communities* (Grand Rapids: Eerdmans, 2003), 141-69; R. M. Kidd, "Titus as *Apologia*: Grace for Liars, Beasts, and Bellies," *HBT* 21 (1999): 185-209.

Rome's sway and was made a province in 71 B.C.E. Its history is that of an island located well for sea trade, a home to piracy, the famous (legendary) hundred cities, and much inter-city fighting (see the commentary at Titus 1:5, 12). Its legal code accorded women certain freedoms not enjoyed by women elsewhere in the Greek and Roman world. The religious landscape was as diverse as that of any Roman province; but it is notable for its unique retelling of the story of Zeus, whom Cretans claimed was born and died (!) on Crete. This became a part of the source of the widespread sentiment that Cretans are liars (Titus 1:12-13). Equally noteworthy for reading the letter to Titus is Crete's reputation (including its religious deceitfulness), going back centuries, as a self-indulgent, belligerent, wild, immoral society. Sexual promiscuity, gluttony at feasts (where immoral activities frequently took place), and lying ("cretanizing" meant "lying") characterized what was widely held to be the way of life on Crete: to speak of a "Cretan point of view" was to speak of deception.

The ethical instruction of the letter to Titus starts from this Cretan background. Instructions in ch. 2 to older men, older women, young women, and younger men all assume a basic clash of the Christian message with the current value system. The teaching of opponents, who are somewhat less prominent in the letter than in 1 Timothy, is labeled deceptive and dangerous in exactly the same way that philosophers often categorized the manipulative words of clever orators who made their living off smooth public speaking or teaching in households. It was not uncommon for Jewish teachers to come under the influence of pagan culture and to become forceful teachers of secular values. The picture painted in Titus 1:10-16 envisions Christian teachers (Jewish: "especially those of the circumcision") who refuse to break free from the value system corrupting Crete and so in the churches become opponents of the apostle and his mission. But it is this reluctance to disengage from Cretan ways that Paul seems most to concentrate on, rather than doctrinal aberration.

The fit of what can be reconstructed of Cretan culture during Roman rule with the situation assumed in the letter to Titus is a close one. The difficulty comes in creating the space in Luke's or Paul's telling of the mission story for the mission to have reached the island and the churches to have been planted (see the reconstruction below). Paul need not have been personally present to have "left" (better, "assigned"; see the commentary at 1:5) Titus to the straightening and completing of the task already underway. In any case, the strong Cretan flavor invites reading the letter in the historical setting it depicts for itself. As for Pauline association with the churches, the question ultimately will be whether the only solution is the verdict of "fictional" pseudepigraphy; silence on the part of Luke and elsewhere in Paul does not lead inescapably to this conclusion.

2. Elements of Historical and Cultural Setting

a. False Teaching/Opposition/Cultural Movements

If there is one thing about these letters on which scholars do agree, it is that they purport to address church or mission situations in which false teachers or opponents figure quite prominently. Here too there is the danger of assuming that the letters envision a rather unified front,[104] while we should rather expect the telltale signs of discontinuity at least when the situation in Ephesus is set alongside that of Crete (see below). There remains, of course, the sort of explanation offered by Dibelius — that the author constructed a paradigmatic fictional heresy that had nothing to do with actual historical circumstances in Ephesus or Crete; in this way the letters could function as a sort of handbook for the church for combating heresy whenever and wherever it should crop up.[105] But more scholars today are inclined to view the opposition as actual (whatever the relationship of Paul to the letters), and the letters consequently as a response to the rise of heretical opponents in these Pauline churches at some point in time (or in others for which the scenario dreamed up for Ephesus and Crete serves as a model). In any case, there is clearly more to the local situations depicted in the letters than the element of opposition or heresy, but the place to begin an examination is with this feature.

The theme is easily detected.[106] 1 Timothy addresses the matter in a series of texts: 1:3-7, 18-20; 4:1-5, 6-10; 6:2b-10, 20-21. And in other texts (see the commentary), the influence of the opponents or their teaching may be latent (e.g., 2:1-7, 11-15; 5:15). Verbal indicators of the movement include the language of "false teaching" (1:3; 6:3) and the labeling of this teaching as "myths and genealogies" (1:4) or "myths" (4:7) or "demonic doctrines" (4:1-2), in addition to explicit mention of opposition leaders (1:20: Hymenaeus and Alexander).

2 Timothy presumably depicts the same opposition, though it may be at a later stage of development. Relevant passages taken up with the opposition are 2:14-26; 3:1-9; 4:1-5. The term "myth" bearing the same pejorative meaning recurs in 4:4. And an extended discussion of heresy as an eschatological symptom, backed up by a traditional paradigm, is given in 3:1-9. Continuity with the situation described in 1 Timothy is suggested not only by the person of Timothy and the evidence that opposing the rebels still falls to

---

104. Cf., e.g., Mounce, lxix-lxxvi, who describes the heresy (depicted in each letter) under the single category "The Ephesian Heresy."

105. Dibelius and Conzelmann, 66; H. Koester, *Introduction to the New Testament* (Philadelphia: Fortress, 1982), 2:297-305; Trummer, *Paulustradition,* 163-64.

106. See Towner, *Goal,* 21-42.

him, but also by further mention of a certain leader named Hymenaeus alongside one named Philetus (2:17), and a possible second reference to Alexander (4:14).

Titus also treats the issue of opposition, but the view taken is quite different from that of 1 Timothy despite the use of the same sort of disparaging vocabulary to label the rebels and their message (1:9-16; 3:9-11). In this case, 1:14 labels the opposing message as "Jewish myths," and the term "genealogies" is also applied to the contents (3:9). Arguments and disputes linked to the false teaching are termed "battles over the law" (3:9), and the same sort of disruption is linked to the opponents' activities (e.g., 1:10-11).

The identification of the respective opposing fronts continues to be debated. But some guiding conclusions can be drawn once older paradigms have been briefly explained and evaluated.

(1) Gnostic Elements

We begin not with the more easily supported assertion of Jewish elements, but with the more widely held view that Gnosticism in one form or another is being combated. One of the conclusions drawn by some in the critical school in the early days following Baur was that the letters were based on a presumed response to Gnosticism of the second century. References to *gnōsis* ("knowledge"; 1 Tim 6:20), "myths and genealogies" (1 Tim 1:4),[107] ascetic tendencies (1 Tim 4:1-3; Titus 1:15),[108] and realized views of eschatology (2 Tim 2:18) could all be explained by this framework. Study of the Nag Hammadi finds, however, determined among other things that the Jewish contribution to Gnosticism is significant,[109] and this led to a more pliable reconstruction of the heresy as an admixture of Jewish (Judaizing) and Gnostic (or Gnosticizing) elements. For the most part, the label "Gnostic" was applied in modified fashion in most discussions of Pauline treatments of ethical and theological aberrations. Or, rather, the category was enlarged to include items (theological and ethical) that bore similarity to tendencies that would appear in association with later, mature Gnostic movements.

But still today some interpreters link the opponents with Gnosticism, placing the letters at the beginning of the second century. W. Schmithals is

---

107. Irenaeus, *Against Heresies,* 1.pref.

108. Irenaeus, *Against Heresies* 1.24.2 makes mention of Gnostic views of marriage.

109. See R. McL. Wilson, "Addenda et Postscripta — I," in U. Bianchi, ed., *Le Origini dello Gnosticismo: Colloquio di Messino, 13-18 April 1966* (Leiden: Brill, 1966), 691.

perhaps the most persistent proponent of this hypothesis,[110] but J. Roloff, L. Oberlinner, and others[111] observe what they take to be the distinctive vocabulary of Gnosis (*gnōsis* in 1 Tim 6:20) and connect this reference to "knowledge" with the realized resurrection doctrine in 2 Tim 2:18 and other indications of ascetic enthusiasm, dualism, and a salvation bent on redemption from an evil world. In Roloff's reconstruction all of this is already evident to some degree in the contexts of other Pauline churches. But advancing the thesis in the letters to Timothy and Titus requires playing down considerably the Jewish elements that appear far more obvious than Gnostic ones in the letters. Further, the presence of other features in the letters that bear much closer resemblance to developments in Corinth and Colossae, and the absence of the more dramatic elements of later Gnosticism (the systems of archons, the demiurge, etc.), recommend looking in a more lateral direction to other opposing movements in the Asian Pauline churches for help in understanding the situations depicted in the letters to Timothy and Titus. As Marshall points out, drawing on the consensus of the Messina colloquium and of those who continue to explore the Pauline letters, the better tag for the mix of elements (from ascetic tendencies to enthusiastic elements of theology and soteriology) is "pre-Gnostic" in the sense that certain developments visible in the Pauline letters correspond to those that would later come together to form the second-century Gnostic matrix. There is simply too much missing from the descriptions of opposing beliefs in these letters and those written to churches to support the Gnostic hypothesis. At the same time, what seems a more typical blend of Jewish (or Judaizing) and Christian (sometimes enthusiastic or pneumatic) elements, as appears in Corinth and Colossae with additional glimpses elsewhere, can account for the whole package confronted in the Pauline mission context.[112]

(2) Jewish Elements

Jewish elements are clearly in evidence. The self-claim to be "teachers of the law" (1 Tim 1:7; see commentary) should be linked with the speculative

---

110. W. Schmithals, "The Corpus Paulinum and Gnosis," in A. H. B. Logan and A. J. M. Wedderburn, eds., *The New Testament and Gnosis: Essays in Honour of R. McL. Wilson* (Edinburgh: T&T Clark, 1983), 107-24.

111. See esp. G. Haufe, "Gnostiche Irrlehre und ihre Abwehr in den Pastoralbriefen," in K. W. Tröger, ed., *Gnosis und Neues Testament* (Gütersloh: Mohn, 1973), 325-40; Roloff, 234-38; Oberlinner, *Pastoralbriefe,* 52-73; M. Goulder, "The Pastor's Wolves: Jewish Christian Visionaries behind the Pastoral Epistles," *NovT* 38 (1996): 242-56.

112. See esp. W. Thiessen, *Christen in Ephesus: Die historische und theologische Situation in vorpaulinischer Zeit und zur Zeit der Apostelgeschichte und der Pastoralbriefe,* TANZ (Tübingen: Francke, 1995), 317-37.

use of the law indicated in the language "myths and endless genealogies" (1 Tim 1:4; see commentary). Shifting to Titus, the identification of the rebels with the phrase "those of the circumcision group" (1:10) and the description of their activities as "quarrels about the law" (3:9) indicate the Jewish or Jewish-Christian impulse of the movement. The situation in Crete calls for its own qualifications and precautions in defining the opposition. But probably in neither case should we explain all features on a purely Jewish basis.[113]

(3) An Amalgam of Jewish, Christian, and Ascetic Elements

As in some of the developments in other Pauline contexts, we are better off to conclude that the heretical fronts evident in the letters contain elements from various sources, an observation that connects them with a broad phenomenon. Further, the groups are linked loosely by the fact that the leaders (at least) seem to be Jewish Christians, who, though possibly itinerant teachers, seem to have secured for themselves a place within the church communities in view.[114] But in each locale different emphases and influences are present, just as we would expect of movements separated by the geographical and cultural distances that distinguished Ephesus from Crete.

The whole matter of reconstructing the heretical views is complicated by the fact that the author engages the problem indirectly, and, despite naming certain leaders, only a few of their practical and theological tendencies emerge in the course of the letters. We are not without some useful information, but the profiles of the opposing movements that can be constructed from that information remain frustratingly provisional. We may be misled by commonalities in the polemics that runs through the three letters, however, to assume that different chapters of the same "movement" are indicated. It is not warranted to import elements from the Cretan description to fill out the Ephesian profile, and vice versa. The exception comes in 2 Timothy, which may be regarded as continuous with 1 Timothy. In any case, common characteristics should be treated cautiously.

Beginning with the Ephesian church depicted in 1 Timothy, the false teaching may have been introduced into the communities by wandering prophetic groups of some sort (or by Paul's Jewish-Christian opponents). But by the time the letter was written, the opposition clearly had found a home within the house churches and was exerting considerable influence at all levels, especially among women (1 Tim 5:15; 1 Tim 2:11-15; cf. 2 Tim 3:6) and perhaps

---

113. See the views of Spicq, 85-119; and esp. F. J. A. Hort, *Judaistic Christianity* (London: Macmillan, 1909).

114. Towner, *Goal*, 25-26.

among some church leaders (1 Tim 5:17-25).[115] The opponents were active in church meetings and in the context of the household (2 Tim 3:6). The Jewish law seems to be central to their mode of teaching, and this they expounded with the aid of speculative exegetical methods. They regarded themselves as "teachers of the law" (1 Tim 1:7) and possibly preferred to think of their teaching as "knowledge" (*gnōsis;* 1 Tim 6:20). Related in some way to their doctrines and, perhaps, behavior was speculation on the OT (most likely focusing on the stories of creation and OT heroes; see 1 Tim 1:4; 4:7; cf. 2 Tim 4:4; Titus 1:14; 3:9). The author's disparaging description of this activity as "myths and genealogies" (1 Tim 1:4; 4:7; 2 Tim 4:4; cf. Titus 1:14; 3:9) sheds little light on the process by which the false teachers developed their doctrines,[116] but it does locate the movement within a Jewish or, more likely, a Jewish-Christian context. To this evidence may be added the apparent preoccupation with asceticism, which may have involved a predilection for ritual purity (the prohibition of marriage and certain foods in 1 Tim 4:3; Titus 1:15) and the self-designation "teachers of the law" (1 Tim 1:7). There is an elitist bent among them, for they claim "to know God" (1 Tim 6:20) and seem inclined to frustrate the universal Gentile ambitions of the Pauline mission (2:1-7). It is somewhat less clear (see the commentary at 1 Tim 2:11-15; 4:1-5) how the role of women/wives, childbearing, and a disparagement of marriage and foods should be linked to their doctrines and values.

Christological aberrations might be back-read out of the various theological statements (e.g., Docetism from the strong incarnational tone of 1 Tim 2:5; 3:16).[117] But it is very difficult to be certain whether these formulations were corrective of such specific theological errors; when taken as a whole, the creedal statements do, however, consistently reinforce belief in the present reality of salvation in Christ.[118] When taken letter by letter, however, Christology is fashioned to give expression to three distinct themes that correct and subvert prevalent views and support the course of action Timothy is to take (see below and see the commentary).

But a soteriological aberration emerges in the allusion to the over-realized view of the resurrection of believers in 2 Tim 2:18. This suggests a view of the times and of eschatology that might underlie approaches taken to practical social/sexual matters in a Christian community in which a fuller experience of salvation and the Spirit is proclaimed (see the commentary at 1 Tim 6:20; 2 Tim 2:18). But theologically the statement of 2 Tim 2:18 is something like the tip of an iceberg. In fact, what is most distinctive about the false teach-

115. See the discussion in Fee, 8.
116. See the discussions in the commentary.
117. See the approach of Oberlinner, *Pastoralbriefe,* 69-71.
118. Towner, *Goal,* 75-119.

ing in Ephesus is the way it conveyed a view of salvation that made much of the cognitive or "spiritual" dimension of life. Paul indicates that the opponents claimed to possess "knowledge" (1 Tim 6:20-21). In contrast to these claims, Paul's attack on their impious outward conduct identifies a misconception of spirituality that concentrates almost wholly on the cognitive experience.

The specific shape of the doctrine taught by the opponents is impossible to reconstruct fully from the few clues that the documents give up. In the case of the movement in Ephesus, the teaching that the resurrection of believers had already occurred was a central feature (2 Tim 2:18). Similarities between the descriptions of this doctrine in 2 Tim 2:18 and the description of the false teaching called *gnōsis* in 1 Tim 6:20-21 suggest at least that the specific resurrection doctrine was the type of belief that would come under the category of the heretical "knowledge" (whether or not the doctrine described in 2 Tim 2:18 is already in view in 1 Tim 6:20).[119] The basis for this doctrine is uncertain, but as in the case of the similar misunderstanding addressed in 1 Cor 15:12-58, something in their understanding of theology had apparently led them to the belief that spiritual fullness was attainable now, so much so that in the minds of the enthusiasts any future eschatological event was reduced to a symbol of what had already occurred, when for Paul it remained fundamental to the completion of salvation. Such a doctrine was possibly the result of a misunderstanding of Paul's association of baptism with participation in Christ's resurrection (Rom 6:3-8; 1 Cor 4:8; Eph 2:5; Col 2:12; 2 Tim 2:11-13), or perhaps grew out of the belief that Jesus' resurrection had fully ushered in the new age and mature believers were to live the life of the age to come.[120] E. Schlarb has argued that references to the prohibition of marriage and abstinence from certain foods might reflect the attempt to return to the manner of life prior to the fall — before marriage and the eating of meat were sanctioned.[121] Whatever the relationship between these ascetic tendencies and the false resurrection doctrine, it is clear that the opponents were under the influence of some sort of mistaken eschatology.

The situation to be faced by Titus in Crete shares some of these characteristics. We are introduced to the opponents, who are Jewish or Jewish Christian (Titus 1:14) and more apparently prone to insist on matters of ritual purity (1:15). They are equally argumentative (1:11), wrangle about the law (3:9), and advance a quality of teaching that can also be labeled "myths"

119. See the commentary at 1 Tim 6:20-21. Cf. P. H. Towner, "Gnosis and Realized Eschatology in Ephesus (of the Pastoral Epistles) and the Corinthian Enthusiasm," *JSNT* 31 (1987): 104-6; E. Schlarb, *Die gesunde Lehre: Häresie und Wahrheit im Spiegel der Pastoralbriefe* (MTS 28; Marburg: N. G. Elwert, 1990), 121-22; Oberlinner, *Pastoralbriefe*, 54-57.

120. See the discussion at 2 Tim 2:18; Towner, *Goal,* 31.

121. Schlarb, *Die gesunde Lehre,* 83-133.

(1:14). No leaders of the movement are named, and this suggests either a bit more distance from the situation, or an opposition that has yet to evolve into a force within the church, operating more effectively on its periphery. This might comport with what is said about how they have gained a hearing in the households (1:11), which also conforms to what may be known about smooth-tongued rhetoricians of the day and the ways in which they "taught" with material support as a goal. The absence of explicit reference to the sort of asceticism linked to the movement in Ephesus may place these teachers into another category. Paul is so concerned to remove these young churches from the perverse clutches of Cretan culture that it is quite possible that these Jewish-Christian teachers present their danger in the form of a gospel that has been tainted by Cretan values that Paul finds to be at odds with his (authentic) gospel. If this is so (see the commentary), then the opposition on Crete is better described in terms of rebellious teachers who reject Paul's authority and continue to ply the communities with a lowest-common-denominator Christian faith that makes plenty of room for Cretan vices.

The uniformity of the polemic carried out by Paul is more indicative of his method than of any necessary continuity of the heretical movements.[122] In each locale, although the activity of teaching appears to be central to the opposing movements (1 Tim 1:3; 6:3; 2 Tim 2:17-18; 3:7; 4:3; Titus 1:9), the results these opponents achieved in the communities are more typically characterized by disruption, arguments, and disputes (1 Tim 6:4; 2 Tim 2:14; Titus 3:9). As for their teaching, Paul denounces it in the strongest terms as foolishness, godless talk, speculation, demonic doctrines, and utterly useless speech (1 Tim 1:6; 4:1-2, 7; 6:20; 2 Tim 2:17, 23; Titus 3:9). The opponents themselves are liars and hypocrites "whose consciences have been seared" (1 Tim 4:2), devoid of understanding (6:4) and truth (6:5; 2 Tim 3:13). They are depicted as impious and immoral (Titus 1:18; 2 Tim 3:1-5), and as motivated by greed (1 Tim 6:5-10; Titus 1:11). Paul portrays both the doctrine and behavior of the rebels in terms of paganism (1 Tim 1:20; cf. v. 13), and in the case of the Cretan opposition he sets this out very boldly (Titus 3:3). Paul generally suggests that the immorality of their thought and behavior can be traced to corrupted consciences and minds (1 Tim 1:19; 4:2; Titus 1:15); that is, visible signs of paganism among these false believers are linked to the cognitive and spiritual level of life.

(4) A Cultural Factor

But just as it is inappropriate to meld the three letters into a continuous corpus, so it is ill advised to make the reconstruction of the local situations rest solely on

---

122. Cf. L. T. Johnson, "II Timothy and the Polemic against False Teachers: A Reexamination," *JRS* 6-7 (1978-79): 1-26.

the presence of heresy. Heresy is a dominant element for understanding the *Sitz im Leben* both in the letters to Timothy and Titus, but part of Paul's polemical repertoire opens a window on another element at work alongside the heretical oppositions in Ephesus and Crete. The language and conceptual framework within which wives and widows are addressed in 1 Tim 2:9-10, 15; 5:3-16 and in which older and younger groups of husbands and wives are addressed in Titus 2:1-8 have been linked to a discourse that developed in the Roman Empire from Augustus onward in reaction to a movement among particularly wealthy women (often supported by influential philosophers and teachers). Characteristic of this movement was a throwing off of the dress code (apparel, adornment, hairstyles) that symbolized respectability, sexual modesty, and fidelity to one's husband. Equally characteristic was the desire of influential women to acquire for themselves and enjoy the freedoms, normally restricted to men, to explore multiple sexual liaisons in association with dinner parties and banquets. Pursuit of sexual freedom required remaining unencumbered with children, so the ancient discussions include references to the practices of contraception and abortion. What might appear less drastic were the desires of women to take active roles in public life, in legal contexts sometimes functioning as advocates; but in some cases this simply took the form of speaking up in the presence of men/husbands, offering opinions, teaching, and philosophizing. All of this represented a breach of the traditional codes of respectability endorsed by the status quo. A network of activities and drives are thus all linked to what has been termed the movement of the "new Roman woman."[123]

What is most interesting in the application of this to Pauline studies is the observation that in urban contexts such as Corinth and Ephesus, where wealthy women were numbered among church members, the new movement had apparently made inroads. Matters of the dress and behavior of women in Pauline churches were therefore quite likely to have been influenced by the model of the new liberal woman. If the background proves sustainable, then we find Paul reacting to trends in Corinth that threatened to link the gospel message with a rejection of all the old rules of modesty. This would effectively associate Christianity with immorality in a way that would thoroughly discredit the gospel. The suggestion goes as well for the passages indicated in 1 Timothy (for Ephesus) and Titus (for Crete). While Winter suggests that the penetration of this "new woman" ethos lies behind the corrective (or preventive) comments to women in these letters, what remains to be explored is whether or not specific elements and aims of the false teaching might have converged with the new morality — that is, whether perhaps certain clever opponents were endorsing and exploiting the new values as part of their agenda — to encourage women to behave in ways that Paul and wider soci-

123. Winter, *Roman Wives.*

48

ety regarded as sexually immodest, disrespectful of husbands, and a threat to the gospel and the church's mission (see further the commentary at 1 Tim 2:9-15; 5:3-16; Titus 2:1-10).

(5) Lateral Relationships, Influences, and Comparisons

I have already suggested that an amalgamation of influences probably best explains what erupted especially in Ephesus as a heretical movement. The cultural factor just identified complicates the landscape further. It remains to point out that the best models for this kind of development and thought are not to be found in later Gnosticism or some permutation of Judaism but rather in situations such as we find depicted in 1 Corinthians. Paul's instructions seem to address unsanctioned activities among some women (1 Tim 2:9-15; 5:15; 2 Tim 3:6), and perhaps also unrest among slaves (1 Tim 6:1-2; cf. Titus 2:9-10). The institution of marriage (1 Tim 4:3) and the sanctity of widowhood (5:15) were under pressure from the opponents and perhaps also the "new woman" cultural forces working in the social life of the church or possibly being exploited by the opposition. Without resorting to the Gnostic hypothesis, the more natural parallel is the situation described in 1 Corinthians, where, in an atmosphere of Spirit enthusiasm that might have included overrealized eschatology, linked in some way to a misunderstanding of the resurrection and of the incomplete nature of the present age, the validity of marriage was being called into question and certain excesses of behavior among women and charismatic enthusiasts were also visible (1 Cor 4:8; 7:1-16; 11:2-16; 14:22-25; cf. 7:21-24).[124] The degree to which such aberrations were theologically motivated in either Corinth or Ephesus is uncertain, but in the latter community the influence of the false teachers is obvious in some cases and less so in others. The involvement of women in teaching within the assembly (1 Tim 2:11-12; see commentary) stems in part from the influence of the heresy, as the reference to the deception of Eve (2:14) would seem to require. In Corinth, too, the presence of the "new woman" morality is thought to have been present.

How much of the Corinthian excess can be shown to have been theologically motivated or culturally conditioned is disputed. And certainly it need not be the case that the same connections between elements of theological misunderstanding and manifestations of behavior were made in each case. It is enough to see the parallels, both in terms of the theology/ethics interrelationship and the cultural dimension. The point is that we need not step out of the context of Pauline history to assess this movement, and the field of comparison is broader than 1 Corinthians. First, some form of a resurrection misunder-

---

124. Discussion in Towner, "Gnosis and Realized Eschatology."

standing is evident in 1 Corinthians, as we noted, and also in Philippians.[125] Second, Paul's encounters with opposing Judaizing tendencies to stress a confidence based on the law are well known from Romans, Galatians, Philippians, and Colossians. Third, food restrictions are addressed in Romans, 1 Corinthians, and Colossians, and sexual asceticism is evident from 1 Corinthians.

Therefore, although it may be difficult to explain the mixture, what we find, then, in these letters is evidence of an opposition of the broad type Paul encountered elsewhere, even if it is not to be thought of as genetically related to other groups of opponents. It is clearly here in the Pauline mission history, where Paul's teaching took up a complex mix of theological interests and cultural trends, that we should look for parallels to help explain the opposition in Ephesus and Crete, not in later Gnostic movements.

b. The Organization of the Churches

Another historical factor often advanced as evidence of the post-Pauline setting of the letters is the church organization depicted in them. Several observations are germane. First, some writers have overemphasized the place of church structure in these letters and the degree to which this differs from community situations reflected in Paul's letters to churches.[126] 2 Timothy does not take up the matter. Two sections in 1 Timothy (3:1-13; 5:17-25) and one in Titus (1:5-9) address the issue of church leadership, and in doing so, although the churches envisioned are at different stages of development, they share a common nomenclature of leadership. This includes "overseer" (episkopos; 1 Tim 3:1, 2; Titus 1:7) and "elder" (presbyteros; 1 Tim 5:17-25; cf. 4:14; Titus 1:5); the term "deacon"/"deaconess" (diakonos) is limited to 1 Tim 3:8, 12. What is often dismissed rather quickly is the fact that the language (Rom 16:1; Phil 1:1) and the phenomenon of authoritative church leadership (e.g., Rom 12:8; 1 Cor 6:2-6; 12:28; Phil 4:3; 1 Thess 5:12) are present elsewhere in Paul. Furthermore, very little of the actual structure of the church in Ephesus is evident from 1 Timothy. In both 1 Timothy and Titus, instructions regarding leaders and their selection focus mainly on matters of character and behavior. And in the case of Ephesus, the importance of character is seen against the background of the defection of some leaders from an already existing church.

But in spite of the similar nomenclature, the churches reflected in

125. Philippians 3 alludes to people who claim to be already "perfect," in response to which Paul speaks strongly of his aspiration to attain to the resurrection. See the discussion in Marshall, 751-54.

126. Cf. the approach of J. Roloff, Die Kirche im Neuen Testament (NTD 10; Göttingen: Vandenhoeck & Ruprecht, 1993), 250-67; or Dibelius and Conzelmann, 5-10; with Towner, "Pauline Theology or Pauline Tradition in the Pastoral Epistles," TynB 46 (1995): 287-314; or Johnson, Paul's Delegates, 13-16.

1 Timothy and Titus are at different stages of development. The churches in Crete (probably house churches in a number of towns throughout the island; 1:5; see commentary) are depicted as being under the guidance of Titus, still, presumably, fairly young, but nevertheless having reached the stage where Titus must select elders/overseers from the house fellowships to lead them (cf. Acts 14:23). This surely seems to be the picture of an ecclesiastical situation (in one geographical area) characterized by decentralized leadership, with the qualification that each local community might be presumed to be under the founding apostle's authority. Given this picture, it is rather difficult to explain, as proponents of pseudonymity must, how the letter would have functioned years after Paul or Titus, when some sort of leadership would already have been in place and instructions that are so specific would have been completely irrelevant. The church setting depicted in the letter to Titus is completely at odds with theories of late authorship.

1 Timothy depicts a more developed ecclesiastical situation (cf. 3:6). The leadership structure of the house churches of Ephesus includes the role of overseer (3:1), which may be a position occupied by a plurality, elders (4:14; 5:17-25), who may or may not be equivalent to the overseers, and deacons/deaconesses (3:8-13; see the commentary at 3:1). The saying in 3:1 ("whoever aspires to be an overseer desires a noble task") has led many to the conclusion that the author assumes the existence of the monarchical episcopate as he writes. But the lack of clarity in the use of the terms "overseer" and "elder" (cf. the writings of Ignatius) suggests that neither a rigid hierarchy nor a highly complex level of organization had yet evolved in Ephesus. Widows (5:3-16) may have played some part within the churches' ministry (vv. 5, 10), but the main issue regarding widows was their support by the church. While the presence of a support structure for them within the church, with a system of provision and evaluation of need, might suggest a more mature community with a broader support base, it is not clear that such a description requires a late dating (cf. Acts 6:1-4).[127] In fact, the church's financial resources were put under pressure by the number of widows.

2 Timothy presumably assumes the church order depicted in 1 Timothy, but apparently the interests and situation of the letter precluded any such discussions. 2 Tim 2:2 envisages the appointment by Timothy of replace-

---

127. That "widows" comprised an office within the church (along with bishops/elders, deacons/deaconesses), rather than a social category, is difficult to demonstrate from the passage. Bassler, 93-94, has argued that part of the problem in the church was caused by the expansion of the category to include not just women whose husbands had died, but also young virgins and divorced women who had taken a vow of celibacy, which had become a defining characteristic of this group; cf. B. W. Winter, "Providentia for the Widows of 1 Timothy 5,3–16," *TynB* 39 (1988): 83-99. This may have been the case, but such a development is also not datable.

ments for those who had deserted Paul or who were to continue the work once he had gone to Rome (1:15; 4:9, 16), but these may well have been mission team members instead of church leaders (see the commentary).

c. The Addressees: Timothy and Titus

If taken at face value, the letters to Timothy and Titus are the only letters written by Paul to individual coworkers. According to 1 Timothy and Titus, the coworkers are to represent the absent apostle as his delegates in the church and mission settings to which they were sent.[128] 2 Timothy is far more personal and, as discussed above, probably follows the form of a parenetic-protreptic letter. Timothy's assignment to represent the apostle in Ephesus (1 Tim 1:3) corresponds to tasks related to Thessalonica, Corinth, and Philippi (1 Thessalonians 3; 1 Cor 4:16-17; 16:10-11; Phil 2:19-24). We know that he had a crucial place within the Pauline mission, which may have included some degree of involvement in the writing of five undisputed letters.[129] He was much loved by Paul (1 Cor 4:17, "my true son in the faith"; cf. 1 Tim 1:2, "my dear son"; 2 Tim 1:2). Descriptions of him as a minister (Phil 1:1; 1 Thess 3:2; 2 Tim 2:24) and of his ministry (1 Thess 3:2; 1 Tim 4:12; 6:2; 2 Tim 2:14; 4:2) follow a consistent line from the undisputed Pauline letters to these letters to him. Even Paul's concern that Timothy's youth, unimpressive presence, and lack of confidence would affect his reception by the churches follows this line (1 Cor 16:10-11; Phil 2:19-23; 1 Tim 4:12; 2 Tim 1:6-8).

Our knowledge of Titus is more limited. From Galatians we learn that he was a Gentile (2:3) who had been with Paul as early as (perhaps even prior to) the time when Barnabas went to Tarsus to bring Paul back to Antioch (Gal 2:1; cf. Acts 11:25-30).[130] Despite the epithet "my true son" (Tit 1:4), we would have to say that he did not enjoy the privileged position that Timothy did. However, he served Paul as a trusted colleague. It was Titus whom Paul called on to represent him in the troublesome situation in Corinth, with corrective measures, and in the matter of the collection for poor believers in Jerusalem (2 Cor 2:3-4, 13; 7:6-16; 8:16-24). His assignment among the churches in Crete appears to have been equally to serve as Paul's representative and delegate — to appoint leaders in the churches, to rebuke rebellious opponents, to teach, to remind, to discipline, and above all to lead the Cretan Christians to a

---

128. Cf. Towner, *Goal*, 228-29; Johnson, 94-96; W.-H. *Ollrog, Paulus und seine Mitarbeiter* (WMANT 50; Neukirchen: Erziehungsverein, 1979), 23; J. Roloff, *Apostolat–Verkündigung–Kirche* (Gütersloh: Mohn, 1965), 250; Kelly, 13; Jeremias, 1-2.

129. 2 Cor 1:1; Phil 1:1; Col 1:1; 1 Thess 1:1; 2 Thess 1:1, and Phlm 1. See Prior, *Paul the Letter-Writer,* 37-50; Johnson, 94-96.

130. Cf. R. Riesner, *Paul's Early Period: Chronology, Mission Strategy, Theology* (Grand Rapids: Eerdmans, 1998), 269.

break from the Cretan value system (Titus 1:5, 13; 2:1, 15; 3:1, 8, 10). As in the case of Timothy, the profile of Titus's role in the letter written to him corresponds to the picture that emerges from other Pauline correspondence.

There may be reasons for questioning the authenticity of the letters. But it cannot be said that one of those reasons is that the roles of Timothy and Titus portrayed in them fail to conform to patterns described in the undisputed letters. It has been wondered why trusted workers needed the sort of instruction these letters contain. But skepticism of this sort bears little weight since the letters, incorporating mandate elements, served to endorse the delegates to the receiving communities as well as to set out their authoritative job descriptions for public appraisal.

C. UNITY AND DIVERSITY OF THEOLOGICAL AND THEMATIC ELEMENTS

If, as this commentary maintains, these three documents are to be read as individual letters that also manifest the signs of linguistic and thematic attraction, to what degree is it useful or misleading to introduce "the theology of the Pastoral Epistles"? Johnson chooses to emphasize the individuality of each letter's message and so refrains from a collective presentation of theological features that might be regarded as unifying elements in the three letters that distinguish them as a cluster within the Pauline corpus. As a corrective to the corpus reading of the modern consensus his procedure was most welcome. But at the risk of losing some of the ground gained by Johnson's presentation, I will seek to introduce the theological emphases in a way that does some justice to both the unity of the cluster and the diversity of the individual letters. At the same time, I will assess recent work to determine a distinctive centering Christology of the "PE," and, where necessary, I will "decenter" the themes employed. (See the commentary for detailed arguments.)

1. Shared Elements of Theology

a. Salvation in Jesus Christ

A shared feature of the theology of the letters to coworkers is the theme of salvation.[131] This much can be discerned from the poetic periods in which his own teaching or traditional materials appear throughout the letters (1 Tim 1:15; 2:4-6; 2 Tim 1:9-10; 2:8-13; Titus 2:11-14; 3:4-7). Each text announces

---

131. See Towner, *Goal*, 75-119; F. J. Matera, *New Testament Christology* (Louisville: Westminster/John Knox, 1999), 158-59; Marshall, 291-92.

that salvation is a present reality because Christ entered history and accomplished his redemptive work.

Within this sweep of redemptive action, several dimensions of traditional Christology intersect in the "epiphany" theme (*epiphaneia;* 1 Tim 6:14; 2 Tim 1:10; 4:1, 8; Titus 2:11, 13; 3:4). This theme is sometimes inaccurately regarded as the central unifying theme of the three letters (see below), but for the moment a discussion of its occurrence in each letter is appropriate here. The "epiphany" concept is not unknown elsewhere in the Pauline corpus (2 Thess 2:8), but its preponderance in the letters to coworkers marks a departure from Pauline emphases in the letters to churches. It portrays Christ's earthly ministry and future parousia as divine "appearances" of grace, salvation, and help (see the Excursus at 1 Tim 6:14). In this concept the deity of Christ is probably implied. The epiphany Christology also presumes the preexistence of Christ, a notion that may be indicated in 1 Tim 1:15 (cf. Phil 2:5-11; Col 1:15; cf. John 9:39; 11:27; 16:28; 18:37). Christ's first epiphany is equated with his incarnation and human existence, a connection amply confirmed by texts bearing other themes (1 Tim 2:5; 3:16; 6:13; 2 Tim 2:8; cf. Rom 1:3; Gal 4:4).

Accompanying the dominant epiphany theme is use of the title "Savior" for both God and Christ. This is another theme in need of "de-centering" (see below), but it is not out of place to consider the theme provisionally in a global way here. The close association of God and Christ made through the epiphany concept[132] is reinforced by Paul's designation of each of them as "Savior" in conspicuous juxtaposition (Titus 1:3-4; 3:4, 6; see also 2 Tim 1:10 [of Christ]; cf. Eph 5:23; Phil 3:20; and 1 Tim 1:1; 2:3; 4:10; Titus 2:10, 13 [of God]).

Other soteriological emphases complete the picture. The connection of the sacrificial self-offering of Christ's death "for us" and redemption from sin is depicted in Pauline fashion (1 Tim 2:6; Titus 2:14; cf. Gal 1:4; 2:20). The strong abnegation of human effort in the salvation process (2 Tim 1:9; Titus 3:5) also corresponds to the Pauline gospel, which explored this misconception both in terms of "works of the law" (e.g., Rom 3:27-28) and, as in 2 Timothy and Titus, in the more general sense (cf. Rom 9:11-12; Eph 2:4, 8).[133] In contrast to certain tendencies of the opposing message in Ephesus, which endorsed an optimistic view of the present age and an overrealized view of salvation that diverged from the Pauline gospel (e.g., 2 Tim 2:18), the letters to coworkers follow Pauline lines, holding in tension the evil and transitory nature of the present age in which salvation has begun to unfold (1 Tim

---

132. A. Y. Lau, *Manifest in Flesh: The Epiphany Christology of the Pastoral Epistles* (WUNT 2.86; Tübingen: Mohr-Siebeck, 1996), 260-79.

133. Towner, *Goal,* 96-97.

4:1; 2 Tim 3:1; cf. Rom 12:2; 1 Cor 10:11; Gal 1:4). Equally evident is the necessity of the return of Christ for the completion of salvation (1 Tim 6:13-15; 2 Tim 4:1; Titus 2:13; cf. 1 Thess 2:19; 2 Thess 2:8; Phil 3:20).

b. The Pauline Gospel and Mission

The importance of the gospel message and the missionary enterprise is underscored in these letters. Two factors shape the way in which the apostolic teaching is described. Terms such as "sound doctrine" (1 Tim 1:10; 2 Tim 4:3; Titus 1:9) and "word of truth" (2 Tim 2:15, 18) reflect the conflict with opponents and the need to set the Pauline gospel in stark contrast to the false or incomplete teachings being spread in the churches. The term "deposit" (parathēkē) views the gospel as a commodity entrusted by God to Paul and by Paul to Timothy (and others; see the commentary at 1 Tim 6:20). In 2 Timothy (1:12, 14) this conception is part of the broader theme of handing over the Pauline mission and gospel to Timothy. The function of this description includes protection from the dangers posed to the message by heresy (1 Tim 6:20). This parathēkē language reflects some development in the notion of "tradition" as compared with other Pauline discussions. Elsewhere reflections on "tradition" focused on "accepting" and "maintaining" the apostolic gospel (1 Cor 11:2; 15:1; Gal 1:14; Col 2:6; 2 Thess 2:15; 3:6). However, in the letters to Timothy, and particularly in 2 Timothy where the imminence of the apostle's departure and the threat posed by heresy are in view, the accent shifts to the idea of the secure transmission of "the deposit" to the next generation. The concept is absent from Titus.[134]

In various ways, the three letters articulate a theology of mission. First, the threat to the gospel and the mission is very much what 1 Timothy and Titus respond to: 1 Tim 2:1-7 (2:1–3:16) grounds the universal mission in the fact that Christ died for "all" (2:5-6). Equally, the Gentile mission of Paul provides the framework for the letter to Titus (1:1-3). The witness motive that underlies much of the ethical teaching demonstrates one important way in which the Christian communities are to participate in the mission to the Gentiles (1 Tim 3:7; 5:14; 6:1; Titus 2:5, 9; 3:2, 8). This point is strengthened by means of a subtle but detectable allusion to the OT in 1 Tim 2:8. There, following the theological argument for universal mission made in 2:1-6, capped off by the strong reminder of Paul's calling to the Gentiles in 2:7, men are commanded (literally) "to pray in every place." The phrase "in every place" (en panti topō) appears to be rather ordinary until one realizes that it occurs, in the NT, only in Paul (1 Cor 1:2; 2 Cor 2:14; 1 Thess 1:8), in each case in relation to the proclamation of the gospel of Jesus Christ in ways that

---

134. Cf. Towner, Goal, 124-26.

pick up the theme announced in Mal 1:11 of the future universal Gentile worship of God ("For from the rising of the sun to its setting my name is great among the nations, and *in every place* incense is offered to my name, and a pure offering; for my name is great among the nations, says the LORD of hosts"). These echoes place the Ephesian church in the salvation-historical position of "fulfillers" of the OT promise that the nations would worship God — Paul's own mission to the Gentiles (2:7; 2 Tim 1:11) has become the church's mission as well (see commentary).

Then, instructions to Timothy develop his role in terms of the Pauline mission, and 2 Timothy is written specifically to prepare the younger coworker to carry on with the apostle's mission (2 Tim 1:6-14; 2:1-7; 3:10-17; 4:1-5, 6-18). In fact, the command to Timothy not to be ashamed (2 Tim 1:8) is extraordinarily "missiological" and eschatological. On the one hand, in this command and with the "shame" language, Paul consciously connects Timothy and the younger man's ministry with himself and his stand for the gospel (1:12), and, as he does so, the echoes of Rom 1:16 are impossible to miss. From there, on the other hand, the "I am not ashamed" announcement echoes OT themes associated with God's promise to vindicate his people (Ps 24:2; Isa 50:7-8; 28:16), which Paul sees as being fulfilled in the revelation of God's righteousness in the gospel he preaches.[135] Thus Timothy stands in the same line of fulfillment of the eschatological promise that Paul linked to his mission to the Gentiles.

c. The Holy Spirit

It is often held that the Spirit, so dominant in Paul's letters to churches, is lacking in the picture of ministry and the spiritual life that emerges from the letters to Timothy and Titus. But the five references to the Spirit reflect a Pauline understanding (1 Tim 3:16; 4:1; 2 Tim 1:7, 14; Titus 3:5). Titus 3:5 considers the role of the Holy Spirit in salvation — as the agent whose "washing" brings about "regeneration" and "renewal." 2 Tim 1:6-7 depicts the Spirit as the source of power for ministry, with possible echoes of Romans 8 and Joshua 1. 2 Tim 1:14 speaks of the Spirit's indwelling of believers. In 1 Tim 4:1 the Spirit is seen in traditional mode as the Spirit of prophecy. Finally, 1 Tim 3:16 characterizes the resurrection existence of Christ with the term "in the Spirit" (cf. Rom 1:4). Thus the Spirit is not absent from these letters, even if other themes are employed to articulate a theology of the Christian life.[136]

---

135. R. B. Hays, *Echoes of Scripture in the Letters of Paul* (New Haven, CT: Yale University Press, 1989), 38-39.

136. Towner, *Goal*, 56-58; Marshall, 105.

d. The Christian Life

In a way similar to Paul's teaching in Phil 4:8-9, though more extensively, these letters use Hellenistic vocabulary to construct a model of the Christian life. Three concepts describe the whole of the Christian life — "faith," "godliness," and "good works" — of which the most striking is godliness (or piety; *eusebeia*). This term conceptualizes Christian existence as a balance of faith in God/Christ and the appropriate response of love and service toward others (see the Excursus at 1 Tim 2:2). The term "piety" had already been adapted for use in Hellenistic Judaism to describe a life lived in response to God's covenant lovingkindness, so there is no reason to think it is at odds with Pauline theology. At the same time, the letters employ various other terms that were well known in secular ethics to describe the outward life (prudence, moderation, discretion, and self-control [*sōphrosynē;* see 1 Tim 2:9, Excursus]; seriousness or respectability [*semnos;* see 1 Tim 2:2, Excursus]), along with "love," "patience," "endurance," and "hope," taking care to explain that all of these characteristics of faithful living are grounded in the event of Christ's appearance and the salvation it introduced (Titus 2:11-14). Whether through magnifying the cognitive and "spiritual" dimensions of the faith or through rigid adherence to matters of ritual purity, the opponents had driven a wedge between faith and practical living. We may ask why Paul chose such a distinctively Greek way of articulating this aspect of his message, but the difference between this expression and that of Phil 4:8-9 is only one of degree; the thought is continuous.[137]

e. Church and Leadership

Theological description of the church is most evident in 1 Timothy, where household imagery provides the dominant components. The church is God's household (3:15; *oikos theou*). This concept ties together related themes in key places to describe God's rule in life in terms of household order (1:4; *oikonomia theou*) and the overseers' leadership in terms of household management (3:4-5).[138] Subsequent discussion of relationships pertinent to both household and church shows how the fundamental social institution has come to serve as a model for understanding the obligations of believers within the community of faith. The concept is not stressed to the same degree in Titus (1:7): in this letter the household is the place where Christian faith must first take root, altering "Cretan" behavior patterns into those that will endorse the gospel, though there may be some degree of overlap with behav-

---

137. See the commentary at 1 Tim 2:2, 9-10; Titus 2:1-10; Towner, *Goal,* 145-65.

138. Cf. Towner, "Pauline Theology or Pauline Tradition in the Pastoral Epistles," 287-314; see the commentary at 1 Tim 3:14-15.

ior in the Christian community (2:2–3:2).[139] In 2 Timothy the household metaphor (2:20) serves a different purpose.

2 Timothy was written to prepare Timothy for joining the apostle in Rome. This included preparation for suffering (1:8; 2:3; 4:5) and instructions to ensure that gifted leaders were selected to join the Pauline mission work in Asia Minor (2:2). Here ministering gifts are stressed, while in 1 Timothy 3 and Titus 1 they are not. Essentially, the leadership profile in these letters to coworkers includes three related perspectives: qualifications for leadership, personal commitment to the mission, and personal holiness. Timothy himself is to follow the example of Paul by persevering in godliness, suffering, and trust in God (1 Tim 4:6-16; 6:12-14; 2 Tim 1:6-14; 3:10-17; 4:1-5).

f. The Authority and Use of Scripture

2 Tim 3:16 makes a very strong statement about the authority of Scripture and its use. We are probably to understand the declaration of Scripture's divine inspiration to be directed against the tendency of the false teachers to put forward strange teachings, which Paul categorizes as "myths" (4:4), and as directing Timothy to be diligent in his use of the OT writings. The point of the statement in 3:16, which underlines the divine nature of Scripture, is to demonstrate the superior effectiveness of the OT for teaching and correction in the church. The implications about Scripture in general contained in this passage need not be denied, but Paul's aim at this juncture was not to propound a doctrine of Scripture as such.

Nevertheless, his view of the OT's supreme usefulness in teaching is amply demonstrated in various ways throughout his letters to churches; and the same is true of these three letters to coworkers. Although there are no sustained quotations such as distinguish Romans within the Pauline corpus, short direct citations occur at 1 Tim 5:18-19; 2 Tim 2:19. OT allusions and echoes, sometimes produced by words and phrases rather than whole texts, are more numerous, even if they are more difficult to spot and, therefore, open to question.[140] Some allusions may be incidental, arising simply from the use of scriptural language. But use of language that links to OT texts is often intended to evoke the readers' recollection of those OT texts. The allusion to Mal 1:11 at 1 Tim 2:8 illustrates this intentional echoing of OT themes in order to interpret the present situation in the light of prophetic

---

139. Cf. Marshall, 231-36.

140. E.g., 1 Tim 2:8, alluding to Mal 1:11 (see above); 6:1, alluding to Isa 52:5 (cf. Rom 2:24); 6:7, alluding to Job 1:21 and Eccl 5:14; 6:16, alluding to Exod 33:20; 2 Tim 2:7, alluding to Prov 2:6; 4:16-18, containing several allusions to Psalm 22; and Titus 2:14, connecting with Exod 19:5; Deut 7:6; 14:2; Ps 130:8; and Ezek 37:23.

promise. The concatenation of echoes in Titus 2:14 invites readers to understand the death of Christ as the outworking of God's faithfulness to his covenant promises.[141]

It is somewhat less clear how the apostles understood the teaching of Jesus, or, for that matter, apostolic correspondence, in relation to the authority of the OT. But we do know from 1 Cor 7:10; 11:23-26 that Paul regarded the Lord's teaching as authoritative; yet where that accepted tradition did not touch on the local situation, he spoke equally authoritatively as an apostle (7:12) and believed the source of his teaching to be the Lord (2 Cor 13:3; cf. 1 Cor 7:40). What we find in 1 Tim 5:18 (see commentary), which discusses the support of ministers, is an intertextual web woven of an explicit OT quotation in 5:18a ("Do not muzzle an ox while it is treading out the grain"; Deut 25:4), followed in 5:18b by a saying of Jesus in which he alluded to related teaching about the rightful wages of the Levites in Num 18:31 ("workers deserve their wages"; Luke 10:7; cf. Matt 10:10). Interestingly, Paul employed this same combination in 1 Cor 9:9-14. The assumption of some that the formula preceding the quotation of Deut 25:4 ("For Scripture says") encompasses the Jesus material as Scripture is neither likely nor, from the standpoint of authority, necessary. Although the Jesus tradition was no doubt already being written down and collected, and regarded as authoritative (as in Paul), the canonical Gospels had not yet emerged. This is not to say that the teaching of Jesus would be accorded a subscriptural authority — the Messiah was the supreme interpreter of the Scriptures; it is simply the case that what is not written cannot, in the strictest sense, be regarded as Scripture. In this repetition of a pattern, Paul adds to the authority coming from the OT and the Jesus tradition that which comes from his own apostolic use. Timothy, the immediate recipient of this letter, would surely have known the force of Paul's argument (cf. 1 Cor 16:10). Since Paul wrote 1 Corinthians from Ephesus, it is reasonable to assume that the Ephesian believers would also follow the echoes to the other situation of authoritative apostolic teaching.

2. In Search of a Christological Center: Savior and Epiphany

As the modern consensus has developed, proponents have increasingly come to recognize the pseudepigrapher/author as a creative theologian in his own right.[142] With this recognition has come the desire to locate as precisely as possible the author's theology. Several scholars have identified his interest in

---

141. See the commentary throughout; see also P. H. Towner, "The Old Testament in the Letters to Timothy and Titus," in Carson and Beale, eds., *Commentary on the Use of the Old Testament in the New Testament.*
142. Turning in a new direction from Dibelius and Conzelmann, 9.

the theme of salvation in the present age.[143] But the spotlight has fallen on Christology, and the two elements often thought to unify and distinguish the Christology of the PE are the depiction of Christ as Savior and the epiphany concept.

If the letters are considered as a corpus (PE), it is perhaps accurate enough to say that in it both God and Christ are identified with the appellation "Savior." A general processing of these data indicates that the title designates God as "Savior" in the sense of being the architect and initiator of the salvation plan (1 Tim 2:3; 4:10; Titus 1:3; 2:10, 13; 3:4; cf. 1 Tim 1:1). Christ as "Savior" is the means by which this plan is implemented in history (2 Tim 1:10; Titus 3:6; cf. 1:4). But when the actual occurrences are evaluated letter by letter, this becomes less a unifying theme and more one that causes the Christology of one letter to stand out. In two important passages in Titus God and Christ are each named Savior in close proximity (see esp. Titus 1:3, 4; 3:4, 6).[144] This has the dramatic and thematic (see below) effect of identifying Father and Son as co-sharers of this title. In 2 Timothy "Savior" occurs only in reference to Christ (1x). In 1 Timothy the title is used only of God (3x). It is surely arguable that the activity associated with the "Savior" designation is implicitly attributed to Christ in and through use of the *sōzō* ("salvation") word group and other theological formulations of the Christ event (e.g., 1:15), but suppressing the title as a christological category suggests an intentional reticence to make the claims associated with it; in the case of 1 Timothy the choice to emphasize other elements of Christology (see below) may have led to its omission.

More typical of recent scholarship is the tendency to type the PE on the basis of an "epiphany Christology." And there is some merit to this, for the distinctive *epiphaneia* word group occurs in each of the three letters (see the Excursus at 1 Tim 6:14). Yet interpretations vary. V. Hasler, the first to follow this lead, detected in the author's use of "epiphany" a retreat from Paul's apocalyptic outlook and new interests in God's transcendence and the complete futurity of salvation.[145] L. Oberlinner argued that the concept shifted the focus in eschatology decisively from the parousia to the presence of salvation in the world.[146] Neither view, however, balances with the eschatology of these letters.[147] A. Lau more helpfully concludes that the concept

---

143. See above on salvation: IV.C.1.a.

144. In the case of 2:10, 13, both references are to God (see the commentary).

145. V. Hasler, "Epiphanie und Christologie in den Pastoralbriefe," *TZ* 33 (1977): 193-209.

146. L. Oberlinner, "Die 'Epiphaneia' des Heilswillens Gottes in Christus Jesus," *ZNW* 71 (1980): 192-213.

147. See Towner, *Goal*, 66-71; Marshall, 293-96.

represents a reconfiguration of traditional Christology for a Greek audience rather than a Hellenizing departure from it.[148]

Both the noun *epiphaneia* (1 Tim 6:14; 2 Tim 1:10, 4:1, 8; Titus 2:13; cf. 2 Thess 2:8) and the verb *epiphainō* (Titus 2:11; 3:4 in the aorist) refer to an "appearance." The secular background to the language parallels that of "Savior." In Hellenistic religious discourse, the terminology described the appearance of a god on behalf of his worshipers. The emphasis in the term on divine assistance made it an effective device to explore the Christian belief that God's salvation intervened in history in a person. Hellenistic Judaism (LXX) used the concept to retell the stories of Yahweh's interventions in the world, providing some precedent for its later Christian use (see further 1 Tim 6:14, Excursus).

In these letters, the "epiphany" concept has two foci. Most clearly demarcated is the future appearance of Christ. In 1 Tim 6:14 and 2 Tim 4:1, 8, *epiphaneia* is effectively synonymous with *parousia* (cf. 2 Thess 2:8). In the case of Titus 2:13, however, the same event (the parousia of Christ) is described with epiphany language as "the appearance of the glory of our great God and Savior" (see commentary). But when the noun describes the historical appearance of Christ as Savior (2 Tim 1:10), the attending phrase "through the gospel" delays the closure of the "epiphany," as its extension into (or its effects upon) present human life is considered (cf. Titus 1:2-3). Use of the verb in reference to appearances of God's grace in Titus 2:11 and 3:4 (descriptive references to the Christ event) is similar. In these cases, Marshall argues, that "the past epiphany is not restricted to the actual historical event of the life of Jesus but encompasses the ongoing effects that are brought about by the gospel . . . one epiphany inaugurated by the coming of Jesus and continuing throughout present and future time."[149] Or perhaps such texts view the formative epiphany as being reenacted in the proclamation of the gospel. Such perspectives may be appropriate if a metaphorical extension of something concrete (the Christ event in history) is meant.[150] Titus 2:11 and 3:4 refer obliquely to the Christ event in order to view the event from theological and ethical perspectives. In any case, the relationships are such: God's grace "has appeared" in the epiphany of his Son; it is being revealed in and through the church's proclamation of the gospel; and it will be revealed finally and ultimately in the future epiphany of Christ (= "the glory of God" in Titus 2:13).

148. Lau, *Manifest in Flesh.*

149. Marshall, 295; cf. L. Oberlinner, *Titusbrief,* 156-57; K. Läger, *Die Christologie der Pastoralbriefe* (Hamburger Theologische Studien 12; Münster: Lit, 1996), 111-19.

150. There is the potential here to confuse the event of Christ's coming with its ongoing effects on people (right into the present and future) through proclamation of that event (see Towner, *Goal,* 70-71).

Attaching to the epiphany concept as used of Christ is preexistence sliding toward deity. Use of the concept represents a christological "experiment" by which Paul explores the link between God's salvation plan and its manifestation in and through a preexistent Savior, the Messiah (2 Tim 1:9-10; cf. 1 Tim 1:15).[151] Epiphany, in combination with the accumulation of epithets and activities formerly associated with Yahweh (Savior, judge, Lord, recipient of a doxology [2 Tim 4:18]), reflects a Christology shaped to encompass deity.

Finally, epiphany Christology also reconceptualizes the relation between eschatology and ethics. By establishing, with a single word, that the historical past "epiphany" introduces salvation and the future "epiphany" completes it, the present age between these poles comes fully under the influence of "epiphany." This is especially noticeable in Titus 2:11-14 and 3:4-7; but in 2 Tim 1:10 and Titus 1:3 the role of proclamation in influencing the present age strikes a similar note.

With the epiphany language and category, God's story is retold in Hellenistic christological dress in a way that forces a rethinking of common categories. As with "Savior" (see the commentary at 1 Tim 1:1), epiphany language is deployed deliberately to engage the dominant religious-political discourse. Perhaps the challenge posed by co-opting the dominant language of emperors is profound enough. But use of the term in reference to the past human experience of Christ (2 Tim 1:10) sharpens the subversive point. "Epiphany" called to mind power and divine intervention (in secular Greek thought, in Hellenistic Judaism, and in the Roman Empire). But in the epiphany of Jesus Christ, divine power and presence are disguised in human weakness, suffering, and death (cf. 2 Corinthians 12). The added allusion to preexistence heightens the paradox.

3. The Trajectories of Christology in the Three Letters

Consequently, in varying degrees Christology in these three letters is oriented to this dual salvation/epiphany theme. But the attraction created among the letters by applying such language to Christology does not force Christology in each case into a unified trajectory. In fact, as the letters are read individually, the visibility or attraction of the theme varies, and other literary goals decide the degree to which Christology serves this theme. The best illustration of this is 1 Timothy, which, for its own reasons, noticeably suppresses the "Savior" title and limits "epiphany" to one occurrence (see below; cf. 2 Thess 2:8). The decision to adapt this elevated, politically loaded language to Christology (to one degree or another in each letter) may reveal

---

151. See Lau, *Manifest In Flesh*, 279.

the intention to take the dialogue with the powers of the culture to another level. But in each letter Christology assumes a distinctive shape.

a. Christology in 1 Timothy: "Christ Jesus, himself human"

Under the control of the opening image of *oikonomia theou* (1:4), through which Paul views Christian existence as God's design for human society, Christology in 1 Timothy acquires a distinctively "human" shape. Four creedlike or commemorative texts combine to present a picture of Christ that supports engagement in this world ordered by God (for what follows, see the commentary). Of these, 2:5-6 best characterizes the christological trajectory of the letter. It occurs within the carefully constructed discourse about salvation (2:1-7), and grounds Paul's assertion that God's will is to save "all" people (2:3-4). Within this context, it is Christ's humanity that shapes Christology: he mediated between God and people as a "human being" (v. 5) and executed this function through his self-offering (v. 6). The formulation establishes clearly the necessity of Christ's complete participation in humanity in order to accomplish the work of mediation intrinsic to God's universal salvation plan.

In the remaining christological texts the humanity of Christ is similarly to the fore. 1:15 centers on Christ's entrance into the world and links salvation to his human history. The so-called Christ-hymn of 3:16, given to explain "the mystery of godliness," begins by affirming his humanity ("he appeared in a body [flesh]"). And though the reflections on his resurrection/ vindication (line 2) and entrance into glory (line 6) indeed fill out the picture of his earthly history, the latter allusion to the ascension is a reminder that the vindicated Messiah represents humanity completed through his suffering and resurrection. And it is as the completed human that Christ is the content of the gospel proclaimed and believed in the world (lines 4-5). Christology again seeks to bind Christian existence and mission inextricably to the humanity of Christ. At the core of the church's present existence and mission is the vindicated human Christ.

A last glimpse of the humanity of Christ, alongside a reference to his future epiphany, is given in 6:13-14. A striking conjunction of thoughts occurs. On the one hand, in the ethical and admonitory context, solemnity is added by reminding Timothy of the presence of God and (the exalted) Christ. But, on the other hand, the dominant pattern of faithfulness that is the focus of the entire commissioning text is the human witness of Christ in weakness before Pilate.

Christology in 1 Timothy assumes a human trajectory. It is shaped to explore the theme of God's design for humanity by allowing various glimpses of the human work and experience of Christ. In this way he becomes the template for faithfulness in ministry, suffering, and vindication, as reflections on his own work in the world provide the pattern for present gospel ministry.

b. Christology in Titus: Christ Jesus, Co-Savior

Christology in the letter to Titus assumes a different trajectory. A careful look at the language and conceptual world of the letter (see the commentary) reveals that it was written specifically and intentionally, not just notionally, to the Cretan context, where a nascent church was adrift in a rude social and ethical environment. Paul's discourse is designed to engage the Cretan cultural story and an opposition that was bound by Crete's sub-Christian value system. Once this tactic is recognized, the emergence of the Cretan stereotype at various points in the letter, as a negative backdrop, makes sense (see commentary at 1:2, 12; 2:11; see below). In the background is a Cretan view of Zeus, alleged to have been born and to have died on Crete and to have received divine status for his benefactions to humans. Christology in Titus intentionally collides with the cultural myth by playing down the human features of Christology (e.g., 1 Tim 1:15; 2:5; 3:16) and insisting that Christ "appeared" among humans from above, not from below, and conferred gifts (salvation, a life of virtue).

This elevated view of Christ provides the dramatic christological brackets that shape the main part of the letter. In the opening and closing christological texts God and Christ are depicted as co-sharers of the title "Savior" (1:3-4; 3:4, 6).

Within this frame a high Christology is developed. In 2:11-14 theological material grounds the ethics of the new existence (2:1-10). The themes of Savior (2:10) and epiphany converge to describe Christ's historical ministry as the "epiphany" of God's grace (2:11). His eschatological return is described as the "epiphany of the glory of our great God and Savior." Christ is the source of present Christian existence and hope for its completion.

Paul's Christian epiphany story subverts (by employing the current language and symbols) the cultural "epiphany" stories. For the oblique reference to Christ's entrance into the human sphere as the epiphany of "God's grace, bringing salvation" trumps the similar stories about gods, heroes, and even the emperor. Paul further exegetes the Christ event in Hellenistic terms as "education in culture" (paideia), describing the effects of this truly divine epiphany, in opposition to the Cretan stereotype, in terms of a "Christian civilization" where the cardinal virtues can indeed be realized (2:12). Allusion to a second epiphany in 2:13 plays equally on the typical theme of epiphanies of Hellenistic kings, gods, and Roman emperors ("the glory of our great God and Savior"; tēs doxēs tou megalou theou kai sōtēros). Into that theme Paul defiantly inserts the name "Jesus Christ" as the one whose "epiphany" will embody God's glory. As the commentary will explain, Christ does not here explicitly acquire the status of *theos*. But implicitly he very nearly does, and he nevertheless displaces other claimants to deity by appearing as the embodiment of the divine glory.

In the attached tradition about Christ's self-offering (2:14; see 1 Tim 2:6; Gal 1:4; Eph 5:2) a christological critical mass is reached. OT allusions (Exod 19:5; Deut 7:6; 14:2; Ezek 37:23) facilitate a christological transfer of saving actions originally expected of YHWH to Jesus Christ himself. Human salvation is pinned on Jesus Christ, who in his past epiphany embodied the grace of God the Savior and in his future epiphany will express divine glory.

In 3:3-7 the same story is retold with a slight thematic adjustment. Paul again describes the Christ event in terms of divine epiphany and the beneficent gifts ("kindness and love") bestowed by a ruler on his subjects (3:4). The benefactor is God the Savior, while the gift and the new life it produces are in subsequent statements located precisely in the redemptive ministry of "Jesus Christ our Savior." The Cretan quality of life (cf. v. 3) is thus rejected by God (v. 4), who manifests his life-altering beneficence in the person of Christ. Now, however, the antidotal newness of life is described in terms of the Holy Spirit (3:5-6).

Consequently, the letter to Titus constructs a Christology of the same conceptual bricks and mortar (Savior, epiphany) used in the letters to Timothy. But specifically in Titus the resultant Christology follows a higher trajectory designed to sharpen the gospel's penetration into Cretan culture: it is the story of the elevated Christ, who in his divine past "appearance" is Savior and in his future "appearance" is "the glory of our great God and Savior."

c. Christology in 2 Timothy: The Lord Jesus Christ, Paradigm of Suffering and Vindication

It can surely be said that the Christology of 2 Timothy employs the same distinctive materials already introduced. But a marked use of the title "Lord" adds a dimension not stressed in the other letters. This dimension, in addition to the literary function and more personal nature of 2 Timothy, sets Christology on a distinct trajectory.

First, the title "Lord" *(kyrios)* is dominant in this letter (16x; cf. 5x in 1 Timothy and 0x in Titus).[152] In one case it occurs in a discussion of suffering ("the testimony about our Lord"; 1:8). But it predominates in reflections on Christ the resurrected Lord. He is the object of the church's faith (2:22)

---

152. 2 Tim 1:2, 8, 16, 18(2x); 2:7, 19(2x), 22, 24; 3:11; 4:8, 14, 17, 18, 22; 1 Tim 1:1, 12, 14; 6:3, 14 (6:15 of God).

and the servant's source of wisdom (2:7) and identity (2:19, 24; 4:22). More notably Paul looked to the Lord for deliverance and strength (3:11; 4:17-18) and especially for vindication (4:8, 14; cf. 1:16, 18). The *kyrios*-emphasis in 2 Timothy may be linked to Paul's location in Rome, where the dominant religious use of the title would have been in reference to the emperor. It is certainly not unlikely that Paul would voice a subversive objection to the powers in this way. But within the story of Paul that this letter brings to a conclusion, it is the association of Christ's Lordship with resurrection and vindication (cf. Rom 1:4) — and especially in view of Paul's personal fixation on these promises in anticipation of his death — that suggests the relevance of a *kyrios*-Christology to the message of 2 Timothy.

The twin themes of resurrection and vindication run throughout the letter. The first theological piece (1:9-10) utilizes Savior and epiphany language to describe Jesus' redemptive ministry in history. Although the co-sharing of status between Christ and God comes close to emerging through the *sōzō-sōtēr* wordplay ("[God] *saved* us . . . because of his grace . . . through the epiphany of our *Savior,* Jesus Christ"), the context of this and other christological statements in the letter shows the more dominant interest to be in the suffering *and especially* resurrection of the Savior. Thus here the epiphany of Christ in history is viewed from the results it achieved: he "destroyed death" (Rom 6:6, 10; 14:8-9; 2 Cor 4:10; 1 Thess 5:10; cf. Heb 2:14). But the emphasis is on resurrection ("brought life and immortality to light"). Paul's christological interest in this letter will hover at this intersection of the Lord's life and death, where the door to eternal life has been opened.

This way of characterizing "epiphany" entails a surprise that is meant to encourage Timothy not to be afraid. An unbeliever would scarcely think of the life, suffering, and death of Jesus Christ in terms of a divine "epiphany," for the elements of weakness and shame (1:8, "the testimony about our Lord"; v. 12) strike a discordant note. The divine and powerful effects of the cross are realities evident only to faith (cf. Rom 8:24). For those outside the faith or those challenging the place of suffering within the faith (see commentary), this use of the concept turns common notions inside out and makes a radical claim for the Christian gospel. Christ in death and resurrection embodies God's grace powerfully yet in and through utter human frailty — a paradox that faith alone resolves.

It is the application of this Christology to Timothy in this second letter that distinguishes its trajectory from the trajectories followed in 1 Timothy and Titus. With the gospel mission hanging in the balance (1:8, 14), the christological reflection of 1:9-10, supported by Paul's own testimony (1:8, 11-12), assures Timothy that neither suffering nor death poses an ultimate threat to the gospel or its representative.

Christology in 2:8-13 makes the same connections. Its message is for

Timothy ("remember," v. 8). It begins its retelling of the gospel with the resurrection theme, emphasizing resurrection and vindication in the process. Paul's own suffering is then related to this gospel (v. 9), but suffering will not bring the mission to a halt (v. 10). The intentional resurrection emphasis (cf. Rom 1:3-4; see commentary) accords with the parenetic function of the passage. Paul recommends a course of action and supports this by means of models — first Jesus, then himself. The following faithful saying (2:11-13) reminds Timothy particularly of the promises associated with the eschatological future: death with Christ will mean life with Christ, (faithful) endurance now will mean sharing in his reign then. In all this, the resurrection/vindication of Jesus infuses the parenesis with the hope and inspiration needed for Timothy to take up the dangerous role to which Paul is calling him.

Final Christological references create an eschatological picture of Christ the Lord ruling in his kingdom, judging and vindicating his people (4:1, 8, 14). For the faithful, modeled by Paul (4:8), the eschatological "epiphany" (4:1, 8) will mean fulfillment and vindication. The intervening final charge to Timothy to fulfill his ministry with its suffering (4:5) reveals again the distinctive note sounded by Christology in this letter. The final focus on the eschatological event suits the thrust of the letter that is to close the Pauline story. Paul's suffering for the gospel will end in his death, and for obvious reasons the eschatological vindication looms largest in his thinking. But Christ established the pattern he follows, and Christ's historical resurrection/vindication (the past epiphany) substantiates his own hope for this outcome in the eschatological epiphany. Timothy is to find himself in this same pattern, for the continuation of the gospel ministry (which reveals these truths) is a continuation of suffering, death, and vindication.

d. Unity and Diversity in the Christology of the Letters to Timothy and Titus

Within each letter Christology is constructed partly from elements shared by all letters. This includes the Savior and epiphany categories, as well as the habit of expressing Christology in poetic bursts of text. But the unique literary goal of each letter requires that Christology in each case follow a unique trajectory. This should not really surprise us, but the tendency to read these three letters as a three-part corpus has muted their separate messages. Christology in 1 Timothy follows a distinctly human trajectory. Christology in Titus soars higher to subvert a peculiarly Cretan religious and cultural story. 2 Timothy adds the *kyrios*-dimension as it constructs a Christology around the promises of resurrection and vindication, and the eschatological functions of Christ the Lord as a way of interpreting the suffering and death associated with the gospel mission and encouraging faithful endurance.

The argument of this introductory examination and of the commentary itself is that the epiphany and Savior concepts "unify" the Christology of these three letters only in the most qualified way. The data speak for themselves. In 1 Timothy, where the focus is on the humanity of Christ, only God is designated "Savior" (3x), and "epiphany" occurs only once in reference to the eschatological event of Christ's parousia. In 2 Timothy only Christ is designated "Savior" (1x), and "epiphany" occurs in reference both to the past event and to the future event. Additionally, *kyrios*-Christology is employed in a way not seen in the other two letters. Distinctly in Titus we find a noticeable co-sharing of "Savior" (in two pairings) and the "epiphany" concept applied by means of both verb and noun (in reference to past and future events respectively). Consequently, while the christological messages share certain common components, they nonetheless assume distinct shapes in each letter — shapes, moreover, that cannot be fully appreciated unless the letters are read as separate literary entities.

Within the broader Pauline corpus, the decision to employ these Savior and epiphany concepts does represent a new step of christological experimentation that was somehow pertinent to the writing of these three letters to co-workers. While one could overplay the search for connections with the Christology of other Pauline letters (in fact, I have played this down in the interest of reading the letters individually), one could underplay it as well. The distribution of the "epiphany" and "Savior" language (along with other linguistic and lexical features) links these letters loosely into a distinctive cluster among the other epistolary clusters that comprise the canonical Pauline corpus.

D. THEOLOGICAL PERSPECTIVE, STRUCTURE, AND MESSAGE IN THE LETTERS

From the observation that each of the three letters exhibits a unique christological trajectory, it is a logical and necessary step of introduction to identify briefly the controlling theological themes and the literary structure by which these themes develop into messages.

1. 1 Timothy: The Oikonomia Theou and Oikos Theou

a. The Theological Perspective of 1 Timothy

Johnson has argued persuasively that the theological perspective of 1 Timothy is shaped by the concept of *oikonomia theou* with which the letter opens (1:4; see the commentary). The term envisions a divinely organized pattern of life — God's ordering of reality — and the opening instruction suggests that it is apprehension of this pattern and the appropriate faith response to it that this letter will seek to explain.[153] As Paul applies it to Christian existence, the term is expansive, encompassing the whole social, political, and religious world in much the same way that the emperor would take to himself the role of the father or householder and regard the empire and its inhabitants as his household. Understood in this way, the whole of life is subject to the divine will (or is meant to be). The implications for a Christian understanding of the church in the world and mission are enormous.

Use of a term like this implies that Paul regards the social structure as continuous with God's ordering. On the one hand, therefore, 1:4 announces that the opponents stand in opposition to this divine ordering. And indications of an elitist disinterest in the world outside of the church (2:1-7), of an asceticism grounded on a misunderstanding of creation (4:1-5), and other elements of disruption will emerge to explain this allegation as the letter proceeds.

On the other hand, it is in keeping with this divine pattern *(oikonomia theou)* that the church is named the *oikos theou*, "the household of God," in 3:15. The metaphor makes the people of God the microcosm or paradigm of a world obedient to God's ordering; and its mission is to extend this reality beyond its walls so that God's way of ordering life can be known and obeyed by more and more of the unbelieving world. The whole world is God's world, and present social obligations are therefore still meaningful within Christian households. Consequently, men and women, husbands and wives (2:8-15; 5:1-2), widows and their relatives (5:3-16), and slaves and masters (6:1-2) must not ignore the social rules that determine respectability in their quadrant of human culture; but they must also live in full awareness that God's presence is redeeming, renovating, and reshaping the impulses for behavior within these relationships.

It is the centrality and control of this *oikonomia theou* perspective that determines the trajectory that Christology assumes in the letter. If the church is to give expression to the reality of *oikonomia theou,* it can do so only by engagement in all aspects of social and political life. Christological expressions repeat the refrain that the fully human Jesus entered the world and gave himself for it. The salient implications for the delegate and the church addressed by the letter are first and foremost missiological. Paul remembers his redemptive encounter with the Christ who entered history and discovers a pattern for all unbelievers (1:12-16). The same human Christ event is the basis for the uniquely Pauline universal mission to the world (2:1-7). Moreover, proclamation of this divine incursion into the human sphere has already brought results (3:16). And Timothy for his part is to be as fully engaged in ministry to this world as Jesus was (6:13).

153. Johnson, 147-54.

A combination of heretical and cultural elements stands in the way of this full redemptive engagement in human life. Timothy's task is to communicate Paul's vision of Christian existence as *oikonomia theou* in the church of Ephesus. This will include correction of opponents, instruction in doctrine, and adjudicating in matters of church leadership and administration, all in the effort to ensure that this church will effectively be God's household in society — the visible emblem and physical medium of his redemptive presence in the world.

b. The Structure and Message of 1 Timothy

   I. Opening Greeting — 1:1-2. The opening is designed to establish Paul's and, in this case, Timothy's authority for a church that has come to question the apostle's teaching and mission.

  II. Body of the Letter: (1:3–6:21a)

    A. Ordering and Organizing God's Household: Part I (1:3–3:16)

Several sections are discernible in this first half of the letter.

     1. Regarding False Teachers and False Doctrine (1:3-20). This first section divides into four subsections.

      a. Charge to Timothy: Engaging the Opponents (1:3-7). Paul begins by commanding his coworker to engage the false teachers. The directive contrasts true and false teaching and begins the defamation of the heresy on mainly ethical grounds. It emerges that the false teaching is in substance ("myths and endless genealogies") Jewish in nature (1:7)

      b. The Law and Paul's Gospel (1:8-11). Consequently, it is necessary to spell out the usefulness of Torah.

      c. Paul's Calling as a Pattern of Conversion (1:12-17). Paul draws on his own conversion from rebellion against God to ministry and bases his change to obedience on the traditional apostolic gospel.

      d. Charge to Timothy Resumed (1:18-20). Timothy's own calling is then linked to Paul's, and engagement with the false teachers is placed first on the agenda in Ephesus as this section comes full circle.

     2. Regarding Appropriate Prayer in the Church (2:1-7). The second section takes up the matter of prayer for all people. This is prayer in support of Paul's worldwide mission to the Gentiles (v. 7), which has apparently encountered a debilitating elitism that rejects Paul's mission to the Gentiles. The

very redemptive will of God is produced as evidence of God's desire to save all people, and the mission of the human Christ Jesus (2:5-6) underscores the church's commitment to engagement in the world.

3. Regarding Men and Women (2:8-15). The theme shifts to the conduct of men and women (husbands and wives), with the emphasis lying clearly on problems that have arisen in the case of some women (vv. 9-15) influenced both by a cultural trend (the "new woman") and the presence of false teachers. Paul responds by prohibiting wives in this context from the ministry of teaching within the church assembly.

4. Regarding Overseers, and Deacons (3:1-13). Also as a result of the heresy, no doubt, 3:1-13 addresses the need to select (new) leaders. The church in Ephesus had grown large enough to require a more complex leadership structure. Overseers/bishops and men and women deacons are to be carefully selected. 3:1 affirms the high calling of such leaders, perhaps in order to reassure the church after some of its leaders had defected. The codelike material of 3:2-7 parallels that found in Titus 1:6-8, suggesting that Paul may have used a traditional list of qualities for leaders. As in Titus, the accent falls on qualities that prove one's character rather than on abilities or gifts that might be associated with leading, the whole of which figures in the general qualification of "blamelessness" or "irreproachableness." A proven track record in household leadership and a good testimony among those outside the church form brackets around which a listing of Christian qualities and attitudes are given. Unlike the situation in Titus (due to the relative age of the churches), new believers are specifically exempted from consideration (v. 6). Qualities to be found in the qualified deacons are parallel, though commitment to the faith (assumed in the case of overseers, v. 2) is specifically mentioned (v. 9).

6. The Church and the Faith (3:14-16). The first part of the letter is summed up in a final call to live in a way that is appropriate for members of God's household (3:14-15). Christology expressed in the Christ hymn of v. 16 declares that this very manner of life ("godliness") in the world is indeed a possibility because of the Incarnation and mission to the world that it launched. The implicit call to the church to continue the Messiah's mission in the world flows from Jesus' full engagement in human life.

71

B. Ordering and Organizing God's Household: Part II (4:1–6:21a).
This section explores further the practical implications of the
oikonomia theou and *oikos theou* themes. The contents are parallel with those of the first half of the letter, except that Timothy's own disposition toward groups, their situations and problems, and the instructions to be given are somewhat more
pronounced in the second half. This section also falls into easily
discerned subsections.
1. Regarding Heresy, Godliness, and Timothy's Responsibility
   (4:1-16). The section heading is purposely broad to encompass the three loosely connected topics.
   a. The Emergence of Heresy (4:1-5). The eschatological na-
      ture of the heresy and some of its specific errors are intro-
      duced. Its asceticism is identified and refuted by means of
      a theology of creation accessed by intertextual echo.
   b. Sound Teaching and Godliness (4:6-10). Paul's enjoinders
      to Timothy to pursue "godliness" uncover a false notion of
      "godliness" linked somehow with the false myths and per-
      haps physical training (vv. 7-8). Timothy and the apostolic
      teaching are set in contrast to the opponents and their
      false doctrine: the basis for this mission is the "faithful
      tradition" that affirms that God is the Savior of the whole
      world (v. 10).
   c. Timothy: Paradigm of the Healthy Teacher (4:11-16). This
      turn to mission and ministry leads directly into a section
      devoted to Timothy's behavior and ministry practice. Con-
      tinued practice of identity-forming Scripture reading and
      exposition in the church by ministers such as Timothy
      with exemplary ethics serves as an antidote to the present
      dilemma.
2. Regarding Other Groups in God's Household (5:1–6:2a). The
   next broad section shifts attention to specific groups within
   the community.
   a. Proper Treatment of Age Groups (5:1-2). Timothy is to
      exercise his leadership in ways that reflect appropriate re-
      spect for age and gender differences. The continuity be-
      tween the Christian and the human community implied in
      the *oikonomia theou* theological category is again evident.
   b. Proper Treatment of Widows (5:3-16). An apparently sig-
      nificant practical problem needing attention is the adjust-
      ment of the system for meeting the needs of widows. A
      system (v. 11) was in place in the church of Ephesus for

the maintenance of widows. But what had started as a means of seeing that the subsistence needs of genuinely needy widows were met had been exploited by any and all widows, regardless of character, family support, or age. Younger widows had probably also absorbed the "new" values of a cultural trend, resulting in promiscuous behavior. Paul thus imposes guidelines to ensure that the needs of widows are met in a way that does not leave the church open to accusations of encouraging immoral behavior.

   c. Proper Recognition and Discipline of Elders (5:17-25). In the case of the church's administration of its elders, there was the need both to remunerate those who were serving well (v. 17), for which scriptural authority is provided, and to discipline fairly those who had fallen into sin (vv. 20-21; in this case probably by association with the opponents). The church was to take the selection of replacements seriously, in order that only those with sound reputations would be chosen.

   d. Expectations of Slaves (6:1-2a). The presence of slaves in the church required sensitive oversight. Some had masters who were not believers, while others probably worshiped in the same assembly as their Christian masters. Some slaves were taking the message of the gospel as grounds for ignoring the status of their owners. Paul requires slaves instead to serve their masters, whether believers or not, in exemplary fashion. But at the same time, with a subtle shift in language, Paul injects into the instruction a redemptive-subversive interpretation.

3. Regarding False and True Teachers: Godliness, Greed, and the Correct Use of Wealth (6:2b-21a). The final section addresses a number of issues, framed by the concern to confront the opposition and by the theme of wealth and alternative ways of viewing it.

   a. Charge to Timothy: Confront the False Teachers and Their Lust for Wealth (6:2b-10). Paul denounces the opponents' teaching of false doctrine and charges that they teach for profit. He distances genuine godliness from material acquisition and explores a proper view of material wealth.

   b. Recasting Timothy's Commission: Genuine Character and Motive for Ministry (6:11-16). In contrast, Timothy is to pursue the things that lead to eternal life, to fulfill his ministry until the return of Christ (v. 14). The testimony

73

of the human Jesus before Pontius Pilate is paradigmatic for Timothy's faithfulness in the world mission. Just as Paul's reminiscence of calling concluded with a doxology (1:17), so here Timothy's calling is punctuated by a solemn declaration of God's sovereignty (6:15-16).

    c. A Corrected Perspective on Wealth (6:17-19). Instructions for the wealthy of the community correct the misunderstanding of the greedy opponents. Paul stresses their responsibility to share material wealth in a way that calls to mind the emphasis on "equality" in 2 Corinthians 8.

    d. Repeating the Charge to Engage the Opponents (6:20-21a). The final instruction of the letter mirrors the one that opened it. It stresses the importance of guarding the apostolic gospel, upon which the Pauline mission and the church's health depends.

III. Closing Benediction (6:21b). The final brief blessing reveals the public scope of the mandate message to Timothy.

2. Titus: The God Who Does Not Lie and the Cultural Deception of Crete

a. The Theological Perspective of Titus

The key to deciphering the theological strategy of Titus lies in recognizing the opening reference to "the God who does not lie" (*ho apseudēs theos;* 1:2) as a polemical challenge to the Cretan story.[154] The message unfolds from there as Paul identifies the true God as the source of the eternal life proclaimed by his gospel, while he rejects and condemns the compromised value system of Cretan culture. Reaching high points at 2:11-14 and 3:4-7, the presentations of God and Christ converge to force a subversive rethinking of the categories (Savior, grace, epiphany, salvation, civilization, divine beneficence) so often applied to the gods and the emperor.

    Paul's subversive technique leaves no doubt as to the layered message this letter intends to communicate. First, the appalling cultural value system (1:12; see also the commentary at 1:6-9, 10-11; 2:2-10; 3:1-3) is aptly linked to a perverted mythology. Second, when Cretan (Jewish-)Christian teachers propagate a view of the faith still encumbered with perverse cultural baggage, they stand condemned for their willful opposition to Paul's mission and for their fulfillment of the decadent Cretan stereotype. It is lifting the church from this cultural morass that forms part of Titus's teaching mission on the island

---

154. See above on Christology, 64-65.

(1:5). Third, in keeping with the sweeping claims of Paul's theological polemics, the authentic source of the virtues heralded by Greek and Roman culture and of true education in civilization (*paideia;* 2:12) is the God who caused the grace-gift of Christ to "appear" in human history (2:11; 3:4). Paul's none-too-veiled claim is that in comparison with the "epiphany" of Christ (past and future; 2:13) all other alleged "epiphanies" pale in significance.

From this theological perspective, the letter to Titus becomes less a pastoral document and much more a polemical and subversive crafting of the gospel into a directive to a Pauline coworker (and to those churches in which he will work) that denounces the utter deception of Cretan religion and life. And, in response, the church's task in this context is to embody the grace of God in so full a way that its life, from household to community (authentic Christian existence), is as radically different from the depraved expectations and values of Cretan culture as the truthful God of Paul's gospel is from the lying Zeus of Cretan lore.

b. The Structure and Message of Titus

   I. Sources and Background Information on Crete

  II. Opening Greeting (1:1-4). It is always a temptation to pass quickly over the opening comments of Paul's letters in order to get to the meat of his message. But it is also a dangerous thing to do. The opening greeting of Titus is one of the longest, most carefully and theologically constructed of Paul's letters.

     A. Paul and His Apostolate (1:1-3). In addition to identifying himself in terms of his apostolic office and authority in relation to God and Christ, Paul briefly defines the main goal of his ministry (1:1-2) and establishes that his ministry is the outworking of God's redemptive plan (1:2-3). The point of this is not simply to discuss the theology of preaching or salvation, but rather to establish the theological and eschatological framework within which Titus's specific ministry in Crete is to be understood and to situate this on the foundation of "the God who does not lie" (1:2; see above, and see the commentary). What applies to Paul and his ministry also applies to his coworker's activities in the Cretan churches. The strategic function of the opening is demonstrated as its key terms and concepts are developed later in the letter.[155]

155. "Faith" (1:1, 4, 13; 2:2, 10; 3:15), "godliness" (1:1; 2:12), "hope" (1:2; 2:13; 3:7), "eternal life" (1:2; 3:7), "Savior," "save," "salvation" (1:3, 4; 2:10, 11, 13; 3:4, 5, 6), and the concept of divine disclosure (1:3; 2:11; 3:5).

B. Titus: The Recipient (1:4). The close linkage between Paul and
his colleague is further established as v. 4 describes the addressee as a "true son" who shares a "common faith."

C. The Greeting (1:4b)

III. Body of the Letter (1:5–3:11).

A. Instructions to Titus (1:5-16). The body of the letter divides into
two main sections, the first of which separates into three subsections addressed most directly to Titus.

1. The Overarching Instruction to Titus: Putting in Order and
Finishing Up (1:5). Titus was to remain on assignment in
Crete to accomplish a twofold task: to complete the work already begun through initial stages of church planting and to
correct certain defects that had come to light (v. 5a).

2. Appointing Church Leaders Able to Instruct the Church and
Correct Opponents (1:6-9). One part of this command involved the selection of leaders, for which Paul provides guidance similar to that given Timothy in 1 Tim 3:1-7. Paul refers to the leaders as "elders" and "overseers" (bishops) in
rapid succession (vv. 5, 7). As the emphasis falls on elements
of personal and interpersonal character (they are to be
"blameless"), on private and public reputation, it becomes
clear from the language used that the "unfinished" business
is that of extracting this church from the clutches of Crete's
immoral value system. At v. 9 attention shifts to ministerial
duties, as Paul stresses commitment to the apostolic gospel
and the ability to teach and envisions the ongoing work of
engaging a resistant trend.

3. Naming and Engaging the Opponents (1:10-16). Transition is
made to a subsection that identifies the presence of opponents who are apparently rebellious Jewish-Christian teachers
unwilling (or unable) to evaluate cultural assumptions critically (v. 10). These had gained a hearing in Christian households and disrupted their adherence to the higher goal of
Paul's gospel (v. 11). Paul "types" these rebels by reference
to the distasteful "Cretan" stereotype (vv. 11-13a) and disparages their inferior teaching about ritual purity as "Jewish
myths" and human traditions. They deny their claims to
know God by their behavior (v. 16).

B. Instructions for the Church (2:1–3:11).

1. Some Local and Formal Matters of Introduction. The second
main section of the letter body, though still addressed to Titus, is taken up with instruction that is more directly oriented

to the believing community. The agenda of 1:5 is still in mind as the thought turns at 2:1 to positive teaching designed to foster stability in the churches (2:1-10) and a respectable public profile in the larger society (3:1-8). 3:9-11 returns to the matter of dealing with the opponents as a matter of church discipline. Each main section of the teaching is supported by theological material (2:11-14; 3:4-7). The theology is intended to provide the basis for the teaching about the way Christians ought to live, and it does so, pointedly, in a way that distances Paul's view of "godliness" from Cretan patterns of behavior. Paul's style of instruction from 2:1 to 3:2 is influenced by a traditional form he has made good use of in other letters (Col 3:18–4:1; Eph 5:21–6:9; cf. Rom 13:1-7) — the household code — though here the application is expanded somewhat to include life and relationships in the church. Christian living is thus viewed from the perspective of the various social stations in which believers find themselves within the household and society. Use of the form also underlines Paul's concern for behavior within the church that is generally respectable, and would be regarded as such even by those observant and critical outsiders to the faith. Paul is concerned not just that the churches rise above the Cretan value system, but also that they communicate positively a good witness in the world.

2. Christian Living within the Household (2:1-15). 2:1-15 addresses life in the church, which, to judge from v. 1, had been ethically compromised under the influence of the culture and resistant Jewish-Christian teachers who were quite comfortable with the Cretan status quo.

   a. Living in Accordance with Sound Doctrine (2:1-10). With an awareness of the conventional patterns of respectability, the instructions address Christians' ordinary situations in life (in the household) according to social positions, gender, and age. Older men are to be the paragons of virtuous behavior, while older women are to avoid stereotypical Cretan character defects so that they can impart to younger women the domestic qualities that will make them exemplary wives. At this juncture it is possible to see the mark of the "new woman" trend, which challenged women to let go of dress codes and pursue promiscuity, spreading throughout the empire. Younger men, to which category Titus also belongs, are to live in such a way that

they are models of good character and good deeds. Slaves,
similarly, are to be faithful in all their service to their
masters. Three times Paul underlines that the lifestyle he
enjoins is not simply the correct outworking of the faith
but also meant to enhance the church's reputation and witness in the world (vv. 5, 8, 10).

  b. The Basis of This Life (2:11-14). The theological rationale
follows the ethical instructions. In defiance of the cultural
myths and the Roman story, this passage asserts that true
godliness (and the life characterized by the virtues, 2:12)
is the outworking the epiphany of God's grace in Christ.
There can be no mistaking how different from the cultural
myth Paul's gospel is, for the passage emphasizes that it is
the traditional message of Jesus Christ's atoning death that
forms the basis for God's plan of redemption (2:14).

  c. Summary Command to Titus (2:15). Titus is to insist on
this subversive message in these churches that have been
influenced by a depraved culture and conflicting messages
(v. 15).

3. Living as the Church in the World (3:1-8). 3:1-8 invites the
readers to consider their existences as the Christian community in the world, and to do so with the church's mission
very much in mind.

  a. Christian Living within Society (3:1-2). The public profile
of the church includes its recognition of secular authorities, and the life of service it is to lead in public is understood by Paul to be its responsibility both to God and to
the state (3:1-2).

  b. The Theology That Generates This Life (3:3-7). The capacity to live in society without being compromised by its
pervasive value system is also linked to the change
brought about by the epiphany of God's gracious kindness
in Christ (3:3-4). The theological statement (3:4-7) should
not be taken as a mere rehearsal of salvation data, but
rather as the theological foundation of the Christian life of
witness in the world.

  c. The Motive (3:8). The missiological intention of this life
closes the section, and Titus is to "insist" on this dimension of the traditional gospel, in order that the requisite
observable behavior to be exhibited by believers ("good
deeds") will influence positively those who stand outside
the faith.

78

    4. Disciplining the Opponents in the Church (3:9-11). The return to the matter of the rebellious teachers forms a bracket within the letter that underlines Paul's concern for their unsettling influence in the Cretan churches. Much stands to be lost if this corrupt influence persists. Titus is to deal decisively with anyone associated with the opposition.

IV. Personal Notes and Instructions (3:12-14). As is typical of Paul's letters, the closing section includes personal information about travel. In this case, the notes indicate that Paul is moving about freely. Titus is to join Paul once his replacement has arrived in Crete.

V. Final Greetings and Closing Benediction (3:15). In a truly personal note, Paul conveys the greetings of the team members traveling with him specifically to Titus, and asks Titus to greet, on behalf of Paul and the team, those in Crete who stand firm in their support of the apostle. And, as in the case of 1 Timothy, Paul's closing wish reflects the intention — consistent with its use of elements of the *mandata principis* document form — that the letter to Titus be read in the churches in which he has been assigned.

3. 2 Timothy: Suffering and Succession

a. The Theological Perspective of 2 Timothy

Although some of the concerns that emerged in 1 Timothy stretch across to this letter, 2 Timothy addresses them according to its own unique agenda. Its authorship may be questioned (and its literary and theological purposes as well), but the letter presents itself as Paul's last. It depicts Paul in prison in Rome facing execution, and expresses none of the optimism so characteristic of the Prison Epistles. From the perspective of the Pauline corpus, or the Pauline story, this is the final chapter. And in it Paul weaves together a pattern of suffering and vindication by reference to his own experiences and those of Christ. This pattern is set before Timothy not just as Paul's delegate who would represent the apostle to a church (e.g., 1 Cor 4:7) but as the one who must persevere in his ministry in the new scope and urgency created by the nearness of Paul's departure from this life.

    The letter belongs to the parenetic-protreptic genre. Its personal address and numerous exhortations are often backed by reference to Paul's example. But it is the application of that example, in which Paul has followed Jesus into suffering out of faithfulness to the gospel, to Timothy who must "not be ashamed of the testimony about our Lord or of [Paul] his prisoner" (1:8), who must "join with [Paul] in suffering for the gospel" (1:9), who must "keep the pattern of sound teaching" received from Paul and "guard the good deposit" (1:13-14), that determines the theological perspective of the message. This multiple summons to mission and to suffering in the letter's opening sections is repeated in various ways as the discourse unfolds. The key to endurance and to courage is the Holy Spirit (1:7, 14), given as gift and empowerment when Timothy came to faith. But much of the ethical force of the commands comes in the realization that the coworker has a history with God and with Paul (1:3-6, 13-14, 15; 2:8-13; 3:10-15).

Endurance (2:12; 3:14; 4:15) and suffering (1:8; 2:3; 4:5) are the themes woven together to guide Christology and the presentation of Paul's personal reflections in the letter. Paul's calling and willing suffering for Christ mirror Christ's own experience of death (1:8-10; 2:8-10). And in the climactic conclusion (4:16-18), Paul engages the Messianic Psalm 22 (MT; LXX Psalm 21) in such a way that his impending death and the Gentile mission that his death crowns conform to and in some ways more fully complete the OT paradigm of suffering and vindication with which the early church interpreted the passion of Christ. But these vignettes do not simply serve to create a Pauline hagiography, as certain contemporary commentators allege. Rather, they mark the path that Timothy is to follow, in full awareness of the suffering ahead and the promises of relief and vindication, as he takes up (or resumes) his ministry with renewed heart in the knowledge that Paul's course is finished.

b. The Structure and Message of 2 Timothy

I. Opening Greeting (1:1-2). The opening is a near repetition of 1 Tim 1:1-2.
II. Body of the Letter (1:3–4:8). The decision to close the body of the letter after 4:8 is based on the fact that the sections leading up to this point have focused primarily on instructions to Timothy, with Paul serving as the model intermittently, that reached their culmination in the charge of 4:1-5 and its rationale in 4:6-8. However, the subsequent section (III. Closing Instructions and Personal Information), 4:9-18, is a deeply theological section that is equally crucial to the letter's central message.
A. The Call to Personal Commitment and Spirit-Empowered Ministry (1:3-18). The first major section of the letter divides into three subsections. Following the opening greeting, Paul weaves together in the first section of the letter several kinds of material designed to impart to Timothy a renewed sense of calling.
1. Thanksgiving for Timothy's Faith (1:3-5). Paul begins with a statement of thanksgiving in which he reaches back into his own and Timothy's past and links his coworker to himself on the basis of this shared heritage of faith.

2. The Renewed Call to Boldness and Faithfulness in Ministry (1:6-14). Building on this mutual relationship and faith, the next subsection mounts the argument for Timothy's continued participation in the mission.

   a. The Call to Action (1:6-8). Paul begins from the reality of the Holy Spirit in Timothy. This gift is the basis of the power and courage, and the Spirit's presence in his life is the platform for a renewed call to suffer for the gospel (vv. 6-8).

   b. The Gospel for Which We Suffer (1:9-10). The core of the gospel itself is reason enough for such commitment. But the emphasis on death's abolition and the risen Christ's accomplishments in this reflection launch a Christology that is meant here and throughout to foster the courage and hope needed to face suffering.

   c. The Apostolic Model for Timothy and the Call to Succession (1:11-14). The pattern of the apostle's own life underlines the necessity of suffering for the mission. Timothy must therefore prepare himself to renew his efforts in this task from Paul, in the full knowledge of the Spirit's power (vv. 11-14).

3. Models of Shame and Courage (1:15-18). Contrasting images illustrate both betrayal and the kind of loyalty Paul has had in mind. The contrasting technique will continue, as it now becomes clear what is at stake in Timothy's decision either to heed or neglect Paul's call (vv. 15-18).

B. Called to Dedication and Faithfulness (2:1-13). The next section begins to chart the renewed coworker's course. It is characterized by the repetition of the themes of power (2:1; cf. 1:7, 8) and suffering (2:3, 9, 11; cf. 1:8, 12).

1. Carry Out Your Ministry with Dedication (2:1-7). Instructions are first given concerning the practical matter of choosing faithful teachers (2:2), some of whom are needed to replace those who have turned back from Paul, to take Timothy's place in Asia, so that he can travel to Rome. Then the repetition of the call to join in suffering develops into a threefold description of perseverance and single-mindedness (2:4-6).

2. Reasons for Enduring Suffering (2:8-13). The preceding images of soldiers, athletes, and farmers and the perseverance and devotion they convey are fully animated by the flesh-and-blood illustration of Paul's own experiences for the gos-

pel. Here again, within this context given to the hard realities
of ministry, christology concentrates on resurrection and vindication for the faithful (2:8, 11-13). The section closes on a
solemn note with promises of reigning with Christ, for those
who suffer with him, woven together with warnings of denial
by Christ, for those who deny him (2:11-13).

C. Addressing the Challenge of Opposition in the Church (2:14-
26). In a fairly discrete section, Timothy is set to the task of engaging opponents in the church and the confusion they have set
in motion. Two opponents are identified — Hymenaeus and
Philetus — along with the major aspect of the false doctrine
they have been teaching — the belief that the resurrection of
believers has already occurred. The reality of heresy in the
church is an unsettling thought; Paul assures Timothy that the
Lord knows those who belong to him and that his church will
stand firm (2:19-21). Timothy's methods of engagement include
avoidance of futile arguments (2:14, 22-26); he is rather to correct patiently with a view to repentance and renewal.

D. Prophecy, Commitment and Call (3:1–4:8). The final main section of the body addresses three topics.

1. The Heresy in Ephesus in Prophetic Perspective (3:1-9). At
3:1 Paul begins to locate the opposition on the eschatological
map (3:1-7). It is a "sign of the times" and the repetition of
an age-old opposition to God. Conveying this premise is the
traditional story about the two magicians who opposed Moses in Pharaoh's court (3:8-9), and the caricature created in
this way stands as a reminder for Timothy and believers that
God's truth and power will prevail.

2. The Way of Following Paul (3:10-17). By way of contrast,
Paul offers his own life as a model for the faithful coworker
to follow. Paul's model lifestyle forges the essential link between ministry and suffering (3:10-11). Moreover, his experiences are interpreted as typical of faithfulness and godliness
in general (3:12). With Paul as his model, Timothy is to hold
firm to what he has learned, the authoritative Scriptures being his standard tool (3:15-17).

3. The Final Charge to Timothy (4:1-8). The renewed call to
ministry, then, follows in 4:1-5. From the perspective of the
Pauline story, this is a call to "take up where Paul is leaving
off." If desertion and false teaching are a more prevalent issue than in earlier years — a mark of the postapostolic age
— the appropriate response is faithful proclamation of the

apostolic message by Timothy and those who stand with him in this work. His calling from God is certain; it is to continue the mission to the Gentiles that Paul must relinquish. The apostle has done his part faithfully, and his end is at hand. All that is left is to ensure that the work is placed into hands that are ready for the work and suffering that must continue to be experienced for the sake of the gospel (4:6-8).

III. Closing Instructions and Personal Information (4:9-18). Clearly 4:9-18 is a section of personal instructions and news similar to Titus 3:12-14. But it is not for this reason lacking in theological importance. On the one hand, Timothy must join Paul in Rome (4:9); this is the main concern of the letter, and it is theologically motivated by Paul's understanding of his universal mission. On the other hand, more than creating a tone of finality, by allusion to the Messianic Psalm (21 LXX), 4:16-18 overlays Paul's experiences with those of the suffering Christ. But in the light of Christ's resurrection, the apostle sees through the desertion he has experienced to the certainty that the mission to the Gentiles is being accomplished (4:17). This note of hope is Timothy's lifeline as he accepts his part in mission and suffering.

IV. Closing Greetings, Instructions, and Blessing (4:19-22). The closing has more the look of closings in Paul's letters to churches. Among the people on Paul's mind at this crucial moment in his life, eight specific individuals are named. His concern for friends made over the years and thankfulness for their support come through clearly. The closing benediction first blesses Timothy specifically; then Paul again looks briefly beyond the main addressee to the community within which the coworker represents the apostle.

V. PAUL AND THE LETTERS TO TIMOTHY AND TITUS: DEFINING THE PARAMETERS

At last, after discussing the main lines of the modern approach to these three letters and devoting several pages to how they should be read in historical context, it is time to state clearly how that discussion will affect the approach of this commentary. I have spent enough time with these letters — and even more time with interpretations surrounding them — to know that one way or another questions of authorship have controlled their reading. The authorship problem as such cannot finally be solved. But neither has anything like a compelling case been made, individually or collectively — one that substantiates questionable presuppositions and starting points and responds to the oversights and logical dead-ends discussed above — to exclude the reasonable possibility that the letters are actual, individual letters to historical persons and situations. It is this shortcoming of the majority program, and not dogmatic or faith-based assumptions, that urges some of us to read the letters as they purport to have been written. Now with the briefest of summaries I will set out the framework for the commentary and reading of the letters.

A. PAUL AND THE LETTERS TO TIMOTHY AND TITUS

The question that all scholarship on these three letters has sought to address is that of their relationship to Paul. It should be obvious at this juncture that this commentary is not going to follow the course plotted by the majority, not because authenticity is more provable than inauthenticity, but rather because the majority view (pseudonymity in one permutation or another) assumes a historical reconstruction (a "construal," in Johnson's language) that remains largely hypothetical at numerous critical junctures and has yet to address adequately numerous methodological questions.

To review briefly the developing critical view, most recent German scholars, followed by the British and North Americans, regard the "PE" as prime evidence of a transition between generations, normally identifying the transition as from third to fourth generation (or later). The writer's goal was to reestablish the line between his church and Paul via the characters of Timothy and Titus. Elsewhere I questioned this "solution" to the Paul and PE problem by arguing that if in fact transition (conceptual, linguistic, ecclesiastical, etc.) is visible in the letters, it is just as probable that the shift in view is from first generation (Paul) to the second (his coworkers).[156] But the shift or movement evident from a comparison of the letters to coworkers with the undisputed letters to churches may instead be a lateral one within the same historical scope — that is, movement indicative of changes in the situation, context, and purpose of the writer and/or of the presence of unique circumstances in the case of the recipients.

Several additional conclusions bear repeating. A reevaluation of "style" and the realities of ancient letter-writing advise the need for some latitude in reconstructing the authorship process.[157] Document forms and gen-

---

156. Towner, "Pauline Theology or Pauline Tradition in the Pastoral Epistles," 287-314.

157. For a helpful discussion of this matter, see B. Witherington III, *The Paul Quest: The Renewed Search for the Jew of Tarsus* (Downers Grove, IL: InterVarsity Press, 1998), 89-129.

res available to Paul open up new possibilities for explaining the genre of the letters to coworkers and raise questions about "standard" comparisons made with the undisputed letters to churches. Examinations of assumptions about what might constitute a normative Pauline letter have long been avoided. Equally, chronologies derived from Acts or from Paul need to be held rather loosely in view of the certainty that gaps exist. These essential observations lie behind the decision to read the letters to Timothy and Titus as letters from Paul to his coworkers.

The suggestion is that through recent probing of the substructure of the majority view, a degree of reasonable doubt has been established. This means that some significant room to maneuver has been created for the position that these letters reflect another dimension of the letter writing and ministry of the Pauline mission. Perhaps these letters reveal the extension of Pauline themes in some directions not attested in the letters to churches (employment of new vocabulary and concepts). The question is whether the character of the letters, addressed to coworkers in unique church and mission settings, can account for these seemingly new directions.

B. PAUL'S LETTERS WITHIN HIS MISSION: LETTERS TO CHURCHES AND LETTERS TO COWORKERS

There is wide agreement that Paul wrote letters and sent them as substitutes for his actual authoritative presence.[158] Even if this much is agreed, as pointed out, the actual process by which he wrote is far less certain. And the degree to which the presence of co-senders ("co-sponsors"), differences in situations addressed, changed circumstances of writing, genre choice, and so on would have affected the literary product (lexical choice, grammatical-syntactical elements, conceptual shift, register) is impossible to calculate, unless some sample of Pauline letters is assumed to represent "the way Paul wrote." Working, then, from the assumption that attempts to establish "the way Paul wrote" have not achieved reliable results, I will regard the letters to Timothy and Titus as follows.

Among the thirteen canonical Pauline letters, ten[159] were written to churches and three, the letters to Timothy and Titus, were written to individ-

---

158. See S. K. Stowers, *Letter Writing in Greco-Roman* Antiquity (Philadelphia: Westminster, 1986), 58, 68-69, 144; cf. the helpful discussion in Johnson, 93-94; Collins, *Letters That Paul Did Not Write,* 69-75.

159. This holds as well for the Letter to Philemon, which, while addressing Philemon as the head of the house church and employing the second-person singular pronoun throughout, nevertheless expressly names among the addressees other individuals and the church as a whole.

ual coworkers. To judge from what we know of Paul's apostolic and mission *modus operandi* and of the functions performed by his mission colleagues (Rom 16:1-3; 1 Cor 4:17; 2 Cor 8:23; Phil 2:19; Eph 6:21; Col 4:7-8; 1 Thess 3:2), the instructions communicated to Timothy and Titus and the roles they were to play within the communities to which they had been dispatched conform perfectly to a Pauline pattern. It is perhaps the fact that the coworkers had been assigned to represent the apostle in churches where his authority was under fire, and where opposition and false or inferior teaching had fully emerged, that led him (in the case of 1 Timothy and Titus) to incorporate elements showing affinity for the mandate form of writing that allowed both direct communication with the delegates and indirect communication with the communities. But whatever motivated Paul to write to his colleagues (he may well have done so in other situations), the fact remains: that he would have so written does not conflict with what we know to have been his perception of his relationship with his churches or the representative functions his coworkers carried out in them in his absence.

C. THE AUTHORSHIP ENIGMA: OPEN QUESTIONS

If the letters are to be read as historical letters to coworkers, how shall we understand the authorship process by which they came to be written? Here I choose to allow open questions to remain open. Among those who have argued for authenticity, however, the most popular scenario is the amanuensis/ secretary hypothesis.[160] Often two factors lead scholars to this conclusion. First, Paul is known to have employed assistants whose task it was to do the actual writing of the letter (e.g., Rom 16:22; cf. 1 Cor 16:21; Gal 6:11; 2 Thess 3:17). Paul's use of such a technique was by no means unusual,[161] but the degree to which an amanuensis might influence the shape of the letter remains an open question, as is the degree to which others named as cosenders might also influence the shape and content of writing.

Second, the assumption that the three letters are "different" from the rest of the Paulines makes the amanuensis hypothesis the default explanation. Mounce illustrates this thinking:

---

160. See the excellent discussion (with refs. to the literature) in Mounce, cxxvii-cxxix.

161. See discussions in Prior, *Paul the Letter-Writer,* 46-48; Sherwin-White, *The Letters of Pliny,* 538-46; R. N. Longenecker, "Ancient Amanuenses and the Pauline Epistle," in R. N. Longenecker and M. Tenney, eds., *New Directions in New Testament Study* (Grand Rapids: Zondervan, 1974), 281-97; cf. E. R. Richards, *The Secretary in the Letters of Paul* (Tübingen: Mohr [Siebeck], 1991).

There are differences between the PE and the rest of the Pauline writings, just as there are differences among the other Pauline writings. The questions are, how different are they and what is the significance of those differences? The Amanuensis Hypothesis best explains the internal and external evidence. It accounts for the differences between the PE and the other Pauline letters and does not introduce its own set of problems.[162]

Consequently, a survey of the commentaries maintaining authenticity reveals Tychicus (2 Tim 4:12; Titus 3:12)[163] and more frequently Luke (2 Tim 4:11)[164] as the likely possibilities to have served as Paul's amanuensis in the writing of these letters. If instead of insisting on authenticity one is satisfied with the argument for the historicity of the letters proposed by Marshall ("allonymity"; see above), then the final authorial group might include Timothy and Titus themselves.[165]

The only point to be made here is that the amanuensis hypothesis is attractive mainly because of the second factor noted above — it explains how these three Pauline letters could be different from the remaining Pauline letters and still be Pauline. Here again it can only be said (and Mounce admits as much) that the set of "differences" that distinguish the letters to coworkers from the letters to churches corresponds to other sets of differences that distinguish the various Pauline clusters from one another. The fact remains (even if we do not know entirely what to do with it) that, whereas other Pauline letters seem to name co-senders or co-sponsors, the letters to Timothy and Titus refrain from naming any. This may not necessitate the conclusion that Paul penned these three letters on his own, but it opens up the possibility — a possibility that might account for certain linguistic and lexical peculiarities when compared with other Pauline letters or clusters of letters.[166]

162. Mounce, cxxix.

163. Jeremias, 8.

164. This has been by far the most popular suggestion, largely because of the correspondence in vocabulary between Luke-Acts and these three letters. See A. Strobel, "Schreiben des Lukas? Zum sprachlichen Problem der Pastoralbriefe," *NTS* 15 (1968), 191-210; C. F. D. Moule, "The Problem of the Pastoral Epistles: A Reappraisal," in *Essays in New Testament Interpretation* (Cambridge: Cambridge University Press, 1982), 113-32; Fee; Knight; Spicq. For the argument of post-Pauline Lukan authorship, cf. S. G. Wilson, *Luke and the Pastoral Epistles* (London: S.P.C.K., 1979); J. D. Quinn, "The Last Volume of Luke: The Relation of Luke-Acts to the Pastoral Epistles," in Talbert, ed., *Perspectives on Luke-Acts,* 62-75. But see I. H. Marshall, Review of *Luke and the Pastoral Epistles,* by S. G. Wilson, *JSNT* 10 (1981): 69-74; Johnson, 88-89.

165. Marshall, 92.

166. See Prior, *Paul the Letter-Writer,* 57-59 (for 2 Timothy); see also Fee, 26, who suggests the possibility.

At any rate, it is my view that the question of the authorship process in the case of these letters must remain open. In fact, the circumstances of the authorship of these three letters may well differ from letter to letter.[167] Given the complex nature of the authorship process that gave us the Pauline corpus, there is nothing to be gained by insisting on a particular theory of composition for the three letters to coworkers. The view of this commentary is that, just as with the remainder of the Pauline letters, Paul is the author of these three letters however much or little others contributed to their messages and composition.[168]

D. FAREWELL TO "THE PASTORAL EPISTLES"?

To be consistent with the line I have taken above, one final observation seems appropriate. It may be time to say farewell to the nomenclature "the Pastoral Epistles." This term, which many trace back to Paul Anton in the eighteenth century,[169] has become something of a restraining device. Its use to describe the contents of the letters is benign enough, but the assumptions about the letters and their intention on which it rests already betray a tendency toward restraint. R. F. Collins cites Anton's rationale: ". . . the three epistles contain 'divine instruction for all church servants and the true original of a church constitution according to God's will.'"[170] Even if Anton cannot be faulted for emphasizing the ecclesiastical thrust of the letters, the degree to which this theme represents their essence must be questioned, and the tendency to "corpus read" the three letters to yield such a theme was already emerging in his assessment. In the final analysis, subsequent use of the term "the Pastoral Epistles" (PE, *Pastoralbriefe*) would eventually force the letters into a restrictive interrelationship that they were never intended to have.

It is time to uncouple the letters from this device that restrains them, and from one another, or at least to acknowledge that whatever their interrelationship within the Pauline ministry, each letter nevertheless retains its status as an independent literary entity. Johnson has been recommending this with increasing resolve since at least 1987.[171] My similar suggestion to bid

167. O. Roller, *Das Formular der paulinischen Briefe* (BWANT 4.6; Stuttgart: Kohlhammer, 1933), 20-21, maintained that the conditions of imprisonment presumed in 2 Timothy were such as would necessitate an amanuensis.

168. See further the discussion in L. T. Johnson, *Writings of the New Testament: An Interpretation* (2d ed.; Minneapolis: Fortress, 1999), 253-59; Johnson, 58-60.

169. Anton, *Exegetische Abhandlung der Pastoralbriefe Pauli an Timotheus und Titum.*

170. Collins, *Letters That Paul Did Not Write,* 88.

171. Cf. Johnson, *1 Timothy, 2 Timothy, Titus,* 7-9; see also Prior, *Paul the Letter-Writer.*

the collective term "farewell," slower in coming, is in the form of a translation from German of the pronouncement made by another scholar who came to the same conclusion for the same reasons.[172]

The term "PE" is no longer helpful, even if it is convenient, for what is gained by economy of reference is more than lost by the weight of the baggage the term has accumulated along the way. It constantly conjures up the notion of an indivisible unit, in the way that terms like "the Corinthian correspondence" or "the Thessalonian letters" do not. One may argue that the designation PE might be used only as a convenience without intending the additional baggage, but there comes a time when compromised language must be discarded in favor of alternatives free from unwanted implications. Although it will seem more cumbersome when compared to "PE," when there is reason to refer to "the letters to Timothy and Titus" in some other way as a cluster in distinction from the other letters of Paul, I will attempt to apply consistently the designation "letters to coworkers" in contrast to the "letters to churches." It is my intention with such a term to indicate both the individuality of the letters and their cluster relationship.

172. See R. Fuchs, *Unerwartete Unterschiede: Müssen wir unsere Ansichten über die Pastoralbriefe revidieren?* (Wuppertal: R. Brockhaus, 2003); see the subtitle of his ch. 4: "Abschied von 'den' Pastoralbriefen" (175; "Farewell to 'the' Pastoral Epistles").

The First Letter
to
TIMOTHY

Text, Exposition, and Notes

I. OPENING GREETING (1:1-2)

1 Paul, an apostle of Christ Jesus by the command of God our Savior and of Christ Jesus our hope, 2 To Timothy my true son in the faith: Grace, mercy and peace from God the Father and Christ Jesus our Lord.

According to ancient literary conventions, all of Paul's writings qualify as letters. But the "letter" category in antiquity was a broad one, containing writings of various degrees of formality and intimacy and a range of purposes. Paul's letters are not all identical in terms of genre and function; they tend rather to vary with the situations and recipients addressed. But they do share the basic social intention of the letter, which was — as a stand-in for oral communication that distance or social status (protocol) prohibited — to engage the recipient(s) in a conversation, dialogue, or some other act of communication.[1]

The only essential formal feature of a letter was the greeting. Typically it identifies the sender and the recipient and adds a salutation. A glance at Paul's letters shows how flexible the greeting might be; in fact, Titus 1:1-4 represents one of the most extensive Pauline greetings (cf. Rom 1:1-7). Variations often reflect directions in which Paul will move as the letter unfolds, as well as the tone he desires to adopt with the readers (see discussion at Titus 1:1-4). Thus the greeting in Galatians is heavy on the origin of Paul's apostolic office, while in Philippians the greeting strikes a different note by passing over this topic altogether. And each of these letters develops according to the lead given in the greeting.

---

1. See D. E. Aune, *The New Testament in Its Literary Environment* (Philadelphia: Westminster, 1987), 158-82, esp. 158.

More than just opening the conversation, the greeting also establishes the social context for the communication. Just as in oral communication, two parties will address one another according to rules of social status and degrees of relationship, so in the written substitute the greeting sets that stage, identifying the relative positions of the sender and the recipient.[2] In the case of 1 Timothy (and 2 Timothy and Titus), the reality of the literary situation continues to be debated. But whether the relationship between the sender and the recipient was fictional or actual, it was meant to be understood as if it were really Paul and really Timothy engaged in this exchange.

Apart from prior assumptions, there is nothing in the greeting to indicate other than a real instance of written communication between Paul and Timothy. Yet the mixture of materials to follow in the letter — some private, for Timothy; some public, for the church — has suggested to some that "Timothy" must be some sort of fictive paradigm or literary device through which teaching for the church and its leadership could be conveyed authoritatively. As we noted in the Introduction (31), among other features this tendency to alternate between private and public instruction has an analogue in a type of Hellenistic diplomatic document called the *mandata principis* (mandates of the ruler). Essentially a memorandum, the document from a ruler or government official set out instructions for his posted delegate (duties and obligations) and addressed the receiving community's responsibilities both to the ruler and his delegate. 1 Timothy represents a letter in which this genre feature has been incorporated. Consequently, both the direct second-person address and the wider public discourse of the letter should be taken at face value.

A. THE WRITER

Paul's first task in the greeting is to identify himself. He does this by stating his name and his office, and explaining something about the basis of his office. We begin with Paul's name. While there is by no means complete uniformity in the greetings of Paul's letters,[3] all of them begin with the name "Paul," identifying the writer as the converted Pharisee and apostle of the Gentiles.[4] Notably, Paul identifies only himself as the author of this letter and

2. See S. K. Stowers, "Social Typification and the Classification of Ancient Letters," in J. Neusner and H. C. Kee, eds., *The Social World of Formative Christianity and Judaism* (Philadelphia: Fortress, 1988), 78-89.

3. For the self-designation "apostle," cf. Rom 1:1; 1 Cor 1:1; 2 Cor 1:1; Gal 1:1; Eph 1:1; Col 1:1; 2 Tim 1:1; Titus 1:1. 1 and 2 Thessalonians lack a self-designation. Romans, Philippians and Titus use the term "slave" to define Paul's relationship to Christ (see discussion at Titus 1:1).

4. As the beginning of each of the Pauline letters indicates, the apostle typically

94

gives no indication of additional co-sponsorship, a situation that may apply otherwise only to Romans and Ephesians.[5] Rather than see this as a sign that the letter is a forgery that seeks to exalt Paul,[6] interpreters have little cause to set aside the possibility that this letter is one of those that, for whatever reasons, was written (or sent) solely by the apostle himself.

Paul next designates himself "apostle of Christ Jesus."[7] In doing so, he signals primarily that the letter with its teaching falls under the category of apostolic authority. "Apostle" in its most technical usage in the NT describes one who had seen the risen Lord and was appointed by him to preach the gospel. While the term also identified some who had been appointed to carry out specific tasks by the churches (Phil 2:25), it is the first sense that applies to Paul (cf. Galatians 1).[8] His status is therefore that of an authoritative leader, one to whom a divine commission has been given. Paul, his coworkers, and those in his churches would have known well the event that marked this calling to office (Acts 9:1-19 pars.; Gal 1:15-16) and indeed the specific Gentile directions in which this calling took him (1 Tim 2:7; 2 Tim 1:11). This history conferred on Paul the obligation and right to adjudicate, as Christ's "sent one," in all matters of church life. The note of authority was presumably not vitally necessary for Timothy to understand his own subordinate status, but as in all of Paul's letters, in this case matters to be addressed in Ephesus by Paul's delegate — corrections to be instituted, discipline to be meted out, leaders to be chosen — carried more force with apostolic weight behind them. It would be critical that the Ephesian believers recognize not only that Timothy was accountable to Paul but also that they were accountable to Timothy as the apostle's authorized delegate in the church.

The association of Paul's apostolate with "Christ Jesus" is standard for Paul.[9] The genitive relationship indicates the source of his commission

---

used the name Paul (Παῦλος was probably his surname or cognomen; cf. Acts 13:7), which best suited his work in the Gentile context; Saul (Σαῦλος) is found only in Acts. See M. Hengel, *The Pre-Christian Paul* (Philadelphia: Trinity Press International, 1991), 6-15; C. J. Hemer, "The Name of Paul," *TynB* 36 (1985): 179-83.

5. Timothy is named as co-sender in 2 Cor 1:1; Phil 1:1; Col 1:1; Phlm 1; Silas and Timothy in 1 Thess 1:1; 2 Thess 1:1; Sosthenes in 1 Cor 1:1; and unnamed colleagues occupy this position in Gal 1:2. See the discussion in Prior, *Paul the Letter-Writer,* 37-50; Johnson, *Writings,* 254; Marshall, 355.

6. So Oberlinner, 1-2.

7. For the order of names, "Christ Jesus," see 2 Cor 1:1; Phil 1:1; Col 1:1; Phlm 1 (cf. Eph 1:1, where the textual evidence is split).

8. Gk. ἀπόστολος. The literature is enormous. Some of the more accessible studies of the concept are H. D. Betz, "Apostle," n.p., *ABD on CD-Rom.* Version 2.1a. 1995, 1996, 1997; C. K. Barrett, *The Signs of an Apostle* (Philadelphia: Fortress, 1972); K. Rengstorf, *TDNT* 1:407-47; J.-A. Bühner, *EDNT* 1:142-46; P. W. Barnett, *DPL* 45-51.

9. Gk. ἀπόστολος Χριστοῦ Ἰησοῦ; see 1 Cor 1:1; 2 Cor 1:1; Eph 1:1; Col 1:1;

and authority (Gal 1:12) and the fact that he is sent to proclaim the gospel (= "Christ Jesus"; cf. 1 Cor 1:23).[10]

Thirdly, Paul sets out the basis or origin of his calling to be an apostle. In doing so, he identifies the action of God and Christ that lies behind his calling but also introduces a key element in the theology and Christology of this letter. In the prepositional phrase "by the command of God . . . and of Christ Jesus . . ." (cf. Titus 1:1), Paul defines his calling in terms of divine "command."[11] The thought differs slightly from that expressed in the phrase "by the will of God" in 2 Tim 1:1. In the present passage, "command" focuses on the active outworking or expression of the divine will, and God and Christ are co-participants in this act. In the alternative phrase ("by the will of God") it is God's will alone that determines Paul's ministry. The decision to bring out the more active perspective on the event lies, almost certainly, in the upcoming allusion to Paul's calling to be an apostle and Christ's revelatory role in that episode (1:11-16).

In this reference to God, Paul introduces a striking theological theme with christological implications. For the first of three times in this letter, God is called "Savior" (2:3; 4:10).[12] "Savior" had already become a well-known appellation of Yahweh in the Greek OT,[13] where the exodus was the archetypal salvation event. In NT usage, "savior" depicted God as saving the

---

2 Tim 1:1. Titus 1:1 reverses the order of names (cf. the variant in Eph 1:1). See further the note on 1 Tim 1:2. In 1 Timothy the order of names, "Christ Jesus," occurs far more frequently (12x) than "Jesus Christ" (2x); however, the two minority occurrences (6:3, 14) each have the name in collocation with the phrase "our Lord" according to the overwhelming preponderance of instances of this collocation in earlier Pauline writings (40+ occurrences; Paul's only true variation is Phil 3:8; for the rest, the order "Christ Jesus" occurs with "our Lord" only when the name is governed by the preposition ἐν; Rom 6:23; 8:38; 1 Cor 4:17; 15:31; Eph 3:11; Col 2:6; in view of this, the configuration in 1 Tim 1:2, which combines "Christ Jesus" with "our Lord" [Χριστοῦ Ἰησοῦ τοῦ κυρίου ἡμῶν], belongs to the category of Phil 3:8).

10. Marshall, 354.

11. Gk. κατ᾽ ἐπιταγήν; ἐπιταγή ("command, directive, order") is Pauline in the NT, used of the commands issued by the apostle and his coworkers (1 Cor 7:6, 25; 2 Cor 8:8; Titus 2:15) and, as here, in relation to Paul's calling to preach (Rom 16:26). Elsewhere the term is used of divine (*Psalms of Solomon* 18:12; Wis 18:15; 19:6; for the exact combination κατ᾽ ἐπιταγήν, used of Zeus, see Polybius 12.26.2) and royal decrees (Dan 3:16; 3 Macc 7:20); see further G. Delling, *TDNT* 8:36-37; W. Grimm, *EDNT* 2:41.

12. Gk. σωτήρ; see W. Foerster and G. Fohrer, *TDNT* 7:1003-21; K. H. Schelkle, *EDNT* 3:325-27; Quinn, 308-13; Spicq, *TLNT* 3:354-56; K. Läger, *Die Christologie der Pastoralbriefe* (Hamburger Theologische Studien 12; Münster: Lit, 1996), 119-26; Dibelius and Conzelmann, 100-103; I. H. Marshall, "Salvation, Grace and Works in the Later Writings in the Pauline Corpus," *NTS* 42 (1996): 39-58.

13. E.g., LXX Deut 32:15; Pss 23:5; 24:5; 27:9; 41:6; Isa 12:2; 17:10; 43:3; 60:16; see Towner, *Goal,* 75-77 (and notes).

world through the gift of his Son. Use of the title for Christ, however, was slow to develop in the NT and limited to the later Paul (Ephesians; Philippians; 2 Timothy; Titus) and 2 Peter. Perhaps ambivalence about the term's use in the Imperial cult for the deified emperor[14] delayed its Christian application. When it was finally applied to Christ, drawing meaning from the biblical tradition, it may well have been in response to the escalating influence of the stories, symbols, and expectations of the Imperial cult on the church and culture. Given this environment especially, and the earlier use of the language of Hellenistic kings, heroes, and gods,[15] we should not imagine that a Christian co-opting of such politically loaded language was simply a matter of convenience — the language was chosen deliberately to make a point.

In these three letters God and Christ Jesus are both designated "Savior." God is "Savior" in the sense of being the architect and initiator of the salvation plan (1 Tim 1:1; 2:3; 4:10; Titus 1:3; 2:10, 13; 3:4). Christ is "Savior" in that he is the means by which this salvation plan is implemented in history (2 Tim 1:10; Titus 3:6; cf. 1:4).

But when these letters are viewed individually, three distinct patterns of usage influenced by separate christological portraits are visible (see Introduction, 59-67). In Titus, where Christology is at its highest and God and Christ are presented as coequals, both God and Christ bear the title in intentionally close proximity (Titus 1:3, 4; 3:4, 6). In 2 Timothy, where Christology provides a pattern for hope and vindication, the title is reserved for Christ alone (2 Tim 1:10).

What is striking about the "Savior" title in 1 Timothy is its suppression as a christological category. Only God is designated "Savior" (1:1; 2:3; 4:10). It is true that the activity associated with the "Savior" designation is implicit in and through use of the "salvation" *(sōzō)* word group and other theological formulations of the Christ event (e.g., 1:15). Yet the absence of the title as a christological reference reflects the decision not to make the claims associated with it in this letter; the choice to emphasize other elements of Christology (see below on 2:5-6) determined this course.[16]

Christ Jesus, seen here as sharing in that act commanding Paul to

14. On this see D. L. Jones, "Roman Imperial Cult," n.p., *ABD on CD-Rom.* Version 2.1a. 1995, 1996, 1997; P. Wendland, "Σωτήρ: Eine religionsgeschichtliche Untersuchung," *ZNW* 5 (1904): 335-47.

15. A title of honor for men of renown (Xenophon, *Agesilaus* 11.13); of Zeus (Plutarch, *Moralia* 830B); of Ptolemy (Plutarch, *Moralia* 361F); of Antiochus (Strabo, *Geography* 11.10.2); see further Dibelius and Conzelmann, 102-3.

16. See P. H. Towner, "Christology in the Letters to Timothy and Titus," in Richard N. Longenecker, ed., *Contours of Christology in the New Testament* (McMaster New Testament Studies 7; Grand Rapids: Eerdmans, 2005), 219-44.

ministry, is described as "our hope."[17] The phrase, which envisions Jesus as the embodiment and summation of Christian hope, is similar to the description in Titus 2:13. The reference point of hope in Paul is eschatological salvation (1 Thess 5:8).[18] In these letters (as also widely in the NT), the noun and related verb reflect on hope from various specific vantage points. It is the determined expectation, grounded in the certainty of God's past faithfulness (cf. Titus 1:2; Rom 5:5), that God will save his people (1 Tim 4:10) and in other ways come to their aid (5:5), that Christ will return to complete our salvation (Titus 2:13), that eternal life awaits (Titus 1:2; 3:7).[19] Alternative human or material objects of hope are always discouraged (1 Tim 6:17; LXX Ps 43:7; Jer 17:5). Here these perspectives converge as Christ personifies and sums up this hope: his death and resurrection declare with certainty that he has overcome sin and death and secured eternal life for us, and his return will complete the promise.[20] The pronoun "our" is not to be taken lightly — it defines this hope as a shared and binding element of the Christian experience.

B. THE RECIPIENT

Secondly, Paul identifies Timothy[21] as the addressee of the letter. Within Paul's letters and missionary circle, he is found in a number of situations. Frequently Paul refers to him as a traveling companion, coworker, and often as a co-sponsor of Paul's letters.[22] The situation in which we find him here corresponds to the numerous other references to him as being on assignment somewhere away from Paul.[23]

In the accompanying phrase, "my true son in the faith," Paul identifies both the degree of relationship within which Timothy will receive the message and the ground of that relationship. The description of Titus is practically equivalent (Titus 1:4). The dominant thought in the phrase "true

17. Gk. ἐλπίς (Titus 1:1; 2:13; 3:7); see also verb forms in 1 Tim 3:14; 4:10; 5:5; 6:17.

18. Rom 5:2; 8:24-25; 1 Cor 15:19; 2 Cor 1:10; 3:10-12; Col 1:5, 27; see esp. G. Nebe, 'Hoffnung' bei Paulus (Göttingen: Vandenhoeck und Ruprecht, 1983), 169-70.

19. See also Spicq, TLNT 1:480-92; R. Bultmann and K. H. Rengstorf, TDNT 2:517-33.

20. For similar references to God as the hope of Israel, see LXX Pss 64:6; 70:5; Jer 17:7; Psalms of Solomon 5:11; 15:1.

21. See the Introduction, 52.

22. Rom 16:21; 2 Cor 1:1; Phil 1:1; 1 Thess 1:1; 2 Thess 1:1; Phlm 1; cf. 2 Cor 1:19.

23. 1 Cor 4:17; 16:10; Phil 2:19; 1 Thess 3:2, 6; cf. Acts 17:14, 15; 19:22.

son" ("loyal child"; NRSV)[24] is that of kinship, with Paul being the implied father-authority figure. Paul drew on this relationship regularly in referring to Timothy and other coworkers and converts.[25] The expression certainly implies a close relationship of care and intimacy, but more of that is perhaps seen in the phrase "my dear son" that expresses this relationship in the more personal second letter (2 Tim 1:2). In the literal context of discussions about ancestry and birthrights, the adjective here translated with the term "true" ("genuine") established the legitimacy of the child.[26] Extended figuratively to the fictive relationship (cf. Phil 2:20), the authenticity implied by the term guarantees Timothy's faith and right to represent Paul in Ephesus,[27] as it also underlines his obligation to serve the father with authentic commitment (Phil 2:22).[28] While it is tempting to see in the language a reference to Paul's influence in the conversion of Timothy (cf. Phlm 10), there is not enough evidence to be sure that he was converted as a direct result of Paul's preaching.[29]

The locus of their relationship was their shared belief in Christ. The prepositional phrase that describes this, "in faith,"[30] is Pauline shorthand for being a Christian; here it describes the sphere in which Timothy is Paul's child, the common bond that unites them as family (cf. Titus 1:4, "in our common faith"). It is about the equivalent of the reality described by the other Pauline phrase, "in Christ," with "in faith" viewing that reality from the perspective of the activity (and content) of belief.[31] Along with the thought of

24. For τέκνον ("child") elsewhere of the metaphorical relationship of coworkers and others to Paul, see, for individuals, 1 Cor 4:17; Phil 2:22; Phlm 10; and frequently for groups of believers, e.g., 1 Cor 4:14; 2 Cor 6:13; 12:14; Eph 5:1; 1 Thess 2:11; G. Schneider, *EDNT* 3:341-42.

25. Cf. 1:18; 2 Tim 1:1; 2:1; 1 Cor 4:17; Phil 2:22; Phlm 10.

26. Gk. γνήσιος; see BDAG, s.v. 1.

27. The term is used widely in classical and Hellenistic literature in all senses (infrequent in LXX [4x] for sincerity, genuineness). Its use to describe Aristotle as the legitimate interpreter of Plato or elsewhere in reference to transmitters of revelation (so Dibelius and Conzelmann, 13; *Corpus Hermeticum* 13.3; see also Philo, *On the Special Laws* 4.184 for assistants to shepherds) suggests to some that a similar relationship is being imagined between Paul and Timothy here (cf. Marshall, 132), but the fictive father-son relationship is most dominant. See further Spicq, *TLNT* 1:136-38, 296-99; F. Büchsel, *TDNT* 1:727; LSJ, s.v.

28. On this see Philo, *On the Confusion of Tongues* 72.

29. Acts 16:1-3 is the relevant background (cf. 2 Tim 1:5 and discussion); cf. Marshall, 356; Oberlinner, 5 n. 10; but see Knight, 63-64; Fee, 36.

30. I diverge here from the TNIV translation "in the faith" (NRSV), which emphasizes to too great an extent in this context the content of what is believed as the ground of this relationship between Paul and Timothy.

31. Gk. ἐν πίστει. "Faith" language occupies a dominant place within the con-

authenticity of relationship already expressed, this additional scope establishes that the faith of the apostle is equally the faith of the delegate dis-

---

struction and expression of Christian existence in these letters to coworkers. Words from
this group occur over fifty times in the three letters.

(1) The noun, πίστις, is most dominant (1 Tim [19x]; 2 Tim [8x]; Titus [6x]), occurring in various configurations. It appears most frequently with the article (1 Tim 1:19;
3:9; 4:1, 6; 5:8, 12; 6:10, 12, 21; 2 Tim 1:5; 2:18; 3:8; 4:7; Titus 1:13; 2:2). In some of
these instances, "the faith" refers to the content of what is believed, summing up the
Christian faith in terms of a fixed body of teaching (e.g., 1 Tim 4:6; 5:8; 6:21), a usage that
already appears in the earlier Paul (Gal 1:23). Implicit within this category is the necessity
of an active "belief" in or commitment to "the faith" (1 Tim 1:19; 3:9), seen also in the
way rejection of "the faith" serves as a measurement of apostasy (1 Tim 4:1; 6:21). But it
is oversimplifying to conclude that all articular occurrences bear this objective meaning,
for in 2 Tim 3:10 and Titus 2:2 πίστις with the article denotes the action or posture of believing, and the anarthrous use sometimes denotes that which is believed (1 Tim 2:7; cf.
3:13; 2 Tim 2:13). The context and choice of verb should decide the meaning.

In other constructions, usually without the article, πίστις depicts the life determined by belief in Christ (or in the gospel, or in "the truth") in terms of active and healthy
"believing" or trust (1 Tim 1:14; 2:15; 5:12; 2 Tim 1:5; 3:15; Titus 2:10; 3:15). The origin
of this belief is conversion (1 Tim 1:14), but authentic Christian existence is a matter of
ongoing belief in the apostolic gospel. A number of times, "faith" occurs in lists constructed of a series of other characteristic Christian virtues (1 Tim 1:5, 14, 19; 2:7, 15; 4:6,
12; 6:11; 2 Tim 1:13; 2:22; 3:10-11; Titus 2:2); in such lists, "faith" might seem to be no
more (or less) important than other characteristics of the Christian life, but its consistent
presence in the lists and the development of the concept in other configurations underline
its fundamental role in relation to the other items listed. Its frequent pairing with ἀγάπη is
traditional (in nine of the lists); as in the earlier Paul, "faith and love" could serve as an adequate summary of Christian existence (Gal 5:6; 1 Tim 1:5, 14; 2 Tim 1:13; Phlm 5), or be
nestled into longer lists of spiritual virtues.

The phrase ἐν πίστει (1 Tim 1:2; Titus 1:4; etc.) describes the new reality of Christian existence brought about by coming to faith in Christ. It is equivalent to the phrase ἐν
Χριστῷ ("in Christ") that reflects similarly on the new existence from a christological perspective (see esp. Rom 16:3, 9-10; Gal 1:22; Phlm 16, 23). The phrase ἐν πίστει views
Christian existence in terms of active and continual believing (in the gospel or in Christ),
as compared with the broader, objective view of that life (as a result) expressed by "in
Christ."

(2) The verb πιστεύω (6x) describes the action of believing in God, Christ, or the
gospel (1 Tim 1:16; 3:16; 2 Tim 1:12) and characterizes Christian existence in terms of
the past and abiding decision to believe (Titus 3:8). On two occasions, the passive
ἐπιστεύθην reflects on Paul's calling to ministry in terms of being "entrusted" with the
gospel (1 Tim 1:11; Titus 1:3; cf. 1 Cor 9:17; Gal 2:7; 1 Thess 2:4).

(3) The adjective πιστός (17x), when describing the believer (9x), regards the person in terms of one who trusts or believes in God, Christ, or the gospel (= "a Christian";
1 Tim 4:3, 10, 12; 5:16; 6:2a, 2b; Titus 1:6). The term is not a mere formality, for it retains
the sense of an active and healthy belief or commitment (see esp. 1 Tim 4:10; cf. 6:2; Titus
1:6). It can denote "faithfulness" in the broader sense of Christians (1 Tim 3:11) and of

patched to Ephesus. In view of the challenges to be faced, the statement of this relationship in shared faith would not only encourage Timothy but also announce his credentials to the receiving community.[32]

C. THE GREETING

In the greeting, which is identical to the greeting in 2 Tim 1:2, Paul essentially offers a prayer or wish that God and Christ Jesus will bless Timothy. "Grace" and "peace" appear customarily in Paul's greetings.[33] The terms were already linked in blessings, in non-epistolary contexts, in Judaism, and the form occurring in Paul's greetings approximates the benediction or blessing he might have pronounced orally in person to a church.[34] The form in which they appear here, without the connecting conjunction "and" (2 Tim 1:2; 2 John 3) and with the addition of "mercy" (as in 2 Tim 1:2; but cf. Titus 1:4), diverges from the pattern present in the Pauline letters addressed to churches.[35]

Christ (2 Tim 2:13); yet in such cases, too, this posture is rooted in a basic disposition towards God. For the adjective in the phrase πιστὸς ὁ λόγος, see the discussion at 1 Tim 1:15.

(4) The α-negatives of this word group are equally thematic for the contrasting profile of unbelief and apostasy developed in the letters. ἀπιστία describes preconversion existence (1 Tim 1:13). When this unregenerate or apostate life is regarded from the perspective of ethical conduct or the act of unbelieving, the adjective ἄπιστος (1 Tim 5:8; Titus 1:15) and the verb ἀπιστέω (2 Tim 2:13) come into play.

The allegation that in the PE the role of "faith" in the Christian life has diminished in comparison with its role in the earlier Pauline writings (e.g., H. von Lips, *Glaube–Gemeinde–Amt*, FRLANT 122 [Göttingen: Vandenhock und Ruprecht, 1979), 72, 281; Easton, 103, 203-4) is unfounded. Texts such as 2 Tim 1:9 and Titus 3:4-7 reveal the central importance of belief as the appropriate human response to the gracious act of God in Christ. The greater attention to faith (in various ways) in the PE can be explained, undoubtedly, by the intense concern for apostasy from the faith and the struggle with heretics and false teaching that underlie each letter to one degree or another. The role of faith in Christian existence is continuous from Paul's church letters to these three letters to Timothy and Titus. See further Towner, *Goal*, 121-29; Marshall, 213-17; Quinn, 271-76.

32. See also Marshall, 357; Fee, 36; Oberlinner, 5.

33. Rom 1:7; 1 Cor 1:3; 1 Cor 1:2; Gal 1:3; etc. See also Rom 15:13; 16:20.

34. See esp. J. M. Lieu, "'Grace to you and peace': The Apostolic Greeting," *BJRL* 68 (1985): 161-78.

35. The form of Paul's greeting when directed to churches is typically χάρις ὑμῖν καὶ εἰρήνη ("grace to you [pl.] and peace . . ."), followed by reference to the divine source of these blessings; here we have χάρις ἔλεος εἰρήνη ("grace mercy peace [to you (sg.)]"). While it is arguable that these differences point to a different author (e.g., Lieu, "Grace," 170-72), they may indicate equally a different literary situation (see further the Introduction, 52).

"Grace," in Paul, is often laden with theological meaning, and probably even in the customary framework of a letter opening it does more than simply satisfy the requirements of epistolary etiquette.[36] Within its broad range of meaning, which includes "graciousness, good will, thanks, and loving care,"[37] it is the LXX use of the term to express the idea of God's favor shown to his people (in various contexts) that Paul has developed into his theology of salvation.[38] Paul thus asks that Timothy experience God's favor in a way continuous with the nature of salvation.

"Mercy," in the LXX, is the frequent translation of the dominant Hebrew term *chesed,* which describes the lovingkindness of God that undergirds his covenant with Israel, as Paul well understood.[39] Within Paul's letters, the insertion of "mercy" between "grace" and "peace" is unique to the greetings of the two letters to Timothy (2 Tim 1:2; 2 John 3; Jude 2), though in one place he does connect the thoughts of peace and mercy (Gal 6:16). If it is assumed that "grace and peace" is the "standard" Pauline greeting, then this threefold formula is of course unique.[40] But that observation tells us nothing other than that Paul wished here to add the notion of "mercy" to his personal letters to Timothy. The fact that in each letter to Timothy "mercy" is developed into a significant theme within the opening discourses (1 Tim 1:13, 16; 2 Tim 1:16, 18) may explain the addition to the greeting in these

36. In Hellenistic letters the standard word of greeting is χαίρειν (1 Macc 10:18, 25; 11:30; 12:6, 20; 3 Macc 3:12; *Letter of Aristeas* 41; Diogenes Laertius, *Lives of Eminent Philosophers* 2.141.2; etc.; see also Johnson, 158). It is likely that Paul's choice of χάρις (shaped by its use with "peace" in Judaism) transposes the greeting into a pronouncement of blessing.

37. The usage of χάρις in these letters is not significantly different from that in other Pauline letters (in greetings and benedictions: 1 Tim 1:2; 6:21; 2 Tim 1:2; 4:22; Titus 1:4; 3:15; in statements about salvation or the Christ-event: 1 Tim 1:14; 2 Tim 1:9; Titus 2:11; 3:7; and in a construction in which it means "thanks": 1 Tim 1:12; 2 Tim 1:3 [cf. the use of χάρις with the dative for "thanks to God" elsewhere in Paul: Rom 6:17; 7:25; 1 Cor 15:57; etc.]).

38. Spicq, *TLNT* 3:500-506; H. Conzelmann and W. Zimmerli, *TDNT* 9:397-99; K. Berger, *EDNT* 3:457-60.

39. Gk. ἔλεος ("mercy"; see Spicq, *TLNT* 1:471-79; Towner, "Mercy," *EDBT,* 520-23; idem, "Mercy/Compassion," in T. D. Alexander and B. S. Rosner, eds., *New Dictionary of Biblical Theology* [Leicester: Inter-Varsity Press, 2000], 660-63), in noun and verbal forms, is an important theme in these three letters: it forms the basis of salvation for Paul and others (1 Tim 1:13, 16; Titus 3:5) and describes other aspects of God's gracious help and protection (2 Tim 1:16, 18). Cf. Rom 9:23; 11:31; 15:9; Gal 6:16; Eph 2:4.

40. For speculative explanations of the insertion of "mercy" as a departure from this standard, see Knight, 66 and Spicq, 318 (who link it to Jewish practice, Timothy's Jewish background, and unique pressures to be faced by Timothy); Dibelius and Conzelmann, 14 and Kelly, 41 (who see it as a replacement for the usual "you" [pl.] of Pauline greetings).

two instances.[41] Paul wishes for Timothy a deep sense of God's sustaining protection.

"Peace," in NT usage, also owes most to the development of the concept in the Greek OT background. In reference to individuals or groups, it denotes harmony or tranquility within and without, the source of which is God, and especially his salvation.[42] As with "grace," the importance of "peace" (both inward and outward) for the situation Timothy would be addressing in Ephesus would seem obvious; no less obvious was the need for the experience of God's peace in the churches generally.

As is typical in Paul's letters, God the Father and Christ are named together as the source of the blessings just mentioned.[43] The prepositional phrase "from God [the] Father and Christ Jesus our Lord," exactly replicated in 2 Tim 1:2, differs from the standard Pauline phrase in giving the order of the names as "Christ Jesus" and in moving "Lord" to the end of the sequence. Since Paul's preference is to use the name "Jesus Christ" in connection with the "Lord" attribution,[44] this may represent a divergence from the pattern (cf. 6:3, 14 where the pattern is maintained). One possible explanation for this deviation might be the dominance of the order "Christ Jesus" in the letters to Timothy.[45] But attention to the pattern "Jesus Christ" in the two other combinations with "Lord" (6:3, 14) suggests that either the shift to "Christ Jesus" was influenced by the order of the names in the preceding verse, or it has resulted from the placement of "Lord" after the names (cf. Phil 3:8).

The designation "Father" for God is restricted in these three letters to the two greetings to Timothy (2 Tim 1:2).[46] Nevertheless, it still establishes at

41. Cf. Roloff, 55.

42. Gk. εἰρήνη; see Spicq, *TLNT* 1:424-38; G. von Rad, *TDNT* 2:400-417. Cf. Rom 15:33; 16:20; Phil 4:9; Col 3:15; 1 Thess 5:23; 2 Thess 3:16.

43. See Rom 1:7; 1 Cor 1:3; 2 Cor 1:2; Gal 1:3; Eph 1:2; Phil 1:2; 2 Thess 1:1; Phlm 3.

44. In 1 Timothy the order of names, "Christ Jesus," occurs far more frequently (12x) than "Jesus Christ" (2x); however, the two minority occurrences (6:3, 14) each have the name in collocation with the phrase "our Lord" according to the overwhelming preponderance of instances of this collocation in the earlier Pauline writings (40+ occurrences in which most have the order "our Lord Jesus Christ" [but see the order "Jesus Christ our Lord" in Rom 1:4; 5:21; 7:25; 1 Cor 1:9]); Paul's only true variation from this pattern is Phil 3:8 ("Christ Jesus *my* Lord"); for the rest, the order "Christ Jesus" occurs with "our Lord" only when the name is governed by the preposition ἐν; Rom 6:23; 8:38; 1 Cor 4:17; 15:31; Eph 3:11; Col 2:6; in view of this, the configuration in 1 Tim 1:2 (2 Tim 1:2), which combines the order of names "Christ Jesus" with "our Lord" (Χριστοῦ Ἰησοῦ τοῦ κυρίου ἡμῶν), belongs to the anomalous category of Phil 3:8.

45. 1 Timothy (12x to 2x for the reverse), 2 Timothy (12x to 1x); see Johnson, 158.

46. Gk. πατήρ; G. Quell and G. Schrenk, *TDNT* 5:945-1014; O. Michel, *EDNT* 3:53-57.

the outset the familial framework within which Timothy is to define his Christian identity, which Paul will then develop through the more dominant themes of God as Savior (1:1; 2:3; 4:10) and householder (1:4; 3:15). The attribution of lordship to Christ Jesus[47] even in this stock phrase implies his vindication by God through resurrection and his authority over the church (as throughout Paul and the NT). With the attached pronoun "our," Paul indicates that the Lordship of Christ is intrinsic to the church's experience and belief.

II. BODY OF THE LETTER (1:3–6:21A)

A. ORDERING AND ORGANIZING GOD'S HOUSEHOLD: PART I (1:3–3:16)

The body of the letter commences at 1:3 with an opening charge to Timothy. While this charge is indeed in effect throughout the entire letter, the culmination of teaching in the theology of 3:14-16 and the new beginning of 4:1-5 suggest the basic twofold division of the body as set out above (see Introduction, 70). The difference between the two main divisions is more one of accent than of new directions, so the outline should be regarded as a matter of dividing the text into manageable, topical units for discussion and not as holding the clue to the letter's message. Under the influence of the charge to Timothy and the programmatic statement about God's household administration, the first main section takes up the matter of the opponents and the need to engage them, turning next to matters of behavior and organization within the church. The teaching of the whole section is finally set into a theological perspective by means of a brief discussion of the nature of the church and the message by which and for which it exists.

1. Regarding False Teachers and False Doctrine (1:3-20)

This opening section falls into a loosely constructed chiasm. The opening charge to Timothy and accompanying instructions concerning the false teachers (1:3-7) is mirrored by the brief repetition of the charge given against the backdrop of the heresy (1:18-20). Between these brackets Paul distin-

---

47. Apart from reference to God with the traditional phrase "Lord of lords" (κύριος τῶν κυριευόντων), κύριος is, in Pauline fashion, applied solely to Christ: 1:2, 12, 14; 6:3, 14; 2 Tim 1:2, 8, 16, 18(2x); 2:7, 19(2x), 22, 24; 3:11; 4:8, 14, 17, 18, 22. The more striking emphasis on Christ's and God's co-sharing of the title σωτήρ in Titus may explain the absence of the title "Lord" from this letter.

guishes himself and his ministry from the opponents in two ways. First, he discusses the usefulness of the law and the false teachers' misunderstanding of it (1:8-11). Second, he reflects on his experience of divine mercy and calling, which made him a paradigm of the saved sinner (1:12-17). While the literary structure remains loose, the overall effect of the various contrasts made between Timothy/Paul and the false teachers, the gospel and false doctrine, and the relative results of the competing messages is to produce a scathing denunciation of the heresy. The structure itself is rescued from too much disarray by means of the closing bracket, which repeats the charge to Timothy.

a. Timothy's Commission: Engaging the Opponents (1:3-7)

3 *As I urged you when I went into Macedonia, stay there in Ephesus so that you may command certain persons not to teach false doctrines any longer* 4 *or to devote themselves to myths and endless genealogies. Such things promote controversial speculations rather than advancing God's work — which is by faith.* 5 *The goal of this command is love, which comes from a pure heart and a good conscience and a sincere faith.* 6 *Some have departed from these and have turned to meaningless talk.* 7 *They want to be teachers of the law, but they do not know what they are talking about or what they so confidently affirm.*

Paul opens the body of the letter by reminding Timothy of his assignment. Within the paragraph, we learn of the location of the work, its main focus, and the theological framework (and central theme of the letter) within which the message and work of Timothy and the opponents can be measured. As we will observe throughout the letter, Paul relies heavily on the persuasive power of contrast — the technique, which compares closely with the polemics found in the philosophical writings of that day, intended to expose and denounce the dangers of the opposing group and its teaching. The technique was designed to leave no doubt about the matter of the superiority and authority of the apostolic teaching and its representatives. This is just the beginning of the critique, but its uncompromising tone is clear from the outset.

3 The section begins with a roughly formed incomplete sentence. "As"[1] introduces a dependent clause that technically requires at some not-too-distant subsequent point an independent clause to anchor it. Instead, it is

---

1. The Gk. term καθώς ("as, just as") here lays a basis (rather than introducing a comparison) for what ought to follow, in the sense of "just as I commanded you . . . so go and do it" (cf. Paul's frequent use of the conjunction in this way; Rom 1:17, 28; 2:24; 3:4; etc.; cf. BDF §453.2).

followed by a clause identifying the purpose of the earlier command. The TNIV and NRSV can be consulted here as examples of attempts to resolve the difficulty. Presumably, Paul started out to say something like: "Just as I commanded you . . . so then complete the task." But after explicitly laying down the basis for the renewed command (namely, that he had previously commanded Timothy to follow a course of action), he either simply assumed that Timothy knew what was to follow,[2] or became so caught up in what he was saying that he forgot to pull the syntactical trigger and complete the thought.[3] The latter is most likely,[4] and the implication is that Timothy clearly understood that the prior instructions alluded to were still in effect.[5] At v. 18 Paul will finally and explicitly close the communication gap. This technique of couching present instructions in a previous command may be influenced by the "mandate" features of this letter.[6]

The language of this past command, "I urged you," is collegial enough in tone, but in this context of conveying binding instructions,[7] it carries the weight of apostolic authority and is intended to persuade and ensure compliance.[8] With this in mind, the first part of the command, still in effect, is to "stay in Ephesus."[9] At the time of writing, Paul was either starting out or already en route to Macedonia.[10]

The historical scenario alluded to requires a situation in which Timothy has either already been dispatched on his own to Ephesus (from somewhere else on duty either with Paul or with others),[11] or in which Paul left him there as

2. Thus Lock, 7.

3. Cf. the REB, which leaves the reiteration of the command implicit. See discussion in Marshall, 362-63.

4. And not at all unlike Paul, who was known for some substantial digressions (Rom 5:12-18; Gal 2:4-6; Eph 3:2-13).

5. On which see Marshall, 363; Roloff, 62-63; Oberlinner, 11.

6. Cf. the examples cited by Wolter, *Paulustradition,* 180-81.

7. As elsewhere in Paul's commands to coworkers and church leaders/members (1 Tim 2:1; 1 Cor 16:12; 2 Corinthians 4; 12:18; 1 Thess 4:1, 10; cf. 1 Cor 16:12); and of Timothy and Titus to the congregations (1 Tim 5:1; 6:2; 2 Tim 4:2; Titus 2:6, 15).

8. Gk. παρακαλέω; see C. J. Bjerkelund, *Parakaleō* (Oslo: Universitets-forlaget, 1967); von Lips, *Glaube,* 132-35; J. Thomas, *EDNT* 3:23-27.

9. Gk. προσμεῖναι ἐν Ἐφέσῳ; in this geographical reference, προσμένω (5:5; Acts 11:23 in the nonlocal sense of "persevere, continue") has the sense "to stay on, remain in"; for the verb cf. Schlarb, *Die gesunde Lehre,* 17, who suggests the meaning "persevere."

10. The present participle, πορευόμενος, in the phrase πορευόμενος εἰς Μακεδονίαν, coordinates the action with the verb it modifies ("urged"), leaving some ambiguity (cf. NIV, "when I went"; REB, "when I was starting for"; NRSV, "when I was on my way").

11. Variously, Simpson, 27.

he himself went on to Macedonia.[12] The ambiguity of their relative locations here is similar to the command to Titus concerning Crete (cf. Titus 1:5). And any attempt to locate the place in Paul's travels in which this assignment most likely occurred remains provisional.[13] Barring the theory of a release from Roman imprisonment (cf. Introduction, 10-14), the sequence of Paul's and his coworker's movements reported in and around Acts 20:1-3 is perhaps most promising. At this point, in close connection with the Ephesian and ongoing Corinthian stages of Paul's work, Paul is reported to have left Ephesus for Macedonia (Acts 20:1), after which he arrived in Greece and stayed for three months (20:2). Timothy's location is not stated at this juncture, though in 19:22 Luke reports that he had been dispatched to Macedonia. If Timothy had returned, or was redirected by Paul back to Ephesus, the scenario assumed by the language of 1 Tim 1:3 of "staying" on assignment in Ephesus just becomes a possibility during that brief period. After his brief stay in Greece, Paul then makes his way back to Asia Minor via Macedonia, and Timothy is reported to have accompanied Paul from Greece to Troas at this point, all of which assumes that Timothy again left Ephesus in order to return to Paul. As Johnson points out, "the window of opportunity for 1 Timothy" presented by the account of Acts is not substantial.[14] But Paul's frequent travels back and forth between Asia Minor, Achaia, and Macedonia and his practice of dispatching delegates to churches are clear from his letters, so the kind of assignment envisioned here is not at all unlikely. If neither Acts nor Paul's letters allow certainty in the question of the timing of such an assignment of personnel, the incompleteness of each source must also be recognized. We will assume that 1 Timothy addresses Timothy in his work at Ephesus sometime during Paul's active pre-imprisonment ministry in these regions.[15]

---

12. See Dibelius and Conzelmann, 15; Fee, 39.

13. See Introduction, 10-14.

14. Johnson, 137.

15. The argument mounted by proponents of pseudonymity is that the apostle's "leaving behind" of coworkers (expressed differently in 1 Tim 1:3 and Titus 1:5), in contrast to the genuine Paul's practice of first planting churches, then "sending" coworkers to further the work (e.g., 1 Cor 4:17; 16:10; 2 Cor 2:4-7), is a literary device that reveals the postapostolic situation of these letters to Timothy and Titus (esp. Trummer, *Paulustradition,* 124; Wolter, *Paulustradition,* 180-84; see also discussion in Marshall, 364). While the Pauline strategy adduced from his letters to churches seems clear, the interpretation of 1 Tim 1:3 and Titus 1:5 on the basis of some sort of comparison with other letters to churches is obviously wholly dependent upon prior assumptions about the nonhistorical and inauthentic character of the letters. If one considers for a moment the possibility that these are in fact two of only three letters (of the extant Pauline collection) that Paul addressed to individual coworkers (with the wider audience of the churches anticipated), and that Timothy and Titus were assuming their place as 1 Tim 1:3 and Titus 1:5 suggest (thus explaining the past tense), one has to ask how else Paul would have de-

Timothy's reason for staying in Ephesus emerges in the purpose clause *(hina)* that begins here and continues into the next verse. It is chiefly to confront the false teachers. First, the term "command"[16] (4:11; 5:7; 6:13, 17) belongs to the technical vocabulary of didactic and corrective activities associated with the apostolic mission and teaching within the church (see discussions at 4:11; Titus 1:9, 13; 2:1, 15). The term implies the delegate's authority to issue commands on behalf of Paul[17] (the content of which follows) and equally that those being thus commanded are within the jurisdiction of this authority. This means that those referred to indirectly as "certain persons,"[18] most likely to demean them before the whole community, were members of the church and therefore accountable to Paul.[19]

The content of the command is expressed negatively as a prohibition by means of two parallel infinitive verbs. The first of these prohibits the activity of "teaching what is false" before continuing to prohibit the useless speculation that lies behind and fuels the activity itself. The verb "to teach what is false" is rare, occurring in the NT only in this letter (6:3).[20] The allegation closely parallels one made in Gal 1:6 (cf. 2 Cor 11:4), where opponents are identified with the same indirect demeaning tag ("some people," Gal 1:7; cf. 2 Cor 10:2). Paul's main concern at this point is less with the teaching style or methods of the opponents (i.e., some sort of speculation and

---

scribed their appointments, which were already in effect. The function of the instructions to Timothy and Titus not only reminded the coworkers of their task, but also the communities of the coworkers' authority as apostolic delegates.

16. Gk παραγγέλλω; the term is used frequently of Paul's authoritative teaching in the churches (1 Cor 7:10; 11:17; 1 Thess 4:11; 2 Thess 3:4, 6, 10, 12; W. Radl, *EDNT* 3:16-17; Lips, *Glaube,* 130-31; Marshall, 364; Roloff, 63) and belongs to the didactic vocabulary by which this ministry is described.

17. Although Marshall, 364, makes the point that Timothy here is called on "to carry out the task of a church leader," there seems little reason to think that the coworker has ceased to function in his capacity as an apostolic delegate, despite the fact that he is here ministering within a particular church.

18. Gk. τινες (the pl. indefinite pron. from τις); this technique is intentional (1:6, 19; 4:1; 5:15, 24; 6:10, 21; 2 Tim 2:18), is found also elsewhere in the Pauline letters (Rom 3:8; 1 Cor 4:18; 5:1; 2 Cor 3:1; 10:2; Gal 1:7; 2:12; Phil 1:15; see also Heb 10:25; Ignatius, *To the Ephesians* 7.1; 9.1; *1 Clement* 1.1), and in the letters to Timothy is used specifically for the opponents. See further Johnson, 162; Roloff, 71; Marshall, 365.

19. See Fee, 40, who suggests that erring elders are specifically in mind; Towner, *Goal,* 24-27.

20. Gk. ἑτεροδιδασκαλέω; see also Ignatius, *To Polycarp* 3.1. The term, and other *hetero*-combinations, occurs more frequently in the Fathers, but first-century (and earlier) use of such compounds is also evident (Josephus, *Antiquities* 10.281; *Jewish War* 2.129; Plato, *Theaetetus* 190E). For the combination of ἑτερο- ("different") with other verbs to form similar compounds, see 1 Cor 14:21; 2 Cor 6:14.

108

perhaps argumentation, though elsewhere this too is specifically denounced; 1 Tim 6:4; 2 Tim 2:14; Titus 3:9),[21] and mainly with the substandard content that is being taught. The choice of this devaluative verb sets the stage for the series of contrasts that will extol and endorse the apostolic gospel as the standard ("the gospel," "the sound teaching," "the sound words of our Lord," etc.) and deprecate the message of the opponents as a counterfeit.

4 A closely parallel[22] second part of the prohibition addresses what is probably the root of the problem. The verb "to be devoted to" ("occupied with")[23] suggests that the opponents have become absorbed in the extraneous materials that make up their doctrines (4:1; Titus 1:14). The object of their attention, "myths and endless genealogies," is where we catch a glimpse of the substance of this false doctrine.

This phrase[24] is problematic and resists precise interpretation. Nevertheless, certain precedents allow us to close in on Paul's sense. The term "myth"[25] has a long history of use prior to the NT, through which it comes to mean a fable or far-fetched story, often about the gods; most importantly, it can stand as a category meaning essentially falsehood.[26] Here the term is in the plural, as throughout the NT, which contains a negative evaluative assessment in itself (namely, spurious, contradictory, human) in contrast to the divinely imbued singularity and unity of the gospel.[27] Paul employs the plural term to label the teaching emphatically as falsehood. But the history of the term's use goes another step: Plato, for one, used the term to denounce cer-

---

21. As with the technical term "the teaching" (διδασκαλία), as it occurs in these letters, either the activity or the content of "teaching" may be in view (cf. Lips, *Glaube*, 39 n. 39; Towner, *Goal*, 26-27).

22. The Gk. particle μηδέ ("and not," "nor") coordinates the following action ("to be devoted to") with the preceding action ("to teach false doctrines").

23. Gk. προσέχω; in this particular context (see also 4:1; Titus 1:14), the verb denotes at a minimum the depth of interest or attention that leads one to be convinced (see Plutarch, *Nicias* 10.5.6); in the case of wine, the term denotes what amounts to addiction (3:8; cf. *EDNT* 3:169-70).

24. For the whole phrase, μύθοις καὶ γενεαλογίαις ἀπεράντοις ("myths and endless genealogies"), cf. Polybius, *Histories* 9.2.1; Plato, *Timaeus* 22A, which show the linkage of these two terms to be traditional.

25. Gk. μύθος; in the NT always in the plural (4:7; 2 Tim 4:4; Titus 1:14; 2 Pet 1:16; see also Sir 20:19; *2 Clement* 13.3; cf. Bar 3:23; Ignatius, *To the Magnesians* 8.1).

26. See, e.g., Plato, *Republic* 376D-377A; Epictetus, *Discourses* 3.24.18 (also with the verb προσέχω); on the whole matter, see Spicq, *TLNT* 2:528-33; G. Stählin, *TDNT* 4:762-95; F. F. Bruce, *NIDNTT* 2:643-47; Johnson, 162-63; Marshall, 206; Dibelius and Conzelmann, 16-17.

27. Cf. the plural descriptions "teachings of demons" (4:1; cf. the pl. formulations in 6:20; 2 Tim 2:16; Titus 1:11, 14). References to the gospel or the teaching (in various terms) are consistently in the singular.

tain stories not simply as false but also deceptive, in that they were told so as to lend credence to immoral behavior or practices by linking them to ancient stories about the gods.[28] The apparent link between certain extreme ascetic aspects of behavior and the false doctrines in Ephesus (1 Tim 4:1-3; cf. discussion at Titus 1:14-15) suggests that Paul also drew on this nuance of the term's polemical use. Thus rather than identifying the content of the teaching, the term "myths" evaluates it as false and pernicious.

"Genealogies," however, with the help of other contextual clues, takes us in the direction of actual content. This term also has a long history of use, describing lists of family names (family trees), and the process of constructing them, that served various purposes.[29] Within Judaism, genealogies played the key role of establishing a person's bloodline and link to a particular family and tribe: rights by birth determined in this way allowed, for example, entrance into the priesthood. As its use in Philo demonstrates, the term could refer to the accounts of people in the early parts of Genesis.[30] This usage especially opens up the possibility that Paul is identifying the practice among the false teachers of speculating on stories about the early biblical characters as well as actual genealogical lists such as occur there or in other more speculative noncanonical Jewish writings (e.g., *Jubilees*). Speculation fitting roughly into this category was known to have been practiced in Jewish communities,[31] and the reference in 1:7 to the opponents' aspirations to be "teachers of the law" helps to locate the sources of this practice within the repository of Jewish literature (cf. Titus 1:14 and the reference to "Jewish myths").[32]

The adjective "endless" attached to "genealogies" might have been a literal reference to long-drawn-out speculations, or may be meant in the sense of "pointless," "contradictory," or "inconclusive."[33] Its force is

28. E.g., Plato, *Laws* 636C-D; 12.941B (ὑπό τινων μυθολόγων πλημμελῶν; "being led astray by certain tellers of myths"); *Republic* 376E-383C; see also Quinn, 245; Marshall, 206.

29. Gk. γενεαλογία; for the noun, as here, see Plato, *Cratylus* 396C; Josephus, *Antiquities* 11.71; for the verb ("to trace one's ancestry"), see Herodotus 2.146; Plato, *Timaeus* 23B.

30. Philo, *On the Life of Moses* 2.47 (and Colson's note in Loeb, VI, 606, which argues for the association of the term with persons in history as against impersonal aspects of history); see further Quinn, 245; Marshall, 335-36; Spicq, 93-104; F. Büchsel, *TDNT* 1:663-65; Schlarb, *Die gesunde Lehre,* 86-90.

31. E.g., 1QapGen; Pseudo-Philo; see also Schlarb, *Die gesunde Lehre,* 86-92; G. Kittel, "Genealogia des Pastoralbriefe," *ZNW* 20 (1921): 49-69; Quinn, 245-46; Marshall, 335.

32. See Schlarb, *Die gesunde Lehre,* 83-93.

33. Gk. ἀπέραντος; only here in the NT (in positive descriptions see LXX Job 36:26; 3 Macc 2:9); in a similar derogatory sense, see Philo, *On the Preliminary Studies* 53; Spicq, *TLNT* 1:159; Marshall, 366; Fee, 42.

clearly polemical, meant to discredit the protracted arguments that go nowhere.

We can go little beyond deducing that these early stories were somehow mined for (or reshaped to yield) clues they contained about the deeper sort of piety the false teachers laid claim to.[34] Nevertheless, it is clear that Paul regarded this teaching as deceptive and dangerous. Quite possibly the extreme practices alluded to in 4:1-3 (see the discussion) were grounded in this speculative interpretation of Israel's early history, all of which was being served up in the guise of authoritative doctrine (1:7).

In the next phrase, Paul supplies an important reason[35] why Timothy is to prohibit this false teaching. It consists of a contrast between the wheel-spinning futility of the deceptive speculation and the direction of God's mission. The first half of this reason is clear: the obsession with myths and genealogies "promotes controversial speculations." The verb[36] is neutral and also governs the positive side of the contrast to come. But the term that follows, "controversial [or useless] speculations,"[37] is one of several that belongs to Paul's polemical repertoire in these three letters to coworkers drawn on to discredit the opposing doctrines and behavior as being everything from foolish

34. Arguments to the effect that the false teachers were tampering with the lineage of Jesus (as given in Matthew; B. T. Viviano, "The Genre of Matt. 1–2: Light from 1 Tim. 1:4," *RB* 97 [1990]: 31-53) or sought by study of their own genealogies to place themselves well with Judaism (Schlatter, 34-35), or that Christ's ancestry was being challenged to some end by them (so Quinn, 245-46, chiefly in reference to Titus 3:9), have little to commend them. Corroborating evidence is also lacking for the once popular (yet still influential) view that "myths and genealogies" (especially the latter term) refers to the systems of Gnostic emanations or aeons, documented only after the first century, that made some use of the biblical genealogies (see, e.g., Irenaeus, *Against Heresies* 1.pref.; 1.30.9; Easton, 112-13; Dibelius and Conzelmann, 16-17; G. Haufe, "Gnostische Irrlehre und ihre Abwehr in den Pastoralbriefen," in K.-W. Tröger, ed., *Gnosis und das Neue Testament* [Gütersloh: Mohn, 1973], 325-39; see discussion in Oberlinner, 14; Towner, *Goal,* 28; Marshall, 336, 366; Johnson, 163).

35. The indefinite relative αἵτινες refers to the preceding "myths and genealogies" (taking its gender from the feminine γενεαλογίαις), intending to categorize them by the result they produce ("of a kind which"; see BDF §293.2).

36. Gk. παρέχω; 6:17; Titus 2:7.

37. Gk. ἐκζήτησις; the variant ζητήσεις, meaning "disputes," appears in a majority of the MSS (see discussion in Metzger, 571; Elliott, 18; Marshall, 362), and it is indeed a word that Paul uses in each of these three letters (1 Tim 6:4; 2 Tim 2:23; Titus 3:9; cf. verb in 2 Tim 1:17), while ἐκζητήσεις ("speculations, investigations") is extremely rare, limited to this instance in the NT and LXX (Johnson, 163, refers to 2 Kgs 4:11, but this appears to be in error) and infrequent in secular Greek (the related verb is common). The harder reading ("speculations") is more likely the original, having been corrected ("disputes") to accord with what was thought to be the author's vocabulary. Marshall, 362, suggests that ἐκζήτησις ("speculation") may include the thought of disputation.

nonsense to disputatious and pernicious.[38] It is clearly these latter characteristics and their danger to the church that most concern Paul as he writes (6:3-4).

In contrast,[39] the text implies that correct and authoritative teaching will promote "God's work." However, the TNIV translation is questionable. The Greek term is *oikonomia theou*.[40] It is translated in various ways in the versions: "the divine training"[41] (NRSV); "God's plan for us" (REB; cf. TEV); "God's work" (TNIV; NIV); and there are numerous other variations.

Of these attempts to render the term, the first is unlikely. Most who propose the meaning "God's plan" narrow the focus to salvation, and draw on the use of the term *oikonomia* in expanded phrases, especially in Eph 1:10 and 3:9 (cf. 3:2).[42] While this can be made to fit the present context,[43] it is perhaps a better fit in Ephesians.

The TNIV rendering, "God's work," might mean a couple of things, such as what God himself does, or what the church (empowered and led by God) is to do for God. In any case, the focus in this translation is on "work" (mission work, church work, gospel work), and it is again possible to see this as an apt counterpart to the speculations promoted by false teaching.

This menu of options suggests a continuing state of uncertainty. Johnson and Marshall have suggested that the key to interpreting *oikonomia* here lies in the household terminology, which Paul employed elsewhere and which is thematic in 1 Timothy. To begin with, *oikonomia* refers to the organization and ordering of a household or the responsibility of management that maintains the order. This is how Paul describes his mission to the Gentiles in 1 Cor 9:17; that is, he understands himself to have been entrusted with management of a household (presumably God's; cf. 1 Cor 4:1). The description of his ministry in Col 1:25 follows the same line: "I have become a minister according to the responsibility to manage God's house [*oikonomia tou theou*] that was given to me." Within 1 Timothy household language links several things together into a complete pattern. Leaving 1:4 aside for the moment, in 3:15 the church is depicted as "God's house" (*oikos theou;* cf. 2 Tim

---

38. See the discussions of language at 2 Tim 2:23; Titus 3:9; see also Towner, *Goal,* 24-25; Schlarb, *Die gesunde Lehre,* 59-73; Marshall, 334-35.

39. The combination μᾶλλον ἤ (2 Tim 3:4; Acts 4:19; 5:29; Gal 4:27) means "rather than."

40. Gk οἰκονομία θεοῦ (Eph 3:2; Col 1:25).

41. See also Dibelius and Conzelmann, 17-18; Hanson, 57; Oberlinner, 14-15, for the sense "the training which leads to salvation." This sense of the phrase is attested much later in Clement of Alexandria.

42. See Kelly, 45; Fee, 42; Arichea-Hatton, 17; Brox, 103.

43. But see Roloff, 65, and Marshall, 367, who maintain that within the contrast, "God's plan of salvation" is an unlikely counterpart to "useless speculations"; however, this may overstress the precision intended.

2:20-21), and by derivation overseers are to understand their task in terms of stewardship (see 3:4-5; in Titus 1:7 the term *oikonomos theou* ["God's steward"] is used).

This brings us back to the phrase *oikonomia theou* in 1:4. Surely it is correct to define the concept within the sphere of household management and duties from which the language emerged. At this point, we note the slight difference in the final results of Johnson and Marshall. Marshall focuses on the activity of management, which leads him to interpret the contrasting image as follows: "rather than [promoting] the performance of the duties of stewardship" (associated with God's house).[44] The duties envisioned include all those to be done by the leaders of the church.

Johnson, however, emphasizes the idea of order: "God's way of ordering things." He interprets Paul as contrasting the speculations of the false teachers, which produce disruption and a flawed understanding of behavior and of God's will, with "faithful attention to" God's way of ordering his creation. The teaching then that Paul will give the church concerning everything from prayer to women in the church, to elders and widows, and behavior in the household and leadership is all designed to explicate "God's way of ordering things." This "ordering" of church and society, two entities or spheres that Johnson rightly sees as continuous and equally "ordered" by God, has been misapprehended by the opponents. In any case, the essential starting point for Johnson is Paul's setting of the whole letter under the rubric of the ordering of life by God. Paul's point is then that "by faith," that is, through acceptance of the correct apostolic preaching and teaching, this divine arrangement can be apprehended and implemented.[45]

In the absence in 1:4 of a direct statement by Paul to the effect that the *oikonomia theou* is that which has been entrusted or given to Paul (emphasizing specifically stewardship, responsibility, and the activity of management; 1 Cor 9:17; Eph 3:2; Col 1:25), it seems best in this case to increase the emphasis on the pattern and order that is to be implemented. That is, the first thought is not of administration as ministry and responsibility, but of the shape of things and the ordering of life to be achieved through the various activities of ministry and service.

The attached comment about faith adds a crucial condition to the un-

44. Marshall, 367. See Knight, 75-76, for the combination of this with the idea of God's salvation plan: "the outworking, administration, or stewardship of God's plan of salvation through the gospel and its communication."

45. This use of the term *oikonomia* seems closest to its use in Eph 1:10 (3:9) for God's all-encompassing plan. There, too, where a christological perspective is of course dominant, *oikonomia* must be understood to refer not just to "salvation plan," but rather to the implementation of the divine ordering of things/life/creation through the Christ-event (i.e., "salvation plan" in its widest sense).

derstanding of the divine pattern.[46] Although it is rendered instrumentally by the TNIV — "which is by faith" — it may denote somewhat more broadly the sense of sphere: "in faith." In either case, it says something more about "the way God has organized life." To be "in faith" is to be in the sphere of authentic faith (see the note on 1:2), and its attachment to the preceding phrase here will encompass the apprehension of God's ways and patterns as well as any actions taken to implement them. The point Paul makes, however, is polemical. It is genuine faith, namely, that faith associated with his gospel, which has access to correct understanding of the will of God. The fundamental condition for understanding the way God has organized life (his *oikonomia*), and for carrying out the activities in the community and world that bring them into alignment, is adherence to genuine faith. As he is about to say, it is Timothy's task of teaching what is true and correcting what is false that will give insight into the *oikonomia* of God.

5 Beginning a new sentence that will carry on for three verses, Paul now presents Timothy's task as a contrast ("but"; *de*) to the negative results produced by the speculation of the false teaching. This new thought is loosely linked with what has preceded, and will soon serve as another measurement of the opponents' shortcomings. Paul's aim is first to show that the task entrusted to Timothy, which is an extension of Paul's own mission, does in fact promote God's *oikonomia*.

He does this by focusing on the "goal" of the command to Timothy.[47] Although there continues to be some debate about which "command" is in view,[48] the context (1:3, 18) requires that the reference be to the charge given to Timothy, of which the task outlined in this section forms the core of his whole mission in Ephesus.[49]

The goal itself is "love." Properly understood, and seen in connection with the three qualifiers that follow, this statement acquires thematic importance within the framework of Christian existence Paul seeks to construct in these letters to Timothy and Titus. The term is *agapē,* which in Paul can serve as shorthand for the entire visible, outward life produced by genuine faith

46. The Gk. phrase τὴν ἐν πίστει is an example of the attachment of a qualification to an anarthrous noun (οἰκονομίαν) by following it with the article and the qualifying phrase (see also 1:14; 3:13; 4:8; 6:3; 2 Tim 1:13, 14; 2:10; 3:15; Titus 1:1); it makes the qualification somewhat emphatic (Marshall, 368); see further BDF §269.3.

47. For τέλος in the sense of goal, see Josephus, *Antiquities* 9.73; Epictetus, *Discourses* 1.20.15; discussion in G. Delling, *TDNT* 8:49-56.

48. Gk. παραγγελία; 1 Tim 1:18; Acts 5:28; 16:24; 1 Thess 4:2. Cf. the views of Brox, 103 (the apostolic preaching and teaching in general; see also Knight, 76; Dibelius and Conzelmann, 15) and Roloff, 66 (a reference to instructions that go with church office; Oberlinner, 16).

49. See also Marshall, 368-69; Johnson, 164; Fee, 42.

(e.g., Gal 5:7). The term is frequently found related to "faith" (as here),[50] with the two concepts together comprising what might be thought of as the invisible (posture of belief in God/Christ) and visible (faith's outworking in life) dimensions of Christian existence. In this construction, love is the concept that Paul uses to summarize the goal to be achieved by correct teaching and preaching. It stands for active response to God's grace, expressed in sacrificial action done on behalf of others. Thus what is noticeable from the outset is the concern for the observable and measurable dimension of Christian existence and its origin in the apostolic gospel. It is this interrelationship of message and agape-life that is in mind as Paul goes on to show that love is the end product of authentic conversion that renders the human interior faculties capable of producing the manner of living God intends.

How is such love produced? Paul considers this source[51] from the perspective of three interior features of genuine belief. The first perspective is the "pure heart" (2 Tim 2:22). This phrase depicts the inner dimension of Christian existence in its entirety. Within Paul's anthropological teaching, and continuous with the biblical tradition and cultures that influenced him, the heart was regarded as the locus of the human personality and origin of the emotions and intentions.[52] It is with the heart that people relate to God, and with the heart they may call upon the Lord (cf. 2 Tim 2:22) and express either worship, or resistance and rejection.[53] In the latter case (sin, rebellion), the OT already expressed, in similar language, the notion that the heart needs to be cleansed for worship and restored in relationship with God.[54] The Jesus tradition affirmed this fundamental thought (Matt 5:8). In this particular setting, the thought is of an action (cleansing) that has already taken place, with the assumption being that God has acted to purify the inner person who has come to faith by the gospel (cf. Eph 5:26). The probable connection of the figure of "cleansing" to the rite of baptism[55] may also suggest the backward

---

50. For ἀγάπη (1:14; 2:15; 4:12; 6:11; 2 Tim 1:7 [without πίστις], 13; 2:22; 3:10; Titus 2:2), see further Spicq, *TLNT* 1:8-22; G. Schneider, *EDNT* 1:8-12; W. Gunther, H.-G. Link, and C. Brown, *NIDNTT* 2:538-51; for the linking of "faith" and "love," see Towner, *Goal,* 162-63, 165-66.

51. The Gk. preposition ἐκ ("from") expresses the source of ἀγάπη.

52. Gk. καθαρὰ καρδία (for the phrase, see Towner, *Goal,* 159). For καθαρά ("clean, pure"), see 3:9; 2 Tim 1:3; 2:22; Titus 1:15(3x). For καρδία ("heart") in Paul, see Rom 1:24; 5:5; 1 Cor 4:5; 2 Cor 4:6; Eph 1:18; F. Baumgärtel and J. Behm, *TDNT* 3:604-14; T. Sorg, *NIDNTT* 2:180-84; R. Jewett, *Paul's Anthropological Terms* (Leiden: Brill, 1971), 448; Lips, *Glaube,* 65-66; Marshall, 370.

53. Cf. LXX Deut 4:29; 5:29; 6:5; 10:12; 11:13 with Deut 29:3; 30:6.

54. LXX Ps 50:12 (καρδίαν καθαρὰν κτίσον ἐν ἐμοί ὁ θεός); Sir 38:10 (ἀπὸ πάσης ἁμαρτίας καθάρισον καρδίαν); Deut 30:6; cf. Gen 20:5, 6; Ps 50:12.

55. Titus 2:14; 1 Pet 3:21; so Marshall, 370; Roloff, 67-68.

look here to the event that marked the profession of faith. Love, the authentic outward expression of Christian faith, issues from the person whose emotional and volitional center has experienced cleansing by God.

The second term for the source of love, "good conscience,"[56] overlaps to some degree with the first. The focus in "good conscience," however, is on the organ of decision that facilitates the process by which a person may move from some norm (in this case that existing in the gospel, the faith, the sound teaching, etc.) to appropriate behavior. The qualification of conscience in these letters as either "good" (1:5, 19) or "clear" (3:9; 2 Tim 1:3) in the case of believers, and as "seared" (4:2) or "corrupted" (Titus 1:15) in the case of unbelievers, is a theological development from other Pauline use in which the term was employed as a neutral concept (see the Excursus below). That is, Paul regards the condition of the human conscience as ultimately affected positively by adherence to the apostolic gospel or rendered ineffective by rejection of it. And following from this, the false teachers' rejection of the gospel makes moral goodness unattainable, while acceptance of the gospel opens up this possibility for authentic believers. "Good," as in the case of "good deeds" (see on 2:10), in Paul's vocabulary refers to an intrinsically positive benefit stemming from conversion. Consequently, Paul regards an effectively functioning conscience to be intrinsic to the process that is to lead from teaching to the goal of love.

The third and last aspect in this description of the source of love is "sincere faith." Within this context ("in faith"; 1:4), "faith" again (1:2 note) describes Christian existence as a posture or state that consists of active believing in God and the apostolic gospel, rather than standing as a measurement of the purity of what one believes.[57] The attached adjective, "sincere" (anhypokritos),[58] stresses the integrity and authenticity (and complete lack of deception) of this commitment, primarily as seen in the response of lifestyle that accompanies belief. Its emphasis on authenticity is suggested by the use of the antonym "hypocrisy" (hypokrisis) to describe the deception of the false teaching (4:2).

These three Christian realities bring into alignment the faith relationship with God and the effects of that relationship in cleansing the inner person for perception of truth and the processing of it into appropriate action. The organization of ideas in the sentence suggests that Paul is exploring the

56. Gk. καὶ συνειδήσεως ἀγαθῆς; 1:19; Acts 23:1; 1 Pet 3:16, 21; cf. Heb 13:18.

57. See Marshall, 370-71; cf. U. Wilckens, *TDNT* 9:570-71, who concentrates on the sense of orthodoxy.

58. Gk. ἀνυπόκριτος; in the NT (cf. LXX Wis 5:18; 18:15 of the Lord) the term is found in several ethically focused texts, describing, as here, the quality of the faith commitment (2 Tim 1:5), sincerity of love (Rom 12:9; 2 Cor 6:6), or brotherly love (1 Pet 1:22), or on its own as being one of several Christian qualities (Jas 3:17). See further Spicq, *TLNT* 1:134-36; 3:412-13.

source of Christian behavior; but at the center of the underlying components is faith in God as mediated through the gospel he preached.

Excursus: Conscience in the Letters to Timothy and Titus

The term "conscience" (συνείδησις) occurs 14 times in other Pauline letters, with the heaviest concentration in the Corinthian correspondence (8x in 1 Corinthians; 3x in 2 Corinthians). And his use probably explains the term's appearance in the early church's technical language for anthropology (Jewett, *Paul's Anthropological Terms,* 421-26; C. Maurer, *TDNT* 7:914; J. Stelzenberger, *Syneidesis im Neuen Testament* [Paderborn: Schöningh, 1961], 51-95). There is not really a background for Pauline usage in the LXX (Wis 17:11; Job 27:6 [verb]; cf. Sir 10:20), but there is wide use of the term in the secular literature, in which, up to Paul, it is related mainly to the consciousness (or lack thereof) of having committed a wrong (see esp. H.-J. Eckstein, *Der Begriff Syneidesis bei Paulus* [Tübingen: Mohr, 1983]). The tendency to qualify the "conscience," for example, in terms of a "good conscience," begins to occur in secular Greek from the second century C.E. onward, though comparable ideas are expressed in Philo (*On Rewards and Punishments* 79-84; *On the Special Laws* 1.203) and Josephus (*Jewish War* 2.582) with the σύνοιδα word group.

Concerning Pauline usage outside the letters to Timothy and Titus, it is frequently commented that Paul's tendency is to employ the term as a neutral concept. It is not limited to any one group of people, but functions as a control for behavior by bringing an assessment of behavior to consciousness on the basis of a known norm (Eckstein, *Syneidesis,* 312). This general definition applies to Rom 2:15; 9:1; 13:5; 1 Cor 8:7, 10, 12; 10:25, 27, 28, 29 (2x); 2 Cor 1:12; 4:2; 5:11. In the case where Paul does qualify the term in a way approaching its use in the letters to Timothy and Titus, he does so less directly by means of participial modifiers (1 Cor 8:7: ἡ συνείδησις αὐτῶν ἀσθενὴς οὖσα μολύνεται; cf. v.10; 8:12: αὐτῶν τὴν συνείδησιν ἀσθενοῦσαν), though the distance from this particular sort of reflection on the conscience in 1 Corinthians to its theological use in the letters to Timothy and Titus cannot be very great. In this usage, the conscience is neither a source of power for correct behavior, nor the source of the ethical norms meant to guide behavior. As Eckstein argues (*Syneidesis,* 314), for Paul the conscience acts as a neutral judge of behavior, according to a norm, that brings its judgment, either positive or negative, to the awareness of the individual by criticism or affirmation.

The main question has to do with the concept as it appears in the letters to Timothy and Titus and whether and how it is related to usage elsewhere in Paul (see esp. Marshall, 218-27; Towner, *Goal,* 154-58; Lips, *Glaube,* 57-65). Compared with the independent use of "conscience," in these letters the qualified term (good/clean, seared/defiled) reveals a theological development of the concept. The polemical context, and especially the application of the term to the matter of apostasy from and faithfulness to the faith, determines the directions in which the term is taken. Particularly in the case of the opponents, the "seared consciences" (1 Tim 4:3; see discussion) and the "defiled consciences" (Titus 1:15; see discussion) are set alongside statements that relate the conditions of their consciences to their dispositions toward the faith: 1 Tim 4:1, "some apostatized from the faith"; Titus 1:14, "having turned away from the faith." Thus Paul's argument is that rejection of the faith has in some sense rendered the "conscience" ineffective, and the chief result is seen in behavior (possibly extreme in the sense of asceticism or immorality) that runs counter to that approved by the apostolic tradition as being "godly."

Corresponding to these connections is the relationship between the good/ clean conscience and adherence to the apostolic ("sound") teaching. But as Marshall, 225 (following Arichea-Hatton, 73), helpfully suggests, a distinction should be maintained between the two positive categories of the Christian conscience. As the context of 1 Tim 1:5, 19 shows, the "good conscience" may pertain mainly to the ability to make decisions effectively about behavior (which leads to love), while in the case of the "cleansed conscience" the focus may veer slightly to the inner approval that no wrong has been done and that actions have been properly motivated (3:9; 2 Tim 1:3). This is, however, a rather subtle distinction (which is not rigidly maintained in uses of the same or similar constructions in Acts 23:1; 1 Pet 3:16; Heb 13:18), and the possibility should perhaps be left open that in 1 Tim 1:5 συνειδήσεως ἀγαθῆς ("good conscience") was selected as the second object of the preposition ἐκ instead of καθαρᾶς συνειδήσεως ("clean conscience") for stylistic reasons, to avoid the repetition of the adjective ("clean"). Nevertheless, as the terms stand in 1 and 2 Timothy, the "cleansed conscience" (in the construction ἐν καθαρᾷ συνειδήσει) in 1 Tim 3:9 and 2 Tim 1:3 seems to depict something like the conviction of innocence (with respect to some nearby action) as a ground of confidence that consistency between faith and action has indeed been achieved. The difference between the two expressions is one of perspective: the "good conscience" having to do with the effectiveness of the process (sound norms/data, effective movement from norms to action), and "clean conscience" having to do with an assessment of the outcome (a state of consistency having been achieved). Notably, the term "bad conscience," which would presumably refer to the conscience that has sent the signal of the need for change (cf. "evil conscience" [συνειδήσεως πονηρᾶς] in Heb 10:22), is not used of the opponents, precisely because Paul's point is that their rejection of the gospel (the approved norm) has destroyed the capacity of their consciences to make reliable decisions (see also Marshall, 225).

When we compare the term's use in Paul's letters to churches and in these three letters, we should note certain differences, then. (1) In some respects the "good conscience" appears to have been influenced by the concept of the "cleansed heart" so that both realities are the result of conversion (1 Tim 1:5). (2) "Conscience" in the letters to Timothy and Titus seems to operate in a way more comparable to "the mind" (νοῦς) in undisputed Paul. (3) Here too it is treated not simply as a neutral inner organ, but instead shows the results of theologizing (cf. the assessments of Roloff, 69-70; cf. Dibelius and Conzelmann, 20; M. E. Thrall, "The Pauline Use of ΣΥΝΕΙΔΗΣΙΣ," *NTS* 14 [1967], 118-25). There is, however, nothing in the theological use that could not, given the right circumstances, have grown out of the more neutral use in the undisputed letters (see also Johnson, 165-66; Trummer, *Paulustradition,* 236). Marshall, 225, makes the point, for instance, that the notion of the heart and conscience being cleansed through conversion in 1 Tim 1:5 (as part of a broader effect on human personality implied in Titus 3:5; see also 2:12) differs little from the implications contained in the statement about the mind being "renewed" in Rom 12:2.

If anything, the theological development observable in the concept would seem to be the result of two things: (1) a new or far more intensive situation in which members of the church have rejected the gospel and embraced questionable ethical practices because of that rejection; (2) further theological reflection on the implications for anthropology of the renovation of the human being through the gospel and Spirit-indwelling. In this situation, Paul insists that the conscience "stands on the line connecting correct belief and corresponding conduct," and in the case of the false teachers, "repudiation of the apostolic faith" rendered the conscience ineffective (Towner, *Goal,* 156). Thus the issue lying behind the use of the concept of the "good/clean conscience" is precisely that of commitment to (belief in, embracing of) the apostolic faith as a basis for godliness in life. (Cf. also A. C. Thiselton, *The First Epistle to the Corinthians* [NIGTC; Grand Rapids: Eerdmans, 2000], 640-44; Spicq, *TLNT* 3:332-36; C. Maurer, *TDNT* 7:898-919; Jewett, *Paul's Anthropological Terms,* 402-46.)

---

6 This positive expression of Timothy's goal becomes the next platform for denouncing the opponents. The return to this mode is signaled by the second demeaning reference to them as "some" (see on 1:3). But the force of the argument lies in the contrast drawn between the "goal" just stated and the actual quite different orientation and results of the false teachers. With the contrast Paul intends to underline their deviation from the approved norm.

Their deviant course is described by a combination of two terms, each belonging to Paul's polemical vocabulary, which stress erratic movement away from the "goal" just mentioned.[59] The TNIV translation expresses the sequential nature of the two interrelated acts of deviation. But the translation

---

59. The connection with the list of items in 1:6 is created by the use of the gen. rel. pron. ὧν (so also 1:19, 20; 2:7; 6:4, 10; 2 Tim 1:7).

can be sharpened somewhat by bringing out the cause-effect relationship. Coming first is the adverbial participle that identifies the likely source or cause of this departure — "because [some] missed out on" the items mentioned in the previous verse (see also 6:21; 2 Tim 2:18).[60] The meaning of this verb in almost all of its uses relates to misdirection, missed targets, and so on. And this sense is very much in evidence in each of its occurrences in the letters to Timothy; but as Paul uses the term, the target, goal, or path that has been deviated from is always related to the faith in some sense. The second term describes the effect of this deviation: they "turned away to" a goal of their own devising. This verb, in three of its four occurrences, describes similarly the results of the false teaching in terms of a divergence from the apostolic faith (see also 5:15; 2 Tim 4:4).[61]

Finally, the end of this misdirection, the "goal" arrived at by wandering lost, comes to expression in the prepositional phrase that describes the useless false teaching as "meaningless talk."[62] Though capable of various translations (see the versions), this term disparages the false teaching as belonging to the category of things that are pagan (see on Titus 1:10). For this reason it is substandard. It belongs similarly to Paul's rather long list of derogatory expressions for the uselessness of the alternative doctrine.[63]

7 Paul develops this thought further[64] by underlining the irony created by the opponents' lofty desire ("to be teachers of the law") and the contraindications of their ability to achieve it. This specific desire locates these opponents within an extreme (enthusiastic) Jewish-Christian orbit, already hinted at in the reference to "myths and genealogies." The term "teachers of the law"[65] appears to be a Christian term for Jewish teachers.[66] Although

---

60. Gk. ἀστοχέω; limited to these three occurrences in the letters; see LXX Sir 7:19; 8:9.

61. Gk. ἐκτρέπομαι (Heb 12:13). In 6:20 the verb is used to direct Timothy to avoid the false teaching. For similar terms in the polemical repertoire, see 1:19; 4:1; 5:15; 2 Tim 4:4.

62. Gk. ματαιολογία is a biblical hapax (Polycarp, *Philippians* 2.1; see ματαιολόγοι in Titus 1:10).

63. Other terms of this sort include βέβηλος (1 Tim 1:9; 4:7; 6:20; 2 Tim 2:16), κενοφωνία (1 Tim 6:20; 2 Tim 2:16), μωροὶ ζητήσεις (2 Tim 2:23; Titus 3:9); ἀνωφελής, μάταιος (Titus 3:9), ἀπαίδευτος (2 Tim 2:23), γραωδής (1 Tim 4:7), ἀντιθέσεις (1 Tim 6:20), ἐντολαὶ ἀνθρώπων (Titus 1:14). See further, Towner, *Goal,* 24-25; Schlarb, *Die gesunde Lehre,* 59-73; O. Bauernfeind, *TDNT* 4:519-24.

64. The sentence continues with a participial phrase that describes the "some" of v. 6 in terms of a lofty desire and contradictory results.

65. Gk. νομοδιδάσκαλοι (pl.); Luke 5:17; Acts 5:34. For some the fact that only Luke uses the term elsewhere in the NT suggests Lukan influence in the writing of these letters (see Wilson, *Luke and the Pastoral Epistles*).

66. So, e.g., K. H. Rengstorf, *TDNT* 2:159; see also Roloff, 71. For the view that

against this background the term may express a critical view of their aspirations rather than being a self-description on their part, it still shows that the OT law is central to their teaching activities, and probably that they sought to have the role within the community equivalent to Jewish teachers. Thus they sought an authoritative place within the community and regarded that authority to be linked to teaching the law.

Their failure, however, is not in their aspiration, but in their complete ignorance of the subject matter they are dealing with. Paul underlines this with the emphatic qualifying statement: "they do not know what they are talking about or what they so confidently affirm." Two items should be stressed. First, Paul initiates here the theme of ignorance:[67] with a variety of language, he insists that rejection of the gospel leads to ignorance of the will of God (1 Tim 6:4, 20; 2 Tim 2:23; 3:7; Titus 1:15; 3:9). Second, Paul's condemnation is sweeping: the development from "what they say" to "what they so confidently affirm" places all of their teaching activities under the category of ignorance.[68] The effect in Paul's argument is to render all of their speaking activities null and void.

In this opening restatement of Timothy's commission (vv. 3-7), Paul has set out the goal his coworker is to pursue, and underscored that the opponents' ministry in the community runs contrary to this goal. Paul has not provided a detailed critical analysis of the false teaching such as we might have wished for, but by naming the goal and linking it to the apostolic gospel, he establishes at the outset that the opponents in Ephesus are in direct opposition to his and Timothy's mission. By stating the goal — love — Paul focuses the critique of the heresy on visible Christian living. What these opponents teach and the disputes resulting from their teaching run counter to God's order of life. The opponents, in fact, are incapable of understanding God's purposes or of serving them because they have departed from the gospel and lack the inward components (cleansed heart, good conscience, and sincere faith) that take the believer from apprehension of the gospel to authentic Christian love. Although Paul stops short of making all the connections, it seems clear that a rejection of the Pauline gospel is somehow tied to misunderstanding of the OT and the purpose of the law within God's will. The next step is to identify the real usefulness of the law (in contrast to the false teachers' use of it) and its relation to the gospel entrusted to Paul.

---

the desire to be "teachers of the law" indicates that the false teachers are non-Jewish, see Schlarb, *Die gesunde Lehre,* 91.

67. Gk. μὴ νοοῦντες (νοέω; 2 Tim 2:7); see J. Behm, *TDNT* 4:948-51.

68. For this, the Gk. rhetorical device μήτε . . . μήτε (= "neither . . . nor"; see Marshall, 373) establishes a range or scope (in this case beginning with "saying" and ending with "professing dogmatically") within which the condition under discussion is true. Cf. Matt 5:35; 11:18; Acts 23:12; 27:20; 2 Thess 2:2.

b. The Law and Paul's Gospel (1:8-11)

> 8 *We know that the law is good if one uses it properly.* 9 *We also know that the law is made not for the righteous but for lawbreakers and rebels, the ungodly and sinful, the unholy and irreligious; for those who kill their fathers or mothers, for murderers,* 10 *for the sexually immoral, for those practicing homosexuality, for slave traders and liars and perjurers. And it is for whatever else is contrary to the sound doctrine* 11 *that conforms to the gospel concerning the glory of the blessed God, which he entrusted to me.*

As Paul has already begun to show, authentic Christian existence expresses itself in love that emerges from the inner being of the genuine believer (1:5). He will go on very soon to link this to faith in the gospel. But before doing so, he adds an important element to the contrast between the false teachers and his own ministry and understanding. His critique of their use of the OT and their desire to be "teachers of the law" has been unequivocal. But it raises a question or two that must be addressed. In case his critique be mistaken for a total dismissal of the law, he affirms its usefulness and defines the parameters in which this is so. But his chief point, following from 1:5, is that the law is not of use for the Christian but rather for the unbeliever. This understanding is similar to that in other texts in Paul, where he urges that love is central to the fulfillment of the law but stops short of dismissing the law completely. In Paul's estimation, the opponents have missed the point of the law: study of it will not produce the love that marks genuine faith.

The issues here are twofold. First, what is the appropriate use of the law? Second, more implicitly, how does the false teachers' use of the law reflect a failure to grasp its purpose? In one long sentence, Paul will continue the series of contrasts, as he discusses the function of the law against the background of misunderstanding. He will also turn from his conclusion about the law to an affirmation of the gospel. The discussion here is limited to the situation of misuse and misunderstanding, so we should not expect it to cover every detail of the law's meaning and intention.

8 Paul leads off with what amounts to a backhanded allegation of misuse of the law. The opening phrase, "we know that," is a formulaic appeal to accepted tradition (resumed in v. 9: "we also know").[1] By opening the appeal in this way, Paul places himself on the side of authoritative tradition and the false teachers outside the mainstream.

When it comes to the tradition that is here affirmed, we are faced with

---

1. Gk. οἴδαμεν δὲ ὅτι; the formula is used widely in Paul in various configurations; e.g., so also in Rom 2:2; 3:9; 8:28; cf. Rom 5:3; 6:9; 1 Cor 15:58; see further Marshall, 374 n. 37.

two problems. The first is the content of the tradition. The second is the strong tendency among modern interpreters to insist that this could not be a Pauline statement.

As for content, the preceding context requires that the statement, "the law is good," refer to the Jewish law as expressed in and through the OT.[2] To call it "good"[3] is to place it into the same sort of category as "deeds" and other things that are intrinsically good or derive their virtue from divine authority and so serve God's purposes. The whole phrase may echo the earlier discussion of one of the law's uses in Rom 7:12-25, and it may consciously recall what Paul said in that discussion about the moral function of the law: "I agree that the law is good."[4] For Timothy and presumably the Ephesian Christian community, such an allusion to Paul's teaching would certainly count as an appeal to apostolic tradition.

As for the insistence of some that this cannot be a Pauline view of the law, it need only be said that this is a limited discussion of the law's function in relation to determining what is morally right and wrong. In Galatians and Romans the specific issue Paul seeks to expose and correct is a Judaizing insistence that Gentile believers observe certain elements of the law (circumcision and rites of purification) as indicators of righteousness (membership in God's people). But in 1 Timothy the abuse of the law indicated by 1:4-6 (cf. 4:1-3) is different in nature. The law as a topic is not central to this letter; where it is briefly under the microscope, the point of comparison is Romans 7, which shares an interest in its moral usefulness. Once this correspondence is seen, it is unnecessary to differentiate this positive evaluation of the law from the similar understanding of the law that occurs in Romans.

The following condition or qualification is what determines the meaning of "good" in this discussion. The law is "good" within the scope of appropriate use: "if one uses it properly." Paul will go on to delineate this appropriate application. But here he indicates that the matter at hand is precisely the sort of use to which the law ought to be put, and, as we shall see, for whom that use is relevant.[5] The backdrop to this is the strained appli-

---

2. Most commentators hold this view. There has been a tendency (Hanson, 59-60; Roloff, 73; Merkel, 19; Hasler, 14) to interpret ὁ νόμος as a reference to Roman law, but this does not seem to fit the context.

3. Gk. καλός (1:18; 2:3; 2 Tim 4:7).

4. Gk. σύμφημι τῷ νόμῳ ὅτι καλός (Rom 7:16); for similar clear affirmations of the law, cf. Rom 7:12, 14.

5. The combination of the adv. νομίμως (which here means "appropriate or proper"; W. Gutbrod, *TDNT* 4:1088-89) and the verb χρῆται ("to use or apply"; A. Sand, *EDNT* 3:471-72) expresses appropriate use or application, and not something like "observance of the law"; the term is mainly Pauline (1 Tim 5:23; Acts 27:3, 17; 1 Cor 7:21, 31; 9:12, 15; 2 Cor 1:17; 3:12; 13:10).

cation of the law within the false teachers' speculative program of "myths and genealogies" (v. 4).

9-10 What is the appropriate use of the law? The participial phrase delineates the framework for this particular understanding of the law, appealing a second time to accepted knowledge: "knowing this. . . ."[6] The mistake at issue is in knowing for whom the law was established,[7] and Paul asserts that it was not for Christians ("the righteous") but for unbelievers. In this context, "the righteous" ("upright, just"; Titus 1:8) are Christian believers who through their genuine conversion produce the self-giving love (1:5) that fulfills the law.[8] It is tempting to make all of the connections here (via the "righteousness" word group) back to Paul's theology of justification by faith (cf. Titus 3:7), but this precise sense is probably not intended here.[9] He simply means authentic believers, for whom the law as a written moral code serves only a very limited purpose.

If not for believers, for whom, then, was the law enacted? Since a misunderstanding about this was at the center of the false teachers' activities, Paul eliminates any ambiguity by employing the rhetorical device known as a vice list. This technique was designed to characterize and exemplify the elements of socially and morally unacceptable behavior and to type people known for it.[10] In this application, the list identifies not vices (as in Rom 1:29-31) but rather the people known for them (cf. 1 Cor 6:9-10). This personalized slant emphasizes moral character and creates a portrait of godless human activity that is precisely the opposite of the image of Christian activity characterized in 1:5 by love.

The list describes extreme lawbreakers: it is given in four pairs, followed by a series of six individual terms, and concluded with a general catch-all category. There is a striking correspondence to the Decalogue from the reference to "killing fathers and mothers" through to "liars and perjur-

---

6. The Gk. phrase εἰδὼς τοῦτο (see also 2 Tim 2:23; Titus 3:14) modifies the immediately preceding clause "if one uses it properly" (cf. the decision of the TNIV to begin a new sentence that links the participle with "we know that the law is good"), pointing forward to the content (τοῦτο) of what is known.

7. Gk. κεῖμαι, here with "law," means "to enact" or "establish" (Aristophanes, *Plutus* 914; see further LSJ, s.v. III.3; F. Büchsel, *TDNT* 3:654). It forms a wordplay with ἀντίκειται in v. 11 that serves to heighten the contrast and force the issue of the law's real intention.

8. For δίκαιος as an appropriation of OT language for Christians, see Heb 12:23; 1 Pet 3:12; 4:18. See also Johnson, 175; S. Westerholm, "The Law and the 'Just Man' (1 Tim 1, 3-11)," *ST* 36 (1982): 79-95.

9. See F. Thielman, *Paul and the Law* (Downers Grove, IL: InterVarsity Press, 1994), 233; Marshall, 377. But cf. Mounce, 34-35; Kelly, 49.

10. J. T. Fitzgerald, "Virtue/Vice Lists," n.p. *ABD on CD-Rom.* Version 2.1a. 1995, 1996, 1997; Towner, *Goal,* 160-61 (see refs. to literature there).

ers."[11] The first three pairs of sinners have also been thought to reflect the earlier parts of the Decalogue,[12] but the precision of these connections is not quite so compelling, and correspondence is rather to be found in the impression of opposition to God that these early vices collectively produce, and in the sequential listing, evident in the Decalogue, of sins against God followed by those perpetrated against fellow humans. The list echoes the Decalogue in such a way that the relationship is close enough not to be missed and broad enough to appeal to the Hellenistic ear of the church that would have overheard this letter.[13] Calling on the Decalogue at this point makes perfect sense since as the core of the Torah it establishes the essential criteria for making sin against God and people known (cf. Rom 7:7) — the appropriate use of the law that Paul has in mind.

Illustrating this appropriate use of the law is the first function of the list. The sins portray graphically a depth of depravity so clearly different from Christian godliness that the irrelevance of the law (as Paul is thinking of its usefulness here) for believers is immediately felt. But there is also a polemical strategy in this discourse. It may be that Paul implies that misuse, misunderstanding, and false teaching of the law are precisely what gives rise to such sinful behavior — that he thus accuses the false teachers of heading inevitably in this direction.[14] In any case, it is certain that the opponents and the behavior linked to their teaching are included among the indicted in the closing catchall phrase, "whatever else is contrary to the sound doctrine."[15] They should be allowing the law to critique their own behavior instead of using it as they have been doing. In Paul's mind and in his theology, the other-directed love that characterizes authentic Christian existence (1:5; Rom 13:10) is to be found in and through conversion and the indwelling Spirit, not in a superficial reading of the law as a moral code.

"Lawbreakers and rebels" head the list as general illustrations of behavior that expresses disobedience and rebellion to God and lies at the root of all other lawbreaking. The first term sometimes refers to Gentiles as those outside the law (1 Cor 9:21), but here it means the culpable violation of the

---

11. See esp. W. Nauck, "Die Herkunft des Verfassers der Pastoralbriefe: Ein Beiträg zur Frage der Auslegung der Pastoralbricfc" (unpub. diss., Göttingen, 1950), 8-16; Marshall, 378-79.

12. Knight, 84, suggests that (1) the first pair, "lawbreakers and rebels," is introductory; (2) the second pair, "ungodly and sinful," corresponds to not honoring God and worshiping idols, respectively; (3) the third pair, "unholy and irreligious," corresponds to not respecting God's name and breaking the Sabbath, respectively. Cf. Johnson, 169.

13. See Oberlinner, 27; Marshall, 379; cf. Dibelius and Conzelmann, 23.

14. N. J. McEleney, "The Vice-Lists of the Pastoral Epistles," *CBQ* 36 (1974): 203-19, 210; cf. Oberlinner, 27.

15. See the discussion in Marshall, 378.

(God's) law.[16] The second term signifies an attitude of insubordination and here indicates rejection of God's authority (Titus 1:6, 10).[17]

The next two terms, "the ungodly and sinful," are often found together in descriptions of behavior that is impious and blatantly wrong and that expresses arrogant rejection of God.[18]

Comprising the third pair, the terms "unholy and irreligious" are near synonyms for unholy behavior that occur elsewhere in these letters as part of the polemic against opponents. The pair occurs also as a polemical description of Ptolemy's impious and idolatrous disregard for the Jews in 3 Macc 2:2. "Unholy" depicts things that are inappropriate to the worship of God, profane or not consecrated, and in opposition to sacred norms of worship and behavior.[19] "Irreligious" elsewhere describes the false doctrine in terms of its distance from and foreignness to God (4:7; 6:20; cf. 2 Tim 2:16), with its use in the LXX for various kinds of ritual defilement and for foreign profane acts determining the sense here.[20]

Thus far the list takes the direction of behavior that traditionally characterized rebellion, idolatry, pagan profane acts, and opposition to the worship of Israel's God.

16. Gk. ἄνομος; the use of the adj. in 1 Thess 2:8 is comparable; see also the noun ἀνομία in Titus 2:14; Rom 6:19; 2 Cor 6:14; W. Gutbrod, *TDNT* 4:1086-87.

17. Gk. ἀνυπότακτος; the term does not occur in the LXX. It can denote a positive quality of independence, but here (and only in 1 Tim 1:9; Titus 1:6, 10; cf. Heb 2:8 for the meaning "outside of one's control") the negative sense (the opposite of the quality described by ὑποτάσσω/ὑποταγή; 2:11; 3:4) is intended (G. Delling, *TDNT* 8:47).

18. Gk. ἀσεβέσι καὶ ἁμαρτωλοῖς; for the combination see LXX Ps 1:1, 5; cf. Rom 5:6, 8. "Ungodly" (ἀσέβεια; 2 Tim 2:16; Titus 2:12; Deut 9:5; Isa 59:20; *1 Enoch* 1.9; Rom 1:18; 11:26; Jude 15, 18) belongs to the dominant εὐσέβεια word group that figured prominently in Jewish polemics directed towards Greek culture (Prov 1:7; 2 Macc 2:31-32). It functions similarly in these letters to Timothy and Titus. Together the negative term, which describes idolatrous behavior, and the positive term, which serves to describe the life engendered by and appropriate to the covenant relationship with YHWH, encompassed the two possibilities of life. See the discussion of εὐσέβεια at 2:2; Marshall, 135-44; W. Foerster, *TDNT* 7:185-91. The adj. "sinner" (ἁμαρτωλός; freq. in LXX and NT for those who do wrong in the sight of God; Gen 13:13; Pss 1:5; 9:18; 10:2; Isa 1:28; etc. Matt 9:10; Rom 3:7; 5:19; 7:13; Gal 2:15, 17; etc.) covers the ground from "guilty," to "sinful," to "wicked," occurs frequently in opposition to such ideas as "the righteous," and denotes the "sinner" as one who rejects the relationship with God and stands condemned by the law (see further K. H. Rengstorf, *TDNT* 1:317-33).

19. Gk. ἀνόσιος (2 Tim 3:2); its place within descriptions of idolatrous/blasphemous worship (as generally intended here) is seen in LXX Ezek 22:9. See also Philo, *On the Life of Moses* 2.199; Wis 12:4; 2 Macc 7:34; 8:32.

20. Gk. βέβηλος (LXX Lev 21:9; 2 Macc 5:16; *Psalms of Solomon* 4.1; 8.12; Heb 12:16). See Spicq, *TLNT* 1:284-86; F. Hauck, *TDNT* 1:640-41.

With the last pair in the sequence, "those who kill their fathers or mothers,"[21] crimes against people come into view. The combination is traditional[22] and belongs with the word "murderers" that follows. Some suggest that it corresponds to the fifth commandment, to honor father and mother (Exod 20:12), in which case murdering parents would be an extreme example of violating this command (cf. Rom 1:30).[23] It may, however, in conjunction with the following reference to "murderers," correspond more closely to the sixth commandment condemning murder (Exod 20:13).[24] Or, as seems more likely, Paul may make use of the traditional abhorrence of the crime of murdering parents in a way that brings the fifth and sixth commandments together, including the more common crime of murder in the term that follows. In any case, the extreme reference corresponds to the exaggerated degree of depravity emphasized in the list. "Murderers" (Exod 20:15; Deut 5:18) describes evildoers who are hardly less heinous. This term occurs only here in the NT and is rare in the LXX, where its association with blasphemy and impiety establishes its place in the profile of the archetypal enemy of God.[25] In the wider Greek literature it occurs with the preceding pair.

Verse 10 continues the list with two terms that refer to sexual sin. The first term, "the sexually immoral," is more general, being used to describe those who commit adultery and fornication (i.e., unsanctioned sexual activity outside of marriage).[26] More specific is the term that the TNIV translates as "those practicing homosexuality."[27] It denotes, unequivocally, the activity of

---

21. Gk. πατρολῴαις καὶ μητρολῴαις (both are biblical hapaxes); they appear elsewhere with various spellings (on which see Johnson, 170; Marshall, 380 n. 58; BDF §26; 35.2; 119.2).

22. See, e.g., Plato, *Phaedo* 114a (which mentions the pair in connection with ἀνδροφόνος); Lycius 10.8; 11.4.

23. Marshall, 380. Others, perhaps more interested in substantiating the link with the Decalogue, think that the idea of murdering parents is too extreme and, based on the language (πατρ [μητρ-] + ἀλοάω ["to hit or smite"]), take the terms as meaning to dishonor father and mother (e.g., Knight, 85; Simpson, 31). But the use of the term in Greek writings argues against this (Josephus, *Antiquities* 16.356; Plato, *Phaedo* 114a; *Laws* 881A; Diodorus Siculus 21.7.1).

24. Cf. Johnson, 170.

25. Gk. ἀνδροφόνος: 2 Macc 9:28; 4 Macc 9:15 (verb). In reference to the Mosaic law, Philo, *On the Special Laws* 3.83 (ἀνδροφονία), 84, 87; in legal discussions, Plato, *Phaedo* 114a; Aristotle, *Nicomachean Ethics* 1107A.

26. Gk. πόρνος, in the NT, covers this basic range of sexual immorality (1 Cor 5:9, 10, 11; 6:9; Eph 5:5; for the noun πορνεία, see 1 Cor 5:1; 6:15,16; Gal 5:19). See F. Hauck and S. Schulz, *TDNT* 6:579-95.

27. An improvement on "perverts" (NIV 1984); "sodomites" (NRSV). The Gk. term ἀρσενοκοίτης (1 Cor 6:9, not in LXX) is rare and more typical in post-NT Christian writings (for the verb, see *Sibylline Oracles* 2.73).

male homosexuality, and the view of this practice adopted in this text corresponds to that of Paul elsewhere (Rom 1:27).[28] In terms of correspondence to the Decalogue (to the degree that this is intended), the connection would be found in the command covering adultery (Exod 20:14; Deut 5:18). But the expansion in Lev 18:22 and 20:13, which may be more closely related, regards male homosexuality as a deviation from the Mosaic moral code. Contemporary arguments that advocate the legitimacy of homosexuality cannot resort successfully to the biblical texts and etymology. The exegesis of these passages is not in question, and the fate of the current debate about homosexuality will rest on hermeneutics.[29]

"Slave traders" (or "kidnappers"; only here in biblical Greek) denotes those engaged in the business of kidnapping or stealing people and selling them into slavery.[30] According to the pattern of presenting worst cases of Decalogue violations, this activity would correspond to the commandment that condemns stealing (Exod 20:15).[31]

The last two terms make contact with the ninth commandment, which condemns bearing false witness (Exod 20:16). "Liars and perjurers" takes up the matter of deceptive speech, first indicating the general activity, then presenting a specific example of it. The term "liar," which has three Pauline occurrences (Titus 1:12; Rom 3:4/Ps 115:2), describes one who speaks in a deceptive manner.[32] A "perjurer" (only here in the NT; Zech 5:3; Wis 14:25) is one who takes an oath and then breaks it by lying.[33] Lev

---

28. The derivation of the term ἀρσενοκοίτης is in question. The term as Paul uses it was most likely coined from the Greek translation of the Hebrew phrase, "lying with a male," that occurs in Lev 18:22; 20:13 (for which the Greek OT has [18:22] καὶ μετὰ ἄρσενος οὐ κοιμηθήσῃ κοίτην γυναικός· βδέλυγμα γάρ ἐστιν ["you shall not lie with a man as with a woman, for it is an abomination"] and [cf. 20:13] καὶ ὃς ἂν κοιμηθῇ μετὰ ἄρσενος κοίτην γυναικός). See R. B. Hays, *The Moral Vision of the New Testament* (San Francisco: HarperCollins, 1996), 382-83. See further the exchange in D. F. Wright, "Homosexuals or Prostitutes: The Meaning of ΑΡΣΕΝΟΚΟΙΤΑΙ (1 Cor 6:9; 1 Tim 1:10)," *VC* 38 (1984), 125-53; W. L. Petersen, "Can ΑΡΣΕΝΟΚΟΙΤΑΙ Be Translated by 'Homosexuals'? (1 Cor 6:9; 1 Tim 1:10)," *VC* 40 (1986): 187-91; D. F. Wright, "Translating ΑΡΣΕΝΟΚΟΙΤΑΙ (1 Cor 6:9; 1 Tim 1:10)," *VC* 41 (1987): 396-98.

29. See L. T. Johnson, *Scripture and Discernment* (Nashville: Abingdon, 1996).

30. Gk. ἀνδραποδιστής; of selling captive into slavery, see, e.g., Plato, *Republic* 344b; Xenophon, *Memorabilia* 4.2.15 (ἐξανδραποδίσηται); etc.; see also the cognate noun, ἀνδράποδα (3 Macc 7:5, "one taken captive in war and sold as a slave"; for the sense of kidnapping, see Xenophon, *Memorabilia,* 4.2.14; Philo, *On the Special Laws* 4.13.

31. Philo, *On the Special Laws* 4.130; see also Johnson, 171; Marshall, 380. Later Jewish discussions linked it with murder (see Jeremias, 14; StrB 1:810-13).

32. Gk. ψεύστης (cf. 4:2); see the discussion at Titus 1:12; H. Conzelmann, *TDNT* 9:594-603.

33. Gk. ἐπίορκος (see the verb in Matt 5:33).

19:11-12, in reflecting on the Decalogue, discusses these two activities in the same order. They were also typically present in Greek and Jewish ethical discussions.[34]

On the assumption that Paul did intend the list to make contact with the Decalogue, it is noticeable that he omitted any counterpart to the command about coveting. Perhaps it was his strategy of depicting commandment violations in the most extreme way, and the fact that coveting is rather general and so widespread, that determined its omission.[35] Whatever the reason, it would surely be implied (along with other sins) in the broad catchall category that concludes the list: "and whatever else is contrary to the sound teaching."

Paul's strategy mirrors his conclusion to the discussion of love as the fulfillment of the law in Rom 13:8-10. The catchall element in the statement here (lit. "and if there is any other [crime]") is virtually identical.[36] Since it is with this phrase and its stress on "opposing"[37] (cf. Titus 1:9) that Paul turns attention to the false teachers, the term "other" *(heteron)* may echo the preceding reference to "teaching other doctrine" *(heterodidaskalein,* 1:3). Otherwise, the parallel with Rom 13:8-10 is notable. In the Romans passage, Paul assembles a list of commandments concerning adultery, murder, stealing, and coveting and closes it with the catchall phrase, all to argue that they are summed up in obedience to the command to love one's neighbor as oneself (Lev 19:18). There the point is that the individual commandments are now fulfilled in the new agape-orientation in Christ and the Spirit and no longer to be followed as so many individual ethical requirements (Rom 13:10). What Paul says here is a true mirror image — opposite but continuous — for in this discourse the individual commandments are viewed from the standpoint of violations, and for these the law functions to bring unregenerate tendencies to light. The centrality of love within Paul's ethic has already been announced in 1:5, and that goal establishes another link to the Romans text.

What is different in the two texts is the intention: here Paul uses the goal of love and the discussion of the appropriate use of the law to establish the variance of the law-centered approach of the opponents from his gospel. So, the apostle's standard of comparison is clearly stated: ". . . contrary to the sound teaching" (or "doctrine," TNIV). There are several things to notice about this term. First, in general, within Paul, the term "teaching," and re-

---

34. Wis 14:28; Philo, *On the Special Laws* 1.235.

35. Cf. Marshall, 380; Roloff, 77.

36. Gk. καὶ εἴ τι ἕτερον; Rom 13:9, καὶ εἴ τις ἑτέρα ἐντολή; cf. 1 Tim 6:3; Phil 3:15 (with a verb).

37. Gk. ἀντίκειμαι; see 5:14; 1 Cor 16:9; Gal 5:17; Phil 1:28; 2 Thess 2:4; Spicq, *TLNT* 1:129-30.

lated didactic language, dominates in these letters to Timothy and Titus.[38] This corresponds to the emphasis on teaching tasks assigned to the coworkers as apostolic representatives within these contexts rather than to an alleged later postapostolic conceptualization of "the faith" as a fixed body of doctrine. A fixed or accepted and authoritative apostolic teaching is indeed in view in the various terms used for "the teaching," "the faith," "the gospel," and so on, but not in a way unknown elsewhere in Paul.

Second, "the sound teaching," always in the singular, is a technical term in these letters for the authoritative apostolic doctrine.[39] Its singularity stands in intentional contrast with the substandard plurality of the opponents' "teachings" (4:1; see on "myths" at 1:4).

Third, the adjectival participle "sound" ("healthy") introduces an evaluation that strengthens the polemical impact. In its basic use, the word group is medical language that means "healthy," and this is the sense used consistently elsewhere in the NT (Matt 15:31; Luke 5:31; 7:10; 3 John 2).[40] But in these letters to coworkers, the language describes the quality of what is said or taught[41] or of a person's faith or spirituality.[42] The background of this application is the secular philosophical debates, in which the word group acquired a figurative sense.[43] Applied within moral teaching, the term "sound" described behavior or teaching that was virtuous, and evaluated the teaching as being logical or compelling and not necessarily carrying the meaning of healthy in the sense of positively health-producing.[44] But this fuller sense of health-producing (with the opposite sense of noxious, diseased, and dangerous to health), though extended figuratively beyond discussions of physical well-being, is also found in discussions of teaching.[45] It is this latter sense that explains its meaning in these three letters, particularly where the term also describes the state of one's faith (Titus 1:13; 22). Thus "sound teaching" is a way of describing the approved apostolic teaching, which is positively health-producing. The implied polemical contrast is that

38. The singular, διδασκαλία, occurs fourteen times (1:10; 4:6, 13, 16; 5:17; 6:1, 3; 2 Tim 3:10, 16; 4:3; Titus 1:9; 2:1, 7, 10); elsewhere in Rom 12:7; 15:4; Eph 4:14; Col 2:22.

39. Gk. ὑγιαίνουσα διδασκαλία; for the whole phrase, see 1 Tim 6:3; 2 Tim 4:3; Titus 1:9; 2:1.

40. For the original sense of physical health (from Plato to Philo), see the references and discussion in Johnson, 172.

41. 1 Tim 1:10; 6:3; 2 Tim 1:13; 4:3; Titus 1:9; 2:1, 8.

42. Titus 1:13; 2:2.

43. A. J. Malherbe, "Medical Imagery in the Pastorals," in *Paul and the Popular Philosophers* (Minneapolis: Fortress, 1989), 121-36.

44. Malherbe, "Medical Imagery," 121-36; see also Johnson, 172.

45. See Philo, *On Husbandry* 164.5; *On Abraham* 223, 275.

the opponents' "other" doctrines are infectious, diseased, and capable of destroying the spiritual health of those who come under their influence.

11 As the Greek sentence continues, Paul introduces the source and standard of the "sound teaching."[46] In the Roman world of Paul's day, the term "the gospel" ("good news") was part of the fixed political vocabulary associated with the Imperial cult, describing news of military and political successes, especially those of the emperor.[47] While Paul and the early church may also have been drawn to the use of the verb in association with the announcement of peace, salvation, and "good news" in Isaiah (40:9; 52:7; 61:1-2),[48] Paul's dominant use of this term and an array of others was calculated to force a confrontation between the Christian claims about salvation and Lordship and those of the dominant Imperial ideology.[49] In content, "gospel" denotes the good news that the Messiah had come, bringing salvation.[50] The fundamental nature of the gospel for Christian existence is affirmed in texts such as Rom 15:16 and 1 Cor 9:14, and it is its priority, in some sense, to the sound teaching that explains its presence here as a normative source.

When Paul owns the gospel in a unique way, he is referring to the specific mission he has been given to accomplish. The main reason for this reference to the gospel is to close this section by turning the discussion to the topic of his mission and message. It is his mission and message that establish the benchmarks of authentic gospel and faith. His gospel (Rom 2:16; 16:25; 2 Tim 1:10), in contrast to the opponents' activities and teaching, is definitive for Christian faith and behavior — that is, for the "sound teaching" that articulates the appropriate ethical response to God.

More problematic is the intended meaning of the string of three genitives[51] that in the Greek follow "gospel" and in some way define it. Al-

46. For the preposition κατά, in this sense, see BDF §224; BDAG, s.v. B.5. For the view that the prepositional phrase grounds the whole of 1:8-10, see Marshall, 382; Roloff, 79; Brox, 108.

47. For secular refs. and discussion, see S. R. F. Price, "Rituals and Power," in R. A. Horsley, ed., *Paul and Empire* (Harrisburg, PA: Trinity Press International, 1997), 48, 53; P. Stuhlmacher, *Das paulinische Evangelium* (Göttingen: Vandenhoeck & Ruprecht, 1968), 1:196-206.

48. See P. T. O'Brien, *Gospel and Mission in the Writings* of Paul (Carlisle: Paternoster, 1995), 77-81; J. D. G. Dunn, *The Theology of Paul the Apostle* (Grand Rapids: Eerdmans, 1998), 164-69.

49. See esp. N. T. Wright, *What Saint Paul Really Said* (Grand Rapids: Eerdmans, 1997), 41-44.

50. Gk. εὐαγγέλιον (2 Tim 1:8, 10; 2:8; Rom 1:1, 16; 2:16; etc.; Spicq, *TLNT* 2:82-92; G. Strecker, *EDNT* 2:40-74, 73; G. Friedrich, *TDNT* 2:707-37.

51. Gk. τὸ εὐαγγέλιον τῆς δόξης τοῦ μακαρίου θεοῦ (the lit., somewhat stiff translation is: "the gospel of the glory of the blessed God"); for similar strings of genitives, see, e.g., Titus 2:13; 2 Cor 4:6.

though such strings are notoriously imprecise and tend to function best by giving a broad sense of meaning, the resultant differences in the English versions suggest the need for some explanation. The main question is with the first genitive, "glory." The two basic translation strategies are to treat the noun as an adjective or as a genitive of content.

Functioning adjectivally, it may modify the preceding noun "gospel" ("the glorious gospel of the blessed God"; NIV, NRSV)[52] or the following noun, "God" ("the Good News from the glorious and blessed God"; TEV, CEV, REB).[53] While word order perhaps favors the first arrangement, Paul more typically thinks of "the glory" of God or Christ.

However, as in the case of Titus 2:13 ("the appearance of the glory of God"; see discussion), the analogical function of the term "glory," which describes the qualities of God in visible and revelatory categories, favors understanding "glory" as being "of God" and the whole as descriptive of the gospel's content: "the gospel concerning [declaring] the glory of . . . God" (TNIV).[54] Thus the combination "the gospel of the glory of God" describes the message of salvation as that which unveils or declares the visible glory (and associated qualities of power, majesty, etc.) of God in the Christ-event.[55]

In the NT, the intervening adjective, "blessed" (cf. 6:15; Titus 2:13, discussion and note), is more typically used of people who experience God's blessing. Here, as an appellation of God, it creates a connection with Greek religion that was avoided in the LXX but taken up in Philo and Josephus.[56] The gods were "happy" in that they, in contrast to mere humans, were immortal. Such epithets were known in the Imperial cult, which suggests the possibility that the emergence of the term in reference to God here and in Titus reflects a new degree of polemical dialogue with the political powers on the part of Paul.[57]

But Paul's main point about the gospel is that he was entrusted with it

52. Johnson, 172.

53. Rom 1:23; 3:23; 1 Cor 2:8; 2 Cor 3:18; 4:6; 1 Tim 1:17; 3:16. For the noun functioning as an adj., see 1 Cor 2:8; Eph 1:17; Jas 2:1.

54. See also Roloff, 79; Fee, 47; Kelly, 51; Dibelius and Conzelmann, 25. As Johnson points out (172), in combinations like "the gospel of God," the genitive "of God" (τοῦ θεοῦ) may be subjective in meaning (or describing source; e.g., "the gospel from God") or objective (or describing content; e.g., "the gospel about God"), or, indeed, both at once. With the emphasis on the gospel as the criterion or standard of "the sound teaching," I have placed the emphasis on content (the objective sense).

55. Variations on this sense (some of which tend to the imaginative) can be explored in Marshall, 383.

56. Gk. μακάριος. Of the Greek gods (Homer, *Iliad* 1.339; *Odyssey* 10.299; etc.; Philo, *On the Special Laws* 1.209; 2.53; 3.1; *On the Immutability of God* 26; Josephus, *Antiquities* 10.278).

57. See Spicq, *TLNT* 2:439.

in a unique way in his calling to preach to the Gentiles. Throughout these letters to coworkers he emphasizes his link to the gospel[58] as a way of creating distance between his message and false teaching and of identifying his mission with the true message of God.[59] This way of describing the link between apostle and message is Pauline. The language of entrustment is reminiscent of 1 Cor 9:17 and Gal 2:7 (Titus 1:3; cf. Rom 3:2),[60] texts in which Paul discusses his commissioning by the Lord, with the passive verb underlining God's role in the process that called Paul to ministry and invested him with authority. Within the developing argument, Paul has thus connected the authentic gospel with his (and in this context his alone) apostolate. If this seems an extraordinarily egotistic estimation of his place in God's plan,[61] it must be placed alongside similar statements that aimed to establish the authenticity and authority of the Pauline gospel and mission to the Gentiles for readers whose views of him were uncertain (Rom 2:16; 1 Cor 9:16; Gal 2:7; 1 Thess 2:4). The appearance of this word group here marks the transition to the apostolic testimony below (vv. 12-16) in which "faith" language forms a significant theme.

c. Paul's Calling as a Pattern of Conversion (1:12-17)

12 *I thank Christ Jesus our Lord, who has given me strength, that he considered me trustworthy, appointing me to his service.* 13 *Even though I was once a blasphemer and a persecutor and a violent man, I was shown mercy because I acted in ignorance and unbelief.* 14 *The grace of our Lord was poured out on me abundantly, along with the faith and love that are in Christ Jesus.*

15 *Here is a trustworthy saying that deserves full acceptance: Christ Jesus came into the world to save sinners — of whom I am the worst.* 16 *But for that very reason I was shown mercy so that in me, the worst of sinners, Christ Jesus might display his immense patience as an example for those who would believe on him and receive eternal life.* 17 *Now to the King eternal, immortal, invisible, the only God, be honor and glory for ever and ever. Amen.*

---

58. See 1 Tim 2:7; 2 Tim 1:8, 10-11; 2:8-9; Titus 1:1-3.

59. Cf. Roloff, 80.

60. Gk. ὃ ἐπιστεύθην ἐγώ; for this sense of "entrust," see also Xenophon, *Memorabilia* 4.4.17; 1 Macc 8:16; 4 Macc 4:7; Josephus, *Jewish War* 4.492; 5.567; Luke 16:11. G. Barth, *EDNT* 3:91-98, esp. 92.

61. See, e.g., the argument in Roloff, 80; Wolter, *Paulustradition,* 27 (et al.) that such comments reflect the hand of a later Paulinist who seeks to advocate Paul as the guarantor of the gospel for the later church.

Having asserted his unique connection with the gospel, Paul goes on to authenticate his faith and calling in a testimony of gratitude that incorporates his personal experience of salvation into a gospel saying. We discover not only that his gospel is the paradigm of sound teaching, but also that his own experience of coming to faith provides a blueprint for measuring the authenticity of any who would oppose him. This section corresponds to the thanksgiving sections of other letters. The present needs created by opposition to Paul's authority, message, and mission determine the selfward turn of Paul's gratitude.[1]

Verses 12-16 form a tightly knit unit. Paul blends personal history with salvation history in a way that sets him as an apostle squarely into God's plan. His calling to be an apostle is authenticated, and his own experience of mercy and salvation become the paradigm for all believers. As noted above, this section forms a contrasting counterpart to 1:8-11. The intentional contrastive link with what has gone before is signaled by the Pauline self-references that close vv. 8-11 and then commence vv. 12-16.

Two themes shape Paul's discussion. The first employs the "faith" word group (see 1:2, note). Building on the transition to this section that employs the concept of "entrusting" *(episteuthēn)* the gospel (v. 11), Paul identifies himself as "trustworthy" ("faithful"; *pistos*) in v. 12. This application of the adjective to Paul is the first of seven uses in this letter in reference to the believer.[2] But before conversion, he was "in unbelief" *(apistia;* v. 13).[3] This and related antonyms characterize existence outside of the faith, which Paul here identifies with ignorance of the gospel. Next, in v. 14, Paul describes authentic Christian existence as an ongoing experience of "faith" *(pistis)* and love in Christ Jesus. Then, in v. 15, the adjective "trustworthy" *(pistos)* evaluates the gospel that the apostle endorses. Finally, in v. 16, the verb "to believe" *(pisteuein)* expresses the requirement of belief in Christ for salvation. Thus the various ideas expressed by the word group are all made to revolve around the pivotal Christ-event (see note at 1 Tim 1:2).

The second theme indicated by the clustering of the name "Christ Jesus" (vv. 12, 14, 15, 16) is christological. It reaches its climax in the gospel saying in v. 15, where the event of Christ's coming into the world is made the basis of salvation. The fundamental nature of that redemptive event was,

---

1. The personal and mission elements in this thanksgiving make it somewhat parallel to Rom 1:8-15 and 2 Cor 1:3-7; otherwise, such sections focus on the churches (1 Cor 1:4-9; Phil 1:3-11; Col 1:3-8). For the variety and contextual fit of the Pauline thanksgiving, see P. T. O'Brien, *Introductory Thanksgivings in the Letters of Paul* (Leiden: Brill, 1977).

2. Gk. πιστός; 3:11; 4:3, 10, 12; 5:16; 6:2; cf. 2 Tim 2:2; Titus 1:6. See Towner, *Goal,* 79, 146.

3. Gk. ἀπιστία; 5:8; cf. ἄπιστος (5:8; Titus 1:15) and ἀπιστέω (2 Tim 2:13).

however, apparently being redefined by the false teachers or by the community under their influence. Paul's gospel statement is therefore not simply a bit of appropriate liturgical noise to supplement his appeal. It is rather a retelling of the story of salvation (brief though it is) that presents a Christology that emphasizes the earthly, human character of Christ and his work. As the Christology unfolds throughout the letter (1:15; 2:5-6; 3:16; 6:13-14), it becomes evident that Paul was attempting to reestablish a better theological balance.

In the scholarly literature promoting the modern post-Pauline view of these letters, this passage of testimony has emerged as one of the keys to interpreting the so-called "portrait of Paul." The presence of personal reflection or testimony in the undisputed letters to churches is of course well known (Rom 1:1-7; 1 Cor 15:8-11; 2 Cor 11:22-23; Gal 1:13-15; Phil 3:4-11). While these self-reflective texts might seem to set the precedent for our passage, their relationship to the present text is debated. Scholars in the mainstream suggest either that the author was dependent upon these undisputed texts[4] or, as is now more the fashion, that he intentionally reworked them.[5] Reconfiguring "Paul" in this way was part of the program designed to salvage the theology or reputation of the apostle for the later church, or to establish him as the guarantor of the faith. But only the *assumption* that these letters are inauthentic and late sustains the theory. The letter itself determines the reason for this testimony, and so for the earlier examples.

In the critique of the opponents that has been launched, Paul's testimony serves several purposes. First, to authenticate his position as an apostle he provides the personal history behind the claim just made about entrustment with the gospel. As he does this, he sets his ministry strategically into the salvation-historical drama of the outworking of God's promises to the Gentiles. Second, he offers his experience of salvation as a proof of the gospel he preaches. Third, his story establishes the priority of faith in salvation (and implicitly reduces any function of the law to that discussed above). To argue on the basis of some other autobiographical passage that Paul is limited to saying this or that about his past is special pleading. When one bears in mind the differences between this letter to a coworker and his other letters to churches, he should certainly be allowed a certain amount of leeway in self-description.

Paul's weaving of the two themes mentioned above determines the shape of this reflection, but discerning his intention requires the use of both a sharp and a soft focus. Overarching the text is his desire to contrast his author-

---

4. E.g., Trummer, *Paulustradition,* 116-20.

5. Wolter, *Paulustradition,* 27-64; Roloff, 85-88; R. F. Collins, "The Image of Paul in the Pastorals," *LTP* 31 (1975): 147-73.

ity and calling with the character and challenge of the opponents. The text itself at this point places Paul's experience into "gospel" context as follows:

> v. 12 expresses gratitude for his calling to ministry (past/present);
> v. 13 reflects on the former life from which he was redeemed;
> v. 14 describes the present life in theological terms;
> vv. 15-16 expound the gospel and his personal experience of it, relat-
> ing it finally to his ministry and the future hope.

What is crucial to see (v. 15) is that Paul's emphasis is on salvation as a present reality, illustrated in his own experience and ministry, and grounded in a
depiction of the Christ story that anchors salvation in the humanity of God's
Messiah. Undoubtedly something about the heresy (its theology, eschatology, Christology, ethics, etc.) had shifted the balance decisively away from
thinking about engagement in the world (see below on 2:1-7). Paul begins to
redress this shift by telling his own story of the gospel's relevance.

12   Gratitude is the dominant and opening note of this testimony: "I
thank Christ Jesus our Lord." The shape of the thanksgiving is for two reasons not typical of Paul's letters to churches. First, he uses a Greek combination here (consisting of the noun for thanks, *charis,* and the simple verb
"to have") that, while common in Hellenistic writings, diverges from the
pattern found elsewhere in his letters to churches.[6] It is, however, similar to
his formulaic expression, "thanks be to God," which occurs several times
(Rom 6:17; 7:25; 1 Cor 15:57; 2 Cor 2:14; 8:16; 9:15). Little should be
made of the difference, though it is worth noting that Paul's intention in
other opening thanksgiving passages is generally to express his commitment
and fellowship to the churches, while here it is a statement of commitment
to Christ Jesus.[7]

Second, Paul directs his thanks to Christ Jesus, whereas the object of
such thanksgiving elsewhere is typically God. This is explained by two factors in Paul's reflection. On the one hand, as already noted, the passage is
heavily christological, with three additional references to "Christ Jesus"[8]
still to come, and the theological climax coming in the gospel saying about
Christ Jesus in v. 15. On the other hand, Paul's opening reflection (see below) looks back on the event of his calling in which Christ Jesus played the
decisive role.

---

6. Gk. χάριν ἔχω (Luke 17:9; Heb 12:28; Josephus, *Antiquities* 4.316; 7:208 [to
God]); see Spicq, *TLNT* 3:503-6. In the letters to churches, Paul prefers the verb of thanks,
εὐχαριστέω (Rom 1:8; 1 Cor 1:4; Eph 1:16; Phil 1:3; Col 1:3; 2 Thess 1:3; 2:13; Phlm 4).

7. But see the discussions of nuances in Spicq, 340; Oberlinner, 2:13-14.

8. On the order of names and frequency, see the notes on 1:1, 2.

Standing between the act of thanks and the recipient, Christ Jesus, is a participial phrase that further describes Christ: "who has given me strength."[9] This phrase, which is deceptively simple in appearance, invites closer inspection. The verb from which the participle is formed is used of divine empowerment (2 Tim 2:1; 4:17; Eph 6:10), and has a traditional link with Paul's early postconversion ministry experience (Acts 9:22). The aorist tense of the participle corresponds to an event of empowerment somewhere in Paul's past. Considering the thrust of the present context, the Damascus Road experience of conversion and calling is probably in mind (Acts 9:22, 26).[10] The association of divine empowerment with calling, Spirit-filled ministry, and revelatory episodes is well known in Paul's own writings and in the biblical tradition.[11] Furthermore, in Pauline and wider biblical theology the agent of empowerment in this sense is the Holy Spirit (2 Tim 1:7).[12] As in his similar reflection in Galatians 1, the role of the Spirit is taken for granted.[13] In contrast to the opponents, who seek to be "teachers of the law" (1:7), Paul places himself into the tradition of the prophetic call to ministry.

This distinction is developed further as Paul gives the reason for his thankfulness: Christ's personal decision to appoint him to ministry. Here the reflection back on his encounter with the risen Christ is even clearer (Acts 9:1-22; 22:6-16; 26:12-20), as Christ is also seen as the initiator of the apostolate to the Gentiles.[14] Summing up this calling is the generic term for "service" that was applied to various kinds of God-ordained "ministry" (1 Cor 12:5) and that Paul used frequently in reference to his mission.[15]

But the reason behind his calling raises two questions. First, although Paul is imprecise in the way he relates the assessment ("considered[16] me trustworthy") and the act of appointment ("appointing me to his ser-

---

9. Gk ἐνδυναμόω (aor. ptc., "to strengthen, empower"; 2 Tim 2:1; 4:17); see W. Grundmann, *TDNT* 2:284-317; Marshall, 388-89; H. Paulsen, *EDNT* 1:451.

10. Roloff, 92; Fee, 50; Wolter, *Paulustradition,* 38.

11. Cf. Isa 41:10; 42:6; Acts 1:8; 3:12; 4:7-10; Rom 15:19; 1 Cor 2:4-5; 2 Cor 4:7; 6:7; 12:9; 13:4; Phil 4:13.

12. Isa 11:2; 42:1; Mic 3:8; Luke 4:18; Acts 1:8; 10:38; Rom 15:9; 1 Cor 2:4. The lack of an explicit mention of the Spirit at this point is sometimes held to be further evidence of the non-Pauline character of this reminiscence; so esp. Wolter, *Paulustradition,* 40-45; J. D. G. Dunn, *Jesus and the Spirit* (London: SCM, 1975), 347-50.

13. There is no indication that the present text adopts a later "ecclesiastical" (and unpneumatic) view of ordination (*contra* Wolter, *Paulustradition,* 40-45).

14. The role of this event in Paul's letters to churches is already evident (1 Cor 15:8; Gal 1:16).

15. Gk. διακονία; 2 Tim 4:5, 11; Rom 11:13; 12:7; 15:31; 2 Cor 4:1; 5:18; 6:3; see also his use of διάκονος ("minister") as a self-description (1 Cor 3:5; 2 Cor 3:6; 6:4; 11:23). H. W. Beyer, *TDNT* 2:81-93.

16. Gk. ἡγέομαι (in Paul, see 6:1; 2 Cor 9:5; Phil 2:3, 6, 25; 3:7, 8; etc.).

vice"),[17] he is probably much more intent on attributing his calling to Christ than he is of making trustworthiness the condition of appointment.

Second, and more puzzling, is the sense in which "trustworthy" should be understood within this calling testimony. The term operates on two levels in this discourse. On the one hand, it features in the technical vocabulary of these three letters to describe authentic believers from the standpoint of faithfulness, believing, or both (1:2, note). Here the sense is of that faithful commitment to God's commands and word expected of leaders (2 Tim 2:2; cf. 1 Cor 4:2; 7:25). On the other hand, within the historical reflection, Christ's assessment would have been something of a forecast. The possibility of an echo of 1 Cor 7:25 should not be ignored: "but I give a judgment as one who by the Lord's mercy is trustworthy."[18] There, as here, the issue is of Paul's teaching a correct view of things, and the condition of being "trustworthy" (the same "faith" word that occurs here) is linked to the Lord's "mercy" (see below, 1:13). These links, as well as the affinity with the Corinthian situation (see Introduction, 41-52), suggest how the association of divine calling, trustworthiness, and authoritative teaching serves to distinguish Paul from opponents who were attempting to undercut his position. Paul is not arguing that Christ foresaw that in spite of his sin Paul would prove himself faithful; rather, the sense here is of the potency of divine calling to achieve certain results in human lives. As Paul reflects on the process, his argument is that his ministry to this point has demonstrated the effectiveness of Christ's choice in appointing him apostle to the Gentiles.

13 As the explanation of thankfulness continues, Paul describes his conversion. Although this statement is in the guise of a concession that accentuates the scale of Christ's mercy,[19] Paul shapes this part of his testimony in such a way that his conversion becomes a salvation-historical pivot point. The signal for this is the "formerly–now"[20] formula initiated here explicitly and completed implicitly in the "now" of Paul's experience of mercy. As

---

17. Gk. τίθημι (aor. ptc.; in the sense of appointment; 2:7; 2 Tim 1:11; 1 Cor 12:28; see further C. Maurer, *TDNT* 8:152-58); the ptc. might indicate either attendant circumstance (two events) or an action more integrally related to the assessment.

18. Dibelius and Conzelmann, 26; Roloff, 85. The language of 1 Cor 7:25b presents two striking points of contact with this text in the reference to "mercy" (cf. 1:13) and in the term "faithful": γνώμην δὲ δίδωμι ὡς ἠλεημένος ὑπὸ κυρίου πιστὸς εἶναι.

19. The present ptc. ὄντα ("being") modifies the preceding verbal pair, "considered, appointed," introducing a concession ("even though").

20. The adverbial phrase τὸ πρότερον, introducing a description of Paul's moral past, begins a sequence that is completed with the clause ἀλλὰ ἠλεήθην ("but I was shown mercy"), which describes his present situation in Christ. The device corresponds to the more typical ποτε . . . νῦν[ι] ("formerly . . . now"; Titus 3:3-4; Rom 6:20-22; 11:30-32; Gal 1:23; 4:8-9; Eph 2:1-22; 5:8; Col 1:21-22; 3:7-8; Phlm 11; 1 Pet 2:10).

elsewhere, the device, in one configuration or another, is ethical in orientation.[21] It supplies a contrast between two ways of life with the focus on the Christ-event as the moment of change. The striking thing about this application of the schema is the way Paul has deeply personalized each element (Gal 1:23). His sins become illustrative of the "former" time; his experience of grace and mercy takes the place of an explicit reference to the Christ-event, though v. 15 supplies the christological referent in due course; his experience of faith and love characterizes the "now" of Christian existence.

This personalizing of the eschatological transformation will serve two purposes. It prepares the way for Paul's presentation of himself as the pattern of salvation (to which the opponents do not conform). It also links his conversion to God's plan to reach the Gentiles. Thus both purposes are polemically weighted: Paul's conversion included liberation from a Torah-absorbed interpretation of life, and his apostolate to the Gentiles is the eschatological outworking of God's promise.

To describe the former life, he employs a brief vice list (cf. Titus 3:3; Col 3:5) enumerating three sins specific enough to fit the Pauline self-testimony and general enough to occur in lists of impious conduct elsewhere (Rom 1:30; Col 3:8). In this context, however, it is notable that the opponents are also charged with blasphemy (1:20), making this an implicit allegation that they still live as unbelievers and are caught in errors from which Paul himself had been rescued.[22] The "blasphemer" was one who denied God by speaking the name of YHWH carelessly or disrespectfully.[23] In relation to Paul's history, this will refer to his scorn for the messianic claim about Jesus and his hostility toward the followers of Jesus.

The next term, "persecutor," is not used elsewhere either by Paul or in the NT.[24] But as frequent use of the cognate verb shows, the identification comes straight out of Paul's preconversion profile (1 Cor 15:9; Gal 1:13, 23; Phil 3:6; cf. Acts 9:4-5).

Corresponding to the first two sins is the description of rude arrogance contained in the term "violent man." This describes the seething attitude of insolent anger and boastful pride that often fills the void caused by fear and insecurity and produces the worst acts of behavior.[25] The language is rare in the NT (Rom 1:30), but widespread in the Greek OT. The phenomenon itself is part of the stock description of uncivilized behavior in Greco-Roman culture.

21. See the discussion in Towner, *Goal,* 63-64.
22. Oberlinner, 37.
23. Gk. βλάσφημος; 2 Tim 3:2; for the verb, see 1:20; 6:1; Titus 2:5; 3:2; for the noun "blasphemy" see 6:4. H. W. Beyer, *TDNT* 1:621-25; O. Hofius, *EDNT* 1:221.
24. Gk. διώκτης; *Didache* 5.2; *Barnabas* 20.2; A. Oepke, *TDNT* 2:229-30.
25. Gk. ὑβριστής; G. Bertram, *TDNT* 8:295-307; cf. the discussion of "pride" in Spicq, *TLNT* 3:390-95.

Paul's self-description is severe enough to place him into the worst of categories.[26] If it seems out of balance with statements he made elsewhere to the effect that before his conversion he was "blameless" (Phil 3:6),[27] it should be kept in mind that he was not maintaining his moral innocence in such statements, but rather his commitment to the Torah and the rituals that assured his covenant purity as a Jew over and against the defilement of the Gentiles. Zeal in the form of persecution against the upstart messianic sect (though ultimately an act of sinful, ignorant, and arrogant disrespect for God) could even be justified on such a basis. Yet the apostle had long since come to regard his zeal as sin of the worst sort (1 Cor 15:9; Gal 1:13), which suggests that there is no contradiction between the sentiments expressed here and those belonging to the undisputed reflections.[28]

Having offered this personal illustration of the sinful "former" times, Paul makes the transition ("but")[29] to the "now" of salvation history. For him the change was the result of divine grace. "But I was shown mercy" is a way of describing the experience of salvation from the perspective of the initiative and expression of God's kindness and compassion (see esp. Rom 11:30).[30] God steps in and does what a person neither deserves nor is capable of doing. The thought of faithfulness to the covenant that is often attached to OT discussions of "mercy" (in connection with *chesed*) may recede somewhat here but not altogether (cf. 2 Tim 1:9-10).

But that is not the end of the explanation. Paul attaches the reason: "because I acted in ignorance and unbelief." The reason raises two questions. The first is that of meaning. Presumably, by pleading "ignorance" Paul means to place his preconversion errors into the Torah category of sins done "unintentionally or unconsciously," and the language here corresponds closely to that of Lev 22:14.[31] "In unbelief" identifies the sphere (before coming to faith in Christ) in which Paul did these things. But pleading igno-

---

26. See Marshall, 391, who identifies this category as that of the classical "enemy of God" (θεομάχος).

27. Stressed by many, e.g., Dibelius and Conzelmann, 27-28; Roloff, 93; Hanson, 60.

28. *Contra* Oberlinner, 38-42; see further Marshall, 392; Johnson, 178-79; Fee, 55.

29. Both the presence and force of this schema are lost in the translations (see TNIV; NIV; NRSV).

30. Gk. ἐλεέω (here in the aor. pass. reflecting the activity of God); 1:16; cf. R. Bultmann, *TDNT* 2:477-87. See the discussion and note at 1:2 and Titus 3:5 for "mercy."

31. Gk. ὅτι ἀγνοῶν ἐποίησα; cf. the category in LXX Lev 22:14: κατὰ ἄγνοιαν (Acts 3:17); cf. Num 15:22, 27 (cf. *m. Ker.* 1:2). See also W. Schmithals, *EDNT* 1:21 (for "without premeditation," but this qualification surely does not apply to Paul's persecution of the church).

rance does not lessen the degree of guilt (Eph 4:18; cf. Wis 13:8-9); it merely categorizes it and "qualifies" those who are guilty in this sense for God's forgiveness (Luke 23:24; Acts 3:17; cf. Wis 13:1-7). Paul is saying that he sinned as an unbeliever.

This leads to the second question: What is the intention of the admission? For this the controlling feature of the whole discourse is the contrast between Paul/Timothy/sound teaching/gospel and false teachers/false teaching. In contrast to Paul, who sinned before coming to faith in Christ, the false teachers are portrayed as believers (or those who profess to believe) who by their sin have rejected their faith (1:19; cf. 2 Tim 2:17-18).[32] Paul's preconversion sin and that of the opponents, though remarkably similar in the preference for Torah evident in both cases, belong to different categories: Paul's sin predates the enlightenment provided by the risen Lord, while the false teachers' sin postdates their enlightenment by the gospel. The consequences for the latter are much to be feared (Heb 6:4-6; 2 Pet 2:15-22).

14   Still within this testimonial reflection, Paul toggles back to his experience of salvation. He now enlarges on the experience of "mercy" by means of the language of "grace": "the grace of our Lord was poured out on me abundantly." "Grace" overwhelmed his sin. "Grace" (see on 1:2) refers to God's kind intention toward humanity. Here, and often in Paul, it depicts Christ's saving work (1:12-13) as a gift for us ("of our Lord").[33] He uses the language of overflowing abundance; the compound verb occurs only here in the NT, but both components of the word are usual for Paul, as is the tendency to describe the superlative effect of God's grace with such constructions.[34] The sequence, moving from the effects of sin to the supereffects of grace, closely resembles Rom 5:20: "and where sin increased, grace superabounded" (cf. 2 Cor 4:15).

Authentic Christian existence bears unmistakable marks (1:5), and Paul's personal experience of grace bears testimony to that reality.[35] Al-

---

32. The explanation that the plea of ignorance is part of the literary fiction of the PE, in this case designed to sanitize the Pauline story (Collins, "Portrait," 168; Brox, 110), deconstructs in 1:15, where the voice of Paul declares the apostle to be the "chief sinner." See further Roloff, 94; Marshall, 393.

33. For the whole phrase, Gk. ἡ χάρις τοῦ κυρίου ἡμῶν, see Rom 16:20; 1 Cor 16:23; 2 Cor 8:9; 13:13; Gal 6:18; Phil 4:23; 1 Thess 5:28.

34. Gk. ὑπερπλεονάζω (*Psalms of Solomon* 5.19); for Pauline uses of the simplex πλεονάζω, see Rom 5:20; 6:1; 2 Cor 4:15; 8:15; for other compounds using ὑπέρ, see Rom 5:20; 7:13; 8:26, 37; 2 Cor 3:10; 10:14; 1 Thess 3:10; 4:6.

35. The prepositional phrase μετὰ πίστεως καὶ ἀγάπης ("with the faith and love . . .") expresses a loose relationship (an attendant loosely connected phenomenon) between these things and the preceding outflowing of grace, but the cause/effect relationship is clear enough from the ordering of the sentence, and "grace" is the preeminent factor (see also Marshall, 395).

though usually in these letters "faith" and "love" form the core of more extensive lists of Christian virtues (2:15; 4:12; 6:11; 2 Tim 2:22; 3:10), here and in 2 Tim 1:13 the combination occurs alone. In the letters to churches, Paul frequently aligns these qualities,[36] with their use in Gal 5:6 (". . . faith working itself out through love") as a summary of Christian existence showing us the sense here. Together the two terms encompass the vertical relationship of trust in God and the horizontal outworking of this in service to others. Starting from the transition in v. 11, this is now the fourth occurrence of "faith" language within this section shaped by the faith theme. The reference to "love" invites the hearer to think back on 1:5 where it characterizes Timothy's charge (which mirrors Paul's own ministry).

Although it may seem unnecessary to say so, Paul goes on to locate this new manner of existence "in Christ Jesus." The phrase is used nine times in the letters to Timothy.[37] Despite less diversity in application when compared with Paul's usage in his letters to churches, there is little to suggest that these letters to Timothy reflect a non-Pauline use of the phrase.[38] Two times the phrase occurs in connection with a verb (2 Tim 1:9; 3:12), stating the sphere (of faith or life "in Christ Jesus") in which the actions take place. In the remainder of occurrences the phrase functions to relate certain qualities intrinsic to Christian existence ("faith and love," 1 Tim 1:14; 2 Tim 1:13; "faith," 1 Tim 3:13; 2 Tim 3:15; "life," 2 Tim 1:1; "grace," 2 Tim 2:1; "salvation," 2 Tim 2:10) to the experience that can only be described by "in Christ Jesus."

What is meant? Probably no single answer can be given. As elsewhere in Paul, the phrase defines Christian existence by bringing together the fundamental act of God in Christ that begins the relationship, the ongoing present mystery of union with Christ (in the Spirit), and the sense of new and renewed status that results. In other words, the phrase expresses a dynamic existence that is eschatological, relational, and existential. Its application in 1 and 2 Timothy lays stress on the character of the life that union with Christ produces and sustains. As such, the configuration encountered here — definite article (for relative pronoun) followed by the phrase — effectively means "which is/are intrinsic to Christian existence." The fact that the context makes it plain that the opponents have departed from things like "faith and love" (1:6, 19) strongly suggests that Paul employs this phrase as an identity tag of authentic belief in the apostolic gospel, and that in doing so he

36. See the discussion and references in Towner, *Goal*, 165-66.
37. 1:14; 3:13; 2 Tim 1:1, 9, 13; 2:1, 10; 3:12, 15.
38. *Contra* J. A. Allan, "The 'in Christ' Formula in the Pastoral Epistles," *NTS* 10 (1963): 115-21. See M. Harris, *NIDNTT* 3:1192-93; K. P. Donfried and I. H. Marshall, *The Theology of the Shorter Pauline Letters* (Cambridge: Cambridge University Press, 1993), 138-44.

excludes those who reject his gospel and supply another (legalistic and Torah-based) standard of godliness. In Paul's thinking, the direction taken by the opponents back into Torah and Torah speculation is retrograde. Not only does it nullify "faith" as the basis for salvation and holy living (the reason for the "faith" theme of this reflection), but also in terms of salvation history it marks a retrograde step.

15 Now Paul lays the capstone of his argument for the authority and relevance of his gospel for this world. He begins with a formulaic appeal to the gospel that urges the hearers to accept his articulation of the gospel as authoritative. The formula, "here is a trustworthy saying that deserves full acceptance,"[39] continues the theme of faith/faithfulness in the term translated "trustworthy." Now the gospel itself comes to be seen as the source of the theme. In the NT it is only in these letters to coworkers that this formula is found. Its stable form (expanded here and in 4:9 by the addition of "that deserves full acceptance"), however, suggests it is either widely known or will be perfectly understood. Its purpose is to authenticate Paul's immediate expression of the gospel as apostolic and to be accepted as true. Although implicit in each occurrence of the formula, the expansion "that deserves full acceptance"[40] emphasizes the need for hearers to make an appropriate rational response to embrace and esteem what is said and to act accordingly.[41]

Excursus: The "Trustworthy Saying" Formula

The formula occurs five times in these letters. The core phrase is πιστὸς ὁ λόγος ("the saying is trustworthy"), which occurs without expansion in 1 Tim 3:1; 2 Tim 2:11; Titus 3:8. The expanded form πιστὸς ὁ λόγος καὶ πάσης ἀποδοχῆς ἄξιος ("the saying is trustworthy and deserving of full acceptance") occurs in 1 Tim 1:15 and 4:9. The expansion phrase serves as reinforcement, stressing the need to affirm as true the cited material when (perhaps) the material did not elicit this affirmation clearly on its own (Knight, *Faithful Sayings,* 29, 144).

---

39. The literature on the so-called "faithful sayings" is considerable. For useful and accessible discussions, see G. W. Knight, *The Faithful Sayings in the Pastoral Letters* (Kampen: Kok, 1968); R. A. Campbell, "Identifying the Faithful Sayings in the Pastoral Epistles," *JSNT* 54 (1994): 73-86; Marshall, 326-30; Quinn, 230-32; Spicq, 277; Mounce, 48-49. See also Nauck, "Herkunft," 45-52; Dibelius and Conzelmann, 28-29; Roloff, 88-90. See further the excursus below.

40. Gk. καὶ πάσης ἀποδοχῆς ἄξιος; for πᾶς ("full," or "complete") as intensifying the action of ἀποδοχή (4:9; metaphorical for "acceptance"; W. Grundmann, *TDNT* 2:55-56), see the use in 6:1 (see also Knight, *Faithful Sayings,* 25-29; Marshall, 397).

41. See the discussion in Spicq, *TLNT* 1:176-77.

In the Hellenistic world, the phrase is attested in Dionysius of Halicarnassus (*Roman Antiquities* 3.23.17; 7.66.2) and Dio Chrysostom (*Oration* 45.3; see further Spicq, 277) and serves the same basic purpose of affirming its referent, but it does not appear to be formulaic as such (but see Quinn, 230-32). The only Jewish parallel reported ("The Book of Mysteries" = 1Q27 1:8; see the discussion in Nauck, "Herkunft," 50) is no more than a parallel. This leaves the occurrences in the letters to coworkers as the first "formulaic" use (Marshall, 327). For some the origin of the phrase has been thought to rest in the similar description of God as faithful: πιστὸς ὁ θεός (1 Cor 1:9; 10:13; 2 Cor 1:18; cf. 1 Thess 5:24; 2 Thess 3:3; Heb 10:23; cf. Fee, 52). While the trustworthiness of the "saying" in each context surely owes to its divine origin, that factor would seem to be somewhat farther back in Paul's thinking and the desire to continue to draw the line between the sound teaching encapsulated by the sayings and the false teaching by means of the πίστις word group more to the fore (cf. Schlarb, *Die gesunde Lehre,* 214).

Both the direction and extent of the "sayings" referred to by the formula in 1 Tim 3:1 and 4:9 are disputed (see further the commentary on each text). Most are agreed that in 1 Tim 1:15 and 2 Tim 2:11 the formula precedes the saying and that in Titus 3:8 it follows, but the extent of material encompassed by the formula in the case of Titus 3 (vv. 3-7, 4-7, 5-7, or 5-6?) is debated. It is not clear that the formula uniformly refers to salvation texts, or, indeed, that this should be the criterion for determining the substance of the *logos* in question (*pace,* e.g., Campbell, "Faithful Sayings"; Young, *Theology,* 56-57; Johnson, 203, but cf. 250).

What are "faithful sayings"? The answer to this question revolves around that of the function of the formula. Does it mean to affirm the truthfulness of what is said (Marshall, 328-29; Donelson, *Pseudepigraphy,* 150-51; Trummer, *Paulustradition,* 204)? Or does it mark off the material to which it refers as part of the accepted tradition (Dibelius and Conzelmann, 28-29; Brox, 112-14; Spicq, 277; Hanson, 63)? Or is it both of these at once (Knight, *Faithful Sayings,* 19-20)? The majority considers the affirmation of truthfulness to be most significant, with the application of the material being intended (cf. Roloff, 90). The contents of the saying introduced or concluded by the formula, however, do not appear to be fully explained by the category of "accepted tradition." Most of the sayings have been formulated, or significantly shaped, for use in their present contexts, so it is unlikely that Paul has drawn on a reservoir of "tradition" in the usual sense. Rather, with the formula, Paul emphasizes the authentic correspondence of the saying and its authority with the apostolic tradition, the (his) gospel, the sound teaching, and so on. From the outset, Paul identifies the problem as a collision of his gospel with an opposing teaching (1:3; 2 Tim 2:14-18; Titus 1:11). And in each community Paul's gospel had come under heavy fire. The "trustworthy saying" formula is a technique by which Paul, in one motion, rearticulates his gospel (and corresponding aspects of teaching), asserts its authen-

144

ticity and apostolic authority, and alienates the opposing teaching that, by implication (and this is the polemical significance of the πίστις word group), does not belong to the category denoted by the term πιστός ("trustworthy").

The content of the "saying"[42] is a gospel statement consisting of a traditional verb and purpose statement: "Christ Jesus came into the world to save sinners."[43] The broad appeal of this saying may be seen in the way it resonates in varying degrees with Jesus' mission statements preserved in both the Synoptic and Johannine traditions:

> 1 Tim 1:15: Christ Jesus **came into the world to save sinners**.
> Luke 19:10: For the Son of Man **came** to seek and **to save** what was
>   lost.
> Mark 2:17: I have not **come** to call the righteous, but **sinners**.
> John 18:37: and for this I **came into the world**, to testify to the truth.

Perhaps the strongest affinity is with the saying in Luke 19:10, which shares the verb-infinitive combination "came to save" but lacks the phrase "into the world."[44] The name "Christ Jesus" corresponds to the dominant pattern in this letter (see note 1:1). Mark 2:17 includes the verb "come" and makes reference to "sinners," but the purpose is expressed differently as "calling."[45] Johannine tradition shows ample use of the phrase "into the world" in combination with the verb "to come" (9:39; 11:27; 12:46; 16:28; 18:37; cf. 1 John 4:9),[46] but the salvific purpose statement found here is never attached to the Johannine statements, and it is certainly not clear that Paul is indebted to this strand of theology in developing his view of incarnational Christology.[47] Clearly, the gospel saying in 1:15 is not a verbatim quote of

42. Gk. λόγος (3:1; 4:5, 6, 9, 12; 5:17; 6:3; 2 Tim 1:13; 2:9, 11, 15, 17; 4:2, 15; Titus 1:3, 9; 2:5, 8; 3:8); its use is varied: "saying" (1:15; 3:1; 4:9, etc.); ordinary "speech, conversation" (4:12); "message, teaching, what is to be preached" (2 Tim 2:17; 4:2; Titus 2:8); "the word of God" as divine revelation (4:5; 2 Tim 2:9; Titus 1:3; 2:5); "words" (in the pl.) that represent what has been preached (6:3; 2 Tim 1:13; 4:15). Schlarb, *Die gesunde Lehre,* 206-29. Cf. G. Kittel, *TDNT* 4:100-141; H. Ritt, *EDNT* 2:356-59.

43. Only this faithful saying is introduced by the recitative ὅτι ("that").

44. Gk. ὅτι Χριστὸς Ἰησοῦς ἦλθεν εἰς τὸν κόσμον ἁμαρτωλοὺς σῶσαι (1 Tim 1:15); ἦλθεν γὰρ ὁ υἱὸς τοῦ ἀνθρώπου ζητῆσαι καὶ σῶσαι τὸ ἀπολωλός (Luke 19:10). See Kelly, 54; Brox, 111.

45. Mark 2:17: οὐκ ἦλθον καλέσαι δικαίους ἀλλὰ ἁμαρτωλούς.

46. See, e.g., John 9:39: εἰς κρίμα ἐγὼ εἰς τὸν κόσμον τοῦτον ἦλθον; see H. Windisch, "Zur Christologie der Pastoralbriefe," *ZNW* 34 (1935): 221-22.

47. See the discussion in Dibelius and Conzelmann, 29; Roloff, 90-91.

any text extant to us. Given Paul's louder echo of Lukan material in 5:18, probably the stronger case can be made for some sort of reworking of the Jesus tradition known to Luke. But whatever preexisting materials Paul drew on, he has fashioned a new statement, continuous with existing tradition, which exceeds it by placing the salvation work of Christ Jesus into historical relief as a divine work carried out in the human context. Let's explore this claim further.

Paul's shaping depicts the Christ event as a matter of historical record. Jesus' salvific mission was often, as we have seen, described as "coming," and the locus or sphere of his activity was described as "the world." Aorist verbs ("he came," "to save") view the event of Jesus' advent as past and historical, and the implication is that the purpose of his mission, "to save" (from sin),[48] is also, therefore, a present reality underway. The evidence for this is the existence of the church of Jesus Christ, which, according to Paul's gospel, exhibits, increasingly, social equality among all people and a new quality of life together and in the world. "World" in this context means the community of humankind in its need for salvation; Paul and John agree that it is this sphere into which Jesus came and in which salvation takes effect. This gospel statement further specifies the inhabitants of the world with the term "sinners" (see on 1:9; cf. Rom 5:8, 19).

Although often debated, in this gospel saying the thought of preexistence, and hence the divine origin of salvation, is implicit.[49] But the christological weight of the statement is on the human history of Christ and its significance. As elsewhere in Paul, this statement telescopes the whole earthly experience of Jesus into the event of his coming (cf. Rom 8:3-4; Gal 4:4-5). Furthermore, the location ("into the *kosmos*," the world in need of God) and declared target of this "coming" ("to save sinners") disclose the relevance of this tradition for the present church. This implication is expanded as the ongoing relevance and authority of this story is stressed by its application to the experience of Paul.

Elsewhere Paul expressed his identification in the sin for which

---

48. Gk. σῴζω (2:4, 15; 4:16; 2 Tim 1:9; 4:18; Titus 3:5); see Towner, *Goal,* 75-76; W. Foerster and G. Fohrer, *TDNT* 7:1003-21; J. Schneider and C. Brown, *NIDNTT* 3:216-21; K. H. Schelkle, *EDNT* 3:325-27; Spicq, *TLNT* 3:344-57; I. H. Marshall, "Salvation, Grace and Works in the Later Writings of the Pauline Corpus," *NTS* 42 (1996): 339-58; Läger, *Christologie,* 119-26. The present effects of "salvation" within the human community are as important as the promise it holds for eternal life.

49. For the view that preexistence is not implied, see Collins, *Letters That Paul Did Not Write,* 118; Dibelius and Conzelmann, 29; see also H. Sasse, *TDNT* 3:888; and see the classic argument for an adoption Christology in Windisch, "Zur Christologie der Pastoralbriefe," 222. But see the discussion in H. Stettler, *Die Christologie der Pastoralbriefe* (WUNT 2.105; Tübingen: J. C. B. Mohr [Siebeck], 1998), 328-34.

Christ died by using the plural pronoun "our" (1 Cor 15:3; 2 Cor 5:21). Here and on into v. 16 he exemplifies the relevance of the statement by applying it dramatically to himself: "of whom I am the worst" ("foremost," NRSV). Of course, this is a return to the earlier theme (1:12-14), and the application to self is clear. Yet despite the wide agreement of the English versions (TNIV; NRSV; GNB), the intention of self-application in the use of the predicate adjective "worst, foremost, chief, first" *(prōtos),* repeated again in reference to Paul in v. 16, is less clear. The double use of the term is important for Paul's point, and it is best to evaluate the two references to *prōtos* together.

Most translations understand each reference to mean "first" in a qualitative or hyperbolic sense: "worst," "foremost," and the like. This has the advantage of treating the dual usage consistently. The second occurrence draws the implication of the first occurrence into the later part of the argument: Paul's sin serves as a paradigm for those yet to believe by virtue of its immense proportions, not its priority in time. However, in light of the dialogue being carried on with the false teachers and the way in which Paul has already set his conversion and ministry into a salvation-historical mode, the second occurrence must also bear a temporal sense: Paul, as "worst" and "first," is the example not only of what one might be saved out of (degree), but also of what one must believe to be saved (manner; the gospel Paul preaches).[50]

We have already seen that this testimonial passage reflects contact with similar texts in the letters to the churches (1 Corinthians 15 and Galatians 1), and the use of *prōtos* may represent a reverse twist on the theme employed elsewhere to describe Paul as "the least of the apostles" (1 Cor 15:9; Eph 3:8).[51] In each case Paul is the persecutor of the church, but here,

---

50. Other variations can be found in the translations and scholarly literature. See, e.g., REB, KJV, which take the first occurrence of πρῶτος as qualitative and the second temporally as more descriptive of the "first in a sequence." Typical of the modern approach to these letters is the view that this "first . . . first" argument aims to establish Paul as the sole guarantor of the gospel. I will not belabor this because the view is so tenuous; but it is so current that some evaluation is necessary. Essentially, it is the contrast between genuine Paul's self-estimation to be least of the apostles (and therefore inferior) and these allegedly later "firsts" that seem to accentuate his role here. Taking each *prōtos* as temporal (but see Roloff's version of the argument, 95-96, in which temporal and qualitative aspects merge, with the temporal being more dominant in v. 16), proponents notice the shift from the earlier opinion of Paul as "least" to a Paul who is now regarded as the exemplar of and authority for the gospel. In fact, it is argued that Paul's own experience of salvation has become the essence of the gospel: Paul's whole life, according to this view, has been "gospelized" (so esp. Wolter, *Paulustradition,* 49-61, who argues that v. 16 links the salvation of those who follow to Paul's exemplar rather than to the verb "believe"; see on v. 16).

51. Marshall, 400.

where he is measured against not other apostles but false teachers, the application is different.

The double *prōtos* advances Paul's argument about the effectiveness of his gospel; it does not serve to make the claim to Pauline exclusivity. However, to the degree that Paul is defending his specifically Gentile-shaped message and mission against those who have turned back in some degree to a kind of Torah–elitist-based approach, his conversion does represent a salvation-historical benchmark in this sense: as the apostle to the Gentiles, he was the first to comprehend and experience the grace of the gospel he would then articulate in his teaching and ministry to the Gentiles. The immensity of his sin proves the effectiveness of this salvation, and since the revelation of this gospel is associated with his experience of salvation and calling, he can stand as the exemplar of salvation to the Gentiles. It is best, therefore, to take the first *prōtos* as a qualitative statement that reflects again on the immensity of Paul's sin against God and the church, and the second *prōtos* as primarily qualitative (following from the first) and yet also temporal within the logic of its own statement. We have assumed the content and logic of that statement and must now fill in the details.

16 The return to the theme of Paul's sin (cf. v. 13a) brings with it the countertheme of mercy (v. 13b). The repetition of this contrast with the identical statement "but I received mercy" intentionally links Paul's past experience specifically with the gospel statement just made. The addition of a forward-pointing reason, "because of this,"[52] allows the thought of Paul's prototypical role in salvation history to continue developing.

In this case, however, the function of the contrast is to draw attention to the purpose statement that follows. Within the purpose statement it is clearly important for Paul's argument that he keep his own preconversion status in focus. But he develops a neat christological balance that prepares the way for a shift toward fuller reflection on Christ. This requires explication.

First, the Greek word order and repetition of the adjective *prōtos* ("so that in me as the foremost") establish the continued focus on Paul. But with an immediate shift of actors, from Paul to Christ, the perspective on the human dilemma shifts under the new christological lens. From this new vantage point, Paul's experience becomes a (salvation-historical) spectacle, a "display of the immensity of Christ's patience." Elsewhere in Paul, the verb[53] de-

---

52. The TNIV and NRSV translate the causal prepositional phrase διὰ τοῦτο as "but for that very reason," as if the preceding statement were the reason. But the following ἵνα-clause suggests that it supplies the reason for the mercy shown to Paul; i.e., "but I received mercy for this reason, namely, that in me Christ might display. . . ." For the pattern, cf. Rom 4:16; 2 Cor 13:10; Eph 6:13; 2 Thess 2:11-12; Phlm 15.

53. Gk. ἐνδείκνυμι; 2 Tim 4:14; Rom 2:15; 9:17, 22; 2 Cor 8:24; Eph 2:7; Heb 6:10, 11 (in 2 Tim 4:14 and Titus 2:10; 3:2, the term refers to human demonstrations of

scribes various "displays" of God's qualities, but here, in keeping with the christological focus of the whole passage (vv. 12, 14, 15), the subject is Christ. Counterbalancing the emphasis on the immensity of Paul's sin "as the foremost" is the adjective that underscores the immensity of Christ's patience.[54] There is a rich OT background to this image of the divine patience that holds off wrath so that the people might repent.[55] Its application in the NT follows suit (Rom 9:22; 1 Pet 3:20; 2 Pet 3:9). Here "patience," so closely associated with divine mercy and kindness (cf. Rom 2:4), is quantified in terms of the results it produced — the converted Paul was a living illustration of divine patience.

Secondly, the description of this display is too full to be simply of personal importance to Paul. In keeping with the eschatological "formerly–now" pattern already applied by Paul to himself (v. 13), both the contrasting elements ("the foremost sinner" and the dramatic "immensity of Christ's patience") and the rich description of this display of mercy continue to view his conversion and ensuing ministry in terms of the great events of salvation history. The next prepositional phrase moves more clearly in this direction. The purpose[56] of Christ's display in Paul was to provide an "example [pattern, model][57] for those who would believe on him [Christ] and receive eternal life."

What is meant by this "example" or "pattern" is answered from both sides of the term. Clearly, the "pattern" being conveyed in and through Paul is that of experiencing Christ's merciful patience: Christ bore with the persecuting, ignorant Saul until the time was right to save him. But wrapped up in this is the revelation that came to Paul about saving faith in Jesus as the Messiah of God. The nature of this faith is intimated in the attached description of those who will conform to this pattern. Paul's experience of mercy will be replicated in the lives of those who also come to faith through the gospel he

---

good or evil); used of demonstrations of character and power (Josephus, *Antiquities* 7.212); see further H. Paulsen, *EDNT* 1:449-50.

54. Gk. τὴν ἅπασαν μακροθυμίαν; ἅπας is intensive (BDF §275.7; BDAG, s.v.); the NIV rendering, "His unlimited patience," is rightly corrected to "his immense patience" (TNIV).

55. Gk. μακροθυμία; Exod 34:6; Num 14:18; Joel 2:13; Jonah 4:2; Sir 5:4 (2 Tim 3:10; 4:2, of Paul and Timothy); elsewhere it is a characteristic of the Spirit to be found in believers in general (Gal 5:22; Eph 4:2; Col 1:11; 3:12). See further F. Horst, *TDNT* 4:374-87; H. W. Hollander, *EDNT* 2:380-81.

56. Indicated by the preposition πρός (BDF §239.7).

57. Gk. ὑποτύπωσις; in the NT only here and in 2 Tim 1:13; of the range of meanings it might convey (a sketch or outline [Philo, *On Abraham* 71; Strabo, *Geography* 2.5.34] in contrast to the finished or complete work, pattern, model, example, or prototype; see E. K. Lee, "Words Denoting 'Pattern' in the New Testament," *NTS* 8 [1962-63]: 167-73; L. Goppelt, *TDNT* 8:248), pattern, model, or example best suits the context.

preaches. The combination of the verb "to believe"[58] and prepositional phrase "on him" depicts saving faith as creating a personal relationship with Christ[59] rather than formal adherence to a dogma. What must not be missed in this reference to "believing" is that this "faith" word concludes the theme initiated in v. 12 (v. 11). In this conclusion, Paul implicitly links saving faith in Christ to the gospel he preaches — the implications for the law-obsessed false teaching are obvious.

Salvation itself is viewed from the common NT standpoint of its eschatological goal, eternal life.[60] Although the widespread use of the expression might suggest that it has become formulaic, in this letter Paul stresses the link between the goal of eternal life and faithfulness in this life that includes adherence to the gospel he preaches (4:8; 6:12; cf. 2 Tim 1:10; Titus 1:2; 3:7). This interrelatedness of present life and promise shows that "eternal life" is the "spiritual life" that is proper to the resurrected Lord and extended to those who place faith in him;[61] it is relevant to both the present and the coming world.[62] In the sequence he sets out here, "the pattern" (Paul) must come first, requiring a futuristic, or relative time, reference to those who fill out the pattern;[63] but this is not to be mistaken as a reference to predestination.

Now several strands need to be brought together. From the reference

---

58. See the extended note at 1:2; Towner, *Goal*, 81.

59. For the combination of πιστεύειν and ἐπ᾽ αὐτῷ, see Rom 9:33; 10:11; 1 Pet 2:6 (all citing LXX Isa 28:16); cf. Luke 24:25. See further, Towner, *Goal*, 81; R. Bultmann, *TDNT* 6:211-12.

60. Matt 25:46; John 3:36; 4:14, 36; Acts 13:48; Rom 2:7; 5:21; 6:22.

61. Gk. ζωή (4:8; 6:12, 19; 2 Tim 1:1, 10; Titus 1:2; 3:7) can refer to either ordinary human life (1 Cor 3:22) or the spiritual life. Although it can be viewed from present or future aspects, when it is conceived of as God's gift of eternal life (i.e., a sharing in life that is proper to God alone), it is a unity, and the present experience can be understood as an anticipatory experience of final salvation. Various terms qualify ζωή to add the theological accent, but the most frequent qualifier (as here; 6:12; Titus 1:2; 3:7; cf. ἀφθαρσία ["incorruptible"] in 2 Tim 1:10) is αἰώνιος ("eternal"); G. von Rad, G. Bertram, and R. Bultmann, *TDNT* 2:832-72.

62. Gk. αἰώνιος; as part of a time expression (2 Tim 1:9; Titus 1:2; Rom 16:25), the meaning is of long periods of time preceding the present one; but it is often descriptive of some qualitative aspect of God's character (6:16; 2 Tim 2:10; Rom 16:26), or the life he bestows (6:12; Titus 1:2; 3:7). Through these close associations with God, the term, when applied in some way to believers (esp. through "eternal life"), conveys aspects of God's own quality of existence. Cf. Marshall, 125; H. Sasse, *TDNT* 1:208; H. Balz, *EDNT* 1:46-48.

63. Gk. μέλλω. The present participle τῶν μελλόντων (gen., indicating those who conform to "the pattern"; 2 Pet 2:6; similarly 1 Tim 4:12; 1 Cor 10:6), with the present infinitive forms a periphrasis equivalent to the future participle (BDF §356). For μέλλειν, see also 4:8; 6:19; 2 Tim 4:1.

to Paul's entrustment with the gospel in v. 11 Paul has turned the spotlight on his own experience (viewed from various perspectives). The "faith"-theme that permeates the passage suggests that this gesture was calculated to discredit the false teaching, which had diverged from Paul's faith/grace trajectory, and to regain support for his ministry and message. Thus the apostle is as an example or illustration. His experience of Christ's immense patience, his conversion, and knowledge of his gospel form the pattern for those to whom his mission reaches.

But what sort of pattern does it supply? For this we must bear in mind the whole drift of this discourse, its combative and corrective aims. First and foremost, Paul's experience and the magnitude of his sin exemplify the magnitude of Christ's mercy and patience: if Christ can reach and enlighten the zealous persecutor, he can reach others who hear the gospel, and this need not exclude Paul's opponents if they repent.

Second, Paul's experience forms a pattern of belief in Jesus as the Messiah who came from God into the world to save sinners by faith apart from adherence to Jewish ritual or moral requirements. While this latter is certainly not explicit in the text, it was nevertheless the core of Paul's gospel, and some sort of law-inclined (enthusiastic) turn from Paul's understanding of the faith is very much the issue in the context. Consequently, he takes pains to recount his conversion story (vv. 12-14, 15c-16) in a way that affirms and demonstrates the authorized gospel he preaches (v. 15ab).

Therefore, third, Paul's conversion forms the salvation-historical pattern both of the enormous way Christ intervenes in human lives and of the content of saving faith. In this respect his conversion, in which he also experienced his call, forms a defining moment in his own (and ultimately the church's) understanding of a universal mission to the whole world. But at no point in this depiction of his gospel and his role as an apostle does he confuse his experience with the gospel. Faith must be in Christ, and the gospel is about Christ, not about Paul. However, in the polemical contest, where his mission and authority are under fire (cf. 2 Corinthians, Galatians) and the church has been placed in danger of missing or distorting the truth of the gospel, Paul is not slow to put his call to apostleship and his understanding of the gospel on the line. He insists that only the gospel he endorses is true; God ordained his mission and calling; and his own experience of Christ's mercy demonstrates the power of the gospel he preaches and his authority to do so.

17   It is not exaggerating to say that Paul regarded his ministry as the fulfillment of God's promises to save the nations. It was for this reason that he was shown mercy, converted, and entrusted with the gospel. And the closing statement of v. 16 depicts both the power and the success already evident in his gospel. It is for this reason that the section closes with a doxology in praise to God. Not only does the shift of focus to God establish a balance with the heavily christocentric testimony just concluded,[64] but it also reveals Paul's deeply theological presuppositions about salvation in Christ (cf. Romans 9–11; 2 Cor 5:19). The need Paul felt to emphasize the humanity of Christ in the salvation plan does not diminish his belief in God as the author of salvation (2:3-4; 4:10).

Paul's reflection on God's power and grace in salvation and on his own place within this redemptive plan often welled up in thanksgiving and praise expressed in the form of a doxology (esp. Rom 11:36; 16:27; Gal 1:5; Eph 3:20-21; cf. Phil 4:20). The device goes back to Hellenistic Judaism (Tob 13:7, 11), where, as here, the writer, or the speaker in a communal setting, expresses high praise in a way that induces all to join in.

Paul strings together four descriptions of God. "The King eternal" is a traditional Jewish appellation of God[65] that is limited in Paul to doxological expressions in this letter (6:15).[66] Human rulers were also called "king" (2:2; 2 Cor 11:32), so the addition of the adjectival expression "eternal"[67] seeks the appropriate distinction between human and divine power. Whether this intends a further explicit challenge to the claims of the emperor is harder to determine; but trumping such counterclaims of pagan rulers had become a common part of Hellenistic Jewish liturgical expression and was probably also a common function of the early church's doxological expression.[68] That is to say, some degree of polemics is an inevitable part of the dialogue with the pagan world that the church sustained through its proclamation and expressions of worship (cf. 1 Cor 1:26-29).

The next three terms owe their place within Jewish doxological expressions to the Jewish-pagan dialogue. "Immortal," borrowed from Greek categories by late Jewish writers, in the NT, describes God directly only here and in Rom 1:23, where it is clearly shown to be a quality proper to God alone.[69] The "invisibility" of God (Col 1:15; Heb 11:27)[70] is more widely af-

---

64. See Roloff, 98; Marshall, 404.

65. Gk. Βασιλεὺς τῶν αἰώνων; Tob 13:7, 11; Jer 10:10 (MT); Rev 15:3 (variant reading); cf. Sir 36:17; LXX Ps 9:37. The use of "king" for God seems especially prevalent in prayer formulations (LXX Pss 5:2; 23:7-10; 43:5; 46:3; 94:3).

66. The concept is of course present in "kingdom of God" (βασιλεία τοῦ θεοῦ; Rom 14:17; 1 Cor 4:20; 6:9; 15:50; Gal 5:21; 2 Thess 1:5).

67. The plural genitive configuration τῶν αἰώνων ("of the ages") is probably to be understood adjectivally ("the eternal king"), indicating the unending tenure of God's rule (past, present, into eternity; see T. Holtz, EDNT 1:45; H. Sasse, TDNT 1:201; Knight, 105).

68. See Spicq, 346; and the various arguments for this in R. A. Horsley, ed., Paul and Empire (Harrisburg, PA: Trinity Press International, 1997).

69. Gk. ἄφθαρτος; the term appears only late in Jewish writings (Wis 12:1; Philo, On the Life of Moses 2.171; On the Unchangeableness of God 26) and was borrowed from Stoic thought (T. Holtz, EDNT 3:422-23).

70. Gk. ἀόρατος; Philo, On the Special Laws 1.20; 4.31; On the Cherubim 101

firmed in the NT in various constructions. As a quality of God it emerged especially in the polemic of Hellenistic Judaism against the materialistic views of gods in pagan idolatry.[71] Equally, the phrase "the only God" (6:16; cf. 2:5) represents a fundamental affirmation of belief that goes back to the *Shema* of Deut 6:4 ("Hear, O Israel . . . the LORD is one") and became standard theology in the early church.[72] The original affirmation contested pagan polytheism, which in Deuteronomy was symbolized in Egyptian idolatry; it was later developed and used widely in the running debate with paganism.[73] In a purely worship setting, the epithet would draw attention to the supremacy of God.

The expression of praise in the doxology[74] comes in the dual phrase "honor and glory" that has become standard in the NT.[75] Greek culture had elevated the importance of these elements of good reputation to the highest degree, with the ruler being the epitome of one worthy of such an acclamation. "Honor" is a public acknowledgment of worth.[76] "Glory," in this context, refers similarly to the recognition of honor that is owed to a deserving person of high repute.[77] In the set combination, the terms function together to elevate the esteem that is rightly owed to God.[78] Accentuating the immensity of honor even more is the prepositional phrase "for ever and ever"[79] that forms the standard conclusion to doxologies. Neither the plural form (lit. "for

---

(as an epithet for God after the NT, see *PGL*, s.v. B.1-2); as a category of things or powers pertaining to God or to the spiritual realm, Rom 1:20; Col 1:16; in 2 Macc 9:5 of an action of God.

71. See esp. Philo, *On the Embassy to Gaius* 290, 310, 318; *On Abraham* 75-76; J. Kremer, *EDNT* 2:528-29; Spicq, 347; the conviction is expressed in various ways (1 Tim 6:16; John 1:18; 5:37; 6:46; 1 John 4:20).

72. Gk. μόνος θεός; Rom 16:27; more widespread in the NT is the similar εἷς θεός formula (Rom 3:29-30; 1 Cor 8:4-6; Gal 3:20; Eph 4:5-6; and discussion at 1 Tim 2:5).

73. 2 Macc 7:37; Josephus, *Antiquities* 8.335; P. Dalbert, *Die Theologie der hellenistisch-jüdischen Missionsliteratur unter Ausschluss von Philo und Josephus* (Hamburg: Reich, 1954), 124-30.

74. The verb to be supplied is a form of "to be" that fits the implicit request that the items of praise and appellation be acknowledged.

75. Gk. τιμὴ καὶ δόξα; for the combination, see LXX Exod 28:2; Pss 8:6; 95:7; Rev 4:9, 11; 5:13; cf. Heb 2:7, 9; 2 Pet 1:17.

76. Gk. τιμή ("honor, esteem, price, value"; 5:17; 6:1, 16; 2 Tim 2:20); H. Hübner, *EDNT* 3:357-59; J. Schneider, *TDNT* 8:169-80.

77. 1:11 (see discussion there); 2 Tim 4:18; Titus 2:13 (see discussion); H. Hegermann, *EDNT* 1:344-48, 345; Thiselton, *The First Epistle to the Corinthians,* 834-37.

78. Hübner, *EDNT* 3:358.

79. Gk. εἰς τοὺς αἰῶνας τῶν αἰώνων (or the short form, minus the added gen.: εἰς τοὺς αἰῶνας); 2 Tim 4:18; Rom 16:27; Gal 1:5; Phil 4:20; Heb 13:21; 1 Pet 4:11; 5:11; Rev 1:6; 5:13; 7:12.

the ages of the ages") nor the repetition in this longer form reflects precise measurements of time.[80] Rather, the Hebrew idiom functions to stretch the praise of the doxology beyond all limits to eternity.[81] The concluding "amen" (6:16; 2 Tim 4:18) gives Timothy and the church the invitation to join in the acknowledgment.[82]

It is here that we too enter this story Paul told about Christ and himself. His apostleship and experience of mercy are the fruits of the work of the Messiah who lived as a human, and this fact must remain central to an understanding of the gospel. Paul's own experience is drawn on to assure Timothy of Christ's human relevance. Whatever else Christology so shaped might mean, it certainly requires that gospel ministry be carried out in the present sinful world and expects that salvation will have its effect in changing this world from within. The overall profile of the false teaching includes a tendency toward elitism or self-absorption that must have posed a threat to the mission as Paul understood it. But built into the gospel message, rooted as it is in the OT promises to bring in the whole world, is the centrifugal thrust that reaches beyond the church. We today are invited to view the Pauline "pattern" and to replicate it. Our own experiences of conversion and calling contain promises for those around us who do not yet know Christ's mercy. Yet they will come to know it only if the gospel is communicated meaningfully to them — if we resist our own tendencies to become absorbed in what we already have instead of reaching out with what others need to have.

d. Charge to Timothy Resumed (1:18-20)

> 18 *Timothy, my son, I am giving you this command in keeping with the prophecies once made about you, so that by recalling them you may fight the battle well,* 19 *holding on to faith and a good conscience, which some have rejected and so have suffered shipwreck with regard to the faith.* 20 *Among them are Hymenaeus and Alexander, whom I have handed over to Satan to be taught not to blaspheme.*

In this closing bracket to the section, Paul resumes the charge to Timothy with which the section began (1:3). The earlier emphasis on instructions shifts here to personal responsibility and motivation. Before, the command to Timothy was portrayed from the standpoint of action he was to take; here the

---

80. See esp. J. Barr, *Biblical Words for Time* (2d ed.; London: SCM, 1969), 67-71.
81. T. Holtz, *EDNT* 1:44-46, 45.
82. Gk. ἀμήν; in doxologies see LXX Ps 40:14; 3 Macc 7:23; 4 Macc 18:24. In the NT see Rom 16:27; 2 Cor 1:20; Gal 1:5. See further H. Schlier, *TDNT* 1:335-38; H.-W. Kuhn, *EDNT* 1:69-70.

personal stakes are increased as he is reminded of the divine acknowledgment of his calling. Timothy's commission in Ephesus is to be seen as the corollary of his authentic faith. The continued pattern of contrast allows us to see what becomes of leaders who let go of that faith.

18   The resumption of personal instruction is evident from Paul's twofold use of the second person pronoun "you" and in the personal way he addresses his coworker ("Timothy, my son"; cf. 2 Tim 2:1).[1] As with the first reference to "the command" in 1:5, there is some debate about the content of the more specific reference to "this command" here.[2] The translations illustrate the disagreement: "I am giving you these instructions" (NRSV), "I am giving you this command" (TNIV). By broadening the Greek singular to a plural, the NRSV apparently understands the reference to be to the instructions throughout the whole letter.[3] However, the singular is intentional. The original commission given to Timothy was to oppose the false teachers (1:3); it is this task that is subsequently referred to with the term "command" or "instruction" in 1:5. While we may be sure that Paul's instructions from 2:1 onward relate in some way to Timothy's task of opposition and correction, they also probably exceed that task. Consequently, what Paul does at this point is to refer back to the original task, resuming the original thought as a way out of the testimonial digression, to add motivational material before moving on to related topics.

The verb of conveyance employed here ("I am giving, entrusting") further suggests a reflection back on the original commissioning. Here it expresses the sense of "entrustment" associated with receiving a commission (2 Tim 2:2) in a way not noticeably different from the simplex cognate verb "to appoint" that Paul used of his own appointment in 1:12 (2:7; 2 Tim 1:11).[4] This link, along with the bracketing of the instruction to Timothy around the Pauline testimony, ensures that Timothy will feel the weight of his commission.

---

1. For discussion of the epithet "(my) child" (Gk. τέκνον), see above on 1.2a.

2. Gk. ταύτην τὴν παραγγελίαν (see on 1:5); in these letters, the demonstrative pronoun οὗτος more frequently refers backward.

3. So also Bassler, 45-46. In the commentaries, attention is sometimes drawn to the verb of "commission" here, Gk. παρατίθεμαι (mid.), which is cognate to the important term παραθήκη (6:20; 2 Tim 1:12, 14). Since the latter is used to describe the passing on of the apostolic tradition/message/mission to Timothy, it is argued, via the related verb, that "this command" refers extensively to "the apostolic message" (cf. Dibelius and Conzelmann, 3; Roloff, 101; P. Trummer, *EDNT* 3:22; see the discussion in Marshall, 408).

4. Gk. παρατίθεμαι (2 Tim 2:2; Acts 14:23; 20:32; 1 Pet 4:19; Trummer, *EDNT* 3:22) is cognate to the verb indicating appointment in 1:12 (θέμενος; ptc.). See Johnson, 184.

The following prepositional phrase, "in keeping with the prophecies once made about you," motivates by establishing the context of authority for the present command: Timothy's earlier appointment. The role of prophecy in defining Timothy's calling and authority is confirmed by 4:14 (see discussion), but neither the procedure envisioned nor the time is entirely clear. As for procedure, the best analogy is probably Acts 13:2, where, in the Spirit, words of confirmation and calling were uttered by the group of prophets and teachers praying for Barnabas and Paul.[5] As for time, the translation above suggests that the reflection here is on an earlier[6] episode in which multiple prophecies,[7] mutually confirming, were declared "upon"[8] Timothy.[9] It is not possible to locate this event with certainty. 4:14 might seem to indicate that Timothy's authority was confirmed in the local Ephesian setting,[10] or there and here the reference may be back to some earlier occasion(s) either at the outset of Timothy's career (Acts 16:2), or as marking the commencement of this present assignment.[11] Either way, Timothy is thus bound to his commission (1:5, 18a) by the divine decision communicated to him in the presence of others.

The purpose *(hina)* of Timothy's commission, given earlier in terms of commanding and correcting the false teachers (1:3-4), is repeated here in a vivid military metaphor: "fight the battle well" (lit. "fight the good fight").

5. Cf. Fee, *God's Empowering Presence,* 758-61.

6. The verb προάγω (here in the ptc. τὰς προαγούσας) is best taken in a temporal sense, "earlier" (rather than in a local sense as "leading to or going before"; for which see Knight, 108).

7. Gk. προφητεία (4:14; Rom 12:6; 1 Cor 12:10; 13:2, 8; 14:6, 22; 1 Thess 5:20); see esp. D. E. Aune, *Prophecy in Early Christianity and the Ancient Mediterranean World* (Grand Rapids: Eerdmans, 1983), 247ff.; H. Krämer (et al.), *TDNT* 6:781-861; F. Schnider, *EDNT* 3:182-83; C. M. Robeck, *DPL* 755-62.

8. The syntax of the phrase κατὰ τὰς προαγούσας ἐπὶ σὲ προφητείας is problematic. It is possible to take the prepositional phrase as dependent upon the participle ("the going before you prophecies"; see Knight, 108 and preceding note). But on the model of 4:14 (τοῦ ἐν σοὶ χαρίσματος; "the gift in you"; article/prepositional phrase with personal pron./noun), the sense would be "according to the prophecies [prophesied] upon you" (with κατά, "in accordance with," indicating that the prophecies are being fulfilled as Paul gives the commands to Timothy), with the participle simply indicating the time frame. See the fuller discussion in Marshall, 409.

9. The view that "prophecies" refers to words spoken at a formal ordination (Bassler, 46; Roloff, 102) is anachronistic and surely, in view of such precedents as Acts 13:1-4, not required by the texts.

10. Cf. Brox, 118.

11. Fee, 57-58; see discussion in Marshall, 409. As Johnson, 184, points out, the "mandate" function of the letter, which sets out for the receiving community the authority and instructions for Timothy in assuming his role in Ephesus, might suggest that the event took place as Paul sent Timothy off.

The saying seeks to elevate the urgency of the action to be taken by Timothy in the same way that the athletic metaphor in 6:12 does (2 Tim 4:7). The combination of the verb and cognate noun portrays Timothy's calling as that of a soldier (2 Tim 2:4) engaged in a military campaign.[12] Although Hellenistic writers used the metaphor of military struggle widely to describe life in general or in ethical contexts to characterize moral effort,[13] the usage here is continuous with that in other Pauline letters. The combination of verb and noun occurs also at 2 Cor 10:3-4 in a similar discussion about opponents, and a wider array of similar imagery is frequent in Paul.[14] The addition of the adjective "good"[15] specifies that this is the authentic war of faith. But not to be overlooked in this description is the continuing role of the prophecies that accompanied Timothy's commission. It is "by recalling them" that the war will be successfully fought, a reference both to the binding commitment and to the promise of divine help involved in Timothy's commission.

19   As the Greek sentence continues with a participial phrase,[16] Paul returns to the profile of authentic Christian existence in 1:5 to underline the means by which Timothy will be able to wage the good war. In doing this, he is returning to the contrast between his understanding of authentic Christianity as the inward cleansing of the heart that enables the believer to process God's law internally (new covenant) and the heretical notion of spirituality as adherence to an external framework of law. The concepts of "holding on ["having," "keeping"] to faith" and to "the conscience" are expressed elsewhere in the NT.[17] But here the close interrelation of the two items belongs to Paul's schematic of the inner workings of the genuine believer worked out especially in these letters to coworkers. "Faith" is that posture of trust in God that animates the individual's personal relationship with God (see on 1:2 [n.], 5). The "good conscience" is the organ of decision (1:5, Excursus), by which

12. For the verb στρατεύομαι, see 2 Tim 2:4; 1 Cor 9:7; 2 Cor 10:3; for the noun στρατεία, see 2 Cor 10:4. For the verb-object combination see 4 Macc 9:24. See also O. Bauernfeind, *TDNT* 7:701-13; Johnson, 185.

13. Cf. Epictetus 2.4.17; 3.24.34; Plutarch, *Moralia* 204A.

14. 1 Cor 9:24-25; 2 Cor 6:7; Phil 1:27-30; 3:12-14; Eph 6:11-17; Col 1:28–2:2. See also V. C. Pfitzner, *Paul and the* Agon *Motif* (Leiden: Brill, 1967), 157-64.

15. The TNIV rendering of the adjective καλός (in the art./adj./noun combination τὴν καλὴν στρατείαν) as an adverb ("fight the battle well"; cf. NIV, "the good fight") is puzzling and fails to capture the import of the καλός word group in these letters for categorizing aspects of the authentic faith. See the discussion of "good" at 1:8 and "good works" at 2:10. Towner, *Goal*, 153-54.

16. TNIV shows the close relationship of this clause to the preceding by incorporating it into v. 18.

17. For the verb ἔχω with "faith" as its object (Rom 14:22; 1 Cor 13:2; Matt 17:20; 21:21; Acts 14:9; Jas 2:18), with "conscience" as its object (Acts 24:16; Heb 10:2; 13:18; 1 Pet 3:16).

the Christian may move from knowledge of the faith (considered from the standpoint of objective content) and sound teaching to appropriate conduct. Particularly in this theological configuration, the "good conscience" is an ethical description of what the Spirit does within the believer to apprehend God's law. The condition of the conscience is determined by one's disposition toward the gospel (by conversion), which suggests the ordering of "faith" followed by a "good conscience." Paul is obviously setting faithfulness to his gospel as the prerequisite of Timothy's success. Together, then, these two items link the ministry of opposition Timothy is to be engaged in to godly faith and behavior, just as they distance authentic Christian ministry from the activities of the opponents.

In fact, this distance between authentic and inauthentic faith is now explained in terms of the opponents' act of rejection. Just as Paul in 1:5-6 first sets out the authentic shape of faith and then shows how the opponents have veered from it, so here, with the same device,[18] he first establishes the benchmark of authenticity and then the deviation from it. The verb describes a deliberate act of rejection[19] and coincides with other terms describing the culpable deviation of the opponents from sound doctrine.[20] In this case the grammar makes it clear that they have let go of a "good conscience."[21] If we have followed the discourse thus far, we know that Paul is here alluding to the heretical decision to return to an external, law-based (and ascetical) "faith" (1:3-4, 7, 8-10a; 4:1-3). Essentially, their rejection of the Pauline conception of the faith, with its insistence on the internalizing of the norm of godliness, for an external law structure without the Spirit, rendered their conscience incapable of discerning authentic from inauthentic doctrine and conduct (4:2): the law functions to reveal sin, not to empower for holy living (1:8-10a). "Rejecting the good conscience" is neither a reference to specific immoral tendencies that destroyed their faith, nor to a dualistic absorption in the cognitive dimension of faith that ignores practical ethics.[22] But as in 1:5-6, here too the stress is more on the integrity of the whole Christian person: the parts are interdependent, and the failure of any one will affect the other. The false teachers exchanged Paul's understanding of salvation and Christian living for a materialistic approach that relied on novel exegesis of the OT instead of the inner working of the Spirit in a converted heart. This decision of rejection does indeed have practical and visible results in the form of

---

18. The relative pronoun followed by the derogatory indefinite pronoun (ἥν τινες; 6:21; 2 Tim 2:18).

19. Gk. ἀπωθέω (ptc. "to reject, repudiate"; Acts 7:27, 39; Rom 11:1, 2).

20. 1:6; 4:1; 5:15; 6:21; 2 Tim 2:18; 4:4; Titus 1:9.

21. The antecedent of the feminine singular relative pronoun ἥν is the immediately preceding feminine noun ἀγαθὴν συνείδησιν. Cf. TNIV ("which some have rejected") and NRSV ("by rejecting conscience").

22. See Schlarb, *Die gesunde Lehre,* 122-34; see the discussion in Marshall, 412.

behavior that does not conform to godliness, but the root error seems to have been rejection of Paul's gospel.

The consequences of this rebellion were severe. Employing the aorist tense, Paul speaks historically of an event that has already occurred that he will link to two characters. The well-known metaphor of "shipwreck" signifies the catastrophic scale of damage caused by their rejection.[23] But what (or who) has suffered shipwreck? The prepositional phrase "with regard to the faith"[24] defines the context of the disaster. Some take this impersonally as a reference to damage caused to the gospel mission or to "the faith" by the false teaching.[25] But a personal reference to damage caused to the opponents' own faith in some sense is more likely.[26] The most decisive factors are probably the verb itself, whose subject is the collective "some" (about to be narrowed to two individuals), and the main topic of this closing subsection. The verb, whether literally or figuratively, is consistently intransitive, describing a state of the subject, and so means "to suffer shipwreck or disaster" but not "to cause something to be shipwrecked."[27] In this construction, it is the heretics who suffer shipwreck, and the added prepositional phrase is required to describe that in relation to which the figure of disaster is to be measured — it is too indirect to serve as a direct object (even if the verb could take one). This means that in whatever sense "(the) faith" is taken, it must still be seen in connection with the false teachers' personal disaster. Then, the immediate context is taken up with repeating the charge to Timothy, after a long (but carefully planned) digression, and with motivating him. Just as reference to his earlier commissioning and attendant obligations is meant to encourage faithfulness, so too is the warning of possible disaster. Consequently, either

23. Gk. ναυαγέω (2 Cor 11:25, lit.); the verb is intransitive and does not take an object but sometimes takes prepositional phrases that define the context (e.g., Dibelius and Conzelmann, 33 n. 12); for the figurative use, see also Philo, *On Dreams* 2:147; *On the Change of Names* 215.

24. Gk. περὶ τὴν πίστιν (for the construction cf. 2 Tim 2:18).

25. See Fee, 58; Mounce, 67. This requires taking the verb transitively to mean "to cause shipwreck." The main considerations are: (1) the articular form of "the faith" in the prepositional phrase (as in the identical phrases in 6:21 and 2 Tim 3:8) tends to refer to "the Christian faith" as opposed to personal faith; (2) in context, Paul's first concern is for his and his mission's authority in Ephesus. This has come under attack by those who have reverted in some sense to a Judaizing faith; (3) the sin of the two named individuals, "blasphemy" (v. 20), could be understood as an attack on the gospel.

26. Johnson, 186; Marshall, 412; Arichea and Hatton, 41-42.

27. Mounce, 63, 67, takes ναυαγεῖν as a transitive verb but without evidence that it functioned this way. In fact, in each of the περὶ τὴν πίστιν phrases (1:19; 6:21; 2 Tim 3:8), the verb or verbal idea governing the prepositional phrase functions intransitively (6:21; cf. 2 Tim 2:18: ἀστοχέω = "to miss the mark"; 2 Tim 3:8: ἀδόκιμοι), and so requires the preposition to define that in respect of which the state (shipwreck, bad aim, etc.) exists.

the "some" have suffered disaster with respect to "their own faith" (the standard for which is the authentic faith just referred to), or they have suffered disaster "so far as the Christian faith is concerned."[28]

20   In the finale to this section, Paul, without breaking the sentence, underlines the gravity of the danger just mentioned by identifying two of the larger group ("some")[29] who have rejected good conscience and suffered the faith-consequences. The effect of this concrete illustration is both to emphasize the warning to Timothy and to convey to the receiving Ephesian community Paul's official censure of the opposition.

"Hymenaeus and Alexander" were obviously known to both Timothy and the church. Explicit reference to their names probably indicates that they were prominent in the church. Within the NT, the name "Hymenaeus" is the rarer of the two,[30] occurring only here and with the resurrection heresy in 2 Tim 2:18. From the latter reference, it seems that, despite the action taken against him (see below), he apparently continued to operate in opposition to the Pauline mission in the later setting reflected in 2 Timothy. The present context suggests that he was one of the teachers of false doctrine (1:3, etc.), and 2 Tim 2:18 may indicate the sort of distortions the heretical speculation was capable of producing.[31]

The name "Alexander" was more common and often taken by Jews.[32] Four occurrences of the name in the NT have something to do with Paul (Acts 19:33[2x]; 2 Tim 4:14) and are all, even if coincidentally, linked to Ephesus. On balance, though some maintain that the additional reference to his trade in 2 Tim 4:14 intends to distinguish between two people bearing the same name,[33] it seems just as plausible that the additional information supplied at a later time was meant to identify the same opponent who, because of Paul's disciplinary action (see below), moved to a new location and posed a new level of threat to Timothy.

In the disciplinary action taken by Paul, his apostolic authority is

---

28. Arichea and Hatton, 42. See also NRSV. This latter solution is perhaps better supported by the other occurrences of the phrase περὶ τὴν πίστιν (6:21; 2 Tim 3:8).

29. For the use of the genitive relative pronoun to indicate part of the whole (ὧν ἐστιν . . .), see also 1:15; 2 Tim 1:15; 2:17.

30. Gk. Ὑμέναιος, frequent in Greek mythology (see BDAG, s.v.; cf. *Acts of Paul and Thecla* 14).

31. For the view that the heresy denying the resurrection was already current when Paul wrote 1 Timothy, see Towner, *Goal,* 100-107; Schlarb, *Die gesunde Lehre,* 179-82.

32. Gk. Ἀλέξανδρος; see M. C. Pacwa and Joel Green, "Alexander," n.p., *ABD on CD-ROM.* Version 2.1a. 1995, 1996, 1997. Of Jewish men, Acts 4:6; 19:33(2x); 2 Tim 4:14; cf. Mark 15:21; BDAG, s.v.

33. See Quinn-Wacker, 804; cf. Marshall, 413.

clearly in view. The first-person verb "I have handed over" suggests a more direct role in the activity than the parallel text in 1 Cor 5:5, where, with the same language, Paul instructs the Corinthian church to "hand this man over to Satan." The difference is, however, minimal[34] since in both situations it is his authority as an apostle that is to compel the church to take action and since the past (aorist) time of the action alluded to here does not rule out the church's participation in the event. What the language of each text makes clear is that an established disciplinary act — "handing over to Satan"[35] — was known in the Pauline churches.

"Satan" (5:15)[36] refers to the supernatural nemesis of God and the church (Mark 4:15; 1 Thess 2:18), who is here seen as serving God's purposes by overseeing the chastisement of sinners (Job 2:6). This rather curious relationship was apparently a way of explaining the presence of evil in the lives of God's people in a way that compromised neither God's holiness nor the priority of God's purposes for his children (Job 2:6; 2 Cor 12:7; cf. Matt 4:1-11).

The nature of the disciplinary procedure is less clear. Several texts (see also Matt 18:15-17; 1 Cor 5:5; 2 Cor 2:5-11; 2 Thess 3:14-15) would seem to indicate that "handing over to Satan" involved a last stage in which the unrepentant sinner was turned out of the church to be treated as an unbeliever (see esp. 1 Cor 5:5, 9, 11). This was probably envisioned as removal from the sphere of God's protection into the world where Satan still held sway. The situation of even more extreme punishment involving death inflicted directly by God is not in view (Acts 5:1-11; cf. 1 Cor 11:30).

As elsewhere (1 Cor 5:5), the goal of such discipline is reclamation of the erring person. Here that is implied through the purpose *(hina)* of "handing over," namely, "that they might be taught not to blaspheme." The term translated "teach" (TNIV) included both instruction and discipline and envisioned a process (possibly very severe) that brought improvement.[37] Here the verb defines the process of "handing over to Satan" above as a disciplinary/

---

34. It is unlikely that the different perspectives should be interpreted as reflecting different degrees of church involvement in the measures taken in keeping with the alleged theme of Paul as guarantor of the gospel in the PE (*pace* Roloff, 105-6; Brox, 121).

35. Gk. οὓς παρέδωκα τῷ σατανᾷ (1 Cor 5:5: παραδοῦναι τὸν τοιοῦτον τῷ σατανᾷ). The language describing the action of "handing over" is modeled on the episode in Job 2:6, in which God hands Job over for testing (LXX Job 2:6: εἶπεν δὲ ὁ κύριος τῷ διαβόλῳ ἰδοὺ παραδίδωμί σοι αὐτόν; "And the Lord said to the devil [MT = "Satan"], 'Behold, I hand him over to you'"). For the use of παραδίδωμι in this sort of action, see the discussions in MM 483; F. Büchsel, *TDNT* 2:169-72.

36. Gk. Σατανᾶς (*b. Sanh.* 89b for Satan's part in testing Abraham); see V. P. Hamilton, "Satan," n.p., *ABD on CD-ROM.* Version 2.1a. 1995, 1996, 1997; W. Foerster and K. Schäferdieck, *TDNT* 7:151-65.

37. Gk. παιδεύω (see discussion and notes at Titus 2:12).

educative measure designed to correct the sinners. The positive thrust of the action is apparent (2 Tim 2:25), as is the way Paul subtly distances himself from the process. The passive form of the verb "be instructed" either locates the remedial education in God (who never loses control over Satan) or more blandly locates it in the whole process.

The categorization of their sin, which must have included false teaching and rejection of Paul's authority, in terms of "blasphemy" (see discussion at 1:13) forms a link back to the behavior of the preconversion Paul (1:13). Apparently, Paul viewed the legalism and speculative exegesis of this movement in a way similar to his own pre-enlightened Torah zeal. The identical charge of blasphemy, in its religious sense (the meaning is not simply "slander" as in 6:4), places the whole of their activities under the category of behavior that disrespects God by distorting the truth and opposing his agents. Thus the note of denunciation is unequivocal. Yet it is Paul's hope that expulsion from the fellowship will bring these two leaders to their senses and from the position of opposition to alignment with Paul's gospel and work.

2. Regarding Appropriate Prayer in the Church (2:1-7)

> 1 *I urge, then, first of all, that petitions, prayers, intercession and thanksgiving be made for everyone — 2 for kings and all those in authority, that we may live peaceful and quiet lives in all godliness and holiness. 3 This is good, and pleases God our Savior, 4 who wants all people to be saved and to come to a knowledge of the truth. 5 For there is one God and one mediator between God and human beings, Christ Jesus, himself human, 6 who gave himself as a ransom for all people. This has now been witnessed to at the proper time. 7 And for this purpose I was appointed a herald and an apostle — I am telling the truth, I am not lying — and a true and faithful teacher of the Gentiles.*

From this point on in the letter, a number of specific issues will receive attention. The context throughout will continue to be that of false teaching and opposition to the Pauline mission. As Paul treats matters related to the worship gathering and the organization of leaders, and gives instructions concerning various groups, the church will often still feel the presence of opponents and their teaching activities, and the latter will come up for specific treatment in several places (4:1-5; 6:3-10, 20-21). But we will see that the local culture is also exerting pressure on community life in a way that causes Paul to intervene forcefully.

He begins with the matter of prayer in the church. In treating this text, the interpreter typically encounters two misconceptions. The first is one that persists in many quarters of the church today. Paying attention to the broad introduction to this topic, the church has often understood the text to lay down a broad commission to pray for all people and for government leaders without really stipulating what direction such prayer ought to take. But the real concern, as close attention to the argument will show, is for the prayer that supports the church's universal mission to the world. That is, Paul urges Timothy to instruct the Ephesian church to reengage in an activity it had apparently been neglecting — prayer in support of Paul's own mandate to take the gospel to the whole world.

The second misconception was introduced by Martin Dibelius[1] and is still at work in the scholarship of many who have exercised more caution and balance.[2] Dibelius saw this text as introducing the new shape that Christian existence took following the departure of the apostles and as a result of the disappointment over the delay of Christ's return. In his estimation, prayer for all and for those in authority sought the goal of the quiet and peaceful life — that is, a Christian existence characterized by outward behavior conforming to secular notions of "good citizenship." As the logic goes, with the delay of Christ's return, the church came to the conclusion that it was bound to be around for some time to come, and the only way to ensure its longevity in a hostile world was to adopt an approach to living in the world that would be acceptable to the world. This interpretation claims to explain best the use of numerous Hellenistic ethical terms in these letters and what is thought to be the author's endorsement of a life for Christians that seeks little more than the goal of respectability (for which see the rest of the commentary). The point here is that Dibelius ignored the way in which the reference to the quiet and peaceful life is set within the instruction about prayer and the theology that backs it up.

A better way of understanding the instructions to pray in this passage is to place them within the dialogue evident in Romans 13 (and 1 Peter 2). There Paul lays down a theology of the church-world dialectical reality in which the church is to find itself in a position of missiological service to society. Past interpretations of that text that argue that Paul was basically urging a quietistic, "low profile" approach to Christian living in society must be revised in light of Paul's subversive use of the cultural features of benefaction and good works and the very real presence of missionary motivation surrounding the instructions.[3] In our text with its specific evangelistic focus, it

1. Dibelius and Conzelmann, 39-41.

2. See the discussions in Towner, *Goal,* 9-16, 201-5; R. M. Kidd, *Wealth and Beneficence in the Pastoral Epistles* (SBLDS 122; Atlanta: Scholars Press, 1990).

3. For Romans, see 12:20 (and P. H. Towner, "Romans 13:1-7 and Paul's Missiological Perspective: A Call to Political Quietism or Transformation?" in S. K. Soderlund and N. T. Wright, eds., *Romans and the People of God: Essays in Honor of Gordon D. Fee on the Occasion of His 65th Birthday* [Grand Rapids: Ecrdmans, 1999], 149-69; idem, *Goal,* 202-3); for the parallel text 1 Pet 2:13-17, see 2:11-12.

may be argued that the church's commitment to acknowledge the secular power structure and society's expectations is to be expressed in its prayer for salvation and effective political leadership.

In this section, close attention must be paid to the way Paul develops his argument. The whole of 2:1-7 is a coherent unit of thought. Both the overall structure of the argument and the controlling thematic use of the term "all" determine the soteriological-missiological thrust of the prayer enjoined in vv. 1-2.

A. The command, vv. 1-2a.

> I urge . . . petitions,
>> prayers,
>> intercession
>> thanksgiving for *everyone*
>>> for kings and *all* those in authority,

>>>> that we may live peaceful   (purpose of
>>>> and quiet lives   prayer for
>>>> in *all* godliness and holiness. leaders, v. 2b)

B. Prayer for *all* is grounded in God's will to save *all,* vv. 3-4.

> This is good,
> and pleases God our Savior,
>> who wants *all* people to be saved
>> to come to a knowledge of the truth.

C. God's will to save *all* is given theological backing, vv. 5-6a.

> For there is one God
> and one mediator between God and human beings,
>> (=) Christ Jesus, himself human,
>>> who gave himself as a ransom for *all* people.
> This has now been witnessed to at the proper time. [transitional]

D. Paul's mission linked to God's will to save all, v. 7.

> And for this purpose I was appointed a herald and an apostle —
> I am telling the truth, I am not lying —
> and a true and faithful teacher of the Gentiles.

The structure of the text yields four basic points. First, Paul commands that prayer be given for all people and for those in authority. What seems puzzling is that the purpose of prayer for all people is left implicit. As we will see below, the purpose clause in v. 2b explains the subsequent prayer focus on those in authority. But the greater interest emerges as the passage unfolds. Second, Paul sets out God's will concerning salvation, and this in fact determines the thrust of the prayer and of the whole section. The concern is for salvation. But, third, this statement of God's will is surprising enough, or important enough, to call for its own justification. For this Paul draws on traditional theological concepts and christological materials that demonstrate God's universal salvific will. Fourth and finally, Paul relates the prayer for the salvation of all to himself and his mission to the Gentiles.

Sharpening the soteriological point of the passage is the repeated use of the term "all." The term occurs six times in ways that clearly underline the universal scope of the discussion. In vv. 1-2 "all people" and "all who are in authority" are to be prayed for, and the outcome of prayer for government is to be a life lived in "all godliness and holiness." In v. 4 God's will is that "all people be saved," which then resonates with the declaration in vv. 5b-6a that "the human being, Christ Jesus, gave himself for 'all.'"

The theological interests and the universal theme reveal that the prayer practice Paul sought to reinstate in Ephesus had the evangelistic mission to the Gentiles as its target. What is less clear is why this had to be urged. Probably the speculative views of the false teachers or the general atmosphere surrounding the approach to the faith they promoted fostered either some sort of elitism or indifference to those outside the church. The evidence of an excessively realized view of salvation (see Introduction, 41-52) might have heightened the church's sense of separation from the world, and it is worth noting that the similar situation in Corinth apparently spawned similar separationist tendencies (1 Cor 5:9-10).

1-2   Following the brief detour in 1:19b-20, Paul signals his return to the parenetic mode he had resumed at 1:18 ("then, therefore").[4] To do this he employs his typical command verb, "I urge" (Rom 12:1; 1 Cor 1:10; 2 Cor 10:1), to issue instructions in a personal and collegial tone that are nevertheless to be understood as bearing full authority and so to be carried out.[5] If the church has discerned the mandate character of this letter, it understands that Timothy's task is to ensure that these instructions be implemented.

The "first" thing to be addressed (either in sequence or priority of importance)[6] is the church's prayer practice, and its "first-mention" placement in the letter indicates the importance in Paul's mind. The instruction identi-

---

4. This is the sense of the conjunction οὖν, namely, to make the turn to parenesis/ exhortation after there has been a break (see 2:8; 3:2; 5:14; 2 Tim 1:8; 2:1). Otherwise, there is no sense in which 2:1-2 forms a logical conclusion to the preceding passage.

5. See the discussion at 1:3.

6. Gk. πρῶτον (3:10; 5:4; 2 Tim 1:5; 2:6; see discussion at 1:15-16); it is to be taken either as a superlative ("first" in importance) or simply as an indication of the "first" in a series of items (typical of Greek letters; see Spicq, 356). There is no way to be sure which nuance Paul intends, but often the first item mentioned is of greatest importance or urgency.

fies two interrelated objects of prayer: "everyone" and "kings and all those in authority." The nature of their interrelationship is crucial to an understanding of the passage, and this needs to be teased out from the logic and flow of the argument.

Four terms for prayer combine to express the subject of the passive infinitive "to be made" that supplies the content of the exhortation.[7] Rather than understand the four terms as descriptive of a systematic liturgy of prayer, the thought is one of completeness — every dimension and action of prayer being focused on the need at hand. Three of the terms are widely used by Paul and occur together in Phil 4:6. The variety evident in the English translations shows the range of meaning covered by the terms, and there is a good degree of overlap.

"Petitions" ("requests," NIV) accurately captures the sense of the first term. It describes a direct request made to God to intercede in some way for his people.[8]

"Prayers" translates the most generic term for communicating petitions or requests for intercession to God,[9] and includes all aspects of prayer from petition to thanksgiving. But this general coverage does not make the term a reference to a general prayer request ("petitions" being the more specific). These first two terms sometimes occurred together (e.g., 5:5; Eph 6:18; Phil 4:6), and probably do so here with the intention of describing prayer activity in the fullest way possible.[10]

"Intercession" (pl.; 4:5) is limited to this NT letter. It referred originally to formal petitions made among people and usually directed to one of higher rank, and gradually took its place within the church's prayer vocabulary.[11]

"Thanksgiving" (pl.; 4:3, 4) refers to prayers that express thankfulness to God. Paul's letters to churches reveal how fundamental thanksgiving

---

7. Gk. ποιεῖσθαι is probably passive (TNIV; NRSV; BDF §392.4), taking the subsequent accusative nouns as subject. A middle voice meaning is possible (see Luke 5:33; Phil 1:4; BDAG, s.v. δέησις and ποιέω; see Marshall, 419), but there is little difference in meaning.

8. Gk. δέησις (for Pauline usage see 5:5; 2 Tim 1:3; Rom 10:1; 2 Cor 1:11; 9:14; Eph 6:18[2x]; Phil 1:4[2x], 19; 4:6); H. Greeven, TDNT 2:40-41.

9. Gk. προσευχή; also used widely by Paul (Rom 1:10; 15:30; Eph 1:16; Col 4:12; etc.). See J. Herrmann and H. Greeven, TDNT 2:775-808; H. Balz, EDNT 3:164-69.

10. Maintaining a rigid distinction between δέησις ("petition") as a specific request (or the request made by an individual) and προσευχή ("prayer") as a general request (or one made communally by the congregation) is not possible in light of such texts as Phil 4:6 and 1 Tim 5:5. But cf. Oberlinner, 66; U. Schoenborn, EDNT 1:287.

11. Gk. ἔντευξις; for formal petitions to people of rank, see Josephus, Antiquities 16.12; 2 Macc 4:8; Philo, On the Embassy to Gaius 276.2; in reference to prayer, see the later Shepherd of Hermas, Mandates 5.1.6; 10.3.2-3; 10.11.9. See further Spicq, TLNT 2:6-10; O. Bauernfeind, TDNT 8:238-45; MM 218.

was to his practice.[12] Within the church's holistic practice of prayer, thanksgiving not only bolstered confidence by focusing reflection on God's past responsiveness to petition, but also was an expression of confidence in anticipation of God's future response (Phil 1:3 [cf.1:6]; 4:6; Col 3:17).

This multifaceted prayer is to be made first of all "for everyone." As noted, the term "all" is intentionally universal in thrust (cf. vv. 2, 4, 6; 4:10), and probably calculated to counter a tendency toward insular thinking in the Ephesian church brought on by an elitist outlook or theology.[13] While in the NT this universalism is possibly most graphically expressed in this passage, Paul was also pushing forcefully in this direction in other contexts (Rom 15:11; 1 Cor 9:22; 2 Cor 5:19; cf. Acts 1:8). The purpose of this first prong of the prayer effort, delayed until vv. 3-4, will link it with the Gentile mission (cf. v. 7). Opposition to Paul's authority placed this mission in jeopardy, and enlisting the Ephesian church's active support in this way was designed to ensure the uninterrupted progress of the gospel.

Verse 2 adds a second parallel[14] prayer object — "for kings and all those in authority" — and follows it up immediately with a statement of its purpose. Generally, Paul has in mind all those who would fit into the structure of civic or government authority (cf. Rom 13:1; 1 Pet 2:13), whose office would be filled at the pleasure of the emperor. The term "king" had wide usage at this time throughout the Hellenistic world for certain local rulers (e.g., various of those in the Herodian line, Mark 6:14; Acts 12:1; 25:13; the ruler of the Nabateans, 2 Cor 11:32).[15] But its first reference for those in Asia Minor in the first century, where the Imperial cult was the fastest-growing religion, would have been to the emperor. The plural reference to "kings" would signify successive reigns of emperors[16] (i.e., pray for

12. Gk. εὐχαριστία; note Paul's use of the verb in describing his thanksgiving to God (Rom 1:8; 1 Cor 1:4; Phil 1:3; etc.); for the noun in the same sense, 1 Cor 14:16; 2 Cor 4:15; 9:11; Phil 4:6; Col 2:7; 4:2; 1 Thess 3:9. Spicq, *TLNT* 2:9.

13. Given a too fully realized eschatology (understanding the present experience of salvation to be fuller than it actually is), a number of factors (such as are more evident in the Corinthian situation) could persuade the church to view itself as a closed society; see Towner, *Goal,* 33-42. There is no basis for the view that a Gnostic disregard for the state (v. 2) was specifically being addressed (W. Schmithals, "The Corpus Paulinum and Gnosis," in A. H. B. Logan and A. J. M. Wedderburn, eds., *The New Testament and Gnosis* [Edinburgh: T&T Clark, 1983], 117).

14. Both objects of prayer are indicated by the repeated preposition ὑπέρ ("on behalf of"), followed by genitive objects.

15. Gk. βασιλεύς; see also Josephus, *Antiquities* 17.188; 18.273; *Jewish War* 2.20; Spicq, *TLNT* 1:264-65.

16. As in Josephus, *Jewish War* 3.351; 4.596; 5.563. In light of Josephus, it is unlikely that the plural "kings" is a specific reflection of the later situation in which there were co-emperors in Rome (i.e., post C.E. 137).

the current emperor). Nevertheless, prayer for the local or regional representatives of imperial power is also included in the broad addition "and for all
those in authority." The breadth of the command takes in all kinds of officials. The key term in the phrase "in authority" indicates those in a position
of status and corresponds to those holding various imperial appointments
throughout the empire.[17]

Where did this sense of responsibility originate? The precedent for
the practice of God's people praying for pagan rulers goes back to Israel's
exile experience. In this context we find the prophetic instruction to display
loyalty to the surrounding power structure: "But seek the welfare of the city
where I have sent you into exile, and pray to the LORD on its behalf, for in its
welfare you will find your welfare" (Jer 29:7; cf. Ezra 6:9-10; 1 Macc
7:33).[18] This could perhaps be dismissed as an expedient measure designed
to help the displaced Jewish people make the best of temporary difficulties.
But lying behind the prophetic instruction and evident in the prophetic and
wisdom writings[19] was a developing theological (and eschatological) awareness that with the exile the lines of Israel's religious world were being redrawn. YHWH now accomplished his will through pagan leaders whom he
called his "ministers" and "servants" (Isa 45:1; Jer 25:9; cf. Isa 5:26-29;
7:18-20; 8:7-8; 13:4-5). In exile Israel's vision had to expand to encompass
all the nations, and it is chiefly in the body of literature that emerges from
and after this experience that God's universal redemptive intentions become
increasingly clear. It was a logical (and theological) step for Paul to interpret
the church's prayer responsibility on the basis of the prophetic instruction,
because he knew that the very existence of the church was linked to the universal promises that came to expression in writings of those times. Also
stemming from this development was the awareness of an extensive obligation to serve society (Titus 3:1-2; Rom 13:1-7; 1 Pet 2:13-17).[20] Within

---

17. Gk. καὶ πάντων τῶν ἐν ὑπεροχῇ ὄντων (for ὑπεροχή as "excellence," 1 Cor
2:1; 2 Macc 5:13; as "position of authority," 2 Macc 3:11; Polybius 5.41.3; Josephus, *Antiquities* 9.3); cf. the similar language of Rom 13:1 (πᾶσα ψυχὴ ἐξουσίαις ὑπερεχούσαις
ὑποτασσέσθω), where the parallel term for "authority" is ὑπερέχω (1 Pet 2:13). See MM
653-54; G. Delling, *TDNT* 8:523-24.

18. See also Bar 1:10-13; *Epistle of Aristeas* 44-45; Josephus, *Jewish War* 2.197,
409; Philo, *On the Embassy to Gaius* 157, 317; E. Schürer, *The History of the Jewish People in the Age of Jesus Christ* (rev. ed. by G. Vermes, F. Millar, and M. Goodman; Edinburgh: T&T Clark, 1973-79), 2:311-13; H.-W. Bartsch, *Die Anfänge urchristlicher
Rechtsbildungen: Studien zu den Pastoralbriefen* (Hamburg: Reich, 1965), 34-39; Johnson, 195-96; Marshall, 421-22.

19. Prov 8:15-16; Isa 41:2-4; 45:1-7; Jer 21:7, 10; 27:5-6; Dan 2:21, 37-38; 4:17,
25, 32; 5:21; Sir 10:4; 17:17; Wis 6:3.

20. See Towner, "Romans 13:1-7."

this setting, prayer "for kings and all those in authority" cannot be severed from Paul's conception of Christian existence as witness and service in the world.

The purpose statement given to explain this prayer seems also at first blush to be an expedient designed to ease the various pressures the church might experience in a hostile society. It divides into two parts. The first part depicts an ideal set of circumstances or environment in which the church might live: "that we might live peaceful and quiet lives." The second part describes the observable manner in which such a life is to be lived: "in all godliness and holiness." The two parts must be seen as a whole, but for convenience we shall consider each part separately.

Paul characterizes a "life"[21] that is observable, lived among people in society in a way that registers.[22] The two terms ("quiet and peaceful")[23] that initially describe this life express the Hellenistic ideal (conveyed variously) of a tranquil life free from the hassles of a turbulent society.[24] It is obvious enough that Paul envisions the state, with God's help, as being capable of ensuring the conditions that would make such a life possible.

The next phrase, "in all godliness and holiness," describes this life's character and observable shape. The language Paul uses gains its effectiveness from its currency in Hellenistic ethics and from the Christian interpretation he gives it. Many modern commentators have emphasized the former element of the language and ignored the latter, resulting in the conclusion that the writer was endorsing an ethic that conformed to the Hellenistic ideal of respectability. Yet when the theological reshaping of these concepts is taken into account, it becomes clear that Paul had other aims — namely, to express the theology of a dynamic Christian ethics by means of the language of the day. This technique would of course ensure intelligibility. But Paul almost certainly intended also to reinvent the language and subvert alternative claims about the nature and source of godliness associated with politics and religious cults in the empire.

"Godliness" ("piety") is a crucial concept in the letters to cowork-

21. Gk. βίος ("life, activities of life, the means to live"; 2 Tim 2:4; Luke 8:14, 43; etc.); H.-J. Ritz, *EDNT* 219; BDAG, s.v.

22. The Gk. verb διάγω carries the same sense in Titus 3:3; see the discussion and references in Roloff, 116 n. 43.

23. Gk. ἤρεμον καὶ ἡσύχιον; the adjective ἤρεμος occurs only here in the NT and is rare in Greek literature (LSJ, s.v); the adjective ἡσύχιος occurs elsewhere in the NT only at 1 Pet 3:4, but the related verb and noun occur in 1 Thess 4:11 and 2 Thess 3:12 respectively, where Paul encourages pursuit of the same ambition of leading the quiet life.

24. See BDAG, s.v., for the occurrence of the sentiment in the closely similar statement "living a quiet and calm life" (ἤρεμον καὶ γαληνὸν τὸν βίον διαγότων); see also Josephus, *Antiquities* 13.407; Philo, *On the Life of Moses* 2.235.

ers.[25] It serves to describe the whole of Christian existence as the vibrant interplay between the knowledge of God and the observable life that emerges from this knowledge (see the Excursus below). As Paul understands it, the potential to live this life characterized by the integration of knowledge and behavior (faith and deeds) is linked to the appearance of Christ in human history (Titus 2:11-12). What should not be confused here are the ideal circumstances for life sought in prayer for the state ("the quiet and peaceful life") and the authentic Christianity called for. "Godliness" as authentic Christian existence is expected in all situations, tranquil or turbulent (2 Tim 3:12). Prayer for the tranquil setting is prayer for an ideal set of social circumstances in which Christians might give unfettered expression to their faith in observable living. This distinction allows us to place the second prayer (for leaders) into the missiological grid of the passage: the church is to pray for the salvation of "all," and it participates in that mission by making God present in society in its genuine expression of the new life for all to see.

The second term in the phrase is better translated "respectability" ("holiness," TNIV), for it conveys the ideas of "seriousness" and "appropriateness"[26] by which respectability was measured. Although not lacking an inward origin, it focuses more on behavior that is deemed acceptable by other people. Together the pair of terms ("godliness and respectability") describes Christian existence as a holistic experience of new life produced by faith in God and lived out observably in human society. While not denying the degree to which the testimony of Christ might antagonize unbelievers (2 Tim 3:12), the language Paul chooses and the emphasis on observable respectability describe the Christian life as a life of engagement in society that is worthy of respect. It is a life that truly communicates the realities of faith in Christ in a language understood by all, while it also challenges secular notions about the source of such qualities.

Paul's choice of this current ethical language was designed with communication of the gospel in mind. Far from compromising the uniqueness of the gospel and its claims, by employing the common terminology Paul established the relevance and challenge of his message for the culture. The language of "godliness" (eusebeia), among other crucial theological terms that have their place in Paul's lexicon ("epiphany," "Savior," "God," "Lord"), was

25. Gk. εὐσέβεια ("godliness, piety"); the word group occurs a handful of times in Acts (3x) and 2 Peter (5x) but most prominently in these letters (13x).

26. Gk. σεμνότης. This word group, also significant within Greek ethics, has an important role in developing a view of Christian existence in 1 Timothy and Titus. For the noun σεμνότης, see 1 Tim 2:2; 3:4; Titus 2:7 (not used elsewhere in the NT); for the adjective σεμνός, see 1 Tim 3:8, 11; Titus 2:2 (elsewhere in the NT only at Phil 4:8). The word group envisages a particular deportment (translated by a wide range of English terms) of seriousness, dignity, respectability, and holiness.

so closely linked to the Artemis cult in Ephesus that his choice of this term to define the essence of Christian existence would directly confront the cultural story (see the Excursus below). The point would be clear: authentic *eusebeia* was neither to be found nor expressed in association with Artemis, but only by faith in Christ.

Excursus: Godliness and Respectability

Godliness

The concept of "godliness" or "piety" that comes to expression in the εὐσέβεια word group is prominent within the ethical framework of Christian existence constructed by Paul in these letters and therefore central to their interpretation: for the noun εὐσέβεια (1 Tim 2:2; 3:16; 4:7, 8; 6:3, 5, 6, 11; 2 Tim 3:5; Titus 1:1; elsewhere in the NT only Acts 3:12; 2 Pet 1:3, 6, 7; 3:11); for the verb εὐσεβέω (1 Tim 5:4); for the adverb εὐσεβῶς (2 Tim 3:12; Titus 2:12); see also the adjective εὐσεβής (Acts 10:2, 7; 2 Pet 2:9). Its dominance in these letters and currency in Hellenistic ethical thought led many scholars to the conclusion that by the time these letters were written the Pauline churches had embraced a secular ("bourgeois") ethic. But this conclusion is drastically simplistic and deeply flawed.

The history of this term's interpretation reflects a diversity of approaches and results (W. Foerster, *TDNT* 7:175-85; Quinn, 282-91; Marshall, 135-44; Towner, *Goal,* 147-52; idem, "Piety in Chinese Thought and in the Biblical Tradition: *Li* and *Eusebeia,*" *Jian Dao* 5 [1996]: 95-126; Lips, *Glaube,* 80-87; J. J. Wainwright, "*Eusebeia:* Syncretism or Conservative Contextualization," *EQ* 65 [1993]: 211-24; S. C. Mott, "Greek Ethics and Christian Conversion: The Philonic Background of Tit. II, 10-14 and III, 3-7," *NovT* 20 [1978]: 22-48). Against the Hellenistic background, some commentators define the concept as indicating attitudes and behavior honoring to God (Spicq, 482-92). In the German discussion, εὐσέβεια indicated either the degeneration of earlier Spirit-filled Christian living into a rather insipid "nontheological" morality (good works plus respectability) that suited the church as an institution in the world (Holtzmann, 176-79), or it was the intentional expression of a more radically conceived "bourgeois" Christianity — peaceful coexistence with the world (based largely on the occurrence in 1 Tim 2:2) — brought on by the delay of the parousia and subsequent secularization of the church (Dibelius, 39). Some, indeed, sought to find a better theological basis for εὐσέβεια in these letters. Foerster (*TDNT* 7:175-85; "ΕΥΣΕΒΕΙΑ in den Pastoralbriefen," *NTS* 5 [1958-59]: 213-18), while unfortunately linking it too closely (as Dibelius did) to behavior in relation to the orders of the world (overemphasizing 1 Tim 2:2; 5:4), argued that "godliness" was grounded in "faith" (πίστις). Too much dependence upon two occurrences of the term in 1 Timothy and a disregard for developments in Jewish thought limited this interpretation. Later responses to Foerster (Brox, 174-77, and especially Lips, *Glaube,* 80-87; Roloff, 117-19) were more thorough in observing the term's occurrences, deepened exploration of the theological basis of the concept's adaptation by the author, and regarded the Christianizing of the concept more seriously. But "godliness" in these letters was still thought to derive its shape chiefly from its use in Hellenistic ethical thought, and developments in Hellenistic Judaism were ignored.

In Greek culture εὐσέβεια referred to an attitude of reverence expected in relation to a number of persons and things (ancestors, living relatives, rulers, esp. the king, and the legal code). This wide application lent the term the broad sense of respect for the orders of life. It acquired its religious orientation (reverence and cult) by virtue of the belief that all these "orders" of life were under the care of the gods.

But especially noteworthy here is the place of the concept in the cult of Artemis at Ephesus (P. R. Trebilco, *The Early Christians in Ephesus* [Tübingen: Mohr-Siebeck, 2004], 19-30; G. H. R. Horsley, S. R. Llewelyn, R. A. Kearsley, et al., *New Documents Illustrating Early Christianity* [Grand Rapids: Eerdmans, 1997-98], 2:82.19; 4:80-81). An inscription dating to 104 C.E. (IvEph 27, lines 344-45), in which "godliness" and "epiphany" concepts are connected, describes one person's "reverence for the most manifest goddess Artemis": [εἴ]ς τε τειμὴν καὶ εὐσέβ[ειαν τῆ]ς ἐπιφανεσ[τάτης θεᾶς] Ἀρτέμιδος (see translation in G. Rogers, *The Sacred Identity of Ephesos: Foundation Myths of a Roman City* [London: Routledge, 1991], 173). Moreover, in the first century C.E., the Kouretes, wardens of the mysteries of the Artemis cult who also were part of the city's governing structure, were titled εὐσεβεῖς (IvEph 1008; see Rogers, *Ephesos,* 247-50). Consequently, such language was very much a part of any Ephesian discourse about "godliness" and rooted in the fundamental worship of Artemis.

The Roman equivalent to εὐσέβεια was *pietas,* which covered about the same range of objects toward which the obligation of respect was to be paid (so Cicero, *De natura deorum* 1.116; see Quinn, 288-89).

While the currency of the concept of "godliness" in the Greco-Roman environment, and specifically in connection with the Artemis myth in Ephesus, probably explains Paul's decision to employ it in these letters, it is its use in Hellenistic Judaism that readied the concept for Pauline use. Quinn, especially, argued that Hellenistic Judaism was engaged in the task of converting OT concepts into Greek modes. Rather than seeing the process of producing the Greek OT (LXX) as simply unreflective translation of Hebrew/Aramaic into Greek, at many points — and the concept of εὐσέβεια represents one of these — we should understand the Diaspora Jewish community as involved in the conscious attempt to interpret its faith for contemporary non-Jewish society.

Within the LXX the noun εὐσέβεια occurs 59 times (4x in canonical books, Prov 1:7; Isa 11:2; 33:6; 5x in the Apocrypha, 1 Esdr 1:23; Wis 10:12; Sir

49:3; 2 Macc 3:1; 12:45; 3x in 3 Maccabees, 1:9; 2:31, 32; 47x in 4 Maccabees). In translating Prov 1:7; Isa 11:2, and 33:6 (יראת יהוה = "fear of the YHWH"), εὐσέβεια brought together the core ideas of covenant loyalty and the appropriate behavioral response to the law, while the Isaiah texts added the dimension of the "knowledge of God" (cf. θεοσέβεια in the same sense in Gen 20:11; Job 28:28; Sir 1:24; 4 Macc 7:6; 16:11; the adj. θεοσεβής was used of Jews and sometimes of women in Jewish contexts [John 9:31], and is found in Greek contexts of people describing themselves as worshipers of the true religion; J. Murphy-O'Connor, "Lots of God-Fearers? *Theosebeis* in the Aphrodisias Inscription," *RB* 99 [1992]: 418-24). "Fear of YHWH," with all of its cognitive and behavioral implications, is the Hebrew term that comes closest to the English term "religion," and εὐσέβεια contained the breadth of meaning in the Greek world (though Judaism's adaptation developed new emphases) to express in Greek the essential interrelationship of the knowledge of God and corresponding conduct. (The adj. εὐσεβής occurs 10x in canonical writings, 28x in deuterocanonical ones; it often stands for "righteous" [e.g., Prov 12:12; Isa 24:16; 26:7]; the verb εὐσεβέω is limited to deuterocanonical writings [Susannah 63 ; 4 Macc 9:6; 11:5, 23; 18:1].)

Even in those Jewish writings generally thought to reflect stronger Greek influence (Sirach, 4 Maccabees, Philo), the presence of Jewish theology in the use of εὐσέβεια remains high. "Piety" in Sirach is set in opposition to sin (13:17; 33:14), and is linked with knowledge of God (43:33), "righteousness," and commitment to the law (37:12). And εὐσέβεια defines Israel's proper response to the covenant (49:3). In 4 Maccabees, the adjective is employed in the concept "godly reason" to describe εὐσέβεια in action (the whole complex of the knowledge of God and its correct human response = Jewish religion); it dominates the emotions to lead one to worship and other aspects of appropriate (Torah-based) conduct (esp. 5:22-24). Philo, like the Greeks, elevates εὐσέβεια to the status of a virtue, in fact making it the source of virtues (e.g., *On the Special Laws* 4.135, 147); but the place of the OT law and the relationship with God in "godliness" is also clear (*On the Unchangeableness of God* 69; Foerster, *TDNT* 7:180-81; cf. Josephus, *Against Apion* 1.60). Thus use of this language in Diaspora Judaism reflects not hellenization (Foerster, *TDNT* 7:182) but something more dynamic, on the order of contextualization (e.g., Quinn, 287-88; Marshall, 141).

This combination of components in the εὐσέβεια word group (the knowledge of God, fear of the LORD, and requisite conduct), seen in Hellenistic Jewish writings and not secularization, determines its meaning in NT use. In Acts the word group describes the "God-fearers" (10:2, 7), who are known as such by their outward acts of service and worship (cf. 10:35), and the demeanor and actions of Peter and John (3:12; 17:23 might represent its use by Paul on pagan terms). 2 Peter follows the pattern of Sirach in deploying the word group to describe the "godly" (2:9) over against the "ungodly" (ἀσεβής; 2:5-6). Otherwise it is more narrowly a virtue that believers are to exhibit (1:6, 7; 3:11) and more broadly a term representing the whole Christian life made possible by God (1:3).

In the letters to Timothy and Titus the word group is a dominant feature of the theological-ethical portrait of authentic Christianity. The noun describes the life itself, the adverb the manner of that life that is lived in response to genuine faith. The theological origin of "godliness" is clear from several occurrences (1 Tim 3:16; 2 Tim 3:12; Titus 2:12), and its dependence upon a correct knowledge of God (or the gospel, the truth, etc.) emerges in 1 Tim 6:3, 5, 6, 11; Titus 1:1. It describes comprehensively the integration of the outward and inward dimensions of life, and is to be lived actively (1 Tim 4:7-8) and intentionally (Titus 2:12). Its outworking in life takes practical shape (1 Tim 5:4). And in exhorting believers to pursue such a life, it can be compartmentalized as one of several Christian virtues to be possessed (1 Tim 6:11). This description (much like the presentation of "faith" alongside other aspects of "fruit" in the list of Gal 5:22-23) should not, however, cause us to relegate εὐσέβεια to the rather sterile status of one of the virtues (cf. Mott, "Greek Ethics," 22-48). The whole of the data strongly confirms its function of describing, in one term, authentic Christian existence as the interplay of the knowledge of God (variously expressed) and its observable outworking in behavior that is appropriate to that knowledge.

Within the polemic carried out by Paul in these letters, εὐσέβεια, in reference to authentic Christianity, is played off against its antonym ἀσέβεια, in reference to the Pauline opponents (e.g., Titus 2:12; 1 Tim 1:9; 2 Tim 2:16; cf. 2 Pet 2:6). In this, Paul follows the polemical technique of Hellenistic Judaism (Prov 1:7; 3 Macc 3:31-32). What his opponents presented to the churches as "godliness" Paul exposed as being superficial and empty of a genuine knowledge of God, despite their assertions to a better knowledge of the divine.

Why the concept emerges with such force in these letters is debated. Use of the language in 1 Tim 6:5 and 2 Tim 3:5 suggests to some that Paul seized the word from the opponents' vocabulary in order to make some necessary corrections in thinking about "godliness" (Fee, 63; cf. Lips, *Glaube,* 82-83; Towner, *Goal,* 148-49). But the extensive use of the concept in these letters (not just in polemical passages) and the currency of the concept in the Ephesian Artemis cult (as well in connection with the Imperial cult and widely in Greek ethics) make it look less like a heretical catchword and more like one of the many features of the cultural story that Paul sought to subvert by penetration of the gospel. εὐσέβεια, in the tradition of Hellenistic Judaism, defines genuine Christian existence as the ongoing interplay of faith in Christ (= knowledge of God) and the manner of conduct issuing from that relationship. In deploying the word group in this way, it is hard not to see Paul presenting contemporary culture with the challenge that this highly prized Hellenistic cardinal virtue is truly attainable only in Christ.

Respectability

In secular Greek and Hellenistic Jewish writers, the σεμνότης word group often describes outward or visible dignity, seriousness, respectability, and reverence detectable through one's conduct and speech (see Spicq, *TLNT* 3:248; Herodotus 2.173; Josephus, *Antiquities* 6.332; Philo, *On the Embassy to Gaius* 296). Within Judaism the term describes that which calls forth worship and respect for the holy (LXX Prov 8:6; 15:26). Respect for the Maccabean martyrs could be so described (2 Macc 6:28; 4 Macc 5:36), and in this usage, perhaps, the sense of the meaning of "holy, holiness" (= worthy of religious respect), sometimes used to translate the term, can be understood (see esp. W. Foerster, *TDNT* 7:194; TNIV at 1 Tim 2:2). The term either describes the measurable/observable virtue (that produces "dignity," etc.) or considers the end result of behavior to be "deserving respect."

Paul's use of the adjective σεμνός in a list of virtues Christians are to pursue (Phil 4:8) is clearly in touch with secular perceptions of dignity and respectable behavior. It calls for attention to the way Christians project themselves in public. This is also true of leaders in 1 Tim 3:4, 8, 11, where respectable, dignified conduct is contrasted with aspects of behavior that were widely condemned (insincere speech, public drunkenness, dishonesty, slander; see 3:8, 10, 11). But its relevance for all believers is obvious from its use in 1 Tim 2:2 and Titus 2:2, 7. The focus of the term on outward, observable conduct is especially clear from the purpose statement given in Titus 2:8, and consistently implicit elsewhere. The degree to which a mission-witness motive should be understood in this emphasis on outward respectability continues to be questioned (see the discussion in Towner, *Goal*, 235, 253-54; Trebilco, *Early Christians in Ephesus*, 376-79). But given the missiological concern of 1 Tim 2:1-7 and Titus 1:1-4, the absence of such an intention (i.e., the endorsement of outwardly dignified behavior for the sake of its own intrinsic value) would be surprising, especially if Paul has authored these letters. Setting Paul's use off from his secular contemporaries is his understanding that this quality is to be linked to the Christ-event and "sound teaching" (Titus 2:2; the theology of 2:11-12 makes the whole of the life described in 2:2-10 dependent upon the Christ-event). In this way the inward spiritual orientation of the quality can be appreciated (cf. Philo, *On the Special Laws* 1.317; *On the Decalogue* 133; W. Foerster, *TDNT* 7:194), along with its ability to transcend external circumstances inimical to its expression. See further Spicq, *TLNT* 3:244-48; W. Foerster, *TDNT* 7:191-96; Marshall, 187-89; Towner, *Goal*, 163-64; W. Gunther, *NIDNTT* 2:91-93; R. Schwarz, *Bürgerliches Christentum im Neuen Testament?* (Klosterneuburg: Osterreichisches Katholisches Bibelwerk, 1983), 61-62.

3-4   Paul proceeds directly to demonstrate that prayer for the salvation of all accords with God's will. He does this in two stages. First (v. 3), he places the church's prayer into an OT cultic framework whereby prayer becomes the latter-day acceptable sacrifice. Second, in v. 4 he goes on to spell out God's salvific will.

With only minor changes, the language of this assessment[27] ("This is good and acceptable in the sight of God our Savior")[28] reflects the statement found several times in Deuteronomy that affirms certain practices as in accordance with the law and thus pleasing to God: "Do what is pleasing and good in the LORD's sight" (Deut 6:18). Against this background, the term "good" (*kalos;* 1:8) signifies "goodness" or "rightness" of behavior as the Lord measures it. The second term, "acceptable," marks a slight word shift (from the term "pleasing") as the formula is accessed; it calls to mind the use of the word group in Leviticus to describe sacrifices as "acceptable" to God (see also Rom 15:16; Phil 4:18; 1 Pet 2:5).[29] The effect of placing the activity of prayer into this OT legal and cultic framework is to underline its intrinsic importance to God and to his people by comparing it with the role of sacrifices in the old system. Prayer has replaced sacrifice for the messianic people of God,[30] another subtle reminder to the Torah-based opponents who resist the shape of the New Age.

Still in touch with the OT formula, the prepositional phrase concludes the first stage of assessment: "in the sight of God our Savior." Although the local or visual sense of the term sometimes recedes, the thought of being in God's presence and under his inspection is often attached in descriptions of behavior like this.[31] The motivational force of the reminder of God's proximity is obvious. The final shift from the OT formula is seen in the designation "God our Savior" (see discussion at 1:1). The title is apt, for the controlling theme of the passage is salvation, and "Savior" depicts God as the source and architect of the plan to rescue humanity through Christ. It is worth noting that in such close proximity to the prayer for rulers (especially the emperor), both the attribution of salvation to God and worship of him as "Savior" represent a direct challenge to the Imperial cult's claims to such things. Alongside worship of Artemis, the Imperial cult was a dominant religious-political fixture in Ephesus at this time.[32]

27. Here I depart from the more compact translation of the TNIV to establish the link with the OT formula.

28. Compare the Gk. of 2:3 (τοῦτο καλὸν καὶ ἀπόδεκτον ἐνώπιον τοῦ σωτῆρος ἡμῶν θεοῦ; cf. 1 Tim 5:4) with the LXX formula τὸ καλὸν καὶ τὸ ἀρεστὸν ἐναντίον κυρίου τοῦ θεοῦ ὑμῶν (Deut 6:18; 12:25, 28; 13:19; 21:9).

29. Gk. ἀπόδεκτος (only here in the NT); for δεκτός of acceptable sacrifices in the LXX, see Lev 1:3, 4; 17:4, 22:20, 21; see also similar uses of the word group in Rom 15:16; Phil 4:18; 1 Pet 2:5. See further Spicq, *TLNT* 2:137-38; W. Grundmann, *TDNT* 2:58-59.

30. H.-G. Link, *NIDNTT* 3:744-46; Marshall, 425.

31. Gk. ἐνώπιον (for the LXX ἐναντίον); for the same sense, see 1 Tim 5:4, 21; 6:13; 2 Tim 2:14; 4:1; Rom 3:20; 14:22; 1 Cor 1:29; 2 Cor 4:2; 7:12; 8:21; Gal 1:20. See H. Krämer, *EDNT* 1:462.

32. S. R. F. Price, *Rituals and Power: The Roman Imperial Cult in Asia Minor*

Thus Paul explains that prayer for the salvation of all people, and specific prayer for the effectiveness of the civic powers, conforms to the will of God. It is not simply an optional church practice that pleases God, but a practice as integral to the church's life with God as was sacrifice in the time before Christ.

But the enormity of what Paul calls for — a kind of prayer that encompasses the whole world — elicits a specific elaboration of the will of God concerning salvation (v. 4). The added relative clause not only describes the preceding "God our Savior" (v. 3), but also explains why the prayer for all people is good and acceptable to him. The reason is that God "wants [wills] all people to be saved." There are several points to consider.

First, the verb "to will" should be understood in the strongest sense as indicating God's will.[33] In this statement of God's purpose for humankind, however, the element of human response to the gospel is not minimized within the process. It is God's universal intention, as opposed to some form of exclusivism, that is mainly in mind.

Second, the purpose of the reference to "all people," which continues the theme of universality in this passage, is sometimes misconstrued. The reference is made mainly with the Pauline mission to the Gentiles in mind (v. 7). But the reason behind Paul's justification of this universal mission is almost certainly the false teaching, with its Torah-centered approach to life that included either an exclusivist bent or a downplaying of the Gentile mission.[34] This kind of corporate self-centeredness was at least latent in other Christian communities to which Paul addressed letters that argued for Jew-Gentile equality and the divine origin of his calling to the Gentiles (Galatia, Rome). Here the presence of an overly realized view of salvation may have encouraged the belief that Christians are not part of this world (see also 1 Corinthians; Introduction, 41-52).

Third, the meaning of God's will to save "all people" has been equally

---

(Cambridge: Cambridge University Press, 1984), 53-100; Trebilco, *Early Christians in Ephesus,* 30-37.

33. Gk. θέλω can express the weaker sense of "desire," and for some this sense is preferable to a statement about God's will that human indecision can thwart (see M. Limbeck, *EDNT* 2:137-39; D. Müller, *NIDNTT* 3:1015); but the stronger sense is best (see Rom 9:18; 1 Cor 4:19; 12:18; etc.; cf. the noun θέλημα (2 Tim 1:1; 1 Cor 1:1; Col 1:9; G. Schrenk, *TDNT* 3:44-62; Marshall, 427). See further P. H. Towner, "Will of God," in W. Elwell, ed., *Dictionary of Biblical Theology* (Grand Rapids: Baker, 1996), 820-22.

34. The view that a Gnostic exclusivism underlay this emphasis (Roloff, 119; Oberlinner, 72-73; Bassler, 52; Kelly, 63; J. Sell, *The Knowledge of the Truth* [Frankfurt: Lang, 1982], 11-16) is not supported by the evidence (see the discussion in Towner, *Goal,* 22-24).

problematic. As a statement of the breadth of God's will about salvation,[35] it echoes Paul's statements in Rom 3:27-31 and 11:26-32. There and here the chief concern is to clarify that God's salvific intentions fully include the non-Jewish world, and that Paul's unique mission to reach that world is indeed God's means to fulfill his universal redemptive promises (v. 7).[36] But this salvation statement is not simply about life after death. As Johnson maintains, Paul's statement "is less about future destiny ('eternal life') than about present location."[37] "Salvation" in its theological sense here (following "Savior") carries the full meaning of deliverance from sin (1:1; 1:15; Titus 2:14; 3:5-7). Yet Paul's focus is on building a people of God who incorporate all people regardless of ethnic, social, or economic backgrounds, and who are characterized by a manner of life that is qualitatively different from that of society at large (v. 2). In Pauline thought the presence of this combination of features (deliverance from personal and social sin) is present salvation. While the theological and eschatological elements of salvation persist, the primary concern in Ephesus is for a church that has tilted off this Pauline axis or is in danger of doing so.[38]

From the human side, the process of salvation, of coming to faith, can be described in various ways. Paul explains the process here by means of the phrase "to come to a knowledge of the truth."[39] The term translated "knowledge" (or "recognition") is frequent in Paul, and especially in this phrase with the verb "to come to" it reflects the cognitive process of knowing (here the content is "truth").[40] In these letters to coworkers the term occurs only in the technical phrase "knowledge of the truth" (1 Tim 2:4; 2 Tim 2:25; 3:7; Titus 1:1),[41] which, with appropriate verbs,[42] expresses the idea of conversion

35. For the meaning of Gk. σῴζω, see the discussion at 1:15; see also Quinn-Wacker, 180-81.

36. See also Marshall, 426-27; Knight, 119.

37. Johnson, 191; see also idem, "The Social Dimensions of Sōtēria in Luke-Acts and Paul," in E. H. Lovering, ed., The SBL 1993 Seminar Papers (Atlanta: Scholars Press, 1993), 520-36.

38. The possibility that this text expresses a thoroughgoing "universalism" (God will save all people regardless of their disposition toward the gospel; e.g., V. Hasler, "Epiphanie und Christologie in den Pastoralbriefe," TZ 33 [1977]: 204-7) is removed by the consistent emphasis on faith for salvation in 1 Timothy (1:16; 3:16; 4:10; cf. 2 Tim 1:5).

39. The conjunction καί ("and"), which links the two parts of v. 4, is epexegetical (see BDF §442.9): ". . . all people to be saved, that is, to come to a knowledge of the truth"; or even "all people to be saved by coming to a knowledge of the truth" (cf. BDAG, s.v. 1.δ).

40. Gk. ἐπίγνωσις; see Rom 1:28; 3:20; 10:2; Col 1:9-10; 2:2; 3:10; Phlm 6; R. Bultmann, TDNT 1:689-714.

41. Gk. ἐπίγνωσις ἀληθείας; see also Heb 10:26. The verbal equivalent occurs at 1 Tim 4:3.

42. From the human side, the action is described with the verb "to come to" (Gk. ἐλθεῖν; 2:4; 2 Tim 3:7; in 1 Tim 4:3 the verbal form of the formula is equivalent); from

as a rational decision to embrace "the truth."[43] It may also regard authentic Christianity from the perspective of one's understanding of and commitment to "the truth" (so 1 Tim 4:3).

"Truth" language (2 Tim 2:15; Titus 1:1, 14), as used by Paul, is intentionally polemical, inviting the reader/hearer to distinguish between his assessment of the gospel (= the truth) and fallacious competing claims (cf. 6:20). The same standard of measure was employed in Qumran to determine genuine membership in the Sect on the basis of a commitment to "the truth" that separated the community from corrupt mainline Judaism.[44] However much he was indebted to this tendency, Paul's other letters suggest that he first deployed the "truth" category in Christian mission. He applied it, among other overlapping concepts, with various verbs of perception to emphasize the divine origin of his message over against pagan falsehood.[45] In these letters to coworkers, "truth" stands for God's authoritative revelation (as represented in Paul's gospel). The polemical intention is clear from the descriptions, which employ various key verbs, of the opponents' departure from "the truth."[46] Consequently, "coming to the knowledge of the truth" combines a statement about the quality of the gospel message and commitment to it. In the Ephesian context of false teaching, Paul emphasizes that salvation and adherence to the apostolic message are inseparable. God's will is that all people will commit themselves in faith to the truth about Christ.

5-6   At this point, Paul inserts a supportive (*gar,* "for") theological piece crafted from traditional theological and christological statements. Three emphases will emerge. First, the theme of universality and open access to salvation continues to direct the thought. But, secondly, this is juxtaposed

---

God's side the action is described in terms of a gift: "to grant them repentance to the knowledge of the truth" (2 Tim 2:25).

43. See esp. Sell, *Knowledge of the Truth,* 3-7 et passim; Quinn, 276-82; Dibelius and Conzelmann, 41.

44. For the parallel Hebrew phrase דעת אמת, see 1QS 9:17-18. The polemical thrust of this use of "truth" is clear: "The Instructor must not reprove the Men of the Pit, nor argue with them about proper biblical understanding. Quite the contrary: he should conceal his own insight into the Law when among perverse men. He shall save reproof — itself founded on true knowledge and righteous judgment — for those who have chosen the Way" (1QS 9:16b-19a; Wise, Abegg, Cook). For the place of "truth" in the Sect's self-identity, see 1QS 6:15, where initiation into the Sect is described as "returning to the truth."

45. See 2 Thess 2:10, 12, 13-14; Eph 1:13; Col 1:5-6 for the combination of "truth" with "word," "gospel," and "faith," and verbs such as "to hear," "to believe," "to know" (ἐπιγινώσκω) and "to receive." Marshall, 122; Wolter, *Paulustradition,* 71.

46. Thus in 1 Tim 6:5, "robbed of the truth" (ἀποστερέω); 2 Tim 2:18, "wandered from the truth" (ἀστοχέω; cf. 1 Tim 6:21); 2 Tim 4:4; Titus 1:14, "reject the truth" (ἀποστρέφω).

to exclusive theological and christological claims that locate the means of salvation for all in a single person. Third, as theology turns to Christology, Paul again places the heaviest accent on the humanity of Christ (see discussion at 1:15).

Paul begins with theology to ground God's universal will to save. "There is one God" (v. 5a) is a formulaic abbreviation of the *Shema* (Deut 6:4) that goes back to the Jewish mission and the polemics of Diaspora Judaism against the many gods of the Gentiles.[47] "God is one" was a denial of the existence of any other gods. Taken up by Paul, the formula could have such a polemical application (1 Cor 8:6). But it is his use of it in Rom 3:29-30 in support of the argument for Gentile access to God's justification that explains our text (cf. Gal 3:20; Eph 4:5-6).[48] In Paul's missiology, the formula "God is one" yields the logical corollary, "therefore all have access to his salvation, both Jews and Gentiles." It corrects Jewish or Judaizing exclusivist tendencies. The formula functions similarly here, supplying theological proof for the statement that God wills to save all people.

From here, Christology takes over, and the universal claim is attached to a very particular person. "One mediator" accomplishes the universal plan of the one God (v. 5b). The term "mediator" derived from the Hellenistic commercial and legal world to describe a negotiator who helped two parties to make some kind of transaction.[49] Paul's use of it is more directly influenced by religious applications of the concept. In the OT the term can describe how God relates to people,[50] but a closer comparison exists in the *Testament of Dan*, where the angelic mediator "between God and people" intercedes for the peace of Israel (6:2). Use of the concept in the wider church to depict Christ as the mediator of the new covenant (the antitype of Moses; Heb 8:6; 9:15; 12:24) may suggest the implication of covenantal ideas here, despite the lack

47. Gk. εἷς θεός ("God is one," or "There is one God"); W. Kramer, *Christ, Lord, Son of God* (London: SCM, 1966), 95-98; Towner, *Goal*, 50-51; E. Peterson, *HEIΣ THEOΣ* (Göttingen: Vandenhoeck & Ruprecht, 1926); Marshall, 428-29; Dibelius and Conzelmann, 41; A. Oepke, *TDNT* 4:623. For the polemical use of the formula in Judaism, see esp. Dalbert, *Die Theologie der hellenistisch-jüdischen Missions-Literatur*, 124-30; M. Hengel, *Jews, Greek, and Barbarians* (London: SCM, 1980), 78.

48. The occurrence of the formula in Eph 4:4-6 may reflect liturgical worship language, but the sense of universality (if not the Jew/Gentile issue) remains. For the formula outside of Paul, see Matt 23:8, 10; Mark 12:29, 32; John 8:41; Jas 2:19; 4:12. Cf. μόνος in 1 Tim 1:17; 6:15.

49. Gk. μεσίτης; there is nothing intrinsic in the term or the concept of mediation that determines the kind or depth of relationship that existed between the mediator and the parties involved; see further A. Oepke, *TDNT* 4:598-624, 619; Spicq, *TLNT* 2:465-68; Marshall, 429-30.

50. LXX Job 9:33; *Testament of Dan* 6:2; cf. the religious use of the term in Philo, *On the Life of Moses* 2.166; *Who Is the Heir?* 206.

of the term "covenant."[51] In any case, unlike the rather negative use of the concept elsewhere in Paul that associates the reception of the law with a certain distance from God (Gal 3:19-20), the present use is clearly a positive description of Jesus. Whether the result is described in terms of reconciliation or the new covenant, "the mediator" has brought God and people into a new relationship that could be accurately described with a number of metaphors: new covenant, adoption, redemption, salvation, and so on.

A subtle paradox results as the one mediator is placed in immediate juxtaposition to the one God: "and [there is] one mediator between God and human beings." "One God" implies universal access to salvation, and this implication is transferred via the concept of "singularity" to the mediator; that is, "one mediator" implies equally that all have access to what he mediates. But just as the note of universality is sounded, "one mediator" narrows that universal accessibility down to a single means. Paul anchors universal access to God's salvation in the one act of redemption and the one message about it.

The identity of the mediator receives special attention. First, nothing inherent in the term "mediator" suggests that equivalence with God is being emphasized. His position relates him both to God and humankind and qualifies him to negotiate the transaction. But, secondly, the thrust of the statement is to locate the "mediation" accomplished by Jesus precisely in his humanity. This is clear from the phrase that immediately follows the reference to humankind, which I prefer to translate according to Greek word order: "the human, Christ Jesus" (v. 5c).[52] This phrase establishes the central thrust of the christological formulation — namely, the association of salvation with the humanity of Christ, which the subsequent appeal to the Jesus tradition (v. 6a) will complement by stressing the substitutionary and representative nature of Jesus' human death and the universal extent of the results ("for all"). Some scholars trace this unusual use of *anthrōpos* for Jesus to Pauline Adam Christology.[53] But while Christ's human death as representative (v. 6a) coincides with the Adam analogy, this link is not enlarged upon in any identifiable way.[54]

---

51. See Dibelius and Conzelmann, 42; A. Oepke, *TDNT* 4:619.

52. Gk. ἄνθρωπος Χριστὸς Ἰησοῦς; cf. Kelly, 63; Brox, 128. On the order of names, see the discussion and notes at 1:1-2, above.

53. See Rom 5:15: τοῦ ἑνὸς ἀνθρώπου Ἰησοῦ Χριστοῦ ("the one man Jesus Christ"; cf. 1 Cor 15:21-22, 45); e.g., Kelly, 63.

54. See the discussion in Marshall, 431; Towner, *Goal,* 55. Still less likely is the view that "man" (ἄνθρωπος) represents the Grecizing equivalent of the Semitic phrase "son of man" (ὁ υἱὸς τοῦ ἀνθρώπου) at the head of the Marcan logion (10:45) that lies somewhere behind v. 6a: Mark 10:45: ὁ υἱὸς τοῦ ἀνθρώπου . . . δοῦναι τὴν ψυχὴν αὐτοῦ λύτρον ἀντὶ πολλῶν (so J. Jeremias, *Abba* [Göttingen: Vandenhoeck & Ruprecht, 1966], 226-29; Trummer, *Paulustradition,* 197). Too little of the Jesus tradition is reproduced (however it is accessed; see below) to be sure; see Towner, *Goal,* 55; Marshall, 431.

More significant in describing the mediator with this phrase is the link Paul establishes with the theme within developing messianism of "a man to rule the nations" (LXX Num 24:7, 17) and "a man who will save" (Isa 19:20).[55] Several themes and ideas link the two OT discourses together and make the combination an attractive and clever interpretive framework for reflecting on the extent of Christ's work. First, each text reports the contents of a vision (*horasis;* Num 24:4; Isa 19:1). Second, whether incidental or not, Egypt and the exodus figure in each discourse (Num 24:7; Isaiah 19 throughout), and so do the Assyrians (Num 24:22; Isa 19:23-25), though of course the reflections on events, people, and places are from different historical and theological vantage points. Third, and of obvious interest to Paul, each OT vision explores Israel's role in relation to "the nations." Balaam's third oracle casts Israel in the role, under the leadership of "the man," of subjugator or conqueror of the nations. Isaiah's oracle concerning Egypt resumes this theme but adds the dimension of Egyptian worship of God: God's smiting of Egypt is followed by its healing and coming to know God (Isa 19:19-22). Finally, the central actor in each drama is "the man" *(anthrōpos)*. In Num 24:7 the man shall come out of the seed of Israel to rule the nations; 24:17 employs the apocalyptic-like image of a "star rising out of Jacob" and then returns to the more mundane description of "a man" to describe the ascent of this figure to power and victory over the nations. Isa 19:20 records God's promise to the Jews in Egypt: "he will send them a man who will save them; he will judge and save them." The MT at Num 24:7 lacks completely the first reference to "a man"; at 24:17, where the prophecy of "the star rising out of Jacob" does appear, it is subsequently described with the imagery of a "rod" or "scepter," likewise omitting any reference to "a man." There is closer agreement between the Greek and Hebrew of Isaiah 19. However, where the LXX has "a man who will save," the Hebrew has "a savior" *(moshia)*. If the OT background suggested here does lie behind Paul's reference to *anthrōpos,* it is most likely the LXX that he accesses.

But what is gained by describing the mediator in a way that recalls this background? First, Paul strengthens the argument for the universal gospel, based on the statement of God's will (v. 4) and the *heis theos* ("God is one") formula (v. 5), by depicting Christ, the mediator, as the fulfiller of this OT promise of "a man." Second, Paul in effect completes the development of the messianic "man" theme by depicting the death of Christ as the means by which "the man" takes up his rule, and by transforming early OT images of subjugation and judgment into the picture of salvation for the nations, via the gospel, in terms already emerging in Isaiah. As we will see shortly, in 2:8 it is

---

55. See W. Horbury, *Jewish Messianism and the Cult of Christ* (London: SCM, 1998), 44-45.

precisely this sense of the church standing in the midst of salvation's outpouring to the world that defines not only Paul's mission but also that of the church. "The human Christ Jesus" resumes and completes the messianic theme initiated in the Greek translation of Numbers and Isaiah. Paul invites the church of Ephesus to view its own location within God's redemptive story and its responsibilities in relation to the appearance of this "human."

The emphasis on "the human Christ Jesus" is the high point of this traditional piece. The placement of the *anthrōpos* designation between "mediator" and the tradition cited in v. 6a is intended to locate the mediating activity of Christ Jesus specifically in his humanity. What Jesus did to execute God's universal will to save he did as a human being, in complete solidarity with the human condition.

In v. 6a Paul's argument concludes with a christological explanation of Christ's act of mediation: "who gave himself as a ransom for all people." The form of the saying found here represents a retelling of the tradition of Jesus' self-giving that in earliest form is found in Mark 10:45.[56] Paul had already adapted this tradition, with various omissions and substitutions, so we cannot be sure how closely he draws on the Marcan logion at this point. Nevertheless, if we start with Mark 10:45 as a base, Paul's adaptations are easily seen:

Mark 10:45 — For even the Son of Man did not come to be served, but to serve, and *to give his life as a ransom for many.*
Gal 1:4 — who gave himself for our sins
Gal 2:20 — who loved me and gave himself for me
Eph 5:2 — and gave himself up for us
1 Tim 2:6 — who gave himself as a ransom for all people
Titus 2:14 — who gave himself for us.

The key elements of the saying in each application are a verb denoting "giving," the reflexive pronoun "himself" that lays emphasis on the voluntary self-offering, a preposition that conveys the effects of his offering to others, a recipient, and an indication of purpose (variously expressed). Paul's usual preference to apply the work of Christ to "us" (Gal 1:4; Eph 5:2; Titus 2:14) is shifted to "all."[57] While this shift might be regarded as a clarification of the Marcan tradition's "many," we should rather think that Paul's widening of the scope from his more typical "us" to "all" is determined by the universal thrust of the passage. His choice of the preposition "for" *(hyper)* instead of

---

56. Cf. the relevant phrases: 1 Tim 2:6a — ὁ δοὺς ἑαυτὸν ἀντίλυτρον ὑπὲρ πάντων; Mark 10:45 — δοῦναι τὴν ψυχὴν αὐτοῦ λύτρον ἀντὶ πολλῶν.
57. Gk. πάντων = "all"; cf. πολλῶν = "many" in Mark 10:45.

Mark's "for" *(anti)* is normal, and his consistent use of the reflexive pronoun "himself" in place of the Semitic "his life" is an improvement in the Greek.[58] Where the saying most resembles the Son of Man logion is in the interpretation of the giving "as a ransom."[59] For this, Paul replaces Mark's *lytron* with the rare compound *antilytron.*[60] This shift may intensify the sense of substitution (already present in Mark 10:45), or render the idea into more suitable Greek; but it expresses the same sense of a ransom payment that secures release (of someone or something).[61]

This portrayal of the act of mediation contains several elements. First, the saying interprets Jesus' death as a voluntary act of self-sacrifice. The common verb "to give" in some contexts expressed the idea of a martyr's death,[62] and came to be used to describe Jesus' death as an act of sacrifice he intentionally undertook.[63] As the statement is constructed here (active substantival participle referring to Jesus; cf. the divine passive in Rom 4:25), it portrays Jesus as the responsible actor. The reflexive pronoun "himself" makes Jesus the object of his own action, reinforcing the idea of selflessness.

Second, the prepositional phrase "for all [people]," perhaps strengthened by the rare form of "ransom," underlines two interrelated elements in the theology of Jesus' self-offering: he died as both a representative and a substitute. The preposition (Titus 2:14) occurs frequently in Paul and

---

58. Gk. ἑαυτόν replaces Mark's τὴν ψυχὴν αὐτοῦ.

59. This is accomplished in Titus 2:14b with the verb λυτρόομαι ("to redeem, set free").

60. Gk. ἀντίλυτρον; the term is rare (see BDAG, s.v., for occurrences; cf. Josephus, *Antiquities* 14.107, for the similar phrase employing the simplex form: λύτρον ἀντὶ πάντων = "ransom for all"). Paul's preference seems to be for ἀπολύτρωσις ("redemption"; Rom 3:24; 8:23; 1 Cor 1:30; Eph 1:7, 14; 4:30; Col 1:14), which views the result of ransoming. See F. Büchsel, *TDNT* 4:340-56, 349; Spicq, *TLNT* 2:423-29 (423 n. 10).

61. The interpretation of the λύτρον word group in Christology has generated a great deal of discussion. For the question of substitution and the meaning of ἀντίλυτρον in 1 Tim 2:6a, see esp. Marshall, 432; Büchsel, *TDNT* 4:349; K. Kertelge, *EDNT* 2:366; D. Hill, *Greek Words and Hebrew Meanings* (Cambridge: Cambridge University Press, 1967), 76-77; L. Morris, *The Apostolic Preaching of the Cross* (32d ed.; London: Tyndale, 1965), 51-52.

62. Gk. δίδωμι; 1 Macc 2:50; 6:44; Thucydides 2.43.2. See F. Büchsel, *TDNT* 2:166.

63. Titus 2:14; Mark 10:45 (Matt 20:28); Luke 22:19; Gal 1:4 (sometimes in the compound form παραδίδωμι; Rom 4:25; 8:32; Gal 2:20; Eph 5:2). See N. Perrin, "The Use of *(para-)didonai* in Connection with the Passion of Jesus in the New Testament," in E. Lohse et al., ed., *Der Ruf Jesu an die Antwort der Gemeinde* (Göttingen: Vandenhoeck & Ruprecht, 1970), 204-12.

184

throughout the NT to describe the effects of Jesus' actions on others.[64] In doing so, the sense of his solidarity with the intended recipient ("all," "us") is implicit; here, following the phrase "the human Christ Jesus," the emphasis is on his solidarity with the human race. Just as important is the fact that in this demonstration of solidarity, Jesus not only represented humankind but also stood in its place as substitute for its benefit.[65] And here the circle that began with universality has run its course through particularity to arrive again at universality: what Jesus has done he has done "for all people."

Christology in this statement finds expression at a very human level. While nothing of the higher elements of Christology is necessarily sacrificed (for all that is implicit remains), the formulation establishes clearly the necessity of Christ's complete participation in humanity in order to accomplish the work of mediation intrinsic to God's universal salvation plan. As stressed elsewhere in Paul (Rom 5:12-21), it is this full participation in the human experience that makes representation and meaningful self-sacrifice possible, and it is as a human being (not as an object of belief) that Jesus is the mediator of salvation to all people.[66] The very nature of Christ's self-offering, as told and retold in the church's growing tradition, verifies the universal scope of God's salvation.

The closing phrase of v. 6 is problematic, as both the modern translations and the ancient variants demonstrate.[67] The problem is caused largely by asyndeton, since (lit.) "the testimony (made, given) at the right time" is simply appended without connectors to indicate the relation to the preceding statement (vv. 5-6a). Without this information to aid us, we must rely on the two components of the phrase and the context to guide us. The way in which v. 7 links to it suggests its transitional function as well as its meaning.

In the NT mission context, the term translated "testimony" (or "witness"; cf. 2 Tim 1:8) denotes either the content of the testimony (equivalent

64. Gk. ὑπέρ; Mark 14:24; Luke 22:19; John 10:11; Rom 5:6, 7(2x), 8; 8:32; 14:15; 1 Cor 11:24; 2 Cor 5:15(3x), 21; Gal 2:20; 3:13; Eph 5:2, 25; Heb 2:9; 1 Pet 2:21; 3:18; etc. See further M. J. Harris, *NIDNTT* 3:1196-97; H. Riesenfeld, *TDNT* 8:507-16; R. E. Davies, "Christ in our Place: the Contribution of the Prepositions," *TynBul* 21 (1970): 71-91.

65. On the combination of representation and substitution contained in ὑπέρ, see esp. Harris, *NIDNTT* 3:1197; N. Turner, *Syntax* (Edinburgh: T&T Clark, 1963 [vol. 4 of J. H. Moulton, ed., *A Grammar of New Testament Greek*]), 258, 271; M. Hengel, *The Atonement* (Philadelphia: Fortress, 1981), 52.

66. Cf. Johnson, 197.

67. The variants represent attempts to improve the situation: ℵ places the connective καί ("and") before "testimony" to make it part of what Christ "gave"; more witnesses (D* F G, etc.) precede the statement with the relative pronoun οὗ ("of which, to which") and the verb ἐδόθη ("it was given") to relate the statement to the preceding and clarify the meaning: "to which testimony was given at the appropriate time."

to the gospel; 1 Cor 1:6) or the act of giving testimony (proclamation; 2 Tim 1:8; Acts 4:33; 2 Thess 1:10).[68] A reference to the time of this testimony is given in the dative phrase "in its/his own time."[69] In each of its occurrences in 1 Timothy and Titus, the plural Greek term behind this translation should be understood as a singular period of time. The attached adjective identifies the time as that which is appropriate in God's plans (cf. "now" in 2 Tim 1:9-10).[70] Together, then, the two elements in the statement refer to God's time for making known the testimony.

The reference is still vague. But the way in which Paul moves from this statement to a rehearsal of his appointment "for this testimony" (v. 7) suggests the probable solution. As in Titus 1:1-3, where Paul equates his apostolate with the manifestation of God's word "at the right time," so here the statement "the testimony given at the right time" refers to Paul's apostolate called into being by God "at the right eschatological time" to bear witness to the event described in vv. 5-6a.[71] "Testimony" is a suitable term for the apostolic mission (2 Tim 1:8; Acts 4:33; 2 Thess 1:10), and the Pauline mission (prayer for it) underlies the whole passage.

7 The closing statement of this passage brings the whole of the prayer instructions and backing theology into the sphere of Paul's apostolic calling. It has a polemical ring to it, especially in its insistence that Paul is telling the truth. This is not accidental, nor is it done just to lend authority to the teaching. As in the case of 1:11-16 (Titus 1:1-3; cf. 2 Tim 1:11-14), Paul's explicit linking of his apostolate with the traditional gospel is calculated to substantiate and reinforce his own claim to be the authoritative apostle to the Gentiles. The would-be teachers of the law already encoun-

---

68. Gk. μαρτύριον; see L. Coenen and A. A. Trites, "Witness, Testimony," n.p., *NIDNTT on CD-ROM*. Version 2.7. 1999; Spicq, *TLNT* 2:447-52, esp. 450; H. Strathmann, *TDNT* 4:502-4.

69. Gk. καιροῖς ἰδίοις; 1 Tim 2:6 and 6:15; cf. 1 Tim 4:1; 2 Tim 3:1; 4:3; "at his appointed season"; NIV.

70. The term καιρός cannot be distinguished rigidly from χρόνος; each can conceive of time as a point or a period, and Barr, *Biblical Words for Time,* has shown that καιρός is not to be understood in terms of "opportunity" or specifically as God's decisive time. The adjective ἴδιος, in these contexts, refers to God (and not to καιρός or λόγος, which might yield the impersonal idea of "its own time, the proper time"; Marshall, 129; Johnson, 124; Towner, *Goal,* 61); in this relationship it defines the "time" of action as uniquely God's appointed time (cf. Spicq, *TLNT* 2:205-11; H.-W. Bartsch, *EDNT* 2:171-72).

71. So TNIV; NRSV; see Marshall, 433; Johnson, 192-93; J. Beutler, *EDNT* 2:393. The alternative is to understand Christ's self-giving as God's own testimony to the world (NIV; GNB; REB; Dibelius and Conzelmann, 43; Arichea and Hatton, 50-51; G. Delling, *TDNT* 3:461), but this thought sits less naturally in the context, especially in view of 2:7.

tered in 1:3-8 had apparently challenged his position or his understanding of the gospel (which amounts to the same thing). In this passage, the instructions to pray for all people (and for government rulers) and possibly the view of God's will and supporting theology he endorses here (stressing the humanity of Christ) were corrective in thrust. Paul calls for prayer for all people, and it only makes sense to see this within the context of Paul's own mission to all people. The problem of a narrow prayer outlook was not an isolated matter, but rather part of the wide-ranging effect of the law-centered opposition's penetration into a Pauline church that undermined the apostle's authority. Consequently, in 2:7 Paul attempts again to convince the church of the divine origin of his mission and gospel as the authoritative guide for faith and practice.

First, Paul establishes his authoritative link to the gospel for the Gentiles (i.e., 2:5-6a). With the same phrase that he uses in 2 Tim 1:11,[72] and the same verb of appointment as in 1 Tim 1:12 (1 Cor 12:28; 2 Cor 5:19), he underscores the fact that his appointment to ministry was God's choice.[73]

Second, Paul defines the scope of his commission with three nouns that also occur in 2 Tim 2:11: herald, apostle, teacher.[74] The first of these terms, "herald," picks up language that Paul often used of the act and message of proclamation.[75] However, the noun "herald" is infrequent in the NT (2 Tim 1:11; 2 Pet 2:5), owing perhaps to strong religious associations with the secular herald, but the sense of one who proclaims the message is clear.[76]

"Apostle," Paul's usual term of self-description (see 1:1), comes second in the list. With it he distinguishes his position on the basis of the divine origin of his ministry and appointment. Its placement after "herald" suggests

72. Gk. εἰς ὃ ἐτέθην; see 1:12. Cf. Eph 3:7; 1 Tim 1:11 for similar expressions.

73. The first-person pronoun ἐγώ is emphatic, and the passive voice of the verb implies divine agency.

74. Gk. κῆρυξ καὶ ἀπόστολος . . . διδάσκαλος; cf. 2 Tim 1:11: κῆρυξ καὶ ἀπόστολος καὶ διδάσκαλος.

75. For Gk. κηρύσσω ("preach"), see 1 Cor 9:27; Gal 2:2; 2 Tim 4:2; for the noun κήρυγμα, see Rom 16:25; 1 Cor 11:21; 15:14.

76. Gk. κῆρυξ. In the Greek world, the term "herald" described a variety of messengers whose task was to proclaim a message. In service of the royal court, heralds carried out diplomatic missions under the protection of the country they represented and the deity. Political and religious functions overlapped; they pronounced at the time of sacrifices and other cultic activities. Qualities needed by the herald included a loud voice and faithfulness to the message to be communicated. Philosophers could be called heralds of the gods (for refs. and further discussion, G. Friedrich, *TDNT* 3:683-96; J. Roloff, *Apostolat–Verkündigung–Kirche* [Gütersloh: Mohn, 1965], 240-44; 251-52; idem, 124 nn. 79, 80; Spicq, 368-69; Mounce, 92; Dibelius and Conzelmann, 43 nn. 54, 55). Roloff, 124, points out that it is equivalent to "evangelist" (2 Tim 4:5; see also Marshall, 434; Mounce, 92).

that proclamation is uppermost in Paul's mind, which is in keeping with the missiological interest of the entire passage.[77]

Between the second and third nouns, Paul inserts the emphatic affirmation of truthfulness: "I am telling the truth, I am not lying." The statement bears a close resemblance to Rom 9:1.[78] These statements, along with shorter forms of the truth claim (2 Cor 12:6) and the denial of lying (2 Cor 11:31; Gal 1:20), occur in contexts where Paul's claim to be the apostle to the Gentiles, or to authority, was being challenged. The emphasis on truthfulness may apply to the whole statement, or specifically to the preceding claim to be an apostle. But its placement just before the final, more elaborate description, alongside the concern of the whole passage for the universal mission, suggests that the affirmation underlines the certainty of his specific responsibility to the Gentiles.[79]

The term "teacher" fills out the job description of the "apostle." The task of teaching was integral to the Pauline ministry and churches, and was carried out both by him and by others (3:2; 5:17; 2 Tim 4:2).[80] The difference between teaching and preaching (cf. 5:17) was probably more a matter of audience or purpose than of the content communicated or the degree of authority invested in the communicator or message.[81] Paul was known as the apostle of the Gentiles (Rom 11:13; Gal 2:7-8; cf. Acts 13:47), and in this context in which "the teaching" was in dispute and being compromised through the activity of false teachers, and in which the openness of the gospel to the Gentile world was in some sense being threatened, the description "teacher of the Gentiles" reminds the readers that Paul is the one who has received authority to preach and teach in the Gentile churches. This information was not needed by Timothy;[82] but bearing in mind the public dimension of the letter commending the coworker to the Ephesian church, we should almost expect Paul

77. Marshall, 434.

78. Gk. ἀλήθειαν λέγω, οὐ ψεύδομαι; cf. Rom 9:1: ἀλήθειαν λέγω ἐν Χριστῷ, οὐ ψεύδομαι. The view that this represents a later author's attempt to re-create "Paul" for a later church (Roloff, 112; Trummer, *Paulustradition*, 120-23; Hanson, 70) depends solely on a late dating of this letter.

79. Marshall, 434; Fee, 67; Guthrie, 83; Roloff, 112.

80. Gk. διδάσκαλος; for Paul as a teacher, see 1 Cor 4:17; Col 1:28; for others in this role, see Rom 12:7; Col 3:16; for the place of teaching in Pauline churches, see 1 Cor 12:28-29; Eph 4:11, 21; Col 2:7; 2 Thess 2:15. See also K. H. Rengstorf, *TDNT* 2:157-58.

81. J. H. McDonald, *Kerygma and Didache: The Articulation and Structure of the Earliest Christian Message* (Cambridge: Cambridge University Press, 1980), 5, 135 n. 28; K. H. Rengstorf, *TDNT* 2:162; K. Wegenast, *NIDNTT* 3:771; Towner, *Goal*, 123.

82. Although Paul is identifying the unique nature of his authority in the Gentile mission, it is not necessarily the sort of "canonizing" that some attribute to a late "Paulinist" (but see Roloff, 124; Wolter, *Paulustradition*, 77-78).

as that church's founding apostle to underscore his authority in all matters — an authority that extends to his delegate, Timothy.

Due to the range of meaning covered by the "faith" word group in these three letters (see 1:2, note), the prepositional phrase that completes the description ("in faith and truth") is potentially ambiguous. Some translations regard it as a comment on the content of Paul's teaching (in the sphere of faith and truth; "a teacher of the true faith to the Gentiles"; NIV).[83] Others see it as a comment on Paul's adherence to the message given to him by God: "faithfully and truthfully" ("a true and faithful teacher of the Gentiles"; TNIV).[84] The reference to "truth" or "truthfulness" resonates both with the polemical description of the apostolic gospel as "the truth" in 2:4 (see note) and Paul's insistence that he is telling the truth in 2:7b. Generally, in these letters the "in faith" construction focuses on a life that reflects faith in action ("faithfulness"; see 1:2, note), and it is probably that sense that is meant here. By claiming to discharge his mission to the Gentiles "faithfully and truthfully," Paul aligns himself with the OT prophets, who bore these same marks as proof of their divine calling.[85] The polemical distinction Paul draws between his calling/message/character and that of the false teachers has ultimately to do with their distance from God and his proximity.

Paul has come full circle in this section. The allusion to his apostolate given in the instructions to pray for "all people" is now made clear in his claim to be the authoritative and faithful apostle to the non-Jewish portion of the "all." However important this dimension of prayer was for the early church, and is for us today, the instructions were not isolated from his more immediate concern for his own standing in Ephesus. The parochial tendencies of that church were related to the false teaching that Paul saw as an immediate challenge to his authority and his gospel. Using the importance of prayer as a foil, he set out a theological and christological argument that substantiated the universal scope of God's redemptive concern. Simultaneously, he also demonstrated that it is his own calling that embodies the gospel message and is accomplishing this universal will of God. The church was to revive its support for his worldwide mission (vv. 1-2): his mission (in contrast to the opponents' teaching) represents and delivers God's saving "truth" (vv. 3-6) and he bears the marks of God's chosen apostle (v. 7).

Our place in the continuation of this ministry to the entire world should be obvious. Quite apart from our need to wake up to our own tendencies to insulate ourselves from the outside world, a rather elite club of the initiated, we must set our prayers for government officials in relation to the task

---

83. See also Fee, 67; Lock, 29.
84. Hanson, 70.
85. On this see Wolter, *Paulustradition,* 70-82; Marshall, 435.

of mission. Just as Paul regarded his mission as the key to accomplishing God's salvation plan, so too we must see the embodiment of the gospel in our preaching and involvement in the world around us as a requirement of Christian existence.

3. The Behavior of Men and Women in the Public Worship Assembly (2:8-15)

At 2:8 Paul resumes the theme of prayer initiated at 2:1. What is most noticeable about the treatment of this passage in the commentaries is the emphasis placed on vv. 11-15, which address the issue of women teaching in the assembly. These verses have been overused in the modern church by some who have sought to demonstrate a return by one of Paul's students to a patriarchal system inimical to the Pauline gospel, and by others to prove the unsuitability of women for the role of teaching in the church. But this span of text is not an addendum treating a separate topic; it occurs within the textual frame indicated by repetition of the key ethical term "propriety" in vv. 9 and 15 (sōphrosynē) and within the cultural frame of the expectations governing the behavior of women in public. Understanding the cultural frame seems even more crucial in light of recent work on the paradigm of the "new woman" that emerged in the Roman Empire in this era (see below). For now it need simply be said that ancient criticism of this movement drew attention to the same sort of dress code and behavior code breaches that Paul addresses here. If this forms part of the background to Paul's instructions concerning women, then prevailing interpretations need to be reappraised.

Several introductory issues should be briefly aired in preparation for treating the text itself.

The "Public" Dimension of the Instruction

From 2:1 onward Paul has been preoccupied with activities and behavior within the worship assembly. But this observation is somewhat more significant for the present discussion. Recent assessments of epigraphic and literary evidence have documented the emergence of a "new Roman woman." She exercised freedoms and opportunities for participation in public life (political and legal activity, patron and benefactor roles) that far exceeded those of the traditional Greek woman, who has long been the model drawn on by NT scholars. Moreover, the ancient evaluation of her patterns of dress and behavior locate her within something of an ancient "sexual revolution."[1] We will consider the negative effects of this trend below. For the moment, it is its im-

---

1. Winter, *Roman Wives*, 1-74, 173-211.

pact on the public life of women that concerns us, and by extrapolating from the ancient commentary on wealthy women the potential developments affecting Christian wealthy women can be reconstructed.

As B. Winter points out: "Christian women . . . operate[d] in a grey area, for the church met in the main reception room of homes, which was its public area. However, it is clear that women were not relegated to the private rooms in the house in the first century, any more than their secular sisters were. . . . Limited though the evidence may be for Christian women, the filtering down of the new roles for women enabled Christian women to contribute to a wider sphere of service."[2]

Christian worship, carried out in the reception room or atrium of a house, was essentially a "public" activity. As C. Osiek and D. L. Balch explain, the reception area of the atrium-house, which was one of the important settings for Pauline churches, was open to everyone: "everyone has the right to enter a vestibule, atrium, and peristyle, reserving as private space for the family only bedrooms, dining rooms, and baths!"[3] However this open access to the public might strike modern Western sensibilities, Paul apparently could envision the scenario of "unbelievers coming into" a worship meeting, perhaps uninvited (1 Cor 14:23). The point is this: the activities that combined to form a Christian worship meeting were essentially, therefore, public, and it is precisely the public nature of the activities addressed in 2:8-15 and the reactions of observing outsiders that concerned Paul.

What needs to be decided, as far as possible, is what behavior specifically was under assessment. And the greater challenge comes in the matter of women teaching (2:11-12): was the issue the very principle of women teaching men, or was it rather some variation of women teaching men in such a way that they showed disrespect to husbands/men or association with a questionable movement (see below), or both? We will argue the latter line below, but the public nature of the assembly and the potential damage to the church's reputation form a critical frame of reference for understanding this passage. But that frame needs further definition.

---

2. Winter, *Roman Wives,* 204. Winter considers Phoebe and Junia (Rom 16:1, 7) and suggests that they reflect Christian women whose area of operation corresponded generally with the wider range open to influential Roman women. While the evidence stops short of filling in all the details of status and activity that would remove any lingering doubts, it can nevertheless be reasonably surmised that wealthy Christian women in Ephesus too, by virtue of these cultural shifts (and legislative responses to them), had greater presence in the public sphere.

3. C. Osiek and, D. L. Balch, *Families in the New Testament World: Households and House Churches* (Louisville: Westminster/John Knox, 1997), 17 (see 5-35); they cite Vitruvius, *De architectura* 6.5.1.

The Form of the Teaching

The interest in a social pair (husbands/wives; men/women), the standard language (of submission; see the transitional adverb "likewise" ["also," TNIV]; Titus 2:3, 6; cf. 1 Pet 3:1), and the focus on conventional respectable ethics locate this passage within the household code tradition.[4] Throughout the NT this style of teaching (Ephesians; Colossians; 1 Peter), adapted from the culture's reflection on household ethics, and related applications (Rom 13:1-7; 1 Cor 14:33-35; Titus 2:1-10; see discussion), typically resorted to the conventional role configurations of the household (superior and subordinate roles) to settle or prevent disturbances. The language of submission and obedience figures prominently in these discussions, though in NT use of the tradition, parallel secular values were tempered in the direction of justice and fairness in the case of the subordinate. Equally apparent within this sort of parenesis is the emphasis on sexually prudent behavior and dress of wives/women (Titus 2:4-5; 1 Cor 11:5-10; 1 Pet 3:2-4).

While in certain cases such teaching may simply have been standard fare, in others it may have been applied where churches were caught up in movements of Spirit enthusiasm. In descriptions of Corinth and Ephesus, which were closely linked in Paul's ministry, flutters of emancipation can sometimes be detected behind the apostle's discourse. Spirit enthusiasm in Corinth, accompanied by an overrealized sense of salvation (1 Cor 4:8) and inattentiveness to ethics, may have carried over to Ephesus. By the time we reach 2 Timothy, a full-blown overrealized eschatology has emerged (2:18). The degree to which all of this can be linked to a popular interpretation of Paul's equality principle (1 Cor 12:13; Gal 3:28; Col 3:11) is uncertain; but the widespread and traditional nature of that gospel policy cannot be denied,[5] which makes a misunderstanding of it on the part of enthusiasts of various sorts a primary suspect in explaining elements of disruption in Paul's churches and his response.[6]

Recognition of the traditional shape in which the teaching is given — the household code — suggests two directions of Paul's thinking. First, the household codes enjoined a pattern of behavior that sought a respectable showing in and interaction with society. They do not reflect a wholesale adoption of a secular ethic, but rather a Christian adjustment (in terms of motive and goal and supporting theology) that nevertheless aims at producing

---

4. See P. H. Towner, *DPL*, 417-19; D. L. Balch, *ABD* 3:318-20; Marshall, 231-36.

5. See B. Witherington, *The Paul Quest* (Downers Grove, IL: InterVarsity Press, 1998), 218-29.

6. P. H. Towner, "Gnosis and Realized Eschatology in Ephesus (of the Pastoral Epistles) and the Corinthian Enthusiasm," *JSNT* 31 (1987): 95-124; Schlarb, *Die gesunde Lehre*, 93-131; Johnson, 144-45.

and maintaining a respectable public image. Second, this outward sensitivity to secular observation and expectations suggests that concern for the outsider's opinion of church behavior is a crucial motivation in the instruction. However much this passage seems designed to settle a community disturbance, it is ultimately the missionary necessity of maintaining dialogue with culture that drives Paul to seek a reasonable solution in the case of the behavior of men and women.

Pauline Tradition?

Attempts to locate the teaching of this passage within Pauline tradition typically limit the discussion to 2:11-15 and comparison with 1 Cor 14:33-35:

> 2:11 A woman should learn in quietness and full submission. 12 I do not permit a woman to teach or to have authority over a man; she must be quiet.

> 14:34 Women should remain silent in the churches. They are not allowed to speak, but must be in submission, as the law says. 35 If they want to inquire about something, they should ask their own husbands at home; for it is disgraceful for a woman to speak in the church.

Some connection seems evident: (1) silence/quietness (14:34; 2:11, 12) is stressed in each case; (2) central to each text is a prohibition of speaking/ teaching (14:34, 35; 2:12); (3) the correct demeanor is described in each case with the language of submission (14:34; 2:11); and (4) the verb "to inquire" sets out the approved activity with some variation in application (14:35; 2:11).

Three main suggestions prevail. First, some regard 1 Cor 14:34 as the earlier basis for 1 Tim 2:11-12.[7] Slight differences, as the texts are compared, might suggest that the earlier general statement is more narrowly interpreted in the later setting. Of course this interpretation is often influenced by assumptions about the authorship of 1 Timothy and the dating and sequence of the letters; differences in the expression of the teaching could as easily owe to differences in the situations addressed.

Second, most recently Fee revived the view that the text in 1 Corinthians 14 is an interpolation based on 1 Tim 2:11-12,[8] which effectively reverses

---

7. Trummer, *Paulustradition,* 144-51; cf. Roloff, 128; U. Wagener, *Die Ordnung "Hauses Gottes": Der Ort von Frauen in den Ekklesiologie und Ethik der Pastoralbriefe* (Tübingen: J. C. B. Mohr [Siebeck], 1994), 103-4; B. Witherington, *Women in the Earliest Churches* (Cambridge: Cambridge University Press, 1988), 90-104.

8. Fee, *God's Empowering Presence,* 272-81; Oberlinner, 93-94.

the direction of literary dependence. Behind this is the textual question: some early Western witnesses (including D F G) placed vv. 34-35 after v. 40, suggesting uncertainty about the originality of the text as preserved by ℵ A B (et al.) and the possibility that it crept in as a late expansion. Against this explanation is the fact that no manuscripts are known to have omitted the text.[9]

Third, Ellis argues that a direct literary relationship between the two texts is less likely than a common tradition upon which each drew.[10] If a tradition of instruction dealing with social relationships (e.g., the NT household code tradition, but tradition could well have been mainly oral) did in fact exist and had circulated, such a catechetical tradition might account both for the similarity of shape and the variation of the two texts.

The last suggestion may have more in its favor than the first two. But if 1 Corinthians and 1 Timothy are both Pauline, and given the close relationship between Corinth and Ephesus, it is not really necessary to posit anything more than that in two different situations involving the public speaking of women Paul took a similar tack in restricting women from engaging in a public behavior that had reached a level of abuse and was causing disruption (see further below). What we cannot tell without further probing (and some speculation) is whether this measure ran counter to another Pauline pattern, evident in some places, of allowing women greater freedom in participating in speaking ministries. In any case, in both Corinth and Ephesus the measure taken apparently sought to resolve or avert a disturbance.

A Complex Background

Reconstructing the social and historical backgrounds of occasional letters (among other types of ancient written documents) is admittedly a procedure that often has to be carried out with less information than we could wish to have. It requires reading between the lines, or guessing what lay in the shadows of Paul's comments, provoking them, and determining their meaning and significance. Internal clues are an obvious starting place. But for Paul's letters the social and cultural realities that determined the shape of life and values of the Christian communities often come best to light through secular sources. Yet which are relevant, and how can we be sure? Piecing together the situations that gave rise to a letter of Paul is artwork, or perhaps something more on the order of art restoration, where the restorer must access ev-

---

9. C. Niccum, "The Voice of the Manuscripts on the Silence of Women: The External Evidence for 1 Cor 14:24-25," *NTS* 43 (1997): 242-55.

10. E. E. Ellis, "The Silenced Wives of Corinth (1 Cor 14.34-35)," in E. J. Epp and G. D. Fee, *New Testament Textual Criticism: Its Significance for Exegesis* (Oxford: Oxford University Press, 1981), 214-15.

ery useful bit of information to fill in the gaps and retrieve a reasonable facsimile of the original. Without the original as a basis for comparison, any copy or reconstruction will always bear a "provisional" rating, and plausibility remains open in certain respects. But I would argue that even if certain questions must remain open and reconstructions can only be provisional, the sort of documents left to us by Paul cannot be read usefully apart from some attempt to piece together the social and historical situation that gave rise to them in the first place.

In the case of the Ephesian situation that frames 1 Timothy 2, numerous attempts at reconstruction have been made. And S. M. Baugh has recently debunked one of the more popular scenarios that posited a uniquely Ephesian feminist movement, grounded in a feminist principle, surrounding the Ephesian Artemis cult, and giving rise to a local movement that 1 Timothy 2 was custom-designed to address. Rather, Baugh maintains, since what can be discerned of Ephesian culture and women at this time was "typical" of Hellenistic culture, the teaching of 1 Timothy 2 may also be regarded as standard Pauline fare. The local situation gives up no significant clues from which to argue that Paul was addressing a unique problem in a unique way.[11] This is tantamount to saying that the passage has no discernible *Sitz im Leben,* or at least that he has discovered nothing in the course of his thorough investigation to justify the claim that local factors give the teaching to women any unique coloration. On this understanding the interpreter must proceed without the aid of any but the broadest of backgrounds to guide. It need only be said in response that such a conclusion holds only for the extreme feminist background he has debunked. But to think that other local or, indeed, culture-wide elements cannot have placed these wealthy Ephesian women into a unique situation that Paul addressed in a unique way exceeds the scope of his findings. Uncertainty about the social context of a text such as this, or negative findings when one particular (idiosyncratic) reconstruction has been investigated as in the case of Baugh, is not an invitation to give up the search but rather an incentive to renew efforts.[12]

But the possibility that the social situation that gave rise to a letter like 1 Timothy contains more complexities than we can completely unravel must be faced. And what is possible and likely for the message of a letter as a whole is not necessarily less so for any particular passage, even if we could hope that a shorter span of text was likely to address a more discrete topic. In both Corinth and Ephesus there was more at stake, and indeed more on Paul's mind,

---

11. S. M. Baugh, "A Foreign World: Ephesus in the First Century," in A. J. Köstenberger et al., eds., *Women in the Church: A Fresh Analysis of 1 Timothy 2:9-15* (Grand Rapids: Baker, 1995), 13-52.

12. See Winter, *Roman Wives,* 98.

than the public speaking in which some women were engaged. As mentioned, Winter has assembled the evidence pointing to the emergence in the Roman Empire of the first century of a "new" kind of woman.[13] This innovative paradigm expressed itself in an extremely negative stereotype constructed of various kinds of generally prohibited behavior. Some women of means and position (married and widowed), supported in some cases by free-thinking males, flouted traditional values governing adornment and dress and sexual propriety. The emergence of this movement was so disturbing to the status quo that Augustus issued legislation against it. Associated with the new paradigm was behavior that gave it the look of an ancient sexual revolution, with wealthy women displaying themselves in permissive clothing and hairstyles and seeking the sexual freedoms normally reserved for men. The Roman Imperial woman had greater access to the public sphere of life (in contrast to that of women under Greek conventions), increased presence in certain public speaking situations, and occasional roles in the legal setting and in commerce. And this mobility made the presence and impact of the "revolution" impossible to ignore. The practice of contraception and abortion by the new women, although condemned by numerous writers and an offense against the traditional value placed on the household/family, became increasingly widespread because of this new woman's desire to pursue the free life unencumbered.

Given the existence of the "new woman" in Roman society, it is not surprising that Christian women would also be drawn to the movement.[14] Perhaps the most notable symbol of the movement was outer adornment and apparel, and that of the new woman transgressed the traditional dress code of respectability. Winter plausibly maintains that this was precisely the issue in 1 Corinthians 11. New women/wives removed the veil — the symbol of the faithful Roman wife — and appeared in public (especially in what would be regarded as a religious ceremony), endangering the church's reputation in the process.

1 Tim 2:9-10 (v. 15) also belongs to this stream of teaching (cf. 5:11-15; Titus 2). This text addresses a group of wealthy women (probably wives for the most part) for whom respectability and regard for an approved dress code (apparel, hairstyles, jewelry, respectable demeanor) were apparently not high on the agenda. If Winter is correct to bring this development to bear on a reconstruction of the church situation, then Paul was faced with cultural development influencing the behavior of well-to-do Christian women in worship that posed a risk to the church's public image.

The public dimension of the behavior addressed has already been mentioned. But as a concern that complicates the situation, its significance must

---

13. Winter, *Roman Wives.*

14. See B. W. Winter, *After Paul Left Corinth: The Influence of Secular Ethics and Social Change* (Grand Rapids: Eerdmans, 2001), 153-57.

be reemphasized. Wealthy women in the empire were finding greater scope for public movement. And the participation of "connected" women in the life of the city *(politeia)* signaled a relaxing of conventions and some innovation in the activities of women. Their activities and conduct in that sphere were often noted in the sources. Dress codes pertained to the public sphere. Following the general enlargement of the woman's public sphere, Christian women had full access to the church meeting, and perhaps, for the wealthy and influential (anyway), an increasing scope of public activities. Therefore, the dress and activities of Christian women gathered for worship in the larger reception rooms became a matter of public observation and propriety. But an enlarged public profile would expose them to the same secular critical eye that looked with suspicion and disdain on the antitraditional new woman. Paul would not want Christian women to be typed as "new" women since that would bring the church's witness and mission into jeopardy. In Paul's churches Spirit-gifting undoubtedly forced some innovation in the public roles of women. But inappropriate behavior (rude or disrespectful use of a teaching position) that could be linked with the dangerous image of the new woman would necessitate temporarily curtailing these activities, and extreme abuses would not unreasonably call forth teaching in the form of prohibitions.

The effect of Winter's research is to place the activity of teaching in this passage within the more dominant framework of Paul's response to a group of well-to-do Christian wives/women flirting with the image of the new woman. But there is one more element of background that further complicates the picture.

The Presence and Shape of the Heresy

Although it is widely agreed that the existence of a heretical opposition in Ephesus determines much of the shape of the letter, it is impossible to say how much influence the false teaching had at every point. It is in fact not clear how far we can speak with assurance about a solidified heretical front within the church (or on its fringes), though, in comparison with the Cretan situation (see Introduction, 41-49), Paul seems to attribute to the opposition in Ephesus a greater degree of coherence and definition.

Several scholars have noticed similarities between the sorts of problems addressed in 1 Corinthians and in 1 Timothy and suggested, as a lowest common denominator, that an overly enthusiastic eschatology might underlay each development. While an "elitist" interpretation can be seen to be at work in each case, in 1 Timothy Paul addresses this in terms of heresy (1:3). Here the apparent absence or downplaying of eschatological enthusiasm should be noted (see the discussion at 6:20-21a), but emancipatory tendencies (women, young widows, slaves) that parallel the Corinthian situation are in evidence; in 2 Tim 2:18, however, what might have been a nascent over-realized view of the resurrection of believers in the purview of the first letter is now in full bloom.[15] In any case, Paul's treatment of socioethical developments in each context shows enough similarity to suggest linkage with a prevalent alternative theology. And in 1 Timothy Paul has named names in a way that distinguishes the challenge as a heretical movement.

Can it be proved that the women addressed in 2:9-15 were actually teaching the heresy? Probably not. But the very real presence of the heresy, its almost certain effect on the institution of marriage (4:3) and the value of childbearing, its misreading of OT stories,[16] coupled with the attraction for some wealthy women and young widows of the "new woman" paradigm, point in the direction of a background in which the influence of both the heresy and of this new woman movement combined in some mixture to affect the wealthy women addressed in this text (see further below). An additional reason to suspect some connection between the opponents and wealthy women can be surmised from the reference to greed on the part of the false teachers (6:5-10), who would stand to profit from ingratiating themselves in various ways to influential wealthy women in the church.

Mission

The presence of an overarching "mission" theme provides yet another element of the frame surrounding the whole of 1 Timothy 2. This emerged first in the emphasis on the universality of salvation constructed in 2:1-7. It carries over into the present passage by virtue of the resumption of instruction about prayer in 2:8 (presumably the same prayer mentioned in 2:1 is in mind). But the theme is refreshed, deepened, and explored from the perspective of the observing and responding non-Christian ("Gentile") world by means of an intentional echoing of the OT in 2:8 (see below). Consequently, the elements of witness — that is, of the outsider's response to the present behavior under consideration — and of Christian public image are to the fore in Paul's instructions to men and women.

The Interpretive Landscape

Interpretive approaches to this passage can be divided into three basic categories. First, the traditional hierarchalist position[17] concludes that women are

---

15. See Towner, "Gnosis and Realized Eschatology in Ephesus."

16. Among which may well be the early chapters of Genesis; see above on 1:4; see below on 2:13-15a; 4:1-5.

17. The preference of proponents today to describe their position as "complemen-

prohibited from teaching men because of the implications of divine creation. Key to this interpretation is the use of Genesis material to ground the instruction. And this also determines the universal applicability of the teaching in the entire church throughout the generations.[18]

Second is the interpretation associated with the feminist reconstruction of the early church, within which this and similar texts are held to be deficient in authority because they interfere with the actualization of human liberation. In this case, 1 Timothy 2 (along with texts diminishing the rights of women in Ephesians, Colossians, and even in the undisputed Pauline letters) reflects a return to a patriarchal social structure that stands in defiance of the earlier Pauline gospel goal/ideal of equality (Gal 3:28). While admitting that the alleged move might well have been made out of concern for the criticism of outsiders and its effect on the church's well-being or on the mission, proponents nonetheless regard the whole development as retrograde and devoid of the original gospel inspiration. On such a reading, the teaching of the text cannot be resuscitated, but must rather be jettisoned in order to get back on the earlier track.[19]

Third, a broader group of scholars regard certain Pauline statements about the equality of women and men and indications of fuller involvement of women in ministry as a fundamental hermeneutical starting point for treating this passage. Within this group there exists a spectrum of views, some of which attempt to limit either the prohibition, or the activity prohibited, or the scope of the grounding rationale in the effort to salvage the passage's instruction, and even to allow that Paul permitted women to teach in Ephesus if they did not teach the heresy. Others limit the effect of the text (its normativity) to the situation, but see the trajectory of NT teaching about women and ministry as moving in the direction of equality. This trajectory makes the present treatment by Paul either an exception to his own equality rule forced upon him by

---

tarian" is noted; but the heart of this view (however such language hopes to soften the blow) is hierarchy.

18. See esp. A. Köstenberger et al., eds., *Women in the Church: A Fresh Analysis of 1 Timothy 2:9-15;* Mounce; Knight. For a historical survey of the interpretation of the passage, see D. Doriani, "Appendix I: History of the Interpretation of 1 Timothy 2," in Köstenberger, *Women in the Church,* 213-67. For a thorough bibliography of literature treating this passage, see Marshall, 436-37; Mounce, 94-102; T. R. Schreiner, "An Interpretation of 1 Timothy 2:9-15: A Dialogue with Scholarship," in Köstenberger, ed., *Women in the Church,* 105-54; W. J. Webb, *Slaves, Women and Homosexuals: Exploring the Hermeneutics of Cultural Analysis* (Downers Grove, IL: InterVarsity Press, 2001), 281-86.

19. Most recently, Wagener, *Die Ordnung "Hauses Gottes"*; Bassler; E. S. Fiorenza, *In Memory of Her: A Feminist Theological Reconstruction of Christian Origins* (New York: Crossroad, 1983), 260-66, 285-342; see the assessment in P. H. Towner, "Feminist Approaches to the New Testament," *Jian Dao* 7 (1997): 91-111.

circumstances, or a historical snapshot of a place that Paul never rose above in spite of the implications of his gospel for equality, but that in any case the movements of cultures and passage of time have now rendered obsolete.[20]

Within this framework, the line I will argue shares most with the third group. In my opinion, what most invites strenuous efforts in reconstructing the background to the situation is the evidence elsewhere that women did have an increasingly public role to play in Paul's churches and, indeed, the presence of what I regard to be a fundamental equality principle within the Pauline gospel. As difficult and frustrating as it is, the *Sitz im Leben* of the text must be probed, and the elements assembled and reassembled, in the effort to place the text in a Pauline mission trajectory.

The local situation, however, will be assessed differently. First, Paul's concern will be viewed within the context of what constituted public respectability. The influences of the heresy and the emerging redefinition of women and women's roles in public (the new woman) will be seen to intertwine to vex Paul and elicit from him a response that seeks to safeguard the church's reputation. Second, the issue of women teaching men will be considered within the broader framework of respectability, not as a separate or isolated, or even as the central issue of the parenesis. Third, the Genesis material given in some way in support of the prohibition will be considered as a correction of a heretical use of the same kinds of scriptural material by the heretics (or by women themselves).

In the end, Paul prohibits a group of wealthy women from teaching men. The factors leading to this prohibition include: (1) public presentation — outer adornment and apparel and arrogant demeanor give their teaching a shameful and disrespectful coloration; (2) association with false teaching — they may actually have been conveying or supporting heretical teaching. Their actions may have copied a secular trend, and false teachers may have actively or passively encouraged them. Moreover, because this behavior is public and contrary to what was still the traditional status quo, Paul moved to stop the behavior to protect the church's witness. It might be said (though this must be drawn from the implications of Paul's letters and his gospel elsewhere) that under different circumstances the experiment of women, according to giftedness, taking on more and more roles within the church could have continued were it not for the combined detrimental effects of the heresy and the emerging controversial trend among wealthy women.

8 *Therefore I want the men everywhere to pray, lifting up holy hands without anger or disputing.* 9 *I also want the women to dress modestly, with decency and propriety, adorning themselves, not with*

20. For the latter, see esp. Johnson, 208-11.

elaborate hairstyles or gold or pearls or expensive clothes, 10 but with good deeds, appropriate for women who profess to worship God.

11 A woman should learn in quietness and full submission. 12 I do not permit a woman to teach or to assume authority over a man; she must be quiet. 13 For Adam was formed first, then Eve. 14 And Adam was not the one deceived; it was the woman who was deceived and became a sinner. 15 But women will be saved through childbearing — if they continue in faith, love and holiness with propriety.

8   At this point, Paul engages the congregation according to gender groups. In this adaptation of a household code, he takes the men first and speaks to them authoritatively,[21] enlarging on the instruction about community prayer[22] initiated at 2:1. There are several issues to be addressed. First, in Greek the term "men" is ambiguous and could mean "husbands" or "men." Typically either a standard modifying possessive pronoun or similar device will clearly indicate "husband" (e.g., 3:2, 12; 5:9; Titus 1:6; 2:5; Eph 5:22; 1 Pet 3:1), or something else in the context will specify the meaning. The absence of such a signal might support the more generic reference,[23] but the context nonetheless suggests that the husband/wife relationship is largely in view (especially when discussion of the women is considered; see below). On the one hand, the norm for men and women was marriage, and this is the assumption in reference to women and childbearing in v. 15. On the other hand, the language and content of the proscribed "sumptuousness" of wealthy women in 2:9-10 have in mind mainly a trend among wealthy married women (and widows; see on 5:6, 11-15) to adopt a new liberated lifestyle of dress and sexual promiscuity (see below). If this is the case, the generic categories of "men" and "women" are almost certainly intended to express more precision.

Second, Paul is specifically concerned about the holiness and demeanor of men when they pray. This is set out in positive terms first by refer-

---

21. Gk. βούλομαι ("I desire, wish"; 5:14; Titus 3:8) is used in these letters to co-workers only of the apostle's commands and gives them a binding force; Lips, *Glaube* 86 n. 208; G. Schrenk, *TDNT* 1:632; H.-J. Ritz, *EDNT* 1:225-26; Roloff, 130.

22. Gk. προσεύχομαι is the general verb covering all kinds of prayer (see discussion of the noun at 2:1); Rom 8:26; 1 Cor 14:14; Eph 6:18; etc.

23. Cf. E. E. Ellis, *Pauline Theology: Ministry and Society* (Grand Rapids: Eerdmans, 1989), 72-75 (on the basis of the parallel with 1 Cor 14:34; Titus 2:5; 1 Pet 3:3-6, where husbands and wives are more clearly in view). Gk. ἀνήρ ("man, husband"; 2:12; 3:2, 12; 5:9; Titus 1:6; 2:5). In both Hebrew and Greek, the article, a possessive pronoun, or something similar makes clear in the context whether "man" ("woman") or "husband" ("wife") is meant; e.g., Titus 2:5; Eph 5:22; 1 Pet 3:1, "their husbands" (τοῖς ἰδίοις ἀνδράσιν); Col 3:18, "your husbands" (τοῖς ἀνδράσιν). Cf. the similar alternation between "man" and "woman" and "husband" and "wife" in Gen 2:21-23 and 2:24-25.

ence to the symbolic gesture of raising the hands in prayer (coupled with allusion to the rite of hand washing to signify purity). The background is the
biblical tradition in which prayers in various contexts (invoking God's intervention, pronouncing blessing on others) were accentuated by the raising or
extending of hands.[24] Within Israel's cultic regimen, the actual outward act of
washing the hands was a fundamental preparatory step for priests to enter the
Tent of Meeting (Exod 30:19-21). The visible public act of purification signified the presumed inward condition of purity/holiness of those about to engage in ministry.[25] From the act and its significance, the image of "purified
hands" acquired metaphorical status in its reference to moral purity (e.g.,
1 Clement 29.1; LXX Pss 25:6; 72:13) just as the image of "bloody" or
stained hands signified metaphorically the reverse (Isa 1:15). The combination of the adjective "holy/pure" and the symbolic gesture depicts one who is
completely (outwardly and inwardly) ready for ministry.

Measured negatively, the holiness that facilitates acceptable prayer is
devoid ("without"; 5:21) of attitudes and actions that put relationships at risk.
Here Paul highlights two such things. First, the presence of "anger" indicates
the absence of patience, kindness, and forgiveness, all of which are requisite
to the maintenance and fostering of relationships.[26] Consequently, refusing to
harbor anger (and related feelings) toward other people (Eph 4:31; Col 3:8),
along with taking the positive step of forgiveness (e.g., Mark 11:25), is a condition of effective prayer. Second, hostile feelings issue in hostile actions,
and Paul illustrates this with a very relevant reference to "disputing."[27] This
is an almost certain reference to the *modus operandi* of the false teachers,
whose false doctrines and teaching style engendered disputes and division in
the community.[28] But in the nearer context a reference to some kind of vola-

24. For the combination of Gk. ἐπαίρω ("to lift") and χείρ (pl. "hand") as a prayer
gesture, see Luke 24:50; cf. LXX Pss 133:3; 140:2; (and with a cognate verb) 27:2; 62:5.
The equivalent phrase/gesture, "stretching out the hands" (Isa 1:15; 2 Macc 14:34; etc.) is
also frequent. See Nauck, "Die Herkunft des Verfassers der Pastoralbriefe," 78; Spicq,
373-74.

25. Gk. ὅσιος (Titus 1:8); see R. Meyer and F. Hauck, *TDNT* 3:421-26; Marshall,
164-65.

26. Gk. ὀργή ("anger, wrath"; as a human flaw, inappropriate because it is generated by selfishness and sin, only in Eph 4:31; Col 3:8; Jas 1:19, 20; overwhelmingly used
of God's righteous response to sin, expressed in various ways, ultimately in the eschatological judgment: Matt 3:7; Rom 1:18; Eph 2:3; etc.). Cf. G. Stählin et al., *TDNT* 5:419-46
(esp. 419-21).

27. Gk. διαλογισμός (in the negative sense of "quarreling, arguing, disputing," see
Rom 14:1; Phil 2:14; cf. Luke 24:38; the positive sense of "reasoning, thinking" [Rom
1:21; 12:1] does not fit). G. Schrenk, *TDNT* 2:93-98; G. Petzke, *EDNT* 1:308.

28. Cf. 3:3, 8, 11; 5:13; 6:11; 2 Tim 2:24; Titus 1:7; 2:3; 3:2; Towner, *Goal*, 26-
27; Spicq, 374.

tile interaction between men and women (who teach) may also be in mind. For the thought that one's moral condition will affect one's prayer, positively or negatively, see Jas 1:19-20 and 1 Pet 3:7.

Third, a subtly inserted phrase often overlooked in translations and commentaries, "in every place" ("everywhere," TNIV), initiates an OT echo designed to invite the readers/hearers to understand the significance of their entire worship activity in the eschatological framework of God's redemptive promise to save the nations.[29] In the NT the phrase is Pauline, restricted elsewhere to three occurrences (1 Cor 1:2; 2 Cor 2:14; 1 Thess 1:8). Notably, in each of these instances either Paul's prayer (1 Cor 1:2) or his preaching mission (2 Cor 2:14; 1 Thess 1:8) is in view. Both of these features and the sense of universality suggest that the phrase originated in and consciously echoes Mal 1:11:

> For from the rising of the sun to its setting my name is great among the nations, and in every place *(en panti topǭ)* incense is offered to my name, and a pure offering; for my name is great among the nations, says the LORD of hosts.

Within Judaism, Mal 1:11 was associated in the Targumic tradition with prayer.[30] *Didache* 14.3, perhaps influenced by the interests in 1 Tim 2:8 and certainly by those of Judaism, later conflated Mal 1:11 and 14 to construct a citation, attributed to the Lord, that instructed those quarreling to reconcile before praying.[31] But in the OT context, "prayer," that is, the offering of incense and declaring of God's name, is not the sole topic; it is rather symbolic of the gracious outward turn of God to the nations and pronouncement of judgment on the corrupt temple-centered worship.

---

29. Gk. ἐν παντὶ τόπῳ; for the phrase, see 1 Cor 1:2; 2 Cor 2:14; 1 Thess 1:8. As it occurs in 1 Tim 2:8, this phrase is often understood as a local reference (= "in all the house churches [in Ephesus]"). But this fails to notice its role in continuing the theme of the universal gospel initiated in 2:1 and carefully developed with various forms of the term "all" (vv. 1, 2, 4, 6) and other devices to this point (Bartsch, *Die Anfänge urchristlicher Rechtsbildungen,* 48; Brox, 131; Roloff, 130-31; Towner, *Goal,* 205-7; Marshall, 444-45).

30. *Targum of Pseudo-Jonathan to the Prophets;* Justin, *Dialogue with Trypho* 117.2; R. P. Gordon, "Targumic Parallels to Acts XIII and Didache XIV 3," *NovT* 16 (1974): 285-89.

31. *Didache* 14.3: "For this is the sacrifice concerning which the Lord said, 'In every place and time [ἐν παντὶ τόπῳ καὶ χρόνῳ] offer me a pure sacrifice, for I am a great king, says the Lord, and my name is marvelous among the nations.'" Mal 1:11, 14: "For from the rising of the sun even to the going down thereof my name has been glorified among the Gentiles; and in every place [ἐν παντὶ τόπῳ] incense is offered to my name, and a pure offering: for my name is great among the Gentiles, saith the LORD Almighty. . . . for I am a great King, saith the LORD Almighty, and my name is glorious among the nations."

The function of the echo in the Pauline texts is to explore the implications of this prophetic promise in the new eschatological reality of the church. Viewed within this line of OT promise, the churches' prayer (1 Cor 1:2; 1 Tim 2:8) and Paul's apostolic ministry (2 Cor 2:14; 1 Thess 1:8; 1 Tim 2:7) become signs of the fulfillment of God's promise to offer salvation to "the nations." Equally, the church in its proclamation and prayer becomes the vehicle by which the promise is fulfilled. This is exactly the eschatological perspective Paul had of his ministry (Romans 9–11; 15:9-13; Gal 1:15-16),[32] so it is hardly surprising to find it extended here to a discussion of the church's prayer responsibility within the Pauline mission.[33] Within the broader context of 1 Tim 2:8, this echo of Mal 1:11 resonates with the theme of universality and prayer in support of Paul's mission (2:1-6) and Paul's self-understanding of his calling to the Gentiles ("herald, apostle . . . teacher of the Gentiles"; 2:7) to underline the intrinsic place of prayer within the gospel ministry and the ministry of this church. Paul's audience would have been sensitive to the thematic cue. But equally this missiological frame forces the conduct of both Christian men (holiness) and women (modesty) to be evaluated in terms of its effect on observant outsiders.

9-10 The house code transition marker, "likewise" ("also," TNIV),[34] shifts attention to the second member of the pair. At the same time, it requires that the previous verb of command ("I wish"), or possibly the larger verbal idea including "prayer," be carried over. In the latter case,[35] the assumption is that the unifying or thematic factor is "prayer," so that Paul is ultimately concerned with the manner and outward demeanor in which this activity is carried out in the worship meeting by both men and women. However, since the infinitive "to be adorned" completes the thought adequately, there is no real reason to assume that "prayer" is the unifying theme. Marshall suggests that without the connection provided by prayer, the instruction to women "is an unmotivated digression."[36] But house code instruction frequently shifts from one member in a social pairing to another without such linkage (1 Pet 3:1-7). And

32. Cf. M. Hengel, *Between Jesus and Paul* (London: SCM, 1983), 49-54.

33. Towner, *Goal*, 205-7.

34. Gk. ὡσαύτως (3:8, 11; 5:25; Titus 2:3, 6; equivalent to ὁμοίως in 1 Pet 3:1, 7; 5:5).

35. See Witherington, *Women in the Earliest Churches*, 119, 263 n. 203; Marshall, 447-48; Barrett, 55; Dibelius and Conzelmann, 45. The argument is that either the entire phrase βούλομαι προσεύχεσθαι ("I wish [men/women] to pray") is to be supplied from v. 8, with appropriate adornment serving as the counterpart to holy hands and demeanor, or that the adjectival ptc. προσευχομένας is to be added alongside γυναῖκας, giving the sense, "Likewise [I wish] women [in prayer] to be adorned. . . ."

36. Marshall, 447. The more fundamental topic from 2:1 onward is the activity and behavior of believers in the worship meeting.

if the instruction about adornment addresses a trend of behavior involving wealthy women in the community (the "new woman"), then it is hardly "unmotivated." The issue with "women," with the focus on wealthy "wives,"[37] is their adherence to or breach of the respectable dress code.

In material and outward terms, Paul will set up a contrast between modest appropriate dress and the style of adornment to be avoided (v. 9). Following this, he will shift to a definition of spiritual adornment (v. 10). The language, contrast, and spiritual direction taken compare closely with those in 1 Pet 3:3-5, and it is likely that the instruction applied here had acquired a set shape within the early church.[38] As Winter demonstrates, however, what Christian authors have done is to press into service language and themes drawn from the secular critique of the "new woman." It was the operative principle of that critique that clothing and outer appearance were a reflection of moral values, so that "adornment" became "the descriptor of the modest wife,"[39] and the language of adornment in this discourse was concerned not with clothing and jewelry as much as with behavior.

Consequently, the instructions to women/wives begin with an exhortation to "appropriate adornment."[40] As Paul develops this thought, the infinitive "to dress" refers first to outward physical adornment (v. 9) and then shifts to refer to inward beauty (v. 10).[41] A particular dress code was in effect because, with her outer dress, the woman would signal either modesty and dignity or promiscuous availability. At this time the widely approved apparel of the wife was the *stola,* a robe-like garment made of much cloth. As a sign of marital fi-

---

37. Gk. γυνή (2:10, 11, 12, 14; 3:2, 11, 12; 5:9; Titus 1:6); the same ambiguity observed in the case of "men/husbands" is in play; see the discussion above at v. 8.

38. Towner, *Goal,* 208-9 and n. 31 (verbal parallels: κοσμέω, κόσμιος/κόσμος; ἱματισμός/ἱμάτιον; χρυσίον; πλέγμα · ἐμπλοκῆς τριχῶν); see E. G. Selwyn, *The First Epistle of St. Peter* (London: Macmillan, 1946), 432-35; L. Goppelt, *A Commentary on 1 Peter* (Grand Rapids: Eerdmans, 1993), 217-18.

39. Winter, *Roman Wives,* 101. Winter has processed the work of numerous specialists on ancient Greco-Roman culture, and his illustration of the evidence from the secular sources is unparalleled. Much of the following discussion of the cultural and local setting is indebted to his contributions.

40. Gk. ἐν καταστολῇ κοσμίῳ; the phrase combines a reference to "clothing" (καταστολή; of clothing, as here, see LXX Isa 61:3; Josephus, *Jewish War* 2.126; cf. K. H. Rengstorf, *TDNT* 7:595-96) and the adj. κόσμιος (3:2; expressing a range of meanings, but here in reference to a dress code emphasizing "decorum, modest, orderly"; cf. H. Sasse, *TDNT* 3:895-96; Spicq, *TLNT* 2:330-35).

41. Gk. κοσμέω ("adorn, put in order, beautify"; Titus 2:10; 1 Pet 3:5); in reference to dress or hairstyle, see Rev 21:2; physical adornment of various sorts, Luke 21:5; Rev 21:19; see further Spicq, *TLNT* 2:330-35; H. Sasse, *TDNT* 3:867; for the metaphorical sense of inward beauty, 1 Pet 3:5; Sir 48:11 ("adorned with love"); Diodorus Siculus 16.65.2 ("adorned with virtues").

delity and respectability, the *stola* presented an intentional contrast with the often more revealing and colorful clothing *(toga)* of the prostitute, designed to signify her shame but frequently used instead to advertise her wares.[42]

The attached prepositional phrase, "with decency and propriety," connects acceptance of the dress code with a deeper set of values. There are two things to notice about the language as Paul uses it. First, the word translated "decency" occurs in the writers in and around this time in discussions of the modesty (in dress and comportment) of wives.[43] "Propriety" (or "self-control") was the central cardinal virtue applied to wives, setting them apart as most able to honor their husbands (signifying the discretion and stability of the sexually prudent wife; see the Excursus below).[44] Paul's use of the language is clearly in touch with current secular topics.

But secondly, in applying this language to Christian ethical concerns, Paul reaches an even more profound depth in the way he links the ethical concepts to authentic faith. "Self-control" (the *sōphrosynē* word group) becomes central to Paul's description of Christian behavior in these letters to coworkers. As a Christian virtue it has a basis in the Christ-event (cf. Titus 2:12), and so here it is fittingly associated with the profession of godliness (v. 10). The importance of "self-control" in the present discussion can be seen from the way it brackets this parenesis to women (vv. 9, 15); moreover, its currency in the secular discourse gives it double value for Paul, who with it calls Christian wives *away from* the popular movement and *to* an expression of Christian life that is characterized by Spirit-inspired "self-control."

Excursus: Self-Control

The σώφρων word group plays a central role in Paul's expression of visible Christian life in these letters to coworkers. The noun σωφροσύνη occurs only in 1 Tim 2:9, 15 (Acts 26:25); the adj. σώφρων in 3:2; Titus 1:8; 2:2, 5; the verb

---

42. Winter, *Roman Wives,* 42-43.

43. Gk. αἰδώς ("modesty, discretion, propriety"; only here in the NT), typically linked with σωφροσύνη (Spicq, *TLNT* 1:41-44; R. Bultmann, *TDNT* 1:169-71) and part of the paradigm of the respectable matron (Winter, *Roman Wives,* 101; S. R. Llewelyn, ed., *New Documents Illustrating Early Christianity,* III [Grand Rapids: Eerdmans, 1978/97], §§8, 11, 13). For the link to sexual temptation and sin, see Josephus, *Antiquities* 2.52.

44. Gk. σωφροσύνη. Cf. U. Luck, *TDNT* 7:1097-1104; Spicq, *TLNT* 3:359-65; D. Zeller, *EDNT* 3:29-30; S. Wibbing, *NIDNTT* 1:501-3; R. Schwarz, *Bürgerliches Christentum im Neuen Testament?* (Klosterneuburg: Osterreichisches Katholisches Bibelwerk, 1983), 49-51; Towner, *Goal,* 161-62; Quinn, 313-15; Marshall, 182-84; Winter, *Roman Wives,* 101-2.

σωφρονέω in Titus 2:6 (Mark 5:15; Luke 8:35; Rom 12:3; 2 Cor 5:13; 1 Pet 4:7; the verb σωφρονίζω in Titus 2:4; the adv. σωφρόνως in Titus 2:12; and the noun σωφρονισμός in 2 Tim 1:7.

As in 1 Tim 2:9, in Greek writers (esp. Clement) the virtue of σωφροσύνη is often found alongside αἰδώς. ("A range of meaning was covered, beginning with reference to a "sound mind" or "rationality" and moving then to cover aspects of behavior that exhibited such thinking: prudence, self-control, restraint, modesty). It was sometimes included as one of the four cardinal virtues (in Stoic writers), along with wisdom (σοφία), courage (ἄνδρεια), and uprightness (δικαιοσύνη). In reference to women (Winter, *Roman Women,* 101-2 and refs.), "self-control" (= chastity) takes in behavior and dress that signifies the restrained and modest wife, able by it to protect the honor of her husband.

In the biblical tradition, the virtues and values expressed by the word group emerge only in the LXX (4 Macc 1:3, 6, 18, 30, 31; 2:2, 16, 18; 3:17; 5:23; 15:10; Wis 8:7). It occurred in lists of virtues and sometimes as the quality responsible for controlling emotions. Hellenistic Jewish reflection understood the qualities expressed by the language to be grounded not simply in reason or control of the mind, but in Torah (4 Macc 5:23); see esp. 2:21-23 for the incorporation of Hellenistic categories within a Torah matrix: "Now when God fashioned human beings, he planted in them emotions and inclinations, but at the same time he enthroned the mind among the senses as a sacred governor over them all. To the mind [νοῦς] he gave the law; and one who lives subject to this will rule a kingdom that is self-controlled [σώφρονα], just, good, and courageous." This deepening of categories undoubtedly lies behind Paul's adaptation.

In the NT writers, use of the word group clearly seeks contact with the Hellenistic worldview. A list of cardinal virtues may occur in attenuated form in Titus 2:12 (see discussion), as in Philo (representing Hellenistic Judaistic thinking), but elsewhere they appear sporadically (Titus 3:8; Luke 1:17; 1 Cor 16:13; Eph 1:8; 5:13).

Specifically in these letters to coworkers, the meaning of the word group, covering the same range from prudence and self-control to moderation, discretion, and so on, is evident. But the Christ-event is now determinative for attaining the quality of behavior enjoined by the language. Titus 2:12 makes this most explicit, linking authentic Christian existence as described by three of the cardinal virtues (σωφρόνως καὶ δικαίως καὶ εὐσεβῶς ζήσωμεν) with the appearance of the grace of God (= Christ). It is worth noting that four other uses of the word group in the passage grounded by 2:11-12 also give expression to the shape of the new life in Christ. 2 Tim 1:7 makes "self-discipline" (σωφρονισμός) a by-product of the gift of the Spirit, and in 1 Tim 2:9 the close link between "self-control" (σωφροσύνη) and the profession of godliness (θεοσέβεια) is moving in the same direction. Given this theological orientation, use of the language in reference to overseers (1 Tim 3:2; Titus 1:8) will follow suit.

Consequently, use of the σώφρων word group (as well as other Hellenistic ethical terms) reflects engagement with the culture at some level. What the Greek ethicist saw as the goal of education (παιδεία; see on Titus 2:12), namely, inculcation of Greek "civilization" marked by the cardinal virtues, Paul saw as the jurisdiction of the grace of God in Christ. In each case, moral change is central; but in Paul's use of the Greek language and categories for exploring this change, conversion, faith in Christ, and commitment to the apostolic gospel lift the concept of morality to a more dynamic level. The virtue described by "self-control" (and related terms) is a product of faith and therefore a component of authentic Christian existence.

If, in the case of the Roman wife, appropriate apparel was necessary for signaling modesty and respectability, inappropriate outer adornment — flouting the acceptable dress-code — was sure to raise suspicions of promiscuity and immoderation. Paul draws on a widely published depiction of wealthy and immoderate women in constructing the list of proscribed items of adornment and fashion. The secular sources cited by scholars show a fairly widespread critique.[45] Winter has located the source of the critical discourse in the "sumptuary laws" going back to the pre-Christian Roman republic and later revived by Augustus. Originally, the legislation was meant to discourage ostentation and encourage frugality. It naturally dwelt on the various ways in which ostentation might be shown, including the dress and adornment of wealthy women. Paul lists four items.

First to be mentioned is "elaborate hairstyles." The term that means literally "braiding" refers to the complex and fancy styling of hair — plaiting and piling it on top of the head — preferred by fashionable wealthy women of a certain sort.[46] This style presented the exact opposite to the modest, simpler styles traditionally associated with the model Imperial women as displayed in the statuary. The modest Imperial style was meant to set the cultural trend, but many women of means did not follow suit.[47]

After referring to hairstyles, Paul shifts to jewelry. As Winter points

---

45. E.g., Plutarch, *Moralia* 141E; Seneca, *On Benefits* 7.9; Epictetus, *Enchiridion* 40. So also in Judaism, Philo, *On the Virtues* 39-40; *Testament of Reuben* 5.1-5; *1 Enoch* 8.1-2. See further Winter, *Roman Wives*, 104-7; D. M. Scholer, "Women's Adornment: Some Historical and Hermeneutical Observations on the New Testament Passages," *Daughters of Sarah* 6.1 (1980): 3-6; Baugh, "A Foreign World."

46. Gk. πλέγμα ("braided, plaited"; only here in the NT = ἐμπλοκὴ τριχῶν in 1 Pet 3:3); Josephus, *Antiquities* 2.220.

47. See the discussion in Winter, *Roman Wives*, 104, citing Juvenal, *Satires* 6.501-3: "So important is the business of beautification; so numerous are the tiers and storeys piled one upon another on her head." See further J. V. P. D. Balsdon, *Roman Women* (Westport: Bodley Head, 1962), 252-58.

out, "jewelry epitomized sumptuousness" and was regarded as emblematic of the shameful woman.[48] "Gold" was the most valuable of metals and the precious metal of choice by women who practiced ostentation and men who desired to bring attention of this sort to their wives. It came further to be linked with the dress code of highly paid prostitutes.[49] "Pearls" also occupied a place in the caricature of imprudent ostentation.[50]

"Expensive clothes" completes the profile of the immodest Roman wife.[51] Modest clothing associated with propriety and respectability was simple and full. What is envisioned by this description, found widely in the literature, is the showy expensive apparel that came to be associated with the woman drawing attention to herself — the prostitute and the promiscuous woman.[52]

The critique is precise. It prohibits the kind the dress and adornment that would associate Christian women with the revolutionary "new woman" already in evidence in the East. Were that connection to be made, the church would be open to allegations of endorsing this departure from traditional values.

For this reason, v. 10 contrasts ("but"; *alla*) the unseemly outer adornment just condemned with a standard of "adornment" appropriate for Christian wives. Moreover, Paul's language implies that the standard was known and generally accepted.[53] At first sight, the shift from apparel to conduct ("good deeds") seems abrupt, but as already pointed out, in this kind of ethical discourse "adornment" was code for behavior. The shift allows a fuller description of the modest adornment encouraged for Christian women in v. 9.

First, he characterizes Christian wives as those "who profess to wor-

---

48. Winter, *Roman Wives,* 104-5, citing Juvenal, *Satires* 6.458-59: "There is nothing that a woman will not permit herself to do, nothing that she deems shameful, when she encircles her neck with green emeralds, and fastens huge pearls to her elongated ears. . . ."

49. Gk. χρύσιον (1 Pet 3:3; Rev 17:4; 18:16); see the discussion and secular sources in Winter, *Roman Wives,* 104-5.

50. Gk. μαργαρίτης (Matt 7:6; 13:45, 46; Rev 17:4; 18:12, 16; 21:21[2x]); see further Winter, *Roman Wives,* 105-6.

51. Gk. ἱματισμός ("clothing, apparel"; Luke 7:25; 9:29; John 19:24; Acts 20:33) πολυτελής (adj.; "of great value, expensive"; Mark 14:3; 1 Pet 3:4).

52. Philo, *On the Sacrifices of Abel and Cain* 21; Josephus, *Jewish War* 1.605; Spicq, *TLNT* 3:134-35; Winter, *Roman Wives,* 107-8.

53. The ellipsis is noted by commentators (Marshall, 451): the adversative plus relative clause, "but that which is fitting for . . ." (ἀλλ' ὃ πρέπει), assumes repetition of the preceding infinitival phrase "to adorn themselves" (κοσμεῖν ἑαυτάς) from v. 9. Gk. πρέπω ("to be seemly, suitable"); the language "that which is fitting" (ὃ πρέπει; Titus 2:1; 1 Cor 11:13; Eph 5:3; in the LXX: Pss 32:1; 64:1; 95:5; Sir 32:3; 33:30; 1 Macc 12:11; 3 Macc 3:20, 25; 7:13, 19; C. Brown, *NIDNTT* 2:668-69) intentionally calls to mind an accepted norm or code and impresses it upon these wives (see Winter, *Roman Wives,* 91-94, for discussion and refs. to literature).

ship God." The language of "professing" suggests a serious and perhaps public claim to be believers.[54] The content of the claim is expressed with the term *theosebeia*.[55] It is equivalent to the term *eusbeia*, which defines authentic Christian existence as the integration of faith in God and the behavior that demonstrates this (2:3 and Excursus). Its selection here over the more frequently used term may correspond to the specific reference to wives (or to the language of the claim they were making), but in any case it indicates a claim to be authentic worshipers of God.

Second, he redefines appropriate adornment (the infinitive "to adorn" is still in effect) in terms of "good deeds,"[56] which is shorthand for the visible dimension of authentic faith — action done as the outworking of faith to benefit others. In Paul's formulation of the concept the inner reality (knowledge of God, faith) and outer action come together in a life of service in accordance with God's truth. The sphere in which wives/women are to perform these deeds of faith is not limited to the worship setting, but would include the household and more public places of life.

The whole of the parenesis in vv. 9-10 thus forms a challenge to a group of well-to-do Christian wives for whom the emerging trend of the new Roman woman, with its emphasis on outer show and rejection of cultural norms of modesty, was becoming a potent attraction. The language of the prohibition identifies this cultural trend rather specifically. Equally, reference to modesty and self-control identifies the dress codes and symbols of modesty and chastity that the new women were spurning, though as Christian virtues they have been deepened by the Christ-event. Ultimately, Paul calls these Christian wives to give proof of their claim to godliness (1) by dressing modestly, (2) by living a life characterized by modesty and self-control, and (3) by doing works of Christian service.

Excursus: Good Deeds

The term "good works" in its various configurations is an integral part of the description of Christian existence in these letters to coworkers. In relation to con-

---

54. Gk. ἐπαγγέλομαι (in 6:21 the false teachers distinguish themselves by their professing to have knowledge"; see also Wis 2:13; in Philo, *On the Virtues* 54, it is the profession to have divine healing; BDAG, s.v. 2; MM); see Wolter, *Paulustradition*, 265-66. For the meaning "to promise," see Titus 1:2.

55. For Gk. θεοσέβεια (only here in the NT; LXX Gen 20:11; Job 28:28; Sir 1:25; see the adj. θεοσεβής in John 9:31), see also the Excursus on εὐσέβεια ("godliness") at 2:3.

56. Gk. δι' ἔργων ἀγαθῶν ("by means of good deeds"); διά expresses instrumentality (1:5). See the Excursus below.

cepts such as "faith" (πίστις; see note at 1:2) and "godliness" (εὐσέβεια; see Excursus at 2:3) its focus is on the believer's response and interaction on the visible and horizontal plane of life. The term is formed around two words meaning "good" in various senses: καλός and ἀγαθός. The use of each term should be set out first.

By far the favored of the two words, καλός occurs 24 times in these letters. In the Greek world it could describe moral perfection or goodness, but it ranged more widely to refer to inward orderliness or nobility of character, also applied to physical order and beauty (W. Grundmann and G. Bertram, *TDNT* 3:536-56; J. Wanke, *EDNT* 2:244-45; E. Beyreuther, *NIDNTT* 2:102-5). In Jewish use of the language (LXX), its relation to the moral life dominates and (as later in Paul) it becomes nearly synonymous with ἀγαθός, which also means moral goodness.

In these letters, outside the term "good works," καλός describes what accords with God's will (2:3) and what is acceptable to people (Titus 3:8). In slight contrast with ἀγαθός, which refers consistently to inward and inherent moral goodness, καλός, with its wider range that includes outward beauty or nobility, may accent the observable "good" that makes something like a way of living "attractive" (Marshall, 228). In these letters, it describes things that are generally "good" or "excellent" (1:8; 3:7, 13; 4:4, 6a; 6:19; 2 Tim 2:3), but often the theological underpinnings of a statement will lead to the conclusion that again acceptability to God, or "goodness, excellence" in the sense of corresponding to a divine pattern, may well be intended, as in the use of the term to approve various things and activities related to the faith: "the good warfare/contest" (1:18; 6:12a; 2 Tim 4:7); "the good teaching" (4:6b); "the good deposit" (2 Tim 1:14); "the good confession" (6:12b, 13). The remaining eight occurrences are in the "good works" configuration: 5:10, 25; 6:18; Titus 2:7, 14; 3:1 (sing.), 8a, 14.

The term ἀγαθός (consistently an inward and ethical measurement of approbation) occurs ten times in these letters (W. Grundmann, *TDNT* 1:10-18; J. Baumgarten, *EDNT* 1:5-7). Outside of the term "good works," it combines two times with "conscience" to give the theologically determined idea of the "good conscience" (Gk. συνείδησις ἀγαθή; 1:5 [Excursus], 19), once in description of authentic belief (Titus 2:10), and once to characterize young Christian wives (Titus 2:5). The remaining six occurrences are in an alternative expression of the "good works" concept: the tendency is to generalize the singular into a concept (= a habitual activity) in the phrase "every good work" (πᾶν ἔργον ἀγαθόν; 5:10; 2 Tim 2:21; 3:17; Titus 1:16; 3:1); but the plural phrase "good deeds" occurs in 1 Tim 2:10 (ἔργα ἀγαθά).

In the less disputed Pauline letters the singular ἔργον ἀγαθόν occurs most often (Rom 2:7; 13:3; 2 Cor 9:8; Phil 1:6; Col 1:10; 2 Thess 2:17). But the plural phrase does occur in Eph 2:10. The generalizing idea of "every good work" occurs in 2 Cor 9:8; Col 1:10; 2 Thess 2:17. The use of the term καλός with ἔργον is unattested in Paul outside of these letters to coworkers; but note the use of the plural configuration in Matt 5:16; 26:10; Mark 14:6; cf. John 10:32-33. Notably when Paul uses the phrase to describe the life of faith in terms of activity and response, he regards "good deeds" ("every good work") as the result of faith and salvation (Towner, *Goal,* 153-54; G. Bertram, *TDNT* 2:652; W. Grundmann, *TDNT* 1:16; Marshall, 228).

This sense clearly applies also to the phrase's use in the letters to coworkers. Titus 2:14 links the life of faith characterized by the doing of "good deeds" directly to the design of the self-offering of Christ. The parallel with Eph 2:10, where "good deeds" (with ἔργα ἀγαθά) designates the goal of salvation, is noticeable. Further on in the same letter, with the Christ-event still dominating (2:14; 3:3-7), it is salvation in Christ that forms the basis of the command in 3:8, where believers are to "devote themselves to good deeds." And in 1 Tim 2:10, "good deeds" are linked inextricably with the Christian wives' profession to be authentic believers (= θεοσέβεια; see the Excursus on εὐσέβεια at 2:3).

These examples show the theological basis for the concept of "good deeds." The phrase becomes shorthand for describing the whole of Christian existence in its observable dimension, in terms of the fruit produced by authentic faith (Towner, *Goal,* 153-54; Marshall, 229). When it appears in various practical contexts (1 Tim 5:10 [family]; 6:18 [sharing wealth]; Titus 3:14 [providing daily necessities]), it is simply a corollary of the belief that faith in Christ is intended to produce a manner of existence that applies to every facet of life. Far from being another alleged indication that the author of these letters endorsed a secular, respectable social ethic as an end in itself (*contra* Dibelius and Conzelmann; J. Wanke, *EDNT* 2:245; etc.), what the new emphasis on observable Christian living in the phrase "good works" seeks rather to do is to position authentic Christian existence within the world as that manner of life determined by faith in Christ that is in accordance with the values and aims of God. It falls within the overarching missiological theme of Christian existence as a life that is lived with a concern for the observation of the outsider (cf. Rom 12:17; 13:1-7; 1 Thess 4:12), within which "good deeds" as an expression of that life will be recognizable and even ideally acknowledged as such by unbelievers (cf. Rom 13:3; 1 Pet 2:12).

11-12 At this point, a subtopic is initiated that remains within the brackets established by the concept of self-control (vv. 9, 15b). While the shift in topic is noticeable,[57] it is not appropriate to treat vv. 11-15 in isolation from the preceding instructions to wives. Above all, this suggests that the same situational concern (that Christian wives might be following a dangerous cultural trend) continues to be in view, and that the public perception of church activity is supremely in mind. In this situation, vv. 11-12

---

57. The change of topic is signaled by asyndeton (i.e., the absence of connective material; BDF §§459-63) and the shift to a more generic singular "a woman/wife."

prescribe the appropriate behavior for wives in the church meeting. This is done by setting up a contrast between (in barest essentials) learning (encouraged) and teaching (prohibited). But of course there are additional expansions and qualifications that have kept commentators of all interpretive persuasions busy late into the night. And in the end the stakes seem to be measured in terms of limited applicability versus universal applicability. For the traditionalist or hierarchicalist the trump card has always been the subsequent appeal to the Genesis account (vv. 13-14), which is held to indicate an understanding of role relationships in the church inherent in the creation plan of God and therefore universally applicable. For the egalitarian the unique dimensions of the situation itself and Pauline statements and practices elsewhere suggest that something more limited to the occasion and culture is in view.

Verse 11 opens by shifting from the plural "wives" to the singular (generic) "wife" (see discussion at v. 9) in order to state a general principle. It will be questioned (again) whether wives per se are in view or whether this is rather instruction addressed to women in general (see above). The assumption here is that it was specifically the bearing of wives (modesty in dress and purity in behavior) that in that cultural setting was likely to attract the attention of outsiders and critics. The norm was for women to be married, and the approved pattern of behavior is expressed in distinctively domestic terms (v. 15a). One element of the false teaching was a prohibition of marriage (4:3) and the fact that certain young widows were apparently content to remain unattached (5:11-15), or led by sexual impulses to marry unbelievers. To the degree that any of these developments figures in this instruction, v. 15a still closes the circle by endorsing the typical domestic vocation for women. If this seems to leave a loophole in the case of other single women in that culture who would have had Paul's blessing to remain single, or in another culture and time, so be it; but in any case Paul was not dealing with the social realities of twenty-first-century Western life. From all appearances, he was addressing a uniquely complicated situation in Ephesus.

The role of wives in the church meeting is set out simply in terms of the quiet learner. The activity of "learning" was that of formal (more or less) instruction in the church by gifted teachers.[58] And the core of this activity would have been instruction in "the faith" (exposition of the gospel, of the OT) with reference to all aspects of living (4:6; 2 Tim 3:14). While the instruction to the wife to assume the role of learner is indeed positive, by it Paul is not staking out any particularly new territory, as if it were a new thing

---

58. Gk. μανθάνω (Titus 3:14; cf. Rom 16:17; 1 Cor 14:31; Eph 4:20; Phil 4:9; Col 1:7); K. H. Rengstorf, *TDNT* 4:390-413.

for Christian wives to be allowed to learn. The contrast sometimes drawn between women in Judaism and in the church has been overstated,[59] and in the Greco-Roman world women (especially) from wealthy families often had access to education.[60] The emphasis in this instruction is on learning as opposed to teaching (i.e., on "learning in quietness"), not on learning in and of itself.

It is in relation both to learning and to the proscribed activity of teaching (v. 12) that the qualifying prepositional phrase, "in quietness," is to be understood. The term translated as "quietness" ("silence"; NIV) can range from absolute silence to quietness (or peacefulness) of spirit to silence (or quietness) in respect of some speaking activity (here teaching, but elsewhere of being silent while another speaks, Acts 22:2).[61] The context will determine the sense, and there are two elements to this context.

First, in the immediate literary context, "in quietness" describes the posture and attitude of appropriate deference to the teacher. It does not exclude wives from participation in certain speaking activities such as praying, prophesying, or speaking in tongues; but it is unclear what other activities related to the teaching event (discussion, raising questions) a wife might appropriately engage in.

Second, the social context may add clarification. Winter points out

---

59. While a situation of inequality between men and women certainly existed in Judaism at this time, a rather skewed view of misogynistic chauvinism is frequently reconstructed from certain rabbinic texts and held inaccurately to be the widespread norm: e.g., the oft-cited *y. Soṭa* 3:4; 19:7: "Better to burn the Torah than to teach it to a woman" (also assembled to demonstrate this view are *m. Soṭa* 3:4; *Qidd.* 29b, 34a; *b. Sanh.* 94b); but *m. Soṭa* 3:4 and *Ned.* 4:3 seem to allow the possibility. On the whole, a more balanced picture of women learning in Judaism is achieved by R. B. Edwards, *The Case for Women's Ministry* (London: SPCK, 1989), 29; see also B. Witherington, *Women in the Ministry of Jesus* (Cambridge: Cambridge University Press, 1984), 6-10; as Marshall, 452 n. 134, points out, "Women had to fulfil certain aspects of the Torah and must have been taught it to some extent." Cf. T. Ilan, *Jewish Women in Greco-Roman Palestine* (Peabody, MA: Hendrickson, 1996), 190-204.

60. See the discussion and references in Winter, *Roman Wives,* 112-13.

61. Gk. ἡσυχία (2:12; Acts 22:2; 2 Thess 3:12; for the verb ἡσυχάζω, see Luke 14:3; 23:56; Acts 11:18; 21:14; 1 Thess 4:11; for ἡσύχιος, see 2:2, note and 1 Pet 3:4; BDAG; M. J. Harris, *NIDNTT* 3:111-12). The range of nuances is easily seen. In the situation envisaged in Acts 22:2, the term indicates the silence required of listeners so that another can speak. The verb ἡσυχάζω is relativized in Acts 11:18 (meaning "grew silent" with respect to disputing with Peter [see v. 2], for here coincident with "silence" is "glorifying God, *saying*"); 21:14 similarly specifies a certain kind of "growing silent" (in respect to "begging and weeping"), for coincident is a reference to "remarking." See W. A. Grudem, *The Gift of Prophecy in 1 Corinthians* (Washington, D.C.: University of America Press, 1982), 244, 250-52.

that the participation of Roman wives in the various secular gatherings held in homes (the philosophical *symposia* and banquets) drew harsh criticism from certain men threatened by the trend of new women. Such engagement in philosophical discourse was unbecoming a modest wife whose attention should have been concentrated on running the household. In this case, if the encroachment of the new woman paradigm was in view, "learning in quietness" may have been measured to restrict women from engagement in any give-and-take or argumentation during the lesson. The parallel situation in Corinth should be noted. With a similar mix of theological and cultural influences most likely at work in the community,[62] the stricter injunction of 1 Cor 14:34-35 called for wives/women to be silent in the worship meeting (or some portion of it) and restricted learning to the home. In view of the prophetic and prayer activities apparently allowed to women by 1 Cor 11:5, the subsequent ruling may have applied to a particular kind of speech activity (i.e., unrestrained exercise or interpretation of tongues, vv. 28-29, or unrestrained exercise or discernment of prophecy, vv. 29-32), or, as seems more likely to have been the point, the focus may have been on speech that involved dialogue or interaction with men (14:35). In any case, what the comparison of the two texts (and communities) suggests is that in contexts sharing certain "enthusiastic" theological and cultural phenomena, different specific disturbances involving speaking activities of wives/women in the presence of husbands/men elicited differently gauged restrictions from Paul.

Parallel with "in quietness" is a second prepositional phrase, in "full submission." The language of "submission"[63] links this instruction on appropriate roles to the house code tradition, which typically aligned relationships in a vertical configuration.[64] Its application in the present context is something of an adaptation of the tradition, however, since it is not the wife's submission to the husband that is in view (cf. 1 Cor 14:34), but rather her submission either to the instructor[65] or generally in the instructional setting.[66]

While a tradition is being adapted, it is ill advised to think that the typical language of organizing roles (i.e., "submission") expresses the same

---

62. See Towner, *Goal,* 33-36; Winter, *Roman Wives,* 77-96.

63. The noun ὑποταγή occurs instead of the more typical verb ὑποτάσσομαι (Titus 2:5, 9; 3:1; 1 Cor 14:34).

64. Gk. ὑποταγή (3:4; 2 Cor 9:13; Gal 2:5); G. Delling, *TDNT* 8:39-48; see E. Kamlah, "*Hypotassesthai* in den neutestamentlichen 'Haustafeln,'" in O. Böcher and K. Haacker, eds., *Verborum Veritas* (Wuppertal: Theologischer, 1970), 237-43; Towner, *Goal,* 213-14.

65. Marshall, 454.

66. See Winter, *Roman Wives,* 113-14.

nuance in each case.[67] A range of usage is apparent in the NT,[68] and in cases where human relationships are in view, any sense of rigid hierarchy is moderated somewhat by the note of willingness (expressed in the middle voice) in the act of submitting.[69] The point is, to define the position (role, attitudes, etc.) of the learner in terms of "submission" is not necessarily to apply all that "submission" might imply when descriptive of other relationships (master/slave; husband/wife).

Nevertheless, that the wives/women in view were to assume the posture and attitude of learners in the worship assembly (as opposed to teaching) is clear. The parallel phrases suggest that this meant quiet and attentive listening (in quietness) and complete ("all") acceptance of the authority of the teacher to teach and the willingness to embrace what was being taught. As applied here, both "quietness" and "subjection" relate to the teaching situation, not to life and relationships in general: together these stipulations describe the learner (wife or husband, woman or man) in contrast to the teacher, and within a community authority structure (2 Cor 9:13); it does not seem clear that the submission of the wife to the husband, or the woman to the man (per se), is at issue in the phrase "in all submission."[70] What remains to be seen is whether this instruction to wives was corrective, preventative, or universal.

Verse 12 backs up the positive injunction of v. 11 ("a woman [wife] should learn") by issuing a clarifying prohibition. The prohibition consists of the verbal phrase "I do not permit" and two complementary infinitives, "to teach" and "to assume [exercise] authority over." The implications of this verse are at the center of the discussion of this whole passage, and each term and its relation to the other must be examined.

The present tense verbal phrase "I do not permit" falls within the register of apostolic authority initiated by the opening verb in 2:8: "I desire" (see

67. L. Goppelt, *Theology of the New Testament* (Grand Rapids: Eerdmans, 1982), 2:168, argued that the basic sense of the word group was to be derived from its root (*taxis* = "order"; or *tassesthai* = "to order oneself") and less so from the prefix (*hypo* = "under"), and that contextual considerations would decide the specifics of the organizational structure (expectations and freedoms) in view. Where disturbances in the community were at issue, the goal of submission (i.e., of establishing order) was generally the recovery of harmony (1 Cor 14:32-40); cf. G. Delling, *TDNT* 8:43-45.

68. For a rather well-defined hierarchy, see Rom 8:20; 1 Cor 15:27-28; Eph 1:22; in reference to Christ, 1 Cor 15:28; in reference to wives in relation to husbands, Eph 5:21-22; Col 3:18; Titus 2:5; 1 Pet 3:1; used of wives/women in the worship setting, 1 Cor 14:34; 1 Tim 2:11; in reference to slaves in relation to their masters, Titus 2:9; 1 Pet 2:18; in reference to believers in relation to the state, Rom 13:1, 5; Titus 3:1; 1 Pet 2:13.

69. See Kamlah, "*Hypotassesthai* in den neutestamentlichen 'Haustafeln,'" 241-43; M. Barth, *Ephesians* (New York: Doubleday, 1974), 2:708-15.

70. Cf. Marshall, 454; Winter, *Roman Wives,* 113-14.

the discussion and note).[71] While some interpreters have sought in the verb and its aspect some way of restricting the scope of the instruction (e.g., "I do not permit at the present time," etc.),[72] the grounds for this are lacking. The personal language seems instead to express either a new command that does not rely on tradition (cf. 1 Cor 14:34)[73] or an ad hoc solution to a newly encountered situation.

The prohibition is completed by two infinitives, the first of which is "to teach." This letter to Timothy reflects the serious concern for the transmission and protection of the apostolic gospel. Correspondingly, Timothy receives instructions about teaching in this church (4:11; 6:2). And the list of qualifications for the position of overseer/bishop stipulates the ability to teach (3:2; cf. 5:17). The noun "the teaching" *(didaskalia)*, in various formulations, refers to the authoritative apostolic gospel. Consequently, the verb "to teach" *(didaskō)* that occurs here can be safely taken as a reference to the authoritative activity of teaching in the worship gathering.[74] The gift of teaching, like that of apostle, prophet, and evangelist, was held to be limited to certain persons (cf. 5:17; 2 Tim 2:2).[75]

As Marshall points out, the verb "to teach" does not necessarily reflect on the quality of the contents.[76] In this context it may convey the idea of "assuming the office or role of teacher." The question is why Paul issues the

71. Schlarb, *Die gesunde Lehre,* 276 n. 3.

72. Gk. ἐπιτρέπω (Acts 28:16, 1 Cor 14:34; 16:7; Heb 6:3; etc.). Other commands that are binding in nature or universal are expressed in the present tense (1 Cor 7:10; 1 Thess 4:1, 10; 5:14); cf. T. R. Schreiner, "An Interpretation of 1 Timothy 2:9-15: A Dialogue with Scholarship," in A. J. Köstenberger et al., eds., *Women in the Church,* 126-27; Marshall, 454-55. Nor is it the case that ἐπιτρέπω was used only in situations of limited scope (Heb 6:3; *1 Clement* 1.3; Josephus, *Antiquities* 20.267).

73. Marshall, 455. See Witherington, *Women in the Earliest Churches,* 120. Cf. the impersonal third-person singular formulation in 1 Cor 14:34: οὐ γὰρ ἐπιτρέπεται αὐταῖς λαλεῖν ("it is not permitted . . ."), thought to be based on a rabbinic formula (S. Aalen, "A Rabbinic Formula in 1 Cor. 14,34," *SE* II [1964], 513-25).

74. Gk. διδάσκω ("to teach"; 4:11; 6:2; 2 Tim 2:2; Titus 1:11). The word group, and the ministry function it describes, is important in these letters: διδάσκαλος ("teacher"; 1 Tim 2:7; 2 Tim 1:11; 4:3); διδασκαλία ("the teaching"; 1 Tim 1:10 [see discussion and note]; 4:1, 6, 13, 16; 5:17; 6:1, 3; 2 Tim 3:10, 16; 4:3; Titus 1:9; 2:1, 7, 10); διδακτικός ("able to teach"; 1 Tim 3:2; 2 Tim 2:24); διδαχή ("instruction, the activity of teaching"; 2 Tim 4:2; Titus 1:9). Paul regards the activity as a spiritual gift (Rom 12:7; 1 Cor 12:28-29; Eph 4:11).

75. See further H. Greeven, "Propheten, Lehrer, Vorsteher bei Paulus: Zur Frage 'Amter' im Urchristentum," in K. Kertelge, ed., *Das kirchliche Amt im Neuen Testament* (Darmstadt: Wissenschaftliche Buchgesellschaft, 1977), 325-26; B. Holmgren, *Paul and Power* (Philadelphia: Fortress, 1978), 99-100.

76. Marshall, 455.

prohibition. Hierarchicalists declare that it makes no difference what the women were teaching (or even if they were teaching); Paul simply rules out the possibility based on the creation order.[77]

Whether or not such a view does justice to the whole Pauline picture of gospel equality and women in ministry, let alone the evidence from 1 Timothy (slim as it is), is another question. What I wish to do here is to reshape an earlier reconstruction[78] by inserting some new insights into the local and cultural situations.

First, the evidence that women took part in various aspects of ministry in the Pauline churches is sparse but important. Teaching in some authoritative sense is indicated in Titus 2:3 (see the discussion), though it may be limited to the household situation. Acts 18:26 indicates that both Priscilla and Aquila engaged in teaching Apollos, and the priority of Priscilla's name in the pairing should be noted (cf. women in prophetic ministry in Acts 21:9; 1 Cor 11:5). Reference to Junia as an apostle (Rom 16:7) and to other women involved in ministry could also be cited (Rom 16:1-3; Phil 4:2),[79] and where reference is made to the presence and exercise of charismatic gifts in the assembly (1 Cor 14:26), gender distinctions are not a consideration.[80] Teaching situations that might have involved a public exchange of ideas may have been more gender sensitive.

Winter makes the same point with reference to Roman wives/women in speaking and educational roles in Roman society.[81] He cites evidence that wives were becoming advocates, and notes the critical comments disparaging women who would speak up in public meetings and banquets. But there is no evidence of women attaining the post of teacher in the great houses or philosophical schools. Reference to their educational role in the household is evident enough: upper-class women would take part in the education of their sons, and if the husband died, this educational responsibility fell solely to the wife.

Christian women, as evidenced by Junia and Phoebe, may have shared some of the mobility enjoyed by their secular counterparts. Again it is not clearly known what shape their ministries took. But it does seem clear that they were entrusted with various important responsibilities, and generally women were present in the Christian public meetings, not hidden away in

77. See esp. Schreiner, "1 Timothy 2:9-15."
78. See Towner, *Goal,* 209-22.
79. See A. J. Köstenberger, "Women in the Pauline Mission," in P. Bolt and M. Thompson, eds., *The Gospel to the Nations: Perspectives on Paul's Mission* (Leicester: Apollos, 2000), 221-47; C. S. Keener, *Paul, Women and Wives* (Peabody, MA: Hendrickson, 1992), 237-57.
80. The masculine ἕκαστος ("each one") includes both men and women.
81. Winter, *Roman Wives,* throughout, with references to the secular sources.

some side room of the house. New trends in society surely opened up new options for movement and service for women, especially wealthy women, in the church, even though the new sexual mores also associated with the new trend presented serious dangers.[82]

Though the evidence is slender, the suggestion here is that in some Pauline churches space was being cautiously created for a fuller participation of women (and slaves) in the worship setting. Ephesus, perhaps owing something to the precedent set earlier by Priscilla (Acts 18:19), may have been one of those churches. At the same time, the Christian community cannot have been immune to other cultural influences. Those progressive, forward-leaning values assembled around the "new woman" paradigm would most appeal to the mobile wealthy (the new trends in adornment), and greater freedoms would seem to resonate with the freedoms implied by Paul's gospel. It is not hard to imagine wealthy Christian women (such as are at the center of this instruction), perhaps with the encouragement of "progressive" men (or false teachers), adopting aspects of the trend (styles of clothing and adornment, new values, sexual promiscuity, etc.) and even supplying a gospel foundation for the moves being attempted.

I have argued elsewhere that the equality statement of Gal 3:28 (1 Cor 12:13; Col 3:11) cannot be ignored when attempting to reconstruct a Pauline view of Christian existence and ministry. Implementation (in combination with other local factors) could be accompanied by overexuberance and excess. Misunderstandings about eschatology (1 Corinthians; 1 Timothy) could lead men and women to attempt to implement promised freedoms in advance of the appropriate time, or without the appropriate balance.[83] And a number of Pauline letters seem more intent to rein in those caught up in such exuberance than to encourage implementation of all that the gospel promised.[84]

1 Timothy is such a letter. In spite of the fragmentary nature of the evidence, I would nonetheless suggest that three convergent forces lie behind Paul's prohibition of women from teaching. First, whether owing directly or indirectly to the false teachers, some wealthy women had come under the influence of a too fully realized eschatology (see discussions at 6:20-21; 2 Tim 2:18). Second, they may well have been encouraged to step into the role of teacher by some element of the heresy. It can hardly be accidental that Paul encourages the domestic path of bearing children (v. 15) while the false teachers prohibited marriage (4:3; i.e., sexual relations). Third, coinciden-

82. Cf. Winter, *Roman Wives,* 173-204.
83. Towner, "Gnosis and Realized Eschatology in Ephesus"; *Goal,* 29-36; cf. Witherington, *The Paul Quest,* 218-29.
84. Towner, *DPL* 417-19.

tally adding momentum was their contact with the cultural trend of the new Roman woman. Wealthy women in the church, women whose mobility and freedom in society had been increasing, were encouraged by the trend to take a more public role in the church's assemblies. It is not possible to unravel all the details, but it seems inescapable that some of these wealthy women had in fact been teaching in public settings in which husbands/men were also present (or were becoming so vocal as to make it a next unavoidable step). If, on top of this, they were responsible for communicating (or, by their behavior, seeming to endorse) elements of the heresy, an injunction after the pattern of 1 Cor 14:34, restricting them to the role of learner, is understandable. But perhaps it was simply this wealthy circle's association with the promiscuous "new woman," through dress and adornment (and denigration of the traditional household values of bearing children; v. 15) that led Paul to put a stop to the teaching activities of Christian women.

The second infinitive completes the prohibition as it adds another dimension to their behavior. The relative rarity of the term (occurring only here in the NT), the range of meaning possible for its word group, and its situation in the debate about this passage's view of the role of women in the church have combined to make this verb — *authenteō* — almost a household word. Fortunately, with the aid of the *TLG*, several recent studies have overcome somewhat the limitations of the pre-computer lexicons.[85] The semantic range of the word group has been more accurately charted,[86] but it is even clearer now that the bulk of occurrences are in Christian sources later than 1 Timothy, which raises questions of methodology in applying the findings to the single NT occurrence of the word.

As the studies have shown, the word group covers a range that can be broadly categorized as follows: to rule/reign; to control/dominate; to act independently; to be the originator of something; to murder.[87] From this range, most interpreters settle within the area of "the exercise of authority." The

---

85. Gk. αὐθεντέω (only here in the NT; BDAG; MM). See esp. H. S. Baldwin, "A Difficult Word: αὐθεντέω in 1 Timothy 2:12," in Köstenberger et al., eds., *Women in the Church*, 65-80 (and his assessment of previous studies); idem, "Appendix 2: αὐθεντέω in Ancient Greek Literature," in Köstenberger et al., eds., *Women in the Church*, 269-305; L. Wilshire, "The TLG Computer and Further References to AYΘENTEΩ in 1 Tim 2:12," *NTS* 34 (1988): 120-34; G. W. Knight III, "AYΘENTEΩ in Reference to Women in 1 Timothy 2.12," *NTS* 30 (1984): 143-57; cf. R. C. Kroeger and C. C. Kroeger, *I Suffer Not a Woman: Rethinking 1 Timothy 2:12 in Light of Ancient Evidence* (Grand Rapids: Baker, 1992), 84-104, 185-88; C. Osburn, "AYΘENTEΩ (1 Timothy 2:12)," *ResQ* 25 (1982): 1-12; cf. Marshall, 456-60; Winter, *Roman Wives,* 116-19.

86. See esp. Baldwin, "A Difficult Word," 73.

87. This analysis comes from Baldwin, "A Difficult Word"; see further the interaction of Marshall, 456.

neutral sense is expressed with the translation "to have authority over"; degrees of inappropriateness in the acquisition or exercise of authority might be implied in the mild expression "to assume authority" (TNIV) and are clearly emphasized in the options "to domineer, to usurp authority, or to abuse authority."[88] The case for the former neutral view can certainly be made, but the evidence supporting the claim that this was the basic meaning of the word is not so clear.[89] The negative range of meaning possible for the verb probably owes to the strong meanings sometimes expressed by related nouns; for example, *authentēs* can mean "murderer."[90] The verb expresses the negative sense of "abuse of authority" or "domineering" in Chrysostom, but it is largely the context that slants the meaning in this direction.[91]

Winter enlarges on the importance of context or semantic field for determining the appropriate nuance, and brings several examples to bear on the use of the verb in our passage.[92] He notes Hesychius's *Lexicon* (fifth century C.E.) in which *authenteō* is a synonym for the more widely used *exousiazō*, meaning "to have authority" (e.g., 1 Cor 6:12; 7:4a, 4b). Let it be noted that in Pauline discussions of "authority," the noun *exousia* and related verb *exou-*

88. The conclusions of Kroeger and Kroeger, *I Suffer Not a Woman*, must be judged as idiosyncratic. The strength of this treatment is the effort to reconstruct the Ephesian background as a way of understanding the difficulties of the passage (see P. H. Towner, "Feminist Approaches to the NT: 1 Tim 2:8-15 as a Test Case," 91-111). Kroeger's several studies have led her through the more striking meanings of the term (violence, murder, seductive power) and background studies in the fertility cults. The last stop for this developing interpretation took up the semantic range of authorship and origination (attested in, e.g., *2 Clement* 14.3); against the background of Ephesus's Artemis cult and the heresy in the church, this exploration resulted in translating αὐθεντεῖν as "proclaim herself the originator of" — i.e., Christian women under the mixed influence of the Artemis cult and a heretical distortion of Genesis material were rewriting the creation story and asserting their authority as "originators" in a way that overturned the social status quo. Parallels for this kind of belief are later and Gnostic.

89. This is the view of Knight; Baldwin is content to allow a range of possibilities with the exercise of authority (in some sense) as the basic meaning. See the challenge to Knight posed by Wilshire; cf. Witherington, *Women in the Earliest Churches,* 121.

90. For αὐθέντης in this sense, see Hesychius, *Lexicon* 63, 64; Herodotus 1.117; see Wilshire, "The TLG Computer," 125-26. The verb bears this meaning only much later. See further Marshall, 457. Winter, *Roman Wives,* 118, helpfully supports this transference or attraction of meaning by citing a second-century-(C.E.) objection of Phrynichus that αὐθέντης (which Phrynichus insists means "one who murders by his own hand") should not be used for δεσπότης ("master, one who controls another"), as the legal rhetoricians were doing.

91. Chrysostom, *Homily 10 on Colossians* (PG 62:366; cf. *PGL* 262); cited by Witherington, *Women in the Earliest Churches,* 121. See Wagener, *Die Ordnung des "Hauses Gottes,"* 100.

92. Winter, *Roman Wives,* 116-19.

siazō are the standard terms.[93] He also notes that Hesychius linked *autodikei* ("to have jurisdiction over, to have power over another") to *authenteō* as a synonym. Further, if it is thought that such exercises of authority (whether expressing simply a neutral power concept or rather the negative sense of domineering) simply would not apply in the case of women exerting force over men, Winter has unearthed several other instances in which words in the semantic domain of *authenteō* (e.g., *archō,* "to rule"; *stratēgeō,* "to command"; *kyrieuō,* "to exercise authority over") were applied to describe the power women sometimes exercised over men.

In the final analysis, given the range of meanings possible for *authenteō,* the decision to assign a neutral value ("to have authority over") or to see it as making a negative valuation ("authority assumed or exercised inappropriately," "domineering abuses of authority") rests on the reading of the context, not on the simple tallying of occurrences in search of a statistical bulge. And this means reconsidering the two dominant elements that converged to form the background to this text.

First, there is the heresy in combination with a misunderstanding of eschatology, which I have attempted to sketch above. Here it need only be said that in an overcharged pneumatic situation (such as at Corinth or at Ephesus) it is not hard to imagine Christian women and slaves behaving in ways that would allow them to realize more fully the implications of gospel freedom. In the time of the Spirit's fullness, the Genesis curse on women (Gen 3:16) might be regarded as lifted, or in need of being thrown off. The false teachers' re-reading of Scripture and tampering with social institutions may not account for everything, but neither can the possible influence of these activities be excluded. It simply needs to be kept in mind that the combination of an overrealized outlook and some degree of heretical influence might have pushed women to assume roles in ways that disrespected husbands and men.

Second, there is the possible contact with the cultural movement that Winter has documented. If the values of the "new woman" were in fact being countered by Paul in vv. 9-10, then there is already in the text sensitivity to the disruption to traditional values addressed by numerous ancient writers. Some decades ago Wayne Meeks set out the argument for the emergence of an emancipation trend in Greco-Roman society.[94] Winter's arguments for the existence of the trend of the new Roman woman, and his application to the

---

93. For the noun ἐξουσία, see Rom 9:21; 13:3; 1 Cor 7:37; 9:4, 5, 6; 11:10; 15:24; 2 Cor 13:10; 2 Thess 3:9; for the verb ἐξουσιάζω, see 1 Cor 6:12; 7:4(2x).

94. See W. A. Meeks, "The Image of the Androgyne: Some Uses of a Symbol in Earliest Christianity," *HR* 13 (1974): 180-204; cf. W. den Boer, *Private Morality in Greece and Rome* (Leiden: Brill, 1979), 256-62.

Pauline communities, is somewhat more pointed. Rejection of the dress codes synonymous with modesty and chastity, the emergence of well-to-do married women in the Forum and the courts, and rejection of the values of the stable household (expressed in a desire to avoid or terminate pregnancy) add up to a movement with values capable of disrupting the church. In such a context, where in the public setting of the church meeting the practice of wealthy wives/women assuming a dominant (teaching) role *vis-à-vis* husbands/men is envisioned, *authenteō* is likely to have carried the negative valuation of inappropriate exercise of authority (perhaps "domineer").

While Winter suggests that this instruction was preventative (whereas in the case of young widows such behavior had already erupted), the presence of the heresy, its influence on some women (cf. 5:14), and the reference below to the deception of Eve suggest rather that women for a combination of reasons had been engaging in the activity of teaching, and were exercising their gifts in a way that could be seen as heavy-handed or disrespectful of husbands/men. The threat posed and confusion caused by unveiled wives in Corinth and disturbances in their public gatherings (1 Corinthians 11; 12–14), owing possibly to the same mix of causes, provided Paul all the history needed to warrant the drastic action taken in Ephesus.

A. Köstenberger emphasizes rather the syntactical and literary context. He argues that the particular "neither/nor" construction that frames the infinitives in the verbal phrase "I do not permit women . . ." will attribute either positive meaning to each part or negative. His conclusion, assuming a positive meaning for "to teach," is that Paul denies two positive activities to women: "to teach" and "to exercise authority over a man." Furthermore, on this understanding of "to teach," Paul would have had to select the term *heterodidaskalein* ("to teach falsely"; as in 1:3) if in prohibiting women from teaching he envisioned them teaching error.[95] While the grammatical observation may be granted, his assertion that the verb "to teach," when used absolutely in the NT, is always regarded positively by the respective writer is far too confident and somewhat artificial. The context, not just an expressed object, may supply the "content."[96] If, as Marshall suggests, Paul is addressing

95. As Marshall, 458 n. 157, comments, the implications for men of a prohibition phrased according to Köstenberger's requirements (i.e., "I do not permit a woman to give false teaching") are rather alarming (and at least amusing). Without completely restructuring the parenesis, ἑτεροδιδασκαλεῖν simply would not work.

96. In my opinion, from the standpoint of lexical-semantic requirements, once a verb such as διδάσκω is used in a negative sense (i.e., to teach something inferior, substandard, untrue, or contrary to the law, as in Matt 5:19), it is quite capable of implying as much in a case where what is being "taught" is left implicit, if the context warrants. The ground rules are the same as those that apply to διδάσκω used of positive constructive teaching, with or without content expressed.

women who have been involved in teaching the heresy, then "teaching" is here under a negative evaluation. But even if the problem is that they have assumed the role inappropriately (whatever they teach) out of a desire to dominate in the public meeting (or out of a desire to enact gospel freedom), their assumption of the teaching role is under a negative evaluation.

In strong contrast ("but"; *alla*) to the inappropriate appearance or expression of domination by wives/women over husbands/men through teaching,[97] Paul restates the demeanor (and hence the role of learner) they are to assume: "but (*alla*) let them be in quietness."

Feminists and egalitarians may debate whether this was a retrograde move on Paul's (or the author's) part. Hierarchicalists assume that Paul was simply applying a creation ordinance. Textual and background considerations suggest, however, that the presence and influence of a circle of wealthy women in the church were at issue. Their flouting of the traditional dress code suggests a link with the broad trend of the promiscuous wealthy Roman wives that Winter has described. Other yearnings for power and public presence make the paradigm of this "Alpha" Roman female a possible background to the grasping wealthy wives depicted here. The presence of the heresy and its probable influence on the household and women/widows, and its revision of values, complicate the background. But even if a neat reconstruction is beyond our reach, tantalizing points of contact present themselves as we consider the heretical reading of the OT, prohibition of marriage, and the greed (6:5-10) that might have led the opponents to befriend and beguile this circle of wealthy wives and widows (potential patronesses) so attentive to secular trends.

13-15a Verses 13-15 provide backing for the preceding instructions. But questions abound, beginning with the extent of this material's backward reach. The TNIV has so structured the passage into paragraphs that the reader will immediately conclude that vv. 13-15 supply grounds only for vv.

---

97. It is debated whether the οὐκ . . . οὐδέ ("neither . . . nor") construction indicates two separate activities related to leadership in the community ("teaching" and "exercising authority"; see Köstenberger, "A Complex Sentence Structure," 90-91) or whether exercising authority is a further description of teaching (Wagener, *Die Ordnung des "Hauses Gottes,"* 74-76; J. B. Hurley, *Man and Woman in Biblical Perspective* [Leicester: Inter-Varsity Press, 1981], 201). The structure of vv. 11-12 suggests that each central activity (learning, v. 11; teaching, v. 12) is accompanied by an appropriate/inappropriate attitudinal disposition (quietness and submission, v. 11; disrespectful display of authority, v. 12). The abrupt shift following αὐθεντεῖν ἀνδρός back to the disposition of the learner (ἀλλ᾽ εἶναι ἐν ἡσυχίᾳ; "but let her be in quietness") shows further that learning/teaching (and relative attitudes) are at issue. Thus αὐθεντεῖν ("to domineer, misuse authority") here describes something about the way in which διδασκεῖν ("to teach") was being done (Marshall, 460).

11-12.[98] While this conclusion is probably correct, it must be borne in mind that the description of the wealthy women's extravagant adornment (and its sexual overtones) is one part of a larger description that includes their assumption of the teaching role and inappropriate exercise of authority.

Next, the presence of a complex OT allusion in 2:13-14 is recognized by all. There is less agreement whether the allusion continues into v. 15a with the statement "but she shall be saved through childbirth," or whether it is simply the concluding positive instruction setting out the acceptable role of women. I will give grounds for the former view below.

Still more disputed is the intention of drawing on the story of the creation and fall: does it "ground" the prohibition of women from teaching, or rather "illustrate" by forming a link between the OT story and the church's present dilemma? The connecting particle *(gar)* can emphasize logical reasoning or simply introduce something more on the order of an explanation,[99] but its presence alone gives little to go on. Directly related is the question of the motive for drawing on the Genesis story and presenting it in the shape in which it appears.

The supporting material alludes to and draws together two parts of the Genesis story, three if v. 15a is also allusive: (1) the story of the creation of Adam and Eve (2:13; Gen 2:7-8, 15), (2) the story of Eve's temptation (2:14; Gen 3:6-13), and (3) the pronouncement of judgment on the woman as a result of her role in the event (2:15a; Gen 3:16).

Verse 13 is a retelling of the creation account of Genesis 2. In addition to the clear general reference to this familiar account, specific links are established by means of the names "Adam" and "Eve" and the choice of verb "to form." The name "Adam" occurs first in Gen 2:16 and nine times thereafter in the chapter.[100] In the LXX, the name "Eve" does not actually occur until Gen 4:1; thereafter it appears sparingly throughout the OT and NT.[101] But the

---

98. See, however, M. Küchler, *Schweigen, Schmuck und Schleier: Drei neutestamentliche Vorschriften zur Verdrängung der Frauen auf dem Hintergrund einer frauenfeindlichen Exegese des Alten Testaments im antiken Judentum* (NTOA 1; Freiburg: Universitätsverlag, 1986), 13, who argues that all of vv. 9-12 is addressed by vv. 13-15 (see assessment in Marshall, 460-61); cf. J. M. Holmes, *Text in a Whirlwind: A Critique of Four Exegetical Devices at 1 Timothy 2.12 15* (JSNTS 196; Sheffield: Sheffield Academic Press, 2000).

99. Cf. Witherington, *Women in the Earliest Churches*, 122; P. B. Payne, "Libertarian Women in Ephesus: A Response to Douglas J. Moo's Article, '1 Timothy 2:11-15: Meaning and Significance,'" *TrinJ* 2 (1981): 176.

100. Gk. Ἀδάμ (2:14; Luke 3:28; Rom 5:14a, b; 1 Cor 15:22, 45a, b; Jude 14). J. Jeremias, *TDNT* 1:141-43.

101. Gk. Εὔα (cf. MT 3:20, חַוָּה [*chuah* = "life"]; LXX Ζωή [*Zōē*]); Gen 4:25; Tob 8:6; 2 Cor 11:3; Philo, *Allegorical Interpretation* 2.81; Josephus, *Antiquities* 1.36, 49; *Sibylline Oracles* 1.29); BDAG.

name was clearly well known, and so not surprisingly is back-read naturally into the creation story here. Apart from the characters and the general content of the story, it is the verb "to form" *(plassō)* that links the reflection to the account in Gen 2:7-8, 15:[102]

> 1 Tim 2:13: "For Adam was formed *(eplasthē)* first, then Eve."
>
> Gen 2:7: "God formed *(eplasen)* the man from the dust of the ground. . . ."
>
> Gen 2:8: "And there [in Eden] he put the man whom he had formed *(eplasen).*"
>
> Gen 2:15: "The LORD God took the man whom he had formed *(eplasen)* and put him in the garden."

The verb *plassō* is not used in the Genesis account of the process by which Eve came into being, but in later retellings of this story it is typically applied to the creation of both the man and the woman.[103] Notably, while the sequence of creation is clearly important to Paul ("first . . . then"),[104] the notion taken up and stressed in 1 Cor 11:8, of woman's creation being derivative, is absent. The sequence "first[105] . . . then" corresponds to Adam as the first created human and Eve as the second or subsequent human.

The question is, How did Paul intend the allusion to be understood? Indebtedness to Judaism or to rabbinic argumentation is sometimes thought to hold the clue. The basic argument for the superiority of the first created — that is, from the priority of creation — offered in v. 13 (in support of vv. 11-12) is found widely in Greek and Jewish and rabbinic sources.[106] The rabbinic reasoning of "first is best" (cf. 1 Cor 11:8-9) can be seen in the following example:

> *Exodus Rabbah* 21.6: "Moses . . . went to divide the sea, but the sea refused to comply, exclaiming, 'What, before you shall I divide? Am I not greater than you? For I was created on the third day and you on the

---

102. Gk. πλάσσω (here in aor. pass. ἐπλάσθη; rare and Pauline in the NT, Rom 9:20; *Sibylline Oracles* 3.24).

103. 2 Macc 7:23; Josephus, *Antiquities* 1.32; *1 Clement* 33.4.

104. Gk. πρῶτος . . . εἶτα (Mark 4:28; cf. 1 Cor 15:46; 1 Thess 4:16).

105. See Hermas, *Vision* 3.4.1; *Similitude* 5.5.3.

106. For the argument in Greek writers, see Plato, *Republic* 412C; *Laws* 11.917A; for the argument in Judaism particularly linked to creation, see *Exod. Rab.* 21.6; *Midr. Ps.* 114§9; *Sipre Deut.* 11, 10 §37[76a]; see StrB 3.256-57; 626, 645; J. Jervell, *Imago Dei* (Göttingen: Vandenhoeck & Ruprecht, 1960), 71-121; and esp. Nauck, "Die Herkunft des Verfassers," 95-97; Küchler, *Schweigen, Schmuck und Schleier,* 17-32; Dibelius and Conzelmann, 47; Roloff, 136-38; Oberlinner, 97-99.

sixth.'" (Cf. *Sipre Deuteronomy* §37: "This is also true concerning God's actions — whatever is most precious comes first.")

If Paul was applying the argument "first is best," he does not appear to have cited a rabbinic formula that made use of Genesis 2. His indebtedness to rabbinic thought is limited to the method of argumentation, and for all we know, his application of it to men and women by way of allusion to Genesis 2 is novel (cf. 1 Corinthians 11). It is often pointed out that in Judaism and Greco-Roman cultures, the subordinate status of the woman was assumed. Josephus states emphatically: "[The law] says, 'A woman is inferior to her husband in all things. Let her, therefore, be obedient to him; not so that he should abuse her, but that she may acknowledge her duty to her husband; for God has given the authority to the husband.'"[107] This being the assumption, the question why Paul strove to make such a point via Genesis 2 becomes all the more acute.

The tendency among those holding to a biblical feminist perspective has been to play down this element of the argument in v. 13 and focus more on v. 14.[108] But the point from creation seems too central to bypass; nevertheless, the heresy and the possibility of women's involvement in it is an interpretive wildcard that calls for caution in determining what Paul's point was.

First, many understand v. 13 to be Paul's (or a Paulinist's) rather straightforward application of a creation principle with which he was in full agreement. For those who maintain Pauline authorship, he is regarded here as insisting on the view that he uniformly held (e.g., 1 Cor 11:3-16; 14:33-35), which, based on the creative will of God, proscribed women from teaching and holding positions of authority over men in the church.[109] Where the letter is regarded as the work of a Paulinist, application of the Jewish argument is held to reflect the return to a patriarchalism that the Pauline gospel had challenged (Gal 3:28), a return designed perhaps as an answer to women who (under the influence of an overrealized eschatology or an overly enthusiastic implementation of an equality principle [Gal 3:28]) had asserted themselves in ways that caused a disturbance in the community.[110] Although neither variation on this view requires all of the rabbinic and wider cultural chauvinistic

---

107. *Against Apion* 2.200; cf. Philo, *Apology for the Jews* 7.3.

108. See the discussion in Towner, "Feminist Approaches to the New Testament."

109. Schreiner; Mounce; Knight; et al.; cf. Webb, *Slaves, Women and Homosexuals,* Appendix A, 257-62. Johnson, 206-7, sees in this method of argumentation a reflection of the "limits to Paul's egalitarianism" and "cultural conservatism" (207), and finds 1 Tim 2:11-15 to be consistent with 1 Cor 14:33-35. Unlike traditionalists, however, Johnson's hermeneutic does not necessitate regarding the instruction as universal.

110. Variously Roloff, 128-30; Fiorenza, *In Memory of Her;* Wagener, *Die Ordnung des "Hauses Gottes,"* 110-13.

assumptions to be in the author's mind, the view suggests that the author drew quite naturally on the assumptions of the day, including the principle that first created is best.

Second, the creation account may have been drawn on, not for its universal applicability to any and all man/woman situations, but rather in order to combat a specific view or correct an interpretation of the creation account somehow linked with the false teaching.[111] This approach takes various shapes that tend to agree that 2:13 must be taken seriously. One reconstruction suggests that speculation on the creation accounts (cf. "myths and genealogies," 1:4; 4:1, 7) in an atmosphere charged with eschatological enthusiasm produced a pre-fall paradigm for present Christian living (celibacy, vegetarianism; 4:3). Both the eschatology and the retreat to a pre-fall (pre-curse) model could go to the support of a progressive view of women's roles in the community. The apostle's response involves returning to an orthodox, correct reading of the Genesis material (vv. 13-14) to reorient the church's thinking around a view of the present that accounts properly for both creation and the realities of sin and redemption.[112] Of course, attempts to explain OT allusions as corrections of heretical misreadings face the daunting challenge of plausibility. In this case, however, the role of the OT in the heresy and the movement's influence on women make the challenge unavoidable, even if some questions must remain open in the end. The likelihood that women were also drawn in some ways to the popular secular trend set out above (the new Roman woman) complicates both the background and the apostolic response. But its influence on women and possibly the opponents as well should be kept in mind.

Verse 14 picks up the Genesis story at the episode of the woman's temptation given in Genesis 3. Sequence of action is again an important feature of the presentation. In the case of the temptation and transgression, however, the sequence is reversed to emphasize the priority of the woman's deception and action in relation to the man's; this is done not by reversing the order of occurrence of the names, but (by means of the negative) by locating the initial deception and transgression with the woman.

> 1 Tim 2:14: "And Adam was not deceived (*epatēthē*), but the woman was deceived (*exapatētheisa*) and became a transgressor."
> Gen 3:12: "Adam said, 'The woman you gave to be with me — she gave to me from the tree, and I ate.'"
> Gen 3:13: "And the LORD God said to the woman, 'What have you

---

111. Cf. A. C. Wire, *The Corinthian Women Prophets* (Minneapolis: Fortress, 1990), 116-34, 122.

112. Schlarb, *Die gesunde Lehre*, 123-24; Towner, 75-81; Marshall.

done?' The woman answered, 'The serpent deceived *(ēpatēsen)* me, and I ate.'"

Again the OT account is accessed generally by simple reference to the well-known episode. Specific access is made by means of a thematic verb, "to deceive," which occurs, as in the LXX account (Gen 3:13), first in the simplex form *(apataō)*[113] and secondly, in reference to the woman (a departure from the OT account), in the compound form *(exapataō)*.[114] The switch to the compound form of the verb is probably stylistic, serving to set the woman and the man apart in the fall and to stress the priority of the woman's deception. Intensification is not the likely force of the change; the compound had already found its way into the traditional account of this scene (2 Cor 11:3) without any specific added nuance to the deception (i.e., in the sense of sexual deceit). In any case, her deception is followed directly by her fall into "transgression" ("became a sinner"; TNIV). Paul's selection of this term for wrongdoing is not determined by the language of Genesis 3; but its depiction of sin as "overstepping an established boundary" aptly characterizes Eve's violation of God's commandment.[115] In combination with the perfect tense verb of being, this breach has become her resultant condition.[116]

A second intentional verbal connection with the divine interrogation of Gen 3:12-13 may also be present in the decision to refer for a second time to the personal name "Adam" (as in Gen 3:12) but in the case of Eve to the impersonal "woman" *(gynē;* as in Gen 3:13). Within the present passage, this shift also allows readers/hearers to make the appropriate association back to the "wives" addressed in the plural in vv. 9-10, then in the singular of vv. 11-12, and prepares them for the singular reference to come in v. 15.

But what is the force of this argument? The story of Eve's deception and sin attracted a good deal of attention in speculative strands of Judaism. Moreover, the way this story is retold, v. 14 with its apparent emphasis on the woman (cf. the Adamic emphasis in Rom 5:12ff.) bears at least a superficial resemblance to Jewish retellings based on the same Genesis material. While these developments are worth exploring as a way of establishing the context

113. Gk. ἀπατάω (Eph 5:6; Jas 1:26; Jdt 9:3; 12:16; 13:16; cf. Josephus, *Antiquities* 12.20. A. Oepke, *TDNT* 1:385-86; A. Kretzer, *EDNT* 1:117.

114. Gk. ἐξαπατάω (ptc.; Rom 7:11; 16:18; 1 Cor 3:18; 2 Cor 11:3; 2 Thess 2:3).

115. Gk. παράβασις ("transgression, crossing the bounds"; Rom 2:23; 5:14; 14:15; Gal 3:19; Heb 2:2; 9:15); M. Wolter, *EDNT* 3:14-15; J. Schneider, *TDNT* 5:736-44.

116. Marshall, 464. Gk. γέγονεν; the perfect tense verb of being indicates that an enduring state has been entered; the prepositional phrase ἐν παραβάσει that modifies the perfect tense verb defines that state as "in transgression" (for γίνομαι with ἐν, cf. Luke 22:44; Acts 22:17; 2 Cor 3:7; Phil 2:7).

of Paul's thought (cf. 2 Cor 11:3), the dating of some of these is far from certain, and a pattern of development is difficult to fix.

(1) Sir 25:24 bears no material relation to the form or language of 2:14 ("From a woman sin had its beginning, and because of her we all die"). But it offers an interpretive reflection on the origins of sin and death, for which the woman takes full blame, based on the Genesis account, which could be thought to lie behind the second statement of rationale for women not teaching or holding authority over men.[117]

(2) Philo may not have developed the idea, but he gave a certain elegance to the traditional link between the soft and weak feminine nature and her gullibility and vulnerability to deception.[118] Philo's further reflections on Gen 3:16-19[119] are too allegorical to fit precisely within the deception of Eve motif, but the way he interprets the character of feminine human nature as intrinsic to the process leading from the serpent's deception to the man's eating of the forbidden fruit fits in well with his statement on her inborn susceptibility to falsehood. His thinking is more or less reiterated by certain conservative scholars today who distinguish between the rationality of men and the relational, nurturing bent of women and draw conclusions about their relative strengths and weaknesses with regard to "preserve[ing] the apostolic tradition."[120]

(3) Far more provocative and exotic is the development in the speculation on the fall by which Eve's temptation and sin came to be regarded as sexual in nature. Such views are widespread, though the dating of these texts is not always certain. 2 Enoch 31.6 and 4 Macc 18:6-8 almost certainly reflect on the deception of Eve as an event of sexual seduction, and rabbinic and later Christian sources do so as well.[121]

(4) Texts preserved in later Gnostic writings demonstrate an interest in Eve as the prototype of the superior woman.[122]

117. Nauck, "Die Herkunft des Verfassers der Pastoralbriefe," 96-98; but see Holmes, *Text in a Whirlwind*, 268-72.

118. *Questions on Genesis* 1.33; *Pirqe R. El.* 13 (StrB 1.137-38).

119. *Allegorical Interpretation* 3.59-61.

120. E.g., Schreiner, "An Interpretation of 1 Timothy 2:9-15," 145-46; D. Doriani, "Appendix I: History of the Interpretation of 1 Timothy 2," in Köstenberger et al., eds., *Women in the Church*, 263-64.

121. *Yebam.* 103b; *Gen. Rab.* 18:6; *Protevangelium of James* 13.1; *Barnabas* 12.5; *Diognetus* 12.8; see Küchler, *Schweigen, Schmuck und Schleier*, 44-50; A. T. Hanson, *Studies in the Pastoral Epistles* (London: SPCK, 1968), 65-77.

122. K. Rudolph, *Gnosis: The Nature and History of an Ancient Religion* (Edinburgh: T&T Clark, 1983), 211-12, 215-16, 270-72; for the possible relevance, see Kroeger and Kroeger, *I Suffer Not a Woman*, 105-25.

Those who detect this sort of background behind 2:14, especially (1)-(3) above, often depend upon the capacity of verbs of "deception" (*apataō* and especially *exapataō*) to refer to sexual deceit.[123] While this need not be disputed, the compound verb in question already has a nearer corollary in 2 Cor 11:3, where, in another Pauline use of the deception-of-Eve motif, it served (similarly) to raise the question of the Corinthian church's vulnerability to false teaching. Neither Pauline case reflects the sort of rabbinic elaboration that goes beyond the basic thought of "deception" to something as specific as sexual deception.

But numerous conservative scholars nevertheless read vv. 13-14 within the traditional Jewish grid, asserting that Paul operated from a creation blueprint, even if the gospel (or some other influence) had rubbed off the rougher edges of chauvinism (Gal 3:28). Verse 13 addresses enthusiastic claims and desires on the part of women in the role of teacher (or wanting to be) by reasserting a divinely willed ordering of genders applicable to the household and the church (at least insofar as teaching and preaching go). Verse 14 then comes into play, and what might seem (to some of us) to be a rather reasonable and apt illustration of women being deceived by false teachers is plumbed for a more fundamental truth. What results is an assertion of the inherent gullibility of women, and, by extrapolation, a "created" inaptitude for teaching, appreciating, and formulating doctrine, that would have warmed Philo's heart.[124] Even if one could imagine a Paul so agitated by the extreme behavior of some women, with his back to the wall, resorting temporarily to such argumentation (and a text such as Gal 5:12 illustrates the rhetorical extremes Paul is capable of reaching in difficult situations),[125] it seems highly questionable, in view of the roles of women in Pauline churches,[126] that he endorsed such a view as the general principle.

Consequently, despite the background questions that remain open, it seems more conceivable that vv. 13-14 represent a pointed retelling of the Genesis story in answer to a current distortion of it. First, speculation on the OT and a rereading of the early chapters of Genesis were core elements of this heresy (1:4; 4:1-5, discussions). Second, there are indications that women were involved in or influenced by the heresy and thus either propa-

---

123. See esp. Hanson, *Studies,* 72-73; Küchler, *Schweigen, Schmuck und Schleier,* 44-50.

124. E.g., Philo, *Questions on Genesis* 1.33, 46. Cf. Webb, *Slaves, Women and Homosexuals,* Appendix B, 263-68.

125. Of course the feminist view attributes this retrograde appeal to Jewish chauvinism to a Paulinist retreating to a safer patriarchal environment.

126. Teaching, Acts 18:26; prophesying, 1 Cor 14:26; some level of leadership/ministry status, Rom 16:1, 3, 7, etc.; cf. Keener, *Paul, Women and Wives,* 237-57. See also on Titus 2:3.

gated elements of it or assumed the role of teacher on its basis, perhaps with support from the opponents. Third, there are strong indications that certain features of the traditional role of women (marriage and childbearing) were being set aside on the basis of the false teaching. Fourth, if the overrealized views alluded to in 2 Tim 2:18 were at all within the purview of 1 Timothy,[127] then all the theological chemistry necessary to unloose traditional values would have been present. Add to this mix, fifthly, the likely influence on this circle of wealthy wives (and widows) of the emancipationist, progressive "new Roman woman" trend, and a critical mass fueled by theological enthusiasm and aberration and cultural innovation can easily be imagined, even if the historical and social interweaving of these forces makes the task of unraveling them extremely difficult. It should be noted that the devaluation and avoidance of pregnancy (including the practice of contraception and abortions) associated with the new movement suggests a point of convergence with the heretical prohibition of marriage (4:3); by being agents of such a "liberated" view, wealthy wives could have been unwitting purveyors of the heresy.

In such an atmosphere of enthusiasm and innovation, where the operative concept was "reversal of roles," if wives/women were usurping the public role of husbands/men and exerting authority in a way that disrespected their male counterparts, v. 13 is a reminder that the Genesis story properly read in no way legitimates the reversal or the behavior.[128] If heretical speculation on the early chapters of Genesis (fueled by imbalanced eschatology) somehow influenced women to think they were free from the constraints and limitations brought on by the fall into sin,[129] v. 14 not only reminds women of their complicity in the fall and of the present unfinished nature of Christian existence, but it does so in a way that aptly illustrates the deception of wives/women in Ephesus by false teachers (2 Cor 11:3). The application of this motif to the attraction of wealthy wives to a permissive and materialistic cultural trend is equally apt, though the focus on a deviant use of Genesis is probably to the fore.

The situation Paul addressed was a complicated confluence of both cognitive and practical factors. He may have been looking in two directions

---

127. Towner, *Goal*, 29-42; Schlarb, *Die gesunde Lehre,* 117-31.

128. Omission of the mitigating factor included in 1 Cor 11:12 is understandable where women have already stepped over the line. Kroeger's attempt to match 2:13 to a specific articulation of false doctrine (the claim on the part of woman to be the originator of man, which she links to the Artemis cult) remains speculative because it is verifiable only from later Gnostic sources (see Kroeger and Kroeger, *I Suffer Not a Woman;* and assessment in Towner, "Feminist Approaches to the New Testament").

129. Or more specifically if they appealed to the Adam-sinner model of Romans 5 to make their better claim to the right to teach (see Marshall, 467).

at once — toward heretical developments and cultural influences. Some wealthy wives/women either emerged as teachers, or were functioning in such a way in the church's public assembly that they would be regarded as teachers, and teaching in a way that abused authority and disrespected husbands and men. A heretical reading of the creation story somehow supported their progressive, role-reversal inclinations. Paul's response was to prohibit these wives from teaching and to refute the fallacious reading of Genesis.

Verse 15a apparently prolongs the Genesis echo: "but women [lit. she] will be saved through childbearing." The main reason for suggesting this possibility is the term *teknogonia* ("childbearing"), which may well be a re-fashioning of the idea expressed in the verb-object combination *texē tekna* ("you shall give birth to children") in Gen 3:16. Also, by extending the allusion to this clause, which retains the singular as in the Genesis 3 account, we may be helped to explain why the shift to the plural (from "she" to "they") is delayed until the subsequent clause (v. 15b).

> 1 Tim 2:15a: "but she will be saved (preserved) through childbearing (*teknogonia*)";
> Gen 3:16: "And to the woman he said, 'I will greatly multiply your pains and your groaning; in pain you shall bring forth children (*texē tekna*), and your submission shall be to your husband, and he shall rule over you.'"

The meaning of the statement is disputed for several reasons. First, the verb "to save"[130] is capable of physical and spiritual meanings. Its assumed subject (now in the singular) is probably the (singular) woman of vv. 12-13, but a dual reference made by way of intertextual echo that includes Eve in some paradigmatic way is not at all impossible. If spiritual "salvation" is envisioned, the meaning will range along a spectrum from "conversion" to "perseverance in present salvation" to "final eschatological deliverance." The physical sense would imply safety and well-being through the experience of giving birth.

Second, the preposition that links "childbearing" to "salvation" *(dia)* could express the means of salvation or indicate more loosely an accompanying circumstance.[131] Means would probably correspond more closely to a

---

130. See the discussion at 1:15. σῴζω (here in fut. pass.: "she will be saved") has the spiritual sense rather uniformly throughout these letters to coworkers (I. H. Marshall, "Faith and Works in the Pastoral Epistles," *SNT [SU]* 9 [1984]: 203-18, esp. 206) and the NT epistles.

131. On the range of meaning of the Gk. preposition διά (here with gen. obj., "through, by"), see M. J. Harris, *NIDNTT* 3:1177.

spiritual sense of salvation (cf. 1 Cor 15:2), but the sense in which "child-bearing" could serve as a means is open to question (see below). A looser reference to accompanying circumstances would correspond to salvation in the sense of physical safety.

Third, an allusion to Genesis in the term "childbearing" will unavoidably call to mind in some way the curse on the woman and perhaps other elements of that scene as well. I will adopt a position below. But the sense of the term "childbearing" will be central to a solution. Regardless of its echoing function, it is a medical reference to pregnancy, which possibly extends from the basic sense of pregnancy and giving birth to the raising of children.[132]

The intentional linkage to the Genesis account partly explains what is an otherwise unexpected turn of Paul's thought in v. 15a. Winter, however, rightly draws our attention to another tendency within the new woman movement — "the aversion to having children by rich or progressive wives"[133] — that suggests that Paul continues to look in more than one direction as he assesses and addresses the behavior of wealthy wives in Ephesus. As suggested above, it may well be that in this particular element we see the convergence of the heresy, with its objection to marriage (i.e., to sexual relations), and the cultural movement. By adopting and popularizing this radical departure from the traditional value of childbearing, wealthy wives in Ephesus (whether intentionally or not) endorsed one element of the heresy.

Consequently, as the instructions reach a conclusion, it is the puzzling addition of v. 15a-b that brings the discourse fully home to these women. Bearing in mind again the intertwining of elements in the background, v. 15a addresses both an element of the heresy and an element within the secular "new woman" paradigm. Its allusion to Gen 3:16 serves two related purposes. First, in response to confusion about the times and women's roles, it prolongs the allusion to Genesis 3 in a way that establishes the eschatological "location" of the Ephesian Christian women — as still being in that paradoxical place of pain (struggle, tension, sin, etc.) and divine promise. Secondly, it reinforces the continuing relevance, importance, and value of the traditional role model being subverted both by the heresy (4:3) and by the values of the "new women." The statement's affirmation of pregnancy and childbearing may also specifically counter the deviant prohibition of marriage

132. Gk. τεκνογονία (only here in the NT; cf. the verb τεκνογονέω in 5:14; τεκνοτροφέω ["raising children"] in 5:10); for secular references, see esp. A. J. Köstenberger, "Ascertaining Women's God-ordained Roles: An Interpretation of 1 Timothy 2:15," *BBR* 7 (1997): 107-44; S. E. Porter, "What Does It Mean to Be 'Saved by Childbirth' (1 Timothy 2.15)," *JSNT* 49 (1993): 87-102; Winter, *Roman Wives,* 109-12. For the wider meaning (including raising a family), see Dibelius and Conzelmann, 48; Fee, 75; Kelly, 69.

133. Winter, *Roman Wives,* 109.

(4:3; cf. 5:14) and disclose one element of doctrine being taught by these wives.[134]

From the list of possible interpretations,[135] the language of the phrase and the background considerations suggest that (one way or another) Christian women were not to forego or avoid pregnancy. Willingness to become pregnant (and perhaps to see it through to childbirth) was apparently a very real concern. Whether or not the term *teknogonia* ("childbearing, pregnancy") is meant to typify the whole of the domestic life (bearing children and raising them), the appended phrase (v. 15b) with its final reiteration of "self-control" (cf. v. 9) effectively widens the scope to include the respectable wife's proper attention to household responsibilities. Bearing children will not be a means of earning salvation, and it is doubtful if "saving" means simply physical safety through childbirth.[136] Rather, Paul urges these Christian wives to re-engage fully in the respectable role of the mother, in rejection of heretical and secular trends, through which she may "work out her salvation."[137]

Winter sees in the instruction a more precise reference to the option of aborting a pregnancy — possibly an attractive alternative for a progressive Roman woman who found herself pregnant: "the Christian wife would be preserved by continuing in her pregnant condition (and thereby bearing a child) instead of terminating her pregnancy."[138] Presumably, his "preserved by" is a reference either to continuing in salvation or escaping from a temptation (from Satan?) to take some action that would put her faith in jeopardy (e.g., terminating her pregnancy).[139] But this amounts to the same thing: the role in which the Christian wife is to persevere so as to actualize salvation ("she shall be saved through") is the traditionally valued domestic role typified by childbearing.

Reversing the false teaching regarding marriage (and the cultural trend) was one crucial part of the solution. But as vv. 9-10 indicated, a broader rejection of Christian values was at stake in the dress and behavior of

---

134. *Contra* Schreiner, "1 Timothy 2:9-15," 151. The reference to "childbearing" is made not only because it is most representative of the role of women (in absolute distinction from men); it also specifically counters an implication of the heresy and (possibly) a cultural trend among wealthy wives.

135. For which see Porter, "What Does It Mean?" 87-102; Marshall, 468-70.

136. But cf. Barrett, 56-57; Keener, *Paul, Women and Wives,* 118-20.

137. Marshall, 470; Kelly, 69; Fee, 75; Moo, "1 Timothy 2:11-15," 71-73.

138. Winter, *Roman Wives*, 109-12, 111.

139. He cites approvingly the expanded translation of A. Köstenberger, *Studies in John and Gender* (New York: Peter Lang, 2001), 307, cited on 320: "She (i.e., the woman) escapes (or is preserved; gnomic future) [from Satan] by way of procreation (i.e., having a family)."

these wives. Therefore Paul stresses in closing that to ensure the outworking of salvation these women must "continue in"[140] the manner of living characterized by the marks of authentic Christian existence. The shift back to the plural applies the general teaching given in the singular (vv. 11-12, 14) to the whole circle of wives/women (pl. in vv. 9-10). The set pairing of "faith and love" (see the discussion at 1:14) summarizes the whole of the Christian life in terms of one's relationship with God and its outworking in sacrificial service in the human sphere. "Holiness" indicates separation from sin and probably implies sexual purity (1 Thess 4:3, 4, 7) in contrast to the promiscuity associated with the prohibited dress code.[141]

Finally, with a concluding prepositional phrase, Paul brackets the whole discussion by repeating and emphasizing the importance of "self-control" ("propriety"; TNIV), the cardinal virtue that anchored the opening description of respectable feminine adornment (v. 9, Excursus).[142] This second reference to the feminine cardinal virtue ties together the whole discussion of adornment, speech, and attitudes toward marriage, household, and childbearing. The dress and behavior of these prominent Christian women would create either a positive or a negative perception in the public mind. The prohibited style of dress and the grasping for dominance would communicate an undesirable message to those who observed these wealthy Christian women in public places.

Methodology and Application

The line argued above seeks to reconstruct a set of circumstances that called forth Paul's instructions, and suggests that the creation material accessed served other than simply a universalizing paradigmatic purpose. While I do not feel the text needs to be jettisoned or abandoned, either because it is non-Pauline (and of secondary authority) or because of its failure to express a liberating perspective in regard to women, I do feel the traditional understanding of the text fails to account for a more fundamental liberating and egalitarian trajectory within the gospel that determines the Pauline program of mission. The feminist dialogue's evaluation of the liberating potential of this gospel is, I think, correct. But as I have endeavored to explain above, its un-

---

140. For Gk. μένω ("to remain, stay, abide") in the sense of "continuing in," see 2 Tim 3:14; 1 John 4:16; 2 John 9. Cf. F. Hauck, *TDNT* 4:574-76.

141. Gk. ἁγιασμός (Rom 6:19, 22; 1 Cor 1:30; 2 Thess 2:13; Heb 12:14; 1 Pet 1:2); H. Balz, *EDNT* 1:17-18.

142. The dominance of σωφροσύνη among the items listed is established by setting it into its own prepositional phrase (in this case with μετά); see Johnson, 203; Marshall, 471.

derstanding of the motives leading to this text's divergence from that gospel impulse (the chauvinistic return to patriarchy) is, I think, in error.

If the teaching of 1 Tim 2:11-15 is set properly within the broader frame that includes vv. 8-10, then the public dimension of the circumstances is more easily seen. If, moreover, the teaching is set equally within the discourse initiated at 2:1, from which point Paul's mission and the church's participation within it (see also v. 8) assume a place of priority within his treatment of community matters, then the public nature of the instructions to wives/women reflects a mission and witness coloration.

The point of raising questions about the traditionalist/hierarchicalist interpretation is not to challenge the text's authority, but rather the way in which the text's authority is to be exercised within the church.

The Role of the Equality Tradition

Some questions need to be asked of the methodological framework of both the extreme feminist position and the hierarchicalist position introduced above, and we turn first to Gal 3:28. Of the latter view, I will simply say that the indications of the equality tradition (Gal 3:28; 1 Cor 12:13; Col 3:11) in Paul's theology seem to me to bear more directly on the matter at hand (i.e., wives and women participating in activities typically restricted to men) than often allowed. This can be challenged, but it seems doubtful to me that 1 Tim 2:11-15 closes the case.

But I am more concerned here with establishing a balance, and so those at the other end of the spectrum need to be asked next whether Paul in penning a text such as Gal 3:28 clearly meant it as a proclamation of liberty to be experienced immediately and fully in all dimensions of life. It seems to me that it cannot be this simple, or Paul would have been far more forthright in pursuing its implementation. Gal 3:28, for instance, addresses three kinds of fundamental relationships or distinctions — racial, economic (perhaps), and gender. But are all these relationships to be viewed on the same basis? Slavery was already common to Hebrew culture when the covenant was made with Moses. The law provides guidelines for its regulation. It may be argued that racial distinctions between Jews and Greeks (Gentiles) were encouraged for a time, but clearly bigotry and exclusive claims to spiritual superiority have human origins. Of the three pairs, only distinctions related to gender trace directly back to the record of God's creative activity. This is not to say that Gal 3:28 has no bearing on the issue. In fact the reverse is true. The liberating and equalizing intentions of the gospel announced in Gal 3:28 have been initiated, and a trajectory is clearly detectable. This must be the implication of the tradition's citation in Galatians, where only the question of Jew-Gentile inequality is in view. But the view that this text is a straightforward declaration calling for the immediate eradication of all social distinctions is too simple. Paul's own approach to the three relationships suggests that a number of factors would come into play to determine the timing and degree of the equality-change to be implemented in any given context.

There are at least two other questions that might well be raised in this context of a Pauline or NT approach to social institutions and movement in the direction of freedom, or in the direction of patriarchal bondage, as the more radical feminist views it.

Christianity and Culture

The first has to do with an understanding of and sensitivity to culture. On the one hand, Paul and other NT writers seem to have viewed their world and its structures as part of God's design. They could encourage the church to "submit to" the institutions of the world (1 Pet 2:13) and (as far as possible) through generally acceptable behavior to make a redemptive impression in it (1 Thess 4:11-12; 1 Tim 3:7; 6:1). But this view was held in tension with a firm belief that the world is an evil force opposed to God. The church was by no means to allow culture or society to dictate its policies (Rom 12:2; 1 John 2:11-17); yet, where possible, peaceful coexistence would help the church's evangelistic mission. The NT household codes give some evidence of social awareness and cultural sensitivity, but they never advocate conformity for conformity's sake. Ultimately, it is reasonable to think that Paul or any other NT writer would have stopped short of advocating the immediate abolition of, for example, slavery because the culture might perceive it as a threat.[143]

Eschatology and Salvation

Another question is: How did the NT (or Pauline) conception of salvation affect the implementation of gospel freedom? For feminists in the tradition of Fiorenza (as with Liberation Theology in general) salvation here and now means liberation. And the church's brief is to actualize it now. But there is another picture of salvation — often characterized with the phrase "already and not yet" — that is a combination of things to be realized progressively in this life (victory over sin, growth in godliness) and promises to be fulfilled only with the full arrival of the Eschaton (the resurrection, the final victory over sin). It is my view that God's salvation in Christ as it comes to expression in the social life of the church (as well as in relation to personal sanctifi-

---

143. On the need and justification for cultural analysis in the matter of the role of women in the church, see esp. Webb, *Slaves, Women and Homosexuals*.

cation) is best regarded as progressive, underway but not finished, "already" but "not yet."

If this is so, then in principle the term "progress" (as opposed to immediate actualization) might also apply in the matter of achieving equality for women in ministry. The factors determining the balance between speed of implementation and caution in experimentation will include society's readiness to absorb innovative shock, because the nonnegotiable of Paul's agenda was mission. When he seems to draw back from innovation in the case of women (and slaves?), such as we see in 1 Tim 2:11-12, fear for the church's reputation and witness may well be supreme. As we have seen, the complicating factors of a suspicious cultural trend among women and some link to the heresy make it plain that the matter at hand was not simply that of innovation or gospel freedom, but rather an exploitative and dangerous exercise of it. But in any case, in the end experimentation with greater freedom in women's ministry activities might, for the sake of the church's mission, need to move in concert with cultural trends. What this means for Christianity in traditional Asian or Muslim contexts is that too much too fast could endanger the church's witness and credibility. But in much of the Western world, too little too slow could neutralize the church's impact in society just as effectively.

4. Regarding Qualifications of Overseers and Deacons (3:1-13)

Within this two-part section, two categories of leader in the church are considered. Both the order of treatment and the more elaborate introduction to the table of qualifications of the overseer suggest that it was this role that presented the more pressing need. Each leadership role is regarded from the standpoint of qualifications, not duties, and from this it is clear that Paul's stress was on the quality of the leaders' character, though the presence of suitable gifts and abilities would be an assumed requirement.

From one subsection to the next (3:1-7, 8-13), there is a good deal of overlap in the qualities linked to each person, and in each case these go to describe the same general requirement of an irreproachable (blameless) reputation. Behind this concern was either an actual or anticipated leadership crisis, perhaps related to the activities of the false teachers. It seems clear that the emergence of opponents in the church would have caused a number of problems related to leadership. Some of the opponents themselves may have been elders, whose defection would not only create a vacuum in the leadership ranks but also promote competition to fill their spots. This kind of disturbance might also have planted seeds of doubt about the leadership positions and the people filling them.

The need to consolidate the church at this level calls forth from Paul both an endorsement for the positions, and guidelines to ensure that godly people are selected to occupy them. The nature of the qualifications set out and the broad concern for the leaders' reputations suggest that respectability of the sort that would sustain or establish the church's credibility in society was uppermost in mind.

Before exploring the teaching in depth, it will be necessary to introduce two elements that will shape our understanding of the nature and role of leadership in Ephesus: the form of the teaching, and the official nomenclature.

The Form of 3:1-7

Most scholars agree that the section 3:2-7, following the faithful saying endorsement, 3:1, represents what may be termed loosely a "duty code." Its shape is noticeably similar to Titus 1:6-9, which suggests that traditional materials have been employed, though by no means slavishly, or at least that Paul worked with a particular duty code pattern in addressing overseers and elders in the two letters.[1] And it bears a resemblance to secular list-codes that provide instructions for various occupations.[2] Within this overseer code, positive qualities and negative vices occur in lists, a characteristic that links it to the wider presentation in these letters of ethical virtues and vices in lists.[3] This practice is found throughout Paul, and probably reflects the influence of Greek ethics upon Hellenistic Jewish literature.[4]

The comparable features of the two codes include the following items. First, a specific introductory line appears in each code; here I depart from the TNIV rendering since it fails to capture the parallelism:

> 1 Tim 3:2: Therefore it is necessary for the overseer to be above reproach *(anepilēmpton).*
> Titus 1:7: For it is necessary for the overseer to be beyond reproach *(anenklēton).*

---

1. There is of course no reason why Paul could not have devised the codes himself; the similarities and differences are most explainable if the same person wrote the letters at about the same time to different situations.

2. See the references and discussion in Dibelius and Conzelmann, 158-60; Easton, 197-202; Schwarz, *Bürgerliches Christentum,* 88-95.

3. For virtue lists outside the duty codes, see 1 Tim 4:12; 6:11, 18; 2 Tim 2:22, 24; 3:10; Titus 2:2, 3, 5, 7-8, 9-10; for vice lists, see 1 Tim 1:9-10; 6:4-5; 2 Tim 3:2-4; Titus 3:3.

4. Rom 1:29-31; 1 Cor 5:11; 6:9-10; Gal 5:19-21; Eph 2:1-2; Col 3:5-9. On the question of background, see the surveys in J. T. Fitzgerald, "Virtue/Vice Lists," n.p. ABD on CD-ROM. Version 2.1a, 1995, 1996, 1997; for further discussion and references, see Towner, *Goal,* 160-61.

The differences are minor. Differing connecting particles are required by the contexts into which the materials are inserted.[5] And the different predicate adjectives for "blamelessness" are synonymous.[6]

Second, the joining of "blamelessness" and fidelity in marriage in each setting also suggests a linkage of some sort between the two duty codes:[7]

> 1 Tim 3:2: above reproach, husband of one wife
> Titus 1:6: blameless, husband of one wife.

Finally, there is a general compatibility of the various qualities (adjectives and nouns) endorsed and vices discouraged in leaders.[8] Dibelius has argued that the kinds of qualities enumerated in the lists are too general to be associated with any particular local sitiuation.[9] But the additions and subtractions seem rather to point to a specific shaping of the instructional material for the respective contexts (see below and at Titus 1:6-9). What may be more significant is the fact that most of the qualities concentrated in the duty codes are elsewhere applied to believers in general. The effect of gathering the traits together in these parenetic texts is to stress that leaders are to be models of the behavior described for everyone in the church.

In the code of 1 Timothy 3, the sentence structure of 3:2 shows that irreproachability is the broad requirement. Concrete positives and negatives follow to fill out the meaning.[10] These will span the leader's private and public personal behavior and consider his ability to lead in the household.

Overseers and Elders

The occurrence of official titles and the relative concern in 1 Timothy and Titus for church organization has led to various hypotheses to explain the situa-

---

5. In the case of 1 Tim 3:2, the code of instructions follows logically from 3:1 (οὖν), while Titus 1:7 (with its following list of items) is more appropriately joined to the requirements given in 1:6 with γάρ (see the discussion at Titus 1:6-7; see Quinn, 85; Marshall, 148; D. C. Verner, *The Household of God: The Social World of the Pastoral Epistles* (Chico, CA: Scholars Press, 1983), 104-6; Towner, *Goal,* 225.

6. The choice of ἀνέγκλητον in Titus 1:7 may be conditioned by the term's occurrence in 1:6.

7. Verner, *Household of God,* 70, 72; P. Trummer, "*Einehe* nach den Pastoralbriefe: Zum Verständnis der Termini *mias gunaikos anēr* und *henos andros gunē,*" *Bib* 51 (1970): 473-74; Schwarz, *Bürgerliches Christentum,* 76-78.

8. See the comparisons in Dibelius and Conzelmann, 133.

9. Dibelius and Conzelmann, 99.

10. See Towner, *Goal,* 230-31.

tion. Often the developed three-tiered ecclesiastical organization found in Ignatius's letters (c. 110 C.E.; a single bishop presiding over elders and deacons) has been the benchmark by which these two letters have been assessed. Simply put, however, there is very little indication in them of a degree of church organization that comes very close to the scenario depicted in Ignatius. But it has been common to place them in the line leading from charismatic (non-official) leadership to the later monepiscopal model.

Our knowledge of church structure and the organization of authority at the time Paul wrote to Titus and Timothy, as well as to churches, is very limited — in fact, it is so limited that it is impossible to determine anything more than the broadest parameters of the authority structure of a local Pauline church.[11] We know of churches that met in households (1 Cor 16:19; Phlm 2), and churches associated with cities (1 Cor 1:2). But we do not know the precise relationship between them, nor very much about the details of their running. What seems to be clear from the two relevant letters to coworkers[12] is that neither Timothy nor Titus exercises a local church role. Timothy appears to relate to the single Ephesian church in the capacity of apostolic delegate (1:3). Titus, however, in the same capacity appears to be in charge of at least several churches associated with Cretan towns (Titus 1:5). The increased interest in leadership and church structure might indicate a period of development or transition, from a looser, more informal model of leadership to a more rigid and formal model. But the evidence in support of this conclusion (primarily the occurrence of titles and instruction in letters presumed to be late over and against a focus more on charismatic gifts and practical functions in letters presumed to be earlier; but see Phil 1:1) is not the sort that that sufficiently fills all the gaps. The language of function and role was flexible, and undoubtedly within an overarching unity plenty of diversity existed from one local setting to another. And there seems to be no such thing as a straight-line development from a so-called informal Pauline church organization to the sort of setup indicated in Ignatius's writings.

Whatever shape church order in Asia Minor or Rome eventually took, what may be reconstructed from Paul's letters bears a closer resemblance to what may be generalized as typical of leadership and authority structures in both the Greco-Roman and Jewish cultures.[13] For example, within the Jewish orbit, in the case of the Qumran sect and the Diaspora synagogue management, oversight and the exercise of authority involved both individual leaders and councils. Qumran writings describe the

11. Rightly Johnson, 222.
12. 2 Timothy does not consider church order.
13. For this summary, I am indebted to Johnson, 218-19.

mebaqqer, whose tasks overlap significantly with those of the overseer described in 1 Timothy and Titus.[14] Assisting him with oversight, in some sense, was apparently a council of twelve men and three priests (1QS 8:1-4). Details are sometimes lacking, but the general sense of leaders and councils seems clear. What little is known about synagogue organization and management suggests that a council of elders (*gerousia* usually, not *presbyteroi*) worked in concert with the one (or more) designated as the "ruler(s) or the synagogue" (*archisynagogos;* e.g., Acts 13:15; 18:17). Though it has recently been stressed that the Jewish elders of the people had little responsibility within the religious life of the communities and more in civic life, it is misleading to distinguish too rigidly between religious and civic dimensions of life in ancient Judaism. Equally, outside of Judaism, various organizations in the Greek and Roman world depended upon administrative boards for financial and cultic management. In both contexts, it was natural that the successful heads of households — those having social prestige, honor, and wealth — would gravitate to the positions of authority within the various communities and groups. While it is not necessary to think that the Pauline communities would have followed these patterns rigidly, it is reasonable to believe that what was customary would naturally have exerted a significant influence on matters of organization. The point is this: what we see of community structure and leadership in 1 Timothy and Titus corresponds generally to the models in both Judaism and Greco-Roman culture. And the same is true of the undisputed Paulines.

Differences between the picture of organization that emerges from 1 Timothy and the one (say, from 1 Corinthians) normally thought to typify "the Pauline church" may be more imagined than real. It is sometimes argued that the emergence of the "offices" (if this term is even appropriate) reflects a transitional stage from charismatic ministry to "official" ministry, as if the two concepts could not exist side by side.[15] But texts like 1 Cor 16:15-16 and 1 Thess 5:12 certainly at least blur this distinction, although the emphasis on "function" should be noted. In any case, despite the absence of official language (for reasons quite beyond our retrieval), the coexistence of these two entities from early on is more than a remote possibility.

First, in one of his earliest letters, Paul in writing to the Thessalonian church uses the same language to denote "the exercise of leadership" that occurs in 1 Timothy (3:4; 5:17) and distinguishes those who lead from those

14. See B. Thiering, "*Mebaqqer* and *Episkopos* in the Light of the Temple Scroll," *JBL* 100 (1981): 59-74; H. W. Beyer, *TDNT* 2:618-19; R. A. Campbell, *The Elders: Seniority within Earliest Christianity* (Edinburgh: T&T Clark, 1994), 155-59.

15. So, e.g., H. von Campenhausen, *Ecclesiastical Authority and Spiritual Power in the Church of the First Three Centuries* (Stanford: Stanford University Press, 1969).

who do not. And these leaders appear to have functioned in comparable ways (1 Thess 5:12).

Second, 1 Corinthians is often held up as the model of a charismatic, Spirit-led community. But there is ample evidence of the existence of those recognized as authority figures, who are to adjudicate wisely in disputes, who are to be respected community members, who are able to lead and carry out practical service (6:1-6; 12:28; 16:15-18). The existence of an abundance of gifts in that community, and the filtering of much of Paul's discussion about ministry through this "charismatic" language, does not disguise the overlap of the Corinthian church's leadership structure and the Ephesian church's as presented through a different filter in 1 Timothy.

Third, Romans shares this charismatic filter (12:7-8), but the gifts include those having to do with ministering *(diakonia),* teaching *(didaskalia),* exhorting *(paraklēsis),* and leading *(proistamenos),* things that also aptly describe the functions of the overseer/elder/deacon (cf. 1 Tim 3:2-4; 5:17; Titus 1:9). Moreover, 16:1 names Phoebe a "deacon" (of the church at Cenchreae, near Corinth; cf. Phil 1:1).

Fourth, Gal 6:6 indicates the existence of paid teachers, which in turn says something about the formality of church structure in other Pauline churches.

Consequently, in 1 Timothy the conclusion that seems most supported by this survey is that the charismata related to leadership would be expected of the overseers and elders (Rom 12:7-8; 1 Cor 12:28; cf. 1 Tim 3:5; Titus 1:9). But there is no indication that participation in ministry was necessarily limited to those named overseers, elders, and deacons, or that the charismatic gifts had been absorbed into the roles designated by those titles. There is little reason to argue for fluidity in the case of the undisputed Paulines and rigidity in the case of 1 Timothy and Titus. Allusions in the latter to Spirit-filled ministry going beyond the official leadership structure are few but nonetheless telling (1 Tim 4:14; 2 Tim 2:2). Most likely what is found in 1 Timothy is a greater concern to stabilize and restore a leadership structure that was battered and depleted by the heresy. Titus seems more concerned to establish this model of leadership in fledgling churches to assist them with the task of settling into an unstable culture, though the growing presence of opposition from rebellious teachers is also evident.

But what more can be said about church structure in 1 Timothy and Titus? The term "overseer" *(episkopos)* occurs in reference to a church leader four times in the NT (Acts 20:28; Phil 1:1; 1 Tim 3:2; Titus 1:7). It seems preferable to avoid the translation "bishop" since this term carries so much later ecclesiastical baggage with it. In Greek life, the overseer was one who supervised or led in various situations. The term was taken into the LXX to describe a range of leaders in charge of civil and/or religious affairs.[16] Whether or not LXX use of the term led to the Greek-speaking church's later adoption of it, it is probably the currency of the term in Hellenistic society that accounts for its appearance in the church's leadership nomenclature.

What can be discerned of the duties of the overseer suggests that he (either singly or as one of a number of overseers) had oversight of teaching in the church and correction and refutation of false doctrine. The requirement of integrity with money may also imply responsibility for financial matters (3:3-4). Household imagery, such as the term "steward" *(oikonomos),* provides a helpful analogue to place the overseer and his responsibility (to people, acting on behalf of God) within the church. The authority to discipline, adjudicate in certain matters, and give various kinds of guidance fell to the overseer. But the reality of the analogy, and the distinction between household and household of God, must be maintained.

The occurrence of the term "elder" alongside of "overseer" in these letters should be considered. The Greek term "elders" *(presbyteroi)* was used in Hellenistic Judaism to refer collectively to the older members of the community. It was mainly a term that denoted status or prestige rather than function.[17] The term *gerousia,* which was preferred in Greek culture to describe comparable councils of older men, overlaps in usage with *presbyteroi* and at least in some cases appears to be identical (cf. 1 Macc 12:6 with 14:20; Josephus, *Antiquities* 13.5, 8). The body described by either term has power to represent the people and to preside over administrative matters (1 Macc 7:33; 11:23; 12:35; 13:36; 14:20, 28). The preference for the term *gerousia* in Greek culture probably suggests a Jewish background for the early church's adoption of *presbyteroi.*[18] As suggested above, while the Jewish elders of the people may have exerted their influence in civic and social matters, and less obviously in purely religious matters, it is misleading to think that they, or their presence, played no role in religious leadership. The point is well made, however, that the elders that emerge in the early church seem to have taken to themselves religious authority that in contemporary Judaism normally resided in other figures. Nonetheless, the formalization of the Christian category "elders as leaders" appears to have been a natural development that occurred in the church (Acts 11:30; 15:2). As in Judaism, where the status of seniority and prestige was acquired through age, family, and probably also social standing as heads of households, so too in the early church these same factors, including economic status, put certain people into a better position to function as leaders in a household church. In this way, the sense of the term "elders" in the early

16. See Beyer, *TDNT* 2:611-14; Johnson, 217-20.
17. See the discussion in Marshall, 172-74; Towner, *Goal,* 223-25.
18. Johnson, 218-19.

church slid between that of older men and that of leaders, eventually gaining the more specific "official" denotation (though not to the exclusion of the original reference to age and prestige; cf. 1 Tim 5:1).

Much has been made of the fact that the term *presbyteroi* does not occur in the undisputed Pauline letters,[19] while Paul does know the terms *episkopoi* and *diakonoi* (Phil 1:1). Luke's associating of the term with Paul's mission (Acts 14:23; 20:17) does not necessarily reflect Paul's lexicon. And it is not necessary to pit the language of Luke's recounting of Paul's ministry against Paul's own. Perhaps the term was not typical in the majority of Paul's churches, or not the one he would typically use (though for discussions of "official" structure we are limited to Phil 1:1 anyway, which hardly suggests a useful sample). Luke's description of the Ephesian church (Acts 20:17, 28) does suggest that the terms *presbyteroi* and *episkopoi* were both known and used, or at least that the setup was adequately described with this language. In that case, where the terms seem to be interchangeable, the term "overseer" views the leaders from the perspective of function (oversight), while "elder" views the leader from the perspective of position or status.

In the letters to Timothy and Titus, *presbyteroi* occurs in reference to leaders in 1 Tim 5:17, 19 and Titus 1:5. Some of those so named carried out the functions of teaching and preaching (1 Tim 5:17), but the implication is that the primary function of the elders was to exercise leadership *(proestōtes)* in the church (5:17). In Titus 1:5(6) "elders" also carries the meaning of leader, and seems to be interchangeable with the term "overseers" (1:7). But it is notable that the term can still designate simply older men (1 Tim 5:1; cf. Titus 2:2), and it is probable that the older men were still the more likely to be leaders in the church (cf. 1 Tim 4:12).

Often the matter of church order in 1 Timothy and Titus teeters on the question of the number of overseers thought to be the norm and on the relationship between "overseers" and "elders." Let us consider both matters as briefly as possible.[20]

In 1 Tim 3:2 and Titus 1:7, the term "overseer" *(episkopos)* is singular, while "elders" seem to be regarded as a plurality (1 Tim 5:17; Titus 1:5) and reference is made to a council of elders *(presbyterion;* 1 Tim 4:14). Reference to the leadership position *(episkopē)* in 1 Tim 3:1 gives no clue as to the number of those who occupy the position in a given church. Bearing in mind the limits of our data, we will set out two reasonable possibilities here.

First, most scholars regard the singular reference to "overseer" to be generic — that is, determined by the duty code that is drawn upon to set out

---

19. See Jas 5:14; 1 Pet 5:1, 5; cf. Dibelius and Conzelmann, 54-57; Roloff, 169-89.

20. More comprehensive discussions of these issues can be found in Towner, *Goal,* 223-41.

the instructions.[21] Drawing on Titus 1:5-7; Acts 20:17, 28, and Phil 1:1, they often come to the conclusion that "overseer" (referring to function) is the equivalent of "elder" (referring to position/status), that they are interchangeable terms, and that the churches in 1 Timothy and Titus envision a plurality of overseers/elders.[22] Some interpreters refine this somewhat, maintaining that overseers, while numbering more than one, were nevertheless a subset of the larger leadership group known as elders.[23] What must be kept in mind in the case of the two texts cited is the unknown element of the relation between house churches and city churches and what collective references to house churches might imply (or not imply) about the number of leaders.

Second, in light of the caveat just expressed, it also seems reasonable to explore another possible model. As Johnson suggests,[24] the simplest interpretation of the data from 1 Timothy yields a picture of church structure in which a single overseer leads in concert with a larger council of elders (4:14) of which he is a part. This singularity of the overseer was probably a practical necessity in the case of the nascent Cretan situation (see the commentary at Titus 1:5-7). In any case, what needs to be noticed in 1 Timothy is that leading was the basic function of the elders (1 Tim 5:17): it may be implied in the case of the overseer, but only specifically in the case of his household (3:4-5); other duties such as teaching and preaching will fall to some of the elders, but they are requisite in the case of the overseer (3:2).

Finally, it is important to stress again the degree of uncertainty in this matter. A church of longer history, such as the church(es) of Ephesus compared with Crete, may well have developed a more complex structure. But this may have meant a development from singular leaders to a plurality of leaders rather than the traditionally argued line of plurality to monarchical episcopacy (Ignatius). It is also important to stress that the information pertaining to leadership found in these letters to coworkers does not diverge significantly from what can be discerned of leadership in the letters to churches to which Paul wrote.

a. Qualifications of Overseers (3:1-7)

> 1 *Here is a trustworthy saying: Whoever aspires to be an overseer desires a noble task.* 2 *Now the overseer is to be above reproach, faith-*

21. Cf. the singular references that describe generic situations in 5:1, 9.

22. See Fee, 22; Kelly, 13, 73-74; Towner, *Goal,* 223-27 (and further refs.).

23. Often equated with those elders worthy of double honor in 1 Tim 5:17; G. Bornkamm, *TDNT* 6:668; H. W. Beyer, *TDNT* 2:617; Brox, 150-51; J. P. Meier, "*Presbyteros* in the Pastoral Epistles," *CBQ* 35 (1973): 324-29. For further refinement yet, see Campbell, *Elders,* 176-209. And see Marshall, 179-80, for assessment.

24. Johnson, 218.

ful to his wife, temperate, self-controlled, respectable, hospitable, able to teach, 3 not given to drunkenness, not violent but gentle, not quarrelsome, not a lover of money. 4 He must manage his own family well and see that his children obey him, and he must do so in a manner worthy of full respect. 5 (If anyone does not know how to manage his own family, how can he take care of God's church?) 6 He must not be a recent convert, or he may become conceited and fall under the same judgment as the devil. 7 He must also have a good reputation with outsiders, so that he will not fall into disgrace and into the devil's trap.

1 The section opens with the second occurrence of the "faithful saying" affirmation formula: "the saying is trustworthy." However, the direction of this formula's reference continues to be debated. Many insist that it actually concludes the preceding section (2:15), emphasizing the reliability of the statement about the salvation of women.[25] If the faithful sayings are indeed all statements about salvation (see the note at 1:15), then the reference may be backward. But it has to be said that 2:15 seems more corrective and ad hoc in nature and unlike a saying. Others, therefore, take the formula to be introductory of the statement lauding the position of the overseer.[26] The decision here to follow the latter course remains somewhat tentative. The additional weight of affirmation it lends to the office may have been intended to shore up support for the church, whose leadership had come under attack for a failure to address the heretical movement or because some of its membership had gone over to the opposition.

The content of the saying is expressed with the generalizing "if anyone . . ." construction ("whoever"; TNIV). In this usage it sets out a condition worthy of fulfillment.[27] In this way, Paul endorses the role of the overseer *(episkopē),*[28] and encourages those who "aspire" to exercise it.[29] The way in

25. NA[27]; Knight, 152-53; Dibelius and Conzelmann, 51; Johnson, 203; see also Schlarb, *Die gesunde Lehre,* 208-10 (in ref. to 2:11-15).

26. Most English versions; Marshall, 475; Fee, 79; P. Ellingworth, "The 'True Saying' in 1 Timothy 3,1," *BT* 31 (1980): 443-45. The variant ἀνθρώπινος, which occurs in place of πιστός in a few MSS (D* b d g) and is certainly secondary, suggests that it was the nontheological character of the statement about overseers (to which the formula refers) that occasioned the scribal correction (Metzger, *TCGNT,* 572-73).

27. For the εἴ τις . . . construction used to induce a positive action, see also 3:5; 5:4, 16; Titus 1:6; to discourage harmful behavior, see 1 Tim 5:8; 6:3; cf. 1:10.

28. Gk. ἐπισκοπή; see Num 4:16; Acts 1:20; H. W. Beyer, *TDNT* 2:606-8. See further the discussion of offices and nomenclature above.

29. For the verb ὀρέγομαι ("to strive for, aspire to"), see Spicq, *TLNT* 2:591-92; H. W. Heidland, *TDNT* 5:447-48.

which Paul frames the thought here should not be taken as evidence that the process of selection somehow excluded divine guidance. It rather aims to increase the value of such leadership in the eyes of the community.

To conclude the positive condition, Paul resorts to language that in these letters slides between the theological and the ethical: "[he] desires a noble task" (or a good work).[30] Here the language of "good deeds," which in the plural figures so prominently in the discussion of the visible Christian life (see on 2:10), is less theological. The adjective stresses the positive and constructive nature ("good, noble") of the "task" under discussion (that of the overseer). Oversight in the church is a ministry that makes a positive contribution to the life of the believing community and, done well, brings honor to the leader. Wouldn't this be fairly obvious instruction? Yes. But again the heresy may have spawned distrust for leaders and a reluctance to take up the responsibilities such leadership required.[31] Paul, however, would not sanction an indiscriminate filling of the role for its own sake. The saying encourages the desire to serve as a leader on the ground that the task is worthy (and of urgent importance). The importance of the task determines the focus of the rest of the leadership code.

2 The code of qualifications for the overseer begins formally with the opening phrase, "therefore the overseer must be."[32] As noted above, the replication of this phrase (with slight modifications) at Titus 1:7 suggests that Paul has adapted (or created) a standard set of instructions to both situations. The conjunction "therefore" shows that the requirements to follow are commensurate with the importance of the office (i.e., they follow from v. 1). The verb expressing "necessity" and its infinitive "to be"[33] continue to be in effect through v. 7, and should then be repeated at v. 8 with the new subject "deacons."

At the head of the list of qualifications is the term "above reproach" (6:14; cf. 5:7; = "blameless" in 1 Tim 3:10; Titus 1:6, 7). It has in mind mainly aspects of behavior (inward and outward) that have observable results,[34] and

---

30. The verb in the apodosis, ἐπιθυμέω, is synonymous with the preceding verb and to be taken in a positive or neutral sense ("to desire, long for"); cf. H. Hübner, *EDNT* 2:28.

31. Cf. Spicq, *TLNT* 2:591-92; Marshall, 476.

32. On the departure from the TNIV ("Now the overseer is to be"), see above on the set form of the phrase. Comparison with the TNIV's rendering of Titus 1:7 ("An elder must be") reveals a decision to relax slightly the sense of "necessity" that opens the code in 1 Tim 3:2. A similar variation is evident in the NIV.

33. Gk. δεῖ (3:15; 5:13; 2 Tim 2:6; Titus 1:7, 11[2x]); for the combination of δεῖ plus εἶναι, cf. Luke 2:49; Plutarch, *Moralia* 4B, 7C. W. Popkes, *EDNT* 1:279-80; W. Grundmann, *TDNT* 2:21-25.

34. Gk. ἀνεπίλημπτος; as a description of the way one lives, see Philo, *On the Creation,* 142; Schwarz, *Bürgerliches Christentum,* 45-46.

as a measurement it signifies that no grounds for reproach or blame have been found. Its placement within the opening phrase and its wide scope suggest that this is the essential requirement for candidacy. Within the overseer code it is equivalent to the requirement of a "good reputation with outsiders" with which the instructions conclude (v. 7). Together these bracketing requirements frame and magnify the concern for the leader's public image.[35] This high ideal parallels the concerns of secular lists that enumerated similar qualities to be found in leaders,[36] which reveals something of Paul's sensitivity to the expectations of wider society. The leader's reputation must be able to withstand assaults from opponents inside or outside the church (v. 7). But each broad concept requires concrete explanation, for which the intervening specifics of character and behavior are provided.

Paul begins with six positive attributes. The first (and most contentious) of these considers the overseer's marriage. The phrase translated "faithful to his wife" (TNIV) is literally "husband of one wife" (Titus 1:6).[37] But the NIV had "the husband of but one wife," and the NRSV has "married only once," so the ambiguity of the phrase is evident. Was it meant to rule out polygamists[38] or to exclude unmarried men from holding the office?[39] Did it intend to prohibit remarriage, either after the death of a spouse[40] or after a divorce?[41] Various considerations make these specific interpretations less than likely,[42] and the broader interests of the passage suggest that fidelity in mar-

---

35. Towner, *Goal,* 230.

36. See esp. Dibelius and Conzelmann, 158-60.

37. Gk. μιᾶς ψυναικὸς ἀνήρ (cf. ἑνὸς ἀνδρὸς γυνή, "one man woman"; 5:9); see esp. Marshall, 155-57; C. H. Dodd, "New Testament Translation Problems II," *BT* 28 (1977): 112-16; Towner, *Goal,* 231-32; S. Page, "Marital Expectations of Church Leaders in the Pastoral Epistles," *JSNT* 50 (1993): 105-20; Trummer, "Einehe nach den Pastoralbriefen," *Bib* 51 (1970): 471-84; Wagener, *Die Ordnung des "Hauses Gottes,"* 172-77.

38. Justin, *Dialogue with Trypho* 134; Simpson, 50; Calvin, 223-24; cf. Lock, 36-37; Knight, 158.

39. Dibelius and Conzelmann, 52.

40. Kelly, 75-76; Verner, *Household of God,* 130-31; Spicq, 430-31.

41. Hanson, 78; A. Oepke, *TDNT* 1:362 n. 11, 788; Jeremias, 24.

42. 1. Prohibiting polygamists from the office of oversight: although polygamy might have been practiced in some Jewish circles (cf. CD 4:20–5:6; Josephus, *Antiquities* 17.14; Str-B 3:648-50), monogamy was the generally accepted norm in Greco-Roman and Jewish culture by this time, and prohibition of polygamy in Christian circles would have been unnecessary (Hanson, 78). Furthermore, assuming a corresponding meaning for the phrase in 5:9, a prohibition of polygamy here would necessitate a prohibition of polyandry there, a practice unknown in that culture. 2. Excluding unmarried men from office: this is thought to be a response to the heretical prohibition of marriage (4:3), but under certain conditions celibacy is endorsed in the Pauline churches (1 Cor 7:32-40), and this interpretation makes a tautology of the corresponding phrase in 5:9. 3a. Excluding from

riage (understood to be monogamous and acceptable in the eyes of the community) is meant.[43] This would assume the inappropriateness of any form of sexual immorality or marriage/remarriage in breach of accepted patterns, though sexual immorality as such is not the sole concern.[44] The domestic assumptions of the code, which may respond to a heretical tendency (4:3), present the overseer as a husband and father. In such a context, the candidate's conduct within the marriage relationship (i.e., faithfulness to his wife) would be an anticipated topic.[45]

Second, the overseer must be "temperate" (3:11; Titus 2:2).[46] The question is whether the term is to be taken as a literal reference to the virtue of moderation in the use of wine (3:3, 8; Titus 2:2, 3)[47] or rather as a figurative reference to balanced, sober thinking.[48] The unequivocal reference to literal sobriety in 3:3 suggests the moral sense of being balanced in thought here. The overseer is to maintain command of his reason, to be watchful and observant of things going on around him, and balanced in his assessments.

Third, "self-control" (see 2:9, Excursus) is required of the overseer. One of the cardinal virtues in Greco-Roman ethical thought, it was appropriated by Hellenistic Judaism and supplied with a theological basis in the Torah (see on

---

leadership those who remarried after the death of a spouse: this view is often based on inscriptions lauding women who remained single after the death of their husbands (Latin: *univira;* Greek: *monandros;* see M. Lightman and W. Zeisel, "Univira: An Example of Continuity and Change in Roman Society," *CH* 46 [1977]: 19-32). However, the evidence is limited to women, and the Greek phrase in question (μιᾶς γυναικὸς ἀνήρ or ἑνὸς ἀνδρὸς γυνή) does not appear in the inscriptions. Furthermore, remarriage was not prohibited in the Pauline churches (Rom 7:1-3; 1 Cor 7:8-9, 39-40), and prohibition of remarriage in the case of leaders is at odds with the encouragement to younger widows to remarry (5:14). 3b. Excluding from leadership those who remarried after a divorce: while this view would allow remarriage in the case of death, it emphasizes texts such as Mark 10:11 (in comparison with more open-ended opinions as in Matt 19:9; 1 Cor 7:15) to posit a higher standard for leaders. Or it may exclude the man who had formerly married an unbeliever, divorced her, and married a believer (so Easton, 212-15). On the whole, this kind of specificity is not at all obvious from the phrase.

43. So most; Fee, 80-81; Marshall, 156-57; Trummer, "Einehe nach der Pastoralbriefe," 471-84; Barrett, 58-59.

44. See Quinn, 86.

45. See the discussion in Trummer, "Einehe nach der Pastoralbriefe," 477-82; Towner, *Goal,* 232.

46. Gk. νηφάλιος ("temperate, sober"; figurative, "self-controlled, soberminded"); BDAG, s.v.; MM, s.v.; see O. Bauernfeind, *TDNT* 4:936-41; Marshall, 186-87.

47. See Philo, *On Sobriety* 2; *On Drunkenness* 123; Josephus, *Antiquities* 3.279; Marshall, 186-87.

48. Philo, *On Abraham* 260; cf. Paul's use of the cognate verb νήφω for "soberminded, clear-headed, free from confusion" (2 Tim 4:5; 1 Thess 5:6, 8; Plutarch, *Moralia* 800B). See Schwarz, *Bürgerliches Christentum,* 48-49.

Titus 1:8). Paul deepened this basis by linking it to the Christ-event (Titus 2:12). The term covers a range of meaning (prudence, moderation, sobriety), but gives the general sense of control over one's behavior and the impulses and emotions beneath it. Although it appears here as a requirement for leadership (Titus 1:8), it was expected of all believers (2:9, 15; Titus 2:2, 4, 5, 6).

The fourth attribute, "respectable," is almost predictable (see 1 Tim 2:9). It occurs frequently alongside "self-control" in the literature,[49] the two together completing a picture of honorable and dignified bearing.[50]

Fifth, the leader must be "hospitable" (Titus 1:8).[51] Hospitality, like most of these qualities, was a practice required of all believers in general,[52] which leaders were to exemplify. Within Hellenistic culture, the hospitable householder was esteemed, and practicing hospitality was a matter of honor. Given the dangers of travel in the empire and the economic uncertainties faced by many believers, the early Christian mission and churches depended on those who would open their homes and share their goods.[53] It seems to be an assumption that overseers were often also householders (vv. 4-5), so it is natural that the church should look to them to model this virtue.

The sixth quality is skill in teaching (2 Tim 2:24; cf. Rom 12:7).[54] This is really the only ministry skill or gift enumerated among the aspects of character that fill out this leadership profile (1 Tim 5:17). Titus 1:9 spells out the requirement in more detail, showing that it would encompass not only instruction but also discipline and correction. And while there is no need to limit the gift to the overseer (cf. 2 Tim 2:2), it is certainly not unexpected that church leaders would be chosen from among those who display this gift.

3 The public life of the candidate comes more clearly into view as the list continues with a mix of prohibitions and positive traits. The first pair of prohibited activities — "not given to drunkenness,[55] not violent"[56] — is replicated in Titus 1:8. Their close association is traditional, revealing the

49. Philo, *On the Special Laws,* 3:89; Spicq, *TLNT* 2:332.
50. See further Schwarz, *Bürgerliches Christentum,* 51.
51. Gk. φιλόξενος; see Spicq, *TLNT* 3:454-57; Stählin, *TDNT* 5:1-36.
52. Rom 12:13; Heb 13:2; 1 Pet 4:9.
53. For the importance of hospitality to mission, see Acts 16:15; 21:7; 28:14; Rom 16:4; *Didache* 11.2, 4; cf. esp. Goppelt, *1 Peter,* 299; Quinn, 90-91.
54. Gk. διδακτικός; K. H. Rengstorf, *TDNT* 2:165; Schwarz, *Bürgerliches Christentum,* 52-53.
55. Gk. πάροινος ("addicted to wine, drunkard") occurs only here and in Titus 1:7 in the NT; not in the LXX. It sometimes refers to behavior characteristic of being drunk (Josephus, *Antiquities* 4.144), but is surely a reference to literal excessive drinking here. See BDAG, s.v.; MM, s.v.
56. Gk. πλήκτης; also limited in the NT to this text and Titus 1:7; not in the LXX. See BDAG, s.v. The word occurs several times in Plutarch's ethical writings. Schwarz, *Bürgerliches Christentum,* 54.

wide acknowledgment that excessive drinking leads to violent behavior.[57] The degrees and modes of violence that the word might express are numerous (bullying, verbal abuse, angry pushing and shoving), and the prohibition should be regarded as widely as possible.

In contrast, a second pair of adjectives, also descriptive of the good Christian testimony in Titus 3:2, supplies qualities that ought instead to characterize the candidate for leadership: "gentle, not quarrelsome." The adjective "gentle" (and the related noun, Acts 24:4; 2 Cor 10:1) covers such a wide range of meaning that precision is difficult to obtain.[58] In the LXX the word group describes a quality of God ("forbearing in justice"), and in secular writings it is also a virtue of legislators ("tolerant and conciliatory") and kings ("showing clemency").[59] As a human virtue it can almost subsume all virtues into itself,[60] coming to mean a "virtuous equilibrium" that expresses itself in a balance between honesty, tolerance, and gentleness. If we attempt to narrow the focus, the context here has human interaction in mind, where in the activity of supervision and leading this quality would express itself in reasonableness, courtesy, and tolerance that involves the ability to give way to others (Phil 4:5; Jas 3:17; 1 Pet 2:18). The link between this quality and Christ (cf. 2 Cor 10:1) assures us that Paul's notions of ethics are theologically determined (Titus 2:11-12).

Closely associated is the adjective meaning "not quarrelsome" ("peaceable").[61] This theme seems to grow out of the disputes that characterize the heretical opponents in each letter to coworkers.[62] As a Christian virtue to be cultivated (cf. Matt 5:9; Rom 12:18), this irenic, constructive demeanor would heal rifts caused by bitter argument, aid in uniting the congregation, and positively contribute to the leader's public reputation.

Closing this second series of qualities is the adjective "not greedy" ("not a lover of money").[63] Paul enumerates this characteristic consistently in

57. See, e.g., Plutarch, *Moralia* 132D (Schwarz, *Bürgerliches Christentum,* 54; Quinn, 80).

58. Gk. ἐπιεικής; Spicq, *TLNT* 2:34-38.

59. For the adjective ἐπιεικής, see Phil 4:5; 1 Tim 3:3; Jas 3:17; 1 Pet 2:18. For the word group used of God, see 2 Macc 2:22; 10:4; in association with mercy, Ps 86:5; Dan 3:42; Bar 2:27. Of political figures, see Philo, *Virtues,* 148; *On the Special Laws* 4.23; *On the Embassy to Gaius,* 119. Of kings, Josephus, *Antiquities* 15.14, 177.

60. Aristotle, *Poetics* 13.1452b; Herodotus 1.85; Philo, *On the Confusion of Tongues* 37 (where the compound form ἐπιεικέστεροι means "well bred").

61. Gk. ἄμαχος; O. Bauernfeind, *TDNT* 4:527-28; Schwarz, *Bürgerliches Christentum,* 57.

62. Note the use of the cognate terms for "fighting" in Titus 3:9 (μάχη); 2 Tim 2:23-24 (μάχομαι).

63. Gk. ἀφιλάργυρος (Heb 13:5); BDAG, s.v.; Spicq, *TLNT* 1:245-46; Schwarz, *Bürgerliches Christentum,* 57-58.

connection with leadership (3:8; Titus 1:7; cf. 1 Pet 5:2) because the temptation to greed in the case of teachers was widely criticized and the vice was traditionally denounced in Jewish and Greco-Roman writings; generosity, its positive counterpart, was highly esteemed.[64]

4-5 A syntactical change (from the string of adjectives to a participial phrase) signals a shift in perspective from the overseer's personal qualities to his proficiency in "managing his own household." Although in the phrase to follow this requirement resolves itself into family leadership (TNIV), and "family" is the modern equivalent in Western culture to the ancient household concept *(oikos),* the stipulation here initially exceeds issues of parenting and husbanding to include management of slaves, property, business interests, and even maintenance of important relationships with benefactors/patrons or clients.[65] Given the fundamental importance of the household within Greco-Roman culture (the microcosm of the empire),[66] it is not surprising that the householder's reputation would hinge on his success (or failure) in this domain. This domestic activity is not minimized or spiritualized, even though the image of the household will superimpose itself on that of the *ekklēsia* ("the household of God, church of the living God") in 3:5 and 3:15. While caution should be exercised, the assumption of this set of instructions is that overseers would be householders — that is, men of at least sufficient enough means to have houses, to run them, and manage their affairs.[67] The verb of "management" is the same one that describes the task of "leading" in the church (5:17; Rom 12:8; 1 Thess 5:12; cf. 1 Cor 12:28).[68] The analogy of the church as a household

---

64. Diogenes Laertius 4.38; Diodorus Siculus 9.11.12; see further Johnson, 215; Prov 11:25-28; 15:16; 16:8; Sir 29:10-11; Wis 5:1; 1 Cor 16:1-4; 2 Cor 8:9; Jas 5:1-6.

65. Gk. τοῦ ἰδίου οἴκου (3:5, 12; 5:4). The precision of the phrase ("his own household") makes it clear that it is the domestic entity, and not the church, that is of concern. See the discussion preceding Titus 2:1. On the household concept in Greek culture, see Osiek and Balch, *Families in the New Testament World;* Verner, *Household of God;* W. A. Meeks, *The First Urban Christians* (New Haven: Yale University Press, 1983); A. Strobel, "Der Begriff des 'Hauses' im griechischen und römischen Privaterecht," *ZNW* 56 (1965): 91-100; P. H. Towner, *DPL* 417-19.

66. See Towner, *DPL* 417-19.

67. It is not likely that Paul was thinking "inclusively" here (cf. the strategy of, e.g., CEV, which, while hermeneutically sensitive to modern Western realities, may show less exegetical sensitivity to the situation envisioned in the text [GNB]). He was rather spelling things out in terms of the broad norms of society. However (see Marshall, 840 n. 22), we cannot be certain that he would have ruled out the possibility of women householders serving as overseers.

68. Gk. προΐσταμαι (with gen. obj.); six of the eight NT occurrences of this term are in 1 Timothy and Titus (1 Tim 3:4, 5, 12; 5:17; Titus 3:8, 14), otherwise Rom 12:8; 1 Thess 5:12; in most cases it means "to lead" but also implies "care for" (see B. Reicke,

already present in Paul (Gal 6:10; Eph 2:19-22) is, as Marshall points out, here expanded beyond ideas of membership and identity to include a model of leadership (Titus 1:7).[69] The dominance of the *oikos* in shaping patterns of leading, management, authority, and responsibility within the cultural framework made it the natural model for defining the overseer's position.[70] The adverb "well" (3:12, 13; 5:17), attached to the verb of management, establishes the high standard of proficiency Paul expects in candidates for church leadership.[71]

One rather obvious measurement of the candidate's household management ability is stressed: "see that his children obey him." The implications are left vague, but the language (lit.) "keeping his children submissive" ("obedience"; cf. TNIV)[72] clearly reflects the assumed patriarchal top-down sense of order in the household (and society more generally). The head of the house was to exert his authority downward along clearly defined lines, and those beneath were obligated to submit. Given the situation of heresy in Ephesus, this probably includes the children's commitment to the faith. In the pioneer situation addressed by Titus 1:6, the faith of the leader's children is set as a prerequisite; here in another setting, perseverance in faith is the appropriate counterpart. The overseer's fitness to lead the church is thus measured on the basis of his ability to maintain the submissiveness of his children, including encouraging and "keeping"[73] them in the faith.

The additional stipulation, "with all dignity" ("seriousness, respectability"),[74] either defines the demeanor expected of the overseer's children (NIV; NRSV) or the way in which the father is to exercise the authority necessary to maintain his children in submissiveness (TNIV; REB). The proximity of the phrase to "children" favors the former solution.[75] But the dignified bearing of the overseer has already been a point of emphasis (3:2), which, in view of the traditional concern in Hellenistic culture for the appropriateness

---

TDNT 6:701-3; *EDNT* 3:156; Lips, *Glaube,* 130-31). For the meaning (unlikely here) of "concern for, devoted to," see Titus 3:8 (and discussion), 14.

69. Marshall, 480.

70. Meeks, *First Urban Christians,* 74-139; Osiek and Balch, *Families,* 91-222; Lips, *Glaube,* 126-43; Schwarz, *Bürgerliches Christentum,* 58-59.

71. Gk. καλῶς (προϊστάμενον); 3:12,13; 5:17. For the whole sentiment, cf. Diogenes Laertius 1.70: μανθάνειν τῆς αὐτοῦ οἰκίας καλῶς προστατεῖν ("one must learn to manage his own house well"; c. 200 C.E.); cf. BDAG, s.v. 1.

72. Gk. ἐν ὑποταγῇ (see 2:11).

73. The sense of the participle ἔχοντα ("having, keeping") is that of actively maintaining; cf. Marshall, 480.

74. Gk. μετὰ πάσης σεμνότητος; see the discussion at 1 Tim 2:2 (note). For the phrase, see Josephus, *Life* 258.

75. See also Fee, 82.

and dignity of the father's bearing toward his children,[76] suggests that the manner in which authority is exercised over the children by the father is a measure of his suitability to exercise authority over church members.[77] Paul's understanding is that this (and other observable aspects of conduct) has both an inward and a theological/spiritual origin (2:2, Excursus).

The point of this household examination is made by way of an analogy that is introduced in v. 5 with a conditional statement.[78] The analogy itself is straightforward and need not detain us long. But two observations should be made. First, management in the household becomes something of a template for management in the church. This logic essentially reflects the widespread conviction in Paul's day that one's private behavior determines to some degree one's potential to lead in the public arena.[79] This axiom was at least implicit in the requirement just considered in v. 4; here in the conditional statement, the link is made clear. In the protasis ("if anyone does not know how[80] to manage his own household"), the verb for management is repeated from v. 4 (see the discussion), and it carries the same active sense of "leading." There is, however, a shift in verbs in the apodosis ("how can he take care of God's church"?) that expands the scope of "management," which might be limited to a rather mechanical view of supervision, to include the more compassionate activity of "caring for."[81] Paul's choice of this verb was apparently made for him by the traditional analogy he is making, since this is the verb used to describe the father's responsibility within the household.[82]

Second, the image of "household" already introduced in 1:4 is now superimposed more specifically on the image of "church." Paul's term for "the church" (3:15; 5:16) is standard in the letters to churches,[83] and as in most cases there, here the reference is to a local Christian community (cf. the universal sense in 3:15).

What the analogy contributes to the instructions is, therefore, an em-

---

76. E.g., Plutarch, *Moralia* 13D.

77. Cf. Johnson, 216; Marshall, 280.

78. For the style of argument, see 1 Cor 14:7, 9, 16; for the negative in a condition of fact, see BDF §428.1.

79. E.g., Plutarch, *Moralia* 70C; see Dibelius and Conzelmann, 53 (and notes).

80. For the Gk. verb οἶδα plus the infinitive in the sense of "know how to," see Phil 4:12; 1 Thess 4:4; A. Horstmann, *EDNT* 2:494.

81. Gk. ἐπιμελέομαι; elsewhere in the NT only in Luke 10:34-35; see also Gen 44:21; Prov 27:25; 1 Esdr 6:26; 1 Macc 11:37; Sir 30:25; Spicq, *TLNT* 2:47-53.

82. E.g., *Philo, On Sobriety* 91; cf. Marshall, 481.

83. Gk. ἐκκλησία (θεοῦ); Paul's term in the letters to churches is often ἐκκλησία τοῦ θεοῦ; see 1 Cor 1:2; 10:32; 11:16, 22; 15:9; 2 Cor 1:1; Gal 1:13; 1 Thess 2:14; 2 Thess 1:4; cf. Acts 20:28. See M. E. Thrall, *2 Corinthians* (Edinburgh: T&T Clark, 1994), 1:89-93; K. L. Schmidt, *TDNT* 3:501-36.

phasis, derived from the traditional social axiom, on the importance of the candidate's proven responsibility within his household. The stakes for the church are twofold. On the one hand, Paul's concern is to ensure that leaders will be selected who will effectively manage the community and meet the needs of its members. But on the other hand, just as the honor and reputation of the householder depend on his successful discharge of his duties of care and oversight, so in the case of the overseer, this social axiom links the public image of the church (witness) directly to the reputation of its leaders.

6-7   The listing of requirements resumes, adding two final specifically Christian items accompanied by purpose statements to explain them. First, the overseer was not to be chosen from among new converts.[84] The church in Ephesus, a Pauline church with at least a few years under its belt, had the luxury of being more selective in its choice of leaders than was the case in the pioneer situation in Crete.

The advantage of this requirement is seen in two related dangers that maturity should help leaders to avoid. First, although the versions consistently translate the first danger as "conceit" (TNIV; NIV; NRSV), Paul's association of this flaw with the false teachers (6:4; 2 Tim 3:4) may suggest that he is thinking more of the fascination with authority that went with the position of the teacher that deluded and then led the opponents astray.[85] Either way, the hope is that with experience in the faith and age would come the maturity and sense of proportion that would prevent leaders from self-absorption with position and authority.

Second is the danger of the judgment or condemnation that follows from this delusion or conceit. Paul portrays this as a situation into (or under) which someone might "fall" (3:7; 6:9),[86] and the term "judgment, condemnation" includes not only the condemnation of guilt but also the punishment that follows (5:12).[87] This is further described by the genitive phrase "of the devil,"[88] and the sense of the genitive is ambiguous. Translating this as an ob-

---

84. Gk. νεόφυτος; lit. "newly planted"; then "infant" (LXX Pss 127:3; 143:12; Isa 5:7); used only here in the NT. The application of the term here to the "new convert" may reflect current Christian vocabulary (so Roloff, 160); in any case, it continues in Christian writings (MM, s.v.).

85. Gk. τυφυθείς (ptc. from τυφόω, "blinded, deluded, conceited"; cf. Spicq, *TLNT* 3:388-89; Schwarz, *Bürgerliches Christentums,* 60); of the false teachers in 6:4; 2 Tim 3:4.

86. Gk. ἐμπίπτω; for this figurative sense, see also Luke 10:36 (cf. 6:39); Heb 10:31; Spicq, *TLNT* 2:1-2.

87. Gk. κρίμα; see M. Rissi, *EDNT* 2:317-18.

88. Gk. διάβολος, elsewhere and as an adjective meaning "slander, slanderous" (3:11; Titus 2:3), it refers to "the devil" (3:7; 2 Tim 2:26), the personal enemy of God and his people. Cf. Eph 4:27; 6:11; Heb 2:14; Jas 4:7; 1 Pet 5:8; Rev 2:10, etc.

jective genitive, Paul is understood to mean that the deluded, conceited over-seer is headed for the same condemnation/punishment "as the devil" (TNIV; cf. Matt 25:41).[89] An alternate strategy translates the phrase "of the devil" as a subjective genitive: "falling under the devil's condemnation." This implies that the devil, in one role or another (as God's agent, as provocateur who de-mands justice, as the great enemy of Christians who aims to seduce them into sin and judgment), having successfully tempted the overseer, actively pro-nounces the condemnation he has designed for God's people.[90] Although in choosing one solution over the other little is lost, the active role of the devil in 3:7 favors putting him into an active role in this statement. With the fall of the false teachers in the background, Paul expresses his fear and a warning to Timothy and the church against putting ill-prepared new converts, who are more vulnerable to the schemes of the devil, into positions of leadership.

In addition to experience and maturity in the faith, v. 7 adds the re-quirement of a "good reputation with outsiders." As noted above (v. 2), the "good reputation" serves as the closing bracket to the whole set of character requirements.[91] It reflects on "blamelessness" more specifically from the broad perspective of public image. To get at the idea of "reputation," the lan-guage of "testimony/witness" is used (Titus 1:13). This places the accent on the truthful evidence given by one person in assessment of another;[92] it comes to mean the ongoing "evidence" about people that attaches to them in the sense of a reputation. The term "good" (3:1; see the discussion and note at 1:8) emphasizes that the reputation required in the case of the candidate must establish unequivocally that he is regarded well in society. In fact, it is his wider reputation that is chiefly in mind. "Outsiders" are unbelievers.[93] Paul registers this concern for the opinion of outsiders variously and widely in these letters to coworkers and also in the letters to churches.[94]

But why this concern for the leader's good witness, and more broadly

---

89. Cf. NIV; GNB; CEV; REB; Johnson, 217; Knight, 164; Fee, 83.

90. NRSV retains the ambiguity; variously Kelly, 79; Spicq, 437; W. Foerster, *TDNT* 2:81; Roloff; Hanson, 76.

91. Note the repetition of the parenetic verb of necessity, δεῖ δὲ καί . . . ("He must also be . . ."), which adds emphasis to the closing requirement.

92. Gk. μαρτυρία, "testimony," usually positive; cf. 3 John 12; Spicq, *TLNT* 1:83; 2:447-52; H. Strathmann, *TDNT* 4:474-508; 1 Tim 2:6; 2 Tim 1:8; 1 Cor 1:6; 2 Cor 1:12; 2 Thess 1:10; for μαρτύριον in this sense, cf. Marshall, 204; see the discussion of μαρτυρία in Titus 1:13. Cf. Mounce, 398.

93. Gk. οἱ ἔξωθεν; as a reference to "those who do not belong to the group," see Mark 4:11 (variant); Herodotus 9.5; Diodorus Siculus 19.70.3; Josephus, *Jewish War* 4.179; *Antiquities* 15.316; MM, s.v. Cf. 1 Cor 5:10.

94. 1 Tim 5:14; 6:1; Titus 2:5, 8, 10; 3:2, 8; 1 Cor 10:32; Col 4:5; 1 Thess 4:12; cf. 1 Pet 2:13, 15; 3:1, 16.

for the church's public image? On one level, the purpose clause explores this question with immediate and personal concerns in mind. Paul first thinks in terms of the leader's social environment, in which a good reputation guarded a person from "falling into [public] disgrace."[95] Envisioned is the disparagement that would come from "those outside" for behavior, or a standard of morality, that was unacceptable in society. The guidelines given in vv. 2-5 are intended to steer the leader clear of this danger. But failure to achieve and maintain the good testimony (according to the profile) would be accompanied by dishonor and shame and a complete loss of credibility in the wider social context. And following the leader's derision would be the derision of the church. It is this concern, the church's public image in society, that is the bottom line for Paul. Some scholars insist that sensitivity to outsiders begins and ends with the church's simple right to continue to exist (i.e., self-defense).[96] But in this letter the importance of the church in God's plan of redemption (2:1-6; 3:15-16) and the concern to protect the integrity of the gospel suggest that Paul's ultimate motive is missionary in thrust.[97] As much as individuals are important, it is the threat to the evangelistic mandate that would follow from the church falling into disgrace by association (with false teachers and overseers whose reputations are compromised by immorality) that would most trouble Paul.

The spiritual consequences of failure come in the second parallel pitfall: "fall . . . into the devil's trap." The figure, literally that of "falling into a snare" (6:9; 2 Tim 2:26), is traditional for succumbing to various human foibles.[98] In this case, however, "the devil" is depicted as setting the snare,[99] indicating the role of this character in tempting and leading the person into the kinds of sins warned against above and so into disrepute. It is a way of warning the leader to resist temptations outside the church (including false teaching) where the devil's domain lies (cf. 5:14-15).

---

95. Gk. ἵνα μὴ εἰς ὀνειδισμὸν ἐμπέσῃ (for the verb, see 3:6); ὀνειδισμός is generally used in the NT of the unjustified insults and criticism that believers are to endure (Rom 15:3; Heb 10:33; 11:26; 13:13; LXX Neh 1:3; 3:36; Ps 68:10). In this case, reproach for actual misbehavior is meant (LXX Neh 5:9; Isa 47:3, etc.); see further Spicq, *TLNT* 2:585-87; J. Schneider, *TDNT* 5:241-42.

96. Esp. P. Lippert, *Leben als Zeugnis* (Stuttgart: Katholisches Bibelwerk, 1968), 32-33; see the discussion in Towner, *Goal,* 232-33.

97. Towner, *Goal,* 232-33; W. C. Van Unnik, "Die Rücksicht auf die Reaktion der Nicht-Christen als Motiv in der altchristlichen Paränese," in *Sparsa Collecta* (Leiden: Brill, 1980), 2:307-22.

98. For the Gk. phrase ἐμπίπτειν εἰς παγίδα; see Prov 12:13; Sir 9:3; Tob 14:10; cf. Sir 27:26; for παγίς ("snare, trap") in this figurative sense of a human danger, see Rom 11:9; LXX Pss 56:7; 68:23; Prov 21:6; Wis 14:11; Sir 9:3.

99. See 2 Tim 2:26.

In all of this, it is not hard to see the failure of the false teachers behind these qualifications for leadership. If indeed some of them had been young teachers in the church, overcome by pride or arrogance and led astray into ungodly behavior in one way or another, Paul's concern is to shore up the church's leadership and protect the church's testimony in society. Replacements would have to be found who could undo the damage done by the apostates to the church and its reputation. For those leaders who have not fallen, the instructions warn of the danger, but also positively encourage perseverance in the standard of behavior and administration that will project a winning testimony in society.

b. Qualifications of Deacons (3:8-13)

Following the instructions concerning selection of overseers is a parallel and continuous[1] section taking up requirements for the selection of deacons. Verse 11 abruptly introduces women deacons (see below) as being on an equivalent basis with deacons in general, after which v. 12 returns to a final consideration of male deacons. Most of the qualities enumerated are parallel with the overseer code, suggesting again that in the Ephesian context (disruption caused by certain false teachers) public reputation and respectability were regarded as better indicators of qualification to take part in ministry than simply abilities or gifts.

> 8 *In the same way, deacons are to be worthy of respect, sincere, not indulging in much wine, and not pursuing dishonest gain.* 9 *They must keep hold of the deep truths of the faith with a clear conscience.* 10 *They must first be tested; and then if there is nothing against them, let them serve as deacons.*
> 11 *In the same way, the women are to be worthy of respect, not malicious talkers but temperate and trustworthy in everything.*
> 12 *A deacon must be faithful to his wife and must manage his children and his household well.* 13 *Those who have served well gain an excellent standing and great assurance in their faith in Christ Jesus.*

Deacons The position of deacons in the NT churches is attested clearly in just two cases, Phil 1:1 and 1 Tim 3:8-13; cf. Rom 16:1. The noun *diakonos,* denoting a person designated for ministry in the church, limited

---

1. The term translated "in the same way" (Gk. ὡσαύτως; see on 2:9) indicates the continuation of this parenetic section, launched at 3:2. The verbal phrase expressing the necessity of "blamelessness," δεῖ ἀνεπίλημπτον εἶναι ("[deacons] must be beyond reproach"), should be supplied in translation.

though this usage is, derives its meaning from a broad background. The word group[2] describes various kinds of Christian ministry and workers, such as in Paul's letters to churches,[3] and has a central place in describing the role of Jesus (Mark 10:43-45; pars.).

The precise sense of the term in its formal application in the church is more difficult to establish, mainly because of the wide range of meaning usually associated with the word group: including humble service, sacrificial service, and specific kinds of service such as "table waiting." Applied to the position that stands in relation to the overseer (1 Tim 3:8-13; Phil 1:1), two other features become equally, if not more, relevant. First, one who served as a *diakonos* in non-church settings did so by commission or order of a superior, and as such both represented and operated with the authority of the superior.[4] This clears the way for an understanding of deacons in the church that incorporates both the authority that comes with commissioning and the importance (rather than secondary nature) of the ministry they executed. What is less clear is who (God or the overseer) is to be regarded as the source of the commission.

Second, however, the sense of service as an assistant to a supervisor also becomes clear in the two cases in which the formal meaning of "deacons" is clearly meant. In each case, the term occurs in relation to and following the term "overseers." In 1 Tim 3:1-13, where the most reflection on positions in the church occurs, the order of treatment and the greater attention given to the overseer suggest that the role of deacons should be regarded as a subordinate position and an assistantship in some sense. The roots of the formal position of the deacons are not easily linked to the table-waiting seven in Acts 6:1-6. The broad use of the term for gospel ministry sustains its use independent of the formal church meaning (at least at this point in church history) as a reference to ministers in general (e.g., 1 Tim 4:6). Probably with the position(s) of overseers and elders already in existence, the need for greater specialization in some churches of more significant size and longer history led to the establishment of a group commissioned to support the ministry overseen by the *episkopoi* and *presbyteroi*.[5]

As in the case of the overseer, the instructions relating to the deacons have mainly to do with aspects of character, which makes attempts to define

2. Gk. διάκονος, διακονία, διακονέω; see H. W. Beyer, *TDNT* 2:81-93; A. Weiser, *EDNT* 1:302-4; Campbell, *Elders,* 132-35, 199-200; J. N. Collins, *DIAKONIA: Reinterpreting the Ancient Texts* (New York: Oxford University Press, 1990); J. Gnilka, *Der Philipperbrief* (4th ed.; Freiburg: Herder, 1987), 32-39.

3. Of ministers including Paul (Rom 16:1; 1 Cor 3:5; 2 Cor 3:6; 6:4; 11:23; Eph 3:7; 6:21; Col 1:7, 23, 25; 4:7; cf. 2 Cor 11:15).

4. Esp. now Collins, *DIAKONIA.*

5. Cf. Schwarz, *Bürgerliches Christentum,* 39; Marshall, 487.

"diaconal" duties difficult. This focus makes it unwise to assume that tasks of teaching and preaching were excluded from the diaconate, or that the ministry of deacons consisted mainly of practical duties in the church.[6] Almost certainly the insistence that candidates for the diaconate be deeply committed to "the mystery of the faith" (3:9) presumes participation in the ministry of teaching and preaching. And the requirement of proficiency in household management in 3:12, parallel to 3:4-5, suggests leadership responsibilities in the church. As pointed out above, we should probably understand the deacon's task as being that of assisting the overseer/supervisor in administration, leadership, and teaching within the church. The arrangement in Ephesus was apparently that of a group of deacons (note the plurality) serving the church as assistants either to the overseer (singular) or team of overseers.[7]

8   After inserting the same parenetic introduction to the new instructions ("deacons must be beyond reproach"), the shape of the continuing instructions follows the earlier syntactical pattern and in briefer fashion intends to cover the same basic ground. A combination of an initial summarizing positive trait ("respectability") and prohibitions fill out the implied broad requirement of irreproachability; this is later summarized with the synonym "blameless" with which the instructions reach a first conclusion in v. 10.

The instructions begin by summarizing several individual qualities expressed in 3:2 with the broader requirement of "respectability, dignity" ("worthy of respect," 3:4; 2:2).[8] It envisages an observable quality of behavior with an inward source and, just as importantly for Paul, a theological origin (2:2, note).

Three prohibitions follow.[9] First, "insincerity" of speech (lit. "not double-tongued") is to be guarded against.[10] The rare term originally refers to repetition in speech and then comes to describe the shortcoming of "deceitfulness"; the thought is of saying one thing to one person and another thing to an-

---

6. For which see Beyer, *TDNT* 2:90.

7. On the model of the synagogue, in which the head worked in conjunction with a subordinate "servant" (Beyer, *TDNT* 2:91), Campbell, *Elders,* 199-200, suggests that the deacon was the head of a household church who assisted the overseer (himself having responsibility for a cluster of house churches) by managing the household under his care. This reconstruction has, however, no historical precedent (cf. Ignatius, whose letters show that deacons were assistants of overseers within a single congregation).

8. The argument followed here understands Gk. σεμνός (see note on 2:2) to be summarizing the sort of traits listed in 3:2, e.g., νηφάλιον, σώφρονα, κόσμιον, φιλόξενον ("sober-minded, self-controlled, respectable, hospitable").

9. To avoid the idiom and achieve smoothness, apparently, TNIV/NIV have transformed the first prohibition ("not double-tongued") into the positive "[deacons are to be] sincere."

10. Gk. δίλογος ("double-worded, double-tongued"); only here in the NT (cf. Polycarp 5.2). Cf. Schwarz, *Bürgerliches Christentum,* 63; BDAG, s.v.; Johnson, 227.

other, that is, to be "duplicitous," which is condemned in Proverbs, Sirach, and Philo as a danger to the community and relationships.[11] A leader afflicted by this weakness would be a threat to the trust and stability of the community.

Second, an addiction to or excessiveness (lit. "not devoted to"[12]) in the consumption of wine is prohibited. This shortcoming corresponds to the differently phrased requirement in 3:3 and Titus 1:7, and is also condemned in older women in Titus 2:3. While this prohibition pertains to all believers, as evidence of a lack of self-control that would ruin the reputation of the leader and the church it is especially warned against in the case of deacons and overseers.

Third, integrity with money is encouraged with the prohibition against "pursuing dishonest gain" (Titus 1:7).[13] It is noteworthy that this vice is developed at length in the allegation made against the opponents (6:5-10; cf. Titus 1:11),[14] which suggests that Paul may be extra sensitive to this danger in the case of selecting new leaders in the troubled Ephesian church. Nevertheless, the concern for a dispassionate regard for money on the part of church leaders is widely recorded (cf. 1 Tim 3:3; Titus 1:7; 1 Pet 5:2). And while allegations of greed and teaching for gain typically made against false teachers may suggest that the chief concern was to guard against the danger of mixed motives for ministry (e.g., 1 Pet 5:2),[15] the reference is general enough to encompass most kinds of financial misjudgment and abuse.[16]

9   The next requirement is generally applicable to all believers, but it is stressed here in the case of deacons because of the situation of false teaching. Deacons "must keep hold of the deep truths [lit. "the mystery"] of the faith with a clear conscience." As this translation suggests, "the faith" here means the content of what is believed (see the note at 1:2).

But what does Paul mean by "the mystery of the faith?" Elsewhere Paul developed the "mystery" concept, drawing on Hebrew backgrounds,[17] to conceptualize the Christ-event as the revelation of God's secret plan.[18] The

---

11. The more widely used term is δίγλωσσος ("bilingual, double-tongued"); Prov 11:3; Sir 5:9, 14, 15; 28:13; Philo, *On the Sacrifices of Cain and Abel* 32.

12. The Gk. verb used here, προσέχω, denotes a depth of interest that indicates obsession or addiction (see 1:4, note). Cf. the language of "enslavement" in the parallel phrase in Titus 2:3.

13. Gk. αἰσχροκερδής; cf. Spicq, *TLNT* 1:65-68.

14. See the discussion in Schlarb, *Die gesunde Lehre,* 325-26.

15. See Goppelt, *1 Peter,* 336.

16. See Marshall, 490; Roloff, 162-63.

17. See Dan 2:18.

18. Gk. τὸ μυστήριον; in Paul, see 1 Cor 2:7; 4:1; 13:2; 14:2; 15:51-52; Eph 1:9; 3:4; Col 1:26; 2:2; 4:3; cf. Mark 4:11 (par.). See esp. M. N. A. Bockmuehl, *Revelation and Mystery in Ancient Judaism and Pauline Christianity* (Grand Rapids: Eerdmans, 1997), 129-210; G. Bornkamm, *TDNT* 5:802-28; H. Krämer, *EDNT* 2:446-49.

term occasionally stood alone (Rom 16:25; Eph 3:3, 9; Col 1:25) or, as here, in a genitive construction that helps to define the mystery ("the mystery of God," 1 Cor 2:1; "the mystery of Christ," Eph 3:4; "the mystery of his will," Eph 1:9, etc.).[19] Here the closest parallel is "the mystery of the gospel" (Eph 6:19), where the content of what is proclaimed is defined as being that mystery of God's plan to save in Christ that was revealed in history. The shift to "the faith" is understandable in this context as occasioned by the threat of heresy in this church that Paul conceptualizes in a broader way as à danger not just to the gospel (i.e., to Paul's mission) but to the whole present and future of the church (3:14-16). So here the term "mystery" describes the apostolic faith in Pauline terms as the revelation of salvation in Christ as proclaimed in his gospel. The false teachers had distorted or rejected this version of God's plan, and Paul wanted to ensure that leaders be chosen from among those who held firm to the gospel/faith that Paul had delivered to the church.

The attached prepositional phrase, "with a clear conscience," adds the thought of ethical wholeness to the qualification. This is a technical concept for Paul by which he defines authentic Christian existence as adherence to the approved gospel and sound behavior, and by which he measures deviance from the apostolic norm (see the Excursus at 1:5). Standing in the background is the ethical lapse of the false teachers brought about by their rejection of the faith and their consequent ineffective consciences (1:19; 4:2). The two terms "good conscience" and "cleansed or clear conscience" are evaluative and theological: they describe the conscience of one whose belief is sound as being effective ("good") because of God's cleansing. As a result, it gives the verdict of "innocence" in relation to actions that have been taken. Thus the qualification stipulates that the candidate's adherence to the faith ("holding to it") is to be unquestioned, and his conduct is to be appropriate to the faith he professes.[20]

10 With a change in style,[21] the instructions pause to emphasize that the whole process of assessment under consideration is mandatory. Just as is implied in the case of overseers,[22] the aspiring deacon is first to be

---

19. The genitive relation may be understood differently from case to case; but in the case of Eph 6:19, "the mystery of the gospel" (τὸ μυστήριον τοῦ εὐαγγελίου), and 1 Tim 3:9, "the mystery of the faith" (τὸ μυστήριον τῆς πίστεως), the genitive expresses apposition ("the mystery that is the gospel/faith"; cf. BDF §167; Marshall, 490).

20. See Marshall, 491; Lips, *Glaube,* 67-68.

21. Two impersonal third-person plural imperatives (δοκιμαζέσθωσαν . . . διακονείτωσαν; "let them be tested . . . let them serve as deacons") are used, breaking from the original δεῖ εἶναι pattern of 3:2, perhaps to create a greater sense of summing up.

22. The connecting conjunctions, "and . . . also," "but . . . also" (καὶ . . . δέ), are treated rather loosely by the translations (omitted by TNIV and NIV; "and . . . ," NRSV). However, they probably coordinate the testing procedure (hence vv. 8-9) with the implied

tested,[23] then[24] (if he/she passes the test) to be allowed to serve. This is not some new or additional, unspecified test, but rather (as the desired outcome, "if they are blameless," shows) it is the assessment of the candidate's life and testimony on the basis of the qualifications set out in the code that is in mind. "Blameless" (TNIV, "nothing against them") is synonymous with "beyond reproach," the term that describes the general requirement for the overseer in 3:2 (for which "blameless" serves in Titus 1:6-7).[25] With the legal sense of the term in the background, it means to be free of any charge of civic or domestic impropriety.[26] The candidate's reputation both inside and outside the church must pass the test. To determine this, the preceding concrete requirements were laid down. This does not mean that false accusations are grounds for ineligibility, but rather that uncorrected tendencies toward misbehavior ought not to be found in the candidate's background. If the candidate passes the test, he may "serve as a deacon."[27]

11   Rather abruptly the focus shifts momentarily from male deacons to "the women [who are deacons]."[28] The active role of women in the church

requirement of testing for the overseer (see NEB, "as well as bishops"); see Schwarz, *Bürgerliches Christentum,* 64-65; Fee, 87.

23. Gk. δοκιμάζω ("test, examine, prove, approve") for examination and approval is widely used (1 Cor 3:13; 11:28; Gal 6:4; 1 John 4:1); for formal examinations before entering public duties, see the discussion and references in Spicq, *TLNT* 1:357 n. 22 (353-61); W. Grundmann, *TDNT* 2:255-60.

24. The emphatic "first . . . then" sequence (πρῶτον/εἶτα) underlines the mandatory nature of the process.

25. Gk. ἀνέγκλητος; only in Paul in the NT (1 Cor 1:8; Col 1:22); 3 Macc 5:31; Josephus, *Antiquities* 10.281; 17.289. Cf. W. Grundmann, *TDNT* 1:356-57; A. Vögtle, *Die Tugend- und Lasterkataloge im Neuen Testament* (Münster: Aschendorff, 1936), 55.

26. See MM, 40; W. Grundmann, *TDNT* 1:356-57. In 1 Cor 1:8 the term's use in the legal setting is more apparent; here the informal, though related, sense of free from accusation in public or civic matters is a better fit. The modern parallel would be the sort of scrutiny applied to the political candidate's past activities and involvements that might shed light on his or her character.

27. Gk. διακονέω (see BDAG, s.v.) basically means "to serve," but the range of activities it can cover is wide, and each context will determine the more specific sense in which it is intended; cognate to διάκονος ("deacon"), it is used of Christian "ministry" or "service" in a general way (2 Tim 1:18; Rom 15:25; 2 Cor 3:3; 8:19-20), but here the verb acquires almost the technical sense to "serve as a deacon" (A. Weiser, *EDNT* 1:302-4; TNIV; NIV; NRSV).

28. Regrettably, in the TNIV edition of 2005, "the women" marks a retreat to the ambiguous literal Greek from the bolder TNIV edition of 2001, "women who are deacons," which was an improvement on the NIV rendering, "their wives." For the less likely view that "women" (Gk. γυναῖκες) refers to wives of deacons, see (predictably) Mounce, 202-4 and Knight, 170-72; see also Hanson, 80-81; Lips, *Glaube,* 117-18; NIV (but cf. TNIV); NEB (but cf. REB); GNB. The most convincing argument that wives rather than

has already been implied in the discussion of the prohibitions issued by Paul in response to the excess of some women (2:11-12). Whatever their status as Paul addressed them here (probably under at least a temporary restriction from teaching and holding authority), women had apparently occupied some role in relation to preaching and teaching.[29] The instructions here, however, enumerate in the same order the aspects of character and behavior we have already seen in the case of the male deacons in 3:8. And equally the goal is to define in more concrete terms the meaning of the general requirement, also in effect here, of "blamelessness" (3:10).

First, as in 3:8, the term "respectability, dignity" ("worthy of respect"; see the discussion at 3:8; 2:2, Excursus) loosely encompasses a number of qualities spelled out specifically in 3:2 that measure respectability.[30]

Second, parallel to the concern for speech in 3:8, the woman deacon's speech habits are to be scrutinized. Specifically, she is not to be known as a "malicious talker" (lit. "slanderer" = "double-speak" in 3:8), which implies positively that she should be known rather for telling the truth. This is the same term translated "devil" in 3:6-7 (2 Tim 2:26 and widely in the NT), but here it refers to the spreading of lies for which the devil was known.[31]

women deacons are in view is the abrupt placement of the reference in the midst of qualifications for male deacons. However, several factors strengthen the alternative reading adopted here: (1) in similar parenetic contexts, the adverb ὡσαύτως ("likewise"; 2:9; 3:8; Titus 2:3, 6) that changes the topic to "women" serves to introduce a new but related case. As in the case of "deacons" in 3:8 (see discussion), the verb of necessity plus infinitive (δεῖ εἶναι) should be supplied from 3:2. (2) While it is true that γυνή seems too common a term to describe an office, the term "deaconess" (i.e., a fem. form of διάκονος) did not exist, and within a code listing requirements for an office, a reference to "women" (γυναῖκες) would have sufficed to direct attention to female candidates for the post. (3) While it is true that the Gk. term γυνή can refer to "women" or "wives," if "wives of deacons" was meant, it would have been more common to indicate this with either a possessive pronoun or the definite article (e.g., 1 Cor 7:2, 3; Eph 5:22; Col 3:18, 24; 1 Pet 3:1; see discussion and note at 2:9; see Towner, Goal, 212 and nn. 48, 50; see also B. L. Blackburn, "The Identity of the 'Women' in 1 Timothy 3.11," in C. D. Osburn, ed. Essays on Women in Earliest Christianity [Joplin, MO: College Press, 1993], 1:303-19). (4) The omission of a parallel instruction to wives of overseers makes it still less likely that "wives of deacons" would be singled out. (5) Finally, the reference in Rom 16:1 to "Phoebe, a deacon of the church at Cenchreae" (Φοίβην . . . διάκονος) demonstrates both the existence of women deacons and the use of the masculine term to refer to a female deacon.

29. It is remotely possible that the very design of the code (i.e., the brevity and placement of the instructions) reflects the curtailment of the duties and authority of women deacons, some of whom had joined in the false teaching (so Oberlinner, 141-43); but cf. the response by Marshall, 494.

30. For σεμνός (here fem.) of women, see Spicq, TLNT 3:247-48.

31. Gk. διάβολος (Prov 6:24; Sir 19:15; 26:5; 2 Macc 3:11; 14:27; 3 Macc 6:7; Josephus, Antiquities 10.51; 16.81; 19.201; Jewish War 1.633). Cf. W. Foerster and G. von

Third, the term "temperate," which in 3:2 (see the discussion) refers to level-headedness, here probably means avoidance of drunkenness, as the parallel qualification in 3:8 (Titus 2:2, 3) indicates.

Fourth, the catchall phrase "trustworthy in everything," employs the important "faith" word group that, as we have seen, can focus on either belief or trustworthiness.[32] In this case, the broad scope indicated in the phrase translated "everything" (2 Tim 2:7; 4:5; Titus 2:9, 10; 2 Cor 11:6)[33] suggests the latter and emphasizes complete reliability.[34] It is not necessary, however, to separate this quality from the woman deacon's faith; it is her adherence to the gospel (3:9) that produces her "trustworthiness" in carrying out whatever tasks she is set.[35]

12 At this point, Paul resumes instructions concerning male candidates with the two domestic aspects already set out for overseers. Deacons must be faithful to their wives (see the discussion at 3:2; Titus 1:6). They must also exhibit skillful management in the household.[36] The elements of household management mentioned first in 3:4 are shortened and given in reversed order. The order, "let them manage their children and households well," distinguishes between offspring and slaves, suggesting that the deacons, like the overseers, were (generally) householders, people of means and position in the social structure. The concern for this management ability suggests that deacons carried out significant leadership duties in service to the overseers, or perhaps (if overseers supervised a cluster of house churches in a locality) on a par with overseers but in a more limited sphere (the house church; see above).

13 Paul concludes the list of requirements for deacons, both men and women, with a statement of motivation that is on a par with (and perhaps intentionally parallel to) the positive estimation of the position of the overseer in 3:1. In this case, "those who serve well as deacons"[37] stand to obtain two rewards. The rewards are linked to and commensurate with the deacons' initiative and performance (middle verb and dative pronoun, "gain for them-

---

Rad, *TDNT* 2:71-81 (esp. 72-73); O. Böcher, *EDNT* 1:297-98. See the discussions at 2 Tim 3:3; Titus 2:3.

32. Gk. πιστάς (fem.; adj. πιστός); see the note at 1:2.

33. For ἐν πᾶσιν ("in all things") in this sense, see also 2 Tim 2:7; 4:5; Titus 2:9, 10b; 2 Cor 11:6. Cf. the similar use of "all" to widen the meaning of "good work" into an all-encompassing behavior; 2 Tim 2:21; 3:17; 1 Tim 5:10; Titus 1:16; 3:1.

34. See Marshall, 495; Schwarz, *Bürgerliches Christentum,* 66-67.

35. See Roloff, 165-66.

36. For the verb of management (Gk. προΐσταμαι), see the discussion at 3:4.

37. As in 3:10 (see discussion), the participle οἱ διακονήσαντες ("those who serve") reflects the specific technical sense of the verb for the service of the deacon. For the adjective καλῶς ("well") for the standard of excellence, see on 3:4.

selves").[38] The phrase describing the first reward is capable of a number of meanings,[39] but most likely promises an "excellent standing" (i.e., to be esteemed, or held in high regard) in the church.

Similarly, the precise sense of the second reward, "great assurance," is potentially ambiguous. "Assurance" ("boldness") often occurs in connection with speaking activities and particularly proclamation,[40] but also more generally of confidence in various situations. In this case, the prepositional phrase that follows describes the context of this reward and makes "assurance" a better fit. "In faith" here means the deacons' active believing/trusting (see the discussion and note at 1:2), with the subsequent phrase, "in Christ Jesus," indicating both the object of faith and the relationship that this believing sustains (see the discussion at 1:14). Thus the second reward promises that faithful service will deepen the deacon's faith and further strengthen the relationship with God and Christ.

Applying the Leadership Codes in the Modern Church

If the interpretation of the overseer and deacon codes offered above has hit somewhere near the mark, it should be obvious that the qualifications for service are deeply rooted in the value system of first-century Greco-Roman culture. The general requirement, "above reproach, blameless," and concrete items that serve to fill out the general picture in each case (apart from the few

38. Gk. περιποιέομαι (Luke 17:33; Acts 20:28); ἑαυτοῖς is a dative of advantage; cf. Spicq, *TLNT* 3:100-102.

39. Gk. βαθμός (for the accompanying adj. καλός ["good, excellent"] in this sense, see 2:3; 3:1, 7 and discussions) occurs in various contexts; relevant semantic possibilities include "rank" (Josephus, *Jewish War* 4.171; Spicq, *TLNT* 250-52); and its use in Gnostic writings for levels of advancement (Clement, *Stromateis* 2.45.4); a parallel concept related to degrees of status is posited in Qumran (1QS 2:20; 5:23-24; 1QSa 1:17-18; W. Nauck, "Probleme des frühchristlichen Amtsverständnisses," *ZNW* 48 [1957]: 200-220). Again the possible Gnostic connection is ruled out on the basis of the general absence of discernible Gnostic tendencies. "Advancement" in some sense is envisioned: (1) in spiritual understanding (discussed in Roloff, 166-67; Oberlinner, 144; Marshall, 495-96); (2) to the rank of overseer (see discussion in Marshall, 496; Knight, 174; Roloff, 167). Neither of these options has any compelling connections in the text; the latter is ruled out logically because deacons are being urged to serve well *as* deacons, not to work themselves out of a lowly rank. The reading adopted in the commentary (acquisition of a good standing, respect, and esteem in the community) makes sense of Paul's concern to endorse the offices (see on 3:1) and encourage those qualified to participate in them; see *1 Clement* 54.3; Mark 10:43-44; Luke 22:26-27; Marshall, 496; Dibelius and Conzelmann, 59; Kelly, 85.

40. Gk. παρρησία; Acts 4:29, 31; 28:31; Eph 6:19; on the range of usage, see Spicq, *TLNT* 3:56-62; H. Balz, *EDNT* 3:45-47.

that are Christian) come straight out of that society's expectations of the ideal, a respectable householder whose reputation is sound. The minimal attention given to ministerial abilities and gifts does not mean that these things are unimportant as much as that they were most likely assumed. But the extensive emphasis on character, spanning the scale from fidelity in marriage to fiscal integrity, from wise household management to public reputation, requires maturity and virtue from the prospective leader that touches all parts of life. The qualities explored above in reference to overseers and deacons are those that outfit them to project the image of responsible leadership (from the household model) both inside and outside the church. They enable the leader to deal patiently and constructively with people in conflict in such a way that relationships are preserved and strengthened instead of further threatened and destroyed. In this profile, selfish attainment and advancement have no place. Sacrificial service, a style of leading that benefits the whole group at considerable cost to the leader, is to the fore. The leader is not denied pleasurable activities, but they are to be pursued in moderation and not addictively, and virtues such as the practice of hospitality are emblematic of a charge being executed for the sake of others.

Most significantly, fitness to lead is linked to maturity in the faith, and 3:6 rules out the newly baptized/converted believer. Even if this requirement is an ideal and in some mission situations may not be applicable (cf. Titus 1:6-9), the wisdom of it is not something that should be dismissed too quickly as a cultural feature. Today, as Johnson points out,[41] candidates for leadership in the church are often measured by the sort of criteria applied in the corporate setting, where education, innovation, and a youthful, energetic image (not to mention attractive, fashionable outward appearance) govern the "professional" profile. This is a power profile that, however applicable to corporate life with its high esteem for mobility and innovation, is drastically superficial and at odds with the kind of values that frame leadership in these texts. Surely in many respects it can be argued that respectability is measured differently in the modern West than in the ancient Mediterranean world, but with just a few adjustments and perhaps some additions there is no reason why the entire profile cannot be useful to the church today.

This includes the emphasis on the leader's public reputation — that is, with those outside the church. To the evangelically minded, this might seem to be incongruous. Why should God's people be concerned with the estimation of the church's leadership by those critical of the faith? But to ask such a question already suggests the existence in much of Christendom today of a vast divide separating the community of faith from secular society. Separation in terms of values and ethics is one thing; this of course is precisely the

41. Johnson, 224.

"distinction" from profane and ungodly things and practices that is intended in the theological meaning of "holiness," and in this sense the church should keep miles between itself and the secular world. But geographical distance is inimical to the church's original gospel impulse as well as to its ongoing mission responsibility. Paul's churches operated in households, in which the peristyles and atriums were open to the public when worship and teaching meetings took place. Paul expected close contact between believers and unbelievers, and the evaluation of those onlookers (3:7; 1 Cor 14:23) of what could be seen and known about the church was crucial to the mission of the church. Consequently, the emphasis on the prospective leader's public respectability and reputation was a function of the interface that the believing community was to have with the surrounding world. The line that divides public from private activities and life is drawn differently in different cultures. But wherever that line is drawn, the church is to be at the intersection. And it is for this reason — for the reason of the public legitimacy of the gospel — that leaders must be able to project a reputation of integrity and seriousness beyond the church's walls.

5. The Church and the Faith (3:14-16)

> 14 Although I hope to come to you soon, I am writing you these instructions so that, 15 if I am delayed, you will know how people ought to conduct themselves in God's household, which is the church of the living God, the pillar and foundation of the truth. 16 Beyond all question, the mystery from which true godliness springs is great:
> He appeared in a body,
> was vindicated by the Spirit,
> was seen by angels,
> was preached among the nations,
> was believed on in the world,
> was taken up in glory.

At this juncture in the letter, Paul both sums up what has gone before and prepares for what is still to come. On the one hand, 3:14-16 does indeed look backward primarily to the section of teaching about church life (2:1–3:13). Paul explains his reasons for writing: his absence and possible delay, and the need to live appropriately in "God's household." The latter description introduces a reflection on the theology of the church that calls forth a unique manner of behavior. But the real high point of the section comes in the Christ hymn of 3:16. This exposition is given, as we will see, to explain the meaning of "the mystery of godliness." The answer to the questions invited by that phrase comes in the form of a strongly missiological depiction of the Christ-event that stresses both the humanity of Christ and the universality of salvation. The link back to the equally missiological section, 2:1-7, is seen both in the universal thrust and the repetition of the term "godliness," which first appears in 2:2.

On the other hand, however, the function of this section is not exhausted by the backward reference. Similar links forward suggest that it also provides a grounding that anticipates discussions to come. The stress on Christ's humanity ("he appeared in a body"; lit. "in flesh") may prepare for the engagement with the anti-marriage and anti-creation inclinations of the false teachers (4:1-5). The thought of the universality of salvation connects with 4:10, and six more occurrences of the term "godliness" (4:7, 8; 6:3, 5, 6, 11) find their theological anchor in the crucial connection between behavior and the Christ-event established by the hymn of 3:16. Then, another depiction of Christ that stresses his humanity will come in 6:13-14. Finally, the church-related teaching that dominates the second half of the letter is served just as well by the theology of the church laid down in this section.[1]

All of this suggests that attempts to limit Paul's reference in "these things I am writing" to some range of preceding material (e.g., 2:1–3:13) will be to miss the profound way in which the Christ hymn, as the rhetorical and theological high point of the letter, integrates missiology (the worldwide gospel) and Christian living ("godliness") into a dynamic vision of Christian existence that originates in the incarnation and vindication of Christ in human history.

14-15 The return of the letter to parenesis addressed specifically to Timothy, last seen at 1:18, is signaled by the resumption of the second-person singular in v. 14 (the pronoun "you" [2x]; see 1:18) and the second-person singular verb in v. 15. In this way, Paul establishes the basis for the teaching Timothy is to deliver to the church.

It was not at all unusual for Paul to use the letter as a means of communicating parenetic instruction to a church while absent from it. In fact, the language and style of this note are completely consistent with similarly intended notes in other Pauline letters.[2] The formula that extends to v. 15, "I am writing you these instructions so that . . . ," is also found in 2 Cor 13:10[3] but was more widely typical of didactic letters. Here it serves a formal purpose

---

1. Cf. Lau, *Manifest in Flesh,* 107-14.
2. For the ordinary use of ἐλπίζω ("hope") for future desires in travel statements, see Rom 15:24; 1 Cor 16:27; Phil 2:23. The phrase ἐν τάχει ("quickly, soon") establishes the sense of imminence and urgency that suggests determination; cf. the similar use of various forms of ταχέως in the travel statements of 1 Cor 4:19; Phil 2:24 (of Paul) and Phil 2:19; 2 Tim 4:9; Heb 13:23 (of Timothy).
3. Gk. ταῦτα . . . γράφω . . . ἵνα . . .; cf. 2 Cor 13:10: διὰ τοῦτο ταῦτα ἀπὼν γράφω, ἵνα . . . ("on account of this, I write these things while absent, so that . . .").

corresponding to the mandate dimension of the letter, mainly to remind the wider readership of Timothy's role and authority as the apostle's delegate in the community. This sort of role for Timothy is also indicated in 1 Cor 4:17, which is followed by Paul's intention to come to that church "quickly" (4:19; 16:10-11). Similar patterns and language are repeated in Rom 15:24 and Phil 2:23-24. In short, the increasingly popular assessment of this note as part of the supposed literary fiction[4] is a convenient way of dealing with a Pauline trait.

Paul provides two reasons to explain the need to communicate "these things" ("instructions," TNIV, NRSV) via the medium of a letter. As pointed out, the scope of the reference in "these things" is uncertain.[5] While in a strictly formal sense the reference is probably to the preceding section of teaching concerned with church life, 2:1–3:13,[6] the practical scope of the reference will extend to cover instructions that will flow from both this reason and the purpose and theology contained in this section.

The first reason is situational. Paul's allusion to intentions and travel plans, taken in conjunction with 1:3 (see also 4:13), does not, unfortunately, help us to locate him with precision, but it does nevertheless establish the situation of the letter. In fact, he is absent from the church. Both this absence and his announcement of his plans to come quickly produce the context (the so-called "apostolic parousia") within which the letter gains its authoritative force as the apostle's presence in spite of his absence, in this case further strengthened by the presence of the apostolic delegate. But it is in case Paul is "delayed" (v. 15)[7] that he sends Timothy in his place bearing the letter that sets out his function along with instructions for the community. The function of Timothy in such a situation, representing the absent Paul, is similar to the situation described in 1 Thess 3:1-6.

The second reason is expressed with the purpose *(hina)* clause: "that . . . you will know how people ought to conduct themselves in God's household." This in effect categorizes all of the instructions already given from 2:1 to 3:13 (and possibly those still to come) as representative of the "conduct" appropriate to life in "God's household." And it injects the note of necessity or "oughtness" characteristic of Paul's sense of God's claim on the behavior

---

4. E.g., Wolter, *Paulustradition,* 132; Trummer, *Paulustradition,* 123-25.

5. Gk. ταῦτα, in these letters to coworkers, more often refers backward to summarize what has just been said; see the discussions at 1:18; Titus 2:15.

6. In this case, the present demonstrative pronoun ταῦτα reaches only as far back as the similar summarizing conclusion in 1:18, where the last occurrence of a second-person singular (σοι, "you" = Timothy), accompanied by a summarizing anaphoric ταύτην, appears. Cf. Marshall, 505.

7. The possibility is expressed with the abrupt insertion of the conditional statement ἐὰν δὲ βραδύνω ("but if I am delayed"); see 2 Pet 3:9.

of his people (1 Thess 4:1; 2 Thess 3:7).[8] The term for "conduct" is not adequately translated alone with a term like "behave," which might suggest the
need to obey a handful of rules at certain times. It figured in secular discussions about the "manner of living" that fundamental principles called for.[9]
Paul uses the term similarly (2 Cor 1:12; Eph 2:3),[10] referring to a prescribed
manner of living (i.e., Christian living) in which "conduct" is to assume a
specific shape because of theological realities: it occurs here in the typical
combination of the verb and a prepositional phrase that more nearly defines
in some way the scope of such conduct.[11]

It is in the prepositional phrase that the theological framework that demands the particular conduct emerges. Two further descriptions of the church
will elaborate on the primary one: "the household of God." This phrase
brings into sharp focus the concept of the household that has overshadowed
the letter from 1:4-5 (see above), where it provides the general framework for
understanding God's way of organizing life. Here, in more limited scope, the
domestic metaphor describes the church. The background to the concept is
the Greco-Roman household.[12] Paul uses this image, as he has elsewhere,[13]
with its associated aspects of identity, authority, and responsibility, to shape
the instructions concerning Christian life in 1 Timothy. Use of household
codes (2:1-15; 6:1-2), the concern for children (1 Tim 3:4), widows (1 Tim
5:3-16), and slaves (6:1-2), and especially the interest in the church leader's
performance in the household (1 Tim 3:4-5, 12) all conform to the household
pattern of church identity. Just as there are rules of accepted behavior, relationships to observe, and responsibilities to fulfill within the household, so

8. For the same combination of interrogative adverb and verb of necessity, πῶς
δεῖ, in this context, see 1 Thess 4:1; 2 Thess 3:7 (cf. Col 4:6).

9. Epictetus 1.9.24; Josephus, *Antiquities* 15.190; see further the discussion and
references in Johnson, 231.

10. Gk. ἀναστρέφομαι (inf.); Heb 10:23; 1 Pet 1:17; 2 Pet 2:18 (noun in 1 Pet
1:15); Spicq, *TLNT* 1:111-14; G. Bertram, *TDNT* 5:941-43.

11. See BDAG, s.v.3.b.

12. See esp. Verner, *Household of God;* Roloff, 197-99; idem, "Pfeiler und
Fundament der Wahrheit: Erwägungen zum Kirchenverständnis der Pastoralbriefe," in
E. Grässer und O. Merk, eds., *Glaube und Eschatologie* (Tübingen: J. C. B. Mohr [Paul
Siebeck], 1985), 236-37; Lips, *Glaube,* 143-50.

It is unlikely that "household of God" is the equivalent of "temple of God" (ναὸς
θεοῦ; for which view, see esp. B. Gärtner, *The Temple and the Community in Qumran and
the New Testament* [Cambridge: Cambridge University Press, 1965], 66-71; P. Weigandt,
EDNT 2:501-2; O. Michel, *TDNT* 5:129). Temple imagery is of course employed by Paul
to describe the church (1 Cor 3:16; 6:19; 2 Cor 6:16; Eph 2:21-22). In these instances
God's people have become the new temple, the new dwelling place of God. This equation
is absent from 3:15, and the opening stress on household management (1:4) and the shape
of the ethical instruction speak against the temple association in "household of God."

273

there are analogous patterns to be observed in God's church. Believers must therefore know how to behave in God's household.[14]

Next, a relative clause[15] ("which is the church of the living God") expands the discussion of the church by moving out of the metaphorical category of household and into the more familiar territory of the *ekklēsia,* the assembly of God's people. The term "church of God" has already been encountered in reference to the local assembly of believers (see 3:5 and discussion; 5:16). In this context, Paul seems to be thinking of the church in universal terms.

It is less clear what the familiar appellation "living God" (4:10)[16] adds to the concept. The OT background is clear. In 4:10 the stress is on God as the life-giver (Deut 5:26; Sir 18:1), and in other texts the phrase's polemical denial of the dead "gods" of pagan idolatry is carried over from Judaism (Acts 14:15; 1 Thess 1:9; LXX 1 Sam 17:26, 36; Isa 37:41). But here the designation probably carries more the sense of God's reality and presence in the community (Num 14:28; Josh 3:10; Matt 16:16; Heb 3:12; 9:14; 10:31; 12:2).[17] Whether or not "church" ("assembly"; *ekklēsia*) still bears any of the dynamic sense of "being called out, gathered" (by God),[18] in this combination it nevertheless stresses the church's unique identity as that assembly of people who enjoy the presence of God in its midst.

Finally, a last phrase in apposition to the one just considered,[19] "the

13. The language of household management figures prominently in Paul's thinking. In 1 Cor 4:1, οἰκονόμος ("steward") and οἰκονομία ("stewardship") describe respectively the minister and the ministry. Gal 6:10 employs the household image to emphasize responsible behavior among "members of the household of faith" (τοὺς οἰκείους τῆς πίστεως). Eph 2:19 employs the household image in a mixture of metaphors to assure Gentile readers of their identity as "members of God's household" (οἰκεῖοι τοῦ θεοῦ). See further Towner, *DPL* 417-19.

14. See Lips, *Glaube,* 122.

15. Gk. ἥτις (fem. by attraction to the following noun, ἐκκλησία), referring to the preceding "household," is the indefinite relative taking the place of the simple relative pronoun.

16. Gk. θεοῦ ζῶντος; Rom 9:26; 2 Cor 3:3; 1 Thess 1:9; etc.

17. Cf. M. J. Goodwin, "The Pauline Background of the Living God as Interpretive Context for 1 Timothy 4.10," *JSNT* 61 (1996): 65-85; Marshall, 509. The view of Roloff, 198 and n. 441, that the phrase is a reworking of 2 Cor 6:16 ("for we are the temple of the living God"; ἡμεῖς γὰρ ναὸς θεοῦ ἐσμεν ζῶντος) is unlikely; neither the identification of the people with the temple nor the term "temple" (ναός) occurs in 3:15 (see P. H. Towner, "Pauline Theology or Pauline Tradition in the Pastoral Epistles: The Question of Method," *TynB* 46 [1995]: 308-9).

18. See Towner, *Goal,* 129-30.

19. This reading is syntactically more viable. Johnson, 231, suggests that the phrase is in delayed apposition to the statement of purpose, "how it is necessary to behave." This makes "pillar and support for the truth" a metaphorical description of the community's behavior. The point is implicit, anyway, in the reading adopted here.

pillar and foundation of the truth," extends the definition of "the church" from the thought of its unique experience of God's presence to function and ministry. Both "pillar"[20] and "foundation"[21] are architectural terms, though each can be extended figuratively to refer to other ideas, as they do here in reference to the church. Thus "pillar" frequently describes the cloud of God's presence (Exod 13:21-22; 14:24; 33:9; etc.), and stands metaphorically for leaders (Gal 2:9). In this case, where it combines with "foundation" and functions in respect to "the truth" (i.e., "the gospel"; see 2:4), the sense will be that of visible "support" such as the "pillar" lends to a building.[22] The term translated "foundation" also signifies firmness and steadfastness. Together (perhaps in the sense "supporting foundation")[23] the two terms depict the church, in the combative setting of heresy, as existing to provide a powerful and steadfast support for "the truth."[24]

Some maintain that this striking picture of the church marks a departure from Pauline theology. But with respect to language, this is not a non-Pauline use of "foundation" terminology (cf. 1 Cor 3:11; Eph 2:20, where a different term, *themelios,* figures in discussions of the church's origins); it is rather a new configuration, with new language for a completely different situation (that of heresy) in which Paul employs the architectural language to underscore the church's responsibility to guard the gospel and proclaim it.

Neither is the theology of the church here discontinuous from that in Paul's other letters. Allusions in the imagery to permanence, strength, immovability, and so on are thought to be at odds with Paul's stress on growth (Eph 4:15-16; Col 2:19; cf. 1 Cor 3:6-7) and the indwelling of the Spirit (1 Cor 3:16; 2 Cor 6:16). But the imagery here is not designed to present the church as a permanent historical institution in the world. In any case, the thought of permanence, properly understood, is not missing from Paul (cf.

20. Gk. στῦλος; LXX 1 Kgs 7:3; Ep Jer 1:58; Josephus, *Antiquities* 8.77.

21. Gk. ἑδραίωμα; only here in the NT; see the cognate adjective ἑδραῖος ("steadfast, firm") in 1 Cor 7:37; 15:58; Col 1:23; E. Stauffer, *TDNT* 2:363-64; Lips, *Glaube,* 98-99.

22. Roloff, 200-201 (Lips, *Glaube,* 99; Hanson, 82-83), draws attention to the OT sense of "pillar" of cloud as a sign, suggesting that here it designates the church's responsibility to testify "the truth" to the world. The church's witnessing function is surely implicit, but the more dominant nuance will be that of supporting strength.

23. For the possibility that the phrase is a hendiadys (two terms creating one idea), see Lips, *Glaube,* 98.

24. For the comparable description of the Qumran community and its role in relation to "the truth," see 1QS 8:5; cf. 8:8; 9:3-4 (in the sense of "the true temple of Israel"); Roloff, 200; Gärtner, *The Temple and the Community in Qumran,* 68-69; O. Betz, "Felsenmann und Felsengemeinde: Eine Parallel zu Mt. 16,17-19 in den Qumrantexten," *ZNW* 48 (1957): 49-77, 57. It is not possible to prove that the imagery in 1 Tim 3:15 is in any way dependent on Qumran. See Towner, *Goal,* 131; Marshall, 510-11.

Rom 8:31-39). It is, however, permanence in the sense of the assurance of immovability that comes through God's promise (cf. 2 Tim 2:20); this immovability is the mark of the new people of God, and it assures the church that apostasy and heresy will not bring the church to ruin. The uncertainty of the eschatologically determined present ("already–not yet") still applies to every local expression of the church; but the fulfillment of God's plan for the church in history and eternity is assured because of his promises.

16 This powerful combination of ideas is followed by an equally powerful confession of faith. The Christ hymn (v. 16b) now introduced is the rhetorical and christological high point of the letter. It expresses a very strongly missiological interpretation of Christian existence that draws its meaning from a Christology that stresses the humanity of Christ. Both these dimensions are perfectly consonant with the christological and missiological themes of the letter already under construction (1:15; 2:1-7). These themes both point to and emanate from this central confession of "the mystery of godliness."

While the confession, with its capsule summary of the gospel, appears to expand on the notion of "the truth" (= gospel) that concluded the description of the church,[25] the opening call to acknowledge the greatness of the mystery releases the confession to stand as a more independent conclusion to the entire description of the church and the call to appropriate conduct of v. 15.

The opening word, translated in various ways ("assuredly, indubitably"),[26] serves as a call for affirmation. In this context of church-related teaching (2:1–3:15), the liturgical tone of a call to confession should be retained.[27] All in Ephesus are called to acknowledge the truth of the confession.

The confession itself follows in two parts, first prose and then poetry. The first part is the acclamation of greatness, which I translate differently from the NIV: "Great is the mystery of godliness." "Great" (6:6; 2 Tim 2:20; Titus 2:13), here, is a measurement of superior quality, but it may also have a specific religious connotation (see below). As a way of describing the following "mystery"-event, the adjective places the mystery into a (divine) class of its own. "Mystery" recalls the statement just made concerning the deacons

---

25. Marshall, 521.

26. The TNIV/NIV and the NRSV render the term in a declarative sense, removing the liturgical tone ("beyond all question, without any doubt").

27. Gk. ὁμολογουμένως ("adverbialized" ptc.; see Josephus, *Antiquities* 1.180; 2.229) is traced to rhetorical and legal contexts, where the certainty and necessity of affirming a truth are stressed (Spicq, *TLNT* 2:583-84). Some find the term to be "academic" or polemical (see Hanson, *Studies*, 21-28; cf. S. E. Fowl, *The Story of Christ in the Ethics of Paul* [JSNTS 36; Sheffield: JSOT Press, 1990], 182-83). But in the religious context, the community call to confession seems more appropriate; O. Michel, *TDNT* 5:213; cf. Johnson, 232 ("we confess").

who must adhere to the "mystery of the faith" (see 3:9, discussion). In each case "mystery" is descriptive of the unveiled (previously hidden) plan of God, and the two phrases are not far apart in meaning. But "godliness" is the term Paul uses in these letters to coworkers to describe the wholeness of Christian existence as the integration of faith and behavior, and the choice of the term "godliness" in this case (see 2:2, Excursus) is determined by the broader focus on a kind of life suitable to God's household (and as descriptive of all that is dealt with in 2:1–3:13), whereas the concern in the case of the deacons is more specifically fidelity to the apostolic faith. Consequently, the "mystery of godliness" means the revelation of Jesus Christ in which Christian existence has its origin.[28]

Given the Ephesian setting, whether or not the famous riot associated with Paul's ministry (Acts 19) was still fresh in mind, it is impossible not to hear in Paul's statement a subversive echo of the city's bold claim, "Great is Artemis of the Ephesians" (Acts 19:28, 34; cf. 19:27, 35). And in calling the church to confess so extensive a claim — "Great is the mystery of godliness" — it would be quite appropriate for Paul to intentionally hijack the pagan rhetoric to rewrite this bit of the local religious story in terms of the gospel-promise of a new mode of existence, in Christ.[29]

Now the mystery is spelled out in the theological and historical terms of the hymn — at least most scholars describe the genre of the subsequent material in this way. Unfortunately, despite the generous amounts of attention given to the source and background of this piece, nothing can be said for certain about its origins or structure.[30] Its hymnlike or poetic character is clear from the structural consistency of the clauses (passive verb followed by prepositional phrases employing the preposition *en* plus an anarthrous dative object; only the third line breaks the pattern omitting the preposition), as well as by the assonance created by the presence in each line of the passive verb ending *-thē*.

Attempts to organize the lines further generally divide them into either two strophes of three lines each,[31] or three strophes of two lines each.[32]

28. See Towner, *Goal,* 87-89.

29. For the Artemis cult in Ephesus, see Trebilco, *The Early Christians in Ephesus,* 19-30.

30. See R. Deichgräber, *Gotteshymnus und Christushymnus in der frühen Christenheit* (Göttingen: Vandenhoeck & Ruprecht, 1967), 133-37; J. T. Sanders, *The New Testament Christological Hymns* (Cambridge: Cambridge University Press, 1971), 81-96; Fowl, *The Story of Christ in the Ethics of Paul,* 155-94; the discussion in Marshall, 497-504.

31. See UBS[4], Fee, *God's Empowering Presence,* 767-68; idem, 93-96; Lock, 45.

32. Dibelius and Conzelmann, 60-63; Kelly, 92; Deichgräber, *Gotteshymnus und Christushymnus,* 133-37.

In the former case, each half consists of two lines of opposing nouns (flesh/ Spirit, world/glory), with the third line of each half serving as a kind of refrain. In this way the hymn describes salvation history: the gospel-creating events of Christ's death and resurrection/vindication being followed by gospel-preaching events. While this arrangement allows for the parallelism between lines 4 and 5 ("preached among the nations"/"believed on in the world") to have full weight, it perhaps pays too little attention to other noun pairings. In the latter case, more attention is given to the three contrasting pairs of nouns: flesh/Spirit, angels/nations, world/glory. While the pairs seem obvious enough, there is no overarching meaning-frame to explain them. In the end we are left with the unsatisfying conclusion that while clearly being a poetic piece, in its present state the organization of its six lines cannot be reduced to either of the most popular schemes. But this need not hinder an effective reading of the hymn. The interests in salvation history, mission, and gospel are all detectable no matter how the lines are arranged.

More significant is the fact that each line views these interests through a christological lens, forcing the whole of salvation history, as well as the preceding "mystery of godliness," to be understood christocentrically. The hymn accomplishes this by leading off with the masculine relative pronoun "who" ("he"; TNIV),[33] which, in reference to Christ, becomes the subject of each of the six verbs of the hymn. Technically, given its neuter antecedent "mystery," the relative pronoun should be neuter as well, and this causes some syntactical awkwardness in the transition from "the mystery" to the hymn.[34] Since, however, Paul's point is that "the mystery" is a person (which the hymn verifies), the masculine pronoun creates the better sense.[35]

Line 1

After the relative pronoun, the first line of the hymn describes Jesus' manifestation as a human being (or among humankind). The passive verb "was manifested" (implying God is the actor) bears some attraction to the theme of "mystery" just announced (Rom 16:26; Col 1:26). What emerges by connecting the two concepts is that authentic Christian existence ("godliness") is

---

33. Gk. ὅς. The relative pronoun was used to insert traditional pieces into NT letters (Titus 2:14; Rom 8:32; Phil 2:6; 1 Pet 2:22-24; 3:22).

34. This can be seen in the late variants for the original ὅς: the change to ὅ (D* and Vg plus some Latin Fathers) was a gender adjustment to accord with τὸ μυστήριον; another late solution was the change to θεός (ℵ² Aᶜ C² D² Ψ 1739 1881 TR vlgᵐˢˢ), which supplies the antecedent thought to be lacking in ὅς.

35. The shift, *ad sensum*, to an appropriate gender pronoun is common enough (John 6:9; Gal 4:19; Phil 2:15; BDF §296).

linked to the divine unveiling of Christ "in flesh." The verb of revelation,[36] rare outside the NT, has a number of uses in relation to God and Christ (John 2:11; 9:3; Rom 1:19), of things they have revealed (2 Tim 1:10; Titus 1:3), and of the gospel/mystery (Rom 16:26; Col 1:26). A dominant use of the term portrays Christ's human history as a divine manifestation (John 1:31; Heb 9:26; 1 Pet 1:20; 1 John 1:2; 3:5, 8).[37] And this is its function here. As the broad salvation-historical thrust of the hymn suggests, the interest in this line is not on his entrance in human history per se (i.e., incarnation as birth), but on the fact of his humanity and the arena of humanity as the place in which he did his work.[38]

The phrase "in flesh" delimits the manifestation. The question is, how? "Flesh" in numerous cases denotes Christ's preresurrection humanity in one sense or another. One has only to compare Rom 1:3-4, which introduces the similar flesh/spirit contrast as lines 1-2 of this hymn, to appreciate the general way in which the category functions.[39] There are few data here to suggest that "in flesh" might focus more precisely on a particular point in Christ's life, though attempts at greater precision have been made.[40] The phrase can be understood to indicate either the mode (as a human being; "in a body" [TNIV] blurs the distinction intended by the flesh/ Spirit antithesis)[41] or the local sphere (among humankind)[42] of Jesus' his-

36. Gk. φανερόω ("to manifest, make manifest, reveal"; for which the TNIV translation, "appeared," is rather bland).

37. Cf. M. N. A. Bockmuehl, "Das Verb φανερόω im Neuen Testament," *BZ* 32 (1988): 87-99; idem, *Revelation and Mystery,* 210-14; P.-G. Müller, *EDNT* 3:413-14.

38. See also R. H. Gundry, "The Form, Meaning and Background of the Hymn Quoted in 1 Timothy 3:16," in W. W. Gasque and R. P. Martin, *Apostolic History and the Gospel* (Exeter: Paternoster, 1970), 210; Kelly, 90. The view, based on Luke 24:39 and Acts 10:40 (which employ forms of φανερόω), that line 1 refers to Christ's post-resurrection appearances to people (see B. Schneider, "'Kata Pneuma Hagiōsynēs' [Rom 1.4]," *Bib* 48 [1967], 367, 384-85; and J. Dupont, Σὺν Χριστῷ: *L'union avec le Christ suivant Saint Paul* [Bruges: Nauwelaerts, 1952], 108-10) is too narrow to fit the broader sweep of the hymn and the more typical use of "flesh" for Jesus' preresurrection existence (see further Towner, *Goal,* 89).

39. Gk. ἐν σαρκί (E. Schweizer et al., *TDNT* 7:98-151; Spicq, *TLNT* 3.231-41; A. Sand, *EDNT* 3:230-33); John 1:14; 6:51ff.; Rom 8:3; 9:5; Eph 2:14; Col 1:22; Heb 5:7; 10:20; 1 Pet 3:18; 4:1; 1 John 4:2; 2 John 7; cf. Cranfield, *Romans,* 1:60.

40. For the view that σάρξ ("flesh") implies human weakness and so refers to Christ's death, see D. M. Stanley, *Christ's Resurrection in Pauline Soteriology* (AnBib 13; Rome: Pontifical Biblical Institute, 1961), 237; W. Stenger, *Der Christushymnus 1 Tim 3,16* (RST 6; Frankfurt: Lang, 1977), 90.

41. See J. D. G. Dunn, "Jesus — Flesh and Spirit: An Exposition of Romans 1.3-4," *JTS* n.s. 24 (1973): 62-64.

42. See Gundry, "Hymn," 210; Kelly, 90.

torical manifestation. The former seems more in keeping with the stress on Jesus' humanity already evident in 1:15 and 2:5, as well as with the reference to his Spirit-stage of existence about to be made (see below). Thus the most obvious sense of the line is as a celebration of the fact of Jesus' incarnation. As elsewhere in the NT (Rom 8:3; Phil 2:7-8), the crucifixion is to be understood as the ultimate purpose and climax of this stage of existence, and it forms the natural line of demarcation between the images projected in lines 1 and 2.[43]

Line 2

Whatever is decided about the structure of this piece, line 2 is a response and a completion of the events encapsulated in line 1. It is a response in that within this salvation-historical profile of the Christ-event and the gospel, it portrays Jesus' vindication, God's response to the crucifixion. It is a completion in that the affirmation of line 2 completes the portrait of Christ's existence by depicting its second stage.

The verb of line 2 is correctly translated "was vindicated" (Titus 3:7), against the OT background of the term,[44] and indicates God's demonstration of Jesus' innocence. The early church consistently regarded the resurrection/exaltation of Jesus to be the historical event in which God demonstrated his Son's vindication.[45] But a fuller story is implied in the prepositional phrase that follows.

TNIV translates "by the Spirit," which understands the prepositional phrase to be identifying the Holy Spirit as the agency of the vindication/resurrection (GNB; cf. Rom 8:11).[46] However, this does not account satisfactorily for the antithesis created in lines 1 and 2 by the phrases "in flesh" and "in Spirit." The antithesis occurs widely in the NT and tends to stress a distinction between human and supernatural modes or spheres of existence, the latter of which is characterized by the presence and power of the Spirit.[47] With this in mind, "in [the] Spirit" better expresses the second stage of Jesus' hu-

43. See also Marshall, 524-25.
44. Gk. δικαιόω; the model for this is Rom 3:4 (= LXX Ps 50:6); 8:33; Luke 7:35; *Psalms of Solomon* 2:16; 3:5; 4:9; 8:7; *Odes of Solomon* 17.2; 25.12; 29.5; G. Schrenk, *TDNT* 2:211-19.
45. Acts 2:22-36; 3:11-15; 4:10-12; 10:34-43; Rom 1:4; 1 Cor 2:1-9; Eph 1:20-21; Phil 2:5-11; Col 2:8-15; 1 Pet 3:21-22; cf. Dibelius and Conzelmann, 62; Marshall, 525.
46. Barrett, 65-66; Jeremias, 29.
47. Gk. ἐν πνεύματι; cf. Matt 26:41; Mark 14:38; John 3:6; 6:63; Rom 1:4; 8:4, 5, 6, 9, 13; 1 Cor 5:5; 2 Cor 7:1; Gal 3:3; 4:29; 5:16, 17(2x), 19; 6:8; Col 2:5; Heb 12:9; 1 Pet 3:18.

man existence, which he entered by means of the resurrection.[48] This is not to say that the Spirit was not fully operative in Jesus' earthly ministry; rather, it stresses his complete entrance into a final stage of existence for which all believers are destined.

The fuller story alluded to above is simply this: Jesus' human existence cannot be understood solely on the basis of line 1, which ends in death. Line 2 is God's response not only to Jesus' weakness and death, in the sense of a reprieve; it is all the more the completion of Jesus' humanity, as through resurrection the limited authority of death is overcome by resurrection power and the destined Spirit-abode of humanity is entered. What the tradition goes on to declare is that the Christ-event was both a pattern for believing humanity (thus it forms the "mystery of godliness" = Christian existence), and the content of the gospel by which people enter into that pattern. The humanity of Christ in its two stages is the means by which God's salvation mystery is revealed.

Line 3

TNIV's "seen by angels" (NRSV; TEV; CEV) regards line 3 as a passive experience of Christ. However, the passive verb employed frequently depicts an active exhibition of the one so described,[49] which recommends the translation, "who appeared to angels." While it is possible to take "angels"[50] as a reference to human witnesses of the resurrection,[51] this is a far more likely reference to the rich tradition of Christ's resurrection appearance(s) before angelic powers. Beyond this, it is impossible to be completely precise. The

48. Towner, *Goal,* 89-90; Schweizer, *TDNT* 6:416-17; *TDNT* 7:126-28; W. J. Dalton, *Christ's Proclamation to the Spirits* (Rome: Pontifical Biblical Institute, 1965), 127-32; Fowl, *Story of Christ,* 159-62; Marshall, 525-26; Roloff, 204-5; Oberlinner, 165-66; Fee, *God's Empowering Presence,* 765-66. Gundry's attempt ("Hymn," 211-14), based on a presumed link to the tradition of a preresurrection *descensus* in 1 Pet 3:18-19, to interpret "in spirit" as a reference to Christ's "vivification distinct from and prior to resurrection" presses the general language into far too precise a statement (for fuller discussion, see Towner, *Goal,* 91; Fowl, *Story of Christ,* 161-62).

49. Gk. ὤφθη (aor. pass. from ὁράω); Gen 12:7; 17:1; Exod 3:2; Judg 6:12; Matt 17:3 (pars.); Luke 1:11; 22:43; Acts 7:2, 30, 35; of resurrection appearances, Luke 24:34; Acts 9:17; 13:31; 26:16; 1 Cor 15:5-8; of parousia, Heb 9:28; W. Michaelis, *TDNT* 5:358.

50. Gk. ἄγγελος (5:21); only infrequently of people in the NT (Mark 1:2 [pars.]; Luke 7:24; 9:52; Jas 5:21; possibly in 1 Cor 11:10; Revelation 2–3; see further G. Kittel, *TDNT* 1:89; D. F. Watson, "Angels [New Testament]," n.p. *ABD on CD-ROM.* Version 2.1a, 1995, 1996, 1997).

51. E.g., A. Seeberg, *Der Katechismus der Urchristenheit* (München: C. Kaiser, 1966 [1903]), 119-20. The verb is used in describing some resurrection appearances to humans, e.g., Luke 24:34; Acts 9:17.

NT contains the tradition of Jesus' display of victory before fallen powers.[52] But a more general and positive tradition commemorates Christ's triumphant exaltation to the heavenly realm and his display of victory there,[53] and this background coincides better with the tone of the hymn.

In continuing the theme of vindication (implicitly), line 3 extends the thought of line 2 by displaying the meaning of resurrection for the heavenly powers. It may even be regarded as continuing the historical sequence of salvation-historical moments (human life/death; resurrection; manifestation to angelic powers). At the same time, the emphasis on display, exhibition, or communication reveals a link with the next line, as the implications of the Christ-event are proclaimed in the human sphere.

Line 4

Lines 4 and 5 shift the hymn's focus to the effects of "the mystery" among humankind. Christology develops naturally into missiology. The shift is hardly unexpected, especially within a Pauline rendition of redemption, for the proclamation of the gospel "among the nations" represents the fulfillment of God's OT promises and the purpose of the Pauline mission — a theme already encountered (2:1-7, 8). "Preached among the nations" regards the human experience of Christ (still the subject of the passive verb) more obliquely as the content of the gospel, with lines 1-2 providing a rough version of the gospel. The aorist passive verb "preached, proclaimed"[54] intends to summarize the execution of the church's evangelistic mission to this point. The prepositional phrase that follows ("among the nations") explicitly emphasizes the universal scope of the gospel and (with the verb) the prophetic fact of the gospel's penetration into the Gentile world.[55] Thus the hymn sounds the very Pauline theme of the fulfillment of the divine promise to reach the whole world with the gospel (2:1, 7, 8). It may be true that the lan-

---

52. Eph 2:6-7; 3:9-11; Col 2:8, 15, 20; cf. Gal 4:3, 9. See Gundry ("Hymn," 219) for the view that this exhibition took place prior to the resurrection during the *descensus;* cf. Easton, 136-37.

53. Eph 1:21; Phil 2:9-11; Heb 1:3-4; 1 Pet 3:22; Rev 5:8-14; cf. *Ascension of Isaiah* 11.23.

54. Gk. κηρύσσω (2 Tim 4:2); standard in Paul for the activity of preaching (Rom 10:8, 14, 15; 1 Cor 1:23; 9:27; 15:11, 12; etc.); correspondingly, the preacher is κῆρυξ (1 Tim 2:7; 2 Tim 1:11), and the message is κήρυγμα (Rom 16:25; 1 Cor 2:4; 15:14; 2 Tim 4:17).

55. Gk. ἐν ἔθνεσιν (2:7; 2 Tim 4:17); in Rom 15:9 this phrase occurs in a quotation by Paul, remarkably similar in thrust ("therefore I will confess you, O Lord, among the Gentiles"; διὰ τοῦτο ἐξομολογήσομαί σοι ἐν ἔθνεσιν κύριε; LXX Ps 17:50; cf. 2 Sam 22:50), that establishes the OT pattern of his ministry to and success among Gentiles. See also Marshall, 528; Fee, 55; Läger, *Christologie,* 52-53.

guage of "nations" or "Gentiles" "does not necessarily exclude Jews,"[56] for the Pauline mission was always directed to Jews and Gentiles.[57] Nevertheless, as a salvation-historical benchmark, the phrase "among the Gentiles" intends to make another eschatological point. In the Pauline mission, the gospel has begun to achieve the universal proportions for which it was designed, and "among the Gentiles" echoes the promise of "the fullness of the Gentiles" (Rom 11:25-26). Final achievement of this is the condition of the fulfillment of Israel's hopes;[58] it requires the continuation of this universal mission, and the church's full involvement in it (2:1-7).

Line 5

"Was believed on in the world" parallels the preceding line, adding to the hymn the necessary stress on the effectiveness of the Christian mission. Christ as the content of the proclamation is now the one in whom "belief" is placed.[59] The arena of this mission fruitfulness, "in the world," also stands parallel with "the nations" in line 4. "World" here means the community of humankind in need of God (1:15); the fact that Christ has entered this world underlines the church's continued responsibility to be active in ministry within it. Together, lines 4-5 create the missiological necessity emerging from the Christ-event: just as "belief" is the human response to the Christ-event, proclamation is the Christian responsibility. While the hymn indicates success and progress in both the breadth and results of proclamation, it stops short of announcing the completion of God's redemptive plan.

Line 6

The hymn ends on the note of Christ's exaltation: "taken up in glory." The verb suggests an allusion to Christ's ascension.[60] But the stress is certainly

56. Marshall, 528.

57. P. H. Towner, "Mission Practice and Theology under Construction (Acts 18-20)," in I. H. Marshall and D. Peterson, eds., *Witness to the Gospel: The Theology of Acts* (Bletchley, U.K.: Paternoster and Grand Rapids: Ecrdmans, 1998), 417-36.

58. See J. Moltmann, *The Coming of God* (trans. M. Kohl; Minneapolis: Fortress, 1996), 198.

59. For Gk. πιστεύω (aor. pass.), see the discussion and note at 1:2. "Belief" is the appropriate response to the gospel (G. Barth, *EDNT* 3:93); in the aorist passive, ἐπιστεύθη conveys the sense of placing trust in, believing on some object (BDF §312), in this case Christ (the rel. ὅς is still the subject).

60. Gk. ἀναλαμβάνω (aor. pass.); Mark 16:19; Luke 24:51; Acts 1:2, 11, 22; cf. Luke 11:51; see esp. G. Lohfink, *Die Himmelfahrt Jesu* (München: Kösel, 1971), 213; G. Delling, *TDNT* 4:8. See also Marshall, 528-29; Roloff, 210; Oberlinner, 169.

not on the event as a chronological terminus; for if chronology were the organizing theme of the poem, we would expect a line dedicated in some explicit way to hope in the parousia (cf. Acts 1:11). Rather, it is the symbolic value of the historical event that predominates: it represents the exaltation of Christ. "In glory" might refer to the destination to which Jesus was exalted ("the heavenly sphere, God's right hand"),[61] but it is a more likely description of the status of "glorification" conferred in and through exaltation.[62] While the reference frustrates a neat chronological sequence of the events depicted in the hymn, this last allusion to Christ's exaltation, via the ascension, reinforces the link between the present exalted status of the Lord and the vindication of his humanity.

How then does the hymn function? The first mistake to avoid in answering this question is that of attempting to read the six lines as a discrete piece of dogma. This is a temptation caused not only by the fact of its neat poetic structure (and naming it a "hymn"), which causes it to stand out from the surrounding discourse, but also by tradition- and literary-critical attempts to discern its source and internal structure. These disciplines might indeed shed some light on the meaning of the lines and their interrelation, but all too often they give the impression that the piece, as employed here, has a life of its own.

In fact, the function and message of the hymn must be sought in its relation especially to what has preceded it. This means, first of all, that it serves as the climax of the whole concluding section, 3:14-16. As such, it takes its cue from 3:15, which underscores the present behavior of believers as members of God's household. Secondly, in serving this purpose, it also concludes the entire section beginning (at least) at 2:1 — a long section taken up with the aspects of present Christian living that 3:15 intends to summarize as conduct appropriate to God's household. But what can the Christ hymn say to this?

As we have seen at 1:15 and 2:5-6, Christ's humanity is a theme of importance in this letter. It has sometimes been suggested that the Christology that emerges from these statements was calculated to correct some form of Docetism (a denial of the humanity of Christ) being taught by the heretics.

---

61. So Roloff, 210; Kelly, 92.

62. Gundry, "Hymn," 216; G. Kittel, *TDNT* 2:237, 247-49. Gk. ἐν δόξῃ (for the phrase in the NT, see Luke 9:31; 1 Cor 15:41, 43; 2 Cor 3:7, 8, 11; Phil 4:19; Col 3:4). Marshall (525 n. 99) points out that the preposition εἰς would be expected to express the destination of a verb of motion (cf. Heb 2:10); following the action of the verb (ἀνελήμφθη ἐν δόξῃ; "taken up in glory"), the sense of the prepositional phrase may correspond to its use in 1 Cor 15:43 (ἐγείρεται ἐν δόξῃ; "raised in glory"), where a quality or character of status (i.e., "glorification"), rather than a destination, seems indicated. Cf. Fowl, *Story of Christ,* 169-70.

While there is really no way to prove or disprove this assertion, it seems on the whole unlikely, since we might have expected a stronger reaction by Paul. I would suggest that the emphasis on the humanity of Jesus Christ, especially as Paul has anchored the gospel precisely in the Messiah's human experience, intended rather (1) to revive the church's interest in gospel ministry in the world, outside of the Christian community (see esp. the discussion at 2:1-6), and (2) to counteract the antiflesh views of the opponents (4:1-5) that may well have influenced the church's theology.

The hymn can be seen to gather together these concerns. First, it continues the theme of the humanity of Christ, reemphasizing his full participation in human weakness (line 1). But, secondly, the ground of Christian hope, which has thus far been left as an unnamed assumption, is now more fully expressed — that is, vindication of Christ through resurrection (lines 2-3). In these two or three lines it emerges that human experience does not end in weakness, suffering, and death, but on the contrary in life and vindication. But this dimension of Christ's existence remains for the church in the present an aspect of hope. Without it, present struggle has little purpose; with it, present struggle is the "suffering with him" (2 Tim 2:11-12) that carries great hope. The real clue that this hymn is about Christian existence, and not just about Christ's existence — that it truly does explicate "the mystery of godliness" and provide a christological foundation for "conduct in God's household" — can be seen in lines 4-5. These lines fully implicate human beings in the salvation plan of God, not just as undeserving recipients of God's grace (line 5), but first of all as messengers who announce the truth en-fleshed in the Messiah. The aorist tenses are not to be read as signaling completion, but rather fact. In God's salvation drama, Paul (and the church) has proclaimed the gospel, and the mission has produced results. But the ministry and results are characteristic of the church's present age — as the age continues toward the end, so must the activity.

The hymn establishes a balance that rightly begins with the fundamental Christ-event. But the central place of human response and responsibility in mission is essential to the salvation plan of God. It is actually almost a misnomer to call this piece a "Christ hymn," for its solemn purpose is to reiterate in the present context the intimate connection that exists between Creator and creation — a connection that God has reestablished through the incarnation and death of his Son (see further 4:1-5). It is thus a hymn about restoration and wholeness — the reconciliation of the divine and the human into a unified relationship through the human experience of Christ. At present, the church is to identify with the experience of Christ in suffering and witness (lines 1, 4), its hope made sure and purpose for doing so grounded in the fact of his resurrection, vindication, and glorious exaltation.

B. ORDERING AND ORGANIZING GOD'S HOUSEHOLD: PART II (4:1–6:21A)

Following the climactic summary and conclusion of the hymn, in the last half of the letter Paul returns to addressing a mix of practical issues. The numerous second-person singular verbs or pronouns show Timothy to be either the direct recipient of the instructions (4:6-16; 5:1-2, 22-26; 6:11-16, 20a)[1] or the mediator of them to various groups in the church (5:3-16, 17-21; 6:1-2, 17-19),[2] in which case third-person plural verbs indicate responsibilities to be carried out by group members. The exception is seen in the descriptive-polemical sections (4:1-5; 6:3-10), designed mainly to identify (for all) and denounce the beliefs and practices of the false teachers. Even in these sections, Timothy remains in view as the one who would see that the refutation of the opponents was carried out on the basis of Paul's denunciation (1:3, 18; 6:12, 20), and that the fellowship was duly instructed in the errors of the heretical teaching (4:6)

1. Regarding Heresy, Godliness, and Timothy's Responsibility (4:1-16)

Although the division of what is really a continuous long section of the letter into smaller units is more a matter of convenience than rhetorical necessity, shifts in topic and resumption of commands establish three subsections in 4:1-16. At v. 6 the shift from description and argument in vv. 1-5 to the second-person singular and imperatival tone reveals the first seam. Two second-person imperatives at v. 11 mark similarly the transition from the theological summary that rounds off vv. 6-10 back to parenesis to Timothy.

At 4:1-5 Paul returns to the topic of the false teaching troubling the community. The subsection consists of two essential parts. Verses 1-3, which form a single sentence in the Greek, categorize the heresy in general and specific terms. A prophetic word of the Spirit essentially puts a theological or eschatological name to the movement and sets it into the framework of redemptive history (in "the last times"), and locates the source of its doctrines (the demonic). This eschatological interpretation slides easily into an evaluation of the character of those who are promoting and being influenced by the heresy. And as the description closes, Paul identifies two specifics of the heretical teaching (v. 3a), and transitions into theological refutation that centers on the last item (abstention from certain foods; v. 3b). Verses 4-5, the second sentence of this subsection, first substantiate Paul's counterassertions with

---

1. Second-person indicators are present in 4:6, 7, 11, 12, 13, 14, 15, 16; 5:1, 22, 23; 6:11, 12, 13, 14, 20a.

2. 5:3, 7, 11, 19, 20, 21; 6:2b, 17.

argument from the Genesis creation accounts demonstrating God's creational intention. He follows this with a reminder of how the believing community may "by the word of God and prayer" activate its divinely intended privilege to eat all foods.

a. The Emergence of Heresy (4:1-5)

1 *The Spirit clearly says that in later times some will abandon the faith and follow deceiving spirits and things taught by demons.* 2 *Such teachings come through hypocritical liars, whose consciences have been seared as with a hot iron.* 3 *They forbid people to marry and order them to abstain from certain foods, which God created to be received with thanksgiving by those who believe and who know the truth.* 4 *For everything God created is good, and nothing is to be rejected if it is received with thanksgiving,* 5 *because it is consecrated by the word of God and prayer.*

1-3a   To neutralize the threat posed by the false teachers' confusing and clever arguments Paul seeks to demystify the movement. He does so by giving a name to this heresy — by naming it as God does and placing it into a theological grid — which also underlines the real dangers it presents to the unwary in the church. The opening phrase, "the Spirit clearly says," establishes the prophetic character of the assessment to follow.[3] This is the only reference in this letter to the Spirit's present ministry in the church.[4] His function here is to convey (as source and divine enabler) a prophetic word.[5] The whole phrase may be something of a Christian formula, with the now fully present Spirit occupying the gap experienced by the OT prophets who announced, "Thus says the LORD" (cf. Rev 2:7, 11, 17, 29; 3:6, 13, 22).[6]

3. The TNIV correctly chooses not to translate the weak connective δέ; rather than intending a sharp contrast with 3:16, it serves simply to link the new topic to the preceding discourse of the letter.

4. Gk. πνεῦμα; 3:16 (and notes); 2 Tim 1:7, 14; Titus 3:5 (of "deceiving spirits," Tim 4:1b; the human spirit, 2 Tim 4:22); see the discussion in Towner, *Goal,* 57-58; Introduction, 56-57.

5. 2 Sam 23:2; Acts 21:11; 2 Thess 2:2.

6. The whole phrase, "the Spirit clearly says" (τὸ δὲ πνεῦμα ῥητῶς λέγει), compares with the statement describing prophetic messages embedded in the seven appeals to the churches of Revelation 2–3 to "hear": "Let anyone who has an ear hear what the Spirit says" (ὁ ἔχων οὖς ἀκουσάτω τί τὸ πνεῦμα λέγει; Rev 2:7, 11, 17, 29; 3:6, 13, 22); the phrase that introduces the prophecy of Agabus in Acts 21:11, "the Holy Spirit says" (τάδε λέγει τὸ πνεῦμα τὸ ἅγιον), is similar in ascribing prophecy to the Spirit, but is otherwise fashioned after the OT "thus says the Lord" (τάδε λέγει κύριος; e.g., Isa 22:25; 30:1; 31:9) formula (cf. Rev 2:1, 8, 12, 18; 3:1, 7, 14).

Paul does not indicate clearly whether this was a prophetic word revealed directly to him, in the past or immediate present (Acts 16:9; 18:9-10;
2 Cor 12:1),[7] or whether he passes on revelation that has come by way of
Christian prophets and has circulated in the churches for some time (1:18;
4:14; Acts 21:9; 1 Cor 14:29; Rev 2:7; 14:13; 22:17).[8] Both options are possible,[9] and the more important feature of the statement is the affirmation of
the authority of the Spirit's prophetic word.

The present relevance (but not necessarily present time) of this Spirit-
word is indicated by the present tense verb "says."[10] It is worth noting that
Paul presumes the ongoing operation of the Spirit of prophecy in the congregation.[11] The attached adverb, "clearly, expressly, unambiguously,"[12] sharpens the sense of authority and relevance by removing any possibility of
vagueness from what is being said.

The phrase that opens the prophetic word is temporal in appearance but
theological in meaning: "in later times." This particular configuration is a
variation on the theme more usually expressed with the phrase "in the last
days" (as in 2 Tim 3:1).[13] It identifies the eschatological time of the Spirit and
salvation (thus = "the last days"), but does so here specifically by describing
an element of the dark reality of sin, struggle, and danger that coexists with
the Spirit in this age of incompleteness. In this case, he adapts the general
theme of a falling away, an increase in evil, deceit, and disorder that would oc-

7. Paul's farewell warning to the Ephesian elders about apostasy recorded in Acts
20:29-30 may lie behind this (Towner, *Goal*, 58; see Mark 13:22 [par.]; J. D. G. Dunn, *Je-
sus and the Spirit* [London: SCM, 1975], 453 n. 14; D. Hill, *New Testament Prophecy*
[London: Marshall, Morgan & Scott, 1978], 140). Cf. D. E. Aune, *Prophecy in Early
Christianity*, 289-90, 292. Typically, proponents of pseudonymity argue that the post-
Pauline author made use of the Acts record to lend authority to his "Pauline" criticism of a
Gnostic movement (e.g., Hasler, 33-34).

8. See Fee, *God's Empowering Presence*, 769.

9. The language would seem an unlikely reference to the teaching of Jesus (but
see Knight, 188), for which cf. 1 Cor 7:10, 12; see also Marshall, 537.

10. Gk. λέγω; cf. this sense in similar statements about Scripture (5:18; Rom 4:3),
David (Rom 4:6; 9:15), and God (Rom 9:15; Heb 1:6-7).

11. *Pace* Roloff, 220.

12. Gk. ῥητῶς (only here in biblical Greek); BDAG, s.v.; Marshall, 537; Roloff,
219 n. 6; Knight, 188; e.g., Philo, *Allegorical Interpretation* 1.60 (with a verb of speaking); Josephus, *Antiquities* 1.24. The absence of any indication of a direct quote makes the
more specific sense of "in these words" unlikely (but cf. Lock, 47; e.g., Philo, *Allegorical
Interpretation* 1.60 [possibly]; Plutarch, *Moralia* 1041A).

13. Gk. ἐν ὑστέροις καιροῖς ("in later times"; prep. + comparative adj. + pl. noun;
cf. 1 Pet 1:5: ἐν καιρῷ ἐσχάτῳ) more typically is one of the "last days" variations: Isa 2:2;
Acts 2:17: ἐν ταῖς ἐσχάταις ἡμέραις ("in the last days"; cf. Jas 5:3; *Didache* 16.3; *Barnabas* 4.9); following ἐπί in the genitive: Deut 32:20; Heb 1:2; 2 Pet 3:3.

cur in the last days, a warning to the faithful who are to persevere in spite of such opposition.[14] The tendency of some to treat the phrase as a literal temporal reference ("in the future," "in days to come")[15] ignores the parallel description in 2 Tim 3:1. Not only do the same general events appear to be in mind (a falling away, deceivers), but in both passages a shift from the initial future tense ("some will fall away," 1 Tim 4:1; "terrible times will come . . . people will be," 2 Tim 3:1-2) to discussions of the present underlines the present relevance of what is being said. These patterns strongly suggest that the two phrases are functionally equivalent and that the reference to "the later times/ last days" is to the eschatological period of the Spirit.[16] What is happening in the church corresponds to the prophetic tradition: believers are to recognize the movement, not panic in surprise, and respond accordingly.

After establishing the eschatological framework of the message, Paul comes to the main substance. He depicts the movement in Ephesus in terms of apostasy from the faith. The Greek verb "to fall away" ("turn away," 2 Tim 2:19; "abandon," TNIV), often with a genitive as here, acquired the technical meaning "to apostatize."[17] As in 1:3 (see the note), 6, and 19, the vague subject, "some (people)," is an intentional expression of disrespect. It refers to the false teachers and to those who are accepting their doctrines.[18] And in this acceptance is rejection of "the faith," understood as the sum total of the Christian way (see 1:2, note).

Next, a participial phrase describes the means by which these have fallen away (NRSV; or possibly more loosely an attendant circumstance, TNIV). Beginning with the language that characterizes the commitment of the opponents in 1:4 ("to be devoted to, pay attention to"; see the discussion at 1:4), the phrase goes on to describe apostasy in terms of the source and con-

---

14. 1QpHab 2:5-6; 1QS 3:22; *Testament of Dan* 5:5-6; Mark 13:22 (par.); Acts 20:29; 2 Thess 2:1-12; 1 John 2:18; Revelation 13; cf. discussion in Quinn-Wacker, 350-52.

15. E.g., Spicq, *TLNT* 3:427-31 (esp. 431).

16. See further Towner, *Goal,* 65; Marshall, 537-38; Mounce, 234. W. L. Lane, "1 Tim iv. 1-3: An Instance of Over-Realized Eschatology?" *NTS* 11 (1964-65): 164-67 (164), cites *Acta Carpi* 5 for the phrase in reference to a period of time.

17. Gk. ἀφίστημι; Josh 22:23, 29; 2 Chron 28.22 *Psalms of Solomon* 9.1; Jer 39:40 LXX; 1 Macc 2:19; Luke 8:13; Heb 3:12 (ἀπὸ θεοῦ); Hermas, *Vision* 3.7.2; H. Schlier, *TDNT* 1:512-13.

18. Fee, 97 (see also Marshall, 538), argues that τινές must refer not to the false teachers but to "members of God's household" being duped by them; but the next phrase, "devoting themselves to deceiving spirits and doctrines of demons" (προσέχοντες πνεύμασιν πλάνοις καὶ διδασκαλίαις δαιμονίων), which further describes the group in view, seems closely parallel to the description of the false teachers in 1:4, which employs the same verb (προσέχω) to describe their devotion to "myths and genealogies." What 4:1 does is to assign those myths to a demonic source. Cf. Johnson, 239.

tent of the heretical message that diverts them from the faith. "Deceiving spirits," a part of the eschatological paradigm,[19] are demonic influences or forces believed to be actively at work promoting the falsehood of the heresy.[20] The internalization of this activity in the opponents can be seen in 2 Tim 3:13 (see discussion), where the cognate verb is central in Paul's caricature of the false teachers.

Parallel with "deceiving spirits" is the second object of the participle, "things taught by demons." The phrase does not really add anything new to what has just been said, but the accent now shifts to the content of the false doctrines. The plural form, literally "teachings" ("doctrines"), creates an intentional, traditional contrast with the singularity (and therefore authority and truthfulness) of the apostolic doctrine (LXX Isa 29:13).[21] The genitive should probably be rendered "of demons,"[22] indicating the source of the doctrines as being the demonic realm.[23] Johnson has shown that the allegation of complicity with demons was typical in first-century Jewish polemics,[24] and the tactic may be one used by Paul as well (cf. Rom 16:20; 2 Thess 2:9). However, the temptation to write this off as rhetoric should be resisted in view of the strong sense present in especially the Corinthian letters and 1 Timothy that the Christian community lived under the constant real threat of Satanic attack (1 Tim 3:6-7; 1 Cor 5:5; 7:5; 10:20-21; 2 Cor 2:11; 11:14; 12:7). Belief in the demonic was a fixture in the early Christian worldview, and this kind of statement in this passage is part of the attempt to "locate" the heretical movement within the eschatological demonic opposition to God. In fact, together the whole phrase, and its indictment of the false doctrine as demonic, indicates a claim on the part of the opponents to be recipients of revelation (cf. 1 John 4:1-6).

Verse 2 adds two phrases that implicate the false teachers in the demonic deception. But as the Greek sentence continues, the strain on syntacti-

19. For the plural πνεύματα ("spirits") as evil, demonic spirits, see Luke 4:36; 1 Pet 3:19; cf. 1 John 4:6 (sg.). For their place in the traditional picture of end-times evil, see *Testament of Judah* 14.8; 20.1; *Testament of Reuben* 2.1-2; *Testament of Simeon* 6.6; 3.1 (sg.); for the role of the demonic in the eschatological deception, see *Testament of Dan* 5.5; *Testament of Benjamin* 3.3; 1QS 3:18-22; CD 2:17; 1QpHab 10:9; Rev 16:14; 18:2; cf. 2 Cor 4:4; 11:3; Jas 3:15.

20. For Gk. πλάνος (adj.) in the active sense of "deceiving, leading astray," see the adjective for noun use in Matt 27:63; 2 Cor 6:8; 2 John 7(2x); H. Braun, *TDNT* 6:249-50.

21. See 1:10; Titus 1:14 (discussion); Matt 15:9 (Mark 7:7 = Isa 29:13); Col 3:22; cf. Eph 4:14.

22. Gk. δαιμόνιον; elsewhere in Paul only in 1 Cor 10:20, 21 (showing again the attraction between 1 Corinthians and 1 Timothy); for the activity of demons in the world (and the collocation πνεύματα δαιμονίων), see esp. Rev 16:14; cf. W. Foerster, *TDNT* 2:1-20.

23. TNIV's "by demons" stresses instrument or agency.

24. See esp. L. T. Johnson, "The New Testament's Anti-Jewish Slander and the Conventions of Ancient Polemic," *JBL* 109 (1989): 419-41; Johnson, 239, 245.

cal continuity increases. First, a prepositional phrase, "with [by] the hypocrisy of those who speak falsely," is only loosely connected to the preceding description. The connections are uncertain, as various translation strategies illustrate. The strategy of the TNIV begins a new sentence and links the phrase to the nearest action, which is inherent in "teachings" (v. 1): "Such teachings [of demons] come through hypocritical liars."[25] An alternative strategy regards the phrase as adding (loosely) some accompanying information ("in connection with").[26] The confusing thing about the phrase is the double reference of hypocrisy: the whole prepositional phrase indicates something about the means of distributing the demonic "teaching"; but the "hypocrisy" itself, as a character flaw, belongs to "those who speak lies." A better translation strategy at this point will begin a new sentence at v. 2, regarding the statements about people as further description of the "some" in v. 1: "In hypocrisy they speak falsely. . . ."[27] However, it is well to keep in mind the implicit connections: "In hypocrisy they [i.e., these who have fallen away] speak falsely [i.e., teach the demonic doctrines]."[28] In any case, the phrase shifts the focus from the demonic source of the teaching (v. 1) to the involvement of human minions and their moral condition.[29] Thus what is demonic in origin involves human duplicity in execution; it is this collusion that makes heresy both appalling and perilous.

While the appropriateness of the label "liars"[30] is immediately obvious, the sense in which "hypocrisy"[31] is applied is less clear.[32] In view of the next statement about consciences, which have to do with regulating behavior, Paul is probably alluding to a disconnect of some sort between claims they made (to be Christian teachers, to possess godliness, to possess a better reve-

---

25. So Fee, *God's Empowering Presence,* 768 n. 59.

26. For the preposition ἐν in this sense (where the classical simply used the dat.), see BDF §198.1 (2 Tim 1:13; Marshall, 539).

27. Johnson, 238.

28. See TNIV, which does a better job of supplying implicit information about the teachings than it does linking the "liars" with the apostates in v. 1.

29. Marshall, 539, rightly points out that the following prepositional phrase ("whose consciences have been cauterized"), in reference to the preceding noun, "liars" ("those who tell lies"), indicates that the individuals in view in v. 2a are humans, not demons.

30. Gk. ψευδολόγος (NT hapax); Josephus, *Antiquities* 8.410; see Spicq, *TLNT* 3:517.

31. Gk. ὑπόκρισις (Matt 23:28; Mark 12:15; Luke 12:1; Gal 2:13; Jas 5:12 [v.l.]; 1 Pet 2:1). The word only gradually acquired the meaning, such as we encounter in NT usage, of "two-faced, pretentious, deceptive," i.e., of portraying oneself one way outwardly while being another way inwardly (Gal 2:13). See Spicq, *TLNT* 3:406-13; U. Wilckens, *TDNT* 8:559-71.

32. See the discussion in Marshall, 540.

lation, etc. as perhaps demonstrated in ascetic practices) or things they said/taught and what they actually were doing (teaching falsehood). The allegation of "hypocrisy" amounts, then, to the charge of deception: they were not who they said they were, and their teaching was not what they claimed it to be. The use of the term in ancient polemics (and in the NT) suggests that intentional, rather than accidental, deception is implied.[33]

The description of the false teachers continues with a participial clause formed on a rare verb. It means "to sear, to cauterize, to brand."[34] As a perfect participle it indicates that the condition in view has come about and is enduring. But the imagery employed here is open to question. As a medical operation, "cauterizing" or "searing" a wound deadened the pain, and applied to the conscience, the sense would be of rendering it insensitive, ineffective.[35] If the action of "branding" is in mind, as some maintain,[36] then the imagery is of marking the conscience, either to show ownership (i.e., Satan's) or as a penalty. The "conscience" itself (see on 1:5 and Excursus) is the organ of decision that allows the translation of the normative faith into appropriate behavior. Given Paul's concern here about the purity and effectiveness of the conscience in relation to a sound faith (1:5, 19; 3:9), where a rejection of faith is linked to demonic doctrines and bizarre patterns of behavior, the "seared conscience" refers to the ineffective, scarred conscience of the false teacher. Prior decisions to depart from the faith (4:1; cf. Titus 1:15), in which they refused to obey their consciences, left them unable to align their behavior with the faith.

At v. 3a Paul continues the description of those with "seared consciences" by attaching a participial phrase ("who forbid marriage") followed by an elliptical infinitive construction ("[ordering] abstinence from foods"). The first phrase, with its genitive participle, may intend to explore the behavior that led to "searing," or may simply illustrate the character of the liars by adding information.[37] The latter is suggested by the TNIV, which relieves the

---

33. Marshall, 540; Towner, *Goal,* 155. For the place of this charge in ancient polemics, see Johnson, 239. But cf. Fee, 98.

34. Gk. καυστηριάζω (Strabo 5.1.9 [v.l.]; NT hapax; noun καυστήρ = "cauterizing apparatus"; see Lampe, *PGL,* s.v.) is apparently a spelling variant of καυτηριάζω (corresponding nouns are spelled with or without the sigma). The textual variants that arise at this point represent (1) a misreading of the reduplicated κεκαυστηριασμένων as καὶ καυ-[σ]τηριασμένων (F 0241), and (2) the non-sigma spelling preference of κεκαυτηριασμένων (C D G I Ψ TR etc.). NA[27] has the harder reading (following ℵ A L etc.). See further Elliott, 62; Marshall, 536.

35. Marshall, 540-41; Johnson, 239-40; Knight, 189.

36. Cf. the views of Roloff, 221-22; Dibelius and Conzelmann, 64; Fee, 98-99; Kelly, 94-95; Lock, 48. Collins, 114, combines the images.

37. Gk. κωλυόντων γαμεῖν; κωλύω is "to hinder, prevent, forbid," depending on the context (Acts 16:6; Rom 1:13; 1 Cor 14:39; 1 Thess 2:16; S. Légasse, *EDNT* 2:332-33). For

syntactical strain by commencing a new sentence. In any case, the added phrase indicates that among their practices was the forbidding of marriage. Unfortunately, nothing more is said, but we can surmise that abstinence from sexual relations was the intent, which declining to marry would achieve for the unmarried, though it is not clear what course was encouraged for those already married (see further below).[38]

As indicated, the second phrase concerning foods is elliptical,[39] omitting a participle to parallel "forbidding." Since the infinitive "to abstain" makes no sense with the preceding participle "forbidding," the best solution is to supply the matching verbal idea, "ordering, to order," to complete the thought as the TNIV has done: "and order them to abstain" (cf. "demand abstinence," NRSV); presumably, the similarly spelled previous participle, "forbidding," would have immediately called "ordering" to mind.[40]

But what do these practices signify about the false teachers? Some scholars continue to attribute the restrictions concerning marriage and foods to Gnostic dualism, noting especially the second-century debates about sexual relations and marriage.[41] Others point specifically to the apocryphal *Acts of Paul and Thecla,* in which Paul is made the proponent of the sort of ascetic lifestyle combated here.[42] But nothing in the text suggests the need to go beyond what are surely more suspicious parallels much nearer to Ephesus in the Pauline era. According to Philo and Josephus, the Essene movement included a branch that practiced celibacy.[43] But there is nothing to indicate that such strict food asceticism should be linked to the Essenes/Qumran.

---

the infinitive γαμεῖν ("to marry"), see 5:11, 14; 1 Cor 7:9(2x), 10, 28(2x), 33, 34, 36, 39 (E. Stauffer, *TDNT* 1:648-57).

38. See Marshall, 541.

39. Gk. ἀπέχεσθαι βρωμάτων; for ἀπέχομαι (middle voice) in the sense of "to abstain from" in ethical contexts (as here), see Acts 15:20, 29; 1 Thess 4:3; 5:22 (Spicq, *TLNT* 1:162-68, esp. 166-68). Βρῶμα (pl. here) is generally "food," or "solid food" (as in the contrast to "milk" in 1 Cor 3:2; Heb 9:10).

40. Thus the readers were to take their cue from the supplied participle κωλυόντων ("forbidding") and fill in the blank with κελευόντων ("ordering, commanding"); this particular type of ellipsis is called "zeugma" (see BDF §479.2; Marshall, 542). Cf. the alternative strategy of Johnson, 240.

41. Most recently, Collins, 114-17; Kelly, 236; Schmithals, "Corpus Paulinum," 116; Trummer, *Paulustradition,* 166-68. See Irenaeus, *Against Heresies* 1.24.2; Epiphanius, *Panarion* 45.2.1; Rudolph, *Gnosis,* 258-60.

42. *Acts of Paul and Thecla* 6; 12; 23; 25.

43. Philo, *Apology for the Jews* 11.14-17; Josephus, *Jewish War* 2.120-21; *Antiquities* 18.21. See also Pliny, *Natural History* 5.17. See CD 7:6-7. For Josephus's concession that some did marry, see *Jewish War* 2.160-61; G. Vermes, *An Introduction to the Complete Dead Sea Scrolls* (Minneapolis: Fortress, 1999), 123, 124, 126, 162-63, 187-88, 228, 238-39.

Looking instead within the orbit of the Pauline ministry and just beyond, we should note the following data. Generally, Paul's letters bear witness to the fact that the issues of sexual relations and rules about foods were items of lively debate as his churches sought to understand the implications of salvation and the Spirit for Christian living in the last days (Rom 14:13-21; 1 Cor 7:12-16; 8:1-13; 10:25-31; Gal 2:11-14; Col 2:16; 1 Thess 4:3-6). And in none of these cases do we know all the elements at work in the debates: Jewish tendencies and sensibilities, Spirit enthusiasm, a too-realized view of eschatology.

More specifically, first, the Jesus tradition could speak favorably of celibacy in the service of God (Matt 19:12), and Paul regarded it as appropriate in certain situations and possibly ideal (1 Cor 7:26-35). But the teaching of neither of these evolved into the blanket prohibition mentioned in 1 Tim 4:3. Second, intrachurch problems that arose between Jewish and Gentile Christians over the propriety of eating meat that had been offered to idols, as well as tension surrounding a Jewish-Christian adherence to kosher food rules, are very much a part of the Pauline church phenomenon (Romans 14; 1 Corinthians 8–10; Col 2:16-23). Third, in Corinth questions about the propriety of marriage and sexual relations were being raised, with such options as abstinence within marriage, divorce or separation of married believers from each other, divorcing unbelieving partners, and celibacy for virgins being entertained (1 Corinthians 7). What all of this indicates is that matters such as marriage and dietary restrictions, linked with questions about the ongoing usefulness of the law, are not unusual in Paul's ministry.

But perfect paradigms, by which the developments in one church might be explained on the basis of those in another church, do not exist in Paul. We have situations that overlap, but in most cases each contains unique elements not apparent in even the most comparable church situations. The combination here, enforcement of celibacy and abstention from certain foods, is perhaps unusual, and may have required some unmentioned catalyst to bring them together. There is evidence of a Jewish-Christian element in the opposition, but circumcision and laws of purity are not a focal point of the opposition. What seems more central is a sense of elitism, separatism, claims to special knowledge. Johnson suggests that the aberrations mentioned in 4:3 might be misunderstandings of Paul's own statements (celibacy as an ideal, 1 Cor 7:1; his willingness to forgo meat for the sake of another, 1 Cor 8:13) worked into a new piety.[44] If so, Paul does not redress the misunderstandings as he did in 1 Corinthians.

The connections between 1 Timothy and 1 Corinthians compel me in another direction. In each case, the communities had adopted a severely real-

44. Johnson, 247.

ized (or overrealized) eschatology, although in the case of Ephesus of 1 Timothy, this may have been in the early stages.[45] To this outlook, in some way, may be linked questions about marriage and sexual relations and their appropriateness to life lived more fully in the Spirit (1 Corinthians 7). The chief difference is that in 1 Corinthians the sense of living in the Eschaton/age of the Spirit was accompanied by an inordinate compulsion to express personal freedom in matters of food, while in 1 Timothy the "initiated" had apparently equated "piety" with food asceticism. This difference may be the result of differing hermeneutical systems in each case. While in the case of the Corinthian enthusiasts it seems to be chiefly the presence of the Spirit that leads to a super-Pauline realized eschatology, for some reason in the Ephesus of 1 Timothy a system of OT interpretation, which Paul terms "myths and genealogies," appears to play a central role in arriving at certain dualistic conclusions about piety and the present life that stressed avoidance of certain elements proper to creation. What spiritual insights the Corinthians may have been relying on the Spirit for directly (via wisdom, knowledge, prophecy, tongues, etc.) are sought (or at least grounded) by the Ephesian opponents through "spiritual" exegesis of certain OT stories about creation and early history.

The response Paul is about to give from Genesis to the dietary restrictions may well be aimed at a prime example of just such a manipulation of the Genesis materials to undergird a call to return to pre-fall patterns of living. The assumption is that this was regarded as the pattern most suitable for preparation for the arrival of the Eschaton — that life in Eden is the paradigm for life in heaven. Before the fall into sin, sexual relations had not been initiated, and meat was not sanctioned for food until Gen 9:3.[46] While such an OT paradigm might have served as the foundation for the preparatory ethic, it is not without gaps.[47] But while precision is not possible, after the extreme use of Genesis is accounted for, most of the gaps can be filled once the connections of this teaching with tendencies current in Corinth and Colossae, and in religious society at large (e.g., generally asceticism and spirituality were compatible ideas), are made. Even Jesus' teaching about marriage and the resurrection (Matt 22:30) might provide a helpful subtext for the heretical disparagement of marriage.

---

45. The clearest evidence of this comes in the resurrection of heresy alluded to in 2 Tim 2:18. This is not mentioned explicitly in 1 Timothy, though the presence of one of its proponents, Hymenaeus (1 Tim 1:20; 2 Tim 2:17), suggests that the teaching and the enthusiasm or theological grounds for it may be latent. See further discussion at 6:20-21.

46. See the discussion at 1 Tim 2:13-15; Schlarb, *Die gesunde Lehre,* 132-33; Marshall, 534-35; Towner, *Goal,* 36-38.

47. As Marshall, 534 n. 10, points out, Gen 1:27-28 would seem to contradict the claims made about celibacy.

3b-5 Having identified these two elements in the false teaching, Paul renders his theological response. It consists of an opening counterassertion (v. 3b) that initiates consideration of God as Creator and also the need for community response to this truth in thanksgiving. Then v. 4 adds a more formal theological basis for the counterassertion that expresses the same two elements: creation and thanksgiving. The importance of the latter response is drawn out in v. 5, where the effectiveness of prayer is underlined. Finally, the core of the response is an apostolic interpretation of the early chapters of Genesis. We shall look at each aspect of this response in turn.

First, in v. 3b Paul's counterassertion begins with a relative clause and an attached prepositional phrase indicating goal: "which God created to be received. . . ." The relative pronoun limits the reference grammatically to the last named "foods."[48] Paul's previous affirmations of marriage (2:15; 3:2, 12), coupled with the upcoming encouragement to young widows to remarry (5:14), provide a sufficient correction to the marriage prohibition. But this context suggests that views of marriage and foods are each the products of a heretical understanding of creation; so response to the latter also implies response to the former.

Second, the core of the response, as we will explore in greater depth below, is the assertion that God is Creator.[49] This brief statement (effectively repeated in v. 4) taps into the creation story and puts the argument on theological ground. It is this activity of God, applied to "foods" as the test case, which the heresy has failed to account for. The creation of food was designed to meet human needs, as any straightforward reading of Genesis could not fail to apprehend (see below). And the term Paul uses to express this "reception" ("sharing") may indicate that he has the corporate life of the church in mind; by implication, the stringent asceticism of the heretics poses a threat to the common life and commitments of believers who give expression to this fellowship by sharing in the gifts of God.[50]

---

48. The neuter plural relative ἅ has the neuter plural βρωμάτων as its antecedent. To understand the relative pronoun as referring to both foods and marriage (cf. Johnson, 240) is grammatically unlikely (see Fowl, *The Story of Christ*, 185 n. 3; Marshall, 542).

49. Gk. ὁ θεὸς ἔκτισεν; the selection of the verb κτίζω reflects the preference for this verb (over ποιέω, "to make") in the Hellenistic-Jewish (Wis 9:2; 13:5; 14:11; Sir 39:16, 25-27, 33-34; 3 Macc 5:11) and NT discussions of creation (Matt 19:4; Mark 13:19; Rom 1:25; 1 Cor 11:9; Eph 2:10, 15; 3:9; 4:24; Col 1:16a; 3:10; Rev 4:11[2x]; 10:6); see Towner, "The Old Testament in the Letters to Timothy and Titus," in Beale and Carson, eds., *Commentary on the Use of the Old Testament in the New Testament* (Grand Rapids: Baker, forthcoming). See W. Foerster, *TDNT* 3:1000-1035; G. Petzke, *EDNT* 2:325-26.

50. Johnson, 240. For the Gk. μετάλημψις ("sharing, receiving"; NT hapax), see the cognate verb in 2 Tim 2:6; Acts 2:46, and G. Delling, *TDNT* 4:10 11.

But, third, the appropriateness of reception and use of God's creation on the part of believers (and this is the issue at hand) is subject to a single condition: "thankfulness." "Thankfulness" in this context implies the understanding that foods are the gracious gift of the Creator God. Paul is of course not saying that only believers may eat; but he is saying that authentic believers ought to acknowledge their dependence on God in their heartfelt response of thanks. The vehicle for expressing thanksgiving is the grace prayer said at meals.[51] The attached description of believers — "by those who believe[52] and who know the truth" — purposely links (authentic) belief with the process of "coming to a knowledge of the truth" (see the discussions at 1:4; 2:4). This is the process of coming to faith as viewed from the angle of the individual's rational reception and perception of "the truth" and the accompanying decision of commitment to this truth. The polemical intention of the "truth" language should not be missed in the passage where Paul offers an apostolic version of teaching in response to that of the opponents. Notably, use of the perfect tense in this description of believers as those who "have come to a knowledge of the truth"[53] indicates that Paul has full-fledged authentic believers in mind; in precise contrast to the orders of the false teachers, believers in fact are free to partake of God's creation. What the opponents are offering as "teaching, knowledge, or truth" Paul regards as symptomatic of unbelief.[54]

Verse 4 establishes the general creation-theological basis that allows freedom in the use of foods: "For everything God created[55] is good [see on 1:8], and nothing is to be rejected if it is received with thanksgiving."[56] The first half of this reason intentionally echoes the summary statement of Gen 1:31 (see below), broadening the argument from the creation story of Genesis.

Following from the creation pronouncement is the important deduc-

---

51. Gk. εὐχαριστία is generally "thanksgiving," often in the sense of prayers of thanksgiving to God (2:1 [see discussion]; 4:4; 1 Cor 14:16; 2 Cor 9:11, 12; etc.). For the practice of table prayers, see Rom 14:6; 1 Cor 10:16, 30; 1QS 6:4-5; 10:14-15. Neither here nor in 4:4 does μετὰ εὐχαριστίας mean the celebration of the Eucharist (pace Hanson, Studies, 96-109; Holtz, 102).

52. The Gk. dative τοῖς πιστοῖς (in the sense of "believers," 4:10, 12; 6:2; see 1:2 and note) is either to be translated as "by those who believe," as expressing the agent of "receiving" (as above), or as "for those who believe," a dative of advantage, showing for whom foods were created.

53. Gk. ἐπεγνωκόσι τὴν ἀλήθειαν; cf. the formulations in 1 Tim 2:4; 2 Tim 2:25; 3:7; Titus 1:1.

54. Cf. Oberlinner, 181.

55. Gk. κτίσμα θεοῦ (Jas 1:18; Rev 5:13; 8:9; cf. Wis 9:2; 13:5; 14:11; Sir 39:16; etc.) means "things created by God" (see 4:3 and note).

56. The Gk. ὅτι clause is most likely explanatory (1:12, 13; 2 Tim 1:16); it might be taken as a noun clause defining the content of the preceding "truth," but the phrase "knowledge of the truth" is normally not further defined.

tion about foods. "Nothing" (i.e., no food) is to be "rejected"[57] (i.e., considered ritually or otherwise unclean; see v. 5; cf. Mark 7:15; Acts 10; Rom 14:14; 1 Cor 10:26; Titus 1:14-15). Again, as far as this applies to believers, the stipulation of thanksgiving is appended by means of a prepositional phrase.[58] Believers are indeed free in Christ to make use of all foods, but this is done within a relationship in which the gift nature of food is acknowledged by the recipients' response of gratitude.

The "mechanics" of this thanksgiving prayer become clearer with the rationale ("for"; *gar*) added in v. 5. The implied subject ("it") of the passive verb "is sanctified" is the aforementioned "nothing" (= no food). Paul's point is that the stipulated prayer response in some sense "sanctifies" the food in question. There are two things to notice. First, the language of "sanctification" (2 Tim 2:21)[59] suggests that the false teachers regarded the banned foods as unclean in some sense. It is not clear that they were simply insisting on Jewish regulations about foods. And it is not likely that meat offered to idols was the specific issue, for Paul had gone on record already, having drawn the line, on the one hand, at eating such meat in the context of pagan worship (1 Cor 10:19-21),[60] and, on the other, outside of such a context, declaring all things clean as long as one had faith to accept this dictum (Rom 14:14). Paul's argument here suggests other grounds for banning certain foods.

Second, how should "sanctification" be understood? The language means "to make holy" or "to set aside," and in some contexts the act identified the suitability of something to be used for religious/cultic purposes, or of someone to serve God.[61] The root of this is the idea that things or people are brought within the sphere of God's presence or influence. The dynamic of prayer is not to be understood as taking the place of God's pronouncement ("Everything created is good"), or even adding any special, mystical grace to it. It is rather that through prayer (and the dual agency about to be mentioned)

57. Gk. ἀπόβλητος (cf. the cognate noun ἀποβολή in Rom 11:14), a NT hapax (Philo, *On the Special Laws* 2.169; see LSJ, s.v.).

58. Gk. μετὰ εὐχαριστίας λαμβανόμενον; for λαμβάνω ("take, receive"; 2 Tim 1:5) in the specific sense of "to take and eat food" (as probably intended here; see Marshall, 545), see Mark 15:23; John 19:30; Acts 9:19. The relation of the participle λαμβανόμενον to the verbal idea ("nothing is to be rejected") is loosely adverbial, and the sense is uncertain: "since (as, when) it is received with thanksgiving." The conditional translation, "if it is received with thanksgiving" (TNIV), may give the impression that prayer renders food usable. Cf. Marshall, 545; Johnson, 241-42.

59. Gk. ἁγιάζω (here pass.); O. Procksch, *TDNT* 1:111-12.

60. See B. Witherington, *Conflict and Community in Corinth* (Grand Rapids: Eerdmans, 1995), 225-27.

61. Of things, LXX Exod 29:27, 37; 30:29; etc.; Matt 23:17-19; of people, Exod 28:41; 30:30; 1 Cor 6:11.

the community acknowledges and activates what God has declared to be true. To draw on another Pauline passage about foods (Rom 14:14), through prayer (and Scripture, teaching, preaching, etc.) believers develop an awareness and conviction of the truth that "nothing is unclean in itself."

The means of sanctification, initially attributed to prayer, is now expanded along two related lines. First, sanctification is "by the word of God." This might refer to a specific divine logion (cf. Rom 3:4; 9:6), in which case Gen 1:31, or the entire early section of Genesis, or a word of Jesus (Mark 7:1-23) might come to mind.[62] Or "word of God" (see 1:15, note) might be understood in the sense of the gospel message.[63] In this case, sanctification comes by way of proclamation and teaching of the Christian message that enlightens people concerning God's will.[64] A decision between these two alternatives is difficult.[65]

Second, in conjunction with "the word of God," sanctification comes by means of "prayer." This word for "prayer" ("intercession, entreaty, request") technically differs from "thanksgiving," though both are grouped together in the cluster of "prayer" words given in 2:1 (see the discussion). "Thanksgiving" in 4:3-4, associated with table prayer elsewhere in Paul (1 Cor 10:30), is the acknowledgment of God as the creative source of the gift of food. Possibly in this context "prayer" ("intercession") should be understood as a generic term for prayer[66] not to be rigidly distinguished from "thanksgiving." In any case, the function of prayer is to acknowledge consciously God's provision and his people's acceptance of the gift of food in the awareness of his presence and in fellowship with other believers.

The entire logic of Paul's engagement with the heretics at this point is dependent on his utilization of the Genesis creation story. As we saw, at 4:3 Paul begins to denounce the opponents for their abstinence "from certain foods, which God created to be received with thanksgiving." The corrective assertion draws upon and in two ways alludes to the story of creation and its elaboration in the early chapters in Genesis. First, the argument adapts Gen 9:3 specifically since it negates the erroneous limitations (i.e., "to abstain

---

62. Cf. Marshall, 546; Collins, 118; Dibelius and Conzelmann, 64; Kelly 97; Spicq, 500.

63. Cf. 2 Tim 2:19; Titus 1:3; 2:5; 1 Cor 14:36; 2 Cor 2:17; 4:2; Col 1:25; 1 Thess 2:13.

64. See Roloff, 227; Johnson, 242.

65. Other less likely possibilities include the recitation of a blessing, words of consecration spoken at the Eucharist, "the Word" as a reference to Jesus (see Marshall, 546, for discussion and refs.).

66. As in Hermas, *Mandates* 5.6; 11.9; *Similitude* 2.6-7. See also Johnson, 242; but cf. Marshall, 547, who suggests that the shift to ἔντευξις envisions the possible request to God to cleanse meat that had been offered to idols.

from foods"; Gk. *brōmatōn*) on the basis that God gave everything for food ("Every living reptile shall be meat for you [Gk. *eis brōsis*]; as the green vegetables, I have given everything to you [for food]").[67] Paul's argument also recalls the stress on divine initiative in the earlier affirmation of God's provision ("God gave") of vegetables "for food" (*eis brōsin* in Gen 1:29 and 2:9; *brōsei* in 2:16; cf. 3:2; cf. Deut 26:11). Thus a simple verbal allusion taps into a broader stream of tradition about the source of foods.

Secondly, in the counterclaim about foods, "which God created," the subject/verb combination that asserts God's role as the Creator recalls the account of creation. As pointed out, use of the verb "to create" (Gk. *ktizō*) in 4:3 reflects the preference for this verb in the Hellenistic-Jewish and NT discussions of creation.[68] In the LXX of Genesis, the verb "to make" (*poieō*) predominates in the early chapters,[69] with *ktizō* entering only in 14:9. The replacement by *ktizō* to access the early accounts of God's creative activity is not problematic; it prepares the way for the polemical *coup de grâce* in 4:4a.

In 4:4a Paul gives the foundation for the previous counterassertions: "for everything God created is good" *(hoti pan ktisma theou kalon)*. In this statement, which itself quite obviously echoes the divine assessment that closes Genesis 1, the specific connections are made by the adjective "all" *(pan)*, by reference to the Creator "God" *(ktisma theou)*, and by the predicate adjective "good" *(kalon)*:

> 1 Tim 4:4a: "For the whole *(pan)* creation *(ktisma)* of God *(theou)* is good *(kalon)*."
>
> Gen 1:31: "and God *(theos)* saw all the things that he had made *(ta panta hosa epoiēsen)*, and behold they were very good *(kala)*."[70]

Again the shift from the *poieō* word group to *ktisma* reflects preferences shaped by the tradition. The logic of Paul's polemical response to the heretical food asceticism is completed in the following statement: "and nothing is to be rejected if it is received with thanksgiving." The same argument — permitting the consumption of all foods with the proviso of thanksgiving — was made in 1 Cor 10:26, 30. And the logic here is not hard to follow.

---

67. Cf. 1 Tim 4:3a: ἀπέχεσθαι βρωμάτων, ἃ ὁ θεὸς ἔκτισεν εἰς μετάλημψιν; LXX Gen 9:3: καὶ πᾶν ἑρπετόν ὅ ἐστιν ζῶν ὑμῖν ἔσται εἰς βρῶσιν· ὡς λάχανα χόρτου δέδωκα ὑμῖν τὰ πάντα.

68. Wis 9:2; 13:5; 14:11; Sir 39:16, 25-27, 33-34; 3 Macc 5:11; Matt 19:4; Mark 13:19; Rom 1:25; 1 Cor 11:9; Eph 2:10, 15; 3:9; 4:24; Col 1:16a; 3:10; Rev 4:11(2x); 10:6.

69. In the NT, see Matt 19:4; Mark 10:6; Acts 17:24, 26.

70. Cf. 1 Tim 4:4a: ὅτι πᾶν κτίσμα θεοῦ καλόν; LXX Gen 1:31: καὶ εἶδεν ὁ θεὸς τὰ πάντα ὅσα ἐποίησεν καὶ ἰδοὺ καλὰ λίαν.

In 4:3-4, there is no doubt that Paul has drawn on Gen 9:3 as a historical/theological precedent for the specific eating of meat, subsequently backing this by allusion to the more fundamental statement in Gen 1:31 of the goodness of God's creation. The tougher question is why.

For that we need to think creatively about the heretical teaching alluded to in 4:2 (cf. discussions and references above at 4:3a; 2:13-15a; Introduction, 41-49). Assuming a link between these ascetic tendencies and the opponents' speculative exegesis ("myths and genealogies"; 1:4), in the sense that the former were somehow grounded in the latter, Paul possibly gives his authoritative interpretation of OT Scripture to counter the opposition's novel exegesis of Genesis. Other patterns of their outlook, such as an overly enthusiastic (too realized) eschatology, which led them to anticipate the end by living according to a pre-fall pattern, could provide the theology fueling the asceticism. The effect of Paul's counterargument would be: (1) to affirm the ongoing relevance of the pattern of life reflected in Gen 9:7, (2) to discourage (or deny implicitly) attempts to live beyond the present realities (including the ongoing presence of sin), and yet (3) to affirm freedom in Christ (note the emphasis on thanksgiving and prayer, vv. 4b-5) to partake of all foods because of their created basis. While it remains conjectural that Paul specifically corrected aberrant exegesis of Genesis texts, it is nonetheless certain that the argument from Genesis intends to counter the practice of abstention from certain foods (= meat), as well to affirm by implication the creation basis and sanctity of marriage.

b. Sound Teaching and Godliness (4:6-10)

> 6 *If you point these things out to the brothers and sisters, you will be a good minister of Christ Jesus, nourished on the truths of the faith and of the good teaching that you have followed.* 7 *Have nothing to do with godless myths and old wives' tales; rather, train yourself to be godly.* 8 *For physical training is of some value, but godliness has value for all things, holding promise for both the present life and the life to come.* 9 *This is a trustworthy saying that deserves full acceptance.* 10 *That is why we labor and strive, because we have put our hope in the living God, who is the Savior of all people, and especially of those who believe.*

At v. 6 Paul closes the preceding subsection and opens a new one. The shift back to parenesis to Timothy is apparent from the changed direction of Paul's discourse to "you," and this movement from general to specific is also evident as Timothy is addressed. Although Timothy's role as a teacher is doubtless in the background, his own behavior comes mainly into focus, and in this context of opposition, this is measured by his own commitment to the apostolic gospel. For this reason, the text is built around commands to Timothy, but the opponents remain in view.

The argument — the indirect way in which the opponents are challenged and the concluding reflection on Paul's mission — though somewhat differently focused, can be compared with 2:1-7. The first command is an implicit one about teaching (v. 6a), embedded in the summarizing transition that is backed by the exhortation to excellence, all linked to continued adherence to the "good teaching." While it marks a new beginning in the parenesis to Timothy, it is nevertheless developing in some sense from the engagement with the false teachers just concluded in 4:5. The second command specifically urges avoidance of the false doctrines (v. 7a), while the third command, in contrast, calls for pursuit of godliness (v. 7b). The views and failure of the opponents are alluded to in the derogatory reference to "godless myths" and the opposite way Timothy is to proceed.

"Godliness" emerges as the central interest in the subsection, and reflection on it helps undergird its importance within the view of authentic Christian existence Paul seeks to develop. For this reason its meaning is carefully measured against a traditional emphasis on physical exercise (exemplified in the asceticism of the heretics) and woven into a proverbial statement (v. 8). Paul's use of the logic is then reinforced with the "faithful saying" formula (v. 9).

At v. 10, Paul concludes by affirming the role of his mission and message in the salvation plan of God. According to the order of interests, his gospel is made the source of Christian behavior (= godliness), and his mission the conveyor of the Savior God's salvation in the world. In this case (cf. 2:4, 7), Paul's main concern is to stress that those manifesting the godliness that promises eternal life are the authentic believers referred to in v. 10b, and not the opponents. Ultimately, the truth of the gospel and its power to impart an authentically spiritual life in those who believe are the realities that insist on the continuation of Paul's mission. The necessity of Timothy's ongoing faithful service is thus grounded in the gospel and shaped by the situation of conflict in Ephesus.

6-7a The new section resumes instructions to Timothy. Typical of a transition from an apostolic statement to parenetic response, Paul first commends the tradition just stated, incorporating it into Timothy's assignment, and then moves out in related directions (cf. 4:11, 15; 5:7; 6:2; 2 Tim 2:2, 14). In this case, it is particularly the creation theology just set out in response to the heresy (4:3b-5) that is commended to Timothy.[1] On the one

---

1. Gk. ταῦτα ("these things"; see discussion in 3:15; Titus 2:15). The scope of its reference is debated (2:1–4:5, Fee, 110; 4:1-5, Oberlinner, 188). But the apostolic re-

hand, he is to convey it to the church members (lit. "brothers"; but the translation "brothers and sisters" is appropriate here).[2] The means of communication is somewhat open, and translations of the verb range from "point out," to "suggest," to "recommend" or "teach." This might reflect the more congenial setting of giving instruction among fellow believers, which could take more the form of leading in a didactic discussion, as opposed to commanding or correcting (in the case of engagement with the false teachers).[3] But undoubtedly Timothy's authority to convey the apostle's teaching is implied.[4] On the other hand, in keeping with the interest in Timothy's behavior, it is by passing on the apostle's teaching faithfully to the church that he will demonstrate his "excellence" ("good" = divine approval; see the discussions at 1:8; 2:3) as a "servant of Christ Jesus" (NRSV).[5]

Before moving on to the false teaching again, Paul first pauses to deepen the definition of the "good servant of Christ." He adds a participial phrase to emphasize the fundamental[6] importance of saturation in and conti-

---

sponse to the heretical teaching about marriage and foods just laid down is more likely the material Timothy is to convey to the church (see also Marshall, 548).

2. Gk. ἀδελφός (pl., 6:2; 2 Tim 4:1; lit. as a male sibling in 5:1). Limiting the reference to leaders (so Schlarb, *Die gesunde Lehre,* 282, 289; cf. E. E. Ellis, *Prophecy and Hermeneutic in Early Christianity* [Grand Rapids: Eerdmans, 1978], 13-22) is unnecessary; "brothers" regards Timothy's relationship in familial, not authoritative terms (Oberlinner, 189). Use of the masculine term as a description of a congregation (or group) without regard for gender is idiomatic (or perhaps chauvinistic), and should be understood to mean "fellow believers" (or "brothers and sisters"; frequently 1 Cor 2:1; 3:1; etc.; see also P. Ellingworth, "'Men and Brethren . . .' [Acts 1.16]," *BT* 55.1 [2004]: 153-54; I. H. Marshall, "Brothers Embracing Sisters," *BT* 55.3 [2004]; Marshall, 549 n. 66; Fee, 102). See J. Beutler, *EDNT* 1:28-30; H. von Soden, *TDNT* 1:144-46.

3. Gk. ὑποτίθημι (act. in Rom 16:4); participle (showing means) in the middle voice (only here in NT; lit. "by commending these things, you will be a good servant of Christ Jesus"); BDAG, s.v. Philo, *On the Life of Moses* 2.51 (in contrast to "command"). Kelly, 98, cites Chrysostom (PG 62:559) for the meaning "suggestion." Hanson's view (89-90), that in the post-Pauline context this term implies a limitation of authoritative teaching (as expressed through other terms) to ordained ministers (e.g., the "bishop"), is not supported by the text.

4. See Oberlinner, 188-89; as in the use of the term for Moses (Philo, *On the Posterity and Exile of Cain* 12).

5. Gk. διάκονος (see discussion at 3:8; here in the sense of "servant," typical of Paul's ministry nomenclature, 1 Cor 3:5; 2 Cor 3:6; 6:4; 11:23). I prefer to steer away from the "ministerial" translation of the TNIV.

6. The relationship of the participle to the "good servant" predicate, or the whole preceding thought, is loose: the sense is either: "If you commend these things, you will be a good servant and demonstrate that you are nourished in the faith . . ."; or simply adds description: "you will be a good servant, (showing you are) nourished. . . ." Technically, the opening participle ὑποτιθέμενος and this participle ἐντρεφόμενος can be construed as

nuity with the apostolic teaching. By teaching what Paul requests, Timothy will show first that he has been (and is being) "nourished on the truths of the faith and of the good teaching." Paul uses language that had already been adapted (from the image of feeding and rearing children) to the educational sphere in Greek ethics: "nourish, rear, bring up."[7] The present tense reflects not primarily on Timothy's prior education (cf. TNIV/NIV, CEV) but more emphatically on his ongoing intake of the "nourishment" ("continually nourished on").

The source of spiritual nourishment is described with two phrases. The first phrase is literally "the words of the faith." It is equivalent to several other expressions that conceive of the Christian faith as a body of tradition articulated in teachable doctrine (5:8; 6:21).[8] From this perspective, the gospel is the approved standard. The second phrase, "the good teaching," is equivalent to another set of terms (specifically "sound teaching," 1:10 [discussion]; "sound words," 2 Tim 1:13) that describes the gospel polemically as measurably superior to the false teaching. From this perspective, the truth of the apostolic gospel, as opposed to the falsehood of the heresy, is stressed. A contrast is intended with "teachings of demons" in 4:1.

Timothy's qualification, as well as his distinction from the heresy, is finally stressed in the relative clause that is attached: "which [teaching] you have followed." The verb of following envisions thoughtful commitment to a course or path (teaching) and in the perfect tense suggests a process begun in the past and continuing in the present (see the same verb at 2 Tim 3:10).[9]

Having affirmed Timothy's course, at v. 7a the sentence continues by shifting to a description of that which he is to avoid.[10] Here a true imperative,

---

parallel, each modifying "will be a good servant," the first indicating the means of "being a good servant," the second more likely simply adding descriptive detail of what a "good servant" is.

7. Gk. ἐντρέφω (the pres. ptc.; ἐντρεφόμενος is either mid. ["nourishing yourself"] or pass. ["educated in, instructed by"] only here in the NT); for spiritual instruction, see Philo, *On the Embassy to Gaius* 195; on its use in Stoic education, see Hanson, 89; Epictetus 4.4.48.

8. For the technical sense of the articular ἡ πίστις, see the discussion at 1:2; Towner, *Goal,* 121-26.

9. Gk. παρακολουθέω (perf. in 2 Tim 3:10); the dative relative pronoun ᾗ (referring to "teaching") is normal for the verb. See further G. Kittel, *TDNT* 1:215-16. See further references in BDAG, s.v. 3.

10. Although most translations, preferring to avoid long sentences, justifiably begin a new sentence with v. 7 (TNIV/NIV; NRSV; GNB), NA[27] links v. 7a to v. 6 with a semicolon, suggesting greater continuity between the two contrasting statements. The GNB expresses this connection best by translating the connective δέ ("but") as indicating true contrast.

"reject, avoid,"[11] taken from Paul's polemical and disciplinary vocabulary (5:11; 2 Tim 2:23; Titus 3:10), increases the sharpness of the command tone implicit in the exhortation to excellence just given. Specifically, the coworker is to steer clear of the false teaching, for which Paul repeats the pejorative term "myths" (1:4, discussion; 2 Tim 4:4; Titus 1:14). Although the preceding discussion about marriage and foods in 4:1-3 might mean that some particular "retellings" of the OT are in mind, generally the term categorizes the heresy as false and deceptive in its moral implications.

Two terms complete the description of these myths. First, they are "godless" ("profane"; see the discussion on 1:9), which separates them as defilement completely from God. Second, the teaching under discussion was, not to put too fine a point on it, "characteristic of elderly women." In the philosophers, the adjective (e.g., "old wives' tales," TNIV/NIV, NRSV) was derogatory, typical of the male-dominant cultural stereotype of women, and applied to trivialize a competing view. This is the most likely application in this polemical context (cf. 2 Tim 3:6: "silly women").[12] Together the two terms portray the heresy as pagan in its thrust and insignificant in its contribution.

7b-8   Timothy is take the alternate route of godliness (v. 7b). The third command employs language typical of Greco-Roman ethical teaching: "train yourself." It was first applied to the effort and exercise involved in physical contexts, and transferred naturally to describe the work of progressing toward virtue in the moral and spiritual sphere.[13] Here the language of training paves the way for the development of the next comparison of bodily exercise and godliness.

The purpose or intended result[14] of this training is "godliness." This term, first surfacing in 2:2 (see Excursus), defines Christian existence as the interplay of the knowledge of God and of the truth (cf. 4:3) and the observable outworking of that knowledge in appropriate ways. The contours of this

---

11. Gk. παραιτέομαι; with an accusative thing as object ("myths," 4:7a; "controversies," 2 Tim 2:23), the meaning is "to reject, have nothing to do with, avoid"; where the object is a person (5:11; Titus 3:10), the sense of dismissal or refusal (to do something) is intended (see BDAG, s.v. 2.b.α.β.; G. Stählin, *TDNT* 1:195).

12. Gk. γραώδης (only here in biblical Greek); for the connection with μύθοι ("myths"), see esp. Plato, *Republic* 350E; *Gorgias* 527a; see Spicq, *TLNT* 1.285 (and n. 5); Marshall, 550; Collins, 121. For the view (discussed and rightly rejected by Johnson, 243-44) that the term presupposes a later social situation (e.g., that described in the *Apocryphal Acts*) in which women had the role of transmitting the heresy in one form or another, see S. L. Davies, *The Revolt of the Widows: The Social World of the Apocryphal Acts* (Carbondale, IL: Southern Illinois University Press, 1980), 95-129.

13. Gk. γυμνάζω; physical effort: 2 Macc 10:15; Josephus, *Antiquities* 6.185; mental/moral/spiritual effort: Heb 5:14; 12:11 (cf. 2 Pet 2:14); Josephus, *Antiquities* 3.15; Philo, *On Dreams* 2.63; *On the Life of Moses* 1.48; A. Oepke, *TDNT* 1:775-76.

14. On the Gk. preposition πρός, see BDF §239.7.

life of genuine spirituality would include all of the ethical teaching contained in the letter, but we are invited immediately to consider the elements spelled out in 4:11-16. It is highly probable, in this context where Paul has firmly denounced certain behaviors of the opponents (4:1-2), that "godliness" is being advanced in contrast to the misshapen spirituality of the heretics. But Paul will rely on traditional paradigms and implicit comparisons as he finishes his brief exposition of "godliness."

Verse 8 provides grounding ("for"; *gar*) for the command to pursue godliness. It consists of a contrast between the value of bodily or physical training and godliness. Although the reference to bodily training *(gymnasia)* was anticipated by the preceding reference to "training" *(gymnaze)*, the comparison might be proverbial and had possibly found its way into Christian teaching by this time from either secular or Hellenistic-Jewish sources.[15] "Physical training" is generally that which pertains to the body, and the language suggests immediately a background in the athletic culture of Greco-Roman society.[16] Paul admits that such exercise has "some value" (cf. 1 Cor 9:24-27),[17] but the purpose of saying this is mainly to limit its relevance within this discussion and shine the brighter light on "exercise in godliness."

The question often asked of this text is whether the reference to "physical exercise" in what is perhaps a well-known comparison coming from the philosophical schools (in which physical training is understood in the Greco-Roman sense of athletic training) is simply a way of highlighting the greater significance of "godliness,"[18] or whether the term specifically zeroes in on the asceticism alluded to and challenged in 4:3.[19] In my opinion, this remains an open question, though the force of the contrast (clearly elevating godliness to the highest level) cannot be missed. Although the traditional maxim would suffice to emphasize the greater importance of godliness, it does not seem farfetched that the ascetic practices of 4:3 are at least

---

15. See Marshall, 551 (citing Merkel, 37); Roloff, 246 (a Hellenistic-Jewish maxim). In any case, the comparison between bodily and mental efforts was already popular and expressed in a variety of ways (e.g., Josephus, *Against Apion* 2.217-18).

16. Gk. γυμνασία (only here in NT); alone it can also be used figuratively for religious suffering or debating (4 Macc 11:20; Plato, *Laws* 648C). Gk. σωματικός (adj.; Luke 3:22); "bodily, in reference to the body" in contrast to noncorporeal (see BDAG).

17. The predicate adjective ("is useful, of profit"; ὠφέλιμος, 2 Tim 3:16; Titus 3:8; the word group was used by ancient ethicists to underline the goal or practical value of teaching or profession; Johnson, 249-50) is limited by the prepositional phrase πρὸς ὀλίγον ("for a little," or "for a little while"). For a similar sentiment, cf. the Cynic *Epistles of Crates* 3, "Take care of your soul, but take care of the body only to the degree that necessity requires" (Malherbe, 55).

18. So Marshall, 552.

19. Towner, *Goal*, 149-50; Johnson, 249; Kelly, 100; Roloff, 246.

obliquely in view (how could they not be?), perhaps regarded by Paul as an extreme example of the category defined by "physical exercise." Paul's denunciation of the opponents' excessive measures with regard to marriage and foods is unequivocal, so there is no need to address them specifically again. But they do nevertheless fall at least somewhere within the category of those physical activities (including athletic exercise) that, in comparison with exercise in godliness, can only offer limited benefits.[20] In turning the instructions to Timothy to his pursuit of godliness, Paul shifts to the level of larger principles. It is difficult to ignore the alter-image of the heretics and their practices (vv. 3, 7) as this shift is made.

The contrast indicating the better course to be pursued is expressed with an almost perfect parallelism, as a literal translation shows:

8a: For physical training is of some value,
8b: but godliness is valuable for all things.

8a: *hē gar sōmatikē gymnasia*   *pros oligon*   *estin ōphelimos,*
8b: *hē de eusebeia*   *pros panta*   *ōphelimos estin.*[21]

In place of physical exercise (whether ascetic rigor is meant or not), exercise in "godliness,"[22] that holistic life encompassing faith and visible behavior, is set out as the first priority (2:2; 4:7). Its superiority stems from its far-reaching value ("for all things"), in contrast to the limited value of the former. This value is then explained in terms of eternal life: "holding promise for both the present life and the life to come." The phrase "promise of life" is almost technical, identifying this "life" as that which is specifically associated with the salvific pledge of God (2 Tim 1:1; Titus 1:2).[23] Given the inher-

---

20. Marshall, 552, makes the valid point that γυμνασία is not attested in the sense of "asceticism." The question is whether in the development of the discourse the reader/hearer is intended to understand the contrast between bodily exercise and godliness as also, by semantic extension if not by etymology or prior use, applying to the previous discussion.

21. The parallel is clearly noticeable in the Greek:

ἡ γὰρ σωματικὴ γυμνασία πρὸς ὀλίγον ἐστὶν ὠφέλιμος,
ἡ δὲ εὐσέβεια   πρὸς πάντα ὠφέλιμός ἐστιν.

22. The athletic metaphor of exercise, initiated in 4:7 and repeated with the noun γυμνασία in v. 8, is still in mind (i.e., we should read, "for bodily exercise is of some value, but exercise in godliness . . ."; cf. Marshall, 553 n. 80).

23. Gk. ἐπαγγελία; with the genitive of content, "of life" (ζωῆς); for a similar thought see Heb 9:15; 1 John 2:25. The association of "promise" with God is so natural that the genitive of source (θεοῦ; e.g., Rom 4:20; 2 Cor 1:20) is expressed only when the source is emphasized; in this case, it is omitted to emphasize the place of "godliness." Use of the "promise" concept, in various connections, in Paul is widespread (Rom 4:13, 14,

ent unity in the concept of life associated with God's promise (both now and to come; see discussion at 1:16), it is unlikely that Paul is distinguishing rigidly between physical life ("now") and spiritual or eternal life ("to come").[24] The point is rather that the practice of godliness will lead the believer into the experience of God's promise of eternal life in the present age that carries on into the "age to come."

In the letters to Timothy and Titus it is typical of Paul to hold tightly together the present age ("now")[25] of Christian activity and the "coming"[26] age (here the life associated with it), the result of which is an ethical tension. On the one hand, Paul insists that the future promise of God is being realized "now" in the present age, changing it and opening up new possibilities for those in faith. On the other hand, this fact, linked to the fact of the past Christ-event, obligates believers to "put on" the new reality. Here this entire network of ideas is consolidated into the concept of "godliness." Practice of it is anticipation of the fullness of blessing to come. Its value transcends that of bodily exercise — and in this the behavior of the opponents is flatly denounced — not simply because bodily exercise pertains only to life here and now but because godliness is the outworking of God's eschatological promise of life that has broken into the present age.

9 Rather abruptly, there occurs at this point in the discourse the expanded version of the faithful saying formula: "This is a trustworthy saying that deserves full acceptance" (1:15). Paul intends the formula as an authentication of the apostolic authority of his teaching, and the expansion emphasizes the need to respond by embracing the teaching. But to what does it refer? Some connect the formula to v. 10 or v. 10b,[27] but this seems unlikely. Verse 10 (esp. v. 10a) has the feel of a "personal statement" more than that

---

16, 20; 9:4, 8, 9; etc.). See the discussion of the verb in Titus 1:2. G. Friedrich and J. Schniewind, *TDNT* 2:576-86; A. Sand, *EDNT* 2:13-16.

24. As Marshall, 554 n. 83, points out, the double use of the article need not intend a distinction between two kinds of life; it may instead be called for by the two different constructions (art. with adv.; art. with ptc.).

25. Gk. νῦν; for the use of the adverb to describe the present age, see 1 Tim 6:17; 2 Tim 4:10; Titus 2:12; Towner, *Goal*, 62.

26. For Gk. μέλλω (ptc.; see discussion and note at 1:16) in various references to eschatological events, see Matt 12:32; Eph 1:21; Heb 2:5; 6:5; 13:14; 1 Pet 5:1; Towner, *Goal*, 62.

27. Collins, 126-27; Guthrie, 107. Roloff, 240, argues at some length that v. 10 is a reworking of Col 1:28-29, and so is more pronounced in the passage than v. 8, and a more likely "faithful saying" (see discussion below). Mounce, 247, 254, argues that v. 10b, with its salvation theme, is the more likely "saying" (so apparently NIV; but cf. TNIV) and that v. 10b gives the "ultimate reason that Timothy should pursue godliness — salvation." This latter reasoning is highly subjective since "life" as explored in v. 8b is hardly less pivotal an idea than salvation in v. 10b.

of a "doctrinal statement."[28] And v. 10b is isolated from the formula by the grammar and intention of the intervening comment of v. 10a (see below): "for to this end we labor and strive, because . . ." (NRSV). Consequently, the formula most probably reflects on the teaching just given in v. 8. But it is not certain whether the saying includes all of v. 8a-b[29] or simply the positive endorsement of godliness in v. 8b.[30] In either case, the force of the faithful saying formula is to underline both the need to pursue godliness and the instruction's apostolic authority, and thereby to embrace authentic Christian living in contrast to the fragmented and ascetic approach being tried by the opponents.

10 To round off this section, Paul adds a conclusion that links his and Timothy's mission efforts backward to the value of "godliness," as well as to the salvation plan of God. The connections are in two directions, with v. 10a relying on godliness (v. 8b) as its reason, and v. 10b providing further grounds for ministry effort now expanded into soteriological language.

First, the connecting phrase "for this reason" ("that is why," TNIV; "for to this end," NRSV) points backward, gathering up what has been said about "godliness" and its promise of eternal life as a reason for Paul's missionary efforts.[31]

Second, a very Pauline combination of terms describes the gospel mission. The first term conveys the sense of "labor," "toil," or "hard work" and occurs several times in reference to Paul's mission work.[32] The second term, "to strive, struggle,"[33] probably continues the athletic contest imagery initiated in the "training" *(gymnaze, gymnasia)* sequence above (vv. 7b-8a),

28. So Marshall, 554. See also Fee, 104-5. The presence of γάρ connecting v. 10 with v. 9 is not necessarily problematic (cf. 2 Tim 2:11 and discussion). However, as Johnson, 250, and Bassler, 84, point out, γάρ makes v. 10 appear to be an explanation of v. 9.

29. Knight, 198; Barrett, 70; Brox, 177; Lock, 51.

30. Fee, 104-5; Kelly, 101; Johnson, 250 (apparently).

31. Gk. εἰς τοῦτο γάρ (for the combination, see Mark 1:38; Acts 26:16; Rom 14:9; 2 Cor 2:9; 1 Pet 2:21; 4:6). Depending on the translation, the γάρ may or may not be expressed. In this case, a backward reference is preferred since it helps to tie v. 10 to the preceding discussion of godliness, and allows the pursuit of godliness to be seen as a reason for Paul's efforts (see also Marshall, 555; Dibelius and Conzelmann, 68-69). But the matter is somewhat open. Mounce, 254, understanding the "saying" to be v. 10b, takes εἰς τοῦτο γάρ as a forward reference, which, with the two succeeding verbs, intervenes between the formula and saying "to emphasize the significance of the faithful saying." The possibility of this is remote.

32. Gk. κοπιάω; in reference to ministry see 5:17; Rom 16:6, 12[2x]; 1 Cor 15:10; 16:16; Gal 4:11; Phil 2:16; Col 1:29; 1 Thess 5:12; for other kinds of work see 2 Tim 2:6; 1 Cor 4:12; Eph 4:28. See Spicq, *TLNT* 2:322-29; F. Hauck, *TDNT* 3:827-30.

33. Gk. ἀγωνίζομαι; for background and references, see esp. Pfitzner, *Paul and the* Agon *Motif;* E. Stauffer, *TDNT* 1:135-40; G. Dautzenberg, *EDNT* 1:25-27.

though a military background is also possible.[34] From the original athletic/ military background, the term was applied in Greek discussions about the pursuit of moral virtue and in Jewish reflection on struggling for the law.[35] Paul applied this term to descriptions of his labor (2 Tim 4:7; Col 1:29), or to the Christian life in general (1 Cor 9:25). In the present text Paul depicts the great effort and risk involved in the work of the gospel (Phil 1:30; Col 2:1; 1 Thess 2:2). The pairing of the terms might be a traditional or formulaic way of characterizing the degree of effort and commitment required for missionary work (Col 1:29).[36] It is the great value of the promise of (eternal) life contained in godliness that justifies the hard work and exposure to risk and danger that goes with the Pauline mission.

Verse 10b makes what can only be called a gospel statement as further reason ("because"; *hoti*) for the effort of Paul's missionary ministry. It begins with an almost personal confessional statement of the certainty of the gospel message: "because we have put our hope in the living God." The decision to "place hope in" God is typically associated with the gospel and salvation in the NT (see the noun "hope" at 1:1 [and notes]; Titus 1:2; 2:13). In the perfect tense (2 Cor 1:10), the verb envisions a past decision that has resulted in a present condition.[37] "Hope," in Paul's missiological vernacular, implies the unfinished nature of Christian salvation (Rom 8:24-25), but also the firm anticipation that the object of hope (in this case the living God) will act according to divine promise (Titus 1:2). It is precisely the promise of life (v. 8) associated with godliness, and fundamentally also with the gospel, that determines the meaning of the appellation "living God" in this context: he is the life-giver, whose promise of life through the gospel is sure (see the discussion at 3:15).

Reference to "the living God" calls forth a specifically salvation-oriented description of God and his will to save people. The designation of God as "Savior" is thematic in this letter (see 1:1; 2:3). He is thus the originator of the salvation plan through Christ and the one who bestows this gift according to his will.[38]

---

34. Pfitzner, *Paul and the* Agon *Motif,* 92-98, stresses the use of this language in a military setting, and suggests that the gospel ministry is conceived of in battle terms (especially in view of the opponents). See also Roloff, 247.

35. For the term's use in Judaism for the effort of following the law, see Wis 4:2; 4 Macc 9:23-24; Philo, *On Husbandry* 113.

36. See Roloff, 247, for the view that the author employs a transformed version of Col 1:29 (based on the occurrence of the combination of κοπιάω/ἀγωνίζομαι, an opening εἰς phrase, and the reference to "all people" in Col 1:28). An intentional echo is possible.

37. Gk. ἐλπίζω (perf. tense); see also the perfect tense in 5:5; 6:17; 1 Cor 15:19. For the link of the verb with salvation, see esp. Rom 8:24-25.

38. The view of some (e.g., Guthrie, 108; Barrett, 70) that in the broad statement

In keeping with the theme of God's universal salvation already announced in 2:1-7, here too "all people" are within the scope of the Savior God's concern (cf. esp. 2:4). Appended to this affirmation, however, is the brief phrase "especially those who believe," which intends to sharpen (somehow) either the preceding genitive qualifier ("of all people") or the overall statement. And it has become problematic for interpreters. Many commentators conclude that Paul (or the author) has divided humanity into two groups: "all people" to whom, through the gospel, salvation is offered, and "those who have believed" in the gospel and so responded to the offer.[39] Another solution depends on the alternative translation for the term rendered "especially," that is, "namely, I mean,"[40] which then in effect narrows the meaning of "all people" to "believers": "who is the Savior of all people, I mean of those who believe."[41]

Bearing in mind, however, Paul's earlier engagement with the opponents' exclusivist claims about salvation in 2:1-7, where he countered with the bold affirmation of God's universal salvific will (2:4), we are on firmer ground to read this closing statement of the section with the polemical battle in mind. First, the ascetic requirements refuted in 4:4-5 (also utilizing the "all"/universal argument) would conform to the presence of a Judaizing exclusivism at work in the community. Second, "godliness" was affirmed as the authentic life associated with Paul's gospel in both 2:2 and 4:7-8. Third, this reality and the rejection of the Pauline gospel by the opponents led Paul in 2:7 and 4:10a to insist on the authority of his (universal) mission to the Gentiles and by implication the authority of his gospel as the true expression of God's will and only source of "godliness." This pattern of themes suggests that the potentially confusing statement ("who is the Savior of all people, especially of those who believe") should be read in the light of 2:1-7 and especially 2:4.

Therefore, "God is the Savior of all people, especially of those who believe" replicates almost perfectly the affirmation of 2:4: "who desires all people to be saved and to come to the knowledge of the truth." In the earlier setting, God's universal will (salvation for all according to Paul's gospel and in correction of exclusivism and laziness) is followed by the provision that links salvation to a response to the gospel (a rational decision — "coming to

---

"Savior of all people," "Savior" must be limited to a meaning that can indeed apply to all human beings regardless of their faith commitments ("sustainer, preserver") neglects the thematic use of the term for God.

39. There is some variation; see Kelly, 102-3.

40. Gk. μάλιστα (5:8, 17; 2 Tim 4:13; Titus 1:10); see especially R. A. Campbell, "Καὶ μάλιστα οἰκείων — A New Look at 1 Timothy 5.8," NTS 41 (1995): 157-60; T. C. Skeat, "'Especially the parchments': A Note on 2 Tim 4.13," JTS n.s. 30 (1979): 173-77.

41. Marshall, 556-57; Knight, 203.

the knowledge of the truth"). So too, here universal access to the gift of salvation is reaffirmed in the "Savior" statement, which is followed by a variation on the earlier gospel provision ("particularly, those who believe"). The point made in this way is that God's universal salvific will is realized "particularly" through proclamation of and belief in the gospel. Consequently, Paul says again (as in 2:1-7): (1) God's salvation is universal in scope (v. 10b); (2) it is linked to the gospel Paul preaches (vv. 6, 10a) and distinctly severed from the opponents' message (vv. 1-3, 7); (3) the authentic spiritual life ("godliness") is associated with Paul's message and Paul's ministry (vv. 7-8, 10a) and distinctly severed from the opponents' teaching and behavior (4:1-3, 7), it is the mark of those who believe (v. 10b), and by it (and by believing) God's universal will to save comes to realization.[42]

There is no division here based on limited and unlimited atonement, and no need to posit two shades of meaning for the term "Savior." Rather, in this primarily missiological and polemical conclusion, Paul brings his own ministry again to the fore, linking salvation and godly living to it. In so doing, he denounces both the extreme exclusivist claims and ascetic rigors of the heresy.[43]

c. Timothy: Paradigm of the Healthy Teacher (4:11-16)

> 11 *Command and teach these things.* 12 *Don't let anyone look down on you because you are young, but set an example for the believers in speech, in conduct, in love, in faith and in purity.* 13 *Until I come, devote yourself to the public reading of Scripture, to preaching and to teaching.* 14 *Do not neglect your gift, which was given you through prophecy when the body of elders laid their hands on you.*
>
> 15 *Be diligent in these matters; give yourself wholly to them, so that everyone may see your progress.* 16 *Watch your life and doctrine closely. Persevere in them, because if you do, you will save both yourself and your hearers.*

Having highlighted the role of his mission in the salvation plan of God, Paul again takes up parenesis to Timothy. Ten imperatives in a short span of text establish the genre and set the tone. Timothy's own behavior and activities as a coworker form a pattern of the godliness just reflected on. Central to this

---

42. Cf. the slightly differently framed interpretation of Johnson, 251: "The point is . . . that God's 'desire that all human beings should be saved' . . . is 'particularly' realized among the faithful, those who in fact have 'come to the recognition of the truth' (2:4; see also 4:3)" (apparently also Collins, 127-28).

43. See also Bassler, 85.

section is the instruction about Timothy's "gift." This links the power of the Holy Spirit to the life he is to lead. At the conclusion of the subsection it becomes more apparent that the coworker's demonstration of godliness (in various personal and public ways) is also to be linked with Paul's mission concerns: Timothy's own salvation and the salvation of others depend on his faithfulness (v. 16).

11   The dual imperative, "Command and teach these things," creates the almost formulaic link (6:2; Titus 2:15) between a preceding apostolic statement and a parenetic section calling the coworker into action as a teacher.[1] The reflection is backward, summing up what has just been said.[2] The term translated "command" (see on 1:3) describes the authoritative activities of "ordering, exhorting, and instructing" carried out by Timothy and Paul, and here envisions apostolic insistence on the implementation of the preceding discussions. The second term, "teach" (see on 2:12), refers to the equally authoritative instruction in the congregational setting (of the *didaskalia;* see 1:10; both theology and ethics); this activity will consist of doctrinal instruction and perhaps a more structured pedagogy. Together these two terms, overlapping to some degree, summarize the actions Timothy would take to apply the sort of apostolic discourse given in response to specific doctrinal and ethical errors or more generally to community needs (6:2). As throughout 4:1-10, instruction intended for the believing community is often interlaced with refutation and correction of heretical notions.

12   Paul apparently thought Timothy would encounter the same sort of obstacle he anticipated in the Corinthian church. Although the mandate dimension of this letter (written to Timothy but also for the church) differs from that of 1 Corinthians (written directly to the church), the closest parallel to the kind of concern expressed here is 1 Cor 16:10-11:

> When Timothy comes, see to it that he has nothing to fear while he is with you, for he is carrying on the work of the Lord, just as I am. No one, then, should refuse to accept him. Send him on his way in peace so that he may return to me. I am expecting him along with the brothers.[3]

The issue of Timothy's relative youth is not specifically mentioned in 1 Cor 16:10-11, but the possibility that the Corinthian church would scorn or despise him if he were sent in Paul's place is paralleled in this text in the term

---

1. 1 Tim 4:11; 6:2; Titus 2:15 stress teaching and exhortation.

2. In this case, ταῦτα must point backward either to all of 4:1-10, or possibly to 4:6(7)-10 (see Lips, *Glaube,* 95 n. 4).

3. Cf. also the double commendation of Timothy in 1 Cor 4:17, given to prepare the way for his acceptance in the community: "For this reason I have sent to you Timothy, my son whom I love, who is faithful in the Lord."

"to look down upon" (cf. Titus 2:15).[4] The sense of the command, "Don't let anyone look down on you because you are young," may compare his age to Paul's, or to that of older people in the church over whom he would exercise delegated apostolic authority (1 Tim 5:1). Each possibility would apply, as well as the simple fact that he was standing in for Paul in a situation where anti-Pauline sentiments might have been on the increase. In any case, if the noun translated "youth, state of youthfulness" is a reference to an age group, Timothy would probably have been less than forty years old.[5] Attempts at greater precision are speculative since we do not know his age at the time he was called.[6] But the possibility that "youth" means here simply "younger than me" or "younger than the elders in the church" should not be ruled out. Either way, the parallel in 1 Cor 16:10-11 (Titus 2:15) suggests that Paul's practice of dispatching coworkers authorized to act in his place (instructing, disciplining) meant putting them into very ticklish ministry situations.[7] In this case, the explicit reference to Timothy's youth adds the burden of crossing the cultural line of age veneration.[8]

To overcome any liabilities associated with youth, Paul urges Timothy to become an "example for the believers" (Titus 2:7).[9] The task of "modeling" was intrinsic both to formal and informal ancient education.[10] Paul assumed this role in relation to Timothy (1 Cor 4:17) and within the

4. Gk. καταφρονέω; for a similar description of youth being despised, see Diodorus Siculus 17.7.1; Rom 2:4; 1 Cor 11:22; Spicq, *TLNT* 2:280-84; C. Schneider, *TDNT* 3:631-32. The situation faced by Titus, which the similar command of 2:15 addresses, may not be precisely that of youthfulness; see the commentary.

5. Gk. νεότης (elsewhere in the NT always in the set phrase ἐκ νεότητος ["from youth"], Mark 10:20; Luke 18:21; Acts 26:4). Among the various Greek schemes (more or less detailed) for classifying age groups (e.g., Dio Chrysostom 74.10; Philo, *On the Creation* 105; cf. *On the Embassy to Gaius* 227), a more basic distinction between "young" and "old" existed that placed youth at the age of forty and under (e.g., Irenaeus, *Against Heresies* 2.22.5; see also Josephus, *Antiquities* 18.197; cf. *1 Clement* 21.6-8). See further Marshall, 239.

6. But cf. Simpson, 69 (35-40 years old); Easton, 146 and Collins, 128 (20s); Jeremias, 34 (30s).

7. For the situation behind Paul's instruction in 1 Cor 16:10-11, see Fee, *1 Corinthians,* 821-22.

8. Paul's own insistence on the selection of older leaders (3:6) underlines the potential for disrespect in the case of the younger Timothy. For the veneration of age in Greco-Roman culture and Hellenistic Judaism, see Spicq, 511-12.

9. Gk. τύπος (Rom 5:14; 6:17; 1 Cor 10:6; cf. ὑποτύπωσις in 1 Tim 1:16; 2 Tim 1:13). For Gk. πιστός (here gen. pl. meaning "to or for believers," as in 1 Cor 10:6; 1 Pet 5:3), see the note at 1:2.

10. See examples in Wolter, *Paulustradition,* 192; discussion in Witherington, *Conflict and Community in Corinth,* 144-46; for the ethical use of τύπος ("pattern, model"), see Spicq, *TLNT* 3:387; L. Goppelt, *TDNT* 8:246-59.

churches (Phil 3:17; 1 Thess 1:7; 2 Thess 3:9), and in these letters to delegates, Timothy and Titus were to do the same (Titus 2:7).[11] Elsewhere it was a responsibility to be taken up by believers in general (e.g., 1 Thess 1:7), and expected of church leaders (1 Pet 5:3). To be a model or set an example meant more than simply presenting a pattern that others were to mimic: "The more a life is moulded by the word, the more it becomes *typos,* a model or mould."[12] It was a case of living out life as faith in the gospel had shaped it.

Paul depicts this life by attaching a string of five short prepositional phrases enumerating five of its elements. The first phrase, "in speech,"[13] is thought by some to refer to the specific kind of speech involved in preaching or teaching (e.g., 5:17; Titus 1:9).[14] But while this might be included in the sense of what one professes, alongside of "conduct," the broader sense of "speech" is more likely.[15] "Conduct,"[16] that is, manner of life, how one lives, was a natural counterpart to "speech" in Greek and Jewish moral teaching.[17] Together they encompassed most of the observable life, and especially for the teacher, the manner of life was to correspond to what was professed. In Timothy's case, coherence of speech and behavior was to command the respect of one assigned to represent the apostle and his teaching in the community.

The next two qualities in effect repeat the more widely used "speech/conduct" model specifically in terms of Christian maturity. Paul frequently summed up authentic spirituality in terms of "faith" (= belief in God; see on 1:2) and "love" (= the outworking of faith in service; see on 1:5; 1:14).

Added to this pair is the fifth phrase, "in purity." In this context, the reference is either to the sexual purity (chastity) required especially of young

11. Those who regard these letters to be pseudonymous argue that in the fictitious setting of these letters the characters of "Timothy" and "Titus" serve as "types" of the ideal believer (e.g., Wolter, *Paulustradition,* 191-95). But the "model" concept applied in the undisputed Pauline letters corresponds perfectly with its use here (Titus 2:15), and can just as well be viewed as an aspect of verisimilitude.

12. Goppelt, *TDNT* 8:250.

13. For Gk. λόγος see the note at 1:15 in reference to conversation or speech.

14. Roloff, 253.

15. 1 Cor 4:20; Col 4:6; see Johnson, 252; Collins, 128.

16. Gk. ἀναστροφή (see verb at 3:15): Gal 1:13; Eph 4:22; Heb 13:7; Jas 3:13; 1 Pet 1:15, 18; 2:12; 3:1, 2, 16; 2 Pet 2:7; 3:11; 2 Macc 6:23; Tob 4:14; Spicq, *TLNT* 1:111-14; G. Bertram, *TDNT* 7:715-17.

17. For the sentiment, see Philo, *On the Life of Moses* 2.48, where life lived according to the arrangement of the universe involves a "perfect harmony and union, between his words [λόγους] and his actions [ἔργων] and between his actions and his words"; Plutarch, *Moralia* 1033B.

men (5:2),[18] or to purity of motives.[19] Given the concern that Timothy not give grounds for his youth to be criticized, emphasis on the need for sexual probity is most fitting.

Paul calls Timothy to display a balanced and authentic Christian lifestyle. It will not only bear the traditional marks of consistency (speech/conduct), but also the stamp of spiritual coherence (faith/love) from which the opponents had deviated in their teaching and behavior. Any lingering questions related to Timothy's relative youth were finally to be laid to rest by his refusal to slip into unchaste tendencies of speech, conduct, or inappropriate interaction with members of the opposite sex (see below on 5:2).

13-14 Although the importance of personal character within this profile will reemerge below (4:15-16), the next two imperatives take up three aspects of ministry in the church that Timothy is to carry out (v. 13), and then reflect on the charismatic basis of these activities and its implications (v. 14). The historical context for this instruction is Paul's absence ("until I come"; cf. 3:14-15), which requires Timothy as apostolic delegate to represent the apostle in his stead. Anticipation of Paul's arrival[20] serves both as a motivation for Timothy and a signal to the church that Paul will shortly back up his extended authority in person (cf. Phlm 22). The brief statement is pregnant with possible meaning. Clearly, Timothy does fully represent Paul in Ephesus; what Timothy is to do, Paul would do himself if he were present. By indicating his forthcoming arrival (the time is uncertain but not the fact), Paul establishes continuity both of his apostolic authority over the church (in spite of his absence) and of his work of proclamation, teaching, and correction.

Three ministry commands, all based on the single imperative, "devote yourself to, pay attention to" (see on 1:4), provide a framework for the ministry related to the Scriptures that Timothy is to execute in the church. These were certainly not innovations in the worship service,[21] but rather activities that needed to be continued (or possibly resumed) in view of the disruption caused by the false teaching.

The first of these activities is correctly translated "the public reading

18. Polycarp, *To the Philippians* 5.3; Philo, *On Abraham* 98; Johnson, 252; Hanson, 92.

19. Marshall, 562, Spicq, 513.

20. The sense is possibly, "while I am coming" (cf. John 21:22, 23); see E. D. W. Burton, *Syntax of Moods and Tenses in New Testament Greek* (3d ed.; Edinburgh: T&T Clark, 1898/1976), §328.

21. The presence of the definite article with each item (τῇ ἀναγνώσει, τῇ παρακλήσει, τῇ διδασκαλίᾳ) suggests that each was already a fixed activity in the church; see P. H. Towner, "The Function of the Public Reading of Scripture in 1 Tim 4:13 and in the Biblical Tradition," *SBJT* 7 (2003): 44-54; Marshall, 562.

of Scripture" (TNIV, NRSV).[22] This refers to the practice, inherited from temple and synagogue worship, of the public reading of the OT (Deut 31:11-12; Neh 8:7-8; 1QS 6:6-8),[23] and while the emphasis here is on the regular performance of the activity, underlying the instruction are certain assumptions about Timothy's ability to read well.[24] It is not certain whether the Jewish schedule of readings, which included selections from Torah and the prophets according to a three-year cycle (cf. Acts 13:15; 2 Cor 3:14),[25] was followed. But it is likely that the OT (with some fluidity of content in this period), in Greek translation (in Paul's churches), would have been the main focus of this public reading. The synagogue readings would have expanded naturally to include the stories in the Gospel tradition and the Pauline letters, as texts such as 2 Cor 7:8; Col 4:16; 1 Thess 5:27; and 2 Thess 3:14 suggest for the latter.

It is normally assumed, apparently, that the primary function of the public reading of Scripture in the worship setting was to lay the groundwork for the preaching and teaching to follow (corresponding to practices of Scripture reading in many nonliturgical traditions today).[26] This is a partial explanation, and indeed in Jewish worship the public reading was followed by preaching/teaching. Yet the public reading of the Scriptures served a deeper social function as well. Modern studies of narrative and human social experi-

22. Gk. ἀνάγνωσις (Acts 13:15; 2 Cor 3:14); Spicq, *TLNT* 1:101-2; R. Bultmann, *TDNT* 1:343-44.

23. Towner, "The Public Reading of Scripture." Cf. Mounce, 200, who, while acknowledging that a public reading is envisioned with synagogue practices in the background, nevertheless sees the focus in "reading" to be on Timothy himself: "Timothy is to immerse himself in the biblical text. . . ."

24. Certain discussions that speak of the difficulty of reading and the importance of the task begin a Greek background sketch. Epictetus wrote: "When you say, 'Come listen to a reading that I am going to do,' make sure that you do not grope your way through" (3.23.6; see also Plutarch, *Alexander* 1.1; 23.3). Apprenticeship to the scholar began in the school (Plato, *Laws* 810B), and if the pupil misread a syllable or stumbled in the reading, he often experienced extreme embarrassment (Plautus, *Bacchides* 423ff.). Training in reading became a fundamental element in rhetorical education because in the recitation-declamation component of the official examination, the student had to give critical comment on the text that was sight read (Plutarch, *De audibilibus Poeta*). The point of such references is simply that reading was an act the success of which was measured by its accuracy in communicating the content of a written discourse exactly. Reverence for the biblical texts in the case of ancient Jewish culture assures the same level of concern within the Jewish context. Those called on to read in a Christian church, whether in Palestine or the Diaspora, would be expected to conform to high standards of quality control.

25. See Towner, "The Public Reading of Scripture," for a discussion of reading patterns; Schürer, *History of the Jewish People,* 2:448.

26. Cf. Marshall, 563; Collins, 129.

ence and of the role of reading and readers within the broader discussion of hermeneutics and communication events work from very different bases and arrive at different assessments of the place of the reader/hearer in the determination of meaning.[27] But while almost all aspects of the related discussions continue to be under construction, a point of convergence that seems to have emerged whether the individual reading event (N. Holland) or the corporate/public reading event (D. Bleich, S. Crites, D. H. Kelsey, S. Hauerwas) is considered, is that reading/hearing certain significant texts influences the formation, shaping, defining, and redefining of individual and corporate identity.[28] The significance of this observation for understanding the role of the public reading of Scripture in the Jewish and Christian tradition may be invaluable.[29]

27. Cf. the different programs of N. Holland, *The Dynamics of Literary Response* (New York: Oxford University Press, 1968); idem, *5 Readers Reading* (New Haven: Yale University Press, 1975); D. Bleich, *The Double Perspective: Language, Literacy and Social Relations* (New York: Oxford University Press 1988); S. Crites, "The Narrative Quality of Experience," *JAAR* 39 (1971): 291-311; D. H. Kelsey, "Biblical Narrative and Theological Anthropology," in G. Green, ed., *Scriptural Authority and Narrative Interpretation* (Philadelphia: Fortress, 1987), 121-43; S. Hauerwas, *A Community of Character* (Notre Dame, IN: University of Notre Dame Press, 1981).

28. In addition to Crites, Kelsey and Hauerwas (just cited), see also Johnson, *Scripture and Discernment,* 28-33.

29. The practice and function of public reading in the Greek religious sphere, including both the more publicly relevant Delphic Oracles and the more private mystery cults, might be regarded as a useful backdrop to reading Scripture in the Pauline churches. The institution of the Delphic Oracle, more relevant to the classical period, provided Greek society with a divine touchstone, embracing the religious, moral, and political facets of Greek life. Its role in reinforcing the sense of corporate Greek identity (normally segmented into city groups) in these terms cannot be overestimated (see the discussion in E. Ferguson, *Backgrounds of Early Christianity* [Grand Rapids: Eerdmans, 1987], 166-71). The broad religious category of the so-called "Mysteries" is potentially more relevant to the NT period, but as a category it does not represent a religious or cultural phenomenon that is particularly unified, stable, or predictable, and thus great care is needed in assessing the data that have come to light (see Ferguson, *Backgrounds,* 197-240). Our knowledge of the liturgical practices of the ancient religious cults is fragmentary at best, and often ancient writers intentionally withheld from their descriptions the very details from which our reconstructions could most profit (D. E. Aune, "Prolegomena to the Study of Oral Tradition in the Hellenistic World," in H. Wansbrough, ed., *Jesus and the Oral Gospel Tradition* [Sheffield: Sheffield Academic Press, 1991], 59-106, 83-85; see refs. to the sources). Nevertheless, glimpses of practices in this setting provided by the ancient writers suggest that various readings and recitations (of materials at first perpetuated in an oral tradition but eventually written down and read) did play a part in the groups' communal activities. Of greatest interest is the observation that a myth (e.g., surrounding Dionysius or Mithras; cf. the *Hymn to Demeter*) that would be "recited and enacted" (Pausanias 8.6.5) lay at the center of a group's identity. The central myth celebrated by a

318

From the perspective of the historical description of the practice as noticed in the OT and NT records (as well as in other relevant literature in Judaism), it may be suggested that the Scriptures were intentionally read as a way of answering the always present and pertinent question: Who are we? Related but subsidiary questions — if this is who we are, how should we live, what should we do, etc.? — were equally ever-present and addressed as the didactic response to the regular public readings of the holy texts (in the form of Targumic expansion "preaching and teaching"). Although the question of identity was always the given subtext, the need for a particularly relevant re-expression of the answer clearly became more acute whenever situations that threatened the community's well-being presented themselves, whether internal in the form of idolatry or rebellion against God, or external in the form of attacks from the outside.

The public reading of Scripture becomes a point of emphasis at crucial or crisis moments. The sort of events depicted in Nehemiah, in the story of Josiah (2 Chron 34:18-19, 30, with both public and private settings in view), and in 1 Timothy all share a common theme that sheds light on at least one common feature of the function of community Scripture reading. In the OT incidents mentioned, Israel is in crisis, either back from exile and puzzling about her identity, or coming back to God after a time of spiritual exile (as in the case of Josiah). The people are being recalled to their God; their identity as the people of the covenant is being restated, redefined for a new generation. These exceptional incidents explain the function of Scripture reading by relating the activity to the corporate identity of the people. Assuming the practice of regular reading of the text, in some organized fashion, almost certainly the practice is to be linked to the sort of command found in Deut 31:11-12:

> 11 when all Israel comes to appear before the LORD your God at the place that he will choose, you shall read this law before all Israel in their hearing. 12 Assemble the people — men, women, and children, as well as the aliens residing in your towns — so that they may hear and learn to fear the LORD your God and to observe diligently all the words of this law.

While Deuteronomy may be a later reflection of the covenant and practices associated with it, the public reading of Torah was apparently designed to remind the people of their origin in YHWH, their continued existence within a covenant relationship, and their obligations within that rela-

---

given cult was not a secret, whereas the initiation rites were indeed kept secret, and, in addition to the central myth, the withholding of the initiatory revelation was paramount to a group's distinctiveness and sense of identity (see Ferguson, *Backgrounds,* 197-240).

tionship. The content of the formative "story" to be read grew to include the prophetic writings and Psalms (as the relevant Mishnah and NT texts confirm). But then the sense of living in YHWH's story necessarily entailed a lengthening of that story to ensure that the present people of God, in any place and time, not only knew where their identity came from but also where it was at present and where it was headed. In response to the new realities presented by exile and eventual resettlement in the land, weekly synagogue readings, along with other heavily symbolic cultic acts, served to tell and retell the story that kept Israel's faith and identity alive.

The function of Scripture reading in the NT era within the Christian movement undoubtedly served the same basic purpose. Again new realities are absorbed into the growing story of Israel's salvation. Now regular public reading of Scripture also served to locate the new identity in Christ being experienced by various non-Jewish converts in the story that had been in process for centuries. And the Christ-event, particularly its core-forming elements of crucifixion and resurrection, became the relocated story-"center," not displacing the event of the exodus but rather prolonging the meaning of that formative covenant-founding event and bringing the salvation it proclaimed to a new point of climax.

Crisis points continue to underline the importance of what could easily be mistaken for a simple liturgical fixture. In fact, were it not for crisis, habituated activities such as the public reading of Scripture would come up only for passing references (cf. Acts 13:15; 15:21; 2 Cor 3:14 of synagogue practices). Given the OT examples cited, it does not seem surprising that, in the context of a church being led away from a focus on a traditional reading of the Scriptures to disputes and speculation engendered by new readings of certain texts (1:3-4; 4:7) and a new interpretation of "Christian identity" (4:1-3), Timothy would receive the command to "be devoted to" an activity that would remind the community of its identity in Christ and its covenant relation with God. A different sort of crisis from those seen in the OT, perhaps, but it was again a crisis situation that brought to light something of the function of the practice of the public reading of Scripture.

As pointed out, questions related to identity as the people of God — how should we live, what should we do? — were addressed by way of deeper exploration and application of the Scriptures. And from this perspective, the public reading of Scripture set the stage for the next two activities. "Preaching" (which is perhaps too generic a translation) or "exhorting" is listed next.[30] This is use of the Scriptures (or apostolic teaching) to bring instruction (6:2), to exhort, encourage, or console, and generally has in mind

---

30. Gk. παράκλησις (freq. in Paul of both "consolation" in general and for the activity of exhorting through the Scriptures: Rom 12:8; 15:4, 5; 1 Cor 14:3).

the implementing or changing of behavior, on the basis of the Scripture's sense or intent.[31]

Connected with exhortation is "teaching" (5:17). This is the activity of instruction and discussion that is associated with the body of apostolic instruction also called "the (sound, good) teaching" (4:6, 16; 6:1, 3); this latter association suggests that this function was not simply another mode of applying the particular Scripture texts read publicly. As the noun *didaskalia* suggests (1:10, discussion), the activity of "teaching" (see on 2:12) is instruction in the authoritative doctrine, which stands over and against the competing views of the opponents (4:1).[32]

Taken together, in this crisis context the three activities serve to remind believers of their identity in the people of God and what behavior and behavioral changes that identity entails. The currency of confusing and contradictory doctrine calls for ongoing instruction in the apostolic traditions (theology and ethics) to ensure conformity with the will of God as understood by the apostle.

Verse 14 shifts logically from the exercise of spiritual gifts (Rom 12:6-8; cf. 1 Corinthians 12) to a reflection on Timothy's giftedness. The command "do not neglect" is typical of this kind of parenesis from a superior to a subordinate.[33] It stresses first of all that Timothy must regard his "gift" as carrying with it the responsibility to put it to proper use; he must live up to his God-given potential and exercise the authority that goes with the gift. In fact, this is an image of the potency of the Christian life open to all believers; J. Moltmann refers to the "courage to be" as a "key to being," which is faith to embrace the invisible reality of God.[34] But in this case, Paul also undoubtedly sent a message to the church to receive Timothy as his authorized delegate.

The meaning of "gift" will be determined by Pauline usage of the term, which, apart from general references to God's various gracious gifts, normally refers to workings of the Spirit.[35] In this context, it is either a reference to a particular manifestation or manifestations of the Spirit for service,[36]

31. Note how Acts 13:15-41 combines appeal to the OT and the gospel tradition to bring about change in faith and ethics; cf. the frequent use of the verb in this sense; 2:1; Titus 1:9; Rom 12:1; 15:30; 16:17; etc.; 2 Macc 7:24; 15:11. On the verb (παρακαλέω), see the discussion and notes at 1:3. See J. Thomas, *EDNT* 3:23-27; Lips, *Glaube,* 132-35.

32. See Oberlinner, 207, Marshall, 563; Johnson, 253.

33. Gk. ἀμελέω (Matt 22:5; Heb 2:3; 8:9); on secular usage, see Wolter, *Paulustradition,* 185-89; Spicq, *TLNT* 1:87-91; Johnson, 253.

34. J. Moltmann, *The Crucified God* (New York: HarperCollins, 1991), 335.

35. Gk. χάρισμα ("gift"), mainly Pauline in the NT (1 Pet 4:10), is infrequent before the Christian era (LXX Ps 30:22; variants in Sir 7:33; 38:30); see Lips, *Glaube,* 206-23; H. Conzelmann, *TDNT* 9:402-6; K. Berger, *EDNT* 3:460-61; Roloff, 255-57.

36. Rom 12:6; 1 Cor 1:7; 7:7; 12:4, 9, 28, 30, 31; 1 Pet 4:10; *1 Clement* 38.1.

or a reference to the Holy Spirit as God's "gift."[37] Marshall suggests that the distinction between a particular gifting associated with the Spirit and the Spirit himself as a gift is artificial since the two things are indivisible in these letters.[38] Greater precision, however, may be possible. In any case, the increasingly popular understanding of the "gift" as commissioning to office (making Timothy the paradigm of later church officers to whom the gifts and authority for ministry were limited)[39] is out of place in this text.[40]

The language of *charisma* and the phrase "in you," which describes the location of this gift, suggest a connection with the indwelling Spirit (2 Tim 1:14). But the preceding reference to particular gifts of ministering strongly suggests that here "the gift in Timothy" refers to his giftedness or empowerment for ministry (including the activities just listed), though admittedly the indwelling of the Holy Spirit (i.e., the gift of the Spirit) is not far from mind.

Timothy's giftedness from the Holy Spirit is said either to have been conveyed[41] or recognized (and so confirmed as authoritative) by two closely related activities. We must consider each activity, their interrelation, and the participants in the event. The action of the giving of the gift is defined first by the activity of prophecy. The phrase translated "through prophecy" employs a preposition *(dia)* that can cover a range of senses: here, with the genitive singular,[42] it will either indicate the "means" by which the gift was given or more generally refer to prophecy as an accompanying activity or feature of

37. The gift of the Spirit (esp. 2 Tim 1:6: τὸ χάρισμα τοῦ θεοῦ) would be included in general references to God's gracious gifts: Rom 5:15-16; 6:23; 11:29.

38. Marshall, 564. This is apparently based on his reading of 2 Tim 1:6-7 (696-97) in which he understands Paul first to refer (v. 6) to "the gift of God" = "spiritual equipment for ministry" and secondly (v. 7) to identify this with the Holy Spirit.

39. Oberlinner, 208, 211; Roloff, 255; cf. Bassler, 88-89.

40. The language here and in the parallel text 2 Tim 1:6 will not bear the strain imposed by making χάρισμα into "office." As Fee, *God's Empowering Presence*, 772-73, points out, even if in 4:14 the idea of neglecting an office is reasonable enough (though can an office be "in you"?), the imagery of fanning into flame the "gift of God" cannot be applied sensibly to an "office" (773). See also Marshall, 564-65.

41. The verb "to give" (δίδωμι; here aor. pass.) appears in similar statements in 1 Cor 12:7, 8 and 2 Tim 1:7. The main question is how this action relates to the two succeeding prepositional phrases: "through prophecy [on account of prophecies], with the laying on of hands by the presbytery."

42. Gk. διὰ προφητείας is ambiguous, either accusative plural ("on account of prophecies," or "with the accompaniment of prophecies"), or (as most TNIV/NIV, NRSV, REB) genitive singular ("through, by means of, accompanied by prophecy"). The latter gives the better general sense (cf. 1:18, discussion, where, however, the pl. occurs) of "through prophecy" in the sense of words of confirmation issuing from the Spirit, communicated at the event by prophets (see Fee, *God's Empowering Presence*, 773-74).

the event. On the model of 1:18 (see the discussion; Acts 13:1-2), where the role of prophecy figures in a similar context, the latter, looser sense of accompanying prophecy is probably best (the plural, "prophecies," is grammatically possible though the sense of this is vague). Prophecy itself will not have been the "means" or cause of conveyance; the passive verb "was given" indicates the action of God/the Spirit. It is probably rather a reference to words of the Spirit spoken by a prophet(s) that confirm and identify Timothy's giftedness and thereby authorize his ministry in the community.[43]

Closely connected in Paul's description of this event is the laying on of hands. This action is also linked by a preposition *(meta)* that can cover a range of meanings. Here, with a genitive object, the general sense of accompaniment links this action loosely with the activity of prophecy ("with the laying on of hands"; e.g., NRSV).[44] The ceremonial or social act of laying hands on a person occurs several times in the NT in a variety of contexts for differing reasons (2 Tim 1:6; Acts 8:18; Heb 6:2).[45] Presumably, the imposition of hands for the communication of healing (or the invoking of God's benevolent intervention; Mark 6:5; Luke 13:13; Acts 28:8), of blessing (Gen 48:14; Mark 10:16), of spiritual gifts or skills (Acts 8:17; 19:6; 2 Tim 1:6), and of various more official kinds of authorizations and appointments (Num 27:18-23; Deut 34:9; Acts 6:6) belongs to the basic category of symbolic social or cultic action. The former benevolent significance can be found outside the biblical tradition, but it was mainly within the OT, Judaism, and the NT that the signification of "authorization" became a dominant function of the rite.

What is less clear is how the act is to be associated with the communication of the particular commodity to the recipient — does the action literally function as the means of conveyance (Deut 34:9), or rather as an acknowledgment that God has already given it (Num 27:18-23)? While in many cases (blessing, healing) the laying on of hands is assumed to be a public sign of invoking God to act, in other situations the function is left ambiguous. In this case of an appointment to service, where the preposition *meta* fosters ambiguity, two possibilities remain. Either the laying on of hands is to be regarded as the visible human counterpart to the inward action by which God really confers some gift or blessing, or it is (similarly) the public, visible action signify-

43. For the range of meaning possible for διά, see M. J. Harris, *NIDNTT* 3:1177, 1182-83; Marshall, 468.

44. The NEB translation "through" (expressing means) is incorrect; the TNIV/NIV translation "when" extracts more from μετά than it can actually give, and suggests a sequence that is unwarranted (first laying of hands, then prophecy; cf. the REB for the reverse sequence).

45. Gk. ἐπιθέσεως τῶν χειρῶν (2 Tim 1:6; Acts 8:18; Heb 6:2; see also Philo, *On the Special Laws* 1.203; *Allegorical Interpretation* 3.90. In other language, Acts 6:6; 8:17; 9:17; 19:6.

ing recognition of what God has already done within an individual, thereby expressing community authorization. The concurrence of a prophetic word from the Spirit does not resolve the ambiguity, but it does suggest that the confirming/authorizing act at least works in concert with the Spirit's guidance.

The term describing the group that laid hands on Timothy is *presbyterion.* It occurs three times in the NT; in the other two occurrences the reference is to the council of Jewish elders (Luke 22:66; Acts 22:5), and it was later adopted to describe a council of Christian elders within the church.[46] This is the likely sense of its use in this text as well, its application to Christian leadership nomenclature paralleling that of *presbyteros* to designate a church leader.[47] Consequently, Paul has admonished Timothy not to neglect his giftedness for and to ministry; the elders of the Ephesian community have played a part, by relating a prophetic word and laying on hands, in recognizing and confirming the gift (rather than in actually conveying it to him).

This conclusion is not in itself necessarily problematic, but the fact that here this "gift" is said to be conferred in some sense through the imposition of hands by the elders, while 2 Tim 1:6 appears to speak similarly of "the gift of God" coming to Timothy through Paul's hands alone does raise a question for interpretation. How are these two texts and events to be reconciled?

One solution maintains that the same event is in view in each passage and that Paul and the elders participated in the event of laying hands on Timothy. In accordance with the unique requirements of each literary situation, the event is reflected on from differing perspectives. 1 Timothy is written both to Timothy and the Ephesian church; thus Paul not only reminds Timothy of this event and the gifting and confirmation of authority to minister, but he also addresses the elders themselves as a way to ensure their continued allegiance to Timothy and the apostolic mission. 2 Timothy is more

---

46. Gk. πρεσβυτέριον; Ignatius, *To the Ephesians* 2.2; 4.1; 20.2; *To the Magnesians* 2.1; 13.1; *To the Philadelphians* 4.1; 5.1; 7.1; *To the Smyrnaeans* 8.1; 12.2; *To the Trallians* 2.2; 7.2; 13.2. G. Bornkamm, *TDNT* 6:651-80; J. Rohde, *EDNT* 3:148.

47. See Meier, "*Presbyteros* in the Pastoral Epistles," 340-44; Dibelius and Conzelmann, 71; Towner, *Goal,* 227; Marshall, 567-68; Johnson, 253; Lips, *Glaube,* 241-42. D. Daube (*The New Testament and Rabbinic Judaism* [London: Athlone, 1956], 244-46) and J. Jeremias ("*Presbyterion* ausserchristlich bezeugt," *ZNW* 48 [1957]: 127-32; "Zur Datierung der Pastoralbriefe," *ZNW* 52 [1961]: 101-4), on slightly different grounds, suggested that the term πρεσβυτέριον with its phrase denotes something like "investiture with the rank of elder." Apart from the fact that elsewhere Timothy is not regarded as an "elder" (and due to age may not have been qualified; see Fee, 111), the rabbinic practice allegedly behind the phrase seems overly obscure for the Ephesian context, especially in view of the collective meaning present in Ignatius; for further discussion, see also Meier, "*Presbyteros,*" 340-42; E. Lohse, *Die Ordination im Spätjudentum und im Neuen Testament* (Göttingen: Vandenhoeck & Ruprecht, 1951), 28; Marshall, 568-59; Bornkamm, *TDNT* 6:666 n. 92; Roloff, 258-59; Towner, *Goal,* 227.

personal, and since it is taken up with the relationship between the apostle and the coworker, reference to Paul's participation in the event alone is fitting. This is a reasonable way to reconcile the differences between the two descriptions, but it depends on the assumption that the events (and the "gifts") are identical. However, evidence will be given at 2 Tim 1:6 that suggests that the reference to "the gift of God" there is not identical with the "gift" referred to here.

A second solution, which in view of the differences between the texts seems marginally preferable, regards the two texts as reflecting on two different episodes in the life of Timothy. In 2 Tim 1:6 (see discussion), Paul recalls for Timothy the more fundamental moment in which he received the gift of the Holy Spirit "through the laying on of Paul's hands." This event may have coincided with Timothy's call to participate in the apostolic mission, which is entirely relevant to the theme of succession developed throughout 2 Timothy. The present passage reflects instead on a subsequent episode in which Timothy's authority to act on behalf of Paul was publicly recognized and endorsed by the Ephesian church leadership. Whether Paul was present for this rite or not is impossible to say, but it could have been carried out at his command in his absence on Timothy's arrival in Ephesus sometime after Paul's departure during those turbulent times referred to in Acts 20:1-4. Acts 13:1-3 provides the model for this sort of "appointment" to a temporary post in conjunction with prophetic guidance and with conferral or recognition of gifting/authority for the work.[48]

In all likelihood, then, Paul reminds both Timothy and the leadership in Ephesus that the coworker is duly authorized to represent the apostle and take the appropriate action in Ephesus (1:3). As reflection on a past ceremony implies, that church had already acknowledged Timothy's authority at an earlier time.

15-16 Paul now adds an exhortation that gathers the preceding thoughts together and looks at how Timothy's actions will affect others. Verse 15 appears at first to be superfluous since it adds no new content. Its function is to repeat the command of v. 14, which was cast in terms of the Spirit's gifting, and to shift the focus to Timothy's dedication.

The parallel imperatives, extending the theme of devotion already underscored in the imperatives of vv. 13-14 ("devote yourself to," "do not neglect"), reveal the emphasis: "be diligent in these matters," "give yourself

---

48. The view that the event is simply part of the fictitious aim of the letter to set Timothy up as the model minister, to provide apostolic endorsement for a later ordination rite and so on (see Oberlinner, 210; Hanson, 121; Brox, 42-46; et al.) depends entirely on the nonhistorical reading of the letter. Historical precedents for the sort of rite described (Acts 13:1-3, etc.) are easily (if not logically) ignored (cf. Roloff 257 n. 183; Bassler, 89).

wholly to them." The reflection is backward to the commands regarding Timothy's conduct and work (vv. 12-13). The first imperative *(meleta)* forms an assonant link to the immediately preceding imperative of v. 14 *(mē amelei)* that reinforces the continuity of the whole subsection. At the same time, its role in philosophical and moral contexts can be to enjoin cultivation or practice.[49] This emphasis on "doing" what has been set out as instruction links thematically with the exercise motif *(gymnaze/gymnasia)* used in support of godliness.[50]

The second imperative statement calls for Timothy's full devotion to these things.[51] With the same instructions in mind, nothing new is added but the stress on dedication ("be absorbed with, i.e., live and breathe these instructions and duties").

While Timothy's devotion to his good conduct and his duties would certainly have personal benefits, Paul attaches a purpose clause *(hina)* that focuses instead on the observations of others. Dedicated pursuit of "these matters" is to yield observable "progress."[52] This term figured in a current philosophical debate in which the Stoics stressed that moral progress or growth was the result of steady advancement through instruction and character development, while the Cynics were impatient with such tedious attention to Stoic dogma and the traditional religions.[53] Whether or not Paul was consciously taking sides, his view of "progress" (that the goal of parenesis was growth in the practice of moral conduct) and his parenetic style place him within the sort of didactic framework that shaped the Stoic approach, with certain key nuances (the Christ-event, the power of the Holy Spirit) needing to be factored in. The reference to the Spirit's gifting in v. 14 assures that Paul is not thinking of human effort alone in this process.[54] Instead, in keep-

49. Gk. μελετάω; the range of meaning includes "to meditate, reflect upon, plan" (Job 27:4; Sir 6:37; Acts 4:25), "to try, endeavor, take care to" *(Barnabas* 19.10), "to take great pains, practice, cultivate" (Epictetus 1.1.25; 2.1.29; *Barnabas* 21:7); BDAG; Marshall, 570 n. 140; *EDNT* 2:403.

50. See Epictetus 1.1.25.

51. For the imperative of εἰμί (ἴσθι; "be") in the sense of "be devoted to, occupied with" (BDAG, s.v. 3.c.), see Prov 23:17. The sense appears to be the result of a form of εἰμί modified by the preposition ἐν (as in Prov 23:17; Josephus, *Antiquities* 2.346; cf. N. Turner, *A Grammar of New Testament Greek* (ed. J. H. Moulton), Vol. 3: *Syntax* (Edinburgh: T&T Clark, 1963), 265.

52. Gk. προκοπή (Phil 1:12, 25; for the cognate verb, see 2 Tim 2:16; 3:9, 13); G. Stählin, *TDNT* 6:703-19; Spicq, *TLNT* 3:185-88; W. Schenk, *EDNT* 3:157-58; Lips, *Glaube,* 163-65.

53. See the discussions and references in Johnson, 254; Marshall, 570; see also Ferguson, *Backgrounds of Early Christianity,* 275-77, 285-87; T. Engberg-Pedersen, *Paul and the Stoics* (Edinburgh: T&T Clark, 2000), 36, 47, 57, 70-71, 109.

54. Cf. Stählin, *TDNT* 6:714, who places this statement within a broader NT

ing with his development of the "godliness" conception of authentic spirituality, he stresses that "progress" in this sense bears "visible"[55] marks (1 John 3:10; but cf. Gal 5:19). The watchful and critical eye of others in the church is already in mind (4:12); but now this becomes something of an audience (or flock)[56] capable of being influenced and presumably shaped by what is observed. Paul regards Timothy's development in the things he has set out as crucial not only to the mission's credibility in the apostle's absence but also to the growth of the congregation.[57]

Verse 16 brings together the concern for Timothy's own welfare and that of those among whom he works. Paul begins with Timothy, and the dual imperatives repeat what has already been said in other ways above. The first imperative, "watch closely" or "pay attention to,"[58] is applied to two aspects of Timothy's existence: "your life and doctrine." Probably, in this summary, Paul is dividing the parenesis above into two elements or categories. Thus on the one hand, Paul urges attentiveness to Timothy's own personal conduct and character (i.e., lit. "yourself"). On the other hand, Timothy is to be equally attentive to his faithfulness in communicating the apostolic teaching in the church.[59] The term translated "doctrine" is *didaskalia,* which may focus on the content or the activity of teaching, or, as here, hold the two elements in close conjunction (see on 1:10). The need for balance between these facets of the coworker's life (what one professes and how one lives) has already been evident in the parenesis (cf. 4:6-7, 12-13).

But the second summary command explicitly assembles these aspects of Timothy's life into a unified whole: "persevere in them."[60] The ref-

---

understanding of προκοπή as a grace gift of God (he also points out that for Philo, who took up the Stoic language, "the first and last source of all προκοπή is God Himself," 710).

55. Gk. φανερός (pred. adj.; Rom 1:19; 2:28[2x]; 1 Cor 3:13; 11:19; Phil 1:13). Cf. P.-G. Müller, *EDNT* 3:412-13; R. Bultmann and D. Lührmann, *TDNT* 9:2-3.

56. The dative plural adjective πᾶσιν can be construed as either neuter ("in all [things], in every respect") or, as in most translations (TNIV/NIV, NRSV), masculine ("to everybody").

57. The placement of the genitive pronoun "your" (σου) emphasizes the importance of Timothy's commitment in the situation; this is a case where I might opt for a translation using the passive voice to bring out the slight emphasis: "so that your progress might be visible to everyone [might be seen by everyone]" (cf. NRSV, TNIV/NIV).

58. Gk. ἐπέχω, when intransitive as here, means "pay attention to" (Luke 14:7; Acts 3:5); cf. the transitive sense "hold on to" (Phil 2:16).

59. "Paying attention to the teaching" (for Gk. διδασκαλία, see discussion at 1:10) might refer to Timothy's personal commitment to the apostle's teaching for his own spiritual growth, but the interest in Timothy's appointment and responsibility to teach (4:6, 13) suggests the interpretation followed here.

60. Gk. ἐπιμένω is literally "to stay" in a place (1 Cor 16:7, 8; cf. προσμένω in

erence in the neuter pronoun "them" will be either to the two aspects of Timothy's life just mentioned, or possibly to the whole of the teaching reflected back on in v. 15 ("these things"). Either way, it is the gathering together of Timothy's faithfulness as a teacher and in moral conduct into a coherent pattern of life that summarizes all of 4:6-16a. It is this pattern of life and ministry that holds so much promise for Timothy himself and for those to whom he ministers.

After the theological pause of 4:9-10, where Paul's mission and God's salvation were linked, it is not surprising to find a similar connection between Timothy's responsiveness and salvation. Paul closes the subsection by explaining ("for"; *gar*) that doing what has just been commanded (persisting in attention to himself and his teaching) will make Timothy an instrument of divine salvation. Although this thought of human instrumentality in God's salvation might seem at odds with 4:10 ("God is the Savior of all people"; cf. 2:3-4), the thought is thoroughly Pauline, echoing texts such as Rom 11:14; 1 Cor 7:16; 9:22. The gospel ministry is the effective means by which God saves people, and it is in this sense that Timothy may "save" (see on 1:15) himself and others.

The future tense of the verb ("will save") is not a denial that salvation is also a present aspect of Christian existence (cf. 1:15; 2 Tim 1:9);[61] rather, Paul envisions the potential influence that Timothy's life and teaching hold both for his own and the church's greater realization of God's salvation. Tying the fortunes of these two parties together is also Pauline (1 Cor 10:33; 9:22); as Paul's delegate, Timothy exists to serve others, and his realization of the fullness of salvation is incumbent on a faithfulness that stretches from personal character to the quality of his teaching and service to others.

Thus salvation through Christ, as mediated by the gospel and "the teaching" to "those who hear" responsively,[62] is a present reality. Authentic Christian existence, endangered by the false teachers, involves stepping into this experience in ever fuller ways. While there may be many ways to facilitate this growth, the chief elements are an understanding of the apostolic teaching (the gospel, doctrine, and its application in ethics) coupled with teachers whose lives reflect the transforming truth of what is taught. Conversely, the inattentiveness to life and teaching on the part of someone like Timothy (e.g., the false teachers) could have adverse effects (cf. 1 Cor 9:27).

1:3), but is figurative here, "to persist or persevere" in some course of action (Rom 6:1; 11:22, 23; Col 1:23; BDAG, s.v. 2).

61. Towner, *Goal*, 75-119.

62. Gk. ἀκούω ("to hear, listen"); it is Pauline to characterize believers as participants in the redemptive communication process, conceived of as proclamation and teaching of Christian truth and "hearing" it (2 Tim 1:13; 2:2, 14; 4:17; Rom 10:14; 15:21; Eph 1:13; Col 1:6, 9, 23).

2. Regarding Other Groups in God's Household (5:1–6:2a)

At this point, Paul shifts attention to other groups in the church. The continuation of the second-person singular imperatives (5:1, 3, 7, 11, 19, 20, 21, 22, 23) underscores Timothy's role as apostolic representative in the church and as primary recipient of the letter. There is greater emphasis in the instructions on his behavior or the care he takes exercising his leadership role in 5:1-2 and 17-25; otherwise, third-person singular and plural verbs show that the teaching concerning widows (5:3-16), elders and their assessment (5:17-25), and slaves (6:1-2a) is to be received and acted on by members of the groups addressed and, in some cases, by the larger community as a whole. 5:1-2 takes up Timothy's appropriate demeanor toward age groups. 5:3-16 addresses the matter of widows in the church. In 5:17-25 Paul gives instructions to guide Timothy in the administration of elders. Finally, 6:1-2 adapts traditional parenesis to Christian slaves for the local situation.

a. Proper Treatment of Age Groups (5:1-2)

> 1 *Do not rebuke an older man harshly, but exhort him as if he were your father. Treat younger men as brothers, 2 older women as mothers, and younger women as sisters, with absolute purity.*

This brief set of instructions consists of a single Greek sentence. Although it exhibits syntactical symmetry,[1] the first and last groups receive greater attention. The significance of appropriate demeanor toward age groups is explained partly by the attention paid to age and gender groups in Greek moral teaching,[2] and partly, in this case, by the sensitive issue of Timothy's age already raised in 4:12. This latter observation suggests one of the links between this subsection and what precedes it. But there would be different dynamics at work as Timothy crosses the various generational and gender lines. In the case of older men, peers, and older women, the issue would be that of a younger man having authority to teach and what that means for the rules of respect in the case of elders and peers. There is an additional concern where Timothy would come into contact with younger women — that of safeguarding sexual purity.

---

1. After ruling out adopting a harsh disciplinary attitude toward older men, one positive verb governs all the groups considered, with the fourfold use of the conjunction ὡς ("as") in each case describing the fictive relationship Timothy is to adopt toward each age and gender group. The TNIV/NIV decisions (1) to break the sentence after "father" and (2) to change the positive verb from "exhort" to "treat" disturb the symmetry unnecessarily (cf. NRSV).

2. For examples from the literature, see Dibelius and Conzelmann, 72; Marshall, 572-73.

At the same time, the following detailed treatment of widows may well grow out of the brief reference to "older women" in v. 2.[3] And to the degree that "elders" as church leaders overlaps with "elders" as older men in the community, 5:1-2 also serves as a general introduction to vv. 17-25. Similarly, in the fictive family context envisioned in 5:1-2, with its rules of interaction, slaves and their relationship to masters can easily be contained. Consequently, the decision to isolate 5:1-2 is largely one of convenience: the specific instructions given to guide Timothy's interactions with the various household groups establish the general framework for 5:3–6:2a.

On the whole, the impression is that the fellowship is to operate with the notions of respect and intimacy proper to a family. In this case the kinship is fictive (thus the repeated use of "as"), but the force of the dynamic of kinship would strengthen the cohesion of the otherwise diverse group of believers and provide the church with the structural and behavioral paradigm of family responsibilities and rules for relating.[4] Just as the life and activities of the blood family were carefully patterned according to age and gender, so the faith family was to be ordered. This fictive transference of kinship and family dynamics to other groups goes back to earlier moral writings.[5]

1 Paul first addresses Timothy's way of relating to men. "Older" *(presbyteros)* in this context is primarily a comparative category of age (1 Pet 5:5).[6] A precise age-range is difficult to pin down (see 4:12 and note; Titus 2:2-3), but depending on which classification of ages Paul followed, an "older man" would be at least older than forty and possibly older than fifty. However, despite the breakdown of age and gender groups that seems to require "older" here to be generic and not a reference to status, two things complicate the interpretation. First, Paul has just used a cognate term, *presbyterion,* in reference to the committee of elders who lead the church (4:14), and in 5:17 and 19 these elders will be mentioned again. Second, in that later reference there will be discussion about the disciplinary process to be followed in the case of erring elders. It is germane here to point out that probably part of Timothy's task in Ephesus was to correct the leadership, which had come under the influence of the false teaching. That leadership would have consisted of men drawn from the age range above Timothy's. And since the activity Paul prohibits as the younger coworker relates to older men could

---

3. Cf. the discussion in Johnson, 269.

4. See Osiek and Balch, *Families in the New Testament World,* 165-66.

5. E.g., Plato, *Republic* 5.463C.

6. John 8:9; Acts 2:17. For πρεσβύτερος, see the discussion at 3:1. See the related term πρεσβύτης in Titus 2:2; Phlm 9; cf. Titus 2:3. Quinn-Wacker, 411, suggest that the singular, "older man," which envisions a man-to-man confrontation, is thus distinguished from the leader or "elder," who is to be corrected publicly (5:19-20).

describe a "harsh disciplinary rebuke,"[7] it seems possible that Paul at this point is thinking ahead to 5:19 and how Timothy should exercise his authority to correct elders. The precise reference in "older man" therefore remains unclear. In any case, Timothy's appropriate action and attitude are described with a term that encompasses "exhorting, urging, encouraging, consoling and comforting" (see 1:3, discussion and note; cf. Acts. 16:39; 1 Cor 4:13; 1 Thess 2:12). Here it will involve correction that is done in a conciliatory and positive way, one that seeks to restore fellowship rather than to isolate those in error.

The comparison "as a father" contributes the underlying moral logic. Within the Greco-Roman (and Jewish) family, the father was owed complete respect (cf. Sir 3:12-14). The application of the kinship model transfers household degrees of respect to the church. Elsewhere, in a similar way Paul took up the fictive position of father in relation to the converts (= children) in his churches (1 Thess 2:11-12; see also the qualification "as a father"). In this instance the situation is reversed, and Timothy is called on to treat even older men in need of correction with a certain deference and politeness that will ensure that the correction is unifying rather than divisive.

In the case of "younger men,"[8] which here means "those younger than the older men," Timothy is to exhort and correct in the same way (the one verb governs all the objects). But the fictive relationship that shapes his demeanor in this case is that of "brother." The term was used widely to describe the status of believers as siblings in God's family (see 4:6, discussion). Its effect on the instructions is to imply an attitude of mutuality such as might be expected among peer-members of the same group. This does not reduce Timothy's authority as the apostle's delegate, but rather shapes how that authority will be expressed.

2 Women in the church are also considered in the categories of older and younger, and the instructions are parallel to those shaping Timothy's demeanor with men. Within the fictive family framework constructed here, Timothy is to exhort "older women"[9] with the deference a son should show to a "mother."[10] The respect is the same as Paul reflects in Rom 16:13, and also corresponds to the high esteem in which the wider culture held mothers.[11]

"Younger women," corresponding to younger men,[12] are to be ex-

---

7. Gk. ἐπιπλήσσω (only here in NT; Josephus, *Antiquities* 1.246; Philo, *Allegorical Interpretation* 2.46); MM, s.v.

8. Gk. νεώτερος (masc. comparative of νέος, Titus 2:6).

9. Gk. πρεσβυτέρα (fem. form of πρεσβύτερος, only here in NT; LXX Gen 29:26; Ezek 16:16; see πρεσβῦτις for "older women" in Titus 2:3).

10. Gk. μήτηρ; see 2 Tim 1:5.

11. E.g., Philo, *On the Decalogue* 120; W. Michaelis, *TDNT* 4:642.

12. Gk. νεωτέρα (fem. comparative of νέος, 5:11, 14; cf. νέας in Titus 2:4).

horted as "sisters."[13] The relationship of brother-sister implies mutuality of obligation. But Paul immediately adds the prepositional phrase, "with absolute purity." This phrase repeats the concluding trait Timothy is to model before his dissenters who mistrust his "youth" (see on 4:12), but it also intensifies the requirement by adding the adjective "all" ("absolute, complete, utter"; cf. 2:2, 11; 2 Tim 4:2). Undoubtedly, the added stipulation refers to sexual purity and seeks to prevent Timothy from getting into a situation in which his propriety could be called into question. The subsequent reference in 5:11 to the sensual appetites of certain "younger widows," quite possibly under the influence of the trend of the "new Roman woman," suggests that in the present situation Paul regards the danger of sexual impropriety (or accusations to that effect) as being especially acute for Timothy.

b. Proper Treatment of Widows (5:3-16)

3 *Give proper recognition to those widows who are really in need.* 4 *But if a widow has children or grandchildren, these should learn first of all to put their religion into practice by caring for their own family and so repaying their parents and grandparents, for this is pleasing to God.* 5 *The widow who is really in need and left all alone puts her hope in God and continues night and day to pray and to ask God for help.* 6 *But the widow who lives for pleasure is dead even while she lives.* 7 *Give the people these instructions, so that no one may be open to blame.* 8 *Anyone who does not provide for their relatives, and especially for their own household, has denied the faith and is worse than an unbeliever.*

9 *No widow may be put on the list of widows unless she is over sixty, has been faithful to her husband,* 10 *and is well known for her good deeds, such as bringing up children, showing hospitality, washing the feet of the Lord's people, helping those in trouble and devoting herself to all kinds of good deeds.*

11 *As for younger widows, do not put them on such a list. For when their sensual desires overcome their dedication to Christ, they want to marry.* 12 *Thus they bring judgment on themselves, because they have broken their first pledge.* 13 *Besides, they get into the habit of being idle and going about from house to house. And not only do they become idlers, but also busybodies who talk nonsense, saying things they ought not to.* 14 *So I counsel younger widows to marry, to*

---

13. Gk. ἀδελφή; of a literal sibling (Acts 23:16; Rom 16:15); of a female believer (Rom 16:1; 1 Cor 7:15).

*have children, to manage their homes and to give the enemy no oppor-
tunity for slander.* 15 *Some have in fact already turned away to follow
Satan.*

16 *If any woman who is a believer has widows in her care, she
should continue to help them and not let the church be burdened with
them, so that the church can help those widows who are really in
need.*

Paul's teaching concerning widows in the church is the most extensive treatment of a group in the whole letter. While this indicates a problem of some
scope and urgency, the nature of the situation that Paul addressed continues
to be debated, and a brief introduction to the discussion will help focus the
treatment of the text to follow.

Essentially, there are questions of history, identification, and structure
that need to be addressed. Within the first category, the question is raised
whether the passage assumes the existence of an order or sisterhood of widows in the church.[14] Several lines of evidence are offered in support. First,
5:3 refers to the "honor" that is due the "real" widow, which, on the model of
5:17, where the cognate noun "honor" includes the thought of remuneration
in some sense, might be understood to refer to payment corresponding to an
office.[15] Second, the reference in 5:9 to "enrollment" on a list might suggest
formal acceptance into an order of widows.[16] Third, the similarity between
the lists of requirements pertaining to the widows (5:9-10) and those pertaining to the bishop and deacon (3:1-13) might indicate that enrolled widows
were regarded in the same official and formal sense.[17] Fourth, 5:12 is taken
by many to infer a vow of celibacy as a condition of enrollment, indicative,
yet again, of an official order.[18]

Some of these data are incorporated into the feminist reconstruction
that discovers in the instructions a reflection of the author's patriarchal suppression of an active women's ministry in the church — his goal being to
limit access to the group and restrict its activities to the domestic sphere. The

14. E.g., Bartsch, *Die Anfänge urchristlicher Rechtsbildungen,* 112-43; Dibelius
and Conzelmann, 73-74; Verner, *The Household of God,* 161-66; B. B. Thurston, *The
Widows: A Women's Ministry in the Early Church* (Minneapolis: Fortress, 1989); J. M.
Bassler, "The Widow's Tale: A Fresh Look at 1 Tim 5:3-16," *JBL* 103 (1984): 23-41;
Bassler, 92-98; Wagener, *Die Ordnung des "Hauses Gottes,"* 114-233.

15. J. Müller-Bardorff, "Zur Exegese von 1 Tim 5:3-16," in G. Delling, ed., *Gott
und die Götter* (Berlin: Evangelische Verlagsanstalt, 1958), 114-15; Lips, *Glaube,* 119;
Johnson, 260-61 (honor in the form of financial support); cf. Bassler, 92.

16. Bassler, 96; Müller-Bardorff, "1 Tim 5:3-16," 118-19.

17. Müller-Bardorff, "1 Tim 5:3-16," 120-21.

18. Verner, *Household of God,* 164; Roloff, 285-86; Bassler, 97; Hanson, 98.

development and formalization of the women's order, as the argument goes, was at least partly a response to oppressive patriarchal tendencies to sideline women; the group provided a framework for the affirmation and freedom of women.[19]

However one reads the data (see below), the question is whether either permutation of this interpretation is really necessitated by the text. Viewing the passage instead within the social worlds of Judaism and Greco-Roman culture suggests a rather more straightforward understanding of the parenesis. From Israel's earliest times, God was known as the defender of widows (Deut 10:18; 24:17). "Doing justice" was at least partly measured by the treatment of widows (Isa 1:17). And honoring God's concern for widows became an intrinsic element in the keeping of the covenant, which the early church recognized as one of its responsibilities (Acts 6:1; Jas 1:27). In Jewish communities, the synagogue and wider community leadership provided an institutionally structured mechanism for ensuring that both daily and longer-term requirements of the needy were met.

In the Greco-Roman world, generally, the female obtained her status and social identity by virtue of being "embedded" in a male — first her father, and then passing from his household and that "embedding" to "embedding" in her husband and his family. This was at least how things were understood in the traditional mainstream. As Malina explains, "Females are always perceived as embedded in some male unless they find themselves in the anomalous situation of being a widow or divorcée without kin."[20] It is precisely this "anomalous situation" that Paul seeks to address, but an additional cultural trend outside the mainstream — that of the new Roman woman already considered in 1 Tim 2:9-15 — may make the background to this text still more "anomalous" (see below). In any case, various solutions were open to the church to ensure that widows were not dishonored, and providing church support was only one of those options. The death of a husband raised questions about the disposition of the dowry (given by the wife's family to the husband for oversight). The widow might find herself without support if the dowry, as part of the husband's property, were to pass directly to his children, if she were too old or otherwise unable to remarry (the normal recourse), or if there were neither dowry nor family to provide for her needs. In such cases, the state would provide *providentia*.[21] But in Judaism and Greco-

19. See Bassler, "Widow's Tale"; Wagener, *Die Ordnung des "Hauses Gottes"*; cf. the discussion in Johnson, 270-72.

20. B. J. Malina, *The New Testament World: Insights from Cultural Anthropology* (rev. ed.; Louisville: Westminster/John Knox, 1993), 143.

21. B. W. Winter, "*Providentia* for the Widows of 1 Timothy 5.3-16," *TynB* 39 (1988), 83-99; idem, *Seek the Welfare of the City: Christians as Benefactors and Citizens* (Grand Rapids: Eerdmans, 1993), ch. 3.

Roman society it was first the responsibility of the family to provide for its widows.

Given the sensitivity of the church to its widows, it is reasonable to assume that the church as a community would mobilize itself to meet the needs of widows who had neither private means nor family to care for them. Acts 6:1-6 reflects one such instance of community care for widows, as well as an example of the sort of complications that might arise. And later Christian writings suggest that care for widows was regarded by the church as an ever-present responsibility.[22] We can see in 1 Tim 5:3-16 evidence not only of problems but also of measures taken to care for widows that place the text into what we know to have been the social framework of that time. Family support of widows was expected as a first line of care (5:4, 8, 16), though this responsibility was also apparently being neglected (5:8). But the passage assumes the existence of a community mechanism for the support of widows (a list or roster of eligible widows; 5:9), and suggests that some form of abuse of this mechanism had occurred. On the one hand, younger widows, quite possibly caught up in the new definition of "woman," who could have remarried were choosing a more liberated, single path, and still receiving support from the church. Not only did this add to the financial strain on the church, but their questionable behavior (subsidized by the church!) was threatening the community's reputation with those outside. On the other hand, the financial strain itself on a small church, caused by supporting increasing numbers of widows, needed to be relieved. To address these matters, Paul gives instructions to limit church support to those who prove to be "real widows."

This leads to the question of identification. In view of the factors just introduced, Paul instructs Timothy how to define the "real widow" and thus reduce the ranks of those receiving support. Various requirements aim to shorten the list: genuine financial need (lack of family to support); sixty-year minimum age. Younger widows are to be excluded. To the standard criteria cited for this exclusion — (a) still vital physical drives will make them want to remarry, (b) their reliance on community support encourages idleness, (c) possibly some association with the heresy — should be added the further complicating possibility that these young widows were caught up in a radical trend of behavior associated with the emergence of the "new woman" in the Roman Empire (see on 2:9-10; see further below).[23] In this case, young (and wealthy) widows present a problem that is not just the incidental outcome of an unwise allocation of church support, nor necessarily one that is linked

22. Ignatius, *To the Smyrnaeans* 13.1; Ignatius, *To Polycarp* 4.1; Polycarp, *To the Philippians* 4.3; *Didascalia Apostolorum* 14.

23. Winter, *Roman Wives, Roman Widows*, 128-37.

only with the heresy. Rather, as the treatment of certain well-to-do women in 2:9-10 suggests, a convergence of factors lay behind the problem. Some attraction to and exploitation by the opposition may well be present, but the language and the behavior Paul associates with these young widows place them within the framework of that emerging libertarian movement of women whose values and aims suggest something approaching a sexual revolution. In the case of young widows — young vital women, now released from the confines of marriage — their possible absorption into this trend can be posited on the basis of their behavior and promiscuous lifestyle characterized by the sexual freedoms typically granted to men. It has never been sufficient to explain this pattern on the basis of involvement in the heresy itself; but it is not beyond thinking that the opposition could have had something to gain by encouraging young widows not to reenter marriage.

It hardly needs to be said that the characteristics of this free-wheeling promiscuous lifestyle were at odds with the values by which the church sought to be known, and by which Paul identified authentic Christian existence. The apostle's concern is both to staunch the flow of promiscuity and to protect the Christian community's reputation.

Consequently, young and wealthy widows were not to be supported by the church, but were rather to reenter an appropriate marriage. In the case of other needy widows, the bottom line again appears to be Paul's insistence that the church step into the gap where the "anomalous situation" (a widow without kin) truly existed.

Paul, then, envisions three categories of widows. The first category consists of the "real widow" who will be genuinely without support and meet the age and moral requirements (vv. 3, 5, 6, 7, 9, 10, 16b). Second is the widow who is not necessarily young but who has family members to care for her (vv. 4, 6, 16a). Third is the category including the young widow and the wealthy widow with sufficient resources to live a life of luxury (vv. 6, 11-15). This group presents a particular problem or set of problems. They are described by Paul as "turning away to follow Satan." This is the sort of language Paul will use to denounce false teachers; but similarities in the tone of his polemical language need only mean that he has painted young widows and heretics with the same brush (see below). The actual degree to which involvement with the false teaching is the source of their problems is, again, not clear. While certain neutral requirements can be applied to rule out supporting this third category (e.g., age, remarriageability, etc.), it must be recalled that remarriage and reentry into the domestic sphere was designed equally to stop their active participation in the "new woman" trend and distance them from the heretical front.

The passage forms a unitary whole, bracketed at each end by the concern for "the real widow" (5:3, 16b), who is also defined by the requirements

336

in 5:9-10.[24] Within the passage, Paul addresses indirectly three clusters of people, who cycle in and out of view.

> 5:3 — Support "real widows"
> 5:4, 7-8, 16a — Family responsibility toward widows
> 5:5, 9-10 — "Real widows"
> 5:6, 11-15 — Young (and loose-living) widows
> 5:16b — The church will support "real widows"

The paragraphing of the TNIV translation supplied above corresponds to this cycling through topics. Two translational problems should be noted. First, the TNIV's attempt at v. 8 to neutralize the NIV's gender-specific "if anyone . . . *his* . . ." with the inclusive alternative "anyone who . . . *their* . . ." is unnecessarily awkward (cf. NRSV), though the intention is surely correct. Second, the rendering of the opening command, "Give proper recognition to" (cf. NRSV, "honor"), while open enough to interpretation, is perhaps a little too tentative to catch the material implications of the command.

3 Paul opens this section by laying down the controlling instruction, which is translated here literally for the moment: "Honor widows who are in truth widows." The command immediately raises two questions — the first occasioned by Paul's choice of the verb "to honor"; the second is a question Paul purposely addresses to the community.

The "honor" word group occurs three times in the longer section: as a verb in 5:3, and as a noun in 5:17 and 6:1.[25] The verb can cover a range of meanings, and the best translation will both fit the present context and make sense of the background. A reference to the acknowledgment of "respect" clearly does not do full justice to the intention of the passage.[26] On the one hand, it would be unlikely that Paul would restrict "respect" in this sense only to one category of widow. On the other hand, the passage draws out the implication of "honor" in very material terms. Consequently, while it is incorrect to interpret the verb as commanding "payment" to qualified widows,[27] "honor" should be understood to mean something like "provide the

24. See Towner, *Goal,* 180-82. For other explanations of structure, see Verner, *Household of God,* 161-66 (esp. 161).

25. Gk. τιμάω (noun in 1:17 [see discussion]; 5:17; 6:1, 16); see J. Schneider, *TDNT* 8:169-80; H. Hübner, *EDNT* 3:357-59; A. Sand, "Witwenstand und Ämterstruktur in den urchristlichen Gemeinden," *BibLeb* 12 (1971): 193-97.

26. But cf. Hanson, 96; Oberlinner, 223-24; Dibelius and Conzelmann, 73.

27. *Contra* Wagener, *Die Ordnung des "Hauses Gottes,"* 144-49; Bartsch, *Die Anfänge urchristlicher Rectsbildungen,* 118; Müller-Bardorff, "1 Tim 5:3-16," 115. Appeal to later church orders (esp. by Bartsch), in which the term does indicate payment, is anachronistic and fails to observe the interpretative help provided by the parallel state-

support that honor demands."[28] That is to say, the subtext of the "honor" command is explicitly material. This is borne out additionally by the parallel statement in v. 16b, where "honor," already developed in terms of practical support (vv. 4, 8), is paraphrased with a verb meaning "to assist or aid."

In addition to the well-defined concern for widows that had become emblematic of covenant faithfulness (Deut 10:18; 24:17; Isa 1:17; Acts 6:1; Jas 1:27), Paul may intentionally echo the similarly framed fifth command-ment ("Honor your father and mother") that in Greek translation utilizes the same verb (Exod 20:12; Deut 5:16; Mark 7:10; 10:19; Luke 18:20; Eph 6:2). This commandment assumed the responsibility of the children to provide for their elderly parents; its quotation in Mark 7:10 is central to the discussion of a problem of withholding support from parents. If in our passage an allusion to this commandment seems more pertinent to 5:4 and 8, where blood rela-tives are in view, it should be recalled that 5:1-2 already extended family re-lationships and responsibilities in a way that allows Timothy and the rest of the church here to view "real widows" as mothers. As we will see, the re-sponsibility to provide for widows falls first to actual blood-family members; but in the absence of family members, the church is to view "real widows" within the framework of the fifth commandment.[29]

The second question that concerns us is the one implied by Paul's stipulation: "widows who are really in need." The term "widow" might ex-tend to include more than just those women whose husbands had died (e.g., women practicing celibacy, virgins, and wives who were abandoned by hus-bands, or who separated from their husbands and families to serve the church).[30] But the requirements concerning faithfulness to one's husband and raising children in 5:9-10 suggest that by "widow" Paul means a woman whose husband had died. By adding the qualifier "real, actual, genuine,"[31] he implies a refinement of the meaning of "widow" as the term or category pertains to material conditions. In what follows he will reveal the relevant criteria; these will include not only the presence of conditions that make her truly in need of church support but also the presence of authentic marks of faith.

---

ment in 5:16b: "so that the church might provide assistance for those who are real wid-ows" (see Towner, *Goal,* 183; Verner, *Household of God,* 163), which moves the meaning of the term away from remuneration and toward support.

28. Johnson, 260-61, 273-74; Marshall, 582; Verner, *Household of God,* 163.

29. Cf. Winter, *Seek the Welfare of the City,* 69.

30. Gk. χήρα (5:4, 9, 11, 16; Acts 6:1; 1 Cor 7:8; Jas 1:27; etc. G. Stählin, *TDNT* 9:440-65). For various attempts to broaden the meaning, cf. Wagener, *Die Ordnung des "Hauses Gottes,"* 132; Bassler, 93-94.

31. Gk. ὄντως (adv. in attributive position = adj.; 5:6, 16; 6:19; 1 Cor 14:25; Gal 3:25; etc.); BDAG.

4 A first conditional statement[32] introduces the basic parameters by which the category of "real" widow can be defined and those outside them can be disqualified. The first consideration concerns genuinely elderly widows who "have"[33] living family members. For those widows who do have relatives, the relatives themselves come under Paul's indirect instruction. Assuming the advanced age of the widow in this case, "children" (see 1:2, note) and "grandchildren"[34] refer to adult relatives who are then able to step in and carry out the responsibilities of the deceased husband.

Specifically, these family members[35] are to "learn" (see on 2:11) what their "first" priority is.[36] Paul first places this within the theological and ethical category of "godliness," and then explores the meaning in more practical terms. Behind the translation "to put their religion into practice" is the infinitive of the verb related to the *eusebeia* word group that Paul employs strikingly in these letters to define authentic Christian existence (see 2:2, Excursus). It is not at all surprising to find the concept drawn on here, since in Greek culture "piety" ("godliness") was at root that attitude of reverence and respect owed to, among others, relatives.[37] The translation just noted attempts to express Paul's expanded theological conception of this attitude, developed from use of the word group to describe faithfulness to the covenant in the LXX. For Paul, "godliness" is the integration of the inward faith-commitment and outward faith-response that should characterize belief in God. Here a particular outward expression of faith is in view, and the impli-

32. See vv. 8, 16; see the discussion at 3:1 and the note.

33. Gk. ἔχω ("have") is here used to express family relationships (3:4; Titus 1:6; BDAG, s.v. 2.a; Winter, *Seek the Welfare of the City,* 72-73).

34. Gk. ἔκγονος (neut. pl. "descendants, grandchildren"; only here in NT; freq. in LXX); BDAG.

35. The shift from the singular widow as subject in the protasis to a plural verb (Gk. μανθανέτωσαν; see discussion at 2:11), taking a plural subject, is somewhat awkward and has led to an alternative interpretation (note the secondary singular reading μανθανέτω, "let her learn," in some Western witnesses; 945 d f m vg), i.e., that the widow is charged to care for her children and so pay back her parents for care she received (Bassler, 94-96; Wagener, *Die Ordnung des "Hauses Gottes,"* 149-54; G. Stählin, *TDNT* 9:453-54; Roloff, 287-88). However, this alternative reading does not sit well with v. 5 or v. 16 (both of which conform to and establish the overall thrust of the passage; i.e., families, first and foremost, are to care for widows and so relieve the church's burden), which (in reference to a widow who is truly alone and without support) makes smoothest sense as a contrast to a widow having a family to support her. Equally, the alternative reading makes the shift from singular verb to plural (from widow as subject to widows) unnecessary (especially when it is observed that a sg./sg. pattern is maintained in the identical "if anyone" conditions in vv. 8 and 16; though cf. 2:15). See further Marshall, 583-85.

36. On this use of πρῶτος ("first, in the first place"), see 2:1 (note), 1:15 (note).

37. See also Spicq, *TLNT* 1:96 n. 6.

cation will be that "godliness" practiced in relation to "their own family"[38] is an outworking of genuine faith.[39] The emphasis placed on this as a "first" priority suggests that it was being ignored.

A parallel infinitive construction ("and so repaying their parents and grandparents") defines the intended aim of caring for widowed relatives and places the obligation within a broader framework of filial devotion. First, this act of godliness is conceived of here, in a rather redundant expression, as a reasonable "repayment of a return."[40] Second, its meaning is completed by reference to their forebears, which here means living relatives born earlier, expressing the counterpart to "children and grandchildren" above (i.e., "parents and grandparents").[41] A family's care for its needy "widows" thus fulfills the obligation of the younger to make a return to older relatives.

This insistence on filial responsibilities pervaded traditional Greco-Roman society, a fact that underlies the caustic criticism of 5:8. But whatever this value might add to the appeal, Paul does not base this instruction on natural law or Greek philosophy. Rather, at this point Paul inserts for the second time in this letter a formulaic reason that makes the will of God as expressed in Torah the framework for ethics: "for this is pleasing to God" (see on 2:3). On the model of the "acceptable" sacrifice from Leviticus, the care of family members for older relatives is behavior that accords with God's will. Here the allusion will again be to the fifth commandment, which came into view in 5:3 (cf. Eph 6:1-2).

5-6 Following the instruction that is to cover widows with family are guidelines that set out consecutively criteria for defining, in contrast, the "real widow" without family and "the disqualified widow." Verse 5 describes the real widow in terms of her critical situation and the dependence on God that this creates. First is the fact that she has been "left all alone."[42] This descrip-

---

38. Gk. τὸν ἴδιον οἶκον (lit. "one's own household"; for the sg. with a pl. verb, see note above; for the phrase and discussion see 3:4, 5); the phrase places care for a widowed relative within the more general category of obligations toward one's household, and the scope of "household" exceeds the limits of the modern Western concept of "family."

39. Pace Roloff, 288, who maintains that the act envisioned is faith-motivated only if the widow is being called upon to serve her family. But Paul has infused the concept with a dynamic theology, so that even if it begins from a common cultural understanding of filial piety, it finishes as an ethical aspect of the Spirit's influence in a believer's life.

40. For the combination, as here, of ἀμοιβή (only here in the NT; "return, recompense," BDAG; Spicq, *TLNT* 1:95-96) and the verb ἀποδίδωμι ("to pay back, return, recompense"; BDAG, s.v. 4; see 2 Tim 4:8, 14), see Josephus, *Antiquities* 5.13.

41. Gk. πρόγονοι; in the NT only here and 2 Tim 1:3 (where it means "ancestors"; cf. Philo, *On the Embassy to Gaius* 54.2; see BDAG). As a description of living parents, see Plato, *Laws* 11.931D.

42. Gk. μονόω (perf. pass.; only here in the NT; "to be left alone, solitary"). Cf. the

tion implies the death of her husband and the absence of a supporting family (children). But the language draws also on the thematic description in Judaism of the widow who has fallen through the social safety net (or has been marginalized): she is bereft of husband and family, unprotected, and poor.[43]

Second, the real widow is the one in this predicament who "has put her hope in God." This is "hope" in the Christian sense of determined trust in God's promises (see 1:1; 4:10). In Paul, the perfect tense of the verb depicts emblematically the unique Christian posture of confident anticipation of God's intervention and provision (4:10; 6:17; 2 Cor 1:10; cf. 1 Cor 15:19). But the background is the psalmists' dominant framing of Israel's faith and worship in terms of "placing hope in YHWH."[44]

Dire circumstances have perhaps accelerated the real widow to a place of faith that is exemplary in a community that is corporately responsible to exercise prayer (Eph 6:18; 1 Thess 5:17). And her posture of hope in God has shaped a life characterized by a steadfast practice of prayer.[45] The TNIV rendering, "to pray . . . to ask for help," translates two words that denote "petitions" (or "requests") and "prayers" (in general).[46] While specific requests might refer to her reliance on God for basic provisions, the second more general term for prayer suggests a wider intercessory scope for this activity. "Night and day" is a favorite phrase in Paul for expressing the idea of devotion and constancy of effort in carrying out some task.[47] As a whole, the description recalls such models of prayer in the tradition of piety as Hannah

---

similar thematic description of the widow (χήρα καὶ μόνη; "widow and alone") in LXX 4 Macc 16:10 (Isa 49:21; Lam 1:1).

43. Wagener, *Die Ordnung des "Hauses Gottes,"* 135-43, insists, largely on the basis of descriptions of Esther and Asenath (Add Esth 4:17[1] [Rahlfs]; cf. *Joseph and Asenath* 11.3, 16; 12.5, 13-14; 13.2), that the language "on her own" is figurative, signifying a degree of spirituality, not material need. It may be suggested, however, that these two figures represent an exception to the broader theme of the destitute and helpless widow whose plight is regularly imagined in LXX Deut 10:18; 14:29; 16:11; Pss 108:9; 145:9; 4 Macc 16:10; etc., which is then applied as a description of Israel in exile (Isa 49:21; Lam 1:1).

44. See LXX Pss 4:6; 5:12; 7:2; 9:11; 12:6; 15:1; 16:7; 17:3, 31; etc.

45. Gk. ῃρουμένῳ (1:3), with a dative of thing (BDAG, s.v. 1.b), indicates continuity of practice (Acts 13:43; cf. 11:23).

46. For the prayer terms, Gk. δέησις, προσευχή, see the discussion and notes at 2:1. The intention of the definite articles before each noun (ταῖς δεήσεσιν καὶ ταῖς προσευχαῖς) is uncertain. For the view that "appointed prayers" might be meant, see Kelly, 114; Lock, 58. But cf. the similar constructions of Phil 4:6 and Col 4:12, where such formality is not implied.

47. Gk. νυκτὸς καὶ ἡμέρας. P. G. Müller, *EDNT* 2:482-83. See 2 Tim 1:3; Mark 5:5; Luke 2:37; Acts 9:24; 20:31 (Luke's description of Paul's devotion in Ephesus); 26:7; 1 Thess 2:9; 3:10; 2 Thess 3:8; Rev 4:8; 7:15; 12:10; 14:11; 20:10.

(1 Samuel 1) and Anna the widow (Luke 2:37; cf. *4 Ezra* 9:44) and, in any case, circumscribes carefully this category of widow.

The widow of v. 6, however, presents a dramatic contrast, and her appearance at this stage is puzzling. Who is she? She is well-to-do and characterized as "living for pleasure" ("living in luxury"), which clearly recalls the women caricatured in 2:9.[48] Some see in this vivid language[49] a reference to sexual impropriety,[50] to self-centeredness,[51] or to selfish indulgence and therefore implicitly a failure to share her wealth with the needy (Ezek 16:49; Jas 5:5).[52] Paul's warnings about wealth (6:6-10) and critique of self-indulgent pretension in the case of a certain group of women (2:9) culminate here in a dramatic contrast to the poor widow. She "is dead even while she lives."[53] Probably all of the above nuances converge as this brief but graphic reference to the luxury of certain widows introduces the image of the widow as "new woman" at this point.[54] The fuller description of the young widows (5:11-15) will develop this image further, but it is needed here for the contrast it presents. This widow's glamorous outward appearance paradoxically conceals a profound state of inward spiritual death. Implicitly, in contrast to the real widow, this woman, whose membership in the church is uncertain, should receive no support from the church, nor should she expect any.

7 Paul pauses ("give the people these instructions"), as he does throughout the letter, to add this material to the growing parenetic curriculum Timothy is to "teach" within the community.[55] The reference to instructions

---

48. *Pace* Mounce, 283, who finds the description synonymous with that of the young widows in 5:11, and argues that wealth is not implied.

49. Gk. σπαταλάω (aor. ptc.; Jas 5:5; LXX Ezek 16:49; Sir 21:15; cf. Prov 29:21); Wagener, *Die Ordnung des "Hauses Gottes,"* 155-61.

50. So Hanson, 97; Easton, 152.

51. Mounce, 283.

52. Marshall, 588; Johnson, 262-63; Collins, 138; Wagener, *Die Ordnung des "Hauses Gottes,"* 155-161.

53. Gk. ζῶσα τέθνηκεν (for similar descriptions, see Rev 3:1; Hermas, *Similitude* 6.1.6; Philo, *On Flight and Finding* 55; see further refs. in Dibelius and Conzelmann, 74 n. 11). Turner, *A Grammar of New Testament Greek,* 4:102, maintains that this oxymoron is distinctive of the style of these letters to coworkers. But Paul surely employs something similar in 2 Cor 6:9: ὡς ἀποθνῄσκοντες καὶ ἰδοὺ ζῶμεν ("as dying and behold we live"). In the latter text, Paul describes his apostolic condition, employing the paradox (with opposite effect) to underscore the more profound reality of the unseen life. The same principle is true in the case of self-indulgent widows, whose real condition (spiritual death) is thinly covered by an outward appearance of life.

54. Cf. Winter, *Roman Wives,* 129-31.

55. Gk. καὶ ταῦτα παράγγελλε. The addition of καί (cf. 4:11) in the sense of "also, as well," and the summarizing ταῦτα (3:14; 4:6, 11, 15; 5:17, 21; 6:2) form the series of instructions into a whole.

(lit. "these things") is imprecise, but the reflection points backward to vv. 3-6 or some part of it.[56]

The purpose of these commands is that "no one may be open to blame." "Blamelessness" (i.e., to be "beyond reproach"; see on 3:2) is a measure of public acceptability, signifying that no grounds for (public) reproach exist, and here in this matter of caring for widows, as in 3:2-7 in the case of the overseer, Paul reflects his sensitivity to the critical eye of secular society. This much is clear.

But whose "blamelessness" does Paul seek to ensure? The TNIV translation offered above ("Give the people these instructions . . .") is a slight reshaping of the text (lit. "teach these things also, that they might be blameless"; see NRSV) that understands the reference as being to the whole church. To others it seems obvious that the widows are in view.[57] Two connections suggest, however, that Paul has circled back at this point to refocus on the families or children of widows. First, as pointed out, the goal, "blamelessness," is a matter of public reputation (= witness), and this concern anticipates what Paul is going to say to insensitive families in v. 8. Second, since v. 8 builds on the thought of v. 4, addressing families of widows, it seems clear that the family's role in this matter is central to Paul's teaching. The didactic pause of v. 7, therefore, has in mind chiefly a concern for the public image (and the positive Christian witness) of the supporting families of widows, and the following expanded translation is suggested: "that families of widows might be blameless."[58]

8 The second conditional statement of the passage is the mirror image of the principle given in v. 4, and effectively brackets the teaching to relatives of widows contained in this section (vv. 4-8) while underlining the theme of supporting families. Whereas v. 4 exhorted (optimistically) household members to express their spirituality ("godliness") in taking care of their widows, v. 8 condemns in the strongest terms household members ("anyone") who fail to do so.[59] As in the case of the instruction of v. 4, v. 8 also locates the specific issue of "provision" for widows (left implicit) within the general framework of household responsibility.

The verb translated "provide for"[60] is Pauline; it can simply mean "to

---

56. Cf. Knight, 220 (5:4); Fee, 117 (5:5-6); Collins, 139; Johnson, 263 (5:3-6 apparently).

57. E.g., Collins, 139; Fee, 117; Roloff, 288.

58. Marshall, 589; Johnson, 263; cf. Mounce, 274.

59. But see Bassler, 95; Wagener, *Die Ordnung des "Hauses Gottes,"* 155-61; Roloff, 292, for the view that the "anyone" in the instruction is the widow belonging to a household who is to discharge her responsibilities in that sphere.

60. Gk. προνοέω (Rom 12:17; 2 Cor 8:21; cf. the noun in Acts 24:3; Rom 13:14; Wis 13:16); J. Behm, *TDNT* 4:1009-11; W. Radl, *EDNT* 3:158-59.

think of beforehand," but here it combines forethought with the appropriate material provision. The language may allude to the institution known as *providentia,*[61] which in this case established that the householder within whose house a widow resided (to whom her dowry had passed for administration) was responsible to "provide for" her.[62] Whether or not a specific negligence of this institution is in mind, "provision" will include the equivalent of financial support.

In identifying the sphere of responsibility, Paul slides from a general or looser designation, "relatives,"[63] to the more specific or tighter designation "of the household."[64] These two spheres are distinguished differently depending on how the intervening phrase is understood ("and especially," or "namely"; see on 4:10).[65] However, on either function of the phrase, some degree of refinement is intended from a broad idea to a specific application of it. With responsible householders in Ephesus in view, Paul ensures that they understand that "provision" for any members of their immediate household (including widows, and perhaps more than one in a household)[66] is their responsibility.

Paul places the capable relatives (presumably householders) who fail in this duty into the category of unbelievers. To understand this, the dynamic and holistic meaning of "godliness" in v. 4, which makes care for family an outworking of genuine faith, must be kept in mind. Shirking this responsibility is, thus, denial[67] of "the faith" (see 1:2, note), an act that reveals a breach

---

61. The Greek equivalent is the noun (cognate to the verb used here) πρόνοια; see J. R. Harrison (S. R. Llewelyn, ed.), *New Documents Illustrating Early Christianity* (Grand Rapids: Eerdmans, 1982-83), 7:106-67.

62. Winter, *Seek the Welfare of the City,* 67-70.

63. Gk. οἱ ἴδιοι (gen. pl. "one's own"); used in a variety of ways to show relationship: e.g., fellow believers (Acts 4:23; 24:23); of relatives (Sir 11:34; see further BDAG, s.v. 4.a).

64. Gk. οἰκεῖος (e.g., metaphorically for believers as God's family members, Gal 6:10; Eph 2:19; for family members, see *Testament of Reuben* 3.5; LXX Isa 58:7; O. Michel, *TDNT* 5:134-35; R. A. Campbell, *"Kai malista oikeiōn,"* 157-60.

65. E.g., Spicq, *TLNT* 1:385 and notes, suggests that οἰκεῖος indicates blood relations (Lev 21:2), implying that the broader designation, οἱ ἴδιοι, would extend to others (like slaves and other salaried domestics); other scholars suggest relatives no matter how widely spread as well as one's immediate family (Verner, *Household of God,* 138; Kelly, 114); any and all family wherever they are and those living specifically at home (Winter, *Seek the Welfare of the City,* 68); and, as a reference to the church (members of God's family, i.e., fellow believers), see Campbell, *"Kai malista oikeiōn,"* 157-60.

66. See Winter, *Seek the Welfare of the City,* 69 and n. 35.

67. Gk. ἀρνέομαι (2 Tim 2:12[2x], 13; 3:5; Titus 1:16; 2:12); H. Schlier, *TDNT* 1:469-71; W. Schenk, *EDNT* 1:153-55; H. Riesenfelt, "The Meaning of the Verb ἀρνεῖσθαι," *ConNT* 11 (1947): 207-19; A. Fridrichsen, "Zu ἀρνεῖσθαι im Neuen Testament

in the integrity of the faith-generated behavior that is authentic Christianity. While this failure is not necessarily linked to the heresy (in 2 Timothy and Titus "denial of the faith" is symptomatic of apostasy), the process and end result are closely similar.

Assuming that the attached assessment is not hyperbole, Paul not only identifies neglectful relatives of widows with "unbelievers" (Titus 1:15; 1 Tim 1:2, note) but actually makes them morally "worse"[68] than those outside the church. The condemnation is a shocking wake-up call, and the parallel with 1 Cor 5:1 is informative. There the issue of a particularly egregious case of sexual misconduct *(porneia)* in the church called forth the ironic comparison with unbelievers who themselves viewed such behavior with disgust; here it is neglect of provision for relatives that is unfathomable even among unregenerate society.[69] Bearing in mind the goal of "blamelessness" in 5:7 and the public image factor implicit in that goal, one of Paul's concerns is for the potential of this refusal of family responsibility to damage the church's reputation with those outside.

9-10   Paul now defines the qualifications for "enrollment" of those widows without family to provide for them.[70] Three criteria emerge: age, marital fidelity, and evidence of "good works," the last of which is expanded in various ways. Verse 9 begins with the matter of "enrollment" ("put on the list"; TNIV). The verb, occurring only here in the NT, often has to do with the compiling of lists and can imply various things in various contexts, and in numerous cases describes selection for membership or enlistment in a group (soldiers, a religious body).[71] While the implication here is that a formal list or roster and related enrollment procedure already existed, which Paul sought to adjust, nothing in the term itself reveals *how* formal the procedure was or in what sort of group the process determined membership.

We saw above that some regard enrollment as being to an order devoted to ministry, which Paul seeks to regulate (or even suppress). But the text suggests that the main theme is *care* for widows, and on that basis enrollment was most likely to the group that Paul calls "real widows" — those

---

insondernheit in den Pastoralbriefen," *ConNT* 6 (1942): 94-96. The Matthean "denial" logion (Matt 10:33) may be somewhere in the background (cf. Marshall, 591).

68. Gk. χείρων ("worse"; comp. of κακός, "bad, evil, morally reprehensible").

69. See Marshall, 591 n. 53, for Greek sources reflecting a high estimation of family obligations.

70. Although the reference to the widow is here generic, χήρα (without the art.), the argument developed to this point in the passage makes it clear that the "real widow" (ἡ ὄντως χήρα; 5:3, 5, 16) is meant; Marshall, 591. But cf. Roloff, 293.

71. Gk. καταλέγω (see LSJ, s.v.: in the act. "to pick out, choose," in the pass. "to be enlisted, enrolled"); Josephus, *Jewish War* 2.226, 576, 584; 4.196; *Antiquities* 2.180; 3.288; 11.68; 14.449; etc. See BDAG; Johnson, 264.

truly needy widows with no family to provide for them (vv. 4-8, 16). This does not preclude some sort of role within the church's ministry. But references to activities in v. 10 are backward reflections on activities that determine character, not references to ongoing service.[72] Furthermore, given the typical life span of that culture and day, the age stipulation would mean that these real widows were in the closing years of their lives, not at a point in which to take up new ministries.

The age stipulation, "over sixty" (or "sixty and over"),[73] is probably designed to trim the numbers significantly on what was perhaps a bulging widow roster. On the one hand, in this way widows of remarriageable age and vitality were eliminated. On the other hand, in the first century when life expectancy was far shorter than that of the modern West, the number of women of this genuine elderly age in a small Christian congregation would not have been large. In any case, sixty years of age would represent a stage of life in which typically they would rely on others to meet their material needs.[74] The age itself was regarded as venerable,[75] but the added requirements show that age itself is not the only factor in enrollment.

After the matter of age is settled, Paul begins to look back over the widow's life. As in the case of aspiring leaders (3:2, 12; Titus 1:6), behavior in marriage is high on the agenda. In the case of the widow, the counterpart to the marriage formula applied to males stipulates that she be known as (lit.) "a one-man woman." The phrase describes marital fidelity and the absence of any sexual immorality.[76]

Verse 10 adds the final category of assessment — a good "reputation." ("well known").[77] The content of this reputation is to consist of acts of Christian service done in faith.[78] This is the meaning of "good deeds" in Pauline thought (2:10, Excursus),[79] and the way the concept brackets this discussion

72. *Contra* Dibelius and Conzelmann, 75.

73. Gk. μὴ ἔλαττον ἐτῶν ἑξήκοντα γεγονυῖα ("having reached the age of not less than sixty years").

74. See Marshall, 593; Kelly, 115.

75. If the biblical model is in mind, Lev 27:7 sets sixty years of age as elderly (Philo, *On the Special Laws* 2.33; cf. CD 10:7-8)

76. See the thorough discussion (and notes) at 3:2. With the appropriate shifts made from overseer to widow, the same considerations are pertinent. See Marshall, 594; Oberlinner, 231-33; Mounce, 287; Dibelius and Conzelmann, 75.

77. Gk. μαρτυρέω (6:13; "witness, bear testimony"; here pres. pass. ptc.) in the passive indicates the status of being well spoken of (as in Acts 6:3; 10:22; 16:2); H. Strathmann, *TDNT* 4:474-508, esp. 496-97.

78. The Greek preposition controlling "good works," ἐν, makes "good works" the basis or reason for the testimony.

79. The concept is expressed in two equivalent ways: for ἔργα καλά, see 5:10, 25; 6:18; Titus 2:7, 14; 3:8, 14.

of reputation shows its thematic character. But what do "good deeds" look like? Paul names four such acts, though the list is only illustrative.[80]

First, she is to be known for having raised and cared for her children.[81] The past tense of the verb suggests a historical reflection: when she was married, she performed honorably the duties of wife and mother.[82] While it is true that the "real widow" is without family to care for her, it seems unnecessary on that basis to restrict the meaning here to caring for the children of other people (or orphans), though this thought might be included.[83] This qualification expresses an ideal, which here underlines the value already placed on normal household duties in 2:15 (5:14; cf. 3:4).

Second, as in the case of prospective overseers (see 3:2) and Christians in general, she must have a record of "showing hospitality."[84] This too is a retroflection on her conduct as matron of the house,[85] showing her practical participation in caring for traveling believers and in this way extending the church's mission.

Third, the "real widow" was also to be known for "having washed the feet of the Lord's people." As the translation of the original, "saints" (NIV, NRSV), suggests, the reference is to believers, and the action in mind is associated with the church.[86] But the nature of the act itself poses a dilemma. The act of washing the feet[87] was widely practiced in antiquity, and in Jewish and Greek cultures it was a typical display of hospitality, normally carried out by slaves or women,[88] or a service performed by the wife for the husband (1 Sam 25:41). It is tempting to understand the act in the context of the im-

---

80. The conditional form of the presentation ("if she . . .; εἰ + verb occurs five times in 5:10) is unusual but probably belongs to the "qualifications" tone of this instruction.

81. Gk. τεκνοτροφέω (only here in the NT; Epictetus 1.23.3, "to bear children").

82. See Johnson, 265; Spicq, 534; G. Stählin, *TDNT* 9:456 n. 153.

83. Cf. Marshall, 595; Dibelius and Conzelmann, 75; Kelly, 116-17.

84. Gk. ξενοδοκέω (only here in the NT; more typically expressed with the φιλόξενος word group as in 3:2; Titus 1:8; Rom 12:13; Heb 13:2; 1 Pet 4:9). See Spicq, *TLNT* 2:55-60.

85. Hospitality was chiefly the responsibility of the wife (and other women) of the household; see Johnson, 265 (and refs.); Mark 1:30-31; Luke 7:36-50; 8:1-3; etc.

86. Gk. ἅγιος, in the plural, is typically a reference to believers (widely in Paul's letters to churches; e.g., Rom 12:13; 15:26; 16:2; 1 Cor 6:1; 14:33; etc.; but here only in the letters to coworkers); cf. O. Procksch, *TDNT* 1:88-115; H. Balz, *EDNT* 1:16-20. Wagener, *Die Ordnung des "Hauses Gottes,"* 188-89, attempts to limit the reference to a specific group within the church, but there is no basis for this claim.

87. The Gk. verb νίπτω (John 13:5, 6, 8[2x], 10, 12, 14[2x]; etc.) is often used to indicate a washing of part of the body (Mark 7:3; John 9:7); cf. F. Hauck, *TDNT* 4:946-47.

88. For the act in the biblical tradition, see LXX Gen 18:4; 19:2; 24:32; 43:24; Exod 30:19, 21; etc.

mediately preceding reference to hospitality.[89] It develops cultic purity associations in connection with the stipulation concerning foot washing in Exod 30:19-20,[90] and it is perhaps this background that gives meaning to the Johannine recollection of Jesus' washing the disciples' feet (John 13). Later church tradition would transform the Lord's act into a ritual.[91] Probably, however, the reference here is to an act that became a symbol for humble service, its metaphorical extension being suggested by the general application here to "the saints."[92]

Fourth, a rather general reference is made to the "real widow's" habit of "helping those in trouble." The verb denotes the "help, care, or assistance"[93] that would be appropriate in the case of those members of the community under the pressures of poverty (5:16) or social pressure (persecution).[94] Both situations are easily envisioned in the Pauline churches (2 Tim 1:8; 2:3; 3:12; 2 Cor 12:10; 2 Thess 1:4), though external hostility is outside the purview of 1 Timothy, and helping the poor may be preeminent. In any case, the widow is seen to be one who is strategically placed to actively bring relief to the afflicted of the community.

The final phrase of v. 10, utilizing a second expression for the concept, resumes the category of "good deeds" with which this list began. It provides a last open-ended condition that describes the acts of service by which the "real widow" will be known. The Pauline phrase "all kinds of good deeds" functions to summarize the visible outworking of faith.[95] The guiding verb adds the thought of devotion (whole-hearted "following in").[96] Since godly women have already been characterized with this language in 2:10, it is not likely that any of the activities specified, nor those others implied by the generalizing conclusion, is to be understood as describing ministerial duties such as might define an "order" of widows. As Marshall points out,

89. E.g., Collins, 140; Bassler, 97.

90. See Philo, *On the Special Laws* 1.206-7; *On the Life of Moses* 2.138; H. Weiss, "Footwashing," n.p., *ABD on CD-ROM*. Version 2.1a. 1995, 1996, 1997.

91. E.g., Augustine; see Fee, 125; Marshall, 596.

92. See R. B. Edwards, "The Christological Basis of the Johannine Footwashing," in J. B. Green and M. Turner, eds., *Jesus of Nazareth: Lord and Christ* (Grand Rapids: Eerdmans, 1994), 371, 378.

93. Gk. ἐπαρκέω; in the NT only in 1 Tim 5:10, 16(2x); 1 Macc 8:26; 11:35.

94. Gk. θλίβω; here in the passive participle in the sense of a condition of pressure, including social pressure and persecution (1 Thess 3:4; 2 Thess 1:6, 7; Heb 11:37), and particularly associated with the gospel ministry (2 Cor 1:6; 4:8; 7:5); cf. H. Schlier, *TDNT* 3:139-48.

95. Col 1:10; see 1 Tim 2:10 (Excursus).

96. Gk. ἐπακολουθέω (5:24; Mark 16:20; 1 Pet 2:21); for the figurative extension, as here, from "following, following after" (e.g., 5:24; 1 Pet 2:21) to "to be devoted/dedicated to," see LXX Josh 14.14; Josephus, *Against Apion* 1.6.

prayer (cf. 5:5) was not mentioned in this list.[97] Consequently, the function of the list is to provide a way of measuring the reputation of the widow on the basis of visible acts understood to be the outworking of faith ("the Spirit"). Assuming that these things were characteristic of her past life, what distinguishes her from godly women in general as a "real widow" and qualifies her for "enrollment" are her age, the death of her spouse, and her situation of destitution.

11-12 Having discussed the qualifications for enrollment, Paul goes on in vv. 11-15 (a new paragraph in the TNIV)[98] to consider the case of younger widows. The paragraph begins by identifying a group to be excluded from the list of supported widows, with backing rationale of two sorts (vv. 11-13). It continues by setting out the approved alternative (remarriage and pursuit of the domestic life; v. 14a), which is considered from the vantage point of social respectability and public witness (vv. 14b-15).

Verse 11 identifies a group of widows unqualified to be enrolled and establishes the grounds for their rejection. Two questions arise. The first concerns their identity. "Younger widows" is a fairly loose description, the scope of which is determined mainly by contrast with those who qualify as "real widows." Obviously, the adjective "younger" (see on 5:2) will mean less than sixty years of age (v. 9). In view of the concerns about a certain kind of remarriage and instructions about marriage and childbearing in v. 14, Paul might have in mind a specific group (or phenomenon) of "younger" (i.e., still capable of bearing children) widows in Ephesus.[99] Yet this is perhaps too restrictive, and "younger" should probably be understood instead to mean simply "eligible for remarriage." The domestic tasks listed in v. 14 might be more representative of the kinds of household duties remarried widows of various ages could attend to, whether or not all apply to each widow.[100] Those widows who are of a (re)marriageable age are to be "rejected" from consideration.[101]

97. Marshall, 598.

98. The adversative conjunction δέ draws a contrast between the widows about to be discussed and the group for enrollment that has just been considered in vv. 9-10. To capture the full intention of the contrast in translation, the topic of "enrollment" (from the main verb of v. 9) should be repeated; e.g., "but reject younger widows from enrollment" (or "refuse to enroll younger widows"; or "as for younger widows, do not enroll them, but reject them"). Cf. the strategies of TNIV; NRSV; see further Marshall, 598; Wagener, *Die Ordnung des "Hauses Gottes,"* 123 n. 44.

99. See Wagener, *Die Ordnung des "Hauses Gottes,"* 200-201, for the view that νεωτέρας is not comparative but indicates a specific age group.

100. Marshall, 598.

101. For Gk. παραιτέομαι ("to reject, refuse, decline, avoid"), see the discussion and note at 4:7. Johnson, 265-66, suggests that in keeping with Paul's concern for Timo-

The reason *(gar)* for rejection that follows poses the more puzzling question. Paul envisions a condition or situation that was apparently being experienced by this category of widow.[102] The problem arises in the verb ("to be overcome by strong desire, to become wanton against") and its relation to its object, "Christ." The compound verb is a true *hapax legomenon,* known only from its use in this text.[103] The simplex form of the verb ("to live in luxury") occurs in Rev 18:7, 9 in descriptions that associate the harlot, Babylon, with a determined pursuit of luxury (in specific contrast to a widow, v. 7) and associate sexual immorality with luxurious living (v. 9).[104] The preposition *kata* added here to the root intensifies the meaning and in this collocation contributes the sense of action "against," of which "Christ" becomes the recipient ("grow wanton against Christ"; or "feel sensuous impulses that alienate from Christ"[105]). The language implies that the young widows had adopted a lifestyle characterized by sexual misbehavior and that this negated their dedication to Christ (cf. 1 Cor 7:34) — that is, their lifestyle contradicted their profession of faith. This pursuit of promiscuous behavior is clearly thematic and strongly suggests involvement in the lifestyle of the "new woman."[106]

But the language and gravity of this description, which might elicit thoughts of sexual immorality, seem at odds with the result: "they want to marry." In what sense is the desire to (re)marry a cause of alienation from Christ? Remarriage is, after all, ultimately encouraged (v. 14), and Paul sanctions it in 1 Cor 7:39, where presumably the same reality of a vital sex drive is also in mind (cf. 7:2). Clearly there is something implicit that Paul and Timothy (and other Ephesian readers) share knowledge of that we must reconstruct (see below). We must either read the desire to remarry as in conflict with a vow committing the enrolled widow to service,[107] or understand the

---

thy's (sexual) purity (4:12; 5:2), and in view of usage elsewhere (4:7; 2 Tim 2:23; Titus 3:10), the sense of the imperative παραιτοῦ might be to urge Timothy to avoid younger widows because of the sexual threat they pose (v. 11b). Whether "avoid" or "reject" correctly reflects the sense, disqualification from enrollment (i.e., from community support) is implied, though the former option would emphasize more Timothy's own stake in the matter.

102. The temporal conjunction "when" (Gk. ὅταν; Titus 3:12) with the aorist subjunctive verb gives the conditional sense of the statement; the apodosis in the present tense ("they wish to marry") depicts a current situation.

103. Gk. καταστρηνιάω; BDF §181; BDAG; C. Schneider, *TDNT* 3:631.

104. Rev 18:7 — "as she glorified herself and lived luxuriously [Gk. στρηνιάω], so give her a like measure of torment and grief. Since in her heart she says, 'I rule as a queen; I am no widow, and I will never see grief.'"

105. Suggested by BDAG, s.v.

106. Winter, *Roman Wives,* 132-33.

107. E.g., prayer for the church in exchange for community support (Johnson, 266), or service in some broader sense (Scott, 61).

disallowed (re)marriage to unbelievers to be in view. Whatever light can be shed by the passage comes from the next verse.

As the Greek sentence continues, v. 12 abruptly shifts to the serious result of surrendering to the impulses to remarry inappropriately: "they bring judgment on themselves" (or condemnation).[108] The question is whether Paul is thinking here of divine judgment (3:6),[109] or rather the condemnation/disapproval of critical public opinion (cf. 3:7; 5:7-8, 14; 6:1).[110] The solution may hinge on the interpretation of the difficult explanatory statement that follows. But in the earlier case of overseers, both the divine court and the court of public approval are parallel concerns (3:6-7).

The rationale for this severe judgment is now explained with a puzzling statement that is capable of two main translations: "because they have broken their first pledge," or "because they have rejected their first/original faith." At issue is something (either a pledge/vow or a commitment of faith) that has a prior claim.[111] The verb ranges in meaning from "to reject, set aside, nullify, ignore, refuse,"[112] and the precise sense (and severity) required will depend on its object. The crux of the problem is the meaning of the Greek noun *pistis,* which in these letters to coworkers normally refers either to one's belief/faith in the gospel/Christ or to the content of what is believed (see on 1:2). More often applied here, however, is the amply attested sense of "vow, pledge."[113] What might this latter sense entail?

If vow or pledge is meant, several more or less formal promises could be in mind,[114] but they begin with a vow to remain single (i.e., not to remarry)

---

108. The infinitive plus accusative object (ἔχουσαι κρίμα) means lit. "to have or bear judgment" (or, in a slightly more futuristic sense, "they incur or bring judgment"; for the sense, cf. Mark 12:40[par.]; Rom 13:2; Jas 3:1, which employ the more usual future form of λαμβάνω) and draws its subject ("they") from the preceding and succeeding third-person plural verbs.

109. Marshall, 599 (who cites Calvin as interpreting this to mean "eternal death").

110. Johnson, 266.

111. Cf. Rev 2:4; discussion of "first" at 2:1; cf. NJB.

112. Gk. ἀθετέω (Mark 6:26; 7:9; Gal 2:21; 3:14; 1 Thess 4:8[2x]; etc.). See Polybius 11.29.3 for its use with πίστις ("pledge"); Spicq, *TLNT* 1:39-40; C. Maurer, *TDNT* 8:158-59.

113. See BDAG, s.v. 1.b. Cf. the translations.

114. We may safely set aside the view that the reference is to an implicit vow attending her first marriage to remain unmarried after her husband's death (see Spicq, *TLNT* 3:112 n. 8). While there is some precedent for this view in Judaism, which praised women who remained unmarried after the death of their spouses (Jdt 8:4; 16:22; Luke 2:36-38), the suggestion is unlikely in view of the positive encouragement to remarry in the case of young widows (as in the case of applying the *univira* inscriptions to the meaning of "one-man woman" in 5:9).

as part of her commitment to ministry in the church.[115] More often this has been adopted with elaborations (e.g., vows of celibacy understood as marriage to Christ) more appropriate to later periods of the church.[116] But quite apart from the question of anachronism, a "vow" of this sort would not be a likely condition of enrollment for widows aged sixty. If, however, *pistis* retains the sense of "faith" more typical of these letters (as its use in v. 8 would recommend), then Paul's meaning is that (re)marriage amounts to rejection of the faith — with some particular element of the local situation remaining to be reconstructed. In this case, the judgment incurred would surely be that which God dispenses. This serious charge could not refer to (re)marriage as such since it is sanctioned in v. 14. And when we put these two texts together, it is clear that two models of marriage are assumed — one that is condemned and one that is sanctioned — and these must be brought to the surface to make sense of this strong condemnation.

It is possible to construe the distinction as turning on the alleged "vow" not to remarry: vv. 11-12 depict remarriage as vow breaking; v. 14 depicts the remarriage of those who have not taken the vow. In such cases those encouraged to remarry in v. 14 are only those young widows who have not taken the "vow."[117] But it seems far less complicated to reconcile the two views of remarriage around the issue of marriage to unbelievers, in keeping with earlier Pauline instructions (cf. 1 Cor 7:39).[118] Apparently, Paul envisions young widows led by their enjoyment of promiscuous behavior to marry unbelievers. Since typically the wife would adopt the religion of the husband, remarriage to unbelievers would involve actual rejection of the widow's "first/prior faith in (commitment to) Christ." Indeed, Winter suggests that abandoning their Christian faith may have been a precondition of marriage to unbelievers.[119] When Paul turns to encourage young widows to remarry in v. 14, he assumes marriage to believers.

13 Having addressed the worst case scenario of remarriage to unbelievers, Paul describes a parallel development[120] involving (apparently) oth-

---

115. Many commentators adopt this sense without straying into later models of celibate orders of women; Knight, 222, 226-27; Johnson, 266; Barrett, 76.

116. E.g., G. Stählin, *TDNT* 9:454-55 (see his use of Philo, *On Dreams* 2.273); Kelly, 117; Roloff, 296-97; Hanson, 98; Spicq, 535-36; Wagener, *Die Ordnung des "Hauses Gottes,"* 202-4.

117. See esp. Wagener, *Die Ordnung des "Hauses Gottes,"* 200-201.

118. Winter, *Roman Wives,* 136-37; Fee, 121; Hasler, 42; Marshall, 600-601.

119. Winter, *Roman Wives,* 137.

120. The connecting combination of ἅμα δὲ καί ("Besides," TNIV, NRSV; "Moreover," Johnson, 259) indicates a parallel or concurrent event (Acts 24:26; 27:40; Col 4:3; Phlm 22); thus Marshall, 601: "At the same time as some are wanting to marry, others are learning to be lazy."

ers among the church's young widows. It is not at all clear how Paul relates these two kinds of problems, but the language allows us to understand two sorts of situations into which young widows were getting themselves.

The new theme emerges through the emphatic first reference to "idleness" at the head of the verse and its repetition in v. 13b.[121] In the first case, "idleness" is described as something that has been learned,[122] the idea being that their enjoyment of church support with little to do has left them with time on their hands.

Their idleness or lack of direction is described as "going about[123] from house to house."[124] It is not entirely clear what this activity amounted to, but there is little to commend the view that the description is of an abuse of a visitation ministry.[125] Rather, without household responsibilities to occupy their time, these young widows were moving through the household terrain where they felt comfortable and had easy access.[126] Probably one of Paul's concerns was for the power they could exert among the women of the households with whom they would have chatted and gossiped. As C. Osiek suggests, this segment of the social structure (women in the household) operated according to its own rules of honor and shame, were adept at keeping confidences, and represented an influential power bloc that could determine or, equally, threaten the community's stability.[127]

121. Gk. ἀργός; for a discussion see Titus 1:12; cf. Dibelius and Conzelmann, 75; Marshall, 602.

122. The construction is difficult: ἀργαὶ μανθάνουσιν (for Gk. μανθάνω, see discussion at 2:11; cf. Titus 3:14). Normally the verb-adjective combination would take an infinitive to create the linkage (e.g., Phil 4:11), and probably the infinitive εἶναι should be supplied (see the examples in Marshall, 602 n. 91; cf. Johnson, 267). But the jarring omission has exercised many commentators (see Jeremias, 39), and Wagener (Die Ordnung des "Hauses Gottes," 204-6), relying on 2 Tim 3:7 as a parallel and capitalizing on the syntactical uncertainty, construes the phrase as a criticism of women learning: something like "Their desire to learn is useless" (cf. Jas 2:20). But each use of the adjective in this sentence is likely to carry the same meaning, and in view of the intensifying construction in the second half of the sentence that repeats the term ἀργαί (οὐ μόνον δὲ ἀργαὶ ἀλλὰ καί; "not only are they lazy but also . . ."), where it describes the young widows themselves, the sense of "lazy, idle" (Titus 1:12) in reference to the women is the more likely meaning.

123. Gk. περιέρχομαι (Acts 19:13; Heb 11:37) means to "go about, wander," sometimes in the sense that a tourist ambles through a city (see P.Oxy. 1033.12 [BDAG, s.v. 1; cf. references in Johnson, 267; Marshall, 602 n. 92).

124. The plural object "houses" is best rendered as "from house to house." Cf. the variant at LXX Job 2:9: περιερχομένη καὶ οἰκίαν ἐξ οἰκίας ("I am a wanderer from house to house . . .").

125. But see Dibelius and Conzelmann, 75; Kelly, 118; Knight, 227.

126. Cf. Verner, Household of God, 164-65; Fee, 122.

127. C. Osiek, "Family Matters," in A People's History of Christianity, vol. 1, ed. R. Horsley (Minneapolis: fortress, 2005).

In comparison with the idleness that may have been the root of this development, the activities in which they went on to engage were the more disruptive: "And not only do they become idlers, but also gossips and busybodies" (NIV).[128] Two rare terms describe this activity. The first can refer to "gossip" or "nonsense,"[129] and while both senses are possible, the probable reference to spreading the false teaching in the phrase to follow (see below) suggests that the accent is on talking nonsense, though the scope of what this might entail is quite wide. The second term describes overly curious, nosy busybodies, and envisions those who involve themselves in affairs that are none of their business.[130] The cognate verb occurs in a very similar Pauline description of idlers who are busybodies in 2 Thess 3:11. This kind of behavior would draw the wrong sort of attention to the church and cast doubt on its credibility (3:7; 5:14; 6:1; cf. 1 Thess 4:11-12).[131]

The closing participial phrase completes the description of this activity: "saying things they ought not to [say]." Although the verb "to say" can mean "to teach" (cf. Titus 2:1, 15), there is no indication that formal teaching is meant in this context. If "teaching" in any sense is meant, the preceding terms suggest that it would be such as would be done through casual, informal conversation (cf. Titus 1:11). But this does not limit the content of what is said ("things they ought not to say").[132] Of the range of possibilities,[133] the particular expression "things that ought not to be said" (cf. the parallel in Titus 1:11)

128. This is the sense of the construction οὐ μόνον δὲ ἀργαὶ ἀλλὰ καί in this context (see 2 Tim 2:20; 4:8; 2 Cor 7:7). For the sake of discussion in the text, I revert here to the NIV since the TNIV rendering presents the adjectives in reverse order ("busybodies who talk nonsense"). This inversion is apparently designed to create a more natural connection to the final phrase, "saying things they ought not to," which also has speaking of some sort in mind.

129. Gk. φλύαρος (adj. only here in the NT); of "foolishness" (4 Macc 5:10; Plutarch, Moralia 39A; Spicq, TLNT 3:466); of "gossiping, spreading malicious lies" (see the verb in 3 John 10; Philo, On Dreams 2.291).

130. Gk. περίεργος (Acts 19:19 of dabbling in magic [BDAG, s.v. 2], which is not in view here, but see Kelly, 118; Hanson, 99). It is difficult to be as specific as, e.g., Wagener, Ordnung des "Hauses Gottes," 208-11 (women ignoring household responsibilities and interfering with men), despite the citations (e.g., Philo, On the Special Laws 3.169-71; Plutarch, Moralia 515A-23B).

131. See Fee, 63, 125-26.

132. Gk. τὰ μὴ δέοντα (cf. the equivalent expression in Titus 1:11: ἃ μὴ δεῖ); for τὰ δέοντα ("things that are necessary"), see LXX Exod 16:22; 21:10; 1 Kgs 5:2; Prov 30:8; 2 Macc 13:20; for δεῖ in reference to what is morally compulsory, see the discussion and note at 3:2.

133. Magic spells (Hanson, 99) can be excluded; but the telling of rumors of sexual conquests (Winter, Roman Wives, 135), the use of coarse language (Easton, 151) and the telling of secrets (Guthrie, 116) are well within possibility.

and the conclusion in v. 15 might suggest that they were spreading (perhaps inadvertently) elements of the false teaching as they went from house to house.[134] If the reflection of 2 Tim 3:6-7 is related to this earlier setting, the case for involvement of some sort in the heresy would be strengthened.

Winter, however, has assembled a profile from the references to idleness, meddling, gossiping, flitting from house to house, and saying things that are not right in the context of secular commentary on the rejection of traditional household values by the "new woman." He plausibly suggests that the gossip and inappropriate speech belong within the semantic domain of sexuality. Consequently, the behavior Paul identifies is not simply that of careless, lazy young women who do not have to work for a living, but specifically that which had become stereotypical of the sexually liberated Roman woman.[135]

14 In response to this trend ("therefore"), with an undisguised tone of authority,[136] he counsels them[137] to remarry and take up the responsibilities of the domestic sphere — that is, to return to the traditionally valued place of the household. Three infinitives describe this life, essentially patterning it after the profile expected of the "real widow" (5:9-10).

First is the command expressed by the simple verb "to marry" (4:3; 5:11), which in this context will mean "remarry." Paul's advice here is sometimes seen to conflict with the teaching of 1 Corinthians 7.[138] However, despite the sense of eschatological crisis influencing Paul's appeal to the Corinthians, he never excluded marriage (or remarriage), and in fact he encouraged it in cases where the strength of the sex drive was a current factor (7:2, 9), and approved it in the case of widows (7:39). While it is surely possible that certain features of the Corinthian situation contributed an extra degree of eschatological tension, the eschatological outlook of 1 Timothy is equally vibrant.[139] At the same time, in addressing the Corinthian situation Paul did not

---

134. Marshall, 603.

135. For secular sources and assessment, see Winter, *Roman Wives,* 133-36.

136. On the strength of the Gk. βούλομαι, see the discussion at 1 Tim 2:8; Titus 3:8.

137. Although the feminine adjective νεωτέρας ("younger") lacks the specifying noun χήρας ("widows"; 5:11), it is highly unlikely to think that Paul has shifted to address younger women in general at this point (but see Lock, 61).

138. Dibelius and Conzelmann, 75-76, argue that the eschatological motive behind Paul's teaching in 1 Corinthians 7 has been replaced by the motive of *"christliche Bürgerlichkeit"* (Christian good citizenship) in 1 Timothy 5. It need only be said that this interpretation (for a description and critique, see Towner, *Goal*) overlooks both the concern for the church's reputation in 1 Corinthians and the presence of eschatological tension in 1 Timothy. Cf. Johnson, 267.

139. Towner, *Goal,* 61-74.

have to face the particular problem concerning widows that he does here; had he been pressed to do so, there is no reason to think his advice would have differed appreciably (cf. Rom 12:18; 1 Thess 4:11-12). His treatment of wealthy women under the influence of the new trend in each case is comparable (see on 2:9-15).

This positive instruction will have been designed to counter not only the devaluation of (re)marriage associated with the ethos and lifestyle of the "new woman," but also the prohibition of marriage linked to the heresy (4:3).

The next two instructions, each expressed through rare verbs, follow naturally from the first. "Bearing children" was the normal and expected role of the wife (see on 2:15).[140] This is also true of "managing the household."[141] The verb takes its meaning from the more widely used cognate noun, which refers unmistakably to the ruler of the household (Matt 13:27, 52) and implies a good deal of authority. When the duty of management is applied to the wife (including oversight of slaves, children, and business interests attached to the household), there is no reason to lessen significantly the sense of authority involved in the role.

A fourth instruction summarizes the previous three by stating what pursuit of the domestic life will prevent. But the syntax of the statement is difficult. We begin with what is clear. Paul believes that a life so lived will "give no opportunity" (cf. 2 Cor 11:12)[142] to some perceived "adversary." But by eliminating the opportunity, what is thereby prevented? And who is "the adversary"? To answer the question "what?" most translations connect the final causal phrase (lit. "on account of reviling"[143]) with the adversary; thus "give the enemy no opportunity for slander" (TNIV; NRSV). But the final prepositional phrase is causal and is better taken as explaining the potential cause/source of the opportunity Paul seeks to prevent; thus "give no opportunity to the enemy on account of reviling."[144] In this case, an additional agent is implied, that is, some unnamed agent responsible for the act of reviling. This will be a person or people since the term used to describe the verbal at-

<hr>

140. Gk. τεκνογονέω (only here in the NT; *Anthologia Graeca* 9.22.4 [of an animal]; cf. τεκνογονία at 2:15).

141. Gk. οἰκοδεσποτέω (only here in the NT; elsewhere of celestial influences on human life, BDAG). The corresponding noun is οἰκοδεσπότης (e.g., Matt 21:33; 24:43; Luke 12:39; 13:25; 14:21; Philo, *On Dreams* 1.149; Plutarch, *Rome and Greece* 271.E.3-4).

142. Gk. ἀφορμή ("occasion, opportunity"; only in Paul: Rom 7:8, 11; 2 Cor 5:12; 11:12[2x]; Gal 5:13; LXX Prov 9:9); G. Bertram, *TDNT* 5:472-74.

143. Gk. λοιδορία (1 Pet 3:9[2x]; for the verb, John 9:28; Acts 23:4; 1 Cor 4:12; 1 Pet 2:23); Spicq, *TLNT* 2:407-9; H. Hanse, *TDNT* 4:293-94.

144. For Gk. χάριν, see Titus 1:5, 11; Luke 7:47; Gal 3:19; 1 John 3:12; Jude 16; cf. Johnson, 268; Wagener, *Ordnung des "Hauses Gottes,"* 213-14.

tacks envisioned here is used of people (cf. Jude 9). Presumably, Paul means those outside the community, and he therefore has the church's public reputation in mind.

This leaves the identity of "the [singular] enemy."[145] It might be a collective reference to the false teachers,[146] or to one of them (cf. the singular in reference to the apocalyptic lawless one in 2 Thess 2:4).[147] But Paul's tendency elsewhere is to use this term in the plural of those who oppose him (1 Cor 16:9; Phil 1:28; cf. Luke 21:15). In view of the reference to Satan in the next verse, "the enemy" here is apparently Satan, who operates against the community in concert with the criticism of those outside (as in 1 Tim 3:7; cf. Rev 12:10).

Consequently, the logic of Paul's instructions to young widows is to ensure that they take their respectable place within the domestic sphere and abandon the promiscuous lifestyle of the new woman. But as in the case of the teaching women in 2:11-15, so here we may have to contend with a convergence of influences on these young widows precisely at the point where the traditional institutions of marriage, childbearing, and managing the household come in (2:15). By following the secular trend, these widows in the church (perhaps inadvertently) also endorsed elements of the heretical view (4:3). The denigrating description of the young widows in v. 15 as "some" and as having "turned away to follow Satan" has all the markings of Paul's polemical categorization. If it is going too far to link the progressive young widows directly with the heresy (but cf. 2 Tim 3:6-7), it is clear from Paul's language that he is at least painting them with the same polemical brush.

In any case, ultimately the church's reputation is at stake, and Paul seeks to prevent outside criticism that the Enemy (Satan) could turn to his advantage against the church. According to the logic, the first line of defense, and the prior concern, is actually for the unnamed agent: those potential critics of the church on the outside. Paul's interest in social order and stability and a respectability that guarantees these things is not to be divorced in some way from theology or, for that matter, from mission. We may assume what is stated more explicitly elsewhere — namely, that protection of the church's reputation in the world has the promotion of the gospel as a significant goal (6:1; Titus 2:5, 10; 1 Thess 4:11-12).

15 Paul's instructions from v. 11 onward can best be described as damage control since some had already fallen. And it is this actual moral

---

145. Gk. ἀντικείμενος ("adversary, opponent"; masc. sg. ptc. ἀντίκειμαι; see discussion and note at 1:10).

146. Cf. G. Stählin, *TDNT* 9:455 and n. 142.

147. E.g., Simpson, 76; Easton, 151.

failure of "some" (see on 1:3) young widows that lends force to the whole approach taken toward them.[148] Paul's employment of the polemical vocabulary reserved for the false teachers places their fall into the category of a "turning away" from the apostolic faith (see 1:6), that is, apostasy. "Following Satan"[149] is the dark alternative to following Christ, and association with Satan (depicted ironically with the same metaphorical language of service to God/Christ) is typical of Paul's denunciation of opponents of the gospel (2 Cor 11:13-15). By pursuing a lifestyle marked by sexual promiscuity and rejection of traditional values (vv. 11-13) they have endangered themselves and potentially the church's reputation.

16 This third conditional statement reverses the logic of 5:4 to form the section's closing bracket. Now the obligation is slightly rephrased so that it is for the believing woman who "has widows"[150] to provide for them. The repetition of this concern for relatives to care for widows is at first glance an abrupt change of topic.[151] But as a conclusion its function is to return to the primary theme of reducing the church's burden to that of caring only for genuinely destitute widows. The matter of excluding younger widows from enrollment (and addressing the problems they had created) is a subtopic; consequently, as a closing note, the return to the main theme is warranted.

The more puzzling questions concern the identity of those addressed and why the responsibility is laid on "the believing woman" alone.[152] Determining her identity is an uncertain task. If, as 2:9 might suggest (see discussion), there existed in Ephesus a particular group of wealthy women, 5:16 may be addressing this group in particular, laying responsibility for the care of widowed family members, or possibly of widows who had been taken into their homes, especially on them (cf. 6:17-19).[153] Paul's letters and Acts bear testimony to the presence of such influential women (householders) in the

148. Gk. ἤδη γάρ is a connecting device used to reinforce an argument (see Wagener, *Ordnung des "Hauses Gottes,"* 218).

149. Gk. ὀπίσω ("after, behind"; in relation to allegiance to leaders, see Mark 1:17; Acts 20:30; Rev 13:3).

150. On the expression, see the note at 5:4.

151. The shift is particularly problematic for those who regard the instructions to be addressed to the widows (and not their relatives) all along (see discussion at v. 4), such as Wagener, *Ordnung des "Hauses Gottes,"* 223-27 (cf. Roloff, 301).

152. Gk. πιστή ("believing [woman]"; nom. fem. adj.; see note at 1:2). The secondary variant, πιστὸς ἢ πιστή ("believing man or woman"; D Ψ TR a b vgmss sy; see KJV; NEB; Easton, 157-58; Elliott, 80), apparently either sought to distribute the responsibility more fairly (Metzger, 642) or reflects a later misunderstanding about the place (householder) women might occupy in the household (Johnson, 268). The longer reading is secondary; the initial "if anyone" (εἴ τις) would have been sufficient to include both women and men (Marshall, 581).

153. Cf. Johnson, 268; Kelly, 121; Roloff, 301; Marshall, 606.

Pauline mission and churches (Acts 16:14-15, 40; Rom 16:1-3; 1 Cor 1:11; 16:19; Col 4:15). Otherwise, Paul may simply be addressing the women in families "having widows"[154] as those to whom the main responsibility of care would have fallen.[155] In any case, while clearly male relatives would not have been excluded from some part in shouldering this responsibility (vv. 4, 8), perhaps, at the close of this subsection focused specifically on the duties of widows (vv. 10, 14), Paul deemed it fitting to emphasize the role such capable and well-to-do women, or the wives of householders in general, might play in reducing the stress on the church.

We have already encountered the verb describing the help/assistance to be given (see the discussion at v. 10). The way Paul applies the verb in this closing statement, first to the believing woman, then to the church, emphasizes again the basic alternatives in this situation and the practical purpose *(hina)* of shifting this care to families where this was possible. If women take on the responsibility of helping widows, then the church (1) will be freed of the responsibility ("burden") to do so, and (2) thus enabled to care for the community's "real widows." Presumably, Paul is thinking of the economic burden involved (cf. 1 Thess 2:9; 2 Thess 3:8), and the idea (from v. 3 onward) was to reduce the drain on the church's limited resources.[156]

Consequently, the final purpose clause, with its very material concerns, returns to the section's opening command to the whole church ("Honor widows who are real widows," v. 3). The category of "real widows" has been carefully defined in economic, practical, and ethical terms, and it is this group that should be enrolled (vv. 9-10) to receive church support: "real widows" are those who, after the various criteria have been applied, and without family or wealthy women to care for them, require the practical and economic safety net of the church family. The complexity of the situation facing the Ephesian church should not be missed. It emerges in various ways, but above all we see how Paul walks the fine line between dealing with what might be regarded as a church-specific problem and the wider society's evaluation of the church. The bottom line is that in this case, too, behavior adopted in the church or sanctioned by the church ultimately affects how those on the outside regard the church. In the case of the Ephesian widows — both from the perspective of the obligation of families to meet their needs

154. Use of the plural "widows" suggests that Paul at least envisions situations in which a single household had more than one widow (mother and mother-in-law of the householder), or alternatively that he thinks of a situation that found wealthy women providing support for more than one widow.

155. Marshall, 606; Knight, 229.

156. Gk. βαρέω; (Matt 26:43; Luke 9:32; 21:31; 2 Cor 1:8; 5:4); for references to economic stress, see G. Schrenk, *TDNT* 1:558-61. Paul's use of ἐπιβαρέω in 1 Thess 2:9; 2 Thess 3:8 is comparable.

and the perspective of how young widows live their lives — Imperial culture stood ready to evaluate the respectability of what would be perceived as Christian behavior.

c. Proper Recognition and Discipline of Elders (5:17-25)

17 *The elders who direct the affairs of the church well are worthy of double honor, especially those whose work is preaching and teaching.* 18 *For Scripture says, "Do not muzzle an ox while it is treading out the grain," and "Workers deserve their wages."* 19 *Do not entertain an accusation against an elder unless it is brought by two or three witnesses.* 20 *But those who are sinning you are to reprove before everyone, so that the others may take warning.* 21 *I charge you, in the sight of God and Christ Jesus and the elect angels, to keep these instructions without partiality, and to do nothing out of favoritism.*

22 *Do not be hasty in the laying on of hands, and do not share in the sins of others. Keep yourself pure.*

23 *Stop drinking only water, and use a little wine because of your stomach and your frequent illnesses.*

24 *The sins of some are obvious, reaching the place of judgment ahead of them; the sins of others trail behind them.* 25 *In the same way, good deeds are obvious, and even those that are not obvious cannot be hidden forever.*

A new section of instruction begins at this point, linked to the previous section by the repetition of the interest in "honor." Although the coherence of the passage has been questioned,[1] in fact two features shape this text into a unit. First, the topic throughout is that of "elders" — community respect and support, procedures in cases requiring discipline, care in selection, and the eschatological framework of church appointments.[2] Second, after the topic is introduced in vv. 17-18, the shift to the second-person singular imperative form in vv. 19-23 causes Timothy's administration in the affairs of elders in Ephesus (discipline and selection) to stand out. The following structure unfolds:

(1) vv. 17-18 take up the matter of "honoring" elders;
(2) vv. 19-21 lay down procedural guidelines Timothy is to follow, with theological backing, in cases requiring that elders be disciplined;

1. Cf. Oberlinner, 260-61; Johnson, 285.
2. See esp. Marshall, 608-9. Cf. Meier, *"Presbyteros,"* 336, whose chiastic scheme (questionable in some respects) reflects the bracketing theme of "elders."

(3) vv. 22-23 underline what is at stake for Timothy in selecting elders, presumably to fill the spots opened by those dismissed for sins (see below), with the high emphasis on purity calling forth an explanatory addendum (often regarded as a digression) to keep Timothy from misunderstanding the intention of the instruction;

(4) vv. 24-25 shift noticeably back to the generalizing third person in setting out the theological and eschatological framework within which Timothy's role as apostolic delegate and administrator (and all church decision-making) is to be exercised.

Despite the shift in topic, this section clearly corresponds to the previous one, not only in the continuation of the "honor" theme, but also in addressing instructions to Timothy (and the church) concerning another specific group in the community. Both sections of instruction fall generally under the introductory framework of household propriety constructed in 5:1-2.[3]

17 The passage begins on a positive note, commanding the community to reward its faithful leaders. But undoubtedly behind this set of instructions lies a complex community situation that has necessitated, on the one hand, identifying those who have exercised leadership with distinction and, on the other hand, detailing strict guidelines for adjudicating allegations of negligence or explicit sin.

First come matters of identification. "Elders" here refers to a recognized group of leaders in the church.[4] The wording of the whole verse may imply different categories within this group, but of the various schemes attempted,[5] only the following alternatives bear consideration: (1) "elders who lead well," within which is a smaller group who also preach and teach, are distinguished from those who have exercised leadership poorly; (2) "elders who lead well" (= those who preach and teach) are distinguished from those who have exercised leadership poorly. Probably, however, too much is made of possible distinctions, and the more crucial elements are fairly visible.

Based on what can be discerned from the instructions and the letter as a whole, the main distinction is probably between those elders who had faithfully discharged their duties (whether leading well and preaching/teaching, or, in the case of some lacking the latter gifts, just exercising leadership), and those who had failed. The instructions imply that one or more elders had been accused of something. Johnson suggests mismanagement of commu-

---

3. Cf. Marshall, 609.

4. See the introduction to 3:1.

5. Attempts to interpret the language as reflecting the introduction by the author of some new leadership setup into an already existing one (cf. Roloff, 305-9; Oberlinner, 249-50; see discussion in Marshall, 611) are entirely conjectural.

nity funds: administration of the church's finances would likely have been included among the elders' administrative duties, and the instruction of 5:17 might be meant to restrict "payment" to those proven to be faithful.[6] In view of the emphasis on preaching and teaching, the element of the heresy should be factored in, though this might well include the dimensions cited by Johnson (6:5-10). In this case, the underlying scenario consists of elders who have gone over to (or indeed instigated) the heresy (see on 1:20). While it is possible that the Ephesian church was suffering a series of unrelated crises, it seems more likely that the heretical movement can best account for Paul's attention to matters of quality control in leadership selection and disciplinary action.

Paul thus draws attention to elders who "lead well." "Exercising leadership" is the element of function that links elders to those called overseers.[7] This term also describes household administration (3:4, 5, 12), and it covers a range of meaning, which in the right context reflects on leadership in various ways. In relation to the church, the notions of guiding, administering, and caring for are all relevant, but the term stops short of "ruling." Here Paul adds the adverb — those who "lead *well*"[8] — which underlines proficiency and, given the context of heresy, faithfulness of service.[9]

Further definition either of this group of elders or of a subgroup of them is added by the loosely connected phrase that closes the verse: "especially those whose work is preaching and teaching." The uncertainty of the relationship stems from the connecting adverb, which might mean "especially, above all" (see on 4:10) or "namely, I mean" (see Titus 1:10). While the second sense would make for greater clarity, the former meaning seems preferable, particularly if the elders are understood to possess a variety of gifts: all faithful elders have "earned their pay," but, especially in the context of a battle with heresy, those equipped to preach and teach, who have persisted in teaching the apostolic faith, receive even more recognition.

The "work" ("labor/ministry"; see on 4:10) described in this way comes under the category of didactic activities. The first is literally "in [the] word" *(en logǭ),*[10] and in connection with the preceding description of this activity as "labor" (= ministry, 4:10), the probable reference is to preach-

6. Johnson, 286-88.

7. See the introduction to 3:1; the discussion and note at 3:4; Rom 12:8; 1 Thess 5:12.

8. Gk. καλῶς προεστῶτες ("exercise leadership well"); cf. the same phrase in 3:12, καλῶς προϊστάμενοι, used of the deacon's skill in household management.

9. Based on the language of 3:12, 13, καλῶς is less likely a reference to added duties (such as preaching and teaching; but see G. Bornkamm, *TDNT* 6:667; Dibelius and Conzelmann, 78; Marshall, 612), or a technical term for "full-time" (but see Kelly, 124).

10. See the discussion at 1:15; cf. 2 Tim 4:1, 2.

ing.[11] How this is to be distinguished from the following term, "teaching," is less certain.[12] Since in terms of content, *euangelion* and *didaskalia* (gospel and teaching) were continuous, the distinction should perhaps be sought in application or audience, the former being directed to unbelievers and the latter to the church.[13]

These faithful elders are to be considered "worthy of double honor." This directive is for the church, and the language ("consider worthy, deserving")[14] creates an intentional link with the identical image of evaluation central to the Jesus-saying about to be invoked (v. 18). As suggested above, the need for such (re)evaluation on the part of the community may indicate a serious decline in the prestige of the offices, whether due to the heresy in some way, or to abuses committed by leaders (cf. on 3:1).

The term "double honor" has produced a good deal of discussion. The backing for the instruction that Paul gives in v. 18 suggests that at least in some cases more than respect in the form of acknowledgment — that is, some form of material compensation — might be meant.[15] Moreover, something on this order for those engaged in ministry was clearly the practice in Pauline churches (1 Cor 9:7-14; 2 Cor 11:8-9; Gal 6:6; 1 Thess 2:7). But it is well to recall that Paul himself did not lean on the material implications for himself, though he did expect to be treated with the respect to be accorded to those in the service of the gospel. The precise meaning of the stipulation "double honor" is difficult to determine.[16] Of the numerous interpretations offered,[17] the Pauline practice just cited and the following OT citation (and adaptation in Paul) and allusion to the Jesus tradition point in the direction of "honor" that could sometimes be expressed in material terms.[18] "Double" might then have

11. But cf. Johnson, 278: those who "labor in speech and in teaching."

12. See the discussion at 1:10; cf. 4:13.

13. See Towner, *Goal,* 121-24.

14. Gk. ἀξιόω (Luke 7:7; 2 Thess 1:11; Heb 3:3; 10:29); W. Foerster, *TDNT* 1:380. Cf. the use of the adjective ἄξιος in 5:18b; 6:1 (elsewhere in the longer "faithful saying" formula, 1:15; 4:9).

15. See Meier, *"Presbyteros,"* 327; G. Bornkamm, *TDNT* 6:667; J. Schneider, *TDNT* 8:176-77. Lips, *Glaube,* 109-10, suggests more specifically "salary." However, the term τιμή is not attested in this sense (see Marshall, 613; Roloff, 308; J. A. Kirk, "Did 'Officials' in the New Testament Church Receive a Salary?" *ExpTim* 84 [1972-73]: 105-8), which suggests that something less formal is in mind. But see Oberlinner, 252-54, for the view that "respect" alone is meant.

16. Gk. διπλῆς τιμῆς (adj. διπλοῦς; see BDAG, s.v., for use of the adj. with "honor" and in similar contexts discussing "double wages").

17. For the view that "double honor" refers to respect *and* remuneration, see Fee, 129; Brox, 199; Arichea and Hatton, 126.

18. The view of G. Schöllgen, "Die διπλῆ τιμή von 1 Tim 5,17," *ZNW* 80 (1989): 232-39, that the reference is to a double portion at the community meal, is certainly possi-

meant literally "twice as much as" some implied or earlier-named group, whether it be other elders who do not teach, deacons, widows,[19] or, figuratively, "great, more, most, or additional" in a superlative sense.[20] Surely elders who were householders and who had "led well" had no need of double pay; but the appropriateness of urging community acknowledgment of their faithfulness is perfectly sensible in the situation of false teaching.

18   To ground the instruction ("for"), Paul cites relevant OT material and early church tradition as authoritative precedents. The opening phrase is the formal introductory formula that initiates the OT proof text: "For Scripture says."[21] The term employed here, literally "the writing," might refer either to a specific text of Scripture or to the whole of Scripture,[22] but in this case the two senses effectively coalesce, that is, "this text of Scripture."[23]

The more popular question has been whether the scope of the introductory formula extends to include the Jesus logion, lending it the status of "Scripture." Since it is separated from the first quotation by the single conjunction "and," many have understood Paul (or the author) to have redrawn the boundaries of Scripture to include Jesus' teaching.[24] While this is possible, it seems more likely at the point in time of this letter that "Scripture" would have normally meant the OT (here in Greek translation), and that the (equally) authoritative Jesus-saying is added as further proof.[25]

The content of the first quotation, "Do not muzzle an ox while it is threshing," is a slightly reorganized rendering of the LXX of Deut 25:4:[26]

---

ble (see the OT parallels and example of the practice in Tertullian adduced by Marshall, 614-15, who adopts this interpretation). But it is not the most natural use of τιμή ("honor"), and the practice of compensation elsewhere in the churches described by terms like μίσθος ("pay, wages," v. 18) and ὀψώνιον ("pay, wages," 1 Cor 9:7; 2 Cor 11:8) offers the better interpretive clue to the term "double honor."

19. For this spread of views, cf. Dibelius and Conzelmann, 78; Meier, *"Presbyteros,"* 327; Roloff, 308-9; Jeremias, 42; Lock, 62; Barrett, 79.

20. See Easton, 159; Brox, 199.

21. The formula λέγει γὰρ ἡ γραφή is identical in form and function to Rom 9:17; 10:11; cf. 4:3; 11:2; Gal 4:30; etc.

22. See examples in BDAG, s.v. 2.a. and 2.b.β.

23. Cf. Marshall, 615.

24. E.g., Roloff, 309; Simpson, 77-78; cf. Collins, 145-46.

25. See Fee, 134; Kelly, 126; Brox, 199-200. See the discussion in Marshall, 615.

26. Cf. the Greek:

Tim 5:18b:	βοῦν ἀλοῶντα οὐ φιμώσεις
Deut 25:41:	οὐ φιμώσεις βοῦν ἀλοῶντα.

Gk. βοῦς ("ox, cow"; 1 Cor 9:9[2x] = LXX Deut 25:4). Gk. ἀλοάω ("to thresh"; 1 Cor 9:9 [= LXX Deut 25:5], 10). Gk. φιμόω ("to muzzle"; "shut the mouth"; 1 Cor 9:9 [variant]; figuratively elsewhere in the NT: Matt 22:12, 34; Mark 1:25; 4:39; Luke 4:35; 1 Pet 2:15).

Deut 25:4: *ou phimōseis boun aloōnta* (gloss: do not muzzle ox threshing)

1 Tim 5:18a: *boun aloōnta ou phimōseis* (gloss: ox threshing do not muzzle).

The shift of the object (threshing ox) to the head of the sentence (so also Philo, *On the Virtues* 145) may simply be in accord with better Greek style, but it probably also corresponds to a different emphasis created in the NT adaptation of the OT command. The word order of the Greek in Deut 25:4 rather slavishly copies the Hebrew, which in the legal setting stresses obedience (and therefore "you," the subject of the verb). But the rearrangement in 1 Tim 5:18b allows for stress to be placed on the "threshing ox," which by analogy stands for the faithfully laboring elders who are the main topic. The Mosaic command envisioned one of the processes by which threshing was accomplished. The ox was driven over a threshing floor, separating the grain from the stalk and chaff with its hooves.

By the time Paul employs the OT principle in this letter, he can assume that its application is clearly understood (which he nonetheless reinforces by adding the Jesus logion). This was perhaps not the case in 1 Cor 9:9-10, where Paul takes the time to disabuse the Corinthian congregation of any simplistic material notions concerning the true import of the Deuteronomy text by drawing on another ethical development of the agricultural logic that promised the plowman and the thresher a share in the harvest (Sir 6:19; Jas 5:7). But in any case, between the original command set down in Deuteronomy, which presumably was given originally out of concern for the proper care of oxen, and the application of the OT text here and in 1 Corinthians 9, the text had passed through the grid of Jewish exegesis[27] to yield finally the analogy that Paul employs here. The argument works, *a fortiori,* by applying the reasoning of the Torah concerning provision for working oxen to the situation of those laboring in the gospel ministry. In both Pauline texts, Paul followed or adapted the Jewish interpretation of the text and applied it to material support for those engaged in ministry.

Notably, the same principle had been pursued and reached along re-

---

27. This commandment had been a well of deeper meaning for rabbinic scholars (see StrB 3.382-99). It was used as a particular illustration of the "lesser to greater" logic that urged that God's concern for animals implied far greater concern for people (*b. B. Meṣ.* 88b; *b. Giṭ.* 62a; 1 Cor 9:9; e.g., Philo, *On the Virtues* 145; see additional refs. in Knoch, 40). Pharisaic interpretation apparently deduced from this text a broader principle: oxen stand for all species of labor including that of humans (D. I. Brewer, "1 Corinthians 9:9-11: A Literal Interpretation of 'Do Not Muzzle the Ox,'" *NTS* 38 [1992]: 554-65), and Paul may have drawn on this *halakic* rule instead of engaging in creative midrash himself.

lated tangents, as the subsequent quotation of the Jesus logion shows: "workers deserve their wages" (Matt 10:10; Luke 10:7). Paul connects this second quotation to the first.[28] In the Greek, the second quotation is an exact replication of the saying of Jesus preserved in Luke 10:7 (Matt 10:10, employing "food" instead of "wages"):[29]

> Luke 10:7: *axios gar ho ergatēs tou misthou autou;*
> 1 Tim 5:18c: *axios ho ergatēs tou misthou autou.*

Both the "worthiness" theme (5:17)[30] and the thrust of the entire statement make it a natural supplement to the quotation from Deut 25:4. The "worker"[31] corresponds obviously to the "ox" and to "elders who lead well." Reference to the worker's "wages," as a return for work accomplished,[32] suggests that material support is at least partly in mind in the reference to "double honor" in 5:17.

It is not possible to know how Paul came by the saying. The exact correspondence with the Lukan wording has of course suggested to some that the "Paul" of this letter wrote at a time late enough to have had access to Luke's Gospel in some form or other.[33] Others maintain that the author of 1 Timothy was none other than the author of Luke-Acts,[34] or that Luke served as Paul's amanuensis in this case (cf. 2 Tim 4:11).[35] But if a written source is required by the exact verbal correspondence, surely it is sufficient

---

28. Gk. καί ("and") elsewhere serves the same purpose: 2 Tim 2:19; Heb 1:10. Cf. Paul's καὶ πάλιν ("and again") in Rom 15:10, 11, 12.

29. Cf. the Greek:

Luke 10:7:	ἄξιος γὰρ	ὁ ἐργάτης τοῦ μισθοῦ αὐτοῦ
Matt 10:10:	ἄξιος γὰρ	ὁ ἐργάτης τῆς τροφῆς αὐτοῦ
1 Tim 5:18c:	ἄξιος	ὁ ἐργάτης τοῦ μισθοῦ αὐτοῦ.

The absence of γάρ (used to connect the saying within Luke's and Matthew's discourses) is immaterial.

30. For Gk. ἄξιος ("worthy, deserving"); taking the genitive object, 1:15; 6:1; Matt 10:10; Luke 10:7; etc.; see the discussion and notes at 1:15; 5:17; 6:1.

31. Gk. ἐργάτης ("worker, laborer"; freq. in the Gospels of farm workers; in Acts 19:25 of tradesmen; fig. of "evildoers" in 2 Cor 11:13; Phil 3:2; of Timothy/laborer in the Gospel, 2 Tim 2:15).

32. Gk. μισθός ("pay, wages, remuneration for work done"); see esp. 1 Cor 3:8, 14; 9:17, 18; H. Preisker and E. Würthwein, *TDNT* 4:695-728, esp. 698, 723-24.

33. E.g., Easton, 161; see the other suggestions of Dibelius and Conzelmann, 79; cf. Knight, 233-34, who suggests that the authentic Paul may have been dependent on Luke's Gospel.

34. E.g., Quinn-Wacker, 462-63; Wilson, *Luke and the Pastoral Epistles.*

35. Spicq, 543-44.

to posit that by this time various written collections of the sayings of Jesus had begun to circulate, and that Paul had access to the version that Luke eventually consulted.[36] However, whatever materials might have influenced the shape of the saying as attributed to Jesus,[37] it was certainly both sufficiently succinct and profound to maintain its shape in the oral tradition. In any case, the saying of Jesus provides supplementary authoritative support for the command to recompense the community's hardworking faithful elders.

19 Attention shifts to another administrative matter. Charges of some sort (collusion with the opponents or involvement in other inappropriate behavior) have been brought against one or more elders, and so Paul sets the parameters of due process in the examination and (if necessary) discipline of elders. Return to the second-person singular address places Timothy, who as coworker/delegate acts with the authority of the apostle, at the center of the action to be taken.

First is the matter of evaluating the charges and gathering evidence. The opening of the instruction emphasizes the protection of elders from an erroneous or unsubstantiated "accusation." This is legal language, and the context is that of a more or less formal hearing.[38] The present tense imperative ("do not entertain an accusation") may recommend the translation "stop accepting accusations,"[39] and may suggest that Timothy (or others before his arrival) already had done so. This is perhaps the rough equivalent of "innocent until proved guilty." But the attached adverbial exceptive phrase introduces the correct procedure to follow ("unless, except");[40] it is a citation of Mosaic legislation that shows the meaning of the banned procedure to be pre-

---

36. Cf. Roloff, 310 (who traces the source to a collection like Q).

37. See LXX Num 18:31 ("And you shall eat it in any place, you and your families; for this is your reward [μισθός] for your services in the tabernacle of witness"); 2 Chron 15:7 ("But be strong, and let not your hands be weakened; for there is a reward for your work [μισθὸς τῇ ἐργασίᾳ ὑμῶν]"); Sir 51:30 ("Do your work [ἐργάζεσθε τὸ ἔργον ὑμῶν] in good time, and in his own time God will give you your reward [μισθόν]"). For secular parallels, see Euripides, *Rhesus* 161-62 (ποιοῦντα δ' ἄξιον μισθὸν φέρεσθαι); Phocylides, *Fragments* 17 (μισθὸν μοχθήσαντι δίδου; "give wages to the one who toils").

38. Gk. κατηγορία (Titus 1:6; John 18:19; Josephus, *Antiquities* 2.49; *Against Apion* 2.137); here in a formal setting; but see Titus 1:6. Cf. F. Büchsel, *TDNT* 3:636-37.

39. Gk. παραδέχομαι (pres. impv.; "accept, receive, admit"); see the legal use with the negative in LXX Exod 23:1: οὐ παραδέξῃ ἀκοὴν ματαίαν ("do not accept a false report"); Mark 4:20; Acts 15:4; 16:21; 22:18; Heb 12:6); see BDAG, s.v. 1 (Sextus 259: διαβολὰς κατὰ φιλοσόφου μὴ παραδέχου: "Do not accept false accusations against a philosopher").

40. Gk. ἐκτός ("except"; 1 Cor 6:18; 15:27; 2 Cor 12:2; etc.); the phrase ἐκτὸς εἰ μή ("unless") is Pauline in the NT (1 Cor 14:5; 15:2; BDF §376).

cisely that which two related Deuteronomy texts prohibited, namely, establishment of guilt on the basis of a single witness.

Rendering the Greek literally, Paul insists that accusations be accepted only "on the basis of"[41] two or three witnesses."[42] The relevant command accessed here is a combination of two texts in LXX Deuteronomy. In reference to sentences of death, Deut 17:6 stipulates:

> "A person shall die on the testimony of two or three witnesses *(epi dysin martysin ē epi trisin martysin);* a person who is put to death shall not be put to death for one witness."

In a more general context, Deut 19:15 insists:

> "One witness shall not stand to testify against a person for any iniquity, or for any fault, or for any sin that may be committed; by the mouth of two witnesses, or by the mouth of three witnesses *(epi stomatos dyo martyrōn kai epi stomatos triōn martyrōn),* shall every word be established."

1 Tim 5:19 describes a specific adversarial setting and "accused": "Do not accept any accusation against an elder," which of course differs from the OT scenario.

In turning then to correct procedure, the phrase "on the basis of two or three witnesses" reflects certain features of both these Deuteronomy texts:[43]

> Deut 17:6: *epi dysin martysin ē epi trisin martysin apothaneitai;*
> ("a person shall die on the testimony of two or three witnesses")
> Deut 19:15: *epi stomatos dyo martyrōn kai epi stomatos triōn martyrōn stathēsetai pan rhēma;*
> ("by the mouth of two witnesses, or by the mouth of three witnesses every matter shall be established")
> 1 Tim 5:19: *epi dyo ē triōn martyrōn;*
> ("on the basis of two or three witnesses").

---

41. For the preposition ἐπί plus genitive in the sense of "on the basis of," see BDF §235.5; *EDNT* 2:22; BDAG, s.v. 8. Heb 7:11.

42. Gk. μάρτυς (6:12; 2 Tim 2:2); here with the legal meaning of "one who gives testimony in legal matters" (Matt 26:65; Acts 6:13; 7:58; Josephus, *Life* 256; BDAG, s.v. 1).

43. Cf. the Greek:

> Deut 17:6:   ἐπὶ δυσὶν μάρτυσιν ἢ ἐπὶ τρισὶν μάρτυσιν ἀποθανεῖται;
> Deut 19:15:   ἐπὶ στόματος δύο μαρτύρων καὶ ἐπὶ στόματος τριῶν
> μαρτύρων σταθήσεται πᾶν ῥῆμα;
> 1 Tim 5:19:   ἐπὶ δύο ἢ τριῶν μαρτύρων.

The conjunction "or" *(ē)* and the omission of the word "mouth" *(stomatos)* reflect the wording of Deut 17:6, but the genitive object of the preposition *(dyo ē triōn martyrōn)* corresponds to Deut 19:15. Assuming that it is the presence of the word "mouth" in the Greek of Deut 19:15 that determines the genitives that complete the object (also present in the Hebrew of 17:6 but absent in the Greek translation at that point), the genitive construction of 1 Tim 5:19 may correspond more closely to the more general application of the multiple witness principle in Deut 19:15, with "mouth" having been omitted to give a smoother expression. Since the death penalty is not under discussion (cf. Heb 10:28), it is not surprising that the broader application of the witness principle in Deut 19:15 would be most relevant.

However, the form of the citation as it occurs here may also have been shaped by the early church's tradition. Notably, Paul clearly cites Deut 19:15 most closely in 2 Cor 13:1, dropping only the repeated phrase, "by the mouth" *(epi stomatos),* but retaining the subject/verb combination, "every matter shall be established" *(stathēsetai pan rhēma).*

> 2 Cor 13:1: *epi stomatos dyo martyrōn kai triōn martyrōn stathēsetai pan rhēma;*
> ("by the mouth of two or three witnesses will every matter be established").

Though lacking the introductory formula, it is nonetheless a formal quote, as the syntax shows. The principle was also known within the Jesus tradition, where Matt 18:16 preserves a slightly more attenuated citation of Deut 19:15.[44] And in reference to the death penalty, Heb 10:28 naturally utilizes the multiple witness principle (with slight modification) as it occurs in Deut 17:6 in connection with the death penalty.[45]

In invoking this OT principle by means of quotation, Paul did not teach in a particularly innovative way. The principle was deeply rooted in the teaching of the early church, as can be seen in the Jesus tradition and numerous other allusions to the law of multiple witnesses (e.g., John 8:17) and apparent applications of it in various practical and eschatological situations (Matt 18:19-20; 27:38; Mark 6:7; Luke 9:30, 32; 10:1; 24:13; John 20:12; Acts 1:10; Heb 6:18; Rev 11:3-4). This principle governing due pro-

---

44. Note the change of conjunctions (from "and" [καί] to "or" [ἤ]) and the change (in a purpose clause) from the future passive to the aorist passive form of the verb "to establish" (σταθῇ). Matt 18:16: ἵνα ἐπὶ στόματος δύο μαρτύρων ἢ τριῶν σταθῇ πᾶν ῥῆμα ("so that by the mouth of two witnesses or three every matter might be established").

45. Heb 10:28: ἐπὶ δυσὶν ἢ τρισὶν μάρτυσιν ἀποθνήσκει ("on the basis of two or three witnesses").

cess in the giving and weighing of evidence was mediated to the early church from Judaism. Josephus (*Life* 256) and the Qumran writings (CD 9:17–10:2; cf. *m. Sanh.* 5:4) demonstrate how the principle was present and applicable in Jewish life in general, and in fact did not need to be quoted to be understood.

Thus Paul gives directions in the two administrative matters in 5:18-19 by drawing explicitly upon OT legislation that had already been appropriated in the early church (especially in Pauline churches) and Judaism. The first principle concerning the support of laborers was accessed, at some point in the tradition (not necessarily originally by Paul, or freshly at this point; cf. 1 Cor 9:9-10), by means of allegorical or midrashic techniques. The second principle involved no such exegetical procedures. Direct quotation of the OT was intended to ensure that the authority of the instructions and the gravity of the situation were properly understood.

20 Still within the OT and early church legal process, Paul gives instructions covering those situations where charges have been allowed to stand and sin has been detected. The transition from the previous statement governing the discovery stage is abrupt[46] and raises the question of how this step of discipline is related to the preceding step. But the logic seems to be continuous.

Elders continue to be in view in the participle rendered by the TNIV as "those who are sinning." This translation is justified in stressing the continuous action of the present tense (cf. NIV, "those who sin"). The implication is that there is indeed an ongoing problem in the community involving sinning elders. Marshall offers the plausible suggestion that this is a further indication that the first stages of the traditional procedure of church discipline (private rebuke; Matt 18:15-17; Titus 3:10) had been ineffective in stemming the elders' misbehavior.[47] Less precision on this point would simply mean that Paul is now referring to those elders who, on the basis of legitimate allegations (v. 19), have been shown to be sinning. "To sin" carries the widespread biblical meaning of "missing the mark" (deviating from) as established by God's law and will; though again precise identification of the acts that constitute sin in this case is not possible, Paul's language categorizes the behavior in terms of unbelief and rebellion against God.[48]

The discipline envisaged is that of the public "rebuke." The term could

---

46. Some copyists (A D* [F G] 1175 and some versions; see TNIV) add δέ ("but, and") to smooth the transition and bring out the connection with the preceding.

47. Marshall, 618.

48. Gk. ἁμαρτάνω (pres. ptc.; Titus 3:11 = ἁμαρτωλός, "sinner," 1:9 [discussion and note], 15). For the noun ἁμαρτία ("sin"), see 5:22, 24; 2 Tim 3:6. Cf. G. Quell, G. Bertram, and W. Grundmann, *TDNT* 1:267-316; K. H. Rengstorf, *TDNT* 1:317-35.

imply a range of possible measures to be taken by Timothy:[49] exposure and convincing of wrongdoing, refutation, correction, reprimand, censure, or discipline. In the letters to Timothy and Titus, the term takes its place within the vocabulary of community discipline (2 Tim 4:2; Titus 1:9, 13; 2:15; cf. the noun in 2 Tim 3:16) for which the Jesus tradition apparently provided the template (Matt 18:15).[50] The content or severity of the rebuke cannot be discerned from the context, but it may have included the threat of removal from leadership (1:3; Titus 1:9) or excommunication (1:20; Titus 3:10; 2 Cor 5:4-5), and the following purpose clause implies a substantial degree of severity.[51]

In this case, the action is to be carried out "publicly," that is, in the presence of the congregation (cf. Gal 2:14).[52] The public nature of the procedure suggests that the Mosaic framework of Deut 19:15ff. is still informing Paul's instructions, though Paul now has moved on to the case of proven allegations. Within the traditional model of church discipline (Matt 18:15-18; 1 Cor 5:4-5; 1 Tim 1:20), public rebuke either indicates (as mentioned above) that private intervention has not been successful and resistant elders are therefore publicly accused and censured, or that in the case of sinning church leaders, whose sin was perceived as a direct threat to the stability of the entire community, public discipline would have been the rule. Probably the first scenario is envisaged here, but in either case the nature of the proceedings is extremely serious.

This is borne out by the purpose clause *(hina)* that defines the logic of the public exposure in terms of what "the others" (both the remainder of the elders and the congregation) might gain from the experience.[53] Deut 19:20 is now in the background: "And the rest of the people shall hear and fear, and never again do such a thing in the midst of you" (LXX). The echo is obvious enough on the level of general associations, but the verbal echo is specifically created by means of the verb "to fear" (Deut 19:20, *phobēthēsontai;* 5:20, *phobon*)[54] and the way of referring to the congregation as "the rest" (or

---

49. The second-person imperative ("you rebuke") envisions Timothy as Paul's delegate administering discipline. If the character of the letter is taken seriously, it seems unnecessary to weaken this sense (but cf. Marshall, 618).

50. Gk. ἐλέγχω; LXX Sir 20:2; 31:31; Prov 9:7; *Didache* 2.7; F. Büchsel, *TDNT* 2:473-76; F. Porsch, *EDNT* 1:427-28. For this term in the church discipline context, see esp. Matt 18:15; 2 Tim 4:2; *Barnabas* 19.4. Cf. Johnson, 279.

51. *Contra* Roloff, 311.

52. For ἐνώπιον (discussion at 2:3) πάντων (lit. "in the presence of all"), see Luke 14:10; Acts 19:19; 27:35; Rom 12:17; for ἐνώπιον in reference to community gatherings, see Acts 6:5; 3 John 6; for a wider forum, see Rom 12:17.

53. Gk. καί, meaning here "also," implies that this purpose is in addition to the effect of the rebuke on the elder himself.

54. Gk. φόβος; for the sense of godly fear intended here, see Acts 5:5; 1 Pet 1:17.

"the others"; Deut 19:20, *hoi epiloipoi;* 5:20, *hoi loipoi).*[55] To understand "fear" (i.e., here of the realization of the gravity of sin on the basis of the censure and discipline carried out) alone as the purpose of this exercise of course stops short of the intention of this clause. The idea is completed by the OT text that explains this godly "fear" to be the preventive to further sin.[56]

21 The fact that Paul is first instructing Timothy in the administration of this process is strengthened by the solemn warning to act impartially in executing "these instructions."[57] The solemn tone is created by two features of the warning. First, the verb means "to charge, warn, or adjure" in this context,[58] and in these letters signifies the very serious nature of the tasks Timothy is given in the community (2 Tim 2:14) and as the apostle's delegate (2 Tim 4:1).

Second, whereas Timothy's administration of discipline was to take place before the congregation, Paul's admonition to Timothy is witnessed by the heavenly entourage: "in the sight of God and Christ Jesus and the elect angels."[59] The gravity of the situation cannot be missed (2 Tim 2:14; 4:1). This witness formula typically includes God and Christ Jesus,[60] but here the third element, "elect angels," is a marked addition that might have been prompted by the reference to "three witnesses" in Paul's OT material.[61] "Elect" normally in the NT designates believers as the "chosen" of God (2 Tim 2:10; Titus 1:1, discussion); its use here of angelic beings depends on Intertestamental apocalyptic developments (*1 Enoch* 39:1).[62] Yet in a related NT development the role of angels in connection with Christ's parousia and the final judgment becomes the more typical NT theme.[63] These images may

55. Gk. οἱ λοιποί (Matt 22:6; 27:49; etc.; BDAG, s.v. 2.b.α; adv. in 2 Tim 4:8). The Mosaic background to this instruction supports extending the meaning of "the rest" beyond simply the circle of elders (for which see Johnson, 280; Roloff, 311) to the whole congregation (Marshall, 619; Knight, 237).

56. Thus the TNIV translation: "so that the others *may take warning*," which gets at the intended goal of the expressed visceral response of "fear"; but it perhaps minimizes the sense of "dread of judgment" often associated with "fear" in such contexts.

57. Gk. ταῦτα ("these instructions"; TNIV/NIV; NRSV) in v. 21b connects this charge with the preceding guidelines of vv. 19-20, as the added stipulation of impartiality indicates (but cf. Dibelius and Conzelmann, 80).

58. Gk. διαμαρτύρομαι (2 Tim 2:14; 4:1; 1 Thess 4:6; etc.; cf. the simplex form of the verb ματύρομαι in Gal 5:3; Eph 4:17; 1 Thess 2:12); H. Strathmann, *TDNT* 4:510-12.

59. Gk. ἐνώπιον τοῦ θεοῦ; for the preposition, see 5:20 (note); for the phrase see 5:4 (6:13; 2 Tim 2:14; 4:1; Rom 14:22; 1 Cor 1:29; etc.).

60. See 6:13; 2 Tim 4:1; for God alone, 2 Tim 2:14.

61. See J. W. Fuller, "Of Elders and Triads in 1 Timothy 5:19-25," *NTS* 29 (1983): 258-63, esp. 261-62.

62. Gk. ἐκλεκτός (see discussion and note at Titus 1:1); for ἄγγελος, see the discussion at 3:16. For the combination, cf. *Odes of Solomon* 4.8.

63. For the presence of angels with Christ at the eschatological judgment, cf. Matt

converge as Paul here evokes the imagery of the divine court, in which God and his Messiah are attended by angelic beings.[64] In any case, in the strongest terms, the warning intends to place Timothy and his faithfulness in the matter concerning elders in the presence of divine witnesses. The solemnity thus created suggests that this task was among the most important Timothy was to attend to.[65]

The content[66] of the warning itself is to follow to the letter (lit. "keep, guard")[67] the instructions on dispensing discipline (vv. 19-20). But Paul extends the warning, in a most emphatic way, to include the element of strict fairness, on the model, undoubtedly, of divine impartiality. Emphasis is created with two parallel phrases containing strikingly similar terms that occur only here in the NT. The first term, in the phrase "without partiality" *(prokrimatos),* is attested later as a legal term that stresses objectivity; it instructs Timothy to administer justice without pre-judging the case.[68] The second term, in the participial phrase "do nothing out of favoritism" *(prosklisin),* describes an inclination or predisposition.[69] Its negative connotation in this kind of context (cf. *1 Clement* 21.7; 47.3; 50.2) is that of giving preferential treatment to a person or persons, which Timothy must not do. Elsewhere Paul prefers other language to describe the impartiality of God/the Lord in judgment *(prosōpolēmpsia;* Rom 2:11; Eph 6:9; Col 3:25; cf. 2 Chron 19:7; Sir 35:12; Acts 10:34). Nevertheless, the human agent of God is clearly to emulate the divine objectivity in the administration of church discipline, without jumping to conclusions before the evidence has been heard, and without discrimination based on personal relationships.

22 The instructions shift at this point, apparently, to address the contingency of appointing new elders to replace those dismissed as a result of the discipline process. "Laying on of hands" was a symbolic act that in the NT and Judaism functioned to signify public recognition of authority, commissioning, and the communication of various divine powers (e.g., healing) and

---

24:31, 36; 25:31; Mark 13:27; Luke 2:13-15; 1 Cor 6:3; 11:10; cf. 1 Thess 4:16; 2 Thess 1:7; etc.

64. See LXX Job 1:6; 2:1; Ps 81:1; Dan 7:9-10; Rev 14:10; for the role of angels as witnesses, cf. *Testament of Levi* 19.3.

65. See Johnson, 280.

66. Gk. ἵνα functions here, with διαμαρτύρομαι, like an infinitive construction to complete the thought initiated by the verb (BDAG, s.v. 2).

67. Gk. φυλάσσω (6:20; 2 Tim 1:12, 14; 4:15); for the sense, cf. Rom 2:26; 6:13. G. Bertram, *TDNT* 9:236-41.

68. Gk. πρόκριμα; the cognate verb προκρίνω is widely attested in the sense of "deciding beforehand, preferring" (LSJ, s.v.). For the preposition emphasizing "absence of," see 2:8. G. Bertram, *TDNT* 3:953.

69. Gk. πρόσκλισις; Polybius 5.51.8; 6.10.11; *1 Clement* 21.7; 47.3; 50.2.

gifts (e.g., the Spirit [Acts 8:17-19; 19:6]).[70] In 4:14 the rite is mentioned in connection with Timothy's appointment to act as Paul's delegate in Ephesus. It will be appointment or commissioning in this basic sense, in this case of elders, that is indicated in this verse,[71] and the second-person singular envisions Timothy as taking the lead in the procedure (though it is not necessary to rule out participation by others in leadership). This interest is not surprising in view of the concern for the qualifications of overseers and deacons (3:1-7, 8-13). Equally, on the assumption that the disciplinary review might have led to the dismissal of some leaders, selection of replacements would be essential.[72]

The cautionary note, "do not be hasty," implies that the same care required in the selection of overseers, deacons, and "real widows" is to be practiced in deciding whom to commission as elders. But the instruction goes on to focus only on the downside of careless appointments and what is at stake for Timothy should he fail to make sufficiently extensive examinations of candidates.

The second phrase follows closely on the heels of the first to explain its meaning.[73] Framing it as a parallel command ("and do not share")[74] and in general language ("the sins of others"), Paul almost seems to be citing a well-known maxim whose application here needs no explanation.[75] The direction of Paul's logic is clear: the language of "sin" already used of elders (see on 5:20)

---

70. Typically with the ἐπιτίθημι word group plus the term for "hands" (χείρ); for the noun, see the discussion at 4:14; 2 Tim 1:6; Acts 8:18; Heb 6:2. C. Maurer, *TDNT* 8:159-61.

71. Marshall, 620-22; Kelly, 127-28; Lips, *Glaube,* 174-77; Knight, 239; W. Radl, *EDNT* 3:462-63.

72. Less likely is the alternative view that the laying on of hands was part of a restoration rite (attested by later writers; Eusebius, *Ecclesiastical History* 7.2; *Didascalia Apostolorum* 10; cf. discussion in Kelly, 128; Spicq, 548; for the view, see Dibelius and Conzelmann, 80; Hanson, 103; Lock, 64; Bartsch, *Die Anfänge urchristlicher Rechtsbildungen,* 101-2). While some later writers understood the passage in this way (e.g., Tertullian; see Spicq, 548), and the preceding context is amenable (for the interest in restoring sinners to the community, cf. 2 Cor 2:6-10; Jas 3:1-7), the following reference to sins (esp. to future sins) is more appropriate to the situation of appointing elders, and the NT does not attest to the other practice.

73. For the close connections formed by Gk. μήδε ("and not"), see 1:4; 6:17; 2 Tim 1:8. Marshall, 622.

74. Gk. κοινωνέω ("to share, participate in"; negatively, as here, 2 John 11; positively Rom 12:13; 15:27; Gal 6:6; Phil 4:15; etc.); BDAG, s.v. 1.b.β.; F. Hauck, *TDNT* 3:797-809.

75. For the combination of thoughts, see Prov 28:24: "He that casts off father or mother, and thinks he does not sin (ἁμαρτάνειν), this one is partner (κοινωνός) with an ungodly man." Cf. 2 John 11; Isa 1:23; See the extrabiblical parallel cited in BDAG, s.v. 1.b.β (Artemidorus 3.51: "partner [κοινωνός] of the sins [ἁμαρτημάτων] of him").

determines the application of the principle to the process at hand — if out of negligence Timothy appoints someone who is unqualified (because of sin), or leaves someone in the position of leadership who continues in sin, he (the appointer) will in some sense share in the sin and guilt "of others" (i.e., the appointee) and bear responsibility for sins overlooked or committed in the future.

Having framed this command negatively in terms of avoidance, Paul restates the instruction positively: "Keep yourself pure." The adjective "pure" echoes the two previous warnings to Timothy about sexual purity (4:12; 5:2). The combination of verb and reflexive pronoun, "keep yourself,"[76] stresses maintaining (present tense verb) a state or condition, in this case "purity." This will mean distance from any involvement with the sins of elders, but, in view of the echo set up with preceding references to this condition, Timothy's sexual comportment may also be encompassed.

23   But what can Paul's next comment mean? It is clearly an independent thought that could stand in a random list of advice for healthy living, but that is not the nature of the present discourse. Marshall notes that "in a modern document it would be a footnote or in parentheses."[77] And TNIV's decision to regard the comment as a separate paragraph effectively underscores an independent function, or at least uncertainty as to its presence in the text.

The sentence consists of two imperatives. The first is negative, and the second is positive, opposed by the conjunction "but" and balanced around the traditional polarity of "water" and "wine."[78] Bodily reasons for the "moderate"[79] use of wine form the second half of the advice. Paul specifies two: "the stomach"[80] and "frequent illnesses."[81] The first of these is a probable

---

76. Gk. τηρέω (see H. Riesenfeld, *TDNT* 8:140-46) covers a range of meanings: in connection with the law, commands, or the faith, "to keep, guard, obey, observe" (6:14; 2 Tim 4:7; Prov 3:1; 23:26; Sir 29:1); of the heart and the person, "protect, preserve" (Prov 13:3; Wis 10:5). For the combination of the verb and a reflexive pronoun, see 2 Cor 11:9; Jas 1:27; Jude 21.

77. Marshall, 623.

78. Gk. ὑδροποτέω (only here in the NT; on χράομαι, "to make use of," see discussion at 1:8 and BDAG, s.v. 1.a; for the verb with οἶνος, see Plutarch, *Moralia* 353B); BDAG suggests the perhaps overly nuanced meaning, "to prefer water for drinking, to drink (only) water" (cf. LSJ, "to drink water"), but in this case, and elsewhere frequently in opposition to wine drinking (e.g., Herodotus 1.71.2; Epictetus 3.13.21; etc.; cf. Dan 1:12), the nuance seems justified.

79. Gk. ὀλίγος; as here, of small amounts (in various senses Luke 7:47; Acts 19:24; 2 Cor 8:15); of drinking and wine and with the verb χράομαι, see Plutarch, *Moralia* 353B.

80. Gk. στόμαχος (only here in the NT) means "stomach" but here effectively "stomach ailments"; Spicq, *TLNT* 3:296-99.

81. Gk. ἀσθένεια (pl. "weaknesses = illnesses, ailments"; e.g., Luke 5:15; Acts 5:15; Gal 4:13; etc.; cf. the verb at 2 Tim 4:20 etc.; G. Stählin, *TDNT* 1:490-93). For the adjective πυκνός ("frequent"), see Luke 5:33; Acts 24:26.

reference to digestive ailments, for which wine was a typical treatment.[82] The second, broader reference to "frequent illnesses" is undetermined, but wine was prescribed for various disorders. We can discern from the language ("stop drinking only water") what Timothy had been practicing, namely, drinking water exclusively, and abstaining from wine. Clearly Paul urges Timothy to alter this pattern for the sake of his physical health. What is not clear is why Timothy was abstaining, or whether Paul had more on his mind than just Timothy's health.

What can be surmised of the situation comes from the description of Timothy's habit in combination with evidence from the text. "Water drinking" was often indicative of asceticism.[83] And Paul's instruction, coming as a counterinstruction ("stop drinking . . . but use . . ."), makes clear that Timothy had elected to abstain from wine. Local reasons suggested by the letter include, first of all, the ascetic practices of the opponents (4:3), though it is clear neither that this included wine, nor (apart from this text, possibly) that Timothy was in any way under their influence.[84] Secondly, injunctions against drunkenness (3:3, 8; cf. Titus 1:7) may indicate a tendency to abuse wine among some of the householders and leaders of the community in response to which Timothy might have chosen to abstain. While precision here is not possible, the sense of the command in the context seems to be to define clearly what "purity" (v. 22) does and does not entail. The preceding command to purity was not, for practical reasons (in Timothy's case) among others, to be understood in terms of asceticism. And following on from the general and wide-ranging command of v. 22, this instruction should be interpreted as a corrective or explanatory note.[85]

24-25 The final comment, now in the third person, apparently offers both Paul's general pronouncement against sinners and a concession to human fallibility in the matter of identifying sin and merit. While this closing statement immediately rounds out the present instructions (vv. 17-23), the safety net it provides for Timothy may extend to the evaluation of widows (vv. 3-16).[86] In assessing people, errors are unavoidable. The present statement therefore puts the procedure Timothy is to execute in the context of divine judgment.

The whole statement is a balanced construction of contrasting elements: within each half is a contrast of obvious deeds with hidden deeds, and

82. For the traditional prescription of wine for various digestive problems, cf. Prov 31:6; Plutarch, *Moralia* 132A-F; Strabo 6.1.14; Spicq, *TLNT* 3:298-99 nn. 12-14.
83. Dan 1:12; Epictetus 3.13.21; *Pirqe Abot* 6:4; cf. *Acts of Paul and Thecla* 25.
84. Cf. Dibelius and Conzelmann, 80-81; Roloff, 315.
85. Cf. Collins, 149-50; Bassler, 102.
86. Cf. Marshall, 625-26; Roloff, 316-17.

then the whole of the statement contrasts the character of those deeds — sins versus good deeds. Its general tone ("some [people]"; 2:1)[87] and careful construction give it a traditional ring, but its application to the elders is clear enough.

First, v. 24 takes up the matter of "sins," mentioned here for the third time in this subsection (see on 5:20, 22). In the first case, the sins of some are "obvious,"[88] that is, in the context, "indisputable," and easily discerned in and through the process of evaluation enjoined above. The image is of a procession, with the sinners' sins "reaching the place of judgment ahead of them."[89] Almost certainly the dominant sense of this first statement — as the eventuality of justice in the cases under discussion confirms — is of divine and ultimate judgment. God's eschatological decision is thus the framework within which Timothy's own act of discernment takes place.[90] The blatant sin of obvious sinners forges the path to the ineluctable eschatological judgment, and one in a role such as Timothy's becomes a participant in the judicial process (cf. Matt 16:19).

Trickier for Timothy is the contrasting situation of hidden sin; thus the addition, "[but] the sins of others trail behind them [to judgment]."[91] From the prior statement and the contrast created, the implication is clear: the sins of some people are not evident and come to light only at the eschatological judgment.[92]

The meaning of this statement for Timothy is debated. But it seems to serve two purposes. First, generally, it does place Timothy's ministry of discernment (decisions about discipline and selecting prospective leaders) into an eschatological context.[93] He works in cooperation with the intention of God ultimately to judge human sin. But, secondly, in the process, since Timothy cannot see into the hearts of people and is bound to err, Paul explains, by way of consolation or to provide some relief, the reality that

---

87. Gk. τις (here "anyone, someone"); it is rare for the indefinite pronoun to take the initial position, as it does in each clause (gen. "of some people . . . of others"; cf. Phil 1:15), probably for emphasis. See A. Horstmann, *EDNT* 3:362-63; BDAG, s.v. 1.a.ε.

88. Gk. πρόδηλος ("obvious, clear, known"; 5:25; Heb 7.14, Josephus, *Life* 22; 212); MM 538-39.

89. Gk. προάγω (1:18; 2 Macc 10:1); for the metaphorical use, see LXX Isa 58:8; *Barnabas* 4.12 (following Isa 58:8 and in the context of judgment). Cf. R. Heiligenthal, *EDNT* 2:50.

90. Gk. κρίσις (2 Thess 1:5; F. Büchsel, *TDNT* 3:921-42, esp. 941-42; BDAG, s.v. 1.a.α); for the view that human judgment is meant, see Knight, 241.

91. See the discussion and note at 5:10; cf. Rev 14:13, of "good deeds following."

92. Matt 10:26; Mark 4:22; Luke 8:17; 12:2; Rom 2:16; 1 Cor 4:2, 5.

93. Cf. Roloff, 316-17.

God's judgment will eventually pull together all the loose threads that elude human administration.[94]

With some subtle shifts,[95] v. 25 applies the same ("in the same way, likewise"; see on 2:9) contrastive formula (obvious/hidden) now to the matter of discerning "good deeds" (2:10, Excursus). If this is a common saying, the language of "good deeds" is generic enough to mean any acts of benevolence. But in the vocabulary of these letters, this is the term Paul uses to quantify those actions done on behalf of others that arise from true faith (5:10). In parallel with the statement about sins, this part of the saying declares with the same adjective that these deeds produced by faith are "obvious" (see on v. 24).

But the situation contrasting with good deeds is also explained: literally, "even those [good deeds] that are not obvious[96] [i.e., not evident] cannot be hidden" (see TNIV/NIV, NRSV).[97] The impossibility of keeping something good "hidden" is vaguely reminiscent of Matt 5:14.[98]

Consequently, vv. 24-25 function as a unit to locate Timothy's task within an eschatological framework that underlines God's ultimate control over these delicate matters of discipline and, especially, selection of leaders. While surely human error is to be avoided (and perhaps much of it can be) by careful administration (according to the rules laid down above), the messy reality is covered by God's own eschatological purposes. The resonance of this closing set of contrasting principles with the Jesus tradition would have strengthened the force of Paul's consolation to Timothy.

94. It is not likely that the saying is meant to urge Timothy to take his time in appointing leaders (*pace* Knight, 241; Mounce, 322), for in the case of those hidden sins, it is not an adequate period of waiting that brings sins to light, but the final judgment (rightly Marshall, 625).

95. The second line about good works omits the dual use of the indefinite pronoun "some" (τις), which might seem to make it an even more general statement ("all good works are obvious"); the shift is apparently stylistic.

96. The verb ἔχω with an adverb (here "otherwise, in another way"; ἄλλως only here in the NT) is intransitive and equivalent to "to be" (BDAG, s.v. 10.a).

97. Some understand the adverb to be creating a contrast between good deeds, in the first half of the statement, and those that are not good, in the second half (Johnson, 282-83; Simpson, 81; Collins, 151 n. 84 [possibly]). But this disturbs the parallelism between v. 24ab (sins evident/sins hidden but ultimately revealed at the judgment) and v. 25ab (good deeds evident/good deeds hidden but ultimately revealed). Cf. Marshall, 626; Mounce, 320; Knight, 241-42.

98. "You are the light of the world. A city on a hill cannot be hidden" (NIV). Gk. κρύπτω (Col 3:3; freq. in the Gospels).

d. Expectations of Slaves (6:1-2a)

> 1 All who are under the yoke of slavery should consider their mas-
> ters worthy of full respect, so that God's name and our teaching may
> not be slandered. 2 Those who have believing masters should not show
> them disrespect just because they are fellow believers. Instead, they
> should serve them even better because their masters are dear to them
> as fellow believers and are devoted to the welfare of their slaves.

This third in the series of "honor" passages also fits within the household framework established by 5:1-2.[1] Paul's instructions shift again to the impersonal third-person imperative that allows direct impact on the group in view. Yet the return to the second-person singular address in v. 2b ("these are the things you are to teach and insist on") makes clear that they are to be mediated by Timothy as Paul's delegate in the community.

The interest in slaves and masters links this teaching loosely to the household code style of parenesis. The slaves in view are Christian slaves. The fact that the masters are not addressed (so also Titus 2:9-10) marks a divergence from the tendency toward reciprocal exhortation evident in Eph 6:5-9 and Col 3:22–4:1 (cf. *Didache* 4.10; *Barnabas* 19.7). Exclusive attention to the slaves can probably be traced back to the specific community situation Paul addresses: present tense imperatives and prohibitions heighten the sense of reality and perhaps stress certain habits, in the case of Christian slaves, that need to be broken.[2] Verse 1 implies that some slaves were guilty of disrespecting their masters. Verse 2 requires even more strongly the same conclusion but in a different context, as we will see; in this case, more elaborate details about motivation are given.

In the early Christian literature, numerous passages instruct those in the situation of slavery, which can only mean that slavery was a difficult problem for the church.[3] A first-century slave's hope for manumission was more than a dream, and the realistic possibility of obtaining freedom[4] served to motivate the slave to excel in service.[5] Within the Pauline churches, the

---

1. The cohesiveness of the teaching from 5:1-2 to 6:1-2a is best seen by retaining the more literal translation "honor" for Gk. τιμή in 6:1 (cf. TNIV at 5:3: verb, "give proper recognition"; noun, "honor"; 6:1, "respect").

2. Cf. BDF §336.

3. 1 Pet 2:18-25; *Didache* 4.10-11; Ignatius, *To Polycarp* 4.3; *Barnabas* 19.7. See esp. S. S. Bartchy, "Slave, Slavery," *DLNTD* 1098-1102; Bartsch, *Die Anfänge urchristlicher Rechtsbildungen*, 146; H. Gülzow, *Christentum und Sklaverei in den ersten drei Jahrhunderten* (Bonn: Habelt, 1969), 101-41.

4. S. S. Bartchy, *ΜΑΛΛΟΝ ΧΡΗΣΑΙ* (SBLDS 11; Missoula: Scholars Press, 1973), 71; see Epictetus 4.1.33.

5. See Bartchy, *ΜΑΛΛΟΝ ΧΡΗΣΑΙ*, 82-87.

teaching of the gospel, with its accent on freedom and equality and its shift away from social stratification (1 Cor 12:13; Gal 3:28; Col 3:11), almost certainly fueled the desire of Christian slaves for freedom. In some cases this desire could have provoked attempts to act immediately on gospel promises with disruptive results for the churches involved and their reputations in wider society. The equality tradition cited above was clearly well-known in Paul's churches, but the matter of implementation in the case of slaves and women is more complex, as Paul's own interaction with Philemon suggests.[6]

Ephesian Christian slaves would have known this equality platform. To judge from the explanation in 6:2, a misunderstanding of Paul's teaching could well have contributed to the development of a disturbance in the church. As in the cases of women/wives, young widows, and even sinning elders, the presence of the heretical opposition within the community does not necessarily rule out Paul's addressing unrelated problems of other sorts.

"Honor," in this case, translates into the "respect" due to the slave's master, manifested in obedient service and faithful devotion (TNIV). Two situations are envisaged in vv. 1-2, which can be divided either according to general and specific rules, or according to the unbelief or faith of the slaves' masters. In either case, the principle of v. 1 will include the case of Christian slaves owned by unbelieving masters. Disobedience in this situation could have extreme consequences for the church's reputation and hence mission. In the second case, slaves with believing masters present an equally explosive set of circumstances. Scholars often feel that it is just this sort of emancipatory activism that caused a post-Pauline author to fall back on the safety of conservative cultural structures.[7] However, two features of the parenesis challenge this "conservative" reading. On the one hand, as we will see, the introduction of a missionary motivation for what might seem to be a retrograde step in an otherwise rather forward-looking and robust Pauline social program (Gal 3:28; etc.) makes the simplistic claim of a retreat to conservatism unlikely. On the other hand, and far more dramatic, is Paul's subversive co-opting of language and concepts that belong to the social institutions of honor and shame and benefaction in order to lay the groundwork for a reversal of values based on his gospel. Suffice it to say, there is more to this set of instructions than meets the eye.

1 Although effectively two categories of slave will emerge from this

---

6. On the whole matter, cf. Witherington, *The Paul Quest*, 174-229.

7. Thus Verner, *Household of God*, 140-45; Bassler, 107; Osiek and Balch, *Families in the New Testament World*, 184-85; Collins, 151; Young, *Theology of the Pastoral Epistles*, 98-99.

parenesis, Paul first gives a general instruction for all who are[8] Christian slaves.[9] The designation "slave" (Titus 2:9) refers to a man or woman who was the property of, in this case, a householder, and typically assigned any range of duties from the menial to those requiring special skills[10] in the household.[11] The further description, "under the yoke" (cf. Gal 5:1), is traditional and stresses the harsh social and existential reality of the person who existed as the property of another (whether of an unbeliever or a believer).[12]

Whatever sort of excitement or activism on the part of Christian slaves had occasioned the instruction, Paul calls for adherence to the social institution as it was defined by that culture. Elsewhere the same sentiment is expressed with the more typical language of "submission" (Titus 2:9; 1 Pet 2:18; *Didache* 4.11; *Barnabas* 19.7) or "obedience" (Eph 6:5; Col 3:22).[13] Here, in keeping with the "honor" theme already being developed, that instruction is translated as "consider worthy of respect."[14] But the honor or respect due a master is understood to be the enactment of submission and obedience in carrying out assigned duties and responsibilities faithfully and without questioning.

Paul, then, sets parameters on this instruction in two ways. First, he intensifies the command with the term "all" (2:11) that underlines the need

8. This is the sense of the plural correlative pronoun: Gk. ὅσοι (= "as many as, all who"; Rom 2:12; Gal 3:10; cf. 2 Tim 1:18). For the suggestion (unlikely in my opinion) that elders who are slaves are being addressed, see Barrett, 82; Hasler, 46.

9. It is possible that v. 1 specifically addresses Christian slaves under non-Christian owners (Marshall, 629 [possible]; Simpson, 81; Hasler, 45; Towner, *Goal,* 175-80).

10. Including education of children and participation in or oversight of the household's economic interests; see Bartchy, *ΜΑΛΛΟΝ ΧΡΗΣΑΙ,* 72-82; Ferguson, *Backgrounds,* 45-48; Osiek and Balch, *Families in the New Testament World,* 174-92.

11. Gk. δοῦλος (1 Cor 7:21-23; 12:13; Gal 3:28; Eph 6:5-8; Col 3:11; 3:22–4:1; Phlm 16; cf. 1 Pet 2:18 [οἰκέτης]; metaphorical in 2 Tim 2:24; Titus 1:1; K. H. Rengstorf, *TDNT* 2:261-80; Spicq, *TLNT* 1:380-86; A. Weiser, *EDNT* 1:349-52).

12. Gk. ὑπὸ ζυγόν ("under the yoke"; cf. Plato, *Laws* 770E: δούλειον ὑπομείνασα ζυγόν; Polybius 4.82.2: ὑπὸ τὸν ζυγόν); see further Spicq, 552. For ζυγός ("yoke") used metaphorically of a burden such as slavery or an obligation, see Matt 11:29, 30; Gal 5:1; G. Bertram and K. H. Rengstorf, *TDNT* 2:896-901. For the view that "under the yoke" designates specifically slaves belonging to non-Christian masters, see Knight, 244; Hanson, 105; but the general language militates against this specificity and, in view of gospel promises, slavery in a Christian household (e.g., v. 2) might even be conceived of as still more cruel. See further Mounce, 326.

13. Cf. E. Kamlah, "ΥΠΟΤΑΣΣΕΣΘΑΙ in den neutestamentlichen Haustafeln," in O. Böcher and K. Haacker, eds., *Verborum Veritas* (Wuppertal: Brockhaus, 1970), 237-43, 243.

14. For the verb ἡγέομαι ("consider, think, regard"), see on 1:12; for ἄξιος ("worthy"), see on 1:15; 4:9; 5:17-18; for τιμή ("honor, respect"), see on 5:3, 17.

for Christian slaves to serve with excellence and complete obedience (i.e., "consider worthy of *full* respect"; cf. Titus 2:10). Second, he restricts the scope of the instruction to "their [own] masters" (2:9).[15] "Master" *(despotēs)* is the technical term for one who owned slaves.[16] Roman law gave wide-ranging powers to the master in exercising authority over the slave. But the narrowing of the instruction to one's "own master" effectively limits application to the household context.[17] At the same time, Christian slaves are thus reminded that household institutions patterned in a top-down manner are not to be ignored.

Ultimately, Christian slaves who are held to be disruptive or insubordinate could damage the church's witness (cf. Titus 2:10). Paul describes this damage in two ways with a purpose clause *(hina)*. First, insubordination, especially in the case of a Christian slave under a pagan master, puts "God's name" at risk of being "slandered" or "maligned" (cf. Titus 2:5).[18] In this context where the church is thought of as God's household, a reference to God's name is a way of referring to his reputation:[19] it will either be honored or dishonored based on the behavior of those who associate themselves with his household. Consequently, the very identity of the church, which is centered on the name of God, is at stake. Also at risk, secondly, is the "teaching," which again refers widely to the Christian message or doctrine by which the church is known (Titus 2:10; see on 1 Tim 1:10; 4:6, 13). The thought is that the social tension being created by slaves might wrongly be attributed to the gospel by the unbelieving slave owners, or by outsiders observing the church through critical eyes.

The sense of this motivation becomes clearer still against the OT background that Paul echoes. As he sees it, the ultimate objective of the slaves' respect for their non-Christian masters is the good testimony (cf. 3:7). The language echoes the LXX of Isa 52:5:

> 1 Tim 6:1b: "that the name of God *(to onoma tou theou)* . . . might not be blasphemed *(blasphēmētai)*"
> Isa 52:5: "Thus says the Lord, 'On account of you, my name *(to*

---

15. For this use of Gk. ἴδιος ("one's own"), see Titus 2:9; cf. Titus 2:5; Eph 5:22; 1 Pet 3:1. H.-W. Bartsch, *EDNT* 2:171-73.

16. Gk. δεσπότης (6:2; Titus 2:9; 1 Pet 2:18; Plato, *Laws* 757A; used of God in Luke 2:29; Acts 4:24; Rev 6:10); K. H. Rengstorf, *TDNT* 2:44-49. Elsewhere, κύριος ("lord") is occasionally used of the slave owner (Eph 6:5; Col 3:22).

17. Roloff, 322.

18. See the discussion at 1:13, 20; cf. Titus 2:5: "that no one might slander the word of God."

19. Gk. ὄνομα (2 Tim 2:19); H. Bietenhard, *TDNT* 5:242-83, esp. 271-76. For the phrase τὸ ὄνομα τοῦ θεοῦ in connection with "blasphemy," see Rev 16:9.

onoma mou) is continually blasphemed *(blasphēmeitai)* among the Gentiles.'"[20]

The thought was thematic. Ezekiel says much the same thing in different words (36:20; cf. CD 12:7-8). Paul himself elsewhere (Rom 2:24) cited the Isaiah text more fully (including the causal "on account of you" and the reference to the Gentiles), making the same change (as here) from the original first person to the third person required by his discourse. The only other alteration required by 1 Tim 6:1b is the shift to the subjunctive form of the verb to suit the preceding conjunction, "in order that" *(hina)*.

According to the OT pattern invoked here,[21] the echo will equate believing slaves with the Jews depicted in the Isaiah text and implicate the unbelieving masters (and outsiders) with the Gentiles of the OT text/tradition: disobedience on the part of the Christian slaves would complete the equation, making them responsible for provoking unbelievers to slander God's name, while in fact the behavior of God's people should rather adorn the Name and make it attractive to unbelievers (cf. Titus 2:10). Although a missionary emphasis is either lacking or remote in the OT texts that utilize this theme, it is dominant in the NT application.[22] And this concern is paralleled in other NT texts that address the issue of the community's witness in the world in various contexts (Jas 2:7; 1 Pet 4:4, 14; 2 Pet 2:2).[23]

2   The crux of the problem with slaves in Ephesus, for which v. 1 provides the corrective fundamental principle, may well be implied in this second situation. Here Paul specifies "[slaves] who have believing masters."[24] In this case, the present tense prohibition of "showing them disrespect" is a command to stop something already underway. The verb essentially means "to

20. Cf. the Greek:

1 Tim 6:1:   ἵνα μὴ τὸ ὄνομα τοῦ θεοῦ καὶ ἡ διδασκαλία βλασφημῆται;
LXX Isa 52:5:   . . . δι' ὑμᾶς διὰ παντὸς τὸ ὄνομά μου βλασφημεῖται ἐν τοῖς ἔθνεσιν.

21. Marshall, 630, suggests that this might have become a "commonplace" in the early church (cf. Jas 2:7; 2 Pet 2:2; Revelation 16; *2 Clement* 13.2; Polycarp 10.3). Paul's specific use of it elsewhere (Rom 2:24) suggests a conscious use of it here.

22. Cf. W. C. Van Unnik, "Die Rücksicht auf die Reaktion der Nicht-Christen als Motive in der altchristlichen Paränese," in *Sparsa Collecta* (Leiden: Brill, 1980), 2:307-22.

23. Bartsch, *Die Anfänge urchristlichen Rechtsbildungen,* 147, 149; Towner, *Goal,* 177; Spicq, 553.

24. The conjunction δέ ("but, and") functions as a weak adversative to set this situation apart from the first (either introducing a second category of slave, or moving from the general conditions to a specific one). For the Gk. adjective πιστός ("faithful, believing") for "believers," see the note at 1:2.

show contempt" (see on 4:12), which in this context is acted out by slaves who fail to acknowledge their Christian masters' authority over them.

Paul's treatment of this situation differs from that envisioned in 6:1 in two respects. First, with a causal clause he explains the basis or reason underlying the disrespect of these slaves. Second, with a parallel causal clause he lays a different type of groundwork for the appropriate demeanor of Christian slaves toward their believing masters. The first of the causal clauses *(hoti)* is potentially ambiguous, but it is best read as supplying the reason for the slaves' show of contempt for their masters: "because they [their masters] are brothers"[25] (cf. TNIV, NRSV). The phrase might almost have been the slaves' slogan: the declaration that the gospel has leveled the playing field within Christian households, so that it is most appropriate now for slaves to disregard the old rules of the slave/master relationship and regard their masters as brothers in Christ.[26]

This disregard, in Paul's opinion, amounts to a show of contempt, even if the gospel has been cited as the authority. The same danger to the church's witness drawn out in 6:1 applies here. Unbelievers observing households disrupted by slaves who claim some sort of gospel privilege would conclude that the foreign "Christian" teaching underlies the disturbance.

Consequently, Paul issues the countercommand to slaves with Christian masters: "[but] instead they should serve them."[27] The present tense command requires Christian slaves to continue to recognize their masters' authority and to give them the quality of service their station warrants,[28] even though they are fellow believers.

25. For Gk. ἀδελφός in the sense of Christian brother, see on 4:6. Some (e.g., Fee, 139; GNB) take the first Gk. ὅτι clause to supply the reason for showing respect ("do not despise masters, for they are brothers and sisters"). But this would make the second ὅτι clause essentially redundant.

26. Towner, *Goal,* 178-79; Verner, *The Household of God,* 142.

27. The Gk. comparative adverb μᾶλλον (1 Tim 1:4; 2 Tim 3:4) either emphasizes a greater degree of something ("but let them serve all the more [even better]"; cf. NRSV, TNIV, BDAG, s.v. 2.a; 1 Cor 5:2; 6:7; 9:15), or heightens the contrast of actions ("but instead [i.e., of showing contempt] let them serve"; Marshall, 631; BDAG, s.v. 3). Johnson, 284, notes the use of μᾶλλον in the parallel advice to slaves in 1 Cor 7:21 (ἀλλ' εἰ καὶ δύνασαι ἐλεύθερος γενέσθαι, μᾶλλον χρῆσαι; "Even if you can gain your freedom, make use of your present condition now more than ever" [NRSV]), suggesting that the instruction of 1 Tim 6:2 is "less ambiguous." The interpretation of 1 Cor 7:21 is problematic (see Bartchy, *ΜΑΛΛΟΝ ΧΡΗΣΑΙ;* Fee, *1 Corinthians,* ad loc.), but I have noted the similarities between 1 Corinthians and 1 Timothy at various points; and if these passages are in fact parallel, Paul's instructions to Timothy in each case place freedom from the constraints of the social institution beneath the higher priority of service to God and the church's mission. Yet Paul does not leave the institution completely intact (see below).

28. Gk. δουλεύω (metaphorical in Titus 3:3; cf. Phil 2:22); here of actual service as a slave (Matt 6:24; Luke 16:13; John 8:33); K. H. Rengstorf, *TDNT* 2:261-80.

Now follows the second causal clause, this time providing the grounds for the Christian slaves' faithful service to their Christian masters. The first part of this reason presents a minor problem, which is best seen in a literal rendering of the Greek before the TNIV's resolution of it: "because they [i.e., the masters] are believers and beloved." Here the language of "belief" (see on 1:2) describes the masters (cf. 6:1). But to call them further "beloved" is either to stress the masters' standing with God (i.e. "loved by God"; Rom 1:7; 11:28) and therefore worthiness to be served by fellow Christians, or possibly the slaves' Christian love for (= obligation to) their masters (cf. "dear to them" [i.e., to the slaves]; TNIV/NIV).[29] Whichever nuance is intended, the most critical thing to see is that the shared bond of faith does not function as the slaves had imagined (6:1b) — namely, as grounds for disregarding and actively dissolving the institution of slavery. Rather, it places the masters, as fellow believers, into the category of those to whom slaves as Christians must render superior service.

It is the second part of this reason, which further describes the masters, that raises the more important questions. All agree that the participial phrase that closes the Greek sentence stands in apposition to the preceding "because they are believers and beloved," and so refers to the masters. But two interpretations are possible, as the translations of the TNIV and NIV illustrate:

> TNIV: "because their masters are dear to them as fellow believers and *are devoted to the welfare of their slaves*";
> NIV: "because *those [masters] who benefit from their service* are believers, and dear to them."

Thus the phrase in question (in italics) either depicts the masters as benefactors who devote themselves to doing beneficence for their slaves or in general (TNIV) or it depicts them as the recipients of benefits proceeding from their slaves' service (NIV, NRSV). Before we resolve this conflict, we must set out the controlling cultural concept of "benefaction."

Behind the two translations observed above is the noun that means "the doing of good" or "the good that is done" (TNIV, "welfare"; NIV, "service").[30] What the translations generally cannot really bring out is the technical meaning this term acquired within the system of patronage and honor that

---

29. Gk. ἀγαπητός; of God's love (Matt 3:17; Mark 9:7; Rom 1:7; cf. Dibelius and Conzelmann, 82), of human (though possibly God-inspired) love (Acts 15:25; Rom 16:5; Phlm 16; cf. Roloff, 324 n. 494). See G. Schneider, *EDNT* 1:8-12.

30. Gk. εὐεργεσία (Acts 4:9); Spicq, *TLNT* 2:107-13; G. Bertram, *TDNT* 2:654-55.

defined so much of social interaction in ancient Mediterranean culture. In the cultural context, the "good deed" *(euergesia)* was an act of benefaction done normally by a person of some means and influence (the benefactor) for someone who was socially inferior, for which in return he would receive honor in the form of public recognition of some sort.[31] Perhaps it is the taming of this term in translation, which effectively removes it from the sphere of benefaction, that has allowed the majority of English translations to think in terms of slaves doing "service" to their masters. But if the term's likely meaning of "benefaction" is acknowledged, then we have to contend with the more surprising possibility that Paul depicted socially inferior slaves as benefactors of their socially superior masters.

The issue revolves around the action expressed in the Greek participle that translations usually render in terms of "devotion to" (TNIV), or "benefit from," depending on which social direction the action is thought to be moving — from the top down or from the bottom up. This term, too, figures in the ancient discussions of the system of benefaction.[32] And within that context, the term will indicate either the giving or receiving of a benefit (or a return on a benefit).

If Paul has employed benefaction language, it would be most in accordance with normal usage to think in terms of the masters (who are social superiors) as those acting on behalf of their slaves.[33] In this case, the instruction would be exhorting Christian slaves to honor their masters as a way of helping them (the masters) in their efforts to be benefactors, which also benefits the church's reputation in the world.[34] And Paul would be viewing the slaves' attitudes entirely from the standpoint of the masters' and (perhaps) the church's reputation. Further, this would represent a return to (cf. Gal 3:28) or reinforcement of a very conservative position.[35]

31. E.g., Plato, *Gorgias* 513E; *Laws* 850B; *Letter of Aristeas* 205; see esp. F. W. Danker, *Benefactor: Epigraphic Study of a Graeco-Roman and New Testament Semantic Field* (St. Louis: Clayton, 1982), 323-24; Kidd, *Wealth and Beneficence in the Pastoral Epistles,* 142-44.

32. Gk. ἀντιλαμβάνομαι (pres. mid. ptc.; Luke 1:54; Acts 20:35); for a thorough discussion of the sources and of this term in relation to benefaction, see esp. Kidd, *Wealth and Beneficence,* 144-56.

33. So Kidd, *Wealth and Beneficence,* 155-56; Verner, *Household of God,* 143-44; Hanson, 105; Dibelius and Conzelmann, 82; Brox, 204; Bertram, *TDNT* 2:655.

34. See esp. Verner, *Household of God,* 144.

35. See Fiorenza, *In Memory of Her,* 279. She argues that the return to conservatism was occasioned by the social tension created by attempts to live out the radically egalitarian values of the gospel: "the praxis of coequal discipleship between slaves and masters, women and men, Jews and Greeks, Romans and barbarians, rich and poor, young and old brought the Christian community in tension with its social political environment. This tension engendered by the alternative Christian vision of Gal 3:28 . . . be-

But quite apart from the questionable adequacy of this ideological reconstruction of the early church,[36] this interpretation (masters as benefactors)
complicates the logic of the text: simply put, the statement that the masters
are "believers and beloved" is a far better reason for the slaves "to act on behalf" of their masters, as most translations have observed.[37] Consequently,
the closing phrase is better taken as an elaboration on the service the slaves
are instructed ("but instead let them serve"; or "but let them serve all the
more") to render.[38]

Yet what sense can it make for slaves to be described as if they are
"benefactors"? Paul has been known to co-opt the language and concepts so
dominant in his culture in his effort to redefine, challenge, and rather intentionally subvert the "givens" of his day on the basis of the transforming truth
of the gospel he preached.[39] However, here in reversing the roles of slaves
and masters and speaking of slaves as benefactors Paul was not thinking entirely in an unprecedented way. Seneca (d. c. 65 C.E.) introduced the possibility of slaves as benefactors (*On Benefits* 3.18-20):[40]

> . . . there are certain acts which the law neither enjoins nor forbids; it is
> in these that a slave finds opportunity to perform a benefit. So long as
> that which he supplies is only that which is ordinarily required of a
> slave, it is a "service"; when he supplies more than a slave need do, it is
> a "benefit"; it ceases to be called a service when it passes over into the

came the occasion for introducing the Greco-Roman patriarchal order into the house
church."

36. See P. H. Towner, "Can Slaves Be Their Masters' Benefactors? 1 Timothy 6:1-
2a in Literary, Cultural and Theological Context," *Current Trends in Scripture Translation*
182/183 (1997): 43-50; idem, *DLNTD* 513-20.

37. Johnson, 288-90; Marshall, 633; Fee, 139; Knight, 247; Towner, "Can Slaves
Be Their Masters' Benefactors?" 39-52.

38. Marshall, 633.

39. See, e.g., Winter, *Seek the Welfare of the City;* R. A. Horsley, ed., *Paul and
Empire: Religion and Power in Roman Imperial Society* (Harrisburg, PA: Trinity Press In-
ternational, 1997); P. H. Towner, "Romans 13:1-7 and Paul's Missiological Perspective: A
Call to Political Quietism or Transformation?" in S. K. Soderlund and N. T. Wright, eds.,
*Romans and the People of God. Essays in Honor of Gordon D. Fee on the Occasion of His
65th Birthday* (Grand Rapids: Eerdmans, 1999), 149-69.

40. Seneca's logic runs as follows: (1) slaves possess human rights and have the
capacity for virtue (3.18.2); (2) the bestowing of benefits is one part of virtue, therefore
slaves must be able to bestow them (3.18.4); (3) the fact that a slave's obedience is an obligation, coerced (the slave is not strictly speaking a client who has entered into a
"patron-client" relationship of his own free will), does not make it impossible for him to
act beneficently: (a) because it is merely the slave's body, not mind, that is owned (3.20);
and (b) "not the status, but the intention, of the one who bestows is what counts"
(3.18.2).

domain of friendly affection. (3.21) . . . And, just as a hireling gives a benefit if he supplies more than he contracted to do, so a slave — when he exceeds the bounds of his station in goodwill towards his master by daring some lofty deed that would be an honor even to those more happily born, a benefit is found to exist inside the household. (3.33.1, Loeb)

Two things call for comment here. First, Seneca has reversed the typical direction of benefaction; the socially inferior one is found capable of bestowing a benefit on a social superior. Second, a part of his argument is that benefaction in the case of the slave involves going above and beyond the normal call of duty, a theme that may be present in 1 Tim 6:2a.

Within the early church's growing body of teaching, the Jesus tradition preserved by Luke also laid the groundwork for the reversal of certain fundamental social realities, and "benefaction" is at the center of his illustration:

Luke 22:25-27: But he said to them, "The kings of the Gentiles lord it over them; and those who exercise authority over them call themselves benefactors. 26 But you are not to be like that. Instead the greatest among you should be like the youngest, and the one who rules like the one who serves. 27 For who is greater, the one who is at the table or the one who serves? Is it not the one who is at the table? But I am among you as one who serves."

If this illustration is taken seriously, then certainly one point of its relevance within the social world of the early church would be to redefine genuine beneficent action in terms of an attitude of humility and its product — genuine service.[41] Could Jesus' "reversal" teaching have found a fruitful testing ground in the Christian slave-master relationship? At least we can conclude that in the light of Seneca and the Jesus tradition the way forward toward a "reversal of roles" thinking had been prepared.

Within the immediate literary setting, the reader of 1 Timothy quickly discovers that Paul is operating on a couple of different fronts. He has been engaging false teaching in the community and addressing the issue of Christian behavior within the structures of society. The latter issue (however much it might have been influenced by the heresy) is most crucial here. All of 1 Timothy falls within the framework of God's order of reality in the world — God's *oikonomia* (see on 1:4). Paul did not rigidly differentiate between God's will understood in this way and the structures of human society, but rather saw the latter structures as continuous with God's order. It is for this

41. Cf. Danker, *Benefactor,* 324.

reason that the household codes, borrowed from secular ethics, could, once adapted to Christian theological realities, be applied to encourage believers to pursue appropriate behavior within the household and the church.

When read sensitively, these codes are hardly evidence of a wholesale return to patriarchal conservatism, or of abandonment of the Pauline vision of equality. But they are evidence that the biblical writers were sensitive to the expectations of wider society, and knew as well as anyone that the household was the basic social unit. Disorder at this level (no matter what the cause) could spell disaster for the church's reputation in the world. The teaching about relationships in the household sought a creative middle ground with secular ethical values. Christian adaptation and grounding assured that the church would not simply capitulate to social conventions. But it must live and move in society in a way that communicated with that world and at the same time articulated and embodied God's *oikonomia*. God's presence in the world aims at reformation and transformation of its structures, never uncritical acceptance of them. Tension is unavoidably created as God's values clash with the world's. Paradoxically, the household codes sought to control the effects of this tension while also sustaining it; they kept Christians engaged in the culture and urged against any radical dismantling of the social structure. Yet the instruction also encourages critical assessment of traditional assumptions and values that shape the institutions, by placing human household relationships under the Lordship of Christ and redefining things such as honor and benefaction with *agapē* and service. The tension in Christian existence remains acute, and it can be easily felt in 1 Timothy, where the church overlaps with the household.

This brings us back to the teaching on slaves in 6:1-2a, teaching that belongs to or grows out of the household code tradition. In the instruction to Christian slaves whose masters are believers (v. 2a), we have the supreme example of a situation in which social obligations belonging to the household come into conflict with the values and goals that shape Christian existence and life in the church. Giving rise to the specific instruction is the dissonance between the Christian ethos of egalitarianism ("because they are brothers") and the cultural household reality of slavery ("they are masters"). In this paradoxical context Christian slaves are told that the common bond in Christ they share with their masters ("because they are brothers") is not legitimate grounds for exercising equality (despising them, showing contempt); but in fact precisely that bond ("because they are believers and beloved") calls the slaves to even better service. Typically (cf. 1 Corinthians 7; Ephesians 6; Colossians 4), Paul refuses to resolve this tension by tampering directly with the structure (e.g., "Masters, release your slaves who are brothers"). Even where Paul comes closest to doing so, in writing to Philemon, he never forces the master to regard the institution of slavery as null and void. Rather, in this case his solution is spiritual, which is not to say ethereal ("Slaves, act as though you were the masters"). This reversal, which is determined in our text by Paul's application of honor and benefactor language in the closing phrase, is both subtle and surprising. The subtlety is seen not so much in the ambiguity of the phrase itself as in the fact that by all appearances the slave-master relationship is kept intact. The surprise comes in the description of the slaves' extraordinary service as a benefaction received by the masters (for which, we have seen, there is some precedent in Seneca and in the reversal teaching of Jesus): "Instead slaves should serve their masters even better because those who receive the slaves' benefaction are believers and loved (by God/by the slaves)."

Paul has turned the tables. The slaves serve, but in God's surprising *oikonomia* they do so from a position of power; nobility and honor, the rewards of benefaction, are accorded here implicitly to the slaves. In all of this, the privileges of honor which that culture reserved for well-to-do patrons, benefactors, and slave owners are not denied; nor are the obligations of slaves to their masters trivialized. But the meaning and value of life lived at that level are relativized by the more fundamental reality of the universal Lordship of Christ within God's *oikonomia*.

3. Contrasting False and True Teachers, Godliness, Greed, and the Correct Use of Wealth (6:2b-21a)

This closing section of the letter bears a remarkable structural resemblance to the opening section in ch. 1 (1:3-20). Most scholars now admit that the structure is intentional,[1] and a brief comparison of the elements will help to introduce the exegesis below. From a global perspective, it is hard to miss the fact that the whole letter is framed by the doxologies of 1:17 and 6:16. Yet more duplication is evident in this closing section.

1:3: Command to Timothy to instruct	6:2b: Command to Timothy to teach

4-7a: Topic/Description: false teachers
   Positive Theme: love
	3-6: Topic/Description: false teachers
	   Positive Theme: godliness

7b-10: Misunderstanding: the law
   [purpose of the law explained]
	5-6: Misunderstanding: godliness/
	   wealth [godliness explained]

	[7-10: Desire for wealth critiqued]

---

1. See esp. J. Thurén, "Die Struktur der Schlussparänese 1 Tim 6,3-21," *TZ* 26 (1970): 241-53. Cf. Dibelius and Conzelmann, 83-91.

11-16: Contrasting Model: Paul	11-15: Contrasting Model: Timothy
[conversion/calling]	[restating Timothy's commission]
[role of the historical Jesus]	[example of the historical Jesus]
17: Doxology	16: Doxology
	17-19: Instruction to the Wealthy
18-20: Timothy's commission repeated	20-21: Timothy's commission repeated.

While perhaps more subtly nuanced structural layouts could be tried, the breakdown offered here allows the repetition of a pattern and the substitution of certain themes to be observed. Most notable is the degree of continuity Paul establishes. The letter to Timothy naturally began with a statement of his commission and instructions concerning Ephesus that are then recapitulated at the conclusion of the opening section. The final section of the letter effectively repeats this pattern, reemphasizing that this is a letter about Timothy's work in Ephesus. False teachers are the central concern within each commissioning section.

But some interesting developments occur from opening to closing sections. First, at the outset Paul described the goal of his gospel in terms of a thoroughgoing love. Now, as he closes the letter, he substitutes the theme of godliness, which throughout these three letters defines authentic Christian existence as the integration of inward and outward elements (faith and love). Second, misunderstanding is a subtheme in each section. In the first case, the law, which the false teachers purport to be teaching, has been misunderstood, so Paul gives correct instruction. In the latter case, godliness has been misunderstood as a means of acquiring wealth, and the motive of greed is intertwined with this misunderstanding. Again Paul gives correct instruction, first, concerning the true gain to be expected in godliness, and, second, in greater detail concerning the danger of striving after wealth.

Most notable in the closing section is the expanded instruction concerning the dangers of wealth. This may seem like a digression, but it is probably to be explained, on the one hand, as falling out logically from the denunciation of the false teachers and their greedy motives, and, on the other hand, as preparation for the later reflection on wealth's appropriate use in the community (6:17-19).

The rhetorical device of contrast (true gospel/false gospel; false teachers/models of true teachers; etc.) figures effectively in each section. But whereas Paul (his conversion and calling) represents the model of truth and faith in ch. 1, in the closing section Timothy takes this place as his commission is restated in overtly ethical terms. This feature of the closing section, along with the restatement of his commission in relation to the false teachers (6:20-21a), reminds us that this letter was first and foremost addressed to the apostolic coworker to direct his work in Ephesus.

a. Charge to Timothy: Confront the False Teachers and Their Lust for Wealth (6:2b-10)

> 2b *These are the things you are to teach and insist on.* 3 *If anyone teaches otherwise and does not agree to the sound instruction of our Lord Jesus Christ and to godly teaching,* 4 *they[2] are conceited and understand nothing. They have an unhealthy interest in controversies and quarrels about words that result in envy, strife, malicious talk, evil suspicions* 5 *and constant friction between people of corrupt mind, who have been robbed of the truth and who think that godliness is a means to financial gain.*
>
> 6 *But godliness with contentment is great gain.* 7 *For we brought nothing into the world, and we can take nothing out of it.* 8 *But if we have food and clothing, we will be content with that.* 9 *Those who want to get rich fall into temptation and a trap and into many foolish and harmful desires that plunge people into ruin and destruction.* 10 *For the love of money is a root of all kinds of evil. Some people, eager for money, have wandered from the faith and pierced themselves with many griefs.*

Despite the interruption of versification, the new section begins at v. 2b with a second-person singular command that reverts to Timothy's role as teacher and apostolic delegate. The first subsection (vv. 2b-10) is framed by three themes: the false teachers, godliness, and wealth. The interrelation of these themes is not precisely clear, but it is apparently some combination of a misunderstanding of "godliness" and greed motives on the part of the false teachers that has led Paul to expand on the dangers of greed at some length.

2. As the apodosis of the "if anyone, then . . ." statement is reached, the TNIV chooses to shift from an original singular ("he" or "she") to the plural "they" in order to get the appropriate gender-inclusive sense. The strategy employed in 5:8, which might give a slightly smoother reading, makes the condition into a statement: applied here it would yield: "Anyone who teaches otherwise . . . is conceited" (cf. the NRSV). The decision not to go this way here was based on the fact that this would turn a case-specific exhortation (i.e., it is spoken in view of the existence of those who are actually teaching "otherwise") into a gnomic one (and 5:8 is arguably gnomic in thrust). In that case, I might choose to pluralize the front reference and stress slightly the present tense of the verb, and render the statement thus: "those who are teaching otherwise [or teaching false doctrine] . . . are conceited."

The TNIV begins a second paragraph at v. 6, where a shift occurs from discussion of the false teachers to a more general but related explanation of godliness and wealth.

2b   The new section is linked to the preceding instructions by the formulaic summary command to Timothy, "These are things you are to teach and insist on," probably referring to the instructions of 5:1–6:2a. The didactic language has already occurred in the letter, and this restatement of the formula differs only slightly from 4:11.[3] Its function (to sum up a section of teaching before a new one commences) is the same. The combination here is sufficient to put Timothy back in a teaching and correcting mode following the community concerns just covered. And it is departure from that pattern of teaching that Paul is about to address.

He will do so from three perspectives. First, Paul defines positively the character of the instructions he has been giving. Secondly, in contrast, he harshly denounces the character of those who teach false doctrine. Thirdly, he links their activities to a misunderstanding of godliness and a materialistic motive.

3   Paul returns to the subject of Timothy's main task in Ephesus. As in ch. 1, he first creates distance between Timothy and the false teachers, and between the apostolic message and the heresy. The well-used "if anyone . . . then" formula functions to identify an actual group of false teachers almost as a wanted poster might do (see on 3:1).[4] Their misdeed, named in specific contrast to the command to Timothy just issued, is "to teach contrary doctrine" (or, stressing the contrast with Timothy, "to teach otherwise"). The verb is repeated from 1:3 and reflects back on that initial allegation of false teaching. The language and the contrast with Timothy place this activity (and those involved in it) in direct opposition to the teaching of the apostle and his delegate (6:2b).

As Paul elaborates on those who teach "otherwise," it becomes clear again (cf. 1:4-7) that the problem is not simply that of disseminating factual errors; it is rather a failure of the heart that involves willful rejection of God's pattern. The other side of false teaching, expressed with the negative, is thus "not agreeing with" (or "lacking in devotion to")[5] the apostolic doctrine.

3. For Gk. διδάσκω ("teach"), see the discussion on 2:12 and the note. Here παρα-καλέω ("exhort, urge, insist"; see on 2:1) replaces παραγγέλλω ("command, instruct"; 4:11) but with little net difference in effect.

4. The εἴ τις ("if anyone . . . , then . . .") conditional formula with following indicative verbs introduces the actual situation as the author sees it.

5. Gk. προσέρχομαι (in the NT usually in the local sense of movement toward; e.g., Heb 4:16, etc.; 1 Pet 2:4); for this sense of intellectual movement toward (= assent, devotion; see TNIV/NIV; NRSV), see (with various objects) Philo, *On Husbandry* 123; *Didache* 4.14; Epictetus 4.11.24; BDAG, s.v. 2. J. Schneider, *TDNT* 2:683-84. Confirming

Paul's renewed deployment of the graphic medical language of "soundness" ("healthiness"; see on 1:10) describes the effect and potency of his gospel. The toxic influence of false teaching will be described in terms of character flaws presently but is otherwise left implicit. The complete combination, "sound instruction" (lit. "words"),[6] occurs here for the first time in the letters to Timothy (see 2 Tim 1:13). It is further defined by the modifying phrase "of our Lord Jesus Christ" (6:14), but the connection is somewhat ambiguous. Given the fact that Paul intends the whole term to cover instructions already given in the letter to this point, a specific reference to the sayings of Jesus is extremely unlikely.[7] The intention of the additional genitive phrase is far more likely to ascribe the origin and, consequently, authority of the teaching to Jesus.[8] The full appellation "our Lord Jesus Christ" anticipates 6:14, where Jesus' final appearance and his authority as judge establish the framework for Timothy's devotion. Here it underlines the absolute authority of the instructions given by Paul.

From the thoughts of authority and origin, Paul shifts to a reflection on the "godliness" that "the teaching" is designed to produce in believers. The TNIV translation, "godly teaching," smoothes out an uncertain grammatical relationship but may lose something in the process: lit. "the teaching that is in accordance with godliness." In these letters to coworkers, "godliness" describes Christian existence as the balance of faith in God/Christ/the gospel and the outward life it produces (see 2:2, Excursus; Titus 1:1). In the phrase in question, the term is attached to "the teaching" by the Greek preposition *kata* (see the note on Titus 1:1). The sense will be to identify godliness either as the standard of "the teaching" ("the teaching that is in accordance with godliness") or as the goal of "the teaching" ("the teaching that produces/promotes godliness"). In this context, the distinction is rather fine since in either case "godliness" as an actual by-product of the apostolic teaching is clearly central to Paul's point. But given that the false doctrine

---

this sense is the secondary reading προσέχεται (ℵ* a few Old Latin MSS), which represents a later "correction" in conformity with the more widely used term (1:4; 3:8; 4:1, 13; cf. Titus 1:14).

6. For the plural use of Gk. λόγοι in reference to teaching, see 4:6. The combination "sound teaching" (with διδασκαλία) is more frequent (1:10; 2 Tim 4:3; Titus 1:9; 2:1; cf. Titus 2:8 of speech), and the independent use of διδασκαλία for Christian instruction is far more frequent than the plural λόγοι (4:6, 13, 16; 5:17 [with sg. λόγος]; 6:1; 2 Tim 3:10, 16; Titus 2:7, 10).

7. But see Lock, 68; Spicq, 557.

8. Rightly Fee, 141; Marshall, 638-39. Some argue for the meaning "teaching about Jesus" (Dibelius and Conzelmann, 83; Kelly, 134; Guthrie, 123; cf. the gen. "the word about Christ" in 1 Thess 1:8); but given the content of the preceding community instruction, a broader sense is warranted.

produces rather different results, and that the measurement of orthodoxy versus unorthodoxy is uppermost in mind, Paul probably appeals to the quality of life ("godliness") as the standard or proof of the authority of his teaching.[9]

4-5   Equally, a life devoid of godliness (and associated virtues) is the benchmark of rejection of the gospel and adherence to false doctrine. To illustrate this anti-life, Paul begins with rudimentary moral flaws, moves on to controversy and other sins, and ends with complete rejection of the truth and confusion about the real meaning of "godliness."

Verse 4 commences the apodosis of the "if . . . then" statement and with it the indictment of those who teach falsely and reject the church's teaching. Paul first follows the lead of ancient polemicists and links inferior teaching and rejection of the truth to a "deluded" or "stupid" state (TNIV, "conceited").[10] Second, Paul rephrases the opening allegation of ignorance (1:7): they "understand nothing."[11] Third, also recalling the opening polemical barrage, strengthened here by repetition of the medical imagery (v. 3), these opponents are sick[12] either because they crave controversy (TNIV)[13] or as a result of involvement in it.[14] The term "controversies" (2 Tim 2:23; Titus 3:9) describes discussions that have gone beyond the stage of a useful exchange of ideas.[15] They result in "quarrels" (lit. "word battles")[16] that serve only to draw out and fuel even baser sinful activity.

Paul gives a short list of typical evil qualities engendered or aggra-

---

9. Paul describes his apostolic calling in closely similar terms in Titus 1:1 ("the knowledge of the truth that is in accordance with godliness"; see discussion).

10. For references to ancient polemics, see Johnson, 292; most versions take Gk. τυφόω (see discussion at 3:6) in the sense of arrogance or conceit (BDAG, s.v. 1); but in the context a hunger for power may be indicated, placing the meaning in the domain of mental illness, delusion, or stupidity (as in Philo, *On the Confusion of Tongues* 106; Josephus, *Against Apion* 1.15; see A. J. Malherbe, *Paul and the Popular Philosophers* [Minneapolis: Fortress, 1989], 123-24 n. 7).

11. Gk. μηδὲν (indef. pron., "nothing"; 5:21) ἐπιστάμενος (masc. sg. ptc. from ἐπίσταμαι, "to know"; here only in Paul, freq. in Acts).

12. Gk. νοσέω (only here in the NT; of spiritual or mental illness in one degree or another, see LXX Wis 17:8; Philo, *Allegorical Interpretation* 3.211: "infected with the disease of foolishness"); cf. Josephus, *Antiquities* 16.244.

13. As in Plutarch, *Moralia* 546F; BDAG. Cf. A. Oepke, *TDNT* 4:1095.

14. See Johnson, 292.

15. Gk. ζήτησις is essentially a neutral term in pre-NT and NT usage for "speculation" or "inquiry" that sometimes slides into the range of "dispute, debate, dissension" (John 3:25; Acts 15:2, 7; Josephus, *Antiquities* 15.135; *Against Apion* 1.11) in later usage (H. Greeven, *TDNT* 2:892-94; BDAG, s.v.).

16. Gk. λογομαχία (only here in the NT; variant reading in Titus 3:9; cf. G. Kittel, *TDNT* 4:143); see the verb λογομαχέω in the same sense in 2 Tim 2:14; and μάχη ("fighting, quarreling, disputing") in 2 Tim 2:23; Titus 3:9.

vated by the opponents' controversies.[17] Some belong to the traditional web of vices often drawn on by Greek ethicists (cf. Rom 1:29; Gal 5:20-21; Phil 1:15), and the polemical intention of the critique is hard to miss. The list extends to v. 5 and includes five moral defects that affect human relationships and threaten unity.

"Envy" (Titus 3:3) does not carry the rather neutral sense that we often give to it. In Greek thought it was a vice characterized by an incessant craving for things or positions possessed by someone else.[18] Aristotle described it as "a certain sorrow" felt by those who lack what others have; it fits well within the traditional medical framework of disease since it gnaws away at the inner person and provokes the hatred toward others that destroys relationships.[19]

Often linked with "envy" in both Paul (e.g., Rom 1:29; Gal 5:20-21; Phil 1:15) and the moral philosophers is the next vice, "strife" (Titus 3:9).[20] The chaotic dissension it envisions goes naturally with the situation of controversy caused by the opponents.

"Malicious talk" (or "slander"; not "blasphemy" in this context) is hardly a surprising addition to the list.[21] It occurs in similar lists elsewhere (Mark 7:22; Eph 4:31; Col 3:8), where abusive and defamatory speech characteristic of life outside the church is denounced. Verbal attacks were apparently typical of the arguments associated with the heresy.

"Evil suspicions" correspond naturally to the climate of sick competitiveness and the stress on social relationships in Ephesus.[22] This is a natural outgrowth of envy, and obviously undermines the trust that determines successful relationships.

Verse 5 continues the list of sins but with a change in style and focus as a climax approaches. "Constant friction" is again easily enough imagined

17. The linking phrase (Gk. ἐξ ὧν), consisting of the preposition "from, out of" plus the feminine genitive plural relative pronoun "which [things]," identifies the two preceding feminine nouns, "controversies and word battles," as the source of what is to follow.

18. Gk. φθόνος (Matt 27:18; Mark 15:10; Rom 1:29; Gal 5:21; Phil 1:15; Jas 4:5; 1 Pet 2:1. Cf. Spicq, *TLNT* 3:434-36.

19. Aristotle, *Rhetoric* 1387B (cited by L. T. Johnson, *The Letter of James* [AB 37A; New York: Doubleday, 1995], 287). See also Plutarch, *Moralia* 536E ("Concerning Envy and Hatred"). On the set topic in Greek moral discourse, see esp. L. T. Johnson, "James 3:13–4:10 and the *Topos ΠΕΡΙ ΦΘΟΝΟΥ*," *NovT* 25 (1983): 327-47.

20. Gk. ἔρις ("strife, contention"; pejorative; see Rom 13:13; 1 Cor 1:11; 3:3; 2 Cor 12:20; Phil 1:15; Sir 28:11; 40:4, 9). Cf. Spicq, *TLNT* 2:69-72.

21. Gk. βλασφημία ("defamation, slander"; see discussions at 1:13, 20; 6:1; cf. Titus 2:5).

22. Gk. ὑπόνοια ("conjecture, suspicion"; only here in the NT; cf. the cognate verb in Acts 13:25); for the combination with the adjective πονηρός ("evil"; 2 Tim 3:13; 4:18), see Sir 3:24. Cf. J. Behm, *TDNT* 4:1017-19.

within this disputatious setting.[23] The emphasis in this sentence is, however, on the further description "between people of corrupt mind, who have been robbed of the truth." The language of "corruption" belongs to discussions of moral and intellectual breakdown,[24] and here it is with respect to the "mind" of people that corruption occurs.

Within these letters to coworkers, each occurrence of "mind" is in reference to the ineffective, corrupted thinking of the false teachers (2 Tim 3:8; Titus 1:15). The language descriptive of this corruption varies,[25] but the effect in each case is to associate this condition with loss of or resistance to "the truth." The "mind" in Pauline anthropology describes the organ or agent of rational discernment and perception through which the revelation of God, "the gospel, the truth," can be understood and processed.[26] In this passage (also 2 Tim 3:8) the alignment of "mind" and "the truth" (= "the gospel"; see on 2:4) suggests that the corrupted mind of the false teacher either stems from rejection of the truth or frustrates correct perception of it.

Paul leaves the precise connection between these things somewhat ambiguous. But the following phrase, "robbed of the truth,"[27] makes it clear that through their teaching and disputing they have cut off any access to understanding the gospel. And taken in conjunction with similar statements in these letters (2 Tim 3:8; Titus 1:14), decisions made against Paul's gospel are directly related to the corrupt state of their minds and the sinful activities that have ensued. Moreover, it is worth noting that the perfect tense of the participles "corrupted" and "robbed" indicates conditions that do in fact exist "now" because of past actions or decisions made. Rejection of the apostolic faith has rendered these opponents incapable of comprehending (theology) and processing (ethics) God's truth.

The next comment, detailing yet another flaw in the heretical outlook, illustrates how profound the opponents' delusion was (v. 5b). A third participle describes the false teachers as those "who think that godliness is a means

---

23. Gk. διαπαρατριβή is a true hapax legomenon (for its derivation, see BDAG; see also Malherbe, *Paul and the Popular Philosophers,* 125 n. 9; Johnson, 293).

24. Gk. διαφθείρω (for various kinds of destruction and corruption, see Luke 12:33; 2 Cor 4:16; Rev 8:9; 11:18[2x]). Cf. G. Harder, *TDNT* 9:93-106. See Johnson, 293, for the use of this term (moral, mental corruption) in ethical literature.

25. Cf. the use of a related verb, καταφθείρω ("to destroy, corrupt"), in 2 Tim 3:8 (ἄνθρωποι κατεφθαρμένοι τὸν νοῦν; "people of corrupt mind"); the term used in Titus 1:15, μιαίνω ("to defile"), belongs to the language of ritual defilement: μεμίανται αὐτῶν καὶ ὁ νοῦς καὶ ἡ συνείδησις; "their minds and consciences are defiled."

26. Gk. νοῦς (Rom 1:28; 7:23, 25; 11:34; 12:2; 14:5; 1 Cor 1:10; 2:16[2x]; 14:14, 15[2x], 19; etc.; cf. 2 Cor 11:3). See further the discussion (and refs.) in Towner, *Goal,* 158-59; Marshall, 210-11.

27. Gk. ἀποστερέω (Mark 10:19; 1 Cor 6:7, 8; 7:5).

to financial gain." The shift to the present tense creates a closer link with the preceding statement, describing one way (at least) in which they have been "robbed of the truth," namely, "in that they think. . . ."[28] The verb of thought frequently indicates a wrong assumption,[29] and that is certainly the case here. Although financial "gain" (or, to be precise, "means of gain") is meant in this first use of the noun,[30] Paul will shift to spiritual "gain" in making his correction below.

The crux of the problem is a misunderstanding of some sort about "godliness" (see 2:2, Excursus). But it is not entirely clear what Paul implies about that misunderstanding. Probably he means that the false teachers were passing themselves off as "godly" Christians in the service of God, and exploiting their own distorted version of "godliness" in order to draw people in who would then support their teaching.[31] This amounts to a financial motive. Paul had to answer such an allegation himself (1 Thess 2:5), and warnings and complaints about teachers with financial motives were widespread (Rom 16:17-18; 1 Pet 5:2; 2 Pet 2:2).[32] In any case, Paul's own exposition of "godliness" as authentic Christian spirituality forms the contrastive backdrop to association of it with the heresy.

6 As indicated by the repetition of the two key terms "gain" and "godliness" and the linking "to be" verb (now moved to emphatic position),[33] Paul turns the negative assessment just made inside out to correct (and further condemn) the heretical distortion of values. While the repetition of thoughts is

---

28. Marshall, 643. Consequently, the NRSV translation is preferable to the TNIV/NIV, which takes the participle as describing an attendant circumstance.

29. Gk. νομίζω (for this use, see esp. Luke 2:44; 3:23; Acts 7:25; 8:20; 14:19; 16:27; 17:29; 21:29); cf. W. Schenk, *EDNT* 2:470.

30. Gk. πορισμός (6:6; LXX Wis 13:19; 14:2); Plutarch, *Moralia* 524D ("On Love of Wealth"); for "means of gain," see references in BDAG; Marshall, 643 n. 18.

31. Alternative interpretations include Kelly, 135, who understands the "godliness" to be that of other unsuspecting believers who feel compelled to support the false teachers (cf. Lips, *Glaube,* 81-83, who suggests that the false teachers had gained access to the mission-support fund); Kidd, *Wealth and Beneficence,* 96-100, offers a more comprehensive reconstruction: the opponents rose to prominence from a wealthy circle in the church in which wealth and leadership became closely linked; a particular notion of godliness (εὐσέβεια) and wealth (as a means of continuing to acquire honor) became interconnected; Paul then seeks to disconnect true godliness from wealth.

32. See Roloff, 333-34.

33. Cf. vv. 5b and 6:

5b: πορισμὸν εἶναι τὴν εὐσέβειαν
6: ἔστιν δὲ πορισμὸς μέγας ἡ εὐσέβεια μετὰ αὐταρκείας.

Marshall, 644, points out that 6:6 presents the only example in these letters in which the verb εἰμί ("to be") is first in its clause.

rhetorically significant, it is the expansions he introduces, and the implicit re-definition of "godliness" that results, that shift the direction of meaning.

First, Paul takes the discussion to a higher level than the heretical understanding is able to reach. The "great gain"[34] he associates with "godliness" exceeds the limited material "gain" sought by the opponents.

Second, his repetition of the term "godliness," bearing the profound meaning of authentic Christian existence, also seeks a higher, spiritual level of meaning. The further qualification of it as "godliness with contentment [or self-sufficiency]" removes godliness from the material limitations of the false teachers' motives and substantiates Paul's spiritual thrust. The qualifying phrase contains a term that was essential to Stoic philosophy (and present also in Cynic and Epicurean teaching), where it expressed the notion of "self-sufficiency," emphasized detachment from things or outside possessions, and stressed independence.[35] Paul was clearly in touch with this theme (2 Cor 9:8; Phil 4:11-12), but supplied a Christian basis for it. By introducing the countermaterialistic concept of self-sufficiency as an element of "godliness," he left no room for the acquisitiveness and financial implications attached by the false teachers. With a slight shift, the term comes to mean the satisfaction or contentment with what one already has.[36] In the present context, the two ideas converge (cf. the adj. in Phil 4:11). Godliness is not about acquiring better and more material things; it is instead an active life of faith, a living out of covenant faithfulness in relation to God, that finds sufficiency and contentment in Christ alone whatever one's outward circumstances might be.[37]

7-8 The following sentence, constructed partly of traditional material echoing Jewish wisdom and conventional wisdom, substantiates Paul's view of contentment/self-sufficiency. The language of 6:7 ("for we brought nothing into the world, and [because] we can take nothing out of it") shows some affinity with the wisdom sayings of Job 1:21, Ps 49:16, and Eccl 5:14. But the thought is so well documented in the ancient world that it is impossible to limit the source of the proverbial saying, as it appears here, to the OT,[38]

---

34. On the Gk. adjective μέγας ("great"), see the discussion at 3:16.

35. Gk. αὐτάρκεια (2 Cor 9:8; see the adj. αὐτάρκης at Phil 4:11). For the theme in Greek moral teaching, see Plato, *Republic* 2.369B; Diogenes Laertius 10.130-31; G. Kittel, *TDNT* 1:466-67; Dibelius and Conzelmann, 84-86; A. J. Malherbe, *Moral Exhortation* (Philadelphia: Westminster, 1986), 112-14, 145.

36. See the word group in LXX Prov 24:30; Sir 5:1; 11:24; 31:28.

37. Cf. Marshall, 644-45; Oberlinner, 278-79; Roloff, 334-35; Fee, 143.

38. Philo, *On the Special Laws* 1.294-95; Pseudo-Phocylides 110-11 [*OTP* 2:578]; *Anthologia Palatina* 10.58 [*The Greek Anthology* 4:33]; Seneca, *Epistle* 102.25; *'Abot* 6:9 [StrB 3.655]; *b. Yoma* 86b; Luke 12:16-21; Hermas, *Similitude* 1:6; see Dibelius and Conzelmann, 84-85; M. J. J. Menken, "*Hoti* in 1 Tim 6, 7," *Bib* 58 (1977): 532-51, esp. 535-36.

though OT wisdom may indeed have played a seminal role in bringing the opinion into the ethical thought of the early church. This particular statement of the principle is later picked up by Polycarp (*To the Philippians* 4.1).[39]

On a close reading, Paul's reasoning could certainly be questioned: that is, given that v. 7 intends to ground v. 6 ("for"; *gar*), how does it substantiate the preceding minimalist (self-sufficiency) view?[40] Material possessions are surely at issue (v. 8), and the couplet aligns nicely the two negative statements: nothing brought into the world/nothing brought out.[41] The arena of this activity is the sphere of human life (*kosmos;* see on 1:15; 3:16), stated clearly in v. 7a and assumed in v. 7b. However, the symmetry is disturbed in a puzzling way by the conjunction that connects v. 7b to v. 7a (cf. TNIV's "and" with NRSV's "so that"). Without some other element (such as a verb of saying or perception requiring an explanatory marker, "that"), we would expect the Greek word *hoti* to mean "because." With some creativity (I adjust the aorist tense of the first verb in translation for smoothness) this might give the right sense: "we bring nothing into the world because we cannot bring anything out."[42] The idea would be that human existence is just this way: "we arrive empty-handed because in fact that is just the way we will leave"; material possessions and advantage cannot pass through the veil, and if they could, we would have arrived better equipped.[43]

To return to the question of Paul's logic, the answer is surely that he addresses in two ways the tendency of acquisitiveness that motivated the false teachers. First, he places life on earth into eternal perspective. While he does not devalue human earthly life in any sense, he does force the reader to view it in temporary terms. Second, following from this, an eschatological understanding of human life as beginning in a temporal mode but destined for an eternal mode invites a rethinking of focus that will accord the appropriate value to each stage of life and a balanced approach to material living.

Verse 8 takes up this matter. It completes Paul's thought by explaining (1) what the self-sufficiency/contentment reference above (v. 6) means and

---

39. *Contra* Dibelius and Conzelmann, 85.

40. See the discussion in Marshall, 646.

41. Cf. the Gk. εἰσφέρω ("to bring into"; Luke 5:18-19; Acts 17:20; Heb 13:11; K. Weiss, *TDNT* 9:64-65) and ἐκφέρω ("to bring out of," here in inf. form with δύναμαι [hence "we are not able to bring out"]; Acts 5:6, 9, 10, 15). Polycarp, *To the Philippians* 4.1.

42. Barrett, 84; Marshall, 648. But the abrupt ὅτι (‫א‬* A F G, etc.), which is original, exercised the early copyists, who emended the text in various ways, usually to enable the conjunction to function as "that" (D* a b; ‫א‬² D² Ψ TR), or omitted it (co Hier Aug Cyril); see Metzger, 576.

43. An ellipsis of some sort is possible; see Marshall, 646-48, for the numerous solutions attempted.

(2) the appropriate perspective on the material life between the two boundaries identified in the proverb.

What Paul means by "contentment/self-sufficiency" is described with an informal condition.[44] It boils down to the basics of life, "food"[45] and "clothing."[46] On the other side of the conditional thought stands another term in the domain of self-sufficiency: "if we have food and clothing, *we will be content* with that."[47] Thus Paul fills out his self-sufficiency concept.

This interpretation of "contentment" in terms of the essential items of life can be found in Jewish and Greek literature.[48] It had also found a place in the Jesus tradition (Matt 6:25; Luke 12:22) and church writings (Heb 13:5), and Paul may be more closely in touch with its adaptation in and through the early Christian movement.

In any case, in explanation of the proverbial saying in v. 7, Paul's interpretation of contentment/self-sufficiency provides his perspective on material living. What he endorses is not poverty, but, as Marshall and Stott aptly point out, a simple lifestyle.[49]

9-10 Having thus spelled out a view of life consonant with "godliness," Paul takes up a critique of acquisitiveness. The sentiments he expresses are certainly general enough to apply anywhere, but the immediate application is to the financial motive of the opponents (v. 5b). He first sets out the dangers of seeking wealth (v. 9), then supports his view of the matter with a proverbial statement (v. 10a), which he finally applies to the local situation (v. 10b).

Verse 9 begins by identifying a group of people. It is probably correct to distinguish this group, "those who want to get rich,"[50] from the group of

44. For the adverbial participle (here ἔχοντες, "having") expressing condition, see BDF §418.2.2.
45. Gk. διατροφή (only here in the NT); LXX 1 Macc 6:49; Josephus, *Antiquities* 2.88; BDAG.
46. Gk. σκέπασμα ("clothing," as in Aristotle, *Politics* 1336a; Philo, *That the Worse Is Wont to Attack the Better* 19, or "shelter," as in Aristotle, *Metaphysics* 1043a); in the context of this discussion of self-sufficiency, "clothing" (TNIV/NIV, NRSV) is the better sense.
47. Gk. ἀρκέω (fut. indic. pass.: "to be content"; Luke 3:14; Heb 13:5; cf. 2 Cor 12:9; LXX 2 Macc 5:15; 4 Macc 6:28); Josephus, *Life,* 244; for the term in philosophical thought, see G. Kittel, *TDNT* 1:464-66 (esp. 465); possibly imperatival in force (Kelly, 137; Roloff, 336).
48. Gen 28:20; Sir 29:21; Plutarch, *Moralia* 155D; see further Dibelius and Conzelmann, 85; see also references to αὐτάρκεια above.
49. Marshall, 649; Stott, 153.
50. For Gk. βούλομαι ("to wish, desire"), see on 2:8; 5:14. Gk. πλουτέω ("to be rich"; 1 Cor 4:8; 2 Cor 8:9; fig. in 1 Tim 6:18; Rom 10:12); cf. the use of the word group in 6:17: noun πλοῦτος ("wealth"), adjective πλούσιος ("a wealthy person"), adverb πλουσίως ("richly"); F. Hauck and W. Kasch, *TDNT* 6:318-32.

those already wealthy whom Timothy is to address in 6:17-19.[51] While it is possible that reference to the financial motives of the opponents above (v. 5) caused Paul to give general teaching on the topic of wealth here, it seems more likely that the opponents are being described in the closing association of eagerness for wealth and wandering from the faith (v. 10b).

Paul describes the dangers of this desire with a series of three terms, almost as a violent chain reaction. The whole image begins with the verb "to fall," which (as in 3:6-7) often depicts the unexpected and unfortunate entrance into an experience or condition that is better avoided.[52] There follows an ineluctable sequence of "falling." First comes "temptation," which here carries the specific passive sense of being lured into sin (Matt 6:13; 1 Cor 10:13; Jas 1:12).[53] The desire for wealth makes one susceptible to corrupt suggestions and unscrupulous opportunities to advance. Second, the next term "trap" (or "snare"; see on 3:7) moves the sequence from enticement to actual entrapment in a predicament.

The third element is more complex and more specific in identifying the inward forces or appetites unleashed by the desire for wealth: "many foolish and harmful desires." "Desires" in and of themselves may be positive and natural (Luke 22:15; cf. the verb in 3:1); but in the present context and frequently in the NT the term describes human desires that have gotten out of balance or are pursued without appropriate restraint.[54] "Many" (see on 3:8) is emphatic of the exceptional danger presented by the hunger for wealth. The two adjectives classify the evil desires as "foolish" (or ignorant) in the sense of reflecting ignorance of God and his wishes (see on Titus 3:3), and "harmful," leading to destruction.[55]

Finally, but still speaking in generalities, Paul extends the note of destruction just sounded with still more graphic language to describe the cata-

---

51. Verner, *The Household of God,* 174-75. But cf. Kidd, *Wealth and Beneficence,* 95-97, for the argument that the same group (the wealthy in the church) is meant in each case.

52. Gk. ἐμπίπτω ("to fall" into the hands of robbers, Luke 10:36 [Epictetus 3.13.3]; into the hands of God [in judgment], Heb 10:31; into sickness, 1 Macc 6:8; a loose woman's snares, Sir 9:3).

53. Gk. πειρασμός (for the act. sense of "tempting," Luke 4:13; for the sense of trial/test, see Luke 8:13; 22:18; Acts 20:19; Heb 3:8; 1 Pet 4:12); Spicq, *TLNT* 3:80-90; H. Seesemann, *TDNT* 6:23-36.

54. Gk. ἐπιθυμία (2 Tim 2:22; 3:6; 4:3; Titus 2:12; 3:3; the verb is neutral, 1 Tim 3:1; Luke 22:15). F. Büchsel, *TDNT* 3:171; H. Hübner, *EDNT* 2:27-28. For the ideal of restraint in the case of "desires," see Plato, *Phaedo* 83B. For the Jewish perspective on "desires" and their results, cf. 4 Macc 1:22-23; Sir 23:5 (prayer for "evil desire" to be removed); Wis 4:12 (the uncontrolled desire); 4 Macc 1:3 ("lust" hinders self-control).

55. Gk. βλαβερός (only here in the NT; LXX Prov 10:26; Hermas, *Similitude* 6.5.5, 6, 7 (of harmful luxuries). Spicq, *TLNT* 1:292.

strophic end result of the chain reaction. The image is of being forced under water ("to plunge, cause to sink"), which is extended figuratively here to mean "to cause disaster."[56] The extent of disaster is portrayed emphatically with two synonyms for "destruction" ("ruin and destruction"; TNIV, NRSV).[57] It is unlikely that they intend to express some distinct nuance of disaster, or refer to stages (present material ruin, followed by eschatological judgment).[58] Rather, each term occurs in contexts discussing eschatological destruction and judgment, and the thought driven home by their combination here seems to be of the complete moral and spiritual devastation that leads (among other things) to apostasy (v. 10b).

Verse 10 brings this discourse on modest living and the dangers of avarice to a conclusion by reciting or formulating a traditional maxim of common wisdom and showing what has happened to some (opponents in the church) who have transgressed it. The dictum linking evil[59] to "love of money"[60] was widely published (with various expressions) by the ancient philosophers.[61] As in some of Jesus' parables (Matt 13:21; Luke 8:13; cf. Rom 11:16-18), "root" functioned figuratively in a wide range of wisdom and ethical writers to depict the source from which sprang either good or evil things.[62]

In this version of the saying, "root" (the predicate of the noun "love of money") is placed in the emphatic position.[63] Since it lacks the definite article ("the"), a question of translation naturally occurs. Several translations and commentators prefer "a root" (i.e., "the love of money is a root of all

---

56. Gk. βυθίζω (of literal drowning, 2 Macc 12:4; for the passive of a boat going under, Luke 5:7); for the figurative extension, BDAG, s.v. 2.

57. Gk. ὄλεθρος ("destruction"; Pauline in the NT; 1 Cor 5:5; 1 Thess 5:3; 2 Thess 1:9); J. Schneider, *TDNT* 5:168-69. For ἀπώλεια, see Matt 7:13; 26:8; Rom 9:22; Phil 1:28; 3:19; 2 Thess 2:3; etc.; A. Oepke, *TDNT* 1:396-97.

58. But cf. Kelly, 137; Knight, 256-57.

59. The plural Gk. combination πάντων τῶν κακῶν ("every evil") might be understood as a generic statement ("every kind of evil"; cf. Knight, 258; Johnson, 296), but the presence of the article makes this less likely (Marshall, 651 n. 51). Gk. κακός ("evil"; 2 Tim 4:14; Titus 1:12) describes something that is either harmful or morally wicked (W. Grundmann, *TDNT* 3:469-87) — in this context and with the plural, both possibilities might apply.

60. Gk. φιλαργυρία ("avarice, miserliness"; 4 Macc 1:26); cf. the adjective φιλάργυρος ("fond of money"; 2 Tim 3:2; Luke 16:14); ἀφιλάργυρος ("not a lover of money"; 3:3); Spicq, *TLNT* 3:446-47.

61. See the citations in Dibelius and Conzelmann, 85-86 (e.g., Diogenes Laertius 6.50: "He called love of money [τὴν φιλαργυρίαν] the mother-city of all evils"); Spicq, *TLNT* 1:45 n. 5; 3:446-47; and the list in Marshall, 652 n. 55.

62. Gk. ῥίζα; see the numerous examples in BDAG, s.v. 1.b; C. Maurer, *TDNT* 6:985; Marshall, 651 n. 48.

63. It is first in the sentence, well in advance of the equative verb ἐστιν ("to be").

[kinds of] evil"; see TNIV/NIV; NRSV; GNB).[64] While the aim of this rendering is apparently to keep Paul from assigning too much blame for evildoing to greed/money, the emphatic position of the term "root" and especially the rhetorical needs of the discourse favor, instead, the bolder translation, "the love of money is the root of every evil." It is the strongest sense that lends the argument the force required to drive home the point that avarice produces devastating results. To tame the translation is to soften the indictment of the greedy opponents.

And it is specifically the intention of sharpening the indictment that Paul achieves in the closing description of those in the community who have fallen in love with wealth. Using the same formula of indictment that appears in 1:19 (1:6; 6:21),[65] the false teachers are again identified with the dismissive "some" (see on 1:3, 6). Despite the widely known peril of pursuing wealth (as set out in the saying), it is just this, "aspiring" (see 3:1 and note) to be rich,[66] that has undone the opponents in view. Their undoing is described in two ways.

First, they have left "the faith." Paul means that whether by rejecting apostolic doctrine or behaving in a way that implies rejection (or indeed both) they have let go of commitment to the content of the Christian "faith" (see the comments on 1:2). The term for the act of apostasy, "wandered away" (so TNIV, NRSV), is perhaps better translated as a true passive, "led astray,"[67] to bring out the element of deception that describes the opponents (4:1; 2 Tim 3:13; cf. Titus 3:3). It belongs to a group of several terms that Paul uses for deviation from the standard authoritative teaching.[68] Lust for wealth is thus depicted as a force that blinds them and causes them to veer off course.

Second, Paul uses the graphic language of impalement ("they pierce themselves")[69] to describe the way in which these people cruelly harm

64. Kelly, 138; Knight, 257; Collins, 159; Mounce, 346.

65. For the combination of relative pronoun/pejorative indefinite pronoun/participle action leading to contravention of "faith" (ἧς τινες ὀρεγόμενοι ἀπεπλανήθησαν τῆς πίστεως), see 1:19 (ἥν τινες ἀπωσάμενοι περὶ τὴν πίστιν ἐναυάγησαν).

66. The feminine relative pronoun (ἧς) at the head of the clause refers to the preceding "love of money," which is modified slightly to mean "money" or "wealth" (see the translations) according to the needs of the resulting statement.

67. Cf. 2 Chron 21:11; Prov 7:21; Sir 13:6.

68. See the discussion at 1:6, 19; 4:1; 5:15; 6:21; 2 Tim 2:18. Gk. ἀποπλανάω (Mark 13:22; LXX 2 Chron 21:11; Prov 7:21; Jer 27:6; Sir 4:19; 13:6, 8; 2 Macc 2:2); for its later use as a technical term for apostasy, see Polycarp, *To the Philippians* 6.1; Hermas, *Similitude* 6.3.3; 9.20.2; *Mandate* 10.1.5). See H. Braun, *TDNT* 6:249-50.

69. Gk. περιπείρω (only here in the NT; for a similar figurative example, see Philo, *Against Flaccus* 1: "he inflicted (περιέπειρε) the most intolerable evils."

themselves[70] in pursuing the dream of wealth. The further description, "many griefs,"[71] is intentionally broad in scope. Any number of things might be included, from the personal emotional torments of unfulfilled dreams (of wealth) and damaged reputations to the relationships destroyed when desire for wealth overrules brotherly love.

Paul has closed the circle begun at v. 3. The opening indictment of the opponents for false teaching developed into a description of the sorts of ungodly behavior associated with their activities. As their misshapen outlook on "godliness" came into view, linked as it was to avarice, Paul pivoted to consider what in fact godliness might look like from the perspective of material wealth. Then, with real circumstances in the church and among the opponents in view, he set out (with some help from traditional materials and sentiments) the simple life that accords with authentic Christian existence. The closing of the parenetic circle required one last contradictory look at the opponents whose culpable lust for wealth had taken them to disastrous places. It would be remiss not to stress the way in which Paul fleshes out "godliness" in very material and practical ways. If we choose a term like "spirituality" to describe what Paul means by the term "godliness" (= authentic Christian existence), we must not fail to see that it describes the life of faith in God as one firmly anchored in the realities of this world and yet at the same time not bound to this world's sinful values and structures. Godliness as a description of existence incorporates the human mind and heart, with which faith and ethical decisions are made, and the physical senses, with which the human being engages the material and social world and produces a visibly Christlike manner of life in it.

b. Recasting Timothy's Commission:
Genuine Character and Motive for Ministry (6:11-16)

> 11 *But you, man of God, flee from all this, and pursue righteousness, godliness, faith, love, endurance and gentleness.* 12 *Fight the good fight of the faith. Take hold of the eternal life to which you were called when you made your good confession in the presence of many witnesses.* 13 *In the sight of God, who gives life to everything, and of Christ Jesus, who while testifying before Pontius Pilate made the good confession, I charge you* 14 *to keep this command without spot or blame until the appearing of our Lord Jesus Christ,* 15 *which God will bring about in his own time — God, the blessed and only Ruler, the*

---

70. Use of the reflexive pronoun (Gk. ἑαυτούς, "themselves") and its initial position in the clause emphasize the self-inflicted nature of this harm.

71. Gk. ὀδύνη (Rom 9:2); F. Hauck, *TDNT* 5:115.

King of kings and Lord of lords, 16 *who alone is immortal and who lives in unapproachable light, whom no one has seen or can see. To him be honor and might forever. Amen.*

From the solemn opening phrase, "[O] man of God," to the closing doxology, this section brings the commissioning and instructing of Timothy to a climax. The liturgical language and tone of this closing call to commitment probably correspond to confessional events in the church (e.g., baptism).[1] Thus though Paul addresses Timothy directly, the language also contains a public "witnessing" element, as others hear Timothy's commission renewed and by implication respond.

Two dominant themes appear to shape the exhortation. First, the thrust of the charge is antithesis and separation. On one level, this is the function of the polemical discourse Paul has been constructing throughout the letter. Having described the devastation experienced by the opponents, Paul propels Timothy in the opposite direction of holiness. The separation from all that is evil (as exemplified in the case of the heretics in 6:3-10) is underscored with two direction-changing devices: "but you" and the following traditional "flee-pursue" formula. And the goal of ensuring that Timothy as Paul's delegate (and counterpart to Paul himself in ch. 1) is measurably different from the opponents (their teaching and lifestyle) is clear enough.

But on another level — that of Christian existence — Paul's employment of antithesis is determined by the contrastive character of holiness as it finds expression in an unholy world. In this sense, the subtext of Paul's instruction — flee/pursue — is "become what you are in Christ," embrace the antithesis that Christ's death and resurrection have introduced into human life. That is to say, in a very real sense the present experience of Christian life is a continual process of flight from and pursuit toward.

Second, also shaping the exhortation is the use of past and future references to focus attention on the present. The parallel Pauline reminiscence in 1:11-16 is similar: Paul looked back to his conversion and calling and forward to eternal life. Now his responsibility is to take hold of (and to proclaim) a present salvation based on Christ's earthly ministry. Here Paul recollects Timothy's past confession of faith (v. 12; baptism?). This past boundary marker was to have determined Timothy's direction in life from that point on. But a future eschatological boundary marker is also indicated — the epiphany of Christ (v. 14). It is between these two boundaries, and in light of them, that the series of present-oriented commands that express Timothy's commission is given. It is not accidental that Paul again draws on the humanity of

---

1. For which, see Roloff, 344 (based on the work of K. Wengst, *Christologische Formeln und Lieder des Urchristentums* [2d ed.; Gütersloh: Mohn, 1973], 124-25).

Christ to provide the exemplar of faithful human confession. In the end, when the details have been examined and reorganized, the human experience of Christian existence is bounded by a past event of grace that is apprehended by faith and a future event of grace that is awaited in hope. The present can then be characterized in many ways, but here the focus is on the ethical quality to be experienced and on the obligation to pursue it.

The work associated with this charge (1:3-7; 6:20-21) is consciously muted so that the ethical character in which Timothy is to perform his tasks can be set in vivid contrast to the scathing list of vices (vv. 4-5) and charge of greed (vv. 5, 10) applied to the opponents.[2] After bringing Timothy back to his formative confession, Paul restates his delegate's terms of commitment, calling the heavenly court as witnesses, and concludes as in ch. 1 with a doxology. Just as in Paul's case it is Christ's decisive saving act that issues in a calling to service, so too in Timothy's it is the reality and authenticity of his faith and salvation that qualifies him to serve.

11 As the restatement of commission begins, Paul turns first to the matter of Timothy's holiness — separating him distinctively from the errorists. He establishes this distinctiveness in three ways. First, he employs (for the first time in these letters to coworkers; 2 Tim 3:10, 14; 4:5; Titus 2:1) the abrupt "but you" transition; this polemical-rhetorical device is designed to emphasize a break with, and to create distance from, the opponents.[3]

Second, Paul distinguishes Timothy in the appeal, "[O] man of God." This title exceeds the rhetorical personalizing function of the similar phrase, "O (hu)man" (Rom 2:1, 3, 20; etc.) by virtue of the addition of the genitive qualifier "of God" that places Timothy into the category of the numerous OT servants of God who were so designated.[4] Equally, the presence of the emotive vocative marker of personal address, "O" (cf. 6:20; Gal 3:1; etc.),[5] distinguishes this title from the similar general reference to "the one who belongs to God" as used in 2 Tim 3:17.[6] The title underwent some development in

---

2. Cf. Thurén, "Struktur," 243-44.

3. Gk. Σὺ δέ (2 Tim 3:10, 14; 4:5; Titus 2:1; cf. Rom 11:17; 2 Tim 2:1); "but you" is emphatic in the expression of the pronoun and its placement at the head of the phrase; the device occurs in parenetic literature (*Epistle to Diognetus* 12 [106.11 in Malherbe]; Socrates, *Epistle* 7.5 [242.26 in Malherbe]); cf. Wolter, *Paulustradition,* 135-37.

4. Cf. the Gk. phrase ὦ ἄνθρωπε θεοῦ with the simple ὦ ἄνθρωπε of Luke 5:20; 12:14; 22:58, 60; Rom 2:1, 2; 9:20; Jas 2:20. For OT usage, see, e.g., Moses (Deut 33:1; Josh 14:6; etc.), David (2 Chron 8:14), prophets (1 Kgs 13:1; 17; 18; 2 Kgs 23:17), and Samuel (1 Sam 9:6).

5. The TNIV omits this marker since (apparently) the English "O" lacks the emotive force of the Greek interjection. On the tone and use of the vocative marker ὦ ("O"), used only with human beings, see BDF §146; Turner, *Syntax,* 33.

6. For various reasons, some interpreters regard the title in 6:11 to refer generally

Philo, who used it to identify a qualitatively different sort of person whose life, patterned in some sense after Moses', was marked by a profound devotion to God.[7] As applied to Timothy, both servanthood (and holy lineage) and devotion to God (a superior quality of godliness) combine in this final address. Paul sets Timothy apart not from all other leaders but from those whose lifestyle demonstrates a false claim to authority.

Third, the traditional "flee/pursue" formula (2 Tim 2:22) draws an emphatic line between behavior that has been denounced ("all this" in reference to the preceding discussion, 6:3-10) and behavior that is to be embraced. The two verbs ("flee, pursue") were stock items in Greek ethical teaching, and were sometimes juxtaposed as here.[8]

Consequently, the transition Paul has made in his discourse is not just one of topic. Rather, in these three ways he shifts from a set of values and aspirations that he has evaluated and rejected to an approved measurement of holiness. He has also set Timothy's character and calling apart from those of the opponents. And he urges Timothy to separate consciously from the things they do and seek, and to "pursue" the authentic virtues of godliness they lack.

The remainder of v. 11 fills out what is meant by the pursuit command in a series of six virtues. Virtue lists, such as this one (2 Tim 2:22-25; 3:10), were a typical feature of Hellenistic ethical teaching that allowed the cardinal virtues to be packaged and presented neatly and concisely.[9] The use of this device by Paul and other NT writers (sometimes alongside a contrasting list of vices) shows indebtedness to the literary and pedagogical fashions of the day.[10] Christian virtue lists also functioned to package neatly the (cardinal) qualities characteristic of authentic Christianity. No single list is exhaustive, and each also intended to call to mind the whole network of behavioral qualities that constitute a life lived in response to God's covenant. The contents of the lists vary, but the "faith/love" pair often forms a noticeable core (see on 1:14), and the Christianizing of a secular device is evident from this critical anchor. Like-

---

to every believer; see A. Sand, *EDNT* 1:103; Karris, 35. While it may be argued that Timothy does serve as a model (and that instructions to him are relevant to all believers and leaders), there is no reason to obscure the primary personal reference in the parenesis.

7. E.g., Philo, *On the Confusion of Tongues* 41; see further J. Jeremias, *TDNT* 1:364-65.

8. Gk. φεύγω ("flee, shun") and διώκω ("pursue"). Apart from classical use (esp. in Aristotle and Plato), for φεύγω see Sir 21:2; Tob 4:21; 1 Cor 6:18; 10:14; for διώκω see Prov 15:19; *Testament of Reuben* 5:5; Rom 12:13; 1 Cor 14:1; 1 Thess 5:15. Rom 9:30 has the traditional combination of "pursue" and "righteousness" (Herodotus 1.96.2; Deut 16:20; Prov 15:9; Isa 51:1; Sir 27:8). For the formulaic pairing, see *The Cynic Epistles* (ed. A. J. Malherbe), 56.3; 64.18, 24.

9. See the discussion and references in Towner, *Goal,* 160-61.

10. 2 Cor 6:6-7; Gal 5:22-23; Col 3:12-14; 2 Pet 1:5-7.

wise the organization of items in the lists follows no discernible pattern, though in the letters to Timothy there is some preference for the first three terms (see also 2 Tim 2:22), and the "faith/love" pair resonates even more widely. Although there is some distance between, this list of virtues forms the polemical counterpart to the shorter vice list of 6:4 that helps put distance between the life Timothy is to pursue and the way chosen by the opponents.

"Righteousness" in Paul's various discussions can be a rather loaded term.[11] In some contexts (e.g., Rom 9:30; 10:3; Gal 5:5; etc.; 2 Tim 4:8), against the law-court background of the OT, it is the resulting status that accompanies the verdict of acquittal handed down by God to those who have placed their faith in Christ.[12] Here, however, it is one way of describing the whole of ethical and observable life. It means moral "uprightness" in the sense of a life lived in accordance with God's law (2 Tim 2:22; 3:16; Acts 10:35; Phil 1:11). This is not to diminish the theological orientation of "righteous" living, but only to place the accent on the behavior that belief in God is meant to produce.

"Godliness" (see 2:2, Excursus), the second term, is broader still. As throughout these letters to coworkers, it characterizes the whole of Christian existence as the combination of faith in God and the observable ethical response to his covenant.

The next three terms, "faith, love, endurance," form a traditional triad that summarizes Christian existence. "Faith" and "love," perhaps the essential pair,[13] effectively interpret the concept of "godliness." "Faith" in this context could mean faithfulness (i.e., to the gospel or the truth) or the ongoing act of believing (see 1:2, note). "Love" (see on 1:5) is the active outworking of belief in sacrificial service to others. But earlier expressions of the "faith-love" combination show how it attracted other important virtues to itself. "Faith, hope, love" appear together in 1 Thess 5:8 and as a distinct triad in 1 Cor 13:3; in 1 Thess 1:3 we can already see how room was made to add virtues such as "endurance" (Rev 2:19).[14] This term also occurs with faith and love in the lists of 2 Tim 3:10 and Titus 2:2. It expresses the determination and perseverance that are needed to support faith and love in the face of adversity,[15] which in all three settings has the conflict with opponents in view (cf. Rev 2:2-3).[16]

11. Gk. δικαιοσύνη; G. Schrenk, *TDNT* 2:192-210; K. Kertelge, *EDNT* 1:325-30.

12. E.g., 2 Tim 4:8; cf. Rom 9:30; Gal 5:5; Phil 1:11.

13. See 1 Tim 1:5, 14 (discussion); 2:15; 4:12; 2 Tim 1:7, 13; 2:22; 3:10; Titus 2:2. W. Günther, H.-G. Link, and C. Brown, *NIDNTT* 2:538-52; Towner, *Goal,* 162-63; Spicq, *TLNT* 1:8-22; G. Schneider, *EDNT* 1:8-12.

14. Towner, *Goal,* 160-61; Marshall, 241.

15. Gk. ὑπομονή; see further Spicq, *TLNT* 3:414-20; W. Radl, *EDNT* 3:405-6. It is used widely in Paul (Rom 2:7; 5:3-4; 8:25; 12:12; 15:4-5; 1 Cor 13:7; 2 Cor 1:6, etc.).

16. See also Fee, 186; Marshall, 241.

Closing the list is the rare term "gentleness."[17] Its place in the list (as with its synonym in 2 Tim 2:25) is to describe the attitude necessary to engage those in opposition in a way that will facilitate their repentance and reconciliation.

Thus Timothy is to pursue a life that, in contradiction to the rebelliousness and factiousness of the opponents, exhibits genuine godliness and compassion for those in error. If Paul seems to be preoccupied with ethical matters, the slippage in the behavior of some of the church's former leaders explains his concern. In any case, what should not be lost on us is that Paul does not isolate elements of human conduct from matters of ministry, but rather seeks to integrate belief and behavior into a holistic pattern of existence. It is not accidental that he began this restatement of Timothy's commission from an ethical perspective: the starting point for ministry is a manner of life that is visibly different from that patterned after the values of the world, which keeps faith and love/conduct bound tightly together.

12 Paul next broadens this ethical base by adding two commands that pertain more specifically to the fundamental health of Timothy's faith and the authenticity of his salvation. The first concern is that he should not fall from the faith as others have done (4:12).

First, therefore, he is to continue to engage in the Christian contest of faith. With minor adjustments, the command to Timothy (in the present tense) employs the same language and athletic metaphor to be used (in the perfect tense) to describe the apostle's own faithfulness in the Christian struggle in 2 Tim 4:7: "compete in the good contest of faith."[18] The application of this athletic language of effort to the pursuit of moral virtue and Paul's various uses elsewhere have already been seen at 4:10.[19] Here it occurs in a more stereotyped formula (2 Tim 4:7, discussion; cf. 1 Tim 1:18), suitable to the confessional/commissioning tone of the section but without diminishing the emphasis on struggle.[20] If we compare the battle formula in 1:18 with the athletic formula here, the contexts suggest a shift in attention from Timothy's ministry to confront the opponents to his need to attend to his own contest of faith (as in Paul's application in 2 Tim 4:7). While this need not exclude aspects of ministry (including confrontation with opponents), the distinction, though fine, should be noted. As in the case of the battle terminology of 1:18,

---

17. Gk. πραϋπαθία (only here in the NT, not in the LXX; see Philo, *On Abraham* 213). Cf. Spicq, *TLNT* 3:171; BDAG.

18. I have chosen to depart from the TNIV translation ("fight the good fight") in order to call attention to the distinction between the two formulas.

19. For the verb ἀγωνίζομαι, see the discussion and note at 1 Tim 4:10.

20. Gk. ἀγωνίζου τὸν καλὸν ἀγῶνα; for the noun ἀγών (2 Tim 4:7), clearly in the sense of a "contest," see Heb 12:1; *1 Clement* 7.1; BDAG, s.v. 1; in the sense of "struggle," Phil 1:30; 1 Thess 2:2; *2 Clement* 7.1, 3, 5. Cf. E. Stauffer, *TDNT* 1:135-40.

"good" identifies the Christian contest as authentic and corresponding to God ("noble, excellent"). With Timothy's stability of faith in mind, it is preferable to translate the genitive qualifying phrase "of [the] faith" as a reference to the essential quality of the Christian life as contest (= persistent believing; i.e., "keep competing in the good contest of faith"),[21] rather than as a definition of the object of the contest with the opponents (= the content of what is believed; i.e., "for/of the faith"; TNIV, NRSV).[22] Paul's concern here is that Timothy not grow weary or complacent in believing, as the false teachers so clearly had done.

Paul's third command, composed of three parts, directs Timothy both forward to the goal of faith and backward to a decisive moment in his personal history. The combination of thoughts complements the previous command as it also underscores the obligation attached to his public confession of faith. First, Timothy is to "take hold of the eternal life to which you were called." In 1:16 (see discussion; Titus 1:2) "eternal life" is described as the goal of belief in the gospel. With the metaphor of athletic effort still in mind, the imperative "take hold of" ("grasp"; 6:19)[23] affirms that for the one who perseveres in faith eternal life begins in a substantial way (is really obtained) in the present. While in the present age believers still wrestle with the invisibility of salvation blessings (Rom 8:24-25), their reality now is nonetheless founded on the certainty of God's past act in Christ.

Second, "eternal life" is stated to be the goal of God's "calling": "to which [i.e., eternal life] you were called."[24] As in Paul and in the formative background of Isaiah, God's act of "calling" (indicated here in the passive voice; Gal 5:13; Eph 4:1, 4) is the means by which he summons people to salvation (2 Tim 1:9).[25] The reflection in Timothy's case is backward in history to his own experience of hearing the gospel and responding to this invitation in conversion.

Third, this direction is confirmed by mention of Timothy's past "confession." The syntax is rough, with the connection between the immediately preceding reference to God's calling and Timothy's confession made ambiguous by the conjunction "and." As the TNIV translation suggests, the in-

---

21. The genitive is appositional; see Pfitzner, *The* Agon *Motif,* 179; Marshall, 659.

22. See the translation of Johnson, 305 ("Engage the noble athletic contest for the faith"). For the range of usage of πίστις, see 1:2 (note).

23. Gk. ἐπιλαμβάνομαι (6:19; Matt 14:31; Luke 9:47; BDAG, s.v. 4).

24. See the identical syntax in Col 3:15; 2 Thess 2:14.

25. Gk. καλέω (Rom 8:30; Gal 1:6; 1 Thess 2:12; 5:24; etc.) in combination with the preposition εἰς ("to, toward, unto") signifying goal; see also 1 Cor 1:9; 1 Pet 2:9; 5:10. LXX Isa 41:9; 42:6; 48:12; 50:2; cf. K. L. Schmidt, *TDNT* 3:487-91; J. Eckert, *EDNT* 2:240-44.

tended sense is probably temporal, indicating that it was *when* he "made the good confession . . ."[26] that he became aware of and responded to God's summons to salvation. The act of "confession" entails agreement, acknowledgment of some fact, and commitment;[27] as with the contest of faith, it is "good" (i.e., accords with God). But Paul omits any description of what has been confessed. The second reference to "the good confession" as that which Christ made before Pilate (v. 13) is clearly to the messianic self-testimony that led ultimately to the cross (see below). In this light and in view of Pauline thought elsewhere (Rom 10:9-10), the allusion is surely to Timothy's own confession that Jesus is the Christ and Lord.

The connection with God's "calling" and the aorist tense of the verb "[when] you confessed" suggests reflection on a particular event in Timothy's life, and that it was probably to Timothy's initial confession of faith at conversion/baptism. The attempt to locate this confession in an ordination ceremony is popular but speculative.[28] Yet it identifies an important element of this injunction. The allusion backward to the initial baptism confession and commitment is clearly made with Timothy's present life and work in view.[29] The time gap is bridged not simply as a way of encouraging the coworker in hard circumstances, but more so in order to remind him of the binding obligations associated with his primal confession that time does not erase. It is for this reason that Paul adds the reference to "the presence[30] of many witnesses."[31] The relating of this past formative event through letter to Timothy and to the receiving church extends the obligation across time as it also extends that group of binding "witnesses" to include the Ephesian congregation itself.

13-15a Once the territory from holiness (v. 11) to faithfulness (v. 12a) has been covered, and the line of obligation has been strung from Timothy's past to the present (v. 12bc), Paul finally restates his delegate's commission. In doing so, he gathers up the twofold charge to Timothy in 1:3, 18 into a concluding reaffirmation of his commission that will echo one last time in 6:20-21. The command tone is authoritative and formal — "I charge"[32] — and suited to the importance of the moment. While the injunc-

---

26. Gk. καὶ ὡμολόγησας τὴν καλὴν ὁμολογίαν; the repetitive wordplay style (verb/art./καλός/cognate noun) is identical to that in v. 12a (ἀγωνίζου τὸν καλὸν ἀγῶνα).

27. Gk. ὁμολογέω (Titus 1:16; Rom 10:9-10; etc.); for the noun ὁμολογίαν, see 2 Cor 9:13 ("the action of confessing"); 1 Tim 6:13; Heb 3:1; 4:14; 10:23 ("the contents of the confession"); cf. O. Michel, *TDNT* 5:210-11; O. Hofius, *EDNT* 2:514-17.

28. E. Käsemann, *Exegetische Versuche und Besinnungen,* Erster Band (Göttingen: Vandenhoeck & Ruprecht, 1960), 101-8; Roloff, 340-45; Knight, 264-65; Barrett, 86.

29. Cf. Oberlinner, 293.

30. See the discussion at 2:3; 5:4, 20, 21.

31. See the discussion at 5:19; 2 Tim 2:2.

32. See the discussion and note at 1:3; cf. 1:18.

tion itself may seem straightforward ("I charge you . . . to keep this command"), the additional intervening descriptions of God and Christ Jesus who attend the charge as witnesses and lend it weight require attention.[33]

First, it is standard to remind Timothy (and other readers) of God's intimate presence in the midst of his people.[34] In another context this truth might be a source of comfort (Luke 12:6; Acts 2:25), but the presence of God is typically invoked to ensure veracity (Luke 1:19) or, as here (5:21), to strengthen the sense of obligation contained in an apostolic command.

The pattern of naming both God and Christ as witnesses is parallel to 5:21 (where the elect angels are added) and 2 Tim 4:1. But each divine witness is described uniquely. God is further styled, with a present participle, either as "the one who gives life to everything" or "who preserves the life of all things." Both meanings of the verb are attested,[35] but the object "everything" (= "the universe," Col 1:16; Eph 1:23) and the anticipation of the allusion to Christ's death and resurrection both call for the meaning of life-giver.[36] God is thus viewed as the creator of life and sustainer of the universe.

Christ Jesus accompanies God the Father in witnessing the charge to Timothy. But in dramatic contrast to the image of creative power drawn on to depict God, the present exalted Christ is remembered in his moment of supreme earthly weakness and vulnerability as his interrogation "before[37] Pontius Pilate"[38] is called to mind. And this allusion concludes the christological emphasis on Christ's humanity in this letter (1:15; 2:5-6; 3:16).[39] The mo-

---

33. The TNIV/NIV and NRSV attempt to get smoothness by moving the long prepositional phrase ("in the presence of God . . . and Christ Jesus . . .") to the head of the verse so that the initial verb, "I charge you," and its complementary infinitive phrase, "to keep the commandment . . . ," can be joined. However, while a more idiomatic and smooth English sentence results, the original abruptness of the transition from v. 12d to v. 13a (shifting to the authoritative verb of command with no intervening connective) probably intends to attract attention.

34. For the technique, see 2:3; 5:4, 21; Rom 14:22; 1 Cor 1:29.

35. Gk. ζῳογονέω (of "sparing life" in Luke 17:33; Acts 7:19; LXX Exod 1:17, 18, 22; Judg 8:19; 1 Sam 27:9; of "making alive, giving life" in 1 Sam 2:6); R. Bultmann, *TDNT* 2:873-74; Spicq, *TLNT* 2:164-65.

36. See Towner, "Christology in the Letters to Timothy and Titus."

37. The interrogation setting favors translating the Gk. preposition ἐπί in the local sense as indicating position "before, or in the presence of" Pontius Pilate (e.g., Mark 13:9; Acts 24:20; BDAG, s.v. 3; Marshall, 663; Roloff, 351) rather than as indicating the temporal sense of "in the time of" Pontius Pilate (Mark 2:26; Luke 4:27; BDAG, s.v. 18a; Kelly, 143-44; Brox, 216).

38. Gk. Πόντιος (*nomen* [middle or tribal name] of Pilate; Luke 3:1; Acts 4:27; Matt 27:2 [variant]) Πιλᾶτος (cognomen, freq. in all Gospels and Acts). Pilate was the Roman governor of Palestine.

39. Towner, "Christology in the Letters to Timothy and Titus."

ment in view is the court scene as preserved in the Synoptic tradition (Mark 15:2; par.), where in answer to Pilate's question, "Are you the King of the Jews?" Jesus answered, "It is as you say." Alternatively, Paul possibly shows knowledge here of the more elaborate tradition that is preserved in John 18:36-38; in John the specific verb "to bear testimony" (*martyreō;* note the shift from the preceding verb "to confess" = *homologeō* used of Timothy in v. 12) occurs on the lips of Jesus.[40] That act of confirming his messianic identity is translated here into the phrase, "he testified[41] the good confession" (see on v. 12). The parenetic application to Timothy is obvious from the repetition of the "good confession" language already used of him: as the charge to Timothy unfolds, he is to find his pattern of faithful service "now" in the risky faithfulness exhibited by the earthly Jesus.

After the divine witnesses have been invoked, v. 14 resumes and completes the charge initiated with the words "I charge [you]" and places the whole of Timothy's ministry in the light of the return of Christ. First, the charge itself is summarized with the infinitive clause: "to keep this command."[42] In spite of a rather surprising amount of discussion about the meaning and scope of "the command[ment]" (better, "the mandate, order, commission"),[43] the reference is surely to what Paul has charged Timothy to do in Ephesus, introduced in 1:3-5 and filled out in the course of the letter.[44]

Second, in another awkward turn of syntax, Paul appends two adjectives, "without spot[45] or blame,"[46] which most translations render as a double accusative. If TNIV (NIV, NRSV, etc.) is correct, the adjectives, modifying "this command," call for Timothy to keep the command intact, to guard its

40. See Johnson, 308. Johnson, however, surprisingly misspeaks when he declares: "Note that the Synoptic Gospels do not have Jesus speaking before Pilate" (but cf. Matt 27:11; Mark 15:2).

41. The shift here to μαρτυρέω (see on 5:10) from ὁμολογέω in the case of Timothy (v. 12) has been explained in various ways. In view of the allusion to bearing (spoken) testimony before Pilate (ὁμολογία), it is an unlikely reference to his death as "martyrdom" (but see Dibelius and Conzelmann, 88). The two word groups were apparently capable of overlapping (e.g., John 1:19-20).

42. The Gk. infinitive τηρῆσαι ("to keep, obey"; see 5:22; often with nouns like "the law," "commandment[s]," "word," e.g., in Matt 19:17; 1 John 5:3; Rev 3:10) completes the thought of the verb of command, παραγγέλλω ("I charge"), that initiated the sequence in v. 13.

43. See the discussions in Knight, 266-68; Marshall, 664-65.

44. Gk. ἐντολή (Titus 1:14) is best rendered here in the general sense as "order, mandate, commission" (cf. BDAG, s.v. 2; Roloff, 352); see further Spicq, *TLNT* 2:11-13; G. Schrenk, *TDNT* 2:544-56; M. Limbeck, *EDNT* 2:459-60.

45. Gk. ἄσπιλος (Jas 1:27 [also as a double acc. with the inf. τηρεῖν]; 1 Pet 1:19; 2 Pet 3:14).

46. For Gk. ἀνεπίλημπτος, see the discussion at 3:2; 5:7.

purity, etc. But the adjectives are more suitable as descriptions of people,[47] which suggests that they might refer instead to Timothy: "keep the mandate (and keep yourself) spotless and irreproachable."[48] The latter rendering, though admittedly teased out of the ambiguous syntax, makes better sense of the initial ethical emphasis of the renewed commission (6:11), but the decision is a fine one. In either case, the addition stresses the degree to which Timothy must be faithful in carrying out his charge.

Third, Paul spells out a time frame of obedience: "until the appearing of our Lord Jesus Christ."[49] The reference is clearly to the eschatological event of Christ's parousia. But the language Paul employs, "appearance" *(epiphaneia),* introduces into these letters (2 Tim 1:10; 4:1, 8; Titus 2:13) a distinctive christological theme.[50] *Epiphany* language characterizes that event as a divine intervention to bring assistance and salvation. The word group had a long history of usage in connection with the military victories of Greek kings, and was absorbed into Roman imperial discourse. Already in the Greek OT and Intertestamental writings, the language had been adopted to describe the covenant God's numerous saving interventions and appearances, and undoubtedly the theological content of the concept as Paul employs it stems from Judaism, where the concept was expressed in various ways. In these letters, both through the noun and related verb, each of Christ's "appearances," past (incarnation) and future (parousia), bears this unique stamp.

47. Cf. "spotless," Jas 1:27; 2 Pet 3:14 and of ritual purity in 1 Pet 1:19; "irreproachable," 1 Tim 3:2; 5:7.

48. Marshall, 665, cites *2 Clement* 8.6 as an illustration of this deferred or deflected reference to the people being addressed; thus the command there, "keep the flesh pure and the seal [of the Spirit] spotless, so that we might obtain [eternal] life," is actually about the moral purity of the people being addressed.

49. 6:3; for other instances of the full name and title of Christ in eschatological texts, cf. 1 Thess 5:9, 23, 28; 2 Thess 2:1, 14; 3:18.

50. Gk. ἐπιφάνεια. R. Bultmann and D. Lührmann, *TDNT* 9:7-10; Spicq, *TLNT* 2:65-68; Hasler, "Epiphanie," 193-209; D. Lührmann, "*Epiphaneia:* Zur Bedeutungsgeschichte eines griechischen Wortes," in G. Jeremias et al., eds., *Tradition und Glaube* (Göttingen: Vandenhoeck & Ruprecht, 1971), 185-99; L. Oberlinner, "Die 'Epiphaneia' des Heilswillens Gottes in Christus Jesus: Zur Grundstruktur der Christologie der Pastoralbriefe," *ZNW* 71 (1980): 192-213; E. Pax, *ΕΠΙΦΑΝΕΙΑ: Ein religionsgeschichtliche Beitrag zur biblischen Theologie* (München: Zink, 1955); F. Pfister, *PWSup* 4 (1924): 277-323; A. Lau, *Manifest in Flesh;* Marshall, 287-96 (esp. 293-95); Towner, *Goal,* 66-71; Schlarb, *Die gesunde Lehre,* 164-72.

Excursus: The Epiphany Concept

The "epiphany" theme, used in differing degrees according to the needs of the letter, is constructed of the noun ἐπιφάνεια ("appearance, appearing"; 1 Tim 6:14; 2 Tim 1:10; 4:1, 8; Titus 2:13; 2 Thess 2:8; cf. *2 Clement* 12.1; 17.4) and the verb ἐπιφαίνω ("to appear"; Titus 2:11; 3:4; Luke 1:79; Acts 27:20). The adjective ἐπιφανής ("splendid, glorious") does not figure in these three letters but occurs in an eschatological comment in Acts 2:20.

In general, in Hellenistic use the noun depicted an "appearance" of something that had been invisible or hidden (from natural occurrences, such as the arrival of dawn, to supernatural occurrences, such as the appearance of gods). In the early Hellenistic ruler cults, the language was applied to the kings, whose appearance in battle (as divine representatives, or even embodiments) brought victory and safety to a city One recurring theme in the use of the concept is the helping or beneficial nature of the "appearance" (Lührmann, *"Epiphaneia"*), though the element of "visibility" (i.e., of "appearance" out of invisibility) also plays a part in the religious development of the concept (Lau, *Manifest in Flesh,* 179-225).

The word group was adopted in the Greek-speaking Jewish milieu to discuss YHWH's theophanic appearances to save his people. The noun occurs in descriptions of God's powerful and glorious saving interventions (2 Macc 2:21; 3:24; 5:4; 12:22; 14:15; 3 Macc 2:9; 5:8, 51; see discussion in Lührmann, *"Epiphaneia,"* 193-96; Pax, *ΕΠΙΦΑΝΕΙΑ,* 159-60). Relevant uses of the verb describe God's appearance to Jacob at Bethel (Gen 35:70), on Sinai (Deut 33:2), and to bring help (Ps 117:27), and in descriptions of his future appearance (Jer 36[29]:14; Zeph 2:11), appearances in the temple (2 Macc 3:30), and appearances in battle (2 Macc 12:22; 14:15). See the adjective in 2 Macc 15:34; 3 Macc 5:35.

In the literature of Judaism, the theme of the Messiah's "revelation" sometimes occurred (*4 Ezra* 7.28; *2 Apocalypse of Baruch* 29.3; 39.7; see also the Targums: *Tg. Jerusalem 1,* Gen 35:21; *Pal. Tg.* Exod 12:42; *Tg.* Zech 3:8; 6:12; *Tg.* Jer 30:21; see M. McNamara, *The New Testament and the Palestinian Targum to the Pentateuch* [Rome: Pontifical Biblical Institute, 1978], 246-52).

From the Jewish (canonical and extracanonical/Judaistic) writings, it is evident that the language of "appearance"/epiphany was quite compatible for discussing God's divine appearances and interventions to save his people. The same range of usage as is evident in Hellenistic contexts pertains in this body of literature, and NT usage will surely have drawn most heavily on the biblical and Jewish traditions in applying the language to the development of christological eschatology.

In NT usage, the "epiphany" concept has two foci. Most clearly demarcated is the future appearance (1 Tim 6:14; 2 Tim 4:1, 8; Titus 2:13), where ἐπιφάνεια refers to the same event as παρουσία (1 Thess 5:23; 2 Thess 2:1; Jas 5:7, 8; etc.). But while the eschatological event might be equally depicted with each term, the character lent by the respective terms to the depiction (and factors motivating lexical choice) may differ to a smaller or larger degree. The second focal point is more surprising. In one instance, the noun describes the historical appearance of Christ as Savior (2 Tim 1:10). In this case, the attending phrase "through the gospel" delays the closure of the "epiphany," as its extension into (or its effects upon) present human life is considered (cf. Titus 1:2-3).

The use of the verb in reference to past appearances of God's grace in Titus 2:11 and 3:4 (descriptive references to the Christ-event as events of divine beneficence) is similar. Does this mean, as Marshall, 295, argues (cf. Oberlinner, *Titusbrief,* 156-57; Läger, *Christologie,* 111-19), that "the past epiphany is not restricted to the actual historical event of the life of Jesus but encompasses the ongoing effects that are brought about by the gospel . . . one epiphany inaugurated by the coming of Jesus and continuing throughout present and future time"? Or is it that this formative epiphany recurs in the proclamation of the gospel? Such perspectives seem legitimate if a metaphorical extension of something concrete is meant. Otherwise it may confuse the past event of Christ's coming with its ongoing effects on people (right into the present and future) through proclamation of that event (Towner, *Goal,* 70-71). Titus 2:11 and 3:4 refer obliquely to the Christ-event (as the cotexts surely support) in order to view the event from theological and ethical perspectives. In any case, the relationships are so: God's grace "has appeared" in the epiphany of his Son; it is being revealed in and through the church's proclamation of the gospel; and it will be revealed finally and ultimately in the future epiphany of the Lord.

An important christological implication attaching to the use of the ἐπιφάνεια concept in reference to his past "appearance" in history is his pre-existence. The connection of ideas in 2 Tim 1:9-10 (note the development from "grace in Christ before the ages" to its "manifestation in the appearance of Christ"; Marshall, 295). Other texts employing different thematic language (1 Tim 1:15; 3:16) corroborate the element of preexistence in the epiphany language.

Quite apart from the question of content contributions to the ἐπιφάνεια theme as applied to Christ is the question of motivation for choosing to employ the term. It might be argued that it finally occurred to Paul to extract a rather rich but hitherto overlooked theme from its source in the Greek OT and Intertestamental Judaism. But it seems more likely that his choice was determined by the role of the language (along with numerous other terms: "Lord," "Savior," "grace," "gospel/good news," etc.; see discussions in Horsley, ed., *Paul and Empire,* in the Imperial and (in the case of the Artemis cult in Ephesus) local discourses. The strategy is that of hijacking or "co-opting," and Paul can be seen to engage the culture at various levels by such a use of the language of current cultural fixtures/institutions that carried significant political/economic/religious freight in the dominant discourse of the empire (see discussion of his use of benefaction language at 6:1-2; see Towner, "Romans 13:1-7 and Paul's Missiological Perspective: A Call to Political Quietism or Transformation?" in Soderlund and Wright, eds., *Romans and the People of God,* 149-69; Winter,

Seek the Welfare of the City). By co-opting the term "epiphany" in reference to Christ (or in reference to the grace of God), Paul challenged the local Ephesian association of protection, prosperity, and importance with Artemis and the Imperial association of peace, power, security, and dignity with the emperor by proclaiming the superiority of the "epiphany" of Christ as Lord.

The question is, Why did Paul choose to employ the concept? First, as with the title "savior," epiphany language must intend deliberately to engage the dominant religious-political discourse. For anyone in Asia Minor at this time, the term "epiphany" would have called to mind first and foremost the victories of Augustus (Savior) that brought an end to the civil wars and introduced the *pax Romana,* with its benefits, to the Imperial provinces. Note the language (esp. in italics) used by the assembly of the province of Asia to honor Augustus:

> Whereas the providence which divinely ordered our lives created with zeal and munificence the most perfect good for our lives by producing Augustus and filling him with virtue for the benefaction of mankind, sending us and those after us a *saviour* who put an end to war and established all things; and whereas Caesar [sc. Augustus] *when he appeared* exceeded the hopes of all who had anticipated *good tidings* [= *euangelion,* gospel], not only by surpassing the benefactors born before him, but not even leaving those to come any hope of surpassing him; and whereas the birthday of the god marked for the world the beginning of *good tidings* through his coming. . . .[51]

The Imperial cult, along with other civic cults (e.g., of Artemis in Ephesus, whose manifestation was described with the term "epiphany"),[52] became the vehicle for communicating the political-social-religious ideals of Rome.[53] Its presence in Ephesus at this time is certain, and its influence reached to all levels of society.[54] Paul's use of epiphany language (along with other terms co-opted from the current cultural discourse and refined for Christian application) forces a rethinking of common cultural categories as it tells God's story in Hellenistic christological dress. And it presents a christological com-

---

51. My italics; adapted from Price, *Rituals and Power,* 54 (he relies on the translation of N. Lewis and M. Reinhold, eds., *Roman Civilization* [New York: Columbia University Press, 1955], 2:64).

52. See *New Documents,* IV, 80-81, §19.

53. See Price, *Rituals and Power.*

54. See Trebilco, *The Early Christians in Ephesus,* 30-37.

plement to the vivid counter-Imperial claims expressed in the striking multi-tiered description of God to come.

Perhaps the challenge posed by co-opting the dominant language is profound enough. But, secondly, the application of "epiphany" to the past human experience of Christ (2 Tim 1:10) sharpens the subversive point. "Epiphany" called to mind power and divine intervention (in secular Greek and Hellenistic Judaism). But in the epiphany of Jesus Christ, divine power and presence are disguised in human weakness, suffering, and death. (Paul's similar discourse in 2 Corinthians comes to mind.) The added allusion to Christ's preexistence heightens the paradox. "Epiphany" language does not just represent thematic development; it seeks to retell the gospel in a most subversive and thought-provoking way.

Thirdly, of immediate relevance to Timothy and the Ephesian church, "epiphany" Christology reconceptualizes the relation between eschatology and ethics. By establishing, with a single word, that the historical past "epiphany" introduces salvation and the future "epiphany" completes it, the present age between these poles (so important in these letters)[55] comes fully under the influence of "epiphany." This is especially noticeable in Titus 2:11-14 and 3:4-7, but in 2 Tim 1:10 and Titus 1:3 the role of proclamation in influencing the present age strikes a similar note. The time between Christ's "epiphanies" is the time of the church, and the time in which the mission mandate is to be carried out. Associated with the return of Christ was, of course, the event of judgment, which lends to the eschatological event a motivational element as well. Elsewhere in ethical passages the forward look to the parousia serves to motivate excellence in living the Christian life (2 Tim 4:1-5; 1 Thess 3:13; 5:23); so too this reference does more than provide a time frame for the mission.

This assumes that the eschatological event of Christ's epiphany was still regarded as in some sense imminent. And despite the emphasis in these letters on living in the present age, the greater focus on church organization and administration, and the new terminology employed, there is no good reason to doubt this.[56] The language of epiphany stresses the expectancy of a real and visible future event of divine intervention. Along with the sense of living in the uncertain present age as "the last times/days" (4:1; 2 Tim 3:1), it is the forward look to the event of Christ's parousia, and the belief that with it salvation will be completed, that makes Christian existence a meaningful ongoing project. There is no reason to doubt that both Paul and Timothy could well have envisioned the event occurring in their lifetime. But even its delay was not a cause for disappointment, for the shape and timing of the entire project of faith are under God's direction.

55. See Towner, *Goal,* 61-74, 118-19.
56. Towner, *Goal,* 71-74.

Verse 15a describes the time of the epiphany in precisely this way: "which [epiphany] God will bring about in his own time." Together with the language of epiphany, the verb "will bring about" (lit. "to exhibit, or show") underscores the fact that the event will be a decisive visible manifestation,[57] not some invisible, slowly growing reality. The concept of "his own time" (i.e., God's eschatological time) was already encountered in Paul's discussion of his mission to the Gentiles (see on 2:6; Titus 1:3). When we combine its use in that context with this application, it becomes clear that Paul conceives of the whole epoch bounded by the two epiphanies and characterized by his mission as subject to God's eschatological "clock."

15b-16 The affirmation of God's sovereign control over eschatological events develops into a multitiered portrait of God rounded off by a doxology. The parallel with 1:17 is evident, though this description is more elegant than its earlier counterpart. Six phrases, adjectives or appellations, formed around OT language and ideas, set God apart from all human powers.

The first phrase repeats divine epithets already used. "Blessed" ascribes to God the divine attributes of immortality and happiness sometimes also attributed to Hellenistic rulers (see on 1:11). The following adjective, "only," echoes the Jewish (then Christian) claim of monotheism (see on 1:17) as it restricts to God the status of "[sovereign] Ruler."[58] The title came to be used of God in Intertestamental Judaism, and it appears in 2 Macc 3:24 in connection with the term "epiphany." The intention of the description is to ascribe (and limit uniquely) to God the blessings and power of authentic divinity. All other claimants to such things are subordinate or false.

"King of kings" repeats but expands the attribution of kingship in 1:17. The title has roots in the OT and Intertestamental Jewish protest against pagan polytheism.[59] A variation of this fuller description occurs in the Maccabean literature, where in 3 Macc 5:35, again in connection with epiphany language, the Lord God is styled the "King of kings," and in the Greek translation of Dan 4:37.[60] Christ acquires this title, in slightly different form,

---

57. Gk. δείκνυμι (John 5:20; with visions, Rev 1:1; 4:1, etc.). See H. Schlier, *TDNT* 2:25-30 (esp. 26); G. Schneider, *EDNT* 1:280; Marshall, 666.

58. Gk. δυνάστης; elsewhere in the NT of human rulers (Luke 1:52; Acts 8:27); of God in Sir 46:5; 2 Macc 12:15; 3 Macc 2:3; cf. W. Grundmann, *TDNT* 2:286.

59. See the similar comparative titles "God of gods" and "Lord of lords" in Deut 10:17; LXX Ps 135:2-3 [MT 136:2-3]; LXX Dan 4:37; 1QM 14:16. The origin of such titles is probably to be located in oriental royal court language (Ezra 7:12; Ezek 26:7; Dan 2:37); from there it enters the Jewish polemic against paganism; cf. G. K. Beale, "The Origin of the Title 'King of Kings and Lord of Lords' in Revelation 17.14," *NTS* 31 (1985): 618-20.

60. Gk. ὁ βασιλεὺς τῶν βασιλευόντων (constructed of the noun followed by the ptc. of the cognate verb βασιλεύω); 3 Macc 5:35: τὸν ἐπιφανῆ θεὸν κύριον βασιλέα τῶν βασιλέων ("the glorious Lord God, king of kings); Dan 4:37: ὅτι αὐτός ἐστι θεὸς τῶν θεῶν

in Rev 17:14 and 19:16. While the phraseology here and throughout may be liturgical (i.e., the common parlance of Christian worship), the blow it strikes against Imperial claims is nonetheless evident.

The background to the attached phrase, "and Lord of lords," is the same.[61] The designation "Lord" is normally applied to Christ in this letter (1:2, 12, 14; 6:3, 14), and the only other NT uses of the equivalent variation on this phrase are reserved for Christ (Rev 17:14; 19:16). Together with the two preceding phrases, they make the resounding claim that God's authority and power to rule over all human powers are beyond compare.

Verse 16 extends the description of God from elements of power and politics to matters of ontology. The fourth phrase, developing the thought of "incorruptibility" in 1:17, sounds the note of divine uniqueness again as it describes God's "immortality" (see on 1:17). While Intertestamental and Wisdom literature know the language and concept, they do not apply the term directly to God.[62] Other gods, military heroes, kings, and Roman emperors were alleged to possess this quality, and it is Hellenistic discourse rather than Judaism from which this language comes.[63] The ascription of immortality to God alone is the Christian refutation of this false claim. Elsewhere Paul describes the resurrection of believers with this language (1 Cor 15:53, 54), indicating that the Christian hope is nothing less than participation in God's unique self-generating life.

The next phrase describes the glory of God's habitation:[64] "who lives in unapproachable light." The imagery of bright light as a description of God's otherworldly glory goes back to the OT Exodus story. The light of the continually burning oil lamp symbolizes God's presence among his people (LXX Exod 27:20; 35:14; 39:16; Lev 24:2). The Sinai theophany, in which Moses was granted just a fleeting glimpse of God's "glory," anticipates later graphic uses of "light" imagery to describe in tangible terms the ineffable appearance of God (Exod 33:18-23). The Psalms develop further the association of God and light, depicting him as "robed with light as a garment" (LXX Ps 103:2; cf. 89:15: "whose countenance is light"). NT reflections on God's glory follow

---

καὶ κύριος τῶν κυρίων καὶ βασιλεὺς τῶν βασιλέων ("because he is God of gods and Lord of lords and King of kings").

61. See the preceding notes. Gk. καὶ κύριος τῶν κυριευόντων (noun followed by the ptc. of the cognate verb κυριεύω, "to rule, master, control," in various contexts and senses, Luke 22:25; Rom 6:9, 14; 7:1; 14:9; 2 Cor 1:24; Spicq, *TLNT* 2:351-52). Cf. the variation κύριος κυρίων (noun followed by gen. pl. noun) in Rev 17:14; 19:16.

62. Gk. ἀθανασία; Wis 3:4; 4:1; 8:13, 17; 15:3; 4 Macc 14:5; 16:13; for the adjective ἀθάνατος, see Sir 17:30; Wis 1:15; 4 Macc 7:3; 14:6; 18:23.

63. Homer, *Iliad* (freq.); Aristotle, *On the Heavens* 279a30; *Sibylline Oracles* 2.150; see Roloff, 356.

64. Gk. οἰκέω; here with the accusative φῶς in the sense of "inhabit" (BDAG, s.v. 2); elsewhere of God's "dwelling in heaven" (Tob 5:17); cf. O. Michel, *TDNT* 5:135-36.

suit (2 Cor 4:6), as statements such as Rev 21:23 and 22:5 declare that God's "glory" is the "light" of the New Jerusalem. The ultimate application of the imagery is finally made in the Johannine tradition, which not only equates God and light (1 John 1:5) but transfers the category to God's Son (John 1:4, 5, 7; 8:12; etc.). The imagery of light is then extended naturally to describe the essence of the Son's kingdom (Col 1:12-13) and of Christian existence within it (Rom 13:12; 2 Cor 6:14; Eph 5:8; 1 Thess 5:5).[65] The specification that God's light is "unapproachable" emphasizes the stark contrast between deity and humanity, and possibly intentionally calls to mind the warning that people were not to approach the mountain because of the presence of God in his glory.[66]

Paul links the sixth description of invisibility (see 1:17), by a relative pronoun, to the preceding description of glory and light: "whom no one has seen or can see." And the connection of ideas is traditional, as the same Sinai story, which the language of this phrase echoes, provides the source both of the idea of God's invisibility and of the inability of human beings to penetrate this veil: Exod 33:20: "You will not be able to see my face; for no person shall see my face and live"; John 1:18: "No one has ever seen God."[67] While the threat of death associated with the Sinai theophany is removed or muted, the affirmation of God's invisibility extends the thought just made of the distinction between God and people.

Clearly from the standpoint of ontology, the God of the covenant is as unlike human claimants to divine glory and honor as can possibly be. OT imagery and concepts combine to spell out the sheer distance that, both in terms of power and character of existence, separates human creation from the eternal God.

All that is left after so majestic a litany is an expression of doxology uttered in awe (cf. 1:17; Rom 11:33-36). This doxology takes the standard form, with the relative pronoun ("to whom") drawing the recipient of praise ("him") from the preceding statement.[68] This confession of God's "honor"

---

65. Gk. φῶς; see Spicq, *TLNT* 3:470-91; H. Conzelmann, *TDNT* 9:310-58.

66. Gk. ἀπρόσιτος (only here in the NT; see esp. the use of the term by Philo, *On the Life of Moses* 2.70 and Josephus, *Antiquities* 3.76).

67. Gk. ὁράω ("to see"; 2 Tim 1:4; of seeing "revelations," Rev 4:1; 5:1). Cf. the language in this tradition:

Exod 33:20: οὐ δυνήσῃ ἰδεῖν μου τὸ πρόσωπον
("you will not be able to see my face");
John 1:18: Θεὸν οὐδεὶς ἑώρακεν πώποτε
("No one has ever seen God");
1 Tim 6:16: ὃν εἶδεν οὐδεὶς ἀνθρώπων οὐδὲ ἰδεῖν δύναται
("whom no person has seen nor is able to see").

68. For this ᾧ, the masculine dative singular relative is typical (Rom 16:27; Gal

repeats the earlier doxology (see on 1:17). Here it is linked with his "might," which was typically attributed to God in Jewish and Christian thought (Eph 1:19; 6:10; Col 1:11; 1 Pet 4:11; 5:11).[69] The ascription is strengthened by extending the validity of the claim to eternity.[70] And the "Amen" invites the agreement of Timothy and the Ephesian church (see on 1:17).

While it is difficult to be sure of Paul's intention in stressing the authority, power, and unique nature of God's existence in closing Timothy's restatement of commission (a tone of solemnity and worship, or that plus a challenge to pagan claims), the possibility that he sought to restate his gospel's challenge to the world forces and their claims should not be too quickly dismissed. The letter was addressed to Timothy and to the church receiving him for service. And that church was subjected to the constant political/social/religious propaganda of the Ephesian myth and the greater Imperial story. It needed to be reminded constantly, and the flow of that discourse needed to be interrupted and subverted intentionally, if the prior and greater claims of God and Christ on human culture were to be understood and embraced. Timothy's commission as Paul's delegate in Ephesus included this ongoing task.

Just as pertinent is the matter of the effect of our culture's "story" upon us and the church's appropriate response. Is there within this deployment of political ideas and language a pattern we should be attempting to replicate today? If so, any effective gospel engagement of the modern world's numerous stories will require more than simply "telling the old, old story." That story will in fact need to be retold within the language range of whatever social and political context that prevails. The potent language and symbols of the present "empire" will need to be decoded, and then turned around, strategically filled with challenging new meaning and delivered in a message that opposes all false claims to power, authority, promise, and hope.

c. A Corrected Perspective on Wealth (6:17-19)

> 17 *Command those who are rich in this present world not to be arrogant nor to put their hope in wealth, which is so uncertain, but to put their hope in God, who richly provides us with everything for our enjoyment.* 18 *Command them to do good, to be rich in good deeds,*

1:5; 2 Tim 4:18; Heb 13:21; 1 Pet 4:11). A form of the verb "to be" will be assumed (see on 1:17).

69. Gk. κράτος (LXX Ezra 8:22; Ps 86:16; Sir 18:5; Jdt 2:12; 9:11; 2 Macc 3:34; 7:17; 11:4; Josephus, *Antiquities* 10.263). For the secular use of the term to describe the gods, see further W. Michaelis, *TDNT* 3:905-10.

70. Gk. αἰώνιος (adj. "eternal"; see on 1:16; 6:12); the single word "forever" serves the same purpose as the longer phrase (εἰς τοὺς αἰῶνας τῶν αἰώνων), on which see 1:17.

and to be generous and willing to share. 19 In this way they will lay up treasure for themselves as a firm foundation for the coming age, so that they may take hold of the life that is truly life.

Following the doxology, Paul issues instructions to Timothy for "those who are rich." The present brief treatment of wealthy people in the church may seem like an afterthought or a displaced piece of teaching.[1] Nevertheless, the section provides a balance with the denunciation of the false teachers' greed motives in 6:3-10,[2] and serves to conclude or round off the instruction of the letter intended for the community.[3] The attraction of this section to the earlier one contrasting godly self-sufficiency with avarice suggests that Paul here fills out somewhat the approved perspective on material wealth stated earlier in principle.[4] Thus, just as Paul earlier played a base, materialistic view of "gain" off against a godly view of "gain," here those addressed are challenged to avoid fixation on material wealth and to acquire the godly wealth that is measured in much different, more enduring terms. At the center of this exposition is the key ethical concept of "good deeds," with its emphasis on faith-generated action. By means of this concept and associated attitudes toward self and others, Paul explores the shape of godliness in the case of those who happen to be materially blessed.

The presence of socioeconomic diversity of this sort in a Christian community is not unusual, but it did pose certain challenges to unity and community relationships across social strata.[5] Some scholars allege that the author took a more relaxed, accepting approach to wealth and the wealthy than that found in the Jesus-tradition;[6] or indeed that this teaching even indicates a shift from an earlier, more stringent Pauline outlook.[7] The former may well be true, but there is no discernible shift in the Pauline emphasis on sharing (with a view to equality) such as appears in 2 Cor 8:13-15 (see below). In any case, Paul accepts the existence of a wealthy circle in the Ephesian church, and does not set out to dismantle it. The group in view might have included some of the householders already addressed (3:4-5), but otherwise it has thus far been alluded to only indirectly (2:9-10; 5:6, 16; 6:2).

17 As we have seen throughout the letter (1:3; 4:11; 5:7), Timothy

---

1. Cf. Easton, 170; Spicq, 575.
2. See Thurén, "Struktur," 242-44.
3. Cf. Rom 16:17-20; Gal 6:11-16; Marshall, 669.
4. Marshall, 669; Kidd, *Wealth and Beneficence in the Pastoral Epistles,* 100.
5. See esp. G. Theissen, *The Social Setting of Pauline Christianity* (Philadelphia: Fortress, 1982); M. Hengel, *Property and Riches in the Early Church* (Philadelphia: Fortress, 1974); Kidd, *Wealth and Beneficence in the Pastoral Epistles.*
6. Verner, *Household of God,* 175.
7. See Hanson, 114; Hasler, 52.

is to convey the apostolic instructions, and the verb used to express this activity (also of Paul, 6:13) indicates that his authority to do so is that of apostolic delegate (see on 4:11). The instructions form a single sentence in the Greek composed of a series of infinitive clauses arranged to fill out the content of the "command." Essentially, within opposing brackets that contrast "the present world" and "the coming age," two themes emerge: hope in God instead of in uncertain riches, and the appropriate behavioral response to God's generosity. A final statement spells out the eternal wealth that awaits wealthy believers who respond faithfully to God.

First to be addressed and adjusted is the basic orientation of "the rich,"[8] who are named up front. To do this Paul employs the related triad — rich (adj.)/wealth (noun)/richly (adv.) — to introduce a mistaken orientation toward wealth and counter it with a correct orientation toward God. And he establishes the extreme limitations of their wealth and their orientation by naming the sphere of its relevance: "in this present world [age]" (Titus 2:12).[9] The phrase is constructed of the typical term "age" (used of eternity in 1:17; 2 Tim 4:18), which is then specified with the adverb "now," the whole of which designates the sphere of time known as "the present" or (as TNIV) "this present world." In these letters to coworkers, "this age" is contrasted with "the age to come" (v. 19; cf. 4:8), the present age being the time in which salvation has truly begun and consequently in which godly living is to be pursued and the present evil attractions to be rejected (2 Tim 4:10). And here the contrast anticipates the admonition that will remind these wealthy believers that their values and goals should be those that transcend the terminal present age and conform to the eternal reality that is already breaking in.

But their superficial orientation is first identified in two negative tendencies. First, the verb "to be arrogant" is a rare word, occurring only here in the NT.[10] But in other language, the ancients often criticized the wealthy for haughtiness,[11] so it is not a surprising assessment of the current attitude. Turned on others, this self-importance would put church unity at risk.

Second is the ironic tendency to place hope in something uncertain.

8. Gk. πλούσιος in the plural, as here, typically designates a social stratum (Luke 6:24; 21:1; Jas 2:6; Rev 6:15; 13:16); see 6:9 and note.

9. Gk. ἐν τῷ νῦν αἰῶνι. For αἰών (period of time, era, epoch, universe, world), here of a period of time, and, as qualified by νῦν (adj. "now"; cf. 4:8), that which defines the present age (2 Tim 4:10; Titus 2:12), see discussions in Towner, *Goal*, 61-63; Barr, *Biblical Words for Time*, 65-67; H. Sasse, *TDNT* 1:197-209; T. Holtz, *EDNT* 1:44-46; H. Balz, *EDNT* 1:46-48; W. Bousset and H. Gressmann, *Die Religion des Judentum im spät-hellenistischen Zeitalter* (repr.; Tübingen: Mohr [Siebeck], 1966), 243-51.

10. Gk. ὑψηλοφρονέω (variant reading in Rom 11:20; see BDAG; BDF §119.5); see the adjective ὑψηλόφρων ("high-minded, haughty"; Plato, *Republic* 550B).

11. *1 Clement* 59.3; see Verner, *Household of God*, 175 n. 64; Spicq, 575-76.

425

We have encountered the verb "to hope" in the more normal theological discourse of 4:10 (cf. 1:1) and 5:5, where the perfect tense describes the condition of firm expectancy in God that characterizes Christian faith. Here in the perfect tense, the wealthy are described, in stark contrast, as those who have "put their hope" (or are in danger of doing so) in something other than God. The noun phrase that expresses their object of hope, "the uncertainty of wealth,"[12] considers human wealth critically and is one of many that express the biblical theme of the transitory character of material wealth.[13] The comment anticipates the allusion to the Jesus tradition preserved in Matt 6:19-21 about to be made; and the implication of this negative tendency is that those so oriented have effectively rejected God in favor of serving another master (Matt 6:24; Luke 16:13).

As Paul counters, God is the only appropriate and reliable object of hope (4:10; 5:5). The picture developed in 4:3b-5 of the generous and kind Creator God and the goodness of creation lies in the background. First, in both texts, the sweeping term "all" is needed to describe the extent of the goodness of creation and God's providence over it (4:5). Second, in both texts, the argument points to God's benevolent willingness to extend creation as a gift: here he "provides[14] everything richly" (Titus 3:6), not in the sense of wasteful excess but as a fitting description of the gracious and sufficient provision that will meet (and continue to meet) every need. Third, in both texts, the act of human receiving of God's gifts is stressed — here, dramatically, in the phrase "for our enjoyment."[15] Finally, in both texts Paul subtly shifts from discussing "them" to reflecting on "us," revealing that a faith relationship is at stake — God's covenant with human beings — requiring the human response of worship in return. The earlier text emphasized the element of thanksgiving in this human response. This text, however, translates acknowledgment of the divine gift into active Christian service that will benefit others (see below). This understanding of God's generosity and desire to provide is a matter of confession, and those hoping in another source of sufficiency are therefore invited to live appropriately within the covenant relationship.

18 Three infinitive phrases expand the initial command, spelling out the appropriate ways in which the wealthy are to express their trust in God.

---

12. Gk. ἀδηλότης (only here in the NT; BDAG; BDF §165); Philo, *On the Virtues* 152; *On the Change of Names* 10.

13. E.g., Mark 4:19 (pars.); Luke 12:13-31; Jas 1:9-12; 4:13-17; 5:2; Rev 18:16. For secular criticism, see Spicq, 576.

14. Gk. παρέχω; here "to grant or provide" (also of God in Acts 17:31); see 1:4 for "to promote"; Titus 2:7, "to show."

15. Gk. ἀπόλαυσις (Heb 11:25; 3 Macc 7:16; *1 Clement* 20.10; see the verb in 4 Macc 5:9; 8:5; Spicq, *TLNT* 1:181-82.

The first two of these resume the emphasis on the observable outworking of faith and quantify it with parallel expressions (5:10) in terms of visible service (2:10; 5:10, 25). "To do good" (i.e., "to benefit others"; Acts 14:17) is a compound verb that combines the components of one of the "good deeds" configurations (2:10, discussion).[16] The specific shape this activity is to take becomes clearer as Paul plays with "wealth" language in the next phrase. In its redeployment of the "wealth" word group, the phrase "to be rich in good deeds"[17] effects the same obvious reversal of values (cf. 6:9) that is achieved in Luke 12:21, a strand of the Jesus tradition about to be further exploited. Together the piling up of "good deeds" expressions (as in 5:10) lays stress on the call to make an observable showing of authentic faith.

But it is the last infinitive phrase with its two objects that instructs how the faith of the wealthy is to be demonstrated: "to be generous and willing to share." The terms are complementary if not synonymous,[18] and encompass the attitude and disposition of liberality and the action of giving. The value of sharing, carried over from Judaism (cf. Tob 4:7-9) and also apparent in Greek thought,[19] was fundamental to all strata in the church (Rom 12:13). What is sometimes regarded as a text that expresses a preferential option for the rich,[20] with (as some amazingly propose!) *"no suggestion* that the rich should share their wealth,"[21] in fact operates on the same basic principles designed to encourage equality and the meeting of community needs as 2 Cor 8:13-15.[22]

19   In all of this there is, to be sure, a return that the wealthy can expect. Paul describes this in two ways, each of which requires viewing wealth and the correct use of it in this age from an eternal perspective.

First, in a participial phrase composed of mixed images, Paul incorporates the Jesus tradition that similarly urged "laying up treasures in heaven" as opposed to accumulating earthly wealth. The language is closest to that of

16. Gk. ἀγαθοεργέω (see discussion at 2:10); cf. W. Grundmann, *TDNT* 1:17.

17. Now in the configuration πλουτεῖν ["to be rich, to abound"; see discussion and note at 6:9] ἐν ἔργοις καλοῖς ("in good deeds"; discussion and note at 2:10).

18. Gk. εὐμετάδοτος ("generous, ready to impart"; only here in the NT; see μεταδίδωμι = "to share," Eph 4:28; MM 263; BDAG, s.v.; Spicq, 577-79. For κοινωνικός ("liberal, generous"), see F. Hauck, *TDNT* 3:809 (of one who "gladly gives to others a share"); Polybius, *Histories* 2.44.1; Josephus, *Jewish War* 2.122 (of the Essenes' communal sharing).

19. See the discussion in Aristotle, *Nicomachean Ethics* 1119b-23a (cited in Spicq, 577).

20. See the view of Verner, *Household of God,* 175.

21. Hanson, 114 (my italics); see also Hasler, 52. Cf. Towner, *Goal,* 190-91; Kidd, *Wealth and Beneficence in the Pastoral Epistles,* 100.

22. Cf. C. L. Blomberg, *Neither Poverty nor Riches* (Grand Rapids: Eerdmans, 1999).

Matt 6:19-20 (Jas 5:3; cf. Luke 12:21),[23] where the related verb, "to lay up as treasure" *(thēsaurizō)* occurs.[24] The compound form of the verb *(apothēsaurizō)* re-creates the Matthean sense,[25] and the dative reflexive pronoun "for yourselves" (see on 2:6; 3:13), reproduces Matthew's "for you." But in place of the object "treasures in heaven" is the odd phrase "a firm foundation." The TNIV's "firm" is the characteristic modifier "good," on which see discussions at 1:8, 18 and 2:3. In a description otherwise devoid of architectural imagery, the presence of "foundation" (see on 2 Tim 2:19) seems puzzling. It probably denotes figuratively a firm base on which an edifice of some kind can be built (cf. Rom 15:20; 1 Cor 3:10-12; Eph 2:20), which here would be the completion of salvation.[26]

Finally, the eternal perspective created by Matthew's "in heaven" is here expressed in language more characteristic of this letter — literally "for the future." The eschatological reach of the time phrase, that is, "the coming age," is seen clearly in the contrast with the "now"-focused time element of 6:17 ("in this present world").[27]

The clause *(hina)* that concludes the passage defines the purpose of laying up spiritual wealth on God's terms. The language repeats with slight modifications the command to Timothy in 6:12 (see discussion and note):

> 6:12: "Take hold of the eternal life";
> 6:19: "so that you might take hold of the life that is truly life."

Hanson, operating with a rather banal interpretation of the theme of "good works," reads the purpose clause as teaching "that it is possible to store up a treasury of merit with God by doing good deeds."[28] But, while the action

---

23. Cf. the Greek:

Matt 6:20:   θησαυρίζετε δὲ ὑμῖν θησαυροὺς ἐν οὐρανῷ;
1 Tim 6:19: ἀποθησαυρίζοντας ἑαυτοῖς θεμέλιον καλὸν εἰς τὸ μέλλον.

24. The tradition is more widely in evidence in related statements about "treasure in heaven" (Matt 19:21; Mark 10:21; Luke 12:33-34) with a background in Judaism (Prov 8:21; 13:22; Tob 4:9; 12:8; Bar 3:17).

25. Gk. ἀποθησαυρίζω ("to store, lay up as treasure"; only here in the NT but widely in Hellenistic lit.; BDAG; Sir 3:4; Josephus, *Jewish War* 7.299).

26. Johnson, 311; for the view that it means "treasury, reserve" (which, when understood figuratively, differs little from the meaning adopted), see Marshall, 673.

27. See 4:8; cf. the phrase in Matt 12:32; Eph 1:21. For the Gk. phrase εἰς τὸ μέλλον, see also Luke 13:9 (of the future); cf. esp. the equivalent phrase formed on the verb, ἐν τῷ μέλλοντι (Matt 12:32; Eph 1:21). Cf. the cognate verb in 1:16; Rom 8:38; 1 Cor 3:22; cf. A. L. Moore, *The Parousia in the New Testament* (NovTSup 13; Leiden: Brill, 1966), 164.

28. Hanson, 115; cf. Lips, *Glaube,* 76 n. 171. Tob 4:9 is cited as an example of

called for in the case of Timothy differs in specifics from that expected of the wealthy, the intention of the clause duplicates the earlier command: it requires not an earning of salvation or eternal life, but rather a demonstration of genuine godliness in the present age.

The previous phrase "eternal life" is described here as "true [or "real"; see on 5:3] life." This distinction continues the reversal of values motif already expressed by contrasting transitory, present-worldly wealth and the divine provision, as well as by the paradoxical assertion that sharing wealth "now" is in reality an acquisition of heavenly wealth. Eternal life is meant.[29] But in the way it is expressed ("the life that is truly life") and by repetition of the verb of v. 12 (which echoes the command to "take hold of"), the real possibility of beginning the experience of eternal life in the present age is confirmed.

As in the case of Timothy, so in the case of the wealthy cadre in the church of Ephesus (as well as men, women, leaders, widows, slaves); authentic Christian existence is the holistic interaction of belief in God and the outworking of that belief in lives increasingly shaped by God's values. For the wealthy this must mean adopting a perspective on temporal material wealth that allows it to be seen as (1) an uncertain and undependable object of hope, and (2) an obligation to be discharged for the benefit of others. While there are surely other equally important aspects of holy living also of relevance to the rich, the exercise of "good deeds" — that observable dimension of Christian existence — must in their case include generosity and sharing to an extraordinary degree. What we Christians in the West (and parts of Asia) today of many tax brackets must come to terms with is the relative wealth we enjoy (with the accompanying implications) when compared with the rest of the global community.

d. Repeating the Charge to Engage the Opponents (6:20-21a)

> 20 *Timothy, guard what has been entrusted to your care. Turn away from godless chatter and the opposing ideas of what is falsely called knowledge,* 21a *which some have professed and in so doing have departed from the faith.*

In this closing summary of the charge to Timothy, Paul reshapes succinctly the opening instructions (1:3-5, 18-20) that so focused on the opposition in

---

such merit theology (cf. Marshall, 673), but in context (4:5-6, 11) "almsgiving," and the promises associated with it, almost certainly requires a nuanced explication so as to be understood within the demands of the covenant.

29. Note the secondary textual variant αἰωνίου (D² 1881 TR etc.; and ὄντως αἰωνίου, 1175 pc), which represents an attempt to clarify on the basis of 6:12 (see Metzger, 577).

the church. Although Timothy's commission included more than engaging the heresy, in this final sentence it appears to be the reality of heresy and apostasy around which his commitment to and execution of the gospel are spelled out. Two concerns, the first positive, the second negative, are vital. The first, which is paramount, takes up Timothy's responsibility to the gospel, which Paul describes with the graphic language of "guarding" and "entrustment." It is paramount because it is Timothy's (and the church's) positive and faithful use of the gospel that constitutes its "guarding." The second instruction repeats the sort of advice given in 4:7 to avoid involvement in the controversies and contradictions of the false teacher. As we will see, this is not a call to disengagement as much as direction to proactive engagement, but on Paul's terms with the tools of the apostolic gospel. The dangers of any other course of action, or of allowing the heresy ("called knowledge") to continue unchecked, are measured by the direct link between adherence to the false doctrine and departure from the faith.

20 Two features combine to create the appropriate solemnity of the conclusion and to regather earlier commands. First, as in 6:11 where restatement of Timothy's commission began, Paul again employs the Greek marker of direct address, "O." The English marker of exclamation, "O," is not really an equivalent, and TNIV (NIV, NRSV) leaves the Greek marker unexpressed (see on 6:11). Second, Paul explicitly names "Timothy" as he did in an earlier statement of command (1:18). Together these devices attract and concentrate attention on the main recipient and purpose of the letter.

Two interrelated commands then follow. First, the literal command, "guard the deposit" ("what has been entrusted to you"; cf. NRSV), introduces language and a concept that require detailed attention. The distinctive phrase — composed of the verb "to guard" in combination with the noun "the deposit" *(parathēkē)*[30] — alludes to the process (in Greco-Roman and Jewish cultures) of entrusting some commodity with a person who is to ensure its safekeeping (and, in this context, proper use) and eventually return it to its owner.[31] Assumed in the process are the ownership of the commodity and the obligation of faithfulness on the part of the trustee.

The language marks a divergence from other discussions of "tradition" in Paul. Elsewhere he employed the more common terminology, "tradition" *(paradosis;* 1 Cor 11:2; Gal 1:14; 2 Thess 2:15; 3:6), with accompanying verbs

---

30. The Gk. phrase is τὴν παραθήκην φυλασσέσθαι; see also 2 Tim 1:12, 14. On Gk. παραθήκη, cf. Herodotus 8.86; 9.45. On φυλάσσω, see 5:21 (discussion).

31. Lips, *Glaube,* 266-68; K. Wegenast, *Das Verständnis der Tradition bei Paulus und in den Deuteropaulinien* (WMANT 8; Neukirchen-Vluyn: Neukirchener, 1962), 143-50; Towner, *Goal,* 124-26; Lau, *Manifest in Flesh,* 18-39; Spicq, *TLNT* 3:24-27; C. Maurer, *TDNT* 8:162-64; Marshall, 675.

"to transmit" (*paradidōmi;* 1 Cor 11:2), "to receive" (*paralambanō;* Col 2:6), "to maintain" (*katechō;* 1 Cor 11:2), and "to hold fast" and "stand firm" (*krateō; stēkō;* 2 Thess 2:15). It is almost certainly a combination of the form in which Paul addresses Timothy (a letter with mandate elements announcing a commission) and the new situation of heresy that force a shift in the language used here with its more obvious emphasis on protection and entrustment.[32] Notably, in this letter, the theme of "entrustment" was initiated with the related verb in the commissioning of Timothy in 1:18 (see note). In terms of content, the scope of the earlier "entrustment" (i.e., the specific commission of 1:3-5) is probably enlarged in this more elaborate and formulaic closing command. But the theme is nevertheless continuous with the earlier instruction to Timothy.

The contents of the *paratheke* itself have been defined in different ways, but the most likely reference is to the gospel for which Paul had been appointed (1:12; 2:7; 2 Tim 1:1). As use of the term in 2 Timothy (1:12, 14), where the actual handing over of the Pauline mission is underway, will confirm, it is the Pauline articulation of the faith/the gospel that is being endangered by heretical distortions, additions, and deletions.[33] Correspondingly, Paul probably regards himself as the official "depositor" (and not God, who has already entrusted the mission and message to the apostle; cf. 1:11), who places the commodity of the gospel/the faith (and associated mission) into the charge of his delegate for the apostolic work in Ephesus.[34] The scope of "entrustment" necessarily broadens in the discussion of 2 Timothy, as Timothy will stand to receive "the gospel" not just for a particular assignment but rather for the task of continuing the Pauline mission to the Gentiles as Paul's successor.

Consequently, the language of "guarding" as applied to this task is somewhat figurative (see on 5:21). It will include the dimensions of "preserving" and "keeping," but it is an active rather than a passive task. The entire package of instructions to Timothy suggests that it is precisely through proclamation and carrying out his various didactic ministries that the apostolic gospel will be preserved intact within the ministry in Ephesus and (presumably) in the church of the next generation.

A second command urges Timothy to maintain a certain distance from the heresy. Paul's choice of verb for this is interesting. The language of avoid-

32. Cf. Towner, "Pauline Theology or Pauline Tradition in the Pastoral Epistles," 306-7. The suggestion that the language shift marks a parallel shift on the part of the post-Pauline author, from the gospel as ground of authority to "Paul" or Paul's apostolate (Oberlinner, 309), is unnecessary.

33. Towner, *Goal,* 125-26; Roloff, 372-73; Marshall, 675-76; Johnson, 311; Maurer, *TDNT* 8:163-64; but see Fee, 161 (Timothy's task).

34. Rightly, Wegenast, *Tradition,* 140; Wolter, *Paulustradition,* 116-19; Roloff, 372-73; see the discussion in Marshall, 676.

THE FIRST LETTER TO TIMOTHY

ance or separation applied to Timothy here occurs elsewhere in reference to the opponents' deviant distance from the truth (see on 1:6; 5:15; 2 Tim 4:4). Timothy is thus to behave in a way precisely opposite to that of the false teachers, avoiding the contemplation of the heresy that might draw him off course.

Paul draws again on his polemical vocabulary to classify the teaching. On the one hand, it is "godless chatter." The adjective "godless" places the teaching into the category of behavior (see on 1:9) and stories (4:7) that are opposed to God. The noun "chatter" is self-explanatory, denouncing the teaching as completely senseless and therefore useless.[35]

On the other hand, the reference to "the opposing ideas of what is falsely called knowledge" may be more revealing of the heresy's content. The phrase itself yields two initial perspectives on the false teaching. First, Paul's assessment, which has been building for some time, reaches a climax. In the past, the term translated "the opposing ideas" *(antitheseis)*[36] was taken by many scholars as a technical reference to one or another sort of teaching (the Marcionite document called *Antitheseis,* or rabbinic-style instruction).[37] But it is rather a description either of the self-refuting nature of the heresy (and so nearly synonymous with the preceding term "chatter") or of its specific tendency to contradict the apostolic tradition.[38] The remainder of the phrase completes the assessment by denying the opponents' claims about the character of their teaching. The assertion is that what they claim to be "knowledge" is only falsely so labeled.[39]

But, secondly, in the negation of the claim, the perspective of the opponents emerges. They applied the term "knowledge" *(gnōsis)* to their system of doctrine.[40] This might explain Paul's preference for the compound

---

35. Gk. κενοφωνία ("chatter, empty talk"; according to Hesychius, *Lexicography* it is synonymous with ματαιολογία [on which see 1:6]; BDAG; MM; Towner, *Goal,* 24-25); the whole phrase τὰς βεβήλους κενοφωνίας is repeated at 2 Tim 2:16.

36. Gk. ἀντίθεσις (only here in the NT; pl. in reference to the false teaching [cf. 4:1, discussion] in contrast to the sg. "sound teaching"); BDAG; Plutarch, *Moralia* 953B; Philo, *On Drunkenness* 187; see Spicq, 113 n. 1.

37. See Roloff, 374; Marshall, 677, for discussion and references.

38. So, e.g., Kelly, 152 ("counteraffirmations"). Schlarb, *Die gesunde Lehre,* 62-66 (E. Schlarb, "Miszelle zu 1 Tim 6.20," *ZNW* 77 [1986]: 276-81), has shown that the selection of the term ἀντίθεσις corresponds to the author's predilection for placing the apostolic mission and faith in opposition with the heresy by means of words built on the τίθημι verb (cf. 1 Tim 4:6 and 2 Tim 2:25; 1 Tim 1:18; 2 Tim 2:2), and by use of the negating α-privative prefixes ἀντί and ἀπό. These observations suggest that the term ἀντίθεσις fits neatly within the polemical lexical repertoire.

39. Gk. ψευδώνυμος ("falsely bearing a name, falsely called; only here in the NT); MM; Plutarch, *Moralia* 479E; Philo, *On the Life of Moses* 2.171.

40. Gk. γνῶσις, in reference here to "what is known"; cf. R. Bultmann, *TDNT* 1:707-8; E. D. Schmitz, *NIDNTT* 2:392-96.

432

form of the term, *epignōsis,* in descriptions of coming to faith.[41] Whatever might be implied about content by the term (see below), Paul may have encountered similar claims to "knowledge" in enthusiastic or heretical movements in Corinth and Colossae.[42] And the term "knowledge" also functioned to describe doctrine, belief, or law in Judaism and Qumran.[43]

But what did the claim imply about the contents of the alternative doctrine? As we have seen, this first letter to Timothy gives up little in the way of solid information about the beliefs of the opponents. We traced a connection to OT stories, with some interest in the creation narrative, and a predilection for the ascetic in the case of foods and marriage (1:4; 4:1-5, 7). Financial motives (6:5, 10) speak volumes about sincerity but tell little about doctrine. Consequently, the term *gnōsis* in this closing comment has attracted a great deal of attention.

There are still those who maintain that it indicates a link between the beliefs of the heretics and those associated with later Gnosticism.[44] But the connection is unlikely since there is no evidence beyond this single word, which as observed had other than "Gnostic" associations elsewhere in Paul, to indicate the systems of archons and emanations that characterized Gnosticism (see further at 1:4). It is also not likely that *gnōsis* indicates a specifically Judaistic or Judaizing doctrine, though the Jewish element is clearly present.

If Paul was criticizing the false teachers' tendency to contradict apostolic doctrine, then the description "falsely called knowledge" would include specific elements of the false doctrine that did so. In addition to the few items already cited, it is possible that at this time in Ephesus the doctrine that comes fully to light only in 2 Tim 2:18 — the belief that the resurrection of believers had already occurred — or at least (and perhaps more likely) the drift toward a too-realized eschatology along the lines of Corinthian developments might already have begun to influence the church. The presentation of Christology (1:15-16; 2:5-6; 3:16; 6:13), I have argued, was intentionally measured to check the tendency toward disengagement from the church's

---

41. See on 2:4; 2 Tim 2:25; 3:7; Titus 1:1; cf. Sell, *The Knowledge of the Truth,* 3-31.

42. 1 Cor 8:1, 7, 10, 11; 13:2, 8; cf. 2 Cor 10.5, 11:6; see R. A. Horsley, "Gnosis in Corinth: 1 Corinthians 8.1-6," *NTS* 27 (1980-81): 32-35. A gnosis-concept of some sort was probably countered in Colossians with the use of ἐπίγνωσις (1:9-10; 2:3, 12; 3:10); P. T. O'Brien, *Colossians, Philemon* (WBC 44; Waco: Word, 1982), 21-22, 95.

43. Hos 4:6; Mal 2:7; 4 Macc 1:16-17; 1QpHab 11:1; 1QS 10:9, 12; 11:6, 15; 1QH 2:18; 11:24; CD 2:4.

44. See esp. Wolter, *Paulustradition,* 265-66; Rudolph, *Gnosis,* 302-3; Haufe, "Gnostische Irrlehre," 328; Schmithals, "The *Corpus Paulinum* and Gnosis," in Logan and Wedderburn, eds., *The New Testament and Gnosis,* 116. See the discussion in Towner, *Goal,* 29-33.

mission in the world that might well be linked to an elitist, overrealized eschatology. But the full blooming of this tendency is clearly visible only in the later reference to the resurrection heresy in 2 Tim 2:18. Was it already at the embryonic stage in 1 Timothy?

The present passage, 6:20-21a, is remarkably similar to 2 Tim 2:15-18. In both cases Paul instructs Timothy to pay careful attention to the gospel: "guard what has been entrusted to your care" (6:20); "handle rightly the word of truth" (2 Tim 2:15). In both cases he is to avoid the false doctrine, which is described identically as "godless chatter" (6:20; 2 Tim 2:16). In both cases adherence to false doctrine ("falsely called knowledge," 6:20; the resurrection heresy, 2 Tim 2:17-18) causes departure from the faith/truth (6:21a; 2 Tim 2:17-18). The similarity of these descriptions may suggest that the more general reference to *gnōsis* in the earlier instance anticipates the more pointed reference to the resurrection teaching. In each case the same verb, "to depart from," accompanied by a participle indicating profession of a doctrine ("professing," "saying"), describes the rejection of the faith and links this development to false knowledge/the false resurrection doctrine. Also, in each case, the pejorative term "godless chatter" (occurring only in these two texts) denounces the false doctrine. Consequently, it is possible that the resurrection heresy, or the theological chemistry out of which it would come, was already brewing when Paul wrote 1 Timothy. The continuity of characters (Hymenaeus, 1:20; 2 Tim 2:17) suggests continuity of thought.[45] But there is no way to be certain how far things had developed at the time of the first letter; if the resurrection heresy was current, his choice not to mention it specifically might simply indicate that he hoped it would be so unlikely to garner support in the community that it would fade.

21a In any case, Paul ends the final charge to Timothy by underlining the danger inherent in "professing" (see on 2:10) this false knowledge. It is the real experience of those labeled "some" (= the opponents; see on 1:3) on which Paul draws. The language resembles that of 1:19, which makes the same basic point by way of reflection on the rejection of an effective conscience and the metaphor of shipwreck. Here that same basic end is described as "departure" or "deviation"[46] from "the faith" (see on 1:2). The process of rejection of the faith here reaches an ultimate stage (cf. 1:6), although the possibility of repentance is not ruled out (cf. 2 Tim 2:25-26).

45. Cf. Schlarb, *Die gesunde Lehre,* 120-22, who argues that the content of the "antitheses" includes: (1) an overrealized view of soteriology (of which the resurrection heresy explicitly mentioned in 2 Tim 2:18 forms a part); (2) a diminished stress on or deprecation of suffering and good deeds; (3) an overly enthusiastic approach to freedom in the Spirit.

46. See the discussion at 1:6, where an earlier stage in the road to apostasy is considered.

III. CLOSING BENEDICTION (6:21B)

21b *Grace be with you all.*

Grace benedictions typically occur as the last words of Pauline letters (Rom 16:20; 1 Cor 16:23; 1 Thess 5:28).[1] Ordinarily the form of these closing benedictions consists of the blessing to be confirmed or bestowed (e.g., "grace," Rom 16:20; 1 Thess 5:28; cf. 2 Cor 13:13 with its threefold blessing), the divine source ("the Lord Jesus," Rom 16:20; 1 Thess 5:28; cf. 2 Cor 13:13 with its reference to Father, Son and Spirit), and the intended recipient ("you all," 2 Cor 13:13; 2 Thess 3:18; "your spirit," Gal 6:18; Phil 4:23; Phlm 25; "you" [pl.], Rom 16:20; 1 Cor 16:23).[2]

The grace benediction that closes this letter is identical with 2 Tim 4:22[3] and all but identical with Titus 3:15. Yet of the three benedictions it appears the most abruptly, with no break between it and the concluding instruction of the letter. The divine source is not mentioned but may be assumed from the pattern elsewhere. And omission of a verb of being or multiplying (cf. 1 Pet 1:2) is standard.

What the benediction represents, far from a literary convention, is a serious and caring prayer of the apostle that Timothy and those to whom he was sent (pl. "you") would experience God's gracious presence among them. A variant reading at this point changes the plural "you" to a singular "you," apparently as an adjustment to the letter's tendency to make direct addresses to Timothy alone.[4] But the wider scope of the blessing corresponds to the adaptation of mandate elements in the crafting of a letter written to Timothy and secondarily to the church receiving him (see Introduction, 31-36). When one draws together the opening blessing of Timothy (1:2) and this closing benediction, it becomes apparent that Paul views his coworker's task and this church's life as equally carried out within the protective and nurturing grace of God. Paul's closing prayer-wish is that they will work and live in full awareness of the Lord's real presence among them.

---

1. See Aune, *Literary Environment,* 186-87.

2. Aune, *Literary Environment,* 186-87; T. Y. Mullins, "Benediction as a NT Form," *Andrews University Seminary Studies* 15 (1977): 59-64.

3. Gk. Ἡ χάρις μεθ' ὑμῶν; for χάρις, see the discussion and note at 1:2.

4. So μετά σου (sg. "with you"; D [K L] Ψ 048 1739 1881 TR, etc.); but the plural reading (μεθ' ὑμῶν) is well attested (ℵ* A F G 33 81, etc.) and, as the original reading, it more readily explains a change to the singular. See Metzger, 577.

The Second Letter
to
TIMOTHY

Text, Exposition, and Notes

I. OPENING GREETING (1:1-2)

1 Paul, an apostle of Christ Jesus by the will of God, in keeping with the promise of life that is in Christ Jesus, 2 to Timothy, my dear son: Grace, mercy and peace from God the Father and Christ Jesus our Lord.

The greeting consists of a single sentence in the Greek. It has the customary threefold structure of the Greco-Roman letter: the name of the sender, the recipient, and the greeting. The form is closely similar to that of 1 Tim 1:1-2 (see discussion). First, in each case, Paul defines his apostleship in relation to Christ Jesus and identifies its origin in the will ("command," 1 Tim 1:1) of God. In each case, too, the meaning of Paul's apostleship is expanded as the allusion to the mind of God develops into a reference to the salvation he himself provides in Christ. Thus Paul's ministry is linked to the plan of salvation. Second, Timothy, the recipient, is described in some sense as Paul's child. Third, the greeting in each letter to Timothy is identical, with the uncharacteristic use of the term "mercy" in the threefold blessing being most often noted. Differences in expression are also noticeable — their significance will be discussed below.

A. THE WRITER

1 The greeting first identifies the writer and then refines that identification by means of two parallel prepositional phrases. The writer is "Paul, an apostle of Christ Jesus." Whatever we make of the question of authorship, the name "Paul" refers to the same person who authored the undisputed Pauline letters — converted Pharisee and apostle to the Gentiles.[1] The phrase functions on two levels. First, for Paul the technical term "apostle" encompasses the whole concept of his calling to ministry. The reference evokes thoughts of the event in which he encountered the risen Lord and subsequently was entrusted with divine revelation. The tradition of this event (Acts 9:1-19 and pars.) associates authority and the special calling to preach the gospel to the Gentiles with Paul's apostleship, and Paul's own use of the phrase "apostle of Christ Jesus," and related phrases, as self-references confirms the presence of these themes. These letters to coworkers in general show no depreciation in this view of the Pauline apostolate: Paul is the recipient of revelation and also of an authoritative ministry to the Gentiles (1:11; 1 Tim 1:11-16; 2:7).

Second, this is an appeal to authority. In the letters attributed to Paul it is typical to find an opening reference to his apostolic office. Exceptions to this pattern are noticeable in those letters in which the motif of friendship plays an important part.[2] Although some scholars find it unusual that such a reference would occur in a letter as personal in tone as this one,[3] there are several possible reasons why a reminder of Paul's station would fit this letter to Timothy. The more obvious one is the need, which emerges as the letter progresses, to remind Timothy to undergo suffering and not shrink back from the responsibilities he has been called to carry out (1:6-8; 2:3, 11-12; 3:10-15; 4:1-5). The importance of faithfulness would be well grounded on the basis of apostolic authority.[4] If the letter were also intended to be read by the church (cf. 4:22), the appeal to apostolic position would serve to legitimate the one being called to carry on the task.[5] In any case, the purpose and tone of the letter easily justify the writer's use of this trump card to ensure that the gravity of the task entrusted to Timothy would not be missed.

The description of the writer continues with two parallel statements that define more specifically the nature of Paul's apostleship. The first prepositional phrase — "by the will of God"[6] — locates the means or agency of this apostolic calling and authority in the will of God. Specifically, Paul occupies the position he does in the church because of divine selection and not because of human decision or chance (cf. 1 Tim 1:1). This is typical Pauline language that in such contexts emphasizes further the authority already im-

---

1. For what follows, see the discussion and notes at 1 Tim 1:1.
2. See Philippians; 1 Thessalonians (cf. 2 Thessalonians); Philemon.
3. E.g., Oberlinner, 6.
4. Cf. Fee, 219; Knight, 363.
5. See Spicq, 697.
6. Gk. διὰ θελήματος θεοῦ; cf. 1 Tim 1:1, κατ' ἐπιταγὴν θεοῦ ("according to the command of God") that creates the effect. For θέλημα ("will") of the divine will, see the discussion and note on the use of the cognate verb θέλω in 1 Tim 2:4.

plicit in the previous designation.[7] The reason behind this emphasis may be, as in the earlier occurrences, the crosscurrents in the churches that left Paul's authority to teach and discipline, especially from a distance, somewhat in doubt. And in the case of 2 Timothy we do well to keep in mind the context of opposition and defection from the faith (1:15; 2:16-18; 3:1-9; 4:10, 16).

Something about the pattern or purpose of Paul's calling is indicated in the second of the two prepositional phrases — "in keeping with the promise of life that is in Christ Jesus." The phrase presents two questions for interpretation: the issue of its reference and the sense in which it describes Paul. The first question hangs on the meaning of the two combinations, "the promise of life" and "in Christ Jesus." By linking his ministry to the promise of life, Paul consciously depicts himself as the one who within God's plan executes "the promise." It is clear from the parallel in Titus 1:1-3, where the same basic connections are made, that God is the one who has made the promise of life.[8] "Life" is the content of the promise; despite the absence of the word "eternal," the meaning is precisely eternal life (see 1 Tim 1:16, discussion and note; 6:12; Titus 1:2; 3:7). The time element in "life" is left open, and we must be careful not to allow the attached thought of "promise" to project our thinking about the time of this "life" into the future.

Paul delimits the reference by interpreting the life as being "in Christ Jesus" (see on 1 Tim 1:14). The phrase is typically Pauline (Rom 3:24; 8:39), and although it can express different aspects of the life of faith and sometimes eludes precise explanation, it functions as a description of the reality of spiritual life in relation to Christ. In this case, the (eternal or spiritual) life that defines Paul's missionary calling is that which God has promised and given to all who are related to Christ (see below on 1:13-14). The time of the promise of life is right now and on into the future (1 Tim 4:8), so that God's gift of eternal life is to be understood as already in effect for those who have believed in Christ.

But the point of this theology is to describe Paul, which takes us on to the second question. The preposition *kata* that introduces the phrase we have been exploring, and which is parallel to the previous preposition "by," creates a relationship between Paul's apostleship and a specific result of God's redemptive plan, "the promise of life." But the sense is unclear. It may mean

7. See 1 Cor 1:1; 2 Cor 1:1; Eph 1:1; Col 1:1.

8. Gk. ἐπαγγελία ("promise"; see discussion at 1 Tim 4:8); Titus 1:2 employs the verb (ἐπαγγέλλομαι). The thought of God's redemptive plan as a promise to be worked out for his people first comes to expression in this language in the LXX (2 Macc 2:18; 3 Macc 2:10), and is fully developed in the NT (cf. the use of the noun in, e.g., Luke 24:49; Acts 1:4; 2:39; 7:17; 13:23; 23:21; Rom 4:13; 9:4; 2 Cor 1:20; Gal 3:18; Eph 2:12; Heb [14x]; 2 Pet 3:9; 1 John 2:25).

generally that Paul's apostleship is "in conformity with" the divine plan as summed up in the promise of life: this is the sense intended by TNIV's "in keeping with" (cf. NIV's "according to").[9] Or the preposition may express one degree or another of purpose or goal — Paul's apostleship is "for the sake of" (NRSV), and therefore for the proclaiming of, the promise.[10] The usage and ambiguity here are similar to those of Titus 1:1. But in each case, the broader goal of the letters, which is to give a mission mandate to the co-workers, suggests that the similar *kata* phrases establish the purpose (or basis) of Paul's calling/mission. In this passage, "the promise of life that is in Christ Jesus" is an abbreviation for Paul's gospel (1:9-11).[11] What the language does here is to describe Paul's calling to preach as being integral to the outworking of God's redemptive plan — the promise of life. It is in understanding this relationship between apostleship/calling and God's salvation that Timothy will achieve faithfulness in his own calling.

Thus Paul's self-description breathes an air of authority — originating in the will of God — and redemptive purpose, in that Paul's gospel is the linchpin in God's plan of salvation. It is easy to see how the modern interpretation of these letters as advocating a kind of Pauline exclusivism could arise. But are these statements about Paul's ministry any stronger than those that occur in his letters to churches? Not in any demonstrable way. More important are the observations that these features establish for the reader the tone and the significance of Paul's ministry. The reason for this is bound up not only with the work that Timothy is being called to take up, but also with Paul's own situation and the shaky status of his mission among the churches in Timothy's orbit.

B. THE RECIPIENT

2 Timothy is the recipient of the letter. The two points of comparison for this description of Timothy (1 Tim 1:1 and Titus 1:4) reveal a curious difference. In 1 Tim 1:1 (see discussion) Paul addresses Timothy as "my true son in the faith." He addresses Titus similarly with the phrase "true son in our common faith" (see on Tit 1:4). Here, as in 1 Cor 4:17, Timothy is called "my dear son" (lit. "my beloved child").[12] Some scholars interpret this as an expression of affection and intimacy, without the legitimizing inference of 1 Tim 1:2 (Titus 1:4)

---

9. For Gk. κατά, see the discussion at Titus 1:1 (and note).

10. Dibelius-Conzelmann, 97; Kelly, 153; Oberlinner, 7; Knight, 364.

11. Brox, 223.

12. For Gk. ἀγαπητός ("beloved"), see 1 Tim 6:2 (note); for τέκνον ("child"), see 1 Tim 1:2 (discussion and note).

present.[13] Yet the cultural dynamic at work in this language requires a slightly more nuanced explanation. Here the term "son" ("child") describes Timothy's relationship to Paul in terms of fictive kinship.[14] With such language Paul often portrayed himself as a father to those converted through his ministry. "Dear" (or "beloved") is also certainly a term of approval, affirmation, and intimacy. When one combines these items, the picture becomes one that involves responsibility (as of a child to a father or a disciple to a teacher) and close filial relationship.[15] Timothy's responsibility — to continue the Pauline mission — will be spelled out through the rest of the letter; the filial obligation and relationship are underlined here as the basis for the exhortations to come.

C. THE GREETING

The substance of the greeting is a prayer or wish that God and Christ Jesus will bless Timothy. The wording and meaning are identical with those of 1 Tim 1:2 (see discussion). Each element — "grace" (1:9; 2:1; 4:22), "mercy" (1:16, 18), and "peace" (2:22) — occurs elsewhere in the letter. The meaning of "mercy," the element that is unique to the greetings addressed to Timothy (1 Tim 1:2), calls for special notice. In 1 Tim 1:13 and 16, it is Paul who, in spite of his sin but owing to his capacity to be obedient, serves as the prototypical recipient of God's mercy. And Paul's mercy-prayer for Timothy in the opening of the first letter, therefore, places the coworker, in contrast to the false teachers, into the apostle's category. Now in this letter, the context suggests a slightly different accent. Note how the mercy-prayer is also made

13. Fee, 220 (although the same description does serve a legitimizing purpose in 1 Cor 4:17; see Fee, *1 Corinthians*, 188-89). Less likely is the view that "beloved child" means "Paul's firstborn" (= heir; for which see Spicq, 698-99, drawing on the use of "beloved" in such discussions; Gen 22:2, 12, 16). The dominant pseudonymous interpretation of such personal notes in these letters to coworkers should be mentioned. In this case, "beloved" becomes a typical part of the "pro-Paul" pattern created by the pseudepigrapher by which the Pauline gospel tradition is authenticated and preserved (over and against other traditions). In support of this post-Pauline project, Timothy must be legitimized for the later churches as *the* chosen conduit or guarantor of the Pauline gospel (see esp. Oberlinner, 8-9; Wolter, *Paulustradition;* Hasler, 55). This interpretation obviously depends on a number of significant prior assumptions about the letters and church situations addressed; nothing in the letter itself automatically requires such an explanation, and in many respects it creates more problems than it solves (see Introduction, 15-24).

14. Cf. Osiek and Balch, *Families in the New Testament World,* 156-67; see further references and discussion at 1 Tim 1:2.

15. See Johnson, 335; idem, *Paul's Delegates,* 45; the closeness of relationship is stressed throughout the letter (1:4; 4:9, 21; Marshall, 686).

for Onesiphorus's household (1:16), and for Onesiphorus himself on the day of judgment (1:18), because he, in contrast to "everyone in the province of Asia," had not been "ashamed" of Paul (1:16, 18). Moreover, the first instructions to Timothy will urge him not to be "ashamed" of the gospel or of Paul (1:8). Consequently, in 2 Timothy the prayer for God's mercy (or covenant-sustaining kindness and concern) is especially pointed to this danger (shame and shrinking back) that Timothy must avoid.[16] The items that Paul entreats God and Christ to grant to Timothy will prove to be intrinsic to the ministry and responsibilities he is called to embrace.

Right from the start it is clear that this is a very personal letter. This observation and the fact that to some degree this opening salutation is a Pauline literary convention should probably caution us against making too much of its theology. However, as the letter unfolds, its relevance for all believers, especially for those facing ministry challenges, will become clear. And this suggests that we will find consolation and encouragement in the same gifts of God and in the Lordship of Christ that Paul brought directly to Timothy's attention at the outset. No, we are not beloved of Paul in the same way that Timothy was. But we are beloved of God, and we are involved in the same mission that this letter was preparing Timothy to take to the next stage. In this respect, everything written to Timothy — every bit of theology, ethical exhortation, and practical advice — was also written (even if unintentionally) to us. We will understand our mission better if we view it in relation to Paul's perspective on his own (v. 1). We will give ourselves to it far more effectively in the knowledge of God's provision of "grace, mercy and peace" for the tasks he has set us. The opening greeting invites us to follow along in this letter of renewal and commission to Timothy and to find ourselves within it.

II. BODY OF THE LETTER

A. THE CALL TO PERSONAL COMMITMENT AND SPIRIT-EMPOWERED MINISTRY (1:3-18)

Paul now begins to address more directly some of the issues that his co-worker must face. He first reaches back into both his and Timothy's personal histories to establish the heritage of the faith they share (1:3-5). This becomes the platform for the first appeal to Timothy — namely, to draw on the gift of the Holy Spirit for courage to face suffering for the gospel (vv. 6-8). A specially formed theological piece is inserted at this point to illustrate the

16. Cf. Johnson, *Paul's Delegates,* 45.

content of Paul's gospel and to expand on the concept of the power of God (vv. 9-10). This develops into an authentication of the Pauline ministry to which Timothy is ultimately linked and called to continue in. With suffering and shame as key concepts, Paul closes this initial appeal by offering both negative and positive models (vv. 15-18).

1. Thanksgiving for Timothy's Faith (1:3-5)

> 3 *I thank God, whom I serve, as my ancestors did, with a clear conscience, as night and day I constantly remember you in my prayers.* 4 *Recalling your tears, I long to see you, so that I may be filled with joy.* 5 *I am reminded of your sincere faith, which first lived in your grandmother Lois and in your mother Eunice, and, I am persuaded, now lives in you also.*

The literary environment that determined the shape of Paul's letters was that of the Hellenistic and Hellenistic-Jewish letters. The thanksgiving-prayer portion of such letters was typical.[1] In the case of Paul's letters, the appearance of the section compares with the broader milieu,[2] but the content of his thanksgiving-prayers was inspired by OT concepts. Two models of structure can be identified in Paul's thanksgiving sections. The more complicated structure, commencing with a verb of thanksgiving, states his intention to pray for the recipients, and concludes with a clause that explains the content of the prayer (cf. Phil 1:3-11). A shorter form (e.g., 1 Cor 1:4) also begins with thanksgiving to God and ends with the reason for giving thanks.[3]

Both letters to Timothy include the thanksgiving paragraph, though the thanksgiving section in 2 Timothy is closer in tone and purpose to Paul's other thanksgiving sections.[4] It is a combination of the two forms noted above, but its way of expressing thanksgiving is identical with that of 1 Tim 1:12 (see below). Verses 3-5 form a single, complex Greek sentence that has given rise to several questions of interpretation. First, does Paul explain why he gives thanks? Second, how are the various phrases related to one another? Finally, what is the function of the thanksgiving-prayer within the developing discourse? A layout of the structure will provide a basis for reconstructing the intended flow of thought and addressing these questions.

1. Rom 1:8ff.; 1 Cor 1:4ff.; Eph 1:15ff.; Phil 1:3ff.; Col 1:3ff.; 1 Thess 1:2ff.; 2 Thess 1:3ff.; Phlm 4ff. See O'Brien, *Introductory Thanksgivings;* Aune, *Literary Environment,* 186-87.

2. Cf. 2 Macc 1:10-13.

3. See P. Schubert, *Form and Function of the Pauline Thanksgivings* (Berlin: Akademie, 1939), 10-39; O'Brien, *Thanksgivings,* 6-15.

4. 1 Tim 1:12-14 is unusually self-oriented; see the discussion there.

(1) I thank God
    (a) [whom I serve, as my ancestors did, with a clear conscience]
(2) whenever I remember you
    (a) in my "night and day" prayers
    (b) (and remembering you and praying for you, I am) longing to
        see you
        (i) because I remember your tears,
        (ii) so that I might be filled with joy
(3) because I remember the sincere faith that is in you
    (a) [which dwelt first in your grandmother Lois
        and in your mother Eunice,
        and, I trust, is also in you.]

The relationships can be explained as follows:

(1) The main statement of thanksgiving
    (a) a relative clause related unambiguously to (1); the reference to
        Paul's heritage and clear conscience is intrinsic to the argument,
        as we will see.
(2) This is subordinate to (1), identifying the time "when" Paul gives
    thanks to God; it is specifically when Timothy comes to Paul's
    mind that Paul gives thanks.
    (a) and that happens during the apostle's regular prayers,
    (b) (result) the remembrance of and the praying for Timothy result
        in a longing to see Timothy again;
        (i) (cause) Paul now fastens on one particular memory — Tim-
        othy's tears;
        (ii) (purpose) seeing Timothy again would complete Paul's joy;
(3) This is also subordinate to (1); it gives the reason for Paul's offer-
    ing of thanks to God — namely, his recollection of Timothy's sin-
    cere faith.
    (a) is a relative clause that is parallel to the relative clause (1)(a);
        note how Paul refers to Timothy's heritage (as he has to his
        own), and that he refers to Timothy as one having good stand-
        ing in the line of faith.

We may now return to our questions. First, why does Paul give
thanks? It will be apparent from the layout above, which follows the Greek
word-and-phrase order, that no English translation is able to render smoothly
the combination of thoughts and relationships without departing from the
original organization of thoughts. This is the reality of translation. In any
case, the basic sentence is: "I thank God . . . because I remember your faith."

The thought of "remembrance" is the key theme in the section, woven into the passage with clever wordplay (v. 3 "when I remember you"; v. 4, "because I remember your tears"; v. 5, "because I remember your sincere faith").[5] And it is precisely this thought of "remembrance" in relation to Timothy's faith that links the statement in v. 5 with the initial expression of thanksgiving. Missing this connection obscures somewhat the relationship Paul is forming between his faithfulness at the beginning of the prayer and Timothy's faithfulness at the end. The bracket formed in the discourse by the discussion of heritage and parentage and the continuity of each character with his line of faithful forebears are the most important features for determining the thrust of this section within the broader story.

Second, how do the parts relate? Within the bracket Paul's first two acts of remembering establish his relationship with and concern for Timothy; he prays for Timothy and is moved by his younger coworker's tears. This relationship forms the basis for the exhortations that will follow. His third remembrance — of Timothy's faith — is not the only reason for Paul's thankful spirit; so is the recollection of a track record that implies certain obligations of the one to whom it belongs. Paul's thinking here is complex and very purposeful. It is not a passage about Paul's prayer life or the need to be thankful toward God.

This brings us to the third question — how does this thanksgiving-prayer function within the broader narrative? The brackets create a paralleling effect — what is true of Paul (faithfulness in accordance with his spiritual heritage) is also true of Timothy (true faith in accordance with his spiritual heritage). But the directions of story movement are noticeably different. Paul announces his faithful service to God, but we know from the whole letter that this service is nearing its end. This announcement is a summary. Paul identifies Timothy's proven pattern of faith, but this affirmation is an open-ended introduction. Even the sequence of characters in v. 5 leaves the reader in the present: grandmother, mother, son. The final statement, "and, I am persuaded, [faith] now lives in you also," is an affirmation, and in fact it is the repetition of the affirmation about Timothy's faith just made.

But the twofold mention of this fact causes the reader/hearer to be wary of implicit signals. Why mention this item twice, and why does Paul underscore his confidence in Timothy? There is built into this double affirmation a reminder or warning to one who may be in danger of betraying his heritage. Paul's confidence in Timothy is not something Timothy is to accept passively. He must rather validate his faith and Paul's confidence in the tasks that lie ahead, the first of which involves a very personal return to spiritual

5. The wordplay is more obvious in the sounds of the Greek words: μνείαν (*mneian*), v. 3; μεμνημένος (*memnēmenos*), v. 4; ὑπόμνησιν (*hypomnesin*), v. 5.

empowerment. Paul's thanksgiving-prayer is, then, the basis for his appeal to Timothy. It supplies encouragement — Paul prays for him and affirms his faith; it implies obligation with a note of warning — there is a heritage that requires loyalty, and a confidence that must be validated.

3 As noted above, the verbal construction of the thanksgiving formula that occurs here is identical with that of 1 Tim 1:12 (see discussion) but different from that typically used in the thanksgiving-prayer sections of Paul's letters to churches. Yet, in keeping with past practice, the object of thanksgiving here is God. As mentioned, the reason for the thanksgiving takes longer to emerge. In this case, the only apparent reason stated comes in the participial phrase of v. 5, referring to Timothy's faith.[6] The particular shape of the argument forces the separation of this reason from the initial expression of thanks by several intervening clauses.

In place of the usual pronoun "my," which emphasizes the apostle's personal relationship to God (e.g., Rom 1:8), is the relative clause that underlines Paul's faithfulness in ministry. It consists of three items: the verb of "service," a backward-looking time reference, and a prepositional phrase that defines the character of Paul and his service.

First, the language describing "service" to God[7] recalls Paul's description of apostolic ministry in Rom 1:9, and a glance back at patterns present in this earlier letter may be helpful. There too a relative phrase relates Paul to God in service. The meaning of the term in the NT is most heavily influenced by the LXX, where the verb denoted the religious ministry and worship of the priests who carried out the sacrifices to YHWH in specific contrast to pagan gods.[8] This meaning is echoed in a number of NT texts that reflect back on OT situations.[9] But the term also came to express the more comprehensive meaning of Christian existence as righteous service to God,[10] for which the OT priestly service to YHWH provided a kind of paradigm. Standing somewhere between these two meanings is Paul's use of the term to refer to his missionary ministry.

Romans 1:9 identifies two important dimensions of this ministry-service that are also developed here, though in different order and with different language: "God, whom I serve in my spirit in preaching the gospel of his Son."[11] First, the experiential "locus" of this activity is the human spirit, by which Paul almost certainly means that dimension of life where he experi-

---

6. Cf. Heb 12:28, where a participial phrase introduces the reason for thanks.

7. Gk. λατρεύω; see Rom 1:9; 12:1; Acts 27:23; Phil 3:3; Heb 9:14.

8. See H. Strathmann, *TDNT* 4:59-63.

9. Acts 7:7, 42; Rom 1:25; Heb 8:5; 9:9; 10:2; 13:10.

10. Luke 1:74; Acts 24:14; 27:23; Phil 3:3; and the noun (λατρεία) in Rom 12:1. Cf. Oberlinner, 15.

11. Rom 1:9: ᾧ λατρεύω ἐν τῷ πνεύματί μου ἐν τῷ εὐαγγελίῳ τοῦ υἱοῦ αὐτοῦ.

ences the Holy Spirit's power and presence.[12] Then, the content of Paul's service is the proclamation of the gospel. This combination of thoughts relates Paul's ministry and his experience of God to the OT in terms of both continuity and transcendence. Paul's calling is the fulfillment of the OT promise to take salvation to the Gentiles, to expand the boundaries of the people of the one true God.[13] But he carries out his ministry in the context of the new covenant in which the Holy Spirit is the key distinctive.

These same connections are latent in this thanksgiving-prayer and explicit in the broader passage, so that it is clear that the verb "I serve" carries the full-orbed meaning that it does in the Romans thanksgiving. The force of the present tense of the verb, determined by the following backward-looking time reference ("as my ancestors . . ."), is to stress mainly continuity and consistency of action — Paul's service to God is something he has been doing in the past and continues to do now. The verb thus links Paul's apostolic ministry intentionally to OT patterns of service to God. But this continuity with the past is established more clearly in another way.

Second, in the phrase that follows — "as[14] my ancestors did [served]" — Paul consciously connects his ministry to the worship of Israel by placing himself into the line leading back to his "forebears."[15] In doing this, he follows the standard cultural practice of establishing one's credentials by association with the authoritative and accepted history. In this case Paul's concern is to make the link to the OT faith, which he conceives of here in ideal terms. "Ancestors" will mean not parents — despite the nice parallelism this would create with the description of Timothy — but "the fathers" to whom the promise of blessing was made by God and through whom the true worship of YHWH was practiced and transmitted through the generations. The same heritage and continuity are emphasized in Paul's speech in Acts 24:14.

The attachment of the phrase "with a clear conscience" (1 Tim 3:9) is thought by some to place this passage and self-testimony at odds with the portrait of Paul in 1 Tim 1:12-16.[16] This is part of the technical vocabulary in these letters to coworkers that describes the various inner aspects of people in relation to their commitment to the apostolic faith (see 1 Tim 1:5, Excursus).

---

12. Cf. J. D. G. Dunn, *Romans 1–8* (WBC 38A; Dallas: Word, 1988), 29; Fee, *God's Empowering Presence,* 485-86.

13. H. Balz, *EDNT* 2:344-45.

14. Gk. ἀπὸ προγόνων (lit. "from my ancestors = as my ancestors did"; BDAG, s.v.); this use of ἀπό (usually showing origin or distance) to express (the source of) a pattern of behavior ("in the same way as") is peculiar in the NT but frequently attested in secular inscriptions; see Dibelius-Conzelmann, 98 n. 3.

15. See the discussion at 1 Tim 5:4. Elsewhere Paul tends to use the term "fathers" (πατέρες) to establish this link; e.g., Rom 9:5.

16. For Gk. συνείδησις, see the Excursus at 1 Tim 1:5. See Oberlinner, 16.

Unlike Paul's use of "conscience" in his main letters, where the term provides a neutral reference to the organ that makes moral decisions according to a set of standards, here the formula "clear conscience" is theologically determined; that same organ is viewed from the perspective of faithfulness to the apostolic gospel.[17] Consequently, Paul is describing himself as one who has served God — as did the fathers — with consistent faithfulness to the message of salvation. The supposed dissonance detected between this testimony and others in which he emphasizes his past rebellion (1 Tim 1:12-16) could also be found in the Lukan portrait of Paul (cf. Acts 9; 23:1; 24:16), and is mainly imaginary. Just as Paul can reflect back on an ideal Israelite faith, passing over the many lapses into sin, so he can characterize his apostolic ministry in terms of faithfulness without reference to his questionable pre-Christian history. The differently oriented portrait in 1 Tim 1:12-16 needs to be seen in the flow of that narrative, where a contrast between Paul and false teachers is drawn, and in which the purpose is to underscore the nature of grace.

Paul's self-identification combines action, history, and character. But what function does it serve in the narrative? To answer this, we should keep in mind that the letter operated on at least two levels. First, as a letter to Timothy, within the narrative that is developing, the conscious paralleling of Paul and Timothy suggests that this self-description serves as a model and a reminder of the kind of testimony to which Timothy himself is to aspire. This function will become more apparent as the letter proceeds and Timothy's call to continue Paul's mission is spelled out clearly.

Second, as a letter to be read also by the church(es) in which Timothy was working, Paul's claim of consistent faithfulness to God and the gospel, and especially his claim to have a "clear conscience," may well be directed to those who are opponents[18] or to those who are being influenced by opponents to reject the apostle's authority. The context (1:8, 12, 15-18) suggests that his imprisonment became grounds for some to disparage the Pauline ministry.[19] Paul's self-reference clearly sets him apart from those who have rejected his gospel.[20]

17. Cf. 1 Tim 4:2; see also "good conscience" in 1 Tim 1:5, 19 (discussion and Excursus).

18. Opponents are categorized in terms of ineffective or malfunctioning consciences in 1 Tim 4:2; cf. Tit 1:15. The primary point of the "good conscience" category is faithful adherence to the apostolic tradition (see the Excursus at 1 Tim 1:5). Cf. Oberlinner, 16.

19. Moreover, if the opponents were Judaizers, the emphasis on continuity with Israel's faith might be similar to Paul's claims in other disputes (cf. Acts 23:1; 24:16; 2 Cor 11:22ff.; Phil 3:2-6); see Kelly, 155.

20. The modern consensus is that this depiction of Paul is a literary feature employed by the third-generation (or later) pseudepigrapher to authenticate the Pauline tra-

As the Greek sentence continues, the thanksgiving-prayer proceeds to a report of the actual prayer for Timothy. The function of this long phrase, "as night and day I constantly remember you in my prayers," which recalls the thanksgiving-prayers of Rom 1:9; 1 Thess 1:2-3[21] (cf. Eph 1:16; Col 1:3), is temporal in relation to the act of thanksgiving.[22] But within the section (vv. 3-5) the prayer-report expresses the benevolent feelings of the writer for the recipient typical of the friendship letter. It is formed of three typical elements. The adjective "constantly" emphasizes the fervency of Paul's prayer for Timothy and reflects on his devotion to God.[23] The intentional act of "remembering" ("making mention") is central to the prayer-report, but also assures Timothy that Paul will not forget him, especially when he prays.[24] The term for prayer indicates specific requests to God for intercession.[25] In this case, a fourth element is added to the prayer-report. The phrase "night and day," which has various applications, adds still more emphasis to Paul's fervency in prayer[26] and piety (see on 1 Tim 5:5). Thus Paul's prayers for his coworker are requests for God's intervention and help in the specific circumstances of ministry; his commitment and friendship to Timothy and his devo-

---

dition as *the* authorized tradition (Oberlinner, 16). 2 Timothy is thought to employ these personal details to create a posthumous "last will and testament" of Paul, through which the Pauline follower receives full authorization to continue the apostle's mission. This literary "Paul" begins to emerge in the opening thanksgiving of the letter, which, employing echoes of the genuine letters, establishes through Timothy the continuity of the ministry in view of Paul's death (Woltcr, *Paulustradition,* 20-25, 240-56; Oberlinner, 1-5; cf. Collins, *Letters That Paul Did Not Write,*124-29; for a critique see the Introduction, 25-27).

21. Cf. 2 Tim 1:3c ὡς ἀδιάλειπτον ἔχω τὴν περὶ σοῦ μνείαν ἐν ταῖς
δεήσεσίν μου;

Rom 1:9c ὡς ἀδιαλείπτως μνείαν ὑμῶν ποιοῦμαι.

22. Whereas in Rom 1:9c the construction (with adv.) and flow of the argument require ὡς to have the meaning "that" (marking discourse content, or "how") and supplying the substance of God's testimony on behalf of Paul (BDAG, s.v. 4); for the temporal function, see BDAG, s.v. 8; BDF §455, 2, 3.

23. Gk. ἀδιάλειπτος (adj.; Rom 9:2), ἀδιαλείπτως (adv.; Rom 1:9; 1 Thess 1:2; 2:13; 5:17) is Pauline vocabulary used mainly to describe devotion in prayer and, hence, commitment to God (Spicq, *TLNT* 1:32-34). Cf. 1 Macc 12:11; 2 Macc 13:12.

24. Gk. ἔχω . . . μνείαν; the combination is idiomatic for "keeping the memory," which is the opposite of forgetting; cf. 1 Thess 3:6; LXX Ezek 21:37; 25:10; Wis 5:14 (see Spicq, *TLNT* 1:32 n. 5; 2:496; O. Michel, *TDNT* 4:678-79). For the more typical construction, μνείαν ποιοῦμαι, see Rom 1:9; Eph 1:16; 1 Thess 1:2; Phlm 4; for μνεία ("memory") in this sense without an expressed verb, see Phil 1:3.

25. For Gk. δέησις ("request, prayer"), see the discussion at 1 Tim 2:1.

26. The RSV connects it with the following "longing" of Paul to see Timothy; but 1 Tim 5:5 (1 Thess 3:10) shows "night and day" to be a typical picture of devotion to prayer. See the discussion in R. Leivestad, *EDNT* 2:434.

tion to God combine to assure the coworker that he will not be left alone or without resources.

4 A second element in the letter's friendship motif is Paul's wish to see Timothy again.[27] This thought is expressed with a participial phrase, "longing to see you."[28] In this continuation of the sentence, the phrase describes Paul's emotional situation as he prays, generated perhaps in the course of the prayer.[29] It was characteristic of Paul to stress the importance of the relationships he had formed with his churches. One way he made this clear was by reminding them of his (or his team's) "longing" for them, either in general terms (Phil 1:8; 4:1) or specifically as the desire to "see" them again (Phil 2:26-28; 1 Thess 3:6; cf. Rom 1:11; 15:23). In fact, with this language of "longing"[30] he also reminded his churches how they were bound to him (2 Cor 7:7) and to one another (2 Cor 9:14). In this case, the wish, which serves the same literary purpose, is directed to an individual and forms a theme that encircles the whole of the letter (4:9, 21), injecting it with a sense of emotion and urgency. Coming at the outset of the letter, the note of friendship helps to reinforce the relationship-obligation factor that is to motivate Timothy's response.

The following participial phrase identifies one specific cause of Paul's longing: "recalling your tears."[31] Here the second note in the theme of remembrance is sounded. The allusion created by "remembering" is intensely personal and emotional,[32] and we are left to wonder what sorrowful event is in Paul's mind. Although it is a stretch, the tearful parting described in Acts 20:37 is sometimes thought to be in mind,[33] but the reference is more likely to some event of which we have no record. The reference strengthens the sense of concern and intimacy.

What Paul hopes to gain from seeing Timothy again is also deeply personal — "so that *(hina)* I may be filled with joy." In contrast with Rom 1:11-12, where Paul's purpose in "seeing" the Roman believers is to exchange spiritual blessings with them in the situation of Paul's imprisonment, the purpose clause defines the benefits entirely from the perspective of Paul's own needs.

---

27. For the discussion of this feature, see Wolter, *Paulustradition,* 209-10.

28. Gk. ἐπιποθῶν σε ἰδεῖν; the infinitive is complementary, the participle and the infinitive functioning together to form a single idea.

29. The present tense stresses that this sense of longing is linked to the time and theme of unceasing prayer for Timothy.

30. Gk. ἐπιποθέω; see Spicq, *TLNT* 2:58-60.

31. Gk. μεμνημένος σου τῶν δακρύων ("remembering your tears"); the force of the perfect participle is durative (1 Cor 11:2; Marshall, 693); for the causal use of the participle, see Moule, *Idiom Book,* 102-4.

32. Gk. μιμνῄσκομαι (1 Cor 11:2); for the emotional potential of the verb (e.g., Heb 13:3), see R. Leivestad, *EDNT* 2:430-41; BDAG, s.v. 3; cf. Spicq, *TLNT* 2:489-96.

33. See the discussion in Hanson, 119-20; Kelly, 156; Spicq, 704.

At the deeper level, the effect is twofold. First, Paul underscores again the identity that exists between himself and Timothy — they are apart, and what Paul wants more than anything is for them to be together. Second, the expression of friendship involves Timothy ever more deeply in the responsibilities that their mutual relationship entails. This relationship, consisting of elements of authority and intimacy, will be the basis for urging Timothy to press on in Paul's work. Although it is clear that "joy" is a characteristic of the people who live in the sphere of God's presence (e.g., Rom 14:17; Gal 5:22),[34] there is no clear distinction between natural "joy" and something like Christian joy in the NT. The thought here is similar to that of Phil 2:2, where Paul called on the Philippian believers to "complete[35] my joy" by growing in love for others — in each case, the appeal flows out of a secure and intimate relationship and aims to satisfy a deep longing of Paul.

5   At this point, Paul begins to close the bracket begun with his self-description in v. 3. Timothy's faith and heritage will now be described in a way that parallels Paul's description. Grammatically, another participial phrase creates the connection with the initial statement. Thematically, it is the thought of "remembrance" that helps forge the connection. Logically, the phrase announces the main reason for Paul's offering of thanks. The word indicating the act of remembering or recalling *(hypomnēsin)* is the third of its type in this section (see *mneian,* v. 3c; *memnēmenos,* v. 4b). The noun combined with the aorist participle[36] probably intends the passive sense "I am reminded."[37] Paul does not indicate a specific reason for this recollection;[38] he simply fastens on a distinctive trait as a prelude to parenesis.

That trait is the quality of Timothy's faith. Two things require discussion — the meaning of "faith" and the force of the qualifier "sincere." "Faith" is a key concept in these letters to coworkers that carries different nuances of meaning in different contexts: often with the definite article it means the objective content of what is believed (the apostolic gospel), but it may describe the existential condition of believing in God or Christ.[39] In this context, "your faith"[40] is probably meant as Timothy's continual disposition of

---

34. Gk. χαρά; H. Conzelmann, *TDNT* 9:359-72; Spicq, *TLNT* 3:498-99.

35. Gk. πληρόω; see G. Delling, *TDNT* 6:286-98. For the figure "filled with joy," see also Acts 13:52; Josephus, *Antiquities* 15.421.

36. Gk. ὑπόμνησιν λαβών; the phrase appears to be an idiom for "having remembrance." For the related verb ὑπομιμνῄσκω ("to remind"), used actively, see 2 Tim 2:14; Titus 3:1; 2 Pet 1:12. Cf. Spicq, *TLNT* 2:489-501.

37. So J. Behm, *TDNT* 1:348-49.

38. But cf. the discussion in Knight, 368-69.

39. See 1 Tim 1:2 (discussion and note).

40. Literally, the phrase (Gk. ἐν σοί [2x]) describes faith as being "in you" (see 1:6; 1 Tim 4:14); it is a Pauline expression (see Rom 1:12 [pl.]).

belief in Christ. The qualifier, "sincere," is more accurately understood as "authentic," as in 1 Tim 1:5 (see discussion and note), in contrast to the inauthentic faith of those who have deserted Paul and who have been involved in spreading false doctrine (2:17-18). And the contrast is probably intended (for the wider readership) to distance Timothy from the false teaching (1:8, 12, 14; 2:2). Timothy's faith is "authentic" in terms of what he believes and the fruit that that belief produces.

Timothy's spiritual heritage is traced back to his grandmother and mother: "which [faith] first lived in your grandmother Lois and in your mother Eunice, and, I am persuaded, now lives in you also." The effect is to create a parallel with the reference to Paul's spiritual heritage in v. 3. The verb translated "to live in" (perhaps more familiarly "to indwell"; 1:14) is Pauline and used uniformly to describe inward spiritual elements of the Christian life.[41] "Faith" is thus depicted as an enduring characteristic of these three lives. The aorist tense of the verb suggests that this state had a beginning, and the reader is invited to see God as the initial cause.

We know nothing of the two women, except that they were Jewish (Acts 16:1).[42] The content of their faith and the sequence in which they came to it and came to know Paul, as Paul envisages it, are matters of speculation among commentators. Paul's self-description leaves some room for the reference to be to a living Jewish faith that readily accepted the gospel.[43] But while this continuity may be necessary for the historical connections in the sequence to make sense, Paul's main interest is in the quality of the faith that now resides in Timothy, which is to be measured by the pure apostolic faith.[44] In any case, we know only that Timothy's grandmother and mother apparently came to faith in the Messiah prior to Timothy and provided an environment crucial to his conversion and spiritual development (cf. 3:15). Of the latter, Paul seems, on the surface, convinced: "And I am persuaded,[45] [the faith] now lives in you also." But, given the context, which implies some de-

---

41. Gk. ἐνοικέω; here of "faith"; of the Spirit's indwelling (Rom 8:11; 2 Tim 1:14; cf. the equivalent in 1 Cor 3:16, οἰκεῖ ἐν ὑμῖν); of God indwelling his people (2 Cor 6:16); of the word of Christ (Col 3:16). Cf. R. Dabelstein, *EDNT* 1:456; O. Michel, *TDNT* 5.135-36 and references. For the similar concept in relation to sin's indwelling, see Rom 7:17, 18, 20 (Gk. οἰκέω + ἐν ἐμοί).

42. The name Lois (Λωΐς) occurs only here in the NT and appears to have been uncommon in the Greek of that time (see Spicq, 705; BDAG). Eunice (Εὐνίκη) is also rare but better attested (Spicq, 705; BDAG). It was not unusual for Jewish women to have Greek names.

43. See Scott; Fee, 223.

44. Kelly, 157; Spicq, 706.

45. Gk. πείθω (perf. pass., "to persuade"). The perfect passive expresses conviction, or certainty (Rom 8:38; 14:14; 2 Tim 1:12); Spicq, *TLNT* 3:66-77.

gree of ambivalence toward the mission on the part of the younger coworker, the rhetorical effect of this statement goes beyond simple affirmation and encouragement to exhortation designed to induce Timothy to demonstrate his faith.[46]

With this statement of Paul's conviction about Timothy, the thanksgiving-prayer comes to a close. It functions to remind him of Paul's true feelings of affection. The thanks to God and prayer offered for Timothy and the fond memories serve this purpose. Equally, the sense of identity created between Paul and Timothy intends to bridge the gap of distance that separates them. But this is not an end in itself. The same paralleling of characters and qualities — apostle and fellow worker — that the bracketing formed by Paul's self-description and Timothy's description emphasizes becomes the basis on which Paul will urge Timothy to take up the work again. At this level, the argument proceeds as follows: "Timothy, in terms of our faith and spiritual heritage, we are cut from the same cloth. The obligations and call to duty that this implies for me also implies for you."

We would pass too quickly over this very personal introduction if we considered only its literary significance. Paul strikes a chord that finds some degree of resonance in all believers. The OT prophets often tell the story of an enslaved people chosen and blessed by God. These people are given privileges and promises and with them the obligation to serve the Lord in every facet of life. But one of the repeating themes of this story is how the people squander their privileges and fail to carry out the obligations that attend the blessings. In preparing the coworker for the renewal of his calling, Paul draws heavily on Timothy's sense of loyalty and responsibility to the faith, which he has as a heritage, to live out his faith in service. He was obligated to exercise the faith in him as a gift, and this included taking seriously the people to whom God had committed him. God mediates that claim of loyalty through numerous relationships in which we have experienced his grace and call to service. Loyalty or faith in modern Western culture often operates more on the intellectual than the interpersonal level,[47] and this puts us at a disadvantage when we seek to understand a passage like this. It boils down to this: authentic faith in God requires more from us than simply adherence to doctrinal ideas.

---

46. For the same language and strategy, see Rom 15:14. See the discussion in Johnson, 341-43.

47. J. J. Pilch and B. J. Malina, *Handbook of Biblical Social Values* (Peabody, MA: Hendrickson, 1998), 70.

2. The Renewed Call to Boldness and Faithfulness in Ministry (1:6-14)

> 6 *For this reason I remind you to fan into flame the gift of God, which is in you through the laying on of my hands.* 7 *For the Spirit God gave us does not make us timid, but gives us power, love and self-discipline.* 8 *So do not be ashamed of the testimony about our Lord, or of me his prisoner. But join with me in suffering for the gospel, by the power of God,*
>
> 9 *who has saved us*
> *and called us to a holy life —*
> *not because of anything we have done*
> *but because of his own purpose and grace.*
> *This grace was given us in Christ Jesus*
> *before the beginning of time,*
> 10 *but it has now been revealed*
> *through the appearing of our Savior, Christ Jesus,*
> *who has destroyed death*
> *and has brought life and immortality to light through the gospel.*
>
> 11 *And of this gospel I was appointed a herald and an apostle and a teacher.* 12 *That is why I am suffering as I am. Yet this is no cause for shame, because I know whom I have believed, and am convinced that he is able to guard what I have entrusted to him until that day.* 13 *What you heard from me, keep as the pattern of sound teaching, with faith and love in Christ Jesus.* 14 *Guard the good deposit that was entrusted to you — guard it with the help of the Holy Spirit who lives in us.*

Paul's confidence in Timothy's faith (vv. 3-5) serves as the basis for the commands to follow. This can be seen from the transition, "for this reason," which forms the backward connection, and from the continuation of the "remembrance" theme, "I remind you." The instructions Paul gives at this point will be seen to lead to the handing over of his ministry to his successor. The passage provides a basis for all that will follow in the letter.

Structurally, vv. 6-14 should be regarded as a single unit. Verses 6-8 create a connection between the Spirit and participation in suffering for the gospel and provide an alternative to being ashamed of the gospel. This theme is repeated in vv. 12-14, where Paul exemplifies the way of suffering for the gospel and explains the task Timothy is to carry out in the Spirit. Between these thematic brackets (Spirit, shame, suffering, gospel), the content of the gospel is presented in a carefully structured exposition (vv. 9-10). The passage raises a number of questions (see below); but the central issue for understanding the function of 2 Timothy is the portrayal of the role of Paul the apostle in relation to Timothy and the later church.

a. The Call to Action (1:6-8)

In this first subsection, Paul makes the transition to instruction. Matters that must concern us include the meaning of "the gift of God," the apostle's role in mediating this gift to Timothy, and the significance of the statement about the Spirit whom God gave. But we begin with the relationship of the whole passage to what precedes.

6 The opening phrase, "for this reason,"[1] forms a clear causal connection to the preceding discussion. It is the reality of Timothy's sincere faith (v. 5) that encourages Paul to expect as much from his coworker as he does from himself.[2] To this end, Paul adds a fourth word of "remembrance" to the chain already established in vv. 3-5, with one important difference: now, on the basis of those memories, Paul turns to "remind" Timothy of his calling. What might seem to be a gentle tone in which to couch a command is actually all the more binding, because a "reminder" draws on shared knowledge and experience and implies that past commitments are still in effect.[3] The effect of the language is to make an appeal to truth that Timothy knows quite well; if it cannot be denied, he is committed to a course of action.

The instruction itself is expressed with metaphorical language. The image of keeping a fire burning ("fan into flame"; NRSV, "rekindle") could apply to Timothy in several ways. But having just affirmed the authenticity of his faith, the vividness of the present tense (verb and infinitive) probably envisions stoking "the fire" to keep it burning brightly so as to maximize its potential.[4] The need to achieve his potential is very much in view since it is the "gift of God" that needs to be burning hotly (cf. 1 Thess 5:19).

But what is "the gift of God" that is to be fanned into flame?[5] Within Pauline thought (see esp. 1 Cor 12:4-11) the "gifts" (pl.) of God refer to the various activities of the Holy Spirit that make ministry possible in the life of

---

1. For the strong causal phrase δι' ἣν αἰτίαν, see BDF §456.4; also 1:12; Titus 1:13; Acts 10:21; 22:24; 23:28; Heb 2:11.

2. Cf. Kelly, 159; Oberlinner, 27.

3. Gk. ἀναμιμνῄσκω; for the technique of obligating by reminder, see Rom 15:15; 1 Cor 4:17; 2 Cor 7:15; Heb 10:32. Cf. H. Patsch, *EDNT* 1:86.

4. Gk. ἀναζωπυρέω; Clement (*1 Clement* 27.3) uses the verb similarly to appeal for a redoubling of faith that is already present: "Therefore let our faith be rekindled within us" (Lightfoot, Harmer, Holmes). But Ignatius uses it of revival from death (Ignatius, *To the Ephesians* 1.1); Lips, *Glaube,* 208-10. See Marshall, 696.

5. Gk. τὸ χάρισμα τοῦ θεοῦ; for the phrase in a different context, see Rom 6:23.

the believing community.[6] Referred to in the singular, and in the present context, "the gift of God" has been explained in three ways.

(1) Some interpreters point out that in these letters to coworkers the only other reference to such "gifting" is again to Timothy (1 Tim 4:14), who in each case receives the gift through the laying on of hands; from this is deduced that at this (later) time in the church the "gift" *(charisma)* was linked to ordination and office and imparted the authority and ability to execute this charge.[7]

(2) Others understand the "gift" as a reference to one or another of the various abilities for ministry provided by God, which Paul often means by "gift(s)" elsewhere.[8]

(3) However, a straightforward reading of the text suggests that v. 7 explains "the gift of God" in v. 6 as being the Holy Spirit given by God. The discussion in the passage is more immediately about Timothy's need for power (to overcome timidity) and love and self-control (v. 7), things that the Spirit provides all believers.[9] What complicates this conclusion is the reference to the laying on of hands and the question of how the event alluded to here relates to 1 Tim 4:14. Before drawing a final conclusion, these factors should be considered.

The remainder of v. 6 consists of a relative clause that defines further the gift just mentioned. It states quite clearly that the gift is "in" Timothy ("you").[10] This location corresponds to the concept of the inwardness of faith in 1:5 and also the "indwelling" of the Spirit in 1:14, suggesting that the Spirit is depicted as residing in the inner person, influencing human thoughts, motives, and emotion, and giving shape to outward and visible activities.

Associated with the gift is Paul's act of laying hands on Timothy.[11] The preposition governing the action indicates either that the act was (somehow) instrumental in conveying the gift of the Spirit to Timothy, or that the act was an accompaniment to the gift.[12] Of these, only instrumentality (in some sense) fits. In view of Paul's preceding rehearsal of Timothy's faith-

6. See M. Turner, *The Holy Spirit and Spiritual Gifts Then and Now* (Carlisle, U.K.: Paternoster, 1996), 103-35; Fee, *God's Empowering Presence*, 151-75.

7. See the discussion in Lips, *Glaube*, 220-23; Oberlinner, 28-29; Brox, 229; Kelly, 159-60; Hasler, 57; Hanson, 121.

8. Rom 1:11; 12:6; 1 Cor 1:7; 7:7; 12:4, 9, 28, 30-31; see Johnson, 344-45, 353-54; Knight, 370-71.

9. Fee, *God's Empowering Presence*, 785-89; cf. Dunn, *Baptism in the Holy Spirit*, 167.

10. Gk. ἐν σοί; 1:5; 1 Tim 4:14; 1 Cor 12:6; Eph 2:2; Phil 2:13.

11. Gk. διὰ τῆς ἐπιθέσεως τῶν χειρῶν μου ("through the laying on of hands"); for the rite, see the discussion at 1 Tim 4:14.

12. On διά with the genitive, see M. Harris, *NIDNTT* 3:1182-83.

heritage (1:5), a reference now to the gift of the Spirit received by Timothy at his conversion seems perfectly natural. Equally, that Paul should urge Timothy to access the Spirit (rather than some specific ministering gift) for the items about to be mentioned (v. 7) also seems perfectly natural. What might give pause is the text's claim that this gift came by way of the apostle's hands. Nevertheless, conveyance of the gift of the Spirit in this way, through the laying on of hands by the apostles, is attested in Acts 8:17-18; 9:12, 17; 19:6. This does not necessarily mean that Paul "channeled" the Spirit to Timothy, but rather that Paul, by laying hands on him, (publicly) confirmed the presence of faith in him (Num 27:18-23), on which acknowledgment God gave the gift of the Spirit.[13] It is not impossible that Timothy received his commission as Paul's coworker at the same time. In view of the renewal of commission that these verses have initiated (see below), an allusion to this past "beginning" would also have been fitting.

This brings us back to the similar description in 1 Tim 4:14 (see discussion and notes) and the question whether the same event (and gift) is in mind. Several differences suggest to me different events.[14] (1) In 1 Tim 4:14 it is the elders who are present at the event and who lay hands on Timothy; Paul is either absent or at least (apparently) did not participate. In 2 Tim 1:6 Paul alone is officiating. (2) Reception of the gift is accompanied or occasioned by prophecy (see on 1 Tim 4:14), and (with a different preposition)[15] by the laying on of hands by the elders. Even assuming that the change of prepositions does not change substantially the nature of instrumentality, the fact that here Paul alone is the agent of conferral represents a significant difference. (3) In 1 Tim 4:14 Timothy is said to receive "the gift," which is preceded by a discussion of specific ministering gifts (4:13). While it may seem to some to be quibbling, here Timothy is said to have received "*the* gift of God," which statement is immediately succeeded by a discussion — accessed by means of an intentional echo of the parallel "Spirit" text in Rom 8:15 (see below) — of qualities ("power, love, self-discipline"), not ministering gifts, produced (in all believers) by the Spirit. "Gift" understood as "ministering gifts" fits the context in 1 Tim 4:14 better than it does here.

13. Fee, *God's Empowering Presence,* 785-89; Towner, 160; cf. Johnson, 53.

14. Those who maintain that a single event is described from two perspectives and stress the differences in the character of the two letters (public/congregational vs. private/testamentary) range from those who endorse the letters' authenticity and stress (e.g., Knight, 209, 371) to those who relate the two descriptions to the two literary functions of the respective pseudepigraphical letters (so, with some variation, Wolter, *Paulustradition,* 218-22; Dibelius-Conzelmann, 71, 98; Brox, 228-29; Hanson, 121; Oberlinner, 29-30; Young, *Theology,* 108).

15. In 1 Tim 4:14, μετά is compatible with the verb ἐδόθη, but it is not suitable with ἐστιν in 2 Tim 1:6 (see Lips, *Glaube,* 251).

Given Timothy's résumé, which included service as Paul's mission coworker and occasional assignments within established congregations (e.g., 1 Cor 4:17), separate references to a congregational commissioning (1 Tim 4:14) and to an apostolic commissioning in conjunction with his conversion/ initiation present no great problem. The literary character of the respective letters corresponds just as well to this situation. In this case, the commissioning event in mind — the handing on of the mission from Paul to his coworker — might quite suitably call for this reminder of the earlier formative event in which the gift of the Spirit came to Timothy. Though the parallel is not quite complete, the traditions of Moses handing on authority to Joshua (see below) and of Elijah passing the mantle on to Elisha may not be far from mind.[16]

7 In order to strengthen the admonition, Paul adds to his acknowledgment of Timothy's genuine faith a theological reason for stepping back into action. This reason ("for"; *gar*) is to be found in the recollection of a theology of the Holy Spirit. The language of this verse is very similar to that of Rom 8:15:[17]

> Rom 8:15 — [For] the Spirit you received does not make you slaves, so that you live in fear again; rather, the Spirit you received brought about your adoption to sonship.
> 2 Tim 1:7 — For the Spirit God gave us does not make us timid, but gives us power, love and self-discipline.

Although the texts are not identical, the latter text must be understood as a conscious echo of the earlier teaching about the Spirit.[18] The text is reshaped to meet the present need. In this ministry context, Paul transposes the concern expressed in Romans for enslavement to the law *(douleias)* to timidity *(deilias)* in the face of opposition.[19] But the intentional shift to a near homophone at the same time opens the door to another echo — this time of the command spoken by the Lord in the commissioning of Joshua:

> Josh 1:9 — I have commanded thee; be strong and courageous, be not cowardly [*deiliasēs*] nor fearful, for the LORD your God is with you wherever you go (cf. 8:1).

---

16. For the background, see Wolter, *Paulustradition,* 218-22.
17. Cf. esp. the Greek:
Rom 8:15: οὐ γὰρ ἐλάβετε πνεῦμα δουλείας . . . ἀλλὰ ἐλάβετε πνεῦμα υἱοθεσίας. . . .
2 Tim 1:7: οὐ γὰρ ἔδωκεν ἡμῖν ὁ θεὸς πνεῦμα δειλίας ἀλλὰ δυνάμεως καὶ ἀγάπης καὶ σωφρονισμοῦ.
18. Cf. Oberlinner, 32; Hanson, 121.
19. Cf. Oberlinner, 32.

The verbal echo, if present, is admittedly faint.[20] But the tone, narrative setting, and intention of the instructions create a plausible match. The effect would be to call on the image of Joshua, who in his commissioning was urged to be strong and courageous and not timid because God would be present. In the Pauline adaptation of the OT promise, Timothy, by virtue of the Spirit in him, can count on the same protective presence of God.

In the end, both the connection to Rom 8:15 and the present language itself[21] make clear that it is God's gift of the Holy Spirit, and qualities associated with this gift, that provides the reason Paul's logic requires.[22] First, the echoing of Romans reveals that the intended backdrop to this teaching is Paul's fundamental teaching about the Spirit and Christian identity — possession of this gift ensures and confirms adoption into God's family (Rom 8:14-17). Corresponding to this is the general description of the recipients of this gift as "us," which is most probably a reference to all believers.[23] Further, the qualities ascribed to the Spirit's presence — "power, love, self-discipline" — are not the type we would normally limit to a discussion of church office or ministering gifts, though here they are applied to the task confronting Timothy. Consequently, as Paul initiates this opening exhortation concerning Timothy's return to ministry, his basis is the fact that Timothy possesses the Spirit that God promised to give to his people.

The description of the Spirit consists of contrasting negative and positive qualities. Presumably, the negative trait that stands in contradiction to the Spirit, "timidity, or cowardice,"[24] does in some sense describe Timothy's situation. The context implies that this weakness has revealed itself in a reluctance to stand openly for the gospel and for Paul, its imprisoned spokesman. While Timothy may have been predisposed to fearfulness (1 Cor 16:10), even a modest reconstruction of the turbulent church situation depicted in

20. But cf. also how Joshua is instructed to "guard" (φυλάσσεσθαι) what Moses commanded (1:7), and Timothy is to "guard" (φύλαξον) the good deposit entrusted to him by Paul (2 Tim 1:14). Cf. the promise that the Lord will never abandon (ἐγκαταλείψω) Joshua (1:5) and the use of the "abandonment" (ἐγκαταλείπω) theme in 2 Tim 4:10, 16.

21. Gk. δίδωμι; the verb "to give" in one form or another typically describes God's action in respect to this gift (Luke 11:13; Acts 5:32; 8:18; 15:8; Rom 5:5; 1 Cor 1:22; 5:5; etc.).

22. In the present context, reference in some sense to Timothy's commissioning in v. 6 has led some to interpret "Spirit of power" in this statement as a specific charisma received with ordination; see Brox, 229; Kelly, 159-60; Hasler, 57.

23. For the broad meaning of ἡμῖν ("us" = believers in general) in doctrinal contexts, see C. E. B. Cranfield, "Changes of Person and Number in Paul's Epistles," in M. D. Hooker and S. G. Wilson, *Paul and Paulinism* (London: SPCK, 1982), 280-89; Towner, *Goal,* 57 and references there. Cf. Rom 8:15, ". . . in whom we cry, 'Abba, Father.'"

24. Gk. δειλία; only here in the NT; for the verb, see John 14:27; for the adjective, Mark 4:40; Rev 21:8; see Spicq, *TLNT* 1:300-302.

1 and 2 Timothy gives enough reason for his reluctance. Opposition to Paul's gospel and rejection of his authority are evident from the overrealized doctrine of the resurrection identified in 2:17-18. If the letter reflects the continuation and growth of problems with false teachers addressed by 1 Timothy, then it is not hard to imagine Timothy, feeling outnumbered and outmaneuvered, with his own delegated authority in doubt, cowering in the face of threats and Paul's declining reputation. "Timidity" parallels the following admonition "do not be ashamed" (v. 8). Timothy's confidence and courage to stand for the gospel had received a hard blow.

In contrast, three positive qualities characterize the presence of the Holy Spirit. The first is "power." This particular quality is central to this entire discussion of Timothy's renewal for ministry (1:8, 12; 2:1).[25] It is a basic characteristic of God (e.g., Josh 4:24; 5:14), and it is so intrinsic to the understanding of the Spirit that it is almost a tautology to speak, as Paul does here literally, of the "Spirit of power."[26] There is no need to narrow the meaning down to any particular manifestation of power in this passage; what is essential is to note the link between the supply of God's power and the experience of sufficient boldness for ministry. In this context "power" is linked to witness and willingness to undergo suffering (1:8).

The second mark of the Spirit is "love" (1:13; 2:22; 3:10; see on 1 Tim 1:5). This is one of several components characteristic of authentic Christian existence as portrayed in these letters that Timothy is especially to pursue and exhibit. It often occurs alongside "faith," identifying the observable dimension of Christianity as service to others done in the power of the Spirit (cf. Gal 5:6, 22-23; 1 Tim 2:15, note).

Third in the list is a quality that can be viewed from several perspectives as either "self-discipline," "self-control," "discretion," "moderation," or "prudence." The word group to which this term belongs is also integral to the interpretation of the Christian life in these three letters, and it was a dominant feature in secular ethical thought (see 1 Tim 2:9, Excursus). It depicts the control over one's actions and thoughts that prevents rash behavior and aids a balanced assessment of situations. In this context, it would apply to Timothy's appraisal of the situation of opposition and confrontation and allow him the clarity of thought necessary to trust in the invisible God despite the threats of very visible opponents.

Paul's logic in vv. 6-7 seems to develop as follows. Reference to "the gift" conveyed in some sense to Timothy by the laying on of the apostle's

---

25. For the cognate verb "empower," see 2:1; 4:17; 1 Tim 1:12 (discussion and note).

26. Gk. δύναμις; Isa 11:2; Luke 4:14; Acts 1:8; 10:38; Rom 15:19; 1 Cor 2:4; Eph 3:16; 1 Thess 1:5; Spicq, 710. See G. Friedrich, EDNT 1:355-58.

hands (v. 6) is interpreted, almost doctrinally with the allusion to Romans, in terms of the gift of Holy Spirit "given" by God to all believers at conversion (v. 7). The reflection/reminiscence seems to be of Timothy's conversion (or of Paul's confirmation of it) when he received the Holy Spirit and his commission to join the mission to the Gentiles. An additional allusion to the Joshua commissioning would reinforce the reminder of Spirit-power and courage. The present exhortation calls Timothy to renew his dependence on the Spirit in him (v. 6), whose presence means "power" for the challenges of the task at hand (v. 7). This "power" will assume the manifestation appropriate for the situation.

8 The general command to resume ministry is now repeated with the mission situation in view, and two alternatives of response are proposed for Timothy — shame or suffering. Justification for taking vv. 8-14 with vv. 6-7 was given above. But the command is linked logically to v. 7: "so" ("therefore").[27] Here we note that vv. 8-12 form one long sentence in the Greek that gives instructions and an exposition of the gospel, and offers the example of Paul's own behavior. The command of v. 8 consists of an alternative to avoid and one to pursue.

Taking the negative first, Paul implies that there is some course of action (or inaction) that Timothy might take when he says, "do not be ashamed of the testimony about our Lord, or of me his prisoner."[28] What that might be is not clear. We can guess that it amounts to a failure to stand boldly for the gospel. Paul categorizes this behavior very strongly in terms of the values of honor and shame that were central to that culture.[29] Honor was accorded to a person or a group on the basis of public acknowledgment that one's family was honorable or had inherited honor, or that virtuous deeds had been done. Often values like strength, courage, wisdom, and generosity were associated with honor. Shame, on the other hand, was the absence of these virtues or the refusal to accord them to someone. Weakness, selfishness, and foolishness were the negative counterparts that were despised.[30] In this setting, the point is not so much that Timothy *feels* embarrassment or shame and so fails to give a witness,[31] but more that by his failure he is discrediting or shaming the ones mentioned. Timothy is cast in the role of one who, on the basis of his

---

27. This is a typical use of the conjunction οὖν; see 2:1, 21; 1 Tim 2:1; etc.

28. The standard prohibition, in the aorist subjunctive μὴ ἐπαισχυνθῇς . . . , forbids a specific action.

29. Gk. ἐπαισχύνομαι; 1:12, 16; Rom 1:16; 6:21; cf. R. Bultmann, *TDNT* 1:189-91.

30. See H. Moxness, "Honor and Shame," in R. L. Rohrbaugh, ed., *The Social Sciences and New Testament Interpretation* (Peabody, MA: Hendrickson, 1996), 19-40; B. L. Malina, *The New Testament World* (rev. ed.; Louisville: John Knox, 1993), 28-62.

31. Cf. Marshall, 703.

463

own identification with or distancing from the gospel, accords either honor or shame to the testimony about Christ and to Paul himself.

The connection of shame with its first object, "the testimony about our Lord," suggests another reflection on what Paul had written to the Romans (cf. 1:16).[32] "Testimony" has the flexibility to refer either to the content of the witness or to the activity of witnessing; in this case the following genitive, "of [or about] our Lord," defines the content as the gospel message (see on 1 Tim 2:6).

The connection of this testimony with the second object, Paul "the prisoner,"[33] suggests that it is the content of the testimony, not the activity of testifying, that is mainly in mind,[34] although the two things are so closely related that it may be difficult to separate them (do not be ashamed of the message, or of me, one of its representatives). In this letter, the independent use of the articular "the Lord" for Jesus is frequent,[35] suggesting that the gospel of the risen Christ is predominantly in view.[36]

Timothy's reason for being ashamed of this message need not detain us long; it is related to the two objects. First, the cross of the Messiah continued to be a scandalous message in both Jewish and Gentile contexts, and to associate oneself with such a message was to participate in the scandal (cf. Rom 1:16; 1 Cor 1:18ff.).[37] Second, specifically within Timothy's sphere of ministry, the Pauline presentation of the gospel had also apparently fallen on hard times due to the preaching of an alternative, "more spiritual" gospel (cf. 2:18) by false teachers.

The other potential object of shame is the prisoner, Paul. Paul describes himself as "the Lord's prisoner" in Ephesians (3:1; 4:1) and Philemon (9), which is an actual reflection of the apostle's situation in Rome. The attached genitive (lit. "of him") defines the imprisonment as for the Lord's sake and intentionally identifies the apostle and his message with the Lord. Perhaps the fact of Paul's imprisonment was being turned against Timothy in that church as evidence that Paul had lost his influence, or lacked the fullness of the Spirit in some sense. As a result, Paul's gospel (1:11; 2:8) and authority had come under fire. In any case, with the request about to be made of

---

32. Cf. Oberlinner, 34.

33. Gk. δέσμιος; this designation is standard for Paul (Eph 3:1; 4:1; Phlm 9) and interprets his imprisonment as being "for the sake of" (here the gen. αὐτοῦ = "our Lord") Jesus Christ. See F. Staudinger, *EDNT* 1:289-90.

34. Cf. A. A. Trites, *The New Testament Concept of Witness* (SNTSMS 31; Cambridge: Cambridge University Press, 1977), 210.

35. 1:16, 18; 2:7, 14, 19a, 19b, 22, 24; 3:11; 4:8, 14, 17, 18, 22; cf. 1 Tim 1:14 (none in Titus).

36. J. A. Fitzmyer, *EDNT* 2:330-31.

37. See M. Hengel, *Crucifixion* (Philadelphia: Fortress, 1977).

Timothy — that he hasten to Rome (4:9, 21) — the coworker is reminded that to be ashamed of this gospel is also to be ashamed of its representatives. Faithfulness to Christ makes no sense apart from faithfulness to those appointed by him and suffering for him (1:11-12).

In contrast to the prohibition ("but"; *alla*), Timothy is commanded to walk in Paul's footsteps. Paul may have coined the term that describes this course: "join in suffering."[38] Suffering for the faith is the lot of all Christians.[39] But with this term stressing joint suffering, and related terms,[40] suffering for the gospel becomes a theme in this letter.[41] In this context proclamation and "suffering for the gospel" are virtually equated. Instead of disengaging himself from the ministry, Timothy is rather to be fully engaged in preaching.[42] The deliberate conjoining of Timothy's ministry/suffering to Paul's ("join with me in suffering")[43] anticipates the full handing over of the Pauline mission to the coworker with instructions to go to Rome (1:13-14; 2:1-2; 4:1-5, 9, 21).

The closing phrase of the verse — "by the power of God" — raises a question. Some maintain that the connection of thoughts is patterned after Rom 1:16, where the cause of Paul's boldness in preaching is the gospel's divine power to save. To sustain such a connection, the Greek preposition employed here, *kata,* would have to be causal in meaning;[44] if so, the sense (playing on Rom 1:16) would be: "suffer with me for the gospel *because* it is the power of God," with the thought of salvation, set out succinctly in Rom 1:16, being developed in the formula that follows.[45] The alternative is to take the preposition *kata* as providing a basis, meaning "according to [or "by"] the power of God," which makes the phrase an explanation of the way in which "suffering" can be endured.[46] In light of v. 7, which introduces the

38. Gk. συγκακοπαθέω; 2:3; not in the LXX or earlier extant secular literature (see BDAG, s.v.; W. Michaelis, *TDNT* 5:936-38; BDF §19).

39. See Rom 8:17; 2 Cor 4:7-15; Phil 1:29; 1 Thess 1:6; 2:14; Jas 5:10; 1 Pet 2:21; 4:15-16.

40. Gk. πάσχω ("to suffer," 1:12); κακοπαθέω ("to suffer evil," 2:9; 4:5).

41. P. H. Towner, "The Portrait of Paul and the Theology of 2 Timothy: The Closing Chapter of the Pauline Story," *HBT* 21.2 (1999): 151-70. Cf. Spicq, *TLNT* 2:238-40; W. Michaelis, *TDNT* 5:936-38.

42. For Gk. εὐαγγέλιον ("gospel"), see 1 Tim 1:11 (discussion and notes).

43. Cf. NIV, NRSV; this seems to be somewhat deflected in the impersonal translation, "take your share in the suffering" (e.g., Johnson, 344, 347).

44. BAG, s.v. 5.a.d (408), points out that in some cases there may be a merging of κατά as the norm of some action ("in accordance with") and as the reason for ("because of") some action.

45. Rom 1:16: οὐ γὰρ ἐπαισχύνομαι τὸ εὐαγγέλιον, δύναμις γὰρ θεοῦ ἐστιν εἰς σωτηρίαν παντὶ τῷ πιστεύοντι; see Oberlinner, 36-37.

46. The phrase κατὰ δύναμιν θεοῦ makes reference to a concept, "the power of

"Spirit of power," and v. 14, which identifies the indwelling Spirit as Timothy's source of enablement, we are probably to understand the phrase to point in the same direction: that is, the logic being, "therefore, join [me] in suffering for the gospel in that power supplied by God." An intentional echo of Romans is still possible, but if so, that text has been reconfigured for the new literary situation. Timothy's calling to preach will entail suffering, but God will supply the power necessary to carry him through the ordeal.[47]

We should not miss the theological connections made in these verses. The presence of the Spirit of power provides a guarantee of the strength, endurance, and courage needed to face the situation. But equally important is the reality of suffering that the gospel ministry will induce. In fact, while certain ministries such as proclamation do make one more visible and perhaps more open to persecution, it is the very presence of the Spirit in the life of the community and the observable characteristics of the life he produces in God's people that promise suffering (3:12). What the Spirit provides is power to endure the stress that comes from bearing witness to God, not removal to some safe place.

b. The Gospel for Which We Suffer (1:9-10)

9-10 What follows is a carefully constructed unit of theology that emphasizes a traditional understanding of salvation. Although the poetic structure is not as symmetrical as that of the "hymn" of 1 Tim 3:16, its more formal character stands out in the context.[48] Some of the elements are reminiscent of Paul's letters to churches: the negation of "works" and the terminology of salvation and calling. Others are more characteristic of these three letters to coworkers: the concept of "appearance" and the designation "Savior." On the basis of content, the piece appears to be a summary of salvation. The emphasis in the piece is created by the transition from that which was designed "before the beginning of time" to that which has occurred "now" in the present time, in the coming of Christ. Through this contrast, the present significance of salvation comes fully into view; the interest in the gospel and proclamation to which this piece leads demonstrates that this is the direction of Paul's thought.

Whether the piece was pre-formed or composed by Paul as he wrote to Timothy, its function is apparently to articulate the gospel for which Timo-

---

God," that carries various shades of meaning in the NT. It is linked to the resurrection of Jesus Christ (Rom 1:4; 1 Cor 6:14), and it can also portray the gospel as the medium of God's saving power (Rom 1:16; 1 Cor 1:18). See further G. Friedrich, *EDNT* 1.356-58.

47. Cf. 2 Cor 8:3; Eph 3:7; Col 1:11, 29; Heb 7:16.

48. Towner, *Goal*, 94, Oberlinner, 37.

thy is to suffer. It accomplishes this by describing God in terms of salvation, as the structure of the piece indicates. It may be helpful to set out that structure (departing from the TNIV slightly to display the syntactical structure):

who has saved us
and called [us] with a holy calling
    not because of anything we have done
    but because of his own purpose and grace.
        This grace was given us
            in Christ Jesus   [manner/sphere]
            before the beginning of time,   [time]
        but it [grace] has been revealed
            now   [time]
            through the appearing of our Savior,
            Christ Jesus,   [manner]
                who has destroyed death
                and has brought life and immortality to light
                    through the gospel.

As the structural layout shows, the description of salvation proceeds in a carefully conceived series of pairs and contrasts, in step-down fashion, beginning with God's activity in salvation, continuing with the basis and ending with the means by which salvation was executed. Although the whole piece serves as an interpretation of "the gospel" just mentioned (v. 8), at two points the means by which it is made relevant to the contemporary community comes to light as well. And this "contemporization" of the gospel for the "present" Christian community is an important dimension of Paul's message that links his ministry to that of those who will follow as it also links God's promise of salvation to the actual experience of Christians in every age.

First, two aorist participles examine the gospel in terms of God's actions. In the first and most basic statement, the gospel declares that God has acted to "save us" (1 Tim 1:15). This statement, in the aorist tense, looks at this action as a finished fact. It is the theme statement of the entire piece that culminates in the reference to the Savior, Christ Jesus. The sequence of the first two participles, "saving" first, then "calling," probably corresponds to a description of the event and the application of it to people.[49] As the piece indicates, salvation is from sin and death and to life; it is to be understood here in its widest theological sense.[50]

The human experience of salvation depends on God's action of "call-

49. Towner, *Goal,* 95-96; Oberlinner, 38.
50. For Gk. σῴζω, cf. Tit 3:5; 1 Tim 1:15 (discussion); Eph 2:5, 8.

ing" — the second participle.[51] Calling can be used in a comprehensive sense to describe salvation as the result of God's sovereign control in summoning people to himself (Rom 8:28, 30). Or it can be viewed from narrower perspectives, such as one of its goals — eternal life (1 Tim 6:12) — as the discussion in v. 10d suggests. Here the calling of God receives further definition with the addition of a cognate noun in the dative, "calling," and the adjective "holy."[52] The precise sense of the dative addition is not clear, but some parallels may help to shed light. It may be a dative of means — "he called us *by means of* or *with* a holy calling," the force of which would probably be to emphasize that it is a calling that comes *from* God (NRSV). The means by which God effectively executes his calling is the proclamation of the gospel (2 Thess 2:14).[53] Alternatively, the sense of the dative might be, as the TNIV has translated it, to describe the goal of calling as "to a holy life,"[54] or to be "those called saints."[55] Precision is impossible in this case, but we would do well to allow the possibility that Paul intends to slip in a reference to God's calling through the gospel in the early going of this salvation liturgy. It is, after all, a reflection not only on the meaning of salvation (i.e., the content of the gospel; v. 10), but also on the reality of salvation and its relationship to the Pauline preaching mission.

Next, the gospel summary describes the basis of this salvation. The next two lines consist of a negative/positive contrast that explains the basis of God's saving and calling. First, on the negative side, is the thoroughly Pauline statement rendered literally "not according to our works."[56] Its effect is to rule human effort completely out of the process. This negation of works corresponds to the sentiment expressed similarly in Eph 2:9. Notably, in each of these passages the discussion centers on salvation, not, as in most passages

---

51. For Gk. καλέω, see on 1 Tim 6:12.

52. The further definition is made by appending to the participle καλέσαντος the cognate noun κλήσει (for Gk. κλῆσις ["calling"], see Rom 11:29; 1 Cor 1:26; 7:20; Eph 1:18; 4:1, 4; Phil 3:14; 2 Thess 1:11), to which is added the adjective "holy" (see 1 Tim 5:10, note).

53. Proclamation or gospel seems much more dominant in the context than the rite of baptism. Oberlinner, 28, and Trummer, *Paulustradition,* 185-86, suggest that the passage 1 Tim 6:11-12, in which "calling" is mentioned in a sacramental baptismal context, determines the sense of "calling" in 2 Tim 1:9. For them the baptismal rite signifies the moment in which people realize the salvation will of God. This emphasis on baptism seems, however, to be more imagined than real.

54. I.e., dative of interest. Cf. Dibelius and Conzelmann, 99. 1 Cor 7:15, using a preposition, provides an example of this. Fee, 229, offers 1 Cor 1:2; 1 Thess 4:7 as illustrations of the intended meaning.

55. A similar thought is expressed in Rom 1:7 and 1 Cor 1:2, where believers are described as "those called saints" (κλητοῖς ἁγίοις).

56. Gk. οὐ κατὰ τὰ ἔργα ἡμῶν. For the preposition κατά expressing reason or basis, see BDAG, s.v. 5.a.d.

in Romans and Galatians taken up with "works of the law," justification. Although it is probable that the basic phrase "not out of works [of the law]"[57] was coined in the Pauline formulation of justification by faith with the debate about the significance of the Jewish law for Christian living in view, it seems equally clear that Paul also discussed the distinctions between divine grace and human effort in a context broader than the Jewish one. In Rom 9:11-12 the choice of Jacob over Esau illustrates God's sovereign independence in election: in that text "not out of works" (v. 12) stands parallel to the preceding "anything good or bad" (v. 11). In any case, there is no compelling reason to see in this generalizing application of the negation of works to a non-Jewish situation evidence of a post-Pauline development.[58]

In contrast ("but"; *alla*), salvation has its positive basis (preposition *kata*) in God's "own purpose and grace." This line emphasizes that God is the initiator of the salvation plan; it does not arise from any human decision or source (the force of the specification "his *own*" is to strengthen the contrast).[59] But the two concepts, "purpose" and "grace," are distinct and should not be merged together. Several times Paul locates the ultimate, prehistorical decision to save humanity in God's own purpose (cf. Rom 8:28; 9:11-12; Eph 1:11; 3:8-11).[60]

The text also describes the way in which the decision was executed — God's grace. In isolation "grace" refers to God's unmerited favor (1:2; see on 1 Tim 1:2, 12; Titus 3:7), and the contrast between human merit and God's purpose and grace celebrates the divine initiative in the salvation of people. However, within this formulation of theology, the mention of "grace" forms the transition to the discussion of the way in which God saved — the redemptive ministry of Christ Jesus in history.

In the last two lines of v. 9 (see above), a participial phrase continues to explore the idea of "grace." Though the believing "us" has been in view from the first lines, at this point the statement that "grace was given [to] us" begins the transition from the lofty and theoretical deliberations about salvation in the mind of God to its reception by people through the work of Christ. First, "grace" (here a near synonym for salvation) is depicted as a gift (1 Tim 1:2). God's "giving" of grace is standard language in Paul for the bestowing of salvation or blessings associated with it.[61] Second, the gift is said to come

57. Gk. οὐκ ἐξ ἔργων (νόμου); cf. Rom 3:20, 28; Gal 2:16(3x); 3:2, 5, 10.
58. Nevertheless, cf. Trummer, *Paulustradition,* 174-91, for the view. See the discussion in Oberlinner, 39; Hanson, 122.
59. See 1 Tim 2:6 (note).
60. Gk. πρόθεσις ("plan, purpose"; 3:10); see H. Balz, *EDNT,* 3:155-56; Towner, *EDBT* 820-22; C. Maurer, *TDNT* 8:164-67.
61. Gk. δίδωμι (here as divine pass. in reference to the preceding χάριν, "grace"); Rom 12:3, 6; 15:15; 1 Cor 1:4; 3:10; Gal 2:9; Eph 3:8; 4:7.

to us "in Christ Jesus" (see on 1 Tim 1:14), which is typical Pauline theology and language for depicting the agency, instrument, or channel of salvation.[62] It states simply the way in which God's grace was made available to people.

Third, the closing phrase — "before the beginning of time" — commences a Pauline "transition of time" scheme,[63] whereby the passage receives a salvation-historical character that allows the unique nature of the present age to be seen.[64] The time phrase itself, literally "before eternal times," drawn from Hebrew thought, distinguishes between the timelessness of God's existence and the temporality of his creation.[65] Although it is therefore not completely logical to place the decision of God to save, as mentioned in this statement, into a time frame, the point that v. 10 will make is that what was conceived prior to creation[66] — the plan to save people — was executed at a point in history in which the grace of God became manifest in history in Christ. But at this point in the text, the theological poem tells us that the plan to save through the work of Christ was made, and in God's mind worked out, prior to creation. In this way, the piece underlines God's sovereignty both in electing his people and in bringing this to pass through Christ's redemptive work.

Once v. 10 is reached, the unfolding of the story of God's grace in history and its present relevance come fully into view. In one sense we are taken from a description of the basis of God's salvation to its outworking in time. And by means of the Pauline transition scheme, initiated by the last phrase of v. 9 here concluded with the "but . . . now" of v. 10a, the thought moves from that "gracious" basis to the experience of the church in present time. As else-

62. Notice the close resemblance to 1 Cor 1:4 (τῇ χάριτι . . . τῇ δοθείσῃ ὑμῖν ἐν Χριστῷ Ἰησοῦ; "the grace . . . which was given to us in Christ Jesus"); see also 2 Cor 5:19; Eph 1:3, 10, 20; 2:6-7; 3:11; 4:32. There is no reason to place this use of the "in Christ" formula outside of Pauline thought (*contra* Allan, "In Christ," 119-20). Harris (*NIDNTT* 3:1192-93) identifies seven nuances of meaning in the Pauline use of the phrase.

63. See the discussion at Titus 1:2.

64. Gk. πρὸ χρόνων αἰωνίων . . . δὲ νῦν ("before the ages . . . but now"); see Towner, *Goal,* 63-64.

65. This tendency to trace eschatological salvation back before creation apparently began when Israel's self-concept as "the elect" was most under fire and its situation under pagan rulers was most tenuous (see *2 Apocalypse of Baruch* 4.3; 57; 1QS 3–4). The church, understanding itself as continuous with Israel, naturally adopted this view (Matt 25:34; Rom 9:23; see Marshall, 126).

66. Gk. χρόνος ("time, period of time, age") usually denotes an expanse or period of time (age, epoch). For Gk. αἰώνιος ("a long period of time"), see 1 Tim 1:16 (note). Together the phrase refers to the whole of time from creation onward, which, modified by the preposition πρό, focuses on God's pre-creation will and activity (cf. Barr, *Biblical Words for Time,* 75; Towner, *Goal,* 63-64; H. Hübner, *EDNT* 3:488). The phrase is about equivalent to Eph 1:4, "before the foundation of the world."

where (see Titus 1:2-3), the effect of the formula is to declare that what had previously been hidden in God's mind has now been revealed. The general fact of the appearance, then, is expressed in the first line of v. 10: "but it [God's grace] has now been revealed." The verb of revelation is a technical term in the NT for expressing the inauguration of the age of salvation in Christ.[67] Here the past tense (aorist participle) indicates that the decisive event of revelation has occurred and, as defined by the term "now," that this event of revelation is particularly relevant to the condition of the present age.

Paul builds on the thought of divine revelation as he explains the means ("through") of revealing God's grace and something of its redemptive nature. The term rendered by the TNIV as "the appearing" (4:1, 8) is the Greek word *epiphany,* already encountered in various forms in 1 Timothy (see 6:14, Excursus) and Titus. In these letters to coworkers, it refers exclusively to Christ, describing either his parousia or, as here, his incarnation and earthly ministry as a divine intervention on behalf of God's people. In this case, the incarnation of Christ Jesus, viewed widely to incorporate his life, death, and resurrection (see below), is the historical reference point of the revelation of grace. Its nature as a saving intervention of God is apparent in the description of Christ Jesus as "our Savior" (see commentary on 1 Tim 1:1). In fact, "salvation" proves to be the central theme of this gospel summary; it is the opening note ("who saved us") and the theme that all subsequent lines seek to explore in one way or another. What was said to flow out of the grace of God is now seen to be executed in the person of Christ, the Savior. And the concluding lines of the piece describe the effects of "the appearing" as they reflect on ways in which Christ Jesus is "our Savior."

The concluding pair of contrasting[68] participles considers the appearance of the Savior in history from the standpoint of the results it achieved. On the negative side, Christ's work is characterized by the destruction of death. The language of "destruction" employed here takes up a dominant theme in the eschatology of the early church, which announces that God will "destroy" or "render ineffective" the things and enemies that belong to this crippled, sinful life and stand in opposition to his purposes.[69] The phrase is reminiscent of 1 Cor 15:26 — "the last enemy to be destroyed is death" — and along with the positive assessment that follows points yet again to a conscious linkage to an earlier Pauline exposition of theology.[70] There death is

---

67. For Gk. φανερόω, see the discussion and note at 1 Tim 3:16.

68. The contrast, implicit in the actions of the verbs, is heightened by the μὲν . . . δέ ("on the one hand, on the other") construction.

69. Gk. καταργέω. This category includes the old covenant and the law (2 Cor 3:14; Eph 2:15) and such enemies as the antichrist (2 Thess 2:8) and the devil (Heb 2:14). See H. Hübner, *EDNT* 2:267-68.

70. Gk. θάνατος is here the termination of physical/natural life, the ultimate cause

depicted as a still reigning enemy whose power will be neutralized at last (15:53ff.). Here the certainty of its destruction is celebrated, even though in the lives of those Christians who heard this letter read, death continued as a reminder of the incompleteness of the present age of salvation. As a reflection on the historical Christ-event, the statement about death's defeat is to be paired with Christ's own death. Elsewhere in the NT, his death is distinguished from his resurrection as *the* event that canceled the power of death.[71]

On the positive side, the parallel, contrasting participle describes the work of the Savior in terms of the eternal life he revealed. Eternal "life" (see on 1 Tim 1:16) in this case is depicted in terms most suitable to a description of God's existence — as "incorruptibility," which in connection with "life" means "immortality."[72] This is a characteristic of God's existence (1 Tim 1:17), and proper to the divine realm, whereas death dominates in the *kosmos*. It is therefore proper, as well as poetic, that the language of "illumination"[73] ("*brought* life and immortality *to light*") should be used to portray the unveiling of eternal life in the midst of darkened humanity. The focus is on triumph over death and the shining forth of eternal life. Such language, belonging as it does to a well-defined network of imagery for depicting the apprehension of invisible realities (especially "through the gospel"), would call to mind the contrasting images of sin as darkness and God as light (cf. 1 Cor 4:5; Eph 3:9; 1 Tim 6:16).

Within the ongoing story of Paul, the description of life as "immortality" closes the circle and connects this exposition of theology with the earlier teaching of Christ's resurrection as the basis for eternal life (1 Cor 15:53, 54).[74] Both passages teach the intrinsic necessity of Christ's resurrection for the hope of eternal life. In this passage, it is the Christ-event that brings the hope across the gulf from promise to fulfillment. The force of the revelatory statement is to underline not the promise of eternal life but its actual manifestation in history in the experience of Christ.[75] Through Christ God reveals the

---

of which is sin (in various ways; see R. Bultmann, *TDNT* 3:7-21; W. Bieder, *EDNT* 2:129-33; cf. J. Moltmann, *The Coming of God* [Minneapolis: Fortress, 1996], 77-95).

71. See Rom 6:6, 10; 14:8-9; 2 Cor 4:10; 1 Thess 5:10; Heb 2:14.

72. Gk. ἀφθαρσία ("incorruptibility") is a Pauline term in the NT (Rom 2:7; 1 Cor 15:42, 50, 53, 54; Eph 6:24; Wis 2:23; 6:19; 4 Macc 9:22; Philo, *On the Eternity of the World* 27); G. Harder, *TDNT* 9:93-106. The two terms "life and immortality" (ζωὴν καὶ ἀφθαρσίαν) form a hendiadys.

73. Gk. φωτίζω; as here, the "enlightenment" that the gospel supplies; see John 1:9; Eph 1:18; 3:9; Heb 6:4.

74. The NT writers uniformly associate Christ's resurrection with the gift of eternal life; Acts 2:27-31; see also W. L. Craig, "The Bodily Resurrection of Jesus," in R. T. France and D. Wenham, eds., *Gospel Perspectives* (Sheffield: JSOT, 1980), 1:60-70.

75. M. Winter, *EDNT* 3:449-50; H. Conzelmann, *TDNT* 9:349.

existence of the alternative reality and opens it up as a human possibility (Titus 1:2-3). This is the essence of the gospel message — the availability of eternal life in Christ. At the same time it is well to bear in mind that the same kind of circumstances and theological misunderstanding that gave rise to the teaching in 1 Corinthians 15 are as likely a background to this restatement of the Pauline gospel (2:18).

In this account of Christology hope for God's people is anchored safely in the vindication of Christ. The suffering apostle portrays the reality of salvation in the terms most relevant to him — as a promise of vindication/resurrection. Yet there remains in the human sphere of history the dilemma of incompleteness as death and sin continue to exist. This is where the concluding phrase "through the gospel" comes into play. The reference is to the ongoing gospel ministry in which Paul has taken part.[76] And the addition of the phrase to the theological material reveals that it is "through the [proclamation of] the gospel" that the past event obtains and retains its present relevance. In a very real sense, from the human perspective it is only "through the gospel" that the "illumination" of the eternal life in Christ can occur. On one level, as we saw, this bringing to light of life from death occurred in Christ's experience of resurrection; now, on the other level of human awareness and experience, the proclamation of that event (interpreted theologically by Paul's material) brings to light the eternal life Christ made available. Thus in a subtle way the closing phrase of v. 10 redirects the theology back to the point (made by Paul) that gave rise to it — "join with me in suffering for the gospel" (v. 8) — and delivers a reason anticipated by the earlier point — Why join in suffering for the gospel? Because preaching it is the divinely chosen means by which God's salvation, crafted in and through the Christ-event, may be made available to the world. From the point of view of the narrative, the closing phrase also forms Paul's transition to a discussion of his own role in relation to the gospel.

c. The Apostolic Model for Timothy and the Call to Succession (1:11-14)

In this closing subsection, Paul illustrates the point he has been making by defining his ministry in terms of the gospel and his trust in the power of God. This illustration is meant as a model for Timothy, to whom, in the light of that model, the charge to ministry is repeated.

---

76. Gk. διὰ τοῦ εὐαγγελίου (for the phrase, 1 Cor 4:15; Eph 3:6; 2 Thess 2:14). In references to "the gospel" (τὸ εὐαγγέλιον; 1 Tim 1:11, discussion and notes), the emphasis may be on the content of what is preached (1 Cor 15:1; 2 Cor 4:4; 11:4, 7; Gal 1:6; cf. G. Strecker, *EDNT* 2:70-74) or, particularly, as here, in the case of the phrase "through the gospel" (διὰ τοῦ εὐαγγελίου; 1 Cor 4:15; 2 Thess 2:14), on the proclamation of that content. In fact, in the latter case the two ideas are inseparable.

11-12 Paul's illustration begins with his own appointment (v. 11). As in 1 Tim 2:7, which this statement replicates with certain omissions,[77] Paul describes his ministry in terms of function and authority. The grammatical link to the aforementioned "gospel" is established with the phrase "unto which I was appointed," which is also a formula for describing Paul's divine commissioning (see on 1 Tim 1:12; 2:7). In each case Paul makes the point that his calling to ministry is to be understood in relation to the gospel message. There is probably no discernible significance in the ordering of "herald," "apostle," and "teacher" except to suggest that the task of proclamation seems uppermost in mind (see on 1 Tim 2:7). The apostolic dimension of this description incorporates the other two and extends beyond them to include other tasks related to the establishment and oversight of churches. Together the terms describe Paul's ministry comprehensively.

But from what follows (v. 12), it seems that the main emphasis of the ministry model falls on the conditions that attend his appointment and the appropriate response to them, rather than on the office to which he has been appointed. What does this model consist of? First, Paul makes clear that his suffering is caused by his calling to preach the gospel: "That [i.e., his appointment] is why I am suffering as I am."[78] On the one hand, this is an interpretation of Paul's present situation as a prisoner in Rome for the gospel, just as it is of all the suffering encountered during his ministry.[79] But on the other hand, this experience is not to be considered unusual or tied exclusively to Paul's apostolic calling. His experience is paradigmatic. Reference to his "suffering" forms a link to the instruction to Timothy to "join in suffering" (v. 8):[80] in Paul's letters, the verb "to suffer" describes the affliction in relation to faith that comes on believers in general (cf. 3:12).[81] The underlying principle is that the gospel ministry and suffering go hand in hand.

---

77. Two items in the longer statement in 1 Tim 2:7 (see the discussion and notes) have been omitted here: the pledge of truth ("I am speaking the truth, I do not lie") and the genitive "of the Gentiles," which qualifies "teacher." It is probably the more personal tone of 2 Timothy that accounts for the alterations. However, the more notable textual variant that occurs here, adding ἐθνῶν after διδάσκαλος (which has better attestation; ℵ² C D F G Ψ 1739 1881 TR latt sy co), is most likely a later adjustment meant to bring the text into conformity with 1 Tim 2:7; cf. Metzger, 647.

78. For the causal phrase, see 1:6 (discussion and notes).

79. Cf. 2 Tim 3:11; 2 Cor 4:7-8; 11:23ff.; Gal 6:17; etc.

80. The verbs συγκακοπαθέω (v. 8) and πάσχω (v. 12) are cognate.

81. Gk. πάσχω (1 Cor 12:26; 2 Cor 1:6; Gal 3:4; Phil 1:29; 1 Thess 2:14; 2 Thess 1:5); W. Michaelis, *TDNT* 5:904-24 (919-21); outside of Paul, it may refer to the sufferings of Christ (e.g., Luke, Acts, Hebrews, 1 Peter) in a way that makes the link between the suffering of Christians and the suffering of Christ more tangible (see J. Kremer, *EDNT* 3:51-52).

Second, the model of ministry contains the component of response to suffering. And in drawing this out, the apostle again links himself closely to his coworker. He too had alternatives to consider. And his conviction comes through in the strong contrast: "yet *(alla)* this is no cause for shame." In Timothy's case, this was expressed as a command to be fulfilled (see on v. 8). In Paul's case, this is a determined mind-set; his condition of suffering has not moved him to feel ashamed for the gospel he has proclaimed.[82] The story at this point calls to mind again the statements about the gospel, shame, power, and salvation in Rom 1:16; Paul's present circumstances stand as proof of his earlier claim and form a fitting conclusion to the apostolic story that developed that theme. Now, however, Paul writes from the other side of experience as he faces execution in a Roman prison.

Paul's faithfulness to his calling has caused his circumstances, but the reason ("because") for his confidence (instead of an experience of shame) is his knowledge of God.[83] There is no reason to distinguish between knowledge about God (i.e., factual and theoretical) and personal knowledge of God, as is sometimes done on the basis of the verb employed.[84] The emphasis in the text is created by alliterative perfect tense verbs, "I have believed" *(pepisteuka)* and "I am convinced" *(pepeismai).* The first, "I have believed," stresses that Paul's knowledge of God has grown out of a steady experience of belief (see on 1 Tim 1:2, 16). This includes knowing what kind of God he is and also that he continues to be constantly involved in all aspects of Paul's life and ministry.

Inseparable from his settled belief is his settled confidence in God's power/ability: "I am convinced" (see 1:5, note). For Paul this conviction could apply quite generally (e.g., 4:17-18; 2 Cor 1:10), but in this case his application is very specific. Continuing the "power" theme (vv. 7, 8; 2:1), Paul grounds his confidence in God's ability *(dynatos)* to "guard" a certain commodity (or "deposit") that has been entrusted. The verb/noun combination, literally, "guard the deposit," alludes to the practice of entrusting a commodity of some sort with a person who is to protect it and eventually return it to the owner.[85] The identification of the deposit as in some sense "my [Paul's] deposit"[86] leaves the meaning of the Greek phrase somewhat ambiguous, as

82. The Gk. verb ἐπαισχύνομαι (pres.), without an object, describes Paul's mind-set.

83. Or possibly Christ — the object of belief implied by "whom" has to be supplied from the context.

84. Gk. οἶδα; the verb is used in the context of discussions of genuine knowledge of God (Titus 1:16; Gal 4:8) and is suitable to express the idea of personal acquaintance with or knowledge of God (1 Thess 4:5; 2 Thess 1:8).

85. See the discussion and notes at 1 Tim 6:20.

86. The Greek is τὴν παραθήκην μου.

the variety of interpretations confirms.[87] Probably most decisive for a solution is the fact that God is the one who is to guard the deposit,[88] which would normally imply that he is the recipient of the deposit entrusted by Paul (thus TNIV's "what I have entrusted"). There is also some evidence that in related discussions the one to whom the deposit originally belongs is identified in the genitive (as Paul is here in the pronoun "my").[89]

What is the content of that deposit? In the two other occurrences of the term (*parathēkē*, v. 14; 1 Tim 6:20), the command "guard the deposit" involves both preserving and proclaiming the apostolic gospel. The use of "good" to describe the commodity in v. 14 almost certainly suggests that the Pauline gospel is primarily in view (cf. 1 Tim 4:6). Within the flow of thought, succession is very much in mind. Paul invokes the "deposit" metaphor at this transitional point, with his departure imminent and false teachers threatening the purity of the gospel. He entrusts the gospel (and by implication the entire Pauline mission) to God, all of which is in preparation for the discussion of the successor in vv. 13-14.

Having determined this much, we should not lose sight of the point Paul makes: in spite of being imprisoned for the gospel, and perhaps being regarded as a failure, Paul stands convinced that the God who called him will indeed guard the message and the ministry until "that day" has been reached. The specific "day" envisaged as the limit is the day of Christ's return and of judgment (1:18; 4:8).[90] At that time, the mission that began with Paul (and is being handed on) will be complete. But more importantly, on "that day" Paul's own faithfulness as an apostle will be assessed and the purity of his suffering will be demonstrated.

13-14 This model of Paul's faithfulness and confidence in God provides the final step in the sequence, which began in v. 6, leading to the call to Timothy to continue the Pauline mission. To rehearse the sequence, Paul began with his convictions about Timothy's sincere faith in which they share an intimate relationship. This and their share in the Spirit of power led to the exhortation to boldness in witness and co-suffering for the gospel. This gospel, which binds the two together, was then articulated, and Paul's calling and confidence in God's vindication are linked to it. But at v. 12 it becomes clear

87. For the view that "the deposit" is something God has entrusted to Paul (i.e., the gospel, the gospel ministry), see Dibelius and Conzelmann, 105; Kelly, 165-66; Guthrie, 144; but see Johnson, 356-57.

88. Fee, 232; Marshall, 710-11.

89. Wolter, *Paulustradition*, 116-18; cf. Lau, *Manifest in Flesh*, 31-32.

90. Gk. ἐκείνη ἡ ἡμέρα; within the letters to coworkers, the phrase, with its decisive referent, is limited to 2 Timothy, in which the day of vindication (as an emblem of hope in suffering) plays a dominant role. See also 2 Thess 1:10; Hos 1:5; Amos 2:16; 8:3, 9; Matt 7:22; 24:19; (pl. in Matt 24:22, 29, 36; 26:29); Towner, *Goal,* 62.

that Paul is not simply calling Timothy to a renewal of previous duties; he is rather preparing Timothy to be his successor in the mission. This call now culminates in two verbs of command that outline Timothy's task in terms of faithfulness to the Pauline gospel and Christian behavior, and dependence upon the Holy Spirit for the ministry he is to inherit. The two verses, which are more or less parallel, combine most of the aspects of the exhortation that began at v. 6.

The first command takes up the matter of the message (v. 13a). Just as the apostle's gospel has bound Timothy and Paul together to this point (vv. 9-10), it is to provide the organic link in the ongoing mission. This is the clear intent of the command "What you have heard from me, keep as the pattern of sound teaching." This statement weaves together three crucial strands. First, Paul describes his gospel ("from me") with language that underscores both its spiritual, health-giving effects and its distance from false gospels (see on 1 Tim 1:10; 6:3). Second, he presumes that Timothy has accepted and embraced it.[91] His commission involves "keeping or maintaining" what he has embraced from the start (see on 1 Tim 1:19)

Third, the Greek word translated "pattern" describes a model, form, or standard (NRSV) that serves as a reliable guide. In 1 Tim 1:16 (see discussion) the term depicted Paul's conversion as an "example" of God's mercy. Although the context is different, that meaning applies in this occurrence as well.[92] The message Timothy is to adhere to in his preaching is the one Paul himself proclaimed. The continuity between Paul's ministry and Timothy's (and of those who will follow; cf. 2:1-2, which uses the same language) is underscored in the phrase "what you heard from me." It is precisely this apostolic continuity that ensures the purity of the message on into the next generation. The liturgical poem of vv. 9-10 illustrates the contents, as do the rest of the theological pieces in these letters to Timothy.

Raising a minor point of interpretation will reinforce further the sense of the unity of the mission begun by Paul and to be continued by Timothy. A comparison of the TNIV ("What you heard from me, keep *as the pattern* of sound teaching") and the NRSV ("Hold *to the standard* of sound teaching that you have heard from me") shows how the word "standard" may be taken differently in relation to the verb of command. Although there may seem to be little difference, the grammar, which favors the NRSV rendering (see also

---

91. Gk. ἀκούω (aor.; "I hear, listen"); in this type of statement (also 2:2; Eph 4:2; Phil 4:9; Col 1:23), "hearing" presupposes belief; G. Schneider, *EDNT* 1:54.

92. See also Knight, 381. The meaning "outline," that is, a pattern that is to be completed (cf. Kelly, 165; Guthrie, 145; Lee, "Words Denoting 'Pattern' in the New Testament," 171-72), is possible but not as likely in this context in which firm adherence to a traditional message is in view.

GNB),[93] accentuates the command's stress on adherence to an established tradition — Paul does not have in mind his message as a general pattern, but, in this context of false teaching, the main point is the specific standard of accuracy his words represent. As indicated, the shadow cast by the false teaching lies behind the description of Paul's message as "sound words" (cf. 4:3). Consequently, maintaining the Pauline form and nature of the gospel has become Timothy's obligation.

But this task is not one to be carried out in a detached, academic manner. The command next takes up the matter of the messenger. The following prepositional phrase, "with faith and love in Christ Jesus" (v. 13b), outlines the manner[94] in which Timothy is to fulfill his mission. "Faith and love" serve as an abbreviation for the authentic life of faith, combining into a unity the dimensions of one's relationship to God and the lifestyle of service produced by that faith-relationship (see on 1 Tim 1:5, 14). In short, for Timothy to "keep" the apostolic message and proclaim it he must at the same time pay careful attention to his own faith in Christ.

Parallel to the first command is the second, v. 14, which reformulates the call in terms of succession. Timothy is to "guard the good deposit." Virtually the same command is given in 1 Tim 6:20 (see discussion). In this case, the repetition of the term *parathēkē* ("deposit"), which in v. 12 described the gospel (and ministry) that Paul entrusted to God, reveals the continuity between the ministry Timothy is taking up and the one Paul is relinquishing. There is no substantive difference between "sound teaching [words]" (v. 13) and "good deposit"; the latter term (as we saw in the case of Paul) simply views the gospel from the perspective of a trust to be kept and, in the context of the commissioning sequence, emphasizes the transmission of Paul's operation to the coworker. The addition of the adjective "good"[95] is undoubtedly occasioned by the desire to preserve a balance with the description of the

93. The question revolves around the function of the anarthrous noun ὑποτύπωσιν ("pattern") in relation to the verb in the phrase ὑποτύπωσιν ἔχε [i.e., "to hold to, maintain"] ὑγιαινόντων λόγων ὧν παρ' ἐμοῦ ἤκουσας. The TNIV/NIV takes the relative clause "what you have heard from me" as the object of the verb (apparently because the noun "pattern" lacks the definite art.; cf. Lock, 89; Dibelius and Conzelmann, 105; Guthrie, 145), treating the remaining "pattern of sound words" as a predicate description of those words; but if this were the case, we would expect the accusative relative pronoun οὕς (and in this configuration there is no good way to explain the gen. case of the rel. pron.). In fact, despite the absence of the article, it is more natural to take the accusative ὑποτύπωσιν (with its description ὑγιαινόντων λόγων) as the direct object, with the genitive of the relative pronoun (ὧν) being the result of attraction to the case of its antecedent (ὑγιαινόντων λόγων).

94. For the Gk. preposition ἐν of manner, see BDAG, s.v. 11; Moule, *Idiom Book,* 78.

95. 2:3; 4:7; see 1 Tim 1:8; 2:3 (discussion and notes).

gospel in v. 13. Just as "sound" contrasts Paul's teaching with the opposing message, "good" signifies God's endorsement of what has been entrusted to Timothy.

The final phrase of v. 14 closes the entire calling sequence by spelling out the means by which "guarding" is to be done — the agency of the Holy Spirit.[96] He is said here to "live in us." There are several things to notice. First, this is the continuation of the theme, initiated in vv. 6-7, of the gift of the Spirit and the enablement he provides believers. Second, reference to the Spirit at this point forms an *inclusio* that brackets the passage and underlines one of the major themes. Third, this statement parallels what was said about God's ability to "guard the deposit," though in this case the power of God is described as that which believers experience through the Holy Spirit's "indwelling." Thus an important principle, which surfaced first in v. 7, then in v. 12, reappears here: it is God himself who ensures the success of his mission.

But what this theme also indicates is that God will achieve that success in and through the cooperation of human agents. This cooperation is possible because of God's presence with his people, which, in thoroughly Pauline thought and language, is described as the Holy Spirit indwelling us (see on 1:5; cf. 1 Cor 3:16).[97] Moreover, this description of the experience of God's presence in the Spirit applies to all believers, as does the teaching about the Holy Spirit above. There is no reason to limit the reference in "in us" exclusively to Paul and Timothy or to "ministers."[98] The application of the general truth is certainly to a specific situation, even an unusual situation — that of the handing over of the Pauline mission mandate to the successor.

96. Gk. διὰ πνεύματος ἁγίου ("through the Holy Spirit"); for the same thought of the Spirit as the agent by whom God manifests himself or his blessings among his people, see Rom 5:5; cf. Acts 1:2; 4:25; Heb 9:14.

97. For the phrase "through the Spirit" (διὰ τοῦ πνεύματος), see 1 Cor 2:10; 12:8; Eph 3:16; elsewhere, Paul uses the language of "indwelling" (Gk. ἐνοικέω) to describe believers in terms of the presence of "God" (2 Cor 6:16), "the word of Christ" (Col 3:16), and "faith" (2 Tim 1:5, see note). For the use of the preposition "in" (ἐν) to describe the Spirit's presence among believers, see Rom 8:9, 11; 1 Cor 3:16; cf. 2 Tim 1:6; 2 Cor 1:22. The possibility that the phrase of Spirit-indwelling echoes Rom 8:11 (1:14b: διὰ πνεύματος ἁγίου τοῦ ἐνοικοῦντος ἐν ἡμῖν; Rom 8:11: διὰ τοῦ ἐνοικοῦντος αὐτοῦ πνεύματος ἐν ὑμῖν) depends on the outcome of the textual problem in Rom 8:11. NA[27] and UBS[4] accept the reading just cited (διὰ followed by genitives indicating instrument or means); but see G. D. Fee ("Christology and Pneumatology in Romans 8:9-11 — and Elsewhere: Some Reflections on Paul as a Trinitarian," in J. B. Green and M. Turner, eds., *Jesus of Nazareth: Lord and Christ* [Grand Rapids: Eerdmans; Carlisle: Paternoster, 1994], 323-26, esp. 324 n. 47), who argues persuasively for the better-attested causal reading διὰ τὸ ἐνοικοῦν αὐτοῦ πνεῦμα ἐν ὑμῖν ("because his Spirit dwells in us"), which shifts the thought away from means.

98. *Pace* Hanson, 125; Kelly, 167-68.

But the power for the work (and the lifestyle) is accessible to all believers, and the ministry we are all to be involved in is the same one initiated by Paul and continued by Timothy (cf. 2:1-2).

3. Models of Shame and Courage (1:15-18)

> 15 *You know that everyone in the province of Asia has deserted me, including Phygelus and Hermogenes.*
>
> 16 *May the Lord show mercy to the household of Onesiphorus, because he often refreshed me and was not ashamed of my chains.* 17 *On the contrary, when he was in Rome, he searched hard for me until he found me.* 18 *May the Lord grant that he will find mercy from the Lord on that day! You know very well in how many ways he helped me in Ephesus.*

It is not unusual for Paul to draw on human experiences to illustrate the truths he is trying to express (Phil 2:19-30). Here he singles out three people and divides them into two categories. Despite the TNIV's decision to break this into two paragraphs, the contrast Paul develops suggests rather a unity.[1] The recurrence of the "shame" theme that Paul uses to link Timothy to himself (1:8, 12) suggests that he included the contrasting examples in 1:15-18 in support of the exhortation to Timothy rather than simply to convey information concerning his present situation.

15 The first sentence of this closing section introduces a negative example. One cannot be sure that Timothy was already aware of the event and people about to be discussed.[2] Nonetheless the relevance of the details to his present circumstances is implied by the reference to "the [Roman] province of Asia" (cf. 2 Cor 1:8), since Timothy's probable location was in or near Ephesus (see also v. 18), the most important city of this province. But the passage contains a number of uncertainties. We cannot be sure of the time and nature of the actual event Paul recounts.[3] But a straightforward reading of the text[4] would suggest that Paul is referring to a defection of his followers in Asia, either from himself ("me") or from the Pauline understanding of the faith.

---

1. The scope of τοῦτο ("this") is probably all of the contents of vv. 15-17(18), whether shared knowledge or news.

2. For the sense of the transitional "you know this" (Gk. οἶδας τοῦτο), see 1 Tim 1:8, 9 (discussion and notes).

3. E.g., some (Spicq, 732; Bernard, 113) suggest that Paul is referring to those from Asia who had been in Rome during his house arrest and trial, apparently assuming that 4:16 reflects on the same situation. Actually, 4:14 may reflect back on this Asian defection.

But is Paul now referring to an event that occurred while he was in Asia, an arrest or re-arrest?[5] Or is he alluding to the effect of his Roman imprisonment and verdict on those in Asia? Or is this a reference to the opposition to his authority and gospel that emerged in Ephesus and more widely? Given the importance of Paul's imprisonment (i.e., "suffering") for the gospel in the development of the passage (vv. 8, 12), and the relationship of "shame" to his "chains" (vv. 8, 16), the defection would seem to be related in some way to his status as a prisoner (or criminal). But the degree to which this turn of events is to be related to the opposition movement is equally uncertain. The verb "deserted"[6] is part of the vocabulary of these letters to coworkers for describing apostasy (4:4; Titus 1:14); but when Paul speaks directly about the heresy (2:17-18), he has other leaders in view. Still, in Paul's mind, rejection of the apostle and/or his gospel is tantamount to rejection of Christ (v. 8), and the defection described may well have been continuous with the falling away from the faith alluded to elsewhere in the letter (cf. 2:17ff.; 4:4). A movement seeking to persuade Pauline churches to reject the apostle's message and authority might well make use of news of his imprisonment in Rome to prove the eclipse of his influence and assert the need for a new and improved gospel (2:18).

What does seem certain is that Paul defines their desertion in terms of their relationship (or former relationship) to himself ("me"; cf. 4:9).[7] Two people are singled out from the larger movement (cf. 2:17; 1 Tim 1:18).[8] The names "Phygelus" and "Hermogenes" are known in the nonbiblical literature,[9] but nothing is known of these two specific characters.[10] Speculation as to their identity is plentiful — Pauline coworkers,[11] opponents of Paul (cf. 4:14),[12] or fictional characters[13] — although there is no good reason to doubt their historicity. Yet both the language of Paul's description ("deserted") and the logical demands of the illustration suggest that the reason they are men-

4. Gk. πάντες οἱ ἐν τῇ Ἀσίᾳ (lit. "all who are in Asia") is a more obvious reference to "those in Asia" than "those from Asia [in Rome]" (for which οἱ ἀπό . . . [Acts 17:13; 21:27; 25:7; cf. Heb 13:24] would be more natural).

5. See the discussion in Marshall, 717.

6. Gk. ἀποστρέφω (aor. pass.); Heb 12:25; Josephus, *Antiquities* 2.48; 4.135; Philo, *On the Confusion of Tongues* 131; see further G. Bertram, *TDNT* 7:719-22.

7. Cf. Dibelius and Conzelmann, 106.

8. In each case the focusing phrase is ὧν ἐστιν ("among whom is/[are]").

9. Gk. Φύγελος ("Phygelus"); see Quinn, 299; BDAG. For Ἑρμογένης ("Hermogenes"), see BDAG, s.v.

10. But cf. the apocryphal *Acts of Paul and Thecla* [E. Hennecke, *New Testament Apocrypha,* ed. R. McL. Wilson (London: Lutterworth, 1963, (1965)], 2.353, 357, where one "Hermogenes" is mentioned.

11. Barrett, Hanson.

12. E.g., Merkel, 61.

13. E.g., Hasler, 60.

tioned is their former association with Paul in some capacity (noteworthy colleagues or church leaders) and their disappointing betrayal either when Paul was in need of moral support (4:14) or as part of an apostasy. What they illustrate negatively for Timothy is the shameful way of willful dissociation from Paul, his hardships, and his ministry.

16-18   The way of loyalty to the apostle and the gospel is exemplified in the person of "Onesiphorus" (4:10).[14] Verses 16-18 form a single sentence in the Greek that consists of two wishes in which Paul identifies four things that set Onesiphorus apart. The first wish is, "May the Lord grant mercy to the household of Onesiphorus" (v. 16a).[15] The background to this wish formula and idiom is the Greek OT.[16] As in Paul's other wish-prayers (v. 18a),[17] the wish is intended as a prayer expressed indirectly to the Lord (Jesus) but directly to the one or ones to be blessed, showing a sense of solidarity and immediacy of concern.[18] This specific wish for mercy to be granted is rooted in the OT understanding of God's desire to help his people (e.g., Deut 13:18; Isa 47:6; Jer 16:13).

The basic meaning of "mercy" (see on 1 Tim 1:2, 12) envisions God (or, in Paul's view, Christ the Lord) seeing someone's suffering and being moved (by compassion) to share in it, bringing help in time of need, when people are incapable of helping themselves. The form that mercy takes will vary with the circumstances, as the two wishes in this passage illustrate — one, v. 18, in relation to eschatological judgment; the other, here, for help in the present. Paul means for the Lord to do for them as he had done for him through Onesiphorus. The emphasis in the wish is on the kind of help that is a necessity and only the Lord can give.

The intended recipients of this mercy are the members of the household of Onesiphorus (4:19). This may indicate something about his social status. A householder or patron could be a man of some means, whose property would typically include slaves and land, which would explain how he was able to be in Rome. Whether the wish also indicates that he was absent from home and so not included is open to question, since a reference to

---

14. Gk. Ὀνησίφορος; *New Documents* IV.181-82 §97; *Acts of Paul and Thecla* [Hennecke-Wilson (see p. 481)] 2.353-60, 364.

15. Gk. δῴη ἔλεος ὁ κύριος. For Gk. δίδωμι ("to give") in association with God, see above, 1:7 (note). For other Pauline wishes in the optative, see Rom 15:5; 2 Thess 3:16.

16. Gen 27:28; 28:4; 43:14; Num 6:26; Ruth 1:9; 1 Sam 1:17; 1 Chron 22:12. The formula includes a reference to God (or possibly someone else), who is to carry out the wish, and the verb "to grant or give" in the optative mood (δῴη).

17. For wishes in this form, see Rom 15:5; 2 Thess 3:16; for other variations, cf. 1 Thess 3:11; 2 Thess 2:16-17.

18. The same is true of curses in the OT; see Num 5:21; Deut 28:24, 25.

one's household might have been sufficient to include the person himself (see below).[19]

But it is in the reason ("because") behind the wish that Onesiphorus's character begins to emerge. Paul stresses two traits that set this man apart. First, he had "refreshed" Paul, which would have included bringing food to him and helping him in other practical ways.[20] Moreover, he had done this many times ("often," "frequently"), which showed his earnestness and depth of commitment to Paul. The cost involved for Onesiphorus is hinted at in the second part of the reason: he "was not ashamed [cf. on 1:8, 12] of my chains,"[21] that is, of Paul's imprisonment. It was no light thing for a person to be associated with a criminal. In doing so, one ran the risk of being regarded by the authorities (as well as by family members, friends, neighbors, and business associates) as a sympathizer and possibly an accomplice and, there-fore, deserving imprisonment or punishment (cf. Matt 26:69ff. and pars.). Paul wore the chains on his hands, a mark of shame in society,[22] as a badge of honor[23] earned by his solidarity with Jesus Christ and refusal to "be ashamed" of the cross. Onesiphorus's wholehearted solidarity with Paul in his circumstances demonstrated the same refusal to categorize imprisonment for the cause of Christ as a social stigma.

The third thing that Paul emphasizes about the character of One-siphorus comes through in his resolve to find Paul in Rome (v. 17). The con-trast drawn with shame implies that he knew Paul was imprisoned, or learned of it after arriving in Rome. There is no way of knowing what brought Onesiphorus to Rome (perhaps business); but the time and place reference, "when he was in Rome,"[24] does not necessarily suggest that he made the trip specifically to visit Paul. What is central in Paul's vivid, epi-grammatic turn of phrase ("he searched hard for me until he found me") is not only his success in finding Paul but the difficulty and the effort ex-

---

19. For Gk. οἶκος ("house, household"), see 1 Tim 3:3-4 (discussion and notes). See esp. 1 Cor 1:16 and the reference to Paul's having baptized the "household of Stephanas"; cf. the discussion in Marshall, 718-19.

20. Gk. ἀναψύχω (only here in the NT); this sense is attested in Josephus (*Antiq-uities* 15.54) and Ignatius (*To the Ephesians* 2.1; *To the Trallians* 12.2); see BDAG, s.v.; Spicq, *TLNT* 1:120-21.

21. Gk. ἅλυσις ("hand fetters or cuffs"; BDAG, s.v.; Acts 28:20; Eph 6:20). See further B. Rapske, *The Book of Acts in Its First Century Setting*, Vol. 3: *The Book of Acts and Paul in Roman Custody* (Grand Rapids: Eerdmans, 1994), 206-9.

22. See Rapske, *Paul in Roman Custody*, 283-312.

23. Acts 28:20; Eph 6:20; cf. Eph 3:1; 4:1; 2 Tim 1:8.

24. Gk. γίνομαι (cf. showing one's location is a common use of the ptc. [γενόμενος]; BDAG, s.v. 10.a; Matt 26:6; Mark 9:33; Acts 7:38, etc.). For Ῥώμη ("Rome"), see Acts 18:2; 19:21; 23:11; 28:14, 16; Rom 1:7, 15.

pended in doing so.[25] Paul's situation was no longer the one we read of in Acts 28:30-31 (see further on 4:16). But beyond this, the statement sheds no light that helps in the reconstruction of Paul's concluding situation. All that can be told is that his location at that time was not widely known, and it took some effort on the part of Onesiphorus to track him down. The reflection on his zeal and perseverance underlines his boldness and willingness to be identified with the apostle whatever the consequences, and fills out the picture of courageous loyalty Paul has been drawing for Timothy.

Before listing the final item in the positive profile, Paul inserts, almost parenthetically, a wish-prayer for Onesiphorus at v. 18a. The language of the wish varies only slightly from the preceding wish for his household. While the parenthesis is almost certainly motivated by Paul's deep sense of gratitude for his friend's loyalty, it may well have been occasioned at this point in the reflection by the use of the verb "find" above. The play on words is obvious: he "found" Paul, and Paul wishes that the Lord will grant to him "to find" mercy.[26] The wish takes up an OT expression, "to find favor," which means to be looked upon favorably by someone.[27] In this case, for some reason Paul's wish-prayer for Onesiphorus is for a good showing on the day of final judgment, which is what "on that day" stands for (see on 1:12; 4:8).

The double reference to "Lord" presents a potential ambiguity. "Lord" is used of both God and Christ in the NT; in Paul, however, "Lord" is used overwhelmingly of Christ, and refers to God only in a few OT quotations. In this instance, the granter of the wish-prayer is best understood as Christ (as in v. 16); the potential awkwardness of a redundant second reference to Christ might indicate that the second anarthrous reference to "Lord" refers to God. But the later reference to Christ as the judge dispensing the crown of righteousness "on the last day" (4:8) might overrule. It is a moot point whether or not the language of this passage indicates that Onesiphorus had died.[28] The time frame of Paul's reflection is clearly past, so it is possible that this was the case. But it is equally possible that he was yet alive, whether away from home, on the way home, or at home. The reference to his household in v. 16 (cf. 4:19) need not exclude a reference to him (cf. 1 Cor 1:16; 16:15).

---

25. Gk. σπουδαίως [Titus 3:13] ἐζήτησεν με καὶ εὗρεν. For the pairing of ζητέω ("to seek") and εὑρίσκω ("to find"), see Song of Sol 3:1, 2; 5:6; Matt 7:7-8; 12:43; John 7:34, 36; Rev 9:6.

26. V. 17, εὗρεν; v. 18a, εὑρεῖν.

27. Gk. εὑρεῖν ἔλεος (see LXX Gen 19:19; Dan 3:38); a practical equivalent in the LXX is "to find favor," expressed with εὑρεῖν and χάριν (cf. Gen 18:3; 30:27).

28. For the possibility that he was already dead, see Fee, 237; Bassler, 137; cf. Oberlinner, 63-64; for the view that he was still alive, see Knight, 386; Dibelius and Conzelmann, 106; Guthrie, 148-49.

Whatever we make of this question, we should guard against reading too much into the verse. If Onesiphorus had died, we should not read into Paul's wish a prayer for his friend's postmortem salvation, as if his spiritual condition at death were uncertain and sufficient prayer might sway the Lord toward mercy; the text is hardly an allusion to anything like the advice given in 2 Macc 12:43-45.[29] Paul seems to be quite clear on this man's standing in the faith. However, two factors should be kept in mind as we consider the import of Paul's wish for his friend. On the one hand, the judgment on "that day" is one in which believers will face the Lord's assessment (1 Cor 3:13). If this is in mind, invoking the Lord's mercy is not at all out of place, for the one thing Paul warns severely against is presumption. On the other hand, certain aspects of Onesiphorus's faith and life recall the Jesus tradition preserved in Matt 25:34-40:

> 34 "Then the King will say to those on his right, 'Come, you who are blessed by my Father; take your inheritance, the kingdom prepared for you since the creation of the world. 35 For I was hungry and you gave me something to eat, I was thirsty and you gave me something to drink, I was a stranger and you invited me in, 36 I needed clothes and you clothed me, I was sick and you looked after me, I was in prison and you came to visit me.'
>
> 37 "Then the righteous will answer him, 'Lord, when did we see you hungry and feed you, or thirsty and give you something to drink? 38 When did we see you a stranger and invite you in, or needing clothes and clothe you? 39 When did we see you sick or in prison and go to visit you?'
>
> 40 "The King will reply, 'I tell you the truth, whatever you did for one of the least of these brothers and sisters of mine, you did for me.'"

On the basis of this teaching, and, indeed, the whole drift of Paul's thought in this passage, Onesiphorus's acceptance by the Lord is already a settled matter. From this sort of perspective, whether he is alive or dead, what Paul wishes for is that the blessing promised to God's faithful servants be fulfilled in the case of his friend. The same concern for the status of believers at the Eschaton can also be seen in passages such as 4:16, where he "wishes" that

29. See the discussion of the development of this view in Oberlinner, 63-64. The classic text in support of prayer to God to deal with the sins of the dead is 2 Macc 12:43-45 ("He also took up a collection, man by man, to the amount of two thousand drachmas of silver, and sent it to Jerusalem to provide for a sin offering. In doing this he acted very well and honorably, taking account of the resurrection. 44 For if he were not expecting that those who had fallen would rise again, it would have been superfluous and foolish to pray for the dead. 45 But if he was looking to the splendid reward that is laid up for those who fall asleep in godliness, it was a holy and pious thought. Therefore he made atonement for the dead, that they might be delivered from their sin." RSV).

the wrongs of those who deserted him will not be counted against them, presumably by the Lord. Equally, 1 Thess 3:11-13 is a typical Pauline wish that his readers might be found blameless at the time of Christ's parousia — the sentiment is not different in substance from Paul's wish for Onesiphorus. What is accented in this wish/prayer by couching it in terms of "mercy" is the divine initiative and compassion involved in salvation.

The fourth thing that Paul recalls about Onesiphorus is the way he served the work at an earlier point. In mentioning this, Paul draws on knowledge that he and Timothy share ("you know very well")[30] as a way of assuring Timothy's confirmation of the portrait of courage and commitment already drawn. The probable reference is to Onesiphorus's participation in Paul's mission in Ephesus during his three-year stay in that city (Acts 19–20),[31] though it is possible that the allusion is to ministry that distinguished Onesiphorus as an ally during the turbulent time of Timothy's ministry in Ephesus (1 Timothy).

What he did in the way of service in Ephesus is less clear. Although the verb might indicate service in the church as a deacon (cf. 1 Tim 3:10, 13), elsewhere the term refers less technically to ministry of various sorts.[32] In any case, Timothy apparently knows what Paul is referring to; the important thing is how Onesiphorus's later service to Paul in Rome combines with his earlier record to form a consistent profile of loyalty in contrast to the behavior of the majority from Asia Minor who proved to be deserters (v. 15).

The contrasting images, of desertion and dedication, shame and courage, presented in this closing section provide a model for all readers. But we should use care in underlining the main issues involved. While it seems clear that Paul measured faithfulness to the Lord by one's willingness to be numbered among his coworkers, he did so because of his own commitment to the Lord. He proclaimed unswervingly a message that brought all people, Jews and Gentiles, within the same category. His concern in extending the church was that the divine plan of a unified people of God whose unity overcame all divisions be realized, not to win for himself any glory or to establish the church as "Paul's" church. His conviction was that the Lord had raised him up

30. Gk. βέλτιον (Acts 10:28 [v.l. D] in the same sense to emphasize complete or better knowledge), adverb, with γινώσκω ("to know"; 2:19; 3:1), either indicates best/complete knowledge ("you know very well"; BDF §244.2; BDAG, s.v.); possibly comparative ("you know better [than I do]"); but usually followed by a genitive (Isa 17:3; Sir 30:16; Josephus, *Antiquities* 18.268). Cf. Dibelius and Conzelmann, 106.

31. This assumption lies behind the textual variant, occurring in a few late MSS and versions, that adds "me" (μοι) as the indirect object of the verb "serve." The variant is secondary. Cf. the similar statement in Phlm 13.

32. For Gk. διακονέω, cf. Acts 6:2; 1 Pet. 4:10-11; see the discussion and note at 1 Tim 3:10.

to bring this OT mission promise to pass within a world divided by race, gender, and socioeconomic differences; when he demanded loyalty to himself and his gospel, he was demanding loyalty to the God of the covenant. Faithfulness to God unavoidably entailed faithfulness to God's universal mission.

B. CALLED TO DEDICATION AND FAITHFULNESS (2:1-13)

Nowhere in this letter do we really depart from parenesis to Timothy. The present section reinforces and summarizes the initial appeal Paul made in 1:3-18, continuing the theme of suffering for the faith, before the letter turns to address Timothy's responsibilities in the local church setting. The TNIV breaks the section rightly into two paragraphs, 2:1-7 and 8-13. Again, however, the method of teaching employed by Paul is that of personal parenesis; it does not depend on a logical progression of concepts, but rather utilizes examples (human and metaphorical) and repetition of themes to guide Timothy in his thought and behavior.

1. Carry Out Your Ministry with Dedication (2:1-7)

1 You then, my son, be strong in the grace that is in Christ Jesus. 2 And the things you have heard me say in the presence of many witnesses entrust to reliable people who will also be qualified to teach others. 3 Join with me in suffering, like a good soldier of Christ Jesus. 4 No one serving as a soldier gets involved in civilian affairs; rather, they try to please their commanding officer. 5 Similarly, anyone who competes as an athlete does not receive the victor's crown except by competing according to the rules. 6 The hardworking farmer should be the first to receive a share of the crops. 7 Reflect on what I am saying, for the Lord will give you insight into all this.

Following the models of shame and courage (1:15-18), Paul resumes direct exhortation to Timothy and the handover of the Pauline mission. It is difficult to find a single word or theme that summarizes the teaching in this paragraph, but there is more than a random listing of commands going on. The three imperatives ("be strong," "entrust," and "join in suffering") are linked verbally to what has gone before. These three commands are not unrelated to one another, but the preceding context is necessary to appreciate their interrelation. By repeating and weaving together the letter's opening themes, Paul creates a new, all-encompassing theme that takes the teaching to Timothy to a higher level. This section perhaps anticipates a question: How can one fulfill faithfully the mission being passed on to Timothy? Repetition of themes was a typical teaching device; by recombining ideas already introduced, Paul seeks to give Timothy the fullest understanding possible. Three imperatives are followed by three illustrations, and here a literary balance is struck in the passage. But the educative purpose of the illustrations is apparently to tease out the implications of the third imperative, which calls for endurance in the face of suffering. Finally, a closing command calls for reflection on these things and rounds off the paragraph.

1 After illustrating the meaning of courage and faithfulness in the life of Onesiphorus, Paul resumes the charge to Timothy. The leading words "you then"[1] signal clearly the transition to direct exhortation and indicate that what has gone before forms a basis for the present instruction. It will become clear that Paul is building on the previous instructions, and we should avoid regarding this section as an isolated piece. First, the personal reference to Timothy as "my son" (lit. "child") re-creates the tone set at the outset (1:2). While this perhaps contributes a note of intimacy, it also reminds Timothy, and any other readers/hearers, that his special relation to Paul lends him a certain authority that positions him to continue Paul's ministry just as it obligates him to serve faithfully (v. 2).

Second, in this initial command Paul returns to the theme of power. In 1:7-8 Paul introduced the theme by connecting power to the Holy Spirit *(dynameōs)* and then to God *(dynamin)*. Here in the command "be strong" the verbal form *(endynamou)* continues the wordplay as it connects this power to "grace" and "Christ Jesus." The verb (see on 1 Tim 1:12) is probably to be taken as a passive, which implies that strengthening for ministry comes through divine agency.[2] It is also in the present tense, which, in view of the aorist tense of the two verbs that follow, marks the action it alludes to and suggests that responding to this command concerning empowerment will somehow be the ongoing key to carrying out the rest.

The theme and the sequence of tenses parallel the development of thought in 1:6-8. There the movement is from the present-tense command to "fan into flame the gift of God," to which is linked the promise of power from the Holy Spirit. Then, there follow the aorist commands "do not be ashamed" and "join in suffering" (1:8). In each sequence, recognizing and accessing spiritual power is preparatory to other activities Timothy is to carry out. In view of the exhortation of 1:6-14, it is not unreasonable to think that a real situation of stress and perhaps some wavering on the part of Timothy under-

---

1. The Greek σὺ οὖν serves the same transitional purpose as the "but you" of 1 Tim 6:11; 2 Tim 3:10, 14; 4:5; Titus 2:1.

2. The verb ἐνδυναμοῦ is possibly middle (see Lock, 93), but the wider passage and 1 Tim 1:12 suggest that empowerment for ministry is the domain of God, Christ, and the Spirit.

lie the whole web of commands in the letter.[3] In the face of the alternatives open to him (to follow or to abandon Paul), he is to seek the power that God makes available so that he can carry out his ministry. The sense of the imperative is really "yield yourself to divine empowerment."

A third link to the preceding admonition comes in the association of power with "grace." In 1:6 "grace" *(charis)* language occurs in the discussion of "the gift *(charisma)* of God." If we make the connections, the *charisma* of God (= the gift of the Holy Spirit) will be understood as the means by which God manifests his grace *(charis)* among his people. The perspective in 2:1 may have shifted slightly, but the connections are similar. In this case, power is linked with "grace," which is further defined as being "in Christ Jesus."

Is the same power under discussion? The links with the preceding passage would suggest so. "Grace" is a term that often refers to God's undeserved favor as the basis of salvation (see on 1 Tim 1:2; Rom 3:24; Eph 2:8). That thought alone is probably too broad for the present statement. Rather, just as the *charisma*/Spirit/power combination focuses the readers on the enabling power and activity of the Spirit in 1:6-7, here the power/*charis* combination probably implies the activity of the Spirit. By describing in this way what, in terms of specifics, is put more clearly in 1:6-7, the emphasis is placed on the gracious nature of the power the Spirit provides.

Access to this gracious power is defined with the code phrase "in Christ Jesus" (see on 1 Tim 1:14). The phrase seems vague because it can convey various shades of meaning, but in general it is Pauline shorthand for the human situation characterized by faith in and fellowship with Christ; in other words, it locates the experience of this grace (and its power) in the context of genuine belief in Christ.

2   As the Greek sentence continues, the second command reaches back to the commands of 1:13-14. There "the things heard" from Paul formed a pattern for Timothy's teaching as well as the substance of what had been entrusted to him. Here virtually the same phrase, "the things you have heard me say,"[4] identifies the commodity Timothy is to pass on to others. That commodity, "the things" (TNIV),[5] refers to the Pauline expression of the gospel.

---

3. But cf. Bassler, 139, who suggests that the ordering of the tenses in each passage is more a reflection of rhetorical technique than Timothy's actual need to return to basics.

4. For the element of belief, see the discussion at 1:13. Only the form of the relative pronoun and the word order are changed: 1:13 — ὧν παρ' ἐμοῦ ἤκουσας; 2:2 — ἃ ἤκουσας παρ' ἐμοῦ.

5. This translation merges the initial relative pronoun ἃ ("which things," the direct object of "heard") and the demonstrative pronoun ταῦτα ("these," the direct object of "entrust") to which it points.

Timothy's hearing (reception and acceptance; see above on 1:13) of it is further defined by the prepositional phrase translated "in the presence of many witnesses" (TNIV, RSV, REB) or "through many witnesses" (NRSV). These two renderings reflect different interpretations of the Greek preposition *dia.* But in view of the explicit reference to Paul as the immediate source of what Timothy "heard" ("from me"), which seems more to underline the direct link between Paul and Timothy (and the distinctive Pauline stamp on the message), the more likely sense of the prepositional phrase in this context is "in the presence of many witnesses."[6] This qualification places the emphasis on the presence of others who can authenticate the message.[7]

Mention of the "witnesses" (see on 1 Tim 5:19; 6:12) suggests to some that the allusion is to a ceremony such as Timothy's commissioning (or baptism) at which he received "the deposit" (1:14; 1 Tim 6:20) along with a charge to proclaim the gospel.[8] In view of the interest in these kinds of events in Timothy's life elsewhere in the letters to him (1:6; 1 Tim 4:14; 6:12), this is a reasonable scenario. However, in any case, the emphasis is on the apostolic origin and shape of the teaching and its authenticity, to which many can attest, whether or not Paul harks back to a decisive moment in Timothy's life.

The command itself, "entrust [*parathou*] [these things] to reliable people,"[9] which comes in the next phrase, picks up and echoes the language of "deposit" and "guarantor" *(parathēkē)* introduced in 1:12-14 and earlier in 1 Tim 1:18; 6:20 to describe the succession of Paul's ministry to his follower. But this continuation of the mission to the Gentiles should not be confused with later notions of "apostolic succession." Rather, some ostensibly historical factors must figure in the command given to Timothy here. First, as the apostle's successor, he must join Paul in his difficult circumstances in Rome (4:9, 21) — the call to suffering issued to Timothy, thus creating the need to prepare those who can carry on in his place. Second, in Ephesus and Asia Minor a vacuum already existed, apparently because of the defection in Ephesus and the desertion in Asia and Rome by a number of followers (co-workers) disheartened by Paul's imprisonment. New workers must be commissioned, and they must be trustworthy. The church leadership ranks were

---

6. Cf. Moule, *Idiom Book,* 57; Johnson, 364-65.

7. Because διά with the genitive typically identifies agency, some see this as an indication that the "Timothy" of this letter was a fictional character who was removed from Paul by a number of intermediaries. E.g., Easton, 48-49. But see Fee, 241, who retains the sense of agency in the preposition but understands the activity it governs to be this group's attestation of the message.

8. Cf. Dibelius and Conzelmann, 108; Bassler, 139.

9. Gk. ταῦτα παράθου πιστοῖς ἀνθρώποις; see further the discussions at 1 Tim 1:18; 6:20.

being depleted, and the itinerant Pauline mission was in danger of grinding to a halt. The command is therefore designed primarily to ensure the continuation of the churches' and the mission's ministry in Asia Minor. "Entrusting" the gospel was not simply a matter of a tap on the shoulder; it would require Timothy to teach and to model the faith (1:11-12; 3:10-17).

Two qualifications are mentioned in connection with successors. The first, having to do with character, is that these be "reliable" people (NRSV, "faithful"; see 1 Tim 1:2, note). Soundness of faith is assumed. This quality has more to do with dependability in relation to the apostolic teaching (in contrast to that of the heretics), loyalty to Christ and Paul (in contrast to those who abandoned him), and commitment to fulfill what one has promised to do (cf. 2:13; 1 Tim 1:12).

In the final clause of the sentence a second qualification related to divine gifting is named — those selected by Timothy must be "qualified to teach others."[10] This ability is an important key to the success of the process envisioned. The activity in view is the authoritative teaching of the faith (see on 1 Tim 2:12), for which the gifting of the Holy Spirit is a practical necessity (cf. Rom 12:7). Following from this the predicate adjective describing the "qualification" or "competency" expected of acceptable candidates implies a divinely bestowed aptitude that makes them sufficient for the task.[11] Nevertheless the text is not at all clear whether formal appointment to church office or to the Pauline mission is meant (presumably Timothy knew).[12] Although the process described is not intentionally open-ended, reaching specifically to future generations, it does provide a pattern for the continuation of the ministry and its expansion. The "others"[13] (1 Tim 1:10) are distinguished from the "reliable" ones who teach them the apostolic gospel, which anticipates the outward growth and movement of the ministry.

3 The third command resumes the main theme of the letter — the

---

10. Gk. οἵτινες ἱκανοὶ ἔσονται . . . διδάξαι. The presence of the future form of "to be" (ἔσονται) in this clause — "who <u>will be</u> able to teach others" — has led some to speculate that a formal succession procedure for the future is in view (*1 Clement* 42.1-4; Scott, 100-101; but cf. Dibelius and Conzelmann, 107-8; Oberlinner, 72-74). But the future tense is logical, required by the fact that Timothy will not have carried out the command at the time of reading and by the fact that those who are selected will teach others after they have learned the sound teaching (see also Marshall, 726).

11. Gk. ἱκανός (see 2 Cor 2:16; 3:5-6; cf. 1 Cor 11:30; 15:9; 2 Cor 2:6; Josephus, *Antiquities* 3.49, verb); see Spicq, *TLNT* 2:220-21.

12. For the debate cf. Oberlinner, 67-68, who (following Lips, *Glaube,* 181-82) maintains that ordination is in view; and Wolter, *Paulustradition,* 234, who sees something less formal with the emphasis lying elsewhere.

13. Gk. ἕτερος (pl. adj.; "other, another different"; BDAG, s.v.); here the meaning is "others besides the original reliable ones," which underlines the distinction.

call to Timothy to "join in suffering" (1:8; 2:9; 4:5).[14] It connects with 1:6-8 by repeating the imperative verb that occurs in 1:8, thereby resuming the command to "suffer" for the faith. The initial command, however, dwelt on that for which suffering is to be experienced — the gospel — and draws the contrast between suffering and being ashamed; this repetition of the call expands on suffering as a requirement of faithful service. To do this, Paul employs three metaphors in the following verses that develop this command. The first of these, the soldier, is introduced at this point in a general way by means of the simile "like a soldier of Christ Jesus." In this image, Christ Jesus is cast in the role of a commanding officer,[15] and the one called to suffer for the gospel plays the role of a professional soldier under the commander's authority.[16] Without pushing the comparison too far, the willingness to suffer seems to distinguish the outstanding soldier ("good")[17] from the mediocre.

4-6 To aid Timothy with this daunting command, Paul develops in three pictures a scenario of the inner requirements that the good soldier must meet. Metaphorical use of the images of the soldier, the athlete, and the farmer to encourage commitment, self-control, discipline, and preparedness occurs elsewhere in Paul (1 Cor 9:7, 24; Eph 6:11-17; 1 Thess 5:8) and more widely in the secular ethical writers.[18] Structurally, each example encourages a specific mode or quality of behavior and links it to a goal that practice of that behavior will obtain.

The picture of the "soldier" (see on 1 Tim 1:18) in v. 4 expands on the military imagery already in mind from v. 3. Of the many things that the metaphor might serve to emphasize in such a teaching context, Paul extracts the quality of single-minded devotion to duty.[19] This particular qualification is arrived at negatively since the illustration urges avoidance of preoccupation with "the affairs of life" (TNIV, "civilian affairs"; NRSV, "everyday affairs"). The illustration envisages a soldier, described by means of a present

14. Some MSS (C³ D¹ Hᶜ Ψ 1881ᶜ TR syʰ) have altered the original συγκακο-πάθησον (ℵ A C* D* F G H* I P 33 81 104 365 1739) to read σὺ οὖν κακοπάθησον (probably under the influence of v. 1; see Metzger, 647). The NIV translation "endure hardship" is weak. It apparently assumes from the illustrations that follow that the meaning intended here is more general than in 1:8.

15. The parallelism with 2:4 identifies Christ's position in the picture as the commander who has enlisted the soldier (ptc. ὁ στρατολογήσας; v. 4); cf. BDAG, s.v.

16. Gk. στρατιώτης ("soldier"; only here in Paul; freq. in Acts and the Gospels); see O. Bauernfeind, TDNT 7:703, 708-12.

17. For Gk. καλός, see the discussion and note at 1 Tim 1:8, 18; 2:3.

18. These metaphors of soldier, athlete, and farmer are also found in the secular diatribe style of, for example, Epictetus (see Dibelius and Conzelmann, 32-33, 108).

19. For Paul's use of military and battle imagery in various connections elsewhere, see Rom 7:23; 1 Cor 9:7; for metaphorical use of weapons and armor, see Rom 6:13; 2 Cor 6:7; Eph 6:11-18.

participle, who is actively engaged or on assignment.[20] At such a time, his priorities must preclude involvement in any outside activities that might distract him from his military duties. Distraction caused by attention to mundane matters related to making a living, buying, and selling is described as "getting involved in civilian occupations."[21] These things are not sinful in and of themselves, but they pose a threat to the soldier since involvement in them would interfere with his military responsibilities.

As the thought shifts to the motive of this resolute mind-set, the military commander enters the picture. He is, literally, the one who enlisted the soldier,[22] and in the illustration he corresponds to the Christian leader's master, Christ. The soldier's goal is to "please"[23] or satisfy the wishes of the commander, who expects nothing less than complete attention to duty so that the military objectives will be accomplished.

Depending on how much of the detail of this picture is brought to bear on the Christian leader, the meaning of the illustration within this section of parenesis has varied among commentators. Some maintain that the metaphor implies the reversal of the Pauline model of a Christian worker earning his own keep and recommends the "professionalization" of the clergy, or that it was at least designed to discourage ministers from engaging in business dealings.[24] Most, however, find the emphasis to be more generally on the need for discipline and single-minded commitment in Timothy's ministry.[25] The subsequent indictment of Demas, who "loved the world" (4:10), would cause readers at that point to think back to this illustration.

---

20. Literally, "no one who is engaged in military service" (οὐδεὶς στρατευ-όμενος); cf. Spicq, 740-41. In the effort to ensure that the metaphor would not be misunderstood, some late copyists added the words τῷ θεῷ ("to/for God") after the initial participle (F G it vg[cl, ww]; Cyp Ambst).

21. Gk. ἐμπλέκεται ταῖς τοῦ βίου πραγματείαις ("entangled in the affairs of life"). In its two NT occurrences (see also 2 Pet 2:20), Gk. ἐμπλέκω ("to entangle") describes involvement in worldly affairs as a cause of interference or even immobilization (cf. Epictetus 3.22.69; BDAG, s.v.). Gk. πραγματεία ("activity, occupation") in the LXX covers all sorts of practical activities (1 Kgs 9:1; 10:22; Dan 6:4; 8:27); in some contexts it refers to "occupations" or means of earning money (Philo, On the Life of Moses 2.211, 219; On the Special Laws 2.65); See Spicq, TLNT 3:149-51; C. Maurer, TDNT 6:640-41. For Gk. βίος ("life, activity of living, means of living"), see 1 Tim 2:2 (note). Cf. Josephus's portrait of the Roman soldier in Jewish War 3.72-108.

22. Gk. στρατολογέω (only here in the biblical writings; Ignatius, To Polycarp 6); in the participial form it refers to the person who recruits or marshals an army (see Spicq, TLNT 3:300).

23. Gk. ἀρέσκω ("to please"); used in Paul for "pleasing God": Rom 8:8; 1 Cor 7:32; 1 Thess 2:15; 4:1; cf. W. Foerster, TDNT 1:455-56.

24. Cf. Hanson, 129; Dibelius and Conzelmann, 108; Spicq, 742.

25. So Marshall, 729; Johnson, Paul's Delegates, 63; Fee, 242; Kelly, 175.

The second metaphor, of the athlete in v. 5, reinforces this theme. Here too Paul might have stressed many things by means of this image. His concern is what it takes to win — "he does not receive the victor's crown *except* . . ." The background to this picture is the competition of professional athletes in the organized games of that day, such as the Olympiad or the Isthmian games.[26] The requirement for winning the competition (the crown) is contained in the phrase "according to the rules" (see on 1 Tim 1:8). This metaphor of the athlete competing according to the rules was also well known in secular writings,[27] owing to the popularity and cultural significance of the games throughout the empire. Paul's earlier use of the image in 1 Cor 9:24-26 (with different language; cf. Phil 3:12-14) to describe his own commitment and self-control links winning, which must be defined in the context in terms of spiritual attainment, with discipline and determination.

In the actual competitions from which this metaphor is drawn the stipulated condition or requirement ("according to the rules") referred either to the rules of the race or to the ten-month period of disciplined training that professional athletes had to complete to qualify for the games.[28] Either is possible, but this ambiguity does not affect the understanding of the application of the metaphor to Timothy. He is to look above in the text to the overriding requirement made of him — suffering. The attempt to avoid suffering, or situations that might lead to suffering, would amount to a breach of "the rules." To accept the stresses and strains on body and mind connected with such situations would require the utmost in self-control and determined commitment to the work. The metaphor therefore repeats from a different perspective the importance of self-discipline for effective ministry.

Finally, the third example of the hardworking farmer is introduced in v. 6.[29] This traditional example was applied to illustrate two main points. On the one hand, the farmer's right to enjoy the produce of the field he worked was often the basis for the broader claim that one had a right to enjoy the fruit of whatever one had done (Deut 20:6; Prov 27:18; 1 Cor 9:7). On the other

---

26. See esp. Spicq, 742-43.

27. In the Gk. conditional sentence ἐὰν δὲ καὶ ἀθλῇ τις, οὐ στεφανοῦται ἐὰν μὴ νομίμως ἀθλήσῃ, the combination of the Gk. verbs ἀθλέω ("to compete"; only here [2x] in the NT; *1 Clement* 5.2; *2 Clement* 20.2; MM 492) and στεφανόω ("to crown"; Heb 2:7, 9; *2 Clement* 7.1; cf. 4.8 for the cognate noun στέφανος ["crown"]), along with the adverb νομίμως ("in accordance with the rules"), is traditional and well documented in extrabiblical literature (Epictetus 3.10.8; 3.22.51; see further BDAG, s.v.). The application of the example underlined the importance of exerting extreme effort to obtain virtue.

28. Cf. the discussion in Kelly, 175-76; Marshall, 730.

29. Gk. γεωργός ("farmer, vinedresser, tenant farmer"); only here in Paul; see Jas 5:7; frequent in the Gospels.

hand, the diligent farmer exemplified hard work; it was this kind of effort that promised to return a crop (Prov 20:4). In this application of the stock example, Paul allows both aspects to converge. The activity of "hard work"[30] connects with the themes of single-mindedness (the soldier) and discipline (the athlete), so that once again the example does not endorse just any kind of activity but specifically diligent and focused activity.

Then, the last half of the verse takes up the thought of the reward this kind of performance "should" (or "ought to")[31] receive,[32] namely, a first share of the crop. As the metaphor is applied to Timothy's situation, the weight contained in the word "first" does more to emphasize the certainty of the outcome than Timothy's priority in receiving a reward (see 1 Tim 1:15, 16; 2:1), but the thought of reward is not incidental.[33] Interpretations of the "share" range from material support from the church[34] to spiritual reward.[35] Since the orientation of the three examples together is toward suffering according to the model of Paul, it is most likely to be the thought of eschatological reward for faithfulness in the gospel ministry that concludes the threefold illustration. Paul's later use of the athletic metaphor to describe the reward coming to him, and to others who have shared his love for the Lord, in terms of a "crown" (*stephanos;* 4:8) would immediately remind the readers of this passage that employs the same metaphor of "receiving a crown" (*stephanoutai,* v. 5) in relation to Timothy's ministry.

Taken together, the illustrations function loosely but nevertheless forcefully to convey a consistent theme. Each links disciplined, diligent performance to obtaining a valuable goal. And as the pictures unfold, the concept of goal develops from the implicit to the explicit promise of reward.[36] While the reality of the suffering Timothy is to face calls forth the repetition of examples to emphasize unswerving commitment, it is the goal (from pleasing the Lord to the promise of reward) that supplies the motivation.

7 Yet the instruction is left somewhat open-ended (cf. 1 Cor 9:7, 24-27), and Timothy is forced to draw his own conclusions as to application. To this end, Paul closes the teaching with two brief statements that urge him and other readers to consider carefully the web of commands and metaphors just woven, and also to think beyond to the road ahead. The command translated

---

30. For Gk. κοπιάω ("to toil, labor"), see 1 Tim 4:10; 5:17 (discussion and notes).

31. For the impersonal verb of necessity, see on 1 Tim 3:2, 7.

32. Gk. μεταλαμβάνω ("to have a share, to receive"); only here in Paul (but see the cognate noun μετάληψις ["a sharing"] in 1 Tim 4:3); Acts 2:46; 24:25; 27:33, 34; Heb 6:7; 12:10.

33. *Pace* Bassler, 141.

34. As in 1 Cor 9:7, 10; cf. 1 Tim 5:17-18; so, e.g., Hanson, 130.

35. See Kelly, 176; Johnson, *Paul's Delegates,* 63.

36. Cf. Bassler, 141.

"reflect on what I'm saying" is a well-known didactic formula[37] — the meaning is simply "pay attention" or, in our modern vernacular, "Listen up!" This refers backward but might also advise care in discerning the meaning of the phrase that follows.

Paul backs up the imperative with a statement of promise: "insight" will come from the Lord. In the language in which the promise is expressed we may detect an allusion to LXX Prov 2:6:

> 2 Tim 2:7: "for the Lord will give you insight into all this" *(dōsei gar soi ho kyrios synesin en pasin)*
>
> Prov 2:6: "Because the Lord gives wisdom, and from his presence come knowledge and insight" *(hoti kyrios didōsin sophian kai apo prosōpou autou gnōsis kai synesis).*[38]

The points of contact are compelling but not conclusive: 2 Tim 2:7 parallels Prov 2:6 in the verb ("to give": *dōsei/didōsin;* see on 1:7, 9), in the designation "Lord" *(ho kyrios/kyrios;* see on 1 Tim 1:2), and in the reference to "insight" *(synesin/synesis).*[39] While reduction, modifications, and the proverbial ring might suggest that 2:7 represents a commonplace distantly linked to a saying like Prov 2:6,[40] contact with the wider discussion in Proverbs 2 strengthens the likelihood of intentional interaction with Prov 2:6. There we notice the contrast between the one (sg. "you"; "[my] son," Prov 2:1, 2, 3,

---

37. Cf. the Greek here, νόει ὃ λέγω, with that of Plato, νοήσατε ἃ λέγω (Plato, *Letters* [Stephanus] 352c; cited by Marshall, 731). On Gk. νοέω ("to think, think about"), see 1 Tim 1:7 and note.

38. Cf.

2 Tim 2:7:   δώσει γάρ σοι ὁ <u>κύριος</u> <u>σύνεσιν</u> ἐν πᾶσιν;
Prov 2:6 (LXX):   ὅτι <u>κύριος</u> <u>δίδωσιν</u> σοφίαν καὶ ἀπὸ προσώπου αὐτοῦ γνῶσις καὶ <u>σύνεσις</u>.

The LXX follows the Hebrew closely, substituting "presence" (πρόσωπον; lit. "face") for "mouth" *(peh)* as the source of knowledge and understanding.

39. Gk. σύνεσις ("the faculty of understanding, comprehension"; 1 Cor 1:19; Eph 3:4; Col 1:9; 2:2; H. Conzelmann, *TDNT* 7:888-96). Differences between the texts are also noticeable: (1) the verb is third-person future in 2 Tim 2:7 (δώσει), third-person present in Prov 2:6 (δίδωσιν); (2) 2 Tim 2:7 personalizes the promise by adding the pronoun "you" as indirect object, while Prov 2:6 is general; (3) "Lord" has the article in 2 Tim 2:7, but lacks it in Prov 2:6; and (4) the threefold reference to wisdom, knowledge, and understanding in Prov 2:6 is reduced to "understanding in all things" (for the phrase ἐν πᾶσιν ["in all things"], see discussion at 1 Tim 3:11) in 2 Tim 2:7.

40. The idea that "understanding" is a divine gift is widely expressed: Exod 31:6; 1 Kgs 3:11-12; Dan 1:17; 2:21; *Testament of Reuben* 6.4; *Testament of Levi* 18.7; Col 1:9; 2:2; Jas 1:5.

etc.), who diligently pursues wisdom, and "those who have forsaken the up-right way" (pl.; *hoi enkataleipontes,* 2:13). In the wider discussion of 2 Timothy, this latter group could correspond to the opponents and to those who have forsaken the apostle, whose desertion is described with the language of Prov 2:13 (4:16: "all have forsaken me"; [*pantes me enkatelipon*]; 4:10: "Demas deserted me" [*Dēmas me enkatelipen*]; cf. 1:15).[41]

If this broader comparison is intended, then in these instructions Paul reconfigures the Wisdom tradition's ideal way of wisdom and uprightness (i.e., according to Proverbs 2, "the fear of the Lord") as the way of suffering for the gospel that the apostle has exemplified and Timothy is to walk in. In the new context, the promise of the Lord's assistance applies first to understanding the immediate teaching (cf. Mark 4:9); but in view of the wide scope implied by "into all this,"[42] and if the Proverbs background is considered, the gift of insight extends beyond the immediate passage to the dangerous path of suffering that still lies ahead for Timothy.[43] As the citation is applied to Timothy, "the Lord" is to be understood as Jesus.[44]

The Wisdom tradition's way of wisdom thus supplies a template for the way of apostolic suffering. In either articulation, the starting point is "the fear of the Lord" (Prov 1:7; 2:5-6), which in 2 Timothy is reshaped in terms of the vital concept "godliness" (*eusebeia,* 2 Tim 3:12). "Godliness" was closely associated with "the fear of the Lord" in (LXX) Prov 1:7.[45] Its use in 2 Timothy to define the authentic life of faith incorporates the goal of the pursuit of God from Proverbs and sets in contrast the opponent who forsakes that way. 2:7 is an OT allusion that invites Timothy to equate the way of suffering in godliness with the gift of God according to Proverbs 2 (cf. 2 Tim 3:12).

Timothy's path was leading to Rome and suffering. It was a hard path in every way. It involved first selecting new team members to fill the gaps caused by those who had left the mission team and who would expand the ministry in Asia. Then the challenge of suffering at Paul's side and in his place had to be faced. Promises of divine enablement, power (v. 1), and insight (v. 7) encircle the instructions, reminding Timothy of the gifts and capabilities he received with the Spirit God had given to him. In the midst of

41. Gk. ἐγκαταλείπω is the verb used in Prov 2:13 (ptc. οἱ ἐγκαταλείποντες) and 2 Tim 4:10, 16 (q.v.).

42. For the Gk. phrase ἐν πᾶσιν ("in all things"; the TNIV/NIV translation, "into all this," is too restrictive), see the discussion at 1 Tim 3:11.

43. The promise is in the future tense (δώσει; "for the Lord will give . . ."), which may simply reflect the difference between Paul's time of writing and Timothy's time of reading, or which may point to the future activity to which Timothy is being called.

44. See above on 1:18; 1 Tim 1:2 (note).

45. See also Isa 11:2; 33:6; see 1 Tim 2:2 (Excursus).

this, however, Paul's instructions and illustrations place Timothy's part in the transaction, the most fundamental aspect of which is the summons to join in Paul's suffering, in the position of emphasis. The appropriate response will take hard work, self-discipline, and unswerving loyalty to Paul and the Lord. The thought of reward for good service is introduced in an open-ended way; the later testimony of Paul (4:8) suggests the sort of eventualities Timothy must anticipate on the way to reward.

The general nature of the illustrations Paul employed tempts one to project the teaching into many situations. As valid as such an exercise would be, I do not want to distract us from our observation of Timothy's specific situation. Suffice it to say that the normative way of wisdom — the Lord's way, the way of the Christian — is a life in which human beings make visible the presence of Christ in mission, rejoice in that visibility, and faithfully accept the opposition that his presence provokes. Is so costly a life worth the effort? This is very much the question the entire epistle seeks to answer, and the next passage takes us deeper into this mystery.

2. Reasons for Enduring Suffering (2:8-13)

> 8 *Remember Jesus Christ, raised from the dead, descended from David. This is my gospel, 9 for which I am suffering even to the point of being chained like a criminal. But God's word is not chained.*
> 10 *Therefore I endure everything for the sake of the elect, that they too may obtain the salvation that is in Christ Jesus, with eternal glory.*
> 11 *Here is a trustworthy saying:*
> *If we died with him, we will also live with him;*
> 12 *if we endure, we will also reign with him.*
> *If we disown him, he will also disown us;*
> 13 *if we are faithless, he remains faithful,*
> *for he cannot disown himself.*

The calling spelled out in the previous passages, from 1:6 onward, contains much that is hard to accept and hard to understand. That the present section[1] continues the theme of suffering and fits generally into the instructions already issued to Timothy is easily enough seen. Paul recounts again elements of his gospel, his experience of suffering for it, and a theology of participation with Christ that makes heavy demands on those who would claim him as Lord. All of this is continuous with what has gone before, though the con-

---

1. A new section is indicated at 2:8, with the resumption of the second-person singular imperative "remember" (μνημόνευε) extending as far as the next (cognate) imperative at 2:14, "remind" (ὑπομίμνῃσκε).

tents, particularly of the formulation in vv. 11-13, add a greater element of danger and hope to the package. Even so, the opening command, "remember," and the promises contained in the saying give the passage a motivational tone, and we should read it accordingly.

The combination of the elements — command/gospel/suffering according to the Pauline testimony/promise of God — is at this point in the letter not unexpected (see 1:8-14). The passage breaks into two main parts: 2:8-10 contains the command to "remember" Jesus Christ and the model he and the imprisoned Paul provide, while 2:11-13 forms the "faithful saying" that serves to draw out the practical and ethical implications of the command and models given in vv. 8-10 and to authenticate them as the formula of trustworthiness implies.

8   The section begins sharply with a command. In the command "remember"[2] Paul takes Timothy backward to things he has already learned, just as in 1:6, inviting him to relive their significance. Verses 8-10 actually form a single sentence in the Greek; thus the content of what is to be recalled includes not just Jesus Christ, whom the gospel message enshrines (v. 8), but also the apostle's willingness to follow the cruciform pattern.[3] These two ideas together set the stage for the saying (2:11-13) that will provide the parenesis with its greatest motivational punch; Paul's main concern throughout the letter is not simply to remind Timothy of the message, but rather to remind him that his responsibility to it requires that he live as Paul (and Jesus) did.

Nevertheless, in v. 8 Paul's depiction of Jesus is of course a primary concern. There are several items to notice. First, the words "Jesus Christ, raised from the dead, descended from David" may represent part of a formula.[4] Second, Paul underlines this core statement's authenticity with the phrase "according to my gospel"[5] (cf. 2 Tim 1:11; 1 Tim 1:11). This authentication might be regarded as a polemical response to a competing heretical message (2 Tim 2:18), but its basic sense was to endorse the message as apostolic and characteristic of the proclamation Paul directed to the Gentiles (Rom 2:16; 16:25).

2. Gk. μνημονεύω ("to remember, recollect; to keep in mind"; Gal 2:10; Eph 2.11, Col 4:18; 1 Thess 2:9; O. Michel, *TDNT* 4:682-83); in the present tense, the verb in this context of setting forth models for Timothy to observe may call for continual "remembering, or conscious reflection upon" (see Johnson, 373; idem, *Paul's Delegates,* 65).

3. In attempting to render Paul's long Greek sentence into understandable and natural English, the TNIV/NIV strategy of opting for shorter sentence units may seem to limit the scope of the imperative "remember."

4. To which the infrequent order of the names "Jesus Christ" (see 1 Tim 1:2, notes) may correspond.

5. Gk. κατὰ τὸ εὐαγγέλιόν μου; cf. 2 Cor 4:3; 1 Thess 1:5; 2 Thess 2:14.

Third, the resurrection of Jesus is naturally central to the gospel (1 Cor 15:4, 12, 13, 14, 16; 2 Cor 5:15). However, the perfect participle "having been raised"[6] affirms that this event is unusual (see below). It perhaps opens up for the reader the way to think more immediately of the lasting significance of Jesus' resurrection — that is, it is not just a historical event to be remembered but a truth holding promise for believers to be rehearsed over and over again (1:10).

Fourth, his descent from David is also a stock element within the gospel tradition (Rom 1:3; John 7:42); although this statement implies the incarnation (see Gal 4:4), it goes beyond to indicate the conviction that Jesus is the Messiah (cf. John 7:42).[7] Commentators have tended to see in this formulation (and in Rom 1:3-4) the reflection of a two-stage Christology that distinguishes rigidly between Jesus' earthly status and his exaltation.[8] But the two parts of the formula should be seen as a unity, expressing the belief that Jesus' messianic identity consists both in his descent from David and in his resurrection: the resurrected one is the Messiah.[9]

The absence of other items from the statement (death for sins, for "us," etc.), even if they are implied, may suggest that Paul draws on a tradition here primarily to present Jesus as a model for Timothy to consider as he contemplates the difficulties he will face and secondarily, if at all, to convey theological information.

This parenetic function of the tradition here may explain why Paul has probably reversed what would have been the more normal, historical, sequence of events. Most scholars, noting the resemblance that 2:8 bears to Rom 1:3-4, argue that the Romans passage stands somehow behind this statement:[10]

Rom 1:3 — [the gospel] regarding his Son, who as to his earthly life was a descendant of David *(ek spermatos Dauid)*

---

6. Gk. ἐγείρω (perf. ptc.; "to raise, to wake from sleep, to cause to rise"; cf. A. Oepke, *TDNT* 2:333-38); the verb (in various forms) is standard in discussions of Jesus' resurrection and the believer's hope of resurrection, esp. in Paul. The 40-plus Pauline uses of the verb are all in this theological sense; usage in the perfect tense is limited to 1 Corinthians 15 (7x) and 2 Tim 2:8, which share a concern to correct misunderstandings about resurrection and emphasize that thus far (historically) only Jesus "has been raised" (perf. tense emphasizing a past act with ongoing significance), not yet his followers.

7. Literally, "from the seed of David" (ἐκ σπέρματος Δαυίδ); the phrase is a reference to descendants. This phrase was a way of referring to Jesus' earthly descent from the line of David and thus also his messianic position (cf. John 7:42); see U. Kellermann, *EDNT* 3:262-64; E. Lohse, *TDNT* 8:484.

8. E.g., Dibelius and Conzelmann, 108.

9. See Marshall, 735, Towner, *Goal,* 101-3.

10. See the discussion and references in Towner, *Goal,* 101; Marshall, 734.

4 and who through the Spirit of holiness was appointed the Son of God in power by his resurrection from the dead *(ex anastaseōs nekrōn)*: Jesus Christ our Lord.

2 Tim 2:8 — Jesus Christ, raised from the dead *(egēgermenon ek nekrōn)*, descended from David *(ek spermatos Dauid)*.

Each passage expresses a twofold view of Jesus' existence in terms of his human descent through the line of David and his resurrection from the dead. Each also employs the order of names, "Jesus Christ." But if Rom 1:3-4 lies behind the statement in 2 Timothy, the material has been rearranged and the ideas somewhat reformulated,[11] with the notion of the installment of Jesus as the Son of God in connection with resurrection being omitted altogether from 2 Tim 1:8.

In fact, the matter of the interrelationship of the texts does not aid us much in understanding the significance of the statement here, but it probably does confirm that Paul has intentionally inverted the two dimensions of Christ's existence in order to emphasize the thought of resurrection. The reason for doing so probably lies in the overall function of the passage, which is parenetic and motivational, recommending a course of action and supporting this by means of models — first Jesus, then Paul. The following faithful saying (vv. 11-13) directs Timothy (and other readers) to the promises associated with the eschatological future: death with Christ will mean life with Christ, (faithful) endurance now will mean sharing in his reign then. Within the message of the saying, the resurrection is the fundamental source of hope. In view of this, Paul's reason for leading off with the thought of Jesus' resurrection in 2:8 must be to anchor firmly in Timothy's mind the accompanying concept of vindication: resurrection must imply the thought of Jesus' suffering that culminated in his crucifixion,[12] but that whole complex of events recalls equally his ultimate vindication and victory over death.

At the same time, we should not be too quick to rule out the possibility that in restating "his gospel" with an intentional resurrection emphasis Paul aimed simultaneously to deconstruct the opposing message (soon to be denounced in 2:18) that was built on the false foundation of the doctrine that the resurrection of believers had already occurred.[13] If so, what Paul has done is to preempt the false belief that "the resurrection has already occurred" (v. 18; perfect tense) by asserting as of first importance that Jesus "has been raised" (perfect participle), and that this event, which is a present

11. E.g., 2 Tim 2:8 uses the participle (ἐγηγερμένον) instead of the noun that appears in Rom 1:4 (ἀναστάσεως) to describe resurrection.

12. Kelly, 177.

13. *Pace* Marshall, 735; see Towner, *Goal,* 102; Oberlinner, 77-78.

501

reality, is to be what galvanizes a believer's hope, rather than the deluded notion that believers have already been resurrected. Timothy, especially if he is to succeed Paul, must come to terms with the fact that the character of the present age that lies between eschatological past event of Christ's resurrection and the eschatological future event of the resurrection of believers includes suffering — an element that is to be embraced by the faithful, not rejected and replaced by false hope. In fact, to do so is tantamount to denial of Christ (v. 13; Titus 1:16), which is essentially what Paul regards the opponents to have done.

9 It is almost formulaic in the letters to Timothy that when a statement of the gospel is "owned" by Paul through one expression or another (cf. 2 Tim 1:11; 1 Tim 1:11), as it is here in the phrase "according to my gospel," an illustration from his own life will follow. In this case, vv. 9-10 project an image of Paul's deep commitment to the gospel's powerful ministry. But it is a paradoxical image that brings suffering, power, and salvation into tense alignment. Verse 9 continues the sentence, now focused on Paul's experience, with a loosely attached prepositional phrase that adds suffering to the apostle-gospel combination ("for which I am suffering").[14] The pronoun ("which," as in most English translations) is best taken in reference to "the gospel" just mentioned.[15] Together with the preposition, the phrase identifies "my gospel" (i.e., the gospel ministry)[16] as the context, sphere,[17] or cause[18] of his suffering. The preposition is slippery but the relationship between gospel and suffering here is similar to that expressed in 1:11-12 ("of this gospel I was appointed a herald . . . that is why I am suffering"). The present tense verb "I suffer" describes Paul's current situation and forms a thematic link with the challenge Timothy is to take on (1:8; 2:3; 4:5).[19]

Although Paul has already defined the character of his ministry in terms of "suffering" in previous sections, at this point he reflects on the actual nature and extent of his hardship and connects this experience closely with that of Jesus. On the one hand, he suffered as a prisoner ("to the point of

14. Gk. ἐν ᾧ κακοπαθῶ; the combination of the preposition with the relative occurs frequently in the NT, expressing various senses (sphere, cause, advantage).

15. But see Simpson, 133, who understands the connection to be to Jesus Christ.

16. As in Paul's references to the gospel in Rom 1:9; 2 Cor 10:14, the accent can fall on the activity of proclamation instead of the content.

17. Marshall, 736.

18. Knight, 398. BDAG, s.v. 9.a, suggests that ἐν ᾧ can be equivalent to ἐν τούτῳ, meaning "because" (John 16:30; 1 Cor 4:4).

19. Gk. κακοπαθέω ("to suffer, bear hardship"; 4:5; Jas 5:13; Josephus, *Antiquities* 12.336; Philo, *On Dreams* 2.181); the simplex verb is required here, but the link with συγκακοπαθέω (1:8; 2:3) is thematic. See W. Michaelis, *TDNT* 5:936-38; Spicq, *TLNT* 2:238-40.

being chained"). Elsewhere the allusion to his fetters[20] was sufficient to indicate his incarceration (Phil 1:7, 13-14, 17; Col 4:18; Phlm 10, 13). It carried the connotation of shame for wrongdoing,[21] even if Paul boldly called himself Christ's prisoner (Eph 3:1; 4:1; Phlm 1).

That Paul deliberately emphasizes the severity of his suffering ("even to the point of . . .")[22] in terms of imprisonment "like a criminal" may indicate the more serious state of his situation as he writes this letter. The term translated "criminal" is used only here outside of Luke's references to the criminals crucified alongside of Jesus (Luke 23:32, 33, 39); it often designated the worst sort of criminals, those headed for crucifixion.[23] Given the seriousness of Paul's imprisonment and the social stigma attached to it, it is perhaps easier to understand why some would desert him (1:15; 4:10, 16). It is hard not to see in this self-description a parallel with the description of Jesus (see also 1:8), who, for his faithfulness to God, was crucified as one of three "criminals" that day, even if the NT does not so describe him. Paul, who has followed his Lord in that same faithfulness, suffers the same fate.

Paul speaks harshly of his condition. But by contrast and clever wordplay, he makes it clear that he sees through the mirage of Rome's power structures to the reality of God's power — that he has experienced the truth that extreme human weakness is the vehicle for the display of God's power (2 Cor 12:9). He may be in bonds *(desmōn),* but *(alla)* "God's word" remains unbound *(ou dedetai,* cognate to *desmōn).* The phrase "God's word" is used here to describe the proclamation of the gospel in dynamic terms,[24] so that the entire surprising contrast underlines that his own proclamation continues to be effective, perhaps even more so, in his situation of suffering (cf. Phil 1:12ff.). Out of death, resurrection; out of imprisonment, the powerful message of salvation.

10 As Paul's self-testimony continues, v. 10 supplies the reasoning behind his willingness to undergo suffering. Two factors are involved — di-

---

20. Gk. δεσμός (see also Acts 16:26; 20:23; 23:29; 26:29) in the plural refers to the condition of being fettered and may be metaphorical for imprisonment (BDAG, s.v. 1.a). For a thorough discussion of chains and bonds in Roman imprisonment practices, see Rapske, *Paul in Roman Custody,* 206-9. Cf. 1:16 (discussion and note).

21. See Rapske, *Paul in Roman Custody,* 283-312.

22. On Gk. μέχρι (prep.) as a marker of degree, see also Phil 2:8, 30; Heb 12:4 (BDAG, s.v., 3).

23. Gk. κακοῦργος (Diodorus Siculus 20.81.3; Philo, *Against Flaccus,* 75; Josephus, *Antiquities* 2.59); Spicq, *TLNT* 2:241-43.

24. Gk. λόγος; for similar uses (in various constructions) for the gospel, Christian teaching, etc., see 2:15; 4:2; 1 Tim 4:5, 6 (pl.); 5:17; 6:3 (pl.); Titus 1:3, 9; 2:5; for the phrase (ὁ λόγος τοῦ θεοῦ), see Titus 2:5; 1 Cor 14:36. See the discussion and references at 1 Tim 4:5, 6; Titus 1:3.

vine power and human need. First, the opening phrase, translated as "therefore" by the TNIV/NIV (NRSV), identifies a reason for Paul's willingness to "endure everything." This reason, just mentioned, is the unstoppable "word of God," which fuels Paul's steadfastness on behalf of the elect (cf. Phil 1:12ff.).[25] Paul's imprisonment is thus interpreted as facilitating the gospel ministry, for it is another opportunity for God to display the gospel's power.

With this backward linkage made, a verbal shift occurs from the term "suffering" (v. 9) to the term "enduring."[26] This term is more general than "suffer" and suits better the inclusive object, "endure everything," which in this context means "all kinds of hardship" (cf. 2 Cor 6:4; 12:12). "Endurance" (3:10) describes an attitude of determined "holding on" in times of struggle; in the NT it is linked with the severest trials (Rom 5:3) and comes to be seen as a sign of apostleship (2 Cor 6:4; 12:12). Moreover, as the present context confirms, "endurance" looks beyond the present trials to a victorious outcome in resurrection.[27]

Secondly, human need also compelled Paul to endure. This factor becomes clear in the parallel reason, "for the sake of the elect" (cf. Titus 1:1). As in the opening of Titus, the question emerges, Who are these "elect" for whom Paul gladly endures imprisonment? A Reformed view of the term understands it to be to those who have not yet come to faith but are destined to do so.[28] But this requires an unlikely use of the term "elect," which in the OT and NT refers to the people of God,[29] and reflects an overly narrow view of the concept of salvation, which in Paul's theology is a process initiated by proclamation and conversion but not concluded until the Eschaton (see on Titus 1:1).[30] This is precisely the perspective on salvation reflected in the last

25. Rightly Marshall, 737; Fee, 247. The phrase in question, Gk. διὰ τοῦτο, is very common in the NT. Some have taken it to refer forward to the "the elect" and the purpose clause (ἵνα) that follows (as in 1 Tim 1:16; see Knight, 398-99). However, while this is possible (especially if the reference is solely to the purpose clause that is then the reason for Paul's action), it is awkward and repetitive and actually obscures the force of the point Paul has just made about the emergence of the gospel's power through (or in spite of) human weakness.

26. Gk. ὑπομένω/ὑπομονή (for the noun see 1 Tim 6:11; 2 Tim 3:10; Titus 2:2; for the verb see 2 Tim 2:10, 12).

27. Spicq, TLNT 3:414-20 (esp. 419-20).

28. E.g., Knight, 399.

29. Gk. ἐκλεκτός; for this use of "the elect" (οἱ ἐκλεκτοί), see LXX 1 Chron 16:13; Pss 104:6; 105:6; Isa 42:1; 43:20; 45:4; 65:9; Sir 46:1; 47:22; see NT Mark 13:20ff.; Rom 8:33; 16:13; Col 3:12; Titus 1:1; cf. 1 Clement 1.1. See further J. Eckert, EDNT 1:417-19; G. Schrenk, TDNT 4:179-92.

30. The intermediate view of Spicq, 747, that both believers and unbelievers are included in the reference, also fails to acknowledge the tendency to use the term "the elect" to refer to those who are at present God's people; see Marshall, 737.

half of the verse and in the faithful saying that follows, and it suggests as the more likely interpretation that Paul thinks of "the elect," without splitting fine theological hairs, as "God's people" for whom he willingly endures whatever afflictions he must to ensure that they receive the constant attention and effective teaching of God's word they need to remain faithful from start to finish.[31]

The purpose clause *(hina)* that concludes v. 10 identifies the point of Paul's perseverance: "that they too may obtain the salvation that is in Christ Jesus." In line with the above identification of "the elect" (= "they"), the other recipients of salvation implied in the TNIV's "too" would be Paul and Timothy.[32] This makes the most sense in the present epistolary context in which Paul is directly addressing Timothy. The goal is for the elect to "obtain" salvation. The verb used here, "obtain," has the sense of receiving something that is out of one's own reach and is thus a gift,[33] and as such can describe the receipt of salvation from a future perspective (cf. Luke 20:35; Heb 11:35).

"Salvation" in the NT can be presented, through the verb or the noun, as either a past fact (e.g., Titus 3:5; Eph 2:5, 8), a present experience (e.g., Phil 2:12), or a future hope (e.g., Rom 13:11).[34] These aspects are woven into a holistic understanding of God's gift of deliverance from the bondage to sin and the destruction of physical, emotional, and social health traced to sin. Here future or final salvation, that is, the consummation of the past and present reality, is held out to believers and linked with the ongoing ministry of the word through Paul and Timothy.

It is specifically located "in Christ Jesus," which in these letters to Timothy is simply a way of linking the blessing (in this case, "salvation") with the genuine faith in Jesus Christ which the proclamation of the gospel makes possible (see on 1 Tim 1:14). In this case, the future or final dimension of salvation is indicated with the added phrase "with eternal glory." "Glory" is proper to God. It is God's deity and eternal power often conceived of in vi-

---

31. See also Marshall, 737; Fee, 247. This is another passage in these letters to co-workers in which some see the development of a "Paulology"; thus Oberlinner, 81 (Läger, *Christologie,* 75-76), maintains that the Pauline testimony, with its use of "the elect" for Christians in general, whose salvation is tied specifically to Paul's gospel, amounts to a "Pauline" claim on the community. This is an unnecessary conclusion to draw.

32. See Marshall, 738; Knight, 399. On the Reformed view of "the elect" as those not yet but bound to be saved, "too" could conceivably have in mind all who have already actually come to faith.

33. Gk. τυγχάνω (cf. Heb 8:6); G. Haufe, *EDNT* 3:372; cf. Marshall, 738.

34. Gk. σωτηρία (noun; also at 3:15); see also the discussion of the verb σώζω at 1 Tim 1:15. See G. B. Caird, *New Testament Theology* (completed and ed. by L. D. Hurst; Oxford: Clarendon, 1994), chs. 5–7.

sual terms as that which identifies his supreme honor (John 1:14) and distinguishes him as divine (see on 1 Tim 1:11). Paul especially depicts the state of humankind in terms of a loss of glory (Rom 3:23; 8:19-21). Consequently, salvation means a regaining, through God's gracious gift, of (or a sharing in) God's glory.[35] The accent is almost always on the future state of affairs to accompany the consummation of salvation, and in this respect the adjective "eternal," which is often used to describe gifts that attend or interpret God's salvation (see on 1 Tim 1:16), meaning "without temporal limits, neverending," provides the contrast with the present state characterized by suffering, hardship, and the invisibility of salvation.[36]

Consequently, Paul lays down for Timothy a pattern of sacrificial ministry shaped after Christ's own. Somewhere in the background of this is the Pauline concept of "completing the sufferings of Christ" (cf. Col 1:24; see below on 4:16-18).[37] What Timothy is to comprehend from this picture is that suffering is a normative part of the gospel ministry, as the lives of both Christ and Paul amply demonstrate. The picture stresses equally the mysterious paradox that makes human weakness the divine crucible from which ministry done in God's power may emerge. This fact alone makes enduring the hardest of afflictions worthwhile, and the completion of the elect's salvation is an urgent motive that Timothy himself must embrace.[38]

11 As we approach what appears to be a theological affirmation, it is important to bear in mind that we are still in the middle of a section of parenesis. The theological material that follows in vv. 11-13 is both supportive and illustrative of the command "remember" given in v. 8. Although Timothy (and other readers/hearers) could deduce from the command and the descriptions of Jesus and Paul where the instructions were headed, this insertion of theological affirmations makes the obligation to join in suffering impossible to miss and too serious to dismiss. Before we examine the contents and their implications, however, some matters of structure and logic need to be considered.

The introductory phrase "here is a trustworthy saying" calls attention to the authority and possibly traditional character of the material about to be

---

35. See Rom 5:2; 8:18, 30; 2 Cor 3:18; 4:17; 1 Thess 2:12; cf. 2 Thess 2:14 for sharing in Christ's glory. For μετά (prep.; "with") as introducing items that accompany, see the discussion at 1 Tim 1:14. For δόξα ("glory"), see further H. Hegermann, *EDNT* 1:344-47; Spicq, *TLNT* 1:362-79.

36. Cf. H. Balz, *EDNT* 1:46-48.

37. So Kelly, 178.

38. See Hanson, 131; Oberlinner, 81-82. The argument (so Läger, *Christologie,* 75-76) that for a later Paulinist the apostle's suffering has come to have a salvific quality as part of the gospel (cf. the discussion in 2 Tim 1:8ff.; 1 Tim 1:12ff.; Wolter, *Paulustradition,* 27-95), is completely read into this passage.

rehearsed (see 1 Tim 1:15, Excursus). If we assume that the formula is meant as a preface,[39] its relation to the lines that follow is loose (cf. 1 Tim 4:9), and its effect within the flow of the passage is abrupt and thus more emphatic. The first line of the "saying" is connected to what precedes with the conjunction *gar* ("*For* if we died with him . . ."); [40] the connection thus forms a logic that bypasses the introductory formula and suggests that the series of conditional statements (vv. 11b-13) draws out the ethical implications of vv. 8-10 (or some part thereof).[41]

Some of the material in vv. 11b-13 does reflect the influence of traditional sources (see below), but it has all the marks of having been shaped by Paul for insertion here: (1) the compound form of the verb "died with"[42] corresponds closely to the "participation in suffering" motif already established and expressed with the similar compound "suffer with" (1:8; 2:3); (2) the vocabulary is typical of the letters to Timothy;[43] and (3) the resonance of the two parts of the passage (vv. 8-10 and vv. 11b-13) and of vv. 11b-13 to the rest of the letter is manifest. All of this is simply to say that while Paul gives the contents of the faithful saying a "formulated," symmetrical look, it is more because of the rhetorical role it plays within this passage than because he is citing a well-known piece verbatim.

The Greek connective intends to link vv. 11b-13 with what has gone before in order to ground the parenetic illustrations (Jesus and Paul) and the model of suffering and endurance in well-known, accepted theological affirmations and warnings. The extent of the preceding material grounded in this way is also debated. But whether we take vv. 11b-13 to be providing a basis

---

39. Most interpreters take the phrase to refer to the more clearly patterned material, with its traditional links, that follows in vv. 11b-13; but see Lock, 96; Ellicott; Holtz; Schlatter. For the view that the phrase is not yet formulaic and, corresponding to the meaning of "the word" (ὁ λόγος) in v. 9 as God's word," means "the word [of God] is trustworthy," see Johnson, *Paul's Delegates*, 65. For full discussion of the formula, see 1 Tim 1:15 (Excursus).

40. Gk. εἰ γὰρ συναπεθάνομεν; literally, "for if we died with [him]."

41. The question of what γάρ ("*For* if we have died with him . . .") intends to connect is answered in several ways. It is common to find the word explained as the remnant of an originally longer hymn or poem of which Paul cites only a portion (e.g., Kelly; Guthrie; cf. Bassler, 142-43). Knight, 401, refines this in suggesting that the saying about Jesus Christ in v. 8 is part of that original hymn and that *gar* referred to this material originally and does so also in the present setting. Neither view, however, is capable of verification.

42. Cf. the form of Gk. συναπεθάνομεν (cf. the use of the simplex in Rom 6:8, ἀπεθάνομεν) with συγκακοπάθησον (1:8; 2:3).

43. For "endure" (ὑπομένω/ὑπομονή), see 1 Tim 6:11; 2 Tim 2:10, 12; 3:10; cf. Titus 2:2. For "disown" (ἀρνέομαι), see 2 Tim 2:12, 13; cf. Titus 1:16; 2:12. For "unbelieving" (ἀπιστέω/ἀπιστία/ἄπιστος), see 1 Tim 1:13; 5:8; 2 Tim 2:13; cf. Titus 1:15.

for all of vv. 8-10 or just for v. 10a,[44] we have already seen how vv. 8-10 form a complex unity, so that v. 10a cannot be easily divided from the preceding; indeed, if we disconnect the command to "remember" (v. 8a) from the illustrations and rationale that follow (vv. 8b-10), the exhortatory nature of the teaching is lost. Paul is not inserting the traditional material simply to remind himself why he "endures" (v. 10a), but to provide a theological basis for the behavior Timothy must seek to emulate.

Paul's symmetrical presentation of the material in vv. 11b-13 gives it rhetorical impact and gravity. Four conditional statements ("if — then") are made in succession, with only the final condition departing from the form in that it supplies a reason for the apodosis (the "then" phrase). The form is similar to that of 1 Cor 15:12-19, in which a forceful argument is mounted by means of a succession of conditional statements. Johnson compares the function of the statements made here with "sentences of holy law" that emphatically reminded readers that human actions call forth appropriate divine responses.[45] In combination with the solemn introductory formula, this genre emphasizes the certainty of the promises and warnings spelled out for Timothy.

The first line of the material enters the mysterious region of "dying and rising" with Christ: "If we died with [him], we will also live with [him]." The carefully balanced compound verbs of each half of the condition ("died with," "will live with") require the inclusion of the implied participant, which, as v. 8 (as well as the tradition) shows, is Jesus Christ. In fact, within the broader section this line forms an interpretive link with the statement about Jesus Christ's resurrection in v. 8; that is, it points to the promise of vindication that Paul wants Timothy to associate closely with the reality of Christian suffering. Strengthening these connections is the conscious interplay of this line with the parallel statement in Rom 6:8 ("Now if we died with Christ, we believe that")[46] with which Timothy (and, in some form or another, probably any Pauline community) was almost certainly familiar (Rom 16:21). The meaning of the line hinges on the answers to two questions.

---

44. Cf. the views of Marshall, 739; Fee, 248, understands vv. 11b-13 to ground all of 2:1-10.

45. Johnson, *Paul's Delegates*, 66. Cf. 1 Cor 3:17; 14:38. Recognition of this device goes back to E. Käsemann, *New Testament Questions of Today* (Philadelphia: Fortress, 1969), 66-81; cf. Fee, *The First Epistle to the Corinthians*, 148.

46. Cf. 2 Tim 2:11b — εἰ γὰρ συναπεθάνομεν, καὶ συζήσομεν; Rom 6:8 — εἰ δὲ ἀπεθάνομεν σὺν Χριστῷ, πιστεύομεν ὅτι καὶ συζήσομεν αὐτῷ.

As the comparison shows, the association of the believer "with Christ" created by means of the phrase σὺν Χριστῷ ("with Christ") in Rom 6:8 is replicated by means of the compound σύν-verbs of 2 Tim 2:11. The language of "dying with" and "living with," which in secular writers tends to apply to literal/local situations, becomes metaphorical and theological in Paul.

The initial verb means "to die with [someone]."[47] It has been taken in two senses. First, in the present context, where Paul's suffering has been a focal point (vv. 9-10) and Timothy is called to follow in that pattern (1:8, 12; 2:3; 4:5), it has been popular to understand the verb to refer to a martyr's death.[48] Typically, this teaching is seen as a post-Pauline application of the Romans passage, which is designed to present Paul here as the martyr whose martyrdom is then elevated to a central place within the gospel. But the past tense of the verb and the time sequence from the first to second lines (past — present) speak against this interpretation and suggest instead a metaphorical "death with Christ."[49] This is not to say that death may not accompany the one who "endures" in the gospel ministry (in fact, that possibility is very much in view), but the thought of martyrdom (or the canonization of Paul's death) as such is not in this text. It is far more likely that the thought of Rom 6:8 is a better guide to the sense intended here. There Paul introduces the idea of "death with Christ" (as a past act, aorist) as a way of identifying the symbolic significance of the baptism–initiation–conversion experience. The aorist tense of the verb in the present text corresponds equally to a past event such as entrance into the faith and the community initiatory event of baptism that signifies participation in Christ's death to sin (Rom 6:6, 7, 12).

As in Rom 6:8, death with Christ is followed by the promise of life with him. For this the antonym of the preceding verb (in the future tense) gives the sense "we will live with [him]."[50] The second question involves the time reference in the future tense — whether it refers solely to the eschatological future[51] or includes the believer's present experience "in Christ," as in Rom 6:8.[52] With the thought of Christ's vindication/resurrection in mind as a model for Timothy (v. 8), the eschatological aspect of this promise is probably uppermost in mind, though this accent need not exclude the implicit understanding that present Christian living is "union with Christ" in his death and resurrection. Nevertheless, the requirements of the parenesis determine the emphasis on the certainty[53] of resurrection as a solid foundation for Tim-

47. Gk. συναποθνήσκω (Mark 14:31; 2 Cor 7:3; cf. refs. in Spicq, 748-49); W. Grundmann, *TDNT* 7:786; Spicq, *TLNT* 3:330-31.

48. Jeremias, 55; Brox, 244; see Läger, *Christologie,* 73-81, Oberlinner, 85; Trummer, *Paulustradition,* 204-7; cf. Young, *Theology,* 124-26.

49. Towner, *Goal,* 104; Marshall, 739; cf. Bassler, 145.

50. Gk. συζάω; Rom 6:8; 2 Cor 7:3; Grundmann, *TDNT* 7:787.

51. Dibelius and Conzelmann, 109; Trummer, *Paulustradition,* 204-5.

52. Knight, 400; Marshall, 740; Fee, 249. On the convergence of the eschatological future and the present in Rom 6:8, see Cranfield, *Romans,* 1:306; A. T. Lincoln, *Paradise Now and Not Yet* (SNTSMS 41; Cambridge: Cambridge University Press, 1981), 122-23.

53. Marshall, 740, detects in the word "also" in the second phrase (for καί: "we will also live with him" [TNIV, NRSV]; καὶ συζήσομεν) a note of certainty (cf. BDF §442,

othy's present endurance; moreover, the "futurity" of this promise's full realization may have served as an antidote to the misconceptions surrounding resurrection being spread by the false teachers (2:18). The first line of the saying portrays the entire scope of Christian existence, from conversion to glorification, in terms of "dying and rising" with Christ.

12 The second line returns specifically to the parenetic purpose of the passage as it proceeds to explore the theology and promise of the first line from the perspective of human responsibility. This is done by several means. First, the repetition of the conditional ("if . . . then") structure of the previous line, which maintains the contact with the theology and the rhythm of its expression there, invites comparison with the first line.

Second, in doing so the transition becomes immediately apparent: the phrase "if we endure" employs the same verb Paul used to describe his own perseverance in ministry in v. 10, but in form it departs from the "with" verbs in v. 11b (since there is no corresponding compound of the verb "to endure"[54]) and thus sharpens the ethical focus as the transition is made from the first line to the second. The effect is almost to ask, "Now what is your part in this?"

Third, the verb "endure" (see on 2:10; 1 Tim 6:11; Titus 2:2) links the behavior expected of Timothy with the model of endurance in the afflictions of ministry displayed in Paul's life, reinforcing again the call to action and the need for appropriate response.

Finally, the present tense is probably intentional, suggesting that endurance in affliction is to be a normal way of life for the believer ("if we keep on enduring"), just as it hints that afflictions will also be normal (cf. 2 Tim 3:12). The pattern for this can be detected in Jesus' teaching, which cast faithful endurance in the turbulent present age in the same role (Matt 10:22: "the one who endures until the end will be saved").[55] Endurance is the Christian response to the sufferings that attend the life of faith (Titus 2:2; Heb 12:7; Jas 1:4; 2 Pet 1:6), and, as seen above, it is especially associated with the commitment required of Paul's coworkers (1 Tim 6:11). With this phrase, the teaching deliberately introduces the idea that future eschatological blessing (however that might be conceptualized) is dependent to some degree on the quality of present human response in history.

---

7); in general, a sense of certainty attaches to the promise from v. 8, the "sentences of holy law" literary background, traditional background, and the form of the condition employed, all of which give the impression that the actuality of the first circumstance will issue in the projected outcome.

54. Marshall, 740.

55. Cf. Matt 10:22: ὁ δὲ ὑπομείνας εἰς τέλος, οὗτος σωθήσεται; and 2 Tim 2:12a: εἰ ὑπομένομεν, καὶ συμβασιλεύσομεν. The conditional sense is implied in Jesus' words; use of the participle ("the one who endures") characterizes the faithful disciple specifically in terms of endurance. In each case, the reward is eschatological.

At the end of the test is the reward, expressed in the apodosis by another *syn*-verb: "we will also reign with [him]." The literal promise of "ruling with the king" broadens out in the NT to the well-known theme of sharing in Christ's eschatological role of king and judge,[56] the source of which was undoubtedly the Jesus-tradition (Matt 19:28 and par.: "I tell you the truth, at the renewal of all things, when the Son of Man sits on his glorious throne, you who have followed me will also sit on twelve thrones, judging the twelve tribes of Israel"; cf. Luke 22:30). The time frame, which is clearly future and eschatological, confirms the future emphasis of the promise of life above. But in the case of this condition especially, the point is the importance of ongoing faithfulness, as here measured by endurance as a prerequisite to obtaining the promise. In spite of this greater emphasis on the human dimension, the promise is equally certain; the conditional formula will not fail to succeed because of anything on the divine side, a point that will be drawn out forcefully in subsequent lines.

But what happens when human disobedience enters the equation? Verse 12b initiates this dissonant theme with a shift in the literary strategy of the poem. From this point on, the protasis ("if" clause) and apodosis ("then" clause) are formed around different subjects: people and their decisions in relation to Christ are placed in opposition to Christ and his actions in relation to these people. Overall, there is also a shift from the positive tone of promise in the first two lines to the threatening tone of warning. What emerges is a legitimate warning[57] based on the reality of the circumstances in which Timothy is situated.

Rejection of the responsibilities enumerated above, "dying with Christ, enduring suffering," is described with the term "to disown."[58] The source of this warning is clearly the Jesus-tradition preserved in Matt 10:33: "But whoever publicly disowns me I will disown before my Father in heaven."[59] The term "disown" assumes that a relationship that involved commitment, obedience, and adherence existed previously.[60] Jesus Christ is the implied object (cf. Titus 1:16 of God), and "disowning" takes its specific meaning for Timothy from either of two current events. The behavior encouraged in the two previous lines suggests that something like the desertion of those mentioned in 1:15;

56. Gk. συμβασιλεύω (1 Cor 4:8; cf. the parallel in Polycarp, *To the Philippians* 5.2); for the theme (with βασιλεύω) see Rom 5:17; 1 Cor 6:2-3; Rev 1:6; 3:21; 5:10; 20:4, 6; 22:5. Spicq, *TLNT* 1:270-71.

57. BDF §371.

58. For Gk. ἀρνέομαι ("to deny, repudiate"), see on 1 Tim 5:8; Titus 1:16.

59. Cf. Matt 10:33 (cf. Luke 12:9): ὅστις δ᾽ ἂν ἀρνήσηταί με ἔμπροσθεν τῶν ἀνθρώπων, ἀρνήσομαι κἀγὼ αὐτὸν ἔμπροσθεν τοῦ πατρός μου τοῦ ἐν [τοῖς] οὐρανοῖς; 2 Tim 2:12b: εἰ ἀρνησόμεθα, κἀκεῖνος ἀρνήσεται ἡμᾶς.

60. See H. Schlier, *TDNT* 1:470; Spicq, *TLNT* 1:199-205 (204-5).

4:10, 16 from the Pauline mission out of fear of imprisonment and shame for Paul is uppermost in mind. And we should note here that the accent in this section of parenesis, in the models and instructions given as well as in the saying of Jesus from which this warning stems, falls mainly on readiness and willingness to undergo suffering for the gospel rather than on adherence to the "sound teaching." At the same time, however, that latter thought is never far from Paul's mind in the letters to Timothy; those alluded to had defected from the apostolic gospel, denied Paul's authority, and might also have been motivated by a desire to discredit the apostle because of his imprisonment. The future tense (rare in a condition that is futuristic anyway) should not be overstressed. The concern is for present patterns of behavior, and the construction conceives of disowning Christ as a very possible eventuality.[61]

The apodosis takes up the severe divine response to that eventuality. Whereas divine blessings were indicated in the two lines above, here divine judgment is threatened: "he will also disown us." The actor in this sequence ("he") is Jesus Christ,[62] as the source (Matt 10:33) and the context demand. The action he will take is described with the same verb that occurs in the protasis, "disown," also in the future tense. While it is possible that such denial would be experienced in some sense in the present life of an apostate,[63] the eschatological sense of the promises above and in the related teaching of Jesus point instead to the final judgment scenario. The meaning is clear: disowning Christ, whether as desertion caused by fear of suffering for the faith or as apostasy, carries fearful eternal consequences.

13 The fourth line, and fourth condition, of the poem continues to develop the thought of the preceding line, as it introduces the last condition around the same opposing subjects. Some features of this line are parallel with the preceding one: the negative tone in the verb of the protasis and the use of the pronoun "he" to refer to Christ in the apodosis. But the effect of these similarities is to give even greater impact to the differences. The tense shifts to the present, and breaking with the pattern, this condition includes a reason (v. 13b).

The verb of the protasis ("if we are faithless") means either "to be unfaithful" or "to be disbelieving."[64] The present tense may project the sense of

61. Unlikely are the suggestions that the future in the protasis expresses remoteness of possibility (*pace* Spicq, 750; cf., e.g., the use of εἰ with the future indicative for a present or imminent situation in 1 Pet 2:20) or that it refers to denial of Christ at the eschatological judgment (see discussion in Marshall, 740).

62. For the form (Gk. κἀκεῖνος is the combination of two words, καί and ἐκεῖνος), see Luke 11:7; 22:12; Acts 5:37; John 6:57; 7:29; 14:12. MM, s.v.

63. See W. Schenk, *EDNT* 1:154.

64. Gk. ἀπιστέω; see the discussion and note at 1 Tim 1:2; Titus 1:6; see also the range of meaning in BDAG, s.v.

continuous behavior, but the question is what sort of behavior is in mind. In this parenetic context, where we should assume a continuous development of thought applicable to Timothy, "unbelief" as such does not really fit. More likely the verb refers here to lapses in loyalty to Christ that amount to unfaithfulness.[65] The wordplay between human "unfaithfulness" *(apistoumen)* and the description of Christ as "remaining faithful [*pistos*]" would seem to confirm this as the chief concern.[66] What "unfaithfulness" might mean in concrete terms and how it differs from the act of "disowning" in the preceding line are problems. If "to disown" is to be understood in terms of desertion because of fear of suffering, then "to be faithless" is possibly meant to express something less grave.[67] Attraction to the other concern of the letter, however, might suggest that the term is descriptive of vulnerability to the false teaching, as will be taken up in the following section (2:14-26).[68] In either case, some interpreters suggest that the "if" clause makes a rather general reference to "the frailty of the believer," to temporary unfaithfulness,[69] as if the solemn warning of v. 12b needs mitigating. But the point may be unnecessary.

The two thoughts of disavowal and faithlessness converge in this letter, and the insertion of the line referring to "faith*less*ness" may be intended rhetorically to set up the contrast with Christ's "faith*ful*ness." Here the rhythm of the faithful saying departs from the "act-consequence" pattern, as the apodosis underlines the certainty of Christ's continuing "faithfulness" in contrast to the reality of human faithlessness.[70] The language of faithfulness is used to describe God and Christ in reference to keeping promises related to the covenant, especially in the context of the trials that make human faithfulness so difficult to maintain.[71] Then the following reason (*gar;* "for") explains why Christ must remain faithful: "For he cannot disown himself." The denial language (as in v. 12b) is redeployed at this point to reinforce the contrast with human faithlessness already made: the faithfulness by which God and Christ are characterized is a matter of the divine nature.

---

65. *Contra* Schlier, *TDNT* 1:470. It should be pointed out that in the context of the letter as a whole, in which both desertion from the Pauline ministry (out of fear) and apostasy in connection with false teaching are discussed, the distinction between "unbelief" and "unfaithfulness" might be marginal, cf. G. Barth, *EDNT* 1:121-23.

66. In reference to Christ, "faithful" is the better translation; see 1 Tim 1:2 (note). See Knight, 406; Marshall, 741.

67. So Marshall, 741; Spicq, 750; Kelly, 180; Towner, *Goal,* 107.

68. Cf. Bassler, 147.

69. So Knight, 406-7.

70. The omission of the καί in the apodosis (cf. κἀκεῖνος in v. 12b) is required by the opposing of negative and positive action.

71. Gk. πιστός (see on 1 Tim 1:2); 1 Cor 1:9; 10:13; 2 Cor 1:18; 1 Thess 5:24; 2 Thess 3:3; Heb 2:7; 10:23; 1 John 1:9; Rev 1:5.

But in this context what does the text imply that Christ is "faithful" to do? If the protasis depicts the general frailty of the believer, Christ is faithful to his promises of salvation to the point that he will save erring believers. That general point, however, is true (cf. 2 Tim 2:25), whether the statement intends it or not. Some commentators think that Christ's faithfulness is to a standard of holiness that requires him to execute judgment on deserters and apostates (unbelievers) without mercy.[72] Others see it as a general statement of Christ's faithfulness that is meant to be taken as a note of encouragement for believers (such as Timothy) who face rejection for the faith and struggles with apostates that whatever befalls the church, Christ will remain faithful to it. This last option, in one sense or another, is probably right. The point may be parallel to the encouragement that emerges below in 2:19-21: even if there are false teachers and false believers in the church, God will not fail to preserve his people; that is, whatever happens to the church and its leadership, God will remain faithful to his covenant.[73] Perhaps the only purpose of the turnabout is to stress the paradoxical nature of God's mercy: by it he can draw the worst of sinners to himself (cf. 1 Tim 1:12-16), open the way of escape when temptation seems irresistible, and surprise the church with a continual offer of repentance (2:25-26). These things are true, and they return the thought finally to God's paradoxical grace with which the parenesis began. Nevertheless, the strength and severity of the warnings equal the hope of the promise of eternal life and reward.

C. ADDRESSING THE CHALLENGE OF OPPOSITION IN THE CHURCH (2:14-26)

At this point, with Timothy still in view, the parenesis shifts to instructions about dealing with the opponents in the church. Timothy will now be depicted as interacting with and living in the presence of the opponents.[1] The passage consists of a number of commands in the second person addressed to Paul's coworker (vv. 14, 15, 16, 22, 23).[2] These, however, have to do primarily with how he is to teach or relate to those involved in the disputes engendered by the heresy. They may be divided into two sequences, each constructed of three imperatives in a negative/positive/negative pattern.[3] Paul provides a rationale for the behavior commanded (vv. 16b-18, 24-26). And in the midsection (vv. 19-21) he develops a strong picture of the church as hav-

---

72. So Lock, 96; Oberlinner, 88.
73. Fee, 251.
1. See Johnson, *Paul's Delegates,* 72.
2. The second-person imperative characterizes the whole stretch of text to 4:5.
3. See Marshall, 743.

ing its foundation in God and in the Lord's knowledge of his own people. Within these supportive and illustrative passages, he also issues commands in the third-person singular.

> 14 *Keep reminding God's people of these things. Warn them before God against quarreling about words; it is of no value, and only ruins those who listen.* 15 *Do your best to present yourself to God as one approved, a worker who does not need to be ashamed and who correctly handles the word of truth.* 16 *Avoid godless chatter, because those who indulge in it will become more and more ungodly.* 17 *Their teaching will spread like gangrene. Among them are Hymenaeus and Philetus,* 18 *who have departed from the truth. They say that the resurrection has already taken place, and they destroy the faith of some.* 19 *Nevertheless, God's solid foundation stands firm, sealed with this inscription: "The Lord knows those who are his," and, "Everyone who confesses the name of the Lord must turn away from wickedness."*
>
> 20 *In a large house there are articles not only of gold and silver, but also of wood and clay; some are for noble purposes and some for disposal of refuse.* 21 *Those who cleanse themselves from the latter will be instruments for noble purposes, made holy, useful to the Master and prepared to do any good work.*
>
> 22 *Flee the evil desires of youth and pursue righteousness, faith, love and peace, along with those who call on the Lord out of a pure heart.* 23 *Don't have anything to do with foolish and stupid arguments, because you know they produce quarrels.* 24 *And the Lord's servant must not be quarrelsome but must be kind to everyone, able to teach, not resentful.* 25 *Opponents must be gently instructed, in the hope that God will grant them repentance leading them to a knowledge of the truth,* 26 *and that they will come to their senses and escape from the trap of the devil, who has taken them captive to do his will.*

Although the versions reflect various attempts to make sense of the structure,[4] the overriding concern is to instruct Timothy how to interact both with opposing leaders (vv. 17-18) and others who have been caught up in the turbulence (vv. 23-26) and to arouse others by indirect commands to repent of their involvement (vv. 21, 25). This suggests a loose unity. It is achieved by the weaving together of contrasts, negative and positive imperatives, and corresponding character portraits. These features are certainly not arbitrary.

4. The NLT breaks the passage into five paragraphs (vv. 14-18; 19; 20-21; 22; 23-26); the TNIV/NIV into three (vv. 14-19; 20-21; 22-26); the NRSV into two (vv. 14-19; 20-26); NA[27] into two (vv. 14-21; 22-26); UBS[4] treats vv. 14-26 as a single paragraph.

Johnson shows how this span of the text, as far as 4:5, reflects the influence of secular parenetic style (chiefly the protreptic discourses), a feature that sets 2 Timothy (and these letters to coworkers in general) off from the earlier writings of Paul.[5] In this section, there is a shift in the didactic strategy from an emphasis on models to instruction with maxims and specific commands. Timothy is the direct recipient of this teaching, as the singular imperatives indicate; the overhearing community members enter the parenetic flow indirectly. There is also the striking presence of antithesis, with caricatures of the opponents serving as background to positive instructions given to Timothy. Where the caricatures prove to be stock descriptions of opponents, the intention of the contrast ("they do this . . . , but you should . . .") is to emphasize the superior character of the life and action that Timothy is to embrace. Additional influence from secular moral teaching can be seen in the use of medical imagery (2:17). The conceptualization of conversion as the turn from vice to virtue (2:19-21) and of the teacher as one who effects this change in others (2:25-26) also has secular parallels. Paul's concern for the way in which Timothy teaches (cf. 2:23, 24-25) is not unusual, as it also resonates with themes taken up in secular ethics.

What emerges as the immediate passage unfolds is an emphasis on the repentance and salvation of erring people, which puts this aspect of the ministry to which Timothy is called into the overall perspective of the Pauline mission to the Gentiles. The bottom line is God's desire to save his creation; achieving this objective involves correcting those who pervert the truth, living a life that authenticates the truth, and interacting with people in a way that invites them to (re-)embrace the truth. But for the argument to be persuasive, Paul must accomplish three things. First, he must ensure that Timothy understands where his responsibilities lie and what is at stake. Second, he must convincingly discredit the opposition and its teaching. Third, he must establish beyond question that the high stakes involved include divine judgment and salvation.

14 The first sequence of imperatives opens with the command that places Timothy briefly in a teaching mode: "Keep reminding God's people of these things." The command, in the present tense and in this context, regards some part of the information above as teaching to be conveyed.[6] Two questions

---

5. For references and illustrations, see Johnson, 389-98; idem, *Paul's Delegates,* 73, 76-78.

6. Gk. ὑπομιμνῄσκω ("to remind, call to mind, recollect"); the usage here corresponds to other parenetic and polemical contexts in which the need to remind readers of accepted teaching has become acute due to the presence of false teachers (2 Tim 2:14; 2 Pet 1:12; Jude 5), elsewhere simply because of the passage of time (cf. Wis 12:2; 18:22; 4 Macc 18:14). In this case (unlike that in Titus 3:1) the verb takes the accusative object of contents (ταῦτα) to be called to mind (BDAG, 1.b.α; see 3 John 10).

arise. The first has to do with the human objects of the reminder and the subsequent warning, which the Greek sentence fails to mention. The TNIV understands the church to be in mind in both instances ("God's people . . . them");[7] in view of the language used and the surrounding interests,[8] this seems a more likely conclusion than to think that Paul has suddenly fixed on some select group for instruction and admonition.[9] Possibly we are to understand a narrowing of focus in the shift from reminder to warning in the next clause, so that the subsequent target group (those to be warned) is now the opponents who engage in polemics (cf. "those who opposed," v. 25). More likely, however, the same

7. See Marshall, 745-46; Johnson, *Paul's Delegates,* 70; Kelly; Dibelius and Conzelmann. The NRSV (NIV) supplies the ambiguous "them" as the object of both "reminding" and "warning."

8. The rough syntax, which omits a human object (cf. Titus 3:1 and note), obscures the meaning, but the language and surrounding interests suggest that we should at least supply the pronoun "them" (after each verbal form: "remind," "warn") to indicate those to whom Timothy is to address this reminder. The added verb of warning tends to indicate a strong appeal made to another party (cf. Acts 18:5; 20:21; 28:23).

For Gk. διαμαρτύρομαι (here ptc.; "to warn or bear witness solemnly"), see 1 Tim 5:21 (discussion and note). *Pace* Prior, *Paul the Letter-Writer,* 158-60, who argues at length that if the human object were someone other than Timothy, it would have been spelled out (as in Titus 3:1), and so opts for the intransitive meaning of ὑπομίμνῃσκε ("remember"; e.g., Luke 22:61). This would seem to fit with the emphasis on Timothy's own behavior throughout the letter. However, Prior does not handle the participle and prepositional phrase that follow (lit. "declaring solemnly in the presence of God"; διαμαρτυρόμενος ἐνώπιον τοῦ θεοῦ) in a convincing manner when he translates this phrase as "as you bear witness in the presence of God, not by engaging in word-wrangling. . . ." Johnson's way of handling the syntax, by breaking the verse into two sentences (383-84, "remember these things as you admonish before God. Do not engage in polemics . . .") is more plausible, but the unambiguous transitive use of the imperative verb ὑπομίμνῃσκε, in what appears to be a similar context in Titus 3:1, favors the transitive sense here and suggests the need to supply the second object, "them."

Notably, textual variants that occur here (though clearly secondary) apparently reflect the attempt to smooth out the bumpy syntax created by the omission of the object. The change from "God" (θεοῦ; ℵ C F G I 614 629 630 1175, etc. a vg^mss sy^hmg sa^mss bo^pt) in the phrase "in the presence of God" to "Lord" (κυρίου; A D Ψ 048 1739 1881 TR b vg sy sa^ms bo^pt) or "Christ" (Χριστοῦ; 206 pc) may reflect the attempt to take the participle διαμαρτυρόμενος in the sense of witnessing before God (for which "the Lord" or "Christ" was better suited; 1:8) instead of as "solemnly warning" or "declaring." Then, the change from the original infinitive "to fight with words" (λογομαχεῖν; ℵ C3 D F G I Ψ 33 1739 1881 TR sy Cl) to the second-person imperative (with the negative, a prohibition; λογομάχει; A C* 048 1175 pc latt) took the prohibition as directed at Timothy (adopted by Johnson, 384). See Metzger, 579.

9. E.g., those Timothy is to appoint (2:2). For the focus has been entirely on Timothy from that point to this, and as the letter was read, these candidates were not yet appointed. But cf. Karris ("church leaders"); Houlden ("the elect" of v. 10).

broader group remains in focus with the shift being one of topic, from that of doctrinal purity ("remind them of the above teaching") to avoidance of involvement in the disputes with the implied opponents.[10]

Second, of what must Timothy remind the church? "These things" is a vague reference, but the probable connection would be back to the theology of v. 8, possibly in combination with the promises and warnings of vv. 11-13. The whole unit (vv. 8-13), including the example of Paul, contains what could conceivably be viewed as corrective, apologetic and admonitory materials useful for calming anti-Paul sentiments such as were probably running high in this church. But here Paul's twofold concern should again be noted. In this personal parenetic letter, the need to deal with the opponents is embedded within the instructions to Timothy, which include adopting the apostle's model (suffering and hardship) and addressing the situation of opposition ("teaching," "reminding") in a particular way. Timothy's behavior and performance are still in focus.

In a formulaic phrase,[11] "warn them before God," Paul encourages Timothy to teach (or reprove) in the same way that he himself does; Timothy is to call on God as an approving witness of what is taught, thus implying that this is God's teaching.[12] What is to be communicated in this way is a prohibition against quarreling (lit. "battling with or about words").[13] This activity belongs to the broad characterization of the opponents' destructive methods in the correspondence to Timothy (1 Tim 6:4; cf. 1 Tim 1:4; 2 Tim 2:23). As a general instruction to the congregation or to the leaders within it, the point is that no one is to employ the tactics of the false teachers or engage them in polemics, not that serious discussion with the false teachers should be avoided. The fact that all verbal forms in v. 14 are in the present tense may suggest the implication "stop quarreling about words," in which case the emphasis of this command is remedial rather than preventive.

The rest of the Greek sentence consists of two prepositional phrases that combine to supply two reasons why such tactics ("quarreling about words") should not be used. The first phrase is difficult in Greek,[14] but the

10. This is the implication of GNB and TNIV; see Marshall, 746-47.

11. Gk. διαμαρτυρόμενος ἐνώπιον τοῦ θεοῦ (4:1; for Gk. διαμαρτύρομαι, see discussion and notes at 1 Tim 5:21; cf. 1 Tim 6:13; Gal 1:20).

12. 4:1; see 1 Tim 5:21; 6:13; 1 Tim 2:3 (and discussion); 5:4.

13. Gk. λογομαχέω ("to dispute about or with words, split hairs"). The prohibition formed with the infinitive plus the negative (μὴ λογομαχεῖν) supplies the content of the warning. Cf. discussions (and notes) of the noun in 1 Tim 6:4 (λογομαχία); cf. Titus 3:9; BDAG.

14. Gk. ἐπ᾽ οὐδέν is most likely dependent on χρήσιμον (thus supplying an explanation for the prohibition "which are useless"; this is a typical relationship in, e.g., Plato, *Laws* 796A; *Gorgias* 480B; see Dibelius and Conzelmann, 110; Marshall, 746) instead of

sense, which is to label such disputing as being "of no value" (= "useless"), comes through clearly enough.[15] Practical "usefulness" was the traditional test of any teaching's quality,[16] and the polemics Paul prohibits do not measure up.

The second prepositional phrase extends this measurement, showing how far from "useful" quarreling (polemics) is: "and only ruins those who listen."[17] Although some exaggeration should be allowed for, extensive damage (not mere setback; cf. 2:18) is indicated in the term "ruin," as its use in descriptions of the judgment of Sodom and Gomorrah illustrates.[18] The situation of foolish controversy linked with the opponents' teaching and methods is now clearly in view, with "those who listen" being believers in the church who are susceptible to this dangerous influence. Verse 18 illustrates one dimension of the "ruin" Paul has in mind.

15   From this discussion of behavior to avoid, Paul proceeds to behavior Timothy is to pursue. He issues the second of the three imperatives and introduces a contrasting profile of ministry approved by God. Two parts characterize this acceptable profile in broad strokes, with the final phrase establishing the narrower concentration on teaching, which is the issue at hand.

First, in contrast[19] to others in view (v. 17), Timothy is to "do his best"[20] to work in such a way that he will stand approved before God. Two characteristic terms in Paul's thought come together here to describe this countergoal.[21] The first is the adjective "approved," which implies that some-

---

on the infinitive, producing an appositional explanation, which is somewhat parenthetical (Marshall, 746; Simpson, 136). Some MSS replace ἐπ' (א* A C F G I P 048 33 1175 1241 *pc*) with εἰς (א² D Ψ 1739 1881 TR) to clarify the sense of result. The harder reading (ἐπ') is to be preferred.

15. Gk. χρήσιμος ("useful, beneficial") occurs only here in the NT, but for the term in a negative context implying "uselessness," see LXX Ezek 15:4. See BDAG; MM.

16. Expressed with a near synonym (ὠφέλιμος, "profitable") in 2 Tim 3:16; 1 Tim 4:8 (see ὄφελος, "benefit"; Philo, *On the Migration of Abraham* 55; Plato, Gorgias 504E); see further Johnson, 384.

17. For ἐπί used with the dative (here καταστροφῇ) to introduce a result clause see BDF §235, 4.

18. Gk. καταστροφή; cf. LXX Gen 19:29; 2 Chron 22:7; Prov 1:18; 2 Pet 2:6; G. Bertram, *TDNT* 7:716 n. 6; BDAG, s.v.

19. There is no adversative conjunction, but the abrupt shift from the disapproved behavior to a new positive thought (the activity Timothy is to pursue), by means of the imperative (σπούδασον; "you pursue"), makes the contrast evident.

20. Gk. σπουδάζω (in this sense, see Gal 2:10; Eph 4:3; 1 Thess 2:17; but see 2 Tim 4:9, 21; Titus 3:12 for the meaning "hurry, hasten"); see Spicq, *TLNT* 3:276-85, esp. 278; G. Harder, *TDNT* 7:559-68.

21. Oberlinner, 94, notes the Pauline parallels and rightly links the interests in this parenesis with the overarching desire to ensure the continuation of the Pauline mission. It is also likely that the example of Paul's own approved service (e.g., 1:12; 2:9-10; 3:10-11;

one will be carefully assessing Timothy's work but also here that he is to pass the test.[22] The second is the language of "presentation" that in ethical passages is sometimes used in the sense of "offering oneself as a sacrifice" (Rom 12:1; Col 1:22) and sometimes in the sense of "presenting someone before a judge" (Rom 6:13; 2 Cor 4:14; Col 1:28).[23] These senses might merge, but in the absence of cultic language, the latter legal sense seems sufficient. Together the presentation and approval language underscores the fact that one is accountable for what one does and that an account must be given (Rom 14:10). It is noteworthy that the presence of God (in this case to judge) is again invoked (cf. v. 14) to inspire personal responsibility ("[you] present yourself") and obedience ("approved"); the casualties depicted in both the near and remote contexts of the letter underline the gravity of the command and raise the specter of a failed test.

The meaning of "approved" (having passed the test) is developed further by the next phrase, "a worker who does not need to be ashamed."[24] The phrase consists of a noun, "worker," and the unusual adjective (lit.) "unashamed." In Paul's letters to churches the association of the term "worker" with the church leader or preacher of the gospel is visible through its sarcastic application, with negative adjectives, to opponents (2 Cor 11:13; Phil 3:2) and through the frequent use of the cognate term "fellow worker."[25] In view of this background, the purely positive use of the term here, then, marks no great step for Paul to take in this letter to a coworker:[26] in 1 Tim 5:18 (see

---

4:7) would come immediately to the reader's mind in reading this command. However, none of these features requires the fictitious distance from the historical Paul that Oberlinner assumes; in fact, the employment here of Pauline features used elsewhere to describe Paul himself, his coworkers, and believers in general identifies the command as being more "typical" than "ideal."

22. Gk. δόκιμος; Rom 16:10; 2 Cor 10:18; see the discussion and references at 1 Tim 3:10 (verb).

23. Gk. παρίστημι. In the case of Col 1:22 (also Eph 5:27), the sacrificial and the legal images have probably merged, as the use of παραστήσωμεν in 1:28 in a judgment scenario suggests (cf. P. T. O'Brien, *Colossians, Philemon* [WBC 44; Waco, TX: Word, 1982], 68-69). Cf. BDAG, s.v.

24. The Gk. phrase ἐργάτην ἀνεπαίσχυντον is either in apposition to the preceding double accusative ("yourself as approved") or related to it as an explanatory predicate ("as an unashamed workman").

25. Gk. συνεργός; in references to church/mission workers see Rom 16:3, 9; 1 Cor 16:16; Phil 4:3; Phlm 1. Perhaps the association of this language with God's work stems from its use to describe the Levites (Gk. ἐργάζομαι, vb.; LXX Num 8:25, 26); see R. Heiligenthal, *EDNT* 2:49.

26. Oberlinner, 94 (see also Heiligenthal, *EDNT* 2:49), argues that the positive usage reflects a non-Pauline tendency, but this fails to see through the irony of the earlier negative uses.

note) the term is loosely associated with the elders by way of the use of the Jesus-tradition (Matt 10:10; Luke 10:7), and the "works" language is applied to gospel and church ministry (2 Tim 2:21; 4:5; 1 Tim 3:1). The adjective "unashamed" occurs only here in the NT but belongs to the "shame" word-group already introduced in 1:8, 12, 16.[27] The point in this passage, however, does not have to do with Timothy's public association with the scandal of the gospel or its representatives, but with the fact that he will stand before God in confidence of receiving approval for having done his job well.

The final phrase of the sentence identifies the specific activity that in this context is to be the criterion of approval before God as an unashamed worker.[28] In short, Paul's concern is for Timothy's teaching. "The word of truth"[29] describes the traditional apostolic gospel. In applying this language to the gospel, Paul categorizes its content, the message about Christ as he preaches it, on the basis of its quality and factualness (2 Cor 6:7; 11:10; Gal 2:5, 14). In these letters to coworkers, the gospel as truth is entrusted to the church (1 Tim 3:15), and conversion is essentially one's understanding and acceptance of the gospel as truth (2:25; 3:7; 1 Tim 2:4; 4:3; Titus 1:1). The polemical intention of this description is apparent from the description of heresy as the rejection of "the truth" (i.e., as falsehood; 4:4; cf. 1 Tim 4:3).

Timothy's responsibility with respect to "the truth" is set out with a seldom-used term that means, literally, "to cut straight."[30] Its history as a metaphor[31] and diversity of application have yielded numerous figurative translations that all take "the word of truth" as the object of the verbal idea: "correctly handle" (TNIV/NIV), "rightly explaining" (NRSV), "keep strictly to" (REB), "rightly dividing" (KJV). As numerous are the interpretations of

27. Gk. ἀνεπαίσχυντος; Josephus, *Antiquities* 18.243; cf. BDAG, s.v.; MM, s.v. See Marshall, 748 (and refs.), for the possibility that the term describes "the workman" as one in whom someone else (God) need not be ashamed.

28. The participial phrase ("correctly handling the word of truth"; built on the accusative ptc. ὀρθοτομοῦντα) is possibly adjectival, further defining Timothy (see TNIV/ NIV), or adverbial, explaining how he is to make a good showing before God (NRSV). There is little real difference between the two possibilities.

29. For Gk. λόγος ("word") see 2:9 (1 Tim 4:5, 6, discussion and notes); Titus 1:3; for Gk. ἀλήθεια ("truth") as a description of the content/quality of this message, see the discussion and notes at 1 Tim 2:4.

30. Gk. ὀρθοτομέω (Prov 3:6; 11:5; see BDAG, s.v.; H. Köster, *TDNT* 8:111-12; Spicq, *TLNT* 2:595; MM 456-57; R. Klöber, *NIDNTT* 3:351-53. The compound is formed of the adjective ὀρθός ("straight") plus τέμνω ("to cut"); for the literal sense of "cutting a road for access through a rough area" (τέμνειν ὁδόν), see, e.g., Josephus, *Against Apion* 1.309.

31. Metaphorical development is traced to Plato, *Laws* 810E, where he employs the concept of "cutting a road" (τετμνημένην ὁδόν; from τέμνω, "to cut") to describe the results of effective speech.

the imagery that might be implied by the metaphor.[32] In the Wisdom literature the metaphor described the effect of wisdom or righteousness as the
"cutting of a (secure) road" for the upright (Prov 3:6; 11:5), and similar metaphors convey the same sense (Ps 106:7; Prov 2:7; 9:15; 16:25; 20:11). But it
is likely that the more graphic element of "cutting" had dissipated, allowing
the remaining emphasis in the prefix "straight" *(ortho)* to reduce the overall
meaning to correct action.[33] In our text, the application of the metaphor to
Timothy's action (not God's or wisdom's) in relation to "the word of truth"
(not to a "road, way") supports the simplification of the metaphor.[34]

But an ambiguity remains. Assuming that "correct action" is called for
on the part of Timothy, is it the action of teaching correctly (accurately) "the
word of truth," or the action of right conduct in conformity with "the word of
truth"? While clearly conduct is a significant topic in these letters to Timothy,
the immediate context is dominated by speech acts[35] and references to Timothy's teaching and the false teaching (vv. 14, 17-18). These factors strongly
suggest that Paul employed the metaphor to underscore the "straightness" of
speech (as opposed to inadequate, arcane, and deceptive formulations; v. 17)
and correctness of meaning (in accordance with the traditional apostolic gospel; cf. v. 18) that were to characterize Timothy's teaching.[36]

32. For the imagery from plowing, see Spicq, 754; Simpson, 137; Calvin suggested that the image of a father distributing food at a meal was in mind; Barrett, the cutting of stones to fit into a building; etc.

33. MM 456-57; Dibelius and Conzelmann, 111 n. 5, draw attention to similar
compound verbs in which a prefixed idea eventually overpowers the meaning "to cut" of
τέμνω. Cf. Köster, *TDNT* 8:112; Spicq, *TLNT* 2:595; Marshall, 748; Fee, 255; Kelly, 183;
Knight, 411-12.

34. See Quinn-Wacker, 676; Marshall, 749.

35. Timothy is to "remind them" (v. 14a); the issue is "word battles" (v. 14b);
community members are described as "hearers" (v. 14d); the message is "the word of
truth" (v. 15c); "godless chatter" (v. 16a) describes their "teaching" (v. 17a), which is
spread by way of "speaking" (v. 18b). Cf. Weiser, 192.

36. With various emphases Weiser, 192; Spicq, *TLNT* 2:595; Marshall, 749;
Oberlinner, 95; Fee, 255; cf. 2 Cor 2:17; 4:2; 2 Pet 3:16. Spicq points further to the use of
ortho- language to describe a criterion of correct speech in ancient rhetoric (λέγειν ὀρθῶς
in Aristotle; ὀρθοέπεια in Plato). For the view that the metaphor emphasizes the alignment of Timothy's ethical conduct with "the word of truth," cf. Köster, *TDNT* 8:111-12;
Mounce, 525; Hasler, 67. Attention is drawn to Paul's use of another *ortho*- compound in
Gal 2:14 (οὐκ ὀρθοποδοῦσιν πρὸς τὴν ἀλήθειαν τοῦ εὐαγγελίου: "they were not acting in
accordance with the truth of the gospel") and to the use of *ortho*- language in Hermas, *Vision* 2.2.6 (ἵνα κατορθώσωνται τὰς ὁδοὺς αὐτῶν ἐν δικαιοσύνῃ: "so that they might direct
their ways in righteousness"). But these verbs are not the same as the one used in 2 Tim
2:15; and the sentence structure is different (note the prep. πρός that determines the relationship between verb and "truth" in Gal 2:14; cf. Weiser, 192); Hermas's statement reflects the shape of the Wisdom theme ("paths of righteousness"), unlike 2 Tim 2:15.

16a   The third of the imperatives in this first sequence returns to the negative side of exhortation as it contrasts the manner of teaching just mentioned with a methodology that Timothy must avoid. This repeats the thought of the first prohibition ("quarreling about words," v. 14), but the repetition is not gratuitous, for Paul will go on to fill in the general descriptions of the results of this kind of foolishness given in v. 14 with specific details of results in Ephesus.[37] The language and structure of the argument parallel the closing charge to Timothy in 1 Tim 6:20-21.[38] "Godless chatter" reproduces the disparagement of false doctrines in 1 Tim 4:7 and especially 6:20 in terms of the futile debating of the opponents and the content that such debates produced. The command "to avoid" such debates is one of several synonymous commands given to the coworkers in these letters to coworkers (2:23; 1 Tim 6:20; Titus 3:9).[39] Although through repeated polemical use language such as "godless" may lose some of its meaning, the sense of "profane" or "secular," that is, "distant from and foreign to (and even "in opposition to") God," should be retained in this discussion of false doctrine and the manner in which it is dispensed.[40] The point is that the heretical nonsense threatens to bring the teaching of the church down to the level of base human teaching.

16b-17a   Paul now makes the transition to material that supports the commands. The basic reason (*gar;* "for") he provides is that with their methods and doctrines, the opponents[41] become increasingly depraved. But in developing the reason, he divides the problem into two parts. He first considers the effects of heresy on the teachers themselves (v. 16b). By their involvement in the so-called godless chatter,[42] the false teachers "become more and more ungodly" (lit. "make progress in ungodliness").[43]

Irony and contrast serve to strengthen the force of this reason. On the

37. Marshall, 750.

38. See the note there; Towner, *Goal,* 30-31.

39. Gk. περιΐστημι (pres. impv.; in the middle voice "to avoid"; Titus 3:9); in this sense of avoiding/shunning teaching, philosophy, sin, etc. see Josephus, *Jewish War* 2.135; *Antiquities* 1.45; 4.151; 10.210. See MM, s.v.; Quinn, 235.

40. See the discussion at 1 Tim 1:9.

41. The plural pronoun in v. 17a ("their"), in reference to specific false teachers about to be named, suggests that the opponents (not people in general, as NRSV implies) are now in view.

42. The instrumentality of the false teaching, implied from v. 16a, can be expressed in various ways (cf. TNIV, "those who indulge in it," and the reordering of thoughts in NRSV: "it will lead people into more and more ungodliness").

43. The plural subject of the third-person plural verb, "make progress," "they," is indicated by reference to the plural pronoun ("their") in the second half of the sentence (v. 17a), which must be plural but is not expressed; the reference to the false teaching in v. 16a is plural, which leads to the translation in the NRSV, "for it will lead people into more and more impiety."

one hand, the concept of "progress" employed in this verse (3:9, 13), here emphasized with the addition of the prepositional phrase "more and more,"[44] was frequently associated with moral and spiritual growth.[45] Here Paul turns the concept into sharp irony to denounce the teaching and methods (and perhaps the claims to godliness) of the opponents as "progress" in ungodliness (see also 3:13).[46]

On the other hand, by describing the effect of this heresy as "ungodliness" *(asebeia)*,[47] Paul places it at the opposite end of the spectrum from the product of the apostolic teaching, which is "godliness" *(eusebeia)*.[48] The reason why Timothy must avoid the disputations of the false teachers is clear: involvement leads progressively and inexorably away from God toward destruction.

Verse 17a, further grounding the command, explains the second part of the problem as the dangerous spread of the teaching, which will continue unabated if the arguments are not stopped. Here the focus changes slightly from the behavior of the false teachers to the effects of their doctrines.[49] Paul again employs contrast to locate the false teaching on a qualitative continuum. While in v. 15 the apostolic gospel was called "the word of truth," here the false teaching is called merely "their word,"[50] a verbal blow directed at its poor quality.

Medical imagery, so typical of this kind of discourse,[51] and a favorite device in these letters to coworkers,[52] delivers the *coup de grâce* as it spells

44. For ἐπὶ πλεῖον ("more and more"), see also 3:9; Acts 4:17; 20:9; 24:4. Cf. 3:13, ἐπὶ χεῖρον.

45. Gk. προσκόπτω (3:9, 13; Luke 2:52; Gal 1:14) see the cognate noun in 1 Tim 4:15 (noun; see discussion and note); Phil 1:25; for the concept in the Wisdom context, see Sir 5:17. For secular use of the concept, see Seneca, *Epistle* (in A. J. Malherbe, *Moral Exhortation: A Greco-Roman Sourcebook* [Philadelphia: Westminster, 1986], 43-46, with discussion). See further Spicq, *TLNT* 3:185-88; G. Stählin, *TDNT* 6:703-19; W. Schenk, *EDNT* 3:157-58; Lips, *Glaube*, 163-65. For the neutral idiom, see Rom 13:12.

46. The ironic use of the concept was already well known; Josephus, *Antiquities* 4.59; *Testament of Judah* 21.8.

47. "Impiety" (NRSV); Titus 2:12; see the discussion and notes at 1 Tim 1:9; 2:2 (Excursus).

48. See 3:5; see 1 Tim 2:2 (Excursus); cf. the similar contrast in 1 Tim 4:7-8.

49. The sentence concludes with v. 17a, which is an independent clause that stands parallel to v. 16b, coordinated by the conjunction καί.

50. Cf. τὸν λόγον ἀληθείας (v. 15) and ὁ λόγος αὐτῶν (v. 17a). Cf. Oberlinner, 96. On the use of λόγος in general for "message, teaching," see 1 Tim 4:5, 6 (discussion).

51. See the discussion in A. J. Malherbe, "Medical Imagery in the Pastorals," in W. E. March, ed., *Texts and Testaments* (San Antonio, TX: Trinity University Press, 1980), 19-35; Johnson, 385-86.

52. For "healthy teaching" (from the verb ὑγιαίνω) see 1 Tim 1:10 (discussion and

out graphically the danger inherent in this substandard teaching. The TNIV translation, "will spread like gangrene," catches the force of the idiom well.[53] "Gangrene" occurs only here in the biblical writings; it may depict a variety of diseases or infections characterized by spreading.[54] Applied to the opponents' false doctrine, it warns of the dangerous way it spreads spiritual sickness. While the metaphor should not be pressed too far, the harmful effects of the false teaching and the virulent danger it poses to the church are underscored to convince Timothy to bring the discussions of false doctrine to an end. Consequently, in support of his argument against the opponents and their methods Paul links the growth of ungodliness (in their behavior?) and the spread of spiritual sickness in the community to their teaching.

17b-18 In this single sentence in the Greek text,[55] two false teachers and the specific teaching they advanced are submitted to illustrate the truth of the premise just laid down. Out of the party implied by the general pronoun noted above ("*their* teaching," v. 17a), two examples are drawn,[56] "Hymenaeus and Philetus" (v. 17b). The name "Hymenaeus" is known from 1 Tim 1:20 (see discussion and note), where, along with an "Alexander" (cf. 4:14), one so named is described as having been put out of the church for his active involvement in the heretical movement. If the same person is in mind, as we should probably assume, then it seems clear that the measures taken to discipline him were unsuccessful. "Philetus" occurs only here in the NT;[57] the fact that the name is used suggests that he had the status of a leader and that Timothy knew him.

With language that nearly replicates 1 Tim 6:20 (see discussion and note), these characters are described in the next clause as having "departed from the truth" (v. 18a). The verb, which originally meant "to miss the

---

notes); 2 Tim 4:3; Titus 1:9; 2:1. For use of the language in reference to lifestyle related to the apostolic gospel, see 1 Tim 6:3; 2 Tim 1:13; Titus 1:13; 2:2, 8.

53. The future of ἔχω ("to have"), which here implies inevitability, functions together with the noun νομή (originally meaning "pasture" [John 10:9], but used figuratively in medical contexts with appropriate verbs for the spreading of disease [see refs. in BDAG, s.v.; Marshall, 751]) to depict the idea of a spreading disease.

54. Gk. γάγγραινα; used widely as a medical term (BDAG, s.v.); metaphorical, as here in Plutarch, *Moralia* 65D; see Spicq, 749; Weiser, 194.

55. The versification is rough. The decision to end v. 17 and begin v. 18 immediately after the reference to Philetus in the middle of a sentence is puzzling. For different translation strategies, cf. NRSV (which reflects well the syntax of the Greek, except that it makes v. 18c, the last clause of the original sentence, into a separate sentence) and TNIV.

56. The genitive plural relative pronoun ὧν with ἐστιν (followed by people named) makes the connection backward and isolates the examples (as also in 1:15 and in 1 Tim 1:20; the combination does not occur elsewhere in the NT).

57. Gk. Φίλητος. The name is attested in the first century; see BDAG; MM; Marshall, 751 n. 23.

mark," can convey ideas ranging from renunciation to denial to going astray.[58] In this case, where a standard of some sort is clearly set out in the phrase "from the truth,"[59] the sense of "deviation from" the standard is specifically meant,[60] although figurative translations that express this deviation in terms of "wandering or swerving" (e.g., from the normal course) are acceptable. The point is that these two men departed from a well-known, standard tradition.

In the following participial phrase (v. 18b), their divergence from the truth is traced to or summed up in one particular error. That error was specifically teaching that the resurrection had already occurred.[61] Although Paul's way of summing up the problem in this one doctrine suggests that it was central to the heresy,[62] there is little in the letter from which to explain it. We must work on the basis of analogy and parallels, but we begin with the immediate context. First, we may assume that the reference is to the resurrection of believers.[63] This topic was already broached at 2:11, which locates the promise of resurrection in the eschatological future and which, as noted, may well have anticipated this discussion of the deviant view. Within the broader passage Paul affirms as central to his gospel the resurrection of Jesus Christ (vv. 8, 11) and the promise (as yet unfulfilled) of the believer's resurrection (v. 11). Consequently, the false view apparently involved a turning ahead of the traditional eschatological clock, so that in some way it could be claimed that believers had already experienced resurrection; the language distinguishes this view from a basic denial of a bodily resurrection.[64]

---

58. For Gk. ἀστοχέω, see the discussion at 1 Tim 1:6; 6:21. Thus the various translations: "departed from" (TNIV); "wandered away from" (NIV); "swerved from" (NRSV).

59. I.e., "the gospel," v. 15; the discussion at 1 Tim 2:4.

60. Cf. Plutarch, *Moralia* 705C. The standard is expressed with the preposition περί ("with regard to"; Moule, *Idiom Book,* 62) and an object, e.g., "the truth" or "the faith" (1 Tim 6:21). In the case of the participle in 1 Tim 1:6, the implied standard is laid down in v. 5. See also Knight, 413-14.

61. The TNIV/NIV translation, "they say . . . ," is too weak; the verb λέγω (here in participial form), followed by the accusative and infinitive (τὴν ἀνάστασιν ἤδη γεγονέναι; cf. Matt 22:23; Mark 12:18; Luke 20:41; Rom 15:8), means "teach." Cf. NRSV, "claiming."

62. Cf. Oberlinner, 98.

63. Gk. ἀνάστασις; used by Paul of the future hope of believers in 1 Cor 15:12, 13, 21, 42; or of Christ's resurrection in Rom 1:4; Phil 3:10. Rom 6:5 also refers to Christ's resurrection but links believers closely to it by means of the promise of sharing in it. Cf. A. Oepke, *TDNT* 1:371-72.

64. Such as the Sadducees maintained (Matt 22:23; Acts 23:8). Spicq's suggestion (757-58) that the false teachers "allegorized" the traditional view of the bodily resurrection in some way to appease Greek sensibilities (belief in immortality of the soul, the irrelevance of physical resurrection) is not in itself impossible, but Paul's description of

2:14-26   ADDRESSING THE CHALLENGE OF OPPOSITION IN THE CHURCH

Attempts to deliver more precision than this move in several directions. (1) Numerous scholars draw on developments in Gnosticism to explain this aspect of the heresy.[65] This view explains that in Gnostic circles the eschatological resurrection would have been reinterpreted as the present reception of divine knowledge *(gnōsis)*. *The Acts of Paul and Thecla* (14) confirms the possibility of such a development: "The resurrection . . . has already taken place; it has come about in the children we have, and knowing the true God we are risen." And other presumably Gnostic teachers deeschatologized the resurrection in other ways. According to Irenaeus, Menander maintained a completely "realized" view of the resurrection: "his disciples obtain the resurrection by being baptized into him [or by him], and can die no more, but never grow old and are immortal."[66] There is also evidence that Pauline teaching was incorporated into the reshaping of the resurrection belief in Gnostic circles, as *The Treatise on the Resurrection* from the Nag Hammadi Library reveals: "Then indeed, as the Apostle said, 'We suffered with him, and we arose with him, and we went to heaven with him.'"[67] The variety in these later sources is evident. On the whole, however, the letters to Timothy lack indications of additional fundamental Gnostic tendencies, which makes Gnosticism an unlikely source for this teaching in the first century.

(2) Jesus' teaching about resurrection (Mark 12:25) and recollections of his postresurrection appearances (and eating habits) are sometimes held to explain the view of the resurrection reflected in this text (and current in Ephesus). On this view, some believers apparently held that Jesus' resurrection catapulted the church into the age to come, which required food restrictions and celibacy (see on 1 Tim 4:1-3) to follow the patterns suggested by Jesus' teaching and behavior. However, while patterns drawn from the postresurrection appearances and Jesus' teaching about marriage in the resurrection might be attractive to a group that believed itself already to be raised, the Jesus-tradition alone seems to lack the essential catalyst: some interpretation of Pauline baptismal teaching (as in later Gnosticism) is a more likely inducement of the claim that the eschatological resurrection itself has already occurred. Thus, other analogies should be considered.

---

the view in 2:18 seems an odd way to accomplish this. For other denials of the resurrection, see Polycarp, *Philippians* 7.1; *2 Clement* 9.1.

65. Oberlinner, 98; Brox, 246; Rudolph, *Gnosis,* 189-90. See Weiser, 210-25, who argues that 2:18 reflects a gnosticizing development more radical than the earlier enthusiasm evident in 1 Corinthians 15 and somewhere on the spectrum between the realized eschatology of Ephesians/Colossians and the extreme developments in the second-century Gnostic systems.

66. Irenaeus, *Against Heresies* 1.23.5.

67. J. M. Robinson (ed.), *The Nag Hammadi Library in English* (Leiden: Brill, 1977), 51.

(3) Some scholars suggest that the unorthodox view of the resurrection was the result of a reconfiguration (or misunderstanding) of Pauline teaching, and this seems the more promising way to go, particularly in the context of a Pauline community.[68] In this there are two important points of contact with the earlier Paul. First, there may be a connection of some sort between the misunderstanding of the resurrection alluded to in 1 Cor 15:12-58 and 2 Tim 2:18. The argument is that the Spirit-enthusiasm in Corinth led to the belief that the End had arrived in a much fuller sense than Paul ever meant to teach. Evidence of this "overrealized" eschatology is spread throughout the letter (1 Cor 4:8) and includes the resurrection misunderstanding alluded to in 1 Corinthians 15 — which is not a Greek denial of bodily resurrection but rather something more like the radicalization of Pauline baptismal teaching through which it could be said that in one sense the community had been "raised with Christ": it seems likely that in Corinth possession of the Spirit (as evidenced in various charismatic activities) became the sign that the eschatological resurrection had taken place, making hope in a future resurrection obsolete.[69]

The second broad Pauline touchstone is the stream of teaching in which he linked baptism with a present (preliminary or anticipatory) participation in Christ's resurrection (Rom 6:3-8; Eph 2:5; Col 2:12); indeed, this may well have figured in creative developments in Corinthian theology. The line Paul drew between present and future realization in this teaching was very fine, and though Paul clearly maintained the tension between the "already" and "not yet" of salvation, it is easy to imagine that in Corinth, with its dramatic experiences of the Spirit, that line could have been crossed. Confusion of the times was apparently not confined to Corinth, as problems addressed in 1 and 2 Thessalonians (e.g., 2 Thess 2:2) confirm. Moreover, Paul may have sought to adjust a too-realized view of the resurrection in Phil 3:10-12.[70] The bearing of all this on 2 Tim 2:18 is that in Corinth and Philippi there had already occurred analogous reinterpretations of the resurrection characterized by the removal of the eschatological or apocalyptic elements but without indication of influence from Gnosticism.

In the present passage, the likelihood that Paul's own baptismal/resurrection teaching had been misunderstood or misused is strengthened by the focus on Jesus' resurrection in Paul's recitation of his gospel (2:8) and his strong affirmation of the futurity of the believer's resurrection promise in the

68. For further details and proponents, see Towner, *Goal,* 29-36; idem, "Gnosis and Realized Eschatology in Ephesus," *JSNT* 31 (1987): 95-124. See also Schlarb, *Die gesunde Lehre,* 97-110.

69. See A. C. Thiselton, "Realized Eschatology at Corinth," *NTS* 24 (1978), 510-26.

70. See P. T. O'Brien, *Commentary on Philippians* (NIGTC; Grand Rapids: Eerdmans, 1991), 413-14.

slightly adjusted language of Romans 6 (2:11). In fact, his thrust in the preceding passage, when connected with this passage, strongly suggests that he sought to reinvest the doctrine of the resurrection of believers with its full eschatological force — to reset the clock in this community's thinking about resurrection. Thus, one way or another, the opponents had come to believe that the eschatological resurrection of believers had already occurred, and they had popularized this view. It seems quite likely that the ascetic tendencies that were current in Ephesus reflect the attempt to reconcile the conviction that salvation was fully realized with the temporal realities that continued to impinge on life in this world (see on 1 Tim 4:3).

The implication of such a teaching for the average believer would have been that the resurrection hope was completely spiritualized into some presently attainable mode of living. In essence, however, it meant the deflation of hope in a substantial resurrection, and meant that salvation became a totally spiritual (as opposed to material) affair. In any case, it marked a confusion of the relation of this temporal stressful existence and future perfection in salvation. For those in the community who could not quite see through the present curtain of distress to the traditional Pauline hope of resurrection, the doctrine of present resurrection offered a compelling substitute, but at the cost of the disruption to their faith.

This is the concern Paul expresses in the final clause of the sentence (v. 18c): "and[71] they destroy the faith of some." The verb certainly has serious disturbance, upset, and (potential) ruination of the belief of Christians in mind,[72] though it is perhaps more remediable than the TNIV's "destroy" would allow. In any case, Paul's language indicates that the situation is extremely serious (as also in Titus 1:11).

19 This observation poses a dilemma for the reader (Timothy first) that has actually been in the making since Paul's paradoxical contrasting of his trials with the unbound "word of God" in 2:9. The tension has been maintained by the positive/negative contrasting of Timothy and the false teachers, and their respective messages: "the word of truth" (v. 15 = "the word of God," v. 9) versus "their word" (v. 17). The strong affirmation of the power of God's word and the contrast technique employed to this point lead to the statement of the danger of the heresy for believers, and to the dilemma: If this danger exists in the church of God, how can the church continue to exist? In the two images that follow, Paul addresses the theological antinomies magni-

---

71. For the use of the conjunction καί ("and") to introduce a result (as in 2 Cor 11:9; 1 John 3:19), see BDAG, s.v. 1.b.ζ.

72. Gk. ἀνατρέπω (Titus 1:11; John 2:15; also of the upsetting of "faith/trust" in Diodorus Siculus 1.77.2); BDAG, s.v. For πίστις (with the art.) for personal faith, see the note at 1 Tim 1:2.

fied by the present stressful situation, not by resolving the tension, but instead by affirming the Lord's control within the situation along with the believer's responsibility to respond positively to that control.

In v. 19a Paul contrasts ("nevertheless") the disruption caused by the heretics with the picture of a strong edifice constructed by God. The architectural term used here, "foundation," reinforced by the adjective ("firm"), has various meanings elsewhere in the NT.[73] Paul applied the term metaphorically in combination with other images in discussions of the formation of the church: in 1 Cor 3:10-13 Christ crucified is the "foundation"; in Eph 2:20, Christ is the cornerstone and the apostles and prophets the "foundation." The term in this passage is left unspecified, which has generated several interpretations of "the foundation."[74] However, the orientation of the other Pauline uses[75] and the parallel architectural description of the church in 1 Tim 3:15 (see discussion and notes) suggest that the reference here is to the church or the people of God.[76] Just as the term could refer to a part of the foundation, the whole foundation, or even to the building,[77] here in figurative usage the language of the part, denoting stability and strengthened by the adjective ("firm"), comes to represent the whole edifice built upon it.

In the *themelios* imagery an echo of Isa 28:16 is probable:

2 Tim 2:19a: "Nevertheless, God's solid foundation *(themelios)* stands firm";

Isa 28:16 (LXX): Therefore thus says the Lord, "Behold, I lay for the foundations *(themelia)* of Zion a costly stone, a choice [stone], a corner-stone, a precious stone, for its foundations *(themelia);* and he that believes on him shall by no means be ashamed."[78]

---

73. Gk. θεμέλιος; for its figurative use see Rom 15:20; 1 Cor 3:10, 11, 12; Eph 2:20; 1 Tim 6:19; Heb 6:1; see W. Grundmann, *TDNT* 7:636-53. For the Gk. adjective στερεός ("firm, solid, steadfast"), see Heb 5:12, 14; 1 Pet 5:9; G. Bertram, *TDNT* 7:609-14.

74. (1) A reference to Christ, by way of the early church's interpretation of Isa 28:16 (Hanson, 137); (2) Christ and his apostles, by way of earlier Pauline use (Lock, 100); (3) the true faith that the church must guard (Gärtner, *The Temple and the Community in Qumran and the New Testament,* 71); (4) a general reference to the certainty of God's eschatological triumph, which might include the church (Fee, 257; Guthrie, 150; cf. Bassler, 153).

75. See the discussion in Johnson, 396-98, of the way in which Paul combines metaphors (household, foundation, temple) in 1 Cor 3:9–4:2; metaphors also overlap in Eph 2:19-21.

76. See Towner, *Goal,* 132; Marshall, 755-56; Brox, 249; Dibelius and Conzelmann, 112-13; Johnson, 396; Bassler, 153 (probably). For the possibility that the church of Ephesus is specifically in mind, see Kelly, 186.

77. Marshall, 755; BDAG, s.v.

78. LXX Isa 28:16: διὰ τοῦτο οὕτως λέγει κύριος, Ἰδοὺ ἐγὼ ἐμβαλῶ εἰς τὰ θεμέλια

In the early church, this OT text became an important OT christo-logical testimony (Rom 9:33; 1 Pet 2:6). Its application here as an eccle-siological testimony appears at first to be a departure from the christological trend, but it is rather an adaptation of it. Paul responds to the turbulent situation facing Timothy by drawing on the part of the well-known OT statement that emphasizes the certainty of God's acts, and applies it to the stability of the church.[79] Yet, as the context suggests (2:8, 11), it is precisely the truth of the resurrection of Jesus Christ that anchors this "foundation" and that can stabilize the tottering "faith of some" (v. 18); and the application of the Isaiah text elsewhere allows its fainter christological echo here to be heard. The reference to Isa 26:13 in the next part of the verse (see below) strengthens the likelihood that this echo of the Isaiah *themelios* text is intentional, however light.[80]

In demonstration of the truth of the statement just made, Paul extends the architectural imagery further by inviting Timothy to imagine a "seal" authenticating the foundation (v. 19b). Seals were used commonly to identify legal ownership of property and, like signatures in modern practice, to guarantee authenticity, genuineness, and integrity or to preserve the secrecy of the contents of a letter or of some product.[81] From the actual custom of placing a seal on something for these purposes (with a signet ring, cylinder seal, or carved stone) there developed the figurative use of the concept. In the NT both the literal (e.g., Matt 27:66; Rev 5:1; etc.) and figurative uses are evident: Paul speaks of the Corinthian believers as his "seal" of authentic apostleship (1 Cor 9:2) and of the Spirit as the "seal" of God's ownership of the believer (verb; 2 Cor 1:22). From ecclesiological contexts such as 2 Cor 1:22; Eph 1:13; 4:30 some suggest that "sealing" is water baptism through which God's ownership was professed and the Spirit conferred,[82] but this is debatable and the linkage between the belief in the gift of God's Spirit to believers and the rite of water baptism remains unclear.[83] In any case, the emphasis is on that which the metaphor of sealing denotes, namely, ownership

---

["foundations"] Σιων λίθον πολυτελῆ ἐκλεκτὸν ἀκρογωνιαῖον ἔντιμον εἰς τὰ θεμέλια ["foundations"] αὐτῆς, καὶ ὁ πιστεύων ἐπ' αὐτῷ οὐ μὴ καταισχυνθῇ.

79. Note that the perfect tense verb ἕστηκεν is idiomatic for "stands firm" (see BDAG, s.v. C.4; cf. Rom 11:20; 1 Cor 7:37; 10:12), which further emphasizes the thought of immovability in the building imagery.

80. See P. H. Towner, "The Use of the Old Testament in the Letters to Timothy and Titus," in Beale and Carson, eds., *Commentary on the Use of the Old Testament in the New Testament;* cf. the discussion in Gärtner, *The Temple and the Community in Qumran and the New Testament,* 71.

81. Gk. σφραγίς; T. Schramm, *EDNT* 3:316-17; G. Fitzer, *TDNT* 7:939-43.

82. Schramm, *EDNT* 3:316.

83. On the whole matter, see Fee, *God's Empowering Presence,* 292-96.

and authenticity. Similarly, in the present passage "seal" is used in a figurative sense to denote God's ownership of "the foundation" (= the church) just mentioned. The metaphor functions flexibly here (for "sealing" did not usually pertain to stones),[84] calling to mind a mark or inscription in the stone of the foundation that identifies the builder. Since the introduction of the imagery into this discourse is meant to assure Timothy of the permanence of God's church despite the presence in it of false teachers and their followers, it is rather difficult to bring baptism into the thought of "sealing."[85]

The content of the "seal" follows in two statements constructed of traditional biblical materials. These statements in effect bring together theology in what is affirmed and ethics in the response Timothy (and others) is called to make in the crisis situation. The first statement is:

> 2 Tim 2:19c: "the Lord knows those who are his" *(egnō kyrios tous ontas autou)*.

This repeats the LXX wording of one part of Num 16:5, making only one change from "God" *(ho theos)* to "Lord" *(kyrios)*:[86]

> Num 16:5: "And he spoke to Korah and all his assembly, saying, 'God has visited and known those who are his *(egnō ho theos tous ontas autou)* and who are holy, and has brought them to himself; and whom he has chosen for himself, he has brought to himself.'"

The reason for that change is debated.[87] But with the "stone Christology" already latent in the discourse, it seems likely that the shift from *theos* to *kyrios* reflects another case in which an OT feature linked with YHWH is transferred by Paul to Christ (cf. Titus 2:14).[88] The anarthrous *kyrios* (frequent in

---

84. Marshall, 756; see also Bassler, 153.

85. But see Hanson, 137; Bassler, 153 (who speaks of a baptismal setting for the saying); cf. Oberlinner, 102. Rightly Marshall, 756; Schramm, *EDNT* 3:317.

86. 2 Tim 2:19b: ἔγνω κύριος τοὺς ὄντας αὐτοῦ; Num 16:5: καὶ ἔγνω ὁ θεὸς τοὺς ὄντας αὐτοῦ.

87. See Dibelius and Conzelmann, 112, for the view that the author knows the text from a Christian recasting of the material (Bassler, 153, suggests a baptismal liturgy). Liturgical transformation of this sort might explain the shift from ὁ θεός to κύριος (in reference to Christ?) in the NT adaptation of the OT material.

88. The Hebrew of Num 16:5 has the tetragrammaton, יהוה (YHWH), which, though normally translated in the LXX with κύριος ("Lord"), is in this case translated ὁ θεός (God). Knowledge of the Hebrew behind the Greek may have led Paul to insert the more normal translation in the citing of the OT material, and so prepare for the christological transference.

the LXX and typical in Numbers) that occurs here is best explained as conforming to the LXX pattern.[89]

Both the OT context and the present context must be compared to appreciate the full weight of the citation's claim that "the Lord knows those who are his." In both cases authority is disputed. Then there is the issue of loyalty — to God in the OT context and to Christ in the present setting (vv. 9-13), and to their appointed servants. The situation in Numbers 16 is one of dispute and confrontation: Moses and Aaron, leaders chosen by God, had been challenged by Korah and his companions (Levites to whom the privilege of the priesthood had not been given), who demanded the right to serve God as priests in the community. In response, Moses declared that God knows those who truly belong to him, meaning the people God had chosen, and that he would make it known. Korah presented a challenge to Moses' and Aaron's authority, and in so doing rebelled against God; God confirmed his choice of Moses and Aaron by the destruction of Korah and all who sided with him.

The reader familiar with the OT background is compelled to view the present situation in a similar light: characters such as Hymenaeus and Philetus with their false teaching present the apostolic ministry with a leadership challenge. So, the points of contact are apparent. But how much of the paradigm is to be brought across to the situation in Ephesus? The result of the OT story was the dramatic destruction of the rebels; it is not hard to see how the story accessed by the citation might function as a warning in the way that the wilderness allusions in 1 Corinthians 10 did for the Corinthian community. The statement of Moses quoted here was a statement of vindication, and pointed forward to judgment. Because God distinguishes, one must ensure one's proper alignment with him. Positively, for Timothy and other readers the force of the citation comes in the reminder that the Lord knows his people personally[90] and will distinguish between true and false followers and preserve the community of faith formed around him. Finally, the OT story serves as a paradigm that acknowledges the rebellion of some within the community and the Lord's continued presence within it; but the statement is both a consolation and a warning. Christ is present as a protector and redeemer but also as a judge who will vindicate his truth and his people. The parenetic force of this reminder for Timothy (cf. 1:6-8) should not be missed.

89. It is doubtful whether the presence or absence of the definite article with κύριος is a valid criterion for determining a reference to Christ or God. Κύριος without the definite article is frequent in the LXX and typical in Numbers. See further the discussion and note at 1:18; 2:24.

90. Gk. γινώσκω; of God's personal knowledge and intimate relationship with his people (see 1 Cor 8:1-3); see W. Schmithals, *EDNT* 1:249; R. Bultmann, *TDNT* 1:706.

The second segment of OT materials (2:19d) serves a function similar to that of 1 Cor 10:14, which follows the OT story there with the admonition to "flee from idolatry." Here the next OT citation completes the content of the "seal":

> 2 Tim 2:19d: "Everyone who confesses the name of the Lord must turn away from wickedness" *(apostētō apo adikias pas ho onomazōn to onoma kyriou).*

Echoes of several OT texts are possible in this statement, and they must be traced as we decide its thrust.

First, "to confess [name] the name of the Lord" is an idiom occurring in the LXX on several occasions.[91] Although presumably the basic sense was to make entreaty to the Lord (more typically expressed with "call upon [the name of] the Lord"; cf. Rom 10:13), it denotes acknowledging the name of YHWH (Isa 26:13) or mentioning the name as if to summon him (Amos 6:10),[92] and in one case it is used to describe blaspheming the Lord (Lev 24:16).[93]

This variety of usage leads to two suggested sources of the phrase cited here. Most regard the reference as an echo of Isa 26:13, where a positive acknowledgment of God is implied:

> Isa 26:13: "O Lord our God, take possession of us: O Lord, we know no other beside you: we name your name" *(to onoma sou onomazomen).*[94]

In this case, the statement, extending the thought of the previous line, calls on the faithful to keep themselves separate from evil and so show their allegiance to God. If, however, "naming the name" intends an echo of Lev 24:16

91. Gk. ὀνομάζω ("to call a name, name"); Gk. ὄνομα ("name, proper name"; 1 Tim 6:1, discussion); here in participial form (ὁ ὀνομάζων τὸ ὄνομα κυρίου); in various forms elsewhere: Lev 24:11, 16(2x); Josh 23:7; Isa 26:13; Amos 6:10; *Odes of Solomon* 5.13 (echoing Isa 26:13); Sir 23:9-10. The more normal phraseology comes to be "to call upon the name of the Lord" (with a form of καλέω or ἐπικαλέω; e.g., Joel 3:5 = Acts 2:21/Rom 10:13/1 Cor 1:2; cf. 2 Tim 2:22); see H. Bietenhard, *TDNT* 5:263.

92. Amos 6:10: "Be silent, that you do not name the name of the Lord" (σίγα ἕνεκα τοῦ μὴ ὀνομάσαι τὸ ὄνομα κυρίου).

93. Lev 24:16: "And he that names the name of the Lord, let him die the death" (ὀνομάζων δὲ τὸ ὄνομα κυρίου θανάτῳ θανατούσθω). But the phrase acquires this negative meaning from 24:11, where naming the Name is accompanied by "cursing": "And the son of the Israelite woman named the Name and cursed" (καὶ ἐπονομάσας ὁ υἱὸς τῆς γυναικὸς τῆς Ισραηλίτιδος τὸ ὄνομα κατηράσατο).

94. LXX Isa 26:13: κύριε ὁ θεὸς ἡμῶν, κτῆσαι ἡμᾶς· κύριε, ἐκτὸς σοῦ ἄλλον οὐκ οἴδαμεν τὸ ὄνομά σου ὀνομάζομεν.

(11), where the phrase is descriptive of blasphemy, the reference would be to the false teachers in the community, who are then to heed the warning of v. 19d and repent before judgment is executed:

> Lev 24:16: "And he that names the name of the Lord, let him die the death" *(onomazōn de to onoma kyriou thanatǭ thanatousthō).*[95]

While the presence of false teachers in the community makes contact with the Leviticus text tempting,[96] an echo of Isa 26:13, where a positive acknowledgment of God is implied, is more likely. That acknowledgment signifies covenant membership. Only here, as in Rom 10:9-13 and 1 Cor 1:2, Christ the Lord has replaced YHWH as the object of confession and the determiner of covenant membership. The renewed contact made with the story in Numbers 16 at its point of climax (see below) strengthens this positive connection. It occurs where the people are instructed to choose sides. The command added to the "naming" text in 2 Tim 2:19d is:

> "turn away from wickedness" *(apostētō apo adikias).*[97]

This command in itself recalls several similar LXX texts, but due to the choice of *adikias* ("wickedness") over *anomian* ("lawlessness") it might seem at first glance closest in form to the citation of Ps 6:9 preserved in Luke 13:27. Three differences from our text are to be noted: (1) Ps 6:9 (Luke 13:27) addresses the command to evildoers; (2) the speaker (David; in Luke it is Jesus describing eschatological judgment) is concerned to be separated from them; and (3) both Luke and 2 Timothy employ *adikias* instead of *anomian:*

> Ps 6:9: "Depart from me, all you who do lawlessness" *(apostēte ap' emou, pantes hoi ergazomenoi tēn anomian);*[98]
>
> Luke 13:27: "Depart from me, all you workers of injustice" *(apostēte ap' emou, pantes ergatai adikias);*[99]
>
> 2 Tim 2:19d: "turn away from wickedness" *(apostētō apo adikias).*[100]

However that lexical choice is to be explained, the main difference is one of perspective. The personal perspective adopted in Ps 6:9 ("turn away

---

95. ὀνομάζων δὲ τὸ ὄνομα κυρίου θανάτῳ θανατούσθω.

96. For this view (and refs.), see Marshall, 758.

97. For Gk. αφίστημι, see 1 Tim 4:1 (note). For the phrase ἀποστήτω ἀπὸ ἀδικίας, cf. the LXX texts Pss 6:9; 33:15; Prov 3:7; Isa 52:11; Sir 17:26.

98. ἀπόστητε ἀπ᾽ ἐμοῦ, πάντες οἱ ἐργαζόμενοι τὴν ἀνομίαν.

99. ἀποστήτε ἀπ᾽ ἐμοῦ, πάντες ἐργάται ἀδικίας.

100. ἀποστήτω ἀπὸ ἀδικίας.

from ME"; "YOU who do lawlessness"; also Luke 13:27) equates "separation" with judgment. The perspective adopted in 2 Timothy, however, compares more closely with that of Ps 33:15; Prov 3:7; and Sir 17:26, which equate "separation" with purity and a return to the Lord, so that "separation" from "wickedness" preserves the Lord's people from judgment:

> Sir 17:26: "Return to the Most High and turn away from wickedness" (*apostrephe apo adikias*).[101]

The sharp focus on God's people, and indeed on their identity as God's people, as well as on their preservation, is produced by the allusion to Isa 26:13 and the image of "naming the Name." The command of separation, although paralleled in various OT texts, is without a precise textual match. But bearing in mind the essential matter of perspective, the climactic command at the end of the story in Numbers (which would have been well known), which orders the people to separate from the rebels, does provide both the thematic (perspective) and verbal contact point (in the verb "turn away").[102] Num 16:26-27 reports the visit of Moses and the elders of Israel, at the Lord's command, to Dathan and Abiram, companions of Korah, to urge the people to get away from the rebels before judgment:

> "He said to the congregation, 'Separate yourselves *(aposchisthēte)* from the tents of these wicked men, and touch nothing of theirs, or you will be swept away for all their sins.' So they *got away (apestēsan)* from the dwellings of Korah, Dathan, and Abiram; and Dathan and Abiram came out and stood at the entrance of their tents, together with their wives, their children, and their little ones."

This concern — for the people of God to demonstrate their purity — exactly parallels Paul's concern in the seal-response portion of 2:19c-d. The initial allusion to Num 16:5 draws Timothy into that dramatic OT story of identity where the specter of impending judgment has been raised. The two situations are sufficiently close, and the Korah story was well enough known in Judaism and the early church.[103] The parallels are obvious: challengers to

---

101. Despite the different verb: ἐπάναγε ἐπὶ ὕψιστον καὶ ἀπόστρεφε ἀπὸ ἀδικίας; Ps 33:15: "Turn away from evil and do good"; Prov 3:7: "fear God and turn away from evil."

102. Cf. ἀποστήτω (aor. impv.; 2 Tim 2:19d) and ἀπέστησαν (aor. act.; Num 16:27).

103. In Judaism the story was applied to enforce proper recognition of authority (e.g., 4Q423, frag. 5; Sir 45:18-19); in the early church it provided a template for rebellious heretics (Jude 11).

God's/the Lord's representatives (Moses/Paul) have been named, and the people must choose sides, thereby establishing their identity. Consequently, the verbal contact in "turn away"/"depart from" should be taken seriously as an echo of the Korah story's climax: the OT story provides a narrative illustration of the concept of "wickedness" *(adikia)* and the narrative source that gives meaning to the command in v. 19d.

Thus following from the warning that supplies the first part of the "seal," the second citation calls Timothy and the faithful of the congregation ("all who name the Name of the Lord") to dissociate themselves completely from the opponents and their teachings *(adikia).* What the rest of the passage confirms, however, is that the fate of the false teachers is not yet fixed, for they too may turn from evil (see below). The general call to separate from evil that occurs throughout the OT is given specific shape in this instance by the intertextual play between the apostasy faced by Timothy (and Timothy's own temptation) and the story of Korah's rebellion in the wilderness. As in the use of wilderness motifs in 1 Corinthians 10, the present passage issues a dire warning by way of Israel's experience of God's wrath. But throughout Paul's churches the christological transfer has been completed, and Christ is the Lord of the church's confession (Rom 10:13; 1 Cor 1:2). The Christ-event and his installation as Lord make it possible for Paul to interact with this OT textual background christologically, and in the process to define covenant identity and purity of faith in relation to Christ. The equal need for the Lord's grace and kindness is not passed over but is left to a later point (v. 25).

20-21   With a shift of metaphor, the need to heed the warning is reinforced. First, the image of the traditional household is introduced as a way of discussing the "mixed" nature of the church (v. 20). But the view expressed in v. 20 is hardly one of resignation, for by extending the metaphor Paul issues a second call to Timothy (and believers; cf. v. 19d) to separate from whatever impurity exists in the church in order to dedicate himself to God (v. 21). Although the images employed in the metaphorical depiction are not particularly complex or abstract, the primary question for interpretation in v. 20 revolves around the implications of the picture and the extent to which the imagery is to be pressed.

While 1 Tim 3:15 drew on the "household" concept *(oikos)* to depict the church as a community in which all members have responsibilities, here the image is of the building *(oikia)* in which the members of the household would dwell.[104] In the present passage, the metaphor of "the foundation" (v. 19) has prepared the way for this metaphor. The adjective "large" (lit.

---

104. Gk. οἰκία. The distinction between οἰκία (i.e., as house) and οἶκος (i.e., as the social household reality) is not hard-and-fast (see P. Weigandt, *EDNT* 2:500-503), but it applies in the use of the terms in 2 Tim 2:20 and 1 Tim 3:15.

"great"; see on 1 Tim 3:16) sets the house in this picture apart from ordinary houses, and the following reference to vessels of gold and silver certainly suggests the house of a wealthy householder. There is little doubt that the house stands for the church,[105] but the description as a whole shows that it is a house that stands for the church, not for the temple.[106]

The real reason for introducing the image of the house is to describe the "articles" within it. Paul does this by explicit contrast ("not only . . . but also . . .")[107] to heighten the distinction already apparent in the materials from which the articles are made. The Greek term for "articles" can describe a range of vessels and other equipment found and used commonly in a house.[108] In the NT, the term occurs in metaphorical passages that compare the human body to "vessels" in various ways.[109] The metaphorical intention is apparent here from the application in v. 21.

First, the household articles are distinguished on the basis of material. Three of the four materials cited (gold, silver, and wood) occur also in 1 Cor 3:12 in a discussion of the church given to architectural imagery and two kinds of building materials that are clearly distinguished (3:14-15). Though the arguments are much different, the overlap in language, the emphasis on the distinction between valuable and common materials, and the judgment setting suggest that Paul here reworks materials he had earlier used in different ways.[110]

In the biblical tradition "gold" especially characterized the splendor of the divine in earthly surroundings (Exod 38:17 LXX; 40:5, 26) and symbolized heaven (Rev 1:12; 5:8; 8:3; 21:15), but it could also serve as a symbol of decadence and greed (Rev 9:20; 17:4); and "gold" and "silver"[111] together could be descriptive of a person's wealth (Acts 3:6; 20:33) and were components of the stereotype by which the wealthy were known (cf. 1 Tim 2:9; Jas 5:3).[112] In this

---

105. So most commentators; see Towner, *Goal,* 134.

106. It is also unlikely that the specific designation "great house" and its plush furnishings are required due to the fact that the house stands for the church (*pace* Oberlinner, 104); the details of the metaphor are required to make the point (rightly Marshall, 759).

107. 4:8; see 1 Tim 5:13 (note).

108. Gk. σκεῦος (cf. Luke 8:16; John 19:29; 2 Cor 4:7; generalizing pl., Mark 3:27; Luke 17:31); see E. Plümacher, *EDNT* 3:250-51; C. Maurer, *TDNT* 7:358-67.

109. Acts 9:15; Rom 9:21-23; 2 Cor 4:7; 1 Thess 4:4; 1 Pet 3:7; cf. Jer 22:28; 28:34 LXX; Sir 27:5.

110. See also Johnson, 396-97.

111. Gk. χρυσοῦς (adj.; "gold, overlaid with gold"; see Rev 1:12, 20; 2:1; etc.); for the cognate noun χρυσίον, see 1 Tim 2:9; Gk. ἀργυροῦς (adj.; "silver"; see Acts 19:24; Rev 9:20).

112. See esp. *The Cynic Epistles* (Malherbe), 234.20.

case, gold and silver articles refer to the various bowls and platters that would decorate the table of the wealthy.

In contrast to these are the articles or implements made of wood and clay.[113] Since such implements were more easily obtained and, in the case of the "clay vessel," more easily broken, these items of much less value were typically put to common, everyday use (e.g., "disposal of refuse"). Paul's figurative use of the earthen vessel image in 2 Cor 4:7 lent itself well to a depiction of human vulnerability and mortality.

Second, this initial classification of the articles leads to their distinction based on purpose.[114] Here a literal translation is helpful to show the rhetorical balance of the statement and its Pauline ring: "some are for[115] noble purposes and some are for ignoble purposes" (lit. "for honor [timēn] . . . for dishonor [atimian]"). The language and use of honor/shame to create a distinction come close to replicating Rom 9:21,[116] and the earlier Pauline text lies somewhere behind the present discussion.[117] But the imagery and concepts have been applied differently.[118] The point of its application here is to reflect on the different purposes or potentials of the various "objects" within "the household" (= church). And in this context, only the positive possibilities will be explicitly emphasized from the analogy (v. 21; cf. Rom 9:22-23). But this softer use of the analogy, in contrast with the earlier stark application in Romans (vessels of wrath vs. vessels of glory), has led some to conclude that the point of the present application has been obscured.

The place to begin to resolve this potential obscurity is with this elaboration on the household objects. The distribution of the categories of "honor" and "dishonor"[119] to the household utensils, to which the language

113. Gk. ξύλινος (adj.; "wooden"); see Lev 11:32; 15:12; Num 31:20; Rev 9:20; Gk. ὀστράκινος ("earthen, clay") see Lev 6:21; 11:33; Num 15:7; Isa 30:14; 2 Cor 4:7.

114. Whether the conjunction καί that introduces the statement and links it with the preceding one is specifically explicative (see C. Maurer, TDNT 7:364 n. 42; cf. Marshall, 760) or simply coordinating in force, the explanatory flow of the sentence is obvious.

115. The preposition εἰς (ἃ μὲν εἰς τιμὴν ἃ δὲ εἰς ἀτιμίαν; lit. "some are for honor, but some for dishonor") expresses purpose or intended result.

116. Cf. Rom 9:21 — ἢ οὐκ ἔχει ἐξουσίαν ὁ κεραμεὺς τοῦ πηλοῦ ἐκ τοῦ αὐτοῦ φυράματος ποιῆσαι ὃ μὲν εἰς τιμὴν σκεῦος, ὃ δὲ εἰς ἀτιμίαν ("one vessel for honorable use, and one for dishonorable") and 2 Tim 2:20 — καὶ ἃ μὲν εἰς τιμὴν ἃ δὲ εἰς ἀτιμίαν.

117. Some proponents of pseudonymity suggest literary dependence: Hanson, 138; Trummer, Paulustradition, 170-71.

118. The distinction based on honor/dishonor is sharpened theologically in the Romans text as the vessels develop into "vessels of wrath destined for destruction" and "vessels of mercy destined for glory" (9:22-23). 2 Timothy makes no use of the "sovereign potter" theme, and there is no apparent relation to the OT source of that theme (Isa 29:16; 45:9; Jer 18:1-11; Wis 15:7-13); see further Towner, Goal, 135; cf. Bassler, 153.

119. Gk. τιμή ("honor"; see discussion and notes at 1 Tim 1:17; 6:1); Gk. ἀτιμία

clearly refers, works out as follows.[120] Generally speaking (surely numerous exceptions could be cited), implements for honorable use are those that by their use, beauty, and value bring honor to the householder, displaying his status; they are used for the public display of foods; through use such vessels obtain honor. Implements that in contrast are common and breakable are used "for dishonorable" purposes and kept out of public view, used for common or dirty purposes (carrying water, refuse, etc.). Having in these parallel statements just separated the implements into two groups, first based on material value and second according to use, the latter twofold division should almost certainly be taken as a further specification of the two categories in the sense "the former . . . the latter . . . ,"[121] instead of as further defining only the second common category of vessel in the sense "some . . . some."[122] To each category in v. 20a belongs a purpose in v. 20b, and these are not to be confused.

A second point of confusion may arise either from an overly subtle reading of the metaphor or from reading the passage in the light of 1 Cor 12:21-26. While it can surely be argued on one level that each category of use is necessary and of value within the household scenario, the metaphor operates on another level; in this context Paul does not intend to develop the categories involved in the metaphor in the direction of the "reversal of honor" theme evident in 1 Cor 12:21-26.[123] Neither does he intend the reader to explore all conceivable permutations the picture might yield: the wealthy householder might indeed have gold-plated chamber pots, and clay bowls might contain the finest of foods. The impact of the house analogy, following

---

("a state of dishonor, disrespect, disgrace"; a Pauline word in the NT: Rom 1:26; 9:21; 1 Cor 11:14; 15:43; 2 Cor 6:8; 11:21); MM; H. Hübner, *EDNT* 1:177.

120. The syntax by which the evaluations "honor and dishonor" are distributed to the preceding costly and common vessels is potentially ambiguous. The device, two successive relative pronouns linked by the correlative μὲν . . . δέ construction (ἃ μὲν εἰς τιμὴν ἃ δὲ εἰς ἀτιμίαν; "some [vessels] for honor, some [vessels] for dishonor") is capable of more or less precision. (1) The construction may distinguish between only the latter named common vessels or refer loosely to both categories at once ("some . . . others"; NRSV; TNIV/NIV); (2) it might distribute according to the order of presentation ("The former . . . the latter"; REB; NJB; but cf. the inverted order of distribution in 2 Cor 2:15-16 [which may owe to chiasm]).

121. Marshall, 761; Johnson, 388; Knight, 418; Kelly, 187.

122. E.g., TNIV/NIV and NRSV (the punctuation of the NRSV is particularly open to this interpretation). We may also rule out the possibility (discussed but not adopted by Marshall, 760-61) that the argument intends that the purposes of honor and dishonor may be distributed to either category of vessel (i.e., there are A and B, and some [of A or B] are for honor, and others [of A or B] for dishonor). The opening division of vessels according to their material value determines the correlation.

123. Cf. the use of the terms ἀτιμότερα and τιμή in 1 Cor 12:23.

from the strong images created by the story of Korah, is created by means of bold contrast, not by excruciatingly subtle syntax.

Two possibilities are opened by the imagery. And whether through the OT lens (Korah) or the imagery of the household, Timothy will see that he must choose to identify either with the false teachers (epitomized in the persons of Hymenaeus and Philetus) or with those who name the name of the Lord.

The point of the extended interaction with the OT and household imagery is reached ("therefore") at v. 21,[124] as the metaphor opens into a general invitation to respond. First, the rigid division into two groups of vessels is replaced by an open proposition. "Anyone" can become an "instrument for noble purposes" no matter what category applied in v. 20. The action required is "cleansing," which, as the object of the action ("themselves"[125]) shows, is an individual decision (cf. 2 Cor 13:5). The verb "to cleanse or remove" is rare in the biblical literature (1 Cor 5:7; LXX Deut 26:13), and belongs to the language descriptive of cultic purity and impurity.[126] Conversion is a cleansing from moral impurities.

Second, however, the language describing the "impurities" (lit. "from these" [things?, teachings?]) is somewhat ambiguous.[127] Two divergent translations illustrate the possibilities: (1) the TNIV/NIV has "from the latter," which identifies the implied impurities with the "implements for dishonor," that is, the false teachers;[128] (2) the NRSV has "of the things I have mentioned," which is a broader reference presumably to the activities and the teachings associated with the false teachers rather than to the people themselves.[129] The sense of the context favors the latter interpretation. On the one hand, in the initial call to separation in v. 19d, the false teachers were characterized by the evil things they do *(adikia),* which encompasses false teaching and practices.[130] On the other hand, in the parallel command to Timothy that

---

124. The TNIV/NIV and the NRSV do not translate the inferential conjunction οὖν ("therefore"), the transition to a conclusion being clear enough from the condition that is laid down.

125. It seems preferable to me to pluralize both elements of the phrase ("anyone" to "all"; "himself" to "themselves") to get gender inclusiveness (as NRSV, "*All* who cleanse *themselves*").

126. Gk. ἐκκαθαίρω; see F. Hauck et al., *TDNT* 3:413-31.

127. Gk. ἀπὸ τούτων (lit. "from these things") indicates specifically that which is to be removed as unclean.

128. Dibelius and Conzelmann, 113; Kelly, 188; Knight, 418.

129. Marshall, 762; Fee, 262; Bassler, 154; Johnson, 397-98.

130. Paul's other use of the verb ἐκκαθαίρω ("to cleanse from") in 1 Cor 5:7 includes separation from both the sinner (in that case intransigent, unrepentant believers) and immoral practices.

follows in v. 22, the theme is flight from harmful attitudes and pursuit of moral qualities, not separation from people (who in fact may yet be saved, v. 25). The cleansing envisaged in v. 21 is such that it allows one to become an "implement for honor," which then opens up the possibility that the "[implements] for dishonor" set off in v. 20 may be among those who become "implements for honor" through cleansing.

Fulfillment of the requirement qualifies one to belong to the class of faithful believer described with the term "implement for honor[able use]." The return to the metaphor might seem confusing if pressed for details, for the picture requires what was once a common object for dishonorable purposes to be transformed into a valuable object for honorable use. What this surprise does, however, is to underline the possibility and importance of change, from wickedness, uncleanness, and dishonor to godliness.

The transformed implement for honor is described in three ways. First, cultic language characterizes the results of the change in terms of "consecration" or "sanctification." One who has separated from wickedness is devoted (as a purified implement is prepared for use in worship), "set apart as holy," to God.[131]

Second, those who cleanse themselves become "useful to the Master." The household metaphor is revived with the term "master" (see on 1 Tim 6:1, 2; Titus 2:9). "Usefulness" *(euchrēstos)* simply means able to do the master's bidding;[132] it may create a wordplay contrast with the earlier cognate term for "uselessness" *(ep' ouden chrēsimon)* applied to the false teachers' ways (v. 14b). The source that inspired the vessel imagery (cf. Rom 9:21-23) stressed the "potter's" authority to decide the use of the article he had made; here within the household metaphor the appropriate counterpart is the "master" *(despotēs)*.

Third, Paul employs the "good works" language typical of these letters to coworkers to summarize the visible outworking of being "holy" to God and "useful": "prepared to do any good work." The phrase parallels 3:17 and Titus 3:1, where the concept depicts authentic faith from the standpoint of the outward service it produces (see 1 Tim 2:10, Excursus).

Consequently, the supporting material laid down in vv. 19-21 consists of an interpretation of the church's situation that weaves together metaphorical images and powerful echoes of a decisive OT experience. As this part of the parenesis plays out, the image of the church's immovability grounded (now in light of the Christ-event) in Christ's knowledge of his people opens to reveal a strong warning to be heeded by all. OT echoes fade, and the illus-

---

131. See 1 Tim 4:5 (discussion and note); cf. Rom 15:16; 1 Cor 1:2.
132. Gk. εὔχρηστος (see 4:11; Phlm 11; Hermas, *Vision* 3.6.7; Hermas, *Mandate* 5.6.6); BDAG; MM 268.

tration is reorganized according to the house and implements metaphor. Here the division of true and false believer is developed further, but thoughts of judgment, still implicit but muted, open out to an invitation to all to seek cleansing and conversion. The purpose of this stretch of metaphors and imagery clearly exceeds the mere giving of consolation to faithful believers such as Timothy who must resign themselves to the perpetual reality of a "mixed" church, though that reality may in fact be implied by the picture (cf. Matt 13:24-30, 36-43).[133] Paul underlines more than anything the goal of producing changed lives so that people within the "household" might be transformed from opposing to serving Christ. Timothy's own behavior and the choices he must make are still in view.

22 Following the illustrative centerpiece of the passage, and in light of the call to conversion just sounded, the second set of three imperatives resumes direct instruction to Timothy. In rough parallel with the first half of the section, the three imperatives in this latter half will be supported with a subsection of rationale (vv. 24-26).

As with the shift back to Timothy in 1 Tim 6:11 (see discussion), the transition here is made by the insertion of a traditional teaching device containing the first two of the imperatives, "flee/pursue." The function of the pair is to contrast behavior to be shunned with behavior to be embraced. Timothy is to flee from "the evil desires of youth."

While this forms a contrast with the "good works" referred to in v. 21, it is not entirely clear what range of behavior or attitudes is covered by "the evil desires of youth." "Desires" may refer to neutral or even positive needs and longings in some contexts (cf. the verb in 1 Tim 3:1), but one development of the term that is prominent in the NT is its reference to negative or neutral desires that, if not controlled, become excessive, and possibly to harmful or evil impulses (see on 1 Tim 6:9). That is surely the case here, but the adjective "youthful"[134] does not limit the scope of the content much. Although Timothy's relative youthfulness is mentioned in 1 Tim 4:12, the reference here is almost certainly not to his own tendencies but to those evident in the church, and especially among the troublemakers. In general, the thought must be of those attitudes or impulses characteristic of youth, and the items to be pursued present a fitting opposite. The present context might imply a tendency to engage in arguments as part of this "youthful" profile,[135] or, on

---

133. Towner, *Goal,* 135-36; cf. Oberlinner, 108-9; Trummer, *Paulustradition,* 168-72.

134. Gk. νεωτερικός; only here in the NT; cf. 3 Macc 4:8; Josephus, *Antiquities* 16.399 links it to presumption or stubbornness (cf. αὐθάδης, "stubborn, arrogant," in Titus 1:7).

135. Kelly, 188-89; Dibelius and Conzelmann, 113; Marshall, 764.

the basis of another development of the term and cognates, "cravings for innovation."[136] In any case, sexual lust does not seem to be the focus, and the plurality of the whole construction suggests a broad pattern of behavior rather than a particular weakness. Various kinds of behavior characterized by impetuous or rash acts without thought to consequences could easily be in view; the context suggests that those related to argument and abrupt innovation would be uppermost in mind.

The second imperative verb impels Timothy positively to "pursue" the alternative life of faith. This life is characterized by a list of four virtues (cf. 3:10-11; 1 Tim 4:12; 6:11). The first three of these, "righteousness, faith, love," also occur in the list of 1 Tim 6:11 (see discussion and notes). "Uprightness" *(dikaiosynē)* was one of the cardinal virtues in Hellenistic thought.[137] Its presentation here in a list of virtues is Greek in style, but its orientation in these letters is specifically grounded in the Christ-event (cf. Titus 2:12). Here it presents a contrast with its antonym, *adikia,* in v. 19.

The next two items, "faith" and "love," occur together nine times in the lists of Christian qualities in the letters to coworkers.[138] Again, while the list-form and some of the items included in the lists correspond to Greek ethical teaching, these two qualities are central to the understanding of authentic Christian existence expressed throughout Paul.[139] Together they sum up the Christian life in terms of the "vertical" or mystical faith relationship with God and the "horizontal" or relational outworking of that faith in other-oriented service (see on 1 Tim 1:5).

The singular occurrence of the fourth element, "peace" (see on 1 Tim 1:2), in an ethical discourse seems to be conditioned by two factors in the immediate context. First, it is an attitude of quiet composure that would have a neutralizing effect on the combative quarreling of the false teachers (vv. 14, 23-24).[140] Second, it corresponds to the disposition of patience and kind concern (see below) that is intended to lead the opponent to repentance.

It becomes clear in the prepositional phrase that finishes the verse that the qualities listed are meant to typify authentic faith,[141] and that "pur-

---

136. See the discussion in Johnson, 399-400; W. Metzger, "Die *neōterikai epithymiai* in 2 Tim 2.22," *TZ* 33 (1977): 129-36. Cf. the use of the cognate νεωτερισμός for revolution and harmful innovation (*Epistle of Aristeas* 101; *Testament of Reuben* 2.2; Philo, *Against Flaccus* 93).

137. G. Schrenk, *TDNT* 2:192-93.

138. 1 Tim 1:5, 14; 2:15; 4:12; 6:11; 2 Tim 1:13; 2:22; 3:10; Titus 2:2.

139. 1 Cor 13:13; Gal 5:6; Eph 6:23; Col 1:4; 1 Thess 3:6; 5:8; 2 Thess 1:3; Phlm 5.

140. Cf. Fee, 263-64.

141. Gk. μετά (prep.) modifies the verb δίωκε and all of its objects, "uprightness, faith, love, peace" (see Fee, 266; Marshall, 764). The alternative of taking the preposition

suit" of them is then to be understood as a standard. Believers are then depicted with two terms. First, the phrase "those who call on the Lord," which was adopted from the OT, is a frequent designation in the early church for God's people.[142] Here it resumes the theme initiated at 2:19; the phrase specifically describes Christians as those marked out by their confession of Christ as Lord ("Lord" = Jesus Christ). This identification of authentic believers is strengthened and more sharply focused in the phrase "out of a pure heart," which views Christian existence from the perspective of the inward cleansing ("heart" = thoughts, emotions, consciousness, volition) associated with conversion (see on 1 Tim 1:5).

23 Finally, in the third imperative of this sequence, Timothy is warned again against engaging in the tactics of the opponents. The command of avoidance repeats v. 16 and adds nothing new. It is expressed in language that is typical of Paul's denunciation of the heretics and their teaching (see on 1 Tim 4:7).

False teaching is depicted critically as "arguments" (TNIV) or "controversies" (NRSV) with the same term used in 1 Tim 6:4 (see discussion) and Titus 3:9 (where avoidance is also urged). In this case, two adjectives are added to seal the indictment. "Foolish" (Titus 3:9) describes the verbal wrangling as frivolous and unskilled because it produces nothing useful.[143] "Ignorant" means literally "uneducated" and in some cases "stupid."[144] The implicit irony or sarcasm sharpens the criticism, suggesting that the result of the false teachers' debates is precisely the opposite of "education" (i.e., *apaideutos*). Notably, in contrast below, Timothy's interaction will be described with its antonym *(paideuō)* as constructive education. Clearly, the coworker is not to avoid confrontation with the opponents, but rather involvement in their doctrinal discussions or the arguments that result. Since their "instruction" has already been criticized with the negative imperatives above (2:14, 16; cf. 1 Tim 1:4; 4:7), the reason for avoidance is (rhetorically) self-evident: "because you know they produce quarrels." Repetition is for emphasis, and

---

with only the last quality in the list, "peace," thus indicating those with whom Timothy should be peaceable (Kelly, 189; Knight, 421), is at odds with the context.

142. Gk. ἐπικαλέω; formed here on the participle (μετὰ τῶν ἐπικαλουμένων τὸν κύριον); cf. 1 Sam 12:17; 2 Sam 22:7; Joel 3:5; Acts 2:21; 9:14, 21; 22:16; Rom 10:12, 13; 1 Cor 1:2; 2 Cor 1:23; see the discussion and note at 2:19. Spicq, *TLNT* 2:41-46.

143. Gk. μωρός (adj.; Titus 3:9; 1 Cor 1:25, 27; 3:18; 4:10); G. Bertram, *TDNT* 4:832-47, esp. 844-47; Spicq, *TLNT* 2:540-41; Quinn, 236.

144. Gk. ἀπαίδευτος (only here in the NT), formed by negating (with α) the παιδευ- stem word-group having to do with instruction, education, discipline, etc. See Prov 5:23; 8:5; 15:14; 24:8; 27:20; Wis 17:1; Sir 4:25; 6:20; 8:4; 21:24; 23:13; 51:23. Mostly descriptive of persons ("uneducated, rude, boorish"); occasionally of words, teaching (BDAG; MM).

the concluding reference to "quarrels"[145] provides a contrast to the description of the servant of the Lord that is coming (vv. 24-25).

24-26 Verses 24-25a present the pattern Timothy is to follow. His behavior is to be decisively different, as the contrast created by wordplay shows (the false teaching produces *machas* ["quarrels"]; but the Lord's servant must not *machesthai* ["quarrel"]). Paul's transition to the third person has the force of categorizing the expectations as "standard operating procedures."

Weightier in terms of motivation, however, is the designation "the Lord's servant."[146] Elsewhere Paul uses similar language in reference to himself (Titus 1:1) and sometimes applies it to his coworkers.[147] Developed from the OT identification of God's servants (Moses and the prophets), it includes the thought of being invested with divine authority for discharging various duties (see Titus 1:1). In the postresurrection appropriation of the OT epithet, the transfer has again been made to Christ, who occupies the place of Lord in the church. Presumably the general reference allows Timothy to imagine Paul as the example of the behavior to be outlined: the servanthood motif underlines the way in which the calling to the ministry of leadership obligates one to the Lord and to the people who must be served.[148]

The archetypal "servant of the Lord" is characterized by three general qualities (no doubt selected because of their relevance to Ephesus) before the instruction is applied specifically to the immediate circumstances (v. 25). First, he is to be an agent of kindness (or peace). This is expressed with a strong contrast ("but"; *alla*) between the activity to be avoided ("quarreling")[149] and the disposition he is to display toward all ("kindness, gentleness, cordiality").[150] In addition to its link with paternal care, "kindness" could also be a characteristic of authority figures, suggesting that authority in this context would lead to seeking to nurture others.[151] The logic of this is drawn out in what follows.

---

145. Gk. μάχη (pl. "quarrels" = "battles but with words"; Titus 3:9; cf. λογομαχία, 2 Tim 2:14; 1 Tim 6:4); 2 Cor 7:5; Jas 4:1; O. Bauernfeind, *TDNT* 4:527-28. Gk. γεννάω ordinarily means "to give birth, beget," but is used figuratively here to express causation (e.g., of fear in Philo, *On Joseph* 254; BDAG, s.v. 3).

146. Gk. δοῦλος κυρίου; only here in the NT. On the OT background, see the discussion at Titus 1:1.

147. As a self-reference, see also Rom 1:1; Gal 1:10; Phil 1:1; of coworkers, Col 4:2; cf. 2 Cor 4:5; cf. Rev 2:20.

148. Marshall, 765, suggests that this picture of the gentle servant may echo the meek Servant of Yahweh in Isa 42:2; 53:7; etc.; but cf. Oberlinner, 115.

149. Gk. μάχομαι; figurative here of quarreling (John 6:52; Jas 4:2), literal in Acts 7:26; cf. O. Bauernfeind, *TDNT* 4:527-28.

150. Gk. ἤπιος (only here in the NT; cf. 1 Thess 2:7, variant); Spicq, *TLNT* 2:174-77; MM 281.

151. See Spicq, *TLNT* 2:174-77.

"Kindness" is followed by two additional adjectives that are also typical features of the leadership profile but are immediately relevant to the combat situation in Ephesus. The "ability to teach" is an essential feature of leadership in these letters to coworkers (see on 1 Tim 3:2; cf. Titus 1:9); it includes positive instruction in doctrine and correction of those in error. Equally essential, especially in this power struggle, is the quality translated variously as "not resentful" (TNIV/NIV), "patient" (NRSV), "forbearing" (RSV). It means literally "to endure evil without resentment,"[152] which in the present context envisions a capacity for tolerance (of insults, contradiction) in the face of opposition, that is, a specific sort of "patience" (cf. 1 Tim 3:3).

In v. 25 the importance of possessing these attitudes and qualities becomes clear as they culminate in a specific course of action that will require them in abundance. That activity is expressed with the participle "to instruct, correct, discipline," but the emphasis is placed on the qualifier "gently" ("in gentleness"), which dictates how the corrective action is to be carried out.[153] This attitude gathers together the qualities of gentleness and tolerance into a disposition of patient openness that is particularly necessary for the Christian response in confrontational situations.[154]

The term of "instruction" employed here is the verb *paideuō*, which covers a range of activity from education (2 Tim 3:16; Acts 7:22; 22:3) to disciplinary action (1 Tim 1:20; Heb 12:9). Somewhere along that spectrum of meanings the term takes on the sense of education with a view to (spiritual) correction or guidance that most suits the present context.[155] The constructive education that Timothy will provide *(paideuō)* will aim to undo the destructive effects of the opponents' foolishness (*apaideutos*, v. 23). Paul describes those in need of this attention, with a rare participle, as being specifically "opponents";[156] the term was chosen, no doubt, because it is formed on

---

152. Gk. ἀνεξίκακος ("bearing evil without resentment" = ἀνέχομαι ["bear or endure"] + κακός ["evil"]; only here in the NT; see esp. Wis 2:19; Josephus, *Jewish War* 1.624); cf. BDAG; W. Grundmann, *TDNT* 3:486-87.

153. Gk. ἐν πραΰτητι παιδεύοντα; the placement of the prepositional phrase ahead of the participle it governs is emphatic (cf. Marshall, 766); for the combination with this preposition, see also Jas 3:13; Sir 3:17; 4:8.

154. Gk. πραΰτης (Titus 3:2; 2 Cor 10:1; Gal 5:23; 6:1; Col 3:12; Jas 1:21; 1 Pet 3:16); see further on Titus 3:2; cf. the synonym in 1 Tim 6:11 (πραϋπάθεια). See Spicq, *TLNT* 3:160-71; F. Hauck and S. Schulz, *TDNT* 6:645-51; Towner, *Goal,* 164. Cf. the cognate adjective πραΰς, through which meekness/gentleness becomes a fundamental of Christian behavior (Matt 5:5; 11:29; 21:5; 1 Pet 3:5).

155. Gk. παιδεύω (see discussion at Titus 2:12); cf. *1 Clement* 21.6; 59.3. G. Schneider, *EDNT* 3:3-4; Marshall, 766. See further G. Bertram, *TDNT* 5:596-625.

156. Gk. ἀντιδιατίθημι ("to oppose oneself, be opposed"; only here in the biblical writings; Diodorus Siculus 34.12; Philo, *On the Special Laws* 4.103). For the view that the participle (τοὺς ἀντιδιατιθεμένους understood as passive instead of middle voice, a minor-

---

the prefix *anti*, which conforms to his polemical vocabulary with its emphasis on resistance to the apostle's message and authority.[157]

But what motivates giving such patient attention to those in opposition? The remainder of the passage (vv. 25b-26) provides an explanation from positive and negative perspectives. First, the positive possibility is raised that God will act for the opposition. The Greek construction that creates this mood[158] in effect asks the indirect question "whether perhaps ["if possibly"] God might grant. . . ."[159] Although a positive outcome is entertained, the idiom couches it in very cautious terms, possibly because those in view are, after all, opponents. Nevertheless, the corrective teaching is intended as a channel through which they would become capable of repenting. This is the act/decision to change one's mind, which in the NT expresses the religious sense of "repentance": in this case Paul envisions a turning from false teaching (acknowledging error) back to the apostolic gospel.[160] But ultimately it is God who "grants" repentance,[161] whether the possibility is presented through the teaching of his servant (cf. Wis 12:10) or God acts more directly to enlighten the mind. In either case, the goal of repentance is the "knowledge of the truth" (see on 1 Tim 2:4) that regards salvation from the perspective of a rational decision to believe the apostolic gospel (i.e., "true" as opposed to false; see on 2:15). The order of events, "repentance leading to a knowledge of the truth," corresponds with other NT texts that make repentance the prerequisite to receiving the gift of salvation (Acts 2:38; 3:19).

Second, the motive of Timothy's teaching (repentance, salvation) just

---

ity view) refers to those affected adversely by the opponents (and not the culprits themselves, who are not to be addressed[?]), see Fee, 267 (following Bernard, 126-27). With only two other ἀντι- terms used to depict the opponents in these letters to coworkers (τοὺς ἀντιλέγοντας, Titus 1:9, and τῷ ἀντικειμένῳ, 1 Tim 5:14; cf. 1:10), Fee's argument from word preference is not easily substantiated.

157. E.g., ἀντιλέγω ("contradict," Titus 1:9), ἀντικείμαι ("resist," 1 Tim 1:10; 5:15); see Spicq, *TLNT* 1:128-30; Marshall, 766; Dibelius and Conzelmann, 113.

158. Gk. μήποτε (adv.) marks the following clause as an indirect question entertaining a possibility (BDAG, s.v. 3.b.β): "[who knows/perhaps] God might grant them repentance" (cf. Luke 3:15; BDF §370.3; cf. Moule, *Idiom Book*, 157).

159. For Gk. δίδωμι ("to give, grant"; δώῃ is subj. in conformity with the connected verb in v. 26) in reference to God "granting," see on 1:16, 18. For the textual problem (of God; aor. subj. δώῃ vs. opt. δῴη [as in 1:16, 18]), cf. the discussions in Marshall, 745; Johnson, 402.

160. Gk. μετάνοια; Rom 2:4; 2 Cor 7:9 (noun); cf. Acts 8:22 (verb). See Spicq, *TLNT* 2:471-77; H. Merklein, *EDNT* 2:415-19; J. Behm and E. Wurthwein, *TDNT* 4:975-1008.

161. For the traditional formulation "to grant repentance" (δοῦναι μετάνοιαν), see Acts 5:31; 11:18; Wis 12:10, 19.

supplied is now viewed from another perspective in v. 26a.[162] Almost with the idea that false teaching is a potent soporific or narcotic, the effect of corrective teaching (namely, repentance) is described as "sobering up," which in moral discussions depicts a "coming to one's senses."[163]

What this means is explained with a rather awkward prepositional phrase that does not seem to follow the verb: literally, "from the trap of the devil."[164] The phrase "trap of the devil" has already occurred as a description of the temptations that belong to Satan's domain (see on 1 Tim 3:7). By implication, those teaching or subjected to the heresy are thought to have strayed into the devil's territory. Decoding Paul's rough syntax, we arrive at the notion that Timothy's teaching will enable a return to sanity or sobriety, bring understanding of the deceptive trap, and stimulate the decision to repent (= escape from the trap of the devil). The equation of the false teaching with the devil's influence is not unexpected (1 Tim 5:15).

When we reach the final comment (v. 26b), we encounter a difficulty caused by Paul's vague use of pronouns: literally, "having been taken captive by him to do his will." The main question is who, the devil or God, is responsible for "taking people captive." Although, as Johnson points out, "God" (who grants repentance) is the last expressed subject,[165] parallel to God is the implicit "they" who "come to their senses." In fact, the nearest antecedent to the phrase "by him" is "the devil," and unless there is good reason why his activity could not be described in terms of "capture," there seems little reason to shift back at this point to the theme of God's activity.[166]

---

162. V. 26 presents a parallel statement to v. 25b (the adv. μήποτε is still in effect, requiring the subj. verb ἀνανήψωσιν); the linking conjunction καί is either explanatory ("thus," or left untranslated; REB, CEV) or coordinating ("and," TNIV/NIV, NRSV).

163. Gk. ἀνανήφω ("to come [back] to one's senses"; only here in the NT; cf. Philo, *Allegorical Interpretation* 2.60, for the verb in connection with "repentance"); BDAG, s.v.; Cf. ἐκνήφω in a similar sense in 1 Cor 15:34.

164. The syntactical problem is created by the attachment of the prepositional phrase ἐκ τῆς τοῦ διαβόλου παγίδος (lit. "from the devil's snare") to the immediately preceding verb ἀνανήψωσιν, which means "to become sober." The punctuation of NA[27] suggests that the verb and prepositional phrase belong together, with the subsequent participial phrase describing further the devil's trap. To smooth the syntactical edges and bring out the sense, the TNIV and the NRSV supply the verb "escape" before the prepositional phrase (assuming it apparently from the following imagery of "capture"; cf. Marshall, 767). Johnson's strategy (399, 402-3) is to ignore the punctuation and take the prepositional phrase with the following participle (giving, "once they have been snatched alive by God from the devil's snare, so that they can do God's will"). If, however, the devil (and not God) is referred to in the following pronouns, this solution fails (see below).

165. Johnson, 403.

166. It is Paul's vague use of pronouns, with at least two possible referents nearby, in the successive prepositional phrases (ὑπ' αὐτοῦ εἰς τὸ ἐκείνου θέλημα; "by him

The whole phrase is governed by the perfect passive participle, "having been taken captive by him."[167] Most scholars treat this as a reference to captivity at the hands of the devil (i.e., "by him," NRSV; "who [the devil] has taken them captive," TNIV).[168] While in some contexts the verb on which it is based can mean "rescue,"[169] it was also used to depict those taken captive in war (LXX Deut 20:16) and often subjected to cruel torture and slavery by the captors.[170] The perfect tense of the participle is perhaps a more apt description of the state of the captives (i.e., in Satan's clutches) prior to escape than it would be of the escape itself (by God) or their conversion (where God is thought to be the captor).[171] Consequently, "having been taken captive by him" both explains the situation from which they escape (by coming to their senses) and further defines the nature of the "devil's trap" as a captivity.

On this understanding, the devil is the captor implied in the first pronoun ("by him"), and the final statement of purpose, "to do his will,"[172] almost certainly sets out the plight of the captives in terms of doing the devil's will.[173] A shift at this point to "God's will" (cf. 1:1) is awkward and rhetorically unnecessary. One of the things at stake from at least 2:19 has been the

---

to do his [that one's] will") and the shift from αὐτοῦ to ἐκείνου that generate the questions. On the one hand, the NRSV (margin) and the REB (margin) suggest as an alternative translation" "held captive by him [the devil] to do his [i.e., God's] will." This shift of thought is not supported by the context. On the other hand, Johnson, 402-3, notes the uncertainty of referents and places more emphasis on the potential of the verb ζωγρέω to mean something more like rescue (Josh 2:13; 6:25), as in the figurative use in Luke 5:10 for the evangelistic activity of "catching people" (see also Lock, 102-3).

167. Gk. ἐζωγρημένοι ὑπ᾽ αὐτοῦ; the TNIV/NIV ("who has taken them captive") collapses the prepositional phrase "by him" (ὑπ᾽ αὐτοῦ), which denotes the agent of the action, into the participle and removes the passive sense, probably to gain smoothness, but the effort loses the emphasis on the fixed state of the captives.

168. So Fee, 266-67; Kelly, 191-92; Dibelius and Conzelmann, 114; Oberlinner, 110; Knight, 426-27; Marshall, 767-68. BDF §291.6.

169. Josh 2:13; 6:25; and figuratively by Luke 5:10.

170. Gk. ζωγρέω (Luke 5:10); Spicq, TLNT 2:162-63.

171. As it is, the participle is adverbial, modifying the preceding verb ἀνανήψωσιν ("that they may come to their senses"), describing the state of captivity by the devil.

172. Gk. θέλημα ("will, wish"; see 1 Tim 2:4, note); often of God's will (2 Tim 1:1; 2 Cor 8:5; etc.) or of human desires (Eph 2:3; 2 Pet 1:21); for the idea of Satan's purposes/will, see 2 Cor 2:11.

173. The shift from personal pronoun (ὑπ᾽ αὐτοῦ; "by him") to demonstrative pronoun (εἰς τὸ ἐκείνου θέλημα; "to do his [that one's] will") does not indicate different referents (but see Barrett, 109-10; Guthrie, 167-68; Bassler, 55-56, is uncertain); the shift might be stylistic or intend some light increase in emphasis (i.e., "to do his will [instead of God's]"; see BDF §291.6; Arichea-Hatton, 219).

clash of opposing figures — Timothy/false teachers, Moses/Korah, implements for honor/implements for dishonor, God/the devil — which finally issues in the image of a struggle between God and the devil for the souls of people. From the parenetic perspective, Timothy enters this struggle as an agent of Christ ("the Lord's servant") to face the agent of the devil (false teachers under his thrall, in his service). What vv. 25b-26 achieve is to set God's salvation through Timothy's ministry in graphic opposition to the effects wrought by the devil through the activities of the false teachers: in Paul's mind these opponents are the devil's agents (cf. 2 Cor 11:15). "Knowledge of the truth" brings the sobriety necessary to escape enlistment in the devil's service.

Paul has emphasized three elements in the whole passage that define Timothy's engagement with the opponents and those who have come under their influence. First, the danger of the false teaching, which is capable of upsetting faith (v. 18), is graphically underlined by linking it to the devil's active campaign to ensnare unsuspecting believers. Second, as the instructions to Timothy reveal, the Lord desires to act, and will act, through the corrective teaching of his servants (in this case, Timothy). What should not be lost in all of this, thirdly, is that the possibility of repentance, conversion, and coming back to one's senses is held open for all (Hymenaeus and Philetus included). The importance of this possibility can be seen in the tremendous amount of attention Paul gives to the demeanor of Timothy (love, peace, kindness, amicability, gentleness), which is gauged to promote the possibility of repentance.

D. PROPHECY, COMMITMENT, AND CALL (3:1–4:8)

At 3:1 Paul changes directions perceptibly to establish another ground or context for the remainder of his instructions to Timothy. The distinction between this part of the letter and the previous one may be seen in the change in perspective from instructions about how Timothy is to engage the opponents — in gentleness with the hope of their repentance (2:14-26) — to a prophetic interpretation of the movement in 3:1-9. This fresh perspective provides the basis for the separate sections of parenesis that follow. Verses 10-17 renew the call to continue the Pauline ministry with suffering (see the link to 3:1-9 in v. 13). And 4:1-8 functions as a summarizing renewal of Timothy's calling as a whole (note how vv. 3-4 echo 3:1-9). As a whole, the section repeats and extends the contrast between the false teaching and Paul's gospel; it underlines yet again the way in which Timothy is to be the successor to Paul; it re-emphasizes the theme of suffering, enjoining Timothy to take on that challenge and strengthening that enjoinder by means of the Pauline model.

1. The Heresy in Ephesus in Prophetic Perspective (3:1-9)

> 1 *But mark this: There will be terrible times in the last days.* 2 *People will be lovers of themselves, lovers of money, boastful, proud, abusive, disobedient to their parents, ungrateful, unholy,* 3 *without love, unforgiving, slanderous, without self-control, brutal, not lovers of the good,* 4 *treacherous, rash, conceited, lovers of pleasure rather than lovers of God —* 5 *having a form of godliness but denying its power. Have nothing to do with such people.*
>
> 6 *They are the kind who worm their way into homes and gain control over gullible women, who are loaded down with sins and are swayed by all kinds of evil desires,* 7 *always learning but never able to come to a knowledge of the truth.* 8 *Just as Jannes and Jambres opposed Moses, so also these teachers oppose the truth. They are men of depraved minds, who, as far as the faith is concerned, are rejected.* 9 *But they will not get very far because, as in the case of those men, their folly will be clear to everyone.*

The theme that is taken up in this subsection is not new; the heretics surfaced in 2:14-26, and Paul characterized them strongly there in terms of the danger posed by their methods and doctrine and from the perspectives of the threat of judgment and the hope of their repentance. A thorough understanding of the opponents, however, requires placing them within the framework of prophecy. The discourse proceeds in two parts. First, vv. 1-5 paint in prophetic fashion a general picture (with some local color) of the evil associated with "the last days." To create a profile of the worst sinners, Paul employs the vice-list technique that was used widely in Hellenistic Jewish and Greek ethical literature to establish deviance from the values that produce virtue. At v. 5b, with the insertion of a warning to Timothy, the picture fades to the present. Second, vv. 6-9 apply that prophetic paradigm to the opponents troubling the church. By drawing again on traditions connected with Moses' leadership, the opponents are typed as pagans in opposition to God and denounced in the strongest terms.

In function, this section parallels 1 Tim 4:1-5, particularly in the way that the present distress is identified as being an expected feature of the last days. In this passage, the literary approach and impact are achieved by the combination of the prophetic element and the vice-list form of denunciation. As Johnson advises,[1] the vice list was not a precise tool; it tended to string together a list of numerous evils (or, in this case, evildoers) to caricature generally and thoroughly whichever opponent was in mind. Such lists were often

---

1. Johnson, 409-10.

crafted for oral presentation, so that repetition of sounds[2] and other rhythmic devices sharpened the impact. The polemical discourse reaches its climax at vv. 6-9, when the opponents step clearly into the spotlight as those who specifically embody the evil associated with the End. The list does not intend to lay each sin mentioned at the feet of the false teachers in Ephesus (i.e., it is not a reliable guide to specifics of their behavior). But the picture it paints suggests that Paul regarded the false teachers as actual deviants from the norms established by his gospel, whose deviance endangered their faith and the faith of their followers.

1   The passage begins by establishing a prophetic point of view for Timothy. The phrase used to catch his attention is similar to that used in 1:15, with an important difference; there Paul called to mind knowledge that Timothy already had ("this [what follows] you know"), here he instructs him with the present tense imperative "know this" (i.e., accept what I am about to tell you).[3] The prophetic framework is not established by means of a verb of prophecy or revelation, but by reference to the times as "the last days" and to warnings about this time that had become traditional (cf. 1 Tim 4:1-2; 2 Pet 3:3).

In this phrase several notions come together about which we must be clear. First, we may hear in the language a reference to the future and events that have not yet unfolded,[4] and Paul's use of it with future verbs in this passage produces that tone to create a prophetic atmosphere.[5] But the term was widely used by NT writers in ways that shed light on Paul's use of it here. As Luke reported it, Peter identified the beginning of the period "the last days" with the outpouring of the Spirit at Pentecost (Acts 2:17). For the writer of Hebrews, "the last days" were aptly characterized by God's sending of the Son (1:2). And in various other ways it becomes clear that the present age of the Spirit (launched by Jesus' ministry, death, and resurrection) is in fact "the last days" (1 Cor 10:11; 1 Pet 1:20; 1 John 2:18). Used in this way, the phrase was understood to imply that with Jesus' appearance, the End, marked by divine intervention, had been inaugurated and would culminate in God's final intervention (in the parousia of Christ) to complete salvation and execute judgment.

---

2. In vv. 2-4, nine words beginning with *a;* the *oi-* ending occurs fifteen times; the *ph-* sound eight times, five of them in compounds built on the stem *phil.*

3. Gk. τοῦτο δὲ γίνωσκε (for the phrase, see Rom 6:6; cf. 2 Pet 3:3). "This" refers forward to the statement about to be made. For the implication of the imperative, cf. K. L. McKay, "Aspect in Imperatival Constructions in New Testament Greek," *NovT* 27 (1985): 201-25, esp. 210.

4. Gk. ἐν ἐσχάταις ἡμέραις. In the OT (Isa 2:2; Dan 11:20), the term sometimes depicts the future time of God's intervention.

5. For the view that the future, not the present, is in mind, see Oberlinner, 119-22.

Second, it was a stock belief in the early church, as inherited from the Jewish apocalyptic tradition, that the time before the End would be characterized by an unprecedented upswing in evil (Mark 13 and pars.; 2 Thess 2:3; Revelation 13) accompanied by a falling away of believers (Matt 24:10; 2 Pet 3:3; Jude 17-19; Rev 13:11-18).[6] Thus Paul is not simply making a reference to future times in the phrase; he is speaking about eschatological events, and focuses primarily on the evil and danger that prophecy has foretold. Although the wider usage of the term suggests that Paul might be viewing the present events as in some sense fulfilling those predictions (the present age as the last days), we will formulate that conclusion after the future tense verbs have been considered.

In accordance with the prophetic tradition, Paul announces that "there will be terrible times in the last days." The verb ("there will come, there will be") is future[7] and speaks of impending events (cf. 1 Cor 7:26), but we should be wary of the prophetic stance Paul is taking with regard to the present (see below). The graphic language emphasizes the severity of the circumstances ("terrible"),[8] which will go on for some time.[9] The emergence of evildoers to be described is the one part of this dangerous scenario (which might include various things from persecution to betrayal) that Paul wishes to exploit.

2-5a The main point of the prophecy comes in the description of its fulfillment — the appearance of evildoers. A second future tense verb ("will be") sustains the prophetic tone of the warning, and the danger has to do with a certain kind of people; as v. 5 makes clear, "people" is not a general reference to sinners but a specific reference to those who apostatize from the faith. Paul describes them with a list of seventeen adjectives that finally gives way to two contrasts before closing with a brief command to Timothy. The items themselves do not appear to be arranged in any specific order,[10] but are rather bracketed by two kinds of misguided love — self-love and love of pleasure. Within this grouping, a broad description of self-centeredness is discernible

6. Cf. 1QpHab 2:1-10; *1 Enoch* 90.22-27; 91.7; 93.9; *Jubilees* 23.14-17; *4 Ezra* 5.1-2, 10.

7. Gk. ἐνίστημι (fut.; of circumstances or events that will happen ["impending, imminent"; 1 Cor 7:26]; Rom 8:38; 1 Cor 3:22; Gal 1:4; 2 Thess 2:2); BDAG, s.v. 3; A. Oepke, *TDNT* 2:543-44.

8. Gk. χαλεπός ("troublesome, hard, difficult"; cf. the versions; of "fierce" demoniacs in Matt 8:28); used in describing horrid diseases (Plutarch, *Moralia* 131B; Josephus, *Antiquities* 13.422) and perilous circumstances (2 Macc 4:4); Spicq, *TLNT* 3:494-95.

9. Gk. καιρός (see 1 Tim 2:6, discussion and note). The plural καιροί carries no automatic theological meaning in this context, but simply refers to an indefinitely long span of time that may or may not be theologically significant (1 Tim 4:1; Acts 3:19; but cf. J. Baumgarten, *EDNT* 2:232-35).

10. But see Knight, 429-30.

in the first four items, followed by various immoral tendencies that draw strength from that basic selfish disposition.[11] But Paul's intention is not to unravel the chemistry of impiety in a precise way. Some commentators see the similar vice list of Rom 1:29-32 behind this list;[12] but the behavior indicated is denounced in similar fashion in Hellenistic and Jewish writings,[13] which suggests that conventional wisdom and traditional values are more at work in the formation of this list than any one specific source. One important point of divergence from the list in Rom 1:29-32 is of course the fact that here the impious behavior, which is generally regarded by all as wicked, is associated not with pagans who have never acknowledged God, but with believers who have defected from the faith. The list intends to create a broad impact on its readers; nevertheless, it will be useful to consider each quality separately.

(1) "Lovers of themselves" is a reference to selfishness.[14] Linked to the following evil by the root *phil-*, meaning "love," it establishes the basic anti-God disposition of the people being described. While love of self was encouraged as a positive attribute in the sense of self-esteem,[15] in excess it becomes egotism and selfishness and in this sense is regularly denounced as a destructive human force. Philo, for example, connected love of self with atheism,[16] which is the direction of this list as well.

(2) "Lovers of money" brings the ideas of avarice and greed into the profile. Its rudimentary influence in corrupting behavior places it early in the list.[17] 1 Tim 6:10 employs the cognate noun (see discussion and note) to develop the common view that love of money, or avarice, is an evil that spawns other evils.

(3) The theme of selfishness continues in the next noun, "boasters" ("boastful" TNIV). This vice was widely denounced by the secular writers and was a weakness often associated with the boisterous, self-aggrandizing

11. See Towner, 191; cf. Marshall, 772.

12. Esp. Hanson, 144; Oberlinner, 123.

13. Philo, *On the Sacrifices of Cain and Abel* 32; 1QS 4:9-11. See the discussions in Johnson, 404-5; J. T. Fitzgerald, "Virtue/Vice Lists," *ABD on CD-ROM.* Version 2.1a. 1995, 1996, 1997; A. Vögtle, *Die Tugend- und Lasterkataloge im Neuen Testament* (Munster: Aschendorff, 1936), 8, 12-15.

14. Gk. φίλαυτος (pl. only here in the NT; Josephus, *Antiquities* 3.190).

15. Johnson, 404, citing Aristotle, *Nicomachean Ethics* 1169A ("so therefore it is necessary to love oneself").

16. See Philo, *Allegorical Interpretation* 1.49 (φίλαυτος καὶ ἄθεος) for the use of this term for arrogant self-regard in opposition to God-centeredness.

17. Gk. φιλάργυρος (adj.; see the noun in 1 Tim 6:10). It goes back to Plato (*Laws* 9.870) and is developed further by Plutarch (see Spicq, *TLNT* 3:446-47, for refs.). In the biblical tradition see Luke 16:14; 4 Macc 2:8; *Testament of Judah* 19.1; *Testament of Levi* 17.11. See also Vögtle, *Tugend- und Lasterkataloge,* 233.

rich and other public figures.[18] This word lends itself well to descriptions of those who in their arrogance take themselves to be gods and in so doing oppose the one true God;[19] human conceit that refuses to acknowledge God and God's hatred of this sin is carried into this list as in the list of Rom 1:30.[20]

(4) Corresponding closely to "boasters" is the next adjective, "proud," which also occurs in Rom 1:30. This, too, was a stock vice that was widely criticized in both secular and biblical writings.[21] The use of the term in Jas 4:6 and 1 Pet 5:5, which each quote Prov 3:34 ("God resists the arrogant and gives grace to the humble"), creates the same fundamental dissonance between impiety and God seen in this term's counterpart, "boaster" (cf. Luke 1:51). This antithesis between human pride and acknowledgment of God is thus imported into the list in this second pair of terms.

(5) "Abusive" is the TNIV and NRSV translation of the Greek term that may mean either "blasphemer" of God in a technical religious sense, or more generally "slanderer" (see on 1 Tim 1:13). In the list it marks the turn from selfish egotism to behavior and attitudes toward other people fueled by self-centeredness. As part of the widely used ethical vocabulary, the general sense of slander prevails in secular usage, and that sense is at least partly intended here; but in a case like this, where, in Christian communication, rude and selfish behavior is being equated ultimately with opposition to God, the distinction is not so clear and both senses may be present.[22]

(6) The archetypal End-time villains are also "disobedient to their parents." At this point in the list, there is a slight shift in the rhythm as two words are used to construct this vice and a transition is made to negative words beginning with the Greek *a*- prefix. "Disobedience" occurs elsewhere in these letters in the vice list of Titus 3:3, where it identifies disobedience to God as one of the characteristics of pagan behavior, and in Titus 1:16, where it describes false teachers. This use mirrors Rom 1:30, which is probably defining paganism as especially marked by a failure to honor parents as taught in the Torah (Deut 21:18-21; cf. Exod. 20:12; Deut 5:16). This offense amounted to rebellion, which could be manifested in any number of ways

18. Gk. ἀλάζων (pl.; Rom 1:30; for ἀλαζονεία = "pride, arrogance," see Jas 4:16; 1 John 2:16). Wis 5:8; Philo, *On the Virtues,* 161-62; *On the Special Laws* 4.170; 2 Macc 15:6; cf. *1 Clement* 21.5. Spicq, *TLNT* 1:63-65.

19. Wis 2:16; 2 Macc 9:8 (of Antiochus Epiphanes); cf. Prov 21:24 and Hab 2:5.

20. See Philo, *On the Special Laws* 1.265.

21. Gk. ὑπερήφανος (pl. adj.; "arrogant, haughty"); for references to secular authors, see Spicq, *TLNT* 3:390-92. See the noun ὑπερηφανία ("arrogance, haughtiness") as a sin originating in the heart but manifested in outward forms (Mark 7:22; Deut 17:12; 1 Sam 17:28; Ps 101:5; Obad 3).

22. H. W. Beyer, *TDNT* 1:624; O. Hofius, *EDNT* 1:220-21; cf. 1 Cor 10:30; Col 3:8; Rev 2:9. Marshall, 773.

and was abhorred within the church and Judaism and in the secular world.[23] And there was a close connection between disobedience to parents and disobedience to God.

(7) Ingratitude ("ungrateful") is the next quality in the list. This deficiency is a general one; there is no specific object of this attitude in mind. It was widely disdained as being evil and barbaric.[24]

(8) Closing v. 2 is the religious deficiency "unholy." The term views these sinners in terms of actions that show disregard for sacred duties or laws, or as people who live in rejection of sacred norms (i.e., those by which the community of faith lives; see on 1 Tim 1:9).

(9) Verse 3 continues the list of evils using *a*-privative terms. "Without love" inclines again to the list in Romans 1 (v. 31).[25] It characterizes the evildoers as lacking in any basic love for people.

(10) The next deficiency of character, "unforgiving" ("implacable," NRSV), occurs only here in the biblical writings. It describes the harshest of attitudes, one that refuses reconciliation and thus leads to the destruction of relationships and lives.[26]

(11) "Slanderous" (better "slanderers" as in NRSV) departs from the pattern of *a*-words. In the singular the term may refer to the devil (e.g., 2:26; 1 Tim 3:6), but in this case it means people who are accusers or maligners who seek to damage the reputation of those who are innocent.[27]

(12) Returning to the *alpha* word pattern, the list continues with yet another character flaw, the lack of self-control. This term identifies the inability to deal with temptation, a complete lack of restraint.[28] And people exhibiting this weakness contrast with authentic believers, who are characterized rather by their possession of the opposite virtue of "self-control," an essential element of true spirituality throughout the NT (Titus 1:8; cf. Acts 24:25; Gal 5:23; cf. 2 Pet 1:6).

---

23. Gk. γονεῦσιν (γόνευς, used only in the pl. in the NT for "parents"; Rom 1:30) ἀπειθεῖς (for ἀπειθής, "disobedient," see Titus 1:16; 3:3; R. Bultmann, *TDNT* 6:10). See Philo, *On the Decalogue* 119-20; *On the Life of Moses* 2.198; Josephus, *Against Apion* 2.206; *Sibylline Oracles* 3.593-94; *Testament of Reuben* 3.8; Epictetus 2.17.31; 3.7.26. Osick and Dalch, *Families in the New Testament,* 165-66.

24. Gk. ἀχάριστος (Luke 6:35; Wis 16:29; Sir 29:25; 4 Macc 9:10; Josephus, *Antiquities* 6.305).

25. Gk. ἄστοργος ("without feeling, unloving"); BDAG; MM.

26. Gk. ἄσπονδος ("unwilling to negotiate, irreconcilable, unforgiving"); included in some MSS in the list in Rom 1:31. See esp. Philo, *On the Virtues* 131; *On the Life of Moses* 1.242.

27. For Gk. διάβολος, see the discussion and notes at 1 Tim 3:11.

28. Gk. ἀκρατής ("without self-control"; adj. only here in the NT; Prov 27:20; Josephus, *Antiquities* 16.399); see W. Grundmann, *TDNT* 2:339-42; Spicq, *TLNT* 1:60-62.

(13) The next adjective, "brutal," typically described wild animals and people who behave like them. Titus 1:12 (cf. Jude 10) employs the same metaphor with more explicit language. There is no way to identify specifics of behavior here; the category, however, smears those so described as belonging to the category of uncivilized barbarians.[29]

(14) The final *a*-trait, "not lovers of good," is another deficiency of character that contrasts with the positive profile of godliness in these letters.[30] This characteristic covers a great deal of ground, but, put simply, it is a lack of appreciation and pursuit of the virtues. Within the list, this "disinterest in good" is the corollary of the first vice, "an excessive interest in self." The willful inward turn of the heart and emotions robs the individual of the capacity to love the good.[31]

(15) At v. 5, the list departs from the *a*-pattern, listing three more single qualities and then introducing the first of two comparisons. The plural noun "traitors" ("treacherous," TNIV, NRSV) describes those who betray a cause to which they had once been committed — Jews who killed the prophets (Acts 7:52), Judas who betrayed Christ (Luke 6:16), those who betrayed the Maccabean revolt (2 Macc 5:15; 10:13, 22; 3 Macc 3:24). They are those who have broken faith, display a complete lack of loyalty, and come to serve the opponents' cause. In later Christian writings, this term becomes closely associated with blasphemers and apostates.[32]

(16) Deficiency in self-control takes another form in the term "rash" ("reckless," NRSV). The meaning of this rare term can be narrowed in its NT occurrences from usage in the Wisdom literature, where it refers to speaking before thinking, and from wider secular usage for hotheaded, impetuous, and overbold acts that end up badly.[33]

(17) The characteristic of being "conceited" that follows is identified in 1 Tim 6:4 as a trait of the opponents. Because of the way it can result from overly high self-estimation, Paul warns against "conceit" in the sketch of leadership qualities (see on 1 Tim 3:6). In both cases where the opponents are

---

29. Gk. ἀνήμερος (only here in the NT; Philo, *Allegorical Interpretation* 3.11); see *The Cynic Epistles* (ed. Malherbe), 292.16, where brutishness and brotherly love are opposed. Cf. Spicq, 776; *Letter of Aristeas* 289; Epictetus 1.3.7; Dio Chrysostom 1.14. Cf. further Vögtle, *Tugend- und Lasterkataloge,* 233.

30. Gk. ἀφιλάγαθος ("without interest in good"; cf. Titus 1:8: φιλάγαθος, "lover of good"); BDAG; MM.

31. Cf. Spicq, 776; W. Grundmann, *TDNT* 1:18.

32. Gk. προδότης; *Letter of Aristeas* 270; Josephus, *Jewish War* 3.354. For later Christian use, see Hermas, *Similitude* 8.6.4; 9.19.1, 3b.

33. Gk. προπετής ("impetuous, rash, thoughtless"; Acts 19:36); cf. Wisdom usage: Prov 10:14; 13:3; Sir 9:18; cf. Philo, *On the Special Laws* 3.175; Josephus, *Antiquities* 15.82; *Life* 170. See Spicq, *TLNT* 3:189-90.

thus described, the perfect passive form is used to denote a fixed condition of conceit involving self-delusion.

(18) The list closes formally with a contrastive phrase that reaches back to the first vice (self-love) and accentuates the basic opposition of all such behavior to God: "lovers of pleasure rather than lovers of God." The tendency in the NT to associate "the seeking of pleasure" *(hēdonē)* with the baser side of life (Titus 3:3; Luke 8:14; Jas 4:1) is duplicated here in the use of the compound term meaning "lovers of pleasure" *(philēdonoi)*.[34] As Johnson illustrates, this was a stock charge against philosophical opponents (to love pleasure above virtue or wisdom).[35] The comparative contrast was also a stock device used to set opposing inclinations completely apart — here, the inclination to pleasure and the inclination to God.[36]

(19) Finally, in v. 5a a second contrastive construction serves both a summarizing and a transitional function. The corollary of their lack of love for God (devoutness) is a superficial "piety." Before we consider the precise thrust of the contrast (which allows that these people have either the appearance or embodiment of "godliness" but lack its power), the transition from general prophecy to the actual situation should be brought out. In his first letter to Timothy Paul stressed the opponents' misunderstanding and exploitation of godliness *(eusebeia)*.[37] With that linkage of ideas in mind, the occurrence of the concept here creates the transition from the general description to the local setting, in which Paul brings the full weight of the disparaging list to bear on the present opposition movement: behavior, attitudes, and motives do not correspond to pious claims. This application is deepened in the verses that follow.

The contrast itself is generally mirrored in Titus 1:16, where Paul asserts that the opponents in view there claim to know God but deny him by their deeds. Here, however, the paradox is expressed in other terms. In the

---

34. Gk. φιλήδονος ("loving of pleasure"; G. Stählin, *TDNT* 2:918) and φιλόθεος ("devout, having affection for God"; Philo, *On Husbandry* 88; BDAG; MM), each occurring only here in the NT. The contrast (φιλήδονοι μᾶλλον ἢ φιλόθεοι, "lovers of pleasure rather than lovers of God") may be traditional; see esp. Philo, *On Husbandry* 88 (speaking of the soul that is φιλήδονον καὶ φιλοπαθῆ μᾶλλον ἢ φιλάρετον καὶ φιλόθεον: "loving pleasure and loving passion rather than loving virtue and loving God"); cf. Epictetus, *Gnomologium* 46.

35. Johnson, 405.

36. For similar contrastive constructions (φιλήδονοι μᾶλλον ἢ φιλόθεοι, "lovers of pleasure rather than lovers of God"), see esp. Philo, *On Husbandry* 88 (speaking of the soul that is φιλήδονον καὶ φιλοπαθῆ μᾶλλον ἢ φιλάρετον καὶ φιλόθεον, "loving pleasure and loving passion rather than loving virtue and loving God"); cf. Epictetus, *Gnomologium,* 46.

37. See 1 Tim 6:5-6; 4:7-8; and 1 Tim 2:2 (Excursus).

first half of the statement, Paul might seem to concede that they have "a form[38] of godliness."[39] But the stress is on pretense and insubstantiality, and the phrase describes the opponents (and people like them) as those who make a strong pretense to being pious, perhaps even claiming to be more "spiritual" than the imprisoned apostle and his colleagues, with insistent teaching and claims to a better knowledge of God, but who in various ways unmask themselves as contradictions and fakes.[40]

Some interpreters suggest that the use of the term *eusebeia* in this connection may indicate that the false teachers in Ephesus had coined it in reference to their notions of spirituality (cf. 1 Tim 6:5-6);[41] while this is a possibility, the point of the whole statement is to contrast the opponents' pretentious claim to piety (or their shallow piety) with authentic Christian existence (= *eusebeia*) on the basis of the thing they lack — "power."

In the term "power," Paul renews a theme initiated earlier in the letter (1:7-8, 2:1) by which the role of the Holy Spirit in generating strength for Christian living, service, and suffering is drawn out. Here too the distinction between what the false teachers might claim and authentic Christian existence is the presence (or absence) of "power" produced in responsive believers by the Holy Spirit. The "people" referred to back in 3:2, who have been in view all along, are said to have "denied its [piety's] power." The verb of denial underlines the culpability of the "decision" to veer from the apostolic faith toward some other alternative and carries overtones of apostasy and desertion (see on 2:12-13; 1 Tim 5:8; Titus 1:16; 2:12). The perfect tense ("having denied") reflects on this action of denial as a settled state.

Consequently, in this closing of the profile of the "eschatological" sinners, Paul sums up their error in terms of a counterfeit spirituality that is actually devoid of the Spirit's indwelling presence. Moreover, he indicts them as culpable in having made the decisions that have brought them to this

---

38. Gk. μόρφωσις (it can mean "form, appearance" or "embodiment, formulation"; BDAG); cf. W. Pöhlmann, *EDNT* 2:443-44; J. Behm, *TDNT* 4:754-55.

39. Gk. ἔχοντες μόρφωσιν εὐσεβείας; the construction is close to Rom 2:20, the only other NT use of μόρφωσις (ἔχοντα τὴν μόρφωσιν τῆς γνώσεως), where the content is knowledge.

40. See the similar charge in Philo, *On Noah's Work* 70: "there are some who make a pretense of piety" (εἰσί τινες τῶν ἐπιμορφαζόντων εὐσέβειαν). An alternative explanation stresses the meaning "embodiment"; the reference is a roundabout one to the teaching (= "the embodiment of godliness") that has been made available to the opponents, the "power" of which they have simply failed to appropriate (W. Pöhlmann, *EDNT* 2:443-44). But with such clear denunciation of the opponents' misuse and misunderstanding of the "sound teaching" elsewhere, it seems unlikely that Paul would be so allusive here.

41. See Fee, 63; von Lips, *Glaube,* 82-83.

point. Hanging over the indictment is the implicit contrast made with authentic Christian spirituality, for which *eusebeia* is the code word linking "godliness" with the Pauline gospel. At the same time, the transition is made from eschatology or prophecy to the actual situation in this closing description, and especially in the command to Timothy that follows.

5b   The present tense command to separate from those indicted ("have nothing to do with such people") reflects the actual situation;[42] the instruction to Timothy is thematic.[43] In this case, the "separation" seems at odds with the redemptive approach urged in 2:23, but the people in view now are probably those who are completely hardened in their opposition — the core of the movement (about to be discussed in 3:6-9) that can no longer be reached. "Separation" possibly means exclusion (or expulsion) from the fellowship (cf. 1 Tim 1:20).[44]

6   Verses 6-9 explain the reason for the command *(gar)* by describing the present apostates. This picture incorporates the same features as the picture drawn in 2:16-19: a description of some aspect of their present activity (v. 6), the futility of the movement (vv. 7, 9), and an indictment of their rejection of divine authority and ungodliness made by associating them with traditional opponents of Moses (v. 8).

Those of the opposition caricatured above who are singled out here are characterized on the basis of the devious methods of their work. The present tense participle translated "who worm their way into" carries the sense of secretive "infiltration,"[45] in this case into houses. In the Ephesian context, the tendency to target households already surfaced in 1 Tim 5:13 (cf. Titus 1:11), and it is just possible that the "gullible women" are those vulnerable young widows (who then go "from house to house"). However, in this case Paul digresses from his main point — the opponents and their tactics — to describe in some length and detail a particular target within the household that the false teachers managed to "gain control over."[46] Many recent scholars link this tendency to prey on women with Gnosticism.[47] But the practice of sin-

---

42. Gk. ἀποτρέπομαι (mid. voice, "to turn away from, avoid"; only here in the NT; 4 Macc 1:33); see the discussion in Towner, *Goal,* 64-65; Dibelius and Conzelmann, 116. The reference to "them" (τούτους) also forms a bridge between the paradigm set out in vv. 2-5 and the description of "those" beginning in v. 6 (ἐκ τούτων) who are fulfilling the prophetic picture in Ephesus.

43. See 2:16; 1 Tim 4:7; 6:20; Titus 3:9.

44. Marshall, 776.

45. Gk. ἐνδύνω ("to enter by devious means, slip in"; only here in the NT; cf. Jude 4, παρεισδύνω; Johnson, 406).

46. Gk. αἰχμαλωτίζω (pres. ptc., "to capture in battle"; Luke 21:24); figurative for "to captivate, deceive" (with ideas) in Rom 7:7, 23; 2 Cor 10:5. BDAG; MM.

47. See, e.g., H. Koester, *Introduction to the New Testament,* Vol. 2: *History and*

gling out women was far more widespread and connected with the belief that they were more easily swayed by novel ideas than were men.[48] In some way or other, this focus on women might have been a compensation for the false teachers' commitment to an ascetical regime (i.e., religious activity among women in place of sexual activity; cf. 1 Tim 4:3).[49] Otherwise, the appeal of the teaching for women is not immediately clear. But from other relevant texts[50] it is reasonable to imagine that the false teaching included a new ascetical approach to the traditional female role in household and community, or endorsed a cultural trend that was influencing Christian women from outside the church (see on 1 Tim 2:9-15).

But Paul's concern is to identify the kind of women among whom the false teachers had success, and in doing so he limits his scope. First, he uses the derogatory diminutive term "gullible women" ("silly women," NRSV).[51] While it might be tempting to read into this usage a low opinion of women on the part of Paul, the term clearly describes a very specific group that has proven especially susceptible to the false teachers' advances[52] and should be balanced with a number of references to women in these letters that contain nothing disparaging (1:5; 1 Tim 2:11; 5:3ff.; Titus 2:3-5). Second, the women who have been so captivated are set apart from women (and others) in general by means of the description of their present sinful state: the perfect tense participial construction "who are loaded down"[53] graphically depicts these women as chiefly characterized by a heavy load of past "sins" under which they continue to struggle in the present. He does not spell out what, or what type of, "sins" are envisaged (see on 1 Tim 5:22); the point seems to be that the influence of sin on the conscience has made these women vulnerable to the lies of the false teachers.

Their weakness against sin is amplified in the next participial phrase, which closes the verse: "swayed by all kinds of evil desires." Here the present passive participle refocuses on the present outworking of the past sinfulness

---

Literature of Early Christianity (Philadelphia: Fortress, 1982), 303-4; Haufe, "Gnostische Irrlehre und ihre Abwehr in den Pastoralbriefen," 331-32; Rudolph, *Gnosis,* 225, 229-30, 291-93.

48. See Josephus, *Antiquities* 18.65-86; and the suspicion about Paul's motives in *Acts of Paul and Thecla* 7-14; see also Dibelius and Conzelmann, 116 n. 10; Fee, 273-74.

49. See Johnson, 411-14; Marshall, 776, who refers to W. Lütgert, *Die Irrlehrer der Pastoralbriefe* (Gütersloh: W. Bertelsmann, 1909), 38-40.

50. See 1 Tim 4:3 and the discussion at 2:9-15.

51. Gk. γυναικάριον (only here in the NT; "little women"); see Epictetus, *Enchiridion* 7; BDAG; Johnson, 411-14.

52. Cf. the technique in 1 Tim 5:15.

53. Gk. σωρεύω ("load up, heap up," and so here "to be loaded down with, overwhelmed"); for a similar sense, see Rom 12:20 (Prov 25:22).

and depicts the effects as an inability to fight off harmful impulses (i.e., rather to be "led" by them);[54] enslavement to "various lusts" was already established as a characteristic of the life outside of Christ (Titus 3:3; cf. 2 Tim 2:22).[55]

7   The futility of these women's situation is finally emphasized, with heavy irony, by describing them as incessant learners who are, however, unable to learn what really matters. The picture drawn depicts them as constantly seeking out every kind of teaching[56] (or of listening patiently to nonsense), to grasping at any and all teaching, with no discernment, in hopes of finding something of meaning. Their inability to arrive at the supreme goal, "a knowledge of the truth," is to be linked to their sin-burdened consciences, which leave them completely unable to search with discernment. As we have seen, in these letters the phrase "coming to a knowledge of the truth" is a polemical conceptualization of conversion; it views the process of coming to faith from the perspective of the cognitive affirmation of the apostolic gospel (see on 1 Tim 2:4). The futility of all the women's striving, and of the false teachers' claims to be able to offer this knowledge, is contrasted openly in 3:15 with the singular capacity of the Scriptures to enlighten unto salvation.

It is worth mentioning again that this select group of disciples and some of the opponents are singled out for very harsh treatment in this passage in a way that seems to rule out the options, stressed in 2:23-26, of correction and repentance.[57] The previous passage shows how those involved in the false teaching might be dealt with, while the present passage sets out the worst-case scenario; perhaps the previous passage should guide our reading of this denunciation (see below).

8   Paul's central interest is in the core group of the opposition. At this point he develops further the indictment begun above by drawing a parallel between them and the traditional opponents of Moses. The shift back to this topic is abrupt, signaled by the phrase "in the manner which" ("just as," TNIV).[58] Two characters from Israel's past are named, Jannes and Jambres, magicians of

---

54. Gk. ἄγω (4:11; pass. "to be led," of good and bad influences; see BDAG, s.v., for refs. connecting the verb with ἐπιθυμία = "lusts").

55. For ἐπιθυμία ("lust, desire") see on 1 Tim 6:9. The language and thought of addiction to sin (ἀγόμενα ἐπιθυμίαις ποικίλαις, "led by various lusts") parallels Titus 3:3 (δουλεύοντες ἐπιθυμίαις καὶ ἡδοναῖς ποικίλαις; "enslaved to various lusts and pleasures").

56. Gk. πάντοτε μανθάνοντα (for μανθάνω see 3:14[2x]; 1 Tim 2:11 [discussion and note]; 5:4, 13; Titus 3:14); the present tense participle strengthened by the adverb "always" underlines the ongoing nature of this incessant activity.

57. See Oberlinner, 133-35; Wagener, *Die Ordnung des "Hauses Gottes,"* 96-97.

58. The Gk. phrase ὃν τρόπον (the conj. δέ need not be translated) is idiomatic, used to introduce a comparison (Matt 23:37; Luke 13:34; Acts 7:28 [citing Exod 2:14]); BAG, s.v.; for examples of the phrase followed by οὕτως to introduce the thing compared, see LXX Josh 10:1; Isa 10:11; 62:5; Acts 1:11.

Pharaoh's court who opposed Moses. The derivation of the names is debated.[59] Jannes may be the Greek transliteration of *Johana,* which is possibly derived from the Hebrew verb *'anah,* meaning "to oppose or contradict."[60] Jambres may be a misspelling of an original *Mambres* (as some Latin and Greek versions have it), which may then be derived (via the spelling *Mamrey*) from the Hebrew *marah,* meaning "to rebel."[61] Whatever the derivation of the names, their link to the tradition is established by the Damascus Document (CD) 5:17-19: "For formerly Moses and Aaron arose by the hand of the Prince of Lights; but Belial raised up Jannes and his brother, in his cunning, when Israel was saved for the first time." Subsequent references are numerous and spread among Jewish,[62] Christian,[63] and secular Latin and Greek writers.[64] What is noticeable, apart from varieties of spelling and variance from single to double mention of the two characters, is the way the tradition elevated their roles to archetypal status. They came to represent Moses' archnemeses, who would counter his displays of divine power with various tricks of their own; and by their association with various stories (such as Balaam's servants or sons, trailing Israel through the wilderness, and instigating the Golden Calf rebellion[65]), they acquired symbolic status as opponents of the truth. Paul's purpose is to place the false teachers troubling the Ephesian church into the same category as those who oppose God's work and who will consequently never succeed, and more implicitly to establish the connection between Moses' authority as YHWH's specially appointed servant and his own apostolic ministry (just as in 2:18-19).

This indicting function of the well-known story[66] is activated against

59. Gk. Ἰάννης and Ἰαμβρῆς; for discussion of the various forms in which these names appear, see A. Pietersma, *The Apocryphon of Jannes and Jambres the Magicians* (Leiden/New York/Köln: E. J. Brill, 1994), 36-42; idem, *ABD on CD-ROM.* Version 2.1a. 1995, 1996, 1997; Dibelius and Conzelmann, 117; Schürer, *History,* 3:2, 781-83; H. Odeberg, *TDNT* 3:192-94; Marshall, 778-79.

60. See H. St. J. Thackeray, *The Relation of St. Paul to Contemporary Jewish Thought* (London: Macmillan, 1990), 221.

61. Thackeray, 220.

62. E.g., *Tg. Ps.-J.* on Exod 1:15; 7:11; Num 22:22; *Exod. Rab.* 9; *b. Menaḥ.* 85a; etc.; see further StrB 3.660-64.

63. See Origen, *Commentary on Matthew* 23:37; 29:9; *Contra Celsum* 4.51; *Acts of Pilate* 5.1 (Hennecke-Schneemelcher, 1:456); etc.

64. See Pliny, *Natural History* 30.1.11; Apuleius, *Apologia* 90; etc.

65. See H. Odeberg, *TDNT* 3:192-93.

66. It is not possible to determine a source for this tradition (Spicq, 779, suggests that Paul learned it from the Targum). The NT attests to the fact that other expansions of OT stories were common currency in the early church's tradition (Acts 7:22, 23, 53; 1 Cor 10:2, 4; Gal 3:19; Heb 2:2; Jude 9). Paul alludes to these figures generally in the way that the rabbinic writers did. His reader(s) presumably knows the developments surrounding these two characters in tradition.

the present opponents in two ways. First, syntactically, Paul "distributes" the charges against the historical characters ("just as") to the contemporary opponents ("so also"). Second, a bit of wordplay substantiates the link between the past activities of Jannes and Jambres and the present activity of the false teachers as each is summed up generally with the verb "to oppose, resist," with the tenses adjusted (aor. first, then pres.) as needed:[67]

> "Just as Jannes and Jambres opposed [antestēsan] Moses, so also these teachers oppose [anthistantai] the truth."

However, the special circumstances surrounding the present challenge require the traditional pattern to be contextualized. Thus in the contemporary setting, it is "the truth" that the opponents oppose rather than Moses. As we have seen, "the truth" is the gospel that Paul preaches (v. 7; see on 1 Tim 2:4). Its authority, already underlined by the polemical identification of it as "the truth," is strengthened by association with Moses. To this point, the opponents of Paul have been charged with standing in opposition to God's truth; they have also been typed as those outside of God's people by association with the traditional figures; and they have been indicted both for their ineffectiveness in leading people to salvation (v. 7) and for practicing outright defiance of the truth.

Two parallel statements add to the denunciation of the present opponents. First, "They are men of depraved minds." In these letters to coworkers this is a stock description of the opponents,[68] whom Paul depicts as people with malfunctioning minds, as revealed (and also probably caused) by their rejection of the gospel (= "the truth").[69] They are unable to discern between error and truth.[70] In this state, it is impossible for them to apprehend the truth of the gospel or its ethical implications.

Second, and more summarily, Paul categorizes these people as those whose faith has been tested and found to be "unfit" ("rejected," TNIV; see the note at Titus 1:16). The commentators and translations are divided over whether the reference point indicated by the qualification "as far as the faith

---

67. Gk. ἀνθίστημι ("to oppose, resist"; 2 Tim 4:15; used of the sorcerer Elymas in Acts 13:8; Rom 9:19; 13:2); from aorist ἀντέστησαν to present ἀνθίστανται.

68. Cf. the Gk. phrases ἄνθρωποι κατεφθαρμένοι τὸν νοῦν; διεφθαρμένων ἀνθρώπων τὸν νοῦν (1 Tim 6:5; see discussion); ἀλλὰ μεμίανται αὐτῶν καὶ ὁ νοῦς (Titus 1:15; see discussion).

69. Gk. καταφθείρω ("to destroy, ruin, corrupt"; perf.; only here in the NT). The perfect tense denotes a present state entered into in the past; the association of this state with their past and ongoing rebellion is surely implied. Cf. 1 Macc 8:11; Spicq, TLNT 2:278-79.

70. See on 1 Tim 6:5; Towner, Goal, 158-59.

is concerned" is the personal faith of the opponents or "the objective faith" (i.e., the Christian faith).[71] On the basis of the closely parallel phrase in 1 Tim 1:19, their failure is measured in terms of their personal faith-relationship with God (or claims thereto), which in the case of the false teachers is worthless, nonexistent, and a sign of their rejection by God, rather than in terms of their substandard doctrine, though the two things are closely related.

As the OT allusion fades momentarily (see below), the appropriation of the archetypes of deception has placed the present reader(s) into the past narrative, and the unity of God's story is understood: what has gone around is now (again, in "the last days") coming around. The pattern established in the early stage of God's story of redemption finds renewed expression in the opposition of "the last days." Equally present in the adoption of the analogy, though more implicit, is a comparison of Moses' authority with Paul's. As in the seminal story, so in the latter days — God's representatives and people will triumph over all opposition.

9 As in the historical duel between Moses and Pharaoh's magicians, the present rebels' days are numbered. Paul returns to familiar patterns of language to describe the movement here in terms of "progress" (see on 2:16; 3:13).[72] In this case, however, there is no irony involved as Paul stresses the end of these opponents. The translations reflect some uncertainty in this statement about progress ("they will not get very far," TNIV),[73] but the sense is probably that in spite of their success in the community, they will not go farther.[74] Paul pronounces their end, and can do so with confidence on the basis of the linkage he has created with the OT pattern.

This narrative reemerges as the interpretive grid as Paul explains the reason (*gar;* v. 9b), which involves to some degree the effectiveness of Timothy's work in the churches and of his encounter with the opponents. Through this prophetic encounter (Moses is the model), which includes the correct teaching and preaching of Paul's gospel and the correction of those who have fallen in with the heretics, the "folly" (Luke 6:11) of the opponents "will become clear"[75] to all. This measurement of their failure is, however, not simply

---

71. Cf. Marshall, 780; following Parry, 63; Knight, 436; NRSV; with Spicq, *TLNT* 1:361; TNIV.

72. Cf. the Gk. here (ἀλλ' οὐ προκόψουσιν ἐπὶ πλεῖον; "but they will not get far") with that of 2:16 (ἐπὶ πλεῖον γὰρ προκόψουσιν ἀσεβείας; "for they will progress more and more in ungodliness").

73. Cf. "they will not make much progress" (NRSV) and "they will progress no further" (e.g., NKJV).

74. The meaning turns on the prepositional phrase ἐπὶ πλεῖον (2:16) in this negative construction (cf. Acts 4:17; 24:4; *1 Clement* 18.3; BDAG, "πολύς," 2.b.β); Kelly, 197; Marshall, 780.

75. Gk. ἔκδηλος (only here in the NT; see 3 Macc 3:19; 6:5; *Letter of Aristeas*

a matter of a lack of teaching; the moral dimension to "folly" is developed fully in the Wisdom and Intertestamental literature;[76] the malfunctioning of their mental processes (v. 8) has yielded error in thought and action for which they are culpable. Their rejection of Paul and his gospel is proof enough of both dimensions (though the vices of vv. 2-5 are not far from mind), and their bold proclamation of a false message is finally equated with the antics of the magicians who opposed Moses. The closing statement compares the folly of the present-day opponents with that of Jannes and Jambres ("as in the case of those men, *their* folly will be clear to all"); the futility of their opposition to the God of Israel was finally demonstrated when they could no longer produce imitations of the miracles worked by Moses (see Exod 7:12; 8:18; 9:11).

Although it is quite clear that Paul wishes to separate the hardened apostates from the rest of the community, and that his method of caricaturing (vice list and use of well-known traditions) intends to put forth a blanket case, we need to read this passage not as so many latter-day "Timothys" but, I would argue, as those whose own potential includes apostasy. What makes an apostate? First, there is one's disposition toward the gospel. In the case of this letter, apostates are those who have not simply deserted the faith but who have remade the gospel into a shape that for some reason they found more accommodating. Certain elements in that remaking emerge, but there is a broader influence that is more useful for us to notice. For whatever reasons, they found Paul's gospel insufficient or uncomfortable, probably because it did not affirm them as they wished to be affirmed, or protect the things that were most valuable to them. Perhaps because of its stress on equality or universality, those whose insecurities depended instead on affirmation of their uniqueness tended to resort to interpretations that underlined limitations and reinforced boundaries. Perhaps because of its stress on the unfinished nature of salvation and the pervasiveness of sin, those who were unsettled by a gospel that continually addressed immaturity and imperfection found it more comfortable to reshape the gospel into the proclamation of a finished salvation now. Whatever reasons lay beneath the production of a false, competing gospel, it must be assumed that the Pauline gospel somehow failed to satisfy some. Only those who had become hardened in their rejection of the traditional apostolic gospel are singled out in 3:1-9, but the tendencies that were

---

85). The future tense "will be" (ἔσται) expresses the statement either as a promise or an assertion, either way stressing the certainty of what will take place (see Burton, *Moods and Tenses*, 33-34; Marshall, 780).

76. Gk. ἄνοια (Prov 14:8; 22:15; in 2 Macc 4:6, 40; 14:5; 15:33; *2 Clement* 13.1); ἄνοια is equivalent to wickedness; in Josephus, *Antiquities* 8.318, it is associated with rude behavior (see also Job 33:23; Ps 21:3; Wis 15:18; 19:3; 3 Macc 3:16, 20). Cf. J. Behm, *TDNT* 4:962-63; G. Harder, "Reason, Mind, Understanding," n.p., *NIDNTT on CD-ROM*. Version 2.7. 1999.

almost certainly at work in bringing them to this point are tendencies with which we ourselves have to wrestle.

Within our churches there exists this kind of apostasy, often passing itself off as doctrinal purity or rigorous adherence to "the traditional faith" or "orthodoxy," be it Reformed, Lutheran, Baptist, or what have you. At the level of movements, at some point in time "the faith" came to be set in concrete, determined by historical councils and the documents and creeds that they produced. While the usefulness of such historical events and documents in helping us to understand the trajectories of the faith and the ways in which historical factors influence theology should not be denied, the habit of setting the faith into concrete is nothing less than a caging of the gospel. At the personal level, the same is true. Whenever one reaches the point where the gospel or "the faith" has been completely systematized, completely molded into a shape that one feels most comfortable to live with, the gospel has been incarcerated. Its teeth have been removed.

But the gospel is untamable, and to "cage" it in this way is really to reach a point where a person or a group does not listen to it anymore. Paul's gospel is wild, it seeks out weak spots in life, it challenges traditions and long-held notions, and it refuses to allow Christians to live too comfortably in their understanding of the faith or to cherish their personal interpretations. It stands over all actions and theologies, and critiques them; and when that critique is not heeded, the road to apostasy has been entered.[77] It is embarrassingly obvious from our own experiences with movements, churches, denominations, traditions, and theologies that reaching such a place in our belief is a very real possibility. But this is also obvious from another perspective. Another glance at the qualities listed in the vice list of 3:2-5 reminds us that these are sins to which all people are prone, and which in contemporary Western society (I will leave other cultures for those who live in

---

77. Cf. the perspective of M. Volf, *Exclusion and Embrace* (Nashville: Abingdon, 1996), 208-9, as he describes the *world of the Scriptures* that (along with the *world of culture*) Christians inhabit: "Is this world best thought of as a 'coherent tradition,' in the sense in which Thomism, for instance, represents a coherent tradition . . . ? I do not think so. The biblical texts are a canonical bundle of overlapping testimonies from radically different contexts to the one history of God with humanity which culminates in Christ's death and resurrection. The Scriptures come to us in the form of plural traditions. The texts and the underlying 'story of the history' which unites them . . . do not offer a coherent tradition. Instead, they demand a series of interrelated basic commitments — beliefs and practices. These commitments *can be developed* into traditions. But such traditions are always secondary phenomena, in need of being interrogated and reshaped in the light of both basic commitments and changing cultural contexts. Christian theologians have their own good reasons to suspect that there is some truth to Nietzsche's aphorism in *Twilight of Idols,* which states that 'the will to a system is a lack of integrity.'"

them) have been easily incorporated into a comfortable, materialistic, appearance-oriented way of life (e.g., "lovers of money, boastful, proud, without self-control, conceited, rash, lovers of pleasure rather than lovers of God"). And just as Paul drew the similar picture of sin in Rom 1:29-31 on his way to the statement that "there is no one righteous . . . there is no one who seeks God . . . all have sinned" (Rom 3:10, 11, 23), so too here Paul more than half contemplates the possibility that the picture he has drawn of End-time villains could just as easily turn out to include any number of lazy, un-wary, uncommitted believers, as well as believers committed to the wrong things. Rather than taking this passage safely as a graphic portrait of "them" in distinction from "us," and so using it to reinforce the boundaries (theologi-cal, social, sexual, economic, cultural) we prefer to live cozily within, it is ca-pable of functioning as a mirror that is ready to reflect unsettling and painful tendencies in our character. The mirror reveals to bring healing and growth, but the one gazing into it must own the reflection for this to happen. The way of Paul's gospel that Timothy is credited with having taken is about to be de-scribed (vv. 10-17); it is a way filled with its own dangers, but it is a better way to go.

2. The Way of Following Paul (3:10-17)

> 10 *You, however, know all about my teaching, my way of life, my purpose, faith, patience, love, endurance, 11 persecutions, sufferings — what kinds of things happened to me in Antioch, Iconium and Lystra, the persecutions I endured. Yet the Lord rescued me from all of them. 12 In fact, everyone who wants to live a godly life in Christ Jesus will be persecuted, 13 while evildoers and impostors will go from bad to worse, deceiving and being deceived. 14 But as for you, continue in what you have learned and have become convinced of, because you know those from whom you learned it, 15 and how from infancy you have known the Holy Scriptures, which are able to make you wise for salvation through faith in Christ Jesus. 16 All Scripture is God-breathed and is useful for teaching, rebuking, correcting and training in righteousness, 17 so that all God's people [or the servant of God] may be thoroughly equipped for every good work.*

Still within the broader framework of parenesis to Timothy (3:1–4:8), this section renews the call to Timothy to follow Paul and share in the apostolic sufferings. It is presented as the antithesis to the ways of the opponents, a technique that Paul uses in each letter to Timothy to denounce error and ac-centuate genuine godliness. To sharpen the contrast, Paul matches the vice list above (vv. 2-5) with a commendatory list of nine virtues and experiences that characterized his ministry. Timothy was already well aware of these things and committed, at least intellectually, to them; they move from theology to ethics and motivation, Christian character, with the last two items exploring the crucial experience of suffering (vv. 10-11). Reference to suffering becomes a transition to a restatement of the paradox that godliness leads to suffering, while evil continues to advance (vv. 12-13). Now that the groundwork has been relaid, the instructions enjoin the coworker to continue without swerving in the way of the faith that he has received from Paul, family, and Scripture (vv. 14-15). Finally, the importance of Scripture, Timothy's touchstone, is examined (vv. 16-17).

10-11 Paul shifts to instruction with the contrastive combination "you, however" (3:14; 4:5; Titus 2:1; see on 1 Tim 6:11). This device creates the typical turnabout, as the contrast is drawn between the road the opponents are going down and the way of Paul that Timothy is to follow. The verb used to describe Timothy's way belongs somewhere on a continuum of meaning from the literal sense of "following behind" to the more figurative derivation "paying attention, following with the mind."[1] Since part of what Timothy is said to "have followed" includes Paul's experiences of sufferings that occurred prior to his joining with Paul (v. 11), the meaning of the term must fall into the cognitive semantic range: knowledge of, perception, and even affirmation.[2] The use of the term in 1 Tim 4:6 also speaks of Timothy's intellectual commitment to Paul's "teaching," which the false teachers have failed to maintain. The statement demonstrates his loyalty to Paul, a loyalty that extends to the whole pattern of Paul's life and ministry.

The device of Pauline modeling (and call to imitate) is certainly implicit, and it is of course accurate to say that Timothy had, by this time, shared many experiences with Paul.[3] But at this stage the parenesis is chiefly laying the groundwork for renewed imitation (see 3:14; 4:1-5), not celebrating Timothy's past success in doing so. In a letter aiming partly (at least) to restore Timothy's confidence and partly to urge him to accept the mantle of the Pauline mission, renewal of his previous commitment to the ministry and leadership is far more obvious in the text than any idealization of Timothy as a church leader or canonization of "Paul" as a moral example on a par with Christ.[4]

What amounts to a list of virtues (in contrast to the vice list above),

---

1. Gk. παρακολουθέω (with διδασκαλία also at 1 Tim 4:6; see note and discussion); cf. Johnson, 416.

2. The TNIV rendering ("you . . . know all about") is unnecessarily vague as it omits (or leaves too implicit) the thought of commitment to what is being described; its rendering of the same verb in 1 Tim 4:6 ("you followed") is preferable.

3. Cf. Brox, 257; Kelly, 198.

4. *Contra,* e.g., Brox, 257-58; Oberlinner, 137-38.

then, enumerates some of the distinctive characteristics that comprise this way of Paul ("my") recommended for Timothy. Nine items are given, with the last two being explored in somewhat greater detail because they correspond to the chief theme of the letter: the need for Timothy to embrace suffering. Effectively, the movement is from the theoretical or objective ("the teaching") to the practical or existential (the rest).

(1) Paul's "teaching" is listed first (3:16; 4:3),[5] since divergence from it is largely the issue in the heresy. It refers to the gospel and attendant doctrinal and ethical developments in various community situations, particularly within the orbit of the Pauline mission. While its contents are difficult to measure, for the tradition would have still been growing, an identifiable body of teaching centered around the message of the death and resurrection of Jesus Christ, such as the entire Pauline corpus gives witness to, is to be understood. Naturally, for Timothy to continue the Pauline ministry, he must be firmly convinced of and committed to the message for which the ministry exists.

(2) "My way of life" is the second item in the list. This term takes us into the realm of daily conduct (cf. 1 Cor 4:17) and suggests, as used of Paul, a life patterned after Christ and lived on the basis of a knowledge of the will of God.[6] Paul implies that his own life and conduct provides an observable template for Christian living, and the items that follow belong to that template.

(3) "My purpose" employs the same term used of God's planning to give the gift of salvation in 1:9 (see discussion and note). As the term applies to Paul,[7] it expresses the ideas of commitment and firm resolve to carry out what he felt called to do. And in his case, and in this context, that involves executing his mission to the Gentile world.

(4) "Faith" (see on 1 Tim 1:2) is a typical Christian virtue found in the virtue lists of these letters to coworkers in tandem with such things as "patience and love" (2:22).[8] Although the term can mean both "faithful" and "believing," Paul probably means that invisible "vertical" dimension of his Christian existence in which he experienced his relationship with God through faith in Christ. Thus he adds the depth of his trust in God to the other qualities that characterize his life.

(5) "Patience" is an aspect of the divine character in 1 Tim 1:16,[9] and

5. See 1 Tim 1:10 (discussion and notes); 4:6.

6. Gk. ἀγωγή ("way of life, conduct"; occurring only here in the NT; cf. Esth 2:20; 10:3; 2 Macc 4:16; 6:8; 11:24; Josephus, *Antiquities* 14.195; of the Christian "way of life" in *1 Clement* 47.6; 48.1). Spicq, *TLNT* 1:29-31; K. L. Schmidt, *TDNT* 1:128-29.

7. Cf. Acts 11:23; 27:13.

8. See the discussion at 1 Tim 1:5, 14; 6:11.

9. See the discussion and note; Rom 9:22; 1 Pet 3:20.

here a quality that the Spirit seeks to produce in all believers (Gal 5:22), which Paul associates specifically with the tasks related to ministry (2 Cor 6:6; 2 Tim 4:3). It is the ability to wait for results and to persevere in the face of opposition.

(6) "Love" (1:7; 2:22) is tied to "faith" as its visible counterpart that takes the form of sacrificial, costly service done for others.[10]

(7) "Endurance" also occurs in the virtue lists used to guide Timothy in pursuing godliness (see on 1 Tim 6:11). In Pauline vernacular, it is a quality that is particularly manifested in the context of suffering (Rom 5:3-4; cf. Jas 1:3; 5:11), and so in his perception came to be an identifying mark of those involved in his mission to the Gentiles (2 Cor 1:6; 6:4; 12:12). Here too it occurs in the list as a foreshadowing of the fundamental element of suffering that is about to be considered.

(8-9) The list concludes in v. 11 with two items that are linked closely together and set off from the preceding items by their plural form and by their reference to actual events (instead of qualities). This is what Paul most wants to highlight. The first is "persecutions," by which he means his specific experiences (thus the plural form) in which he was persecuted for his faith, for proclaiming the gospel (cf. 2 Cor 12:10).[11] Timothy (and his readers) perhaps perceived some level of irony as they recalled the author's self-description, with the related term, "persecutor," at 1 Tim 1:13.[12] But more dominant in the present context is the conclusion that the apostle's trials for the faith have become paradigmatic for all who follow Christ.

The second term, "sufferings," is broader in scope,[13] but in one dominant use still to be linked with suffering as a Christian (Rom 8:18), which Paul again associates closely with his personal experience and apostolic ministry (2 Cor 1:6, 7; Phil 3:10; Col 1:24).[14] In fact, at this point, and in the remainder of the verse, Paul is essentially establishing once again his credentials as an apostle. The three texts just cited reflect his own understanding of the central place of sufferings within his ministry; they were the means by which he identified with and participated in the sufferings of Christ, and it was through them that he would complete his ministry. While Paul undoubtedly regarded his suffering as fundamental (certainly for his apostleship) for

10. See 1 Tim 1:5, 14 (discussion and notes); see on 2 Tim 1:7 and 2:22.

11. Gk. διωγμός. The term is used outside the NT of hostile pursuit of various sorts (see esp. Quinn-Wacker, 741-42, for discussion and refs.), but within the NT (sg. in Matt 13:21; Mark 4:17; Acts 8:1; pl. in Mark 10:30; 2 Cor 12:10; 2 Thess 1:4) and later Christian writings (e.g., *Martyrdom of Polycarp* 1.1; see Lampe, *PGL,* s.v.) it acquires the more precise meaning of persecutions for the faith.

12. Gk. διώκτης (discussion and note at 1 Tim 1:13); so Quinn-Wacker, 747.

13. E.g., Rom 7:5; Gal 5:24 for human "passions."

14. Gk. πάθημα. See Quinn-Wacker, 747-48; W. Michaelis, *TDNT* 5:930-35.

the church and (possibly) as unique among Christian suffering in general (so here Paul draws attention to "my" experiences),[15] this point too is suppressed here in order to demonstrate that his coworker has equally been called to participate in the sufferings that shaped the apostle's ministry and life.

Having drawn attention to this peculiar dimension of his "way," "persecutions and sufferings," Paul makes the transition[16] to an illustration of these experiences from personal history. The defining experiences of Paul's ministry were those that occurred during his first missionary journey (2 Cor 11:25; Gal 4:13-14). Now he turns back to that page in his story to illustrate how "persecutions" and "sufferings" were a typical feature of his calling as apostle to the Gentiles.

Three place names are mentioned. "Antioch" refers in this instance to Pisidian Antioch, which in 25 B.C.E., by decree of Emperor Augustus, had become a Roman colony and thereafter a prosperous and influential city within the empire, with impressive buildings associated with the Imperial cult and citizens (from elite families) who were the first from the eastern provinces to enter the Roman Senate.[17] Paul visited this city during his first missionary journey; after a period of preaching, "the Jews" turned people of influence against Paul and Barnabas and raised up a persecution that forced them to leave (Acts 13:14-52).

"Iconium" was a prosperous city located on a strategic crossroads connecting the cities of the provinces of Macedonia, Achaia, and Asia with the Roman capital.[18] It was in Iconium (Acts 14:1-5), where Paul and Barnabas had again enjoyed initial success among Jews and Gentiles, that the division among the people created by a contingent of Jews finally developed into the threat of harm to the missionaries (stoning; 14:5), causing the team to flee to Lystra.

Also founded by Augustus (26 B.C.E.) as a Roman military colony, "Lystra" was closely linked with Iconium.[19] According to Luke's account (Acts 14:6-19), Paul visited Lystra next in the sequence. Once again due to

15. E. Lohse, *Colossians and Philemon* (Hermeneia; Philadelphia: Fortress, 1971), 72; see also Quinn-Wacker, 747-48.

16. The relative plural pronoun οἷα (οἷος) gathers together "persecutions" and "sufferings" into the subject of the first relative clause ("which things happened to me").

17. Acts 13:14; 14:19, 21. See S. Mitchell, "Antioch of Pisidia," n.p., *ABD on CD-ROM.* Version 2.1a. 1995, 1996, 1997; Quinn-Wacker, 748-50. The name Ἀντιόχεια is shared by several cities founded during the Seleucid era (e.g., Syrian Antioch, Acts 11:20).

18. See further W. W. Gasque, "Iconium," n.p., *ABD on CD-ROM.* Version 2.1a. 1995, 1996, 1997; Quinn-Wacker, 750.

19. See further D. S. Potter, "Lystra," n.p., *ABD on CD-ROM.* Version 2.1a. 1995, 1996, 1997; Quinn-Wacker, 750-51.

the efforts of Jews from Antioch and Iconium who were dogging his trail, Paul actually suffered stoning (14:19; 2 Cor 11:25) and was dragged out of the city for dead.

The point of this return to the past is not to introduce new information, for Timothy probably joined Paul not too many months after these episodes (Acts 16:1), and he would have known well the experiences of Paul in Lystra and Iconium (16:2).[20] What Paul does is to remind him of the pattern that is still in effect; therefore, in a sense, Paul's Roman imprisonment is simply a matter of consistency.

But the reality of suffering must be held in balance with the experience of divine help (cf. 2:8-13) that also characterized the Pauline ministry. Paul establishes this balance by means of two devices — the first rhetorical, the second, theological. First, there are two ways to take the next relative clause, as the differing translations of the TNIV and NRSV illustrate. According to the TNIV, the second relative clause, "the persecutions I endured" (or "which persecution I endured"), repeats the first, in rather redundant fashion, as a way of resuming the train of thought prior to the enumeration of places. The NRSV's rendering, "What persecutions I endured!" takes the second occurrence of the relative pronoun as introducing an exclamation. The latter option is most likely. On the one hand, the repetition of the noun "persecutions" would be unnecessary if the aim were simply to repeat the previous thought.[21] More important, on the other hand, might be the rhetorical value of the repetition of the noun and relative pronoun. The twofold reference *(tois diōgmois . . . hoia . . . hoious diōgmous)* places brackets around the events associated with the three cities and the paradigm they represent that further emphasizes the importance, in Paul's discourse-logic, of this episode, in order to lend even more weight to the statement about divine help about to be made.[22] The verb "endure" is used elsewhere in the NT of "bearing up" under temptation (1 Cor 10:13) and unjust punishment (1 Pet 2:19) in the sense of "holding out, not caving in." The nuance of willingly undergoing trials (i.e., "taking them onboard") rather than avoiding them may be pres-

---

20. It is pointless to argue that a "genuine" Paul would have pointed Timothy back to persecutions experienced after Timothy had joined him (i.e., those recorded in Acts 16–17; Dibelius and Conzelmann, 119). In the first place, Timothy's link to Lystra and Iconium suggests that he would have had knowledge of events that had taken place in Paul's first visits there (Marshall, 785). Secondly (given Paul's own pre-Christian history; Acts 7:57–8:1a), the single experience of having been stoned was clearly etched deeply in Paul's and the early church's minds, which he recalled as fundamental to his apostleship (2 Cor 11:25; cf. Quinn-Wacker, 751). For various theories of Acts dependence on the tradition preserved in 2 Timothy, see Marshall, 785.

21. BDF §304; Marshall, 785.

22. Cf. Quinn-Wacker, 743.

ent;[23] but the main point is to couch these experiences in terms of extreme struggle. The exclamation, "What persecutions I endured!" implies the sequence of events recounted by Luke in Acts — a sequence that culminates in a potentially fatal stoning. As the prelude to a climactic intervention, this scenario provides an ideal setting within which to affirm the Lord's faithfulness to rescue his servants.

Second, a theology of suffering is introduced by way of an OT echo to underline God's protection of his servants and to authenticate again the Pauline mission. Following the exclamation, a contrast ("yet")[24] is introduced:

> 2 Tim 3:11: ". . . what persecutions *(diogmous)* I endured. Yet the Lord rescued me from them all" *(kai ek panton me errysato ho kyrios).*

The wording of this statement corresponds closely to the second half of Ps 33:18 (LXX; MT 34:17-19):

> "The righteous ones cried out, and <u>the Lord</u> heard them <u>and delivered them from all their afflictions</u>" *(ekekraxan hoi dikaioi, kai <u>ho kyrios</u> eisēkousen autōn <u>kai ek pasōn tōn thlipseōn autōn errysato autous</u>).*[25]

Ps 33:20 resumes the language, stating the principle (in the future tense) underlying the act of deliverance celebrated two verses earlier:

> "Many are the afflictions *(thlipseis)* of the righteous, and yet he will rescue them from them all" *(kai ek pasōn autōn rhysetai autous)*[26] (cf. Pss 33:5; 141:7).

The theme of "deliverance" begins in Ps 33:5, but Paul seems to have made his entrance at the point where it is applied specifically to the Lord's intervention on behalf of "the righteous" in 33:18-20. Thus he makes explicit his interest in a theology of suffering built on the OT theme of the righteous sufferer. This theme — the suffering of the righteous and the Lord's promise to vindicate them — was already present in some Jewish circles,[27] and was

---

23. Gk. ὑποφέρω (perf. probably serving for the aor.; BDF §§80-81). See F. Hauck, *TDNT* 4:582.

24. The Gk. conjunction καί is adversative, "but" (e.g., Rom 9:33).

25. Ps 33:18 (MT = 34:19): ἐκέκραξαν οἱ δίκαιοι, καὶ ὁ κύριος εἰσήκουσεν αὐτῶν <u>καὶ ἐκ πασῶν τῶν θλίψεων αὐτῶν ἐρρύσατο αὐτούς</u>; 2 Tim 3:11c: <u>καὶ ἐκ πάντων με ἐρρύσατο ὁ κύριος</u>. See also Pss 33:5, 20; 141:7; Esth 10:3; 1 Macc 2:60.

26. πολλαὶ αἱ θλίψεις τῶν δικαίων καὶ ἐκ πασῶν αὐτῶν ῥύσεται αὐτούς.

27. Psalms 22; 38; 69; Wis 2:12-20; 5:1-7.

taken by the early church in reference to Christ.[28] Paul had already extended the pattern to include Christians (Rom 8:36; 10:16; cf. Acts 13:47), and here interprets his experience according to that pattern. In place of the term "righteous" is the statement in 3:12 that associates "godly living" with "persecution"; 3:12 is thus essentially a contextualized form of Ps 33:20a.[29] Given the importance of the "godliness" language in these letters to coworkers, this transposition is almost predictable. Other changes are incidental.[30]

Consequently, by means of the echo, Paul assumes the role of the OT righteous sufferer and links his sufferings closely to the suffering of Jesus. He allows the theme to interpret his apostolic ministry and extends it to explain the missiological dimension of the church's existence. The appearance of the theme foreshadows Paul's conclusion in 4:16-18, where there is, however, a significant difference in accent. Here, looking backward and toward Timothy's ongoing ministry, Paul's experience of "deliverance" (rhyomai; 4:17, 18)[31] relates to temporal, physical rescue ("from all of them" [i.e., the aforementioned sufferings]). These rescues stand as evidence not only of the Lord's (here Christ's; in the Psalms YHWH's) love[32] but also of the apostle's status as one who stands in the line of righteous sufferers, along with OT prophets, the Suffering Servant, and the Messiah. Seen in this light, suffering is neither meaningless nor hopeless. Paul's suffering (in prison at present or in the past) confirms, rather than denies (as some might have been alleging; cf. 1:16), his divine calling. Sufferings come, but the Lord rescues. Why? The answer comes in the OT

---

28. See, e.g., L. Ruppert, *Jesus als der leidende Gerechte?* (SB 59; Stuttgart: Calwert, 1972).

29. The association of *eusebeia* ("godliness") with *dikaios* ("the righteous") was also taking place in the later OT literature; Prov 13:11; cf. Isa 33:6; 4 Macc 9:24; see 1 Tim 2:2 (Excursus).

30. The replacement of the psalmist's term "afflictions" (θλίψεις) with "persecutions" (διωγμοῖ) and "sufferings" (παθήματα) is incidental and occasioned by Paul's discourse; instead of the feminine form "from all" (ἐκ πασῶν), required by the object "afflictions" (τῶν θλίψεων), Paul uses the masculine form (ἐκ πάντων) in connection with the masculine term "persecutions" (διωγμούς).

31. Gk. ῥύομαι in the NT has a narrower range of meaning (usually for deliverance from people and their schemes; but cf. Col 1:13) than σῴζω; 16 times in the NT; e.g., Rom 7:24; 11:26 (from LXX Isa 15:31; 59:20); 2 Cor 1:10 [2x]; Col 1:13; 1 Thess 1:10; 2 Thess 3:2 [infrequent in contrast to σῴζω, 106x]). Quinn-Wacker, 743-44, suggest that this verb, occurring frequently in the Psalms, has a specifically liturgical connotation in NT usage. More significant, however, is the way this verb creates contact with the theme of suffering and deliverance. Cf. G. Harder, *TDNT* 6:561; W. Kasch, *TDNT* 6:998-1003.

32. Here again "the Lord" (ὁ κύριος) refers to Christ; Paul thus continues to articulate the christological transfer (of actions originally attributed to YHWH to his Messiah) by means of OT echoes.

background: the suffering ones are the Lord's righteous; his pledge is to rescue them completely ("from all of them").

When Paul reaches the end (4:16-18), divine rescue is still his hope, though it will have to be interpreted more broadly. But at this point he lays down a pattern to shape Timothy's thinking.

12-13 Yet however much the suffering of the apostle might be more fundamental to the church God is building, the startling fact (for Paul's opponents and some modern interpreters) is that the pattern of righteous suffering encompasses the whole community of faith. And this fact is intrinsic to a proper understanding of Christian existence. To make this point, the church is now embraced by the same contrast with which Paul has continually distinguished his ministry and message from the beliefs and behavior of the opposition (2:15-22; 3:9-10), which has now been seen in the light of eschatology (3:1-5). The language is by now familiar to us, but the way Paul has implicated the entire church in suffering deserves consideration.

Verse 12 states the corollary: godliness brings persecution. The thought is not a new one[33] but rather belongs within the entire eschatological matrix of thoughts that comprises Christian existence. In this discourse, however, the literary and conceptual connections formed produce a dramatic effect. First, Paul shifts the thought with a surprising and emphatic thrust from Timothy to "everyone," the Greek wording supplying the emphasis on "everyone" ("in fact, everyone," TNIV; "Indeed, all," NRSV).[34] Second, the verb "will be persecuted"[35] picks up a term used twice of Paul's experiences, which at once involves everyone in the Pauline "way" and normalizes it. As a warning, it is open-ended, though Paul's experience underlines the inevitability of the outcome. The only qualification comes in the way believers are described.

Thirdly, Paul's language intends to distinguish between genuine and false believers, in preparation for the next statement. Believers are described in two ways. First, they are those "who want to live a godly life." These are not would-be Christians, but, as the function of the term "godliness" throughout these letters to coworkers indicates, those who are characterized by their resolve[36] to live a life that is a combination of authentic faith in God and ap-

33. Matt 5:10-11; 24:9; Acts 14:22; Rom 5:3; 8:18; 12:14; *Barnabas* 7.11.

34. Placing the adjective "all" between the two conjunctions (καὶ πάντες δέ . . .) gives it emphasis. Cf. 1 Tim 3:10.

35. Gk. διώκω (see discussion and note at 1 Tim 6:11; for the meaning "to persecute," see Rom 12:14; 1 Cor 15:9; BDAG, s.v.). The future passive implies the inevitability of the outcome.

36. LXX Pss 33:13; 62:2. Gk. θέλω ("desire"; see 1 Tim 1:7; 2:4; 5:11; cf. Phil 2:12 for the notion of God's will at work in a human being). For the idea that this "desire" itself is a manifestation of the Spirit, or "the complement of the divine 'will to save'" (so Quinn-Wacker, 751), see *1 Clement* 22:21; Ignatius, *To the Romans* 8.1.

propriate behavior (see 1 Tim 2:2, Excursus). These are at the opposite end of the spectrum from the opponents who have denied the power of true godliness (3:5). Secondly, the phrase "in Christ Jesus" (3:15) indicates, as it has elsewhere in the letter, the source of this life, namely, personal faith in Christ.[37]

On the whole, the fact that this accent is present here suggests two things. First, the modern interpretation that sees this letter as designed to canonize Paul (his message and sufferings), stressing a near equality between his sufferings and Christ's, fails to appreciate the way in which this text incorporates all people in this dimension of life. Second, the point is almost certainly made here to counter the realized eschatology of the opponents, which made suffering completely irrelevant and even odious. Of course, within the parenesis to Timothy, the statement provides further foundation for previous instructions concerning suffering.

Yet this corollary alone does not fully characterize the present evil age. Summing up the exposition of 3:1-9, Paul again contrasts *(de)* the situation of Christians with that of their opponents (v. 13). In so doing, he fits the phenomenon of heresy into the characterization of the church's "now," thus neatly completing the paradox: while the righteous suffer persecution, evil people prosper, getting worse and worse with no apparent hindrance to their evil influence. The OT righteous puzzled and lamented over this injustice, expressing this sentiment in various ways.[38] Paul's expression of the lament here focuses explicitly on the false teachers, whom he contrasts vividly with genuine believers. Three aspects of this contrast require comment.

First, the two descriptions of the people in mind, "evildoers" and "impostors," do not intend to distinguish two classes of sinners. Rather, the focus of the more general reference to "evildoers"[39] is narrowed in the second, more striking reference to "impostors." This rare term ranges in meaning from the technical sense of a "sorcerer" (who deceives by practicing magic and witchcraft) to the broader sense of "deceiver, cheat, charlatan."[40] It is tempting to see in this term a link back to the image of Pharaoh's court sorcerers, Jannes and Jambres (v. 8), who for Paul served as illustrations of opposition, and in this way to import the charge of sorcery or the practice of magic to the opponents in Ephesus.[41] However, the more general meaning of "deceivers" is probably suffi-

37. See 1:1, 9, 13; 2:1, 10; see also the discussion at 1 Tim 1:14.
38. Pss 10:1-5; 37:7; Jer 12:1; Dan 8:25; 11:36; Mal 3:15.
39. Gk. πονηρός ("bad, wicked, evil"; see 4:18; 1 Tim 6:4; Matt 15:19; Luke 11:13; Acts 3:26; Rom 1:29; 12:9 [in contrast to what is "good"]); G. Harder, *TDNT* 6:546-62.
40. Gk. γόης (pl.; only here in the NT; Josephus, *Jewish War* 2.261, 264; 4.85; 5.317; *Antiquities* 20.97, 160, 167, 188; *Against Apion* 2.145, 161; Philo, *On the Migration of Abraham* 83 (see further G. Delling, *TDNT* 1:737). For the cognate noun γοητεία (guile, witchcraft), see 2 Macc 12:24.
41. See Quinn-Wacker, 753; cf. Spicq, 104-10, 783. Marshall, 786-87, allows that

cient in view of the subsequent description of their activities in terms of deceit. In any case, the term is pejorative (they are liars and cheats who pass themselves off as godly teachers), and Paul concentrates on deception and the particular category of false teaching (not magical practices) when he continues the characterization, employing the term as is done in the philosophical debates.[42]

Second, Paul again resorts to irony. As in 2:16, he employs the same "progress" terminology that was often associated with positive education[43] in order to emphasize that these "teachers" are steadily making "gains" but in the wrong direction: they "go from bad to worse" (TNIV; NRSV).[44]

Finally, in a traditional configuration, "deceiving and being deceived," these evil people are blatantly exposed in terms most fitting to the situation of false teaching and apostasy under discussion. "Deception" describes equally well what they do and what they are (cf. Sir 16:23). As false teachers, they actively deceive and enslave others with their false message, while they themselves are equally deceived (1 Tim 1:7; Titus 3:3). This language of deception (see on Titus 3:3) was associated typically with idolatry and false prophecy in the OT,[45] as well as with the phenomenon of heretical Christian movements whose deception, as we have seen, was itself a dominant element in "the last days" scenario.[46] Rhetorically, the use of the traditional derogatory alliteration "deceiving and being deceived" *(planōntes kai planōmenoi)*[47] blackens the negative side of the contrast and makes climactic and memorable the distinction between the persecuted righteous (Paul, Timothy, and believers who recognize their authority) and the opponents who de-

---

an oblique reference to magic used to imitate Christian practices might be included in the picture, or possibly the reference might include false religions and sects outside the church that were associated with magical practices (Acts 8:9; Matt 24:24). But this seems to exceed the demands of polemic employed here.

42. R. J. Karris, "The Background and Significance of the Polemic of the Pastoral Epistles," *JBL* 92 (1973): 549-64; L. T. Johnson, "Timothy and the Polemic against the False Teachers: A Re-examination," *JRelSt* 6-7 (1978-79): 1-26; Towner, *Goal,* 262-63 n. 22.

43. See the discussion at 2:16; cf. 3:9.

44. The notion of "worsening" in general is expressed here, on the model of 2:16, with the prepositional phrase ἐπὶ τὸ χεῖρον (cf. Mark 5:26, where the prep. is εἰς); in 2:16, where "impiety" is the stated "gain," the phrase is ἐπὶ πλεῖον. For the entire phrase, see Josephus, *Antiquities* 4.59; 18.340. G. Stählin, *TDNT* 6:704, 714-16.

45. LXX Deut 4:19; 11:28; 13:6; 30:17; Ps 95:10; Isa 3:12; 9:15, 16; 30:10; 44:20; Jer 23:17, 32; Ezek 14:9, 11; 44:10, 15; Mic 3:5; Wis 11:15; 12:24; Tob[S] 14:6; Bar 4:28.

46. Matt 24:4, 24 [par.]; Luke 21:8; 2 Thess 2:11; 1 John 3:7; 2 Pet 3:17; Jude 11; Rev 2:20; 13:14.

47. Gk. πλανῶντες καὶ πλανώμενοι (see the instances of this configuration in Marshall, 787; Dibelius and Conzelmann, 119; Lock, 109).

ceive out of their own deception.[48] Whatever success they seem to have in the present struggle, compared with the godly who suffer, ultimately their judgment and punishment is certain (Prov 13:9; 21:16; 28:10; 2 Tim 4:1, 10, 14).

14-17 As one contrast concludes, another commences with the same attention-getting device, "but as for you" (3:10; see on 1 Tim 6:11), which points Timothy in a different direction. The instructions, which carry through to v. 17, are carefully constructed: (1) the basic instruction (v. 14a); (2) two causes, motives, or reasons for obeying the instructions, followed by a statement of the Scriptures' salvific power that validates the motives (vv. 14b-15ab); (3) a supporting argument for the power of the Scriptures, based on their nature and function (v. 16); (4) a final statement of the purpose or result of the stated uses of the Scriptures that circles back to Timothy in his situation of ministry and opposition. We will examine the argument piece by piece.

(1) The reference to the deceptive intentions of the opponents in v. 13 forms the immediate background of this instruction to Timothy (v. 14a). Against the tide of opposition with its alternative gospel, Timothy is to "continue in what [he] has learned," to stand his ground and resist going with that flow of innovation and deception. The verb Paul utilizes occurs elsewhere (especially in Johannine writings) to encourage "continuing in" an accepted teaching (1 John 2:24) or "abiding in" the relationship with Christ.[49] Here the first sense is intended, with the attendant relative clause ("what you have learned") identifying that to which he is to remain committed.

Two additional verbs describe Timothy's past and present relationship to the Christian faith. First, he has "learned" (3:7)[50] the contents of the faith,[51] which refers generally to his acquisition through Paul and others of the "sound teaching" (1:13) and the *parathēkē* (1:14). A second verb takes the thought to another level: it either expands on Timothy's deep conviction about the faith ("have become convinced of," TNIV) or comments on his "faithfulness in"[52]

---

48. Cf. Quinn-Wacker, 753.

49. For Gk. μένω, see 1 Tim 2:15 (note).

50. For Gk. μανθάνω ("to gain knowledge by instruction, to learn"), see 1 Tim 2:11 (discussion and notes).

51. The relative phrase ἐν οἷς ("in which things").

52. The translations (NRSV, TNIV) stress the thought of Timothy's firm belief or conviction about what he has learned. Gk. πιστόω ("to be faithful, to be convinced") allows for this; but the sense of the verb is disputed, and the range it covers, from (act.) "to make trustworthy" (cf. R. Bultmann, *TDNT* 6:178-79) to (pass.) "to be convinced" (NRSV, TNIV), or to be made trustworthy, to give a pledge, to be persuaded (3 Macc 4:20), makes narrowing the meaning difficult. The context of the letter suggests that the LXX-attested sense of "to show oneself faithful to; to be true to" (Ps 77:37, cited by *1 Clement* 15.4), as a measurement of faithfulness to the covenant, may make a good fit. Cf. Marshall, 787-88.

580

it. Either option is possible for the verb, but the sense of "faithfulness" or "trustworthiness" in the faith (as evidenced in his life and teaching) corresponds more closely to the contrast developing between Timothy's commitment to the faith and the heretical rejection of it. And it prepares for further reflection on the coworker's responsibility, and the call to him to succeed Paul in the mission.

(2) Now follow, in vv. 14b-15, two reasons or motivations for obeying the instruction. The first of these, dependent on the causal participle "because you know,"[53] consists of the people "from whom[54] you learned it." The force of the phrase parallels the instances of this device in 1:5 and 2:2 and amounts to the argument "the teaching is as good as its teachers"; that is, Timothy should "continue in it" because he knows that the character of those who taught the faith to him verifies the trustworthiness of the contents. Parallel references and the present context (v. 15) suggest that the source includes Paul and others who have taught him (2:2), including family members (his mother and grandmother are indicated in 1:5; cf. 3:15). This equation of the reliability of the commodity and character of those who convey it was a standard way of measuring a truth claim in Paul's culture; and it is the steady and historical dimensions of the gospel (demonstrated by the reliability of the people mentioned) that Paul draws on here.[55] To veer from what had been passed on by trustworthy predecessors, without some good reason, was the exception and not the rule. Novelty had little intrinsic value and was regarded with suspicion.

The second reason (v. 15a) is parallel with the first, pointing to another thing Timothy knows (v. 14b),[56] which reaches back to his childhood. He "knows" that he was raised on the teaching of the Scriptures.[57] The rhetorical thrust of the reference, which intends to stress length of history, is ex-

---

53. Gk. εἰδὼς παρὰ τίνων ἔμαθες ("because you know from whom you have learned it"); the causative sense of the adverbial participle is usual; the preposition παρά, indicating the source of teaching (with μανθάνω), is typical (Sir 8:9; BDAG, s.v. 1).

54. The singular reading τίνος (C³ D Ψ TR lat) is a secondary attempt to limit the reference to Paul. See Elliott, 20; Marshall, 788.

55. For the rather strained view that Timothy is projected here as the "model" of the officebearer or that this passage is to be understood within the author's grand design to canonize an office succession that goes through Timothy back to Paul, see Brox, 259-60. This may have been the intention of the scribe who emended the plural τίνων to the singular τίνος (see Elliott, 20), but it does not correspond to the logic of the passage.

56. The phrase καὶ ὅτι forms the link back to εἰδώς, the καί coordinating v. 14b and v. 15a, with ὅτι introducing the thing known (εἰδὼς . . . ὅτι . . . ; "knowing . . . that . . .").

57. Some wordplay links the two experiences set out in v. 14b and v. 15a: in each case the word expressing "knowledge of" is based on the verb οἶδα: v. 14b, the participle εἰδώς (eidōs) . . . ; v. 15a, the finite form οἶδας (oidas).

pressed well with the phrase "from infancy" (TNIV).[58] Paul apparently draws on his knowledge of Timothy's upbringing in traditional Jewish fashion.[59] From the account in Acts 16:1, which identifies Timothy's father as being a Gentile, we should probably conclude, in conjunction with 1:5, that his Jewish mother and grandmother would have been mainly responsible for his learning of "the holy Scriptures" in the early years.[60]

In the writings of Philo and Josephus the phrase "holy Scriptures" (*hiera grammata;* with or without the definite article[61]) designates technically the Jewish Scriptures or some part of them.[62] But it is not a "title" for the Bible in the early Fathers and occurs only here in the NT.[63] Its reference in our text is apparently a nearly technical one to the OT Scriptures (in Greek translation; LXX),[64] but probably views them from a certain educational perspective. In this context, of course, it does not refer to the entire Christian Bible.

The way in which the term is meant may be seen by analogy with other uses of the seldom-used configuration *hiera grammata*. The adjective "holy" *(hieros)*[65] is seldom used in the canonical OT writings and, apart from its occurrence in compounds (cf. Col 4:13), it appears only in 1 Cor 9:13 (as a substantive) in the NT.[66] The term rendered "Scriptures" by the TNIV is de-

---

58. Gk. βρέφος (BDAG, s.v.); the phrase is formed here with the preposition ἀπό; see Philo, *On the Special Laws* 2.33); cf. Luke 1:41 (of an unborn child); 1 Pet 2:2; rendered "from childhood" by the NRSV.

59. According to *Pirqe Abot* 5:21, a male child was taught beginning at the age of five.

60. Those who allege contradictions between this reminiscence and the account in Acts (Timothy was uncircumcised with a Gentile father) presume to know far more about the actual situation of Timothy's upbringing than Acts reveals; see Marshall, 789.

61. The inclusion of the definite article τά (A C* D¹ Ψ 1739 1881 TR; Elliott, 155; Quinn-Wacker, 764) is uncertain. It is more likely to be secondary (ℵ C² ᵛⁱᵈ D* F G 33 1175 WH; BAG 330; Dibelius and Conzelmann, 120 n. 7; Fee, 281; Marshall, 782), since the anarthrous reading is the harder reading and the occurrence of anarthrous nouns with adjectives or followed by attributives is not unusual in these letters to coworkers.

62. Gk. ἱερὰ γράμματα (cf. Rom 1:2, ἐν γραφαῖς ἁγίαις); for ἱερός, meaning "holy," which occurs only infrequently in uncompounded form in biblical Greek (1 Cor 9:13; Josh 6:8; Dan 1:2; ἅγιος is far more frequent), see G. Schrenk, *TDNT* 3:221-30. For the phrase in reference to the OT Scriptures, see Philo, *On the Life of Moses* 2.290, 292; *On the Embassy to Gaius* 195; Josephus, *Antiquities* 1.13; 10.210; see also G. Schrenk, *TDNT* 1:763-65.

63. Cf. *1 Clement* 43.1; 45.2 for similar configurations, but the language is not technical (Quinn-Wacker, 765).

64. G. Schrenk, *TDNT* 1:761, 765; Quinn-Wacker, 764.

65. Gk. ἱερός (adj.; Josephus, *Antiquities* 16.27; *1 Clement* 43.1 of the Scriptures); G. Schrenk, *TDNT* 3:221-30.

66. Quinn-Wacker, 765, link the relative infrequency of ἱερός, in comparison with

rived naturally from the Greek term *gramma* (meaning "letter of the alphabet"), which in the plural often referred to a writing or document or literature or education in a general way.[67] In the present context, the combination "holy writings" (cf. "sacred writings," NRSV) is sufficient to refer to the writings of the Jewish religion in distinction from other literature.[68] However, the noun *graphē* in 3:16[69] was the more normal term for a passage of Scripture (sg.) or "the Scriptures" (pl.): the plural combination *hagiai graphai* for the OT (e.g., Rom 1:2) is a natural development. Thus the alternative phrase in 3:15, *hiera grammata,* is probably not meant as the equivalent of *hagiai graphai* (or *graphai*), but rather identifies the OT writings (thus the adj. *hiera*) from a more specifically instructional perspective (than the general designation as *graphē* in 3:16 would intend). If instruction in the will of God is the dominant theme, then the background for this phrase may be discussions of the imperative to train Jewish children in the holy literature that they might know the law of God.[70]

The point of this second reason for "continuing" is, then, twofold. On the one hand, training in the holy writings has been a way of life for Timothy, stretching back to his early years. Longevity and tradition are factors bearing intrinsic value. On the other hand, and perhaps the more important feature of the motivation, is the way in which the second reason qualifies the first: what Timothy has learned (from Paul, his family members, and others) is, according to the implications of v. 15a, in accordance with the Scriptures in which he was trained. The Pauline gospel is continuous with the will of God revealed in the holy writings; if the ancient writings are regarded as in some sense authoritative and irreplaceable, so too the revelation of Jesus Christ (and related *didaskalia*) according to Paul's gospel.

Attached to the second reason — Timothy's training in the Scriptures — is an additional incentive (v. 15b). The Scriptures have the ability or power to lead one to salvation, a power that stands in contrast with the impotence of the false teachers (3:5).[71] Several things should be noticed. First,

---

ἅγιος (cf. Schrenk, *TDNT* 1:751; 3:226), to its association with various aspects of pagan religious practice.

67. Gk. γράμμα ("letter of the alphabet"; in the pl. "writings"; BDAG, s.v. 2.c); further references in Schrenk, *TDNT* 1:762, 764.

68. See J. A. Sanders, "Canon, Hebrew Bible, A," n.p. *ABD on CD-ROM.* Version 2.1a. 1995, 1996, 1997.

69. Matt 26:54, 56; Mark 14:49; Luke 24:27; Acts 18:24, etc.

70. See, e.g., *Testament of Levi* 13.2; *Testament of Reuben* 4.1; cf. Spicq, 791 n. 1 (for Philo and Josephus); Quinn-Wacker, 765-66.

71. The Holy Scriptures "are able" (τὰ δυνάμενα) to make wise, while the false teachers have denied the power (τὴν δὲ δύναμιν αὐτῆς ἠρνημένοι) of godliness.

THE SECOND LETTER TO TIMOTHY

Paul is speaking about the same salvation goal[72] as his gospel delivers (Rom 1:16), but is doing so in the first place in terms of the OT writings. The verb "to make wise" echoes the theme expressed variously in the Wisdom literature, that God's law, word, precepts, and the like are the source of wisdom and life.[73] The Pauline gospel may be seen as continuous with the power and intention of the ancient Scriptures, and it is possible that the usefulness of the OT needed to be reaffirmed in the wake of heretical misuse of it.[74]

Second, this continuity is further underlined in the way that salvation is simultaneously rooted in Paul's gospel in the phrase "through faith in Christ" (see on 1 Tim 1:14). The relation of this prepositional phrase is typically taken to qualify either the preceding activity of enlightenment (to make wise by means of faith . . .) or salvation (the means by which salvation may be obtained). There is really little difference between these options, the thought being that Paul guards against any notion of obtaining salvation apart from faith in Christ. Understood in a looser sense,[75] the addition of "through faith in Christ . . ." does not relativize the previous statement of the OT Scriptures' power to lead to salvation. That potential is real. However, it does direct attention to the need to interpret and understand the holy writings by means of the Christian lens and from within a genuine relationship with Christ. For Paul, Christ is the climax of the biblical story, and the biblical story interprets Christ; the OT Scriptures and the Christ-event are integrally related. The whole phrase repeats the pattern seen in 1 Tim 1:14, where "which is in Christ Jesus" identifies the place in which something (here faith, there faith and love) pertains, namely, authentic Christian existence. The syntax is cumbersome, and the logic may seem to verge on the circular; but as in similar constructions (Rom 8:39; Gal 3:26; 1 Tim 1:14), the point is to identify the genuine relationship with Christ as the locus within which various dimensions of spirituality may be experienced (as also v. 12).[76]

It is the life characterized by faith in Christ that releases the potential of the Scriptures for the eyes of faith. False teaching cannot deliver the promise of salvation. Paul's gospel, on the other hand, grounded as it is in the truth of Christ's death and resurrection, completes the ancient revelation in a way that augments and releases its power to save.

---

72. The goal of salvation expressed by the Gk. prepositional phrase εἰς σωτηρίαν ("for salvation") is practically formulaic (Acts 13:47; Rom 1:16; 10:1, 10; 2 Cor 7:10; Phil 1:19; 2 Thess 2:13; etc.).

73. Gk. σοφίζω (act. "to make wise, instruct"; Pss 18:8 LXX; 119; Sir 1:8); cf. U. Wilckens, *TDNT* 7:527-28.

74. See on 1 Tim 1:4; 4:1. Cf. Marshall, 790; Oberlinner, 145.

75. Cf. Marshall, 790.

76. For the view that the phrase "which is in Christ Jesus" expresses the object of faith, see Knight, 444.

(3) The statement that follows (v. 16) clearly adheres logically to the argument that has been developing, supporting the assertion of the Scriptures' power (v. 15b) by emphasizing their divine source and usefulness. It is also a statement whose first three words, primarily (*pasa graphē theopneustos;* "All Scripture is God-breathed," TNIV; "All scripture is inspired by God," NRSV) have received a great deal of attention as a fundamental doctrinal statement (or *theologoumenon*) about the inspiration of Scripture. But this approach to the text has sometimes been only minimally alert to its function within the discourse and has perhaps returned certain results that exceeded the purpose of the argument. From the standpoint of methodology, the present discourse should determine the limits of Paul's intention in making the statement. The question of Paul's meaning in those first three words (as well as in the rest of the statement) hinges on several smaller questions; because of the amount of interest in this text, it will be helpful to work through the issues in some detail.

First, the opening phrase is ambiguous for at least three reasons. (a) The Greek adjective *pasa* can be translated as "all" or as "every" depending on whether it is modifying a collective noun or one that refers to items individually.[77] (b) A solution to this problem thus revolves around the meaning of the second word, *graphē,* which in this context might mean "a scripture" (i.e., a specific text within the OT) or possibly refer collectively to "Scripture" as the whole of the (presumably) OT Scriptures. (c) Complicating the interpretation further is the question of the relation of the adjectives, *theopneustos* ("God-breathed") and *ōphelimos* ("useful"), to the preceding "every [all] scripture [Scripture]," caused in part by the omission of a verb.[78] The second adjective will be in the predicate position: ". . . is profitable." *Theopneustos,* however, might be understood as an attributive adjective modifying *graphē* ("every [all] *inspired* Scripture is useful . . ."), or as a predicate adjective coordinate with "useful" ("every [all] Scripture is *inspired* and useful . . .").

This ambiguity results in the following four basic interpretive options:[79]

(i) "All Scripture is inspired by God [understanding the reference to be at least to the whole OT as a collected unity]."[80]

77. Gk. πᾶς (fem.); thus "all" in Matt 3:15; 28:18; Acts 1:21; 2:36; Rom 11:26; Eph 2:21; Col 4:12; "every" in John 1:9; Eph 3:15; Heb 9:19.

78. A form of the verb "to be" (εἰμί) is assumed, but since it is unexpressed it is somewhat unclear whether it takes both adjectives as its predicate, or just the last one.

79. The possibility that something other than biblical writings is included in the scope of the reference is too remote to consider (as Marshall, 792, points out, γραφή in the NT must refer to Scripture in some sense).

80. TNIV/NIV; NRSV; GNB; REB; Knight, 445; Simpson, 150-51.

(ii) "Every [text/passage of] Scripture is inspired by God."[81]
(iii-iv) "Every/all inspired Scripture is also useful. . . ."[82]

The degree to which these differences actually yield significant differences in meaning (or theology) varies, with (iii-iv) perhaps being open to the most dramatic implications. In any case, deciding between the options will require an analysis of the details.

We begin with the meaning of *graphē*. Above we noted that the terms *gramma* ("letter"; v. 15) and *graphē* ("writing, text") are not interchangeable. They do, however, share the tendency to express a range of meanings. In general, *graphē* denotes something that has been written.[83] With the biblical writings as our context, the term in the singular would normally refer to a passage or text within a book (1 Tim 5:18).[84] Ordinarily, the plural takes the meaning "the Scriptures,"[85] but the singular is not used to refer to a book of the Scriptures.[86] Gal 3:8 and 22 are texts sometimes cited as instances in which Paul employs the singular in reference to the whole of the Scriptures.[87] However, the singular term in 3:8 is easily identified with the specific OT text Paul subsequently adduces to prove his point; 3:22 may seem a broader reference, but in view of Paul's technique in Galatians (and elsewhere), and in view of his normal tendency (along with other NT writers) to distinguish between the singular and the plural, he is more likely to be referring to the implications of the texts he has employed than to the whole body of the OT Scriptures.[88]

If Gal 3:22 is an exceptional use of the singular for the whole, the con-

---

81. G. Schrenk, *TDNT* 1:754; Kelly, 202; Hanson, 151-52; B. B. Warfield, *The Inspiration and Authority of the Bible* (Philadelphia: Presbyterian and Reformed, 1948), 134. For the predicative sense of θεόπνευστος, which is expressed in (i) and (ii), see also Quinn-Wacker, 753; Guthrie, 175-76; Lock, 110; Jeremias, 61; Kelly, 203; Oberlinner, 148-49.

82. Dibelius and Conzelmann, 118; Barrett, 114; REB; E. Schweizer, *TDNT* 6:454; Brox, 261.

83. Gk. γραφή (H. Hübner, *EDNT* 1:260-64; G. Schrenk, *TDNT* 1:749-61); it also applies in some cases to the process of writing, but that is not relevant here.

84. 4 Macc 18:14; Mark 12:10; Luke 4:21; John 7:38; Rom 4:3; Gal 3:8; Jas 2:23; 1 Pet 2:6; etc.

85. Cf., however, 2 Pet 3:16, where the plural (τὰς γραφάς) denotes passages of Scripture without referring to the whole OT.

86. *Pace* Quinn-Wacker, 767. As Marshall points out (citing Josephus, *Against Apion* 2.45), 791, the term ἡ βίβλος would normally be used to indicate a "book" within "the Scriptures."

87. Esp. G. Schrenk, *TDNT* 1:753-55; Quinn-Wacker, 767.

88. Marshall, 791; E. de W. Burton, *Galatians* (Edinburgh: T&T Clark, 1921), 160, 196; but cf. R. B. Hays, *Echoes of Scripture in the Letters of Paul* (New Haven: Yale University Press, 1989), 106-7.

text of 2 Tim 3:16 would still need to determine the precise sense here. In this case it must be noted that Paul has echoed specific OT texts and stories in the near context (2:19; 3:8-9, 11; cf. 2:7; 4:14, 17-18) for the purpose of correction and instruction (see v. 16b), and has referred to the entirety of the Scriptures (albeit uniquely as instructional materials) in the plural in v. 15. Consequently, the singular *graphē* in 3:16 most likely refers to a passage or text within the collected OT Scriptures (primarily in this case the LXX).[89] The scope of the reference is expressed by the term that precedes it.

The choice between "all" and "every" for the adjective *pasa* is determined by the meaning of *graphē* — whether the singular means a text/passage of Scripture or the whole of the Scriptures. There is no other occurrence of the phrase *pasa graphē* in the NT to provide further guidance (cf. 2 Pet 1:20).[90] In view of the decision on *graphē* above, option (ii) is the preferred interpretation. This yields the meaning "every [text of] Scripture."

The scope is extensive, leaving no text of "Scripture" unaccounted for. The only question would be whether the contents go beyond the OT to include writings of the early church already in circulation,[91] but this does not seem very likely. If the whole of the Scriptures is thus included within the scope of the statement, what then is the difference between (ii) and (i)? There is in effect no difference in the scope of the material covered (which is important for the extent to which inspiration applies); the difference lies entirely in the way in which the OT is envisaged. To adapt a distinction applied by Johnson, Paul thinks of the OT here in terms of function and usefulness (and applicability to the church's situation) rather than in terms of ontology,[92] and his own use of it in the course of the drafting of this letter almost certainly shaped his reference to Scripture here.

Consequently, he conceives of it as "useful" text by text, as it were, which is precisely the way in which it is employed in this letter and elsewhere, with the understanding that paradigms discovered in the OT texts (the Exodus story, the Abraham narratives, the story of Korah's rebellion, the Servant Songs, the Psalms, etc.) bear directly on God's people in the present when properly interpreted. Given his use of the OT stories in 2 Timothy, and his desire that Timothy do likewise (vv. 16b-17), as well as the possibility that the false teachers were developing an OT "canon within the canon" (in effect overemphasizing certain kinds of passages and underemphasizing, or even denying the relevance/inspiration of, others),[93] Paul may well have felt

89. See also Marshall, 792; Oberlinner, 147; cf. Johnson, 423.
90. 2 Pet 1:20: πᾶσα προφητεία γραφῆς (= "every prophecy of Scripture").
91. So Knight, 447-48; Spicq, 787-88.
92. Johnson, 423.
93. See the discussion of "myths and endless genealogies" at 1 Tim 1:4; 4:1-5.

the need to affirm that divine inspiration applied evenly to all texts, passages, and stories of the OT, but this anticipates a conclusion to ambiguity (c) noted above.

If *pasa graphē* were to mean "the OT as a whole," which seems less likely, the question of the syntax of the clause would be moot; for it would make no difference whether one said "the whole of the OT, which is inspired," or "the whole OT is inspired," since the reference to Scripture would conceive of it as a whole, not in parts. But in the case where the reference to the texts of Scripture is distributive ("every [text of] Scripture . . ."), the ambiguity in the syntax holds the potential for a rather significant variance in meaning. Again, the function of the first adjective, *theopneustos,* is either predicative (coordinate with *ōphelimos;* ". . . is inspired by God and useful"), or attributive ("Every passage of Scripture that is inspired [or "every inspired passage of Scripture"] is useful").

The solution to the syntactical problem cannot be obtained on strictly grammatical grounds. The *pas* + noun + adjective combination yields examples of both attributive and predicative readings.[94] Drawing on context, some interpreters have argued that since the statement is really about Scripture's "usefulness," "inspiration" is just a thought that is tagged on to the reference to Scripture (as an attribute), or that the term *graphē* requires an attribute (as in the case of "*holy* writings" in v. 15).[95] But neither of these points is sufficient to overrule the clear direction in which logic points. The attributive meaning is unlikely in view of the presence of the conjunction "and" *(kai)* between the two adjectives, "inspired *kai* useful." If attributive, the sense must be "every inspired Scripture is *also* useful." But this would be a completely unnecessary comment, unless the implication is that some Scripture is not inspired. The likelihood of the latter possibility might be greater for second- and third-century Gnostics, but it is too remote even to consider in the case of Paul or a Pauline student. Something verging on a denial of inspiration for parts of the OT might have been the case with the opponents,[96] but that only confirms that the author would not have divided the pie with an attributive adjective here. Once again, given the "functional," distributive way in which Scripture is envisaged, the logical conclusion is that Paul wished to affirm that divine inspiration applies evenly, text by text, to the entire OT. Both adjectives should be regarded as predicates of "every [text of] Scripture."

94. For attributive, see 3:17; 4:18; for predicative, see 1 Tim 4:4; 3 Macc 3:29 (the latter example is the closest parallel, though still not exact, to 3:16; see discussion in Marshall, 793). See Acts 17:26 for both uses.
95. Dibelius and Conzelmann, 120; Barrett.
96. *Pace* Marshall, 793.

The question remains, What is the meaning of *theopneustos* ("inspired by God, divinely inspired")? The term, formed from the two words *theos* ("God") and *pneō* ("to blow, breathe on"), does not occur elsewhere in the biblical writings; and since it is found elsewhere only in later writings,[97] it has been suggested that the author of these letters coined it.[98] Some decades ago it was held that the term was to be taken as an active construction, as if Scripture "breathes God";[99] but it is generally regarded now as passive in the sense of "God-breathed" (= "inspired by God"). The model for the formation of this term can be seen in similar terms such as *theodidaktos* ("taught by God"; 1 Thess 4:9),[100] an adjective describing the result of God's action on people, and various compounds based on *pneō* and *pnoē* (e.g., Acts 9:1).[101] The process envisaged, which gives to the texts of Scripture this character, is almost certainly not to be understood in the strict sense as divine dictation, despite instances of dictation in the OT and the development of this view in Rabbinic Judaism.[102] Rather, more on the order of Philo's conception of the process of Scripture's inspiration,[103] God's activity of "breathing" and the human activity of writing are in some sense complementary (cf. 2 Pet 1:21).[104]

Thus Paul's insertion (coining?) of the adjective at this point is intended to underline the authority of the OT, text by text, on the basis of its derivation from God. For this reason, the OT can be understood and applied with confidence to the current situation, but the need to do so within the hermeneutical framework provided by the Pauline gospel (in contrast to the perverted use of the OT by the opponents) is essential. The view of Quinn that this perspective on Scripture is somehow at odds with (or transcends) a Pauline view (which Quinn characterizes with the Spirit-letter antithesis; cf.

---

97. Gk. θεόπνευστος; see E. Schweizer, *TDNT* 6:454-55; Dibelius and Conzelmann, 120; G. Schrenk, *TDNT* 1:758; Spicq, *TLNT* 2:193-95 for discussion of later (all post 100 C.E.) occurrences of the term.

98. So Marshall, 794; see also Warfield, *Inspiration,* 245-96.

99. See the discussion in Spicq, *TLNT* 2:193-95; E. Schweizer, *TDNT* 6:453-55; Warfield, *Inspiration,* 245-96.

100. See G. Bertram, *TDNT* 3:123; E. Stauffer, *TDNT* 3:121.

101. E.g., for the verb Luke 12:55; John 3:8; 6:18; Acts 27:40 (Acts 9:1; ἐμπνέω); for the noun, Acts 2:2; 17:25 (of breath given by God), cf. Gen 2:7 (LXX). See Quinn-Wacker, 769.

102. See the discussion in E. Schweizer, *TDNT* 6:453-55; and E. Sjöberg, *TDNT* 6:382-83, for the distinction made between the divine dictation of the law and the inspiration of the prophets.

103. The seminal study is that of H. Burkhardt, *Die Inspiration heiliger Schriften bei Philo von Alexandrien* (Giessen/Basel: Brunnen, 1988); see also Marshall, 794.

104. This complementarity can also be seen in OT descriptions of "the Spirit coming upon" a prophet (Num 24:2); cf. the description of the prophet as ὁ πνευματοφόρος (lit. "the one who bears the Spirit") in Hos 9:7.

2 Corinthians 3)[105] fails to account for the fact that this functional view of Scripture (text by text, or as a whole) corresponds precisely with the view of the instructional relevance of the OT expressed in Rom 15:3-4; 1 Cor 9:10 and 10:6, 11 immediately following Spirit-filled adaptations of OT texts to the respective communities (cf. 2 Tim 2:19; 3:8).

But this statement on the divine authority of every text of Scripture is really preliminary to the main topic of the verse, which comes in the second predicate adjective. Inspiration is, in a sense, a platform in the argument about Scripture's "usefulness," so that from the first adjective flows the second. But it is the thought of Scripture's "usefulness"[106] or function that Paul develops. He does this with four prepositional phrases that each employ the same preposition (*pros;* here indicating purpose). Repeating the preposition is not strictly characteristic Greek grammar, but it serves to enumerate the items and stress their individual importance within the overall description: "useful *for* teaching, *for* reproof, *for* correction, and *for* training in righteousness" (NRSV; cf. TNIV, "useful for teaching, rebuking, correcting and training in righteousness"). The items listed might simply apply to the task of Christian ministry in general, for each would have its place within normal congregational or parish life. However, the language used in adjacent instructional sections (2:24-25; 4:2) strongly suggests that Timothy's ongoing duty to engage the opposition constructively is uppermost in mind.

The items are arranged with care, but we will consider the way in which Paul delineates the "usefulness" of Scripture before exploring that arrangement. First in the list is the general term "teaching" *(didaskalia).* We have encountered this term several times already and noted that its reference may be either to the content of what is taught[107] or to the activity of teaching.[108] The latter sense is meant here, though the thought of content (the texts of Scripture properly interpreted; 3:8-9; 2:19) is implicit. As the bedrock of Christian instruction, Scripture's prime function within the community is in relation to teaching (Rom 15:4; 1 Cor 9:10; 10:11).

More specific is the activity described variously in the translations as "rebuking" (TNIV), "convicting of sin," "censure," or "reproof" (NRSV).[109] The term covers a range of activities all related to the process of making

---

105. Quinn-Wacker, 769.

106. For Gk. ὠφέλιμος, see 1 Tim 4:8 (discussion and note); Titus 3:8.

107. I.e., the gospel and attendant doctrine, ethics, etc.; Titus 1:9; 2:10; see 1 Tim 1:10 (discussion and note).

108. See 1 Tim 4:13 and notes; Rom 15:4.

109. Gk. ἔλεγμος (the noun used only here in the NT); to be understood in connection with the activity indicated in the related verb, ἐλέγχω (4:2; 1 Tim 5:20 and discussion; Titus 1:9, 13; 2:15). See F. Büchsel, *TDNT* 2:476.

someone aware of sin, which begins with the educative act designed to produce self-awareness of sin[110] and proceeds to the more immediately disciplinary stage of calling one up short for some specific misbehavior,[111] and finally reaches the point at which "rebuke" is so harsh that it becomes
punitive.[112] The difference is a matter of degree (which context sometimes
helps to determine; see, e.g., 4:2), the purpose of the activity being to make
one conscious of sin in order that a change in behavior might be implemented
(Titus 1:13). For this activity, the OT texts are supremely applicable and effective (2:19; 3:9; 1 Cor 10:1-13).

If convicting is regarded as a negative measure, the activity that follows, "correcting," is positive, aiming at the goal of recovery.[113] The sequence thus far in the list replicates that of the instructions given to the coworkers for engagement with the opponents (2:24-26; Titus 1:13).

Fourth in the sequence of activities delineating the usefulness of
Scripture is the broad term "training" ("education"; *paideia*), which is qualified by the phrase "in righteousness."[114] *Paideia* was a dominant concept in
Greco-Roman culture. It was to result in the attainment of the virtues (self-
control, piety, uprightness, seriousness, etc.), which amounted to "civilization."[115] It included not simply education or instruction, but the negative or
corrective element of discipline (cf. esp. Heb 12:5, 7, 8), which played its
part in the positive development of character. Given the addition of the
phrase "in righteousness," which here means the dimension of Christian existence that can be experienced as visible uprightness of behavior (2:22),[116] the

110. "Conviction of sin"; 2 Tim 4:2; *Psalms of Solomon* 10.1; refutation of error
belongs here, Titus 1:9.

111. Reproof or rebuke; 1 Tim 5:20; Matt 18:15; LXX Lev 19:17; Sir 21:6.

112. LXX Ps 38:12; Jdt 2:10.

113. Gk. ἐπανόρθωσις (only here in the NT); for a similar sequence employing
much the same language ("usefulness," "correction," and "instruction," i.e., ὠφέλιμα,
παιδεία, ἐπανόρθωσις) in an ethical context, see Epictetus 3.21.15, cited in BDAG, s.v.;
see the verb in 1 Macc 14:34; 2 Macc 2:22; 5:50; of "reestablishment"; noun in 1 Esdr
8:52 of "support"; cf. the cognate term ἐπιδιορθόω in Titus 1:5. See Spicq, *TLNT* 2:30-31;
H. Preisker, *TDNT* 5:450-51.

114. Gk. πρὸς παιδείαν τὴν ἐν δικαιοσύνῃ; for the syntax of the repeated article,
see 3:15; 1 Tim 1:14.

115. Gk. παιδεία. See Towner, *Goal*, 110; G. Bertram, *TDNT* 5:602; S. C. Mott,
"Greek Ethics and Christian Conversion: The Philonic Background of Titus 2.10-14 and
3.3-7," *NovT* 20 (1978): 31-32; Quinn-Wacker, 770-71. Cf. Titus 2:12 and discussion.

116. See 1 Tim 6:11 and discussion; not "righteousness" in the sense of "justification by faith," though perhaps one could argue that it is the "actualization" of that gift of
God's righteousness (for which see Quinn-Wacker, 771). For the grounding of "uprightness" (ethical δικαιοσύνη) in the Christ-event, see the discussion at 2:22; 1 Tim 6:11; Titus
2:12; Towner, *Goal*, 163. See G. Schrenk, *TDNT* 2:210; *Barnabas* 4.11, 13.

sense of *paideia* as education is clearly meant (see on 2:25). The OT is equally effective for the task of imparting to believers an ethical framework for the observable dimension of life in community and in society.

The arrangement of the four elements just examined is chiastic in design, following an A-B-B-A pattern.[117] The broadest term is the first, "teaching," which in effect encompasses the rest of the activities. But in its emphasis on education, it corresponds to *paideia,* the fourth activity. Between these two are "conviction" and "correction," which have mainly to do with identification of sin and change. The force of the chiasmus is purely pedagogical, designed to leave hearers with a lasting impression in a context in which the letter would be read aloud. More significant is the archetypal sequence implied by the activities taken in order, which parallels the process envisaged in 2:24-26 (Titus 1:13): "teaching" (a catchall term to refer to Timothy's ministry; cf. 1:11; 1 Tim 2:7) in this context of opposition and heresy involves the stages identified as convicting and correcting, which allow for the next stage of ethical development to take place. This corresponds to Timothy's commission to engage opponents (or those influenced by them) with a view to their becoming aware of their error, repenting, and coming to faith (2:24-25). The sequence would apply equally well in a situation of evangelism, although Paul does not distinguish clearly between the tasks of engaging opponents and engaging pagan unbelievers; in each case, prevailing thought patterns are challenged by the claims of the gospel with a view to the enlightenment of the hearers regarding sin and the need for positive change, followed by positive growth in godliness.

(4) Ultimately, Paul's argument about Scripture's inspiration and usefulness is not an academic matter but a very practical one. In v. 17 he adds a statement that describes the chief purpose *(hina)* toward which his logic has been pressing all along — "that the 'person of God' might be capable, fully equipped for every good deed." The main question for interpretation is illustrated well by comparing the NIV translation of the subject of the purpose clause, "the man of God," with the NRSV translation, "everyone who belongs to God" (and now see TNIV: "all God's people" [or "the servant of God"]).[118] The implication of the latter translation is that the statement of Scripture's usefulness is here applied to all believers. Arguments in support of this view include: (a) the expression "*anthrōpos* of God" is not limited to Christian leaders; (b) the central concern of the passage is that the power of the Scriptures has salvation as its goal, which applies to all; (c) the final re-

---

117. Cf. the less likely suggestions of Knight, 449-50, and Guthrie, 176, evaluated accurately by Marshall, 795.

118. Gk. ὁ τοῦ θεοῦ ἄνθρωπος (see discussion and notes at 1 Tim 6:11); J. Jeremias, *TDNT* 1:364; G. Delling, *TDNT* 1:475-76.

sult of the whole process in v. 17 is "every good work," which is too general in scope to be limited to ministry as such.[119]

However, while what is said about the potency and usefulness of Scripture, as well as the activities specifically mentioned, may be applied in principle to all believers (to one degree or another), the following point suggests that Paul had Timothy specifically in mind. The crucial issue is the intended meaning of the designation "*anthrōpos* of God," and context must have the last say. It is true that the expression "man (better, "person" = *anthrōpos*) of God" may describe any believer, but in the OT it is applied (over thirty times) exclusively to Moses and the prophets who follow in his footsteps (see on 1 Tim 6:11). We have observed how Paul has already established a link between Moses' authority/ministry and his own as he has challenged the opponents (2:19; 3:8-9). When this link is combined with the fact that the primary issue within the discussion of the Scriptures relates to their functionality or use (see above), it seems far more likely that the designation "*anthrōpos* of God" is technical in this case (cf. 1 Tim 6:11).[120] Points (b) and (c) may be conceded, with the provision that it is understood that while salvation and the doing of good works are the rightful domain of all believers, these matters are specifically addressed in this discourse to Timothy; that is, they apply to the one engaged in ministry as well as to the typical believer, but the shape or scope of "good works" may in Timothy's case necessarily include ministerial activities.

Thus the purpose toward which Paul's logic moves is outfitting Timothy for taking over the apostolic ministry (and particularly, though not exclusively, with the opposition and the effective use of the Scriptures in mind). The various uses of Scripture (v. 16b) first make the *anthrōpos* of God "capable," "proficient" (NRSV), or even "complete," that is, fully outfitted for the task.[121] In this case, "full outfitting" or "completion" *(artios)* is to be understood in relation to the functions Scripture can perform, the tools the *anthrōpos* of God must have at his/her disposal for the task. This general statement is then defined further by a play on the word *artios*. The wordplay is executed by the addition of a participial phrase employing a cognate verb (ptc.) *exērtismenos* (from *exartizō*) that repeats the thought of proficiency or completeness just uttered and links it to an appropriate action ("*equipped* for every good work"). There is little difference between the adjective *artios* and the related verb (so the TNIV has combined the thoughts: "so that all God's

---

119. See, e.g., Marshall, 796; Lock, 111; Spicq, 789; Hanson, 153.

120. So also Quinn-Wacker, 771; Kelly, 204; Fee, 280.

121. Gk. ἄρτιος (only here in the NT). Quinn-Wacker, 771, suggest that the term might have the sense of speaking adequately for the need (citing Homer, *Iliad* 14.92; *Odyssey* 8.240); see further Spicq, *TLNT* 2:18; G. Delling, *TDNT* 1:475-76. For "prepared, ready," see Johnson, 421.

people may be thoroughly equipped"). The wordplay simply draws attention to the place Paul wishes Timothy's (and the listening church's) attention to be focused — namely, on the activities in v. 16 with the goal of v. 17.

In the diction of these letters to Timothy, "good works" draws on Hellenistic ethical categories (already adapted by the church) to characterize the visible dimension of Christian existence in terms of service (2:21; see 1 Tim 2:10[Excursus]). It is a general characterization that can be concretized with any number of activities. Here the work of ministry is categorized as a "good work" (1 Tim 3:1), and the specific details of "every good work" may be filled in from the context.

Closing the argument in this way has allowed Paul to bring the discussion full circle back to Timothy in the situation of opposition and ministry. The ground gained in the discourse is specifically related to the use and usefulness of Scripture. As Paul has confronted obstinate challenges to or outright denials of his authority by means of applications of the OT texts, so too must Timothy with confidence and skill. God has ensured that the OT, text by text, has the authority and the power to achieve his desires; Paul's experience in this very use of the Scriptures is Timothy's resource and paradigm (3:10, 14) for continuing the Pauline ministry.

3. The Final Charge to Timothy (4:1-8)

1 *In the presence of God and of Christ Jesus, who will judge the living and the dead, and in view of his appearing and his kingdom, I give you this charge:* 2 *Preach the word; be prepared in season and out of season; correct, rebuke and encourage — with great patience and careful instruction.* 3 *For the time will come when people will not put up with sound doctrine. Instead, to suit their own desires, they will gather around them a great number of teachers to say what their itching ears want to hear.* 4 *They will turn their ears away from the truth and turn aside to myths.* 5 *But you, keep your head in all situations, endure hardship, do the work of an evangelist, discharge all the duties of your ministry.*

6 *For I am already being poured out like a drink offering, and the time for my departure is near.* 7 *I have fought the good fight, I have finished the race, I have kept the faith.* 8 *Now there is in store for me the crown of righteousness, which the Lord, the righteous Judge, will award to me on that day — and not only to me, but also to all who have longed for his appearing.*

3:17 marked the closing of a cycle of parenesis, as the focus shifted dramatically back to Timothy with the designation "*anthrōpos* of God" and indicated that he was completely outfitted for the work. What remains is a summary charge to Paul's coworker. In a tone of solemnity, Paul spells out the terms of ministry and offers his own experience as a model. The structure of the charge, though more compressed, is a familiar one.[1] Verses 1-2 contain the charge itself: its urgent and serious tone is created by the invoking of divine witnesses and eschatological motivation and by means of the solemn command verb employed; this is followed by the specific details of the charge, moving from aspects of ministry to the requisite attitude. Verses 3-4 provide rationale for the instructions and their urgency in the form of a reminder of the eschatological menace already at work in the church. And v. 5 contrasts the present trends with the course to be followed, as the charge is concluded. Verses 6-8 reinforce the charge in two ways: first, Paul, in his steadfast suffering for the gospel, represents a standard to guide the younger successor; second, the disclosure that the apostle's end is drawing near heightens the sense of urgency already expressed in the charge and in the reference to the danger of the local situation.

1-2 This single sentence in the Greek[2] begins the charge by underlining its gravity (v. 1) before setting out the terms of the task (v. 2). The seriousness of the obligation being laid on Timothy is emphasized in two ways. First, the opening phrase of the Greek sentence (reorganized in the TNIV) emphasizes a solemn charge in the presence of witnesses: "I charge [you] in the presence of God and Christ Jesus" (cf. 1 Tim 5:21). In the Greek world formulaic charges of similar tone were made in installment ceremonies.[3] Such charges were also made by Moses, who called on heaven and earth as witnesses (Deut 4:26).[4] The gravity of the charge being spelled out would not be missed.

As we have seen at 2:14 and 1 Tim 5:21, the verb within the formula ("I solemnly charge"[5]) and the appeal to witnesses (v. 1a) create the mood of solemnity that signals a mandatory obligation. Both features have already been examined in the case of 1 Tim 5:21; their use in this context (which at least approximates a commission) is somewhat more formal.

But a second means of emphasis distinguishes this charge from the two other passages cited. Here the formula obtains even greater force in the

---

1. For the loose pattern, consisting of the alternation between command, (often contrasting or exemplifying) illustrative material, followed by command, cf. 2:14-22(26); 3:1-9(10), 10-17.

2. Quinn-Wacker, 772, suggest that the sentence actually runs through v. 4. This is unnecessary, and the punctuation of NA[27]; UBS[4] is to be preferred.

3. So esp. Spicq, 798; see Quinn-Wacker, 772; Marshall, 798.

4. Deut 8:19; 30:19; 31:28; 32:46.

5. I prefer the formality of this translation to those of the TNIV ("I give you this charge") or of the NRSV ("I solemnly urge").

way that, beyond calling on witnesses, Paul expands and adapts it for use here. The expansion creates a motivational horizon consisting of dominant eschatological symbols that are multidimensional and yet form a unified network. Paul first specifically raises the specter of eschatological judgment in the expanded description of "Christ Jesus"; second, he introduces the symbols of Christ's parousia (eschatological appearing) and kingdom. The images evoked by these symbols are strikingly different, as we will see, yet perfectly complementary. Both halves are equally related to the charge, though we should pause to consider how they function for Timothy.

To describe Christ Jesus as one "who will [is about to] judge the living and the dead" is to draw on a traditional configuration by which the early church conceived of the risen Christ's role. The close association of God with Christ in this activity is characteristic of the way these letters to coworkers interrelate the two figures in the redemptive plan of God.[6] The phrase "the living and the dead" initially served mainly as a designation for "everyone," whether dead or alive, though it is always applied in the NT with theological implications.[7] It designates Christ as the judge of all and the Lord of all,[8] and, as perhaps in this instance, envisages the scenario in which the "judgment"[9] Christ executes on his return is received both by those who are alive at that moment and those who have already died (cf. 1 Thess 4:13-16). A sense of urgency, imminence, and certainty is added to this picture by the characteristic futuristic "about to" that occurs elsewhere in similar discussions of the coming Eschaton.[10] Since this element forms just one part of the motivational horizon alluded to above, we must examine the rest of the parts before considering how the motivation is intended to function.

Expanding the description of Christ Jesus is the statement "[and] his appearing and his kingdom." The relationship of this phrase to the preceding statement about judging the living and the dead is somewhat awkward in En-

---

6. See the discussion at 1 Tim 1:1-2; Titus 1:3-4; Towner, "Christology in the Letters to Timothy and Titus"; Marshall, 798. This is another element in the "christological shift" (transfer or sharing of attributes and actions originally linked to YHWH to his Christ) apparent in and through Paul's echoing of OT texts that, by their use of κύριος (or in other ways), can be applied to Christ (see on 2:19; 3:11; Titus 2:14). A classic example of this christological shift/sharing can be seen by comparing 2 Cor 5:10 and Rom 14:10.

7. Gk. ζῶντας καὶ νεκρούς; Eccles 9:5; Sir 7:33; *Letter of Aristeas* 146 (cf. Isa 8:19); Mark 12:27 and pars.

8. Acts 10:42; Rom 14:9; 1 Pet 4:5; *Barnabas* 7.2.

9. Gk. κρίνω; in reference to the eschatological judgment (also the noun), see, e.g., Acts 10:42; 17:31; Rom 2:16; 2 Tim 4:8; 1 Pet 4:5; Rev 18:8; F. Büchsel, *TDNT* 3:921-54, esp. 936-42.

10. For Gk. μέλλω, see the discussion and note at 1 Tim 1:16; 4:8; 6:19; cf. Luke 21:36; Acts 17:31; 24:25; Heb 10:27; Jas 2:12; cf. Rom 5:14; Heb 1:14; 6:5; Rev 6:11.

glish. The phrase is loosely connected to the preceding description by the conjunction "and" *(kai)* but set off by a change to the accusative case. In several occurrences of the strong verb "to solemnly charge" the thing(s) sworn upon (or called on as witnesses),[11] which then guarantee the oath, are given in the accusative (typically "heaven and earth").[12] The combination of elements has the effect of first locating Timothy in the divine presence to hear the charge, with the reference to judgment giving the charge focus; then the following elements of parousia and kingdom serve as the eschatological ground of the charge (perhaps in anticipation of 4:8) and are placed into the accusative case. Both the TNIV and NRSV render this sense smoothly enough into English ("and in view of . . .").[13] Consequently, references to the parousia ("appearing") and the kingdom of Christ, as eschatological realities with significant implications, form quite reasonable grounds for the charge.

Both elements of the added phrase correspond to the eschatological tone of judgment/salvation already introduced. "Appearing" is the Greek word *epiphaneia,* part of the special theological vocabulary of these letters to coworkers that can refer to Christ's past appearance (1:10) or to his future parousia (1 Tim 6:14, Excursus). It characterizes the advent of Christ, past or future, in terms of a divine intervention that brings salvation for God's people and judgment for those who resist him. Here the reference is clearly to the future event of Christ's return in which the thoughts of both judgment and reward/salvation are closely bound up.

Syntactically, "appearing" and "kingdom" may relate to one another closely in the form of a hendiadys, giving something like the meaning, "his

11. So Marshall, 799; cf. Quinn-Wacker, 773.

12. Deut 4:26; 8:19; 30:19; 31:28; cf. Jdt 7:28. The function of "heaven and earth" in the process is the same as that envisaged in Matt 5:34-35.

13. See also Johnson, 428. Quinn-Wacker, 773, suggest another possibility: sometimes the accusative expresses the content of the message indicated by the verb (e.g., Deut 32:46; Ezek 16:2; 20:4), which in Lukan parlance is turned specifically to describing Paul's proclamation of the gospel (Acts 20:21, 24; 23:11), the final instance of which has Paul "testifying the kingdom of God" (28:23). In this Quinn-Wacker detect a possible parallel to the present text. They posit a double use of the verb in the present text, first according to the formula "I admonish in the presence of God and Christ . . . ," then repeating it in a different sense with the subsequent phrase, "[I bear witness to] his revelation and his kingdom." (In smoother form, the translation offered is: "As God the Father looks on, and Christ Jesus who is going to judge the living and the dead, I adjure you, Timothy, while bearing witness to his revelation and his kingdom," 759.) However, despite the similarity to Acts 28:23, from the perspective of the present discourse the overriding factor is the formulaic introduction, which explicitly employs the verb. This solemn-sounding announcement would have programmed the hearer/reader, so that a switch to the verb in the sense of "testifying," where in fact the verb needs to be supplied, introduces a complication into the discourse that would not be easily overcome.

597

appearing through (or in) his kingdom."[14] Whether or not that is so, the appearing of Christ and the eschatological kingdom (4:18) are symbols bearing close relation to one another. In Pauline thought, "kingdom"[15] could be viewed from the perspective of the present experience of salvation;[16] but frequently for the believer it is the symbol of the consummation of salvation[17] and of Christ's final victory, when he takes up his place as universal ruler, savior, and judge. And it is the positive note of triumph that is uppermost in mind here (4:8). The manifestation of his kingdom in this final sense is linked specifically to the event of his parousia (e.g., 1 Tim 6:14; 1 Cor 15:24).

Thus, in support of the verb signaling the solemn adjuration, Paul has constructed a motivational horizon out of dominant eschatological symbols. The way in which this motivation would function depends entirely on what meaning these symbols would have for Timothy and what response they would evoke from him. Of course the witness formula first appeals to the real presence of God and Christ Jesus in the life of the believer. The motivational force of this is not difficult to see (see on 1 Tim 5:21; 6:13). It is with the addition of the explicit reference to Christ as judge that the motivational technique adopts a specific orientation. The symbol of judgment, and image of Christ as judge, functions in one of three ways. First, the thought of judgment may motivate by means of a warning or threat, the sense being to elicit faithfulness from Timothy in view of his own certain judgment; that is, that he might avoid negative consequences (cf. 1 Cor 9:27). The other side of this, secondly, is that the certainty of that day may motivate him positively to labor faithfully in view of the reward that his judgment will announce (assessment; cf. 1:18; 4:7-8). Third, possibly the thought of the judgment of those to whom he must minister is to motivate him (cf. 2:24-26). As this motivation opens out into a positive picture in the next statement, which corresponds to Paul's own expression of hope in vv. 6-8, the judgment scenario is probably held before Timothy in the second sense, as an event to press toward, in faithfulness, in anticipation of vindication and reward.[18]

But the motivational network is still more complex. Paul introduces two further dominant Christian symbols as elements that are sworn upon:

14. BDF §442.16; see the discussion in Quinn-Wacker, 773; cf. Johnson, *Paul's Delegates,* 92, who suggests the alternative "the appearance of his kingdom," which may not place enough weight on the fact that in these letters ἐπιφάνεια is an event of Christ's personal appearing.

15. Gk. βασιλεία; K. L. Schmidt, *TDNT* 1:564-93, esp. 579-90; U. Luz, *EDNT* 1:201-25; L. J. Kreitzer, *DPL* 524-26.

16. E.g., Rom 14:17; 1 Cor 4:20; Col 1:13; cf. 1 Cor 15:24.

17. 1 Cor 6:9; 15:24; Gal 5:21; Eph 5:5; Col 4:11.

18. Cf. Marshall, 799.

Christ's appearing and his kingdom. Within the argument this addition strengthens the certification of the commission and, implicitly, the obligations that go with it. Paul is not resorting to legalism or guilt manipulation that might be associated with the formalities of a public commission. This can be seen by observing the hermeneutical tack Paul follows. In the Christ-event and its association with the gift of the Spirit, Paul's view of the present was reoriented. It came to be marked in so many ways by the future. Future promises, grounded in the past event, were now in the Spirit in the process of fulfillment; God's future had begun to shape the present. In fact, this inaugurated eschatology that stretches the wire from past to future to present is visible in these letters to coworkers precisely in the epiphany concept employed here. The use of one striking term *(epiphaneia)* for both past and future events was not just a matter of lexical economy; nor did it signify the collapsing of these distinctive events into one.[19] Rather, the first appearance of Christ necessitates the second future appearance, and the second appearance is based on the first. What Paul's language implies is that the two events are integrally related, interdependent such that the future event can already make its mark on the present age. The reality of this overlap is not simply a semantic trick, carried off by lexical juggling or carelessness; rather, Paul employs a lexical and semantic device to articulate the interrelatedness of past and future, underlining in the process the way in which the present has been altered by the eschatological realities of past event and future promise.

In commissioning Timothy, Paul's eschatological orientation is clear. He swears (adjures) on these eschatological realities (judgment, parousia, kingdom) because these symbols represent the fulfillment of the bedrock realities that were formerly sworn on — "heaven and earth," and even "Jerusalem" — all undeniable proofs of God's existence, creative activity, and presence among his people. But from Paul's eschatological vantage point, in the Spirit, these bedrock realities were signposts of God's plans for the future (cf. Rom 8:21), already in the process of implementation. Paul took firm hold on the future realities to which they pointed and reoriented present life around them. As Timothy hears the solemn commission, "Christ's epiphany and kingdom" are not simply the temporal boundaries that mark the horizon or the end of his race. They are strong symbols of promise and power, symbols, moreover, of the fulfillment of a power already in effect in his present, that compel him to do and be what God has commissioned (and empowered; 1:6-8; 2:1) him to do and be. The motivational force of these "promises becoming reality" is certainly to encourage, but also to bind him to his task. Paul swears by promises, which the Christ-event has guaranteed.

The certainty and interrelatedness of these three elements — judg-

---

19. *Contra* Läger, *Christologie,* 83-86.

ment, parousia ("appearance"), and kingdom — are in Paul's eschatology able to shine their light into the present of the church already. Salvation has really begun; so, too, the events that await future consummation are capable of shaping Timothy's character and motivating him to faithful fulfillment of this charge.

All of v. 1 is thus a shout to lean into God's certain future that is even now becoming present. But the commission still needs to be filled out in practical terms. Verse 2 begins to do this, outlining with five imperative verbs what the work will entail (v. 5 will continue the description).

First, Timothy must "preach the word." The verb "to proclaim" occurs twice in the letters to Timothy and is a standard term to describe the communication of the gospel about Christ.[20] Designating the gospel message in this case is the term "the word" (see on 1 Tim 1:15). This is the only case in which "the word" serves as the object of this verb, but its reference to the Pauline gospel is easily enough determined from other uses of the term in this letter and elsewhere (2:9, "the word of God"; 2:15, "the word of truth").[21] Although it may be artificial to distinguish rigidly between proclamation to the church and to those outside the faith,[22] this language is the sort associated with the Pauline mission to the Gentiles (1:11), which suggests that its scope is not limited solely to the church (4:5). Timothy is stepping into Paul's place in the worldwide mission.

The second command, "be prepared," employs a verb that expresses a range of meaning from ideas of proximity in place or time ("to stand close, come near"; 4:6; 1 Thess 5:3) to proximity in connection with opportunities of various sorts ("to stand by" in the sense of readiness, LXX Jer 26:14), or possibly "to pay attention to."[23] Here the translations render the term accurately in terms of "preparedness" (TNIV) or "persistence" (NRSV).[24] It thus has mainly to do with Timothy's alertness to opportunities, and this posture will apply to all the activities involved in his work.

Modifying the command verb is the opposing pair of adverbs, *eukairōs akairōs,* which means "when the time is convenient [and] when the

20. For Gk. κηρύσσω, see 1 Tim 3:16 (discussion and note); cf. Rom 10:15; 1 Cor 9:27; 2 Cor 11:4. For the related noun "preacher" (κῆρυξ), see 1:11; 1 Tim 2:7 (discussion and note). For the cognate noun, κήρυγμα, of the message, see 4:17; Rom 16:25; 1 Cor 2:4.

21. Gk. λόγος (cf. Acts 8:4; 11:1; 13:5 etc.; Gal 1:6; 1 Thess 1:6).

22. See the discussion in Oberlinner, 155, who sees no missionary dimension in this command (cf. Marshall, 800).

23. Gk. ἐφίστημι; BDAG, s.v. For the latter, see Johnson, 428 (citing Aristotle, *Metaphysics* 1090A; *Politics* 1335B).

24. See Quinn-Wacker, 759-60. Johnson, 428, rightly argues that the usage incorporates the ideas of readiness and attentiveness.

time is inconvenient." These are rare words in the biblical literature;[25] yet the sense intended is clear enough. One line of interpretation regards the adverbial pair as referring to Timothy's situation: that is, "take advantage of opportunities whether it is convenient for you or not."[26] However, a more likely background for the contrasting adverbial phrase has been shown to be the secular philosophical debates of that time (and especially the polemic against the Cynics), where the need to discern the appropriate time to speak so as to be most persuasive to a particular audience was stressed. The appropriate time was expressed with the term *eukairōs* (or related words) and the inappropriate time with the term *akairōs* (or related words; for the sentiment, consider Sir 32:4 — "Where there is entertainment, do not pour out talk; do not display your cleverness at the wrong time [*akairōs*]").[27] As applied in the present context, the force of the phrase would be to command Timothy to disregard this convention of rhetoricians. Explanations for this advice suggest either that Paul (the author) regarded the audience (chiefly the opponents) as too evil for this fine point of rhetorical strategy to make any difference,[28] or that his concern is rather that the need is so extremely urgent that truth must be addressed to the church immediately and persistently.[29] This latter concern compares closely with the tone of the instructions throughout the letter.

From the range of meanings possible for the third command verb, "convict" seems most suited to the sequence of functions being set down.[30] The task in mind is essentially that of revealing sin, bringing the hearers to the point of awareness and acknowledgment.[31] For those influenced by the false teaching, this step is preliminary to retrieval; for unbelievers, it is the initial step in repentance.

Fourth in the series of commands is a disciplinary action, "rebuke, or reprove."[32] This activity consists of a (verbal) challenge, whereby one is openly or publicly charged with error or sin (cf. the noun in 2 Cor 2:6).[33] It is

---

25. Gk. εὐκαίρως; see Mark 14:11; Sir 18:22 (related forms at Luke 22:6; 1 Cor 16:12; Heb 4:16); Spicq, *TLNT* 2:118-20; for ἀκαίρως, see Sir 32:4 (related forms at Sir 20:19; 22:6); cf. the discussion of *Exodus Rabbah* 15 (76a) in StrB 1.745.

26. Quinn-Wacker, 759.

27. A. J. Malherbe, "'In Season and out of Season': 2 Timothy 4:2," *JBL* 103 (1982): 23-41; see also Marshall, 800; Johnson, 428.

28. Malherbe, "'In Season and out of Season,'" 38-41.

29. Marshall, 800.

30. Or "convince," NRSV; better than "correct," TNIV; 3:16; see 1 Tim 5:20 (discussion and note).

31. F. Büchsel, *TDNT* 2:474; see also Quinn-Wacker, 777.

32. Gk. ἐπιτιμάω (aor. impv.); E. Stauffer, *TDNT* 2:623-27.

33. Used to describe Jesus' opposition to the demons in the Gospels (Luke 4:35, 41; 9:42).

a measure generally reserved for those members of the community who have sinned and stand in need of correction (Luke 17:3). In the context of Timothy's ministry in Ephesus, this command pertains mostly to those who oppose the authority of the Pauline message and ministry.

The first list of ministry activities closes with the broad term "to encourage," which encompasses teaching, encouragement, and exhortation. Throughout these letters to coworkers the term describes the instructional and exhortative ministry of Paul and his colleagues.[34] It encompasses the sort of teaching (from Scripture) that seeks the forward movement of believers toward maturity and is generally positive in tone (cf. 1 Tim 4:13). Unlike the other commands, this one has a phrase appended that expresses the manner in which exhortation is to be done, "with great patience and careful instruction."[35] "Patience" (see on 1 Tim 1:16) is an attitude of composure and forbearance frequently associated with tasks involving teaching or leadership, and specifically linked to the Pauline model (3:10). The added adjective "all" stresses the extent to which this quality must be exhibited in carrying out this task.[36] "Instruction"[37] defines the manner of exhortation. The addition in the Greek of the adjective "all" (probably to be distributed to both nouns in the prepositional phrase) strengthens both the attitude of patience and the activity of instruction: "with *great* patience and *careful* instruction." The model of such patience is Christ,[38] and the activity envisioned is the creative and effective application of the authoritative *didaskalia* for the upbuilding of the community.[39]

3-4 In another single sentence Paul explains what is certainly the most pressing local reason (note the connecting "for") that the ministry activities just outlined are so important. The central danger threatening the community and the Pauline mission is apostasy. Paul's description of it contains four elements, arranged in careful symmetry,[40] that are placed into perspec-

34. Of Paul, 1 Tim 1:3; of Timothy and Titus, 1 Tim 5:1; 6:2; Titus 2:6, 15. See 1 Tim 2:1 (discussion and note).

35. The prepositional phrase, expressing manner, possibly modifies all five imperatives.

36. The model for showing "all" ("the utmost") patience is Christ (1 Tim 1:16; cf. Rom 9:22). It is a quality produced by the Spirit (2 Cor 6:6; Gal 5:22).

37. Gk. διδαχή (Titus 1:9; Rom 6:17; 16:17; 1 Cor 14:6, 26); see 1 Tim 2:12 (discussion and notes).

38. See 1 Tim 1:16; cf. Rom 9:22.

39. Cf. Marshall, 801.

40. The symmetry may be seen in the way that the four descriptive phrases are arranged in contrasting pairs, phrases 1 and 2 (v. 3bc) connected by ἀλλά, phrases 3 and 4 (v. 4ab) by the μὲν/δέ construction. Then there are several verbal links or hooks that contribute a degree of assonance to the whole description: phrases 1 and 2 are linked by the διδασκαλίας/διδασκάλους ("teaching/teachers") pair; phrases 2 and 3 are linked by repeti-

tive by means of contrast with the apostolic message and ministry. As part of the charge given to Timothy, the time element of this development is crucial.

Verse 3 opens by expressing what seems to be a futuristic horizon: "for the time will come" (v. 3a).[41] The effect of the future, however, is to create the sense of fulfillment of eschatological realities, as also in the case of the parallel descriptions in 3:1 and 1 Tim 4:1-3.[42] Although in this case the description of the evil associated with the End is cast in more general terms to correspond perhaps to the commission genre, it remains clear that the same prophetic topic is invoked. Here the force added to the reasoning is eschatological: "for the End is upon us." Strengthening the explanatory force of this reason is the wordplay created by the time word employed here, *kairos,* in resonance with the distinctive preceding phrase *eukairōs akairōs.* The Greek word *kairos* (3:1; 4:6), occurring here in the singular, indicates a point in time rather than a protracted period,[43] and depicts the apostasy as a single element in a larger eschatological scenario. It is the arrival of this "time" that explains the need for Timothy's disregard for rhetorical "appropriateness."

Now the "time" is characterized in four succeeding statements formed around verbs that convey alternating negative and positive ideas, and may envisage apostasy as a sequence of steps.[44] The first distinguishing feature is described in terms of boredom, apathy, or annoyance ("they will not put up with"[45] "sound doctrine," v. 3b). The language implies rejection, or the emotional prelude to rejection. This way of describing Paul's message and teaching is standard in these letters for discussions that emphasize the inferior quality of the heretical message (see on 1 Tim 1:10). Marshall rightly suggests that the response of rejection will be directed as much toward those who teach the message as it is toward the sound teaching itself.[46]

---

tion of τὴν ἀκοήν ("hearing"), and phrases 3 and 4 are linked semantically by the similar verbs ἀποστρέφω/ἐκτρέπω ("turn away/turn aside"). Finally, there is a general syntactical symmetry in phrases 2-4 in the conjunction/prepositional phrase/verb-object order.

41. For Gk. καιρός ("time, point in time"), see 3:1; 1 Tim 2:6 (discussion and note).

42. See discussions at 3:1; 1 Tim 4:1; Towner, *Goal,* 65; Quinn-Wacker, 778-79; Marshall, 801-2. In view of what is clearly the present situation of opposition in the church, the possibility of a real futuristic reference in the future tense, e.g., to prevent Timothy from being surprised (e.g., Knight, 455), seems highly unlikely.

43. Elsewhere in these letters occurrences are plural; 1 Tim 2:6; 4:1; 6:15; Titus 1:3; 2 Tim 3:1. See G. Delling, *TDNT* 3:461-62.

44. The initial link of the characteristics to the opening phrase is created with the temporal conjunction ὅτε ("when"), which serves as a relative pronoun following a noun expressing time (as in Luke 17:22; John 4:21, 23; 5:25; 16:25; Rom 2:16).

45. Gk. ἀνέχομαι (here in the future and negated); of messages 2 Cor 11:4; Heb 13:22; cf. Mark 9:19 and pars.; 2 Cor 11:1, 19; 2 Thess 1:4. H. Schlier, *TDNT* 1:359-60.

46. Marshall, 802.

Second, Paul portrays the contrast of this rejection of "sound teaching" in terms of choosing teachers who "suit their own desires" (v. 3c). The term "desires" in this statement is not neutral (2:22; 3:6); as an expression of their "criterion," it suggests a merely human (or sinful) orientation that is antithetical to the divine will.[47]

Following their desires leads them to the real point of contrast, which Paul identifies in ironic and sarcastic fashion; "instead . . . they will gather around them a great number of teachers." The irony is created by the use of the term "teachers" (didaskalous; see on 1 Tim 2:7, 12). It comes just after (and in strong contrast to, alla) the reference to "sound teaching" (didaskalias), which produces a kind of cognitive dissonance that in effect means "false teachers."[48] The mockery is heightened by means of the striking verb "to accumulate or pile up," which almost gives the impression of stockpiling teachers.[49] At the same time, this verb (episōreuō) sets up an echo that, when followed back to its source in 3:6 (sōreuō), provides the perfect example in foolish, susceptible women burdened by their sins.

In this case, the cause behind their choice of an alternative team of teachers is indicated with a participial phrase containing a metaphor that has two possible senses. Most of the translations take the phrase to mean "because they have itchy ears." Here the picture of an irritation in the ears is extended to depict an appetite for novelty that cannot be satisfied; the metaphor implies that the false teachers will "scratch" (satisfy) the itchy ears for them.[50] A second interpretation reduces the metaphor by half, understanding the term taken as "ears" (tēn akoēn) above to refer directly to the content of what is heard, a message or report.[51] In this case, the image speaks more explicitly of the false teaching (implied by metaphor in the first option) and of a pleasant tickling more than scratching of their ears.[52] Fine distinctions aside, the meaning is clear whichever reading is preferred; this group has a curios-

---

47. Gk. κατὰ τὰς ἰδίας ἐπιθυμίας (for Gk. ἐπιθυμία, see 1 Tim 6:9, discussion and note; Titus 2:12; 3:3; elsewhere also with κατά, Eph 4:22; Jude 16, 18; 2 Pet 3:3).

48. K. Rengstorf, TDNT 2:152; Quinn-Wacker, 780.

49. Gk. ἐπισωρεύω (only here in the NT and LXX); Job 14:17 (Symmachus); Barnabas 4.6; Epictetus 1.10.5; cf. F. Lang, TDNT 7:1094-96.

50. Gk. κνήθω ("to scratch"; only here in the NT; ptc. and causal; see Moule, Idiom Book, 102-3); BDAG, s.v.; MM. Gk. ἀκοή means "hearing, sense of hearing" (e.g., 4:4) and, by metonymy, "ear" (e.g., Mark 7:35; 1 Cor 12:17). For this view, see NRSV; TNIV/NIV; GNB; Johnson, 429; Quinn-Wacker, 780; Dibelius and Conzelmann, 118, 120; Knight, 456.

51. For Gk. ἀκοή in the sense of "report," see Matt 4:24; Mark 1:28; Rom 10:16, 17; Gal 3:2, 5. G. Kittel, TDNT 1:221.

52. See Marshall, 803 n. 122, for the evidence; also REB; Lock, 113; Simpson, 153; EDNT 2:301.

ity so active and a craving for novelty so insatiable that they are driven to extremes and without any discretion for judging between truth and error. The description of this appetite for "teachings" again invites a comparison with the earlier description of the duped women in 3:6-7.

The third element of this characterization (v. 4a) is linked verbally with the preceding phrase by repetition of the term for "hearing" or "message" *(tēn akoēn),* and grammatically with the phrase that follows, by the correlative contrastive *men/de* construction ("on the one hand . . . on the other"; cf. 1:10; 2:20). The verbal link allows this parallel description to deepen and put into fresh relief the criticism just made. Although there is little doubt whom Paul has been describing by employing here the language used earlier for the defection of his team members (1:15), he categorizes this group by defection as well: they "will turn their ears away from the truth."[53] In comparison with earlier uses, where a person (1:15) and "the truth" (Titus 1:14) are objects, the verb here takes "listening" as its object (perhaps as a continuation of the theme from v. 3c), and so describes that same turning away more obliquely.[54] Yet the net result is the same, and the phrase is closely parallel with Titus 1:14. As throughout these letters, "the truth"[55] depicts the apostolic gospel in contrast to the distorted message spreading through the churches. In this case (see v. 3a), reference to "the truth" encompasses the Pauline mission team who communicate it — to "turn away from" the gospel is to "turn away from" those who represent it.

Completing the *men/de* correlation (in a way that parallels the contrasting of the first and second items, v. 3ab), the fourth item in the description identifies what the group will in fact turn aside to — "myths." The whole phrase is stock polemics both for Paul and others.[56] In the letters to Timothy, Paul applies the verb "to turn aside" to the opposition's deviation from truth and decisive turn toward error.[57] "Myths," as we have seen, discredits the false teaching as a whole by implying its deceitfulness and utter implausibility (see on 1 Tim 1:4; 4:7; Titus 1:14).

Thus the elements in vv. 3-4 create a picture of this error-prone group — a picture of movement, emotional and ethical, away from the apostolic interpretation of the faith toward serious and dangerous error. The focus is on this unnamed "group," but the interaction of the opponents with others is alluded to in the reference to "teachers of their own" and "myths." It is made

53. For Gk. ἀποστρέφω, see 1:15 (discussion); cf. Titus 1:14. See Quinn-Wacker, 762.

54. So the discussion in Marshall, 803.

55. 2:15; 1 Tim 2:4; 3:15 (discussion and notes).

56. For the Gk. phrase ἐπὶ δὲ τοὺς μύθους ἐκτραπήσονται; cf. Galen 11.792K: εἰς μύθους γραῶν ἐξετράπετο (cited in Marshall, 803).

57. For Gk. ἐκτρέπω, see 1 Tim 1:6 (discussion and note); 5:15; 6:20.

clear that the decisions leading to this defection were the result of misguided, sinful thinking ("their own desires," v. 3c), and the verbs used throughout suggest that the group are very much the agents of their own demise. The description of the trend forms the case study that determines the necessity and scope of Timothy's ministry in Ephesus; a general susceptibility to the advances of the heretics is to be met by the range of activities included in his commission.

5 As he has done on earlier occasions (3:10, 14; 1 Tim 6:11; Titus 2:1), Paul turns abruptly ("but you") from the description of apostasy to parenesis to Timothy. The bluntness of the contrast is intentional, for Timothy's behavior and attitudes are to be emphatically opposite to the character flaws and disloyalty of those who teach the heresy and those who have succumbed to it. This sentence takes up and concludes the instructional portion of the commission (with illustrative material still to follow), adding four imperative verbs to the five already given (v. 2), three of which indicate further elements of character, commitment, and ministry while the fourth supplies a final summarizing exhortation.

"Keep your head in all situations" (TNIV) renders the first command, which reads, literally, "be sober in all things" (cf. NRSV). The verb "to be sober" occurs only here in these letters to coworkers, but the cognate adjective is part of the ethical instruction for church leaders (1 Tim 3:2, 11) and an aspect of character encouraged in older men in the community (Titus 2:2), and the language belongs to the ethical stratum of Christian teaching.[58] In some contexts (or perhaps in all at least obliquely), the thought of sobriety in the sense of avoiding drunkenness may be intended.[59] However, the chief sense here is the figurative one of mental and spiritual alertness that comes from the practice of self-control. In secular rhetoric the term is linked with the control and balanced speech desired in the skilled speaker.[60] This is likely to be one of the elements intended here, along with the more general sense of observant alertness to the situation implied in the command.[61] This demeanor is one of the qualities that those falling prey to the false teachers lacked. The command is widened and its sense of importance strengthened by the addition of the phrase "in all situations" (or "all things," "all respects");[62] the present tense may underline the normality of this requirement.

---

58. Gk. νήφω (1 Thess 5:6, 8; 1 Pet 1:13; 4:7; 5:8; see ἀνανήφω in 2 Tim 2:26). See the discussion in O. Bauernfeind, *TDNT* 4:936-39; P. J. Budd, "Drunken, Sober," n.p., *NIDNTT on CD-ROM.* Version 2.7. 1999.

59. See Marshall, 803.

60. See Spicq, 802; Quinn-Wacker, 788.

61. The translation suggested by Quinn-Wacker, 788, "keep calm," focuses more on personal composure than outward alertness, and may need to be rebalanced.

62. See 1 Tim 3:11 (discussion and note).

With the second imperative Paul returns to the letter's central theme — suffering ("endure hardship"). At this point, he refrains from the use of the compound form of the verb that called Timothy to "join in suffering" (1:8; 2:3) and opts instead for the simplex form through which he referred to his own suffering (see on 2:9; cf. 1:12; 3:11). The switch may simply represent a generalizing of the requirement to fit the commission style; but the identification of Timothy, as successor, with Paul is also being strengthened now as the time of succession draws closer and the need to understand suffering grows more acute.[63] The place of this theme within the letter suggests that the notion of "suffering" for the gospel was very much a "hill to be taken" in the battle for the legitimacy of the Pauline mission; to shrink back from this demand, which Paul's own team members and, almost certainly, the opponents had done, was to break allegiance with Christ (1:8; 2:8-13) who himself had established the pattern.

The third imperatival phrase identifies a specific category of ministry: "do the work of an evangelist." What is less clear is whether the language designates an office. Elsewhere the term "work, task" is used in relation to the overseer's duties (see on 1 Tim 3:1), but this is not decisive. The rare word "evangelist" *(euangelistēs)* in later Christian writings could refer to one who was a successor of the apostles, or distinguish an itinerant ministry from the local ministry of the pastor.[64] In the NT the term occurs elsewhere in Acts 21:8, in reference to Philip, and in Eph 4:11 as one of the "gifts" to the church. In the case of the reference to Philip, the meaning of the term is closely bound up with his work of proclamation, which is very much an itinerant work (Samaria, on the road to Gaza, in Caesarea; Acts 8:4-40). Eph 4:11 associates the term with a preaching ministry that is distinct, on the one hand, from the ministry of the apostles, and, on the other hand, from localized ministries of shepherding and teaching.[65]

---

63. See also Quinn-Wacker, 781.

64. Gk. εὐαγγελιστής (the noun does not occur in the LXX or the Apostolic Fathers); see Spicq, *TLNT* 2:91-92; G. Friedrich, *TDNT* 2:736-37; Eusebius, *Ecclesiastical History* 3.37.2-4; 5.10.2. For ἔργον ("work, task") in relation to an office of the church, see 1 Tim 3:1. It is doubtful that the verb-object combination "do the work of" (ἔργον ποίησον) distinguishes this duty in a particular way (but cf. Quinn-Wacker, 788-89).

65. Quinn-Wacker, 789-90, represent those who place the term into a post-apostolic scenario (placing Ephesians into a post-Pauline category and dating Acts significantly beyond the period of the Pauline mission) as an interim office between the apostles and the officers of the later monepiscopal church. On this reconstruction of NT history, the term εὐαγγελιστής in NT occurrences exceeds the apostolic church model idealized in 1 Cor 12:28-29. Thus Philip, in Acts, has been linked to the Caesarean church as one of its officers, and Timothy is held to be an "evangelist" in his capacity in the Ephesian church. This, however, is to press the sparse NT evidence into a much more rigid third- or fourth-century framework, and the justification for doing this is not apparent.

Drawing on the widely used verb *(euangelizomai),* we may conclude that the noun refers to the activity of "announcing the good news" ("proclaiming the gospel"). Distinctions apparent in Eph 4:11 and its association with the traveling ministry of Philip suggest that Paul uses the term in v. 5 in a way that envisages Timothy's ongoing work within the apostle's mission to the Gentiles rather than specifically as work within the Ephesian church in a particular office.[66] However, hard-and-fast distinctions between, for example, evangelism and teaching or between local and itinerant ministries are not safely made, as the orbits of these activities would have overlapped to a significant extent.[67] The safer distinction may be one of audience or intention, and the ministry would have been carried out both within the church (Rom 1:15; cf. 2 Tim 2:24-26) and outside of it (2 Cor 10:16). And as "preaching the gospel" could stand as the generic description of Paul's ministry, encompassing various elements of communication (1 Cor 9:16), so this term may well summarize the overall ministry of Timothy, including all that was listed in 4:2 and all that he would do inside this church and elsewhere in pursuit of the Pauline goal for the Gentiles.

In the final imperatival statement, Paul gathers together all of the above, the details of ministry and the sense of obligation, into a summarizing conclusion of the charge. The generalizing term "ministry" *(diakonia)* can cover a lot of ground from "service" to "task" to, in the case of Paul and Timothy, "the task of serving Christ" or "ministry" (see on 1 Tim 1:12). Timothy's commission has been outlined in the preceding three commands. The thrust of this final command is on execution: "discharge, complete, accomplish" emphasizes anew the dimension of obligation contained in the commission.[68] Spicq has shown that in secular use the verb sometimes denotes fulfilling a promise, and even more commonly refers to the repayment of a debt (whether the obligation in view is financial or moral).[69] This latter use corresponds well with the present commissioning text, giving the sense of discharging fully one's responsibility. Paul himself is the model of the resolute commitment that seeks and realizes this goal (4:17).

6-8 A change from second to first person follows the pattern Paul has

---

66. See the discussion in J. Roloff, *Apostolat–Verkündigung–Kirche* (Gütersloh: Mohn, 1965), 251-52; W.-H. Ollrog, *Paulus und seine Mitarbeiter* (Neukirchen-Vluyn: Neukirchener, 1979), 23.

67. See A. Campbell, "'Do the Work of an Evangelist,'" *EvQ* 64 (1992): 117-29; Marshall, 804.

68. Gk. πληροφορέω (aor. act.; with "ministry" and "proclamation" [4:17], the sense is "to complete, or accomplish"; when describing people [pass.; Rom 4:21; 14:5; Col 4:12; cf. Luke 1:1] the sense is "to be fully convinced, assured"). G. Delling, *TDNT* 6:311.

69. Spicq, *TLNT* 3:120-23.

used throughout the letter to develop the parenesis to his coworker and bind him closely to himself.[70] In this way the themes of sharing (in suffering, in character, in lifestyle) converge in the theme of succession. In this last personal note, Paul provides a perspective on his apostolic ministry as a task coming to its conclusion. To do so he weaves together several themes. First is the temporal note, the nearness of the end, which contributes urgency to the preceding discourse (note the "for" [gar] that forms the connection with what precedes). Second, the same statement contains the interpretative element that views his role in terms of sacrifice for the gospel (v. 6). Then, the evaluative dimension stresses both loyalty and success (v. 7). Finally, he sounds the note of vindication (v. 8). It would be easy to become lost in this soliloquy as if it were a discourse to itself; yet the function it serves is seen only in relation to the charge laid on Timothy. Paul's departure requires Timothy to step into the gap. These verses are part of that exhortation, a vital part of the commission. The time element supplies the urgent reason for the commission; the Pauline example is a template for Timothy's commitment and hope.

The language of this section is thought to echo (or depend on) Phil 2:12-18; the passages are comparable in terms of topic (Paul's suffering as sacrifice), and Phil 2:17 contains the only other occurrence of the graphic verb "to pour out [like a drink offering]."[71] However, theories of literary dependence generally presume the author of 2 Timothy could not be Paul, and an excessive tone of self-exaltation is often detected in this depiction of Pauline faithfulness.[72] Whatever the difficulties involved in the argument for authenticity, this kind of criticism is entirely subjective and without weight. Other interpreters have stressed more accurately that this is not an unexpected tone for Paul to adopt;[73] this is particularly true in light of a passage such as Phil 2:12-18. There are indeed grounds for thinking that Paul may be echoing the Philippians letter at this point (and below), just as he has echoed Romans in earlier passages (1:7; 2:11). What should be noticed, however, is the difference in the degree of certainty registered in each text employing the "pouring out" imagery: Phil 2:17 has "if indeed" ("even if"), while 2 Tim 4:6 states definitely "I am already" (cf. also the denial "Not that I have already . . ." of Phil 3:12). What is presented as a distant possibility in the earlier setting has now become an imminent certainty in Paul's mind. For Timothy, who knew the letter to the Philippians (Phil 1:1), the echo of a passage containing Paul's theological evaluation of his crisis would have been all the more poignant a device to enact the handing over of ministry responsibilities.

---

70. As in 1:11; 2:10; cf. 3:10-13 and 3:14–4:5.
71. See Hanson, 155; Bassler, 171; Dibelius and Conzelmann, 121.
72. So Dibelius and Conzelmann, 121; Brox, 265.
73. Marshall, 805; Barrett, 118; cf. Johnson, *Paul's Delegates*, 92-96.

Verse 6 opens with the emphatic personal pronoun "I."[74] This personal reference corresponds to the dramatic summary begun with "but you" in the previous verse. With this shift, Paul grounds Timothy's commission in the urgency of the experience about to overtake him, which is described in strongly theological terms.

Urgency is a product of the time element of the implied event. This is created by signals given in both halves of the sentence. In v. 6a the adverb "already" (2:18; 1 Tim 5:15) denotes an act that is underway or in process, and therefore inevitable, though the conclusion of the act itself may yet be some distance off.[75] This sense of imminence and urgency is then strengthened by the parallel statement that follows in v. 6b. It is a statement that stresses "time," and here the term *kairos* (4:3) envisages a point in time whose nature is about to be defined. The imminence of that event is expressed by means of the verb "to draw near," which appeared in 4:2 (see above) and stressed proximity in time; here the perfect tense "has drawn near" implies the imminent end of a process that has been underway.

But what is the event in Paul's mind, and how does he conceptualize it? Both parts of the sentence allude to Paul's death. The first indication of this comes in the first half of the sentence and the passive verb "to be poured out as a drink-offering," which refers to the libation that was poured out (often) to accompany and complete a (grain, animal) sacrifice.[76] As such, it does not refer to sacrificial death, but the metaphor with its allusion to wine may well intend to evoke the imagery of Paul's blood (i.e., his life) being poured out.[77] And the language clearly places Paul's upcoming death into the sacrificial context as an offering (though the passive verb suggests that it is God who is acting here)[78] that accompanies another, perhaps more fundamental offering. In the present context he possibly sees his death as comple-

---

74. To call the pronoun ἐγώ (1:11; 1 Tim 1:11, 15; 2:7; Titus 1:3, 5) "the apostolic *egō*" (Quinn-Wacker, 791-92) may be a bit melodramatic, but the use of the pronoun is limited in these letters to descriptions of Paul's apostolic ministry or appeals to the authority associated with it.

75. Gk. ἤδη; cf. Spicq, 803-4; Quinn-Wacker, 782. The range of meaning implied in the term — from "already" in the sense of "now at the present moment" (e.g., 1 Cor 4:8 with perf. verbs) to "already" in the sense of a process underway whose conclusion is imminent — is in this case determined by the present tense verb (cf. 2 Thess 2:7) and the conditions set by the context.

76. Gk. σπένδομαι (pass. pres.; Phil 2:17); see the noun (σπονδή) or the verb in LXX Exod 29:40; Lev 23;13; Num 4:7; 29:6; Jer 51:17, 25; Sir 50:15; Philo, *Who Is the Heir?* 183; *On the Life of Moses* 2.150; Josephus, *Antiquities* 6.22. See O. Michel, *TDNT* 7:532.

77. Cf. O. Michel, *TDNT* 7:536; Quinn-Wacker, 792.

78. So it is questionable whether there is any emphasis on Paul's acting "voluntarily" (*pace* Michel, *TDNT* 7:536; Quinn-Wacker, 792); the thought is rather of obedience.

menting the ultimate bloody sacrifice of the Messiah (Col 1:24).[79] Above all, the passive voice and the sacrificial imagery underline that this death is not a meaningless but rather a necessary event in the furtherance of the work of the gospel.

The second half of the verse speaks equally of Paul's impending death but with different imagery. As the time element indicates (see above), an event "has drawn near" that Paul terms a "departure."[80] While the related verb could describe "unloosenings" or departures in various senses,[81] there is sufficient evidence for a figurative use of the term for death,[82] and this is how the majority read this passage. Moreover, the tone of the passage (vv. 7-8, 18) and the use of the cognate verb in Phil 1:23 (where "departing" = death) indicate that the thought of death, not release from prison, is uppermost in Paul's mind as he grounds Timothy's commission.[83]

Thus the impending death of Paul supplies the element of urgency that supports the charge to Timothy. As the description unfolds, it becomes clear that Paul measures the value of his death positively rather than negatively. It is in some sense a completion of another more fundamental sacrifice that is intrinsic to God's redemptive plan. He does not equate the importance of his death with that of Jesus Christ; he perhaps sees it as contributing to the program of church building that involves the human embodiment and ongoing experience of sacrifice for God's truth. The only negative thing about

79. But it is notable that in the other use of the term in Phil 2:17, Paul conceived of his death as completing the service of the Philippian church, which in turn can be seen as its embodiment of the death of Christ (see Marshall, 806).

80. Gk. ἀνάλυσις; for the verb ἀναλύω, see Phil 1:23; Luke 12:36.

81. Polybius 3.69.14 (see LSJ) (unfastening the ropes securing a ship to a dock); Luke 12:36 and Josephus, *Antiquities* 19.239 (departure from a banquet).

82. Philo, *Against Flaccus* 187; *1 Clement* 44.5 (of death); see further LSJ; BDAG; F. Büchsel, *TDNT* 4:337. For the possible influence of nautical imagery, see the discussion in Quinn-Wacker, 792-93.

83. Prior, *Paul, the Letter-Writer,* 98-103, insists that this noun does not mean "death," but rather refers to Paul's expectation of release following a good outcome for his case. His argument depends on turning the first verb, σπένδομαι ("I am being poured out"), and the noun in the second clause ἀνάλυσις ("departure"), away from the meaning of death (see 98-103). While it is true that the verb does not refer to a bloody sacrifice, a dominant usage is for the drink offering that would complete the sacrificial ceremony, and this is the intention in Phil 2:17. It is also true that "departure" need not refer to death (he maintains that when it does refer to death, it is normally qualified; see Secundus, *Sententiae* 19 [LSJ, s.v.]), but Phil 1:27 expresses the idea of death adequately without such qualification (see discussion in Marshall, 806-7), and Prior is not really able to account adequately for the perfective aspect (three perf. verbs in emphatic succession that speak of completion) of the Pauline assessment of life and service in 4:7.

Paul's death is the possible vacuum it would create in the mission to the Gentiles; and so the imminence of this event is a vital reason for Timothy's commission.

As a way of assessing the apostle's life and service and preparing for the statement to follow, v. 7 employs three metaphorical statements of success. The background of the first two metaphors especially is debated (military or athletic or both),[84] but I agree with most scholars that the continuation of the athletic imagery in v. 8 makes it more likely that the dominant theme is athletics.[85] The third metaphor departs from this sphere to create an immediate application to Christian loyalty.

The first phrase, "I have fought the good fight," expressed in the past tense and as a statement of fact, repeats the saying expressed as a command to Timothy in 1 Tim 6:12 (see discussion). The athletic background of the language suggests a translation something more along these lines: "I have competed in the good contest."[86] This stock phrase takes up the athletic imagery favored by Paul to describe committed effort in the spiritual and ethical domains of life (1 Cor 9:25; Phil 1:30; Col 4:12; 1 Thess 2:2). It may have in mind wrestling or running or athletics in general, and it is difficult to narrow the reference, but the imagery of an athletic contest is the main point. Keeping Pauline usage in mind, the application here is necessarily broad, viewing the whole of life as an intense struggle against an opposition in which spiritual power must be matched by personal commitment and resolve to endure to the end of the contest. This is not the language of one about to be released from prison, but rather of one who has contended honorably and well to the end of the contest;[87] it is thus an apt metaphor for life lived responsibly at more than just the physical level.

With the second metaphor, however, "I have finished the race [or

84. See esp. Simpson, 155.

85. See esp. Pfitzner, *The* Agon *Motif,* 183. Some scholars have attempted to explain the relationship of the three metaphors with greater precision. One possibility is that each metaphor has running in mind (Pfitzner, *The* Agon *Motif,* 183); another is that the first refers to wrestling, the second to running (Kelly, 208); the third (perhaps) to the contestant's keeping the rules (cf. Easton, 70; Marshall, 808); finally, the first metaphor is possibly a generic reference to athletic competition, the second illustrative of that general picture, with the third referring to loyalty in one sense or another (Quinn-Wacker, 793-94). There are, of course, those who find the allusion in one of the other of the metaphors to be military (e.g., Spicq, 805-6). Given the variety of uses these sorts of metaphors were put to, it is impossible to be certain about the more elaborate interrelationships suggested above, though it is wise to bear them in mind as possibilities.

86. See Quinn-Wacker, 793; Johnson, *Paul's Delegates,* 203 (but cf. 91, 96!).

87. The perfect tense (cf. τὸν καλὸν ἀγῶνα ἠγώνισμαι [perf., "I have competed"] and 1 Tim 6:12: ἀγωνίζου [pres. impv., "compete"] τὸν καλὸν ἀγῶνα) stresses completion of an activity that has gone on for some time:.

course],"[88] the athletic image sharpens to the event of a foot race, which may have been the climactic event in a first-century Greco-Roman contest.[89] And the imagery may suggest another echo of themes introduced in the Philippian letter with which Timothy was familiar (Phil 2:16; 3:13-14; see on 4:6). The noun is actually first a reference to the course run (or followed) and so serves equally well as a description of the path of the sun (1 Esdr 4:34). It is eventually employed metaphorically to describe the course of a human life (Jer 8:6; 23:10; Acts 13:25);[90] in this sense the whole metaphor (the course of life as a race) attaches to the traditional story of Paul in his final encounter with the Ephesian elders (Acts 20:24).[91] The perfective aspect of the verb ("has completed") indicates that the contestant has finished the race, conforming to the note of finality struck in the previous metaphor. Bringing together the images of athletic effort and the race, Paul thinks not just of the completion of his life but also of his ministry (cf. Acts 20:24).

The third metaphor at its most basic level depicts Paul as having kept a pledge: "I have kept the faith."[92] It may be best to see its reference, if not its point of origin,[93] as keeping the rules of the race.[94] This maintains the athletic theme throughout the series of metaphors.

Within these letters to coworkers, the "faith" word group is a dominant feature of the theological and ethical vocabulary, expressing ideas ranging from "the faith" (noun) as the objective content of Christian belief, to the act of believing in God/Christ (verb), to "faithfulness" (adj.; of believers), to "trustworthiness" (adj.; of sayings; see on 1 Tim 1:2). The importance of this language suggests that Paul here raises the topic of loyalty and faithfulness by means of the pledge or rule-keeping metaphor, but then intends that it be shaped naturally by the mold of his own theology. If this is so, we are still left with a couple of possible references in the phrase at the community level.

---

88. Gk. τὸν δρόμον τετέλεκα; the combination of verb (τελέω, "finish, complete") and noun (for δρόμος, "course, race," see Acts 13:25; 20:24) is found in Homer, *Iliad* 23.373 (see G. Delling, *TDNT* 8:57-61).

89. So O. Bauernfeind, *TDNT* 8:233-34.

90. Gk. δρόμος; Quinn-Wacker, 794.

91. Cf. the Gk. phrase ὡς τελειῶσαι τὸν δρόμον μου . . . ("if only I may finish my race . . .").

92. Gk. τὴν πίστιν τετήρηκα; R. Bultmann, *TDNT* 6:208. For τηρέω ("to keep"), see 1 Tim 5:22 (note).

93. At its most basic level the phrase means simply that one had remained loyal and faithful and could be used in various settings. For the verb/noun combination in this general sense, see Polybius 6.56.13; 7.12; 10.37.9; Josephus, *Antiquities* 15.134; *Jewish War* 2.121 (A. Deissmann, *Light from the Ancient East* [New York: Doran, 1927], 312; Spicq, 806).

94. Cf. 2:5. But see Spicq, 805-6, for the view that a soldier's oath is envisaged; and Guthrie, 181, for the view that it refers to the trustworthy guarding of a deposit.

From the existential perspective, he may mean that he has never faltered in his belief, in his personal faith in Christ.[95] Or he may have in mind more "keeping the faith" in the sense of proclaiming the gospel without perverting it.[96] Paul can certainly think in terms of his own faith in Christ and the life that it requires (1 Cor 9:27); but in the letters to Timothy, where heresy and apostasy are dominant themes, he has raised the ante on faithfulness significantly and interwoven the two dimensions of "faith in Christ" and "faithfulness to the gospel message [the faith]" very tightly. This heightened interest in fidelity to the gospel as a measure of godliness makes it unlikely, in a commissioning setting such as this so sensitive to the dangers of heresy, that Paul would (or, as an apostle, could) differentiate between his own perseverance in the faith and his obligation to preserve the gospel message.[97] In fact, in handing over the ministry to Timothy he must include an account of his faithfulness to the gospel. This is a case where the ambiguity of the reference to "keeping the faith" intentionally invites the wider rather than the narrower of possible meanings: if the widest meaning is intended (the loyalty of the apostle),[98] it must incorporate the narrower specifics. Once again the perfect tense verb emphasizes an activity begun in the past that still holds true in the present; to the degree that faithfulness in proclaiming the gospel is in mind, the implication is that Paul has fully discharged his obligation with respect to the gospel.

Verse 8 concludes the section begun at v. 1 by repeating the theme that initiated the commission to Timothy: final judgment. Now the athletic theme is extended to the point of reward for victory. Bearing in mind how this metaphor functions to articulate theological realities, kaleidoscoping between the athletic contest and the life of Christian service, we may divide the verse into three main thoughts. First, Paul symbolizes the certainty of his "victory." Second, the metaphor opens out into a theological description of the eschatological event that will celebrate the victory. Third, Paul transforms his victory into a picture of hope for all believers and in this context a strong motivational device in the commissioning of Timothy.

The culmination of the account that Paul has been rehearsing is signaled with the adverb that begins the sentence. We might pass quickly over this if it signified merely the logical or sequential conclusion to an argument (2 Cor 13:11). But here the meaning is "from this point on, henceforth," giving the sense "now all that is left."[99] In conjunction with the perfective verbs

95. Kelly, 209; Spicq, *TLNT* 3:112-13; Fee, 289.

96. Oberlinner, 162; Hanson, 155.

97. Cf. Knight, 460, who sees the personal faith as primary and faithfulness with the message as secondary.

98. See R. Bultmann, *TDNT* 6:208; Quinn-Wacker, 794.

99. Gk. λοιπόν (adv. neut. of λοιπός, 1 Tim 5:20); Mark 14:41; Heb 10:13; Moule, *Idiom Book,* 161, 207; BDF §160.

just observed and with what follows, the end of Paul's course and his success are underscored. In comparison with the open-ended time frame implied through the use of related athletic imagery in Phil 3:12, our passage indicates clearly that Paul has reached his goal. All that is left is the celebration and confirmation of that victory.

This eventuality is depicted by the statement about "the crown." The language here is very much that of the games. The verb by itself is not unusual, meaning "to store up, to lay aside, to set aside";[100] its use in this athletic context to depict the prize reserved for the victor is attested.[101] It thus contributes to Paul's statement about the future a sense of certainty and conviction.[102]

"The crown of righteousness" is the centerpiece of this imagery. In the first instance, the crown in the context of athletics is the emblem of victory, awarded to the winner of the contest in public recognition of an outstanding performance (1 Cor 9:26).[103] The athletic imagery, however, gives way immediately to the religious in the addition of the words "of righteousness,"[104] which gives rise to two possible interpretations. In keeping with Paul's belief that "righteousness" was something still to be received in full at the Eschaton (Gal 5:5), the phrase is sometimes taken as a reference to that moment at which the gift (symbolized by the crown) of God's righteousness is fully experienced.[105] In this case the focus is on the source of the crown, God. Other scholars regard the emphasis as falling on the achievement (in some sense) of Paul, so that the crown is truly a reward for his righteousness or holiness of living.[106] Probably it is best not to distinguish too rigidly be-

---

100. Gk. ἀπόκειμαι ("to reserve as reward or recompense, reserve"; BDAG, s.v. 2); Luke 19:20; Col 1:5; Heb 9:27; F. Büchsel, *TDNT* 3:655.

101. See the citation in Dibelius and Conzelmann, 121 n. 20 (Demophilus, *Similitudines* [p. 6, Orelli]: "For those who run in the foot races, there is reserved [ἀπόκειται] for them, at the finishing line, the prize of victory . . .").

102. See Spicq, 806; Quinn-Wacker, 786.

103. Gk. στέφανος ("wreath, crown"; Phil 4:1; 1 Thess 2:19); see further the references in W. Grundmann, *TDNT* 7:624-26.

104. Gk. ὁ τῆς δικαιοσύνης στέφανος (for similar phrases employing genitive qualifiers, see Jas 1:12; 1 Pet 5:4; Rev 2:10). Independent parallels to the language exist. The phrase in 4:8 (ὁ τῆς δικαιοσύνης στέφανος) bears a resemblance to the reward promised to the righteous ones in Wis 5:15-16: "But the righteous (δίκαιοι) live forever, and their reward is with the Lord . . . therefore they will receive a glorious crown (τὸ βασιλείον τῆς εὐπρέπειας) and a beautiful diadem (τὸ διάδημα τοῦ κάλλους) from the hand of the Lord." A closer verbal correspondence is seen in the *Letter of Aristeas* 280: "God having granted you a crown of righteousness" (θεοῦ σοι στέφανον διακαισύνης δεδωκότας). But at best such examples indicate the currency of the imagery; the likelihood of any connection is remote.

105. Knight, 461; Fee, 290; Jeremias, 64; Trummer, *Paulustradition*, 201.

106. G. Schrenk, *TDNT* 2:210; Kelly, 209-10; Hanson, 156.

tween these options. The imagery would seem to demand that a sense of "reward" be maintained, and this is strengthened by the context (vv. 7, 8b). We need to allow Paul to combine several thoughts: (a) righteousness as a gift from God that has yet to be fully received; (b) the need for the believer to "cooperate" in this process by means of his/her faithful response to God in godly living; (c) the concept of "righteousness," including the note of "vindication" (especially if the following reference to the Lord as "the righteous Judge" intends to contrast the divine assessment with that of the emperor). With the symbolism of the crown and athletics, Paul especially combines again the indicative and imperative of Christian living — what God has done and will do is woven together mysteriously with the possibility and necessity of appropriate human response.[107]

In 4:8b depth is added to the picture of reward by reconfiguring the award setting in eschatological perspective. First, the verb Paul selects to characterize the moment is one with a strong sense of "paying out what is due" (4:14),[108] which confirms the reward character of the crown of righteousness. Second, the time frame and setting of the event is the eschatological final judgment. To this end, "the Lord" (= Christ; 4:1, 15; 1:18)[109] is depicted as "the righteous Judge."[110] The adjective "righteous" *(dikaios)* is perhaps occasioned by the reference to the crown of righteousness *(dikaiosynēs)*. But the term "judge" describes God in the OT[111] as well as Christ in the NT (Acts 10:42; Jas 5:9);[112] ultimately, reward and punishment will issue equally from God's justice (cf. 2 Thess 1:5-6).[113] A possible polemical challenge to the imperial judgment handed down against Paul should not be discounted.

The role of Christ as eschatological judge has already been anticipated in the description of Christ in 4:1. Here the day of reward (and judgment) is identified with the term "that day" (see on 1:12). At this point, the

107. Cf. Marshall, 809. In any case, this is hardly a non-Pauline view, even if the present passage with its imagery seems to place more emphasis on the human element *(contra* Hanson, 156; H. Kraft, *EDNT* 3:274).

108. See the discussion at 1 Tim 5:4. The future tense of the verb (ἀποδώσει; "he will award, give") corresponds to the final judgment setting (cf. F. Büchsel, *TDNT* 2:168).

109. See 1 Tim 1:2 (discussion and note); but cf. F. Büchsel, *TDNT* 3:942-43.

110. Gk. κριτής ("judge"; not used elsewhere in Paul; normally of God: LXX; Heb 12:23; Jas 4:12; but see the use of the verb κρίνω to depict Christ as judge: Rom 2:16; 1 Cor 4:5; 2 Cor 5:10. For the phrase ὁ δίκαιος κριτής cf. Ps 7:12; 2 Macc 12:6.

111. LXX Pss 49:6; 67:6; 74:8; Isa 30:18; 33:22; 63:7; Sir 35:12; Heb 12:23; Jas 4:12.

112. Cf. John 5:22, 27; Acts 17:31; Rom 2:16; 1 Cor 4:5; 2 Cor 5:10.

113. See J. A. Ziesler, *The Meaning of Righteousness in Paul* (SNTSMS 20; Cambridge: Cambridge University Press, 1972), 156, 163.

metaphor of the athletic contest has given way to the specifically Christian symbolism of final judgment.

What is a certainty for the apostle can easily function in this discourse as a motivating goal to shape Timothy's response to the challenging commission. Yet in the final phrase of this section (4:8c), Paul explicitly invites "all"[114] believers to anticipate with confidence the same triumph that his experience, certainty, and hope have prepared;[115] for the Lord will give the crown of righteousness ". . . not only to me, but also to all who have longed for his [the Lord's] appearing." The participial phrase "those who have longed for" brings to accurate expression the idea contained in the perfect tense participle of the verb "to love" (4:10).[116] The object of their longing (or love) is potentially ambiguous since the reference to "his appearing" (*epiphaneia;* see 1 Tim 6:14, Excursus) could be to the incarnation of Christ or to his eschatological return. In the present context, the sense is clear, for the theological orientation of the parenesis from 4:1 onward has been consistently eschatological, and the climax was reached only in the immediately preceding phrase.[117] Consequently, the description characterizes those believers who will, like Paul, qualify to receive the reward as people whose lives have been marked by a determined and expectant look forward to the parousia and the consummation of the victory of God (Titus 2:13; Rom 8:23-25; Phil 3:20).

Yet there is more to this way of describing believers than just a belief in the return of the Lord. The phrase reflects a view of Christian living that takes the final judgment very seriously as applying to believers as well as to unbelievers. In a passage that employed the same kind of athletic metaphor, Paul himself drew motivation from the reality of a final substantial assessment of his life, and he even entertained the possibility of failure (1 Cor 9:27). "Longing for" the future event of Christ's appearance implies an awareness of the seriousness of the event and a readiness to face it. Naturally that readiness is the product of a life lived "in the Spirit" in which the rule of Christ is being experienced. But this kind of life involves not just the gracious work of God on behalf of the believer but also the believer's willing response at the level of human life and relationships. In Pauline thinking readiness to face "that day" has nothing to do with misplaced confidence or, as Bonhoeffer called it, "cheap grace."[118]

---

114. Some Western textual witnesses (D* 6 1739* 1881 *pc* lat sy^p) omit "all" (πᾶσι); the evidence for its inclusion is by far the weightier (Metzger, *TCGNT,* 649).

115. The transition is effected with the construction οὐ μόνον . . . ἀλλὰ καί ("not only . . . but also"; 2:20; 1 Tim 5:13 and note)

116. Gk. ἀγαπάω (see discussion of the noun ἀγάπη at 1 Tim 1:5); Jas 1:12; Quinn-Wacker, 799.

117. Cf. Marshall, 810; Quinn-Wacker, 799.

118. *Pace* Oberlinner, 164, who imagines inaccurately that the author here places

With the affirmation of Paul's faithfulness and hope, the commission to Timothy reaches its conclusion. This has not ceased to be a letter written specifically to him, and this section of instructions and motivations relates first to the ministry he was to continue in place of Paul. Both the urgency of the local situation and the imminent departure of the apostle underscore the extreme importance of the work of the Pauline mission. But the closing encouragement reminds all readers that while responsibilities in God's service may differ, all, including the apostle, are called to participate in the same contest, at the same level of faithful performance, with a view to receiving the same reward.

III. FINAL INSTRUCTIONS AND PERSONAL INFORMATION (4:9-18)

9 *Do your best to come to me quickly,* 10 *for Demas, because he loved this world, has deserted me and has gone to Thessalonica. Crescens has gone to Galatia, and Titus to Dalmatia.* 11 *Only Luke is with me. Get Mark and bring him with you, because he is helpful to me in my ministry.* 12 *I sent Tychicus to Ephesus.* 13 *When you come, bring the cloak that I left with Carpus at Troas, and my scrolls, especially the parchments.*

14 *Alexander the metalworker did me a great deal of harm. The Lord will repay him for what he has done.* 15 *You too should be on your guard against him, because he strongly opposed our message.*

16 *At my first defense, no one came to my support, but everyone deserted me. May it not be held against them.* 17 *But the Lord stood at my side and gave me strength, so that through me the message might be fully proclaimed and all the Gentiles might hear it. And I was delivered from the lion's mouth.* 18 *The Lord will rescue me from every evil attack and will bring me safely to his heavenly kingdom. To him be glory for ever and ever. Amen.*

Structurally it is better to divide this section into two parts than to follow the TNIV. The first part, vv. 9-15, is dominated by second-person imperatives to Timothy and information meant to aid him; the second part, vv. 16-18, is characterized by the third person and Paul's focus on himself.[1] The whole is held

---

an un-Pauline amount of emphasis on the role of human love for Christ in salvation. On the contrary, the importance of the human response to divine grace in Pauline thought cannot be emphasized enough.

1. Cf. Quinn-Wacker, 827.

together by its purpose (see below), which continues to be to bring Timothy to Rome and to provide guidance for his behavior and outlook through commands and (positive and negative) modeling. On the surface, this section is not meant to be a closely argued piece; rather, as in other Pauline letters, as the letter comes to a close, the author takes this last opportunity to deal with matters of personnel and logistics, and to write a few personal notes.[2] However, at a deeper level vv. 16-18 weave together echoes of LXX Psalm 21 in a way that interprets the last stage of Paul's ministry theologically and allows these closing thoughts to be read as the "conclusion" to the Pauline story. (Thus I have treated the section of greetings and benediction [4:19-22] as a separate one.)

The purposes of this section relate to the overall functions of letters within the Pauline mission as well as to the literary framework of the letter itself. From the perspective of the macro situation, letters allowed Paul to maintain contact with his coworkers and the churches. A section such as this, then, serves the purpose of organizing the movements of his people in various places, reporting briefly on their whereabouts where that is relevant, providing information that is useful for those who will be on the move, and making personal requests. This is certainly evident in 4:9-15. Timothy is instructed to make a move (see 1:4), the movements of others are reported, a personal request is made, and a very practical warning is given.

From the perspective of the message of the letter itself, Paul may make one last return to the theme(s) developed in the letter. In this case, reference to the desertion of one coworker reinforces the contrastive description of loyalty and shame in 1:15-18. And a final reflection on his own situation in Rome (4:16-18) allows Paul to return to and deepen (by means of OT echoes) the model he has portrayed all along for Timothy, strengthening that connection with a striking verbal cue. Moreover, as just noted, Paul leaves with Timothy an interpretation of this final sequence of events in which, by means of a prominent OT template, he aligns his experience and the progress of the mission entrusted to him with the conclusion of Jesus' earthly ministry.

The authorship of this section of the letter continues to be the source of much debate. Marshall and Johnson are compelled to draw attention to the degree of conformity, especially at this point in the letter, with the undisputed writings of Paul.[3] But numerous scholars have identified problems in the passage and suggest that the details are part of the attempt to create a "Pauline" fiction in which perhaps some genuinely historical traditions along with some that are fabricated are joined together to give the document a sense of life.[4]

---

2. Cf. Titus 3:12-14; Rom 16:1-23; 1 Cor 16:1-23; Col 4:7-18.

3. Marshall, 812-13; Johnson, 445-46; and see idem, *Paul's Delegates,* 97-100.

4. Cf. Dibelius and Conzelmann, 122-28; Houlden, 131-35; Collins, *Letters,* 96-98.

Rather than rehearse all the questions raised by scholars, the material clue to inauthenticity essentially boils down to the supposed inconsistencies in the passage; for example, Timothy is being prepared for continuation of ministry (in Asia Minor) and yet called to Rome; Paul is alone but still able to send greetings from friends. Beyond this, the majority hold simply that this sort of personalia section is precisely what would be included in a pseudonymous letter to create verisimilitude or to lend the composition color.

The alleged material inconsistencies appear rather inconsequential. Paul's concern has been chiefly the absence and especially the desertion of some formerly loyal team members (1:15; 4:9), but this is not to say that he had not made new, local acquaintances (and the names in 4:21 are all new ones). Timothy receives the charge to continue the Pauline ministry in a letter written to him but also to be read in the presence of the church. As the leader chosen to embody the authority and continuation of the mission to the Gentiles in Asia Minor, Timothy must also ensure that sufficient leaders are in place (2:1-2), and there is every reason to think that he would return to Ephesus (or Asia Minor) after visiting Paul. Paul's desire to see him in person and pass the mantle could be viewed as typical of the testamentary style of writing; but there is no reason to think that such a desire would not also serve an important purpose in a historical scenario. Certainly, given the right interpretive framework, this passage could easily be construed as serving the purpose of "canonizing" the already dead apostle Paul. The question one needs to be open to is whether the sorts of details and names, the modeling device, and regrets about the desertion of his team could not also serve the parenetic purpose of a genuine letter to Timothy. What would an authentic last letter to Timothy from the apostle in such circumstances have looked like? On either reading, this section closes the Pauline story, and does so quite dramatically, and these last canonical impressions of his ministry are by no means incidental. Here, however, these details will be read within the context of the historical Pauline mission, and we will see that such a reading (of names, details, and attitudes) is both plausible and useful.

The first subsection (4:9-15) differs from the second (4:16-18) in the use of second-person imperative verbs directed at Timothy. These instructions form a loose network that holds the subsection together and explains the reason for the information included.

9 Dominating the remaining imperatives is the first one, instructing Timothy to travel to Paul: "Do your best to come to me quickly." The language parallels that of the command in Titus 3:12 (cf. 4:21) with the addition here of the adverb "quickly"[5] (1 Tim 5:22), which reinforces the ur-

---

5. Gk. τάχεως (with verbs of motion, "quickly, soon"; 1 Cor 4:19; Phil 2:24; cf. 1 Tim 3:14); see BDF §244.1.

gency contained in the command.⁶ We may assume that the addition of the adverb corresponds to the greater situation of need in 2 Timothy. The command complements and fulfills the wish expressed more obliquely in 1:4 in two ways. On the one hand, it translates the wish of Paul announced earlier into a clear imperative.⁷ On the other hand, implicit in the imperative "make every effort" (see on 2:15) is often the sense of eagerness and willingness (1:17; 2:15; Gal 2:19) that Paul inserts here as a final attempt to overcome any reluctance in Timothy to put himself on the line.⁸ In view of the situation depicted in the letter, the command is clearly meant to be received with all seriousness.⁹ This is the final call to Rome, which Paul may intend as the last step in the process by which Timothy inherits the mission but which may also serve the practical purpose of providing the companionship Paul desires.

10 This last point becomes clear in the reason ("for," *gar*) given for the travel instruction, namely, the movements of three members of the Pauline band. Demas,¹⁰ the first to be mentioned, receives the fuller attention, with his movements of both a moral and geographical nature being described. He is known to have been a coworker of Paul's from references in Col 4:14 and Phlm 24, texts that place him alongside of Luke, Mark, and Aristarchus and assume that he is fully engaged in the team's work. The verb employed in this text (also 4:16), however, describes his departure from Paul in terms of desertion: "he deserted me."¹¹ The causal participial phrase, "because he loved this world [age]," is explanatory of his abandonment of Paul, but the reference is ambiguous. The language of the phrase calls to mind 1 John 2:15, "Do not love the world or anything in the world," both in the use of the verb *(agapaō)* and in the object described: different expressions refer to "the world" from slightly different perspectives.¹² In each case a contrasting set of values is implied — the present age/world and its values versus the

---

6. For the language and construction (verb + inf.), see 1 Tim 3:14 (note).

7. *Pace* Oberlinner, 168, who pays insufficient attention to the indications that Paul through the letter may be preparing Timothy for coming to Rome (1:4, 8; 2:2).

8. See Johnson, 438.

9. Spicq, 810, suggests that the language of this command may be conventional; however, the addition of the adverb, which serves only to strengthen what the verb σπουδάζω ("to make every effort"; 2:15 and note) expresses anyway, suggests that it is meant to be taken seriously here (cf. Quinn-Wacker, 806; Prior, *Paul the Letter-Writer,* 143-46; Marshall, 814).

10. Gk. Δημᾶς; BDF §125.1; BDAG, s.v. See also Quinn-Wacker, 800.

11. Gk. ἐγκαταλείπω; Matt 27:46; Mark 15:34; 2 Cor 4:9; Heb 13:5 (see esp. Spicq, *TLNT* 1:400-403).

12. John's "world" (κόσμος; see on 1 Tim 1:15) and "present age" (νῦν αἰών; see on 1 Tim 6:17); see Towner, *Goal,* 61-63.

age to come/and its promises — as the use of the language in 1 Tim 6:17 and Titus 2:12 reveals (cf. 1 Tim 4:8).

The rhetorical strategy of using word hooks to continue themes already introduced in the previous passage is probably evident here as well. "Love for [*agapēsas*] the world," Demas's downfall, creates a strong contrast with the "longing for [*ēgapēkosi*] the appearance of Christ" (4:8) that promises eternal reward. However, the form that this attraction to "this world" took is not clear. Quinn-Wacker build a case from other uses of the term "love" in connection with wealth and honor and from the admonitions to the wealthy in Ephesus (1 Tim 6:17) to show that "it was the precarious poverty of the apostolate that eroded Demas's zeal," or even that he had "somehow provided for the imprisoned apostle and then left with the purse."[13] Perhaps the former is more likely to fit the vague description. But the second verb in the sequence, "deserted," may by its next use in 4:16 suggest rather that Demas's desertion was motivated more by the fear of being associated with a "criminal" likely to be executed.[14] Certainty is not attainable, but the basic point Paul makes is clear enough; a clash of values occurred in Demas's thinking, leading him to choose comforts (of whatever sort) available immediately instead of those (4:8) at the end of this life's trials.

His geographical movement is charted with the verb that will also govern the next two individuals named: "he has gone to Thessalonica."[15] Paul planted a church in this city in Macedonia on his second missionary trip (Acts 17:1, 11, 13), and his reference to that city in Phil 4:16 suggests that a Pauline community was still in existence. Initially, the church consisted of Jews and Gentiles who had received Paul's gospel. Demas, who was a non-Jew (see Col 4:10-12),[16] is mentioned in association with Aristarchus (Phlm 24) whom Luke names as a Thessalonian (Acts 20:4), which might mean that he had gone to his hometown. This is the assumption of later Christian tradition,[17] but it is not known whether the basis for this assumption goes beyond these few connections. What became of him is not known, but it is noteworthy that the language used to describe his desertion, which stops short of associating him with the opponents, seems closer in tone to that used by Luke to describe John Mark's lapse (Acts 15:38). There is thus no reason to think that his desertion from the Pauline team, as serious as that was in Paul's eyes, indicates his re-

---

13. Quinn-Wacker, 808.

14. Marshall, 815, cites Polycarp 9.2, where a willingness to undergo martyrdom is contrasted with attachment to the present age. On the stigma attached to incarceration, see further on 1:16.

15. For Gk. πορεύομαι, see on 1 Tim 1:3.

16. Quinn-Wacker, 809, raise the possibility that he was a convert from Samaritanism.

17. Chrysostom, PG 62:655; Spicq, 810-12.

jection of the faith or even necessarily his retirement from Christian service.[18] In other words, apostasy as such does not seem to be in view.

Less controversial, though equally felt, were the departures of the next two team members. The name Crescens[19] occurs only here in the NT. Presumably his movement to "Galatia" was on mission business. More problematic is identifying the place it designates. The Greek term *Galatia* was used to designate both the Roman province in Asia (1 Cor 16:1; Gal 1:2; 1 Pet 1:1) and Gaul.[20] Luke's way of referring to "the Galatian region" (Acts 16:6; 18:23; also linking it with Phrygia) may suggest that he desired to avoid any ambiguity, or that he was sensitive to his reader's lexicon.[21] Resolving any ambiguity latent in the term was possibly what gave rise to the textual variant *Gallian* (= Gaul) that occurs at this point in some manuscripts.[22] "Galatia" is the preferred reading since its attestation and ability to explain the variant are superior to "Gaul," but the emergence of the variant tradition may well reflect an exegetical decision about the intended meaning. Later church tradition also believed the reference to be to Gaul,[23] but we cannot be sure what textual tradition was the more influential in that later time and place or the degree to which the later tradition would have been tempted to make corrections to reflect current word use. From the perspective of the historical Pauline mission, if this is a Pauline word use or accurate reflection of a historical scenario (as in the case of the movement assigned to Titus), "Galatia" is probably a reference to Asiatic Galatia.[24]

18. See Spicq, 810-11; Marshall, 816; Kelly, 212-13.

19. Gk. Κρήσκης equals Lat. *Crescens;* see the Latin ending of Polycarp, *Philippians* 14.1; see also *New Documents* 3.91 §78.

20. Gk. Γαλατία; Josephus, *Antiquities* 17.344; see also the discussion in Dibelius and Conzelmann, 122 n. 3; Quinn-Wacker, 809-10.

21. Gk. τὴν Γαλατικὴν χώραν; cf. C. J. Hemer, *The Book of Acts in the Setting of Hellenistic History* (ed. C. H. Gempf; WUNT 49; Tübingen: J. C. B. Mohr [Siebeck], 1989), 120, 204-5; R. Riesner, *Paul's Early Period* (Grand Rapids: Eerdmans, 1998), 285-86.

22. The variant Γαλλίαν (Gaul) appears in א C 81 104 326 pc vg[st ww] sa bo[pt] Eus Epiph. The change from Γαλατίαν is either intentional, to resolve the ambiguity, or accidental (so Elliott, 164; Metzger, 581, leaves the question of cause open).

23. Eusebius, *Ecclesiastical History* 3.4.8; Epiphanius, PG 41:109.

24. Quinn-Wacker, 802-4, challenge the likelihood of this on the basis of Lukan word use and the assumption of the Lukan authorship of these letters. As pointed out, Luke's way of referring to the Asian region of Galatia avoided ambiguity (according to Quinn-Wacker) because he knew that the specific term "Galatia," Paul's term for the province in Asia Minor in his letters, actually referred to Gaul. Thus if Luke wrote the PE, we should expect the reference to be to Gaul. This is certainly special pleading. Quinn-Wacker also assert that other details in the text favor a reference to Gaul: v. 12 states that Tychicus has gone to Ephesus, and it may be that he then carried this letter to Timothy; but

Titus[25] had gone to Dalmatia.[26] This place name, occurring only here in the biblical writings but well attested elsewhere, refers to the southwest part of Illyricum — a Roman protectorate within the larger provincial territory known as Illyricum, which ran along the east coast of the Adriatic Sea from Macedonia in the South to the River Titius in the North (in modern Croatia).[27] Paul's mission had evangelized this area prior to his arrest (Rom 15:19). Assuming that 2 Timothy was written after the letter to Titus, in which Paul had instructed him to join him in Nicopolis,[28] this reference to Titus's movements (Nicopolis was either in Epirus, south of Dalmatia, or in the protectorate itself) is well within the range of historical probability.[29] Apparently, we are to infer that subsequent to that winter meeting, Titus was with Paul in Rome, and then dispatched to the area of Paul's earlier work.

11 Whatever Paul means to say about his present state of abandonment, it is clear that he is not completely alone. The next statement, "only Luke is with me," is apparently a reference to a team member who has not been dispatched on assignment;[30] this specificity is no longer in view when

---

if Crescens were dispatched to the Galatian region, he could easily have stopped in Ephesus on the way, so that there would be no need to send Tychicus. But what was Tychicus's mission? Simply to carry a letter? These arguments are obviously inconclusive. It should be noted that the text indicates a directional orientation: all place names (with the possible exception of Galatia) are eastward of Rome. On the assumption of Pauline word usage, a reference to the Asian region would be more likely. Yet even for Paul, Galatia might mean either place. It would perhaps make an easier reference to Gaul if Paul had visited Spain, and so widened his field considerably, prior to the writing of 2 Timothy. As simplistic as it may seem, the question in the end is more one of what Timothy would have understood "Galatia" to refer to than how later scribes might be prone to read it. Spicq's assertion that these scribes and early church historians gave notice that "Galatia" in the PE did not mean what it did in earlier Pauline usage should be modified to leave room for the possibility that their evaluations may tell us nothing more than what the term could or could not mean to them, not what its range of meaning was for the author and recipient of 2 Timothy.

25. For Gk. Τίτος, see on Titus 1:4; see also the discussion in the Introduction, 52.

26. Gk. Δαλματία; Suetonius, *Divus Augustus* 21, 23; Strabo 7.315; cf. BDAG.

27. See J. A. Pattengale, "Dalmatia," n.p., *ABD on CD-ROM*. Version 2.1a. 1995, 1996, 1997.

28. Nicopolis of Epirus was 200 miles south of Dalmatia, but there were several towns by that name; see the note at Titus 3:12.

29. Cf. Marshall, 816; Quinn-Wacker, 811; Brox, 269.

30. Thus the description μετ' ἐμοῦ ("with me"; Titus 3:15), employing the emphatic personal pronoun (cf. μοι in 4:11b), specifies those who have to do with Paul; cf. Quinn-Wacker, 811. This probable way of referring to those of his team who are present (i.e., Luke) nullifies the charge that this statement is inconsistent with references to other local believers in v. 21.

the broad statement is made about the desertion of believers in general at Paul's trial (4:16).[31] Luke, the author of Luke-Acts, has already been linked to the imprisoned Paul in Col 4:14 and Phlm 24. Because of this statement, Luke is often identified as the single most likely person to have written the letter, either as Paul's assistant or pseudonymously some time after Paul's passing (see the Introduction, 86-87). Suffice it to say here that despite the apparent availability of Luke for the job, there remains insufficient evidence to say who did the actual writing, if in fact Paul himself did not.

Mark was another of Paul's known associates, going back to his early days with Barnabas.[32] He was part of the same team as Luke, being mentioned also in Colossians (4:10) and Philemon (24), but he is most likely to have rejoined the apostle (Acts 12:12, 25) during the later stage of Paul's ministry, after some time apart from him. This development goes back of course to the incident of Mark's abandonment of the early mission recorded in Acts and the falling out between Paul and Barnabas that resulted (15:37, 39). Mark is also associated with the ministry of Peter (1 Pet 5:13). Paul's reason for mentioning him at this point is apparently the depletion of the mission team in Rome. Thus the instruction to Timothy, "bring Mark with you," combines the ideas of conveying him to Paul and traveling with him as a companion.[33] Paul's earlier instructions to the Colossian believers regarding Mark — "if he comes to you, welcome him" (Col 4:10) — indicate that he may possibly have been posted from Rome to Asia Minor, so that when Timothy received the letter he would still have been in the vicinity and more or less on the route Timothy would take to Rome.

Behind the instruction is Paul's assessment that Mark "is helpful to me in my ministry." "Helpful" is literally "useful," the same term employed in 2:21 (see above) of the "cleansed implements" and in Phlm 11 of the converted Onesimus. Along with the indication in Colossians, this brief evaluation suggests something about the measure of each man: Mark, who was able to overcome earlier challenges to develop into a trusted and "useful" coworker in the ministry; Paul, who was able to get past earlier misgivings about Mark's dependability.[34] "Ministry" (4:5; see on 1 Tim 1:12) should be

31. The similarity to the hyperbole of 1:15-18, where Onesiphorus is the exception to the "all," is noteworthy.

32. Μᾶρκος is a Graecized Latin name *(Marcus);* he was Jewish (Col 4:10) and also had a Jewish name, thus Ἰωάννης Μᾶρκος (John Mark, Acts 12:12).

33. For Gk. ἄγω, see on 3:6. Gk. ἀναλαμβάνω (see 1 Tim 3:16 note), of taking someone along on a journey in Acts 23:31; 2 Macc 12:38; cf. BDAG, s.v. 4.

34. Oberlinner, 170-71, suggests that something like this is inherent in Paul's use of the term εὔχρηστος, which in Phlm 11 and 2 Tim 2:21 links improvement to "usefulness." This is not necessarily in mind in other uses of the word (BDAG, s.v.), and there are not enough data to confirm the suggestion.

understood to refer to full-fledged gospel ministry, as normal Pauline usage of the term confirms, as opposed to something more general such as providing practical service to the apostle.[35] Whether this means that Mark is to step in for the departed coworkers in ongoing ministry in the Roman church (in which Paul may have yet played some indirect role) or to come from Rome to assist in taking the mission into new parts is not important. Both aspects of the ministry belong to the Gentile mission, and Paul's awareness that his active part in the mission has been fulfilled (4:6-7) is proleptic enough to allow for his continued burden for the work and even participation, however limited by his incarceration.[36] The whole passage underlines the sense of his awareness that the time of the mission's transition had arrived, and during that period of time there would be the normal overlap of responsibilities and the ebb and flow of emotions until the situation would be fully worked out.

12 The last troop movement to be mentioned is that of Tychicus. According to Titus 3:12 (q.v.), either he or Artemas was to be sent to Crete (to relieve Titus). His link to Paul (in Rome) is known from Eph 6:21 and Col 4:7, texts that identify Tychicus as the bearer of these letters to their intended recipients. Luke confirms the association, mentioning him as one of the Asians who accompanied Paul on his trip from Greece to Jerusalem (Acts 20:4). Paul's comment in the past tense, "I sent Tychicus to Ephesus," may be an instance of the epistolary aorist (the writer's adoption of the time frame of the reader), indicating that he was to be the bearer of the letter to Timothy,[37] and then possibly Timothy's relief. Lending some support to the letter-carrying function is the fact that he had served in this capacity in the past, and perhaps that he is the last one mentioned in the series.

However, the verb (and description) of "sending" implies no such detail, and to be certain of his mission a more illuminating remark would be required in order to suggest that Paul's intent was to have Tychicus relieve Timothy (cf. Titus 3:12).[38] The verb is *apostellō*, from which the term "apostle"

---

35. The parallel description of Onesimus in Phlm 11, 13 (note the phrase "so that he might be of service to me"; ἵνα ὑπὲρ σοῦ μοι διακονῇ) might suggest that "ministry" could include (but not stop at) personal service to Paul, on which see Quinn-Wacker, 813; Spicq, 814; Kelly, 214. Johnson, 440, regards the description "useful to me for ministry" to be ambiguous, implying that Mark was "part missionary, part personal assistant." Cf. Marshall, 817; Oberlinner, 171.

36. Prior's suggestion (*Paul the Letter-Writer,* 146-49) that this sort of request indicates that Paul expected to be released reads more into the language than the surrounding context can bear.

37. I.e., at the moment of writing the "sending" would have been yet future; Quinn-Wacker, 813-14; Jeremias, 65; Marshall, 818.

38. If Timothy is not actually any longer in Ephesus but rather in the vicinity (this is the minimum required by the local references in the letter), having to deal with an oppo-

is derived. Within the Pauline corpus, the verb occurs elsewhere three times, once in an oblique reference to his apostolate (Rom 10:15), once in a direct reference to it (1 Cor 1:17), and once in reference to representatives of his whom he dispatched to carry out his assignments (2 Cor 12:17) in the churches. The noun is twice used of church emissaries dispatched as representatives of the churches to Paul (Phil 2:25) and in the matter of the collection to be carried to Jerusalem (2 Cor 8:23). There has been much scholarly discussion about the whole matter of the apostolate and its authority and the degree to which this use of the verb should be understood as a technical reference to "sending on apostolic mission business," in this case as a representative or extension of Paul himself.[39]

We may assume that Tychicus was sent on apostolic business (cf. 2 Cor 8:18); but the verb itself tells us little more than that he left Paul for Ephesus on Paul's orders, a fact that may have been important in light of the desertion of other team members. With that information known, Tychicus could of course explain in person what his mission involved. If Tychicus was not the bearer of the letter, his trip to Ephesus would have been already underway (to carry out unmentioned purposes) at the time of writing, but the assumption that the notice of his authorized movement is to aid him in his task is probably still correct. In any case, it is a movement that apparently had some relevance to Timothy, even if we cannot be precisely sure what that relevance was.

13   From a report on personnel movements, Paul turns to a request that Timothy "bring" some of his things with him "when he comes" to Rome.[40] Before considering the nature of those items, a matter that has produced a surprising amount of research and speculation, we will explore the historical and geographical implications of the request. Naturally this reference identifies at least one point of the route Timothy would take from his location at or near Ephesus to Rome. The first item at least Paul had left with a person named Carpus at Troas. This town, on the coast of the Aegean Sea in the extreme northwestern part of Asia Minor,[41] is mentioned in Acts 16:8, 11

---

sition that has moved outward from the Ephesian Christian community, then the brief reference concerning Tychicus is less significant.

39. Gk. ἀποστέλλω; see the discussion in J.-A. Bühner, *EDNT* 1:142-46; H.-D. Betz, "Apostle," n.p., *ABD on CD-ROM*. Version 2.1a. 1995, 1996, 1997; K. H. Rengstorf, *TDNT* 1:400-406; for the application of this to the matter at hand, see especially Quinn-Wacker, 813-15.

40. The participial phrase (ἐρχόμενος φέρε) is temporal, expressing an action contemporaneous with its verb; the verb is the present tense form of the imperative (normal for this irregular verb): literally, "when you come, bring. . . ." For Gk. ἔρχομαι, see also 1 Tim 1:15; 3:14 (notes).

41. Troas was a busy and important port town; see the discussion in Quinn-Wacker, 817.

as the place at which Paul received the vision that launched the mission into Europe. Later this becomes the location of the raising of Eutychus (Acts 20:5, 6). Paul mentions another intervening visit to Troas and a time of fruitful ministry there that is to be fit into his movements related to the letters and confusion at Corinth (2 Cor 2:12).[42]

The language ("I left")[43] may imply that Paul's decision to leave things with Carpus was a considered one. But it is not easy to pin down the time at which this off-loading of personal effects occurred. If we limit ourselves to the known visits of Paul to this town, perhaps he left his things with Carpus on his way to Jerusalem.[44] However, if a release from a first imprisonment is posited, along with further travel eastward of Rome, more options become possible. Given the time-sense of the passage, it seems preferable to reduce the time between the leaving of the items in Troas and Paul's present predicament (however the sequence of events and imprisonment[s] be reconstructed). Quinn-Wacker suggest that it was Paul's subsequent re-arrest by Roman authorities that occasioned the decision to leave certain possessions behind with Carpus.[45] This person is not named elsewhere in the NT; the name is Latin, which suggests that he was a Gentile Christian who had apparently put Paul up at some point in his travels.[46] Little else of the details is verifiable.

It is the items themselves that have attracted the most interest. First to be mentioned is Paul's "cloak."[47] This garment was a heavy circular-shaped cape, made from goat hair, hide, or coarse wool, for outer wear, and especially important in the winter months.[48] It was not a garment one took lightly, for it would have been relatively expensive,[49] most men owning only

42. See C. J. Hemer, "Alexandra Troas," *TynB* 26 (1975): 79-112.
43. Gk. ἀπολείπω (here in the simple aor. of a past event); 4:20; Titus 1:5 (see note); Spicq, *TLNT* 1:183-84.
44. So Dibelius and Conzelmann, 123, link the fabrication of the "personal note" to this known event in Paul's ministry.
45. Quinn-Wacker, 817; also suggested by Fee, 295 (esp. in light of the next verse, which suggests that that is where the Alexander of 1 Tim 1:19-20 ended up).
46. For the name Κάρπος, see BDAG, s.v., and the discussion in Quinn-Wacker, 803. It is complete speculation, however interesting, to go beyond this in the manner of Quinn-Wacker, 817.
47. Gk. φαιλόνης; for the derivation and tendency toward metathesis, see the references in Dibelius and Conzelmann, 123; Spicq, 814; and C. Spicq, "Pélerine et vetements (A Propos de II Tim IV.13 et Act. XX.33)," in *Mélanges E. Tisseront* (Civitas Vaticana, 1964), 1:389-417; BDF §§25; 32.2; Quinn-Wacker, 802.
48. W. C. F. Anderson, "Paenula," *DGRA* 2:308-9; Spicq, "Pélerine," 389-417; MM 665-66. For the view that the item in mind was a bag or satchel of some sort (no longer held), see Lock, 118.
49. Quinn-Wacker, 816, suggest the possibility of such a garment costing ten days' wages.

one such piece of clothing, and it doubled as an outer protective covering for sleeping. A person such as Paul, accustomed to travel and to nights in unpredictable situations, would certainly regard this garment as an essential and typical part of his kit,[50] leading to his request to have it back by winter (4:21).

The syntax of the sentence probably indicates that he had also left the other items mentioned, "the scrolls and parchments," with Carpus. Precisely what writings he had in mind is not entirely clear because of the range of written materials covered by the terms and because of the grammar of the clause. "Scrolls" (TNIV/NIV; "books," NRSV) designates a written work in the form of either a scroll (rolls) or a codex (leaves sewn together into something like a modern book) made from papyrus, and could refer to portions of the OT.[51] If small codices are meant, they would have served as notebooks. The second term, translated as "parchments," refers to skins prepared for writing.[52] During this period this material was especially used for the codex form, which was smaller and more convenient for travelers.[53]

Complicating the interpretation is the intervening adverb, which might mean either "especially" (TNIV/NIV; NRSV; Acts 25:26) in the sense of placing emphasis on a subset of the preceding group mentioned, or "namely, I mean," in the sense of specifying the intended meaning of the preceding general reference.[54] Either way, the adverb reveals that the first term is functioning as a generic reference to (at its widest) writings including both scrolls and codices, or possibly just to the latter. An educated guess is required. If two categories of writings are in mind, then it is plausible to think that the OT writings (or some part thereof, for the whole collection would be bulky), perhaps some other writings of the early church, and some of Paul's own notebooks ("the parchments") could be included in the reference. On the view that one set of materials, "namely, the parch-

---

50. See the evidence in Spicq, *TLNT* 3:432-33; E. A. Judge, *Rank and Status in the World of the Caesars and St Paul* (New Zealand: University of Canterbury Press, 1982), 20-23.

51. Gk. βιβλίον (Deut 28:58; Josh 1:8; Luke 4:17; Gal 3:10); cf. A. G. Patzia, *The Making of the New Testament* (Downers Grove, IL: InterVarsity Press, 1995), 118; G. Schrenk, *TDNT* 1:617-20.

52. Gk. μεμβράνα ("parchment"; only here in the NT; BDF §5.1; BDAG).

53. C. H. Roberts and T. C. Skeat, *The Birth of the Codex* (Oxford: Oxford University Press, 1983); E. R. Richards, *The Secretary in the Letters of Paul* (Tübingen: Mohr-Siebeck, 1991); Patzia, *Making of the New Testament,* 118-19; B. M. Metzger, *The Text of the New Testament* (2d ed.; New York: Oxford University Press, 1968), 5-8; Quinn-Wacker, 818-19.

54. For the Gk. μάλιστα, see 1 Tim 4:10 (discussion and note); 5:8, 17.

ments," is singled out, the reference is still potentially rather open-ended but may mean no more than notebooks.[55]

What further can we learn from this reference? From the perspective of the historical Pauline mission, Paul's request reveals that he was a man of letters devoted to the study of the Scriptures, who, if at all possible, wanted to have his writings and writing materials (from notebooks containing personal correspondence to early Christian and biblical texts) close at hand. If the perspective is opened up to include the possibility of pseudonymous authorship, the value of the reference to his personal items tends to be weighed in terms of its function for the later Pauline churches: Paul as the archetypal scholar of the Scriptures and model of simplicity of lifestyle and self-sufficiency.[56] There is, however, nothing to preclude the historicity of the request,[57] and it is far easier to read it in this way.

14-15 Finally, in this subsection, Paul issues a warning to protect Timothy in his travels. It begins in v. 14 with an apparently unrelated piece of information, the relevance of which within this logistical section becomes clear in the verse that follows once a geographical detail is fit into place. Paul singles out one named Alexander, identifies him as "the metalworker,"[58] and alludes to the trouble he caused. "Alexander" was a common name and often taken by Jews (see on 1 Tim 1:20). Four occurrences of the name in the NT have something to do with Paul (Acts 19:33[2x]; 1 Tim 1:20), and they are all, even if coincidentally, linked to Ephesus. In this case, one cannot help but suspect that the Alexander mentioned in this warning is to be linked with the Alexander of 1 Tim 1:20, whom, along with Hymenaeus, Paul describes as having been handed over to Satan to be disciplined for his opposition to the Pauline gospel. That text almost certainly implies expulsion from the church, and suggests that these two persons were recalcitrant leaders of the heresy (see discussion; cf. 2 Tim 2:18). Although some scholars maintain that the

---

55. K. Donfried ("Paul as Σκηνοποιός and the Use of the Codex in Early Christianity," in K. Kertelge, T. Holtz, and C.-P. März, eds., *Christus Bezeugen: Festschrift für Wolfgang Trilling zum 65. Geburtstag* [Leipzig, 1989], 249-56), argues that the term used to describe Paul's trade (σκηνοποιός) refers to the broader category of "leather-working," which may open up the possibility that Paul had experimented with the making of notebooks from parchment.

56. E.g., P. Trummer, "Mantel und Schriften (II Tim 4,13): Zur Interpretation einer persönlichen Notiz in den Pastoralbriefen," *BZ* 18 (1974): 193-207; idem, *Paulustradition*, 86-88; Oberlinner, 167. For the view that the reference to the cloak is an allusion to the Elijah/Elisha type of symbol of succession, see Hasler.

57. For discussion of the argument that the request is part of the fiction (and in fact hardly believable; Brox, 271-74), see Marshall, 820.

58. Gk. χαλκεύς (here only in the NT; LXX Gen 4:22; Isa 41:7; 54:16; Sir 38:28; Hermas, *Vision* 1.3.2), a term that is best understood as metalworker, referring to a common trade; Spicq, *TLNT* 3:496-97.

specification of this Alexander as "the metalworker" is meant to distinguish him from the earlier troublemaker who is simply called "Alexander,"[59] it is perfectly plausible that the description here is meant to identify the same person in a different setting, and his expulsion from the church may have been the cause of his relocation to another place where he continued to oppose the apostle. Quinn suggests that the location of this opponent was Troas, where an association of metalworkers was known to have existed,[60] which would explain why this item was inserted at this point immediately following the instruction that would take Timothy to Troas (v. 13).

Assuming that the same Alexander is in mind, the harm that Paul alludes to here is not likely to have been his opposition in Ephesus. The reference is quite personal ("he did *me* a great deal of harm") and emphatic ("*a great deal of* harm"). The verb has a general meaning, "to show forth, or exhibit," which, as in the TNIV, gives the translation "to do much harm."[61] It may also be used in the legal sense of "to bring charges against, to accuse,"[62] which would lead to a different assessment of the syntax and the translation: "[he] accused me of many evil things."[63] On the basis of the latter possibility, Paul's reference would be to false charges made by Alexander (in Troas) that led to his arrest by the Roman authorities. Naturally this narrower interpretation, which is plausible and should not be ruled out, would tie up some loose ends very nicely. In either case the reference may be to Alexander's part in Paul's arrest and subsequent trial; and apparently it is Alexander's location as Paul writes that makes him a threat to Timothy.

The treacherous role of "Alexander" in the events Paul describes elicited a very strong pronouncement of judgment. In making it, he creates a contrast, by means of the same verb and same tone of certainty, with the statement of his reward in 4:8: "the Lord will award/recompense me" // "the Lord will repay/recompense him."[64] Just as Paul's faithfulness and loyalty assures God's action of vindication on his behalf, so Alexander's treachery

59. Quinn-Wacker, 804,

60. J. D. Quinn, "Paul's Last Captivity," in E. Livingstone, ed., *Studia Biblica* (JSNTS 3; Sheffield: Sheffield Academic Press, 1979), 3:295-96; Quinn-Wacker, 819-20.

61. On Gk. ἐνδείκνυμι, see 1 Tim 1:16 (discussion and note); Titus 2:10; 3:2. Cf. Marshall, 822; Johnson, 441.

62. LXX Dan 3:44; see the references to the papyri in Spicq, 816-17. Cf. H. Paulsen, *EDNT* 2:449-50.

63. The grammar of the sentence certainly allows this option; the accusative κακά ("evil things"; 1 Tim 6:10 and note) remains the object (cf. Acts 9:13), though in a slightly different sense, but the dative μοι ("to/for me") becomes a dative of (dis)advantage instead of an indirect object; the aorist verb would be used to refer to a particular point in time, but it is not decisive. See Quinn-Wacker, 819-20; Fee, 295-96; Hanson, 160.

64. 4:8: ἀποδώσει μοι ὁ κύριος; 4:14b: ἀποδώσει αὐτῷ ὁ κύριος.

assures the Lord's[65] action of judgment on him. The certainty of judgment is affirmed in the future verb, "will repay"[66] (cf. 2 Cor 11:15). The time frame of the first statement, that is, the eschatological "that day," is also envisaged here as the time in which judgment will be executed. As in Rom 2:6 and the tradition behind it, two dimensions of judgment are affirmed here. First, the domain of judgment is clearly marked out as belonging to the Lord (cf. Rom 12:19); although there may also be a hint of Paul's authority to make such a proclamation (cf. 1 Cor 16:22; Gal 1:8-9), it is hedged about with the appropriate recognition of divine prerogative.[67] Second, the standard of judgment that assures impartial justice consists precisely of the deeds of the one judged.[68]

While there may be no conscious attempt to quote or allude to an OT text or texts directly, Paul does have in mind a well-known Jewish principle enunciated variously in a series of OT and Jewish texts. The language of this pronouncement may actually echo Rom 2:6, as other links to that letter in 2 Timothy may suggest (1:7; 2:11). In Romans, the principle is invoked to illustrate the preceding statement about God's fairness of judgment. Here it is invoked because that very "fairness" of God determined that Alexander would get his just deserts. In both texts, it is probably the formulation of the principle in the Psalms and Proverbs that would be most in mind:[69]

> LXX Ps 61:13: "Strength is God's, and mercy is yours, Lord, because you repay each one according to his deeds" *(sy apodōseis hekastō kata ta erga autou).*
>
> Ps 27:4: "Give them according to their deeds *(dos . . . kata ta erga autōn),* and according to the evil of their ways, give them according to the deeds of their hands *(kata ta erga . . . dos),* repay them the recompense due them *(apodos to antapodoma)."*
>
> Prov 24:12: "But if you should say, 'I do not know this person,' know that the Lord knows the hearts of all, and he that formed the breath

---

65. The reference is to Christ (see on 4:8).

66. See the discussion and note at 4:8; 1 Tim 5:4.

67. So also Marshall, 822; Brox, 274; for the view that the apostle is here presented as the determiner of judgment (though there is nothing here that is not also said in 2 Cor 11:15), see Hasler, 80-81.

68. 2 Cor 11:15; 1 Pet 1:17; Rev 2:23; 18:6; 20:12-13. Cf. K. L. Yinger, *Paul, Judaism, and Judgment according to Deeds* (SNTSMS 105; Cambridge: Cambridge University Press, 1999).

69. Pss 27:4; 61:13; Prov 24:12; see also Job 34:11; Jer 17:10; Hos 12:2; Sir 16:12-14; 35:22; *1 Enoch* 100:7; Pseudo-Philo, *Liber antiquitatem biblicarum* 3.10; Matt 16:27).

for all, he knows all things, who pays back each one according to his deeds *(hos apodidōsin hekastō kata ta erga autou)*."

Matt 16:27: "For the Son of Man shall come in the glory of his Father with his angels, and then he will pay back to each one according to his deeds" *(apodōsei hekastō kata tēn praxin autou;* cf. Sir 35:22: "until he repays a person according to his deeds"; *heōs antapodǭ anthrōpǭ kata tas praxeis autou).*

Rom 2:6: "He will repay each one according to his deeds" *(hos apodōsei hekastō kata ta erga autou).*

2 Tim 4:14: "The Lord will pay him back according to his deeds" *(apodōsei autǭ ho kyrios kata ta erga autou).*

Specifically, contact with the tradition in 4:14 is clear from the characteristic verb ("to repay"; *apodidōmi*) and the standard or criterion of recompense ("according to his/her deeds"; *kata ta erga autou*).[70] This application is somewhat unique among the various expressions of the principle because it takes the form of a specific pronouncement (*apodōsei* is future indicative) of judgment on an individual. In this it inclines to the application of the principle in Ps 27:4, and we hear in Paul's pronouncement the sentiments of the oppressed in that text (almost an imprecation, and it would be if the verb were subjunctive or optative, as a few MSS weakly attest;[71] but hardly a "curse"[72]): appeal is made to God to mete out to the oppressor what his evil deeds deserve.

Verse 15 spells out the following instruction and the point of the reference to Alexander. Anticipating Timothy's travel route to Rome (via Troas), the warning about Alexander develops into an instruction: "You too should be on your guard against him."[73] The assumption is that he continues to pose the same threat ("you also") to any member of the Pauline team. The degree

---

70. Cf. esp. (LXX)

Ps 61:13:	σὺ ἀποδώσεις ἑκάστῳ κατὰ τὰ ἔργα αὐτοῦ
Rom 2:6:	ὃς ἀποδώσει ἑκάστῳ κατὰ τὰ ἔργα αὐτοῦ
2 Tim 4:14b:	ἀποδώσει αὐτῷ ὁ κύριος κατὰ τὰ ἔργα αὐτοῦ.

71. A textual variant has the subjunctive or optative form of ἀποδίδωμι (ἀποδωῃ; D² Ψ TR b vg$^{st\ ww}$ Ambst), which would make the pronouncement a wish (or imprecation; cf. the same textual problem at 2:7, 25). The variant is not strongly attested, and the future indicative form creates a contrasting pattern with 4:8.

72. *Pace* Dibelius and Conzelmann, 123.

73. The connection of this thought with the preceding description and then the transition to the imperative are made with the accusative relative pronoun (ὅν), referring to Alexander, and the adverbial καί ("also") followed by the reference to Timothy in σύ (lit. "concerning him also you . . ."). For the verb φυλάσσω (mid. impv. "to be on your guard"), see 1 Tim 5:21; 6:20 (discussion and notes).

of threat is emphasized in the immediate reason ("because, for," *gar*) given for the instruction with the adverb "strongly" ("exceedingly").[74]

But it is the explanation of the threat that may be most helpful in placing Alexander on the map of Paul's opponents. The verb of opposition is the same one employed in the striking adaptation of the story about Moses in 3:8 (q.v.), and it belongs to the vocabulary with which Paul throughout these letters describes the false teachers. The connection back to the story about Moses and Pharaoh's magicians would not be missed. In view of this connection and especially the intention of that story, the object of Alexander's "vehement" opposition can also be seen to place him ideologically into the camp of Paul's opponents: "he opposed our message." Paul's probable meaning is "the message we preached,"[75] referring to the Pauline articulation of the faith.

This is not necessarily to say that Paul's view of things (his theology) diverged drastically from, say, Peter's, John's, or that of any other of the apostles. But at the same time it is without question that he placed the accents on different theological syllables. In the case of his opponents throughout his ministry, challenges were raised at various times to his authority as an apostle, to his lifestyle and methodology, and to his theology. Viewing these letters to coworkers within the perspective of the historical Pauline mission, it is easy enough to imagine that an errant teacher, perhaps an elder, in the church of Ephesus who had refused to be corrected for teaching heretical theology and was expelled, would continue to oppose the Pauline gospel whenever he got the chance. What Paul feared and warns of in the case of Alexander was not simply the opposition to the teaching but rather that he might go to the same lengths as he did in the drastic action he took in opposition to Paul (false, incriminating charges against him to the Roman authorities being high on the list of probable explanations). In any case, Alexander is viewed here as a heretical Christian opponent, not as a pagan persecutor, and as such he fits into the whole pattern of contrasting paradigms that Paul has been creating throughout the letter: Jesus, Paul, Timothy, Onesiphorus, and Moses on the one side; the deserters, false teachers, Korah, the magicians of Pharaoh, and now Alexander on the other. What is most striking at the end of the letter is how in Timothy's immediate historical context Paul himself is contrasted with the epitome of resistance to the gospel, Alexander. Although from a literary point of view, this use of characters is dramatically exploited, the nature of the informa-

74. Gk. λίαν functioning as an adverb; see Matt 2:16; 27:14; Luke 23:8; 2 John 4; 3 John 3; cf. Paul's use of ὑπερλίαν in 2 Cor 11:5; 12:11.

75. Gk. τοῖς ἡμετέροις λόγοις (lit. "our words, message"; for Gk. λόγος, see 1 Tim 1:15, note; for the pl., see 1 Tim 4:6; 6:3, notes); Marshall, 822.

tion provided to the recipient of the letter is most easily understood in a historical framework.[76]

16-18 This historical framework is clearly indispensable to the story line as it shifts to develop Paul's personal reflection on a crucial closing part of it. In the concluding verses of this section, Paul alludes to a "first defense" and to the fact that he underwent it without support. As discouraging (and, for exegetes, frustrating) as this picture might be, he seems to use it as a foil for emphasizing the presence and power of the Lord, which allows him to cast his experience in a very specific OT light. The Lord's faithfulness becomes the closing theme of the section. Nevertheless, Paul has written a closing to his story that operates on two levels. The first is the immediate historical level that includes his present situation and the historical framework. But the description operates at a deeper level as well, giving access to a "metanarrative," configured according to a dominant OT template by which Paul shapes the theological interpretation of his experience. I will argue for the presence and necessity of both these levels in what follows; one must pay attention to each level for the thrust of Paul's conclusion to be felt.

Verse 16 introduces an event that shapes the whole subsection, but as central as it is, it is not an event that is identified without problems with anything that occurred in the last stage of Paul's historical mission: "At my first defense, no one came to my support." There is a certain amount of later evidence that suggests the possibility that Paul was released from a first Roman imprisonment (taking the story onward from Acts). This is one historical possibility, a framework that will affect the interpretation of this passage. What must be kept in mind is that the evidence for this two-imprisonment theory is not indisputable and requires a certain amount of conjecture. Another, more cautious approach (which, however, may err on the side of caution by neglecting the evidence of a release) simply insists that apparent inconsistencies are to be expected when dealing with the evidence that we have — and the state of that evidence is such (Paul did not tell us everything) that we cannot fill all of the gaps with the information at hand. The point is that at the end of the day the presence of gaps and our inability to fill them or to account finally for all of the data do not necessitate the conclusion that the data are spurious. Correspondence with the broader framework of the Pauline mission constructed from the known data is what we seek, but some final answers may remain provisional. In what follows I will

---

76. As Marshall, 822, points out, the pseudonymous interpretation might argue that Alexander is mentioned because he continues to pose some sort of threat to church leaders for whom the letter was created, regardless of the threat he really posed to Paul; but in that case, not enough information about him (i.e., his whereabouts) is supplied to make the warning very useful. It makes far more sense as a historical item.

make an attempt to narrow down the options in identifying the event to which Paul alludes.

It is clear from the language that a very specific event is in mind.[77] The term translated "defense" has the legal sense of an accounting for one's actions (Acts 22:1; 25:16; 1 Cor 9:3; 2 Cor 7:11), and where a specific court action is envisaged, the *apologia* may refer to a technical aspect of the legal process.[78] This is a reflection backward in time, as the adjective "first" reveals; it implies that a "second" legal event has either taken place already or will soon take place. As we look at Paul's story in Acts, it is obvious that several events could be looked back on in this way as "defenses."[79] And if the "first *apologia*" referred to one or all of these events that led Paul to Rome, there would be no historical inconsistencies or gaps. But the demands of the present context seem to limit the event to something much nearer the time of writing, and the time-sense of the discourse should be considered carefully before we proceed with the options for historical reconstruction.

The statement comes at the point of a shift in the discourse from instructions to Timothy to this Pauline personal reflection. Alexander's treachery has just been mentioned, which might imply some association of events.[80] While the information about Alexander is at least partly "news" for Timothy (certainly the warning occasioned by the treachery is), the next statement about Paul's first *apologia* need not be; however, the association of it with the desertion of Paul's colleagues (v. 16b) suggests a time link with events mentioned in the immediate (4:10, with the same verb, "to desert") and more remote contexts (1:15, which may reflect back on the same event). Furthermore, the parenetic function of the similarly oriented statements in 4:6-8 suggests that vv. 16-18 also serve to motivate Timothy, which simply heightens the feeling that Paul is centering on current events rather than on past history. Consequently, the sense is that the "first *apologia*" is not to be removed too far in time from the *prima facie* time of writing. If this is the

77. Note the adjective "first" and the definite article; Gk. ἐν (of location "at"; possibly temporal "during") τῇ πρώτῃ μου ἀπολογίᾳ ("in/during my first defense").

78. Gk. ἀπολογία ("defense speech in court," or "reference to the whole court event"; Josephus, *Jewish War* 1.621 [BDAG, s.v. 2.a], 1 Cor 9:3; 2 Cor 7:11; Phil 1:7, 16; 1 Pet 3:15. Cf. U. Kellermann, *EDNT* 1:137.

79. See esp. Quinn-Wacker, 827-28, for the possibility that the reference is back to "defenses" mentioned in Acts 22:1 and 25:16 (Jerusalem) and 24:10 (the verb, at Caesarea). However, the reference is closely linked to the desertion which seems to narrow the distance from the event to the time of writing (cf. 1:15; 4:11), and the connection with Philippians (on the assumption that it was written earlier from Rome) also suggests a nearer backward reference. As Marshall points out (823), 4:17 suggests a more cosmopolitan setting than the locations mentioned in Acts.

80. See Dibelius and Conzelmann, 124; Kelly, 218.

case, the number of possible events that might be referred to in this way is limited.

First, from the time of Eusebius, when the tradition of Paul's release from his first imprisonment and further travels was already current, one view was that the reference was back to his initial Roman trial — that which Paul awaited at the close of Acts.[81] According to Eusebius, 2 Tim 4:16 refers to that trial, with 4:17 indicating his release ("escape from the lion's mouth [= Nero]") on the decision of a milder Nero to dismiss charges.[82]

Second, more commentators have understood the reference to be to a first hearing *(prima actio),* more or less equivalent to the arraignment in modern trials in the West, to determine that sufficient grounds existed for a trial; this would have included a basic presentation of the case against Paul and his opportunity to give an account.[83] The conclusion of such a proceeding would have been either the decision *non liquet,* meaning "insufficient evidence to proceed," followed, presumably by the decision to release Paul, or the ruling known as *amplius,* indicating that sufficient evidence to proceed existed. The latter decision would then lead to a *secunda actio,* that is, the trial proper.[84]

The language and scenario correspond to what is known of the Roman legal system, making the second explanation most helpful. However, this leaves the historical event in the reference more of an open question, and, in fact, these are not explanations that are mutually exclusive; for if (on the release) theory the reference were to Paul's earlier "first trial," the legal language employed would still suggest that Paul is reflecting on that event as a *prima actio* that led to a *non liquet* decision and his subsequent release. The question is whether we can be more precise in locating that event on the map of Paul's later mission history, and the attempt to do so must account for the additional information that surrounds this reference. At this juncture, it seems reasonable to surmise that Paul has just referred to a past *prima actio.*

Finishing the thought, Paul adds that in this event he was alone: "no one came to my support." The verb ordinarily denotes an arrival or the presence of someone,[85] but here where Paul refers to himself with the dative pro-

81. Eusebius, *Ecclesiastical History* 2.22.2-3.

82. Followed by Lock, 119; Quinn, "Paul's Last Captivity," 296-97; less certain in Quinn-Wacker, 828.

83. Dibelius and Conzelmann, 124; Kelly, 218; Marshall, 823; Guthrie, 175-77; Fee, 296.

84. A. N. Sherwin-White, *Roman Society and Roman Law in the New Testament* (Oxford: Clarendon, 1963), 49-52, 112-117; cf. Ferguson, *Backgrounds,* 49-52.

85. Gk. παραγίνομαι; as in the case of all other NT uses; Acts 10:33; 18:27; 23:16; 24:17; etc. These references are cited by Quinn-Wacker, 822, as parallels to 2 Tim 4:16 in that the "coming" of someone is "to help"; but the additional nuance of helping is

noun (literally) "for me," the verb expresses the specific nuance of a "presence that provides assistance or support" such as would be fitting in a trial situation.[86] We may assume that this "support" might include giving evidence or testimony on behalf of the apostle, in addition to moral support. And we may assume even from this statement that some could have come forward but chose not to do so. This becomes abruptly clear in the strong contrast, "but [alla] everyone deserted me."

This contrast is not simply an indictment, nor is it included merely to prepare the way for the statement of the Lord's faithfulness (for the previous statement serves that purpose well enough). It is a statement that operates on two levels. At the surface level, the alla phrase creates a double contrast, with the statement just made and in the juxtaposing of "everyone" with "me,"[87] which serves to escalate the theme from the sense of isolation and negligence just expressed to the more shocking sense of culpable abandonment. Also at the surface level, the verb "to desert" — the same one that describes Demas's desertion (see on 4:10) — invites the hearers/readers to draw a connection between the two events of abandonment and to place this reference to abandonment within the framework of the statement made about the desertion of the Asian coworkers in 1:15.

If these connections are made, the "first apologia" almost certainly refers to a hearing related to Paul's present circumstances (perhaps resulting from Alexander's treachery), whether 2 Timothy envisages his first or second imprisonment, and we would assume that the outcome was not the dismissal of charges against Paul. However, the repetition of the verb possibly intends rather to categorize Demas's sin as of the same sort that earlier deserters committed under similar circumstances. Either way, working at this first level of the text, complications in the material that follows suggest that we are not out of the woods yet in the placing of the "first apologia."

But this historical reflection on abandonment does not exhaust the contrast statement's function. Rather, it initiates the sequence of allusions to the Psalms, and especially Psalm 22 (MT; Psalm 21 in the LXX), which will form an interpretative grid for a theological reading of Paul's final sufferings.

The verb of abandonment is the same one that occurs in v. 2 of the Psalm ("My God, my God, why have you forsaken me?"), a text that occurs

---

spelled out clearly in the contexts, unlike the present passage (i.e., this is doubtful evidence for Lukan influence).

86. This is the only occurrence of the verb παραγίνομαι with a dative in the NT and LXX (cf., however, Ignatius, To the Trallians 1.1); see MM 481 (for the verb with a dat., see Homer, Odyssey 17.173; Plato, Republic 329B); see LSJ, s.v.; BDAG, s.v.

87. Gk. ἀλλὰ πάντες με ("but everyone [deserted] me").

on the lips of Jesus at the climax of the passion, by which the suffering of Jesus came to be understood (Mark 15:34 and par.):[88]

2 Tim 4:16: but everyone deserted me *(me enkatelipon)*
Ps 21:2: My God, my God, why have you forsaken me? (LXX: *ho theos ho theos mou prosches moi hina ti enkatelipes me?*)
Mark 15:34: *Elōi Elōi lema sabachthani . . . ho theos mou ho theos mou, eis ti enkatelipes me?*

With but a single term serving as the initial cue to an intertextual connection, the question of a Greek or Hebrew source text is in principle open, though Paul's preference for the LXX will be demonstrated again as he extends the OT web. With this allusion Paul (however obliquely) taps into the psalmist's puzzled question and to the theme of the messianic sufferings. His intention is to link up the somber statements of abandonment in the letter, identifying this experience as being symbolic of the cruciform path walked by the Messiah, including the tradition of his passion-abandonment. But the interpretive grid is broader than this, and Paul will incorporate several other items from the Psalm before he is finished.

Yet, having dipped to this level, we cannot ignore the first level, and on that level of the text one thing is clear, that the "all" who abandoned the apostle in his time of need are, regardless of the dangers they faced, nevertheless held responsible for their behavior. Paul does not place them in Alexander's camp, as his brief prayer for them shows. The parallel with the parenthetical statement of judgment on Alexander is striking, particularly because of the difference it expresses in Paul's attitude toward them. The language of the prayer-wish, employing the negative with the verb in the optative mood (the passive voice implying the Lord as the addressee), is formulaic in character by this time. The verb meaning to "count up, reckon" (Lev 7:8; Ps 43:23; Isa 40:17) had already come to be applied figuratively in the LXX to the tallying of sins or righteous acts as personal debits or credits.[89] Paul makes heavy use of the term in this sense in Rom 4:1-12 (8x), citing Ps 31:1-2 directly at 4:8. At the same time, the term for this accounting procedure *(logizomai)* is cognate with the term describing the court event *(apologia)*; if

88. Ps 21:2: ὁ θεὸς ὁ θεός μου, πρόσχες μοι· ἵνα τί ἐγκατέλιπές με; μακρὰν ἀπὸ τῆς σωτηρίας μου οἱ λόγ τοιῶν παραπτωμάτων μου; Mark 15:34: καὶ τῇ ἐνάτῃ ὥρᾳ ἐβόησεν ὁ Ἰησοῦς φωνῇ μεγάλῃ, Ἐλωΐ ἐλωΐ λεμὰ σαβαχθάνι; ὅ ἐστιν μεθερμηνευόμενον· Ὁ θεός μου ὁ θεός μου, εἰς τί ἐγκατέλιπές με. Cf. Mark 14:27 (= Zech 13:7). For Jewish use of this Psalm, see the commentaries at Mark 15:33-39; Matt 27:45-50.

89. Gk. λογίζομαι (here in the sense of "to count against"; Pss 31:2; 105:31; 2 Sam 19:20 [A]; Job 31:28; 2 Cor 5:19); cf. H. W. Heidland, *TDNT* 4:284-92. For the sentiment in the NT, cf. Acts 7:60; 1 Cor 13:5.

the connection is intended, the prayer may request, "In the time of their eschatological *apologia* may they receive the divine *non liquet.*"

The sense of the prayer is clear whether wordplay is intended or not. The prayer is possibly an oblique echo of the Psalm, "Blessed is the man to whom the Lord will not reckon sin, and in whose mouth there is no guile"[90] (Ps 32:2 MT; LXX Ps 31:2). If so, the goal of the prayer for the deserters gains an OT focal point, stressing knowledge of the gracious mercy of God (cf. Rom 4:8), and Paul's look to the Psalms, about to become more overt, begins. Yet this prayer-intervention calls to mind another element in the portrait of Jesus that may be more than coincidental — the prayer for forgiveness. Paul's behavior, as well as his circumstances, presents a rather dramatic parallel with that of Jesus in his last hours — betrayal (Alexander?), abandonment (the Asian team, Demas, "everyone"), trial, prayer for mercy (cf. Acts 7:60) — a parallel that, as we will see, Paul encourages by additional allusions to the Messianic Psalm.

Following a brief prayer for the deserters (4:16b), Paul now uses the strong statement of his experience of betrayal and abandonment as a contrastive backdrop for his presentation of the climax of his ministry (vv. 17-18). The conclusion of the sequence initiated at v. 16 brings together four important elements, each of which is rooted in some way in Psalm 21 (LXX), before the doxology is reached.

First, Paul stresses that abandonment by people was more than compensated for by the Lord's presence and empowering. The first phrase, "the Lord [= Christ] stood at my side" describes an experience of divine presence. The tradition surrounding Paul's ministry made note of similar divine interventions in the apostle's life (Acts 18:9-10; 27:23; cf. 13:2; 16:7; 20:23; 21:11), accompanied, in one case, by the Lord's personal promise of support for his ministry in Rome (23:11); so in itself this is not an unusual feature.[91]

But in making this claim Paul introduces a strong image that evokes a cluster of dominant ideas fundamental to the OT expression of Israel's belief in God. Here again, historical reflection opens the door to a deeper theological and christological level of the text. The language of Paul's claim first

90. Ps 31:2 (LXX): μακάριος ἀνήρ, οὗ οὐ μὴ λογίσηται κύριος ἁμαρτίαν, οὐδὲ ἔστιν ἐν τῷ στόματι αὐτοῦ δόλος.

91. Those who have attempted to place 2 Timothy within the Acts framework (e.g., Lestapis, *L'énigme des Pastorales*) suggest that Paul is here reflecting back on the Lord's encouragement after his arrest in Jerusalem (23:11). Yet the Roman setting of the present statement makes this a highly unlikely reference. Although such past experiences may establish the pattern, the reference here seems to be to another experience of divine presence and assistance, perhaps in connection with a first Roman trial, or a second. A pseudepigrapher interested in composing a fitting conclusion to the Pauline epic might well have stopped with these historical connections.

transports the reader back to the beginnings of Israel's existence. The verb translated "to stand by" in the TNIV means generally "to be present." It first describes the dramatic descent of the Lord in a cloud to "stand by" Moses (LXX Exod 34:5);[92] and Moses' experience becomes one to be enjoyed by any of God's people (Ps 108:31; Wis 10:11), reenacted within the community in the tabernacle and then the temple.[93] Moreover, God's "presence" with his people becomes symbolic of Israel's uniqueness among the nations — a relationship with the Creator God that is characterized by divine "help" and "deliverance" (Exod 15:2; 18:4; Deut 32:38; 33:7; 33:39) as expressed with words crucial to Paul's discourse.[94] These elements become the trademarks of YHWH's presence with his people in the very early going, and their absence is the sign of his displeasure (Deut 28:29, 31).

These concepts are taken into the Psalms in multitude as the liturgists of Israel's middle and later periods shaped the nation's worship on the basis of remembrance of past help and present need (Pss 7:11; 20:2; 21:12, 20; 54:4; 69:2; 70:12; etc.). It becomes typical to find the prayer for God's help and deliverance linked closely to the question of his proximity. This brings us again to LXX Psalm 21, where this cry for help and God's presence is raised twice (vv. 12, 20), and where the Lord's past deliverance of the nation (v. 5) becomes the basis for the prayer for his deliverance from present dangers (vv. 9, 21). And all of this is occasioned by the perplexed opening question of v. 2: "My God, my God, why have you abandoned me? Why are you so far?"

The likelihood that Paul arranged the themes of his closing reflection around Psalm 21 might be questioned if he were limited to explicit quotation to lure his readers to a deeper level. But the theme of the "nearness and help of the Lord" is central in the Psalm, and, as we saw, it is fundamental to the broader OT story; and the evidence will accumulate as we continue. At this point, by saying "the Lord stood at my side," Paul says in effect that in his experience the psalmist's prayers were answered. He, like Jesus, entered the Psalm of messianic travail (indeed, several times, though with the advantage of a postresurrection perspective) and came out of the other end of it (or would do so) in the strength of the Lord's presence. His experiences follow the cruciform pattern established by Jesus (1:8; 2:8-10; cf. Col 1:24), and his vindication, made certain by Jesus' resurrection (2:8), cannot be far off. At the same time, Paul's engagement with the OT paradigm from his position in

---

92. Gk. παρίστημι (intransitive here, "to be present and help"; BDAG, s.v. 2.a.g; cf. the transitive sense in 2:15); LXX Exod 34:5: καὶ κατέβη κύριος ἐν νεφέλῃ καὶ παρέστη αὐτῷ ἐκεῖ ("And the Lord descended in a cloud, and stood near him there").

93. G. Bertram, *TDNT* 5:838-39.

94. For the βοηθέω word group ("help, helper"), see Exod 15:2; 18:4; Deut 32:38; 33:7; 33:39; for ῥύομαι ("to deliver") and σῴζω ("to save"), see below on 4:18.

the salvation drama makes it possible (necessary) for him to execute again the christological shift: Christ (the risen, exalted Lord of Ps 110:1) steps again into the divine role of YHWH by way of the LXX.

The second verb phrase explains that in Paul's situation divine presence/help was experienced as "empowerment."[95] This is the same verb used in the command to Timothy, in preparation for ministry, in 2:1, creating a link that makes the parenetic dimension of this portrait immediately evident: what Paul commanded earlier in the letter for Timothy is substantiated here on the basis of personal experience.

Resulting from this experience of divine help and empowerment ("so that," *hina*) was an event of proclamation that for Paul was symbolic of the completion of his mission (v. 17b). Historically, this is probably a reference to his day in court (the first *apologia*), which, as in the past (Acts 22; 25; 26), he was able to exploit for the gospel.[96] But the connections require explanation. The text identifies specifically an event that marked (literally) "the accomplishment of the proclamation through me." First, the verb stresses completion, as it does in 4:5 in connection with Timothy's ministry.[97] Second, the prepositional phrase "through me," which employs the emphatic personal pronoun in contrast to the unemphatic pronoun of the previous phrase, emphasizes Paul's role.[98] "Proclamation" (see on Titus 1:3) combines the thought of the message and its preaching, with the stress here on the activity. Then, this event is further defined in the phrase "and [that] all the Gentiles might hear it."

But how can Paul interpret this court appearance with such boldness? In what sense have all the Gentiles heard? From all appearances, Paul reflects here on a completed act (despite the subjunctive necessitated by the result/purpose relationship of v. 17ab). The statement (and particularly the verb of "accomplishment") enlarges on the strong statement of fulfillment and completion made in 4:6-8.[99] And the second verb clause of the result/purpose fills

95. For Gk. ἐνδυναμόω, see 1 Tim 1:12 (discussion and note); Phil 4:13.

96. See P. H. Towner, "The Portrait of Paul and the Theology of 2 Timothy: The Closing Chapter of the Pauline Story," *HBT* 21/2 (1999): 166-67; Marshall, 824.

97. For Gk. πληροφορέω, see on 4:5. The passive form of the verb (πληροφορηθῇ) allows "the proclamation, preaching, message" (κήρυγμα) to be placed in the more central role of the subject of the clause.

98. Gk. ἵνα δι' ἐμοῦ; some emphasis is evident in Paul's choice of ἐμοῦ over μου.

99. For the view that Paul here looks forward to a period of future ministry in which he will fulfill the ministry to the nations, see Prior, *Paul the Letter-Writer*, 111-39. His argument depends on turning 4:6-8 into something other than a statement of completion on Paul's part; it is doubtful whether he has made his case, and the more natural reading of 4:6-18 understands Paul to be confirming the completion of his task. To the criticism that the proclamation of v. 17 is too broad in scope to be a reference to a trial *apologia* (125-39; see also Parry, 69-70), it need only be said that the symbolic value of the Roman appearance is not fully appreciated.

out the implication of the first statement: thus "the accomplishment of the proclamation" means precisely that "all the Gentiles [or nations] have heard."

Now to bring this claim back down to earth requires understanding that the phrase "all the Gentiles/nations,"[100] which certainly need not exclude Jewish people,[101] is a theologically loaded term in Pauline thought (Rom 15:11; 16:26; Gal 3:28). It sums up the universal scope of the salvation plan of God, from the Abrahamic promise and institution of the covenant[102] to its full unveiling in the Psalms and prophets,[103] from which Paul clearly took his cue (Romans 9–11; 15:9-13; Gal 1:15-16).[104] It is this deeply theological meaning that suggests the symbolic nature of this statement about his Roman proclamation. Thus what Paul says figuratively in 4:7, "I have competed well, finished the race, kept the faith," now on the historical (and missiological) plane translates into "I have fully accomplished my mission to the Gentiles."

Whether or not Paul ever made it as far as Spain (see the Introduction, 10-14), it is this Roman appearance that signaled for him the end of his course and the successful discharge of his apostolic responsibilities. Rome was for Paul the symbolic cosmopolitan center of "the nations" (Acts 23:11); Spain may have represented the greater geographical challenge (Rom 15:24, 28), but it too was within the sphere of the Roman Empire. Thus its symbolic meaning determines the symbolic meaning of the statement "that all the nations might hear."[105]

Though it serves a different purpose, this statement of results is not

100. Gk. πάντα τὰ ἔθνη (the phrase is formulaic: Acts 14:16; 15:17; Rom 15:11; 16:26; Gal 3:8; etc.).

101. See Prior, *Paul the Letter-Writer,* 115-24; Towner, "Mission Practice and Theology under Construction (Acts 18-20)," in I. H. Marshall and D. Peterson, eds., *Witness to the Gospel: The Theology of Acts* (Carlisle, U.K./Grand Rapids: Paternoster/Eerdmans, 1998), 417-36.

102. See Gen 18:18; 22:18; 26:4; Deut 7:6; 28:10.

103. See LXX Pss 46:2; 71:11, 17; 85:9; Isa 2:2; 66:18; Ezek 38:16; Dan 7:14; Hag 2:7.

104. Cf. 1 Tim 2:8 and its discussion of the phrase ἐν παντὶ τόπῳ ("in every place"). For the view that Paul saw his ministry as the outworking of the OT promise to the nations, see T. L. Donaldson, *Paul and the Gentiles: Remapping the Apostle's Convictional World* (Minneapolis: Fortress, 1997); M. Hengel, *Between Jesus and Paul* (Philadelphia: Fortress, 1983), 49-54; T. Holz, "Zum Selbstverständnis des Apostels Paulus," *TLZ* 91 (1966): 321-30.

105. Gk. ἀκούω means "hearing," with less stress, as sometimes in John's Gospel (see also 1 Tim 4:16, discussion and note), on attendant "believing"; the emphasis here is on the extent of Paul's proclamation, which, made in the cosmopolitan capital city of the empire before the representatives of imperial rule, can be said to have reached its widest audience.

unlike Paul's claim in Rom 15:19: "from Jerusalem all the way around to Illyricum, I have fully proclaimed the gospel of Christ." Now by witnessing faithfully in the Roman courtroom he could claim to have fulfilled his mission to the Gentiles. Questions of overstatement or exaggeration are not to be answered by extending the reference to proclamation to a longer period of time or a wider geographical range;[106] this is a symbolic statement rooted in the significance of "Rome" within the Pauline missiological perspective. The importance for Timothy, who has also been charged to fulfill his ministry (4:5), is that the moment of fulfillment for Paul, Timothy's model, took place while Paul was a prisoner sharing in the sufferings of Christ.

Is the Messianic Psalm still in mind? Again historical reflection finds theological resonance in the background text. As Psalm 21 (LXX) turns from desperate prayer for help (v. 22; and see below) to the beleaguered one's promise to proclaim the Lord's faithfulness (vv. 23-27), the psalmist announces the same promise to the nations that Paul claims here to be fulfilled:

> 21:28-29: "All the ends of the earth *(panta ta perata tēs gēs)* shall remember and turn to the LORD; and all the families of the nations *(pasai hai patriai tōn ethnōn)* shall worship before him, for dominion belongs to the LORD, and he rules over the nations."

The shared themes — the universal scope of salvation ("all . . . all"; *panta . . . pasai)* and the language ("all . . . the nations"; *pasai . . . tōn ethnōn)* — suggest that this is more than a chance allusion.

In rapid succession come three final links to the Psalm: a distinctive metaphor, verbs of rescue, and kingdom language. The second element of the story's conclusion (4:17c) completes the sentence with a metaphorical description of deliverance: "And I was delivered from the lion's mouth." The phrase "lion's mouth" was a strong metaphor for death and functions in this way here.[107] It is a close match with LXX Ps 21:22, and it is the definitive echo of the Psalm in this section and the literary magnet that attracts and orients the other allusions:

---

106. E.g., Prior, *Paul the Letter-Writer,* 113-39; Oberlinner, 178-79, who refers the statement to Paul's successors; Scott, 141-42.

107. See LXX Judg 14:8-9; Ps 21:21; Dan 6:21 (Theod.); Amos 3:12; 1 Macc 2:60. Gk. στόμα λέοντος. The term for "mouth" (στόμα) could refer metonymically to the destructive power of the wild animal (LXX Gen 34:26; Job 36:16; Heb 11:34; K. Weiss, *TDNT* 7:692-701; cf. its use for "the edge of the sword"). One such beast is of course the lion (λέων), which, although sometimes an image of courage and power (W. Michaelis, *TDNT* 4:251-53), often stood metaphorically for stealth and destruction (LXX Num 23:24; Deut 33:20; 1 Kgs 13:24; 20:36; Pss 7:2; 10:9; Heb 11:33; 1 Pet 5:8). No specific reference, such as to Nero or the lion pit, is intended (rightly Marshall, 825).

Ps 21:22: "Save me from the mouth of the lion" *(sōson me ek stomatos leontos)*

2 Tim 4:17c: "And I was delivered from the mouth of the lion" *(kai errysthēn ek stomatos leontos).*[108]

We shall consider Paul's verb selection presently. In the passive "I was delivered," Paul envisions the Lord, Christ, as the agent of deliverance and reflects on a past event. But to what event is Paul referring? The answer hinges on the trial envisaged in the reference to the first *apologia* (see above). If, on the one hand, the first *apologia* refers to an earlier Roman trial followed by release, the metaphor may refer to that trial's successful outcome.[109] But if, after an unmentioned period of freedom, Paul is now expecting the worst, this reflection seems less relevant within the exhortation. If, on the other hand, this statement is to be linked with a proximate "first *apologia*" (= *primo actio*) that is leading to a trial proper (the *secunda actio*), then, as Marshall suggests, the metaphor of deliverance will mean only relative success, or "deliverance" in a very specific (spiritual) sense.[110] For example, he may simply be referring to the fact that he was allowed to make a "defense" at all (in which he proclaimed the gospel), after which the trial turned ugly.

As we now consider the verbs of rescue in the remaining sequence, the scenario of Psalm 21 slides back into focus. In the psalmist's use of the metaphor, the verb of rescue, "to save," is different (but see 2 Tim 4:18b), but the verb Paul selects here, "to rescue, deliver,"[111] and repeats in 4:18a is a dominant feature of the vocabulary of the Psalm (vv. 5, 9, 21), and Paul's selection fortifies the intertextual connection. In fact, the verb pair in 4:18ab *(rhyomai/sōzō)* replicates the alternating pattern of the Psalm (21:5/6, 9a/9b, 21/22):[112]

---

108. LXX

> Ps 21:22:   σῶσόν με ἐκ στόματος λέοντος;
> 2 Tim 4:17c: καὶ ἐρρύσθην ἐκ στόματος λέοντος.

109. E.g., Quinn-Wacker, 834. For the view that the metaphor reflects on past rescues (e.g., 3:11; cf. Acts 23:12-32), see Lestapis, *L'énigme* (on the assumption that 2 Timothy 4 and Acts 28 reflect the same imprisonment); cf. Quinn-Wacker, 834. But a particular event of rescue seems to be in mind, and the point of a much earlier rescue would be lost here.

110. Marshall, 825.

111. Gk. ῥύομαι (see on 2 Tim 3:11).

112. This particular pattern that alternates forms of ῥύομαι/σῴζω, which corresponds to the parallelism of Hebrew poetry, is restricted for the most part to the Psalms (Job 33:28, 30; Pss 6:5; 7:2; 30:2, 3, 16, 17; 58:3; 59:7; 68:15; 70:2; 107:7; cf. Pss 50:16; 85:2; 108:26).

2 Tim 4:17c: "And I was delivered from the mouth of the lion."
   (kai errysthēn ek stomatos leontos)
   4:18a: "The Lord will deliver me from every evil deed."
   (rhysetai me ho kyrios apo pantos ergou ponērou)
   4:18b: "and will save me into his heavenly kingdom"
   (kai sōsei eis tēn basileian autou tēn epouranion)

LXX Ps 21:5: "Our fathers hoped in you; they hoped and you delivered
   (erryso) them."
   21:6: "To you they cried and were saved *(esōthēsan)*."
   21:9: "He hoped in the Lord, let him deliver *(rhysasthō)* him. . . .
   Let him save *(sōsatō)* him because he takes pleasure in
   him."
   21:21: "Deliver *(rhysai)* my life from the sword. . . ."
   21:22: "Save *(sōson)* me from the mouth of the lion. . . ."

In this deliverance litany, Paul has pointed first to some experience of divine presence, empowerment, and deliverance, at least in the form of a reprieve from death long enough to make some kind of defense. But as it continues, Paul's theology deepens as the certainty of his death grows ever stronger.

Without a pause in thought,[113] Paul extends his experience of past rescue into a statement of assurance about the Lord's future rescue and ultimate salvation. In 4:18ab, two parallel future statements of salvation, displaying the psalmist's verb alternation, balance the past statement just made. The first statement measures salvation negatively ("the Lord will rescue me from . . ."). Here the future tense of the verb "to deliver" (see on 3:11), just employed in the past tense (v. 17c), depicts the Lord (Yahweh in the Psalm becomes Jesus in Paul's discourse) in action, "delivering" by removing Paul from the sphere of danger (i.e., future acts of evil). "Every evil attack [deed]" certainly envisages the sort of evil and injustice done to him by the Roman authorities,[114] but the particular configuration also contrasts obviously with the term "good deeds" that characterizes authentic Christian behavior in these letters.[115] This suggests that the behavior of Alexander (4:14) and other acts of evil from Christian opponents would fall into this category. In harmony with the next line, this element of deliverance is to be understood in a final, eschatological sense: echoing the psalmist's confidence, with the vic-

---

113. A few MSS (D[1] F G Ψ TR sy) add καί to the beginning of the sentence, probably to smooth out the syntax; it is secondary (Elliott, 210; Marshall, 814).

114. Gk. ἀπὸ παντὸς ἔργου πονηροῦ; for the combination, cf. 1 Esdr 8:86; John 3:19; 7:7; Col 1:21; 1 John 3:12; 2 John 11. See G. Harder, *TDNT* 6:551-57, esp. 557.

115. See 1 Tim 2:10 (Excursus).

tory of Christ's resurrection also in the background, Paul knows that no evil will separate him from eternal salvation.[116]

The next parallel statement (v. 18b) adds a positive measurement with the future of the verb "to save": "[he] will save me into. . . ."[117] This completes the verb pairing and, with the thought of Paul's impending death, confirms that salvation is now viewed in terms of its ultimate future consummation.[118]

This salvation is ultimately described as entry into "his heavenly kingdom," that is, into the domain of the Lord's rule. As in 4:1 (q.v.), the eschatological manifestation of the Lord's full authority and rule is expressed here with the term "his kingdom." In this case the adjective "heavenly" adds further definition, depicting the kingdom of Christ as presently real but yet future in its culmination, awaiting "that day" when heavenly realities enter fully the earthly sphere (4:8).[119] Notably the way in which Paul has articulated salvation (present experience in anticipation of future consummation) is closely parallel to Col 1:13: "he has rescued *(errysato)* us from the dominion of darkness and brought us into the kingdom of the Son he loves." Here, however, Paul has shifted the accent to the future consummation, though this in no way negates the present reality.

The two-part affirmation of the Lord's salvation promise is in Paul's historical context a thorough rejection of the dominion of evil (rulers or opponents) in view of the reality and supremacy of the Lord's dominion/kingdom. In both the language and the missiological tone, Paul makes his final allusion to LXX Psalm 21, where in v. 29 a claim about God's dominion/kingdom establishes the certainty that "all nations" (as Paul states in 4:17) will turn to the Lord:

> Ps 21:29: "For dominion *(basileia)* is the Lord's, and he rules the nations *(tōn ethnōn)*."[120]

116. For the view that the statement is given in anticipation of future ministry for Paul, see Prior and Oberlinner. Some scholars detect in this language of deliverance from evil the influence of the last line of the Lord's Prayer (Matt 6:13; Quinn-Wacker, 835; Jeremias, 66); but 2 Thess 3:3 employs similar language that complicates the question of intended allusions (πιστὸς δέ ἐστιν ὁ κύριος, ὃς στηρίξει ὑμᾶς καὶ φυλάξει ἀπὸ τοῦ πονηροῦ; "the Lord is faithful, who will establish you and guard you from evil"). In fact, more to the point might be the question of the source of the language and thought of the last line of the Lord's Prayer, which is certainly reminiscent of the prayer-pleas found in the Psalms, and not least in Psalm 2.

117. For Gk. σῴζω, see on 1 Tim 1:15.

118. John 3:12; 1 Cor 15:40, 48(2x); Eph 1:3, 20; 2:6; 3:10; 6:12; Col 1:13; Heb 9:23; H. Traub, *TDNT* 5:538-42; Marshall, 826; Fee, 298; Knight, 472.

119. Gk. ἐπουράνιος (1 Cor 15:40, 48, 49; Eph 1:3, 20; 2:6; 3:10; 6:12; Phil 2:10); Traub, *TDNT* 5:38-42.

120. LXX Ps 21:29: ὅτι τοῦ κυρίου ἡ βασιλεία, καὶ αὐτὸς δεσπόζει τῶν ἐθνῶν.

Consequently, Paul's discourse moves from the historical level to the theological level by making various connections with Psalm 21 (LXX; Psalm 22 MT). The purpose is to interpret his final episode of suffering for the gospel in terms of the tradition of Jesus' passion. By incorporating the psalmist's vision for the Gentiles, this interpretive application of the suffering figure of the Psalm to his apostolic ministry actually takes Paul to a place Jesus would go fully only through the apostolic mission — to the Gentiles. This is in keeping with the place at which the Pauline story begins and ends and the distinctive role Paul plays in relation to God's promise to save the nations. Paul's suffering, the abandonment he experienced, and his impending death all fit the Jesus mold.

In fact, the supremacy of Christ is underlined by the doxology that fittingly concludes the story of Paul's suffering for the gospel. There is much to be thankful for — the fulfillment of Paul's ministry, which means salvation for the Gentiles, and his personal experience of God's presence and help, as well as his assurance of final salvation.

The form of the doxology is standard (Rom 16:27; Gal 1:5; Heb 13:21; cf. 1 Pet 4:11): "To him be glory for ever and ever. Amen."[121] Some commentators are of the opinion that the doxology is offered to God (as in 1 Tim 1:17),[122] but while it is something of a departure from Pauline practice, the relative pronoun "to whom" has the Lord (Jesus) as its most obvious antecedent (cf. 1 Tim 1:12).[123] By means of the doxology, Paul affirms strongly that majesty and dominion (to which "glory" refers)[124] are proper to the Lord. The concluding "Amen" (see on 1 Tim 1:17) punctuates the affirmation as an undeniable fact to which he is completely committed.[125] As a conclusion to the body of the letter, the doxology invites readers to add their voice to Paul's worship.

Some loose ends, both historical and theological, remain. From the historical perspective, as we have already seen, this section of the letter presents us with certain tantalizing pieces of the puzzle of Paul's chronology that require either relaxing the chronology established on the basis of Acts and the earlier Paulines or extending it by positing a release from Roman imprisonment that allows for additional movements. The difficulties are not fully solved by the release-from-imprisonment theory, and I incline away from this alternative toward a single-imprisonment scenario. But even if the

---

121. Gk. ᾧ ἡ δόξα εἰς τοὺς αἰῶνας τῶν αἰώνων, ἀμήν. A form of the verb "to be" (i.e., ἐστιν) is to be supplied.

122. E.g., Oberlinner, 181; Kelly, 220.

123. Quinn-Wacker, 826; cf. Marshall, 826.

124. For Gk. δόξα, see 1 Tim 1:11 (discussion and note).

125. Cf. H. Bietenhard, "Amen, Hallelujah, Hosanna," n.p., *NIDNTT on CD-ROM.* Version 2.7. 1999.

gaps in our knowledge of Paul's pre-imprisonment travels already indicated in the earlier letters and the view of later tradition suggest that we must leave the matter somewhat open, there is nothing to prevent us from viewing the passage within the context of the historical Pauline mission.

The conclusion to Paul's story is heavily laden with christological and theological overtones. In various ways, not least in the contact established with Psalm 21 (LXX), Paul interpreted his final episode of suffering for the gospel in terms of the model left behind by Jesus Christ. We saw that Paul's interpretive use of the suffering figure of the Psalm was able to go beyond Jesus' use by incorporating the psalmist's vision for the Gentiles. Nevertheless, Paul's suffering in no way supersedes that of Jesus; it is rather the complementary outworking of one who has taken to himself the cruciform character and behavior of the Lord. Both in terms of the life lived and the missiological goals implied, Paul's extension of the Jesus-model is not only the pattern for others who will follow (here, chiefly Timothy) but also the critical climax of his own mission.

IV. CLOSING GREETINGS, INSTRUCTIONS, AND BLESSING (4:19-22)

> 19 *Greet Priscilla and Aquila and the household of Onesiphorus.*
> 20 *Erastus stayed in Corinth, and I left Trophimus sick in Miletus.* 21
> *Do your best to get here before winter. Eubulus greets you, and so do*
> *Pudens, Linus, Claudia and all the brothers and sisters.*
> 22 *The Lord be with your spirit. Grace be with you all.*

As Paul closes the letter, he sends final greetings from himself and those with him, whom Timothy apparently knows. He also adds some further information about absent team members, and refines an instruction given earlier to Timothy. A blessing or benediction forms the closing last words. Among other things that might be learned from these details, assuming authenticity, is more of the human side of the writer. At the end, he is concerned for the friendships that he has made over the years, and desires that these friends know of his continued feelings for them in the hardest of times. This kind of concern is also reflected in the addition of the benediction.[1]

---

1. But of course those preferring to view these letters to coworkers as pseudonymous writings evaluate this section in different ways. On the one hand, something like this ending would have to be included to give the letter the right look (Hanson, 163). If, in the attempt to do so, certain inconsistencies are created, well, that is perhaps more to be ex-

19   The greetings section, addressing certain persons or groups indirectly through the letter's recipient(s), was a typical feature of Paul's letters and other NT and early Christian letters (Rom 16:3-16; 2 Cor 13:13; Phlm 23-24; Heb 13:23-24; 1 Pet 5:13-14)[2] and here employs the standard verb.[3] Paul names three people who are presumably still in Timothy's location. Prisca (TNIV/NIV has the diminutive "Priscilla") and Aquila[4] were associated with the Pauline mission from the time of Paul's arrival in Corinth, at which point we learn that the husband, at least, was a Jew (making them Jewish Christians), also a tentmaker (leather worker), originally from Asia Minor (Pontus), who had at some point migrated (apparently) from there to Rome. Subsequently, at the time when Claudius had expelled all Jews from the imperial city (Acts 18:2), they came to Corinth. They also appear in Paul's letters (Rom 16:3; 1 Cor 16:19). When Paul was en route back to Syria/Antioch, they all stopped off at Ephesus, where Aquila and Priscilla were left (1 Cor 16:19) and Paul began to preach (Acts 18:26). By the time Paul wrote Romans, the couple had returned to Rome (Rom 16:3). Yet at the time of this writing they had apparently returned to Asia Minor, probably in

---

pected of a pseudepigrapher than of a genuine Paul. For example, as pointed out above in connection with Paul's reference to being abandoned, the mention of four individuals who are with or accessible to Paul is often thought to be just such an inconsistency. But it is probably best to understand Paul/the writer as distinguishing between close members of his team and Roman Christians, and the four mentioned in v. 21 are notably names that have not occurred elsewhere in Paul. Probably more are of the opinion that the material in this whole last section (vv. 9-22) consists at least partly of genuine Pauline data or fragments, but that they have been inserted without a great deal of concern for the patterns of movements and people established in the genuine letters, and are included more for the purpose of developing various facets of the portrait of the heroic Paul, even if to do so requires the data to form various contradictions. So Oberlinner, 187, suggests that the contradictory picture of companions when isolation and abandonment had been the theme is the result of the author's need to fill out the picture of Paul by adding the dimension of faithful colleagues. Marshall, 827, however, rightly questions whether a pseudepigrapher would risk such inconsistency, and the answer is probably No. We have already seen how acute the need for caution is precisely at the points of discussing the people and movements at this juncture in Paul's history. But there is no need to disregard the details of this closing section of the letter; they do not throw up insuperable contradictions to the circumstances already sketched out by the author.

2. Aune, *Literary Environment,* 186-87. See also the discussion at Titus 3:15.

3. Gk. ἀσπάζομαι (see Rom 16:16; 1 Cor 16:19, 20; 2 Cor 13:12; Phil 4:21, 22; etc.; cf. H. Windisch, *TDNT* 1:496-502). Cf. MM.

4. Gk. Πρίσκα (see also the diminutive Πρίσκιλλα; Acts 18:2, 18, 26) καὶ Ἀκύλαν (Ἀκύλας). For extrabiblical attestation of both names, see BDAG, s.v. The lengthy but inaccurate addition to the text following Ἀκύλαν, found in 181 and 460, of names (which, according to the *Acts of Paul and Thecla,* §2 were the names of Onesiphorus's children) is of course secondary; see Metzger, 650.

the vicinity of Ephesus.[5] It is striking that in four of the six occurrences of the two names, Prisca is mentioned first, as she is here (cf. Acts 18:2; 1 Cor 16:19). This would suggest that she was an important figure, but the degree to which this is a reflection of her social status[6] or greater importance in the church's ministry is impossible to determine.[7]

The next named whom Timothy is to greet is "the household of Onesiphorus." As noted in the discussion at 1:16, where Onesiphorus's household is addressed (there blessed) without separate reference to him, the question of his status at the time of writing is raised. Col 4:15 is cited as a parallel to this greeting of a household,[8] but there it is preceded by a greeting to the householder and the general greeting is to the church that meets in the house, so it is not of much help in determining the implications of this greeting. Ignatius, *To the Smyrnaeans* 13.1-2 presents a closer parallel ("I greet the households of my brothers. . . . I greet the household of Gavia"; cf. 12:1), though the status of the householders is clear in each case. Nevertheless, Paul's comment may indicate that Onesiphorus was not at home at the time of writing (the aorist tenses of 1:16 suggest that Onesiphorus is no longer in Rome; but he may have been en route, or traveling elsewhere, or dead);[9] possibly he is to be understood as included in the greeting.[10]

20 At this point, Paul adds information about two more coworkers. The first to be mentioned is one named Erastus: "Erastus stayed in Corinth."[11] The name occurs twice more in the NT, in Acts 19:22 in reference to one who was dispatched with Timothy from Ephesus to Macedonia, and in Rom 16:23 in reference to one in Corinth who is called "the steward of the city."[12] Scholars

---

5. Cf. A. Weiser, *EDNT* 1:55-56.

6. Going back to Ramsay, as cited in BDAG, s.v.

7. Cf. discussions in J. D. G. Dunn, *Romans 9–16* (Waco, TX: Word, 1988), 892; Fee, *First Epistle to the Corinthians,* 835 n. 10; for the historically improbable view that it is a mere courtesy, see Knight, 475.

8. So Marshall, 828.

9. So Knight, 476; Fee, 301. Quinn-Wacker, 838, suggest that the greeting may be to a house church that included a group of widows presided over by Onesiphorus's widow (relying apparently on their interpretation of the role of Gavia in Ignatius, *To the Smyrnaeans* 13.2 and citing 1 Tim 5:16 as a parallel); this is completely conjectural. The detail supplied by the *Acts of Paul and Thecla (New Testament Apocrypha,* 2:353), that Onesiphorus's home was in Iconium, sheds no light on this passage and raises more questions (such as why Timothy, in Ephesus, or thereabouts, would be asked to greet a household as far away as Iconium).

10. Marshall, 828.

11. The name Ἔραστος was common and, according to Spicq, 822, frequently given to slaves; see BDAG, s.v., for inscriptional evidence. In fact, the name itself gives no clues about his status (see below).

12. See Winter, *Seek the Welfare of the City,* 179-97.

are divided over the question whether these three references are all to the same person.[13] The present reference is often held to be the sort of historical note that would lend credibility to a later telling of Paul's last days. The latter possibility aside, however, the person(s) bearing the name converge on a place, Corinth, and on persons who have a connection with the name, Paul and Timothy.

Corinth was closely associated with Ephesus in the Pauline mission (Acts 18–20); it was a major city in Achaia[14] and a major point of church planting and pastoral headaches for Paul. Furthermore, there was apparently a good deal of exchange between the two churches. In any case, Rom 16:23 and the present text focus on Corinth, a logical stop on the shortest route from Ephesus to Macedonia, which also brings the man and the travel mentioned in Acts 19:22 into the purview of this text.

Another point of convergence comes in the person of Timothy, who is also associated with Erastus as a coworker in Acts 19:22, and was present with Paul and Erastus in Corinth at the time of writing Rom 16:23 (v. 21). While it is possible that Paul had been associated with more than one man bearing the name Erastus, there is nothing to make the identification of the three impossible.[15] Paul's reason for mentioning Erastus at this point is unknown, unless it is simply to explain why he was absent, or to indicate that Timothy might find him en route to Rome.

Trophimus,[16] also a name closely associated with the Pauline mission (Acts 20:4; 21:29), accompanied Paul from Ephesus westward to Macedonia and Achaia, and then on the final trip to Jerusalem. According to Acts (21:29), he was a native of Ephesus and a Gentile, which became the issue leading to Paul's false arrest in Jerusalem. The reference to him in this passage is ambiguous, owing again to gaps in the Pauline chronology. At some point during his travels with Paul or during his ministry assignment at Miletus ("I left Trophimus . . ."),[17] he became ill.[18] The former suggestion,

13. The discussion centers mainly on the references in Acts 19:22 and Rom 16:23; cf. G. Theissen, *The Social Setting of Pauline Christianity* (Philadelphia: Fortress, 1982), 76; Dunn, *Romans*, 911; Winter, *Seek the Welfare of the City*, 196.

14. See D. W. J. Gill, "Achaia," in D. W. J. Gill and C. Gempf, eds., *The Book of Acts in Its First-Century Setting*, Vol. 2: *The Book of Acts in Its Graeco-Roman Setting* (Grand Rapids: Eerdmans, 1994), 448-53.

15. Winter, *Welfare*, 192-97. Marshall, 828.

16. Gk. Τρόφιμος; the name is well attested in inscriptions and papyri (BDAG, s.v.).

17. Gk. ἀπολείπω (aor. "to leave behind"; Heb 4:6, 9; 10) may bear the meaning "to appoint," or "to leave in place" in the sense of an appointment (see discussion at Titus 1:5). Thus Johnson, 447-48, suggests that the text means only that Paul has left Trophimus in place, ministering, in spite of his illness (cf. van Bruggen, *Die geschichtliche Einordnung der Pastoralbriefe*, 57).

18. Gk. ἀσθενέω ("to be weak, sick"; for the latter see Phil 2:26, 27; Jas 5:14;

based on a possible use of the verb (in the sense of "to assign"), would alleviate any of the difficulties involved in reconstructing Paul's travel routes (from his known history) to bring him to Miletus, but the sense of "assignment" in this occurrence of the verb is not as clear as in Titus 1:5, where the same sort of question arises.[19]

Miletus, where Paul stopped on the way to Jerusalem (Acts 20:15, 17), was located on the west coast of the province of Asia,[20] about thirty miles from Ephesus. The proximity of Trophimus to Timothy alone may explain the relevance of the information. But if this is to be regarded as news for Timothy, we might expect that a fairly short period of time had elapsed from Paul's having "left" Trophimus ill at Miletus until the writing of the letter in Rome. If this factor of timing is a requirement (and again the passage itself is concerned with events in near time), then it is not possible that the travel envisaged is that mentioned in Acts 20:4; that text places him with Paul on the trip that eventually takes them to Miletus (20:15); but the fact that he later travels to Jerusalem with Paul requires the reference to be to a later trip or posting to Miletus.[21] But this may simply be a reminder, which explains the reason for Trophimus's absence from Rome at this crucial time, and perhaps an implicit suggestion to Timothy to look in on the coworker as he travels to Rome. Obviously, if the reference implies that Paul and Trophimus were together in Miletus, such a journey fits more easily into a second imprisonment scenario. Once again we are hampered more by our ignorance of the details of Paul's later movements than necessarily by erroneous information.

21 Finally, Paul repeats a command and includes greetings from some local believers. The command is a repetition of 4:9 ("do your best to get here," or, perhaps better in this context, "hurry to get here"), employing the same verb-infinitive combination,[22] while adding a time limit, "before winter." The term translated "winter" can mean either inclement weather,

---

G. Stählin, *TDNT* 1:490-93). The present participle could imply cause ("I left [him] because he was sick"), concession (". . . although he was sick"), or manner (". . . being sick").

19. The difference between this passage, where a reason for "leaving him behind" ("because he was sick") is possibly expressed instead of simply an attendant circumstance, and Titus 1:5, where the "leaving behind" is specifically explained by reasons of ministry, should be noted. Had Paul said here, "I left him in position, although he was sick, to continue ministering," or something along these lines, the "assignment" sense of the verb would be much clearer.

20. See P. Treblico, "Asia," in D. W. J. Gill and C. Gempf, eds., *The Book of Acts in Its First-Century Setting,* Vol. 2: *The Book of Acts in Its Graeco-Roman Setting* (Grand Rapids: Eerdmans, 1994), 360-62.

21. For discussions of Beza's "correction" of the text (to read Μελίτα = Malta), which Paul visited on his journey to Rome (Acts 28:1), see Elliott, 171; Marshall, 827.

22. See 4:9 (discussion and notes).

cold, rainy, windy, and stormy weather generally, or the season of winter.[23] The latter is meant here. Anticipation of the harsh season explains the request for the cloak to be brought to Paul (4:13) and the stipulation that Timothy arrive before the onset of winter. Travel by sea was ill advised in the winter season. Ancient sources confirm that the season for reasonably safe travel concluded on September 14, and beyond November 11 all travel was halted; sea travel began again on February 8.[24] Land travel was also dangerous and unpredictable in the winter months, when mountain passes might become treacherous. Assuming these parameters, the letter was probably meant to reach Timothy by early autumn at the latest, allowing the time necessary to make the trip to Rome before the onset of winter,[25] meaning that it would have been written in the spring or summer.[26]

Having already sent his own greetings, those expressed by local believers are now passed on in typical fashion as the letter reaches its conclusion.[27] Four persons are specifically named (only here in the NT), whom we may guess Timothy knew personally. Of three of them, Eubulus, Pudens, and Claudia, nothing is known.[28] The name Linus (also only here in the NT) attracts somewhat more attention as early traditions associate the name with that of the first bishop of Rome.[29] Rounding off this list of well-wishers is the

23. Gk. χειμών (Matt 16:3; Acts 27:20; with Mark 13:18; John 10:22); Spicq, *TLNT* 2:98.

24. Pliny, *Natural History* 2.122; Vegetius, *De re militari* 4.39. Under extreme circumstances, winter travel on the seas was sometimes chanced (Suetonius, *Divus Claudius* 18.2 (food shortages in Rome); Josephus, *Antiquities* 14.376; Philo, *On the Embassy to Gaius* 190). On the whole matter of sea travel as it affected the Pauline mission, see B. M. Rapske, "Acts, Travel and Shipwreck," in Gill and Gempf, eds., *The Book of Acts in Its First-Century Setting,* Vol. 2: *The Book of Acts in Its Graeco-Roman Setting,* 22-46.

25. Commenting on the time required for Timothy's earlier journey from Rome to Philippi (Phil 2:19), we can estimate that a trip from Ephesus to Rome would require at least a month and a half, depending on how much was land travel and how much sea travel (F. F. Bruce, "Travel and Communication: The New Testament World," n.p., *ABD on CD-ROM.* Version 2.1a. 1995, 1996, 1997).

26. Cf. Marshall, 830; Fee, 301; Jeremias, 67.

27. See also Titus 3:15; Rom 16:21, 23; 1 Cor 16:19-20; Col 4:10, 12, 14; Phlm 23. This secondary communication of greetings, conveyed by means of the third-person verb ἀσπάζεται, is typical of Hellenistic letter closings (Aune, *Literary Environment,* 187). See further the discussion at Titus 3:15.

28. Gk. Εὔβουλος, Πούδης (the Greek for Lat. "Pudens"; cf. BDF §41.2), Κλαυδία. All are well-attested names (see BDAG, s.v., for each; and discussion in Dibelius and Conzelmann, 125). For discussions of these names and attempts to link them to persons in the early church history, see J. B. Lightfoot, *The Apostolic Fathers: Clement* (London: Macmillan, 1890), 1:76-79; C. P. Thiede, s.v., in *Das Grosse Bibellexicon* (Wuppertal, 1988); Spicq, 823.

29. Gk. Λίνος; see Irenaeus, *Against Heresies* 3.3.3; Eusebius, *Ecclesiastical His-*

summary "and all the brothers [and sisters]." The phrase is standard for these closing secondary greetings (1 Cor 16:20; cf. 1 Thess 5:26), with the term "brothers" being understood as shorthand for all who belong to the Christian community in a locale (i.e., "brother and sisters"; TNIV).[30] Again, in the statements above, Paul probably has made a distinction between those members of his mission team who (except for Luke) are absent and the local believers with whom he has had some contact. Why the local believers would not or could not support him at the time of his first *apologia* (4:16), if they are within the purview of that statement, is unknown.

22 The benediction (see on 1 Tim 6:21) is given in two parts, the first of which ("The Lord be [is] with your spirit") is directed to Timothy, the second to a wider group. "The Lord" alone designates both the divine giver and the blessing (his presence; Luke 1:28) to be confirmed.[31] The background to this sort of statement is the OT (Judg 6:12; Ruth 2:4), though by this time it was common NT idiom; it may be less a wish than a prayer confirming the truth of the Lord's presence, which needed only to be embraced.[32] Timothy ("you," sg.) is the sole recipient of this confirmation. The place in which this divine presence is experienced is the human spirit,[33] that dimension of human life which is characterized by the capacity for interrelating with God (Rom 1:9; 8:16; 1 Cor 2:11).[34] The letter itself suggests that the blessing corresponds to the tasks lying ahead for Timothy.

The grace wish ("Grace be with you") is a genuine prayer for the Lord's gracious presence in the lives of the recipients; it is directed toward a broader group (pl. "you").[35] The shift to the plural may be accounted for partly by those previously mentioned (4:19) with whom Timothy is to com-

---

tory 3.2, 13; but cf. Tertullian, *De praescriptione haereticorum* 32, who names Clement as Peter's successor (Marshall, 830).

30. See 1 Tim 4:6 (discussion and note).

31. The variants occurring at this point in some MSS (A 104 614 *pc* vg[st] add Ἰησοῦς; ℵ[2] C D Ψ TR a b f vg[cl ww] sy bo Ambst add Ἰησοῦς Χριστός) are better explained as later improvements on the original, harder reading (ℵ* F G 33 1739 1881 *pc* sa); see Metzger, 650-51.

32. A form of "to be," whether indicative (ἐστίν) or optative (εἴη or πληθυνθείη, 1 Pet 1:2), is to be supplied.

33. Gk. μετὰ τοῦ πνεύματος σου ("with your spirit"); this is thoroughly Pauline (Gal 6:18; Phil 4:23; Phlm 25).

34. Cf. the discussion in J. D. G. Dunn, *The Theology of Paul the Apostle* (Grand Rapids: Eerdmans, 1998), 76-78.

35. Seven variants occur at this point, none of which is more compelling than ἡ χάρις μεθ᾽ ὑμῶν (ℵ* A C G 33 81 1881); Elliott, 172, favors the reading with the singular "you" (ἡ χάρις μετὰ σου; sy[p] sa[ms] bo[ms]), but it is very weakly attested and explainable as an attempt to adjust the ending to fit with the preceding sentence and with the letter's focus on Timothy. See Metzger, 651.

municate Paul's greetings, and partly by those of the church who would hear the letter read (as in the case of 1 Timothy). In form it duplicates the benedictions of 1 Tim 6:21 (q.v.) and Col 4:18 (cf. Heb 13:25), which also omit explicit reference to the divine source of grace, though the implicit meaning is obvious.

It was Paul's pattern to close his letters in this way, but the presence of the pattern does not minimize the depth of feeling he intended to communicate. His benedictions to his churches and coworkers were serious expressions of prayer for his people, that they might know the Lord's presence and help in all situations. In Timothy's case, the need for this gracious blessing from the Lord was linked closely to the challenges ahead of him. If Paul's example of cruciform living and ministry were at all applicable to Timothy, he would not outgrow the need for the helping presence of the Lord and the grace he bestows until he himself passed his ministry on to those who would follow him.

The Letter
to
TITUS

Text, Exposition, and Notes

I. SOURCES OF BACKGROUND INFORMATION ON CRETE

A. The Gods
   1. General Orientation
      - Diodorus 6.2 (first century B.C.E.): two ways of thinking about the gods; some are eternal in genesis and imperishable; others are "earthly gods who have attained undying honor and fame because of benefactions bestowed upon human-kind."
      - Diodorus 5.64.1: The Cretans believed that their race had emerged from the earth, which made them the original Greeks.
      - Diodorus 5.64.2: In contrast to Olympus's claim to be the seat of the gods, Crete countered that those very gods were but men and women of Crete elevated to deity by virtue of benefactions bestowed upon the human race.
      - Diodorus 5.77.3: The Cretans believed their island to be the birthplace of the majority of the gods; Zeus, the preeminent "man become god," was also believed to be buried in Crete. Worship of the gods (according to the Cretans) thus began on Crete.
      - Diodorus's amalgamation of views (from Epimenides and Euhemerus) around 100 B.C.E. reflects what would have been the shape of the general religious climate in Crete in NT times. He says that he is dependent "upon Epimenides, who has written about the gods" (5.80.4). He also gives the best account of Euhemerus's utopian island, Panichaea, to which

659

the human Zeus was supposed to have migrated from Crete to establish his humanistic and enlightened worship (5.42-46).

2. Specific Understanding of the Character of the Cretan Zeus

   a. Attributes associated with him: Diodorus (5.71.1) depicts the Cretan Zeus in terms of an ethical triad — courage *(andreia)*, wisdom *(synesis)*, and justice *(dikaiosynē)* — and says that he surpasses all in these things and "all other virtues." (The closing summary, "and all other virtues," stresses the unity and interdependence of the virtues more than a claim to others — see Philo, *On the Life of Moses,* II)

- Preeminent among these virtues of Zeus is his justice, which he uses for the benefit of the human race by laying down laws to distinguish just from unjust behavior, through establishing courts and judges, and through his persuading the good and punishing the evil (5.71.1).

- In the triad, *andreia* replaces *sophrosynē,* and wisdom stands in the place of *eusebeia. Sophrosynē* had preference over *andreia,* so it is notable that the reverse occurs in Diodorus's description of Zeus . . . especially because Titus emphasizes *sophrosynē* so much.

- *On the Humanity of Zeus:* A fragment preserved by John Chrystosom (part of bk. 6) has Diodorus identifying the Cretan Zeus's human name as Picus (he had been a king of Italy for 120 years, and he had many sons and daughters because he was a debaucher of women [6.5.1]). He apparently assumed godlike characteristics to seduce women, and for this reason some people thought this mortal to be godlike. He was interred on Crete, bearing the epitaph: "Here lies Picus, whom men also call Zeus" (6.5.3).

  - Diodorus 3.61.1-6 is aware of the distinction between the younger Olympian Zeus and the older, less-well-known Cretan one; . . . he confirms that he knows the tradition of his death and burial on Crete.

  - Diodorus 4.9.3 tells the story of Zeus assuming the form of the husband of a woman he is trying but (because of her *sophrosynē*) failing to seduce; he resorts to deception.

  - In light of all of this, Zeus (one who lacks *sophrosynē* and is a liar) forms the perfect backdrop to the characterization of the Christian God ("unlying" [*apseustēs*]; source of the virtues) in Titus.

660

b. Humans confer divine status on the Cretan Zeus for his benefactions to the human race.
- Diodorus 5.71.3: The result of Zeus's placing his virtues in
service of humanity is that he "receives peculiar honors."
- Diodorus 5.71.6: "Because of the magnitude of his bene-
factions and his superior power, all people accorded him
as with one voice both the everlasting kingship that he
possesses and his dwelling on Mt. Olympus."
- On Diodorus, see Kenneth Sacks, *Diodorus Siculus and
the First Century* (Princeton, NJ: Princeton University
Press, 1990).
- Deification is the highest return of honor for benefactions be-
stowed.
B. Crete the Island
- Pliny, *Natural History* 8.83: absence of wild beasts on Crete;
- Plutarch, *Moralia* 86C: contrasts the absence of wild animals on
Crete with the lack of polity that is free from passions that pro-
duce enmity, envy, rivalry, contention.
C. Cretan Lifestyle/Stereotype (from ancient to Paul's present, a dis-
connect has occurred)
- Known for providing mercenary soldiers to various countries and
for their armies' piracy (for both see S. V. Spyridakis, *Cretica:
Studies on Ancient Crete* [New York: Aristide Caratzas, 1992],
43-82, 130-31).
- Polybius 6.46.3; 6.46.9; 6.47.4: on greed, love of gain, and
wealth;
- Suetonius, *On the Right Insult* 13.253: the meaning of *kretizein*
as *pseudesthai*.
An ancient, more positive view:
- Aristotle, *Politics* 2.2.12; 2.7 and Strabo, 10.4.20-22: Both affirm
that the ancient Cretan constitution sought for equilibrium.
- Strabo, 10.4.9: Writers agree that in ancient times Crete had
good laws, worthy to be emulated.
D. Greek Ethical Expression
(Contemporary with Paul)
- Philo, *On the Special Laws* 4.135 (threefold canon);
- Dio Chrysostom, *Orationes* 23.7, 8;
- Lucian, *Somnium* 10;
(B.C.E.)
- Xenophon, *Memorabilia* 4.8.11 *(eusebēs, dikaios, enkratēs,
phronimos).*
E. The Saying in 1:12

- Clement of Alexandria, *Stromateis* 1.59.2 (second century C.E.) attributes it to Epimenides.
- The first extant instance of the whole saying as it appears in Titus 1:12 is this text itself.
- Callimachus, *Hymn to Zeus* 8–9: employs the first line of the saying "The Cretans are always liars" as it appears in Titus 1:12.

F. *Apseudēs* in 1:2

- Callimachus, *Iambis* 12 (Frag. 202) 15-16.

II. OPENING GREETING (1:1-4)

1 *Paul, a servant of God and an apostle of Jesus Christ to further the faith of God's elect and their knowledge of the truth that leads to godliness — 2 in the hope of eternal life, which God, who does not lie, promised before the beginning of time, 3 and which now at his appointed season he has brought to light through the preaching entrusted to me by the command of God our Savior.*

4 *To Titus, my true son in our common faith: Grace and peace from God the Father and Christ Jesus our Savior.*

The opening of the letter to Titus is the longest and most intricate of these letters to coworkers,[1] and it exceeds the openings of most of the other Pauline letters as well. The bulk of the section, a single sentence in the Greek, forms an elaborate theological interpretation of Paul's apostolate (vv. 1-3; cf. Romans 1), before turning to address Titus directly (v. 4). The greeting has the standard Pauline ("Christian") form: it expands the secular letter greetings by grounding the writer's status in various Christian realities; it identifies the spiritual status of the recipient(s) and adds a specifically Christian blessing.[2]

We may guess that the care Paul takes in setting out his ministry has to do with the need to establish and possibly reassert his authority in the sphere of Titus's ministry — this much is suggested from the indications of opposition to the Pauline mission that emerge in the letter. But from the perspective of the thematic development of the letter itself, the salutation functions to introduce a number of key terms and ideas that are later taken up in various contexts. In order of appearance we find: "faith" (*pistis;* 1:1, 4, 13; 2:2, 10;

---

1. Quinn, 19-21, maintains that the length and content of the opening section establish it as the opening of the PE corpus. This view diminishes the significance of the individual letters and is not demonstrable on the basis of the contents of Titus 1:1-4.

2. See the fuller discussion at 1 Tim 1:1.

3:15); "godliness" (*eusebeia;* 1:11; 2:12); "hope" (*elpis;* 1:2; 2:13; 3:7); "eternal life" (*zōē aiōnios;* 1:2; 3:7); "salvation" language (*sōtēr/sōzō/ sōtērios;* 1:3, 4; 2:10, 11, 13; 3:4, 5, 6); and the theme of divine manifestation introduced in v. 3 *(phaneroō)* is later echoed in the language of "epiphany" (*epiphaneia;* 2:12; verbal forms in 2:11; 3:4).[3] These connections invite Titus (and other hearers) to link various sections of parenesis in which these themes occur to the opening exposition of Paul's ministry and authority as the "slave/servant of God." Thus within the apostle's ministry and message, the elements of God's salvation and the life that it opens up to people *(eusebeia)* are inseparable.

To the churches he had planted in Gentile territory, his apostolic authority was preeminent because he brought the message of salvation with the characteristic accent of equal grace to non-Jews. When viewed against the sorts of claims Paul could make in his undisputed letters about his authority as an apostle or the authority of the gospel of grace he preached (1 Cor 4:15; see also the openings of letters in which he concentrates on his own ministry, Rom 1:1; 1 Cor 1:1; etc.), the claim of the opening to Titus is not unusual — in its extent or its content. In fact, if Titus is written to a situation of opposition to the Pauline mission, the letter's opening reflects a Pauline literary *modus operandi* that is quite true to character.[4]

A. PAUL AND HIS APOSTOLATE (1:1-3)

In a long and complicated statement, Paul describes himself and the nature of his ministry. All of this is encased in a literary scheme that emphasizes the disclosure of a divine secret. While this heightens the importance of the author and his position as an apostle, it also defines the eschatological character of the churches that owe their existence to his gospel.

3. See also Towner, *Goal,* 126-28; Johnson, *Paul's Delegates,* 217-19; Marshall, 112.

4. This concentration on the apostle's own role in God's plan of salvation is evidence for some of the post-Pauline nature of the letter. According to this majority view, the opening to Titus (cf. 1 Tim 1:11-15; 2 Tim 1:6-14; 2:8-10) reflects the attempt by later Paulinists to establish the Pauline message as the authoritative interpretation of the gospel for the later church. Taken to its extreme, this view maintains that in the eyes of the pseudepigrapher Paul himself had become the guarantor of salvation, which had been transmitted to the later church through his appointed successors (see esp. Wolter, *Paulustradition,* 82-95; Läger, *Christologie,* 89-92; Brox, 72-74; Roloff, 56). In his letters to churches Paul is perfectly capable of focusing on his unique role in relation to the Gentiles, in exclusion or distinction from other apostles, without attracting the critical attention of later scholars.

Once the structure of the statement is laid out, its thrust will be more easily seen. At certain points, I diverge from the TNIV translation in order to set out the argument according to the Greek structure:

(v. 1)   Paul,
      a servant of God
      and an apostle of Jesus Christ
          (a) *for* the faith of God's elect
             and the knowledge of the truth
               that leads to godliness —
(v. 2)   (b) *on the basis of* the hope of eternal life,
               which God . . . promised before the beginning of time,
                 who does not lie,
(v. 3)   and he has brought to light (disclosed = executed) . . .
             his promise ("word")
               at his appointed season   [time]
               through the preaching   [means]
                   entrusted to me
                     by the command of
                     God our Savior

The relationship between the various clauses is somewhat obscure because of the dense concentration of thoughts, but the layout above suggests the following logical connections.

(1) Paul's self-description as servant and apostle identifies the writer of the letter.
(2) Reference to his office ("apostle of Jesus Christ") then develops into a long interpretation of the apostolate that is constructed around two main prepositional phrases (a) (*kata* — "*for* the faith . . . and the knowledge . . .") and (b) (*epi* — "*on the basis of* the hope . . ."), both of which depend on the activity inherent in the term "apostle" (or perhaps on some assumed verb such as "called as").
(3) The first of these prepositional phrases (a) indicates what might be thought of as the *goal* of Paul's apostolate, which includes the faith of the elect, (their) knowledge of the truth, and godliness.
(4) The second prepositional phrase (b), parallel with the first, then identifies the *basis* or *reason* for Paul's apostolate: the hope of eternal life.
(5) This basis (eternal life) is then expanded on by means of a promise/fulfillment revelation scheme that identifies "the hope of eternal life" as intrinsic to the divine plan of God and confirms that this plan is presently being executed in history.

(6) Finally, the statement comes full circle as it reflects on the place of Paul's preaching in the salvation drama that is unfolding.

Ultimately what Paul has done in this introduction is to place his own apostolate at the center of God's story; his authority and message are essential to it and derive their meaning from it. Thus, Paul is authenticating the ministry of his coworker Titus by establishing his own authority to instruct Titus.

1 From this discussion of structure, it is clear that the development of Paul's thought exceeds the conventional versification given to the text. Nevertheless, in analyzing the long and complex sentence, I will divide the discussion as far as possible according to verses and verse parts.

Verse 1a identifies the author and his relationship to God. Paul's self-reference by means of his Roman *cognomen* (family or surname), *Paulos,* is characteristic of his letters (see on 1 Tim 1:1). More striking is the phrase "servant [slave] of God," which occurs only here as a Pauline self-description.[5] It is more typical for Paul to describe himself as a "servant of Christ,"[6] although the meaning will have been essentially equivalent. In defining his relationship with God in this way, he draws on the OT pattern established by Moses, David, and other prophets who stood in the special position of those who had received revelation from God.[7] Paul, as an apostle, takes his place in that same line of servants, in a way similar to his designation of Timothy in 2 Tim 3:17.[8]

But the essential meaning of the phrase had not faded, as sometimes happens in the development of honorific titles. In the Jewish and Greco-Roman cultures in which Paul moved, the institution of slavery was based on a system of deeply rooted assumptions. The slave (or servant, *doulos*) was the property of the master and had none but qualified (and therefore extremely limited) rights, and a slave's existence was therefore determined by servitude and submission to the authority of the master. This manner of existence was one of complete dependence on the master/owner for subsistence and protection.[9] All of these elements played into the metaphorical applica-

---

5. Gk. δοῦλος θεοῦ (in the pl.) is used by the demonized slave-girl to describe Paul's mission team in Acts 16:17; for Christians in general, see 1 Pet 2:16; Rev 7:3; cf. Luke 2:29; Acts 2:18; Rev 10:7; 11:18; 19:2, 5; 22:3, 6.

6. Gk. δοῦλος Χριστοῦ: Rom 1:1; Gal 1:10; Phil 1:1. As Marshall, 117, suggests, the influence of the exaltation of Jesus as Lord probably led Paul to alter OT patterns by substituting "Christ" for "God" in the phrase.

7. E.g., Moses (LXX Ps 104:26; cf. Rev. 15:3); David (2 Sam 7:4, 8; Ps 77:70); other prophets and leaders (Jer 7:25; 25:4; Amos 3:7; Hag 2:23).

8. See the discussion; cf. Spicq, *TLNT* 1:380-86; A. Weiser, *EDNT* 1:349-52.

9. See 1 Tim 6:1 (discussion and notes); see also Bartchy, ΜΑΛΛΟΝ ΧΡΗΣΑΙ; Osiek and Balch, *Families in the New Testament World,* 174-92.

tion of the institution to describe one in the service of YHWH. And they are equally definitive in the case of the NT carryover of the metaphor, whether in its use to describe the nature of the incarnation of Christ (Phil 2:7) or the nature of the ministry of Paul as an apostle.

The shape of the argument developed in the passage determines Paul's choice of this phrase, "servant of God," over his usual preference, "servant of Christ." His central concern at the outset is to anchor his ministry in the story of the covenant God — thus the emphasis on God: believers are "God's elect"; God has promised eternal life; God our Savior commanded Paul to take up his ministry.[10] With that long story in mind, moreover, it is fitting for Paul to align himself (by the use of the title) with obedient servants of God who preceded him as recipients of revelation.[11] His authority and obedience to God are not to be questioned.

The main point to be explored in this opening section is introduced in the next element of Paul's identity:[12] "an apostle of Jesus Christ." As we have seen, the phrase (allowing for the more typical reversed order of "Christ Jesus") is a normal piece of Paul's literary identification (see on 1 Tim 1:1). In calling himself an "apostle," he meant to draw attention to his authority as one uniquely called in connection with a revelation of the risen Lord. The association of apostleship with Jesus Christ in this way is uniform in the NT, and it caused no problems for Paul to name himself Jesus Christ's apostle even though in some ultimate sense his commission originated in the will of God (v. 3; cf. 1 Tim 1:1; 2 Tim 1:1). Jesus Christ is thus understood to be the Lord of the mission entrusted to Paul.

This mission is explored in the remainder of v. 1 in a long, compound prepositional phrase (see the diagram of the argument above): "*to further* the faith of God's elect and their knowledge of the truth that leads to godliness" (TNIV). How does Paul envisage that goal here? It will be helpful to disassemble this phrase into its component parts. The phrase is composed of two main elements linked by the conjunction "and," the second of which explains the first.

First, the Greek preposition determines the sense in which the phrase describes Paul's ministry as an apostle. In this case, the preposition *kata* almost certainly indicates purpose, which can be rendered in various ways that

---

10. Cf. Marshall, 117-18. A less likely motive for the shift in terminology to "slave of God" is suggested by Quinn, namely, "slave of God" reflects sensitivity to a Jewish-Christian audience (Quinn, 61).

11. Cf. Lock, 125; Hasler, 85; Rev 1:1; 10:7.

12. There is no obvious sense in which the connective δέ is contrastive (*pace* Quinn, 62); it functions as it does in the μέν . . . δέ construction (though here minus the initial particle; see also Jude 1) to introduce information that correlates with and expands on the description already begun in the previous phrase. Cf. Marshall, 118.

link apostleship to "the faith": "for the purpose of, to bring about, or [as in the TNIV] to further."[13]

The object linked to apostleship by the preposition is "the faith of God's elect," but the phrase is somewhat open to question. First, the designation "God's elect" (Rom 8:33; Col 3:12) for the people of God is an OT concept that was readily adapted to the church's situation.[14] Paul implies that those who have come to faith through his apostolate are therefore God's people, "chosen" by him,[15] and continuous with the OT community of faith.[16] As in the case of 2 Tim 2:10,[17] where Paul describes the purpose of his suffering, here "the elect" is not a futuristic reference to all who will come to faith, but rather, corresponding to biblical usage, a reference to those who have already done so. This is in keeping with the rest of the letter, in which Titus is instructed chiefly about the care of the church. Such language probably infers readers (besides Titus) who are sufficiently familiar with Jewish ideas.

Second, the term "faith," which in these letters may refer to the act or state of believing or to the content of what is believed (see on 1 Tim 1:2), is best understood in the former sense. Paul's responsibility as an apostle includes, then, ensuring the vitality of the belief of the people of God. As the next statement will show, a vital faith adheres to the truth taught by Paul and exhibits the appropriate lifestyle response.

Next, this general description of Paul's apostolic purpose (one dimension of it), "the faith of God's elect," is defined more specifically in language

13. Gk. κατά. See NRSV; GNB; BDAG, s.v. B.4; BDF §224; Marshall, 120; Kelly, 226. Allowing for a different arrangement of thoughts in each passage, the combination of ideas is parallel to that in 2 Tim 1:1. There Paul asserts that his apostleship comes "through the will of God" (διὰ θελήματος θεοῦ) and is "in service of the promise of life that is found in Christ" (a statement of purpose; κατ' ἐπαγγελίαν ζωῆς . . .). Here the link of ministry to God's will is established in v. 3, "according to the command of God" (κατ' ἐπιταγὴν τοῦ . . . θεοῦ), following the statement of purpose already made in v. 1. For the alternative view, that κατά introduces a standard ("according to"), namely, "the faith of God's elect and knowledge of the truth" as a measure of the authenticity of Paul's ministry, see Dibelius and Conzelmann, 131; Houlden, 140. This might seem to make sense where the issue is false teaching and the author feels the need to distance his own teaching from it. But since that whole combination is a way of defining salvation in a broad sense, it would be a very awkward statement of a standard of measurement.

14. Gk. ἐκλεκτῶν θεοῦ; LXX 1 Chron 16:13; Ps 105:6, 43; Isa 42:1; 43:20; 65:9. NT: Mark 13:20, 22, 27; Rom 8:33; 16:13; 2 Tim 2:10; etc. The concept of God's special action in forming his people is evident in Paul's earliest descriptions (employing the perf. pass. form ἠγαπημένοι = "beloved") of the church as those who "are loved by God" (1 Thess 1:4) and "loved by the Lord" (2 Thess 2:13).

15. See J. Eckert, EDNT 1:417-19.

16. Fee, 168.

17. See the discussion; cf. 1 Tim 5:21 (discussion and note).

typical of these letters but now with the situation of opposition in view. Paul's goal is *"to further* [the previous preposition *kata* is still in effect] their knowledge of the truth that *leads to* godliness." Just as elsewhere in these letters conversion is described as "coming to" (or embracing) a "knowledge of the truth,"[18] so here without the verb, the phrase "knowledge of the truth" depicts the life of faith in terms of a prior and ongoing apprehension of the truth. The "truth" in mind is of course specifically the truth of the gospel, Paul's gospel, and the polemical thrust of the phrase is intentional.

Characteristic of each of these letters is a conception of salvation that reflects the proper balance between faith in/knowledge of God and the behavior that gives expression to this personal knowledge. The term "godliness" *(eusebeia)* was adopted for that purpose.[19] Here that term is appended to the statement about truth to explain precisely what sort of truth Paul has in mind.[20] The preposition is again *kata,* and is again somewhat ambiguous in sense, as a comparison of the TNIV/NIV ("the truth that *leads to* [*kata*] godliness") and NRSV ("the truth that *is in accordance with* godliness") makes clear. Paul either understands "the truth" (i.e., the gospel) to produce "godliness," or godliness to be the yardstick of "the truth." Given the description of opponents or rebellious Christian teachers in 1:10-16, and the fact that they are denounced for their rejection of "the truth," corrupt behavior, and false claim to know God, the sense of "godliness" (the balance of faith and conduct) as the authentic measurement of truth is probably uppermost in mind. But there is little real difference, and the alternative is also true: the authentic gospel is intended to produce godliness.

Thus Paul has spelled out the goal of his apostolic ministry as being the salvation of God's people in the broadest sense possible: his task is "to further" the faith of God's people *and* the gospel (known by the godliness it produces) that saves. Evangelism may be implied. But far more evident in this statement of purpose is his concern to nourish believers in a way that allows their existence in Christ to be a powerful interaction of faith and action. Titus is in fact involved in this very work among the Cretan churches.

2 Following this statement of purpose, Paul gives the basis of or reason for his ministry (v. 2a). This too is an involved statement that begins with the end product and then retraces the history of its development in God's promise, leading finally and climactically to Paul's part in delivering that

18. For the language and concept, see 1 Tim 2:4 (discussion and note); 2 Tim 3:7; cf. 2 Tim 2:25.

19. See 1 Tim 2:2 (Excursus).

20. For the repetition of the article to resume reference to a preceding noun prior to a further prepositional phrase for the sake of clarity, see BDF §272. Here the feminine genitive article (τῆς) links the prepositional statement specifically to "truth"; for the usage, see 1 Tim 1:14; 2 Tim 2:10; Rom 16:1.

product to the world (vv. 2b-3).[21] This last thought needs to be stressed. While several dominant items of theology are mentioned within this "reason" statement, the main thought is of Paul's ministry: this opening section of the letter begins (v. 1) and ends (v. 3) with that thought. What is contained within these brackets explicates his role.

Now, central within his role (the *raison d'être* of his ministry) is "the hope of eternal life."[22] As we have seen, in Pauline thought and throughout the NT "hope" is confidence in God's promises for the future (see on 1 Tim 1:1). This kind of hope can be the basis of life itself and of various actions,[23] and among the several objects it might take is "eternal life" (cf. 3:7). What thus becomes the basis of Paul's ministry is the promised life that characterizes, in terms of both endurance and quality, God's own existence (see on 1 Tim 1:16, 17). Paul is an apostle because of this hope: it is the reason behind his calling and the promise that motivates his mission.[24]

But to understand the character of this "hope for eternal life" and his ministry in service of this hope, Paul sets it within the framework of God's eternal promise. In this way the credibility of this hope and of his apostolate are established. Several items combine to make the point.

First, the reference to "eternal life" becomes in the following clause the thing that God has promised (". . . God who cannot lie promised it").[25] "Promise" theology of this sort is characteristic of the belief that God lives in a covenant relationship with his people, who are founded on his promises concerning salvation, and who often required obedient waiting for those promises to be fulfilled.[26] In the NT the content of the promise is specifi-

---

21. As the layout above shows, v. 2a consists of a prepositional phrase (ἐπ' ἐλπίδι ζωῆς αἰωνίου; "on the basis of the hope of eternal life"). Its relation to the preceding train of thought is potentially ambiguous, and the TNIV's decision to retain the dash following "godliness" only accentuates the ambiguity. The dash goes back to the earlier NIV rendering ("godliness — a faith and knowledge resting on the hope of eternal life"). The function of the dash may be to offer some relief to the reader (?), but it is not clear that an improvement has been made. NRSV's insertion of the dash at the end of v. 2 may break the thought at a better place; but again its syntactical function is not clear, and it is hard to see how this is more helpful to the reader than a full stop.

22. This use of ἐπί to indicate the figurative ground or base of some activity or state of being is typical (see BDAG, s.v.; BDF §235).

23. Acts 2:26; 26:6; Rom 4:18; 5:2; 8:20; 1 Cor 9:10 (in each case the phrase is ἐπ' ἐλπίδι).

24. Some interpreters have taken the preposition as expressing something more like a goal (see Kelly, 277; Spicq; 593; cf. 2 Tim 2:14)

25. The preceding term (ζωῆς αἰωνίου) is the referent of the relative pronoun (ἥν) and so becomes the object of the verb "promised."

26. Gk. ἐπαγγέλλομαι ("to promise, offer"; in the sense of "to profess," see on 1 Tim 2:10; 6:21); the concept first emerges in 2 Macc 2:17; *Psalms of Solomon* 12.6; *Tes-*

cally linked with Christ (Rom 4:21; Gal 3:13-18). This holds true here as well, though the emphasis is on the way in which the message about Christ is delivered.

More important in Paul's logic here is guaranteeing the veracity of the promise (and his ministry) and initiating, even at this point in the letter, his critique both of the opposition in Crete and of the chaotic Cretan culture. He does this by tapping into and echoing language and concepts that were dominant within the "story" that shaped Cretan culture; in this way, he prompted the audience to begin to form positive or negative associations. In this case, the echo is set up when he identifies God as the one "who does not lie." In principle, to define God in terms of truthfulness is traditional enough and would be widely appreciated among Christians or Jews (Num 23:19; Rom 3:3-4; Heb 6:18). But the application to God of this particular term *(apseudēs)*,[27] which is not made in Jewish or Christian writings but did describe prophetic figures in Greek antiquity,[28] would remind the Cretan recipients of a unique aspect of their pagan heritage. This is surely intentional on Paul's part.

At the outset of the letter, in anticipation of the biting citation to come (1:12 — "Cretans are always liars"), Paul echoes the lurid cluster of traditions that lay at the heart of Crete's deplorable reputation. Most of the reports are secondhand, to be sure, but there is little reason to doubt that they have preserved the spirit and language of figures such as Callimachus (third century B.C.E.). The connecting theme seems to be "lying." Winter has collected ancient evidence that suggests that "Cretans regarded lying as culturally acceptable";[29] and this cultural tendency lies behind the coining of the term *"krētizō"* (from the name for the island, *Krētē* [= "Crete"]), meaning "to play the Cretan," or "to lie."

But a more specific pagan theology may be at the root. Paul's reference to "the God who does not lie" could well lampoon the character of the Zeus of Cretan tales, who in fact did lie to have sexual relations with a human woman (taking the human form of her husband). This same Zeus was also held to be the epitome of virtue (defined by his possession of the cardinal virtues), a dimension of his character that will come more into focus later in the letter.

Equally, the same language skewers the vulnerable character of the

tament of Joseph 20.1; *2 Baruch* 57.2. For the verb in the NT see Acts 7:5; Rom 4:21; Gal 3:19; Heb 6:13; etc. J. Schniewind and G. Friedrich, *TDNT* 2:576-86; A. Sand, *EDNT* 2:14-15.

27. Gk. ἀψευδής ("free from deceit, truthful"); see LXX Wis 7:17; BDAG, s.v.; H. Conzelmann, *TDNT* 9:594-603.

28. See the references in LSJ, s.v. For this whole discussion see R. M. Kidd, "Titus as *Apologia:* Grace for Liars, Beasts, and Bellies," *HBT* 21 (1999): 185-209.

29. Winter, *Roman Wives,* 149-50.

Cretans themselves. They claimed arrogantly that Zeus's tomb was on Crete. This claim, according to Callimachus, was a lie, and it could be introduced as evidence (along with the particular view of the gods that went with it) of the accuracy of the widespread assertion that "Cretans are always liars." Paul's language calls up this background by echoing the retort of Callimachus, who said, "it is speaking without lying [*apseudēs legōn*]" to say that the Cretan tomb is empty.[30]

Consequently, when Paul describes God as "unlying," he uses loaded language. With it he makes his claim about God's veracity on the surface level, while it also raises the specter of the ancient critique of the flawed Cretan religion and morality. In this way, Paul introduces at the outset a conception of God that will sit uneasily and subversively within that culture's story. For the moment, we will focus on the more immediate theological level of Paul's statement, but the tremor set up by this invasive discourse, directed both at certain rebellious Christian teachers and Cretan culture, should not be missed.

Not only is the "unlying" God the source of the promise, but also it is *promise* (in its entire process) that characterizes the present age. Here Paul utilizes a revelation scheme that places his whole thought within the framework of God's eternal will and its outworking in history (2 Tim 1:9-10).[31] The phrase "before the beginning of time" takes the promise back before time began.[32] Consequently, the promise belongs to the divine redemptive plan that was hidden from human perception and understanding until God's time to make it known arrived.[33]

3 The emphasis, however, is not on the fact or the antiquity of the promise but on its fulfillment in the present. In v. 3, the formula therefore turns from concealment to revelation (see the layout above). But in making the turn, Paul introduces a surprise, and several interpretive challenges result from that surprise: What is it that God manifested; what has happened to "eternal life" in this formula; and what time does Paul have in mind?

First, normally in the use of this sort of promise/fulfillment formula what is revealed is the Christ-event or some aspect of it (2 Tim 1:9-10; Rom 16:25). But in this case Paul says that God has revealed "his word." The verb of revelation used here is typical for describing the appearance of Christ or God (1 Tim 3:16), and the aorist tense suggests a reference to a rather dis-

---

30. See the references and discussion in Kidd, "Titus as *Apologia*," 194.

31. Cf. Rom 16:25; 1 Cor 2:6ff.; Eph 3:4-7, 8-11.

32. For the Gk. time phrase πρὸ χρόνων αἰωνίων, see 2 Tim 1:9 (discussion and notes).

33. Thus one effect of the schema is to link salvation and its certainty to the eternal will of God (see Wolter, *Paulustradition*, 85-90; Oberlinner, 9).

crete event such as the incarnation.[34] Here, however, it is "his word" (the word/gospel of Christ's revelation) that has been revealed.[35] In other words, the story is told from the perspective of the gospel ministry.

But, secondly, when Paul's thought veers in this new conceptual direction, the question to be asked is whether or not the thing promised (i.e., eternal life, v. 2a) is actually still in view in the second half of the formula. The formula began by saying that God promised eternal life; now the outworking of that is the statement that he has manifested "his word," that is, the gospel (for this whole discussion, see the layout above). The problem in the Greek text is called anacoluthon.[36] Paul starts out saying one thing about eternal life as a basis in v. 2a, then makes another point about it being promised by God in v. 2b, and apparently meant to link this (by means of the formula and conjunction) to his next statement (vv. 2c-3a). But now he seems to end up somewhere else (a change of object for the second verb; i.e., "his word"). The shift is detectable in the NIV.[37] What we have here is a conflict of interests, and Paul's attempt to resolve it. On the one hand, the constraints of the formula suggest that the content of the promise is somehow still in view when fulfillment (manifestation) is reached. But the direction of Paul's thought requires him to find a way to shift the focus from promise to preaching. To do this he introduces a new object ("his word") that could refer simultaneously backward to the thing promised ("eternal life," which the gospel reveals) and to the means by which the promise reaches fulfillment now ("his word in proclamation"). Consequently, in choosing a new object ("the word") for the verb "manifested," Paul has not moved on to a new subject; he has instead chosen a way of referring to the promise in its fulfillment, that is, the preaching of the gospel.

Third, the time of revelation within the contrast formula is expressed in the dative phrase "at his appointed season."[38] The plural Greek term behind this translation should be understood as a singular period of time. Its function corresponds to the "now" in the similar formula in 2 Tim 1:9-10. But the attached adjective (lit. "its/his own") and other occurrences of the term (1 Tim 2:6; 6:15) confirm that the event is to be understood as a development in God's salvation plan. Thus the whole promise/fulfillment formula has the activity of God at its center.

Again, it is Paul's main goal in this opening section to validate his

34. For Gk. φανερόω (here aor.), see the discussion and note at 1 Tim 3:16.
35. For this use of Gk. λόγος, see 1 Tim 1:15 (note).
36. See BDF §469.
37. The TNIV has apparently attempted to resolve the anacoluthon by absorbing "his word" (τὸν λόγον) into a relative pronoun that makes the preceding "hope of eternal life" (or just "eternal life") the object of the verb "to promise."
38. For the Gk. phrase καιροὶ ἴδιοι, see 1 Tim 2:6 (discussion and note).

ministry. For this reason, he defines the means of revelation/fulfillment as "through the preaching entrusted to me by the command of God our Savior" (v. 3b). The term for preaching is *kērygma,* which can mean the activity or the content of proclamation;[39] but the distinction between these two dimensions is sometimes blurred.[40] The thought is parallel to that of Rom 16:25-26, where Paul situates his gospel and mission to the Gentiles in the prophetic line as the divinely appointed means of God's saving revelation.

But the process of revelation within the scheme is concluded dramatically in the last half of the verse. Paul spells out his understanding of this eschatological proclamation in the language of 1 Tim 1:11: "with which I have been entrusted by the command of God our Savior." He emphasizes three things. First, at the conclusion of the revelation process Paul himself is the recipient of the gospel. This is the point Paul wanted to reach in his opening argument all along. The language of commissioning he uses here ("entrusted to me"; see on 1 Tim 1:11) is typical of statements he makes in other letters (1 Cor 9:17; Gal 2:7; 1 Thess 2:4). In each case the object entrusted is the gospel. The passive verb implies that God is the actor.[41] The point is that Paul's message comes from God within the salvation plan of God.

Second, Paul locates the source of this commissioning in "the command of God."[42] In doing so, he stresses the authority that he is under and that has been given to him by God to carry out this ministry (see the parallel statement in Rom 16:25-26).

Third, Paul describes this God as "God our Savior" (see on 1 Tim 1:1). This first use of "salvation" language initiates a key theme of the letter (1:3, 4; 2:10, 11, 13; 3:4, 5, 6), namely, that God's salvation is a present reality in the life of the church. At the same time, Paul sets the stage for the first christological transfer in this letter of a divine epithet from God to Christ, who will also be called "Savior" (see 1:4b). The appellation corresponds to

39. Gk. κήρυγμα ("proclamation, the message proclaimed"); the prepositional phrase ἐν κηρύγματι means "through or by means of preaching"). The emphasis is usually on the activity of preaching; cf. 2 Tim 4:17; Matt 12:41; Rom 16:25; 1 Cor 2:1, 4; 15:14; G. Friedrich, *TDNT* 3:714-17.

40. G. Friedrich, *TDNT* 3:716-17; Towner, *Goal,* 123.

41. Cf. 1 Tim 1:11, 13, 16; 2:7; 3:16; 6:12.

42. See 1 Tim 1:1 (discussion and note). Wolter (*Paulustradition,* 149-52) draws a sharp contrast between the opening statements in Titus/1 Timothy and 2 Timothy, arguing that locating the calling in the command of God (Titus/1 Timothy) is evidence of a later attempt to revive the authority of the apostle, while locating his calling in the will of God (2 Timothy) shows no such interest (but is more like 2 Corinthians or Galatians). The two phrases probably do function differently in the ways they express commissioning, but the differing functions of the letters themselves (Titus and 1 Timothy more official; 2 Timothy more personal) may account for the different strategies.

the promise of eternal life he made from before creation, the promise he has kept by revealing the gospel and ordering its proclamation through Paul. The reality of salvation "now" peeks through in the addition of the term "our." God's people experience God as the saving God in various ways.

Paul has come full circle in this opening. He has explained his ministry (its goal and basis). He has located it within God's eternal redemptive plan as the means by which eternal life is brought to light now. He has emphasized his authority as the one entrusted with the task of proclaiming the gospel. By derivation Titus, who is charged to carry on Paul's ministry on the island of Crete, shares in that authority. And the extended theological amplification of Paul's mission serves as a basis for the instructions to Titus and (through him) to the churches on Crete.

B. TITUS: THE RECIPIENT (1:4A)

4a Following Paul's extended introduction, the Greek sentence continues by identifying the recipient of the letter before offering the customary greeting/blessing. The technique and language of this statement are parallel to those of 1 Tim 1:2, and they serve two main purposes — to affirm and to define their relationship.

Titus[43] is called "my true son [child]." As in the case of Timothy, the meaning of this phrase is probably to be determined by both the words and the context in which they are used (see on 1 Tim 1:2). That is, "true child," when used literally, described a legitimate child in contrast to an illegitimate one. In this type of figurative application the meaning is "authentic" or "genuine," and the primary implication for those who read or hear the letter is that Titus (and not false claimants) may represent the apostle.

Historically, the description tells us little about Titus. While it is possible that Paul speaks in this way because Titus was a convert of his,[44] the attached qualifier, "in our common faith,"[45] really establishes the spiritual basis for kinship (i.e., faith in Christ rather than blood or legal adoption),[46] with

43. 2 Cor 2:13; 7:6, 13, 14; 8:6, 16, 23; 12:18; 2 Tim 4:10; Gal 2:1. See the Introduction, 52-53.
44. So Knight, 63-64. That the language implies ordination by Paul (Jeremias, 68-69) seems very unlikely.
45. Gk. κοινός ("shared, in common, mutual"; Acts 2:44; 4:32; Jude 3); F. Hauck, *TDNT* 3:789-97. The whole phrase, κατὰ κοινὴν πίστιν ("in accordance with a common faith"), corresponds to the similar faith-sphere of the "genuine" relationship in 1 Tim 1:2 (ἐν πίστει; "in faith"); cf. 2 Tim 1:5. For Gk. πίστις for "that which is believed," see 1 Tim 1:2 (note).
46. See Marshall, 133; Quinn, 72.

the probable implication of Titus's loyalty and fidelity to Paul's gospel.[47] Of course these are important affirmations for Titus.[48] But within this spiritual family relationship, this language of fictive kinship (father/child/son) depicts Paul as father and Titus as son, which affirms more than just the bond itself. Within this relationship, Titus is obligated to serve Paul as a faithful son would a father. Thus both the affirmation of closeness and the implications of obligation set Titus up for the task about to be outlined.

C. THE GREETING (1:4B)

4b   Except for the omission of the term "mercy" and the description of Christ Jesus as "our Savior" instead of as "our Lord," the greeting parallels those of 1 Tim 1:2 and 2 Tim 1:2. There is no special reason why "mercy" is omitted, but the result is a greeting more typical of Paul's earlier letters. In effect a prayer-blessing, "grace and peace" ("from God the Father"), is Paul's request that God may provide what Titus will need to carry out his ministry ("grace" may take many concrete forms) and preserve him in protective calm ("peace") when equilibrium is needed.[49]

Paul's greetings typically place God the Father alongside Christ Jesus as the source of blessings (see on 1 Tim 1:2). In this case, the substitution of "our Savior" for "our Lord" (cf. 1 Tim 1:2; 2 Tim 1:2) is a notable divergence. The designation of God as "Savior" is known from the OT and Intertestamental writings, which stress his deliverance of Israel from her bondage in Egypt and many times thereafter (see on 1 Tim 1:1). In extending the title to Christ, the early church viewed God's activity as savior as being executed through the Messiah's sacrificial work of delivering from sin. While it is mainly in the later NT writings that the use of the title for Christ becomes frequent (especially in these letters to coworkers and 2 Peter). Paul notably and subversively (in view of claims made about the emperor) proclaimed "the Lord Jesus Christ" to be "Savior" in the letter to the church in the Roman colony of Philippi (Phil 3:20). Overall these letters to coworkers reflect a balance in their presentation of God as Savior (1 Tim 1:1; 2:3; 4:10; Titus 1:3; 2:10; 3:4) and Christ as Savior (2 Tim 1:10; Titus 1:4; 3:6); but the latter preference is thematic in Titus.

As we would suspect, sharing the designation links the Father and the Son in the salvation plan, with God being depicted as the source or originator of the plan of salvation (1 Tim 2:3; Titus 1:3; 2:10; 3:4), and Christ as the

---

47. See Quinn, 72.

48. Spicq, 594, regards this as an expression of affection.

49. For the language (χάρις ἔλεος εἰρήνη; "grace, mercy, peace") and the meaning of the entire blessing, see 1 Tim 1:2 (discussion and notes).

means by which the plan is executed. In Christ's past appearance, God's salvation entered human life as a life-changing possibility (3:6; 2 Tim 1:9-10). In his future appearance salvation will be fully accomplished as God the Savior's glory is fully revealed (2:13; cf. Phil 3:20). The present age in which Paul and Titus preach the gospel and the church lives it out is surrounded by these two great events, the one introducing new possibilities, the other promising their completion. The reference to God as savior in the opening discussion of Paul's ministry calls forth this matching reference to Christ as Savior. Salvation is thus underlined as a chief theme of the letter (2:13; 3:6).

But equally dominant in this letter is a high Christology that begins in this initial pairing of "Saviors" (see also 3:4, 6). Eliciting this Christology is that same provocative discourse carried out on more than one level, engaging the Cretan story that still inhabits the minds of the newborn believers and repulsing an opposition that embodies the deception for which Cretan mythology was known (1:12). Once this tactic is recognized, the emergence of the Cretan stereotype at various points in the letter, as a negative backdrop, makes sense.

But both colliding and resonating with this story line was the religious-political discourse of Imperial Rome. At this point in time, the emperor freely took the title "savior" to himself. A Savior Christology, such as Paul constructs powerfully in this letter, would surely also level a subversive blow at this claim (cf. on 1 Tim 6:14).

The Cretan Christians lived and moved in this swirl of overlapping stories, and Paul undercut them where he could in order to reveal the truth of the gospel. He would also exploit them to reveal the flawed character of the renegade Christian teachers. Titus was his man on the scene. His relationship to Paul accorded him the status and authority needed to command the respect of these Pauline communities. But the grace and peace of God and Christ would sustain him in the harsh Cretan environment.

III. BODY OF THE LETTER (1:5–3:11)

In view of the themes that emerged in the concentrated presentation of 1:1-4, it is obvious that Paul crafted this letter with care. For this reason, it is all the more necessary to observe the structure of the letter closely.[1]

---

1. See the discussion of structure and genre in the Introduction. Marshall's treatment of structure (11-40) is exemplary; and Johnson's discussion of literary style and genre features (21-33, 37-41, 105-10, 211-14) is groundbreaking (cf. Bassler, 22-24). Mounce's two pages of Outline (cxxxv-cxxxvi) are supplemented somewhat by introductory treatments of Form/Structure/Setting.

At this point, the body of the letter commences without an intervening section of thanksgiving and prayer (cf. 1 Timothy; Galatians). Instructions to Titus will alternate with the more general instructions of wider, more public application to the churches in which he is working. Two second-person verbs of purpose set out Titus's mission agenda in Crete: "put in order what was left unfinished . . . appoint elders"; 1:5). Then, in reversed order, these two basic instructions are spelled out in greater detail. First, instructions are given concerning the appointment of elders (vv. 6-9). Second, the "unfinished business" and "disorder" alluded to above are addressed by engagement with the unruly opposing Christian teachers (vv. 10-16). In this latter section, there occurs the first of several second-person singular commands that will guide the thought of 1:10–3:11, namely, "rebuke" (1:13): this command will give shape to the immediate discourse (vv. 13b-16), and exemplify the didactic functions introduced in 1:9 ("teach/exhort/rebuke"). Next, 2:1-10 takes up the meaning of "sound doctrine" (1:9; 2:1) in the context of conduct in the household. In the final section of the body, the didactic term "remind" reshapes material of a traditional nature probably already familiar to the churches (3:1-2). Two sections of very Pauline language provide theological foundation for the ethical material Titus is to teach (2:11-14; 3:4-7).

A. INSTRUCTIONS TO TITUS (1:5-16)

5 *The reason I left you in Crete was that you might put in order what was left unfinished and appoint elders in every town, as I directed you.* 6 *An elder must be blameless, faithful to his wife, a man whose children believe and are not open to the charge of being wild and disobedient.* 7 *Since an overseer manages God's household, he must be blameless — not overbearing, not quick-tempered, not given to drunkenness, not violent, not pursuing dishonest gain.* 8 *Rather, he must be hospitable, one who loves what is good, who is self-controlled, upright, holy and disciplined.* 9 *He must hold firmly to the trustworthy message as it has been taught, so that he can encourage others by sound doctrine and refute those who oppose it.*

10 *For there are many rebellious people, full of meaningless talk and deception, especially those of the circumcision group.* 11 *They must be silenced, because they are disrupting whole households by teaching things they ought not to teach — and that for the sake of dishonest gain.* 12 *One of Crete's own prophets has said it: "Cretans are always liars, evil brutes, lazy gluttons."* 13 *He has surely told the truth! Therefore rebuke them sharply, so that they will be sound in the faith* 14 *and will pay no attention to Jewish myths or to the merely hu-*

man commands of those who reject the truth. 15 *To the pure, all things are pure, but to those who are corrupted and do not believe, nothing is pure. In fact, both their minds and consciences are corrupted.* 16 *They claim to know God, but by their actions they deny him. They are detestable, disobedient and unfit for doing anything good.*

1. The Overarching Instruction to Titus: Putting in Order and Finishing Up (1:5)

5 Titus's situation in Crete is not entirely clear from the letter. But this opening set of instructions (v. 5) implies that he is there on mission business. Crete, as we saw in the Introduction, an island in the Mediterranean south of the Aegean Sea, was an important commercial weigh station for the seagoing trade. This meant that it was also a place where most of the current philosophies and religions would pass through at one point or another, undoubtedly leaving their marks. Unquestionably, it would have been just the sort of strategic location where Paul would wish his gospel to find a foothold. And the language of the instructions suggests that the Pauline mission had reached the island, even if Paul himself had not. The verb translated "I left," which might imply Paul's physical presence there (2 Tim 4:13, 20),[2] might also mean "dispatch" or "assign,"[3] and that may be the more important nuance here. Titus is addressed in his role as Paul's delegate, and we know only that he himself is presently in Crete on Paul's instructions. What is clear from the nature of the instructions is that the Cretan churches are still in the fairly early going, and in need of consolidation in two senses.

A purpose clause ("so that," *hina*) containing two verb phrases proceeds to explain the "reason"[4] for Paul's decision as they also lay out Titus's work. The first phrase is constructed in a puzzling way, though the meaning remains basically understandable: "That you might put in order what was left unfinished." This verb "to put in order," "straighten out" (TNIV, NRSV; "straighten out," NIV) is rare, occurring elsewhere in an inscription on Crete (second century B.C.E.).[5] A related verb also occurs in the Cretan legal context in reference to "reforming" treaties and laws (cf. Acts 24:2; Heb 9:10), which may suggest a nuance for our verb.[6] In some sense Paul (possibly in-

---

2. Gk. ἀπολείπω (aor.); see 2 Tim 4:13, 20; cf. Heb 4:6, 9; 10:26; Jude 6; Spicq, *TLNT* 1:183-84; Mounce, 386.

3. See esp. van Bruggen, *Die geschichtliche Einordnung der Pastoralbriefe,* 39-40; Wolter, *Paulustradition,* 183-84; Marshall, 150; Johnson, *Paul's Delegates,* 212.

4. Gk. τούτου χάριν (lit. "because of this"; for the phrase, see Eph 3:1, 15); in this case, τοῦτο is kataphoric, referring to what follows. BDF §216.

5. Gk. ἐπιδιορθόω (occurring here in the aor. subj.); GDI 5039,9 (BDAG); MM.

6. For the related διορθόω, "to make straight, amend," see Dittenberger, *Sylloge*

tentionally) uses language with which the Cretans are quite familiar to empower Titus with the task of reshaping the teaching and behavior of the
Cretan churches.[7]

The puzzle comes in the way Paul further describes this project in the
object, "what was left unfinished."[8] By finishing the thought in this way, Paul
creates a dissonant combination: the main verb of the purpose clause calls for
an object expressing things in need of correction or reform, and the object,
here formed by a participle (lit. "the things remaining [to be done]"), calls for
a verb expressing completion. If one chooses to emphasize only one aspect,
the focus is either on unfinished work (the sense of the object) or the need to
reform and correct something already underway but veering off course (the
sense of the verb). One can easily imagine the first scenario in one sense or
another: (a) the Pauline mission had gotten underway, but then Paul or his
delegate had pulled out before the task was completed, or had run into opposition that impeded progress; or (b) Titus's assignment is to take up where
someone else's work had ended.[9] The second need is equally evident from
the concerns voiced about renegade teachers (opponents). But probably both
nuances are in mind, and the dissonant construction simply draws attention
to both dimensions of the one task. Titus is to complete certain projects (appointing elders, teaching) and also reform or correct other developments
(confronting opposing teachers and those influenced by them and making adjustments in doctrine and community behavior). The rest of the letter will illustrate the scope of the work, but Titus's authority (rooted in his earlier commission by Paul, v. 5c; see below) empowers him to handle whatever the
situations encountered will require.

The second half of the purpose clause singles out the main task needing to be completed[10] — the appointment of elders in every town. Not only
does this assignment reflect the nascent stage of the churches in Crete, but it
also corresponds to the pattern of Paul's mission work described elsewhere
(Acts 14:23). Paul uses a verb that signifies official appointment,[11] but he
does not indicate much more about the procedure and how it is to be carried

---

Inscriptionum Graecarum 581.85 (see LSJ 631; cf. Quinn, 77-78); 1 Clement 21:6; the cognate nouns in Acts 24:2; Heb 9:10; see 2 Tim 3:16 (ἐπανόρθωσις; "correcting, restoration").

7. Pace Mounce, 387; see Marshall, 151.

8. Gk. τὰ λείποντα (pl. ptc. from λείπω; "to leave behind, to be deficient," etc.;
3:13); the participle is a cognate of the compound verb ("I left you behind"; ἀπέλιπον),
which may suggest some level of stylistic crafting (cf. Quinn, 83).

9. On the possible reconstructions, see Fee, 172; Johnson, Paul's Delegates, 212.

10. The conjunction καί is probably epexegetical, meaning "and especially"
(Marshall, 152).

11. Gk. καθίστημι (aor. subj.); see Exod 2:14; 1 Macc 10:20; Luke 12:15; Acts
6:3; 7:10, 27, 35; see also A. Oepke, TDNT 3:444-46.

out. Most of the discussion in the commentaries concerns the degree to which the task is Titus's or to be shared by the church.[12] At a minimum, given the Cretan churches' early state, probably the candidates would have been selected by the communities that knew them best, with Titus's delegated apostolic authority being applied as the final seal of recognition and appointment to leadership (signified publicly by the laying on of hands; cf. 1 Tim 4:14; 5:22; 2 Tim 1:6).[13] But beyond the indication that Titus was to initiate this task, we know little about its actual outworking.

"Elders" is a term that belongs to the vocabulary of Paul's work (Acts 14:23; 20:17; 1 Tim 5:17, 19), and that the early church inherited mainly from the Jewish synagogue (Acts 11:30; 15:2, etc.).[14] As it is used technically here, the reference is to leaders, not "old men" (2:2; 1 Tim 5:1). As we have seen, the elders stand in some relation to the overseers, which is especially clear in this passage where the two terms can describe one leader (vv. 5-7). But we cannot automatically fuse the arrangement depicted here with the one evident in 1 Timothy in which overseers and elders appear to be separate entities. Possibly diversification of leadership into the overseer/elder categories was a luxury reserved for larger, more developed communities (see further below).

Even if we can determine that elders and overseers are the same here, it is less clear how many elders (one or a plurality) in a church would provide the leadership. The pattern elsewhere suggests that plurality of leadership was the rule or the ideal (Acts 20:17, 28; 16:4; Phil 1:1). But the scope of the task — "elders in every town" — offers no sure indication of the distribution of leaders from church to church. Crete was known for its division into city-states during this time,[15] which may account for the description of the task;[16] and the instruction suggests that the church was fairly widespread.

But what was the composition of the church in any area? It may be that the church of a town was understood to be composed of several smaller house congregations (cf. 1 Cor 1:2). In this case, perhaps there would be one elder per house church (which may have been a practical necessity because of size), and the use of "householder" imagery to describe the leader in v. 7 may point in this direction as well.[17] The main point is that elders/leaders are to be appointed for administration of the church or churches in the towns and cities throughout the island.

12. Cf. Lock, 129; Barrett, 128-29.
13. Cf. Knight, 288.
14. See 1 Tim 3:1 (discussion and notes).
15. See, e.g., Homer, *Iliad* 2.649; *Odyssey* 19.172-79; the numbers differ.
16. Cf. Acts 14:23, "elders in each church" (κατ' ἐκκλησίαν πρεσβυτέρους), with the phrase here, "elders in every city" (κατὰ πόλιν πρεσβυτέρους).
17. See Merkel, 90; Marshall, 153; Johnson, *Paul's Delegates*, 224.

The instructions just introduced in the preceding purpose clause, and then funneled into the instruction to appoint elders, are now reinforced with Paul's reflection back to binding orders given to Titus at an earlier time ("as I [myself] directed you").[18] As the ambiguous placement of the phrase (which may refer to what precedes or what follows)[19] and the detailed nature of the instructions that follow suggest, the meaning of "as" in the phrase goes beyond simply making a reference back to an earlier command to include the specifics of the way in which it is to be carried out.[20] The effect is to remind Titus and the wider group of readers of the apostolic authority underlying the specific qualities and priorities that comprise the selection process.

2. Appointing Church Leaders Able to Instruct the Church and Correct Opponents (1:6-9)

From the reflection back on Titus's assignment to the Cretan mission, Paul moves directly to the task of appointing leaders. What appears to be a combination of two leaderships codes (distinguished by the two terms for leaders, "elder," v. 5, and "overseer," v. 7), covering the same ground as the code of 1 Tim 3:2-6a and with much the same language,[21] provides some guidelines for the selection of leaders. As in 1 Timothy 3, the accent falls on qualities that should be evident in the life of the elder/overseer: repetition of the term "blameless" in each part suggests that subsequent qualities serve to define this broader standard of "blameless" (vv. 6, 7; cf. 1 Tim 3:2 — "above reproach"; 1 Tim 3:10 — "blameless"). Thus, in a general sense, the qualification for holding a leadership position is "blamelessness." The specific qualities explore this measurement of character within a concrete framework that includes a person's domestic, personal (and interpersonal), and ecclesiastical (ministry) spheres.

6   A word must first be said about the structure of this sentence. As is often the case when previous or set formulations are adapted, the syntax becomes a bit choppy.[22] Normally the opening "if anyone" clause would be followed by the main clause (1 Tim 3:1, 5; 5:4, 8, 16; 6:3), but in this case,

18. Gk. διατάσσω ("to give instructions"; of binding and authoritative instructions, 1 Cor 7:17; 9:14; 11:34; 16:1; cf. the authoritative βούλομαι ["I wish"] at 1 Tim 2:1, 8 [discussion and notes]); cf. G. Delling, *TDNT* 8:34-35; L. Oberlinner, *EDNT* 1:313-14. In the phrase ὡς ἐγώ σοι διεταξάμην ("as I gave you instruction"), the use of the first-person pronoun is emphatic ("I myself"), and the aorist verb suggests an earlier command.

19. Cf. the GNB, which takes the phrase as introductory of v. 6 ("Remember my instructions: . . .").

20. So Marshall, 153.

21. See the discussion of form and contents at 1 Tim 3:1.

22. See Quinn, 84-85.

just when that main clause is due to come, v. 7 reverts to another relevant piece of teaching, leaving the subject (elders) to be supplied from the context. The TNIV rendering of the opening phrase, "an elder must be blameless" (lit. "if anyone is blameless"), disguises the general and traditional nature of the instruction's opening, as it attempts to resolve the ambiguity caused by the lack of a main clause.[23]

Overall, the leader must be "blameless" (1:7).[24] It is synonymous with the term "above reproach" that identifies the comparable general qualification for the overseer in 1 Tim 3:2.[25] In each case, the reputation of the aspirant is thus brought into view, with the requirement being that there be no grounds for an accusation of civic or domestic impropriety against him. As the concrete qualities will demonstrate, this assessment is not limited to the Christian community but also takes in the opinions of those outside the church.

First, Paul explores the domestic sphere of life, noting two aspects of behavior. As in 1 Tim 3:2, the first matter of concern is the prospective leader's marriage. The phrase translated "faithful to his wife" (lit. "husband of one wife") describes fidelity within marriage and does not specifically delve into matters of polygamy or remarriage (see on 1 Tim 3:2).

Secondly, the candidate's reputation as a father comes under scrutiny indirectly as the behavior of his children[26] is examined in a way not taken up explicitly in the Ephesian context (cf. 1 Tim 3:4). His children are to be either "believing"[27] or "faithful/trustworthy."[28] While it may seem a steeper requirement than we find in 1 Tim 3:4, which does not mention the faith of the children but probably assumes it, the former meaning corresponds better to the range of the "faith" word group in these letters to coworkers (see on 1 Tim 1:2). It is probably the more rugged, pioneer situation of the church in Crete that requires assurance that the leader's household is not a divided one.

23. Such as ". . . let him be appointed" (see Marshall, 154).

24. For Gk. ἀνέγκλητος, see 1 Tim 3:10 (discussion and note).

25. See the fuller discussion at 1 Tim 3:1-7.

26. The requirement addresses what would have been the normal state of affairs — men, elders, would have been married with children.

27. Gk. τέκνα ἔχων πιστά; for Gk. τέκνον ("child"), see 1 Tim 1:2 (note); for Gk. ἔχω ("to hold, have, keep") of children, see 1 Tim 3:4 (note). The question revolves around the two senses ("believing" or "faithful/trustworthy"; see 1 Tim 1:2, note) of the adjective πιστός; for this former, see Marshall, 157-58; Mounce, 388-89; Johnson, *Paul's Delegates*, 220-23; BDAG, s.v. 2.

28. Knight, 289-90: faithfulness to the father (= submissiveness; cf. 1 Tim 3:4) in a nonreligious sense is held to accord better with the items of misbehavior that follow. See also Schwarz, *Burgerliches Christentum im Neuen Testament?*, 67. However, in Paul's mind behavior that is unmarked by these negative traits is characteristic of the life introduced by the Christ-event (2:12).

As a reflection on the father's reputation as a householder, the religious convictions of the children would be expected to conform to those of the master/father.

We might wonder how such a requirement would be measured. In this case, Paul may again draw upon the wild stereotype of Cretan society, as he describes "believing" in contrast to behavior that belies genuine faith: "not open to the charge of being wild and disobedient."[29] The legal language of "accusation" does not here envision a formal legal setting;[30] the sense here is of accusations that might come from any quarter. The first of two genitive terms describing the content of the "accusation," "wild," covers a range of dissolute activity from sexual promiscuity to drunkenness, with excessiveness in the use of money and food lying between.[31] As in Eph 5:18 and 1 Pet 4:4, the widest sense of the word is meant to cover the most ground.[32]

Paul adds "disobedience" (better, "rebellion" or "insubordination") to the uncontrolled conduct.[33] Notably, this is precisely a characteristic of the rebellious teachers troubling the communities (1:10; cf. 1 Tim 1:9), whose behavior Paul will shortly caricature by drawing on the Cretan stereotype (vv. 12-13a). With the household setting in view, the implication is of disobedience that has reached the level of a flagrant disregard for the father's authority. It seems likely that Paul places this behavior on the continuum leading to the misconduct that characterizes the opponents (see 2 Tim 3:2; Deut 21:20).

It may seem a rather excessive requirement to the modern Western mind, but in a general sense within the honor-and-shame framework of first-century Mediterranean culture, a householder's good reputation and respect

29. The negative phrase μὴ ἐν κατηγορίᾳ (the negative particle reflects the action inherent in the adj. which functions as a ptc.; see Moule, *Idiom Book,* 155-56) is taken by most interpreters, correctly, as filling out the meaning of "believing"; however, Mounce, 389, connecting the phrase with the prohibitions that follow in v. 7, regards the phrase as a further description of the elder's behavior. The intrusion of the new introduction at v. 7 — "for it is necessary that an overseer be blameless" — makes this connection unlikely.

30. For the Gk. κατηγορία, see 1 Tim 5:19 (discussion and note). See F. Büchsel, *TDNT* 3:637 n. 2, for the suggestion that the term is a technical one for church discipline, which would give the sense "whose children are not presently under church censure." This seems more specific than the context requires.

31. Gk. ἀσωτία; see in order 2 Macc 6:4; Eph 5:18; 1 Pet 4:4; Luke 15:13; Prov 28:7 (MT). Spicq, *TLNT* 1:220-22; W. Foerster, *TDNT* 1:506-7; BDAG, s.v.

32. As Marshall, 158, points out, the wild behavior of the prodigal son in Jesus' parable (Luke 15) serves as an apt illustration of the profile in mind.

33. For the Gk. ἀνυπότακτος, see 1 Tim 1:9 (discussion and note). The TNIV rendering, "disobedient," is no doubt colored by the domestic context; but while disobedience toward parents is probably in mind, the term seems to stress a more flagrant disregard for authority.

depended on this kind of household solidarity. But at a more basic level, for a church whose first concern was to pull free from the attraction of the rude elements of Cretan culture, its leadership had to point the way. Households that had collectively turned away from that attraction and embraced the value system of the gospel would present an opposing picture in society and counteract the effects of rebellious Christian teachers who were reluctant to separate from Cretan values.

7 This verse appears to introduce a rationale for the requirement of "blamelessness" already introduced. The *gar* ("for") indicates a further explanation in some sense, but the syntax and the repetition *and* alternation have roughened the logic somewhat. As backing or elaboration for the requirement of v. 6, Paul supplies a parallel statement that comes complete with its own term for leadership *(episkopos)* and then repeats the requirement of "blamelessness" with an accompanying list of qualities to explain it (vv. 7b-9). This departure from the pattern of 1 Timothy 3 has raised numerous questions, and our understanding of this passage should be guided by two observations.

First, as seen in the letters to Timothy,[34] the listing of virtues and vices was a typical feature of ethical discourse in Paul's world. In the case of the sort of list employed here, the items themselves, as we shall see, include the stock virtues by which respectability and honor were measured in that culture. Some of them overlap in meaning; but this only creates even further the impression of completeness of virtue, and fine points between them (even if we can be sure of them) are not necessarily to be emphasized. In this format, they were not regarded as so many individual qualifications to be checked off; together they formed an ideal pattern of, for the most part, a life capable of outward, visible assessment. And in extolling an ideal life of virtue, philosophers held forth such lists of virtues to idealize the value of public respectability, and required the leaders in society to be measured against the ideal. For the present passage, the point is this: the device asks for leaders to be those who by their reputation are known to be "respectable." The individual items work together to point in some directions, but they are not to be slavishly exegeted in the hope that they will give up their mysterious secrets to "leadership."

However, while Paul and the early church employed the device and the notion of respectability, they did not do so without theological reflection. For Paul, the language by which authentic Christian existence could be described was the language of the day. The ethical language of these letters to coworkers is in extremely close alignment with the language of Hellenistic ethics. But when Paul employs the language, he stands in a tradition of Jew-

---

34. See the discussion at 1 Tim 6:4-5, 11; 2 Tim 2:24-25; 3:2-4, 10-11.

ish theological reflection that, in the Diaspora, had at least two centuries earlier already taken up the language of Greek ethics to work out the implications of human life according to Torah and in covenant with God. Greek
ethical terms were used to describe human existence in ways that were different and yet still parallel enough with Hellenistic culture that bridges of meaning could be built.

Paul took this task to the next theological stage. Now the life that
could be described with the Greek cardinal virtues, the life of public respectability, was explained to be the result of God's grace in Christ (2:12). Given
this theological foundation for life, the language of ethics, even when super-
ficially comparable to Hellenistic notions, must be understood to describe a
fundamentally different quality of "respectability" or personal conduct, even
if its visible expression appears the same. When Paul provides virtue lists for
Timothy and Titus to assist them in choosing leaders, his intention is that
those chosen be people of undisputed reputation; other specific requirements
(age, ability to teach, etc.) of course reflect the church-specific nature of their
application.

Second, it is clear from a comparison of Titus 1:6-9 with 1 Tim 3:2-7
that there are both similarities and differences. And the differences, we will
see, may open a window onto the situation in Crete. But the most obvious
difference, the apparent identification of the two official terms, elder and
overseer, and the qualification of "blameless" attached to each, should be
considered immediately.

The usual explanation for this repetition suggests the adaptation of
parallel traditions (one using the term "elder," the other the term "overseer").
Their alignment here further suggests either that the two terms were equivalent in Paul's mind (or in some church settings could be), or that the two
church roles they describe were evolving into one. Although Titus 1:6-8 and
1 Tim 3:2-7 are clearly cut from the same cloth, it is more difficult to know
whether traditional duty codes were drawn on and, if so, to what degree Paul
reshaped them. From the combinations of the present passage, one might
even surmise that separate codes existed, each shaped around one of the
leader terms. But literary or tradition history of this sort takes us only so far.
Perhaps more useful is the observation to be made from Acts 20:17-28: apparently within the sphere of the Pauline mission the two terms were already
used in relation to one another to describe one category of leadership.[35] The
function of the "elder" *(presbyteros)* was described in terms of "oversight"
(episkopē).

With these considerations in mind, the topical sequence of our passage suggests that the "blamelessness" required of "the elder" (v. 6) is

35. See the introductory discussion at 1 Tim 3:1-7; cf. Marshall, 177.

closely linked to his calling to oversee the church as God's steward (v. 7 —
note the inferential Gk. particle *gar*). As pointed out above, the logic is not as
smooth as we might like, and perhaps the repetition and shifting are intended
to create a cumulative logic here. There is a movement from the elder considered in the sphere of his household to oversight of the church considered in
the sphere of God's household. An expanded translation might serve to tease
out the logic: "an elder should be blameless in his household [i.e., marriage/
children, v. 6] . . . *for* as an overseer, he must be blameless to serve in God's
household . . ." (i.e., "stewardship," v. 7).

Notably, the syntactical roughness that occurs as Paul seeks to make
this transition (from elder to oversight, and from the domestic household to
the church as a household) is also present in 1 Timothy 3. There, at the juncture of 3:4 and 3:5, a similarly parenthetical comment intrudes into the discourse in order to compare household management with leadership in the
church. Therefore, while the reference to the elder seems to set Titus 1 apart
from 1 Timothy 3, in fact the sequence of ideas in each passage is nearly
identical in linking thoughts of household and church together as the function of oversight is explored. The fact that in Titus 1:7 a second list of qualities follows from the reference to oversight-as-stewardship (vv. 7b-9), given
also in a different style ("if anyone is . . . ," v. 6; "an overseer must be . . . ,"
vv. 7-9), should not obscure the more decisive unity of the teaching and complementary use of the two terms (elder/overseer) for two aspects of the one
reality of leadership (office/prestige and function).

Now in transitioning from the domestic sphere into the sphere of
church function, "blamelessness" (which must still be filled out) continues to
be the overarching requirement. "Oversight" is defined now metaphorically
in terms of "stewardship" in God's household: "Since an overseer manages
God's household, he must be blameless."[36] The equivalence of elder and
overseer is without question,[37] and the singularity of each reference is probably to be understood as a generic reference.[38] In the local situation, an individual elder may out of necessity have led smaller and younger house
churches; but the way he is singled out here is in any case not an indication of
monepiscopacy as such. The style of the requirement ("an overseer . . . must
be blameless") parallels 1 Tim 3:2.

This initial allusion to the household institution sets the pattern for the

36. Following the NIV, the TNIV achieves an economy of syntax in 1:7, but the
metaphor of household stewardship may be diminished a bit too much in the process. The
Greek text overtly compares the overseer with the household steward: "for an overseer
[τὸν ἐπίσκοπον] as God's steward [ὡς θεοῦ οἰκονόμον] must be blameless."
37. For discussion of the background of the term ἐπίσκοπος, see the note at 1 Tim
3:1-7.
38. See the note at 1 Tim 3:1-7.

theology of the church and Christian behavior that will shape much of the letter to Titus (2:1-15; cf. 1:11).[39] The use of the "manager/steward" image to discuss various aspects of ministry is by no means new to the Pauline letters (1 Cor 4:1-2; 9:17; cf. 1 Pet 4:10).[40] A "manager" was charged by the master of the house to carry out certain duties that might range from oversight of laborers to management of money or business interests.[41]

Two features of the imagery are perhaps most appropriate in this adaptation to the role of church leadership. The first is the requirement of faithfulness to the householder (esp. Luke 12:42; 1 Cor 4:2; cf. Num 12:7).[42] While the one appointed as a steward might have impressive representative authority in the affairs in his charge, it was expected that he would execute his duties to the fullest according to the master's wishes. Secondly, as Paul employs the concept elsewhere, the factor of obligation or compulsion may be added. Put simply, stewardship was not an appointment that one took up or laid down at one's own pleasure. In defining the oversight of the elder in terms of stewardship, the picture emerges of the church as a household whose master is God. Oversight is, then, to be regarded as a task, requiring faithfulness and commitment, entered into by God's appointment and carried out on his behalf. For this reason, the steward must be "blameless."

"Blamelessness," now within the sphere of God's household, is defined negatively with five vices (v. 7b) and positively with seven virtues, the last of which is expanded into a detailed duty of the overseer (vv. 8-9). Aspects of personal and interpersonal behavior are essential to fitness for leading.

(1) The first negative trait describes an attitude that is "overbearing," "self-willed," and "arrogant." At the root is a fundamental selfishness that compels one to ride roughshod over others in the effort to satisfy oneself.[43] This is the kind of flaw that typified the opponents (1:12; 2:2; 3:9; cf. 2 Pet

---

39. See the discussion at 1 Tim 1:4; 3:15; 2 Tim 2:20-21.

40. Gk. οἰκονόμος ("manager of household, steward"; Luke 12:42; 16:1, 3, 8; Rom 16:23; Gal 4:2); see Spicq, *TLNT* 2:568-75; O. Michel, *TDNT* 5:149-53; H. Kuhli, *EDNT* 2:498-500; Towner, *DPL* 417-19; see the related discussion at 1 Tim 1:4. For the pre-Christian religious usage, see the discussion and texts cited in J. Reumann, "'Stewards of God': Pre-Christian Religious Application of *Oikonomos* in Greek," *JBL* 77 (1958): 339-49.

41. For the wide range of duties that fall under the category of "stewardship," see Spicq, *TLNT* 2:569-75.

42. Spicq, *TLNT* 2:568-69.

43. Gk. αὐθάδη ("self-willed, stubborn, arrogant"; LXX Prov 21:24; Isa 24:8); on the use of the negative particle μή, see the note on 1:6 above; see Quinn, 80; Spicq, *TLNT* 1:229-30; O. Bauernfeind, *TDNT* 1:508-9.

2:10), and it is antithetical to the behavior that was to characterize genuine Christian faith. It is not paralleled in the list in 1 Timothy 3, which may reflect the coarser Cretan environment.[44]

(2) The next shortcoming, "quick-tempered" ("quick to anger"),[45] was regarded particularly as a liability to human relationships (Prov 2:19).[46] From the use of this term in the Wisdom writings of the LXX, this weakness develops a strong association with the behavior of the godless who are to be avoided (Ps 17:49; Prov 22:24; 29:22).[47] One whose behavior is characterized by this explosive lack of control was unfit for leadership in the church (cf. 1 Tim 3:3).

(3, 4) At this point, the list follows the language and order of 1 Tim 3:3 (see full discussion) in enumerating "drunkenness" and "violence" (or "bullying") among the signs that a person lacks the discipline and composure necessary to lead others. The combination of terms in each passage and associations elsewhere suggest that it was common wisdom that excessive drinking often led to violence.[48]

(5) Another parallel to the list in 1 Tim 3:3 comes in the next term, "pursuing dishonest gain" (or "fond of dishonest gain"). That this specific term belongs both to the list of qualities that described the traditional Cretan stereotype[49] and to the tendencies that characterized the opponents Titus is to engage (1:11)[50] undoubtedly made its selection here most timely. But the wider concern for integrity with money and financially inspired motives on the part of church leaders should be noted (see on 1 Tim 3:3, 8). The prohibition is generally applicable and always relevant for leaders.[51]

8 The list turns to positive traits at v. 8 ("but"; *alla*), identifying six widely valued virtues, before developing the seventh into a specific ministerial requirement.

(1) First, the leader must be "hospitable" (see on 1 Tim 3:2). This practice was expected of all believers (1 Pet 4:9), but its importance cannot be measured by the meaning of the term in modern Western culture. In the

---

44. See the traditional views of Crete in Josephus, *Jewish War* 2.356; 4.94; Polybius 28.14; Strabo 10.49.

45. Gk. ὀργίλος (only here in the NT); see Schwarz, *Bürgerliches Christentum im Neuen Testament?*, 69-70; G. Stählin, *TDNT* 5:419-21.

46. Cf. Epictetus 2.10.18.

47. Cf. G. Stählin, *TDNT* 5:394-95.

48. See Plutarch, *Moralia* 132D (Schwarz, *Bürgerliches Christentum im Neuen Testament?*, 54; Quinn, 80).

49. Gk. αἰσχροκερδής (see discussion at 1 Tim 3:8); Polybius 6.46; cf. Spicq, *TLNT* 1:45-48.

50. In the adjective-noun configuration αἰσχροῦ κέρδους in 1:11.

51. See the discussion in Marshall, 162.

rough, pioneer setting of the early church in Crete, it would have been virtually impossible for the church to survive pressures from the outside,[52] for its
members to worship regularly together (Rom 16:5; 1 Cor 16:19; Col 4:15), or
for the gospel to spread without the generosity of householders who opened
their homes to fellow Christians and travelers.

(2) "Love for what is good" describes the leader generally as one inclined to pursue things and people that are virtuous, inherently good. It was
traditionally contrasted with self-love, and in the Wisdom tradition it was one
of the many facets of wisdom.[53] As Paul applies the term, and its opposites
(2 Tim 3:2, 3), the presence and practice of this selfless quality could stand as
a demonstration of faith (just as it marked the person out as honorable within
secular society), while its absence betrayed not only the selfish unbeliever
but also the false teacher as a pagan (see 2 Tim 3:2-4). This particular rude
trait is not in view in 1 Timothy 3,[54] suggesting yet again that the raw situation in Crete called for more rudimentary education in virtue.[55]

(3) The next character trait, "self-control," is central to the description
of Christian behavior in Titus (see the word group *sōphrōn;* 2:2, 4, 5, 6) and
linked directly to the Christ-event in 2:12.[56] It was heralded in that culture as
one of the cardinal virtues, a restraint over oneself that marked out a person
of true character. The word group covers a range in describing behavior that
(depending on context) includes prudence, sobriety, and modesty. Though
not widely used in the LXX, where the term is adopted eventually in later
writings, it is given a spiritual basis in the law (4 Macc 2:21-23; 5:23) and
held to be the (theological) dynamic that allows control of the emotions. The
step taken in Titus 2:12, where the cardinal virtues are set into a Christian
theological framework, was a natural one for Paul to take: "self-control," and
indeed the whole of the observable life, is linked directly to faith in Christ.
The leader's life was to be exemplary.

(4) "Uprightness" was often the counterpart to "self-control" and was
also one of the Greek cardinal virtues by which Paul characterizes the life of
faith (2:12; see on 1 Tim 1:9; 2 Tim 4:8). In describing the leader, the term
focuses on behavior that is just, fair, and inherently honest in dealing with

---

52. Cf. Quinn, 90-91.

53. Gk. φιλάγαθος (only here in the NT; Wis 7:22; Philo, *On the Life of Moses*
2.9). For the contrast between φιλάγαθος ("loving good") and φίλαυτος ("selfish") in Aristotle, see Spicq, *TLNT* 3:437-39; W. Grundmann, *TDNT* 1:18; for the alignment of
ἀφιλάγαθος ("haters of good") and φίλαυτος ("selfish"), see the discussion at 2 Tim 3:2-4.
See Marshall, 163.

54. The occurrence of κόσμιος ("respectable") in 1 Tim 3:2 comes close.

55. The concentration in this letter of words related to ἀγαθός ("good, beneficial,
useful"; 1:8,16; 2:10, 15; 3:1) suggests a theme directed against Cretan tendencies.

56. For Gk. σώφρων and the related word group, see 1 Tim 2:9 (Excursus).

people. The word group to which it belongs is dominant in the description of Christian existence in these letters to coworkers.[57] The inclusion of the term in this list (it is absent from 1 Timothy 3) again reflects the early stage of the church and the less civil Cretan environment.

(5) Greek thought also linked "holiness" to the preceding two concepts (see on 1 Tim 2:8). This quality does not feature in the list in 1 Timothy 3. In Hellenistic culture, the term would describe one as living in accordance with the wishes of the gods, participating in the worship and life of religious society. But in the OT, "holiness" is an obligation of the people of God (Deut 33:8; 2 Kgs 22:26), and as such it describes the condition of the whole person (Deut 32:4; Prov 22:11; Wis 7:27). Again, the currency of the term in the ethical thought of secular culture should not obscure the theological orientation of the concept in Paul's thought: "holiness" is a condition of inward purity that has outward results.

(6) The final virtue in the string is "discipline" ("self-restraint"), another of the cardinal virtues in Greek thought.[58] In expressing ideas of self-restraint and control over the emotions and passions, the term overlaps with "self-control" but emphasizes more the control of the body and appetites, whereas "self-control" has more to do with the thought life and subsequent behavior. From Paul's use of the concept in a discussion of sexual relations in marriage (1 Cor 7:9) and in reference to his own behavior (1 Cor 9:25), the focus on restraint of physical desires becomes clear. The usefulness and necessity of "discipline" (even when described in terms of the exercise of human effort) was not regarded as inimical within the theology of a Christian life "in the Spirit" (Gal 5:23). Within this list of virtues that have been co-opted and infused with a theological dynamic, "discipline," as a quality required of leaders, should be understood in the sense of the exercise of godly restraint based on a knowledge of God's will.

Collectively, then, the force of this ideal profile of leadership, constructed of stereotypical faults to be avoided and positive virtues to be cultivated, is to project an image of public respectability and good reputation for which Paul co-opts the model of the Hellenistic ideals. The deeper source of this life in its Christian expression remains an implicit part of this discourse (2:12). Paul means, and Titus understands, that leaders of sound reputation,

57. For the related Gk. term δικαιοσύνη ("uprightness, righteousness"), see the discussions at 1 Tim 6:11 (and notes); 2 Tim 2:22; 3:16; 4:8; Titus 3:5. For "justification by faith" see Titus 3:5, 7; 2 Tim 4:8. Cf. 1 Tim 3:16 for "vindication." See further Towner, *Goal,* 163; Spicq, *TLNT* 1:318-47; G. Schrenk, *TDNT* 2:182-91.

58. Gk. ἐγκρατής (adj. only here in the NT; LXX 2 Macc 10:15, 17; 13:13; Sir 6:27; Wis 8:21; etc.). For Gk. ἐγκράτεια (noun; "self-control"), see Acts 24:25; Gal 5:23; 2 Pet 1:6; for the verb ἐγκρατεύομαι ("to control oneself, one's emotions"), see 1 Cor 7:9; 9:25; cf. W. Grundmann, *TDNT* 2:339-42. See further Marshall, 185-86.

who bear the marks of the Spirit, are to be chosen. Leaders of this caliber give no grounds for accusations against them: this is the meaning of "blameless" in this context of respectability and reputation.

9 At v. 9, the leadership profile closes and a transition is made to ministry. First, a requirement is laid down. Then the reason behind the requirement takes us into the areas of teaching the congregation and engaging the opposing teachers. The essential requirement corresponds to the simpler "able to teach" of 1 Tim 3:2 and echoes the additional requirement of commitment to the faith made of deacons in 3:9. The more explicit attention to these details accords with the present situation of inferior teaching and the related need for sound teaching in the church (see vv. 10-16). The two didactic activities about to be mentioned (encouraging and refuting) introduce the two categories that organize the rest of the letter.

The requirement, "He must hold firmly to the trustworthy message," is constructed of a present participle that is loosely attached to the preceding list of virtues. In this context, it expresses the idea of unwavering adherence (to "the trustworthy message" [*pistos logos*]) just as in the prophets it stressed "clinging to" the law (Jer 2:8), the covenant (Isa 56:2, 4, 6), and God himself (Isa 57:13).[59]

If we explore the syntax of the complicated phrase that follows, the object of this commitment is the same divine gospel ("the message") that determined Paul's ministry (1:3). Its definition here establishes its formal and authoritative content. First, moving out from the term itself, the "logos" is "trustworthy."[60] This way of depicting the gospel message places it within the polemical framework typical of these letters. In separate conflict settings, a variety of techniques and adjectives are employed to emphasize the authenticity of the apostolic gospel and to imply the illegitimacy of any inferior substitute.[61] The message is "trustworthy" because of its link to the apostle (which implies its source in God; 1:3).

Second, "the trustworthy message" is further defined with a prepositional phrase (*kata;* see on 1:1) in terms of its content; that is, "as it has been taught" ("in accordance with the teaching"; NRSV).[62] The requirement that the

---

59. Gk. ἀντέχομαι (mid. here in the sense "to cling to, hold fast to, be devoted to"; Matt 6:24; Luke 6:13; for "to be interested in" or "concerned about," see 1 Thess 5:14); H. Hanse, *TDNT* 2:827-28. Cf. Quinn, 81, 92; Marshall, 166.

60. For Gk. λόγος of the gospel message, see 1 Tim 1:15 and note; 5:17; for Gk. πιστός ("faithful, trustworthy"), see 1 Tim 1:2 (note). For this combination in reference to specific "sayings," see 3:8; 1 Tim 1:15; 3:1; 4:9; 2 Tim 2:11.

61. E.g., 1 Tim 1:10, 15; 3:1; 4:10; cf. Towner, *Goal,* 121-26. The stress is not on the need to believe the message (for which see Quinn, 92) but rather on its trustworthiness ("worthiness to be believed").

62. Gk. κατά ("in accordance with"); the prepositional phrase establishes that the

leader is "to hold firmly to" (rather than "be concerned for") the message determines that in this case the reference to "teaching" *(tēn didachēn)* refers to the
content to be taught (Rom 16:17; 1 Cor 14:26; 2 John 9, 10) instead of to the act
of teaching itself (2 Tim 4:2; cf. 1 Tim 5:17).[63] As such, the whole description
("the trustworthy message as it has been taught"), while less economical than
terms like *parathēkē* (1 Tim 6:20; 2 Tim 1:12, 14) or "sound doctrine" (see below), conceives of the gospel as a relatively fixed and authoritative body of
doctrine (cf. Gal 1:23) guaranteed by the apostle.[64] While in the context of opposition and disruptive teaching "holding to" the apostolic faith might be a useful measurement of any believer's loyalty to God, in the case of the leader the
reason for this commitment is related directly to ministry.

The last half of v. 9 supplies the purpose *(hina)* of adherence to the apostolic doctrine. This purpose reveals both the source of effectiveness and the
scope of two didactic tasks (one positive, one negative) to be done by the
overseer. First, the "capability" ("power"; "so that *he can*") to carry out these
tasks is linked (via the purpose construction) to the preceding requirement of
adherence to Paul's gospel.[65] The idea of teaching as one of the charismata
given to the church, and as a gift required by the teacher, is probably to be assumed here (cf. 2 Tim 2:2).[66] But what is stressed is that "effectiveness" in
the task will depend on the purity of the content that is taught.

Two didactic tasks are distinguished, and the subject matter or
"sphere" in which they are to be done is set out. The first, positive activity is
often translated "to encourage"; it can include requests, encouragement, and
instruction with authoritative persuasion.[67] Within the sphere of Christian instruction (where it belongs here; cf. 1 Tim 6:2), the sense is of practical authoritative teaching that compels believers to implement the faith in all aspects of life (2:15).

This latter understanding of "the faith" is intended in the term "sound
[healthy] doctrine" (see on 1 Tim 1:10). "Doctrine" includes both the activity

---

apostolic teaching is *the* measurement of the "word's" trustworthiness; the context of opposition is decisive.

63. Gk. διδαχή (2 Tim 4:2 [discussion]; Rom 6:17; 16:17; 1 Cor 14:6, 26; K. H.
Rengstorf, *TDNT* 2:163-65; H.-F. Weiss, *EDNT* 1:319-20).

64. Cf. Dibelius and Conzelmann, 134; Marshall, 166.

65. Gk. δυνατός (adj.; "able, capable, powerful"; 2 Tim 1:12). The idea of divine
power is often expressed with the δύναμις word group (2 Tim 1:7, 8, 12; 2:1; etc.), but
here the thought is of "capability or adequacy" for a task (cf. 2 Tim 2:2); cf.
W. Grundmann, *TDNT* 2:284-317.

66. Rom 12:7; 1 Cor 12:28-29; Eph 4:11; Towner, *Goal*, 215.

67. Gk. παρακαλέω (here as a complementary inf.: "so that he might be able to
encourage . . ."); see 1 Tim 1:3 (discussion and notes). Used of the coworkers' or the
teachers' task, see 2:6, 15; 1 Tim 5:1; 6:2.

of teaching and the content to be conveyed. In terms of the latter, both "theology" and "ethics" would be included; it is actually rather difficult to distinguish between these categories in the language of preaching and teaching in the NT. In the singular (cf. 1 Tim 4:1) and described as "sound" (i.e., producing health), this term expresses an implicit denial of the claims of all competing "teachings," which are by implication unhealthy and dangerous. This term for the approved authoritative teaching restricts Christian leaders from dabbling in false doctrines or teaching inadequate views of Christian behavior. The implementation of this "purpose" throughout the letter shows (2:1–3:8) that this positive instruction in "sound doctrine" is to be addressed to the churches.

However, the second, negative mode of ministry has the rebellious teachers specifically in mind. "Those who oppose" (or "resist") the "sound doctrine" are false believers (not simply unbelievers) who in their propagation of unworthy doctrine actively oppose ("speak against") the work of the Pauline mission.[68] The task of the overseer is to "refute and rebuke" them. The term that describes this activity includes revealing falsehood, correction, and rebuke.[69] It figures both in the language of church discipline (1 Tim 5:20; 2 Tim 4:2; Matt 18:15) and of mission (John 3:20; 16:8; 1 Cor 14:24), but as throughout these letters to coworkers, engagement of this kind with those who oppose belongs to the category of church discipline. With the situation of an opposing inferior teaching particularly in mind, the correctional and disciplinary dimension of the leader's ministry is viewed more narrowly in terms of condemning the false teaching by insisting on what is correct, and "silencing" the opponents by forceful admonition backed up by apostolic authority (1:11; 3:10; 1 Tim 1:20; 2 Tim 2:25).

Consequently, in comparison with 1 Timothy 3, the requirements and extra attention given to ministry reflect a church situation in Crete that is primitive, harsh, and verging on crisis. Vices are listed that should not need to be discussed in a Christian church, and the reference to dishonest gain draws on the Cretan stereotype. Equally, elementary virtues such as "uprightness," "holiness," and "discipline" ought to have been unnecessary in discussions of leadership. But in the Cretan setting, where (as tradition told) the civilizing influence of Hellenistic culture had failed to establish a beachhead and the Christian faith was in the very early days, ethical formation needed to

68. Gk. ἀντιλέγω (here in substantival ptc.) means "to oppose, speak against, contradict, refuse, be obstinate," depending on the context (cf. 2:9; Luke 2:34; 20:27; 21:15; John 19:12; Acts 4:14; Rom 10:21; there is an element of insubordination in some usages, Spicq, *TLNT* 1:128).

69. For Gk. ἐλέγχω, see 1 Tim 5:20 (discussion and notes). The infinitive ἐλέγχειν, parallel with παρακαλεῖν (linked by the καὶ . . . καί construction), is also complementary to the predicate adjective "able."

begin at the ground floor. The omission of an age/maturity requirement in the Cretan instructions (cf. 1 Tim 3:6) and the explicit instructions regarding the faith of the elder's children both reflect the church at the missionary stage where "mature" believers were nonexistent and mixed households were common. Added to these liabilities was the presence of rebellious teachers who had absorbed so much of the Roman Cretan lifestyle that their teaching either ignored an ethical dimension or endorsed as acceptable aspects of Cretan life that passed as normative in that culture but that fell far short of the standard implied by Paul's gospel. This factor accounts for the greater attention to the leader's commitment to the apostolic gospel and ability to teach/refute. In order to justify the depth of his treatment, Paul goes to some length in the next verses to explain the danger posed by the rebels.

3. Naming and Engaging the Opponents (1:10-16)

In this section Paul explains the reason for the emphasis on faithfulness to the gospel and ability in teaching. He describes a group of opposing teachers in the Cretan churches that is causing disruption (vv. 10-11). The form and content of this characterization make a basic contrast to the description of the overseer just given. Then, in a striking rhetorical move, he links these opponents to the basest element in Cretan society, in effect acknowledging the long-standing Cretan stereotype and suggesting that these rebels epitomize the bestial "Cretan" (vv. 12-13a). This in turn leads directly to the command to Titus to engage the opponents, followed by a sober concluding assessment of their depravity (vv. 13b-16).

10 There is no question here of a hypothetical reflection on opposition or heresy, as the vivid present tense verb "there are" stresses.[70] Both the time frame and the number ("many") combine to create a sense of urgency. The disparaging characterization begins with three terms. First, they are "rebellious" (see on 1:6; 1 Tim 1:9). This repetition of language initiates the conscious contrast between the elder/teacher and the opponent. Thus at the heart of the "opposition" (v. 9b) is a refusal to submit to church and apostolic authority.

The second term begins to address the opponents' occupation. The descriptor "full of meaningless talk" ("idle talker"; NRSV) belongs to the vocabulary that in these letters denounces false teaching as nonsense and its teachers as teachers of nonsense.[71] Although in English translation this pas-

---

70. Gk. εἰμί ("to be"); the Greek phrase εἰσὶν γάρ means "for there are" (cf. the different sense of the phrase in 3:9: "for they are").

71. Gk. ματαιολόγος (only here in the NT; cf. ματαιολογία in 1 Tim 1:6, discussion and notes); see further Schlarb, *Die gesunde Lehre*, 59-73.

time may seem more an annoyance than a crime, the language was used typically to establish the "emptiness" of the beliefs and the futility of behavior that accompanied idolatry and paganism.[72] The comparison made in this way, while consciously polemical and sarcastic, was between truth and error, and far more was at stake than simply wasting time.

In fact, the third term, "[full of . . .] deception" ("deceivers"; NRSV), underlines the culpability of the opponents.[73] As the context makes clear, it is by teaching that the opponents deceive — rather than in telling lies in general, or even in the sense of deceiving themselves[74] — and those led astray are other unsuspecting believers in the churches. Truthfulness and teaching truth for the encouragement of the community have been implicitly and explicitly stressed in relation to elders. Here the contrasting character deficiency continues to widen the gap between the image of the Christian leader just drawn and the rebellious opponent. Simultaneously, the image of the bestial "lying" Cretan superimposes itself on this character ("deceivers" resonates with and helps prepare the way for "liars" in v. 12).

The specific[75] identification of the opposition as "those of the circumcision group"[76] depicts the Cretan churches at the point in time in which the line separating the categories of "Jewish" and "Christian" was still quite permeable, and when the synagogue may still have been one of the significant loci of the emerging Christian community. The term refers to Jewish Christians (Acts 10:45; 11:2; Col 4:11).[77] Although this passage does not indicate that they insisted that circumcision continue to be practiced (cf. Gal 2:12), it is nonetheless clear that "Judaizing" beliefs (related to matters of purification and the law; 1:14, 15; 3:9)[78] played some part in their brand of teaching and ran counter to the Pauline gospel. Extrapolating from observations made elsewhere in the Jewish Diaspora, Winter adds that the overall shape of the

72. Acts 14:15; Rom 1:21; Eph 4:17; Jas 1:26; 1 Pet 1:18; cf. O. Bauernfeind, *TDNT* 4:524.

73. Gk. φρεναπάτης (only here in the NT; lit. "deceiving the mind"); BDAG, s.v.; Dibelius and Conzelmann, 135; MM.

74. But see BDF §119.2, who suggest "self-deceived" and cite the cognate verb in Gal 6:3 as bearing the same meaning (however, it is the reflexive pron. in Gal 6:3 [φρεναπατᾳ ἑαυτόν] that seems to create this sense).

75. Gk. μάλιστα (sometimes translated "especially") should be understood here in the sense of "namely," "specifically," "that is" (etc.), to specify more clearly the general reference that precedes it. See the discussion at 1 Tim 4:10.

76. Gk. οἱ ἐκ τῆς περιτομῆς; here "circumcision" refers to the resulting condition that marked Jews (and Jewish Christians) off from Gentiles (as in Acts 10:45; 11:2; Gal 2:12; Col 4:11); R. Meyer, *TDNT* 6:72-84; O. Betz, *EDNT* 3:79-80.

77. E. E. Ellis, *Prophecy and Hermeneutic in Early Christianity* (Grand Rapids: Eerdmans, 1978), 116-28; Marshall, 195; Quinn, 98.

78. See further the Introduction, 41-52.

allegations (including "meaningless talk," "deception," and "greed" [vv. 7, 11]), which corresponds to the popular criticism of the orators of the day, could well encompass Jewish teachers who had been trained in rhetoric.[79] Jewish communities can be located in Crete from the first century B.C.E. It is therefore more a case of happenstance — than of the Galatian/Romans clash between Jewish and Gentile Christianity — or possibly the result of the Pauline mission strategy, which began in the synagogues, that these rebellious teachers comfortable with Cretan morals were Jewish Christians. What is most unique about this particular glimpse of trouble in the Pauline mission (in comparison with Galatians or Colossians) is that it is indirect, and therefore gives the impression of distance. But this is to be expected of a letter that is written first of all to a coworker who will have to deal with the situation on his own.

11 Where does the real danger lie in opposition movements? Paul's main worry — the main threat posed by the opponents — surfaces here, as the sentence continues with a relative clause to describe the action called for and the reason for it. Whatever the failings of this group might be, the instruction, "they must be silenced," reveals that their "mouths," that is, their teaching, is the main problem. While the term envisages rather graphically an action like "gagging,"[80] the question of method is open. Yet the language of engagement throughout these letters suggests that the Christian leader is to use a combination of positive, corrective teaching and (whenever necessary) authoritative disciplinary methods (rebuking, warning, adjuring; 1:9; 2:15; 3:10; cf. 2 Tim 2:14) to refute and so "silence" the opponents. At this point in the engagement, anyway, there still exists hope that the rebellious teachers can be reasoned with, and it is turning them back, not throwing them out, that Paul hopes to accomplish (1:13). Of course the possibility that this won't be achieved is also entertained (3:10).

Now the second relative clause[81] that follows spells out the danger clearly in two ways. First, Paul describes their teaching in terms of its effects

---

79. Winter, *Roman Wives,* 146-48 (citing Philo, *Allegorical Interpretation* 3.167); for the influence of Greco-Roman education on some Jewish teacher/philosophers, see also B. W. Winter, *Philo and Paul among the Sophists* (2d ed.; Grand Rapids: Eerdmans, 2002), Part I.

80. Gk. ἐπιστομίζω ("to silence, bridle, hinder, prevent"; occurs only here in the NT; cf. Philo, *That the Worse Attacks the Better* 23) was used elsewhere of confuting opponents in the debate situation (Spicq, *TLNT* 2:61-62). Cf. Rom 3:19.

81. The force of the relative pronoun οἵτινες ("which ones, they") may be to gather those who are referred to into a specific class of people, that is, a part of the polemical dialogue and meant to "type" this group ("inasmuch as they . . .", or "these are those who . . .") (so Marshall, 196; cf. 1 Tim 1:4 and note); or it may simply serve as a relative clause (BDAG, s.v.).

on households. In some way, the teaching of the opponents has "disrupted" Christian households. It is not clear how this was done; but it is going too far, as some have, to link the opponents with later Gnostic teachers who disregarded all human institutions.[82] Rather, the language used to describe the disruption ("disrupting, upsetting, ruining"; see on 2 Tim 2:18) is typical of the harmful results produced by heretical doctrine. What follows in 2:1-10 can be read as treating remedially household relationships that had perhaps felt the effects of the opposing teaching. But the reference here may be more generally to the location of the teachers' instruction. The household was, after all, a typical setting for philosophical recitations and rhetorical performance.[83] Dangerous teaching that was tinged with Cretan permissiveness (and other elements more Jewish perhaps) would thus "disrupt" households first.

In any case, the severity of the trouble can be seen in the present tense verb, "they are disrupting," and the extent of the damage being done, "whole households."[84] The point is that, as Paul writes, this activity is still underway and having devastating consequences on Christian households. Since the churches would have met in households, the danger is then also that the church itself will be ruined by the unrest connected with the false teaching.

Second, the instrument of the trouble is traced to their teaching and the content taught. Unfortunately, Paul does not itemize the contents of their teaching, summarizing it only as "things they ought not [to teach]" (but see vv. 14-16).[85] The language of "teaching" (see on 1 Tim 2:11) implies that these teachers were recognized as such in the communities. Moreover, the implication in the phrase ". . . for the sake of dishonest gain"[86] is that the Christian householders supported, to some degree, these opponents, and that

---

82. This view is still widely held, though with modification; Haufe, "Gnostische Irrlehre," 330; W. Schmithals, *RGG* 5:145.

83. Winter, *Roman Wives,* 148 (citing Epictetus, *Discourses* 3.23.23).

84. On Gk. οἶκος, see the discussion and note at 1 Tim 3:4. For the phrase here, ὅλους οἴκους ("whole households"), see Acts 2:2; 7:10; 18:8; Heb 3:2, 5; the stress is on the completeness of the disruption, and therefore the severity of the threat.

85. For the sense of the participial phrase διδάσκοντες ἃ μή ("teaching what they ought not [to teach]"), cf. 1 Tim 5:13, "saying what they ought not" (λαλοῦσαι τὰ μὴ δέοντα). The relative pronoun has no antecedent but rather refers to the commodity assumed in the participle (cf. 2:1).

86. Gk. κερδός ("a gain, profit"; Pauline in the NT; Phil 1:21; 3:7); H. Schlier, *TDNT* 3:672-73. For αἰσχρός ("shameful"; also Pauline), see 1 Cor 11:6; 14:35; Eph 5:12; cf. R. Bultmann, *TDNT* 1:189-91. For χάριν, expressing cause, see the note on 1:5. See Quinn, 106. Some have suggested that the greater crime was that of siphoning off support that was intended for other genuine traveling teachers (Lips, *Glaube,* 81-82; citing the institution as implied in 1 Cor 9:4, 12, 14; Gal 6:6). On the whole question of support in the churches, see M. Hengel, *Property and Riches in the Early Church* (Philadelphia: Fortress, 1974), 35-41.

obtaining support (or financial benefit) was their motive for teaching. Their influence in the households posed a threat to the Pauline mission and the churches on Crete. From the perspective of church health, if Christians were not only listening to the nonsense (which was dangerous enough) but also endorsing and embracing it by their practical support of these teachers, then the defection of whole households from the apostolic faith could not have been far behind.

At the same time, the tendency apparent in Paul's description — teachers/sophists whose primary motivation is money, not education — corresponds to a critical stereotype.[87] Teachers and their motives were widely regarded with suspicion. It is to avoid coming under this blanket criticism that Christian teachers are warned of motives of greed (1:7; 1 Tim 3:3, 8; 6:10; 1 Pet 5:2);[88] and actual cases of teaching for financial motive in the churches (Rom 16:17; 2 Pet 2:3) made the danger more relevant. Paul himself gave answer to similar charges (Acts 20:33; 1 Thess 2:5), so the sensitivity to the criticism is not unusual. Here, as applied by Paul, the traditional criticism helps to place these teachers within the cultural milieu as operating in the way that the stereotypical, self-seeking Sophists did (1 Tim 6:5). The fact that the cultural criticism is adapted and applied by Paul to denounce errant Christian teachers does not mean that he is simply resorting to polemical rhetoric (devoid of historical detail).[89] But it does suggest that the identity and flaws of these teachers, Christian or not, and their *modus operandi* are best sought for within that criticized category of greedy educator, and not solely within the rarified category of the Christian heretic. These teachers were thoroughly immersed in Cretan culture.

The precise language chosen here sets this tendency into contrast with

87. See Winter, *Roman Wives,* 147-48. Cf., e.g., the biting criticism in *The Cynic Epistles,* "Of Socrates" (Malherbe), 1.2: "For no-one will ever find that I have taken anything from anyone ever since I applied myself to the philosophic life. . . . But I give my philosophic instruction in public, and equally allow the one who has much and the one who does not to hear me. But I neither practice philosophy shut up inside, as Pythagoras is said to have done, nor do I go among the masses and demand money from those who want to listen to me, as certain others have done formerly and as some of our contemporaries are still doing"; 1.4: "But I am amazed at the rest, who claim to be making preparations on their own behalf, but who have manifestly sold themselves for the sake of profit [διὰ τὰ κέρδη], and who have little regard for education, but concern themselves with making money. They are indeed admired for their possessions, but they are ridiculed for their lack of education. . . ."

88. Dio Chrysostom 32.10.

89. For the view that this is simply part of the traditional heresy polemic (or topos) and not intended to reveal actual details of the situation, see R. J. Karris, "The Background and Significance of the Polemic of the Pastoral Epistles," *JBL* 92 (1973): 549-64; Dibelius and Conzelmann, 5-8; Wolter, *Paulustradition,* 260-61.

the profile of genuine Christian leadership character (cf. *aischrou kerdous,* "dishonest gain," with *aischrokerdeis,* "pursuing dishonest gain," in 1:7), while also consciously linking this motive with the developing Cretan stereotype. In this aspect of their behavior, too, the opponents typify the worst of Cretan society.[90]

12-13a Having prepared for this next move all along, Paul now springs the rhetorical trap that will vilify the opponents in a way most appropriate for the Cretan church. The citation of the Cretan saying is almost an aside,[91] and at first glance it appears primarily to disparage the Jewish-Christian teachers. Indeed, it does this; but a look at the broader stretch of the letter (esp. 1:5–2:12) suggests that the present section of Cretan echoes, which peaks with the "saying" here, will also prepare the way for a description of Christ designed specifically to engage the Cretan social-religious world (see on 2:12). In any case, Paul taps into the rich social discourse in order to illustrate the meaning of falsehood, and ultimately the meaning of the gospel (see on 2:12), in a way that resonates strongly with a Cretan audience. We must consider some of the historical questions that surround the saying, and also ask how far Paul means to apply it.

The structure of the introduction to the saying (lit. "one of them, a prophet of their own, said") serves two related purposes:[92] it attributes the saying to a member of a group and accords him status in that group. That being said, it also raises two questions: To what group of people does he belong, and who is the "prophet"? Dropped into this setting, the roundabout reference, "one of them, a prophet of their own, said," compares with the device used elsewhere to allude to false teachers in a dismissive, denigrating way.[93] And several translations give the impression that it is the opponents who are referred to in the two genitive pronouns ("of them," "their own") and that the prophet somehow belongs to that circle (NIV; NRSV).[94] However, the saying that follows, which was proverbial with possible links to more than one ancient teacher/prophet in Crete, indicates that the referent in

90. See the indictment of Polybius (6.46.3), who mentions the "Cretan" desire "for shameful gain and greed" (αἰσχροκέρδειαν καὶ πλεονεξίαν); also Cicero, *Republica* 3.9.15.

91. If vv. 12-13a are removed, the text coheres nicely.

92. In the phrase εἶπέν τις ἐξ αὐτῶν ἴδιος αὐτῶν προφήτης, the second αὐτῶν, in combination with ἴδιος, is typical of classical usage (BDF §286), in this case indicating membership (cf. Marshall, 199 n. 128).

93. On this use of τίς see the note at 1 Tim 1:3, 19.

94. Cf. Quinn, 109; or that the saying is that of a Christian prophet (see W. Thiessen, *Christen in Ephesus: Die historische und theologische Situation in vorpaulinischer und paulinischer Zeit und zur Zeit der Apostelgeschichte und der Pastoralbriefe* [TANZ 12; Tübingen: Francke, 1995], 327-28).

"them/their" is supplied first by the following "Cretans." Thus the TNIV rendering gives the better sense: "One of Crete's own prophets has said it." Paul will regard the opponents within that category of humanity. The obvious conclusion that the readers/hearers will draw is that the Cretan celebrity's influential self-testimony is finding fulfillment in the teaching and behavior of the opponents.

If we assume for a moment that "the prophet" in view is Epimenides, Paul is not placing him into the category of the biblical prophet, but rather thinking of him in the way that Plato, Aristotle, and other ancient writers tended to — as a teacher, philosopher, and even (according to some accounts) worker of miracles.[95] "Prophet" would then be a title of honor that attached itself to various historical (and legendary) figures known to have been great teachers and poets.[96]

But in fact the attribution of the saying to this figure is somewhat uncertain. The association of Epimenides with Crete is sound, as is his reputation as a priest and prophet. Depending on who is read (Plato or Aristotle), he can be dated to the fifth or sixth century B.C.E. The Christian-era writers Clement of Alexandria and Jerome linked the saying to him.[97] Other early Christian writers, however, attribute the saying to Callimachus (third century B.C.E.),[98] whose *Hymn to Zeus* (line 8) contains the first phrase of the saying.[99] What is certain is that the saying, as Paul cites it, was held to be linked to a specific Cretan prophet, whatever the actual origin. We have already seen what may be allusions to Callimachus's teaching in the language of 1:2; that Callimachus also cites the "Cretans are always liars" jibe, whoever Paul has in mind as the prophet, only shows that Paul has at his disposal the necessary traditions to construct, through allusion and citation, a virtual collage of criticisms leveled against Cretan culture by some fairly authoritative figures.

The saying itself divides into three parts, and allows Paul to address the way the opponents speak and behave. Part one, "Cretans are always liars," is found verbatim in Callimachus (*Hymn to Zeus* [line 8]; the earliest extant source to preserve the line), who also supplies the reason for this long-

95. Plato, *Laws* 1.642D-E ("divine man"); Aristotle, *Rhetoric* 3.17.10, p. 1418a 23 (see Dibelius and Conzelmann, 136); Cicero, *De divinatione* 1.18; Diogenes Laertius 1.109-12; Plutarch, *Solon* 12.4.

96. For the use of the term, see Aune, *Prophecy in Early Christianity,* 23-48.

97. See also Winter, *Roman Wives,* 151.

98. Theodore of Mopsuestia 2.243 (Swete); Theodoret 3.701 (Schulze in PG 82:861); cf. Marshall, 200.

99. The matter is complex. None of Epimenides' writings is extant, and what we have of his sayings are fragmentary or secondary; cf. Kidd, "Titus as *Apologia*," 188-93; Marshall, 200-201; Mounce, 396-99.

standing opinion of Cretan deceitfulness.[100] This reputation for deceitfulness was, as noted above,[101] widespread and quite possibly linked in a seminal way with the fundamental Cretan religious claim to have the tomb of Zeus on Crete. This in effect reduced the stature of Zeus to that of a human being-become-hero. Behind this Cretan perspective, and the response to it, were opposing "theologies": Crete's was a "theology from below," which maintained that the Greek gods were first men and women. This apparently grew out of the fundamental Cretan belief in its own race as the primal Greek race that emerged from the earth. Cretan beliefs included the view that many of the Greek gods were born on Crete; Zeus also died there. The opposing "theology from above" was the Olympian theology from mainland Greece in which, among other differences, the transcendent status of the gods was protected and the distance between the divine and the human races maintained. Thus the basis of the stereotype was a heretical religious claim.

Part two of the saying equates Cretans and beasts: "evil beasts" (TNIV, "evil brutes").[102] This sort of language was often used to describe rude, wild people.[103] But in the case of Crete, which was in fact noted for its lack of wild animals,[104] the barb acquires an ironic twist. Behind the criticism was the well-known barbaric behavior of Crete, linked to its tradition of warfare between the island's numerous cities, piracy on the sea routes, and the practice of homosexual religious rites.[105] The point of the taunt was to say, "Crete had no need of wild beasts, for its own inhabitants were sufficient."[106] Crete was thus renowned for its wild and dangerous conduct.

The final phrase is usually translated "lazy gluttons" in the English versions.[107] Kidd points out that there is a note of irony here too, since

100. For Gk. ψεύστης ("liar"), see 1 Tim 1:10 (discussion and note); so strong was this association that the verb κρητίζειν (from Κρήτη = Crete [1:5]; Κρής = Cretan; see Acts 2:11), meaning "to lie," eventually developed (Suetonius, *The Right Insult* 13.253, equates κρητίζειν with τὸ ψεύδεσθαι); see further Winter, *Roman Wives,* 149-50; Spicq, 608.

101. See also the discussion and references in Winter, *Roman Wives,* 149-51.

102. Gk. κακὰ θηρία; for κακός ("evil"), see 1 Tim 6:10; 2 Tim 4:14; W. Grundmann, *TDNT* 3:469-81; for θηρίον ("animal, beast"), Mark 1:13; Rev. 6:8; etc.; BDAG, s.v.; W. Foerster, *TDNT* 3:133-35.

103. Philo, *On the Life of Abraham* 33; Josephus, *Jewish War* 1.624, 627; *Antiquities* 17.117, 120.

104. Pliny, *Natural History* 8.83; Plutarch, *Moralia* 86C.

105. Polybius 6.46.9; 6.47.5; 8.16.4-7; 33.16.4 (on warfare and selfishness); Plutarch, *Moralia* 490B (warfare); Homer, *Odyssey* 19.173ff. (piracy); Strabo 10.4.21; Plato, *Laws* 1.636C-D; 8.836B-C (homosexuality and pederasty).

106. Cf. Kidd, "Titus as *Apologia*," 190; Winter, *Roman Wives,* 150.

107. The phrase γαστέρες ἀργαί, is literally "idle stomachs or bellies." The figurative sense of γαστήρ for "glutton" is unusual in the NT ("womb"; e.g., Matt 1:18, 23; Luke 21:23; 1 Thess 5:3; Rev 12:2) but well known in the wider literature (3 Macc 7:11;

Cretans, with their constant involvement in warfare, mercenary services to various armies, and piracy, were hardly "idle."[108] But the phrase complements the sorts of things Polybius and other ancients said about the excessive and uncontrollable appetites of Cretans, who exercised no trace of self-control, gentleness, or uprightness, and who would do anything to turn a profit.[109]

At this point, the main question regards the way in which Paul intended the saying to apply to the local situation. First, the apparent logical conundrum (the so-called "liar's paradox") inherent in the saying ("How can the word of a Cretan who says 'Cretans always lie' be other than a lie"?) should probably be dispensed with[110] — mainly because there is no evidence of any awareness of a logical paradox in this use of the material. The force is that of self-condemnation, reflecting a lack of bias and therefore (especially given the authoritative status of the one to whom the saying is attributed) to be taken as weighty.

But in what sense does Paul apply it to the situation at hand? It is easy enough to see some logical link between the second and third parts of the saying, with the latter complete lack of control somehow fueling the beastly behavior. But it was probably the saying's criticism of the span of Cretan thought and action that appealed to Paul. Throughout the letter Paul condemns both the teaching and behavior of the rebellious teachers (cf. 1:11, 13b-14; 3:9 and 1:15-16; 3:10-11). And it is hardly accidental that the Cretan saying begins with a charge of deceitfulness that stems from religious claims. Almost certainly the second and third parts of the saying intend to indict these teachers for opposing the Pauline gospel by teaching lies and promoting a substandard view of "Christian" behavior that incorporated too much of what passed as acceptable in Cretan culture.[111] Religious lies have been told

---

Philo, *On the Virtues* 182; etc.; cf. the similar use of κοιλία in Rom 16:18; Phil 3:19); Spicq, *TLNT* 1:293-95. For ἀργός (adj.; "lazy, idle" in various senses), see 1 Tim 5:13 (2x); Matt 20:3, 6; Jas 2:20; 2 Pet 1:8; G. Delling, *TDNT* 1:452.

108. Kidd, "Titus as *Apologia,*" 191.

109. Polybius 6.46.3; 6.47.2.

110. But see A. C. Thiselton, "The Logical Role of the Liar Paradox in Titus 1:12, 13: A Dissent from the Commentaries in the Light of Philosophical and Logical Analysis," *BibInt* 2 (1994): 207-23, who argues that the writer intentionally applies the paradox (fully activating it by the assertion in v. 13a that "this testimony is true") simply to underscore that the truth claims of the false teachers and their reckless behavior contradict one another, thereby invalidating the claims.

The "liar's paradox," often connected with this statement (attributed to Epimenides), was also linked to Eubulides, an opponent of Aristotle (Diogenes Laertius 2.108-9; Aristotle, *Sophistici elenchi* 180b2-7), and also to Chrysippus by Plutarch (*Moralia* 1059D-E) and Cicero (*Academicae quaestiones* 2.96). See further the bibliography on this in Marshall, 191.

111. Cf. also Winter, *Roman Wives,* 145-51.

as truth, which, along with impious and reckless conduct, places these teachers squarely into the category of "classical" Cretans who are famously corrupt. Such a statement would not have put off the Cretan Christians, for it would be understood that they should regard themselves as rescued from this perverse lifestyle.

That is one level of Paul's discourse — the polemical level. On another level, by co-opting the famous saying, Paul, the missionary, enters the Cretan religious arena: he submits a challenge to the Cretan religious mind, using the words of a Cretan prophet about religious lies and ungodly behavior, on which he will build with alternative and remedial truth claims (e.g., 2:11-14; 3:4-7).[112]

Still, at this point in the letter it is chiefly the inadequacy and the danger of the rebel teachers' claims and behavior that Paul seeks to disparage. The way he has chosen to do this is perhaps all the more ironical in view of the fact that the opponents are Jewish Christians, whose attachment to the law (whatever they were doing with it) and the synagogue assured them that they stood above the pagan world. Paul's adopted critic suggests precisely the opposite: by implication, these teachers (hyperbolically) embody all that is deplorable in Cretan culture. And Paul authenticates this verdict with the words "he has surely told the truth" (v. 13a; literally, and more formally, "this testimony is true").[113] The purpose of this addition is not to neutralize the Cretan paradox,[114] but rather to confirm the statement and enter it as authoritative evidence ("testimony") against the opponents.[115] The adjective "truthful" echoes Paul's description of the gospel in v. 1 and creates a dissonant connection with the statement soon to be made about the opponents, who reject "the truth" (v. 14).

13b-c Paul now resumes the instruction to Titus: "rebuke them sharply." The "reason" for doing so is their activities and motives (v. 11), which the "Cretan" critique forcefully epitomizes.[116] The remainder of this section (vv. 13b-16) sets out both the purpose of the action Titus is to take ("rebuke them")[117] and the characteristics of the troublesome teachers that call forth the instruction.

---

112. Kidd, "Titus as *Apologia*," 200-201.

113. Gk. ἡ μαρτυρία αὕτη ἐστὶν ἀληθής; Paul appends this statement as a guarantor of the authenticity of the testimony (Spicq, *TLNT* 1:83; 2:450-51).

114. *Contra* Hanson, 177.

115. For Gk. μαρτυρία ("testimony"), see the discussion and note at 1 Tim 3:7; cf. H. Strathmann, *TDNT* 4:474-508; Marshall, 204; Mounce, 398.

116. The phrase δι' ἣν αἰτίαν refers back to the saying and its truthfulness, and establishes the cause of the action Titus is to take; for the construction, see also 2 Tim 1:6, 12; Luke 8:46; Acts 22:24; Heb 2:11 (cf. BDF §294.5; 456.4).

117. The referent in "them" is now, following the insertion of the Cretan saying, narrowed again to the opponents (harking back to v. 11).

Titus is to "rebuke them sharply." The term "rebuke" occurred first in the description of the elder's task (see on v. 9). Consequently, in the action Titus is to take, he is the model for leaders in the Cretan churches. Here the verb resumes the instruction given in v. 11 ("they must be silenced"), but it now places the action clearly within the scope of the duties of ministry laid out in v. 9. Thus the severity of the action to be taken ("sharply"; 2 Cor 13:10)[118] accords with the seriousness of the threat and implies the authoritative character of the action taken up. It will produce an effect, either positively (such as Paul hopes), or negatively in the sense of judgment.

The purpose *(hina)* is set out in the next phrase: "so that they will be (or become) sound in the faith" (v. 13c).[119] This particular application of medical imagery to describe "the faith" of believers is unique to Titus (see also 2:2).[120] Normally, it defines the apostolic message (1 Tim 6:3; 2 Tim 1:13), and most often in its construal as "the doctrine (teaching)" (1:9; 2:1; 1 Tim 1:10; 2 Tim 4:3), in a way that contrasts implicitly with the "diseased" doctrines of the opponents. Here, the intention of the imagery is the same, with "the faith" (see 1 Tim 1:2, note) understood as the matrix of orthodox doctrines, beliefs, and traditions that make up the Christian way. The whole phrase, then, urges a return to healthy belief and possibly restoration for those who have already fallen. To "be/become sound in the faith" describes Christian existence from the angle of belief that is sound — it assumes also the presence of actions that are appropriate, as we might expect given the Cretan saying and the discussion that follows. The goal of the rebuke (stern corrective teaching and chastisement) is thus to restore these opponents to a healthy faith that issues from commitment to the apostolic gospel.

14 What exactly should we expect "healthy" doctrine to consist of? Paul answers that question in various positive ways (e.g., 2:11-14; 3:4-7), but here he defines it in terms of its antithesis, false teaching. First, healthy faith requires "paying no attention" to false doctrine. The verb is the same as is used in 1 Tim 1:4 and 4:1 for attachment or devotion to false teaching (cf. 4:13); it indicates obsession or belief, not simply a flirtation.[121] Healthy faith depends on protection from this contaminant.

---

118. Gk. ἀποτόμως ("severely, rigorously"); in the biblical tradition, this adverb (and related words) occurs in the context of discipline, warning, and judgment (Wis 6:5; cf. 5:20, 22; 11:10; 12:9; 18:15; Rom 11:22), where the severity is descriptive of God's fearful judgment, or the apostle's delegated authority to declare the same (2 Cor 13:10); H. Koester, *TDNT* 8:107-8.

119. Gk. ὑγιαίνω ("be/become sound"); for the word group and application to faith, see the discussion and note at 1 Tim 1:10.

120. The Gk. prepositional phrase ἐν τῇ πίστει ("in the faith") identifies the sphere within which Christians live.

121. For Gk. προσέχω, see 1 Tim 1:4 (discussion and notes).

Then Paul considers the competing doctrine from the standpoints of content and quality in two ways. First, "Jewish myths" identifies the teaching as Jewish (in some degree). When it is taken in relation to "genealogies" (3:9; 1 Tim 1:4), one can likely conclude that the source of these materials is the OT, along with other deuterocanonical Jewish writings.[122] As "myths" these teachings were to be avoided not simply because they were untrue but because they were actually harmful, for such fabricated traditions were often employed to justify immoral practices by linking them to the gods.[123] If 3:9 does lead us to OT stories (see on 1 Tim 1:4), then it is probable that the Jewish-Christian opponents were creating speculative doctrines based on stories of ancient OT heroes and using them to lend the weight of antiquity to certain questionable practices that Paul regarded as ungodly. The rabbinic schools of this era were known for the practice of speculative exegetical methods that often proved the most arcane of details, and the fights over the meaning of the law implied in 3:9 fit well into this context.

Second, Paul also comments on both the source and quality of at least one dimension of the current ethical teaching in referring to it as "the merely human commands."[124] This is a technical term, going back to Isa 29:13, that categorizes teaching as human and therefore substandard, added to God's teaching in a way that obscured the truth.[125] Jesus employed the term in order to contrast the Jewish obsession with rites of purification with the real thrust of God's law (Matt 15:9; Mark 7:7). Paul similarly adapted the term to the Colossian situation in which some were advocating extreme ascetic practices (Col 2:22). The reference here is not only traditional but also pejorative, gaining an ironic force from the fact that "commands" typically refers to divine commands (see on 1 Tim 6:14) but is here diminished to "merely human" or inferior. The use of the plural deepens the contrast between the singular apostolic teaching (from God) and the diverse false teachings (of human origin; as in Mark 7:7-9; see above on 1:9). In view of the reference to purity and impurity (of foods) in 1:15, the focus in these human commands is on ethical practices that contradict accepted Christian standards.[126]

---

122. Gk. Ἰουδαϊκοῖς μύθοις. For the adjective Ἰουδαϊκός ("Jewish"; only here in the NT), see Josephus, *Antiquities* 12.34; 14.228; 20.258; W. Gutbrod, *TDNT* 3:382-83. On μῦθος ("myth"), see the fuller discussion at 1 Tim 1:4.

123. Quinn, 245; Marshall, 206. This was the view of Plato, *Laws* 1.636C-D; 12.941B.

124. The NIV and NRSV tendency to condense the elements in translation ("the commands[ments] of those who reject the truth") obscures somewhat the echo of tradition.

125. Gk. ἐντολαῖς ἀνθρώπων; cf. with τὰ ἐντάλματα καὶ διδασκαλίας τῶν ἀνθρώπων (lit. "the commands and teaching of people"; Isa 29:13; Matt 15:9; Mark 7:7; Col 2:22; TNIV, "merely human rules [commands]").

126. See Quinn, 112.

Finally, Paul establishes the stark difference between these people and their teaching and himself and his gospel. They have become apostates, having consciously "rejected the truth."[127] As in 1:1, "truth" language describes the apostolic gospel and issues the allegation to the opponents that their doctrines are lies; their own disposition toward God is cast in the shape of a decision against him in favor of deceptive, inferior traditions.

15 Traditional logic is applied at this point to counter what must have been a fundamental error of the opponents' teaching about ritual purity and defilement. We may assume that Titus and the churches knew the specifics well enough, but we are left to piece things together based on the few details available to us. The implication of this verse is that these teachers had been requiring observance of rules concerning ritual purity, probably restricting the eating of some foods (cf. 1 Tim 4:3-5); the basis for such views is not stated, but Paul's response and the Jewish character of the opponents would suggest a link to Jewish practices.[128]

Echoes in Paul and the Jesus tradition can establish the background to the basic saying, "To the pure, all things are pure" *(panta kathara tois katharois)*. Working backward, Rom 14:20 employs similar language[129] and logic but applies it to encourage a restricted use of freedom.[130] Each of these texts applies the fundamental point made by Jesus that appears in two linguistic formats in Mark 7:14-20 (Matt 15:11) and Luke 11:41. In each case the argument is that it is not food but that which resides in the human heart that defiles: foods, in fact, are "all clean."[131] We note especially how Mark 7:19 and Luke 11:41 employ forms of *kathara* ("clean or cleanse") together with *panta* ("all"),[132] the same pattern evident in Rom 14:20 and the citation here. The condition mentioned by Jesus in Luke (11:41), "giving alms for

127. For the Gk. verb ἀποστρέφω, see 2 Tim 1:15 (discussion and note); 4:4; cf. Heb 12:25.

128. Some scholars, regarding these three letters as a corpus, argue that the practices alluded to here are Gnostic in character and not limited to food rules, since marriage asceticism (practiced in Gnostic communities) is part of the mixture (1 Tim 4:3; e.g., Dibelius and Conzelmann, 137-38; Brox, 37-38). However, it is not wise to assume that the situations overlap that completely; and the Jewish character of the teachers is more prominent in Titus, though, to be sure, laws of ritual purity may have encompassed more than simply foods.

129. "Everything is clean, but. . . ." Gk. πάντα καθαρὰ τοῖς καθαροῖς; cf. Rom 14:20 — πάντα μὲν καθαρά.

130. See the discussion in Quinn, 113.

131. A number of other passages are clearly also in touch with this tradition, drawing on or developing from one aspect or another of it (Ps 24:1; Acts 10:14-15, 28; 11:8-9; 1 Cor 8:4-8; 10:26; 1 Tim 4:3-5; *Testament of Benjamin* 8.2-3).

132. Cf. Mark 7:19 — καθαρίζων πάντα τὰ βρώματα; Luke 11:41 — καὶ ἰδοὺ πάντα καθαρὰ ὑμῖν ἐστιν.

706

what is in the dish," has been translated into the requirement that the God-given character of all foods be acknowledged through thanksgiving (Rom 14:6; 1 Cor 10:30; 1 Tim 4:4-5), but the principle, though applied in different settings, is not essentially altered. "Defilement" in any meaningful sense comes from within, and Paul here in effect reminds Titus and the opponents that Jewish-type rules defining ritual purity are obsolete and irrelevant, but that essential "purity," that of the person, is indeed a matter of deep concern.

The second part of the saying takes up the matter of personal purity when it refers to "the pure."[133] Here Paul means inner or spiritual purity, and "the pure" are genuine believers (cf. 1 Tim 1:5; 4:3, "those who believe and know the truth"; 2 Tim 2:22). This sense of the reference is confirmed in 2:14, where salvation in Christ is described as a cleansing,[134] and by the contrast in the immediate context between these "pure" and "those who are corrupted and do not believe."[135] The point is clear: believers need not fear contamination from foods, and by implication (but shortly to be made explicit) the situation of those who are obsessed with such matters is more complicated.

In the remainder of the verse, Paul offers a contrasting explanation of those who are really defiled and the source of their defilement. His statements answer several questions: What then is spiritual defilement, who falls into this category and why, and what is its source? First, in contrast to "the pure" who are authentic believers stand those "who are corrupted." The perfect tense participle (lit. "those who have been defiled") indicates a state of being, resulting from prior actions or decisions. The term is used in the LXX for both ceremonial and moral defilement,[136] and in the NT for moral corruption, and the play on each sense is intended here to interact with the misguided beliefs of the opponents. Ironically, the condition of defilement they hoped to avoid by rigorous attention to rituals is precisely the one (only in its deepest sense) in which they find themselves. The condition of "defilement" that is associated with unbelief is the opposite of the "cleansed" condition that comes through faith. Almost certainly the unhappy state of the oppo-

133. For the Gk. adjective καθαρός, see 1 Tim 1:5 (discussion and note; here the art. plus adj., τοῖς καθαροῖς, forms the substantive "[to] those who are pure").

134. "Who gave himself for us to redeem us from all wickedness and to purify (καθαρίσῃ) for himself a people that are his very own, eager to do what is good"; cf. Schlarb, *Die gesunde Lehre*, 84-85; Marshall, 208. *Contra* Merkel, 95, who takes the imagery to refer to baptism.

135. Cf. Oberlinner, 46-47; Marshall, 208. Elsewhere in the letters to coworkers, the term "cleansed heart" depicts the genuine believer's new existence in its totality, from the perspective of the renewed inner person (Towner, *Goal*, 159; Bassler, 190).

136. Gk. μιαίνω; Lev 5:3; 11:44; 13:3; Ezek 9:7; and Num 35:34; Deut 24:4; Ezek 18:6; Heb 12:15; Jude 8; cf. F. Hauck, *TDNT* 4:644-46.

nents is understood to be the result of their rejection of the gospel (thus the description "those who do not believe").[137]

Completing the contrast is the statement "nothing is pure."[138] If everything is pure for those who believe, what can it mean to say "nothing is pure" for those who are apostate and unbelieving? This is probably an adaptation of the logic in Rom 14:14: ". . . no food is unclean in itself. But if anyone regards something as unclean, then for that person it is unclean." But in this different situation we need to appreciate the extra sense Paul gives to the logic here. Now it is not the "weak in faith" but, in this adaptation, "those who are corrupted" by their unbelief. And it is not certain foods that fall within the scope of impurity, but rather, in contrast with "everything is pure," "nothing is pure" to the corrupted ones. Gone entirely is the sense of concession (as in Rom 14:14); in its place is the language of ritual impurity, no doubt current in the opponents' theological vocabulary, but more importantly taken from OT discussions of defilement. In the new light of Jesus' teaching and Pauline exploration of its relevance in the Corinthian and Roman churches, Paul turns the tables on the opponents by stating that their inward moral defilement pollutes everything they touch or do. In this condition, no amount of thanksgiving or attention to rites of purification will render food clean for them, and nothing they can do will please God.[139]

What Paul means by this statement depends entirely on the principle that moral character comes from within the person, not from attention to external rules. And explaining the "corrupted and unbelieving" condition of the opponents is the next phrase: "In fact [what I mean is], both their minds and consciences are corrupted." The verb of defilement, also in the perfect tense, duplicates the previous participle, signaling a state of corruption resulting from past actions and decisions.

Paul explains the inner condition of the false teachers in terms of their "minds"[140] and "consciences."[141] These two terms, along with "heart," describe the interior components of Christian (or human) existence. With them Paul reflects on belief, unbelief, and Christian existence as modes of being dependent on rational decision-making and the system of thoughts that directs this activity. The "mind" (dysfunctional in the case of these teachers; cf. 1 Tim 6:5; 2 Tim 3:8) within Paul's anthropology is the organ that perceives

137. See further 1 Tim 1:2 and note.
138. Gk. οὐδὲν καθαρόν; for the LXX/OT development of this within the cultus, see R. Meyer and F. Hauck, *TDNT* 3:413-31.
139. For useful discussions, see Johnson, *Paul's Delegates,* 228-29; Marshall, 210; Mounce, 401.
140. For a discussion of Gk. νοῦς ("mind, intellect, understanding"), see 1 Tim 6:5 (discussion and note).
141. For Gk. συνείδησις ("conscience, consciousness"), see 1 Tim 1:5 (Excursus).

708

and approves "the truth" (i.e., the gospel or God's revelation). In their defiled condition, the opponents typically not only fail to apprehend the truth but actively "reject" or resist the truth (1:14; 1 Tim 6:5; 2 Tim 3:8).

The reason for this is supplied by an understanding of the term "conscience" in these letters to coworkers. It is the conscience that evaluates the information provided by the mind (norms of behavior, the will of God) and makes the decisions that will produce godly behavior. Again in the case of these rebellious teachers (cf. 1 Tim 4:2), inoperative or dysfunctional consciences render it impossible to make correct decisions about behavior.

Underlying this passage is the assumption that Christian conduct begins with acceptance of the apostolic faith (referred to in various ways). The mind apprehends, endorses, and organizes these data into the cognitive-ethical framework for holy living; and the conscience implements the ethical life by making correct moral decisions. Rejection of "the truth," by perverting or jettisoning the traditional gospel, interferes with the process leading to godly behavior. In its place is a process in which the mind, deluded in unbelief, approves false doctrines that the equally dysfunctional conscience shapes into inferior ethics. In Paul's framework, unbelief (or incomplete separation from pagan ways) or rejection of the gospel seems to be the fundamental error. But as Paul observes and engages unbelief as it has grown into a competing system of thought and way of life, the process has become self-perpetuating: unbelief confuses rational perception and judgment, which produces patterns of behavior and thought that reinforce unbelief.

16 Finally, Paul concludes with a statement that emphasizes the paradoxical nature of the opposition: they claim a better knowledge of God, but their behavior disproves that claim (cf. 2 Tim 3:5). Although previously we gained a glimpse into their exegetical techniques and inclination to ritual purity, here we are in touch with an aspect of their beliefs. At the heart of the opposing views is their "claim to know God." The language indicates a solemn religious "confession" or "profession" (see on 1 Tim 6:12; cf. 3:16) that, from the context, must have been to a higher, more perfect, or even more complete knowledge of God.[142] It is tempting to evaluate this claim to knowledge against the backdrop of similar Gnostic claims to special or deep knowledge of the divine.[143] Yet there is nothing in the context to support such a connection;[144] the

---

142. In the statement θεὸν ὁμολογοῦσιν εἰδέναι, the infinitive construction "to know God" supplies the content of the profession. There is no discernible difference here between οἶδα and γινώσκω ("to know"; for discussion see A. Horstmann, *EDNT* 2:493-94; and note the interchange of terms in Gal 4:8-9). Gk. οἶδα is clearly used to describe the sort of knowledge of God that determines or accompanies faith in God (e.g., Gal 4:8; 1 Thess 4:5).

143. So Kelly, 237; Schmithals, "The *Corpus Paulinum* and Gnosis," 116.

144. Even the use of the term γνῶσις ("knowledge") in 1 Tim 6:20 (see the discussion), in reference to the Ephesian false teachers' beliefs, is no sure link to Gnosticism.

claim to know God was the hallmark of the Jewish identity that distinguished it from the godless nations (LXX Jer 10:25). We are on safer grounds to remain within the context of a Judaizing Christianity that sought to supplement the Pauline gospel and refine Christian living by means of ascetical purification. It is difficult to know what, if anything, their saturation in Cretan values contributed to their confusion.

In this context of religious confession, the precise opposite of "confession" is "denial."[145] And to define impiety and idolatry as a "refusal [denial] to know God," with the same language, is already the practice in Wis 12:27.[146] While normally each verb denotes a speaking activity, Paul, starting from the assumption of the holistic interconnectedness of faith and conduct, insists that their "deeds" (TNIV, "actions") are a rejection of God.[147] The term "deeds," when modified by the adjective "good," is shorthand for the outward, faith-generated dimension of Christian existence (2:7, 14; 3:1, 8, 14).[148] But in the case of the opponents, "deeds" have become the evidence that their claim to know God is empty. In view of the flow of the immediate discussion (vv. 14-15), the reference is perhaps first to the sorts of outward ascetical behavior that their corrupted consciences and minds took for godly conduct, but the principle is general in thrust, and there is no reason to limit the scope of the reference just to asceticism (cf. 1:12-13, 16b).

The remainder of v. 16 completes the profile of "denial" in the harshest and broadest terms, using language honed to a razor edge in the OT discourses treating idolatry and paganism, and also language that belongs to Paul's interpretation of the life of faith. First, the term "detestable" describes them in terms of OT cultic defilement (from ritual impurity and involvement in idolatry[149]) and as those who are "abominable" to the Lord.[150] The note of

145. For Gk. ἀρνέομαι, see 1 Tim 5:8 (discussion and note); 2 Tim 2:12; 3:5. The juxtaposing of ὁμολογέω ("to confess") and ἀρνέομαι ("to deny") is common (Philo, *On Drunkenness* 188, 192; *On the Special Laws* 1.235; Josephus, *Antiquities* 6.151; John 1:20; 1 John 2:23); see further Spicq, *TLNT* 1:202-4.

146. Note the combination of ἀρνέομαι and εἰδέναι θεόν in Wisdom of Solomon's discussion of the judgment on the Egyptians for idolatry: ἰδόντες ὃν πάλαι ἠρνοῦντο εἰδέναι θεόν ("they saw and recognized as the true God the one whom they had before refused to know").

147. For Gk. ἔργον (pl. "deed, action"), see the note at 1 Tim 2:10. Here the dative construction (τοῖς δὲ ἔργοις; "by deeds") indicates the means of "denial" of God ("God" is the object of both verbs — ὁμολογοῦσιν εἰδέναι, "they confess/profess to know"; ἀρνοῦνται, "they deny").

148. See 1 Tim 2:10 (Excursus).

149. For the βδέλυγμα word group, see Lev 11:10, 12, 13, 23, etc.; Deut 27:15. W. Foerster, *TDNT* 1:598-600.

150. For the adjective βδελυκτός (here in the pl.) in this sense, see LXX Prov 17:15 (cf. Deut 23:19).

irony sounded first above in v. 15 is repeated here with greater force: obsessing over ritual purity has not brought them the purity they sought but rather complete defilement.[151]

Second, the term "disobedient" (3:3) places them squarely into the category of pagan unbelievers.[152] False teaching has the same result as unbelief and idolatry (2 Tim 3:2).

Third, this denunciation finishes with a crushing summary crafted with Paul's own language. "Unfit" envisions a test that has been failed. This term describes the compromised faith of the false teachers in Ephesus (2 Tim 3:8; cf. 2 Cor 13:5, 6, 7), and denotes (potential) disqualification because of failure elsewhere (Rom 1:28; 1 Cor 9:27).[153] In this case, a present condition rather than a possible outcome is clearly in mind. And the specific test that has been failed is in the sphere of their observable life: literally, "disqualified with reference to any good deed."[154] Paul employed the phrase "every good deed" with positive force in affirming the intrinsic nature of this dimension of life within authentic Christian existence (2 Cor 9:8; Eph 2:10; see 1 Tim 2:10, Excursus), and in this letter the contrast with 3:1 is evident. In this negative configuration, the scope of their failure, which is perhaps hyperbolic ("unfit for doing anything good"), is extensive, and they are on this basis set outside the people of God: there is nothing acceptable they can do; their "faith" produces no legitimate fruit; they are outside the faith.

It is difficult to know how effective this sort of criticism would have been within the communities. But through Paul's thorough denunciation, the threat they posed to these young churches comes through fairly clearly. In his critique, three potent discourses converged: the current social one with its strong stereotype of Cretan behavior; the OT discourse on idolatry and the polemic against pagans; Pauline reflection on the spiritual life. Presumably, this combination would have had a powerful effect on the readers/hearers, who would have been in touch with each of these backgrounds. What comes through most powerfully to us is the complete lack of compromise evident in Paul's treatment. Additions to the apostolic faith are regarded not as creative interpretation but as rejection of God, and he places these opponents in the place of unbelief. Moreover, the proof of the inadequacy of "novel" interpre-

151. Cf. Marshall, 213; Quinn, 115.

152. For Gk. ἀπειθής, see 2 Tim 3:2 (discussion and note); Luke 1:17; Rom 1:30; for the OT see LXX Isa 30:9; Jer 5:23; Zech 7:12.

153. Gk. ἀδόκιμος (pl. "unqualified, worthless, base"; Rom 1:28; 1 Cor 9:27; 2 Cor 13:5, 6, 7; 2 Tim 3:8); see Prov 25:4; Isa 1:22, where the term refers to the dross in the silver refining process; Spicq, *TLNT* 1:360-61; W. Grundmann, *TDNT* 2:255-60. For the cognate δοκιμάζω ("to test, approve"), see 1 Tim 3:10.

154. The connecting preposition πρός means here "with reference to" (Matt 27:4; John 21:22; BDF §239.6).

tations emerges in the lifestyle to which these are connected. Subtractions or omissions from apostolic Christianity owing to the interference of accepted Cretan values are considered dangerous and intentional. Paul has looked at "the package" (doctrinal and ethical) they are trying to sell and pronounced it unclean and dangerous. This does not mean that he has no concern for the people involved. But Paul names those who profess to believe, pass themselves off as teachers in the communities, and yet stubbornly resist the will of God as unbelievers who must then be treated accordingly. Paul was not slow to sound the alarm; he was not slow to direct Titus and the church leaders under his care to engage these people. While there are certainly numerous areas in belief and practice where modern Christians must allow differences to exist side by side, there are also too many situations where indiscriminate "open-mindedness" has allowed the historical gospel to be diluted to suit modern and postmodern sensibilities. A text such as this one might be regarded as a study in religious bigotry and narrow-mindedness, or it might be read as an authoritative wake-up call for many of us today.

B. INSTRUCTIONS FOR THE CHURCH (2:1–3:11)

1. Some Local and Formal Matters of Introduction

In this second section of the body of the letter, Paul gives instructions to Titus that he is to pass on to the church. He regards the Christian life from two angles. First, Titus is to instruct believers about living within the household (2:1-10). This concern for the *oikos* parallels what can be found in secular ethical writings. But two trends probably converge in this section of teaching. On the one hand, as we have seen, Cretan Christianity had apparently made room for much of the rough and self-indulgent behavior typical of pagan society. Moreover, what Christian teachers in the Cretan communities taught lacked any critical assessment of Cretan culture, and since the teaching took place in the households (1:11), it was there that the impact (or lack of it) was first felt. The Cretan lack of restraint where males are concerned (in public behavior, drinking, and sexual liaisons) is addressed in instructions to older and younger men.

But alongside this lingering Cretan value system, as Paul's "typical" parenesis to women suggests, was the emergence of the new Roman woman with her freedoms and appetites.[1] The topics addressed in chapter 2 align in tone and content with the ancient critical discussion of this new morality associated with wealthy Roman women. Crete had been thoroughly Roman-

---

1. See 1 Tim 2:8-15 (discussion and notes); see esp. Winter, *Roman Wives,* 152-69.

ized, though as the widespread critique of Cretan lifestyle showed, Cretans would have shown little interest in the pursuit of the cardinal virtues. As Winter demonstrates, long before Imperial rule Cretan women enjoyed far more legal privileges and freedoms than their Greek counterparts in Athens. This situation extended to property rights and was visible in legislation about women's rights in sexual offenses, and the greater place of women in Cretan culture could even be detected in the custom of referring to Crete as "the motherland."[2] This higher regard for women would have made Cretan culture a ready-made receptacle for the *avant-garde* mores of the new Roman woman. As we noticed in 1 Tim 2:9-15, one consequence of the movement was a diminished interest in household management (which task normally fell to the woman/wife), for the emancipated woman had other things on her mind, and higher priorities to attend to. Nevertheless, within the empire the *oikos* continued to be held up as the fundamental unit of the social structure,[3] and for this reason innovations, disturbances, evidence of poor management, and the like attracted the attention of conservative-minded observers. In the case of disruption to Christian households, such observation would quickly turn into criticism that would endanger the church's public image and put its reputation and witness within society at risk.

Both the social structure and the physical structures of the ancient household reflect the hierarchical system. Relationships were clearly defined. The father/*kyrios* ("master") was the head of the household. The conception of the household according to clearly defined reciprocal (but not equal) pairs is traditional from before Aristotle, who expressed the system clearly: "master and slave, husband and wife, father and children."[4] One related to one's counterpart either with authority or in subjection. Archaeological studies have shown the houses of the era to be built in ways that facilitated and expressed the system. In urban settings, slaves generally would have been restricted to the drab kitchens and outbuildings in which they worked, and "one dominant imperative in a slave-owning society was to contrast adequately the servile and the seigniorial areas of the house."[5] During parties and the symposia held

2. Winter, *Roman Wives,* 141-44 (citing esp. Plutarch, *Moralia* 792E).

3. The fundamental place of household management was enunciated in Aristotle, *Politics* 1253B.1-3: In discussing the nature of the city, household management was the starting point: "For every city is composed of households" (πᾶσα γὰρ σύγκειται πόλις ἐξ οἰκιῶν).

4. Aristotle, *Politics* 1253b.6-7 (δεσπότης καὶ δοῦλος, καὶ πόσις καὶ ἄλοχος, καὶ πατὴρ καὶ τέκνα).

5. A. Wallace-Hadrill, "Houses and Households: Sampling Pompeii and Herculaneum," in B. Rawson, ed., *Marriage, Divorce, and Children in Ancient Rome* (Oxford: Oxford University Press, 1991), 39 (cited in Osiek and Balch, *Families in the New Testament World,* 199).

by householders, slaves might serve the guests, and traditional Greco-Roman values would have women attending the meals (but generally sitting upright, not reclining like the men) and then departing before discussions began. But the emergence of the new woman in Roman culture saw the woman's place in such meetings enlarged (see on 1 Tim 2:8-15).

Given the public observance of meetings in Christian households, where the gospel made rather egalitarian promises (1 Cor 12:13; Gal 3:28) and worship and even fellowship meals might take place with less attention to social status, the potential for misunderstanding and criticism from outside was very real. One, therefore, might consider what could happen within a single household, where slaves and women (for instance) might feel the influence of various trends, from old Cretan assumptions to new Roman mores, as well as pressure to observe what must have seemed rather arcane rules of purity and impurity concerning foods. The potential for confusion within the household itself would be tremendous — the more so if those charged with preparing foods were believers under this influence and the master of the house was not a believer. The point is, although we cannot be sure precisely how to decipher the background issues Paul has in mind, we can be sure that there were numerous possible and likely ways that disruption could occur in households in which either the Christian gospel or some perversion of it had made an impression, and in which elements of Cretan behavior hung on and the values of the new Roman woman encroached.

What we observe in 2:1-10 is Paul's desire to ensure that the emerging church understands the basics of Christian respectability in society, which would of course begin with the *oikos*. Furthermore, given the resonance of this teaching with secular concerns about the household, it is unlikely that this section is dealing with the church as a gathered community.[6] And one of the important implications of this "household" passage (and similar passages in the NT) is that the life of respectability to be lived at this level is the outworking of the grace of God in Christ and therefore to be lived as an appropriate faith-response to God.

A broader view is taken in the next section, as Titus instructs the church in its engagement with the world (3:1-2, 8). One should note that a distinct statement of theology grounds both sections of ethical instruction (2:11-14; 3:3-7).

If there is a center of gravity in this practical instruction, it comes in the emphasis on respectability in behavior that is outward and public. This has been badly misinterpreted in the past as the reflection of a worldly church whose hope in any significant future intervention by God had faded to a very dull gray (see the Introduction, 15-24). And this bland sort of ethics is also

6. As, e.g., Johnson, 232; cf. Verner, *Household of God,* 171.

said to be part and parcel of the household code style of instruction in which it is couched. This particular interpretative spin could not be farther off the mark.

First, Paul is speaking to these churches in terms they can fully understand with a deliberate view to the continuation of his mission (the influence of the opening, 1:1-4, is still felt here). Both church health and Christian mission (if these aspects of Christian existence can be viewed separately for a moment) depend on the visible message sent by individuals and households in whom faith has generated a quality of life that consistently reflects the virtues and values most prized by the culture. The twofold expression of concern to protect the reputation of the word of God (2:5) and to positively adorn it (2:10) is not accidental. The apostle took his reading of the culture, and so when he utilized the current language of ethics, he adjusted the meanings theologically as necessary. But his goal, in any case, was to communicate to these churches the meaning of the Christ-event for everyday life in the household setting, and his method was to set this reality into their linguistic and cognitive grid. This involved engaging the dominant Cretan stereotype and challenging religious assumptions, in order that the deep significance of the gospel and the radical extensiveness of its claims on human life could be perceived.

Second, neither the form in which this teaching is cast — variously termed a "household code," "station code," etc.[7] — nor the similarity with secular codes is an indication that the ethics is bland and lifeless. New Testament writers adapted the household code, as also loosely in 1 Timothy 2–6, to address instruction to household and community/church groups. As in the case of Ephesians and Colossians where the traditional household members were addressed in their relationships (wives/husbands, children/parents, slaves/masters), so here an adaptation or different development of the didactic tradition finds people addressed according to their ages in the household (in 2:1-10, according to age and gender, and then slaves). The teaching of 3:1-2 regarding the church in society (cf. Rom 13:1-7; 1 Pet 2:13-17) also bears some relationship to the tradition (both form and function), though of course here the church as a whole is addressed concerning its relation to the state.

Two further observations should be made here. First, from a thematic point of view, behind the choice to address ethical teaching to the *oikos* will have been Paul's assessment of the church's situation in Crete. The influence of the Cretan Christian teachers in this sphere (1:11) might figure in the decision; but, if so, it was probably the persistence of Cretan cultural tendencies (including those associated with the "new woman" values) that was being reflected in household situations that Paul sought to redress. These cultural ele-

7. On the whole matter, see now Marshall, 231-36.

715

ments would have blurred the distinctiveness of the Christian message and blunted its effectiveness for life change. Paul insists on thoroughness of change (on conversion), and he goes to the center of social life to complete the mission already underway (1:5). Life within households (normal life in society) is integral to authentic Christian existence.

Second, the function of the household style of teaching has been much debated. But the most compelling background to its application in the NT letters is its development and use in the effort to protect and regulate the institution of the *oikos*/household. This tradition explains the tendency to focus on household positions and to address people in pairs. Yet it is clear at the same time that Christian use of this sort of teaching involved some unique adaptations: no exact parallels to the NT household codes (which themselves reflect considerable variety) exist in secular writings. There is a decided regard for justice and fairness (especially as regards the treatment of subordinates) that exceeds secular usage, and a theological underpinning is supplied. Although their use in a variety of letters and situations suggests that they could be applied for a range of reasons (mission, to quiet unrest or enthusiasm, defense-apologetic), generally the conservative and respectable ethic they tend to endorse reflects in all settings an awareness of the expectations of society and the desire to order Christian life according to accepted standards. Public respectability is therefore one of the goals of this teaching. And both the ethical lexicon employed and the form of the teaching seek to maintain a dialogue with the wider society. The possible reasons for encouraging such behavior — to restore stability shaken by the opponents, to foster a public image that enhances the gospel mission — must be determined from the literary contexts in which the codes appear.

The specific problem of the opposing teachers recedes somewhat into the background at this point, returning briefly at the end where they are viewed within the framework of church discipline (3:9-11). Nevertheless, as we consider the shape of the ethical teaching laid down in these passages, the disruption caused by the "Cretanized" Christian outlook remains part of the background. Thus the deliberate contrast between Titus's teaching and that of the Cretan teachers at 2:1 ("*you, however, must teach what is appropriate to sound doctrine*"; cf. 1:9, 13), and between Christian behavior, which is to be "sound in faith" (2:2; cf. 1:13) and characterized by "good deeds" (2:7, 15; 3:1; cf. 1:16), and their conduct is designed as an implicit polemic that keeps that perilous movement in the readers' minds. Furthermore, behavior that is prohibited will be regarded as characteristic of the opposition.

Yet Paul's discourse follows two tracks. He tagged this movement with a "Cretan" label, but the cultural stereotype serves double duty. Not only does it establish the low caliber of the competing message, but it also resonates with that wider critique of Crete's social character in a way that

716

suggests that the fundamental issue of *the-church-in-the-world* (e.g., 3:1-2, 8) plays its part in this letter as well. These churches are being urged to sink healthy roots deep into the uncertain Cretan soil and to shake loose the cultural elements that have attached to the Christian message, and they are to be as salt and light in this wild frontier.

The tenor of the teaching is Hellenistic, with a heavy emphasis on behavior that would be regarded generally as respectable, honorable, responsible, and so on. It is specifically here in the letter, however, that Paul consciously attributes this quality of life, and indeed the language and concepts employed to describe it, to the historical appearance of Christ (2:11-14).

Titus's role is to take up the ministry responsibility described in 1:9. The language of 2:15, and also the didactic terms in 2:1 and 3:1, places the teaching into the categories introduced in connection with the overseer. In this way, Paul establishes Titus as the authoritative role model, assigned to carry out in the churches the instructions of the apostle. At the same time he exhibits the pattern for subsequent ministry by the overseers. Paul sets out his coworker's activities of teaching and admonition in contrast to the Cretan teaching of the opponents (2:1), a device that serves Paul well throughout these three letters (1 Tim 6:11; 2 Tim 2:1; 3:10, 14; 4:5).

2. Christian Living within the Household (2:1-15)

This subsection is divided into an opening command to Titus that establishes the controlling themes of the passage (v. 1), a series of instructions to groups in the household (vv. 2-10), a section of theological rationale for the teaching (vv. 11-14), and a concluding summary that also bridges from the theology to the next section of parenesis (v. 15).

a. Living in accordance with Sound Doctrine (2:1-10)

> 1 *You, however, must teach what is appropriate to sound doctrine.*
> 2 *Teach the older men to be temperate, worthy of respect, self-controlled, and sound in faith, in love and in endurance.*
>
> 3 *Likewise, teach the older women to be reverent in the way they live, not to be slanderers or addicted to much wine, but to teach what is good.* 4 *Then they can urge the younger women to love their husbands and children,* 5 *to be self-controlled and pure, to be busy at home,*[8] *to be kind, and to be subject to their husbands, so that no one will malign the word of God.*

8. The rarity of οἰκουργούς ("busy at home"; BDAG, s.v.) probably explains the replacement with the better-known classical οἰκουρούς ("staying at home"; א* D² H 1739

6 Similarly, encourage the young men to be self-controlled. 7 In everything set them an example by doing what is good. In your teaching show integrity, seriousness 8 and soundness of speech that cannot be condemned, so that those who oppose you may be ashamed because they have nothing bad to say about us.

9 Teach slaves to be subject to their masters in everything, to try to please them, not to talk back to them, 10 and not to steal from them, but to show that they can be fully trusted, so that in every way they will make the teaching about God our Savior attractive.

1 Paul urges Titus to teach the Cretan believers in such a way that their commitments and behavior will be on an entirely different level from those of the opposing teachers and from Cretan society. This will be achieved through the integration of godly ethics and sound theology. The intention to weave these two dimensions of belief and behavior into a single fabric is signaled in this opening verse; the process is worked out, at least in theory, in the theological section that follows (vv. 11-14). Both acknowledging the need to be distinct and consciously integrating faith and behavior are necessary.

First, Paul contrasts Titus (and implicitly the whole church) with the failed opponents. The transitional phrase "you, however" occurs several times in these letters to Titus and Timothy to indicate a 180-degree change in direction from the false teachers.[9] The device is simple, but it sends the appropriate message of censure as it marks out the start of a new course.

Second, the difference will come through Titus's teaching. The instruction incorporates a term that means "to speak" (2:15) but that in this context draws its specific meaning from the surrounding didactic activities (1:9; 2:6, 15; 3:1), and so means "to teach" or communicate some message.[10] The substance of this message actually comes in the verses that follow, but Paul first establishes the distinct quality of this message.

Third, the content that is to be taught sets Titus's teaching apart from

---

1881 TR). The rare term (harder reading and better explanation for the variant) is perhaps marginally more likely to have been changed than vice versa (but the fit of οἰκουρούς into the vocabulary of respectability of the passage and its comparable MSS evidence make the matter less than clear-cut; see Metzger, 585; Bernard, 167; Marshall, 249).

9. See on 1 Tim 6:11. The NIV translation (simply "You") plays down the note of contrast; but cf. the improved TNIV ("You, however").

10. Gk. λαλέω; for its use in the formal sense of teaching, see Acts 17:19; 18:25; 1 Cor 2:6; 14:6. H. Hübner, *EDNT* 2:335-36. Oberlinner, 105-6, suggests that this verb means here "to converse," because Titus in this setting is to be an example not just for teachers but for all, who will then emulate his "conversation in accordance with sound teaching." This fails to do justice to the intention of the letter to instruct Titus; vv. 2-10 form the content of "teaching that accords with sound teaching."

that of the rebellious teachers. "What"[11] he teaches is to be "appropriate to [to accord with] sound doctrine." This language represents a gauge to measure quality, and it indicates two things. On the one hand, Paul envisions a tight connection between teaching about behavior or Christian living (ethics) and this traditional body of teaching called "sound doctrine." The latter term, as we have seen (1:9), refers to the authoritative apostolic doctrine. This in itself is not to be limited to "theology" or "gospel" as such, but the teaching about the Christ-event, salvation, and so on forms its core element. This statement suggests that there is a Christian ethics that is "appropriate to" ("befitting")[12] the message, contents and claims of the apostolic doctrine.

If one takes "sound doctrine" in its widest sense, one might think that Paul is simply saying, "Let your teaching to the churches be that which conforms to the apostolic norm." This would of course not be wrong. But here the term of correlation ("appropriate to") suggests that in some sense the ethical teaching to follow (2:2-10; 3:1-2, 8) is separate from, though interrelated with, "sound doctrine" (1:9).[13] A slight distinction is therefore drawn between theology and ethics. The distinction should not be pressed too far, for the relation between theology and Christian ethics is dialogical, each dimension implying and depending on the other. Nevertheless, as the kerygmatic passages that follow show (2:11-14; 3:3-7), fundamental statements of theology do indeed form the basis for the observable aspect of Christian existence. And Paul's point is essentially that what Titus teaches in the way of Christian conduct can and indeed must correspond, in some measurable sense, to the apostolic core.[14]

On the other hand, the implication in this instruction and in the use of the term "sound doctrine" is that Titus is to do what the Cretan teachers have failed to do — namely, inculcate an ethic that emerges logically from the truth of the health-giving gospel and is distinguishable from Cretan cultural elements. The disturbance they caused in households (1:11) showed an incomplete separation from secular Cretan assumptions; and the Jewish tinge of some aspects of their teaching (1:14-15) reflects an incomplete grasp of the gospel. Paul thus concluded that the opponents' message stood in contradiction to the Christian ethical teaching already endorsed as authoritative in

---

11. The relative pronoun ἅ designates the implicit object; vv. 2-10 will spell out the content. See the note on 1:11.

12. For Gk. πρέπω ("to be fitting, suitable"), see 1 Tim 2:10 (note); Eph 5:3.

13. For this description of the message, see 1 Tim 1:10 (discussion and note). The dative (of respect) τῇ ὑγιαινούσῃ διδασκαλίᾳ ("for the sound teaching") indicates that by which the appropriateness of the teaching is to be determined.

14. Cf. S. Hauerwas, "On Doctrine and Ethics," in C. E. Gunton, ed., *The Cambridge Companion to Christian Doctrine* (Cambridge: Cambridge University Press, 1997), 21-40.

Paul's churches. The rest of the passage will now reveal the shape of what Titus is to teach.

2 Initially, Paul divides the teaching according to gender and age, combining lists of virtues or prohibited behavior with concrete instructions. In fact, the incorporation of lists into a household code reflects Paul's adaptation of the code to this situation. First to be addressed are the older men. Depending on which ancient classification of age groups we follow,[15] old men are at least somewhere upward of forty years old, possibly into their fifties or sixties. The term does not mean "elders" in the sense of 1:6 (cf. 1 Tim 5:1), but presumably leader-elders would have been drawn from this age group.

In a style similar to that of the code of 1:7-9,[16] Paul enumerates well-known qualities that typify respectability and so should characterize older Christian men. The first three also appear among the virtues associated with overseers and deacons in 1 Timothy 3. First, older men should be "temperate" (*nēphalios;* see on 1 Tim 3:2, 8). The term ranges in meaning from the literal sense of "cautious in the use of wine" to the metaphorical sense of "sober-minded" (1 Tim 3:2). Here the former sense perhaps balances better with the instructions about older women in v. 3,[17] and excessive drinking (along with gluttony) was often the prelude to the display of other vices following the dinners and banquets that instruction such as this aimed to discourage.

Second, they are to behave in a way "worthy of respect" ("seriousness"; *semnos;* see on 1 Tim 2:2). This term is also broad, but it generally denotes an observable bearing or demeanor that commands respect from other people, and was to be especially characteristic of older men.[18]

Third, "self-controlled" (*sōphrōn;* 1:8; 2:5, 12)[19] or "sensible" ("prudent"; NRSV) depicts a measured restraint in all things — the opposite of behavior that might be regarded as foolish or "Cretan." This quality is explicitly identified with the new life made possible by the Christ-event (2:12).

---

15. Philo, *On the Creation* 105, links the term used here, πρεσβύτης (Luke 1:18; Phlm 9), with the age range 50 to 66; see further discussion at 1 Tim 5:1.

16. The instruction is formed from the infinitive verb "to be" (εἰμί) followed by three accusative predicate adjectives. The construction is uncertain. We must either supply a command verb (following the pattern of παρακάλει in 2:6; cf. Oberlinner, 104-5; BDF §389), as, e.g., "teach the older men . . ." (TNIV/NIV), or take the accusative/infinitive combination (πρεσβύτας . . . εἶναι) as dependent upon "teach" (λάλει) in v. 1 (Lock, 139; Spicq, 616); alternatively, Knight, 305, suggests that it may be an example of the imperatival infinitive (Rom 12:15; Phil 3:16; cf. Moule, *Idiom Book,* 126). It is probable that as the didactic verb παρακάλει governs 2:6-10, so λάλει in v. 1 should be understood to control the thought of vv. 2-5. The sense of the instruction is clear, despite the uncertainty.

17. See Marshall, 240; Spicq, 617.

18. See the discussion in Quinn, 131.

19. See on 1 Tim 3:2; and 1 Tim 2:9 (Excursus).

Together, these terms form an overlapping network of virtues that describes a life of respectability free from overindulgence, dissipation, and foolishness. The Christ-event is to be understood as the mystical source of a life so marked, but, as is characteristic of Paul's thought, its manifestation in human society communicates in verbal and non-verbal language understood by all.

The fourth virtue is the most extensive. It is expressed by an accusative participle, "sound," modified by three dative virtues ("in faith, in love and in endurance") that complete the thought.[20] In this case, "faith, love and endurance" form a triad that reflects on the whole of human life. The reference to "soundness" has already taken a specific polemical direction in this letter (1:9, 13; 2:1), so that here too the older men are being called to a life free from the marks of the opponents' "diseased" (i.e., "Cretan-tainted") teaching.

How is soundness measured here? First, "in faith" (see on 1 Tim 1:2) depicts the invisible dimension of Christian existence, focusing on the activity of believing (in the gospel, in God/Christ) that determines Christian identity and expresses the human response to God.[21]

Second, "love" often accompanies "believing" in these letters to co-workers,[22] as it did in Paul's letters to churches.[23] It is meant in the sense of sacrificial service done for another, and therefore represents the visible counterpart to believing.[24] Together these two qualities effectively summarize Christian existence (Gal 5:6), and in the church they already formed a traditional pair.[25]

"Endurance" (see on 1 Tim 6:11; cf. Rev 2:19) (in place of "hope") completes the triad of spiritual health.[26] This element of perseverance could

20. Gk. ὑγιαίνοντας τῇ πίστει, τῇ ἀγάπῃ, τῇ ὑπομονῇ; the whole phrase is adjectival, corresponding to the function of the three preceding adjectives that modify the infinitive εἶναι.

21. The articular ἡ πίστις often means "the faith" in the sense of that which is believed (see discussion in Towner, *Goal*, 121-29; Marshall, 213-17); but here, alongside ἀγάπη and ὑπομονή (see discussion at 1 Tim 4:12; 6:11; 2 Tim 2:22; 3:10), the active sense of "believing" is indicated (Quinn, 132; Marshall, 240; Knight, 306).

22. See the discussion at 1 Tim 1:5; 6:11.

23. 1 Cor 13:13; Gal 5:6, 22; Eph 6:23; Col 1:4; 1 Thess 3:6; 5:8; 2 Thess 1:3; Phlm 5.

24. The point is developed in Towner, *Goal*, 165-66; W. Schrage, *The Ethics of the New Testament* (Philadelphia: Fortress, 1988), 211-17.

25. See further Lips, *Glaube*, 79; Vögtle, *Die Tugend- und Lasterkataloge im Neuen Testament*, 51, 171.

26. In the first occurrence of this triad in Paul (1 Thess 1:3), the virtues "faith, love, endurance" (πίστις, ἀγάπη, ὑπομονή) do not appear alone. Rather, each is linked to the result it engenders: "work produced by faith . . . labor prompted by love . . . endurance

envision the conflict setting[27] or more generally the struggle to live as believers in rough Cretan social conditions (cf. Rom 5:3; Jas 1:3; 5:11). In either
case, it expresses the determination and perseverance that support faith and
love in the face of adversity.

Older men are thus enjoined to live a holistic life of Christian dignity
and dynamic faith. As Paul understands Christian existence, this life will be
measurably distinct ("healthy") from the diminished cultural "Christianity"
endorsed by the opponents, and it will successfully realize the ideals of virtue. But the secret is in the commitment of the person to the truth of the gospel, and the virtues themselves will emerge as the believer's faith expresses
itself in service.

3 The next two groups to be addressed are older women and younger
women. Instructions to older women,[28] set into the same syntactical arrangement as those to the older men,[29] develop through the purpose clause (v. 4)
into instructions to younger women (vv. 4-5). Older women are instructed
with respect to four aspects of behavior. But notably, these are arranged so that
two positively framed virtues bracket two stereotypically negative traits often
associated with the loose behavior Roman women were more free to participate in. Paul is again drawing on both the Cretan and the wider Roman social
discourse as he describes the foibles of some Cretan Christian women.

The first quality, "reverent in the way they live" ("in behavior,"
NRSV), considers the entire demeanor of older women — conduct understood as the interplay of inward and outward realities.[30] As an inward quality

---

inspired by hope." In the present configuration, these relationships may be seen to be tele-
scoped in the concept of "soundness"; thus "sound" = performance/service/behavior that
is good, based on "faith" and "love." "Endurance" will still presuppose hope in the epiphany of Christ (2:13).

27. Towner, *Goal,* 160-61; Marshall, 241.

28. Gk. πρεσβῦτις ("old[er] woman, elderly lady"; only here in the NT; see
BDAG, s.v.; 4 Macc 16:14; Philo, *On the Special Laws* 2.33). The age range covered by
the term "older women" is the same as that for "older men" (cf. 1 Tim 5:2).

29. The connecting adverb "in the same way" (ὡσαύτως; see on 1 Tim 2:9) relates
this command to the preceding one and is typical of this type of parenesis. The same verbal idea (consisting of some verb of instruction + inf. εἶναι ["to be"]) is to be supplied
from v. 2 (see discussion above).

30. Gk. κατάστημα ("demeanor, behavior"; only here in the NT; cf. *Epistle of
Aristeas* 122; 210; 278); the noun is used both of inward deportment, specifically that of
godliness (*Epistle of Aristeas* 210; cf. Josephus, *Antiquities* 15.236) and outward condition (Josephus, *Jewish War* 1.40, of a city). Combining the inward and outward, the term
arrives at a notion of an inward condition that yields an observable result (e.g., Ignatius,
To the Trallians 3.2). See the discussion in Dibelius and Conzelmann, 139-40. The prepositional phrase "in demeanor" (ἐν καταστήματι) denotes the sphere in which "reverent"
applies.

it will give rise to particular observable results that can be emulated. The term describing this condition is translated "reverent" in most English versions. Applied specifically to the behavior seen in priests or priestesses performing duties at religious events, it comes to refer more generally to behavior that is holy or godly.[31] It provides the suitable counterpart to the instruction to older men in which inward realities linked to faith are understood in terms of outward expression (cf. 1 Tim 2:10).[32] Older women, too, must give evidence in their outward life of inward spiritual commitments.

If this holistic spiritual poise is the chief goal of the instruction, getting control of the next two prohibited activities is surely central to obtaining the goal. Here Paul makes contact with the stereotypical and current critical profile of older wives who were prone to drunkenness[33] and loose talk.[34] The descriptor "slanderers"[35] needs little explication; it was often the counterpart to drinking. "Addiction to much wine"[36] was probably more the cause of the slanderous talk; it is emphasized by means of the language of "enslavement" (and adjective "much") that often depicted one who was overpowered by the passions (3:3; 2 Pet 2:19).[37] In our texts slanderous talk and drunkenness are closely linked (1 Tim 3:8, 11) because they were already linked in secular discussions, and particularly, as here, in relation to shortcomings of a certain kind of older wife.[38] What should be noted is that these behaviors, typical of

31. Gk. ἱεροπρεπής occurs only here in the NT (4 Macc 9:25; 11:20 of holiness; cf. Philo, *On the Life of Abraham* 101; *On the Decalogue* 60); see the discussions and references in Spicq, *TLNT* 2:215-16; G. Schrenk, *TDNT* 3:253-54; Marshall, 243-44.

32. Marshall, 244 (Quinn, 134), rightly compares this holy demeanor with the combination σεμνός/σώφρων in the instructions for older men; yet the contact may be more extensive, including the following phrase about soundness in faith, love, and endurance (especially in view of the attraction of κατάστημα for ideas such as εὐσέβεια [*Epistle of Aristeas* 210] and the similar interest in the deportment of women in 1 Tim 2:9-10).

33. For drunkenness, cf. *The Greek Anthology* 2.191, 249; Cicero, *Pro caelio* 55; Ovid, *Fasti* 3.765-66 (cited by Quinn, 135).

34. See the discussion in Winter, *Roman Wives,* 152-54.

35. See on 1 Tim 3:11; 2 Tim 3:3. In these letters to coworkers, as elsewhere, the noun διάβολος can mean "devil" (1 Tim 3:6, 7; 2 Tim 2:26), but here it is the activity for which the devil is known that is in mind (see the discussion in Quinn, 135).

36. I.e., drunkenness; also of leaders; see on 1 Tim 3:8.

37. Gk. δουλόω (perf. pass. ptc.; "to enslave, to make someone a slave"; fig. in Rom 6:18, 22; Gal 4:3; 2 Pet 2:19; cf. Josephus, *Antiquities* 15.91; also K. Rengstorf, *TDNT* 2:279). For the traditional association of this verb with "wine" (μὴ οἴνῳ πολλῷ δεδουλωμένας), see, e.g., Philostratus, *Vita Apollonii* 2.36 (cited in Marshall, 245 n. 32); for the negative view of the effects of wine and the combination οἶνος πολύς ("much wine"), see the examples in BDAG, "οἶνος."

38. See the discussion and examples in Winter, *Roman Wives,* 152-54; Towner, *Goal,* 193, 307 n. 120; K. J. Dover, *Greek Popular Morality in the Time of Plato and Aristotle* (Berkeley: University of California Press, 1974), 95-102.

liberated Roman women at dinners and banquets, were also linked to a loss of "self-control" — *sōphrosynē,* the feminine cardinal virtue that insured sexual fidelity — and sexual promiscuity.[39] These implications were a strong enough part of the social discourse that Paul need not have mentioned them here to have implied them. His intentional echoing of this stereotype is meant to ensure that Cretan Christian older women rid themselves of this "typical" reputation.[40] They were to show themselves as older wives who had successfully emerged from the Cretan way of life.

The fourth quality to mark older women is actually a function that will be explained in the following purpose clause. Most English versions understand the Greek compound *kalodidaskalous* to mean "teaching what is good," with the accent more on the content of "what" was to be taught (2:1) than on the character and responsibilities of who was to do the teaching. But nothing in the term itself supports this decision.[41] The context focuses on the character of older women and perhaps the need to make some changes. This suggests that a better translation here is "good teachers,"[42] and that Paul is calling these older women to a certain quality of performance ("good, excellent") as "teachers." While there is no reason to doubt that this role would include modeling or mentoring in areas ranging from domestic responsibilities to personal godliness (vv. 4-5), Paul nevertheless entrusts to these older women a very significant educative responsibility within the context of the *oikos.*[43]

39. See on 1 Tim 2:9 and Excursus; see also Winter, *Roman Wives,* 152-54.

40. It is not necessary to hold that all older wives addressed here had failed to remove themselves from the Cretan cultural ways; but the tenor of the instructions to follow (see below on vv. 4-5), which suggests that younger wives were indeed caught up in Cretan/Roman patterns of life, implies that the teaching to older wives was not simply preventive.

41. Gk. καλοδιδάσκαλος is not attested elsewhere; it is argued that an emphasis on the quality of what is taught might be surmised from the implications about content in the reverse activities indicated in the terms κακοδιδασκαλέω ("to teach what is bad"; *2 Clement* 10.5) and κακοδιδασκαλία (Ignatius, *To the Philippians* 2.1). See BDAG, s.v.; K. H. Rengstorf, *TDNT* 2:159-60.

42. See also Winter, *Roman Wives,* 155.

43. Mounce, 410, is beating a dead horse when he attempts to distinguish the sort of teaching (he names it "informal, one-on-one encouragement") envisaged here from the sort that would constitute "formal" congregational instruction: "It pictures the older women, those who were experienced in life, marriage and child rearing, taking the younger women in the congregation under their care and helping them to adjust to their responsibilities." What is more at issue is the distinction between public and private spheres and what is considered appropriate for women in each sphere (1 Tim 2:11-15). Here the authority of older women to teach in the household is affirmed, and we must recall that this teaching, though here domestic in nature and culturally respectable in its patriarchal shape, almost certainly involved calling younger women to reject behavior patterns that

724

4 Verses 4 and 5 now state the purpose *(hina)* for which older women are to be "good teachers." The profile of godly "younger women"[44] consists of seven qualities that were widely approved in secular society as the standard accouterments of the ideal respectable wife. The first six items may have been set down in pairs;[45] the seventh repeats the traditional refrain of submission to the husband. But all of them follow, explain, and draw their urgency from the verb that describes the older women's educational role.

The semantic affinity of the verb of instruction in this purpose clause for the last quality of the older women ("teach what is good") suggests that vv. 4-5a serve primarily to explain why older women are to be teachers.[46] Paul shifts from the usual didactic terminology (cf. 2:1, 6, 15) in his selection of the verb *sōphronizō,* which I leave untranslated for the moment. It is cognate to the *sōphrōn* word group that is prominent in the description of authentic Christian existence in the ethical vocabulary of these letters to coworkers (1:8; 2:2, 5; 1 Tim 2:9; 3:2); the emphasis here on respectability in the household as an aspect of this existence might have prompted its choice. But more likely its capacity to express the idea of a figurative, sobering "slap in the face" (i.e., "to bring someone back to his/her senses") determined Paul's choice.

Winter has pointed out that commentators are unsure how to cope with this verb in 2:4. The range covered by the verb is as broad as that of the adjective, expressing variously "moderating excess," "restoring to the senses," "calling someone to responsibility," and "encouraging, instructing and advising."[47] The degree to which the teaching is meant to be corrective (of Roman libertarian excess and Cretan morals) must guide us to the nuance Paul intends here.[48] As Winter has shown,[49] in various settings where people (in moral and

---

might well include sexual promiscuity; absolutely nothing is said about the mode of this teaching (except what might be derived from the term σωφρονίζω in v. 4). See below; cf. Johnson, *Paul's Delegates,* 234.

44. The term "younger women" translates the substantival adjective νέαι. Technically an age group (see J. Behm, *TDNT* 4:896-98; cf. the use of νεώτερος in 2:6; 1 Tim 5:1, 2, 11, 14), the term forms an imprecise comparison with older women in the household, envisioning younger wives who are still occupied with raising children and keeping house.

45. See Knight, 308; Fee, 187; Marshall, 246 (TNIV groups the first four qualities into pairs; but cf. NRSV). The rationale for this is the largely lexical and semantic resemblance of the first two terms, φίλανδρος/φιλότεκνος, but the reasons for pairing successive terms are less compelling.

46. Though there is no apparent reason why the whole of v. 3 could not be understood as serving the need to train younger women.

47. Gk. σωφρονίζω (see 1 Tim 2:9, Excursus). See the references and discussion in Spicq, *TLNT* 3:362-63 n. 18; and esp. Winter, *Roman Wives,* 154-59.

48. See, e.g., Fee, 187, and the suggestion "wise them up."

49. See the examples and references in Winter, *Roman Wives,* 154-59.

behavioral contexts) and even whole cities are in need of being "called back to their senses," Philo and Josephus (as well as Dionysius of Halicarnassus, Dio Chrysostom, and Strabo) employed *sōphronizō* in distinction from other more neutral educative terms. In the present context — given what has already emerged of the substandard Cretan values mixed in with the Christian message and what is suspected of the impact of the new Roman woman ideals — understanding the verb (and therefore the nature of the teaching to be given) as a jolting "call to return to the senses" seems most suitable. The substance of the "wake-up call" is given in the seven qualities that follow.[50]

From the virtues these young wives are to be called back to embrace, the likely impact of the "new woman" morality on the Cretan Christian households can be seen (see on 1 Tim 2:8-15). The values of the "new woman" had little to do with traditional commitments to the household; the new morality they emphasized endorsed the freedom to pursue extramarital sexual liaisons and liberties normally open only to men, which would place marital fidelity and household management at risk. Thus the household was the chief theater of Paul's campaign.

The first two qualities take up her attitudes toward her husband and her children. "Love for the husband" occurs only here in the NT but was regarded as a fundamental proof of the good wife in Hellenistic and Jewish cultures; it was often discussed in conjunction with other elements of behavior belonging to the godly profile in these letters to coworkers.[51]

"Love for one's children," the second term, is also restricted in the NT to this occurrence, and was equally prized in that culture (cf. 1 Tim 5:10). In secular sources it occurs in connection with "love for the husband" as a basic domestic responsibility.[52]

5 This verse extends the thought from domestic responsibilities to

---

50. The present tense verb σωφρονίζωσιν envisions the activities about to be enforced as those that should typify the life of younger women in the household; the verb takes the infinitive εἶναι ("to be") plus accusatives (six adjs. and the acc. ptc. phrase) to express the content of that which they are to be called back to.

51. Gk. φίλανδρος ("having love for a husband"; MM). The importance of this virtue is demonstrated in one of the Cynic writings, *The Epistles of Crates* 30.6 [Malherbe, 80.6]: "I am returning the tunic you wove and sent to me because those of us who live a life of perseverance are forbidden to wear such things, and I do so in order that I may cause you to desist from this task you have undertaken with much zeal *so that you might appear to the masses to be someone who loves her husband* [φίλανδρος; emphasis mine]." See also Philo, *On Rewards* 139; Josephus, *Antiquities* 18.159 (φιλανδρία); for additional references and discussion see Winter, *Roman Wives,* 159; Marshall, 248 n. 42; Spicq, 392 n. 3, 620.

52. Gk. φιλότεκνος (MM). For the combination of φιλότεκνος with φίλανδρος, see Plutarch, *Moralia* 769C; *New Documents* 3.40-43. See also 4 Macc 15:4-6, 11, 23, 25; 16:3; Philo, *On the Life of Abraham* 179; BDAG, s.v. Cf. Winter, *Roman Wives,* 160.

personal qualities. The first of this second pair of qualities, "self-controlled," occurred already in the case of older men (2:2; cf. 1:8; 2:6; cf. 1 Tim 2:9 [of wives/women]; 3:2). But in the case of women, this was the cardinal virtue that defined the modest wife;[53] it was to manifest itself above all in dignified conduct characterized by restraint of the passions and urges that might jeopardize fidelity to her husband. Paul's appropriation of it to address wives influenced by libertarian values was perhaps natural given its currency in ethical thought; but he insists on its theological basis (2:12).

The adjective "pure" ("chaste"; 1 Tim 5:22; see on 4:12; 5:2) completes the pair. It has various applications (e.g., of wisdom, Jas 3:17; of purity of motive, Phil 1:17), but its use in similar passages (1 Pet 3:2; cf. 2 Cor 11:2; Phil 4:8) and in this particular context indicates the meaning of sexual purity in the case of the wife.[54]

Further indication of disruption in the household comes in the third pair of terms that encourage effectiveness in running the household. The first term depicts domestic activity: "busy at home" ("domestic," RSV; "good managers of the household," NRSV). In using this rare term,[55] Paul expresses the ideal in Hellenistic and Jewish cultures that the wife should remain at home and occupy herself in running the household — and in doing so he echoes the complaint of those who criticized the morality of the "new woman."[56]

The final adjective can be translated variously as "good, kind, or benevolent" (etc.). It either qualifies and strengthens the preceding reference to domestic skill ("fulfill their household duties *well*"),[57] or stands alone as a reference to kindness.[58] The syntax favors the latter understanding and suggests that she is to show consideration to those with whom she has contact in carrying out her household duties.[59]

53. See 1 Tim 2:9 (Excursus).

54. Philo, *On the Special Laws* 2.30; 4 Macc 18:7; H. R. Balz, *EDNT* 1:22-23.

55. Gk. οἰκουργός (cf. n. 8 above; here only in the NT; elsewhere only in Soranus, p. 18, 2 [variant; 1-2 C.E.]); a compound of οἶκος ("household") and ἔργον ("work"). (See οἰκουρός, "watching the home," which is a variant here; on this form, see the note above) For the verb οἰκουργέω, see *1 Clement* 1.3.

56. See the discussion at 1 Tim 2:15. For the convergence of the various virtues applied to the younger women here (οἰκουρός/σώφρων/φίλανδρος), see esp. Philo, *On Rewards* 139. The opposite tendency (i.e., to be a gadabout) is criticized (Prov 7:11; 1 Tim 5:13).

57. Gk. ἀγαθός (see 1 Tim 1:5, discussion and note). Normally in these letters to coworkers, the adjective occurs in combination with other terms ("good conscience," 1 Tim 1:5, 19; "good works," 1 Tim 2:10; 5:10; 2 Tim 2:21; 3:17; Titus 1:16; 3:1; cf. "genuine faithfulness," Titus 2:10). For the view that it is dependent on the preceding adjective, see Dibelius and Conzelmann, 141; GNB; CEV.

58. TNIV; NRSV; and most commentators.

59. See the discussion in Marshall, 249.

Finally, the instructions invoke the most fundamental element of the household ethic concerning wives: younger wives must "be subject to their husbands." As we have seen,[60] when the NT writers employed the secular teaching on the household, certain nuances were added that distinguish the Christian from the secular use. The middle voice of the verb *(hypotassomai)* possibly softens the implication to the degree that the wife is to show submission to the husband of her own free will. And the stipulation that submission be shown to one's "own" husband (TNIV, "their") limits the relevance of the instruction. Yet in this application of the tradition, there is a noticeable lack of the attention to theological detail seen in Ephesians and Colossians, which suggests a less thoughtful, less nuanced instruction, or a more rudimentary and volatile situation. Whereas elsewhere in the tradition the wife's right to just treatment by her husband could be seen in the reciprocal address to the husband (Ephesians 5; Colossians 3; 1 Peter 3) and "subjection" is to be "in the Lord," here these notes are lacking (though the theological ground supplied in 2:11-14 should not be overlooked). This truncated application of what is elsewhere a more reflective apostolic use of the Greco-Roman household ethical tradition may indicate a response to a specific problem among young wives, in which the influence of Cretan values in the local teachers' message converged with the *avant-garde* ideals and freedoms of the emerging "new woman." Paul's response parallels the secular traditionalist response to such developments, with a major difference. This instruction for younger wives was designed to stabilize the household by calling them back from promiscuity to godliness and respectability. Yet at the forefront of Paul's thinking was not the collapse of society or the empire, but rather damage to the church's public image and witness.

The only motive expressly stated comes in the attached purpose clause *(hina)* that closes v. 5 (2:8, 10; 1 Tim 6:1). Expressed with a negative, it envisages an effect that is to be avoided: "that the word of God might not be blasphemed ["maligned," TNIV; "discredited," NRSV]." For "blaspheme" in the sense of "slander" (3:2), see on 1 Tim 1:20; 6:1. Paul's language echoes OT texts that lament the slandering of God's name among the nations due to Israel's sin (Isa 52:5; Ezek 36:20-36; CD 12:7-8), except that he shifts the concern to "the word of God."[61] This theme acquires more of a missionary slant in the NT as the concern for witness to outsiders develops (cf. 1 Tim 6:1; 1 Thess 4:12; 1 Pet 2:11-12). The fear is that unbelievers might trace the unconventional (and especially promiscuous) behavior of young women to

---

60. Gk. ὑποτάσσομαι ("to subject oneself"); see the full discussion and notes at 1 Tim 2:11.

61. For ὁ λόγος τοῦ θεοῦ as a reference to the gospel (with emphasis on its point of origin), see 1 Tim 1:15 (note); 1 Cor 14:36; 2 Cor 2:17; 4:2; Col 1:25; cf. Rom 9:6.

the Christian gospel they have embraced and the God in whom this message originated.

All Christian household codes address women and slaves (sometimes passing over husbands or masters) because of the fact that in their respective relationships to husbands and masters, their behavior as Christians would be carefully observed (particularly if their counterpart was not a believer).[62] The master determined the religion of the household, and conventional wisdom alleged that slaves and women were notorious for bringing home all kinds of new-fangled religions from the marketplace.[63] If a new religious conviction entered the equation, the potential for tension and strong reactions by unbelievers inside or outside of the household increased dramatically (1 Tim 6:1; 1 Pet 3:1-2). The negatively stated purpose reflects sensitivity to the kinds of suspicions that would revolve around a household into which the Christian faith had gained access. However, in this case, it was the church's standing, more than simply the husband's honor, that was at stake. As Winter observes:

> The terminology used in 2:4-5 helps provide a composite picture of what young married Christian women were being called upon to abandon and what they were being summoned back to do. They were to operate with modesty primarily in the arena of the "household" . . . which in the first century was distinguished from the other sphere, i.e., "the public place" *(politeia)*.[64]

Young women were married just after puberty, while husbands would be as many as ten years senior. Husbands routinely engaged in extramarital sexual activity, though this cultural norm was clearly opposed by Christian teaching (1:6; 1 Tim 3:2). Now, however, under the influence of the "new woman" paradigm, young Christian wives in Crete were apparently throwing caution and traditional cultural values to the winds, and pursuing sexual freedom. While outsiders to the faith, already suspicious of the Christian groups and their gatherings, would find more fuel for criticism in this unruly behavior of young wives, the Roman government had already proved itself ready to impose bans on any religious group suspected of sexual misconduct.[65] Both risks — to reputation and ongoing existence — could well have been in Paul's mind. But the focus of his concern is clear: behavior in the household was to be an endorsement of the gospel. The similar "purpose" clauses (2:8, 10), the concern for the opinion of outsiders (2:8, 10; 3:1-2, 8), and the strong statement of Paul's missionary calling in 1:1-3 indicate that

---

62. Cf. Bartsch, *Die Anfänge urchristlicher Rechtsbildungen,* 144-59.
63. Cicero, *Laws* 2.7.19-27.
64. Winter, *Roman Wives,* 166.
65. Winter, *Roman Wives,* 166.

the purpose of respectability goes beyond simply preservation and includes mission.[66]

6 The typical adverb "similarly" ("likewise"; 2:3) signals the next group — "young men." In comparison with the instructions that have gone before, young men are instructed very briefly and generally. However, in effect they will continue to be in mind through the discussion of the qualities Titus is to model and the manner in which he is to teach (cf. 1 Tim 4:12; 2 Tim 2:22). The shape of the instructions remains basically the same as those that have preceded; but, having traveled now some distance from v. 1, where the command mode was initiated ("you teach"; *lalei*) and continued with the repetition of the infinitive "to be" (vv. 2, 4 with the transitional "likewise," v. 3), Paul resumes the command explicitly with the imperative to Titus, "you encourage" (*parakalei;* 2:15; see on 1 Tim 1:3; 5:1). There is no significant difference between the two verbs in this setting; Titus's authority to instruct is clear in each case.

Corresponding to the twofold community classification already applied to women, "young men" refers to all the men yet to be addressed (see on 1 Tim 5:1; 1 Pet 5:5). We saw that the age range for the older groups was approximately forty years old and upward; younger men might be from twenty to thirty years of age, with some flexibility at the upward end. Titus is to "teach" young men "to be self-controlled in everything."[67] The verb, drawn from the *sōphrōn* word group and applied widely to all groups thus far (1:6; 2:2, 4, 5), intends the now-familiar range of meanings (self-controlled, sensible, prudent, moderate, etc.) that converge in the balanced, respectable lifestyle approved in the wider society.[68] The scope of its application, "in everything," suggests that this is to be the fundamental characteristic of their outward conduct. Moreover, the self-control called for is equally measured to pull these young men out of the sexually and otherwise indulgent lifestyle that was the norm in Cretan culture.[69] As throughout the passage, Paul re-

---

66. *Contra* Dibelius and Conzelmann, 140-41; see further Towner, *Goal,* 195-96; Marshall, 250; Padgett, "Wealthy Women at Ephesus"; Quinn, 138.

67. Against TNIV; NRSV; GNB; UBS³; Johnson, *Paul's Delegates,* 231; Lock, 141-42; Guthrie, 207, the prepositional phrase that begins v. 7, περὶ πάντα ("in all respects," "in everything") makes a better complement to the infinitive σωφρονεῖν and is an awkward addition to the instruction that follows (NA²⁷; UBS⁴; REB; NJB; Marshall, 253; Dibelius and Conzelmann, 141; Fee, 188; Quinn, 123).

68. Gk. σωφρονέω (see 1 Tim 2:9, Excursus) covers the same range of meaning as the noun and adjectival forms: "good judgment" (e.g., Rom 12:3); "clear-minded, reasonable, serious" (1 Pet 4:7; *1 Clement* 1.3; *Martyrdom of Polycarp* 4.3); "to be sane" (2 Cor 5:13); cf. U. Luck, *TDNT* 7:1103; Marshall, 182-84; Towner, *Goal,* 161-62; Quinn, 313-15.

69. Cf. Winter, *Roman Wives,* 164-65.

gards this manner of behavior from a theological perspective — made possible by the Christ-event and appropriated by faith in Christ (2:12).

7-8   From vv. 7b-8 the attention is focused on Titus, who is set into this context as a model for the young men.[70] Paul divides instructions to him into two categories. First, Paul considers the quality of Titus's observable life: "set them [show yourself to be] an example by doing what is good."[71] The task of "modeling" *(typos)* was intrinsic both to formal and informal ancient education (see on 1 Tim 4:12). Within his churches, Paul assigned himself this task (Phil 3:17; 1 Thess 1:6; 2 Thess 3:9), and Timothy (1 Tim 4:12) and Titus, church leaders (1 Pet 5:3), and believers in general (e.g., 1 Thess 1:7) were instructed to do likewise. In this case, the behavior to be modeled is described with the language of "good deeds" ("doing what is good"; 1:16; 2:14; 3:1, 8). This concept is important within these letters (and esp. in Titus) for depicting the observable dimension of the Christian life that faith produces (see 1 Tim 2:10, Excursus). The importance of this description in this passage can be seen in two ways. On the one hand, 2:14 concludes the theological foundation statement for this whole ethical passage by declaring explicitly that the new life (lit. "zeal for good deeds") is the purpose of Christ's self-offering. On the other hand, in modeling this life Titus will show himself to be the exact opposite of the opponents, whose lives lack any evidence of "good deeds" (1:16).

Second, Paul considers the character of his coworker's teaching in a way that will take in both content and teacher. At this point, the grammar becomes unclear. But we are probably to understand the guiding action still to be the imperatival middle voice participle "show yourself" of v. 7,[72] and the sphere or topic of the subsequent qualities to be "in your teaching" (as the TNIV). Yet within this sphere, as the instruction evolves, the thought moves rather freely between the two poles of teaching as activity and content, both of which can be in mind in the Greek term *didaskalia* (see 1:9); in the final

70. In Paul's day and culture, this task of modeling behavior would have fallen to the teachers/leaders and elders in the community (2 Macc 6:28, 31; Isocrates, *Nicocles* 57; Plato, *Laws* 5.729BC; etc.; cf. discussion in Wolter, *Paulustradition,* 192-93). Timothy qualifies as a model for others, despite his age, because of his status as a leader and coworker of Paul (1 Tim 4:12); in any case, it should not be assumed (*pace* Mounce, 413) that Titus was a νεώτερος; see Oberlinner, 116-17; Marshall, 254.

71. Gk. παρέχω (here mid.: "show oneself to be something"; for the act. form and meaning, see 1 Tim 1:4, note; 6:17) is active in meaning and imperative in force (cf. BDF §316.3). The presence of the reciprocal pronoun "yourself" (σεαυτόν; here as the first of the double accusative) is unnecessary but belongs to the personal exhortative style of these letters to coworkers (e.g., 1 Tim 4:7, 16; 5:22; 2 Tim 2:15; see further Spicq, 622).

72. In this case, the following accusatives "integrity," "seriousness," and "irreproachableness," modified by attendant phrases, serve as additional qualities to be exhibited by Titus in respect to teaching or what is taught.

accusative quality ("irreproachable with respect to the sound teaching," v. 8a) content emerges clearly.

The first qualification on teaching comes in the rare term often translated "integrity" and taken as a reference to Titus's disposition.[73] When one keeps in mind the corrupt motives of the opponents (1:11), a reference to purity of motive would perhaps be fitting at this point; for example, "show yourself to be above corruption in your teaching."[74] But the possibility remains that integrity (i.e., orthodoxy) of doctrine is meant (cf. 1:9).[75] Either way, the intentional contrast with the failure of the rebellious teachers is unmistakable.

Next, however, "seriousness" (or "dignity, gravity") is a clear reference to Titus's manner of teaching (assuming that "teaching," and not conduct in general, is still the sphere). Drawn from the dominant *semnos* word group (2:2; 1 Tim 2:2, Excursus; 3:4, 8, 11), this quality is meant to provide Titus's teaching with the accent of respectability that will distance it from the opponents' rambling arguments (1:10-11; 3:9) and disarm any critics outside the church before they get started (2:8b).

Thirdly (v. 8a), the shift to the content of teaching is made in the last of the qualifiers. The grammar is awkward and, again, less than clear,[76] but the sense is "show yourself to be . . . irreproachable with respect to the sound teaching." This translation conflicts with those of the TNIV and NRSV, which understand Titus's "speech" in general to be under consideration.[77] A transition from teaching to behavior in general, through the reference to "seriousness," is possible. But the use of the term *logos* for gospel is standard in this letter (1:3, 9; cf. 1 Tim 5:17); and medical language frequently describes the faith or gospel throughout these letters ("sound word").[78] Together these two terms (noun, "word"; adjective, "sound, healthy") most likely mean in effect "the authorized gospel."[79] Consequently, with Titus's ministry in view,

73. Gk. ἀφθορία (only here in the NT; "soundness, incorruption"; see G. Harder, *TDNT* 9:103); the semantic range is best determined by the cognate adjective ἄφθορος (BDAG, s.v.); literally "incorruption," it seems to denote "innocence," which may make a better reference to disposition than to content.

74. See Kelly, 242; Mounce, 413; Quinn, 142.

75. E.g., Brox, 296; Schlarb, *Die gesunde Lehre*, 298.

76. The phrase λόγον ὑγιῆ ἀκατάγνωστον consists of three accusatives: the first two are noun and modifying adjective ("sound teaching"), followed by an accusative adjective (pred.) that is the last object loosely attached to the preceding verbal form "show yourself to be" (v. 7, παρεχόμενος). "Sound teaching" is that in respect of which Titus is to be "irreproachable" (for acc. of respect with adj., see BDF §160).

77. So also GNB; CEV; NKJV; NASB.

78. So 1:9, 13; 2:1, 2, 5; cf. 3:8; see on 1 Tim 1:10.

79. Cf. Quinn, 141, separating "irreproachable" from the two preceding words, suggests the meaning "sound in preaching." As Marshall, 256, points out, this interpretation requires too many changes of thought in the sequence (2:7-8) to be likely.

this instruction is a counterpart to the command to older men to be "sound in faith" (2:2).

As an evaluation of Titus's handling of the gospel, especially in this context of opposition and controversy (v. 8b), "irreproachable" (TNIV, "cannot be condemned") will imply the meaning "irrefutable" and almost "unassailable."[80] But it is essential that we understand that this effect will be achieved by commitment to the apostolic doctrine (i.e., purity of what is preached), not by rhetorical prowess. And it is by faithfully discharging this duty (keeping the contract of the letter) that opponents or outsiders will be disarmed: they will have nothing (of substance) to say against his preaching.

This last point is developed into the purpose *(hina)* for the last stipulation and probably for the whole instruction to Titus (vv. 7-8a). Paul is concerned for reputation: "so that those who oppose you [lit. the opponent] may be ashamed because they have [he has] nothing bad to say about us." But the focus of this concern, "the opponent,"[81] and the threat to be neutralized require closer inspection. First, the singular "opponent" in this context could refer to those outside the church (2:5, 10; 3:2, 8),[82] to the opponents inside the church (1:9-16),[83] or to both of these groups together.[84] We have to bear in mind that Paul's concerns in this letter do indeed align themselves along two fronts: the concern for respectability within the culture (2:5, 10), and the concern for the disruption caused in the church by the rebellious Jewish Cretan teachers. But these concerns are by no means mutually exclusive. This section of teaching instructs the church in household behavior that conforms to society's traditional sense of propriety. Nonconformity would bring the Christian message under suspicion (2:5) either for lack of discernment of deplorable Cretan ways, or for seeming to endorse the libertarian values of the "new woman." An equal danger, the one just addressed, is that inappropriate behavior would ruin the reputation of the one who bears that message. The indication of the letter is that the Jewish-Christian teachers were a domi-

80. Gk. ἀκατάγνωστος ("not condemned, beyond reproach"; only here in the NT); the term is rare, occurring in legal contexts (2 Macc 4:47) and in the sense of abiding by the terms of a contract (see refs. to the inscriptions in Spicq, *TLNT* 1:58).

81. Gk. ἐναντίος (adj.; "opposite, against, contrary") is substantivized by the addition of the article in the combination ὁ ἐξ ἐναντίας (definite art. + the prep. + gen. adj.; cf. BDF §241.1) and gives the sense "one who is opposite" (so Mark 15:39 in a purely local sense). For the sense of "opposition" with hostility, see 1 Thess 2:15; 1 Esdr 1:25. The idea of opposition is expressed in several ways in these letter to coworkers (Titus 1:9; 1 Tim 5:14; 2 Tim 2:25, "the one who opposes").

82. Lock, 142; Spicq, 623.

83. Knight, 313; Kelly, 242; Oberlinner, 118.

84. Mounce, 414; Fee, 189; Johnson, 235 (uncertain). Chrysostom regarded the singular as a reference to Satan (PG 62:684; cf. 1 Tim 3:6-7).

nant threat to the Pauline mission, and here the singular "one who opposes" is a more likely reference to them (1:9), and possibly even to a ringleader among them. And Titus's primary task in Crete includes engaging this opposition. But ultimately here too the concern would extend to society at large, where the disruption caused by the convergence in the Christian households of base teaching and cultural movements would be held against the church.

Clearly, there is a lot resting on the shoulders of Titus, for he is instructed to place his conduct and preaching on the line for the Pauline mission team as prevention against the opponents' allegations.[85] "The opponent" is described as already present and making allegations or spreading rumors of some sort. What Paul intends is that Titus's good behavior and teaching will provide no grounds for a charge that will stick (lit. "having no report of our worthlessness").[86] And the strategy is: if the claims of the opponents prove to be empty, their reputation will be discredited ("be put to shame"; *entrapē*).[87] Elsewhere Paul can use the prospect of "shame" (i.e., of losing respect within the community) to bring erring believers back into line (1 Cor 4:14; 6:5; 15:34; 2 Thess 3:14).[88] Here, however, Paul hopes that "shame" will fall to those opponents because their criticism of the mission team proves groundless — their reputation and message will be discredited in society. Paul is also in touch with the reverse of the OT theme echoed in 2:5 — now "All who rage against you will surely be ashamed and disgraced [*entrapēsontai*]; those who oppose you will be as nothing and perish" (Isa 41:11; cf. 45:16).

In any case, the answer to moral disturbance in the churches and Christian households is not to cease mission operations, but rather to continue in them in full awareness of what constitutes culturally superior behavior. And Titus is to exhibit this quality in the context of his ministry as well.

85. Titus's representative role and an already present attack against the Pauline mission (or possibly the whole church) are indicated in the phrase "about us" (περὶ ἡμῶν).

86. Gk. μηδὲν ἔχων λέγειν περὶ ἡμῶν φαῦλον; grammatically, the circumstantial participle (ἔχων; "having") introduces the cause of the opponent's "shame" ("*because [he] has* no bad report about us"). Marshall, 256, suggests that Gk. φαῦλος ("worthless") is actually the charge that they would make if the grounds existed. In NT usage (John 3:20; 5:29; Rom 9:11; 2 Cor 5:10; Jas 3:16), the term describes behavior, but in the LXX it describes speech as well (Job 6:3, 25; Prov 5:3; cf. Quinn, 126), making a general reference to the behavior and teaching of the Pauline mission team likely.

87. Gk. ἐντρέπω (aor. pass., "to shame" [as here "to be put to shame"; 1 Cor 4:14; 2 Thess 3:14] or "to show respect for"). In the sense of embarrassment, see 1 Esdr 1:45; Ignatius, *To the Magnesians* 12.1.

88. See the discussion in D. A. deSilva, *Honor, Patronage, Kinship and Purity* (Downers Grove, IL: InterVarsity Press, 2000), 73-84; Osiek and Balch, *Families in the New Testament World*, 48-54; A. J. Malherbe, *The Letters to the Thessalonians* (AB 32B; New York: Doubleday, 2000), 459-60.

9-10   The final household group to be instructed is slaves (cf. 1 Tim 6:1-2a). As we have seen, it is not unusual for slaves to be addressed in this type of instruction. That masters are not addressed might indicate that the Christian slaves of unbelievers are in view (1 Tim 6:1).[89] Then, again, it may simply have been a case (as with younger wives) that the Cretan situation required that the member of the household pair most vulnerable to criticism or most affected by the disruption be instructed.[90] Slaves were known for their readiness to embrace new religions.[91] While this generally did not disrupt the family religious practices, the intolerant nature of Christianity (and Judaism) became an irritant within the otherwise rather tolerant households,[92] and any religion or teaching that might be seen as disruptive to this sector of society would have been regarded with suspicion. In a situation where the respectability of a household was likely to be under close observation, subordinates would be observed most closely for evidence of nonconformist or unruly behavior. Many have argued that this kind of teaching simply reflects the church's surrender to a cultural status quo, the endorsement of a secular ethic.[93] But this ignores the alternative possibility, argued by myself and numerous others: the purpose statements of these instructions and other textual cues suggest that Paul and other early Christian writers regarded the church's calling in the world as a robust, redemptive role. Elements that (in the absence of the purpose clauses) might reflect secularization are actually evidence of the kind of theological negotiation required by the conviction that the social structure could be more easily redeemed from the inside out.

The specific shape of the instruction is conventional enough until the purpose is reached. The instruction consists of a basic command, "to be subject," followed by four additional commands, given in a brief chiasmus, that spell out "subjection" in this case: positive, negative, negative, positive. Finally, a purpose clause (2:5, 7) sets the respectability of this household institution into a Christian, theological context.

---

89. The church on Crete at this early point may not have had many (or any) members who had the means to be masters (Marshall, 258).

90. Cf. the views: Fee, 190 (slaves in Christian households); Knight, 314; Hanson, 182 (slaves in non-Christian households); Marshall, 258; Mounce, 415 (no specification, general applicability intended).

91. See Cicero, *Laws* 2.7.19-27; Gülzow, *Christentum und Sklaverei,* 74-75; M. I. Finley, *Ancient Slavery and Modern Ideology* (New York: Viking, 1980), 93-122 (cited in Johnson, *Paul's Delegates,* 235).

92. See Osiek and Balch, *Families in the New Testament World,* 83; 1 Tim 6:2; 1 Cor 7:12-16; 1 Pet 3:1; each text reflects the presence of this sort of tension in the household.

93. E.g., Osiek and Balch, *Families in the New Testament World,* 182-85; Fiorenza, *In Memory of Her.*

Society's stricter emphasis on subordination in the case of slaves in relation to their masters can perhaps be seen, in comparison to wives, in the overriding instruction "be subject to their own masters *in everything.*" The same verb that is used of wives, *hypotassomai,* forms the substance of the instruction that began at v. 6 ("encourage/urge . . ."). Within the household-code tradition, the meaning of "subjection" shifts somewhat from one relationship and usage to another, making the shape of the subjection due the authoritative counterpart (rulers, masters, husbands, fathers) different depending on the relationship under consideration (see on 1 Tim 2:11). But on the whole this verb called for observance of the household relationship according to the terms of society. There is also the characteristic limitation placed on the instructions ("be subject to *their [own]* masters"; 2:5; 1 Tim 6:1).[94] But otherwise "subjection" is to be exhibited extensively: "in everything."[95]

This scope is not so much narrowed[96] as it is spelled out in certain details in the four phrases that follow. They are given in contrasting pairs, with the specific negatives supplying the directions for the broader positives.

First, "subjection" to masters means "to please" them. "Pleasing" is a measurement of acceptable service. In the NT, the term is most often used of pleasing God; in the case of a master, the slave will achieve this quality of service by meeting the superior's expectations in acceptable, satisfactory fashion (cf. Exod 21:8).[97]

Second, the shortcoming to be avoided gives definition to the scope of conduct that is "pleasing." In this context (cf. 1:9, note), "do not talk back" aims at avoiding charges of defiance that might be leveled against obstinate, disobedient slaves who question their masters and refuse to do what they are

94. On the term δεσπότης for "master" (of human masters, 1 Tim 6:1, 2; 1 Pet 2:18; of God, Luke 2:29; Acts 4:24; of Christ, 2 Pet 2:1; Jude 4), see the discussion and note at 1 Tim 6:1 (K. H. Rengstorf, *TDNT* 2:44-49). Knight, 314, suggests that the term makes a better reference to non-Christian masters, but 1 Tim 6:2 is surely against this.

95. The Gk. phrase ἐν πᾶσιν ("in all things," "in everything," "in every respect") is rightly taken as modifying the infinitive ὑποτάσσεσθαι (e.g., TNIV), instead of the following εὐαρέστους (NRSV; RSV; GNB). The phrase recalls Col 3:22 ("obey . . . in everything"; ὑπακούετε κατὰ πάντα); taken with the closing phrase of the purpose clause in v. 10 (also ἐν πᾶσιν), "in all things" becomes an *inclusio* that links the fullness of the slaves' submission to the fullness of the endorsement of "God's teaching" that respectable behavior might supply.

96. If in fact the four additional commands are not traditional in character, they probably are meant to develop the general command ("subjection in all things") in ways that will remedy specific problems in the behavior of Cretan Christian slaves, rather than to keep slaves from taking "in all things" so literally that they would do anything their masters might command (*pace* Mounce, 415).

97. Gk. εὐάρεστος (adj.; "pleasing, acceptable"); Rom 12:1, 2; 14:18; 2 Cor 5:9; Eph 5:10; Phil 4:18; Col 3:20; Heb 13:21. Cf. W. Foerster, *TDNT* 1:456-57.

told. This tendency (along with dishonesty; see below) belonged to the cultural caricature of the lazy, good-for-nothing slave.[98]

Third (v. 10), "stealing"[99] from masters formed another part of the traditional caricature of the lazy, dishonest slave population.[100] Undoubtedly, the temptation to improve one's situation in this way was great, and perhaps changes brought about in a Christian household offered more opportunities for theft (cf. Phlm 18). Christian slaves were not to fall to this temptation.

Fourth, the positive contrast ("but"; *alla*) to the stereotypical behavior calls slaves to demonstrate their complete trustworthiness or reliability in the household situation. The wide scope of this instruction ("in every way, in all things") intentionally recalls the breadth of the general call to be in subjection. The syntax is difficult, but in this ethical context, where the basic instruction contrasts a negative aspect of behavior (theft) with a demonstration of good conduct, and where conventional ideals are being crafted into this parenesis, the Greek term *pistis* will be understood as the virtue of "trustworthiness, faithfulness, or reliability" (Gal 5:22), not in the sense of "believing."[101] Paul's choice of verbs, "to show, demonstrate" (3:2; see on 1 Tim 1:16), is in keeping with the emphasis on visible respectability in these instructions, and, as in 3:2, denotes an observable (public) display with the power to convince.[102]

Two adjectives respectively strengthen and then qualify the scope of this display of loyalty. First, "trustworthiness" is strengthened by the addition of "all" ("fully," TNIV; "complete," NRSV) so that it covers all situa-

98. See the references in K. R. Bradley, *Slavery and Society at Rome* (New York: Cambridge University Press, 1994), 28 n. 26, 35 n. 54; See Marshall, 260 (citing Spicq, 625, who establishes this caricature of slaves in ancient comedy).

99. Gk. νοσφίζω ("to put aside for oneself, keep back, steal, pilfer"; here in a subst. ptc.; Acts 5:2, 3; 2 Macc 4:32). The term covers a range of thievery; it denotes, in this context, pilfering or fraudulent use of something (stealing from the boss or misusing something put in one's charge; misappropriation); Spicq, *TLNT* 2:546-47. See the reference to Columella in the following note.

100. On the caricature of slaves, see Osiek and Balch, *Families in the New Testament World,* 80 (citing Columella, *De re rustica* 1.7.6-7 [Ash in Loeb]); Quinn, 149, who assembles the statements from the Jewish, Greek, and Roman writers: *Pirqe 'Abot* (2:8; StrB 4:732); Xenophon, *Memorabilia* 2.1.16; Menander, *Aspis* 397-98; Pliny, *Natural History* 33.6.26-27. See also references in Marshall, 260; Spicq, 625.

101. See on 1 Tim 1:2. So also Quinn, 149; Marshall, 260; Fee, 191. See Dittenberger, *Sylloge* 727.20; for the sentiment see Philo, *On the Decalogue* 167. See below for the discussion of Wallace's interpretation.

102. The "juridical" meaning of ἐνδείκνυμι sometimes implied in the verb ("demonstration of proof"; Rom 2:15; 2 Tim 4:14 [possibly]; Quinn, 149) is not particularly evident here.

737

tions.[103] Thus in effect a positive stereotype is commissioned to counter society's negative caricature.

Second, the addition of the adjective "good, true, perfect" (*agathē;* 1:16)[104] at the end of the sentence has proven more difficult to account for in English translation. The TNIV apparently collapses the two adjectives into "fully," while the NRSV suggests "*complete* and *perfect* fidelity."[105] Possibly, however, the addition of the final adjective (here meaning "genuine, true") was intended to define more precisely what should constitute trustworthiness or reliability in the household, or, rather, what should not. In this case, *agathē* perhaps intends to set moral limits to the wide scope of the instruction, so that the slave will not feel compelled by the duty of loyalty to carry out evil commands given by the master; for example, "but showing complete faithfulness in [with respect to] what is good."[106]

Above we noticed the two purpose clauses that were expressed in the negative. The first (2:5) regarded good conduct as a way of protecting the Christian message from slander. The second (2:8) functioned similarly but with the reputation of the Pauline mission team (and/or perhaps the Christian community) in mind. This third purpose clause *(hina)* provides clearly and positively stated motivation for the slave's behavior (v. 10c) that marks the motivational crescendo of the whole of the household parenesis (vv. 1-10). Logically, any of the *hina* clauses could apply to all of the instructions. In the case of the closing purpose, what is most noticeable, in comparison with the previous two, is the climactic effect achieved by its placement at the end, by its language, and by its missiological thrust. Three aspects of this statement should be considered.

First, the purpose of behavior endorsed is to positively adorn "the teaching about God." As we have seen, "the teaching" *(didaskalia;* 1:9; 2:7) is one of several terms used to describe the Christian message (gospel, doctrine, ethics).[107] Its use here forms a bracket with the reference to "sound

103. For this typical use of the adjective πᾶς ("all"), see also 2:15; 3:2.

104. See 1 Tim 2:10 (Excursus).

105. D. B. Wallace, *The Basics of New Testament Syntax* (Grand Rapids: Zondervan, 2000), 86, 139, cites this phrase (ἀλλὰ πᾶσαν πίστιν ἐνδεικνυμένους ἀγαθήν) as an example of a verb that takes an object-complement combination (i.e., "faith" [πίστιν] is the obj. of the ptc. [show/demonstrate]; and "good" [ἀγαθήν] is the obj.'s complement), yielding "but showing forth all *faith* to be *good.*" While this is a grammatical possibility, the additional conclusion that "if taken this way, the text seems to support the idea that saving faith does not fail, but actually results in good works," rests on a mistaken translation of πίστις, which in this case almost certainly means "trustworthiness/faithfulness," not "faith."

106. See Quinn, 149; Marshall, 261; Ellicott, 185.

107. See on 1 Tim 1:10.

doctrine" in 2:1 that places all of the contents in between into the category of "the teaching."

But in what sense can "the teaching" be "made attractive" ("to adorn")? The language is frequently used of outward adornment and beauty.[108] Applied figuratively to the Christian message, the sense is that the conduct enjoined would augment or draw attention to the beauty that already exists. Spicq has linked this usage to honor, benefaction, and tribute, which suggests that here again (see 1 Tim 6:1-2) Paul is playing subtly with (co-opting and redefining) the very social fixtures he calls Christians to live among: "So slaves . . . *at the bottom of the human hierarchy,* are able, through the splendor of their conduct, to honor God and increase the attractiveness of the gospel in the hearts of pagans."[109] Ordinarily, it was the well-to-do benefactors, not slaves or the masses, who gave "adornments" to cities and leaders in return for public recognition. But life in Christ involved many reversals.

Second, the content of the teaching is described as "about God our Savior." "Our Savior" is a normal appellation for God the Father (1:3; 2:13; 3:4) that expresses the conviction that the church exists because of God's saving action.[110] While this choice of description serves as the transition to the theological statement to follow, its relation to "the apostolic doctrine" that Paul has been teaching implies two things. First, the objective genitive relation of "God our Savior" to the teaching (rightly TNIV; cf. 1:3) does not reduce the content of "the teaching" to a message of salvation. Rather, as this passage reveals, the whole of life comes under the category of salvation, and the whole of life is regarded as a source of knowledge about the God who saves. For this reason, the short phrase "in every way" ("in all things") is repeated from v. 9 (see note) to bring the whole of the slave's life within the scope of this instruction.

Yet, with the outside observer surely in view, it is precisely this behavior — of slaves, but also younger men, younger women, older women, and older men — in accordance with "the sound doctrine" that is able to project an accurate picture of life in relation to the God who saves.

Thirdly, with this observation, the missiological goal of this motivation for Christian living emerges. Life itself — and here it is life lived in very ordinary circumstances with regard to the expectations of secular society — augments, supports, endorses, and illustrates "the teaching about God our Savior." Respectability in the household is not surrender to secular influence

---

108. For Gk. κοσμέω ("to adorn, make attractive, put in order"), see 1 Tim 2:9 (discussion and note).

109. Spicq, *TLNT* 2:330-35 (335; emphasis mine).

110. For Gk. σωτήρ, see 1 Tim 1:1 (discussion and notes).

(the modern interpretation); nor is it a clinging to the ordinary in order to protect the church's existence in a hostile climate. In fact, the household as the center of society was under attack from converging cultural forces. Its central place in life made it the strategic hill to be taken by the gospel if Christianity was going to prove its redemptive capability in the world. The point of the theological passage to follow is that the life Paul expects Cretan believers to live in this context is not an ordinary life in the least; it is the product of the Christ-event. And the implication is that the gospel creates a people capable of living within human society, observing its institutions, speaking its language, embracing its good values, while reshaping and retooling others, in order to bring redemption to it.

b. The Basis of This Life (2:11-14)

> 11 *For the grace of God has appeared that offers salvation to all people.* 12 *It teaches us to say "No" to ungodliness and worldly passions, and to live self-controlled, upright and godly lives in this present age,* 13 *while we wait for the blessed hope — the appearing of the glory of our great God and Savior, Jesus Christ,* 14 *who gave himself for us to redeem us from all wickedness and to purify for himself a people that are his very own, eager to do what is good.*

This section is a densely packed statement of theology that in some ways marks the rhetorical high point of the letter. Owing to the shift in grammar and the elevated language, the reader or hearer will know instinctively that this section is crucial to Paul's discourse for several reasons. First, it is intentionally linked to the preceding passage by the connecting "for" *(gar)* and by the statement that follows in v. 15, which repeats the instructions of v. 1 and forms a closing bracket around the whole of 2:1-15. Second, the language of this section reverberates in such a way that the Cretans will have heard in it a subversive retelling of some dominant parts of their cultural story.

Pauline Christology and Cretan Mythology. At this point in the letter, Paul intensifies the critique (already underway) of various elements of the Greek and Roman story generally pertinent to Crete, while he also takes up a theme only hinted at in the introduction. We saw in 2:1-10 how he played with the current language of ethical discourse in the empire, presenting the Christian life in terms of virtues and aspects of behavior that would be immediately recognizable as traditionally respectable in that culture. This ploy does not reflect a surrender to worldliness, but rather, as the purpose clauses suggest (and this theological section confirms), makes a higher claim to virtue while contextualizing the gospel. This strategy reaches its high point

740

here, as the life already set out among household relationships is summed up with the cardinal virtues and then by means of the Hellenistic concept of *paideia* (education in civilization) placed into a theological setting (2:12). Paul thus claims for the gospel the aspirations of the best of Hellenistic and early Imperial ethics, but carefully explains the difference that exists in authentic Christian living by linking it to the saving act(s) of God.

At the same time, the sheer contrast between the life he has described in 2:2-10 (which reaches a climax at 2:12) and both the Cretan stereotype (1:12) and the values of the "new woman" is unmistakable.[1] Recalling Paul's concern for the cultural influences converging in the community, the conclusion is hard to miss: the life endorsed by the culture-imbued teaching of the Cretan Jewish-Christian teachers lacks the distance from old worldly patterns that would reflect the gracious touch of God (cf. 3:3-7).

But the language of the passage cuts in another decisive direction as it resumes a theme initiated quietly in 1:2-4. On the one hand, the language of "grace," "salvation," "appearance/epiphany," and the title "great God and Savior" all figure in the discourse that surrounded the Imperial cult.[2] Not surprisingly, scholars have argued that here (and in 3:4) God and Christ are depicted in the language used of the emperor (and other hero-gods) as benefactor and savior of the people. If this is the case, the question would be why Paul would choose to do this. Presumably, his intention would be apologetic or evangelistic, and Paul's claim would be a final one: the intended implication of such wordplay would be that the benefaction and gifts of God and Christ exceed those of human emperors, just as the salvation connected with the epiphanies of Christ cause the temporal acts of salvation provided by these human figures to pale in significance.

However, on the other hand, Kidd's research[3] suggests that in the Cretan environment this language would seek to penetrate a more specific religious and political dialogue that in fact must be seen to overlap in some respects with the more widely known Imperial religion. At the start of the letter (see on 1:2) Paul contends that his God is the one who "does not lie," in pointed contrast to the Zeus of Cretan tales who in fact did lie to have sexual relations with a human woman (taking the human form of her husband). Zeus was also held to be the epitome of virtue (defined by his possession of the cardinal virtues). Moreover, in the midst of the humanistic Cretan religious challenge to the Olympian traditionalists — that is, the claim that Zeus was born and died on Crete, the insistence on his humanity — the tendency of Zeus to be portrayed as one who received divine status

1. See Kidd, "Titus as *Apologia*," 185-209.
2. See Dibelius and Conzelmann, 143-46; Danker, *Benefactor.*
3. Kidd, "Titus as *Apologia*," 196-201.

from humans in return for the benefactions he bestowed on them suggests an upside-down approach to "theology" at the popular level that would force a collision between the Christian gospel and the cultural myth. For Paul simply to speak of the Son of God becoming a human being, in traditional incarnational language (e.g., 1 Tim 2:5), would be to open the gospel up to all kinds of Cretan misinterpretation. A Cretan view of the gods made room for such developments. Their truncated views of virtue and the virtuous life made easy use of the language to which Paul appealed in setting out the Christian way of life.

But of course Paul's apologetic starting point in this culture was the one attributed to that Cretan prophet: "Cretans are always liars." What began as a religious lie — that god emerges from humanity — developed into a lie that infected all of life, as the virtues associated with Zeus (and heralded by popular philosophy) proved absent in this culture. And Paul's choice of the ethical language was confrontational and remedial. He did not use the language simply to endorse the lifestyle, but to show that authentic virtuous living — that which was sought by traditional ethical writers and disdained by Cretan values and the "new woman" paradigm — was "taught" by the Christian God. If Kidd is right, and there is much to commend his more focused Cretan interpretation, this theological section aims to oppose wrong theology with right theology: it stresses that Christ, the grace of God (v. 11), and the glory of God (see below on v. 13) "appeared" among humans from above, not from below; and that he conferred gifts in this exalted role, instead of obtaining exaltation (and perhaps deity, but see below on v. 13) in return for his gift/benefaction; and finally the life of virtue that characterizes God is a life that God communicates to his people. They will live the life that exposes the cultural lie (leaders and household members must exhibit the life). At the same time, they must resist the alternative lies associated with Cretan life, the tainted message of the opposition, and the libertarian values of the "new woman": these things, especially when spun into an opposing message, assume the proportions of a religious lie.

The interplay of Paul's discourse may seem overly subtle to the modern eye, but the language and concepts and the religious and political myth brought to expression by them were central to the "story" of Cretan and Roman culture. And the crosscutting intrusions that Paul's gospel made into this story were designed to place the significance of the Christian story of salvation into bold relief within the linguistic and conceptual contours of the existing story.

These introductory observations suggest the need to analyze this passage with sensitivity to more than just grammar, though it is here that we must start. As with some of the other theological pieces in these letters to coworkers, this one consists of a single, complex Greek sentence. Grammatically, the sentence moves steadily from left to right (see below). The noun phrase and main verb in v. 11 actually form the topic, but the participle "teaching" that modifies this topic controls the whole direction of the sentence. A layout of the structure will make the development of thought easy to see. I diverge from the TNIV translation where necessary, in order to set out the argument according to the Greek structure:

"For
1. the <u>grace of God</u> . . . <u>has appeared</u> to all people
    2. <u>teaching</u> us
          ↓
          ↓ 3b. to deny ungodliness and worldly passions,
          ↓ ↓

          3a. <u>to live</u> self-controlled, upright, and godly lives in this present age,
            ↑

          3c. to wait for the blessed hope
               = <u>the appearance of the glory of our great God and Savior,</u>
                       ↑

        . . . . = Jesus Christ,
          who gave himself for us
                  in order   to redeem us from all wickedness
                              purify for himself a people . . .
                                    his very own,
                                    eager to do what is good."

   (i) The past appearing of God's grace (1.) initiated a process of "teaching" (2.);

  (ii) "Teaching" in turn made a particular kind of life possible (3abc.);

 (iii) This life is the focal point, the point toward which the hearer/reader is drawn.

 (iv) When the element of hope is reached (3c.), further definition of the second "appearance" and the Person associated with this event continues the rightward, grammatical movement of the sentence, though thematically there is a return leftward to earlier topics. The parallelism with the opening phrase (1.) is striking: the grace of God has appeared . . . [our hope =] the glory of God will appear.

The grammatical analysis sheds significant light on cause-and-effect relationships. But the language play reveals deeper structures of meaning.

     Thus, read thematically or semantically, the statement can be seen to turn back on itself in a circular fashion that illuminates the character of both the theology and the picture of Christian existence linked to it.

Event — Epiphany: God's grace, carrying salvation, appeared in history;

Process — A closer inspection of the sort of life provided for the present age reveals its Hellenistic conceptualization in terms of the cardinal virtues. This tendency already seen in the ethical vocabulary of the letter determines the choice here to describe the process that stands between the event and the new life as "teaching or training" (*paideia*);

Fulfillment — But in the Christian co-opting of this educative framework some reshaping takes place. The virtuous life acquired through *paideia* is not a discrete product. First, it is contingent on a prior denial of old, worldly ways (conversion; 3b.). Second, it is also dependent on a future epiphany-event for its fulfillment (hope; 3c.). And it is particularly at this point in the statement that Greek thought gives way to traditional Christian theology. In the Eschaton another epiphany-event must occur. It is linked lexically and conceptually to the first epiphany. And when the future event is finally described in terms of the person who will appear — "the glory of our great God and Savior, Jesus Christ" — he is defined (as the ultimate expression of God's glory) on the basis of his past act of self-offering. The purpose of this self-offering is precisely the theological equivalent (redemption/purification leading to ethical renewal) of the results produced by "teaching" (the present virtuous life, 3ab.). Although described obliquely as "the appearing of God's grace," v. 11 has the redemptive appearance of Christ in human history (v. 14) in mind all along.

Understood in this way, the theological passage provides the foundation for the ethical teaching that has just been laid down (2:1-10). Only now what has been prescribed is to be seen clearly as an outworking of grace, linked intrinsically to the death of Christ and the new way of life associated with that event. The language of Greek ethics is indeed sufficient to describe the observable dimension of this life, and it is an effective communication technique (both in Crete and in the wider Greco-Roman culture); but Christian theology is required to explain the power, character, and origin of this way of life that, outside of the faith, remains in the category of "the ideal."

It is a moot point whether this passage (as others in these letters to Titus and Timothy) was a preformed tradition already in use in some setting or other.[4] Surely 2:14 belongs in this category (1 Tim 2:6a; Mark 10:45; see be-

4. See Towner, *Goal*, 108-11; Marshall, 263-66.

low). But enough of the language appears elsewhere in these three letters (and elsewhere in Paul) to suggest that at the very least the passage has been carefully crafted to fit the discussion at this point in the letter. If Paul didn't create the material, he has nevertheless made it his own.

The argument that says that Paul never used this kind of language or these Hellenistic concepts before, and therefore that what we have here is a post-Pauline development[5] simply fails to do justice to the similar kinds of interaction — clashing of stories, co-opting of concepts — that occur elsewhere in the undisputed Pauline writings. New accents and language are chosen to address a new situation.

11 The theological rationale ("for"; *gar*) for the new life begins with a novel reference to the gospel message. "The grace of God that offers salvation" (TNIV) is a roundabout way of referring to the contents of the gospel message. We know from the verb "appeared" that "grace" (see on 1 Tim 1:2) here means the saving act itself as that which gave full expression to "the grace of God." Paul is fond of the phrase "the grace of God,"[6] and often uses it to denote some experience of God's benevolence. Here the further definition, "offering salvation" (or "with saving power"),[7] establishes what Paul means by the phrase by locating it in the salvation associated with the Christ-event. Now he stresses two major points about the gospel.

First, the language of epiphany (here in the verb "appeared"; 3:4) depicts the event (still to be described in the context) as a divine appearance of helping intervention (cf. 2:13).[8] The pluriform background of the epiphany language prepared it for use for Paul. It figured significantly in Hellenistic and especially Imperial religious and political discourse — of gods, heroes, and especially of the emperor — and was descriptive of YHWH's acts in the LXX. Such connections allowed Paul to access and combine the ideas of pre-existence, divine manifestation to save, and royal visitation. All of this gives to the Christ-event the character of a massive incursion of the invisible, divine into visible human history. Moreover, it is not simply a reference to the

5. Dibelius and Conzelmann, 142; Barrett, 137; Hanson, 184; etc.

6. For ἡ χάρις τοῦ θεοῦ, see Rom 5:15; 1 Cor 1:4; 3:10; 15:10; 2 Cor 1:12; 6:1; 8:1; 9:14; Gal 2:21; Eph 3:2, 7; Col 1:6; 2 Thess 1:12.

7. Gk. σωτήριος (here only in the NT; LXX Wis 1:14; 3 Macc 6:31; 4 Macc 15:26; Philo, *On the Embassy to Gaius* 151; for the σῴζω word group, see 1 Tim 1:15, note); here the adjective without the article is a predicate to "the grace of God" (giving "the grace of God appeared with saving power"), not attributive ("the saving grace of God appeared"; see Moule, *Idiom Book,* 114; BDF §269.3). By using a predicate adjective, Paul makes the intention or result of salvation somewhat more emphatic. Cf. W. Foerster and G. Fohrer, *TDNT* 7:1021-24; Spicq, *TLNT* 3:356-57.

8. Gk. ἐπιφαίνω (aor. pass.; "to cause something to be seen, show, appear"; Luke 1:79; Acts 27:20); see 1 Tim 6:14 (Excursus).

appearance of a person but rather of the whole saving event revolving around that person.[9]

Secondly, the event bringing salvation is universal in scope: "to all people."[10] It is not immediately clear why this stress is added;[11] if it was not intended to address a tinge of elitism in the opponents' doctrines or outlook,[12] then it underlines the vastness of the salvation produced by God's grace. It is in any case typical of the presentation of God's salvific will in these letters to coworkers (3:2; 1 Tim 2:1-6; 2 Tim 2:19; 4:17) and accords well with Paul's emphasis on the universality of access to God's grace throughout his letters.

But why does he reflect on the Christ event in this allusive, theocentric way? We began above to consider the intentions of this language, arriving at the suggestion that Paul sought for a way to engage the local, Cretan story of a man-become-god, and specifically to turn this story around by using the same language to make a bold claim about the God of the covenant. In this verse the thrust and parry begins with references to "grace," "God," "salvation," and "epiphany." While all of this would be equally suitable as a response to the specific claims of the emperor cult (see on 1 Tim 6:14), the evidence that Paul has been dialoguing with Cretans all along suggests that he may have been thinking here more pointedly of the still narrower Cretan adaptation of this lexicon in crafting its peculiar "lie." (Yet for Cretan culture the Roman Imperial story would have overlapped with the Cretan mythology.)

In any case, the signal that we were entering into this particular discourse came in the reference to God as "Savior" in 2:10. The language of benefaction and divine prerogative were applied to Crete's Zeus (as also to the emperor), so that his "appearances" among his people (in victory or to bring aid in some way) were marked by "grace" gifts and salvation benefits, all of which demonstrated his virtue to the people.[13] They in turn made a man

9. Here made explicit in the addition of the adjective σωτήριος. See the discussion and excursus at 1 Tim 6:14.

10. The NIV takes the phrase πᾶσιν ἀνθρώποις ("to/for all people") with the verb, yielding "the grace of God that brings salvation has appeared to all men." This is technically an inaccurate statement, corrected in the TNIV; the phrase is best taken with σωτήριος, giving (as also NRSV; cf. RSV, GNB) "the grace of God has appeared that offers salvation to all people" (see the example of Thucydides 7.64.2 in BDAG, s.v.).

11. The view that "all kinds [or classes] of people" is meant, in a way that specifically backs the addressing of different groups in 2:2-10, esp. slaves (e.g., Calvin, 373; Knight, 115; Lock, 143-44), seems foreign to the text.

12. Cf. 1 Tim 2:1-7 (discussion and notes). See Oberlinner, 129.

13. For Gk. χάρις ("grace"; 1 Tim 1:2, discussion and note), in the context of such discussions of benefaction and the like, see further the references in Dibelius and Conzelmann, 144; H. Conzelmann, TDNT 9:375; for "salvation," see the discussion and references in Spicq, TLNT 3:351; Foerster, TDNT 7:1021-22.

into a god. What Paul contends in his application of the language and concepts is that the divine appearance offering salvation, the coming of God's grace among people, was a "from the top down" affair. The ascription of divine glory to the benefactor (not deity in my view; see below) was not, as in Crete and the empire, conditioned on benefaction. Rather, God is the initiator: benefaction (the grace of God offering salvation) is the mercy shown by God to humankind. But the indirect presentation of what soon will become concrete is determined by the further description of the character of this event. In the end, the christological implications in Paul's use of the language and concepts will show that Paul has conceived of the salvation drama — grace, epiphany, benefaction, benefactor, salvation — in theocentric and christocentric terms at the same time.

12 It is, in short, an event that "educates." The present participle ("teaching") and its object ("us") combine to describe, as an ongoing activity, the intention or result of the appearance of God's grace. As pointed out above, it is the educational character or function of the event that stands at the center of what Paul is saying. In this case, the *paideia/paideuō* word group refers positively to training or instruction,[14] and Paul's intention to echo or co-opt the Hellenistic concept of *paideia* is unmistakable.[15] Thus the past appearance of God's grace is seen to be presently effective in the human sphere in an educative sense.

But how is this meant? The *paideia* concept was effectively equivalent to what we would think of as "Greek culture"; that is, the whole process by which human (Greek/Hellenistic) civilization was to become civilized (this civilizing activity being expressed by the verb). For Plato and other thinkers this involved acquiring *aretē* ("virtue"), as quantified in the cardinal virtues, and ultimately involved coming to resemble the divine.[16] This was

14. Gk. παιδεύω (pres. ptc.; "to provide instruction, educate"); Acts 7:22 (received by Moses); 22:3 (by Paul); cf. 2 Tim 3:16. Elsewhere in the NT παιδεία/παιδεύω has the more negative sense of discipline or punishment to correct errant behavior (1 Tim 1:20; 2 Tim 2:25; Rev 3:19), though the amount and kind of "discipline" will vary with the situation (2 Tim 2:25; cf. *1 Clement* 21.6). Since it was the role of the loving father to exercise discipline over his children, within the biblical tradition the term was used to depict God's special chastisement of his children and contributed to a theology of suffering (1 Cor 11:32; 2 Cor 6:4-10; Heb 12:6-7, 10; cf. Trummer, *Paulustradition*, 232-33). See further G. Bertram, *TDNT* 5:596-625.

15. It is really not essential here to answer those who argue that the authentic Paul would never have used παιδεύω in this way (e.g., Dibelius and Conzelmann, 142-43). Yes, this approach to education in Christian spirituality is more akin to OT Wisdom (Bertram, *TDNT* 5:605-23; Fee, 199); but Paul was aware of the thinking and practices of Greek culture and able to turn them to his application when the situation warranted it (cf. Johnson, 241).

16. Cf. Plato, *Republic* 376E; Aristotle, *Rhetoric* 1365B; W. Jaeger, *Paideia: The*

well enough known, even in Crete where it was far from being realized. But in Paul's co-opting of this potent symbol, "civilizing in culture," it is God's own grace-gift that produces the educational, humanizing effect, and it may also be seen in terms of salvation (v. 11).[17] That achieving this goal is conditioned on faith is hinted at in the object "us" that precedes the further description of Christian civilization.

"Civilization" in this sense is now described in three interdependent parts. First, a participial phrase identifies a condition or action that must precede (or possibly coincide with)[18] the positive living out of the new life. That condition is "denial" of ("to say 'No' to") the present worldly way of life. The action of denial (1:16; 1 Tim 5:8; 2 Tim 2:12, 13) might be a fitting allusion to the initial decision and dedication associated with the baptism ceremony.[19] But whether such an allusion is present or not, it is right to regard the attitude of renunciation as a continual set of the mind.[20]

The present or "old" way of the world is described in two terms. The first, "ungodliness, impiety" (asebeia; see on 1 Tim 1:9), creates an intentional contrast with the term "godly" (eusebōs in v. 12c), by which Paul summarizes authentic Christian existence in these letters to coworkers (see 1 Tim 2:2, Excursus). The negative cognate, calling to mind idolatry and associated wicked practices, depicts life in the world as basically irreligious, totally apart from God, determined by unbelief. Secondly, this broad characterization is followed by a reference to "worldly passions" (cf. "youthful passions," 2 Tim 2:22). Although the term "passion" ("desire") is not inherently a negative one

---

Ideals of Greek Culture, vol. 1 (2d ed.; New York: Oxford University Press, 1945), bk. 1; Johnson, *Paul's Delegates,* 240-41.

17. Philo (*On Drunkenness* 140-41; *Concerning Noah's Work as a Planter* 144) had linked παιδεία with σωτηρία. See also S. C. Mott, "Greek Ethics and Christian Conversion: The Philonic Background of Tit. II, 10-14 and III, 3-7," *NovT* 20 (1978): 31-32; G. Bertram, *TDNT* 5:602.

18. Despite the fact that the participial phrase follows ἵνα immediately, the relationship of the aorist participle ἀρνησάμενοι ("having denied") and its objects to the main verb of the ἵνα clause, ζήσωμεν ("[so that] we might live"), with its objects is that of dependent adverbial participle to the main verb (as in 3:7). While the action of "denial" might be construed as in some sense parallel, it is in fact a condition that must be satisfied for the life that grace intends to be lived. If it were simply a parallel command, i.e., a parallel object of *hina,* we would expect ἀρνηθῶμεν. Instead the sentence seems to predicate pursuit of the new life (v. 12c) on renunciation of the old life (v. 12b). For Gk. ζάω ("to live, be living, be alive") in reference to natural life/living, see also 2 Tim 3:12; R. Bultmann, *TDNT* 2:861-63.

19. See Spicq, 638; Jeremias, 72; Brox, 298.

20. Gk. ἀρνέομαι ("to deny, renounce"; see 1 Tim 5:8, discussion and note). For the sense of virtuous renunciation, as here, see Luke 9:23; Heb 11:24 (the sense intended depends on the object). Cf. Oberlinner, 131-32; Marshall, 270.

(cf. the verb in 1 Tim 3:1), its association with "ungodliness" and the description "worldly" shows that "passions" are here regarded as those sinful impulses characteristic of "the world" and its value system in its opposition to God (Rom 1:24).[21] Life summed up in this way is life without God, and pursuit of the life God intends requires that this old life be relinquished.

But the second element of the life Paul envisions, God's civilizing of humanity, takes us beyond the stage of renunciation. In the letting go of old ways, a new life that must be positively pursued presents itself (v. 12c). This is the central goal of the grace of God and of the theological material Paul uses to undergird Christian living. There are three things to notice about this new life.

First, Paul conceives of it in the very terms used by Hellenistic ethics to describe the virtuous life. At this point we need not belabor the meaning of the adverbs that describe the life to be lived: "self-controlled," "upright," and "godly" (2 Tim 3:12).[22] It is sufficient to point out that they represent three of the four cardinal virtues of Hellenistic ethics, and as such they often occurred together in discussions about respectable living.[23] It has been said that the three adverbs express three foci: the self, the neighbor, and God,[24] but the grouping here may be determined more by the traditional presentation of the cardinal virtues in lists than by a desire to intentionally touch on these areas. In any case, together they characterize the life God intends (Christian existence) as one in which the physical appetites are under control, justice is exemplified in behavior, and the knowledge of God is acted on and worked out at the observable level. Paul has refashioned the Greek ideal to reflect Christian truth.

Second, if in translation we express the first-person plural of the verb — literally: "[so that] we might live"[25] — we can see that the subject of the

21. Gk. ἐπιθυμία ("desire, longing, craving") in the NT is often negative (F. Büchsel, *TDNT* 3:168-72; though in principle "desires" may be neutral; cf. the verb in 1 Tim 3:1); defined as it is here by the adjective κοσμικός ("worldly"), the reference is negative, describing "lusts" or "passions" that have become all-consuming. As with the noun κόσμος (Gal 4:3; 1 John 2:16, etc.), κοσμικός (Heb 9:1) acquires the sense of transitory life (as opposed to eternal life) in opposition to God (*2 Clement* 17.3; H. Sasse, *TDNT* 3:897-98).

22. For Gk. σωφρόνως (adv. only here in the NT; Wis 9:11), see 1 Tim 2:9 (Excursus); for δικαίως (adv.; Luke 23:41; 1 Cor 15:34; 1 Thess 2:10; 1 Pet 2:23), see 1:8; 1 Tim 1:9 (discussion and note); for εὐσεβῶς (adv.; 2 Tim 3:12), see 1 Tim 2:2 (Excursus).

23. See *1 Clement* 61.2; 62.1; *Epistle of Aristeas* 37.261; Philo, *On the Eternity of the World* 10; Josephus, *Antiquities* 8.300; see further BDAG, "δικαίως."

24. See Marshall, 271, citing Bernard, 171.

25. Having decided to begin a new sentence at v. 12, the TNIV translates the ἵνα clause as expressing the content of the action of "teaching" contained in the preceding participle (παιδεύουσα); thus, "It teaches us to say 'No' to ungodliness and worldly pas-

intended life corresponds to the object of the *paideia* process — "us." This is a matter of Christian experience, lived in service to God, not human experience in general.

Third, Paul locates this life "in this present age." This time reference is the combination of two elements: the adverb "now," which locates the sphere of activity in time, and the term "the age," which can refer either to "the world or world system" or an epoch of time.[26] In the letters to Titus and Timothy, the whole phrase is part of Paul's eschatological jargon (1 Tim 6:17; 2 Tim 4:10). With it, especially when the added term "now" sharpens the focus, he depicts the present age of human life as transitory (in contrast to "the age to come"; 1 Tim 4:8) and characterized by evil.[27] However, it is also precisely the time of salvation, as this passage makes abundantly clear.[28]

Yet in this setting, the character of the "now" and of the life to be lived now is qualified by the contrast made with the future consummation of hope that follows. In this way, two emphases emerge. First, the new life ("salvation" quantified and exhibited in human society) is a present reality, made possible by the historical appearance of God's grace (in Christ) and is to be taken up "now," not later either in this life or in the Eschaton. Second, this present Christian existence (2:2-10) — salvation here and now — must always be regarded with reference to the future event that will complete the present experience. It is a real but unfinished (contingent) experience of salvation.

13 The third element in this picture of Christian existence is a forward-looking hope. This attitude or posture of expectancy is expressed by the addition of a second participial phrase (parallel to v. 12b). In the present tense, the participle "while we wait," in relation to the verb it modifies ("to live," v. 12), denotes an ongoing activity that is to accompany and direct life in the present age (Jude 21).[29]

---

sions, and to live . . ." (cf. NRSV). The verb παιδεύω is the type that normally requires some complementary expression of contents. The question here is one of focus or emphasis, and whether the ἵνα clause intends to view the process of "education" in terms of purpose/result or rather content. If the former, then the focal point of the clause will be expressed in the main verb of the clause ("[that] we might live"); if the latter, then "denial" and "living" are parallel, though still interrelated, components of the lesson taught by the educative event. Little essential meaning is gained or lost by following either translation strategy.

26. For the Gk. phrase ἐν τῷ νῦν αἰῶνι, see the discussion and note at 1 Tim 6:17; cf. 4:8; 2 Tim 4:10.

27. Towner, *Goal*, 62-63.

28. Cf. Oberlinner, 133.

29. Gk. προσδέχομαι; for the sense of "eager longing," as here, cf. also Mark 15:43; Luke 2:25, 38; 23:51; Acts 23:21; W. Grundmann, *TDNT* 2:57-58. For the same sentiment expressed through other verbs, see Rom 8:23, 25; 1 Cor 1:7; Gal 5:5; Phil 3:20; 1 Thess 1:9-10.

The object of this expectation establishes the vitality of Paul's eschatology. It is expressed by two thoughts that are essentially equivalent in this construction. First, that which is still ahead is described as "the blessed hope." In various ways, with emphasis on one facet or another of the fulfillment of salvation, this sentiment recurs throughout Paul (Rom 8:23-24; Gal 5:5; Eph 1:18; Col 1:27; 1 Thess 2:19). Here, as elsewhere, "hope" requires further qualification by a phrase or a genitive that describes its referent or contents.[30] This is understood here (and explicated in the phrase to follow), as "hope" points to a person or event that marks the fulfillment of something promised earlier (Eph 1:18).

Yet the additional term "blessed" does add peculiar definition. Within the NT only 1 Timothy ascribes "blessedness" to God.[31] More frequently it is used of people who experience God's benevolence in various ways (Matt 5:3, 4, 5, etc.; Rom 4:7; 1 Pet 3:14).[32] Both nuances make sense in this text, and they may both be present. If this phrase is actually equivalent to the person about to be described (see below), then "the blessed hope" is a way of describing Jesus Christ as the very embodiment of hope's fulfillment. Thus "blessed" may be an appellation (such as we find in 1 Tim 1:11 and 6:15) that defines "hope" after the character of God.[33] Or "blessed" may reflect on the event/person in which/whom hope is realized as the means of bestowing blessedness on God's waiting people.[34] In this elevated language it seems best to allow both senses to co-mingle.

Second, on the other side of the equation created by "and"[35] comes a further description of this hope but now in terms of the person who will appear. "Appearance" (*epiphaneia;* see 1 Tim 6:14, Excursus) repeats the dominant epiphany language just used to refer to a past historical event in 2:11. In the letters to Timothy this language is reserved for reflections on the parousia (1 Tim 6:14; 2 Tim 4:1, 8) or incarnation (2 Tim 1:10) of Christ. The precise reference here will need to be discussed (see below), but the epiphany concept again reflects on the parousia as a powerful, divine intervention among

---

30. See 1 Tim 1:1 (discussion and note); cf. Acts 27:20; Rom 8:23-24; Col 1:27.

31. See 1 Tim 1:11 (discussion and note); 6:15. Gk. μακάριος ("fortunate, happy, blessed"); the connection to deity is Greek; the biblical tradition (LXX) apparently intentionally avoided associating YHWH with the Greek gods by steering clear of the usage (F. Hauck and G. Bertram, *TDNT* 4:362-70; Quinn, 154-55).

32. Spicq, *TLNT* 2:432-44; G. Strecker, *EDNT* 2:376-79.

33. See Quinn, 169-70.

34. See Fee, 195; Knight, 321; Oberlinner, 135. This is the sole use of μακάριος ("blessed") in the NT of something other than God or people.

35. The omission of the article after the conjunction and before the second noun (. . . καὶ ἐπιφάνειαν), suggests that καί is epexegetical in meaning (BDF §276.3): "the blessed hope, *that is,* the appearing of the glory of our great God and Savior. . . ."

humanity to bring help. The repetition of the language in this text intentionally links this future event with the past event, making of the two aspects a single complex whole — what began with the first epiphany (2:11) is to be completed in the second. But the epiphany is further described, and here two important interrelated exegetical questions must be addressed.

First, there is the question of what or who, given the complex chain of genitives following *epiphaneian,* we are to understand as the content of the "epiphany"; and solutions proposed will affect conclusions as to the number of persons envisioned in the statement. The nub of the problem is the first genitive, "of glory," and how it qualifies the preceding *epiphaneian;* literally, "the appearance *of the glory* of our great God and Savior." Interestingly, a comparison of the NIV and its recent revision, the TNIV, shows the two possibilities for translating the genitive. The NIV understands "of glory" to be a Hebraic way of saying "glorious," yielding "the glorious appearing of our great God and Savior, Jesus Christ." And this rendering clearly intends the conclusion that "Jesus Christ" is the aforementioned "great God and Savior." The TNIV (NRSV) adjusts this to the more straightforward rendering "the appearing of the glory of our great God and Savior, Jesus Christ." While this translation may also be read to equate Jesus with God *(theos),* it leaves open the option that Jesus Christ is not in fact equated with God, but with "the glory of God" (see below).

The latter translation is to be preferred. The term "glory" *(doxa)* belongs to the analogical vocabulary by which qualities of the invisible God were "translated" into human thinking and language in (usually) visible imagery (see on 1 Tim 1:17). Thus "glory" is often manifested in unearthly bright light — in this context "glory" is the visible expression of God's power and majesty. The analogical character of this sort of language — a strategy for making tangible the ineffable qualities of God — prepares the concept of "glory" for transference to other situations. But how is "glory" to be understood here?

In this case, the stringing together of genitive phrases makes the exact sense of "the appearance [*epiphaneian*] of the glory of the great God and Savior" somewhat ambiguous. On the one hand, if we start from the notion of "epiphany" as eschatological event, we are led to the well-known association of the second coming of Christ and the manifestation of "glory" (with all of the analogical resonances in "glory" of light, divine presence, etc.; e.g., Mark 13:26).[36] Against such a background, the genitive "of glory" in this phrase could be seen to characterize the parousia (the whole cataclysmic redemptive denouement) as the climactic manifestation of "God's" glory (1 Pet 4:13; 5:1) — the eschatological "coming of God" announced by OT and NT prophets. This way of qualifying *epiphaneia* also gives a nice parallel with 2:11,

36. For the connection of ἐπιφάνεια ("appearance") and δόξα ("glory") outside the biblical literature, see, e.g., Epictetus, *Discourses* 3.22.29.

which, though with a different verbal construction, employs a genitive phrase to describe "epiphany": "the epiphany *of the grace of God*."[37] To follow this interpretive path results in taking *epiphaneia* in the rather impersonal sense of an appearance of "glory," the event itself being characterized as the full expression of the divine presence = glory.[38] Yet notably throughout these letters (see also 2 Thess 2:8) the term *epiphaneia* consistently depicts the "appearing" of a person (1 Tim 6:14: "of our Lord Jesus Christ"; 2 Tim 2:10: "of our Savior, Christ Jesus"; 4:1, 8; 2 Thess 2:8: "his").

On the other hand, if we shift the focus in *epiphaneia* slightly from the event to the person in the event (Jesus Christ), we might consider another background in Paul where the identification of God's glory and the person of Jesus Christ is implied. In 2 Corinthians 3–4, where a number of key transitions are under discussion — from Old to New Covenant, from the ministry associated with the law to the ministry associated with the Spirit — and where the resurrected Lord is being viewed in relation to the Spirit and in relation to God, the word "glory" *(doxa)* occurs fifteen times. What most attracts our attention in this discussion of the Pauline ministry in the age of the Spirit is the equation implied in 4:4, 6:

> 2 Cor 4:4: "The god of this age has blinded the minds of unbelievers, so that they cannot see the light of the gospel of the glory of Christ, who is the image of God."
>
> 2 Cor 4:6: "For God, who said, 'Let light shine out of darkness,' made his light shine in our hearts to give us the light of the knowledge of the glory of God in the face of Christ."

4:4 employs an equally challenging string of genitives, describing the content of the gospel as "the glory of Christ," then identifying Christ with "the image of God." Continuing the imagery of light and glory, 4:6, with its own string of genitives ("the light of the knowledge of the glory of God") describes ("the face of") Christ as the repository of "the glory of God." It is not a great distance from these thoughts (esp. 4:6) to a precise identification of Jesus Christ *as* "the glory of God." And against this background, the reference to "the epiphany of the glory of [the great] God" in Titus 2:13 could well be the equivalent way of describing the personal "epiphany of Jesus Christ" (= the glory of God). That is, it is possible that "glory" (or actually the whole of "the glory of the great God and Savior") and Jesus Christ are in apposition.

Marshall contends: (1) that as the sentence stands, apposing "Jesus Christ" to the preceding term "glory" results in an ambiguity (but it should be

37. Knight, 322; Marshall, 275.
38. Cf. Lock, 144; Marshall, 275-76.

noted that actually the apposition is to the whole phrase: "the glory of our great God and Savior"; and to limit the apposition to the term "glory" creates a false impression of syntactical distance between apposed items); and (2) that the insertion of a relative pronoun or similar connective to secure the appositional link could easily have been done (and presumably would have been done if this apposition were intended).[39] But in fact Col 2:2 provides a parallel example of apposition created in this manner. There Christ is set in apposition to "the mystery of God":

> Col 2:2: "that they might know the mystery of God, [that is] Christ" *(eis epignōsin tou mystēriou tou theou, Christou).*

In the Greek text and in the English gloss given, it is simply the comma, the case correspondence of nouns, and the position of "Christ" that indicate the obvious apposition. This structure is no different from Titus 2:13:

> Titus 2:13: "the epiphany of the glory of the great God and Savior, Jesus Christ" *(epiphaneian tēs doxēs tou megalou theou kai sōtēros hēmōn Iēsou Christou);*

at least, it is no different if we allow for (1) the addition of the adjective "great" and possessive pronoun "our," (2) the expansion of the genitive noun "God" to the longer but still unified genitive noun-cluster "our God and Savior" (see below), and if (3) we insert a comma before "Jesus Christ" as I have done above.[40] On this understanding of the syntax, "Jesus Christ" is in the only position it could be in and express apposition to the thought "the glory of [our great] God [and Savior]." Given the background in Paul that allows Christ to be thought of as "the glory of God," the key here is simply to recognize that the cluster "the great God and Savior," selected for its majestic resonance in this passage, was a clear enough titular reference to God (via the LXX; see below). There is no serious impediment to the apposing of "the glory of the great God and Savior" and "Jesus Christ." If "Christ" can stand in apposition to "the mystery of God" in Col 2:2, then "Jesus Christ" can stand in apposition to the longer phrase "the glory of our great God and Savior" just as easily in our text. Any serious ambiguity is avoided as long as the hearers/readers know the code.

In the matter of the reference in "glory," we are left then with two possibilities. Either it describes "the epiphany" impersonally (and hugely) as being the full expression of all that Christ means and is, or Paul draws on a

39. Marshall, 279.
40. *Pace* Marshall, 279.

more precise identification of Christ as the personal manifestation of "the glory of God" that was already in the making (see Eph 1:17 with 1:3; Heb 1:3; cf. Phil 4:19).[41] A decision between the two alternatives must await discussion of the next problem.

Secondly, the question that has attracted more attention divides into three elements: (1) how the final "Jesus Christ" is related to the preceding epiphany and reference to God; (2) whether one or two persons are indicated in the phrase "the great God and Savior, Jesus Christ"; and (3) whether, indeed, the statement calls Jesus "God" *(theos)*. Two basic options are still the most widely promoted, and these will be discussed before a third option is reconsidered.

In the text under consideration, all agree that "Jesus Christ" stands in apposition to some part of the preceding statement. Above I have laid the groundwork for arguing that "Jesus Christ" is in fact in apposition to "glory," which by virtue of the genitive chain of connections means that it is in apposition to the whole phrase "the glory of our great God and Savior." However, most interpreters today regard the whole statement, "our great God and Savior," as a reference to Jesus Christ.[42] And their contest is mainly with some who still consider the appellation to be theologically (christologically) too advanced for Paul (or a Pauline student) and so tend to understand the statement as a reference to two persons — God the Father, and our Savior Jesus Christ.[43] The greater exposure given to the two more widely supported views

41. See M. J. Harris, *Jesus as God: The New Testament Use of* Theos *in Reference to Jesus* (Grand Rapids: Eerdmans, 1992), 173-85, for the view that "the glory of God" became a title of Christ (citing additionally John 1:14; 5:44; 12:41; etc.).

42. Harris, *Jesus as God,* 173-85; Marshall, 279-82; Quinn, 155-56; Towner, *Goal,* 52; Lau, *Manifested in Flesh,* 243-44.

43. Kelly, 246-47; Dibelius and Conzelmann, 142-43; Johnson, *Paul's Delegates,* 236, 238; Windisch, "Zur Christologie der Pastoralbriefe," 226. The main arguments for this view are as follows. First, the designation "God" (θεός) for Christ is said to be unusual and possibly unprecedented in the NT (but see Rom 9:5[?]; 2 Pet 1:1; and see Harris, *Jesus as God,* for discussions of all these texts). Second, a reference to God's epiphany, as strange as that may be, is required by the reference to the epiphany of God's grace in v. 11; but if in fact that earlier reference is an oblique reference to Christ's incarnation, then it is hardly surprising to find Jesus at the center of the statement of the future hope, whether or not the divine appellation applies to him. Third, it is said to be unlikely that both the Father and the Son would be called "God" in the same sentence (vv. 11, 13). But the tendency for God the Father and Jesus Christ to share appellations (esp. Savior; 1:2, 4; 3:4, 6) is already strong in these letters to coworkers (Towner, "Christology in the Letters to Timothy and Titus"), and this was not problematical at other points where Jesus is identified as God alongside of the Father (John 1:1, 18; 20:28-31; Rom 9:5-6[?]; Heb 1:8-9; 2 Pet 1:1-2), so this is not decisive. For more details and discussion, see Harris, *Jesus as God,* 174-85; Marshall, 277-78.

within the debate is, however, more a matter of numerical strength than exegetical persuasiveness. But we will let the argument run its course.

Several lines of evidence favor a single referent and severely weaken the case for multiple referents but do not decide whether Jesus is identified with God or, rather, with the glory of God; of these, three points are most important to note here. A fourth point is added, which, if convincing, requires the conclusion that Jesus is here given the title "God" *(theos)*.

(1) "God and Savior" was a title current in Hellenistic and Jewish religious discourse and usually denoted a single deity. As such, in Jewish writings it was used of YHWH, while elsewhere it was used to express the claims of Greek and Roman rulers (Ptolemy, Julius Caesar), or in connection with cults constructed around worship of one or more of the gods. Given the currency of the title, it seems anachronistic and unwarranted to divide the items between two persons. We have already seen the apologetic potential of this whole presentation of theology — in the Cretan and perhaps also the wider Imperial arena — which makes the adaptation of a current title all the more fitting. The surrounding language — "grace," "epiphany," "great," "bringing salvation," "hope" — is almost set vocabulary for the Imperial cult and numerous other local cults current at the time this letter was written.[44]

(2) To the evidence for unity from popular usage may be added the grammatical argument. In the Greek sentence, one definite article preceding "God" governs the two nouns linked by the conjunction "and" (namely, "God and Savior"), which ordinarily would signify, then, a reference to a single person.[45] The likelihood that the two terms together formed a traditional appellation explains the anarthrous second noun.[46]

(3) The term "epiphany" in the NT is mainly limited to Christ, and in these letters to coworkers, epiphany language is used in reference to both his past and future appearances (1 Tim 6:14; 2 Tim 4:1; 2 Tim 1:10; 4:8). More-

---

44. Note the language and similar tone of the description of Artemis in Acts 19:28, 34 (μεγάλη ἡ Ἄρτεμις Ἐφεσίων). For the background and usage of the title θεὸς καὶ σωτήρ, the seminal study is that of P. Wendland, "Σωτήρ: Eine religionsgeschichtliche Untersuchung," *ZNW* 5 (1904): 335-53; now see Harris, *Jesus as God,* 178-79; cf. 1 Tim 6:14 (discussion and notes).

45. BDF §276. Gk. τοῦ μεγάλου θεοῦ καὶ σωτῆρος ἡμῶν; the point is well explained in Harris, *Jesus as God,* 179-80.

46. Several unlikely explanations for the omission of the second article (which still maintain a reference to two persons) — 1. because "Savior" (Σωτήρ) was a proper name (Bernard, 172); 2. the second article is omitted because the distinction between the great God and [the] Savior, Jesus Christ, was so well known; 3. because Father and Son are in this way shown to be co-sharers in the divine glory, etc.) — are discussed by Harris, *Jesus as God,* 179-82; see also Marshall, 279-81.

over, no NT writer mentions a future epiphany/parousia of the Father.[47] This corroborates what the language has already strongly implied — namely, that "the blessed hope" is (in this argument) the future appearance of one person, Jesus Christ, who in his appearing is the fulfillment of Christian hope and the embodiment of the glory of God.

In view of these three lines of evidence, the possibility that Paul is referring to the appearance of two persons ("the epiphany of the glory of our great God and of our Savior, Jesus Christ") can be ruled out. But a precise identification of the one to appear remains to be made. It is clearly "Jesus Christ" who is in view, but how does Paul's language envisage him?

(4) The term "great" is used in connection with *theos* ("God") only here in the NT, and so some allege that this pattern of use makes "great" a better description of Christ than God. But in fact, apart from a *very* oblique connection of the adjective with Christ in 1 Tim 3:16 ("great is the mystery of godliness") and one other use of the word group (*megaleiotētos*, "majesty") in 2 Pet 1:16, there is little in the NT to support the claim that "great" is more naturally applied to Christ. Against this are the NT uses of the word group in reference to God (Luke 9:43; Heb 1:3; 8:1; Jude 25),[48] and especially the overwhelming use of this language in the LXX as a divine appellation.[49] Its omission as a description of God in the NT has been variously explained;[50] most likely it was used cautiously due to its widespread use in reference to pagan deities and rulers. Whatever sensitivity may have been exercised by the early church in the use of common, current religious language, Paul has clearly thrown caution to the winds in Titus as he shapes his gospel message in a way that will challenge all claims to deity by lesser gods and people. Thus the attachment of "great" to the title "God and Savior" is best explained as part of Paul's intentional engagement with the cultural religious story. But the preponderance of the evidence favors linking the quality "great" with God, not Christ.

47. In the attempt to get around this NT tendency, interpreters sometimes argue that the appearance is not of God himself but of his glory; but as Marshall points out, "the objection misses the point, . . . which is that there is no epiphany of God's glory and grace apart from that in Christ" (281).

48. Gk. μέγας; see, however, the appellation μεγαλωσύνη in Heb 1:3; 8:1; Jude 25; and μεγαλειότης in Luke 9:43 (2 Pet 1:16 of Christ). Cf. W. Grundmann, *TDNT* 4:529-44, esp. 538-40.

49. Exod 18:11; Deut 7:21; 10:17; 11:2; 2 Sam 7:22; 2 Chron 2:5; Neh 1:5; 4:14; 9:32; Pss 47:2; 71:19; 75:2; 76:14; 85:10; 94:3, 4; 135:5; Isa 26:4; 33:22; Jer 39:18, 19 LXX; Dan 2:45; 9:4; Bel 1:41; Tob 3:9; 13:16; 2 Macc 3:34, 36; 3 Macc 1:16; 5:13, 25; 6:18; 7:2, 22; *Psalms of Solomon* 2.29; 4.24; 18.10.

50. Cf. the discussions in Bernard, 172; Houlden, 151; W. Grundmann, *TDNT* 4:540.

Where does the evidence point? First, "great God and Savior" refers to one person, God. But "Jesus Christ," in his eschatological epiphany, is the blessed hope. Second, the remaining question is whether Jesus Christ is in apposition to "our great God and Savior," making this a rare Pauline affirmation of his deity and a rarer still Pauline application of the term *theos* to him (cf. Rom 9:5?), or in apposition to "the glory of our great God and Savior." For the former view: (1) in these letters a significant sharing of the title "Savior" is observable (e.g., 1:3/4; 3:4/6); (2) we are about to see the transference of activities associated with YHWH in the OT to Christ (see on v. 14); and (3) Paul's predominant use of "Lord" *(kyrios)* for Christ and other hints suggest some level of reflection about the divine status of Jesus Christ (e.g., Col 1:15-20; 2:9). In view of these observations it is perhaps not improbable to think that Jesus Christ could be called "God" *(theos),* and the possibility that Titus 2:13 intends this identification should be left open.[51] But the weight of the grammatical, syntactical, and lexical evidence tips the scales in the other direction. Jesus Christ is equated not with God but rather with "the glory of the great God and Savior." And the eschatological epiphany, "the blessed hope," is thus depicted here as the personal appearance of Jesus Christ, who is the embodiment and full expression of God's glory.

Paul draws again from the rich OT/LXX reservoir as he plays with popular religious and political language to describe the future parousia of Jesus Christ as *the* saving/helping epiphany of "the glory of our great God and Savior." In his return, God's glory will be fully and finally revealed. The present passage exhibits again the theological and conceptual transition already observed, by which Jesus Christ comes to be thought of in terms of qualities and titles previously reserved for YHWH (Lord, Savior, and now "the glory of God"). God (v. 11) is seen to be executing his divine plan of redemption, from start to finish, through his Son, Jesus Christ.

14 The explicit identification that closes v. 13 — "the epiphany of our great God and Savior's glory, Jesus Christ" — returns Paul to the past event of salvation with which he began (v. 11). This elaboration consists of a statement that divides into two main parts: (1) a relative clause that incorporates an earlier Pauline interpretation of Jesus' death, and (2) a purpose clause that reflects both negatively and positively on the significance of that action. The whole statement is a thoughtful combination of intertextual echoes of an earlier Pauline saying and OT texts and imagery. The purpose clause especially adapts the Pauline saying for use in the present parenetic setting.

---

51. It is noteworthy that the only other possible Pauline reference to Christ as θεός comes in the equally problematic (grammatically and syntactically) statement of Rom 9:5. See also the textual uncertainty of Acts 20:28.

The traditional character of the opening clause ("who gave himself for us") is indicated by the relative pronoun that attaches this statement to the name Jesus Christ.[52] Although the comment is often traced to the logion in Mark (10:45), this saying of Jesus was clearly picked up very early by Paul and employed in several other contexts (Gal 1:4; 2:20; Eph 5:2; 1 Tim 2:6), and a close look at the elements points us in the direction of Paul's use of the Jesus tradition. If we begin with Mark 10:45, we can see that Paul has made several adaptations:

> Mark 10:45: For even the Son of Man did not come to be served, but to serve, and *to give his life as a ransom for many.*
> Gal 1:4: who gave himself for our sins
> Eph 5:2: and gave himself up for us
> 1 Tim 2:6: who gave himself as a ransom for all people
> Titus 2:14: who gave himself for us

The key elements are a verb of "giving," the reflexive pronoun "himself" that stresses the self-sacrifice in the action, a preposition that distributes the action to others, and the final pronoun "us" (or "many," or "all people"). Characteristic of Paul's use of the tradition is the change from "many" to the more focused "us,"[53] and the choice of the preposition "for" *(hyper)* over Mark's "for" *(anti).* Just as Gal 1:4 interprets Christ's self-giving as "for our sins," so here the expansion will take up the matter of cleansing from sins. The thrust of these elements will be discussed below, but here we need only conclude that Paul cites the gospel tradition in the form in which he had earlier cast it, thereby reminding Titus (and other hearers/readers in the Cretan context) of the authenticity of the Pauline gospel.

First, Jesus' death is seen as an act of selfless sacrifice. The verb "give" is of course common enough, but in certain contexts it acquired the sense of laying down one's life as a martyr,[54] and it is typically used to describe Jesus' death as a conscious act undertaken by him.[55] By leaving the verb in the third person and active voice ("he gave"; cf. Rom 4:25, where

52. The technique is used widely in the NT (1 Tim 3:16; Rom 8:32; Phil 2:6; 1 Pet 2:22-24; 3:22).

53. The exception is 1 Tim 2:6, where, however, the decision to widen the scope to "all" (πάντων), but not to "many" (πολλῶν as in Mark 10:45), is determined by the "all" theme developed in 2:1-5 (see discussion and notes).

54. Gk. δίδωμι (1 Macc 2:50; 6:44; F. Büchsel, *TDNT* 2:166); see further the discussion of this verb in 1 Tim 2:6.

55. So Mark 10:45; Luke 22:19; Gal 1:4; sometimes in the compound form παραδίδωμι (Rom 4:25; 8:32; Gal 2:20; Eph 5:2). See Perrin, "The Use of *(para-)didonai* in Connection with the Passion of Jesus in the New Testament," 204-12.

the passive suggests that this is the Father's action), Jesus is made the responsible actor in this event. The reflexive pronoun "himself" completes the circuit of selflessness by making Jesus the object of his own "giving" action.[56]

Second, the prepositional phrase "for us" emphasizes an important theological duality in Jesus' sacrificial death: Jesus died as a representative and a substitute. The preposition "for" (hyper) occurs frequently to show how Jesus' actions affected others.[57] In such uses, it depicted Jesus as exhibiting a complete sense of solidarity with the intended "us." But more specifically Jesus did this by means of representing humanity in this act and standing in as a substitute for humanity's benefit (see on 1 Tim 2:6).

Thus the crucial historical exhibition of "the grace of God offering salvation" was the self-offering of Jesus Christ. It is important to see that Paul's reflection backward in time on this event is designed as an invitation to Titus and the Cretan believers to find themselves again within this drama ("teaching us," v. 12; "our great God and Savior," v. 13). Christ's death was "for us," and its purpose is therefore determinative for our sense of identity.

The purpose clause that follows (hina) identifies two effects of Christ's death. First, negatively, his self-offering accomplished the removal of "us" from the sphere of sin. To express this aspect, Paul draws on the metaphor of redemption. Behind the metaphor was the practice of buying a slave's or captive's freedom by the payment of a ransom.[58] But the verb "to redeem" was used widely in the biblical tradition of the action taken by YHWH to set his people free,[59] and was already closely associated with his deliverance of the people from Egypt (Exod 6:6; Deut 7:8; 2 Sam 7:23); it had become another way of speaking of God's saving act,[60] and it would have called to mind primarily the OT story of deliverance from Egypt.

From the thought of redemption, the verse goes on to name the hostile

---

56. The pronoun ἑαυτόν ("himself") is a more natural Greek way of expressing the Semitic τὴν ψυχὴν αὐτοῦ ("his life") of Mark 10:45.

57. Gk. ὑπέρ; e.g., Mark 14:24; Luke 22:19; John 10:11; Rom 5:6; 8:32; etc. See further M. J. Harris, NIDNTT 3:1196-97; H. Riesenfeld, TDNT 8:507-16.

58. For λυτρόω (Luke 24:21; 1 Pet 1:18), see F. Büchsel, TDNT 4:349-51; Spicq, TLNT 2:423-29; D. Hill, Greek Words and Hebrew Meanings (London: Cambridge University Press, 1967), 49-81.

59. From enemies, Pss 106 [MT 107]:2; 118 [MT 119]:134; 1 Macc 4:11; Sir 50:24.

60. For the debate over the meaning of λυτρόω, i.e., whether it denotes redemption by payment of a ransom or deliverance as effected by the appropriate offering, cf. L. Morris, The Apostolic Preaching of the Cross (3d ed.; London: Tyndale and Grand Rapids: Eerdmans, 1965), 35; H. Ridderbos, Paul: An Outline of His Theology (Grand Rapids: Eerdmans, 1975), 193, 196 with Hill, Greek Words and Hebrew Meanings, 70; Dunn, Theology of Paul, 227-28.

environment from which people are "redeemed" — "from all wickedness" *(anomia)* — and echoes a chorus of OT texts , beginning with the Greek text of Ps 129:8:

> Ps 129:8: "It is he who will redeem *(lytrōsetai)* Israel from all its iniquities *(ek pasōn tōn anomiōn autou)*";
> Titus 2:14b: "that he might redeem us *(lytrōsetai hēmas)* from all wickedness *(apo pasēs anomias)*."[61]

The changes are basically cosmetic: from "Israel" to "us" (= followers of the Messiah; and thus the substitution of the plural for the collective singular);[62] and from the plural formulation ("from all its iniquities") to a generalizing singular ("from all wickedness").

In both cases, redemption is "from all wickedness" ("lawlessness"). The Greek term *anomia* was used frequently in the OT to depict opposition to God's law (see on 1 Tim 1:9), and in the singular denotes "wickedness" or "sinfulness," which is set in opposition to the concept of righteousness (cf. Rom 6:19; 2 Cor 6:14). Paul uses the term occasionally to describe the state of sinfulness[63] and seems to avoid the plural usage (= "acts of lawlessness"; Rom 4:7). His choice of the phrase was naturally determined by the OT text in mind at this point. But the term *anomia* rings into consciousness the next web of OT texts to be engaged. To this point, the effects of Christ's self-offering are interpreted in terms of redemption from sin's enslavement, which is associated in the OT with God's powerful intervention.

Now with a shift of metaphor Paul makes the transition to another cluster of OT covenantal texts and a positive assessment of the effects of Christ's death: "and to purify for himself a people that are his very own." First, the new metaphor is that of "purifying, washing, or cleansing."[64] A reference to baptism (cf. 3:5; Eph 5:25-26) is certainly not immediately present, though the imagery did come to contain various religious implications in Christian use (Heb 9:14, 22-23; 1 Pet 1:2; 1 John 1:7, 9). Here, however, the sense is that of cultic purification (in relation to the preparation for making sacrifices, etc.), which the OT already expanded to describe God's action of purifying his people, so that they may be his people. The imagery of "purify-

---

61. Ps 129:8 — καὶ αὐτὸς λυτρώσεται τὸν Ἰσραηλ ἐκ πασῶν τῶν ἀνομιῶν αὐτοῦ; Tit 2:14 — λυτρώσηται ἡμᾶς ἀπὸ πάσης ἀνομίας.

62. Doctrine-like sayings are often applied to believers by means of personal pronouns: Titus 3:5; 2 Tim 1:9-10; Rom 5:6; 8:32; etc.; Cranfield, "Changes of Person and Number in Paul's Epistles," 280-89.

63. In the singular, as here, Rom 6:19; 2 Cor 6:14; 2 Thess 2:3, 7.

64. Gk. καθαρίζω (for the cognate adj. καθαρός, see 1:15[3x]; 1 Tim 1:5; 3:9; 2 Tim 1:3; 2:22). See F. Hauck and R. Meyer, *TDNT* 3:413-26.

ing" gives access to a catena of Greek texts from Ezekiel 36 and 37, already anticipated in the *anomia* of the last clause:

37:23: "They will no longer defile themselves with their idols and vile images or with any of their offenses, for I will save them from all their sinful backsliding *(apo tōn anomiōn autōn)*, and I will cleanse them *(kai kathariō autous)*. They will be my people *(kai esontai moi eis laon)*, and I will be their God."

36:25: "and I will sprinkle clean *(katharon)* water upon you, and you shall be cleansed *(katharisthēsesthe)* from all your uncleannesses *(tōn akatharsiōn)*, and from all your idols, and I will cleanse *(kathariō)* you."

36:29: "And I will save you from all your uncleannesses *(tōn akatharsiōn)*."

36:33 "Thus says the Lord God, 'In the day wherein I shall cleanse *(kathariō)* you from all your iniquities *(ek pasōn tōn anomiōn hymōn)* I will also cause the cities to be inhabited, and the waste places shall be built upon.'"

Titus 2:14c: "and he shall cleanse for himself a people of his own" *(kai katharisē heautō laon periousion)*.[65]

Paul's intertextual play may have begun with Ezek 37:23, but the distribution of the term *anomia* and the *katharos* word group makes a single text source impossible to establish. And in the closing reference to "a people that are his very own," Paul strikes another rich thematic vein that incorporates the Ezekiel context but also reaches back to the seminal reflections on the covenant made on Mt. Sinai:

Ezek 37:23: "they shall be to me a people, and I the Lord will be to them a God" *(esontai moi eis laon, kai egō kyrios esomai autois eis theon)*.

Ezek 36:28: "you shall be my people, and I shall be your God" *(kai esesthe moi eis laon, kagō esomai hymin eis theon)*;

---

65. Ezek 37:23: ἵνα μὴ μιαίνωνται ἔτι ἐν τοῖς εἰδώλοις αὐτῶν. καὶ ῥύσομαι αὐτοὺς ἀπὸ πασῶν τῶν ἀνομιῶν αὐτῶν, ὧν ἡμάρτοσαν ἐν αὐταῖς, καὶ καθαριῶ αὐτούς, καὶ ἔσονταί μοι εἰς λαόν, καὶ ἐγὼ κύριος ἔσομαι αὐτοῖς εἰς θεόν.
Ezek 36:25: καὶ ῥανῶ ἐφ' ὑμᾶς ὕδωρ καθαρόν, καὶ καθαρισθήσεσθε ἀπὸ πασῶν τῶν ἀκαθαρσιῶν ὑμῶν καὶ ἀπὸ πάντων τῶν εἰδώλων ὑμῶν, καὶ καθαριῶ ὑμᾶς.
Ezek 36:29: καὶ σώσω ὑμᾶς ἐκ πασῶν τῶν ἀκαθαρσιῶν ὑμῶν.
Ezek 36:33: τάδε λέγει κύριος ἐν ἡμέρᾳ, ᾗ καθαριῶ ὑμᾶς ἐκ πασῶν τῶν ἀνομιῶν ὑμῶν, καὶ κατοικιῶ τὰς πόλεις, καὶ οἰκοδομηθήσονται αἱ ἔρημοι.
Titus 2:14c: καὶ καθαρίσῃ ἑαυτῷ λαὸν περιούσιον.

Exod 19:5: "you shall be a people of my possession out of all the nations" *(esesthe moi laos periousios apo pantōn tōn ethnōn);*

Deut 7:6: "the Lord your God has chosen you out of all the nations on the earth to be a people of his possession" *(se proeilato kyrios ho theos sou einai se autǭ laon periousion para panta ta ethnē;* 14:2);

Titus 2:14c: "and he shall cleanse for himself a people of his own" *(kai katharisǭ heautǭ laon periousion).*[66]

Paul's adaptation draws together the concept of purifying (from *anomia*) and election. The defilement in mind in the purview of Ezek 37:23 and 36:25 is that of exilic and postexilic idolatry, and the application of this to the Cretan context is not hard to see (1:10-16 and the use of the *katharos* word group in v. 15). The wider textual network that Paul contacts also associates purification from idolatry with the event of "becoming" God's people and the ongoing act of "being" God's people by way of the Godward covenant commitments required of his people.

The event of "becoming" is God's covenantal and creative act, and the uniqueness of this people is first seen in this light. Paul sets the identity of the church into the OT context specifically focused on the promise of the new (or renewed) covenant (cf. Ezek 36:26-28). The textual network, beginning with Ezek 37:23, superimposes Christ's purifying act over God's act in the OT. The result is a people whose messianic identity is uniquely imprinted on them.[67] In the OT covenantal transaction, by YHWH's action of purifying (Ezek 37:23) and electing (Deut 7:6; 14:2), and on the condition of the people's faithfulness (Exod 19:5), Israel would be known as "a people for his own possession"[68] — that is, YHWH's "very own" possession, bearing the imprint of his holiness. The quality of uniqueness is emphasized by the selectivity with which Israel was chosen (Deut 7:6); the Greek phrase behind "a people that are his very own" adds the sense of preciousness or costliness to this identity.[69] The histor-

---

66. Ezek 37:23: ἵνα μὴ μιαίνωνται ἔτι ἐν τοῖς εἰδώλοις αὐτῶν. καὶ ῥύσομαι αὐτοὺς ἀπὸ πασῶν τῶν ἀνομιῶν αὐτῶν, ὧν ἡμάρτοσαν ἐν αὐταῖς, καὶ καθαριῶ αὐτούς, καὶ ἔσονταί μοι εἰς λαόν, καὶ ἐγὼ κύριος ἔσομαι αὐτοῖς εἰς θεόν.

Ezek 36:28: καὶ ἔσεσθέ μοι εἰς λαόν, κἀγὼ ἔσομαι ὑμῖν εἰς θεόν.

Exod 19:5: ἔσεσθέ μοι λαὸς περιούσιος ἀπὸ πάντων τῶν ἐθνῶν.

Deut 7:6: καὶ σὲ προείλατο κύριος ὁ θεός σου εἶναί σε αὐτῷ λαὸν περιούσιον παρὰ πάντα τὰ ἔθνη, ὅσα ἐπὶ προσώπου τῆς γῆς.

Titus 2:14c: καὶ καθαρίσῃ ἑαυτῷ λαὸν περιούσιον.

67. The verbal links are (1) Ezek 37:23, "my people" (ἔσονταί μοι εἰς λαόν); Exod 19:5; Deut 7:6; 14:2, "a people for my own possession" (λαὸν περιούσιον).

68. For the phrase λαὸν περιούσιον, see Eph 1:14; 1 Pet 2:9; H. Strathmann, *TDNT* 4:50-57. For the phrase in the OT, see also LXX Deut 26:18; Exod 23:22.

69. See H. Preisker, *TDNT* 6:57-58; Marshall, 286.

ical event that marked this development was the exodus. Now, in the Messianic Age, the death of the Messiah replicates the exodus event and replaces it as the new historical benchmark; and it is the Messiah who, acting on God's behalf, possesses this human treasure and imprints it with a renewed, unique identity.

The act of "being" belongs to the category of response. Titus 2:14d closes the christological statement with the phrase, "zealous for good deeds" (TNIV, "eager to do what is good"). This loosely attached phrase links this christological statement to the preceding ethical teaching (2:2-10), ensuring the close relationship between theology (as anchored in the historical Christ-event) and ethics (the life that this event "teaches"; 2:12). The active noun that opens the phrase is "zealous," meaning "eager, enthusiastic."[70] "Good deeds" is Pauline shorthand (esp. in these letters to coworkers) for the visible outward dimension of Christian existence (1:16; 2:7; 3:8, 14; Eph 2:10).[71]

We should recall that Paul insists that this dimension of Christian identity is something the opponents lack (1:16), for, as we make the connections implied by Paul's logic, they have not been "purified" (1:15) from the effects of Crete's moral chaos. Now in naming the theological source of "good deeds," namely, "purification" (katharisẹ) through Christ's death, Paul takes up language that was apparently central to the opponents' Judaizing doctrines about "purity" (kathara; see 1:15) to anchor Christian purity in God's grace.

Consequently, with this closing phrase ("zealous for good deeds") Paul lifts the entire web of OT reflections into the contemporary situation, rounding off the theological rationale of Christian existence by returning to the ethical vocabulary most familiar to his readers. From the perspective of cause and effect, authentic Christian identity involves a creative act of "becoming" (redemption, purification) that makes a unique quality of "being" possible. Having already established a distinct OT covenant and New Covenant framework for understanding, "zeal for good deeds" can be seen within that frame. The appropriate response to grace was to be devotion to Torah (Exod 19:5; Deut 26:18). From Paul's eschatological Spirit-perspective, the faith response to covenant grace is the Spirit-generated fulfillment of Torah (suggesting the internalization of the law; cf. Jer 31:31-34 [MT], the reshaping of the heart/will to obey; 3:5; Rom 8:1-9; Gal 5:17-18). His web of

---

70. Gk. ζηλωτής; used frequently (noun and verb) to describe devotion to God and Torah (cf. 1 Macc 2:24; 2 Macc 4:2; Josephus, *Antiquities* 12.271 ["if anyone is zealous for the customs of the fathers and the worship of God . . ."]; Acts 21:20; 22:3; Gal 1:14. Cf. ζηλωτὴν καλῶν ἔργων and τοῦ ἀγαθοῦ ζηλωταί (1 Pet 3:13).

71. See 1 Tim 2:10 (Excursus).

Ezekiel echoes — linked by the key themes and word groups of "cleansing," "lawlessness," "nationhood" — encompasses this new Spirit-reality even if he delays explicit reference to the Spirit until 3:5-6:

> 36:25: and I will sprinkle clean *(katharon)* water upon you, and you shall be purged *(katharisthēsesthe)* from all your uncleannesses *(tōn akatharsiōn),* and from all your idols, and I will cleanse *(kathariō)* you.
>
> 36:26: And I will give you a new heart, and will put a new spirit in you: and I will take away the heart of stone out of your flesh, and will give you a heart of flesh.
>
> 36:27: And I will put my Spirit in you, and will cause you to walk in my ordinances, and to keep my judgments, and do them.
>
> 36:28: And you shall dwell in the land which I gave to your fathers; and you shall be to me a people, and I will be to you a God.
>
> 36:29: And I will save you from all your uncleannesses *(tōn aka-tharsiōn).*
>
> 36:31: And you shall remember your evil ways and your practices that were not good, and you shall be hateful in your own sight for your transgressions *(tais anomiais hymōn)* and for your abominations *(tois bdelygmasin hymōn;* cf. 1:16).
>
> 36:33: Thus saith the Lord God, In the day wherein I shall cleanse *(kathariō)* you from all your iniquities *(ek pasōn tōn anomiōn hymōn)* I will also cause the cities to be inhabited, and the waste places shall be built upon.

Making the conceptual shift from "keeping the law" (e.g., Ezek 36:27) to being "zealous for good deeds," Paul has established an OT hermeneutical line that allows Christ's death to be viewed as YHWH's ultimate act of deliverance, and the results to be seen in terms of the New Covenant perspective that emerged especially in Ezekiel. The eschatological wildcard, surely present, as the Ezekiel texts themselves and Pauline theology in general would suggest, but not yet breaking the textual surface, is the Holy Spirit, whose dynamic role in authentic Christian existence will finally be explored in the subsequent section of Titus.

Finally, the attachment of this active phrase ("zealous for good deeds") to the more traditional theology brings the discourse full circle back to the exposition of the observable Christian life laid out in 2:2-10. In Greek terms, the appearance of God's grace "teaches" ("civilizes in") a new way of life; in terms of the biblical tradition, that very life of godliness, lived in the present age until hope has been fulfilled, has proved to be the goal of the Messiah's redemptive self-offering. The life of virtue that the Greeks idealized and the Cretan teachers diluted Paul here declares to be the realistic potential of those who respond to the one true God in faith.

c. Summary Command to Titus (2:15)

15 *These, then, are the things you should teach. Encourage and rebuke with all authority. Do not let anyone despise you.*

It is good at this point, following the intense examination of theology in 2:11-14, to be reminded that the primary concern of Paul's discourse from 2:1 onward has been how believers ought to live. He has been instructing Titus what he is to teach (2:1), fitting it to the contours of Hellenistic respectability and to the demands of the apostolic tradition. At this point, v. 15 does three things: (1) it reiterates the instruction in 2:1, repeating the thematic didactic language; (2) it reminds Titus of his authority as Paul's delegate, and (3) it adds a word of encouragement that anticipates opposition. This return to direct instruction prepares the way for the next parenetic section.

15 Titus's teaching function is first addressed. The reference in "these things" is primarily to the preceding section, 2:1-14.[1] This is indicated by the way the first command verb, "teach," forms a bracket with 2:1.[2] This first verb is the more general of the three, and as in 2:1 it denotes teaching in the widest sense. It alone takes "these things" as its object.[3] The other two didactic terms, "encourage/exhort" (2:6) and "rebuke/reprove" (1:13),[4] recall the job description of the overseer (1:9) that Titus is himself set to doing. They reveal the direction that Titus's teaching will need to move in — the first that of positive exhortation and encouragement, the second that of engaging (correcting, rebuking) those who stand in opposition to the apostolic teaching (1:13).

---

1. Some commentators regard the extent of the reference as 1:5 (e.g., Mounce, 432). For the anaphoric (backward-looking) function of ταῦτα in these letters to coworkers, see 3:8; 1 Tim 3:14; 4:6, 11, 15; 5:7, 21; 6:2, 11; 2 Tim 2:14. For differing views on the scope and on the discourse function of this verse, cf. Quinn, 177-78; Mounce, 432; J. D. Miller, *The Pastoral Letters as Composite Documents* (New York: Cambridge University Press, 1997), 133.

2. Gk. λαλέω (also pres. 2d pers. impv.; see 2:1 and note); see also Marshall, 297; cf. Mounce, 432.

3. The syntax of the Greek sentence (Ταῦτα λάλει καὶ παρακάλει καὶ ἔλεγχε) might suggest that each verb shares the object; however, given the meaning of ἔλεγχε ("refute/reprove"), it is best to understand the syntax as the TNIV and NRSV have done (see also Marshall, 297).

4. For Gk. παρακαλέω ("to exhort, encourage"), see 1 Tim 1:3 (discussion and note); for Gk. ἐλέγχω, see 1 Tim 5:20 (discussion and note).

766

Second, Paul reminds Titus of his authority as an apostolic delegate. Both the turbulent pioneer situation in Crete and the presence of rebellious teachers reluctant to separate from Cretan tendencies are likely reasons for this reminder. Paul has already taken care to link Titus's role to his own as an apostle (1:3-5). Now the language describing Titus's "authority" (or "authority to command"; *epitagē*)[5] recalls Paul's authoritative status as an apostle ("according to the command [*epitagē*] of God"; 1:3), strengthening that link further.[6] The prepositional phrase "with all authority"[7] may intend to back up just the last command verb, "rebuke," but it could well provide backing for all aspects of teaching in the community.[8]

Third, the summary concludes with an indirect command in the third person meant to stiffen the resolve of Titus in anticipation of disrespect: "Do not let anyone despise you."[9] Some scholars read this as directed to the church (cf. 1 Cor 16:11, where the indirect command is to be obeyed by any in the church).[10] But if the role of Titus as the letter's primary recipient is taken seriously, even allowing the letter a wider secondary audience, the force of the command is personal; that is, "Titus, even if someone disrespects your authority, do not be dissuaded from your task." The instruction recalls 1 Tim 4:12 in form and content, with, however, Timothy's youth being mentioned as the cause of disregard. In Titus's case, it is not clear that the cause

---

5. For Gk. ἐπιταγή, see 1 Tim 1:1 (discussion and note).

6. Cf. Knight, 329 and Guthrie, 214, who insist on the divine element inherent in the authority. That point is probably assumed, but in this context the primary interest is in establishing Titus's right to speak for the apostle (Marshall, 297). Those who hold that the letter is pseudepigraphical regard this language as designed primarily to convey a "Pauline" endorsement of the continuing authority of the elders/overseers (esp. Trummer, *Paulustradition,* 137; Lips, *Glaube,* 149; Wolter, *Paulustradition,* 189-91). But a letter employing "mandate" features might also include this reminder for the sake of those whom Titus would be charged to oversee.

7. Gk. μετὰ πάσης ἐπιταγῆς is literally "with every command" but should be understood to mean "with full authority to command" (BDAG, s.v.; see also G. Delling, *TDNT* 8:37).

8. Cf. Mounce, 432: "'with all authority' is appropriate only for the command to rebuke, not the commands to encourage or to speak." This assertion is stated far too strongly and surely downplays the importance of the teaching given in 2:1-14; 3:1-8. In the Crete Paul envisions any such endorsement or inculcation of a vastly "different" way of life would require authority to ensure its adoption by the church, especially where the apostle's authority is under fire. The very use of the term ἐπιταγή in reference to aspects of teaching that would belong to the traditional *paraklēsis* (e.g., Rom 16:26; 1 Cor 7:6, 25; 2 Cor 8:8) cautions against this sort of rigidity.

9. Gk. περιφρονέω ("to have disdain for, look down on, despise, disregard") is found only here in the NT; cf. 4 Macc 6:9; 7:16; 14:1; BDAG; Spicq, *TLNT* 3:103-4.

10. E.g., Brox, 302.

of disrespect would have been his age.[11] More likely Paul anticipates further acts of rebellious opposition to his authority for which the Cretan churches and the teachers troubling them had become known (1:6, 9, 10; 3:10).[12] Titus is to insist on his authority and address the needs of the communities under his charge as the apostle's representative.

3. Living as the Church in the World (3:1-8)

> 1 *Remind the people to be subject to rulers and authorities, to be obedient, to be ready to do whatever is good, 2 to slander no one, to be peaceable and considerate, and always to be gentle toward everyone.*
>
> 3 *At one time we too were foolish, disobedient, deceived and enslaved by all kinds of passions and pleasures. We lived in malice and envy, being hated and hating one another. 4 But when the kindness and love of God our Savior appeared, 5 he saved us, not because of righteous things we had done, but because of his mercy. He saved us through the washing of rebirth and renewal by the Holy Spirit, 6 whom he poured out on us generously through Jesus Christ our Savior, 7 so that, having been justified by his grace, we might become heirs having the hope of eternal life. 8 This is a trustworthy saying. And I want you to stress these things, so that those who have trusted in God may be careful to devote themselves to doing what is good. These things are excellent and profitable for everyone.*

At this point in the letter, Paul resumes the household code style of teaching, as he turns to the traditional concern of the church as a community with responsibilities in the larger society. The way in which the instruction opens out from consideration for rulers and authorities to a wider concern for "all people" is paralleled in the tradition as it appears in Rom 13:1-7 and 1 Pet 2:13-17. As in the last section, a theological statement (vv. 3-7) provides backing for the ethical instruction of vv. 1-2, by explaining the theological realities that make possible the kind of behavior Paul enjoins. In this case, however, the Christ-event is viewed primarily through the lens of the work of the Spirit in applying salvation to God's people. Further emphasis is then supplied through the "trustworthy saying" formula (v. 8a). Then, also following the pattern of the previous passage, Paul finishes the section by reiterating the command to Titus. And in this repetition, both the recurrence of the term "good deeds" ("what is good") and the return to the broad concern for "everyone" ("people") close the thematic bracket begun in 3:1. In this way

11. But see Marshall, 296.
12. See also Bassler, 202; Mounce, 433.

the purpose of the whole section is summed up in missiological terms: when believers devote themselves to "doing what is good" (i.e., the behavior categorized similarly in 3:1-2), the benefit is spread to people in general.

a. Christian Living within Society (3:1-2)

Verses 1-2 form a single Greek sentence that sets out instructions in two parts. Verse 1 addresses the church in its public life *(politeia)* concerning its duties as citizens or residents of the empire. Verse 2 widens the scope of responsibility to include people in general. The question often asked about this instruction and the broader tradition to which it belongs is how Christian beliefs about the corruption of the wider world can be reconciled with this sort of encouragement to live within the world, and especially to recognize its power structures. While various explanations are given for Romans 13, our text is frequently taken as yet another reflection of the author's accommodation ethics. As it is often argued, the "low profile" posture of political quietism and good citizenship endorsed in this parenesis would increase the church's chances of peaceful coexistence with the secular powers. This, however, is not at all the intention of this tradition.

There are two elements of background that illuminate this teaching. First, the entire tradition (cf. 1 Tim 2:1-2) grows out of the reality that dawned in the period of Israel's exile, that YHWH continued to be sovereign in spite of pagan dominion over Israel. This prophetic message fostered hope in God's future, but it also included the obligation to exhibit loyalty to the pagan state: "But seek the welfare of the city where I sent you into exile, and pray to the Lord on its behalf, for in its welfare you will find your welfare" (Jer 29:7; cf. Ezra 6:9-10; 1 Macc 7:33).[1] This obligation of course ran counter to notions of religious and ritual purity and challenged the sorts of barriers (especially Jewish) put up to protect these things. And the theological and practical questions that this gives rise to have continued through the generations. What shape should the church's role in the world take? Demonstrating the subjection and obedience enjoined by the tradition involved the specific activities of prayer (1 Tim 2:1-2) and paying taxes (Rom 13:6-7). But was it just the cultural blinders of Paul and Peter (1 Peter 2:13-17) that made obedience to Rome a natural duty? Did Paul mean to encourage the church to adopt a posture of political quietism for its own preservation? Or is there more to this mundane concern?

Secondly, in the case of Romans 13 and 1 Peter 2 it has been argued, on the basis of the language of "doing good" and "commendation" from the

---

1. See the discussion and references in Towner, "Romans 13:1-7," 149-69, esp. 163.

authorities, that each author co-opted and redefined the cultural convention known as benefaction (i.e., gifts of money given by wealthy citizens to the city-state in return for honor in the form of praise from the authorities).[2] This appropriation of the convention, and expansion of it to include the whole church (not just the wealthy), allowed Paul to define the church's obligation to the larger society in terms of service that "sought the welfare of the city." In this interpretation, Paul implies that the church in apparent weakness and sacrificial service adopts the role of the powerful — a subtle but subversive appropriation of language and conventions that expresses in yet another way the reversal of fortunes that the Christ-event set in motion. The deeper needs of the city-state are addressed as the church lives out its missionary life of Christ in the world.[3]

What is important for us to see as we approach this text and the tradition behind it is that there is more here than meets the eye. It may sound like a cliché, but mission dominated Paul's thought, and this applies to his view of the church in the world as well.

1 Paul sets Titus into the teaching mode again with another in the sequence of didactic imperatives: "remind them [the people]" (cf. 1:13; 2:1, 6, 15; see on 2 Tim 2:14). The choice of the verb suggests that the churches in Titus's charge had already been exposed to this teaching. It was known widely in the church (Rom 13:1; 1 Pet 2:13), and corresponded to Greco-Roman ethics in general. The influence of the rebellious Cretan teachers — whose teaching and praxis reflected too much of Cretan culture and ran counter to the apostolic tradition and caused disruption — explains the need to recall earlier accepted teaching.[4]

Titus is to remind them of an appropriate posture, defined with the verb *hypotassomai* ("to be in subjection"; Rom 13:1, 5; 1 Pet 2:13; see on 1 Tim 2:11), which calls for the recognition and acceptance of authority through appropriate attitudes and actions. Two dative nouns ("rulers and authorities")[5] combine to indicate widely that all official powers are to be shown subjection

---

2. Winter, *Seek the Welfare of the City.*

3. Towner, "Romans 13:1-7."

4. The present tense of the command probably implies the need of continual repetition (cf. 2 Pet 1:12); Quinn, 183.

5. For ἀρχή in the sense of "a person having authority," see Exod 6:25; Hos 1:11; Luke 12:11; 20:20. In the plural, as here, see 4 Macc 8:7; Josephus, *Antiquities* 4.220; *Martyrdom of Polycarp* 10.2. It sometimes refers to heavenly powers (Rom 8:38; 1 Cor 15:24; Eph 3:10, etc.), but that is not the case here. See G. Delling, *TDNT* 1:479-84. For ἐξουσία (pl. "power, authority"; BDAG, s.v.) as those who hold and exercise authority, see Luke 12:11; Rom 13:1, 2, 3; *Martyrdom of Polycarp* 10.2; Josephus, *Jewish War* 2.140. See W. Foerster, *TDNT* 2:562-74. The two terms are often found together (Luke 12:11; 20:20; Eph 1:21; 3:10; 6:12; Col 1:16; 2:10, 15; *Martyrdom of Polycarp* 10.2).

(and obedience), rather than to distinguish between levels of authority. They are followed immediately by the verb "to obey" (cf. Acts 5:29, 32; 27:21).[6] It occurs here without an object,[7] which suggests that "obedience," as opposed to disobedience, will be the general rule. Falling within the scope of this command would be specific actions and behavior (paying taxes, obeying laws) that exhibit the more fundamental posture of subjection.[8]

This use of the tradition is briefer and more general. It lacks such details as reference to the paying of taxes or to the corresponding obligation of the authorities to dispense justice, and the reward of praise for "doing good" is not mentioned. Nevertheless, the wide-ranging third-person infinitival command, which presumably would include such specifics, "to be ready to do whatever is good" does echo the "good deeds" language of the benefaction convention as adapted in Rom 13:3-4 and 1 Pet 2:14-15.[9] But here in another church setting, the command is generalized ("whatever, every"), and the language picks up the thematic use of "good deeds" in these letters to Titus and Timothy as a description of observable, Spirit-filled living (see 1 Tim 2:10, Excursus and note). Simultaneously, this phrase "ready to do . . . good" intentionally strikes again at the moral weakness of the Cretan teachers, who are "unfit for doing anything good" (1:16).[10] With both the negative assessment of Cretan civil life[11] and the opponents' Cretan-like tendencies in mind, Paul's primary concern in this matter of the church's subjection to the state and public behavior is the exercise of a visible Christianity that is free from cultural taint.

The question of the motive or theological rationale beneath the instruction remains. But we may rule out the thought that respectability or pub-

---

6. Although the verb πειθαρχέω can occur without an object (see Dibelius and Conzelmann, 147), the context suggests the sense of "obedience" either to rulers or to the laws they enact and exercise power to enforce (see Spicq, *TLNT* 3:65).

7. But see Knight, 332, who takes both verbs (i.e., "be subject to rulers and authorities, be obedient [to them]"); but cf. Dibelius and Conzelmann, 147.

8. Gk. πειθαρχέω ("to obey"); its sense in a range of contexts (see Spicq, *TLNT* 3:63-65) includes observance of laws or commands of the ruler (Josephus, *Jewish War* 1.454; *Against Apion* 2.293; Philo, *On the Life of Moses* 1.164, 329), which seems most apt here. In some cases, it may carry the sense of "readiness or willingness to obey" (so Quinn, 185).

9. Cf. the phrase πρὸς πᾶν ἔργον ἀγαθὸν ἑτοίμους εἶναι ("to be ready for every good deed") with Rom 13:3 (τῷ ἀγαθῷ ἔργῳ, τὸ ἀγαθὸν ποίει) and 1 Pet 2:14-15 (ἀγαθοποιῶν, ἀγαθοποιοῦντας).

10. Cf. the phrases: 3:1: πρὸς πᾶν ἔργον ἀγαθὸν ἑτοίμους; 1:16: πρὸς πᾶν ἔργον ἀγαθὸν ἀδόκιμοι. Cf. 2 Tim 2:21; *1 Clement* 2.7.

11. Quinn's (185) citation of Polybius's famous slams against Cretan life and politics (*Histories* 6.46.1-47.6) may be slightly overdone, but Paul himself has used this gambit already in 1:12-13, which suggests the relevance of another echo of the stereotype here.

lic image was held to be an end in itself. While the fuller church-in-world theology detectable in Romans is perhaps only anticipated here (possibly delayed so that more fundamental ethical problems could first be addressed), the fact that this text is set into a missiological bracket (vv. 2, 8) and, so, thoroughly grounded in eschatological realities (vv. 3-7) suggests that the church's subjection to the state, worked out in public Christian service, has the redemption of creation as its goal, not simply peaceful coexistence with the secular power structure. The tradition in general bears witness to God's proclamation of reconciliation for the world and to his calling to the church to involvement in that task. The shape and potential of that involvement will vary with the conditions:

> Again and again there have been times when the people of God are persecuted, and martyrdom has been enjoined. Then nothing more is possible in history. That is "the night when no one can work." Then all that is left is to endure to the end, and in that endurance to be saved. . . . the possibilities of history narrow down, and all that remains is the sole decision: to confess or to deny.
>
> Yet again and again there have also been, and are, times of open doors and favourable opportunities for mission, for diaconal service to the poor, and for the liberation of the oppressed. Then we stand face to face with almost unlimited possibilities which can be realized, and we are filled with the "joyful confidence" that this world can be made better . . . the kingdom of God is at hand. Then hope turns into action, and we already anticipate today something of the new creation of all things which Christ will complete on his day. These are the experiences of history's consummation.[12]

2 This verse continues to fill in the content of the reminder Titus is to issue. In doing so it reflects more broadly on behavior to be avoided and pursued, all with a view to protecting the public image of the Christian. First, "slander" ("insult, speak against"; 1 Tim 6:4; 2 Tim 3:2) is generally prohibited.[13] The term can also mean "to blaspheme" (against God, his people, or his appointed servants; 1 Tim 1:13, 20; 6:1; Titus 2:5), but in view of the disputes about teaching and practice that seem to be a concern, the more general meaning is best.[14]

---

12. J. Moltmann, "Hope and Reality: Contradiction and Correspondence," in R. Bauckham, ed., *God Will Be All in All: The Eschatology of Jürgen Moltmann* (Minneapolis: Fortress, 2001), 84-85.

13. The term "no one" (μηδείς) suggests that it is not just slander of civil leaders that is meant here (but cf. Spicq, 647).

14. Gk. βλασφημέω (see discussion at 1 Tim 1:20); but cf. H. W. Beyer, *TDNT* 1:624.

Second, "quarreling" is to be avoided ("be peaceable"). This theme seems to grow out of the disputes that characterize the rebellious teachers in each letter (note the use of the cognate terms for "fighting" in 3:9; 2 Tim 2:23-24). As a Christian virtue to be cultivated, this irenic, noncombative demeanor was to be found in leaders (1 Tim 3:3; see note), and it runs quite counter to the rough Cretan stereotype embodied by the local teachers. Here it is applied generally to a life led in such a way that it causes no offense to other people.

Third, again in contrast to the roughness of the opponents and Cretan behavior in general, believers are to be "considerate" ("gentle, reasonable, forbearing, conciliatory, courteous"; see on 1 Tim 3:3). In view of Paul's desire to claim the fulfillment of the Hellenistic ideal in Christ (2:11-12), he is again arguing that it is the gospel that produces a virtuous human being. Of course within Pauline churches this quality had already been associated with Christ (2 Cor 10:1), which suggests that yet another paradigm is in mind at the same time.

The fourth quality, "gentle" ("humble, meek"; see on 2 Tim 2:25), also occurs with "considerate" in that earlier description of Christ (2 Cor 10:1). While in English usage this quality is often thought to manifest itself in a quiet, passive demeanor that goes unnoticed, the command here calls for its positive demonstration "toward everyone [all people]."[15] This broad applicability — "to all people"   corresponds to the social dimension of this instruction and indicates Paul's concern that believers, in the way they live, send a clear message to the world. The reason for this is not immediately given, but it is almost certainly to be linked to Paul's evangelistic goals for the church (see 3:8, where Christian behavior is said generally to have benefits for "people").

Thus Christian life in the world is to present a vivid contrast to the criticized Cretan image. In the civic arena Christians are to be as responsible as the best citizens. Where believers, more generally, come into contact with other people, they are to embody the highest ideals of human virtue as they imitate the pattern of behavior embodied by Christ himself. But what is the source of this life? How is it possible to live in this way?

---

15. The translations reflect a slight difference in the way the first occurrence of the Greek adjective "all" (πᾶς) functions: NRSV: "to show *every* courtesy to everyone"; NIV: "to show *true* humility toward all men"; TNIV: "*always* to be gentle toward everyone" (cf. RSV, "perfect"; GNB, "always"). The effects are similar: πᾶς calls for the highest degree of meekness to be exhibited (cf. 1 Tim 2:2, note; 2 Pet 1:5; Jude 3). For the sentiment, see 2 Cor 8:24. For the Gk. verb ἐνδείκνυμι, see 1 Tim 1:16 (note); Titus 2:10. For the phrase πρὸς πάντας ἀνθρώπους (also in a witness setting), see Acts 22:15.

b. The Theology That Generates This Life (3:3-7)

A casual reading of this section reveals where the emphasis lies. Paul adapts a well-used conversion formula — "formerly–now" (cf. Rom 6:20-22; 11:30-32; Gal 1:23; etc.)[16] — that creates the same dramatic effect as the revelation formula in 1:2-3 (2 Tim 1:9-10), to focus on the ethical change introduced through the appearance of God's grace in human culture. The former way of life (v. 3) is rough, and though Paul admits that he himself once lived this way ("we"), it is at the same time another allusion to the Cretan image that still persists in the house churches under Titus's charge. Verses 4-7 do not explicitly set out the ethical counterpart for the "now" in Christ, but rather assume the life described in vv. 1-2 in place of the old way, and set out the theological cause behind it. The structure of this lengthy theological section is best set out before its meaning is discussed.

3 At one time [formerly]   [time]

    we too were foolish, disobedient, deceived and   [the old life]
    enslaved by all kinds of passions and pleasures.
    We lived in malice and envy, being hated and
    hating one another.

4 But when [now] the kindness and love of God our
   Savior appeared,   [time]

      5 [he saved us] not because of righteous things
        we had done,   [means negated]

        but because of his mercy.   [means affirmed]

    He saved us   [salvation]

      through the washing of rebirth and renewal   [means of
        by the Holy Spirit,   salvation]
        6 whom he poured out on us generously
          through Jesus Christ our Savior,

     7 so that, having been justified by his grace,   [purpose of
      we might become heirs having the hope of   salvation]
      eternal life.

The statement as a whole consists of two Greek sentences: v. 3 and vv. 4-7. The first sentence, characterizing the former way of life in ignorance of

16. See Towner, *Goal,* 63-64.

God, is fairly straightforward. It sets the stage for the emphasis to be laid on the sequence of events that effected conversion.

However, the second long sentence of theology compresses so much meaning into a single sentence, as it shifts through metaphors depicting salvation, that the grammatical relations are not all perfectly clear. Even so, the movement from God's gracious action in history, through the human experience of it in the Spirit, finally to the ultimate goal of eternal life, comes through clearly and without obstruction.

It is important to note at the outset that a theological piece such as this was bound to evoke a wide range of responses at emotional and cognitive levels. This is not only unavoidable but also probably intentional. Paul's use of current language weighted with symbolic meaning would stimulate the readers'/hearers' imagination in one way; his allusion to OT narratives would move them in another way; and the use of Pauline theological categories already known among his team and churches would provide yet another compass for their imagination. All of this is to say we should expect so theologically and symbolically loaded a text to provoke a potent and complex response. Our task is to establish as many of the connections as we can, in order to allow this statement of theology to speak clearly.

The statement is very Pauline in thought and language. It denies the role of human effort in salvation, describing it rather as God's work, mediated by the Holy Spirit, producing a justification grounded in his grace.

3 The opening phrase ("at one time we too were . . .") signals two things. First, what is to follow undergirds the instruction of the previous section ("for"; *gar*). Second, at this point Paul is reflecting on a "past" time frame ("formerly").[17] He depicts the quality of life before the human history of the Messiah with a vice list that begins with foolishness and ends with hatred. The list can be divided into three parts: the first set of vices focuses on ignorance; the second part draws on the imagery of slavery; the third concentrates on flaws that are base and destructive of relationships.

The first three vices form a rather obvious allusion to the reputation of the Cretan opponents, whose dubious relationship to God is described in three ways. First, in this context the adjective "foolish" (1 Tim 6:9) denotes spiritual obtuseness or ignorance specifically of God.[18]

---

17. The formula usually consists of "formerly . . . but now" (ποτε . . . νῦν[ι]; Rom 6:20-22; 11:30-32; Gal 1:23; 4:8-9; Eph 2:1-22; 5:8; Col 1:21-23; 3:7-8; Phlm 11; 1 Pet 2:10) and tends to be ethical in orientation. In this instance, the "now" is replaced by "but when" (ὅτε δέ).

18. Gk. ἀνόητος ("foolish, unintelligent"); predicate adjective to the copulative verb "we were" (ἦμεν); it can mean "uneducated" (Rom 1:14) but is mostly a negative measurement of a deficient understanding of God or salvation in the NT (Luke 24:25; Gal

Second, the adjective "disobedient" *(apeithēs)* already used of the opponents (1:16; see on 2 Tim 3:2) forms a contrast with the charge to be obedient to rulers in 3:1 *(peitharchein)*. It characterizes the old life (still being exhibited by the rebellious teachers) in terms of a conscious rejection of God and perhaps also Paul, his servant (Eph 2:2; 5:6; Col 3:6).

Third, changing to a participle, those who live this way are "deceived."[19] This is true of all who live in sin without the knowledge of God (Rom 1:27; Heb 5:2; 1 Pet 2:25; Rev 12:9), but it is a special and ironic mark of rebellious Christian teachers in these letters who both lead others astray and are themselves deceived (2 Tim 3:13; 1 Tim 4:1).[20] Both senses are probably meant in this description. This opening triad of character flaws underlines the helplessness of people outside of the sphere of God's grace.

As the list continues, the image shifts to "enslavement" to "various" dangerous impulses.[21] This slavery is to two forces.[22] The first of these is "passions, desires" ("lusts"; 2:12; see on 1 Tim 6:9; 2 Tim 3:6), which, though neutral or even positive in some contexts, here indicate "passions" that have become abnormal in their insatiability. "Pleasures" (or "enjoyment") are evaluated negatively in the NT as having become the primary object of longing (2 Tim 3:4, "lovers of pleasure"),[23] especially of those who either have no knowledge of God (Rom 1:24) or have turned away from God and live life on the visceral level (2 Tim 3:4).

Closing the list are four character flaws that involve other people. They may be organized in terms of a sequence moving from wickedness of thought to outright hatred: but each item is stock in the descriptions of destructive behavior; this pattern forms the perfect contrast to the caliber of life to be lived by Christians in the world (3:2).

3:1, 3; see ἄνοια in 2 Tim 3:9). See J. Behm, *TDNT* 4:961-62. In different words, the idea is well expressed in Rom 1:21-32; Eph 4:17-18; cf. Marshall, 309.

19. Gk. πλανάω ("to deceive"; 2 Tim 3:13; Matt 24:4; etc.); for the word group, see πλάνη ("deception"; Rom 1:27; 2 Pet 2:18), πλάνος ("deceiver"; 2 Cor 6:8; 2 John 7). H. Braun, *TDNT* 6:228-53.

20. Cf. Luke 21:8; John 7:47; 1 Cor 6:9; 15:33; 1 John 1:8.

21. Gk. ποικίλος ("all kinds of") is used to make a blanket reference; see also 2 Tim 3:6 (ἀγόμενα ἐπιθυμίαις ποικίλαις).

22. For δουλεύω in this metaphorical sense, cf. Matt 6:24; Rom 6:6; Gal 4:9 (K. Rengstorf, *TDNT* 2:261-80).

23. Gk. ἡδονή (pl. "pleasure, delight, enjoyment"; Luke 8:14; Jas 4:1, 3; 2 Pet 2:13). The concept is negative in the NT (cf. "lovers of pleasure" in 2 Tim 3:4). Warnings against such powers are found widely in Greek philosophy (Plato, *Phaedo* 83B; see Plutarch, *Lives* [*Pelopidas*] 3.2 for the combination of δουλεύοντες and ταῖς ἡδοναῖς) and Hellenistic Judaism (Philo, *On Husbandry* 83, 84; 4 Macc 5:23). For the combination of these concepts in the NT, see Jas 4:1-3. See further the discussions in F. Büchsel, *TDNT* 3: 168-72; G. Stählin, *TDNT* 2:909-26.

The first two are poisons that begin their work within the person. They occur here in a prepositional phrase that describes the manner in which we used "to live" or "pass our days" (NRSV) before conversion.[24] The noun "malice" ("wickedness"), when referred to in vice lists, depicts life turned toward evil.[25] The related adjective links this characteristic to the Cretan stereotype (1:12). "Envy" is also frequently identified as a flaw typical of unregenerate life (Rom 1:29) that believers are to shun (see on 1 Tim 6:4; 1 Pet 2:1; 5:26). It is the mental outworking of dissatisfaction, associated with "malice" in some cases (as in 1 Pet 2:1; *Testament of Benjamin* 8.1) and with hatred in others.

The last two items, "being hated and hating one another," are correctly regarded as results of malice and envy.[26] Probably the first of the two terms depicts the response evoked in others by those who are malicious and envious, that is, they are considered to be "despicable."[27] The second term, "hating one another,"[28] describes the mutual response of those who belonged to that former way of life.

Thus the "former" life (still very current for those within Titus's sphere) consists of ignorance and active opposition to God and people. In contrast with the life to be pursued by believers, life outside the influence of God's grace is destructive chaos that collapses in on itself under the weight of hatred. But this is not where Paul wishes to concentrate his thought; the good news is that a change has occurred in the world.

4 Within this conversion formula the counterpart to the description of the "former" way of things is a statement describing the "now." Having already

---

24. Gk. ἐν κακίᾳ καὶ φθόνῳ διάγοντες. The present participle διάγοντες (from διάγω, "to spend one's life"; otherwise in the NT only in 1 Tim 2:2 [see note and discussion]) takes the prepositional phrase to describe the manner or scope of "living" (Luke 7:25 [variant reading]; Ignatius, *To the Trallians* 2.2; *Testament of Joseph* 9.3); or frequently in Greek writers, often with the accusative βίον (as in 1 Tim 2:2; Isocrates, *Orationes* 90; Plato, *Republic* 372D).

25. Gk. κακία ("depravity, wickedness") can express the general meaning of evil (Matt 6:34; Acts 8:22); but in the vice lists it personalizes evil or badness in terms of attitudes and feelings that are malicious (Rom 1:29; Eph 4:31; Col 3:8; 1 Pet 2:1); cf. W. Grundmann, *TDNT* 3:482-84.

26. See Marshall, 311.

27. Gk. στυγητός (only here in the NT; in the pass. sense of "despicable, loathsome"; see *1 Clement* 35.6; 45.7; Philo, *On the Decalogue* 131; BDAG, s.v.). The adjective connects loosely back to the copulative verb "we were." But see Knight, 337, who (on the basis of Rom 1:30 [θεοστυγής in the act. sense, "hating God"]; cf. *1 Clement* 45.7) prefers the active sense of "hateful."

28. Gk. μισέω ("to hate, detest"). The language used here, Gk. μισοῦντες ἀλλήλους (pres. act. ptc. with reciprocal pron. as obj.), parallels Matt 24:10, where the thought is of believers coming to hate one another (cf. 1 John 2:9, 11; 3:15; 4:20).

set out the contrasting new life in 3:1-2, Paul proceeds to explain the reason behind it. There are two parts to Paul's argument. First, Paul again draws on the
epiphany concept (2:11-14; 1 Tim 6:14, Excursus) to characterize life "now" in
terms of God's gracious intervention in Christ. However, as in 2:11, this mo-
mentous historical[29] epiphany of Christ is portrayed from a theological (rather
than christological) perspective, and draped in cultural symbolism.

First, expanding on the description of the past epiphany in terms of "the
grace of God" in 2:11, Paul here interprets what "appeared"[30] as being "the
kindness and love of God [for humankind]." The reference to God's "kindness"
("generosity, goodness") and its expression toward people is not unusual in
Paul.[31] The second noun, literally "love for people" *(philanthrōpia),*[32] however,
occurs only here in reference to God's character. Both terms describe virtues
that ought to characterize rulers as they relate to their subjects, and belonged to
the vocabulary current in the Imperial cult and its worship.[33]

The universality of this language suggests that Paul continues to operate on more than one level in this theological dialogue. We have seen him engaged in this task from early on in the letter. First, he again applies the epithet
"our Savior" to God (1:3; see on 1 Tim 1:1), resonating with secular assumptions about royalty and divinity. Second, the very Hellenistic description of
God's attributes makes God the paradigm and source of "royal" or "divine"
virtue. Furthermore, the event through which these attributes are displayed to
the world sets the standard for "kindness and love [for people]." These qualities were widely heralded in Hellenistic ethics (cf. 2:12), and they were to be
observable in virtuous people and were idealized in descriptions of the gods.
But the archetype of "kindness and love" has been expressed in the redemptive work of the Christian God.

Yet the main point in describing the epiphany as a display of these
specific virtues — as a demonstration of God's character — is to explain that

29. The suggestion (e.g., Hasler, 96) that the "epiphany" alluded to here is one
that occurs in proclamation is unwarranted (Towner, *Goal,* 66-71; Knight, 338-40; Marshall, 312).

30. Gk. ἐπιφαίνω (aor. as in 2:11; "to appear") links this reference to the epiphany
scheme.

31. Gk. χρηστότης in Paul is a divine attribute (Rom 2:4; 11:22[3x]; Eph 2:7).
The background to this is chiefly the Greek OT (see LXX Pss 100:5; 106:1; 107:1; Jer
33:11; etc.), though Greek deities were also known as such (cf. Spicq, *TLNT* 3:511-16).

32. Gk. φιλανθρωπία (LXX noncanonical books use it of personal or national benevolence) appears frequently with "kindness" (Philo, *On the Embassy to Gaius* 67, 73;
On the Special Laws 3.155; Plutarch, *Lucullus* 18.9); cf. Spicq, *TLNT* 3:512-13. In the NT
see Acts 28:2; cf. 27:3.

33. E.g., Philo, *On the Embassy to Gaius* 67, 73; cf. also the discussion in Spicq,
TLNT, 3:512-13 n. 8; U. Luck, *TDNT* 9:111, esp. n. 37.

God has communicated the very qualities needed to live the life prescribed in 3:1-2.[34] People are to exhibit these qualities of God in their own lives, and in framing the life of faith in this way a somewhat subversive intention may again be detected: qualities that Greco-Roman culture ascribes to the ideal "ruler" are actually to be exhibited by ordinary Christians in society. The advent of Christ turns assumptions and values on their heads. But how are these qualities communicated to people? The answer is the Holy Spirit.

5 In part two of the argument (vv. 5-7), Paul interprets the life of salvation in terms of the gift of the Holy Spirit. In order to emphasize the exclusion of human effort and the priority of divine mercy in salvation, the Greek text holds the main verb ("he saved") until after these conditions are stated (see the diagram of the structure above). This is awkward in English, however, so both the TNIV and the NRSV move the main verb to the beginning of v. 5, repeating it again in its original location in the sentence. Nevertheless, we begin with the two-part contrasting condition of salvation, diverging at points from the TNIV to reconstruct the syntactical relationships.

First, negatively, the role of human effort is excluded from the equation: "not because of works that we did in righteousness" (TNIV, "righteous things we had done"). The phrase modifies the main verb, "he saved," that will follow. Focusing on the exclusion of works for the moment, most agree that the phrase has a Pauline ring to it.[35] Some are troubled that the excluded "works" are not specified as being "of the law," but this unqualified exclusion of human effort (not just in the specifically Jewish sense) is also present in Paul's letters to churches.[36] The sentiment has a parallel in 2 Tim 1:9.[37] And the verb "to do"[38] occurs often in Paul's discussions of "performing" what the law of God requires.

The qualification that is added to "not from works" is "which we have done in righteousness."[39] But what is the point of this reference to "in righ-

---

34. See Johnson, *Paul's Delegates,* 248.

35. For οὐκ ἐξ ἔργων ("not from works"); cf. the various configurations of the phrase with the genitive νόμου ("of the law"): ἐξ ἔργων νόμου; οὐκ ἐξ ἔργων νόμου (Rom 3:20, 28; Gal 2:16[3x]; 3:2, 5, 10). See Brox, 307; Marshall, 314.

36. See Rom 9:12 and Eph 2:9 for the unqualified exclusion phrase οὐκ ἐξ ἔργων in this sense.

37. Although expressed in slightly different Greek, οὐ κατὰ τὰ ἔργα ("not according to works"), the effect is the same.

38. For Gk. ποιέω ("to do, act, make"; used here within the relative clause that will further qualify the "works" under discussion) in similar contexts, see Rom 2:14; 10:5; Gal 3:10, 12; 5:3. Cf. H. Braun, *TDNT* 6:478-83.

39. For the "spherical" sense of the prepositional phrase ἐν δικαιοσύνῃ, which assigns a quality or character to the action carried out (here "deeds"), cf. 2 Tim 3:16; Eph 4:24; 5:9.

teousness"? In Pauline thought, against the OT legal and covenant setting, righteousness[40] is the status of acquittal or vindication one acquires from God on the basis of Christ's faithfulness to the covenant (= his obedient death for sins).[41] According to Paul's covenantal thought, those with this status (justified by faith) are to live out the righteousness delineated by the "law written on the hearts." For this, the adverb of 2:12 *(dikaiōs)* provides the appropriate description. With this background in mind we might be led to conclude that Paul is again excluding obedience to the Jewish law as the sign of being in the covenant people.[42] Here, however, Paul seeks the lowest common denominator and excludes all "righteous" deeds — whether on Jewish terms, as possibly hinted at in the case of the opponents (1:15), or on Gentile terms — as a way to salvation.[43] He will narrow the thought significantly in 3:7.

With the contrasting "but" *(alla),* Paul reaches the fundamental point of the qualification: "but in accordance with his mercy [he saved us]" (TNIV, "because of his mercy"). What is at issue is a contrast between human effort and God's action in salvation. What God has done is described in terms of "mercy." The phrase "in accordance with [*kata*] his mercy" (1 Pet 1:3)[44] describes both the source of God's act (namely, his lovingkindness directed toward people) and the character of that action (aimed to express that love for those who do not deserve it; Rom 9:23; 11:31; 15:9; Gal 6:6; Eph 2:4).[45] This understanding of the basis of salvation is of course not new for members of Pauline communities, and may possibly have been directed at the Cretan Jewish teachers' preoccupation with rules about purity and defilement and the priority they gave to such things within their understanding of salvation (see on 1:15).

Having anchored the action (about to be mentioned) in God's mercy, we reach the main verb and object of the sentence. As we do so, the thread begun in 3:4 is picked up and the effect of the epiphany event on people is

40. Gk. δικαιοσύνη (and related terms) in these letters to coworkers slides between the sense of moral uprightness, i.e., a life lived in conformity to God's laws (1 Tim 6:11; 2 Tim 2:22; 3:16) and the sense of the verdict of acquittal handed down as a result of the justification process (2 Tim 4:8; cf. Rom 9:30; Gal 5:5). See further the discussion at 1 Tim 6:11.

41. Rom 3:21-31; etc. The literature is enormous, and the discussion of this concept is still in progress: cf. Dunn, *The Theology of Paul the Apostle,* 334-89; Witherington, *The Paul Quest,* 65-69.

42. Quinn, 216; Brox 306-7; cf. Johnson, *Paul's Delegates,* 248, who allows that the qualification might be aimed at opponents who taught a righteousness based on Torah observance.

43. See Towner, *Goal,* 114; Marshall, 315; cf. Mounce, 448.

44. For the preposition κατά, see the note at 1:1.

45. For Gk. ἔλεος ("mercy"), see 1 Tim 1:2 (discussion and note).

stated: "He saved us."[46] This too is well-known language for God's redemption of humankind, expressing in some contexts the thought of future salvation but in others, as here, reflecting on salvation as a past experience with present implications.[47] The reason for the time perspective becomes clear as Paul's focus in this conversion shifts to a description of the way in which people experience salvation: "through . . . the Holy Spirit."

The prepositional phrase that modifies the main verb is densely packed both with meaning and syntactical uncertainty. It is clear from the preposition "through" (or "by"; *dia*) that Paul is talking about the means of the act.[48] Three nouns follow from the preposition, forming the core of the effective action by which people experience salvation: "washing," "rebirth," and "renewal." We shall first take them in order, and then consider the more complicated matter of their grammatical interrelation in this phrase.

"Washing" in everyday usage refers to literal cleansing with water, or to the place of bathing.[49] But here, as in Eph 5:26, the term falls into the metaphorical sphere, with the image of washing referring to a spiritual cleansing.[50] Some have seen in this image a reference to the rite of water baptism, but there is reason to see it rather as a reference to the work of the Spirit in terms of a "washing" (see below) that, then, the outward rite of water baptism might serve to symbolize.

The next term, "rebirth," is in genitive relation to "washing," indicating the result of washing. Of the pair of genitive nouns, this one, *palingenesia,* has stimulated the most discussion primarily because of its alleged

46. The first-person plural pronoun ἡμᾶς ("us") stands for the church as a whole, with immediate application to the readers; cf. Cranfield, "Changes of Person and Number in Paul's Epistles," 280-89.

47. The σῴζω word group ("to save, deliver"; see 1 Tim 1:15, discussion and note) develops in usage from its reference to acts of physical deliverance (from enemies, from sickness = healing) to "salvation" (in Christ, by the gospel) from the effects of sin (1 Tim 1:15; 2:4, 15; etc.); cf. Spicq, *TLNT* 3:344-57; W. Foerster and G. Fohrer, *TDNT* 7:965-98; W. Radl, *EDNT* 3.319-21. The aorist tense of the verb, ἔσωσεν, conceives of salvation as in some sense a past fact (cf. 2 Tim 1:9; Eph 2:8; Rom 8:24), and the present tense reveals it to be equally presently in process (1 Cor 15:2); but the futurity of salvation is also clearly held in tension with the past/present experience of it (Rom 5:9, 10; 9:27; 10:9, 13; 1 Cor 3:15). It is a mistake to think that Paul's view of salvation was wholly future (*contra* V. Hasler, "Epiphanie und Christologie in den Pastoralbriefen," *TZ* [1977]: 207-8).

48. For διά of means/instrument with σῴζω, see 1 Cor 15:2; Eph 2:7.

49. Gk. λουτρόν (elsewhere in the NT only in Eph 5:26) of washing, Song of Songs 4:2; 6:6; Sir 34:25. See further Spicq, *TLNT* 2:410-11; BDAG, s.v.

50. The term is also used of ceremonial washings, and slides into the metaphorical range of washings (of the soul) that remove moral stains (e.g., Philo, *On the Change of Names* 124); see further Spicq, *TLNT* 2:411-12; A. Oepke, *TDNT* 4:295-307; Quinn, 220.

prior or contemporary use in the mystery religions in connection with initiation rites.[51] However, as a background either to this term or to the practice of baptism in the early church, this particular explanation has been laid to rest.[52] In fact, the term was widely in use in all kinds of contexts to express ideas such as restoration, renewal, and rebirth in many senses.[53] In the only other biblical use, it refers to the renewal of the world or the age to come (Matt 19:28). In the present context, the idea of the new birth associated with conversion (symbolized in baptism?) gives the best sense, and the term's widespread use made it adaptable as a metaphor for Christian new birth.[54]

Almost synonymous with "rebirth" is the connected genitive noun "renewal."[55] It stands alone in reference to an event (cf. Rom 12:2, where it takes an object, "renewal of the mind"). The most instructive parallels for this thought are 2 Cor 5:17 ("a new creation in Christ") and Rom 6:4 (where baptism and association with Christ in his death and resurrection lead to "a new life"), both of which express the concept of renewed life in connection with conversion.

The more difficult problem arises in the syntax of this prepositional phrase, and the resultant meaning of the whole. The ambiguity of the original Greek statement illustrates the difficulty:

Literally: "through the washing of rebirth and renewal of (by) the Holy Spirit"

We may think that we know what this means as we read it in English, for we make various connections and insert commas according to our theological upbringing. How much goes with the first preposition, "through"? Does the process of "washing" produce both "rebirth" and "renewal," or is the latter linked only to the following Holy Spirit? Everything depends on where one

51. Gk. παλιγγενεσία ("rebirth"; Matt 19:28); see Mounce, 449; F. Büchsel, *TDNT* 1:686-89; J. Dey, *PALINGENESIA* (Münster: Aschendorff, 1937), esp. 157-76. For the argument of derivation from the mystery religions, see Dibelius and Conzelmann, 148-50.

52. See the discussion in Mounce, 449; G. Wagner, *Pauline Baptism and the Pagan Mysteries* (London: Oliver & Boyd, 1967).

53. See Josephus, *Against Apion* 2.218; Philo, *On the Embassy to Gaius* 325 (for life after death); Philo, *On the Eternity of the World* 9, 47, 76, 107 (for renewal of the world after destruction; cf. Matt 19:28); Plutarch, *Moralia* 996C (of transmigration of souls); see further the references in Marshall, 319; Dibelius and Conzelmann, 148-49.

54. Post-first-century use of the term is predominantly Christian (Lampe, *PGL*, s.v.).

55. Gk. ἀνακαίνωσις; the only other biblical occurrence is Rom 12:2 (Paul is also the first to use the verb ἀνακαινόω; 2 Cor 4:16; Col 3:10); cf. J. Behm, *TDNT* 3:453.

makes the breaks. While there are numerous variations,[56] two main arrangements of the two nouns in relation to "washing" and the preceding preposition have been suggested.

1. through the washing of rebirth
      and
   (through) renewal by the Holy Spirit

In this case, the decision has been made to isolate two operations, the first "the washing of rebirth," and the second (by assuming the repetition of the preposition) "renewal by the Holy Spirit."

2. through the washing of (i.e., that effects) rebirth and renewal,
   (which washing is done) by the Holy Spirit

Here, however, the single preposition *dia* is thought to indicate a single "washing" that produces the complex result, "rebirth and renewal," with the final genitive, "of the Holy Spirit," understood as the agent of the "washing."

Solving this difficulty is not a simple matter. But two factors give the stronger support to the second arrangement. First, the conceptual similarity of the metaphors "rebirth" and "renewal" suggests unity.[57] Second, this implication is strengthened by the fact that they are governed in this instance by the single preposition *dia*.[58] The most likely intention of the phrase is, then, to view a single event from two slightly different, yet interrelated, perspectives.[59] This rules out the possibility that the text conceives of two separate events (either, according to the liturgical traditions, baptism and confirmation, or, according to the Pentecostal tradition, conversion and baptism in the Spirit).

If one complex event is in mind, then the final genitive phrase, "of (or by) the Holy Spirit," despite its location at the end of the phrase, is best understood as attributing this "washing" by which people are saved to the agency of the Holy Spirit. What Paul has done with this material thus far (and will develop further) is to emphasize the present reality of the salvation event by describing it in terms of the gift of the Holy Spirit.

Even before the mention of the Spirit's outpouring (v. 6), this descrip-

56. See the full discussion of views in Marshall, 316-18.
57. See Towner, *Goal,* 115; Spicq, 653.
58. J. D. G. Dunn, *Baptism in the Holy Spirit* (London: SCM, 1970), 156-66; Fee, *God's Empowering Presence,* 781; N. Turner, *A Grammar of New Testament Greek,* Vol. 3: *Syntax* (Edinburgh: T&T Clark, 1963), 275.
59. See also Marshall, 321; Knight, 343-44; Fee, *God's Empowering Presence,* 780-82.

tion of the Spirit's activity echoes OT texts that speak of the New Covenant. In so short a space of discourse, the catena of Ezekiel texts recently summoned (2:14) will not have been forgotten. The epicenter of that network of texts is the promise of renewal by the "in-giving" of the Spirit (36:27). Given the potency of the Spirit-tradition and some verbal and conceptual cues, this language ("the washing [*loutron*] of regeneration," "renewal by the Holy Spirit") would call to mind the vivid images of the Spirit-promise in Ezek 36:25-27 — which included the imagery of sprinkling with water, renewal of the heart, and the gift of the Spirit — and other Spirit texts (cf. LXX Ps 103:30). And the thought of new life implicit in this poem (see 2:14d; 3:1-2) — the Spirit-enabled "doing of the law" — cannot be far from mind. Just as the tradition promised, God's gift of the Spirit would change the way people live. There are a few more connections to be made.

6 While the intertextual echo of the Ezekiel Spirit-texts lingers, Paul now enriches the texture of that story background by echoing yet another OT Spirit-text, at the same time intersecting the Ezekiel passage in a new and rather dissonant way. The purpose is to explain more fully the gift of the Spirit as the outworking of God's mercy. Two theological perspectives converge to explain the fulfillment of this OT promise. The first is the eschatological perspective of promise and fulfillment. The second is Christology, for the role of the Messiah in the event of fulfillment is crucial.

The shift to eschatological fulfillment is cued in by the relative pronoun and verb "whom he poured out on us." Here the in-breaking of the Spirit[60] is described in the rich, graphic vocabulary of the OT promise as an outpouring.[61] It suggests the thought of inundation, which is here emphasized with the addition of the adverb "generously."[62] This language — "he [God] poured out" — parallels the Pentecost tradition preserved by Luke (Acts 2:17-18, 33), where the Joel prophecy is cited:

> Titus 3:6a: "whom he [God] poured out on us generously" *(hou execheen eph' hēmas plousiōs)*
> Joel 3:1: "It will come to pass afterward that I will pour out my Spirit

---

60. The relative pronoun (the direct obj. of the verb) οὗ is genitive by attraction to its antecedent, πνεύματος ἁγίου.

61. Gk. ἐκχέω is used figuratively in various ways (see BDAG, s.v.); here the use (see also Acts 10:45, ἐκχύννω) corresponds to those occurrences that speak of an "outpouring" of mercy (Hos 5:10; Mal 3:10; Sir 18:11) or love (Rom 5:5), or even of God's wrath from above (LXX Ezek 9:8; 36:18; 39:29; cf. Rev. 16:2, 3, 4, etc.).

62. Gk. πλουσίως; the use of the adverb here of a divine action corresponds to the use of the cognate verb and adjective to describe various aspects of God's actions and character (Rom 2:4; 10:12; 11:33; 1 Cor 1:5; 2 Cor 8:9; Eph 1:7; 2:4; Phil 4:9; Col 1:27; 1 Tim 6:17; 2 Pet 1:1; cf. F. Hauck and W. Kasch, *TDNT* 6:318-32.

on all flesh. . . ." *(kai ekcheō apo tou pneumatos mou epi pasan sarka)*

Acts 2:17: "In the last days, God says, I will pour out my Spirit on all people. . . ." *(kai estai en tais eschatais hēmerais, legei ho theos, ekcheō apo tou pneumatos mou epi pasan sarka).*[63]

Although the Pentecost event is somewhere in the mix, Paul (or his material) incorporated just the "outpouring" statement, changing the reference to God from the first person "I" to the third person "he," and the tense of the verb from future to aorist to fit the "formerly–now" agenda of the present argument. But the intertextual link already established with Ezekiel (2:14; 3:5) suggests that Paul wants his readers to think of the "profuse" outpouring of the Spirit against the broader background of Israel's story (cf. Ezek 39:29 [MT]; Zech 12:10).

When the OT promise of the Spirit's "outpouring" is subsequently echoed in 3:6, what must be observed is that in the Ezekiel text's broader context (esp. 36:18), the verb that links the prophetic past as expressed in Joel with the eschatological present as expressed here, "pour out" *(ekcheō),* is in Ezekiel overwhelmingly used of God's wrath.[64] If we allow for the continuing resonance of the Ezekiel Spirit-texts, Paul is possibly creating a striking "reversal of fortunes" theme. In Ezekiel 36, the hearers/readers are to imagine themselves first as victims of the outpouring of God's wrath (for defiling the land) and then as recipients of God's cleansing, of new hearts and the Spirit. And Paul has called up this scenario in 2:14 to dramatize in Ezekiel's prophetic terms the changes that have taken place for the Christians in Crete.

Now, with the audience already immersed in the Ezekiel background, the echo of Joel's prophecy strikes a chord that is at once both harmonious and dissonant. The Spirit-promise attaches firmly to Ezekiel, but the verb describing this event, "pour out," clangs against the dominant use of "outpouring" for wrath in Ezekiel. The newly sounded OT text (Joel) does not supplant the first (Ezekiel), but rather it creates an atmosphere of climax: Paul paints a picture of dramatic reversal. God himself has brought his people from wrath to blessing, from immorality to godliness, by the provision of his Spirit. What was promised to God's people in exile is "now" being enjoyed

---

63. Titus 3:6a: οὗ ἐξέχεεν ἐφ᾽ ἡμᾶς πλουσίως;

Joel 3:1: καὶ ἐκχέω ἀπὸ τοῦ πνεύματός μου ἐπὶ πᾶσαν σάρκα.

Acts 2:17: καὶ ἔσται ἐν ταῖς ἐσχάταις ἡμέραις, λέγει ὁ θεός, ἐκχεῶ ἀπὸ τοῦ πνεύματός μου ἐπὶ πᾶσαν σάρκα.

64. LXX 7:5; 9:8; 14:19; 20:8, 13, 21; 21:36; 22:22, 31; 30:15; 36:18; 39:29; cf. Jer 6:11; Lam 2:4; 4:11.

by God's people in Christ. And in a way continuous with 2:14, the promise of the Joel text is combined creatively with the Ezekiel Spirit-texts and New Covenant prophecy to locate the Cretan Christians within redemptive history.

One further reason to suggest the wider background (Ezekiel and Joel) as a backdrop to the Cretan church's current status is seen primarily in Ezekiel's emphasis on an exhibition of God's holiness to the nations. The vehicle for this demonstration was to be the Spirit-filled, morally renewed people of Israel (36:22, 23, 24-27, 36). In Paul's adaptation this demonstration is to be eschatological, in the process of fulfillment as the outpouring of the Spirit on believers is to effect an exhibition of God's character through the life of the church for the powers and inhabitants of the world to see (3:1-2, 8).

Secondly, Paul centers this moment in high Christology. What the church ("us") has realized has come only "through Jesus Christ our Savior" (cf. 1:4; 2:13; 2 Tim 1:10). This phrase explains that in some sense Jesus Christ has given the Spirit himself (Acts 2:33). The degree to which this event is understood to be the co-action of God and Christ (cf. Acts 2:33) is left vague, but the transference of divine qualities operating in this text suggests something along the lines of the tradition as recorded by Luke. In this text, the second God-Christ equation occurs in the application of the "Savior" title (cf. "God our Savior," 3:4) to Christ (cf. 1:3-4). Equally, the implication is (as also seen in 2:14) that the Messiah has again fulfilled a promise that YHWH made to his covenant people. Finally, the "Savior" appellation makes the whole redemptive ministry of the Messiah the condition (fulfilled) of this action that he has carried out. With ethics and the new life at stake, Paul centers this life-changing development in the Christ-event.

7 As the long Greek sentence of the tradition comes to a close, the ultimate purpose of salvation[65] is stated. Paul shifts in this final statement to the metaphors of justification and inheritance. While this allows two more perspectives on salvation to be seen, the temptation to analyze the whole statement as if it yields a chronological formula or sequence of the experience of salvation must be resisted.[66]

---

65. The precise relationship of the purpose clause (ἵνα) to preceding verbs or verbal ideas (either ἔσωσεν, v. 5; ἐξέχεεν, v. 6; or the whole thought of vv. 4-6) is not clear. The point of the text is not specifically to identify "inheritance" with "the outpouring of the Spirit" in some chronological sense, as if the workings of the Godhead are experienced sequentially as discrete events in the life of the believer. Rather, coming as a culmination of the passage, the thought is clear enough: what God has done in Christ and through the Holy Spirit has made "us" heirs. Cf. Mounce, 451; Marshall, 323 n. 81.

66. The action expressed in the Gk. aorist participle δικαιωθέντες ("[we] having been justified") is coincident with the verbal idea it modifies, κληρονόμοι γενηθῶμεν ("we might be made [become] heirs"), as well as with the main verb of the sentence, "he saved us" (v. 5). In the complex of events being considered, heir-status, with its forward-looking

First, believers are now described as "having been justified by his grace." This is a very Pauline statement (Rom 3:24), and intends to do nothing more than summarize from a different perspective what has already been stated above (cf. Rom 5:1). In this case, the metaphor regards believers as having received the verdict of acquittal or vindication.[67] Also coming through clearly, in the Pauline sense, is the basis of this decision: "by his grace."[68] Whose grace is meant may seem to be unclear; but Paul's choice to employ the emphatic demonstrative pronoun (*ekeinou;* lit. "of that one"; cf. *autou,* "his," in Rom 3:24) suggests that Christ, the nearest antecedent, is meant — and the thought of Christ's grace is not unknown in Paul (1 Tim 1:14; 2 Cor 8:9).[69] Another instance of christological shift is thus evident (cf. 2:14): shifting slightly from Rom 3:24, the enactment of "grace" comes in the redemption accomplished by Christ.

Second, the relationship of this event (literally, "having been justified") to the other aspects of the salvation process is explained in various ways. But by recognizing that the main verb of the whole sentence is "he saved" and that the rest of the material aims to explore that claim, "justification" emerges as a very Pauline alternative for summarizing the whole event under consideration (cf. Rom 10:10). In another text that regards salvation from various perspectives, 1 Cor 6:11, there is no suggestion of a specific sequence of the various metaphors: (Spirit-)washing, sanctification, and justification are for all intents and purposes coincidental. So here, "having been justified" is coincident with "he saved" and also with the following action implied in the purpose, "so that . . . we might become heirs."

In the midst of this twofold reference to being saved ("he saved us . . .

---

reference to eternal life, comes logically as the conclusion. But in fact the distinction created by the use of verbs and metaphors for the single event of salvation is more one of perspective: on one side, we might line up God's decisive actions (saving, washing, justifying, adopting, etc.); on the other side are the positional categories of status (heir, children, etc.).

67. For Gk. δικαιόω in this sense, see Rom 3:24, 26, 28, 30; etc. Cf. G. Schrenk, *TDNT* 2:211-19. For a discussion of those who think otherwise, see Marshall, 323-24. Especially overplayed is the argument that Paul would have connected justification explicitly with "faith" (cf. 3:8); Paul sometimes omits explicit references to faith (though assuming its fundamental importance) in discussions of salvation, justification, and the like (Rom 6:1-11; 1 Cor 6:11; 12:13; 2 Cor 1:21-22).

68. The demonstrative pronoun is emphatic and refers to Christ. The phrase τῇ ἐκείνου χάριτι ("by his grace") mirrors the qualification in Rom 3:24 (τῇ αὐτοῦ χάριτι), but the shift in the pronoun indicates (for the present text) a christological one.

69. Marshall, 323 n. 83. See the same use of the pronoun ἐκεῖνος for Christ in 2 Tim 2:13. Some, however, see the statement as an echo of the Pauline text (or tradition) making God the most likely referent, Rom 3:24 (cf. Titus 2:11; 2 Tim 1:9); Mounce, 450; Quinn, 226.

having been justified") is the Spirit-statement. While this again defines the means by which the "saving" was effected, the Spirit's ministry also communicates the reality of the legal decision. But this is not to say (as some have, construing the sentence as an ordered sequence of events) that justification results from reception of the Spirit, or that it is the prerequisite for receiving the Spirit. Paul's reflection is theological and eschatological rather than chronological, and the theological material he has combined gathers together a number of metaphors to express what transpired in the Christ-event.

The final culminating metaphor is that of "becoming heirs."[70] "Inheritance" serves as another device for illustrating God's salvation. In NT use, the concept emerges from the rich background of the covenant to Abraham. Initially, the promises were material, related to lands to be possessed (Gen 13:14-17; 15:7, 18-21; 17:3-8). But these promises became emblematic of God's favor and blessing, and the whole concept was naturally expanded (2 Chron 6:27; *Psalms of Solomon* 7.2; 9.2) and easily transformed in NT use into a metaphor for salvation (Acts 2:32; 1 Cor 6:9-10; Eph 5:5; Col 3:24). By means of the concept, a writer could establish the tension between the presentness and futurity of salvation at once. Although this status (heir) has already been conferred by the declaration of the Father (Gal 4:7), the believer has not yet come fully into the inheritance. The forward look in hope is an integral part of the imagery. It is typical of Paul to associate the *klēronomoi*-status with such ideas as the work of the Spirit[71] and justification.[72]

In this NT transformation of the concept, the content of the inheritance itself was typically understood to be eternal life (Matt 19:29; Luke 18:18). But related ideas, such as "glory" (Rom 8:17; Eph 1:18), "grace" (1 Pet 3:7), "blessing" (1 Pet 3:9), and "salvation" (Heb 1:14), were also attached. Here the closing phrase, "according to the hope of eternal life,"[73] does not function to identify what is to be inherited (i.e., "eternal life"). "Heirs" is absolute, and the inheritance needs to be inferred (cf. Rom 4:14; 8:17). The function of the phrase is rather to set the promise of inheritance into the broader and more fundamental eschatological understanding of salvation moving toward the goal of "eternal life" (1:2; see on 1 Tim 1:16). That is, Paul qualifies the heir-status not in terms of some content (this is left implicit), but rather in terms of its fulfillment in just the same way as he does

70. Gk. κληρονόμος (Rom 4:13, 14; 8:17[2x]; Gal 3:29; 4:1, 7); W. Foerster and J. Herrmann, *TDNT* 3:767-85.

71. Rom 8:15-17; 1 Cor 6:9-11; Gal 3:14, 18; 4:6-7; Eph 1:13-14.

72. Rom 4:13-14; Gal 3:11-29.

73. In the phrase κατ᾽ ἐλπίδα ζωῆς αἰωνίου ("according to the hope of eternal life"), the genitive combination ζωῆς αἰωνίου modifies ἐλπίδα and not the more distant noun κληρονόμοι (the similar phrase in 1:2, ἐπ᾽ ἐλπίδι ζωῆς αἰωνίου, suggests that this combination is already somewhat formulaic; cf. Marshall, 325).

our possession of eternal life; thus the TNIV translation, "so that . . . we might become heirs having the hope of eternal life." Christians are heirs in process of coming into their inheritance, and the significance of the process is never minimized in Paul.[74]

In fact, it is the process of living that the confessional piece seeks to put into theological perspective. As a backing for the parenesis in 3:1-2, Paul declares that God himself, in and through the epiphany (of his Son), showed his kindness toward people by acting to save "us." The Spirit-perspective adopted in these materials underlines, moreover, that salvation is manifested among people in a new quality of living that originates in the cleansing activity of the Spirit, allowing believers to live according to the just demands of God. This ethical view of salvation makes the Spirit the source of the divine qualities needed to live in the way Paul enjoins: God's kindness and love for people are translated, in and through reception of the Spirit, into a manner of human living that embodies the life lived by the Messiah on earth.

c. The Motive (3:8)

8 Paul's next comment reflects back on 3:1-7 in order to reiterate the command to Titus and draw out more specifically the motivation behind the teaching. The reasons for seeing v. 8 in this relationship to the preceding are: (1) the formula "this is a trustworthy saying" (v. 8a) clearly refers backward to at least 3:[3]4-7; (2) the repetition and reformulation of the command to Titus ("I want you to stress these things") follow the same pattern used in 2:15 (pausing to summarize before moving on), and the term "these things" also points back to material just covered; (3) the purpose of the command (v. 8c) is spelled out in terms of doing "good [deeds]," which forms a verbal link with the description of Christian living in 3:1 ("ready to do whatever is good"); and (4) the closing rationale also reflects backward ("these things" refers to "good deeds") and echoes the concern that Christian character should affect people in general. On this understanding, the transition created at 3:9 ("but [you] avoid . . .") commences a new section (cf. the move from 1:16 to 2:1) that details how Titus should deal with the troublemakers.

What most attracts our attention is not the rhetorical importance of this summarizing statement, but the motive it gives for living the life of the Spirit in the world. Those who believe in God (the "us" who have been saved, washed, and who have received the Spirit, justification, and the status of heirs) have a responsibility to the world.

As we have seen throughout this letter, Paul never loses sight of the Cretan teachers even when issuing commands to Titus. The so-called "trust-

---

74. Cf. Marshall, 324-25; Mounce, 451.

worthy saying" formula is used at this point (as throughout these letters) to authenticate the statement of theology just given as apostolic and therefore authoritative (see 1 Tim 1:15, Excursus). It does not imply that traditional material has been cited, for Paul seems clearly to have given the material its present form, but rather to guarantee the veracity of this articulation, and this, presumably, in view of the challenges to his authority on Crete.

Within this summary and repetition of the command to Titus, the formula has two primary functions. First, its abrupt occurrence (asyndeton) and formulaic ring combine to emphasize the importance of the material to which it refers and to the summary and restatement of the command that follows. The formula refers backward,[75] though the extent of the "saying" is less clear, with scholars including as much as 3:3-7 and as little as 3:5b-6.[76] Since the sentence stretches from 3:4-7, at least that much is probably understood in the reference,[77] though given the variety and flexibility of the materials described by the formula, the whole of the "formerly–now" contrast may be included. Second, it serves to encapsulate the theological basis just laid down in full for the repetition of the instructions about to be given in brief (v. 8b-d).

After authenticating the theological statement, Paul reissues the teaching command above. In doing so, he returns to the official mandate tone in which the letter has been addressed to Titus and those communities under his care (also 1 Timothy; see Introduction, 31-36). The first-person expression of command, usually translated in the versions according to its ordinary meaning of "I want, wish, or desire" (as in 1 Tim 6:9), does not intend to create a mood of collegiality.[78] Rather, the verb expresses the command in the terms and tone of an official edict.[79] Titus's role is to carry out the apostolic edict in the Cretan churches.

The substance of the "edict" is expressed through the infinitive phrase

75. Some have understood the reference to be forward (R. A. Campbell, "Identifying the Faithful Sayings in the Pastoral Epistles," *JSNT* 54 [1994]: 78-79; Scott, 177-78), but the presence of the conjunction καί following the formula, as well as the obvious importance of the preceding content, makes this unlikely (cf. Marshall, 329).

76. The criteria by which these decisions are made become more questionable as the material included becomes smaller: 3:3-7 (Dibelius and Conzelmann, 147; Oberlinner, 181-82); 3:5b-7 (Mounce, 451, 48-49; Easton, 99); 3:5b-6 (Kelly, 254).

77. On this whole matter, see Knight, 347-49; idem, *Faithful Sayings,* 81-86. Cf. Fee, 207.

78. *Pace* Mounce, 452; Fee, 207.

79. Gk. βούλομαι has this formal sense in 1 Tim 2:8; 5:14. For the use, see Josephus, *Antiquities* 11.219; 12.150; 14.319. See the discussion in Wolter, *Paulustradition,* 173-74. In other Pauline letters, the command verb of choice is "I exhort" (παραγγέλλω), and the use of βούλομαι in the sense of "I want you to know" (Phil 1:12) is weaker (for one thing, the verb in these letters to coworkers calls for action; Marshall, 331 n. 93). The distinctive genre of Titus and 1 Timothy may account for the shift in language.

"to stress these things." In the second-person pronoun, Titus is charged to execute the edict. The didactic verb in this case, which occurs elsewhere in the
NT only of the false teachers and their "confident assertions" of falsehood in
1 Tim 1:7, expresses the idea "to insist confidently on."[80] The subject matter
consists of "these things."[81] The authority of the person issuing the edict
might be reason enough to emphasize the manner of teaching; but here the
reason is primarily the apostolic endorsement ("the saying is trustworthy")
given to the teaching Titus is to pass on. "These things" identifies the content
to be taught as broader than the singular faithful logion, including both the
parenesis (3:1-2) and the theology in which it is grounded (vv. 3-7).

In the purpose clause that follows *(hina),* we get another glimpse of
the rather "newborn" and precarious status of the congregations under Titus's
care. As with much of the teaching in the letter, this would probably fall into
the category of elementary Christianity. Titus is to nurture believers who will
commit themselves to bearing visible fruit out of genuine faith. The first
level of interest in this instruction has been and continues to be in those
whose present existence is determined by their recent decision to believe in
God ("those who have trusted in God").[82] That focus will widen shortly, but
for the moment their commitments are central. Insistent instruction is meant
to produce believers who are "careful to devote themselves to doing what is
good" — at least, this seems to be the intention of the combination of the

80. Gk. διαβεβαιόομαι (pres. inf.); for the sense, see Papias 2.3, where the topic is
that of passing on teaching and "guaranteeing" (διαβεβαιούμενος) its veracity. Cf. *Epistle
of Aristeas* 99: "I emphatically assert."

81. Gk. περὶ τούτων, "concerning these things," is anaphoric. Some scholars limit
the reference to the theological material of 3:3-7 (Easton, 101; Schlarb, *Die gesunde
Lehre,* 213), and Quinn, 241, links it to 1:5 and its reference to "the things that remain."
Johnson, *Paul's Delegates,* 250, understands it to include 2:1–3:7, and bearing in mind the
"household code" coherence of this whole span of text, this is a plausible construal. However, the summarizing function of the demonstrative pronoun and the repetition of the
command to teach parallel that of 2·15 (ταῦτα λάλει . . .), which suggests that the summary and recapitulation of 2:15 may also effectively serve as the backward boundary of
this reference; therefore, "these things" in 3:8b probably includes the parenesis of 3:1-2
(as the following purpose spelled out in terms of "good deeds" [3:1] demonstrates) and
the theological grounding of 3:3-7. See Marshall, 330.

82. Gk. οἱ πεπιστευκότες θεῷ (perf. ptc., "those who have believed in God");
Johnson, *Paul's Delegates,* 251, suggests that the perfect tense may emphasize a step only
recently taken. This newness of their faith, however, is better determined from other factors in the context of the letter than from the perfect tense; cf. 2 Tim 1:12; 1 Cor 9:17; Gal
2:7; 1 John 4:16; etc. The combination of πιστεύω (for the πίστις word group; see 1 Tim
1:2, note) and a dative object (θεῷ; but elsewhere with Christ as obj.) is standard in the NT
for depicting the relationship of personal faith in God/Christ (John 6:30; 8:31; Acts 5:14;
16:34; 27:25; Rom 4:3; 10:14; Gal 3:6; 2 Tim 1:12).

verb, meaning "to set the mind on, be intent on,"[83] and the complementary infinitive, meaning "devotion or practice" (3:14).[84] The combination is somewhat uncertain and yields literally the rather wordy idea: "that those who believe might fix their attention on being concerned with [devoted to, active in] good deeds."[85] The combination adds weight and urgency to the command. Titus's teaching is meant to prepare believers who have a strong sense of their responsibility to think through the practical implications of their faith (theology) and put these into action (= "good deeds, or what is good").

Most important for understanding the sense of this intention and action is the key term that denotes Christian action: "doing what is good" ("good deeds"). As pointed out, the term establishes a verbal link with the description of Christian behavior in society in 3:1 — the topic has not changed. But the background to this is the use of this language throughout these letters to depict the visible dimension of Christian existence in terms of service for others inspired by faith (2:7, 14; see 1 Tim 2:10, Excursus). Thus the teaching process (3:1-2, 8) is intended to bring believers to a holistic expression of their faith in God, an expression that incorporates the cognitive (faith) and practical (action) dimensions into a visibly distinct manner of life.

But why? At first glance, the closing statement of the section seems rather pallid and tame:[86] "These things are excellent and profitable for everyone." First, in the demonstrative pronoun "these things" we are again (for the third time in this verse) confronted with the question of an intended anteced-

---

83. Gk. φροντίζω; only here in the NT; in this sense (typically with gen. obj.), see LXX Ps 39:18; Prov 31:21; Sir 8:13; 32:1; 41:12; 50:4; 1 Macc 6:14; 2 Macc 9:21. BDAG, s.v., cites several instances of the verb with an infinitive complement. The word involves both intention and recognition of the responsibility to carry it out (Spicq, *TLNT* 3:467-69, esp. 467).

84. For the construction, see BDF §392.3. Gk. προΐστημι is used variously in the wider literature; the eight NT occurrences are Pauline, with most bearing the meaning "to lead" but also implying "care for" (see B. Reicke, *TDNT* 6:701-3). In Titus 3:8, Quinn, 234, adopts the meaning of "ruling, administration, etc." (1 Tim 3:4-5, 12; 5:17; Josephus, *Antiquities* 8.300), applying it here in the sense of "taking the lead [in doing good deeds]." Dibelius and Conzelmann, 151, note the term's use to express "caring for children." But that hardly fits. Some point out that the term was used for "carrying out a business, engaging in a profession" (Plutarch; Philostratus; see MM 541; Parry, 84); this is applied figuratively to mean, "make good deeds your business." On the whole, in combination with the verb "to set the mind on," the more likely meaning is "to be devoted to, to apply oneself to" (3:14; also with "good deeds" aṡ obj.; in a negative sense in Prov 26:17; cf. Josephus, *Antiquities* 5.90; cf. *EDNT* 3:156-57; B. Reicke, *TDNT* 6:700-703; see discussion in Johnson, *Paul's Delegates,* 250).

85. Cf. Louw-Nida 30.20; Johnson, *Paul's Delegates,* 248-49: "set their minds on engaging in good deeds."

86. Cf. Hanson, 194.

ent. There are three or more possibilities. The nearest possible antecedent is the plural phrase (rendered by TNIV) "what is good" (lit. "good deeds"; v. 8c).[87] The next nearest antecedent is the previous "these things" in v. 8b, encompassing then the whole of 3:1-8c.[88] A third possibility is that the reference is not so much to the specific materials above as to the ministry Titus is instructed to be engaged in ("stress confidently [i.e., teach]"), which is to result in action by believers ("concern to be active in doing what is good").[89] The latter suggestion provides the better contrast with the activities/teaching of the opponents about to be mentioned in 3:9. But the more likely reference is backward to the nearest antecedent, "good deeds." This is sometimes ruled out because the assessment "these things [= good deeds] are good . . ." is thought to result in a tautology. But however it might sound to us in English, "good deeds" *(kala erga)* is heavily coded language for authentic Christian living (see 1 Tim 2:10, Excursus), and it is therefore not a tautology to affirm the concept as "good" or "excellent." On the contrary, such wordplay might be an example of *paronomasia* employed to create a subtle emphasis.[90] If indeed Paul intends this statement to be read in connection with 3:1-2, the attention drawn to "good deeds" in this way would be helpful.

The life referred to in "these things" (i.e., the life characterized by Christian action) is described with two predicate adjectives. "Excellent" ("good"; see on 1 Tim 1:8) in this context is probably an ethical quality, an attractiveness (beauty) that is observable and can be demonstrated.[91] This demonstration is to yield positive results, as the second adjective, "profitable" ("useful, beneficial"), indicates. Paul's selection of this word, which was the criterion of authenticity in Hellenistic ethics (i.e., good teaching will make a positive difference), intentionally places his teaching and the ethical shape of the Christian life into the category of exemplary ethics (see on 1 Tim 4:8; 2 Tim 3:16). For the contrast to this, see the denunciation of the opponents' ways in 3:9.

Those for whom the demonstration of excellence (in good deeds) is meant to be useful are "people" ("everyone," TNIV, NRSV). These stand in contrast to "those who have trusted God" (3:8c) in the same way that "the people" in 3:1 (Cretan believers) stand in contrast to "everyone" in 3:2. The reference is to outsiders to the faith among whom believers are meant to make a positive demonstration of what is truly "good" in the acts they do for

87. Fee, 207-8.
88. Knight, 352; Mounce, 453; Brox, 311.
89. Marshall, 332-33; Barrett, 144-45; REB.
90. See BDF §488; cf. Quinn, 243.
91. For the emphasis on demonstration, see 3:1; cf. 1 Pet 2:12. See also Quinn, 243.

others. The link with 3:1-2, and a backward glance at the purpose(s) for godly living supplied in 2:5, 8, 10, suggests that the entire section, 3:1-8, is motivated by a missionary impulse. Just as Paul could co-opt various Hellenistic symbols and much of the current ethical language in order to set the Christian life alongside of and above the Hellenistic ideals, so here "profitable" comes to mean not simply producing the virtues in people, but ultimately (and theologically) producing the new life of the Spirit that comes through conversion. Paul envisions the Cretan church as an expression in human history and culture of the divine epiphany: in that event God expressed his kindness and love for people, and in the Spirit communicated these qualities to "those who have trusted in God." They in turn become channels for this process to continue in the world.

4. Disciplining the Opponents in the Church (3:9-11)

> 9 But avoid foolish controversies and genealogies and arguments and quarrels about the law, because these are unprofitable and useless. 10 Warn divisive people once, and then warn them a second time. After that, have nothing to do with them. 11 You may be sure that such people are warped and sinful; they are self-condemned.

The decision to begin a new paragraph at this point is based more on content than on absolute discourse markers.[1] The boundary between this last subsection of the body of the letter and the preceding subsection (3:1-8) is not so rigid as to rule out the interplay of ideas, contrast, and so on. These closing instructions address two situations that may or may not be interrelated. Verse 9 concerns Titus's response to the rebellious Cretan teachers. The description of the nature of their teaching and their quarreling over it suggest that this section reiterates instructions given in 1:10-16.[2] The former passage gave only the veiled instruction, "they must be silenced" (1:11), and here Titus is simply told to "avoid" engaging them on their terms. Presumably this does not mean to avoid them altogether, but rather to engage them with sound teaching and a godly demeanor (3:8; cf. the pattern in 2 Tim 2:23-26).[3] The second situation comes under the category of discipline, and the operative imperative in this case, "have nothing to do with them," envisions the last step of discipline in a worst-case scenario.

9 The section opens by introducing a mild contrast ("but"; *de*) with

---

1. So Fee, 210; TNIV; but see NA[27]; UBS[4]; Marshall, 19-25, 325 (3:8-11); NRSV; Quinn, 233; Johnson, *Paul's Delegates,* 248 (3:8b-11); Mounce, 434-43 (3:1-11).

2. For the possibility that 3:9-11 is in chiastic relation to 1:10-16, see Fee, 210.

3. See Wolter, *Paulustradition,* 137-38.

the tone and theme of 3:8. Whereas Titus is to insist on the teaching that leads to good deeds (v. 8b), he is to "avoid" the ways and teachings of the opponents.[4] The language of the command and the description of things to be avoided belong to Paul's polemical repertoire (cf. 1 Tim 4:7; 6:20; 2 Tim 2:23). "Avoidance" (or, more proactively, "shunning") urges nonparticipation in what are considered deceptively dangerous things (false teaching and disputes), but not complete disengagement from debate (cf. 1:14).

Paul lists four things that are in some sense interrelated. The first item, "foolish controversies" (2 Tim 2:23),[5] is a description of the way in which "inquiry" was carried out by the opponents rather than a comment on the content. The polemical adjective "foolish" labels the theological inquiries as frivolous and incompetent, apparently because they produced no worthwhile results (cf. 1 Tim 1:4).

The next term, "genealogies," identifies at least one element of the contents of their doctrines and perhaps also materials that played a part in their art of interpretation (see on 1 Tim 1:4). Although Quinn has argued that the term indicates some dispute about the genealogy of Christ,[6] the more likely reference is to a Jewish type of interpretation based on OT and extra-canonical stories of the biblical heroes and speculation based on family trees.[7] It is less clear how this material figured in the movement, but probably the biblical accounts and other legends formed the basis for certain aspects of belief and practice that ran counter to the apostolic faith. Equally uncertain is the degree to which this aspect of the opposition is related to the similar trend in Ephesus. As in 1:14, the instruction is to give such teaching a wide berth.

Reflecting further on the liabilities of the rebellious Cretan teachers, Paul in the third and fourth terms shifts the focus to the observable chaos produced by their controversies and speculative debates. First, the plural term "arguments" (*ereis;* "dissensions, quarrels"; see on 1 Tim 6:4) depicts the general state of dissension and discord surrounding the movement. In 1 Tim 6:4 the link between dissension and the arcane disputes about interpretation is clear. The use of the term in Hellenistic Jewish and NT vice lists links it with the sort of base ("Cretan") lifestyle that Paul denounced and sought to transform in the fledgling Christian communities on the island.

4. For Gk. περῐΐστημι ("avoid, shun"), see 2 Tim 2:16 (discussion and note).

5. For Gk. ζήτησις (pl., "investigation, controversy, dispute"), see 1 Tim 6:4 (note). For Gk. μωρός ("foolish, stupid"; 2 Tim 2:23, note) used of things, see 1 Cor 1:25, 27; *1 Clement* 39.1; cf. Eph 5:4 (μωρολογία). To judge from 2 Tim 2:23, where the combination also occurs, the adjective μωράς belongs only with the following noun, ζητήσεις.

6. Quinn, 245-46.

7. The view that the term refers to the system of Gnostic aeons and emanations (Dibelius and Conzelmann, 16-17; Hanson, 194; Rudolph, *Gnosis,* 321-22; cf. Irenaeus, *Against Heresies* 1.30.9) is anachronistic. See the full discussion at 1 Tim 1:4.

"Quarrels about the law" alludes to heated arguments about Torah (cf. 1 Tim 1:7).[8] The nature of the quarrels is not completely clear. We may reasonably surmise that the "talmudic" sifting of Scriptures and traditions was applied in support of excessive views about ritual purity (1:14-15); but the whole picture must include the persistent attachment of these teachers to Cretan values that would hardly have sat easily with such Jewish-oriented views. In any case, the disruption implied posed at least part of the threat to the Christian households (1:11) and to the Cretan church's image in society.

Titus was not to wade into this situation as another debater. The reason ("for"; *gar*) for avoidance of the interpretive arguments is their worthlessness. Two near synonyms render this assessment. The first, "unprofitable" (*anō-pheleis;* Heb 7:18),[9] sets up a deliberate contrast with the assessment of "good deeds" as "profitable" *(ōphelima)* in the preceding verse. The proof of the negative assessment can be seen — in stark contrast to the aims of "good deeds" — in the turbulence and fighting generated by these discussions. The second term, "useless" ("empty, vain, worthless, futile"), strengthens the denunciation; in the Greek canonical OT, especially, the term often appears in connection with idolatry, while in the NT it describes a condition apart from God.[10] Together these descriptors measure the fruitlessness of these debates about interpretation in terms of the distance, both ethically and doctrinally, they put between God and people.

10-11 How is Titus to engage the disputants? Verse 10 guides him in the appropriate way to address the problem. The instruction sets out a disciplinary or corrective process that breaks down into three steps, with the assumption that a good response on the part of the offender would bring the process to a halt. The offender (appropriately pluralized in the TNIV) is the "divisive person," the one causing (or promoting) factions in the church. The term *hairetikos* had not yet acquired the technical meaning "heretic" (but see 2 Pet 2:1); nonetheless, in this case divisiveness is directly linked to errant

---

8. Gk. μάχας νομικάς; the noun μάχη ("fighting, quarrels, strife") indicates bitter quarrels that in this context amount to word battles (cf. λογομαχία; 1 Tim 6:4; 2 Tim 2:14); 2 Cor 7:5; Jas 4:1; O. Bauernfeind, *TDNT* 4:527-28. The adjective νομικός ("relating to the law") identifies the subject of the quarrels as the Jewish law (cf. W. Gutbrod, *TDNT* 4:1088); elsewhere in the NT (see 3:13) the term is used substantively for "lawyer" (e.g., Luke 7:30).

9. Cf. Gk. ἀνωφελεῖς (LXX Prov 28:3; Isa 44:10; Wis 1:11; *Psalms of Solomon* 16:8; see further on 1 Tim 4:8, discussion and note) with the cognate ὠφέλιμα, 3:8.

10. Gk. μάταιος ("idle, fruitless, powerless"; 1 Cor 3:20; 15:7; Jas 1:26) belongs to the polemical language of these letters to coworkers; it is used in compounds of the teaching of the opponents (1:10; 1 Tim 1:6). LXX: Lev 17:7; 1 Kgs 16:2, 13, 26; 2 Chron 11:15; Isa 2:20; Jer 8:19; NT: 1 Cor 3:20; 15:17; Jas 1:26; 1 Pet 1:18). Cf. O. Bauernfeind, *TDNT* 4:519-22.

teachings and practice.[11] The phenomenon develops around an opinion (or set of them), belief, or ideology (perhaps including praxis) that a group holds so firmly that it separates from the larger community — thus the sense of factionalism or divisiveness. From the standpoint of the community (even one as small as a household), the danger lies, on the one hand, in fragmentation and resultant instability, which becomes particularly acute if the faction actively proselytizes within the larger community. On the other hand, the activity of such teachers, whose reputations are already marked in society, poses a danger to the public image of the church. People included in this "divisive" category are envisaged as holding to the opposition's views so firmly that they foment further strife in the church.

The corrective process that Paul describes involves confronting the offender with a formal verbal warning. It is an application of the qualification set out in 1:9 with a verb of the word group ("*refute* those who oppose [the sound doctrine]"). Here behind the TNIV's translation, "warn . . . and then warn a second time," is actually the noun meaning "admonition." This includes instruction, correction, and warning with a view to regaining the offender (as in 2 Tim 2:25-26).[12] More than formal accusation, the process includes corrective teaching in the effort to convince the offender of the ethical or doctrinal error and win him/her back.[13]

Recovery of the errant person is a high priority, and the protracted character of the process has precisely this goal in mind. If the first warning is met with resistance, Titus is to make a second attempt to persuade the offender. This procedure may be modeled on the Jesus tradition (Matt 18:15-17), which endorsed an extended disciplinary process for the sake of restoration.

Finally, if a first and second encounter did not bring the offender around, the last measure to be taken was exclusion from the congregation in some sense. The verb indicating this measure has various uses, which makes the sense of this step somewhat unclear ("have nothing to do with them").[14] Probably the severest sense of "drive out, dismiss, discharge"[15] is meant,

---

11. Gk. αἱρετικός; as in the use of the noun for factions or divisions (1 Cor 11:19; Gal 5:20); in the sense of a sect (Acts 5:17; 15:5; 24:5, 14; 26:5; 28:22). For later church use in the sense of "heresy," see 2 Pet 2:1; Ignatius, *To the Ephesians* 6.2; *To the Trallians* 6.1. H. Schlier, *TDNT* 1:184.

12. Gk. νουθεσία (for the noun see 1 Cor 10:11; Eph 6:4; see the verb in 1 Thess 5:14; 2 Thess 3:15); in various instructional and disciplinary contexts (Acts 20:31; Rom 15:14; 1 Cor 4:14; Col 1:28; 3:16).

13. See J. Behm, *TDNT* 4:1022.

14. Gk. παραιτέομαι ("to reject or refuse someone"; 1 Tim 5:11, note; Heb 12:25); "to avoid" (of false teaching, controversies, or death; 1 Tim 4:7, note; 2 Tim 2:23; Acts 25:11). Cf. G. Stählin, *TDNT* 1:195.

15. As in Diogenes Laertius 6.82; Plutarch, *Moralia* 206A (see BDAG, s.v. 2.b.β).

with excommunication from the church in view (see on 1 Tim 1:20). Measures of expulsion such as this were apparently taken to various lengths for various offenses in Qumran.[16] But the procedure to be followed by Titus seems closer to the spirit of the Jesus tradition, and corresponds to the disciplinary measures glimpsed elsewhere in Paul. Above all, the finality of the measure is not addressed. In the present context of controversy and disruption to the fellowship, this last step of discipline is as much a matter of damage control for the community's sake as it is a punitive action calculated to bring the offending individual to repentance.

Justification for this most severe step of exclusion is given in v. 11.[17] There are three elements to Paul's reasoning. First, this kind of person (i.e., one who stubbornly resists a first and second admonition) demonstrates by such resistance that corruption has already set in. The perfect tense verb, literally "has been perverted, corrupted" (TNIV, "such people are warped"), depicts a present state that has arisen out of past actions.[18] The implication is of a hardened state of mind.

Secondly, it follows from this that the offender's present manner of life is characterized by continuing to sin. In this case, the present tense verb "keeps on sinning" (TNIV, "such people are . . . sinful") implies that the warning has been rejected and therefore that the individual, now with knowledge of the error, is culpable (see on 1 Tim 5:20). "Sinning" includes self-deception and error in continuing to embrace the culturally deformed message as true; but it also includes deliberate wrongdoing in leading others astray, disrupting households and the church, and in rebelling against apostolic authority (1:10).

Third, a final participial phrase concludes the assessment of such a person or group as "being self-condemned."[19] The meaning is clear: having been admonished of error (repeatedly), the offender's persistence in the teaching and stubborn refusal to acknowledge the apostolic warning amount

16. 1QS 6–7; 4Q270, frag. 11, col. 11.8-14; 4Q266, frag. 18, col. 4.1-8 *(Damascus Document)*.

17. The adverbial participle εἰδώς (οἶδα) is causal: "because you know." For appeal to "what is commonly known" as a basis for action, see 1 Tim 1:8, 9 (discussion and notes); 2 Tim 1:15.

18. Gk. ἐκστρέφω ("to morally turn aside, pervert"; BDAG; only here in the NT; for the perfect participle in this sense, see Deut 32:20; see the transitive use in Hermas, *Similitude* 8.6.5); cf. Matt 17:17, διεστραμμένη; Acts 20:30; Phil 2:15). For similar uses of the perfect tense, see 1 Tim 6:5; 2 Tim 3:8.

19. Gk. αὐτοκατάκριτος ("self-condemned"; only here in the NT) is rare (see the only other example in F. Büchsel, *TDNT* 3:952; Dibelius and Conzelmann, 151); the adjective is attached to the one under discussion (ὁ τοιοῦτος; "such one"; for the pejorative categorizing use of this demonstrative, see 1 Cor 5:11; 2 Cor 2:6; 2 Thess 3:12) loosely with the participial phrase ὢν αὐτοκατάκριτος (lit. "being self-condemned").

to a self-pronouncement of guilt (cf. Luke 19:22; Gal 2:11). One such as this person is to be removed from the church.

IV. PERSONAL NOTES AND INSTRUCTIONS (3:12-14)

12 As soon as I send Artemas or Tychicus to you, do your best to come to me at Nicopolis, because I have decided to winter there. 13 Do everything you can to help Zenas the lawyer and Apollos on their way and see that they have everything they need. 14 Our people must learn to devote themselves to doing what is good, in order to provide for urgent needs and not live unproductive lives.

In typically abrupt fashion, Paul turns from the closing church-related instructions of the body of the letter to the more practical and personal instructions regarding his own movements and needs and those of the mission team. Although the abruptness may give the impression that this section was dispensable, it was apparently chiefly by this means that Paul maintained the mission network and organized movements essential to its effective ministry (cf. on 2 Tim 4:9-18). The items mentioned conform to the pattern of the closing sections of other Pauline letters (e.g., Rom 16:1-23; 1 Cor 16:1-24; Col 4:7-18; Phlm 23-24),[1] with the movement of personnel, including orders for Titus's redeployment to Paul, at the center. It is not unusual to find scholars who maintain that such details belong to the letter's supposed pseudepigraphical, fictive character, either intended to give the letter a "Pauline" look,[2] or in more nuanced ways to complete the task of extending the apostle's influence to the "third generation" of the Christian mission and church.[3] The view adopted here, however, regards these details within the historical context of the apostle's ministry.

12 First, Paul clarifies his plan for Titus's redeployment. It is contingent on the arrival of one or the other of two people meant presumably to replace Titus.[4] At the point of writing, Paul had apparently yet to decide

1. See the discussion in Marshall, 340.

2. Collins, *Letters,* 125; Donelson, *Pseudepigraphy and Ethical Argument in the Pastoral Epistles,* 23-24; Hasler, 99.

3. See esp. Oberlinner, 193-202; Dibelius and Conzelmann, 152-54; Bassler, 212-14.

4. The temporal conjunction ὅταν, "when, whenever," followed by the subjunctive verb (here πέμψω, aor. subj. "[whenever] I send"), introduces a condition to be fulfilled (but as yet unfulfilled) in the future (see BDF §382); for similar occurrences, see 1 Cor 16:2, 3, 5, 12.

which one he would send. The language of "sending" is typically used to describe Paul's deployment of his team,[5] and we may assume that the two people mentioned are colleagues. The first of these, "Artemas,"[6] is a Greek name otherwise unknown in the NT. About "Tychicus" (also Greek)[7] we are better informed, assuming that he is the same person who traveled with Paul on his third missionary journey, from the province of Asia, named in Acts 20:4; Eph 6:21; Col 4:7 (2 Tim 4:12).[8] The references in Ephesians and Colossians cast him in a similar role as Paul's emissary. It remains unknown which of these coworkers finally received the assignment. One scenario places this letter in very close proximity to 2 Timothy, in which case Paul might have selected Artemas for this assignment since Tychicus was sent to Ephesus (2 Tim 4:12). But an earlier placement of this letter (and 1 Timothy; see Introduction, 37-52) would require another scenario.

Once relief had arrived, Titus was to travel to Nicopolis to be with Paul for the winter. The language of this instruction is identical to that given to Timothy in 2 Tim 4:9: "Do your best to [hurry/hasten to] come to me."[9] The versions opt for the sense of determination (2 Tim 2:15)[10] rather than for speed (2 Tim 4:21),[11] but the time frame probably suggests that, once relieved, Titus is to make his move without delay.

Titus's destination was to be "Nicopolis." Of the various places with that name,[12] Nicopolis of Epirus,[13] on the west coast of the Greek peninsula across from the southern end of the Italian peninsula, is by far the most likely. This location corresponds to Paul's statement about the extent of his ministry (as far as Illyricum [Rom 15:19], which was to the north of Epirus), as well as to the later note that Titus was in Dalmatia (2 Tim 4:10).

At the time of writing, Paul had not yet reached Nicopolis ("I have de-

5. Gk. πέμπω ("to send, dispatch"); for this sense, see 1 Cor 4:17; 16:3; 2 Cor 9:3; Eph 6:26; etc.

6. Gk. Ἀρτεμᾶς is short for Ἀρτεμίδορος ("gift of Artemis"; BDAG, s.v.; BDF §125.1).

7. Gk. Τύχικος (see BDAG, s.v.).

8. See further J. Gillman, "Tychicus," n.p., *ABD on CD-ROM*. Version 2.1a. 1995, 1996, 1997.

9. Gk. σπούδασον ἐλθεῖν πρός με (cf. 2 Tim 4:21: σπούδασον πρὸ χειμῶνος ἐλθεῖν); on the sense of the imperative (either "to hurry" or "to be earnest to"; Gk. σπουδάζω), see 2 Tim 2:15 (note).

10. TNIV, NRSV, GNB, CEV; Quinn, 264; Mounce, 457.

11. REB; Marshall, 341 (and n. 6).

12. Gk. Νικόπολις (only here in the NT). See R. W. Smith, "Nicopolis," n.p., *ABD on CD-ROM*. Version 2.1a. 1995, 1996, 1997; BDAG, s.v.; Spicq, 690.

13. Ptolemy, *Geography* 3.13 (he locates it in Epirus); Tacitus, *Annals* 2.53 (he locates it in Achaia). See further the discussion in Dibelius and Conzelmann, 152-53.

cided to winter *there*").[14] And we are to assume that decisions[15] about his future plans made this busy port town (known for its harsh winters) a strategic spot to spend the winter.[16] The size of the town would have afforded sufficient ministry opportunities among those who were similarly laid up until the passing of the winter months opened up sea travel again. But what Paul had in mind for Titus is not divulged. Presumably, he was to assume another such posting or to assist Paul directly. In either case, the time left to Titus in Crete was apparently sufficient for him to accomplish his duties (1:5; etc.); once his replacement came, however, he had (because of the onset of winter?) to make his way to Nicopolis with speed.

13 Paul next instructs Titus to "do everything you can" to assist[17] two other team members who were due to come to Titus (probably bearing this letter) and then continue on to other places. The verb suggests that his task is to help them in practical ways to be able to continue their journey without delay.[18] In fact, the continuation of the thought in v. 14 suggests that Titus will accomplish this by mobilizing the church to help. And this corresponds to the expectation, linked to this verb's use in Paul's discussions of his and his coworkers' travel plans, that house churches would fulfill the responsibility of extending hospitality to traveling Christians.[19]

Of the two men who are mentioned, "Zenas the lawyer," a Greek to judge from his name, is known to us only here. Speculation as to why the description "the lawyer" is included with his name remains largely just that — speculation.[20] He was undoubtedly a lawyer.[21] His Greek name (meaning

14. Gk. adverb of place ἐκεῖ, "there" (as opposed to ὧδε, "here"), makes this clear.

15. Gk. κρίνω ("to decide, select"; for this ordinary sense of human decision, see also Acts 3:13; 1 Cor 2:2; 7:37; etc.). The perfect tense κέκρικα ("I have decided") suggests that a firm decision was made (Knight, 357).

16. Gk. παραχειμάζω ("to spend the winter"; Acts 27:12; 28:11; 1 Cor 16:6); MM.

17. Gk. σπουδαίως (2 Tim 1:17; Luke 7:4; Phil 2:28). In this case, the adverb (cognate to the command verb of 3:12) stresses "zeal and earnestness" in the action it modifies (G. Harder, *TDNT* 7:559-68).

18. Gk. προπέμπω (impv. "to send on one's way, accompany, escort, assist someone in making a journey"), always in this sense in Paul (Rom 15:24; 1 Cor 16:6, 11; 2 Cor 1:16; cf. Acts 15:3; 3 John 6; 1 Macc 12:4). Cf. *EDNT* 3:160; Dibelius and Conzelmann, 152.

19. See A. J. Malherbe, *Social Aspects of Early Christianity* (2d ed.; Philadelphia: Fortress, 1983), 67-68.

20. For example, Hasler, 99, suggested that this was Paul's attorney, whose legal services, now that Paul had been released, were no longer required. Spicq, 697, suggested that the description was intended to distinguish this Zenas from another by that name also known to Titus (or the church), but this does us little good (and such titles were added occasionally without this intention; Rom 16:23; Col 4:14; Marshall, 343).

21. Gk. νομικός; the non-Jewish usage is well known (BDAG, s.v.; Spicq, 691).

"gift of Zeus")²² suggests that his expertise lay in Greek or Roman law and not in Jewish law.²³ "Apollos,"²⁴ however, is probably the same character associated with Paul in the Corinth-Ephesus stage of the mission.²⁵ While some uncertainty remains with regard to their relationship as reflected in the early chapters of 1 Corinthians, the final reference in 1 Cor 16:12 suggests basic amicability and even cooperation in the mission.²⁶

The purpose of this assistance is given in the *(hina)* clause that follows: "that they have everything they need" (or, literally, "that they lack nothing").²⁷ Paul obviously (see 3:14) has in mind replenishing their material supplies, including money, food, and other practical provisions needed for traveling.²⁸

14 The text suggests that Paul's intention was that this need be met not by Titus alone, but rather by the Cretan Christians themselves, an example of how to extend the practice of "doing good deeds" (3:8) in a direction not anticipated.²⁹ "Our people"³⁰ refers to the Cretan believers as fellow Christians and related in some sense to Paul and Titus. Rather than take this description as deliberately excluding the opponents, it is probably closer to the intention to say that Paul envisages authentic believers who will distinguish themselves as such by practicing their faith in this way. The indirect instruction, "let them learn," means learning by doing (see on 1 Tim 5:4, 13).³¹

And in this case the activity to be learned is described with exactly the

22. Gk. Ζηνᾶς; on the meaning and formation of the name, see BDF §125.1; MM.
23. But see Lock; cf. Mounce, 458.
24. Gk. Ἀπολλῶς is common, being derived from various longer names (see BDAG, s.v.; BDF §§55.1; 125.1).
25. Acts 18:24; 19:1; 1 Cor 1:12; 3:4, 5, 6, 22; 4:6; 16:12.
26. See further Fee, *1 Corinthians,* 823-25; but cf. Schlarb, *Die gesunde Lehre,* 19, 28-36.
27. For Gk. λείπω ("to lack"), see 1:5 (discussion and note). Most English translations (TNIV, NRSV, GNB, CEV, REB), in seeking a smoother sentence, treat the purpose clause as an independent instruction.
28. For various explanations of this note by those who regard the letter to be pseudonymous and the note, therefore, fictitious, see Bassler, 214; Brox, 313; Merkel, 107.
29. Here the meaning of the combination δὲ καί is not completely clear: it either envisions an additional logical application of the earlier command, modifying the verb: "let our people learn *also,*" or it modifies the subject, meaning "let our people [in addition to others (the Pauline coworkers? unbelievers?; cf. Quinn, 267; Lock, 158)] also learn." See the discussion in Quinn, 267; Marshall, 345 n. 17.
30. For the Gk. phrase οἱ ἡμέτεροι in this sense, see 3 Macc 1:27; *Martyrdom of Polycarp* 9.1; Josephus, *Antiquities* 14.228; cf. Spicq, *TLNT* 1:97 n. 1; Quinn, 257-58.
31. As opposed to learning by means of formal instruction. See Quinn, 267-68. For Gk. μανθάνω ("to learn"), see 1 Tim 2:11 (discussion and note).

same language as in 3:8c: "to devote themselves to doing what is good [good deeds]." The obvious significance of the exact repetition of this language is that here Paul gives specific and practical directions as to the practice of the lifestyle defined more broadly in the first occurrence of the term. The instruction is specific in that it has the situation of the two travelers just mentioned in mind. It is practical in that the kinds of needs they were likely to have were to be met in very practical expressions of sharing and hospitality. "Good deeds" in this sense is consistent with the instruction above and the wider use of "good deeds" in these letters to Titus and Timothy — as descriptive of visible acts of service that emerge from genuine faith (see 1 Tim 2:10, Excursus). Thus the goal of this devotion to service (to actualizing one's faith) is "to provide for urgent [daily] needs." The noun-adjective combination[32] is idiomatic, stressing the indispensability or urgency of the needs.[33] The thought is parallel to that in Rom 12:13. The need to be met in 3:13 suggests the scope of Paul's immediate thought as he issued this instruction: "in order to provide for urgent needs [of such Christian travelers]."[34]

From an ethical standpoint, the purpose *(hina)* of learning to behave in this way is to ensure fruitfulness. Expressed negatively here because of the overbearing presence of unfruitful Cretan Christians (opponents),[35] the thought is nevertheless a positive one, as the use of the metaphor throughout the NT demonstrates. One who is connected to Christ, or, in Pauline thought, has the Spirit (3:5-6), bears the corresponding fruit (Eph 5:9; Col 1:6, 10). The shift of metaphors from "good deeds" to "fruit" forms an equation that is already made in Paul (Col 1:10; Eph 5:11); with either metaphor the goal is the same — that the Cretan believers will become holistic Christians whose authentic faith is exhibited in their good acts. Some commentators suggest a connection between this phrase and the later Roman allegation that Christians were "unproductive" *(infructuosi)* in the commercial sphere.[36] Whether

---

32. Gk. ἀναγκαῖος (adj., "necessary"; here in combination with the noun, "pressing, urgent, indispensable"; Acts 13:46; 2 Cor 9:5; Phil 1:24; 2:25; Heb 8:3) plus the Gk. noun χρεία ("that which is lacking, is needed"; e.g., practical necessities such as food, clothing, and shelter; Acts 20:34; 28:10; Rom 12:13; *Epistle of Aristeas* 11).

33. For numerous references to nonbiblical sources, see Spicq, *TLNT* 1:97-98.

34. See also Johnson, *Paul's Delegates,* 253; Marshall, 346. The insertion at this point in the closing notes of a general call to Christians to offer relief in disasters (in the way often done by wealthy benefactors; cf. Hanson, 196-97; Spicq, 693) seems out of place.

35. Gk. ἄκαρπος ("unfruitful, useless, unproductive"; 1 Cor 14:14; Eph 5:11; for the negative term used to describe unproductive believers or unbelievers, see Matt 13:22; Eph 5:11; 2 Pet 1:8); cf. Spicq, *TLNT* 1:56-57. For the Gk. ἵνα μή ("so that not" plus subj. verb) formula of prohibition, see on 2:5; 1 Tim 3:6, 7; 6:1.

36. Lock, 159 (citing Tertullian, *Apology* 42.1); Spicq, *TLNT* 1:57 n. 7; Marshall, 346; Mounce, 459 all mention it.

such a criticism was already being voiced or not, the overall concern for the church's public image (3:1-2, 8) is still in force, and it would have been disgraceful for members of the Christian movement to fail to meet the practical needs of fellow members and especially leaders.

Paul thus uses the practical application (3:13-14) to restate one final time the main point of the letter (1:16; 2:7, 14; 3:1, 8c). In the epiphany of Christ, God communicated grace and gifts to enable his people to live in a qualitatively different way from the rest of the world. The outward dimension of this new existence (attributed to God's grace, to Christ's self-offering, and to the gift of the Spirit) is defined in terms of "good deeds." Transcending the good deeds of Hellenistic culture (benefaction) often done in order to receive back the praise of society's leaders, and revealing the inferiority of the Cretan-tinged version of the faith, these Christian good deeds consist of sacrificial service done for others. This sacrificial action effectively prolongs the epiphany of God's grace so that people outside the faith community might become aware of the reality of Christ among his people.

V. FINAL GREETINGS AND BENEDICTION (3:15)

15 *Everyone with me sends you greetings. Greet those who love us in the faith. Grace be with you all.*

Paul's letter closings vary with the situations. Typically, they include greetings (some more extended with references to colleagues and mutual acquaintances, some quite brief) and a blessing (see on 2 Tim 4:19), and this closing is no different. No names of colleagues or believers known to both parties are mentioned (cf. 2 Tim 4:19-21; Phlm 23-24; etc.), but the expression of greetings underlines the team's love and concern for Titus and those to whom he was ministering (Phil 4:21-22).

15 Reflecting perhaps the mandate dimension of this letter (see Introduction, 31-36) — written to the coworker directly and less directly to the churches to which he had been appointed — greetings are sent first to Titus. The verb of greeting is standard (see on 2 Tim 4:19), and the object is the singular "you" (= Titus; cf. 2 Tim 4:21; Phlm 23; 2 John 13; 3 John 15). Those sending the greetings are Paul's companions: "everyone with me."[1] The most likely explanation for the vagueness of the greeting is that Titus did not know those traveling with Paul. This is hardly surprising (Phil 4:21), and the important thing is the note of concern that the greeting expresses.

---

1. Gk. οἱ μετ' ἐμοῦ πάντες; cf. Phil 4:21: οἱ σὺν ἐμοὶ ἀδελφοί (Gal 1:2).

Paul then instructs Titus to pass on the team's greetings to "those who love us in the faith." The main question in this language is whether Paul intends to differentiate between those who support the apostle and his work (the faithful) and those who oppose it (the rebellious Cretan teachers). First, we should be careful not to make too much of the phrase "those who love us," which was a fixed phrase in letters.[2] Paul is not prone to describe those known by, or well disposed toward, him (and his team) in this way,[3] but the shift in letter form may account for the use of the stock term. It is, nevertheless, Christianized by the addition of the prepositional phrase "in the faith" (see on 1 Tim 1:2).[4] As a description of "love," the phrase indicates either "love as believers" (TNIV; NRSV; CEV; GNB) or faithful love.[5] In terms of epistolary effect, there is really little difference between the two options. In either case, the phrase describes Paul's friends in the Cretan churches, and they will have been those who supported him and recognized his authority. The degree to which Paul intends to separate the sheep from the goats is less clear, but the probability that the opposition is still in mind at the close of the letter seems high.[6]

Finally, Paul ends the letter with a benediction: "Grace be with you all." The language differs from the benedictions of 1 Tim 6:21 and 2 Tim 4:22 (see Col 4:18) only in the addition of "all" (see Heb 13:25). The grace-wish is not a literary formality,[7] but rather a genuine prayer or blessing that desires for the recipients the full experience of God's gracious and loving presence (with all this entails).[8] "All" extends the blessing to the churches under Titus's charge. Given the kinds of moral, social, and ecclesiastical challenges facing the young Cretan churches, and given the goal of actualizing faith in dynamic Christian living that Paul has set before them, this wish for a holistic experience of God's grace was nothing less than a final prayer for strength in battle.

2. Gk. τοὺς φιλοῦντας ἡμᾶς. See the examples in Dibelius and Conzelmann, 155; and a fuller list in G. Stählin, *TDNT* 9:137 n. 214.

3. The more intimate "beloved" (ἀγαπητοί) being preferred (e.g., 1 Cor 10:14; 15:58; Phil 2:12; etc.); G. Stählin, *TDNT* 9:113-46.

4. For the phrase in various senses, see 1 Tim 1:2, 4; 2:7, 15; 3:13; 4:12; 2 Tim 1:13.

5. Arichea and Hatton, 314.

6. This does not, however, imply that Titus is to dole out or withhold greetings within the churches based on his assessment of their loyalty to the apostle (*pace* Knight, 359-60). See Marshall, 348.

7. See the discussion and notes at 1 Tim 6:21.

8. See Oberlinner, 201, who equates χάρις here with "salvation."

INDEX OF SUBJECTS

INDEX OF AUTHORS

811

INDEX OF SCRIPTURE REFERENCES

7:32-40	250n.42		673, 687,	11	196, 223, 227
7:33	293n.37		791n.82	11:2	55, 430-31,
7:34	293n.37, 350	9:18	366n.32		452nn.31-32
7:37	222n.93,	9:21	125	11:2-16	49
	275n.21,	9:22	167, 328	11:3-16	227
	531n.79, 801n.15	9:24	492	11:5	215, 218
7:39	293n.37, 350,	9:24-25	157n.14	11:5-10	192
	352, 355	9:24-26	494	11:6	697n.86
7:39-40	251n.42	9:24-27	306, 495	11:8	226
7:40	59	9:25	310, 612, 690	11:8-9	226
8-10	294	9:26	615	11:9	296n.49, 300n.68
8:1	433n.42	9:27	187n.75,	11:10	222n.93, 373n.63
8:1-13	294		282n.54, 328,	11:12	232n.128
8:4-6	153n.72		598, 600n.20,	11:13	209n.53
8:4-8	706n.131		614, 617, 711	11:14	540n.119
8:6	180	10	533, 537	11:16	256n.83
8:7	117, 433n.42	10:1-13	591	11:17	108n.16
8:10	117, 433n.42	10:2	564n.66	11:19	327n.55, 797n.11
8:11	433n.42	10:3-4	157	11:21	187n.75
8:12	117	10:4	564n.66	11:22	256n.83, 314n.4
8:13	294	10:6	150n.63, 314n.9,	11:23-26	59
9	365		590	11:24	185n.64
9:2	531	10:11	55, 553, 590,	11:28	265n.23
9:3	636		797n.12	11:30	161, 491n.11
9:4	222n.93, 697n.86	10:12	531n.79	11:32	747n.14
9:5	222n.93	10:13	144, 402,	11:34	681n.18
9:6	222n.93		513n.71, 574	12-14	223
9:7	157n.12,	10:14	408n.8, 534,	12	321
	364n.18, 492,		805n.3	12:4	321n.36, 458n.8
	494-95	10:16	297n.51	12:4-11	457
9:7-14	363	10:19-21	298	12:5	137
9:9	364n.26, 365n.27	10:20	290n.22	12:6	458n.10
9:9-10	365, 370	10:20-21	290	12:7	322n.41
9:9-14	59	10:21	290n.22	12:8	322n.41, 479n.97
9:10	364n.26,	10:25	117	12:9	321n.36, 458n.8
	495n.34, 590,	10:25-31	294	12:10	156n.7
	669n.23	10:26	298, 300,	12:13	192, 219, 237,
9:12	123n.5, 697n.86		706n.131		380, 381n.11,
9:13	582	10:27	117		714, 787n.67
9:14	131, 681n.18,	10:28	117	12:17	604n.50
	697n.86	10:29	117	12:18	177n.33
9:15	123n.5, 384n.27	10:30	297n.51, 299-	12:21-26	540
9:16	133, 608		300, 556n.22,	12:23	540n.123
9:17	100n.31, 112-13,		707	12:26	474n.81
	133, 366n.32,	10:32	256n.83, 258n.94	12:28	50, 138n.17, 187,
		10:33	328		

859

INDEX OF EARLY EXTRABIBLICAL LITERATURE

866

Epiphanius
PG 41:109   623n.23

Panarion
45.2.1   293n.41

Epistles of Crates
3   306n.17
30.6   726n.51

Eubulides   702n.110

Euripides
Rhesus
161-62   367n.37

Eusebius
Ecclesiastical History
2.22   11
2.22.2-3   637n.81
3.2   654n.29
3.4.8   623n.23
3.13   654n.29
3.37.2-4   607n.64
5.10.2   607n.64
7.2   374n.72

Herodotus
History
1.71.2   375n.78
1.85   253n.60
1.96.2   408n.8
1.117   221n.90
2.146   110n.29
2.173   175
8.86   430n.30
9.45   430n.30
9.5   258n.93

Hesychius
Lexicon   432n.35
63   221n.90
64   221n.90

Homer
Iliad   421n.63

1.339   132n.56
2.649   680n.15
14.92   593n.121
23.373   613n.88

Odyssey
8.240   593n.121
10.299   132n.56
17.173   638n.86
19.172-79   680n.15
19.173ff.   701n.105

Hymenaeus
1:20   434

Hymn to Demeter   318n.29

Irenaeus
Against Heresies
1.pref.   4n.7, 42n.107, 111n.34
1.20.10   795n.7
1.23.4   4n.7
1.23.5   527n.66
1.24.2   42n.108, 293n.41
1.30.9   111n.34
2.14.7   4n.7
2.22.5   314n.5
3.1.1   4n.7
3.3.3   654n.29
4.16.3   4n.7
5.17.1   4n.7

Isocrates
Nicocles
57   731n.70

Orationes
90   777n.24

Josephus   583n.70, 726
Against Apion
1.6   348n.96
1.11   395n.15
1.15   395n.10

1.60   173
1.309   521n.30
2.137   367n.38
2.145   578n.40
2.161   578n.40
2.200   227n.107
2.206   557n.23
2.217-18   306n.15
2.218   782n.53
2.293   771n.8

Antiquities
1.13   582n.62
1.24   288n.12
1.32   226n.103
1.36   225n.101
1.45   523n.39
1.49   225n.101
1.180   276n.27
1.246   331n.7
2.48   481n.6
2.49   367n.38
2.52   206n.43
2.59   503n.23
2.88   401n.45
2.180   345n.71
2.220   208n.46
2.229   276n.27
2.346   326n.51
3.15   305n.13
3.49   491n.11
3.76   422n.66
3.190   555n.14
3.279   251n.47
3.288   345n.71
4.59   524n.46, 579n.44
4.144   252n.55
4.151   523n.39
4.220   770n.5
4.316   136n.6
5.13   340n.40
5.90   792n.84
6.22   610n.76
6.151   710n.145
6.185   305n.13

Phocylides
Fragments
17   367n.37

Plato   408n.8, 522n.36,
                              700
Cratylus
396C   110n.29

Gorgias
480B   518n.14
504E   519n.16
527A   305n.12
513E   386n.31

Laws
636C-D   110n.28,
                      701n.105,
                      705n.123
642D-E   700n.95
648C   306n.16
729BC   731n.70
757A   382n.16
770E   381n.12
796A   518n.14
810B   317n.24
810E   521n.31
836B-C   701n.105
850B   386n.31
870   555n.17
881A   127n.23
917A   226n.106
931D   340n.41
941B   110n.28,
                      705n.123

Letters
352C   496n.37

Phaedo
83B   402n.54, 776n.23
114A   127nn.22-23,
                      127n.25

Republic
329B   638n.86

344B   128n.30
350E   305n.12
369B   399n.35
372D   777n.24
376E   747n.16
376D-377A   109n.26
376E-383C   110n.28
412C   226n.106
463C   330n.5
550B   425n.10

Theaetetus
190E   108n.20

Timaeus
22A   109n.24
23B   110n.29

Plautus
Bacchides
423ff.   317n.24

Pliny   35
Natural History
2.122   654n.24
5.17   293n.43
8.83   661, 701n.104
30.1.11   564n.64
33.6.26-27   737n.100

Plutarch   252n.56,
                555n.17, 792n.84
Alexander
1.1   317n.24
23.3   317n.24

De audibilibus
Poeta   317n.24

Lives [Pelopidas]
3.2   776n.23

Lucullus
18.9   778n.32

Moralia
4B   249n.33
7C   249n.33
39A   354n.129
65D   525n.54
70C   256n.79
86C   661, 701n.104
131B   554n.8
132A-F   376n.82
132D   253n.57, 688n.48
141E   208n.45
155D   401n.48
204A   157n.13
206A   797n.15
353B   375nn.78-79
361F   97n.15
479E   432n.39
490B   701n.105
515A-23B   354n.130
524D   398n.30
536E   396n.19
546F   395n.13
705C   526n.60
769C   726n.52
792E   713n.2
800B   251n.48
830B   97n.15
953B   432n.36
996C   782n.53
1033B   315n.17
1041A   288n.12
1059D-E   702n.110

Nicias
10.5.6   109n.23

Rome and Greece
271.E.3-4   356n.141

Solon
12.4   700n.95

Polybius
Histories
2.44.1   427n.18
3.69.14   611n.81

INDEX OF KEY GREEK WORDS